INDEX TO
CALIFORNIA HISTORICAL SOCIETY
QUARTERLY
VOLUMES ONE TO FORTY
1922-1961

Index

to

California Historical Society
Quarterly

VOLUMES ONE TO FORTY

1922-1961

chs

CALIFORNIA HISTORICAL SOCIETY

SAN FRANCISCO 1965

© 1965 by California Historical Society

Library of Congress Catalogue No. 25-5895

Designed by Adrian Wilson

Printed in the United States of America
by Anderson, Ritchie and Simon

Preface

The *California Historical Society Quarterly* has appeared continuously since the publication of Volume I, Number 1, in July, 1922. The final number of most volumes has carried an index, and in 1955 a project of combining and editing these for separate publication was begun. This concept was soon abandoned, however, because of the lack of uniformity of the annual indexes and their ultimate inadequacy, and the preparation of a cumulative index of maximum value and usefulness was undertaken.

This Index to the first forty volumes of the *California Historical Society Quarterly* represents the indexing of some 15,000 pages of text. Inevitably, in any undertaking of this magnitude, minor discrepancies and some inconsistencies of style will be discovered; they should not seriously affect the use of this volume, which we believe to be very valuable although less than perfect.

Completion of the Index has been achieved only through the dedicated effort of skilled member-volunteers and the co-operation of the Society's library and editorial staff. All who use this Index are in their debt.

The Society wishes to acknowledge the generous financial assistance for the preparation and publication of the Index provided by the May T. Morrison Trust Estate (Edward Hohfield, Trustee) and by Mr. and Mrs. Richard Y. Dakin in memory of Sara Hathaway Dakin and Mrs. Florence Green Bixby.

DONALD C. BIGGS
Director

Guiding Principles

Because of its expected use the Index stresses the specific over the general and the obscure over the well known. There are more entries for individual hotels than for "Hotels," and more for individual theaters than for "Theaters." Names of Indian tribes, however, are not indexed separately but are listed by name under "Indians." Missions are listed by name under "Missions," ranches under "Ranchos and land grants," and unions under "Unions (labor)." Churches are listed under the name of the church, followed by the name of the city or town. Under the names of some towns and cities is a subheading "churches" followed by page references but not the names of individual churches.

Public institutions, documents, and so forth are those of California unless otherwise stated. "Constitutional Convention" is the California Constitutional Convention. "In California" is understood as part of all generic headings such as "Banks and banking."

ALPHABETIZATION

    1. Entries are arranged letter by letter, not word by word:

This	*Not this*
San Bernardino	San Vicente
Sánchez	San Ysidro
San Diego	Sánchez
Sanford, John Peter	Santa Rosa
Santa Barbara	Santander

    2. French, Spanish, and Italian names of newspapers, ships, companies, books, and plays beginning with an article (*La, Le, L', Les, El, Los, Un*) are alphabetized according to the main part of the name:

        L'Artemise under A
        Les Dominicales under D
        Le Francaise under F
        La Revue Californienne under R
        El Clamor Público under C
        Un Ballo en Maschera under B

    3. Names of business firms containing personal names are alphabetized according to the surname, not the initials or forename. For example:

        H. S. Crocker & Co. appears as Crocker (H. S.) & Co.
        Joshua Hendy Iron Works appears as Hendy (Joshua) Iron Works

4. The modified letters ä, ö, and ü are alphabetized as *ae*, *oe*, and *ue*.

5. Names beginning with "Mc" are alphabetized as "Mac."

Since every entry begins with a capital letter, such names as "de Fremery," "de Roos," and "de Young" appear as "De Fremery," "De Roos," and "De Young."

An effort has been made to provide forenames for persons whose surnames only are given in the text. When these are not available, a clue to the identity is given in parentheses, usually the place and year given in the article in which the person is mentioned.

In some of the diaries printed verbatim many personal names are misspelled. These misspellings have been included if the correct spelling has not been ascertained.

The names of married women for the most part are listed thus: Smith, Mrs. William Hamilton (Jane Baker), and Baker, Jane, *see* Smith, Mrs. William Hamilton. If, however, there are more references in the text to the maiden name, the main entry is that name, with a cross-reference to the married name. Or if the woman is mentioned on only one page in the text, and both maiden and married names are given there, the page number is given after both entries, as: Smith, Mrs. William Hamilton (Jane Baker), 30:45, and Baker, Jane, 30:45, without a cross-reference. Occasionally, for one reason or another, particularly when a husband's forename is not known, a woman's name is given thus: Edna (Smith) Parsons, the Smith being her maiden name.

Anglo-Saxons in Hispanic California are cited by the original forms of their names, not Spanish translations or substitutions, though some of the more firmly fixed Spanish forms are cross-referenced.

Geographical names are entered under the specific part: Lake Tahoe as "Tahoe, Lake" and Mount Shasta as "Shasta, Mount."

Camps and Forts are listed under C and F, respectively: "Camp Baker" and "Fort Tejon."

Contrary to the usual bibliographical and library practice, newspapers are listed under their own names, not under the place of publication. The San Francisco *Daily News* and the San Francisco *Evening Bulletin* appear as "*News, San Francisco*" and "*Bulletin, San Francisco*," without the words "Daily" and "Evening." Under San Francisco, however, as well as under the

names of several other cities, is a subheading "newspapers" followed by page references but not the titles of the papers. Newspapers are not indexed every time they are quoted, but references are indexed if they tell something about the paper's history, editorial position, and so on.

VESSELS

Vessels are listed separately under their own names, in italics, followed by the word "ship" in parentheses, or "barge," "tug," "yacht," for example, if the vessel is too small to be termed a ship. If there is more than one vessel of the same name, however, the kind of ship and the date are, as a rule, put after each name.

Abbreviations

acct.	account	ment.	mentioned
app.	appendix	Mid.	Midshipman
art.	article	Mt.	Mount
assoc.	association	Mtn.	Mountain
b.	born	newsp.	newspaper
Bat.	Battalion	N.W.	Northwest or North West
bk.	book	obit.	obituary
bibliog.	bibliography	p.	page
bldg.	building	Pac.	Pacific
Brit.	British	perh.	perhaps
ca.	circa (about)	phot.	photograph, photographs
CHS	California Historical Society	P.M.S.S.	Pacific Mail Steamship Co.
Co.	Company, County	prob.	probably
Com.	Committee, Commodore	proc.	proclamation
comp.	compiler	proj.	projected
con.	connection	prop.	proposed
Confed.	Confederate	pub.	publisher, published
contrib.	contributor, contribution	Pub.	Publication
cor.	correspondence	R.	River
Corp.	Corporal	regs.	regulations
C.P.R.R.	Central Pacific Railroad	rep.	report
Cr.	Creek	reprod.	reproduced, reproduction
d.	died	rev.	review, reviewed
dept.	department	riv.	river
ed.	editor, edited by, edition	R.R.	Railroad
exped.	expedition	schr.	schooner
fac.	facsimile	S.F.	San Francisco
foll.	following	str.	steamer
Fr.	Father, Fray, French	supt.	superintendent
Ft.	Fort	surv.	survey
H.B. Co.	Hudson's Bay Company	trans.	translated by, translator
hist.	history	U.C.	University of California
illus.	illustration, illustrated	uncl.	unclaimed
incl.	included, including	U.S.N.	United States Navy
Ind.	Indian	v.	versus
introd.	introduced, introduction	Vig. Com.	Vigilance Committee
L.A.	Los Angeles	w.	with
Lt.	Lieutenant		

Standard abbreviations are used for
states and countries.

Volumes of California Historical Society Quarterly

Roman Numerals	Arabic Numerals	Year	Roman Numerals	Arabic Numerals	Year
I	1	1922	XXI	21	1942
II	2	1923	XXII	22	1943
III	3	1924	XXIII	23	1944
IV	4	1925	XXIV	24	1945
V	5	1926	XXV	25	1946
VI	6	1927	XXVI	26	1947
VII	7	1928	XXVII	27	1948
VIII	8	1929	XXVIII	28	1949
IX	9	1930	XXIX	29	1950
X	10	1931	XXX	30	1951
XI	11	1932	XXXI	31	1952
XII	12	1933	XXXII	32	1953
XIII	13	1934	XXXIII	33	1954
XIV	14	1935	XXXIV	34	1955
XV	15	1936	XXXV	35	1956
XVI	16	1937	XXXVI	36	1957
XVII	17	1938	XXXVII	37	1958
XVIII	18	1939	XXXVIII	38	1959
XIX	19	1940	XXXIX	39	1960
XX	20	1941	XXXX (XL)	40	1961

Index

A

Abagge, M., 13:32

Abajian, James de Tarr, "Noteworthy Gift," 34:173-74; comp. "Preliminary Listing of Manuscript Collections in Library of California Historical Society," 33:372-76; bk. rev. by, 38:165-67

Abasa, Serge, 33:2, 6, 149

Abbe, Eleazer, 38:166

Abbot (Carson Hill, 1850), 22:73

Abbot, Charles Greeley, 4:36

Abbot, Samuel Leonard, 21:382-83

Abbot, William A., 2:94; 11:157

Abbot's Hall, Sacramento, 9:34

Abbott, Ann, 9:265, 287, 352

Abbott, Granville S., 27:17

Abbott, John Masterson, 8:347, 360; 9:286-87; family of, 9:287; lawsuit, 10:276, 284

Abbott, Robert O., 34:28, 32

Abbott, Mount, 4:21, 55

Abbott House, Yuba Co., 8:346, 347, 360; 9:265, 286, 353; 10:59, 172

Abbott's Ranch, 33:299, 300, 304

Abeck, François, 11:42; 14:278

Abell, Alexander Gurdon, 9:103; 16:79; 25:259-60, 266

Abella, Ramón, 8:148, 149, 151; 10:30; 15:215, 339; 16:109; 17:249-50; 36:9

Abend Zeitung, San Francisco, 15:175

Aber, Thomas Theophilus and Elizabeth A., 39:55

Abercrombie (Mid. on *Savannah*, 1846), 3:113

Aberdeen, George Hamilton Gordon, Earl of, 18:140, 142, 144; brother of, 17:130; 22:319

Abert, James William, 3:270; 21:194, 221

Abert, John James, 11:123; 19:313, 316; 22:215; 39:84

Abert, Lake, 22:204, 215

Abila, Enrique, 13:349

Abila, Juan, 13:349; *see also* Avila

Above and Below (play); 15:170

Abraham, Charles, 31:378; 32:184

"Abraham Dubois Starr, Pioneer California Miller," by Walter A. Starr, 27:193-202

"Abraham Lincoln and the New Almaden Mine," by Milton H. Shutes, 15:3-20

Abrams, Albert, 40:140, 141, 153

Abrams, Leroy, *An Illustrated Flora of the Pacific States*, rev., 4:88

Abreck (ship), 26:15

Abrego, José María, 13:34, 35, 37, 78; 17:51, 53, 57, 60, 61, 154; 24:372; 29:22, 26; 30:98; 35:104

Academy of Music, San Francisco; *see* Baldwin Theatre; Maguire's Academy of Music; Tucker's Academy of Music

Acadia (ship), 22:169

I

Acalanes, *see* Ranchos and land grants

Acapulco, 1:38, 45; 2:141, 142, 143, 160; 3:4, 218, 316; 6:297, 298, 314; 7:59, 235-45 *passim*, 256, 259, 263-64, 299, 300, 376, 377; 8:15, 34, 45, 47, 50, 68; 14:326-27; 15:225, 382; 19:194, 195, 198; 20:20-21; 23:219, 331, 336; 24:69-70; 27:40, 48; 29:12-13; 32:311; 36:302

Accolti, Michael, 29:139-46; 32:122, 139

"Account . . . of the Plants in the Brackenridge Journal, An," by Alice Eastwood, 24:337-42

Acevedo Texada, Juan de, 7:298-300, 318, 349, 377

Achan in El Dorado, by Scott, 17:173

Ackeman (from N.Y., 1859), 10:169

Ackerman, J. Howard, 1:181; 14:143

Ackerman, John W., 9:19

Ackerman, Stewart, 22:34

Ackerson, Charles H., 15:313-14, 322

Ackey, David B., 15:274

Ackley, Lyman, 10:59, 169, 266; 16:80; 40:212

Ackley, Mary E. (Medley), *Crossing the Plains*, rev., 8:86

Ackley & Maurison, 13:256, 258; 14:160

Acres, Hiram, 5:125

Across the Continent (play), 34:360

Across the Plains by Prairie Schooner, by Bonney, ed. Lockley, rev., 3:89-90

Activa (brig, 1792), 2:282, 292, 306; 10:317, 319, 321, 327, 332-36

Active (str., 1852), 11:302, 305; 15:177; 17:175; 23:339, 342, 343; 33:232, 234

Activities of a Lifetime, by Munk, rev., 3:201-2

Activo (bark, 1803), 24:490

Actress by Daylight, The (play), 9:360, 389

Ada (ship), 16:183; 17:84

Ada Hancock (ship), 16:66; 34:38

Adair, John, 20:22

Adair, Wesley, 14:278

Adalbert, Mme. (S.F., 1851), 28:36; 32:109

Adam Grant Building, San Francisco, 30:210

Adams (S.F., 1851), 34:246

Adams, Mrs. (Sonora, 1855), 35:225, 228

Adams, Capt. (Colorado R., 1859), 22:169

Adams, Alonzo W., 30:131

Adams, Alvin, 15:371; 17:170, 172

Adams, Annie A., 21:241

Adams, David L. and Lydia (Swain), 28:379-80

Adams, Edson, 4:211; 25:382; 30:1; 31:325, 328

Adams, Mrs. Edson (Hannah), 4:211

Adams, Edwin, 21:158, 179, 243

Adams, Emma (Hildreth), 31:24, 25

Adams, Ephraim Douglass, address, "British-American Relations in Connection with the Acquisition of California," 2:258

Adams, F., 15:164

Adams, Frank (Alpine Co., 1864), 30:246

Adams, Frank (Alpine Co., 1864), 30:246

Adams, Frank (prof. at U.C., 1943), 30:322

Adams, George Russell, 33: 1, 6, 7, 12, 159, 161; "Journal," ed. Harold F. Taggart, 35:291-307; phot., 33: opp. 1; family, 35: 305

Adams, Mrs. George Russell (Lillian Hinckley), 35:305

Adams, H. N., 22:250

Adams, J. H., 15: 29, 51

Adams, James Capen, 3:36; 4:13

Adams, Mrs. John Payson (née Vanderbilt), 23:383-84

Adams, John Quincy, 1:16; 24:80

Adams, Dr. and Mrs. John S., 30:246-47

Adams, Lowell, 39:265

Adams, Mrs. Margaret, 17:42, 43

Adams, Maude, 35:142

Adams, N., 11:160, 161

Adams, Oliver, 35:305

Adams, P. R., 19:60-61, 69; 27:316; phot., 19: opp. 59

Adams, R., map by, 14: opp. 224

Adams, Ramon F., *The Rampaging Herd: A Bibliography of . . . the Cattle Industry*, rev., 40:170-71

Adams, Ross M., 21:44-45

Adams, Samuel (S.F., 1850s), 33:372; 35:291

Adams, Samuel ("Steamboat," Ariz., 1864), 22:13-14, 16-19 *passim*, 23, 25

Adams, T. M., 4:310

Adams, Theodore, 29:355

Adams, Will, 18:85

Adams, Point, 9:235; 10:327
Adams & Co. (banking and express),
  11:54; 12:300; 15:169, 177, 185, 192,
  271-79 *passim*, 368, 375; 16:31, 32, 82,
  84, 184, 282, 340-41, 347; 17:168-72
  passim, 176, 180, 182; 19:297; 21:24,
  128; 22:35; 26:195, 199; 27:93; 28:62,
  67, 210; 30:254; 33:375; 35:206, 222;
  37:139, 146, 151
Adams and Co. (grocers), 24:378
Adams *v.* Halliday, 31:328
Adams *v.* Haskell and Woods, 17:170
Adams River, 2:228-35
Adamson, Appolenia, 23:295
Addams, J. P. ("Yankee"), 9:246, 271
Addis, Jacob and Julia (Green), 28:292
Addis, John, 15:179
Addison, John E., 15:173-74; 16:345; 19:236
Addison, William, 19:236
*Address of Vallejo before the Junta of
  1846*, rev., 7:93-94
Adelaide (ship), 31:231
Adelberg, J., 21:325, 326, 331
Adelphi theatres, San Francisco, 4:62;
  14:73, 175; 20:295-98 *passim*, 303;
  22:266; 23:106; 28:36; 31:254, 260;
  33:43
Adelsdorfer Bros., 29:117
Aden, Green, 31:290
Adkins, Richard, 9:144
Adkison, D. Oliver (?), 8:203, 206, 211,
  356; 9:62, 65, 130, 144, 148, 150, 155,
  157, 167, 168, 261, 262; 10:256, 359, 394
Adler, Jacob, "The Spreckelsville
  Plantation . . . Claus Spreckels'
  Hawaiian Career," 40:33-48
Adler, Lewis, 30:322
Admiral (ship), 22:172
"Admission Day," address by Lawrence
  Kinnaird, 24:376
Admission Day celebrations: in 1850,
  3:41; 6:39-41; 8:284; 12:102-3;
  22:249-50; 24:376; 27:232-33; 28:34;
  in 1854, 15:173-74; in 1855, 16:82-83;
  in 1860, 38:338; in 1874, 37:216
Admission of California into Union,
  2:120; 3:41; 6:39-41; 8:273, 284;
  10:140-64, 220-42; 12:102-3; 19:15-18,
  350-51; 22:248-50; 24:116, 199-202;
  26:105-6; 37:361
Admittance (ship), 8:297, 298; 14:343;
  18:35, 51-52; 23:202
Adobe (place), 26:242

Adobe bricks, 4:361-72; 10:303;
  15:89-90; 27:110; illus., showing plant
  content, 4: opp. 361
Adobe buildings, 10:203; 16:132, 134;
  22:183; 25:131; 29:319; Bay Area,
  25:106, 285-86, 373, 382; 30:218-31;
  31:301, 305; Monterey, 16:321-35
"Adobe Houses of California, The,"
  address by Helen S. Giffen, 22:183
Adriance, John, 9:364; 11:57
Adriance's Rancho, 8:199, 208;
  10:173
Adrienne Lecouvreur (play), 10:55, 75,
  77; 20:131
Adsit, L. Burch, 8:200
"Adventures in Manuscript Collecting,"
  address by Edgar E. Robinson,
  26:84-85
"Adventures . . . in the Discovery of
  Humboldt Bay," address by Charles
  P. Cutten, 19:375-76
"Adventures of a Botanist [Alice
  Eastwood]," address by Carol Green
  Wilson, 32:180-85
"Adventures on the Plains," by Charles
  Cardinell, 1:57-71
Advertisements (reprod.): Belding
  Bros. & Co., 31: opp. 336; California
  mining company shares (from French
  newsp.), 39: opp. 16; California Silk
  Mfg. Co., 31: opp. 336; The Chutes,
  33:41; Folsom Estate Sale, 17: opp.
  168; Hawes' Express, 11: opp. 30;
  from Marysville Directories, 8:204,
  339; 9:55, 56; from Marysville
  Herald, 15: opp. 40; "Moving Mirror
  of the Land Route to California,"
  33:35; ships for Trinidad Bay, 5:140;
  strs. for Frazer R., 6:17
"Aél," *see* Lusinchi, Augustin
Aetna Petroleum Co., 31:298
Affleche, Lenora, 10:274-77 *passim*,
  282, 283, 290
"Afterword on Col. Edward Dickinson
  Baker," by Milton H. Shutes, 22:26
Aga-Oglu, Mrs. Kamer, 31:103, 105,
  app. to C. W. Meighan and R. F.
  Heizer, "Archaeological Exploration
  of 16th-Century Indian Mounds at
  Drake's Bay," 31:106-8
Agard, le comte d', 22:299-300
Agassiz, Alexander, letter to, 26:218-19
Agassiz, Louis, 21:368

Agate, Alfred T., 24:321; drawing by, 24: opp. 229
Agave, 25:298, 302; 34:199
Age, Sacramento, 9:275
Agence Américaine, 22:292
Ager, John E., 9:316
Agnese, Battista, 3:265, 312, 313, 325, 374, 376, 378; 7:68; 10:306; 36:171-72, 237; maps by (fac.), 3:377, 379
Agness (S.F., 1851), 6:55
Agnew, Jesse B., 4:41
Agriculture and horticulture, 8:310; 12:282; 13:198, 204; 22:319; in 1848-49, 14:20, 201; in the '50s, 2:65; 5:353, 370; 9:350; 10:292; 23:170-71, 173; 27:236; in 1886-92, 27:113, 118-19, 313, 314; at missions, 2:273, 278; 3:223, 224; 4:361-70; 8:111-12, 237, 310, 319; 23:252; 24:223; in pueblos, 13:201-2, 204; 14:5-11 *passim,* 21; on ranchos, 2:55; 5:135, 136, 257, 273; 12:302; 21:333-34; of Russians, 12:189-96 *passim,* 205-6, 243, 258, 270; *see also* Agricultural colonies; Fruit; Vegetables; Wheat, etc.
Agricultural colonies: in Fresno Co., 25:17-38, 169-77; Los Angeles, 13:198, 201-2, 204; San Jose, 14:4-10
Agua Blanco (White River), 12:8
Agua Caliente, Riverside Co., 12:8, 13
Agua Caliente, San Diego Co., *see* Warner's Hot Springs; Warner's Ranch
Agua Caliente de las Palmas, 15:107, 132, 134
Agua de Hernandez, *see* Resting Springs
Agua de Tomaso (Bitter Springs), 4:37; 14:68
Agua Fria, 28:325, 326, 327, 330; 33:276, 277
Agua Fria Co., 11:245
Agua Fria Mine, 12:75, 76
Agua Mansa, 3:241-42; 12:118-20
Aguanga, 25:298, 299, 307; 26:23
Aguiar, Salvador, 15:359, 360, 361
Aguila, José M., 23:9
Aguilar, Cristóbal, 13:313, 326-27, 333
Aguilar, Francisco de, 30:279-80
Aguilar, José María, 13:212; 15:356; 26:41
Aguilar, Juan de, 3:387; 4:319
Aguilar, María Máxima, 13:200
Aguilar, Martín de, 2:299; 7:299, 300, 328, 334, 347, 369, 377, 379, 383, 385

Aguilar, Rosario, 21:320
Aguilar, Santiago, 12:128, 131-33; 14:258-61 *passim;* 16:240, 354, 355
Aguilar, Simon, 16:224
Aguinaldo Emilio, 31:62, 65
Aguirre, Andrés de, 7:146, 151, 172, 173, 248, 265; letter of, 7:244-45
Aguirre, José Antonio, 8:106; 14:337, 346; 15:128, 138; 18:268, 277; 23:318, 333; 31: 34, 37, 45, 46
Agustín I, *see* Iturbide, Agustín
"Augustín Vicente Zamorano," address by George L. Harding, 13:411
Ah Chow, 23:109
Ah Chun, 23:108
Ah Cow & Co., 9:158
Ah Foey, 23:109
Ah Foo, 13:333
Ah Hem, 9:148; lawsuit, 9:148, 154
Ah Him, 23:112
Ah Hoy, 15:53, 54
Ah Kim (lawsuits, Yuba Co.), 9:148, 154, 158, 159
Ah Kuang, 15:177
Ah Kung, 23:108
Ah Loos, 13:333
Ah Louis (alias Wong On), 37:130-31
Ah Lum, 23:109
Ah Pek, 23:112
Ah Ping, 23:108
Ahrens, J. F., 30:21, 22, 23
Ah Sin (play), 34:362
Ah Sing, 20:133, 134
Ah The, 15:277
Ah Toy, 22:270
Ah Wing, 23:108
Ah Wye, 23:108
Ah You, Charley, 15:276
Ah Young, 23:111
Aich (Yosemite, 1852), 5:332-35
Aiglon, L' (play), 20:138; 35:142
Aiken, J. M., 8:270-71, 273
Aiken, John, 25:256
Aiken and Smith ferry, 25:256, 258, 264
Aikin, Ilo Rafenel, obit., 9:189
Ainsa, Agustín, 19:275
Ainsa, Jesús M., 9:256, 281; 19:274-75
Ainsa v. U.S., 30:328, 337
Ainsworth, Sydney, 13:296
Aisquith, Edward M., 29:302, 306
Aitken, A. G., 24:188
Aiton, Arthur Scott, 6:302
Ajax (ship), 32:191; 34:353
Akenhead, William, 13:32
Akers, Anderson, 25:20

Akins, Alma, 32:376

Alabama (bark, 1851), 25:329

Alabama (Confed. ship, 1862), 8:384; 19:296; 20:114; 26:18; 27:73; 32:312; 33:236

Alabama Bar, 8:338, 342, 355

"Alabama claims," 27:66, 73

Alabama Settlement, 25:24-26

Alamán, Lucas, 24:308; 25:69-72, 78

Alameda, 26:266; 34:330-31; railroad, 26:359, 362

Alameda (ship), 31:158

Alameda County, 12:173-75; address on, 25:373-74; grand jury, 27:267

Alameda County Agricultural Society, 38:27

Alameda County Homoeopathic Medical Society, 33:376

"Alameda County, Past and Present," address by Leslie J. Freeman, 25:373-74

Alamo Mocho, 25:306

Alamos (Antonio S.) & Co., 35:235

Alanis, Máximo, 13:208-9, 212, 223, 234

Alanson, Bertram, 38:4

Alarcón, Hernando de, 1:45, 54; 3:309, 312, 380, 384-86, 387; 6:301, 315, 318, 322; 8:43; 36:218-20

Alarcón, Pascual de, 7:262, 263, 274, 299, 300, 328, 336, 339, 343-49 *passim*, 377, 379, 383, 384, 386

Alaska, 11:306-8, 315-19 *passim*; 12: 191, 195, 217; 30:378-79; 33:10, 147-68; 35:291-307; 36:379; 39:109

Alaska Commercial Co., 33:375; 35:307; 37:182

"Alaska: Historic Links with California," address by Aubrey Neasham, 30:378-79

Alaska Mine, 9:176

Alba, Manuel de, 15:347-48

Alban, W. G., store (illus.), 30: opp. 257

Albatross (ship, 1810), 12:223, 224, 225; 23:216

Albatross (ship, 1889), 31:153

Albernares, José, 23:297

Alberni, Pedro de, 27:337

Alberti, Juan Bautista, 16:43-47

Albertine, Miss (actress, 1851), 20:297

"Albert Little Bancroft," by Henry R. Wagner, 29:97-128, 217-27, 357-67

Albertson, Dean, 28:284; "Dr. Edward Turner Bale," 28:259-69

Albertson, F. C., 26:213, 215

Albertson, Peter, 16:306

Albin, Leonce, 39:146, 153

Albion Hill, 10:169, 193

Albion Lumber Mill, 33:362

Alboni (ship), 16:282

Albornoz, Rodrigo de, 6:296, 306

Albright, Gertrude, 38:2

Alcalá Galiano, Dionisio, 10:81, 313, 315-16, 321; 15:214, 215; 40: 117, 118-19; map, 40: foll. 112

"Alcalde Rule: . . . Local Government in Spanish and Mexican California," by Theodore Grivas, 40:11-32

Alcaldes, 1:25-35 *passim*, 179, 180; 2:151, 353; 3:111; 4:172; 5:146; 8:103, 104, 246; 10:17, 18, 23, 24, 29, 404; 12:151; 13:209, 211; 14:8, 23, 121-22, 150, 229; 16:343; 17:250; 20:14, 121-22, 217; 21:125; 22:57-58; 25:272-76 *passim*; 29:161, 164, 170; 30:333; 31:144; 32:294; 33:50; address on, 33:278-81; art. on, 40:11-32; land grants by, 8:104; 16:343; 17:172; 28:67-68, 266

Alcatraz Island, 5:7; 6:252; 8:239; 17:174; 19:357; 22:331, 360; 23:339; 25:319, 321; 27:293-94; 28:166, 169; 31:51-52; 33:229-38 *passim*

Alcazar Theater, San Francisco, 33:41; 35:142

Alceste (ship), 15:373

Alciope (ship), 14:321, 341, 343

Alcohol, attempt to manufacture, 31:298

Alcorta, Lino I., cor., 13:139-40

Alcott (Del Norte Co., 1862), 26:6

Alden (S.F., 1849), 22:69

Alden, Bradford Ripley, 28:93; 33:372; "The Oregon and California Letters of," 28:199-232, 351-59; memorial tablet, 28: opp. 351, port. opp. 203

Alden, Mrs. Bradford Ripley (Anne Caroline Coleman), 28:200; letters to, 201-24; port. (w. Percy and Sarah) opp. 222

Alden, James, 12:86; 20:276

Alden, Percy, 28:205, 222; port., 28: opp. 222

Alden, Sarah, 28:215, port., opp. 222

Alden, Silas, 2:110, 116, 117, 118, 122

Alden's Branch, 26:74

Alder Creek, Mendocino Co., 4:222, 223; 13:14; 17:179; 23:25

Alder Creek Valley, Nevada Co., 24:74, 75

Alder Grove, *see* Illinoistown

Alder Gulch (Virginia City), Mont., 25:324

Alderman, Isaac W., 4:317, 320, 321

Alderman, M. R., 14:211

Alderpoint, 20:349, 352, 355-56

Alderson, Harry, 32:29

Aldrich (S.F., 1859), 31:246

Aldrich, Daniel, 9:26

Aldrich, L., 7:278

Aldrich, Lewis, 7:278(?); 11:48, 49

Aldrich, Louis, 15:202

Aldrich, Silas, 37:234

Alejo (Indian, 1846), 25:299-300

Alemany, Joseph Sadoc, 8:197; 10:269, 378, 379, 391; 16:283, 344; 18:178, 276; 29:82, 147, 376-77; 31:377; 32:122, 127; 33:75; land claims of, 17:178, 182; 18:178; 23:11; 40:52, 58, 66

Alembique Creek, 31:301

Alendander (Alexander?), David, 23:296

Alert (schr., 1859), 22:169

Alert (ship, 1835), 8:105-6, 294-96; 14:313, 345; 15:226; 19:210, 216; 23:198, 199, 201, 214, 318, 319, 325, 326, 332, 333

Aleuts, 8:233, 324-25; 12:191, 192, 196, 199, 218-38; 13:205; 16:108; 18:328; 29:318; 39:109

Alexander (Dadd's Gulch, d. 1857), 9:136

Alexander, A. B., 31:153-54

Alexander, Annie Montague, obit., 29:378

Alexander, Benjamin, 26:204

Alexander, Clara, 33:274

Alexander, Cyrus, 1:237; 33:63, 64, 65, 71

Alexander, David W., 12:117; 13:223, 325, 329; 17:332, 339; 18:70; 27:108; 29:234; 32:329, 331, 333, 346

Alexander, Emily, 28:292

Alexander, F. H., 29:235, 237, 247

Alexander, Frank, 13:341

Alexander, George, 29:234, 245

Alexander, Henry Nash, 13:335; 29:237, 240-41, 247

Alexander, Mrs. Henry Nash (Feliciana Domínguez), 29:247

Alexander, Jacob, 19:292

Alexander, John, 12:328, 329, 330

Alexander, Joseph D., 29:123, 125

Alexander, Martha Barker, 18:380

Alexander, Remundo, 13:331

Alexander, S., 8:358

Alexander, Samuel T., 18:379, 380; 29:378

Alexander, Mrs. Samuel T. (Martha E. Cooke), 18:379

Alexander, Wallace McKinney, 29:378; obit., 18:379-81

Alexander, Mrs. Wallace McKinney (Mary S. Barker), 18:379-80; 24:379-80; 28:382; obit., 34:184-85

Alexander, William, 29:234

Alexander & Baldwin, 18:380; 40:45

Alexander Barclay (ship), 19:200, 214

Alexander Nevskii (ship), 26:13

"Alexander S. Taylor," by Robert E. Cowan, 12:18-24; as address, 10:91

"Alexander S. Taylor's Map of California Indian Tribes, 1864," by Robert F. Heizer, 20:171-80

Alexandre (of Fr. mining co., 1849), 22:297

"Alexandre Dumas *fils* and the Lottery of the Golden Ingots," ed. and trans. Abraham P. Nasatir, 33:125-42

Alfalfa, 25:29; 27:113, 120

Alford, Landy, 6:152

"Alfred Robinson, New England Merchant in Mexico and California," by Adele Ogden, 23:193-218

Algoa (ship), 31:296

Algodones (place), 21:221; 25:294

Alhambra Restaurant, San Francisco, 3:38

Alhambra Theatre, San Francisco, 20:2; 21:161, 164-71 *passim*, 243, 244; 33:41; *see also* Maguire's New Theatre

Ali, Hadji, 9:305, 307, 315, 319(?)

Alice (schr., 1864), 22:24, 170, 171

Alice (schr., 1872), 31:293-94

"Alice Frivole" (pseud.), 39:243

Alice Haake (ship), 22:154, 173-74; 31:150

Alice Tarleton (ship), 23:279

Alipás, Dionisio, 26:35

Alipás, Gervasio, 13:218-21; 23:324

Alipás, José, 26:32-33

Alisal, *see* Ranchos: "El Alisal"

Alisal, El (Lummis' house), 39:63

Alisal silver mine, 13:60

Aliso (tree), 13:232

Alkali Lake, 22:203, 215

Allan, Charles, 8:17-22 *passim*, 167-68, 172, 178

Allan, George Traill, 28:107, 257

"Alleghanians," 9:359, 388; 10:48, 64, 70

Alleghany, 10:348, 382, 394; 11:240; 28:239; road to, 28:237
Allen, Charles E., 14:164
Allen, Edward Weber, 20:95; comp., "Jean François Galaup de Lapérouse: A Check List," 20:47-64
Allen, Ezra H., 14:278, 280
Allen, Fannie A., 28:294
Allen, Frank, 36:67, 71
Allen, George (Monterey, 1835), 16:335
Allen, George (L.A., 1857), 9:305
Allen, H., 9:42
Allen, H. T., 30:299
Allen, Harvey, 22:77
Allen, Herbert W. and Gertrude (Joliffe), 36:183-84
Allen, Isaac, 9:52, 138, 151, 170, 251; 10:53, 54, 62, 169, 177
Allen, J. H., 21:64
Allen, Capt. James (d. 1846), 21:198, 222
Allen, Gen. James, 8:355; 9:34, 42, 45, 177; 15:152, 153, 154, 273; 19:78
Allen, Moreland, 14:180
Allen, Peter, 23:330
Allen, R. T. P., 13:297; 14:399; 25:266
Allen, Robert, 11:366, 370; 28:162; 29:158; 30:56; 34:4
Allen, Robert N., 13:297; 25:266; 28:193
Allen, Rufus, 14:61, 71, 176-81 *passim*; 22:12-13
Allen, Samuel, 13:32
Allen, Samuel L., 18:109, 110, 134
Allen, Theodore H., 15:177
Allen, W. H., 13:32
Allen & Colbey's, 9:52
Allen (J. E.) & Co., 30:255, 356
Allen & Spier, 30:356
Allgeier, Nicholaus, 5:276; 8:23; 9:395; 11:108-9, 121; 14:202, 205; 23:370
Alli, Hiogo, 9:315
Alliance Française, Los Angeles, 20:140
Allis, Mr. and Mrs. (Yuba Co., 1856), 9:67, 132-35 *passim*, 139-46 *passim*, 166
Allis, George B., 9:61, 130, 132, 156, 165, 172; 10:170
Allis, William, 9:142, 145, 152, 159, 164, 166, 169, 260
Allis & Co., 9:142; *v.* Schultz, 9:139
Allison Ranch, 6:226; 11:244
Allison *v.* Kempton, 10:177, 186
Allman, George, 30:292; 31:50, 57, 65
Allman, Heyman, 5:292
Allred, J. R., 14:278
Allsopp, James P. C., 6:61

Allston, Benjamin, 26:1
All That Glitters Is Not Gold (play), 28:37
Allyne, Edith Winslow, 17:20; 31:185
Allyne, John W., 31:185; 33:372
Allyne, Lucy Helen, 17:20; 31:185
Allyne & White, 31:185
Almanor, Lake, 30:58
Almanza, José Mariano, 24:289, 291, 292, 308; 25:60, 362
Almejas, Punta de (Pt. San Pedro), 14:107
Almond, William B., 15:380; 40:26, 28
Almonte, Juan Nepomucino, 10:9, 111; 13:111; 17:151, 154; 18:225
Almy, A. J., 29:254
"Aloha Farm," 29:100, 101, 363
Alouette, L' (weekly), 39:219, 220, 346
Alpena (ship), 31:295
Alper, Charles, 24:263
Alpha (ship), 23:375
Alpha and Omega, 3:141
Alphonse Fasquelle (ship), 22:303
Alpine County, 30:246, 247
Alsop (Richard) & Co., 13:389; 14:315, 322; 23:311, 312, 313, 325-26, 331
Alta (place), 18:360; 23:121; 35:261
Alta California (province), 31:113-24 *passim*
Alta California (newsp.) San Francisco, 5:86; 7:277-83 *passim*; 8:361-62; 10:139, 143; 13:299; 14:346; 15:9, 13, 15, 18, 32, 208-9; 16:84; 17:81, 177; 19:330; 20:121, 125, 165, 330-39 *passim*; 21:28; 22:37; 23:338-43 *passim*; 24:48, 70; 26:83, 228-33 *passim*, 337; 27:273-74; 28:135, 136; 29:162, 252, 289, 290; 32:221, 224; 33:209, 210; 34:320, 342, 348; cited, 6:12, 14, 16, 34; 10:139, 143-48 *passim*, 163, 240, 241; 12:280; 13:396; 17:183, 262, 264, 311, 314, 315; 20:368; 28:31-45 *passim*; 32:253-54, 299, 350-61 *passim*; 34:41-42, 50-54 *passim*, 58-64 *passim*, 216; 37:366; 40:49, 100, 101
Alta Irrigation District, 25:24
Alta Mira Club, San Leandro, 25:374; 30:224, 229
Altamirano, Juan, 19:243
Altamirano, Lucás Domingo, 38:106, 111
Altar at Mission San José, 37:102, 104-7, 255-58 *passim*; illus., 37: opp. 112
Altaville, 18:22
Alter, J. Cecil, *James Bridger*, rev., 4:290-91

Alter, Samuel, 27:309

Alter, Samuel M., 34:169

Altgeier, *see* Allgeier

Althouse, 19:368, 369, 370; 28:229

Altimira, José, 8:151, 240, 328; 14:123;
  16:100, 110-19; 24:57; 36:241

Altrocchi, Julia Cooley (Mrs.
  Rudolph), 15:100, 187; 28:92;
  "Paradox Town: San Francisco in
  1851," 28:31-46; address, "Quest for
  Pioneers," 17:89-90

Altschul, Charles, 35:272

Alturas Company, 11:242

Alturas County, 9:256, 282; 10:50, 73

Alum, 15:235

Alva, Manuel de, 4:152, 153; 16:354,
  355; 28:259

Alvarado, D., 21:320

Alvarado, Enrique, 29:160

Alvarado, Francisco Javier, 12:223;
  13:217, 223

Alvarado, Francisco María, 21:356;
  33:117-18

Alvarado, Hernando de, 3:264; 6:316,
  317

Alvarado, Ignacio, 21:320

Alvarado, Ignacio Rafael, 20:238

Alvarado, Javier, 12:223; 13:203, 204

Alvarado, José Francisco, 13:198

Alvarado, José María, 26:58

Alvarado, Juan (L.A., 1831), 13:212

Alvarado, Juan (San Pascual, 1846),
  26:41

Alvarado, Juan Bautista (1769), 13:198

Alvarado, Juan Bautista (b. 1809),
  11:342, 343; 12:151, 235, 342, 343;
  13:35, 45, 60, 198; 14:341; 16:223, 231,
  248, 343; 17:68, 146, 151; 27:353;
  29:151, 157, 158, 160; 31:330; 32:267;
  against Micheltorena, 12:147, 288;
  13:229; 15:228-30; 17:156-60 *passim*;
  18:172, 297; 20:147; 28:253; attitude
  toward foreigners, 10:35; 12:342;
  15:116, 224, 225, 238, 240-41; 17:151,
  152, 157, 158; 18:160; 20:234; 21:323;
  28:260; 34:114; 37:63; w. Castro
  against U.S., 3:180, 183, 184; 4:81;
  5:195; 9:82; 12:39, 163; 18:81;
  character, 11:197; 12:342, 343; 17:139;
  27:353; con. w. Graham affair, 14:230,
  255, 318; 15:115-19 *passim*, 126, 130,
  135-36, 238, 240, 241; 18:174; 20:225,
  234; 28:260; 34:114; 37:63, 64, 65;
  contest w. Carlos Carrillo, 13:222;
  16:359; 17:50; 27:337; 29:312; on

council app. by Stockton, 12:345;
  17:231; 27:106; dealings w. Russians,
  12:245-48 *passim*, 252-55, 260-66
  passim, 272-73; 17:63, 66-68; feud w.
  Vallejo, 17:50-62 *passim*; gov.,
  1:30-31; 3:32; 8:100, 110, 113, 120, 127;
  12:133, 134, 147, 280; 14:16, 244-52
  passim; 258-64 *passim*; 15:240;
  16:350-70 *passim*; 17:50-68; 18:320,
  321; 19:214; 20:234; 28:110, 259-62
  passim; 29:313; homes of, 21:322;
  23:348; 31:330; 32:267; 33:280; 37:64,
  65; land grants by, 8:127; 11:69, 349;
  12:111; 14:125; 17:294; 18:295;
  24:92; 26:267; 27:108; 29:314, 318,
  324; grant to, 34:255; negotiations
  w. H. B. Co., 8:100-103, 107, 113, 120;
  17:68; 28:97, 98, 102, 103, 245, 253-58
  passim; relations w. French, 8:116,
  117, 122-23; 11:223; 13:60; 18:316, 326;
  revolution of 1836-38, 10:5; 12:128,
  137; 14:230-44 *passim*, 318-19, 342;
  15:242, 339-55 *passim*; 16:5, 348-49;
  18:70, 320; 23:327-28; sea-otter
  hunting, 12:238; 29:318; 32:267;
  shipowner, 14:341; 19:214; youth,
  16:102-7 *passim*, 217, 221-22; 29:151;
  procs., 12:128, 133, 134; 14:244-45;
  regs., orders and decrees, 3:32; 8:110;
  10:32-33; 14:16; 15:354; 28:107, 110;
  cor., 3:183-84; 12:252-53, 254-55,
  260-61; 14:122, 242-45, 247-49;
  15:341-42; 16:349; 17:51; port. 14:
  opp. 230

Alvarado, Juan de (1540), 6:314, 315

Alvarado, María Antonia, 26:61

Alvarado, Mariano, 29:236

Alvarado, Mascio, 26:54

Alvarado, Miguel, 38:105

Alvarado, Nepomuceno, 13:220

Alvarado, Pedro de, 1:44; 3:389; 395;
  6:296, 303, 308-19 *passim*, 321; 7:141;
  instructions to Zuñiga, 6:324-31; will,
  25:309-10

Alvarado (place), 12:173-75

Alvarado (str.), 18:373

Alvarado y Ruiz, Francisco, 29:236

Alvarez (Mariposa Co. or Yuba Co.,
  1858), 9:358, 363

Álvarez, Juan, 13:202

Alvar Nuñez (ship), 6:312

Alveroni, Giulio, 15:358-59, 365

Alvirez, Juan, 16:348

Alviso, Agustín, 12:173-74; 33:350;
  37:194, 195; 38:101

Alviso, Ángel, 23:254

Alviso, Domingo, 38:183

Alviso, Francisco Javier, 15:134

Alviso, José, 17:258

Alviso, José Antonio, 23:254-55

Alviso, José María, 25:122; 29:262

Alviso, Juan Ygnacio, 15:134; 38:101, 103, 106-11 *passim*

Alviso, Mrs. Juan Ygnacio (Margarita Bernal), 38:108

Alviso, María Loreto, 30:217, 218

Alviso, Melitón, 37:194

Alviso, Nicolás, 15:114, 120, 134; 23:9; 29:337

Alviso, Valentín del Carmen and María Josefa (Livermore), 38:183

Alviso (place), 2:202; 5:353; 8:111; 10:358; 13:256; 14:158, 160, 161, 168, 169, 173; 18:293; 27:130; 28:298, 321; 29:39

Alvitre, Felipe, 13:338; 15:270

Alvord, Benjamin, 21:7; 28:202, 226, 356, 358, 359; letters, 28:224, 351-52, 357-58

Alvord, Charles, 18:201-4, 215

Alvord, William, 27:271, 274; 30:139

Alward, Herbert V., 24:379

Amadis de Gaula, 1:53

Amador, José María, 2:185; 13:167; 28:259; 34:5, 6; 38:110

Amador, Pedro, 2:267, 308; 13:198; 14:111

Amador City, 20:185; 31:283

Amador Dispatch, Jackson, 20:164

Amador Rancho, 24:380; *see also* Ranchos: San Ramon (Alameda Co.)

Amador Weekly Ledger, Volcano and Jackson, 16:339; 20:183, 185

Amargosa Desert and Mountains, 17:214; 18:200, 206, 207, 211, 212

Amat, Thaddeus (Tadeo), 16:342, 344; 29:377

Ambergris, 7:331

Ambrose Restaurant, San Francisco, 10:379, 392

Ambrosio (Indian, 1830s), 14:22

Ambrotypes, 34:294, 297; illus., 34; opp. 296

Amelia (ship), 19:133

Amelotti (Monterey, 1849), 13:280

Ament, Sophronia, 16:143

America (H.B.M. frigate, 1845), 3:108; 5:255; 17:125, 130

America (Cunard str., 1848), 13:250

America (str., 1854), 15:166, 273, 367, 369; 26:1

American (bark, 1854), 15:177, 269, 275; 17:197; 22:95

American (str., 1868), 34:320

American (newsp.), San Francisco, 16:285, 339; 17:81

American Association for State and Local History, 38:75, 76

American Baptist Home Mission Society, 27:9

American Bar, 19:146; 25:4; 29:299, 305

American Bible Society, 32:122-23, 128-29

American Born (play), 21:257

American Brass Band, 16:83

American Brigade, 37:204-11

American Camel Co., 9:302; title page of charter, 9; opp. 336

American Church Missionary Society, 34:317, 319, 320

American Colony, Fresno Co., 25:171

"American Consulate in California, The," by Henry P. Beers, 37:1-17

American Exchange Hotel, San Francisco, 10:276, 290; 16:307

American Express Company, 31:331

American Fur Company, 2:32; 18:292, 309; 22:132

American Hill, 11:234, 240; 29:200

American Home Missionary Society, 28:291, 295; 32:49, 53, 120, 134

American Hotel, Auburn, 9:369, 393

American Hotel, Benicia, 14:364, 367

American Hotel, San Francisco, 11:152; 37:332-33

American House, Napa, 2:136

American House, Sacramento, 24:357

American House, Yuba Co., 10:17; 19:296

American Images of Spanish California, by Hart, rev., 40:250-51

American Korean Electric Co., 30:205

American Mine, 28:234

American National Bank: Los Angeles, 15:195; San Diego, 35:363

"American Occupations of Rancho Santa Margarita y Las Flores," by Jeanne S. Van Nostrand, 22:175-77

American Party, 8:194; 9:38, 39, 100, 102, 103, 108, 112, 115; 16:81, 285; 22:228; 24:169, 170, 171, 176, 180; 27:312; *see also* Know Nothing Party

American Potash and Chemical Co., 17:117

American Protective Association, 19:73
American Raisin Co., 25:32
American Republican Party, 9:17
American River, 2:206; 6:247; 7:7, 8, 14;
    11:107-8, 230; 12:65, 66-71; 13:25, 26,
    168, 174, 264-65; 16:127, 142;
    19:145-46; 22:329, 344; 23:58-59, 60,
    167-70; 24:331; 26:132; 33:330, 366;
    34:19
American Smelting and Refining Co.,
    32:20, 27, 35
American Telegraph Co., 29:345-56
    passim
American Theater, San Francisco, 4:59;
    7:283, 406; 9:179; 10:368, 371, 378, 390,
    395; 15:163-67 *passim*, 181, 186, 266,
    270, 271, 368; 16:81, 83, 184, 283, 285,
    340, 347; 17:81, 315; 20:296, 297, 298,
    304-5; 21:41-47 *passim*, 51, 64, 154,
    161; 22:266; 23:100-101; 28:37, 133;
    34:359; 37:330; 39:298
American Tract Society, 30:255, 265
American Trona Co., 17:117
American Trust Co., 23:190; 25:230,
    241; 32:375; 37:268
American Valley Ranch, 9:69
"Americus" (pseud.), 14:20-21
Ames, Alden, 32:184
Ames, Charles, 10:297
Ames, Charles Gordon, 33:182
Ames, Clark, 14.178, 181
Ames, Dorothy, 33:182
Ames, George Walcott, Jr., 17:288;
    "Horse Marines: California, 1846,"
    18:72-84; coauth., "California
    Preparations to Meet the Walla Walla
    Invasion, 1846," 21:9-21; ed. "A
    Doctor Comes to California: The
    Diary of John S. Griffin," 21:193-224,
    333-57; 22:41-66; ed. "Gillespie and
    the Conquest of California,"
    17:123-40, 271-84, 325-50
Ames, Hiram, 19:132, 138; 29:338, 339
Ames, John Judson, 6:11; 9:196-98, 200;
    11:389; 13:297; 24:275; 31:36; art. on
    press of, 9:193-200
Ames, Julian, 36:128
Ames, Thaddeus Mather, 19:125, 128-29,
    140; 27:226; 30-164
Ames, Thaddeus Mather and Mary Ann
    (Gregson), 19:125, 128, 129, 140
Ames & Pendleton, 31:36-37, 46, 47
Amesquita, Manuel, 14:6
Amesti, Carmen, 29:26
Amesti, José, 29:26

Amesti Ranch, 23:348
Amethyst (ship), 12:226
Amigos, Valle de los, 26:52
"Amity and Enterprise Company,"
    23:276; 30:237-38
Among the Mormons, ed. Mulder and
    Mortensen, rev., 37:369
Amorós, Juan, 16:111, 115; 38:104-5, 111
Amory & Co., 28:360
Amphibians, 12:208, 305
Amphitrite (ship), 15:171, 173, 182;
    16:80; 17:85; 23:192; 27:208
"A. M. Rosborough, Special Indian
    Agent," by Alex J. Rosborough,
    26:201-7
Amsberry (L.A., 1862), 3:165, 167
Amy (Marysville, 1858), 9:345, 347, 350,
    367, 370, 371
Amy, G. & O. (Gustave and Oscar),
    9:51, 69, 266; 30:258, 259; store, illus.,
    9: opp. 62; 30: opp. 257
Amy, Gustave, 30:359; *see also* Amy,
    G. & O.
Amy, John W., 15:29
Amyx, Fleming, 40:311
Anacapa Islands, 7:47, 74, 352-54, 388,
    389; 21:321
Anaheim, 32:328, 340-41, 343; 34:301,
    314; 39:88-89; *see also Gazette*
Anaheim, "the Mother Colony," by
    MacArthur, rev., 39:88-89
Anáhuac, 5:215
Anais (ship), 12:349
Ana María (Indian, 1822), 2:341
Anchorage (old Spanish), San
    Francisco Bay, 25:319-24
Anchor Insurance Co., 26:256
Ancon, definition of, 3:324
Andalusia (ship), 27:366
Andersen, Henry Mattei, 28:188
Anderson (Nevada Co. or Yuba Co.,
    1854, 1857), 8:200; 9:139, 145
Anderson, Mrs. (Marysville, 1858),
    9:347
Anderson, Judge (Nevada City, 1859),
    11:232
Anderson (San Francisco, 1864), 24:263
Anderson (Yosemite, 1869), 5:340
Anderson, A., 34:19, 20
Anderson, Alden, 38:356, 357; 39:21, 22
Anderson, Allen L., 40:350
Anderson, Alexander, 20:366; 34:253
Anderson, Amelia, 33:352
Anderson, Amos, 9:61
Anderson, Bern, *Surveyor of the Sea...*

Captain George Vancouver, rev., 39:368-71

Anderson, Chris, 34:20

Anderson, David, bk. rev. by, 7:287-88

Anderson, David C., 15:169; 21:53, 63

Anderson, Frank, 17:172

Anderson, Frank Barstow, obit., 14:413-14

Anderson, J. T., 36:65

Anderson, James, 10:62, 75; 11:9

Anderson, James H., 27:349

Anderson, James R., 10:52, 75; 21:46

Anderson, John, 3:118

Anderson, John Henry, 21:47-48

Anderson, John Q., 33:284; "Emerson and California," 33:241-48

Anderson, Joseph A., 22:2, 20

Anderson, Ludwig, 9:188

Anderson, Mary, 21:243; 35:141

Anderson, N. E., 18:373

Anderson, Nancy, 28:92-93, 284

Anderson, Robert (dragoon, 1846), 18:77

Anderson, Robert (Ft. Sumter hero), 19:229, 366; 31:203

Anderson, Robert M., 9:42, 45; 15:377

Anderson, Stephen, 6:263; 16:223, 23:206, 210, 216, 217, 303, 305, 321, 331

Anderson, Thomas H., 9:269

Anderson, Vance, 32:12

Anderson, W. A., 23:348

Anderson, Walter, 33:363

Anderson, William (Monterey, 1837), 15:239; 23:348

Anderson, William (Lake Co., 1850), 24:51

Anderson, William C., 24:263; 34:233

Anderson, Winslow, 30:67, 69, 71

Anderson (H. W.) & (H. J.) Seaman, 30:361

Anderson Peak, 34:20

Anderson Valley, phot., 33: opp. 360

"Anderson Valley, Mendocino Co.," by T. Albert Strobridge, 33:361-67

Andes (ship), 8:331

Andre, Louis, 22:347; 23:24

Andrés (Indian, 1846), 25:299

Andres, Chris, 24:263

Andrés, Mateo, 27:310

Andrés de la Asumpción, Fr., 7:274, 298, 300, 337, 349, 357, 359, 367, 370, 378, 379; 8:43, 54; 36:228

Andrew Jackson (ship), 29:106; 38:332

Andrews, Dr. (San Juan del Sur, 1852), 36:143, 144

Andrews, A., 9:172; lawsuits, 9:66, 132, 167, 168, 169

Andrews, A. R., 9:115

Andrews, Allen, 33:256

Andrews, Augustus A. and Rosalía (de Haro), 14:130

Andrews, Charles, 9:390

Andrews, E. C., 4:51, 55, 56

Andrews, Mrs. Frank H. (Rosalie Younger), obit., 19:191-92

Andrews, J. D., 9:149

Andrews, Reuben C., 20:114

Andrews, Thomas, 28:198

"Andrew S. Hallidie as Writer and Speaker," by Edgar M. Kahn, 25:1-16

"Andrew Smith Hallidie," by Edgar M. Kahn, 19:144-56

Andrew Sublette, Rocky Mountain Prince, by Nunis, rev., 40:256-57

Andrew Welch (ship), 27:200, 201

Andromède (ship), 8:317

Andross, Mrs. Albert Knight (née Powell), 26:93

Angel, Andrés, 40:31

Angel, Eugene, 12:11

Angel, Juan, 40:31

Angel, Myron, 1:156; 12:11, 15

Angel family (1847), 16:136, 138

Angeles (ship), 15:359, 360, 361

Angeles Bay, 11:371-72

Angelina (ship), 11:200, 206, 344-45

Angelino, Blas, 11:69

Angelis, David, 28:137

Angel Island, 15:165; 21:312; 27:108, 294; 33:231, 235, 237

Angell, Frank, 37:41

Angell, Horace B., 7:117

Angellotti, Frank Mario, 30:69

Angelo's Ranch, 22:245, 246, 251

Angel's Camp, 11:290, 324, 326; 15:368; 20:101; 22:74, 76-77; 26:2, 10; 27:158, 163; 30:238, 362; 38:309, 362; 40:249

Angel's Creek, 22:71

Angenette (ship), 22:170

Anglin, Margaret, 40:144, 154

Anglo-California Gold Mining and Dredging Co., 12:70, 73-76; 15:179

Anglo Saxon (ship), 30:356

Angola (ship), 3:109; 6:364, 368; 27:300

Angus, James, 21:330

Angwin, Mrs. (Elvira Ellen Mendenhall), 13.12

Angwin (place), 35:159

Anian, Strait of, 1:192; 2:141; 3:218-19, 267; 6:96; 7:233, 234, 240, 249, 250, 264,

296, 305; 8:26-31 *passim*, 38, 51;
10:313; 36:216-17, 238
Animal Life in the Yosemite, by
Grinnell and Storer, rev., 3:299-300
Animals, domestic, *see* Livestock
Animals, wild, 2:58, 200, 287; 5:368;
7:361; 11:114; 12:208, 290-95 *passim*,
304-5; 13:68; 14:103-4, 139, 142; 16:
No. 1, Pt. 2, pp. 30, 44; 17:28, 29;
20:41, 42, 224; 22:198-212 *passim*,
323-43 *passim*; 23:353; 24:329; bk. on,
rev., 3:299-300; *see also* names of
animals
Anita (ship), 27:204; 33:264, 269, 340
Anita Rocks, 25:322, 323
Ankrim, William, 22:2, 20, 21
Ann (ship), 27:163
Anna (ship), 22:309
Anna Bishop Opera Troupe, 14:74
Ann Alexander (ship), 13:7
"Annals of Los Angeles," by J. Gregg
Layne, 13:195-234, 301-54
Annals of San Francisco, by Soulé,
Gihon, and Nisbet, 30:252
Annenthal (warm springs), 13:37
Annis (on *Westward Ho*, 1852), 26:227;
28:322
Annis, Jerome B., 26:171
Anniversary Island, 8:166, 246, 249; *see
also* Dead Man's Island
Ann Welch (bark), 27:190
"Anonymous Narrative," about Francis
Drake, 16: No. 1, Pt. 2, pp. 15, 31;
36:24-25
"Another Huntington Acquisition," by
Henry R. Wagner, 5:196-97
Anselin, Alfred (or Albert), 12:57;
22:52; 29:336; 33:103, 106, 120-23
Anselin (Ancelin or Anselm), J., 6:45,
46; 32:107, 108; 39:10-13 *passim*
Anson, George, 2:309, 311, 321
Antelope (ship, 1854), 9:55, 72, 253,
277; 10:276, 281, 282, 358, 373; 15:179,
273; 16:79, 339, 343; 22:248; 27:302,
307; 30:128; 32:223
Antelope Peak, 34:217, 218
Antelopes, 1:114; 2:200, 236; 5:128;
10:213; 12:290, 305; 13:20, 68, 69;
14:104; 22:200, 201, 204, 211, 214,
327-43 *passim*; 23:19, 33, 36, 37, 38,
123-34 *passim*; 25:3; *see also* Animals,
wild
Antelope Springs, 18:300
Antelope Valley, Kern and Los Angeles
cos., 10:212, 213, 214, 218; 40:216

Antelope Valley, Mono Co., 26:235;
34:213
Anthony, Charles Volney, 26:166
Anthony, Edward G. H., 33:372
Anthony, Elihu, 2:182, 192-96;
26:166-67, 169
Anthony, James, 22:35; & Co., 30:358
Anthony, Thomas R., 13:32
Anthony, Walter, 20:143; 25:240, 244
Anti-Electionists, *see* Democrats
Anti-Know Nothings, 9:35, 43, 73,
103-4, 108, 109
Anti-Lecomptonites, *see* Democrats
Anti-Vigilance movement, 9:249, 250,
251, 260, 275, 276, 283, 284; 10:50, 73;
see also Law and Order
Antillan, Pedro (Pierre Artésien),
12:333
Antiquarian Book Store, San Francisco,
30:254, 255, 356, 365
Antoine Co. *v.* The Ridge Co., 10:363,
364
Anton Hernandez (ship), 6:312
Antonio (Indian, 1846), 5:309-10;
13:104-5
Antonio de la Ascención, Fr. 7:264,
266; 8:51, 52; 23:222, 225; 36:217,
228, 231-32, 235; accounts of
Vizcaíno's voyage, 7:269-73, 295-378;
8:26-40, 55-68
Antonio de la Concepción, Fr. 1:165
"Antonio Melendrez," by James M.
Clarke, 12:318-22
"Anton Roman, Argonaut of Books,"
by Madeleine B. Stern, 28:1-18
Anza, Juan Bautista de, 1:162, 163;
10:214; 14:102; 20:239; 23:372; 27:63;
33:14; 34:195, 229; bk. on, rev.,
11:387-88; *see also* Anza expeditions
Anza expeditions, 1:162-63; 3:100, 225;
10:214, 216; 11:387-88; 14:99; 15:59;
20:235-36, 239; 27:63; 30:2; 33:14;
34:194; 36:4; 38:183; bk. on, rev.,
10:84-85; map showing route, 10:
opp. 211
Anza, Lupita de, 25:192
Ánzar, Juan Miguel, 5:305; 29:26
Ánzar, Mrs. Juan Miguel (María
Antonia Pacheco), 29:26
Anza's California Expeditions, by
Bolton, rev., 10:84-85
Aora (ship), 37:119
Apache, Navaho, and Spaniard, by
Forbes, rev., 40:158-60
Apalátegui, Antonio, 13:217

Apel, John, 23:110; 38:34
Apiculture, *see* Bees
Apis, Pablo, 26:58
Aplin, Marie, 24:232
Apolitana, *see* Politana
Apollo (ship), 22:276; 33:376; 38:40
App, John and Leanna (Donner), 19:96
Appeal, Marysville, 10:296, 394; 21:332; 30:128-30; 33:203-4; 34:60, 61
Appeal-Democrat, Marysville, 14:225
Apperson, Phoebe, *see* Hearst, Mrs. George
Applegarth, Mrs. George Adrian (Gwendolyn Powers), 31:279, 282
Applegate (Empire Mills, 1861), 4:250
Applegate, Charles, 28:228
Applegate, Jesse, 16:53, 55; 21:128, 135; 25:255-56, 263; 28:209, 210, 228
Applegate, Lindsay, 28:228
Apples and cider, 2:273; 5:370, 371, 373; 6:39; 12:193, 199, 200, 205-6, 258; 17:41; 18:120; 20:260; 26:113, 119, 122; 27:119, 122; 28:40; 33:362
Appleton (San Jose, 1850), 27:130
Appleton, David E., 18:333; 30:252
Appleton, John N., 4:26
Appleton, Nathan, 34:361
Appleton, William E., 26:9
Appleton (H. A.) & Co., 9:275
Appleton (William) & Co., 8:297-302 *passim;* 19:48-49, 53, 56; 23:201-2, 215
Appreciation of James Wood Coffroth, An, by O'Day, rev., 5:311-12
"Approach of the Frontiers, The," address by Frederic L. Paxson, 12:367
Apricots, 17:41; 25:31; 27:119
Aptos, 38:259-60
Aqueducts (flumes), 9:78-79; 11:173, 229, 234-42 *passim*, 329-30, 335, 337; 12:327-28; 19:146, 294; 26:104-5; 29:194-96; 35:209, 226, illus., 9:138; 11:239, 325, 334; 29: opp. 200; *see also* Canals and Ditches; Gold mining; Sluicing
Aquila (ship), 25:42; 33:236
Aquilar, Capt. (Colorado R., 1862), 22:170
Aquino, Tomás de, 7:298, 300, 332, 337, 357, 359, 376
Arab (ship), 12:230; 14:127
Arabian (ship), 28:292
Arago (ship), 25:44
Arago, Cape, 10:329
Aram, Joseph, 13:29; 14:18, 163; 29:19, 24; fac. sig., 10: opp. 159

Aram & Belcher, 29:24
"Arañas, Las," 26:33
Aranda, Genevieve (Lafonso), 36:322
Aranzazu (ship), 2:282, 293; 10:318, 322, 338, 340; 15:60, 68
Araujo, Francisco, 13:218
Arbell, Capt. (James Orbell?), 3:115
Arbor, The (restaurant), Marysville, 14:394
Arbor Day (1886), 32:234, 235
"Arboreal Archive, An," by Allen L. Chickering, 34:19-20
Arbuthnot, execution of, 11:19-20
Arcade Hotel, Sacramento, 11:55
Arcade House, San Francisco, 15:280
Arcade Saloon, Camptonville, 9:152
Arcata, 5:145; 21:189, 190; 30:360; 33:67; 34:269; 38:308; *see also* Union Town
Arce, Francisco, 1:82, 134, 170; 3:284; 4:378; 6:137, 144, 145, 272, 364; 7:79; 9:81; 17:164; 21:311, 312, 315-16; 25:122; 27:107, 108; 29:262, 263, 276, 321
Arce, José de, 37:112-19 *passim*, 241-45 *passim*
Arce, José Ignacio, 12:222; 13:124
"Archaeological Evidence of . . . Cermeño's California Visit," by Robert F. Heizer, 20:315-28; 21:82
"Archaeological Exploration of Sixteenth-Century Indian Mounds at Drake's Bay," by Clement W. Meighan and Robert F. Heizer, 31:99-108
"Archaeological Investigation of Sutter Sawmill Site in 1947," by Robert F. Heizer, 26:134-59
Archaeological research, 20:315-28; 25:218; 26:134-59; 31:99-108; 33:87-88
Archambeau, Auguste, 1:125, 131
"Archbishop Joseph Sadoc Alemany," address by John B. McGloin, 29:376-77
Arche d'alliance (ship), 22:300
Archer, Katie, 21:63
Archibald (Colorado R., 1850), 22:20
Archibald, Arnold E., 26:380-81
Archibald, John, 26:229
Archibald Gracie (ship), 15:364; 18:12
"Archibald Menzies' Journal of the Vancouver Expedition," ed. Alice Eastwood, 2:265-340
Architect (ship), 20:31, 45-46

Architects and architecture, 4:395;
    19:250; 25:12; 19:250; 27:173, 174;
    31:27; arts. on, 25:54-56; 38:31-46;
    39:193-207; addresses on, 5:414;
    32:376-78; bk. on, rev., 40:357-59
Architectural Follies in America, by
    Lancaster, rev., 40:357-59
"Architectural Legacy of Sacramento
    ... 19th Century Style," by Joseph A.
    Baird, Jr., 39:193-207
"Architectural Restoration of 'Lucky'
    Baldwin's 'Queen Anne' Cottage,"
    address by Maurice Block, 32:376-78
"Architecture of Santa Barbara
    Mission," address by Rev. Fr.
    Augustine, 5:414
Archuleta, Ignacio, 14:6
Archuleta, Miguel G., 16:103-6
Archulete (or Archilette, place), 10:37
Arctic (ship), 15:183
Arcularius, Frank, 33:189
Arcularius, Genevieve, 33:188-89
Arcularius, William, 33:188-89
Arellanes, "Chino," 18:268
Arellanes, Jesús, 18:261
Arellano, Alonso de, 7:146, 148-50,
    172-73, 182, 191, 192
Arellano, Felipe, 37:207
Arellano, Juan Ramírez, 13:202
Arellano, Manuel, 13:203
Arellano, Manuel Ramírez, 14:6
Arena, Point, 7:25, 26, 57; 9:208; 10:330,
    335; 30:311
Arenas, Cayetano, 21:312; 23:254;
    27:105, 250-52
Arenas, Luis, 13:223; 27:250-51
Arents, Hiram, 9:35
Argelago, Carmen, 33:359
Argenti, Felix, 16:82, 182; 17:174;
    33:372; 34:244, 248, 249; *v.* City of
    San Francisco, 15:186, 282, 366-67,
    370; 16:182; *see also* Metcalf *v.*
    Argenti
Argenti (F.) & Co., 34:244
Argenti, Cavallier & Co., 16:82
Argentina, 16:43-47
Argo, Mrs. Robert G. (Margaret
    Wilson), 26:187
Argo (ship), 11:341, 345, 348
Argonaut, The, San Francisco, 6:35;
    10:64, 96; 15:335-37
Argonaut (ship, 1790), 10:337; 20:80
Argonaut (ship, 1850), 23:366
Argonaut (ship, 1944), 23:189
Argonauts of '49, by Howe, rev., 2:81-83

Argos, Juan, 37:205, 211
Argüello, Concepción, 4:97-98; 27:89;
    40:4
Argüello, Gerónimo, 37:243
Argüello, Gervasio, 12:233; 14:251,
    259-60; 23:252; 27:333
Argüello, José Darío, 2:282; 11:29;
    12:191, 224-25, 231, 236, 241-42;
    15:140; 17:246; 23:2, 251; 25:364;
    36:182
Argüello, Mrs. José Darío (Ignacia
    Moraga), 36:182
Argüello, Luis Antonio, 6:256; 11:74:
    12:224-25, 242; 14:15, 128, 130, 197,
    16:110-11, 114-17; 17:246, 249; 20:239;
    21:378; 23:20, 251, 375; 27:333; 37:117,
    244-45, 248
Argüello, María Antonia, 36:182
Argüello, Santiago, 12:345; 13:223;
    14:235, 237, 245-46, 249-51, 259-60;
    16:216, 223, 226, 230; 17:231; 22:50-57
    passim, 65; 23:333; 26:56; 33:117-18;
    36:121, 182
Argüello, Mrs. Santiago (Pilar
    Ortega), 36:182
Argüello, Santiago E., 13:114, 124;
    14:232, 234, 237; 22:50, 53-57
Argüello, Mrs. Santiago E. (Guadalupe
    Estudillo), 36:182
Arguello, Point, 15:178
Arguello Boulevard Improvement Club,
    San Francisco, 33:376
Argüellos Quiñones, Lope de, 7:267
Argus, San Jose, 14:157
Argus, Stockton, 15:163; 20:162
Ariche, Pedro de, 3:309, 363-65
Ariel (ship), 6:377; 32:312
Arington, J. J., 26:204; *see also*
    Arrington, J. J.
Arizona, 6:31-32, 34-35; 9:301, 307, 308,
    315; 10:305; 12:3-4; 22:1-25 *passim,*
    151-74 *passim;* 34:126-42 *passim*
Arizona (play), 34:364
Arizona (ship), 22:171; 30:211; 31:59,
    60
Arizona and New Mexico Express Co.,
    22:162
Arizona Battalion, Confed. Army,
    6:32-33
Arizona City, 22:158
Arizona Exploring Expedition,
    37:204-11
Arizona Navigation Co., *see* Pacific and
    Colorado Steam Navigation Co.
Arizpe, Ramón, 23:7

Ark (ship), 2:94; 6:214
Arkles, Seth, 9:160
Arlington, J., 22:250
Arlt, Gustave Otto, 29:375
Armand, Capt. (of *Liberato*, 1862),
  19:41
Armand, or The Peer and the Peasant
  (play), 10:57, 77
Armas, Baltazar de, 7:300, 357, 377
Armenians, 30:305
Armer, Morris, 19:293
Armer, Ruth, 38:5
Armer (M.) & Bros., 19:292, 293
Armes, Charles W. and George W.,
  10:291
Armes, William Dallam, 20:141, 145;
  32:237-38
Armistead (d. Panama, 1849), 27:36
Armona, Matías de, 11:275
Armory Hall, Oakland, 19:105
Armory Hall, San Francisco, 15:164;
  29:251
Arms, *see* Weapons
Armsby, Leonora (Wood), 25:284-85;
  "San Francisco Symphony Orchestra:
  First Decade," 25:229-54; obits. of
  Lutie D. Goldstein, 34:181-82; Mrs.
  Sigmund Stern, 35:184-87
Arm's Mountain News Deposit,
  Downieville, 30:366
Armstead (Alviso, 1853), 29:40, 42
Armstrong, "Dr." (on *London*,
  1849-50), 7:213
Armstrong (Nevada City, 1862), 10:385
Armstrong, Edward I., 10:72
Armstrong, George, 14:222
Armstrong, James, 37:198
Armstrong, John, 15:240
Armstrong, John W., 27:134
Armstrong, Mrs. Richard F. (Arabella
  L. Hornsby), 20:114
Armstrong, Sarah, *see* Montgomery,
  Mrs. Allen
Armstrong, Thomas, 15:54
Armstrong, William R., 10:62
*Army Explorations in the American
  West 1803-63*, by Goetzmann, rev.,
  39:83
Army of Californians (1842-46),
  13:43-55, 100, 112, 118, 131, 133, 134,
  227-28; 17:144
Army of the West, 25:291-308; 26:26,
  46, 50, 57; 33:97-124 *passim*, 263, 267
Arnaud, H., 35:315
Arnaz, José, 4:169; 13:227; 18:167, 178

Arndt, Alvin, 4:45
Arnés, Padre, 6:161
Arnhold, Benjamin, 35:124
Arno (ship), 22:166, 169
Arnold, A. S., 33:5, 7-8, 149
Arnold, Benjamin W., 10:43, 357
Arnold, Henry H., 26:285-86; obit.,
  29:83-84
Arnold, John, 29:254
Arnold, Josiah, 14:177
Arnold, Lewis G., 14:364; 16:339
Arnold, Noah Sanford, 22:94
Arnold, Ralph, 37:274
Arnold, Thomas, 9:266
Arnold and Scott, 14:394
Arnold Ranch, San Luis Obispo Co.,
  36:15
Arnstein-Simon, 36:157
Aros, Dolores, 37:195
Around the Horn in '49, by Hall, rev.,
  7:197-98
*Around the Horn to the Sandwich
  Islands and California*, by Lyman, ed.
  Teggart, rev., 4:91-92
Around the World in Eighty Days
  (play), 37:227
Arrah-na-Pogue (play), 21:146
Arrajeta, Joanes de, 2:150
Arrastra, 3:202; 35:43
Arrillaga, José Joaquín de, 2:311-12;
  4:147; 10:345; 12:191, 219, 222, 241;
  14:11, 13; 15:59-60; 16:103; 17:121;
  23:5, 16; 30:316; 36:6
Arrington, J. J., 26:204(?); 31:229
Arrington, William, 17:174
Arrowhead Reservoir Co., 27:113
Arrow Rock, 23:289, 298
Arrowsmith, Aaron, map by, 19:221
Arroyo de la Cuesta, Felipe, 25:135-36;
  36:334-35; 37:305-6
Arroyo Seco, 13:74, 159
Art and artists, 5:198; 10:270, 406; 15:54,
  170, 172, 183, 213-15, 383; 18:180; 21:3,
  327, 329; 22:33-39 *passim*; 23:96;
  24:264, 265, 266; 28:35; 29:276;
  30:136-39; 37:19-38, 89; bk. on, rev.,
  2:173-77; Sloss collection, 37:21-38;
  see also Audubon; Ayres, T. A.;
  Barbieri; Bierstadt; Brookes, S. M.;
  Butman, F. A.; Eastman, Harrison;
  Edouart, Alexander; Hill, Thomas;
  Herrick, William F.; Jewett, W. D.
  and W. S.; Kane, Paul; Keith,
  William; Kern, E. M.; Nahl;

Panoramas; Suría; Tavernier, Jules; *and* Cartoons; Photography
Art associations, *see* Art unions
Arteaga, Ignacio, 40:238
Artémise, L' (frigate, 1839), 8:116, 117; 12:49; 18:315-18 *passim*, 325, 328
Artémise, L' (corvette, 1850s), 15:171, 173; 27:208
Artésien, Pierre, 12:333
Arther (or Arthur), James P., 4:164; 5:132; 23:200, 207, 217, 320, 333
Art, Humor and Humanity of Mark Twain, ed. Brashear and Rodney, rev., 38:368-70
Arthur, J. D., 15:35
"Artifacts from Excavation of Sutter's Sawmill," by Franklin Fenenga, 26:160-62
Artigues, Louis, 21:329
Artillery Company, San Francisco, 15:164, 174
Art of the Old World in New Spain and the Mission Days of Alta California, by Holway, rev., 2:173-77
Artraya, Enrique, 15:40
Art unions, San Francisco, 15:183; 28:35; *see also* California Art Union
Arundel-Harcourt, *see* Harcourt, Thomas Arundel-
Aruz, José, 12:232
Arzaga, Manuel, 13:218-21
Ascención, *see* Antonio de la Ascención
"Ascent of Mt. Shasta in 1861," from Journal of Richard G. Stanwood, 6:69-76
Aschanblan, C., 31:333
Ascher, Leonard W., 15:15, 19, 20
Ashburner, William, 1:13; 4:16, 24; 6:354; 36:45
Ashburner, Mrs. William (Emilia Brewer Field), 36:45, 50-51
Ashby, Eleanor, *see* Bancroft, Eleanor A.
Ashby, George E., 34:337
Ashby, Mark, 17:44
Ashford, Lewis Joseph, 10:178, 183, 188
Ashim, Bark, 17:218
Ashley (Bidwell's Bar, 1861), 29:123
Ashley, Delos R., 9:42, 46, 107; 30:147; 38:314
Ashley, Edward, 30:297, 300
Ashley, William Henry, 3:29; 4:105, 109, 110-28 *passim*, 139, 140, 279; 25:367; 28:119; cor., 37:5-7
Ashley's River, 22:233, 234

Ashton, Tom, 11:58
Asia (ship), 37:258-59
Asiatic-Mexican Company, 25:69-76, 150-68
Askin, Albert, 9:57
Askin, Richard, 9:144
Asmodeus (play), 10:379
Asphalt, 8:157; 10:300; 15:235; 19:203; 23:239
Aspinwall, G. W., 12:75, 16:199
Aspinwall, William Henry, 13:244-47, 251, 386, 389, 397; 15:275; 16:72; 17:308; 26:194, 199; 31:37, 38; port., 13: opp. 389; *see also* Howland & Aspinwall
Aspinwall (Colón), 16:184; 19:290
Aspiroz, Salvador, 15:141
Assai (Arab, 1862), 9:319
Assay offices, 15:244; 16:35-38; 24:183; *see also* Gold
Assembly Rooms, San Francisco, 10:374; 15:369
Associaçao Portuguesa Protectora e Beneficiente, 35:244
Associated Auctioneers, 15:174
Associated Farmers of California, 31:130-31
Associated Veterans of the Mexican War, 24:48
Association for the Protection of Property, 15:163-64
Assommoir, L' (play), 21:256
Asti, 30:309
Astigarribia, Francisco de, 7:173
Astin, Samuel C., 15:369
Astles, John B., 27:185; "Rev. Dr. W. A. Scott, a Southern Sympathizer," 27:149-56
Astor, John Jacob, 12:79, 225; 24:230
Astor House, Monterey, 11:132-33
Astor House (scow), 27:259, 261-62, 265
Astoria, 2:126, 134; 8:98; 17:135; 20:22; 24:231
Astoria (ship), 17:172
Astrea (ship), 3:216
Astrolable, L' (ship), 15:213, 215, 216; 20:51, 52; 26:371
Asumpción, *see* Andrés de la Asumpción
As You Like It (play), 35:142
Atacames, Ecuador, 13:7-8
Atalanta (ship), *see David Paddock*
Atanacio (Indian, 1831), 16:224
Atascadero, *see* Ranchos: Atascadero
Atcha (ship), 39:110

Atchison, Anna, 10:361
Atchison, Ben, 8:211, 362; 9:69
Atchison, David R., 19:361
Atchison, John H., 8:211, 341, 352, 362;
    9:53, 168; 10:177, 181, 182, 189, 260;
    11:54, 55, 56; lawsuit, 10:180; *see also*
    Atchison, John K.
Atchison, John K., 9:50, 58, 69: *see also*
    Atchison, John H.
Atchison, Lizzie, 33:200
Atchison, Sam, 10:359
Atchison, Silas, 8:211, 346, 362; 9:69,
    162, 164, 166, 287; 10:172
Atchison, Mrs. Silas (Emma Phillips),
    9:287
Atchison & Co., 9:63, 136-37, 164
Atchison and Rice's Turnpike, 8:213;
    9:69
Atchison's Bar, Yuba Co., 8:338, 341,
    355; 9:54
Atensio, Gregorio, 26:32
Athenaeum (Negro assoc.), San
    Francisco, 38:303
Athenaeum Reading Rooms, San
    Francisco, 38:314
Athenaeum Saloon, San Francisco,
    22:266-67; 28:37
Athenaeum Theatre, San Francisco,
    20:293
Atherton, Emily, 14:176, 182
Atherton, Faxon Dean, 12:146; 13:192;
    14:320, 343; 22:96; 29:150, 166; 32:185;
    33:372; 38:326-27; letters to,
    28:113-14, 342
Atherton, Florence, *see* Eyre, Mrs.
    Edward L.
Atherton, George H. Bowen, 40:2
Atherton, Gertrude Franklin (Horn),
    17:356; 19:110; 28:33; 36:110;
    addresses, "Rezánov and Concha
    Argüello," 7:95; "The Pageant of San
    Francisco Society," 22:84; obit. of
    Charles Caldwell Dobie, 22:91; art.
    on, 40:1-10; phot., 40: bef. 1
Atherton, Robert, 28:113, 114, 342
Atherton, William, 5:133
Atherton (place), 13:192
Atkins (Sonoranian Camp, 1848 or '49),
    13:384
Atkins, Mary, 16:185; 23:191; 24:63-64,
    72, 165, 179; 26:354; 29:55; 31:86; *see
    also* Young Ladies' Seminary
Atkins, William B., 15:168
Atkinson (on *Westward Ho*, 1853),
    28:322

Atkinson (Kern R. and S.F., 1855),
    15:274
Atkinson, F. A., 29:39, 55; 34:245
Atkinson, M., 14:206, 211, 226
Atlantic (ship), 13:250; 16:77
Atlantic and Pacific Co., 34:209
Atlantic and Pacific Express, *see* Wells
    Fargo & Co.
Atlantic and Pacific Railroad, 22:162;
    27:272, 339, 340
Atlantic & Pacific Telegraph Co.,
    28:285; 39:305
Atlantic Cable, 9:388; 11:306;
    celebration at Marysville, 9:360, 367,
    389
Atmore, Edward A., 5:327
Atole, 15:220
Atondo y Antillón, Isidro, 8:80;
    26:309-19; 27:310
Atrevida (ship), 3:217-18, 232-34, 236;
    15:214
Attai (Chinese slave girl), 32:305-6
Attitiewa, *see* Ottitiewa
Attwood (North Bloomfield, 1871),
    29:204
Atwater, John, 22:243
Atwater (place), 35:242
Atwell, A. B., 31:333
Atwill, Joseph Fairfield, 9:26; 15:176;
    22:31, 33; 28:285; 32:89
Atwill's Musical Repository, San
    Francisco, 28:38; 30:113
Atwood (from Ore., 1848), 13:12-17
    passim
Atwood, H., 29:22
Atwood, Leroy, 34:351-52
Atwood, Melville, 6:341; 11:243, 246
Au, *see* Ah
Aubert, Jacques M., 22:304
Aubertine, Don José Frederico, 29:189
Aubertine, George F., 29:189
Aubertine, Mrs. George F. (Miriam
    Brand), 29:190
Aubichon, Baptiste, 22:217, 222; 23:38
Auble, E. F., 31:127-28
Aubrey (Oroville, 1860), 10:251
Aubry, Francis Xavier, 12:22, 80
Auburn, 2:203-6; 4:258, 259; 9:368, 392;
    11:232, 236; 13:14, 15, 19, 24-26;
    15:364; 18:361-64; 20:331; 30:238,
    260-61, 361; 31:247, 273; 38:38; 39:289;
    newspapers, 18:361; 20:161; 25:380
Auburn City, Ore., 16:40
Auburn Hotel, 18:361-62
Auchampaugh, Phillip G., 32:159

Auckland (ship), 23:336; 28:38
Auclair, Jacquard, 39:342
Auclimbault, Peter, 15:172
Auction Lunch, San Francisco, 16:340;
    17:82; 39:301
Auctions, 8:78-79; 14:388, 402; 15:50;
    38:365-67; in San Francisco, 8:279;
    15:174; 22:273-74; 30:109, 254, 256,
    264, 265, 356, 358, 364; 38:365; *see also*
    "Auction Sales of Californiana"
"Auction Sales of Californiana," 1:96-99;
    2:77-80; 3:191-95; 6:192-94; 7:405;
    8:78-79, 278-79
Aud, Francis L., 9:151, 157, 169-70, 269,
    349, 353, 357; 10:40, 48-49, 57, 62, 66,
    382-83; 14:397; 15:23, 35-36
Audley Clarke (ship), 30:42; 36:309
Audubon, John James, 21:290; 22:67
Audubon, John Woodhouse,
    21:289-310; 22:67, 70-71; 23:168, 176;
    drawings by, 21: opp. 289, opp. 300
Audubon, Victor, 21:290, 302, 303, 304,
    307
Audubon (ship), 15:377; 16:83
"Audubon's Ill-Fated Western
    Journey," by Jeanne S. Van Nostrand,
    21:289-310
Auerbach, Herbert S., ed. Ferris, *Life in
    the Rocky Mountains*, rev., 19:281
Auger, Edouard, 22:273, 274, 276
Augur, Christopher Columbus, 28:202
Augustine, Father, *see* Hobrecht
Aulick, John H., 2:250
Aurélie, L' (ship), 29:81
Aurifère, L' (company), 22:299, 301
Aurora, Nev., 4:67; 7:91-92, 113-19;
    24:277; 26:236-44 *passim*; newspapers,
    7:117; 26:241; illus., 7:114
Aurora (ship), 29:1, 6, 16, 18, 167, 170;
    30:125
Austin, Capt. (Sacramento, 1849), 20:38
Austin, Alexander, 19:237
Austin, Henry, 30:59
Austin, Horace, 11:9
Austin, James, 24:237, 242
Austin, James D. (James Defenbaugh),
    9:245
Austin, Miss M. F., 25:30-31
Austin, Mary (Hunter), 12:77; 30:185
Austin, Mrs. Nat, 16:81
Austin, Samuel C., 9:44, 45; 15:369
Austin & Co., 15:164
Austin, Nev., 6:346, 347-50; 10:394;
    23:260; 28:379
Australia, 19:328-29, 336; 24:169;

26:279-80; 28:277; 30:15-35, 91, 306,
    307; 32:245-47, 259, 273; 33:274
Australian Steamship Line, 27:267
Autenreith, E. L., 8:5, 10, 13
Authors' Carnival, San Francisco, 31:340
"Authorship of the So-Called 'Gordon
    Manuscript,' The," by Helen S. Carr,
    8:374-77
*Autobiography and Memorial of Jacob
    Detweiler*, rev., 2:83-84
Automobiling, early, 32:378-79
Auzerais House, San Jose, 14:167
Avalos, Crecencio, 37:201
Avarice and Revenge (play), 15:48
Aveloss, Mme. (opera singer, 1858),
    9:391
Avenal Land and Oil Co., 31:298
Avenali, Ettore, 31:304
Avenir, L', Los Angeles, 39:342, 346
Avenir National, L', San Francisco,
    39:221, 346
Averett, Alexander, 30:291
Averill, Chester, 4:16; 7:121, 126, 129
Avery, Capt. (Colorado R., 1864),
    22:170, 171
Avery, Benjamin Parke, 9:181; 21:326,
    332; 28:7, 9; 30:361; 33:203; 36:200,
    202; art. on, 30:125-49
Avery, Mrs. Benjamin Parke (Mary A.
    Fuller), 30:130
Avery, Howard, 30:291, 302; 31:62, 166,
    172
Avery, Samuel Putnam and Mary Ann
    (Ogden), 30:125, 139, 148
Avieta, José, 10:30, 31
Ávila, Anastasio, 13:207, 208, 211
Ávila, Antonio Ignacio, 10:36
Ávila, Concepción, *see* Fuller, Mrs. John
    C.
Ávila, Francisca, 1:258
Ávila, Francisco and Encarnación, house
    of, 13:303, 310, 313
Ávila, H., 13:327
Avila, J. B., 35:242
Ávila, José María, 13:211, 212, 213;
    27:337
Ávila, Juan, 12:335; 21:357; *see also*
    Abila
Ávila, Miguel, 12:133; 18:163, 176
Avila, Pablo, 27:92; ed. and trans.
    "Joseph de Morago Commissioned
    Lieutenant," 27:63-64; "Naming of
    the Elector-Designate, Santa Barbara,
    1830," 27:333-38
Avila, Pedro Antonio, 29:237

Avilar, José María, 12:120
Avon (brig., 1830s), 14:314-15, 341, 343; 23:318, 320, 332; 35:197, 199, 200
Avon (str., 1850), 18:9; 39:144
Awan, Adrian, 26:187
Awani (Indian rancheria), 28:333
Awards of Merit, California Historical Society, 38:74-76; 39:64, 71-72
Axe, Ruth (Frey), 29:97; 39:71; trans. "A Trip to the Mining Regions in . . . 1859," by Eduard Vischer, 11:224-46, 321-38; obit. of Mrs. Henry R. Wagner, 36:185-86
Axton, Mrs. Henry (Esther Sweasy), 27:189
Ayacucho (ship), 14:344, 345; 23:303, 305, 318, 320, 328, 331, 332
Ayala, Dr. Juan, 30:226
Ayala, Juan Manuel de, 9:205, 210; 13:180; 23:372; 25:320; 27:293
Ayala, Juan Nepomucino, 14:261; 16:354-55
Ayala, Pablo, 16:351, 359, 368-69
Ayer, Miss (Sacramento, 1859), 10:176
Ayer, Milo J., 22:138
Ayer, Washington, 4:202-5
Ayers, Mrs. (on *Independence*, 1853), 6:358

Ayers, George Washington, *see* Eayrs
Ayers, James Joseph, 39:4; *Gold and Sunshine*, rev., 1:101-2
Ayers, Samuel, 13:330
Aylett, W. D., 10:65
Ayres (Marysville, 1850), 14:215
Ayres, James, 29:237
Ayres, Julia, 29:294
Ayres, Mrs. Maria D., 29:294
Ayres, Thomas A., 1:273; 4:13; 5:336-37; 22:38; 23:376; art. on, 20:275-79; drawing by, 5: opp. 336
Ayres, Venancio, 21:305
Ayres, William, 27:318; 28:55
Ayres, William O., 17:176; 21:366
Ayres, Wot, 15:54
Ayuntamientos, 1:25-34 *passim*; 8:162; 13:209; 14:8, 220, 224; 16:182; 21:125; 33:278-81
Azalene (schr. yacht), 31:154-57 *passim*
Azcárate y Lezama, Juan Francisco, 24:289, 292; 25:267, 362-63
Azevedo (Acebedo or Acevedo), Ignacio, 16:241
Azoreans in California, 35:233, 237-46 *passim; see also* Portuguese
Azusa, 32:328

B

B., de (L.A. to Inyo Co., 1874), 17:99-110 *passim*
"B. T." (pseud.), 24:130, 352
Baash, L. F., 33:381
Babb, Lorenzo H., 14:221, 401; 15:31
Babbitt, E. B., 9:308
Babcock (Yosemite, 1852), 5:332-33
Babcock, E. S., 35:349-50
Babcock, Graham, 35:359
Babcock, Jasper, 11:9
Babcock, William (Ft. Vancouver, 1850), 2:128
Babcock, William (S.F., 1913), 25:249
Babcock, William Fitzgerald, 19:232
Babcock & West, 18:45
Babes in Toyland (play), 33:40-41
Babies' Aid, San Francisco, 31:71; 33:376
Babson, Seth, 38:33

Baby, Frank T., 11:10; 32:310, 312
"Baby, J.," *see* Dupuy, Edouard Joseph
Bacallaos, Strait of, 3:393-96; 6:293
Bach, F. de, 10:382
Bache, Alexander Dallas, 11:300-301, 304, 306; 35:326
Bache, Hartman, 15:374; 35:326-29, 333
Bache, Richard, 16:62, 75
Bachelder, George, 13:32
Bachelier (S.F., 1855), 39:150, 151
Bachelors' Homestead Bill, 38:331-32
Bachelor Valley, 32:364
Bachelot, J. Alexis, 8:132, 133
Bachman, Charles, 29:224
Bachman, Jacob Henry, 21:289-310; "The Diary of a 'Used-up' Miner," ed. Jeanne S. Van Nostrand, 22:67-83
Bacigalupi, E. W., obit. of Henry Carl Maier, 39:355

Bacigalupi, James A., 37:269, 274, 347-48, 352, 353
Backenstoe, Virginia E., 19:139
Backenstos, James, 26:291
"Background of the California Missions," address by Peter M. Dunne, 25:86
Backus, Charles, 9:175, 273; 20:304, 309; 21:42, 64, 65; *see also* Backus Minstrels; San Francisco Minstrels
Backus, G., 9:38; 15:76
Backus, J. S., 27:236
Backus, Rodman, 15:271, 371
Backus & Co., 30:366
Backus & Davis, 8:268, 269, 271
Backus & Harrison, 8:268
Backus Minstrels, 9:175, 262, 273; 15:166, 375; 16:83; 20:304, 309; *see also* San Francisco Minstrels
Bacon (Bostonian, S.F., 1850), 12:98
Bacon (Fr. family, Santa Cruz, 1850), 5:363
Bacon, Edward R., 31:381
Bacon, Frank, 16:134
Bacon, Henry Douglas, 26:193-200; 27:270
Bacon, Mrs. Henry Douglas (Julia Ann Page), 26:193
Bacon, Jacob, 31:381
Bacon, Josiah, 15:376
Bacon, R. H., 17:174
Bacon & Page, San Francisco, 26:195
Badè, William Frederic, 38:251-52; address, "Outdoor Moods of John Muir," 3:207-8; *Life and Letters of John Muir*, rev., 4:292-98; obit., 15:289
Badger, Daisy Florence, 23:90
Badger, George E., 19:170
Badger, William, 36:299
Badger, William Gilman, 15:376; 23:90; 24:266; 36:294, 297-300 *passim*
Badger, Mrs. William Gilman, 24:266
Badger (ship); see *Milton Badger*
Badger, Hill, 28:240
Badger Mine, 20:184
Badillo, Francisco, 18:259-61, 276-77
Badillo, Pedro, 18:260
Badlam, Alexander, 4:393
Baegert, Johann Jakob, 40:199
Baer, Kurt, *Architecture of the California Missions*, rev., 38:273-74
Baer, Warren, 1:285; 22:32, 38
Baggs, Isaac, 9:102
Bagley, David, 10:358

Bagley, John W., 8:365-66; 9:26; 15:371; 16:80, 283; 37:168-69
Bahía Packet (ship), 6:257, 262
Bahnsen, Theodore, 15:277
Baikal (ship), 12:236, 237; 18:347; 39:111
Bailey, Col. (Sacramento, 1849), 20:37
Bailey (S.F., 1851), 28:40
Bailey (constable, Yuba Co., 1857), 9:159
Bailey, Caroline P., 28:293
Bailey, Charles M., 27:93
Bailey, D. B., 11:9
Bailey, G., 2:218, 220; 30:166; 36:120, 123
Bailey, George, 13:296
Bailey, George W., 11:9; 26:247
Bailey, James, 4:245, 246, 269, 300; 5:178; 23:341, 342, 347; 28:40(?)
Bailey, Orrin, 9:29; 15:176, 277
Bailey, Paul, 23:178; 38:371
Bailey, Philip A., 26:187
Bailey, Robert, 18:199, 201
Bailey, S. M., 15:76
Bailey, Theodorus, 2:251
Bailey, William, 15:240
Bailey and Overstreet, 13:319
Baillie, Thomas, 28:252
Baily (or Bailey), James (Monterey. 1792), 2:288, 289
Bain, Susan, 28:294
Baine, A. C., 7:16
Baine, John, 19:286
Baird, Alexander, 30:91
Baird, Daniel, 7:211
Baird, Elias L., lawsuit, 15:266
Baird, John, 7:206, 207, 227, 395, 398, 400, 404; 8:170, 179-81, 262-76 *passim*
Baird, Joseph Armstrong, Jr., 39:270; "The Architectural Legacy of Sacramento, a Study of 19th-Century Style," 39:193-207; bk. revs. by, 40:168-70, 266, 357-59
Baird, Mrs. Mildred, 30:91-92
Baird, Miles, 30:291, 301, 303; 31:50
Baird, Robert, 26:9, 11
Baird, Robert Alexander and Lutie (Cotton), 30:91
Baird, Spencer F., 28:125, 126
Baird, Thomas, 30:91
Baird, Thomas D., 18:201
Baird, William, 30:91
Baja California, *see* Lower California
Bajazon, Dr. (S.F., 1855), 39:142

Bajoux, Capt. (of *Rolant*, 1849), 13:370, 382

Baker (S.F., 1850), 12:94

Baker (Round Tent, 1851), 10:192

Baker (murderer, 1855), 15:365-66

Baker (Marysville, 1858), 9:350

Baker (San Rafael and S.F., 1861), 10:276, 281

Baker, Miss (S.F., 1864), 24:263

Baker, A. G., 31:231

Baker, A. J., trans. "Fray Benito de la Sierra's Account of the Hezeta Expedition," 9:201-42

Baker, Alexina Fisher, *see* Baker, Mrs. John Lewis

Baker, Alfred C., 17:309, 320

Baker, Alonzo, 2:121

Baker, B. A., 15:368; 20:304

Baker, Caroline, 17:309

Baker, Charles K., 13:340-41

Baker, Colin C., 29:254

Baker, E. P., 37:198

Baker, Edward Dickinson, 3:42; 8:370; 9:279, 388; 10:165, 166, 171, 173, 196, 197, 198, 254, 266, 293; 13:188; 14:364, 368; 15:200-201, 205, 267, 272; 16:81, 183, 336, 337; 17:82; 21:27; 24:276, 278; 26:71, 75; 27:102; 28:166, 168; 31:229-40 *passim;* 38:27-28, 301, 312; 39:305, 307; 40:290; arts. on, 17:303-24; 22:26; port., 10: opp. 165

Baker, Mrs. Edward Dickinson (Mary E. Lee), 17:304, 309

Baker, Edward Dickinson, Jr., 22:26

Baker, Emma H., 9:351, 354, 383

Baker, Frank, 17:177

Baker, George Holbrook, 9:275; 10:202; 22:37; 27:369; 34:346

Baker, George W. (S.F., 1850s), 15:169; 22:114

Baker, George W. (1895), 28:49, 50

Baker, Mrs. George W., Jr. (Carmen Ghirardelli), 25:94

Baker, Henry, 27: opp. 97

Baker, Hugh Sanford Cheney, 21:383; 30:191; 31:81; 36:355; 38:367; "A History of the Book Trade in California, 1849-59," 30:97-115, 249-67, 353-67; "Rational Amusements in Our Midst: Public Libraries ... 1849-1859," 38:295-320

Baker, Isaac Munroe, 24:48

Baker, J. E., 22:250

Baker, Capt. James (1792), 2:276, 299; 10:328

Baker, James (Buck Eye Ranch, 1859), 10:171

Baker, Jehiel H., 10:62

Baker, Mrs. Jehiel H., 10:40

Baker, John B., 15:76

Baker, John Lewis, 10:65, 74, 77; 20:298, 303, 304; 21:46-47, 51, 56, 71

Baker, Mrs. John Lewis (Alexina Fisher), 10:65; 20:298, 303, 304; 20:298, 303, 304; 21:46, 71

Baker, Joseph, 2:275, 278

Baker, Judah, Jr., 29:254

Baker, Mrs. L. A., 9:351, 353, 357, 368, 374, 382, 386

Baker, L. L., 24:172, 174

Baker, Lucy, 17:309

Baker, Mary, 34:184

Baker, Newton Diehl, 36:154-55; 39:134

Baker, Peter F., 21:243

Baker, R. S., 10:171, 283

Baker, Mrs. Robert S. (Arcadia Bandini), 1:236; *see also* Stearns, Mrs. Abel

Baker, Sanford Chase, 21:383; 30:191, 365

Baker, Thomas, 18:201

Baker & Hamilton, 15:76; 24:172

Bakers and bakeries, 5:363; 14:398; 24:348; 27:264

Baker's Bay, 8:99, 100; 10:326

Baker's Beach, San Francisco, 37:225

Bakersfield, 12:77; 20:141; 32:2-12 *passim,* 17, 19, 23, 28; newspaper, 8:83

Bakes, Benjamin J., 34:20

Bakewell, J. Howard, 21:291, 305

Balaine, Mrs. G. D., 25:190

Balance, San Francisco, 28:36

Balboa (ship), 31:295

Balboa Park, San Diego, 35:357-58; 36:66-71, 162

Balch family, 36:149

Balcom (Parks Bar, 1851), 25:326

Balda, Francisco de, 7:259

Bald Eagle (ship), 32:209, 212-14, 222

Bald Hill, Mendocino Co., 30:163, 164

Bald Mountain, 10:249, 262, 348

Baldridge, William, 2:62-63, 13:51; 29:134, 267, 269, 320; 31:208, 209; quoted, 2:62-63

Baldwin (S.F., 1856), 15:146

Baldwin, Judge (Aurora, 1862), 26:240, 241, 242

Baldwin, Miss (S.F., 1862), 10:379

Baldwin, Alexander H., 24:37

Baldwin, Alexander Richards, 22:94

Baldwin, Arnold M., obit., 35:82-83
Baldwin, Barry, 5:95; 30:299
Baldwin, C. H., 16:338
Baldwin, Charles H., 29:254
Baldwin, Cyrus G., 28:380
Baldwin, Drury P., 9:42
Baldwin, E. C., 10:360, 369
Baldwin, Elias Jackson ("Lucky"),
    16:86; 21:240-46 *passim*, 254, 259-65
    passim, 274; 25:88; 27:5; 31:20;
    32:376-78
Baldwin, F. F., 40:45
Baldwin, H. P., 40:45
Baldwin, Joseph Glover, 9:381; 10:51,
    70, 74, 199, 251, 264; 11:6-8, 21;
    16:285, 336; 20:167; 30:255; 34:258;
    38:310
Baldwin, Minor, 10:249
Baldwin, Oliver D., 23:191
Baldwin, Roger Sherman, 10:11, 94;
    12:94; 16:30, 31; 30:260, 261
Baldwin, S. D., 9:258; 10:181, 200
Baldwin & Co., 33:375
Baldwin Hotel, San Francisco, 19:225;
    21:241, 274; illus., 21: opp. 259
Baldwin's Academy of Music, *see*
    Baldwin Theatre
Baldwin Theatre, San Francisco,
    20:129-30; 21:241-51 *passim*, 254-63
    passim, 274; illus., 21: opp. 259
Bale, Carolina, 28:265
Bale, Edward Turner, 4:152-54, 177;
    5:127; 8:100; 14:128; 16:129; 17:145,
    155-56; 18:67, 70; 28:259-69; 29:317-18,
    319; 33:103
Bale, Mrs. Edward Turner (María
    Ignacia Soberanes), 4:153; 28:259,
    269; 29:318
Bale Mill, 4:154; 26:159; 29:264; phot.,
    28: opp. 266
Balfour, Guthrie & Co., 27:199; 31:298
Ball, Capt. (of *Olga*, 1848), 14:332
Ball, A. H., 36:245-46
Ball, Charles, 8:202; 10:270; 15:50, 54
Ball, Ella, 10:270
Ball, Frank, 20:249; 25:345
Ball, J. D., 33:363
Ball, Oscar O., 6:12; 8:361; 9:173
Ball, William, 9:132
Ballantine, Mrs. Joseph (Emelia
    Ashburner Christy), 36:46
Ballarat, 17:210
Ballard, Helen Mabry, "San Luis Obispo
    County in Spanish and Mexican
    Times," 1:152-72

Ballard, John W., 39:28
Ballard, S. K., 27:349
Ballast Point, 22:349; 31:155
Ballena (place), 26:25, 28
Ballenas, Bahía de, 7:318, 323, 382,
    383; 8:62; map, 7:324
Ballenas, Punta de, 1:49
Ballenger (Nevada City, 1862), 10:385
Ballestero, Juan de Dios, 1:164, 13:313
Ballestero, Mrs. Juan de Dios (Teresa
    Sepúlveda), 1:164
Ballinger, Richard A., 38:157, 221, 252
Ballo en Maschera, Un (opera), 21:68
Ballona (place), 32:328
Ballou, Sylvester A., 9:260, 269, 278,
    351, 372; 10:43, 62, 187, 246, 254, 259;
    11:9
Ball's Bluff, battle of, 31:229-40 *passim*
Ball's Model of San Francisco, 33:29
Bally (Balley?), W. J., 17:179
Balsas (rafts), 2:271; 3:13, 16, 352;
    8:313; 11:311, 377; 13:69; 14:113;
    20:316, 318, 325; 26:219
Baltic (ship), 11:11
Baltic gold mine, 28:189
Baltimore (ship), 14:291
"Baltimore Fire Laddie, George H.
    Hossefross," by Dolores Waldorf
    Bryant, 23:69-77
Baltimore Hotel, San Francisco, 5:14,
    349
Baly (Sacramento, 1849), 11:35
Bamboozling (play), 9:67, 130-32
Bancroft, Miss (Sacramento, 1861),
    10:277
Bancroft, Alberta, 29:101, 366
Bancroft, Albert Little, 29:97-128, 160,
    190, 217-27, 357-67; 30:82; 31:373;
    32:79; 33:372; port., 29: opp. 97
Bancroft, Mrs. Albert Little (Frances
    Ann Watts), 29:99, 101, 218-26
    passim, 361; 32:79
Bancroft, Mrs. Arthur John, *see*
    Bancroft, Eleanor Ashby
Bancroft, Azariah Ashley, 29:98, 127,
    225, 357
Bancroft, Bert Howe, 29:101, 218,
    225-26, 363, 366; 32:79
Bancroft, Cecilia, *see* Derby, Mrs.
    George H.
Bancroft, Charles E., 29:224-25
Bancroft, Curtis Ashley, 29:221, 225
Bancroft, Curtis Azariah, 29:104, 106
Bancroft, Eleanor Ashby (Mrs. Arthur
    J.), 25:94; "Bibliography . . . Works

Relating to Sir Francis Drake, 16: No. 1, Pt. 2, pp. 49-57; obit. of Ernest A. Wiltsee, 26:377; obit., 35:372

Bancroft, Emily, *see* Palmer, Mrs. Harlow

Bancroft, Francis Watts, 29:101, 221, 226

Bancroft, George, 1:17, 22; 3:188; 10:12; 19:43-58 *passim;* 31:219; 32:293; letters to Sloat, 1845-46, 2:162-72, 247, 249-51, 350-52; letters from Gillespie, 17:125-40, 271-84, 325-50; 18:217-28; 19:53

Bancroft, George Hess, 29:363

Bancroft, Griffing, 29:358; 35:354; 36:182

Bancroft, Mrs. Griffing (née Wood), 35:352

Bancroft, Harlow P., 28:14; 29:221, 225

Bancroft, Hubert Howe, 1:10, 23; 3:250-51; 4:106; 5:287; 6:35; 10:107, 120-21, 123, 126; 12:19, 23, 125, 139, 178; 14:43-44; 17:27, 32; 21:29; 23:94; 24:16, 107; 27:156; 28:7; 29:97-128 *passim,* 149-60, 217-27, 357-67 *passim;* 30:108, 148, 263, 353-54, 356; 31:219-28 *passim,* 355-74 *passim;* 32:65-80 *passim,* 99-100; 35:51; 36:327-31; "Guide to the Colorado Mines," 12:4, 5-10; port., 29: opp. 153; *see also* Bancroft Co.; History Co.

Bancroft, Mrs. Hubert Howe (Emily Ketchum), 29:98, 102-25 *passim;* 31:219-28 *passim,* 355-74 *passim;* 32:65-80 *passim*

Bancroft, Mrs. Hubert Howe (Matilda Coley Griffing), 29:358, 361; 36:181

Bancroft, Hubert Howe, Jr., *see* Bancroft, Bert Howe

Bancroft, John (Karl Augustus), 29:101, 367

Bancroft, Kate Ketchum, 29:122, 221-25 *passim,* 361, 366; 31:369

Bancroft, Mary Melissa, *see* Trevett, Mrs. Theodore B.

Bancroft, Paul, 23:94; obit., 36:181-82

Bancroft, Mrs. Paul (Louise Hazzard), 36:182

Bancroft, Philip, 23:94; 29:363

Bancroft, Sara Cone, *see* Fry, Mrs. Donald H.

Bancroft, William B., 29:225

Bancroft family, 29:97-98, 101, 190, 357-58, 365-67

Bancroft (A. L.) & Co., 29:97-128 *passim,* 160, 220-27, 359-62 *passim;* 38:54

Bancroft (H. H.) & Co., 27:269-70; 29:98-127 *passim,* 217, 219; 30:354; maps by (reprod.), 5:218; 12: opp. 3

Bancroft Co., The, 29:99, 360

Bancroft Library, University of California, 5:287; 26:85-88; 31:190; 36:109-10; 39:97

"Bancroft Library, The," address by George P. Hammond, 26:85-88

"Bancroft's Guide to the Colorado Mines," 12:3-10

Bancroft-Whitney Co., 29:99, 100, 360-61

Band, Charles R., 14:164

"Bandan" (Japanese MS), 32:225, 226

Bandini, Arcadia, *see* Stearns, Mrs. Abel

Bandini, Isidora, 1:236-45 *passim,* 249, 257, 258; 33:109, 261

Bandini, Josefa, 23:217

Bandini, Juan, 1:236; 6:83; 12:111-12, 116-20 *passim,* 319, 345; 13:114, 210, 212, 216, 231, 346; 14:232, 237, 239, 248, 256; 16:225, 227-28, 237-38, 352, 360, 363; 17:161, 231; 21:355; 22:51; 23:197, 199, 213; 26:48; 27:108, 336; 31:37; 33:109

Bandini, Mrs. Juan (Dolores Estudillo), 1:236; 16:227; 33:109, 114

Bandit Chief, The (play), 29:186

Bandits and highwaymen, 8:281-82; 13:327-30, 340-42; 17:115; 18:171, 282; 20:158; 27:247; *see also* Bell, Tom; Boles; Murieta; Vasquez

"Bandits, Borax and Bears," by Edmond Leuba, trans. Allen L. Chickering, 17:99-117

Bandits of the Southern Pacific, by Glasscock, rev., 8:281-82

Bandmann, Daniel E., 21:146, 148, 151, 167; 36:209, 212

Bandmann, Julius, 9:312-13, 329

"Band of Hope," 30:247

Bangor Guards, 38:22

Bangor Trading and Mining Co., 2:90-122

Bangs, E. Geoffrey, *Portals West,* rev., 40:266

Banker, J. D., 22:250

Banker (ship), 14:296, 297, 299

Bank Exchange (saloon), San Francisco, 7:111; 16:199

Bankhead (Brit. Min. to Mex.), 11:200; 18:140, 144, 145

Bank of America, 15:195; 36:112; *see also* Bank of Italy

Bank of California, 5:102; 14:413; 17:79; 21:176; 27:166

Bank of California Tract, Fresno Co., 25:174

Bank of Commerce, San Diego, 35:359-60

Bank of Commerce and Trust Co., San Diego, 35:361

Bank of Gold Hill, Nev., 33:375

Bank of Italy, 15:195; 36:258; 37:267-75, 347-58; *see also* Bank of America

"Bank of Italy and the 1926 Campaign in California," by Russell M. Posner, 37:267-75, 347-58

Bank of San Luis Obispo, 20:269

Banks (Yuba Co., 1855), 8:341

Banks, James A., 9:269; 10:52, 62, 361, 369, 389; 32:216, 223

Banks, Lily, 29:190

Banks, T. C., 19:237

Banks, Mrs. T. C., 19:230

Banks, William, 29:190

Banks (James) & Co., 17:177

Banks and banking, 15:175, 177, 195, 268, 272, 273, 274; 16:37; 17:182; 19:10-13; 22:256; 23:172, 176, 380; 30:342; 32:375; 35:358-64; 37:139, 267-75, 347-58; *see also* names of banks

Bankus, Elmer, 31:125

Ban Mayer, Joseph-Antoine, 22:304

Banner (riv. str.), 22:368

Banning, Phineas, 13:325, 329, 336, 346; 29:234, 236, 237, 245, 246; 32:327-37 *passim*, 340, 341

Banning, William and George Hugh, *Six Horses*, rev., 9:185

Banning and Alexander, 13:325; 32:329, 331, 333

Banning & Hinchman, 29:237, 238, 246

Bannister, A., 27:196, 197, 198-99

Bannister, Edward, 15:186; 31:1, 3; 34:233; 36:349

Bannister, Henry M., 33:12, 159, 167; 35:292

Bannock, Idaho, 15:324; letter from, 16:178-81

Bannon, John Francis, bk. rev. by, 40:76-77

Banta (place), 35:137

Bantam, George, 33:105

Banvard, Lou, 22:178; 23:118

Baptisms, in San Francisco Bay, 15:165, 273, 282; 26:171; 27:233-34, 236

Baptist Association, *see* San Francisco Baptist Association

Baptist churches, 3:37; 12:96, 103; 15:164, 171, 179, 186, 266; 24:263; 26:163, 168-72 *passim*; 27:9-18, 123-31, 229-36, 301-9, 365, 370; 28:291; 29:55, 59; 30:185; 32:120, 123, 139; *see also* names of churches

Baptist Historical Society of California, 27:11

Baptiste (Indian, 1846), 22:221

Baptiste, Jean ("Canada Jack"), 26:62

Baranov, Alexander A., 12:191, 217-29 *passim*, 234, 239, 240; 16:108; 35:236

Barbeau, J. L., 15:367, 369-70

Barbee, J. S., 19:62, 64, 66, 73; 27:313, 315-16

Barbee, John, 10:177

Barber, Arthur S., 15:42

Barber, Ed, 22:244

Barber, Edmund L., 33:74

Barber, Henry Postle, 26:266

Barber, John, 9:374

Barber, Joseph Tillinghast, 6:332

Barber, Matthew O., 30:13

Barber, William, 17:171, 172; 37:155

Barber & Baker, 22:36, 37; 30:258

Barbier, J. Louis, 14:142

Barbieri, Leonardo (Luigi), 18:96; port. of Raousset-Boulbon, 18: opp. 3

Barbour (Sacramento, 1858), 9:248

Barbour, George W., 3:26; 28:328, 330-31, 333, 339; 36:314

Barbour, T. J., 29:208

Barbour, Thomas, 1:19

Barbour, William T., 3:149; 9:350, 352, 353, 363, 367, 372, 380, 381; 10:254-56; 16:80

Barclay (A. J. Barkley?; Marysville, 1862), 10:372

Barclay, John S., 35:77

Barclay (or Barkley), William B., 21:305

Barclay, William P., 10:62

Bard, Cephas Little, 4:169, 10:86

Bard, Thomas Robert, 19:67; 38:355-56

Bardit, Henry, 14:314

Barger, James, 14:269; *see also* Barger, William W.

Barger, William W., 26:113, 114, 115, 120, 122

Barges and barging: Colorado R.: 22:155, 156, 165, 168; Monterey Bay:

28:257; San Francisco Bay: 18:10; 27:263, 264; 28:103; concrete, 31:298
Barham (ship), 23:154
Baric, Charles, 8:120; 11:220, 342; 12:352, 354; 13:58
Barili Thorn, Clotilde, 15:181, 183, 274, 278
Baring, W. M., 26:247
Barkan, Adolf, 25:230, 232
Barkan, Hans, 21:383; obit., 39:356-57
Barker (Feather R., 1849), 27:193
Barker, Charles, 6:214; 8:357
Barker, Charles Albro, 24:188; 27:185; 30:117; "Henry George and the California Background of *Progress and Poverty*," 24:97-115; "Elisha Oscar Crosby," 27:133-40
Barker, J. N., 22:250
Barker, James L., 28:49
Barker, Mary, *see* Alexander, Mrs. Wallace M.
Barker, Mary Louisa, 28:294
Barker, Seth, 14:316; 23:308, 330
Barker, Timothy Leonard, 18:379-80; 24:378; 28:382; 34:184
Barker, Mrs. Timothy Leonard (Mary R. Simpson), 18:379-80; 24:378-79; 34:184
Barker, W. H., 10:393
Barker, William M., 21:44
Barker, Knickerbocker and Bostwick, 30:205
Barker's Ranch, Yuba Co., 8:341, 357
Barkhouse (lawsuit, 1858), 9:360
Barkley, Charles W., 10:325
Barkley Sound, 10:323
Barley (grain), 2:278; 3:239; 4:362-65 *passim*, 368; 5:131, 135, 217; 8:237, 319; 9:358; 12:193, 293, 302; 17:183; 27:163; 32:335
Barlie (Barlee, Barley, Barly; on *London*, 1849), 7:210, 213, 215, 221, 398-99; 8:270
Barlow, Anthony, 21:227
Barlow, Charles A., 19:60, 62, 68, 72; 27:316; 28:51-53; 32:9; phot., 19: opp. 59
Barlow, J. W., 9:15
Barlow, Samuel Kimbrough, 3:89; 10:401-2
Barlow, Wilson, Primrose and West Minstrels, 21:250
Barnaby, William A., 16:282
Barnard, F. W., 14:377, 380
Barnard, Fred, 8:203

Barnard, G. G., 16:82
Barnard, George B., 40:212
Barnes, Dr. (nr. Petaluma, 1855), 26:304
Barnes, George, 21:63, 239, 249-50, 253
Barnes, J. H., 13:296
Barnes, James, 38:41
Barnes, James B., 33:372
Barnes, Stanley Nelson, 25:380
Barnes, William Henry Linnow, 21:174; 24:264; 27:67-68
Barnes' Bar, 30:238
Barneson, John, 30:211-14 *passim*
Barnes, Warner & Co., 31:63
Barnett, Elias, 29:263, 276
Barnett, J. H., 26:297
Barnett, M., 16:338
Barnette, Joseph M., 4:310, 339, 340, 341; 8:82
Barney, Mrs. (N.Y., 1860), 11:11
Barney, James M., 22:152
Barney, Libeus, *Letters of the Pike's Peak Gold Rush*, rev., 39:88
Barney, Samuel, 31:316, 317
Barnstable (ship), 8:297, 298, 299; 14:346; 17:335; 19:49; 23:201, 202
Barnum, Charles R., 28:378
Barnum, Gorham N. and Lorraina (Moore), 28:378
Barnum House, Sonora, 11:169
Barnum's restaurant, Oakland, 35:264
Baronn, Bern, 30:256
Barr, James A., 31:276
Barr, Mrs. James A. (Julia Inez Mann), 31:271, 276
Barr, John C., 9:36, 112; 15: opp. 40; 24:169
Barr, S. S., 32:354, 355
Barra (S.F., 1880s), 39:170, 226, 229-38 *passim*, 333
Barrack Room, The (play), 10:378, 391; 15:48
Barracouta (ship), 27:180; 33:238
Barratt (Barrat, Barritt, 1849), 21:305
Barrela, Cerbulo, *see* Varela, Sérbulo
Barreneche, Juan, 33:13, 15, 16, 19; 34:195; port., 33; opp. 16
Barrett (James B.?; from Ore., 1845), 5:125
Barrett, Judge (S.F., 1850s), *see* Burritt
Barrett, Amos, 15:376
Barrett, Charles, 38:314
Barrett, Herndon, 9:54, 72, 346, 348, 368, 370; 10:53, 184, 251
Barrett, John, 14:224
Barrett, Lawrence, 4:207; 18:370;

21:159, 161, 163, 168, 173, 179, 243; 35:142

Barrett, William H., 13:296

Barrie (Philippines, 1898), 31:58

Barrière, B., 11:203, 213

Barrington, Alexander, 13:281

Barrington, George, drawing by, 10: opp. 252

Barro, Cañada del, 13:373, 383

Barroilhet (S.F., 1850s), 32:110-11

Barron, Eustace Barrow, 8:125; 15:13-14, 129-31, 229, 238-41 *passim;* 17:129; 18:138, 139-40

Barron, George Haviland, 11:295; 36:28; address, "Old Spanish California Families," 3:302-3; obit., 21:378-79

Barron, Michael Columbus and Anna (Haviland), 21:378

Barron, William E., 15:13-14; 29:81

Barron, Forbes & Co., 13:59; 14:346; 15:4, 15; 17:128; 18:12, 14, 18, 140; 23:280

Barron's, San Francisco, 11:10

Barrows, C. H., 8:364

Barrows, David Prescott, 22:287; 25:250; 30:86; addresses, "California in Retrospect," 29:374-75; "Spain Delayed Occupation of California," 26:374-76; *Government in California,* rev., 5:203-4; obit., 33:371

Barrows, Mrs. Frank P. (Julia Smith), 34:66, 82

Barrows, Henry Dwight, 2:37; 13:335; 29:240, 242, 245

Barrows, John and Mrs., 35:354

Barry, Capt. (of *Saracen,* 1855), 26:74

Barry, Dr. (Santa Barbara, 1856), 18:270

Barry, James H. (1850), 6:11, 12

Barry, James H. (1890s), 8:364; 27:312, 316, 318; 28:52; 33:210

Barry, Peter, 7:106; 27:266

Barry, Richard, *see* Bary, Richard

Barry, Theodore Augustus, 6:11, 12; 28:293

Barry, Mrs. Theodore Augustus (Eliza M. Sharp), 28:293

Barry, William, 10:376, 389; 21:63

Barry, William McGill, 27:380

Barry and Patten, 6:11, 12; 15:172

Barry and Sperry, 11:329

Barsman, William, 10:63

Barstow, Alfred, 33:372

Barstow, William, 28:4

Bart, Black, *see* Boles, Charles E.

Bartel, William, 5:125

Bartholomew, Dr. (Yuba Co., 1857), 9:131

Bartholomew, "Mittie," 35:7-8

Barthrop, G., 22:34

Bartine, Alexander, 2:122

Bartleson (John) party, 4:8; 10:34; 17:56, 152; 18:33, 173; 23:289-90; 24:71; 26:235; 32:198

Bartlett (S.F., 1862), 12:12

Bartlett, Annie, 28:293

Bartlett, C. Julian, 9:109; 15:280, 364; 20:337; 27:174

Bartlett, Columbus, 27:174

Bartlett, Edwin, 13:245

Bartlett, F. H., 14:225

Bartlett, Green, 23:296

Bartlett, James W., 20:80; obit., 15:195

Bartlett, Mrs. James W. (Lavinia R. Brady), 15:195

Bartlett, John Russell, 9:14, 15, 301; 13:322; 14:158-59; 21:108; 31:36, 40

Bartlett, Louis de F., 4:49

Bartlett, Washington, 5:287-88; 12:364; 18:331; 19:75; 20:332; 27:171, 174; 30:101; 35:260

Bartlett, Washington Allon, 1:79-81 *passim;* 2:69; 5:305; 6:278, 280, 372; 10:123, 125, 126; 11:133, 134, 137, 300, 301; 12:59; 13:237; 14:100, 149; 16:209-15; 17:226, 229, 295, 302; 20:217, 233; 25:130, 260-62, 266; 30:40, 42; 33:310, 316; 40:23

Bartlett, William Chauncey, 28:8-9; 30:139-40, 148; 33:211; 34:381

Bartlett's Bridge, 7:8, 9; 34:227

Bartlett Springs, 23:296-97, 300; 32:364, 366, 369, 370, 371; phot., 23: opp. 289

Bartol, Abram, 15:174; 28:64, 68

Bartolo, Paso de, 1:148

Barton, Benjamin, 12:122

Barton, George, 9:77; 20:38

Barton, James R., 13:327, 335, 340-41; 29:234, 245, 246

Barton, John, 40:24

Barton, Robert (Yuba Co., 1850s), 9:77

Barton, Robert (Fresno Co., 1882), 25:170

Barton, Thomas, 39:111-12

Barton, Wait, 15:29

Barton, W. B., 21:248

Barton, William, 15:120

Barton Opera House, Fresno, 20:141

Barton's Bar, 9:63, 77

Baruch, Bernard, 24:90; 39:131

Baruch, Frederick, obit., 18:188
Baruch, Isaac, 18:188
Baruh, Marcus M., obit., 21:189
Bary, Richard, 23:206, 216
Basarguire, Capt. (of *Rynda*, 1863),
    26:15
Bascom, L. H., 9:40; 18:384
Baseball, 27:186; 36:296, 299
Base lines, monuments for, 34:1-16
    passim
Bases of Tacubaya, 1:31
Basey, James, 32:265
Basford, Jacob K., 25:285
Bash, L. H., address, "General Persifor
    F. Smith," 6:286-87
Basham, *see* Bassham
Basignano, Clement A., 29:323
Basil, Capt. (U.S. consul, San Blas),
    29:14
Baskets, Indian, *see* Indians: baskets
    made by
Bassani (S.F., 1855), 15:267
Bassett, Charles, 28:325
Bassett, Charles H., 10:280, 293
Bassett, Henrietta (Von Schrader),
    13:80
Bassett, Theo., 13:296
Bassett and Winn, 28:39; *see also*
    Fountain Head; Winn, M. L.
Bassham, William R., 5:308
Bastanchury, Domingo, 13:345
Bastian de Santiago, Felipe, 7:377
Basye, Miss (Mrs. William W. Stuart),
    26:7
Batchelder (Sonora, 1855), 34:293
Batchelder, A. P., 9:149
Batchelder, Adoniram J., 8:201, 202,
    210, 360; 9:148, 153, 169; lawsuits,
    9:165, 166, 167
Batchelor, B. W., 19:63, 66, 72
Bateman, H. L., 15:164, 165, 166
Bateman children, 20:304
Bates, Dr. (Sutter's Fort, 1848), 19:139;
    25:220; 26:123
Bates, A. S., 11:177-78
Bates, C. P., 33:372
Bates, Mrs. D. B., 22:253-254, 268
Bates, Edward, 15:6, 8, 10, 12, 19, 20
Bates, Fordyce, 10:62, 70
Bates, Franklin, 14:211; 16:183; 40:28
Bates, Frank M., 21:160
Bates, Henry, 9:40, 42, 45, 48, 111;
    25:224, 225
Bates, Mrs. Jack, *see* Cowell, Mrs. Effie
Bates, Sam, 17:83

Battaglini, René, 39:316
Battalion of California Volunteers,
    25:127; *see also* California Battalion
Battalion of Mountaineers, First, 26:9
Battle Creek, 22:211, 216, 217; 23:134;
    26:131
Battle Creek Sanitarium Co., 31:15-16
"Battle of San Pascual" (poem), by
    E. D. French, 26:61
Battles of San Pasqual, by Todd, rev.,
    4:291
Batturs, Edward T., 9:26, 29, 108;
    15:280, 281; 28:294, 295
Batturs, Mrs. Edward T. (Eliza
    Waters), 28:294
Bauchet, Louis Auguste, 12:354, 355
Bauchet, Luis G., 29:236
Bauchet, Rafael L., 29:236
Baudry, St. Cintin de, 5:139
Bauer, C. (Carl Baur?), 15:282
Bauer, Patricia M., 33:92; "The
    Beginnings of Tanning in California,"
    33:59-72
Baugh, Theodore E., 22:33
Baur, John E., 31:93; "Los Angeles
    County in the Health Rush,
    1870-1900," 31:13-31; *Health Seekers
    of Southern California 1870-1900*,
    rev., 39:272-74
Bausman, William, 30:128, 359
Bautista, Juan, 3:21
Bauzá Cañas, Felipe, 3:215, 237; 40:118
Baxter, J. H., 31:295
Baxter, Richard, 10:297
Baxter and Monroe, 13:259
Bay, Dr. (Albany, N.Y., 1849), 4:188
Bay, William, 15:370
Bayard, James A., 19:345, 359
Bayard, Le (newsp.), San Francisco,
    39:226, 229-37 *passim*, 346
Bay City (lake str.), 32:366
Bayerque, Jules Barthelmy, 16:341; *see
    also* Pioche & Bayerque
Bayerque, R., 29:198
Bayley, Alden S., 26:125; 30:36
Bayley, Alcander John, 27:282
Bayley, George B., 4:29, 35
Bayley, Thomas S., 30:36
Bayley, Winters & Marshall, 30:36
Baylie (lawsuit, Yuba Co., 1859), 10:188
Baylies, E. M., 37:199
Baylor, John R., 27:170; 34:125, 129,
    130, 131, 142, 153; 40:321
Bay Mill, 38:60-69 *passim*
Bays, John, 34:67

Bays, M. V. B., 26:131
Bay State (ship), 22:121
Bay State House, Coloma, 26:159
Bazaine, Gen. (Fr. Army in Mex., 1864), 13:40, 41; 37:312
Beach (or Beech), Miss (Sacramento, 1858), 9:246, 247, 252; 10:48
Beach, Mrs. (artist, 1859), 30:128
Beach, Chilion, 23:90
Beach, D. S., 11:9
Beach, George H., 10:176; 14: opp. 209, 401; 15:41
Beach, George W., 23:103
Beach, Henry, 10:176
Beach, Horace, 10:257, 361; 14:216, 401
Beach, Mrs. Horace (May Tennent), 10:264
Beach, William C., 13:32
Beach and water lots, *see* Real estate
Beacock, Nelda (Oakes), 28:284
Beadle, H., 36:97
Beal, Benjamin, 19:229
Beale, Edward Fitzgerald, 1:142-43, 146-48, 270; 2:172; 3:122-23; 8:252; 9:7, 182, 183, 277, 303-10, 314; 10:388; 13:343; 15:165, 247, 248, 249, 253; 16:345; 17:177, 340-44 *passim*; 19:183, 231; 21:24, 33, 335, 337, 355; 22:22, 30, 51; 26:24, 28, 30, 34, 47-48, 61-62, 124, 202; 27:215; 28:334, 341; 33:102; 34:152-53, 155; ranch of, 12:6; *see also* Ranchos: Tejon
Beale, Harvey S., 15:104
Bealer (lawsuit, Yuba Co., 1856), 9:67
Beales, Benjamin Bronston, 22:287; "The San Jose *Mercury* and the Civil War," 22:223-34, 355-64
Beall, J. W., 25:169
Beall, Thomas F., 21:130
Beaman (or Beauman), Maj. (d. 1849), 18:113, 114, 115, 135, 243
Beaman (Galena Hill, 1859), 10:167, 170
Beamer, R. H., 28:49
Bean, Col. (Marysville, 1858), 9:362, 373
Bean, Capt. (Colorado R., 1859-72), 22:169-74 *passim*
Bean, J. H., 31:45
Bean, J. M., 33:12, 161, 167; 35:302, 306
Bean, Joshua H., 13:329; 29:245-46
Bean, Robert, 32:263-66 *passim*
Bean, Teehoogah, 15:49, 57
Beans, Rowena, 25:189
Beans, Thomas Edward, 25:189

Beans, 1:166; 4:369; 5:131, 136, 217; 8:237, 319; 14:7; 32:355
Bear (Pine) Creek, Butte or Tehama Co., 22:212; 23:133
Bear Creek, Yuba Co., *see* Bear River
Beard, C. L., 14:164
Beard, Charles, 3:165
Beard, Elias Lyman, 33:302, 308; 34:97, 98, 239-43 *passim*, 253-54, 336
Beard, J. R. (Sacramento, 1859), 10:61
Beard, Joseph and Fannie (Cucamonga, 1862), 3:165
Beard, Joseph R., 11:6, 7, 21; 15:168
Beard, Kennan H., 26:286
Beardslee, A. F., 21:366
Beardsley, Andrew J., 11:174
Beardsley, Buck, 5:337
Beardsley, Fanny, 10:45
Beardsley, Maud E., 14:191
Beardsley, Richard King, 21:96; 25:193, 194, 201, 202, 284; 31:101; "The Monterey Custom House Flag Pole: Archaeological Findings," 25:204-18
Bear Flag, 1:77, 88, 180, 190; 4:287; 6:369; 7:84; 8:258; 9:81, 84; 10:113, 114, 289; 12:337; 14:147-48; 15:231, 237; 16:82, 210; 25:125; 29:265-66, 276-77; art. on, 31:206-17
"Bear Flag Lieutenant: The Life Story of Henry L. Ford," by Fred B. Rogers, 29:129-38, 261-78, 333-44; 30:49-66, 157-75
Bear Flag party, 13:52; 24:54, 57-58, 63, 71-72; 25:123, 124, 125; *see also* Bear Flag revolt
Bear Flag revolt, 1:72-95, 134-35, 171, 179-90, 286-95; 2:63, 69-74; 3:87, 106, 110, 271; 4:286-87; 5:96; 6:134-41 *passim*, 144, 272, 273, 364, 366, 367, 369, 374; 7:79-81, 84; 8:257-58; 9:81-85 *passim*; 10:9-11, 101, 105-15; 12:39, 337; 13:47, 106-11 *passim*; 14:126, 147-48; 15:62, 230-31, 237, 242-43; 16:100-101, 209-10, 212; 17:219-30, 235, 271, 275, 280, 296; 18:75, 83, 172, 298; 19:118, 132; 20:216, 233; 22:367; 24:57-58; 25:122-23; 29:261-73, 321; 31:205-10 *passim*; 40:123; *see also* Bear Flag party
Bear Photo Service, negatives of S.F. earthquake and fire, phot., 39: foll. 182
Bear River, Nevada and Yuba cos., 9:356, 370; 10:183, 184, 192, 297, 347-52 *passim*; 11:105, 109-12 *passim*;

12:292; 13:17-19, 170-71, 174; 19:123; 23:131, 349; 26:132; 28:236; 34:24

Bear River (Pine Cr.), Tehama Co., 23:133

Bear River and Valley, Idaho and Utah, 2:24; 4:282; 10:400; 12:289; 28:300; 32:198, 202, 205

Bear River Water and Mining Co., 31:246-47, 250

Bears and Bear hunting, 1:158, 159, 160; 2:54, 287; 3:136; 4:37; 5:113, 128, 130, 136, 137, 138, 151, 241, 259-62 *passim*, 291, 359; 6:215, 361; 8:145-46, 152, 153, 239-44 *passim;* 10:213; 12:208, 290, 292, 304-5; 13:29, 68; 16:111, 134; 19:200; 20:352; 22:146, 205, 206, 331-40 *passim;* 23:19, 20, 22, 30, 31, 32, 127, 141; 36:2-3; *see also* Bull-and-bear fights; Grizzly bears

Bear Valley, Lake Co., 32:365

Bear Valley, Mariposa Co., 21:326

Bear Valley, Nevada Co., 3:136; 10:347, 350, 351, 352; 12:292-93

Beasley, Jesse, 24:26

Beatitude, *see* Patitoux

Beatrice (ship), 3:93

Beattie, George William, "San Bernardino Valley before the Americans Came," 12:111-24

Beatty, Abraham S., 13:29

Beatty, Henry Oscar and Jessie Appleton (Hooper), 31:302

Beatty, Mrs. J. William, 22:287

Beatty, William Henry, 31:302

Beaubien, Charles, 18:349

Beauchamp, Leander and Medora (Sylve), 28:294

Beaudreau, Charles and Catherine, 39:2

Beaudry, Prudence, 13:345

Beaudry, Victor, 13:345

Beaulieu, Olivier, 4:376; 6:137; 17:220; 36:242

Beaulieu & Co., 14:398

Beaumont, Henry, 40:321

Beaumont, Paul (pseud. Prosper Willaume), 39:345

Beauregard, Pierre Gustave Toutant, 29:240

Beaver, Anna Wheaton, obit., 17:93

Beaver, Frederick Hope, 17:93; 23:94

Beaver, George Washington, 17:93; 23:94

Beaver, Mrs. George Washington (Mary Miller), 17:93

Beaver, 1:113, 114, 117; 2:44, 51, 52, 54,

236; 5:230; 6:102; 8:101, 290; 12:304; 14:196; 16:134; 22:198-214 *passim,* 323-41 *passim;* 23:19, 21, 36, 37, 124-33 *passim,* 307, 309, 311; 28:121, 122, 124, 217, 230, 251, 255; *see also* Fur trade

Beaver (ship), 13:240, 248; 28:105, 247

"Beaver and Sea Otter," address by Charles L. Camp, 6:102

Beaver Creek, River, Valley, Siskiyou Co., 28:217, 230

Beaver Ranch, Yuba Co., 9:52, 70

"Becerillo" (dog, 1540), 3:340

Becerra, Diego, 1:39, 40; 6:298, 307; 20:233-34

Bechdolt, Frederick R., *When the West Was Young,* rev., 5:312-15

Becher, Frederick G., 15:341, 351; 16:247

Becherini, Ernesta, 15:183

Bechtel, Kenneth Karl, 27:310; 34:173-74

Becier, Margaret, 25:221

Beck, Adolph, 24:94

Beck, David L., 9:26

Beck, Peter P., 24:94

Becker, C., 31:157

Becker, George P., 31:231

Becker, Robert H., 34:286; "Mission San José—de Guadalupe?," 34:229-30

Becket (Napa, 1851), 2:136

Becket (ship), 35:196, 199

Beckett, James and Sarah O., 16:81

Beckett, Mary, 10:44

Beckh, Gustavus W., 23:189

Beckh, Walter, 23:189

Becknell, William, 2:10

Beck's Tannery, San Francisco, 33:68

Beckwith, A. C., 16:346

Beckwith, Charles, 10:166

Beckwith, Edward G., 4:11, 242, 248, 249; 38:82

Beckwith, Harvey, 8:196; 9:130, 135, 140, 141, 145

Beckwith, James, 29:23, 28

Beckwourth, James Pierson, 2:204-5; 3:202; 4:10, 126, 128-29, 140; 9:368, 392; 10:37-38; 20:343

Beckwourth Pass, 4:10, 247, 259; 7:13

Bedford, Mrs. (Sacramento, 1859), 10:42, 51, 53

Bedoux, de (S.F., 1849), 5:14, 21, 139

Bedoya, José de, 25:105, 117, 327

Bedwell, William, 6:60

Bee, Albert Wilson, 10:207; 15:95; 29:346, 350

Bee, Mrs. Albert Wilson (Sophronia Clapp), 15:95
Bee, Everett Newton, obit., 15:95-96
Bee, Frederick A., 10:207; 12:323; 15:95; 29:346, 348-50; 30:149
Bee, Henry Jubilee, 14:17; 16:324; 18:74; 30:3-4
Bee, Knights Ferry, 3:91
Bee, Sacramento, 9:382; 19:282; 27:219; 38:75-76; "Souvenir," 38: opp. 321
"Beedatoe," *see* Ten Mile River
Beebee (in mines, 1848), 2:188
Beebee, Alexander M., 27:230
Beebe, Jabez, 26:290
Beebe, Lucius, *Mansions on Rails*, rev., 38:382-83; coauth. *San Francisco's Golden Era: A Picture Story of San Francisco before the Fire*, rev., 40:77-79
Beecher (Yuba Co., 1854), 8:199
Beecher, Henry Ward, 21:247
Beechey, Frederick William, 11:299; 15:213, 215; 20:280; 23:253; 25:320, 324; 30:2-3, 321; 37:305
Beef, 5:136, 274; 14:13, 149; 16:284; 20:120; 23:277, 357; 27:362, 368; corned, 39:110; curing of, 5:274; 6:259; 8:237; 12:194, 293; 14:201; 28:102, 109-10; shipped to Orient, 30:197, 200; *see also* Cattle
Beekman, A., 22:250
Beeks, William, 13:256
Beeman, Truman, 29:22, 27
Beener, John S., 12:29
Beeney (nr. Marysville, 1883), 28:235
Beeny, George W., 10:189
Beers, George, new ed. of his *Vasquez*, rev., 40:260-63
Beers, Henry P., 37:91; "The American Consulate in California," 37:1-17; 38:184
Beers, Hiram W., 34:237
Bees and beekeeping, 17:32; 24:271-75; 31:27, 31
Beeson, Henry (1846), 24:58, 71
Beeson, Henry (1862), 33:363
Beeson, Ike, 33:363
Beever family, 9:70
Begbie, Matthew B., 6:22-28 *passim*
Begg (John) and Co., 6:254-64 *passim*; 8:105, 290; 29:27; 35:107
"Beginnings of Marysville, The," by Earl Ramey, 14:194-229, 375-407; 15:21-57
"Beginnings of Medical Education in

California, The," address by Emmet Rixford, 5:93
"Beginnings of Tanning in California, The," by Patricia M. Bauer, 33:59-72
Begole, Charles D., 4:33-34, 54
Behan (Fr. sailor, d. 1849), 13:370
Behr, Hans C., 32:248
Behr, Hans Herman, 27:346; 31:337; 32:183, 243-62; port., 32; opp. 248
Behr, Mrs. Hans Herman (Agnes Omylska), 32:248
Behrendt, Caspar, 13:335; 20:93
Behrendt, Sam, 19:382; obit., 20:93
Behymer, Linden Ellsworth, 20:139; 26:286
Beideman, J. B., 9:109; 15:281, 364
Beilharz, Edwin A., 30:378
Beith, James, Jr., 39:58
Bekeart, Jules François, 15:96
Bekeart, Philip Baldwin, 26:107; 128-34 *passim; James Wilson Marshall*, rev., 4:89; *Flags That Have Flown over California*, rev., 8:186; obit., 15:96
Belarde, Miguel, 12:117
Belarde, Ramon, 12:117
Belasco, David, 14:411; 21:172, 182, 240, 241, 253-62 *passim*, 269, 272, 274
Belasco, Fred, 33:41
Belcher, Capt. (of *Monterey*, 1855), 22:168, 169
Belcher, Sir Edward, 16:286; 18:344, 346
Belcher, Frank, 35:362; 36:69, 76
Belcher, Frank [Jr.], 36:161
Belcher, Isaac Sawyer, 8:342, 359, 360; 9:374, 396; 10:180, 189, 250, 251, 255, 356, 360, 361, 386
Belcher, Mrs. Isaac Sawyer (Adeline Noble Johnson), 9:396
Belcher, John, 25:12-13
Belcher, John H., 30:66
Belcher, Lewis F., 29:19-25
Belcher, Richard, 8:359; 9:396
Belcher, William Caldwell, 9:396; 10:250, 273, 275, 283, 383; 24:275
Belcher, William J., 9:396
Belcher Mine, 26:196, 199, 200
Bel Demonio (play), 21:146
Belden, David, 9:357, 387; 10:247, 261; 11:54, 56, 142
Belden, Francis C., 32:221
Belden, Josiah, 2:191; 4:8; 8:302-3; 11:142; 12:176; 13:78; 14:17; 16:5; 18:61; 26:264
Belden, L. Burr, 39:211
Belden, Leo V., 37:350

Belfast (ship), 13:390

"Belgian in the Gold Rush, A," by Jean
    Joseph François Haine, trans. Goris,
    37:311-46; 38:141-55

Belgians, in California, 20:68, 76; 22:308;
    37:311-13, 318-26 *passim;* 38:141-42;
    illus., 37: opp. 337

Belgrade (ship), 2:133

Belknap (ventriloquist, 1854), 8:201

Belknap, Charles H., 11:51

Belknap, David Price, 40:204

Belknap, William, 6:11

Bell, A. D., 27:170

Bell, Alexander, 9:42, 45, 104; 13:226,
    230, 316; 26:22; 29:246; 33:345; *see
    also* Bell's Row

Bell, Charles H., 26:16; 33:232-33

Bell, G. W., 15:305

Bell, Horace, 12:178; 13:316, 324, 325,
    328, 329, 352; 33:345, 346

Bell, J. (L.A., 1890s), 38:56

Bell, J. R., 18:201

Bell, John (of Tenn.), 19:270, 344;
    31:201

Bell, John C., 11:9; 38:333

Bell, Joseph de, 14:398

Bell, Joseph Jones, 22:368, 369

Bell, Margaret, 28:294

Bell, Samuel, 9:42; 11:173; 16:343-44,
    346; 27:97, 101; 30:133

Bell, Samuel Bookstaver, 9:354, 386;
    port., 9:355

Bell, Theodore Arlington, 33:372; 39:22

Bell, Thomas, 29:198; 35:134

Bell, Tom (Thomas J. Hodges), 2:205;
    3:158; 8:211; 9:63, 76; 15:380

Bell, W. H., 9:44, 45; 15:369

Bell, William Warren, obit., 22:378

Bell (Alexander) & Co., 16:285

Bella Union gambling saloon, San
    Francisco, 8:273; 20:293; 22:266;
    33:57

Bella Union Hotel, Los Angeles, 12:12;
    13:319; 31:13

Bella Union Hotel, Sacramento, 2:137

Bella Union Melodeon, San Francisco,
    4:59-63 *passim;* 10:276, 290; 21:43,
    65, 154

Belle, Frances P., trans. Paz, *Life and
    Adventures of . . . Joaquin Murrieta,*
    rev., 5:203

Belle (riv. str., 1854), 9:72

Belle (schr., 1854), 18:17

Bellegarde (lawsuit), 21:116

Belle Russe, La (play), 21:256-57, 260

Bellin, Jacques Nicolas, maps by,
    9:206-7, 217, 240

Bellini, Eugenia, 21:159

Bellows, Henry Whitney, 20:266;
    40:302

Bellows, Col. W., *see* Russell, William
    Henry

Bellrude, Jake M., 9:358; 10:176, 177,
    285

Bells and bell casting, 3:241; 8:378; 23:72,
    308; 32:54

Bell's Row, Los Angeles, 13:266, 306,
    310

Bellune, V. de, 27:246

Belmont and Yosemite Railway, 25:174

Belmont Hotel, San Diego, 36:158-59

Belshaw, Mortimer W., 4:33, 34, 35

Belt, George Gordon, 1:267; 4:184, 185

Belted Will (ship), 22:353

Beltran, Xavier, 14:6

Beltzhouver, Daniel M., 31:37

Belvidere (ship), 28:382

Benard, ed. Péron's *Mémoires,* 1:173

Benard de Russailh, Albert, 6:46; 28:37,
    42; 39:3, 7-8, 14; *Last Adventure,*
    trans. Crane, rev., 10:205

Bendeleben, O. de, 33: 12, 153-59 *passim,*
    163-64; phot., 33: opp. 1

Bender, Albert Maurice, 5:90; 11:390,
    392; 12:81, 82, 181-82, 368, 369-70;
    13:94, 189, 284-85, 286, 412, 413;
    14:91-92, 93, 189, 284-85, 411; 15:93,
    94, 193, 194, 287, 288, 385, 386; 16:93,
    94, 189, 190, 287, 381, 382; 17:88, 89,
    189, 190, 286, 287, 357, 359; 18:91, 92,
    93, 185, 186, 187, 283, 285, 377, 378;
    19:82, 189, 283, 285; 38:2; obit. of
    Laura L. McKinstry, 13:414-15; obit.,
    20:92-93

Bender, Jacob, 29:298, 300, 306

"Bendmore," San Mateo Co., 31:301

Benedict (Blue Tent, 1850), 21:127

Benedict (S.F., 1850s), 32:108

Benevolent Friend Society, 32:119

Benevolent Society of California, 35:244

Ben Franklin Mine, 6:230, 236, 332

Benham, Calhoun, 13:39; 14:355, 360;
    15:83, 168, 179; 16:79, 338; 26:345;
    38:49, 214

Benham, D. C., 8:360; 9:395; 10:53, 54,
    57, 59

Benham, John M., 22:37

Benham, Leander, 15:177-78

Benham (D.C.) & Booth (Henry J.),
    9:395

Benicia, 2:52-53, 136-37; 6:146-52 *passim*,
214; 8:17; 9:308; 11:105, 133, 300, 301;
12:27; 13:267-68, 367; 14:144, 202,
357, 372, 399; 15:70-77 *passim*, 85;
16:63, 184, 340; 17:296; 19:22; 20:32,
122, 152, 166, 310; 22:21, 30; 25:327,
328, 329; 27:298, 302-3, 307, 308; 29:15,
16, 159; 30:146, 262, 363; 32:350, 358;
33:301-2; 34:25, 32-35 *passim*; 35:123;
arsenal (*see* U.S. Arsenal); capital at,
11:163; 17:234, 263-67 *passim*; 38:51;
City Hall, 24:64 (*see also* State
House); church, 26:168, 172; 27:302;
founding of, 6:142-43, 146-50 *passim*;
11:133; 12:351; 13:267; 16:340;
17:231-32; 24:63; 27:61-62, 300;
28:267; 30:6, 13; hotel (*see* Solano
House); letters from, 15:83-84;
military hdqrs., 6:287; 12:27; 15:164;
24:62; 34:23; naming of, 6:146; 11:133;
17:231-32, 301-2; 25:340; newspapers,
8:285; 16:340; railroad, 4:225, 226;
5:178; 27:273; schools, 4:214; 23:279;
24:64; 30:262 (*see also* Young Ladies'
Seminary); State House, 17:260-70,
(phot.), opp. 260
"Benicia Boy," *see* Heenan, John C.
Benites, José María, 4:145, 150; 15:379
Benitez, Francisco, 7:262, 274; 8:43
Benitz, William, 12:199-200, 205-6, 288;
17:68; 33:64
Benjamin, E. B., 36:210, 299
Benjamin, Judah Philip, 12:357; 15:6, 16;
17:316-17; 19:265, 345; 20:111; 26:112,
121, 123; 34:45, 46
"Benjamin Parke Avery," by Ernest R.
May, 30:125-49
Benkhouse (Barkhouse?), 9:360
Bennett, Albert A., 9:38; 33:333; 38:32,
33
Bennett, Asahel, 18:202-4, 215
Bennett, C. F., 19:59-63 *passim*, 66;
27:316; phot., 19: opp. 59
Bennett, Catherine, 5:134; 29:135
Bennett, Charles, 12:357; 13:175;
14:273-77 *passim*; 19:124, 134;
26:112-23 *passim*
Bennett, Clarence E., 9:308; 29:243, 248,
249; 40:293, 317, 349
Bennett, Emerson, 4:283
Bennett, Mrs. Frank (Melba Berry),
27:186
Bennett, James, 11:289
Bennett, James M., 16:306; 24:62
Bennett, John, 6:336

Bennett, John E., 15:66
Bennett, Nathaniel, 3:41; 9:116;
20:107-8, 366; 21:331; 22:34; 30:275-76
Bennett-Arcan party, 18:198, 203, 207
Bennett *v.* Brooks, 10:183
Bennett's National Circus, 9:140, 175
Bennett's Ranch, 8:338, 355
Bennett's Restaurant, Sacramento,
23:353
Bennettsville, 4:40
Bennett's Wells, 18:213, 215
Benningham, Miss (Yuba Co., 1858),
9:359
Bensley, John, 11:107; 33:372
Bensley Water Co., San Francisco,
10:391; 17:175; 23:75
Benson, A. G., 37:230
Benson, Eva, 21:379
Benson, Frank H., 39:28, 30
Benson, Harry C., 4:45
Benson, Henry, 10:259, 284
Benson, Henry M., 11:9
Benson, John, 11:127
Benson, Leffert S. (or L.), 21:305
Benson, Octavine, 10:271, 272, 273, 276
Benson, R. F., 37:350
Benson, Robert J., 21:305
Benson, William Ralganal, 11:266-68;
"Narrative," ed. Max Radin, 11:268-73
Bent, Charles, 37:5, 6
Benteen, Frederick W., 34:159
Bentham, George, 18:342, 346
Benton, F. M., 8:213
Benton, Jessie, *see* Frémont,
Mrs. John C.
Benton, John Eliot, 7:410; 10:189
Benton, Joseph Augustine, 2:204; 9:255,
280, 388; 10:189, 292; 12:92, 93; 16:336;
20:44; 22:34, 262, 278; 23:355, 370;
24:165; 26:169-70, 172; 30:251, 263;
33:266, 267, 339; bk. by, 9:280
Benton, Thomas Hart, 1:144, 146, 147,
246; 2:371; 6:89-90, 183, 285, 368;
8:253-54; 10:20, 21, 136-37, 139, 222-36
passim; 11:140; 15:100, 204; 18:298;
19:15, 16, 17, 20, 23, 50-52, 157-61
passim; 21:276, 278; 26:323; 29:30;
30:252, 258; 33:339; 37:3, 5; 40:125-26;
art. on, 13:150-54
Benton, Mono Co., 26:243
Benton City, Tehama Co., 18:298-303
passim, 312
Bent's Fort, 1:124, 125, 136; 3:270
Benzéman (Fort Ross, 1814), 12:193
Berdach, 23:135; *see also* Bindach

Berdue (or Burdue), Thomas, 12:106; 15:34-37 *passim*

Berg, Christian, 19:294

Berger, Emily, 27:190

Bergerot, Jean André, 39:74, 238

Bergerot, Pierre Alexandre, 39:226, 238-43 *passim*, 250-52, 336; obit., 74-75

Bergez, Alexandre, 39:239, 240

Bergin, Thomas I., 21:174; 34:236

Bergson, Ole and Augusta Elizabeth (Kuchel), 28:379

Berial, Capt. (Civil War), 31:234, 236, 240

Bering, Vitus, 23:219, 221

Beritzhoff, Alexander C., 21:309; 22:79, 82, 83

Berkeley, 17:42-49; 27:344-45; 31:328-33; 35:253-54; Bernhardt's visits to, 20:139, 141, 143; St. Mark's Church, 37:51-61

Berkeley, The (hotel), Berkeley, 31:329

Berkeleyan, The (weekly), 33:313

Berkeley Club, 1:13; 27:340-41, 345, 350-51

Berkeley Hills, 27:292, 293, 294

Berkeley Land & Town Improvement Co. *v.* Jacobs, 31:333

Berkeley Musical Association, 29:191

Berkeley plan, 38:354; 39:32

Berkeley Villa Association, 31:329

Berlin, Charles E., 33:174

Berlin, Mrs. Charles E. (Marguerite Jeanne Eugénie Caperon), 33:169, 174

Berlin, Mrs. Irving (Ellin Mackay), 27:95

Bermes, Pedro de, 3:315

Bermudez, Col. (Mex., 1849), 23:262, 266, 268

Bernal, José Cornelio, 21:117-18, 125, 316; 27:107, 142

Bernal, Mrs. José Cornelio (Carmen Cebrian), 16:80; 27:107, 147

Bernal, Margarita, 38:108

Bernal, Zacarías, 20:108

Bernal de Piñadero, Bernardo, 8:52, 54

Bernard, Fred, 8:206

Bernard, Jean, 13:345

Bernard, Sam, 18:265-66

Bernard du Hautcilly, *see* Duhaut-Cilly

Bernardelli (S.F., 1854), 15:174, 179

Bernavette, John, 1:149

Bernhard, Isaac, 19:129, 141

Bernhardt, Lysiane, 20:143

Bernhardt, Maurice, 20:128, 137, 141

Bernhardt, Sarah, 20:126-46; 21:252; 33:45; 35:142

Bernhisel, John M., 6:116

Bernie, P., 22:217-18, 348; 23:134, 140

Bernot (S.F., 1850s), 6:56

Berreyesa, Féliz, 28:264

Berreyesa, Francisco, 16:249

Berreyesa, José de los Reyes, 1:136; 12:56; 15:4, 13, 14; 25:124; 29:266, 270

Berreyesa, José de los Santos, 1:182; 28:264, 265; 36:242

Berreyesa, José Ygnacio, 20:108

Berreyesa, Nazario, 16:249

Berreyesa family, 16:134, 249; 20:108

Berrien, John McPherson, 19:18

Berries: blackberries, 12:306; 15:54; 16:143; gooseberries, 2:278; 5:64; 12:306; 29:173; 32:262; strawberries, 2:116; 9:145; 28:209; 29:40-41, 56; 32:220; sold or traded by Indians, 15:54; 24:231

Berrill, William and Maria (Lucas), 28:293

Berry, Mr. and Mrs. (Empire Ranch, 1849), 8:209

Berry, Benjamin L., 28:116

Berry, Clarence, 27:186

Berry, David M., 31:19

Berry, Daniel K., 29:255-56

Berry, F. G., 25:24

Berry, Harry V., 9:354, 386

Berry, Harvey G., 24:238

Berry, James Richard, 11:75; 19:320, 322

Berry, Jechonias L., 28:337

Berry, Jehu, 10: opp. 48, 62

Berry, John Van Antwerp, 5:293, 294-95; 14:379, 397; 15:28, 33, 38, 45

Berry, Mrs. John Van Antwerp (Catherine Johnson), 5:293-95

Berry, Richard J., 30:381

Berry, Rufus C., 23:191

Berry, T. B., 25:230, 232, 238, 246

Berry, Thomas, 31:329

Berry, William H., 3:118

Berry, William Henry and Alice Edna (Bush), 27:186

Berry, William Jackson, 27:186

Berry (J.) & Co., 15:183

Berryessa, Claudio, 29:27

Berryessa (place), 22:362

Berryessa gang, 29:27

Berryessa Valley, 24:56, 71; 29:276; 32:376

Berryman, H. B., 17:47-48

Berryman, H. J., 37:53, 56

Berry's Saloon, Strawberry Valley, 10:171

Bert, Edward G., 21:66, 168

Bert, Frederick W., 21:168

Bertalot, Julien, 12:352, 353, 354; 22:61

Berteau, Gustav Wilhelm, 12:300-301

Bertha Dolbeer (ship), 38:68

Berthold, Victor M., *William H. Russell*, rev., 8:186

Bertody, Charles, 4:192, 193, 194; 16:283

Berton, Jules, 35:335-44 *passim*

Bertram (play), 16:84

Bertrand (from LaChapelle, 1849), 5:16, 249, 250, 251; 6:46-47

Bertrand (from Paris, 1850), 22:305

Bertrand, Raoul, 39:345-46

Bessie Brady (lake str.), 17:115

Best (C. L.) Tractor Co., 31:89

Beston, Thomas, 11:141

Bestor, Norman S., 33:269, 337, 341

Betsy (ship), 12:217

Betzold, Carrie E., *see* Doheny, Mrs. Edward L.

Beuseman, Chris M., 12:236

Beutler, J. B., 15:165, 167; 25:335

Bevans, Thomas P., 26:232

Beyer, H. Otley, 31:103-5 *passim*

Beylard, E. D., 25:230, 232

Beylard, Mrs. Edward Duplessis (Julia Howard), 27:254-55, 319

B. F. Hoxie (ship), 29:122

B. H. Ramsdell (ship), 31:150

Bianchi, Eugenio and Giovanna, 21:47, 55, 63, 67-71 *passim;* 24:263

Biaz, Francisco, 10:184, 186

Bible societies, 27:127; 32:123, 129, 139

Bibliographical notes, by Henry R. Wagner, on *I Muscoviti nella California*, 1:192-93; on Jerónimo de Ripalda's *Catechismo*

"Bibliography of California," address by Robert E. Cowan, 3:101

Bibliography of California Ornithology, by Grinnell, rev., 3:298-99

"Bibliography Relating to the Russians in California," 12:210-16

"Bibliography . . . Works Relating to Sir Francis Drake," by Eleanor Bancroft, 16: No. 1, Pt. 2, pp. 49-57

Bibliothèque Populaire (weekly), 39:153, 346

Bichi (or Biche), 22:326, 343

Bicknell, H., 13:32

Bicknell, John, 8:200

Bicknell, W., 13:32

Bidault, Dr. (from France, 1850), 22:301

Biddle, James, 1:248; 2:250; 12:346; 19:368; 22:50, 51, 53, 65; 28:342; 33:108-9, 117; 35:108

Biddy, Jonathan, 30:41-44; 36:307

Biden, Charles S., 9:102

Bidwell, John, 1:98, 297; 3:73, 202; 4:8, 14, 155, 161-62, 234, 285; 6:69, 134-35, 366; 10:34, 86, 355, 413; 12:176, 194, 199, 300, 351; 13:12, 230-31; 14:227; 16:57-59, 129, 213, 285, 376; 17:68, 157; 18:296; 19:119; 20:46, 149, 152; 21:82, 372, 373; 22:366, 368; 23:289-91, 298; 24:84; 26:99, 109, 121, 132, 186, 235; 27:136, 139; 28:255, 257; 29:134, 262, 271, 275, 298, 335; 30:54-55, 63, 158; 32:198; 33:372; 36:313-25 *passim;* 38:327; *Echoes of the Past*, ed. Quaife, rev., 8:87-88; rancho, *see* Ranchos: Arroyo Chico

Bidwell, Mrs. John (Annie Ellicott Kennedy), 36:313, 318-23 *passim*

Bidwell (place), 15:169; 30:260, 362

Bidwell-Bartleson party, 26:235

"Bidwell Rancheria," by Anne H. Currie, 36:313-25

Bidwell's Bar, 6:243; 9:69; 13:171, 175; 15:169; 29:104, 205, 299, 305; 30:260, 362; 33:295; illus., 6: opp. 243

Bieber, Ralph Paul, 29:90; 40:161

Biederman, H., 39:343, 344

Bierce, Ambrose Gwinett, 8:83; 19:70, 102, 104; 20:82; 21:257; 27:312, 317; 28:10; 31:286; 35:51, 54; 40:137; quoted, 19:102-3, 104; 27:318

Bierce, Leigh, 4:46

Bierstadt, Albert, 24:265; 30:136; phot., 39: foll. 344

Biesta (Death Valley, 1861), 18:206, 208

Biesta, Federico, 30:357, 366

Biétry-Salinger, Johanne, *see* Salinger

Big Bar, Amador Co., 30:239-40; bridge, 25:382

Big Bar, El Dorado Co., 12:66-68

Big Bar, Trinity Co., 5:177, 219, 221, 227, 230, 236, 246-47; 26:203, 207; Rifle Rangers, 26:203-4

Big Bend hydroelectric plant, 29:203-4

Big Bonanza (ship), 22:353

"Big Eagle of Monterey," *see* Belcher, Lewis F.

Bigelow, Elijah, 40:211

Bigelow, Hardin, 12:105

Bigelow, Henry H., 26:357; 27:166, 167, 270

Bigelow, J. B., 15:24
Bigelow, Richard L. P., 4:51
Bigelow, Samuel Cutler, 26:264
Biger, William, 9:373
Biget, Pierre, 33:174
"Big Four," 4:219, 260-63, 269, 270;
    38:352; *see also* Crocker, Charles;
    Hopkins, Mark; Huntington, Collis
    P.; Stanford, Leland
Biggs, Donald Clair, 33:92; "Melpomene
    on the Half Shell," 33:39-47; phot.,
    39: opp. 80, foll. 182, opp. 360
Biggs, Peter, 13:316-17; 33:255
Bighorn sheep, 22:203, 204, 205
Bigler, Henry William, 6:60-61; 14:269,
    270; 26:109, 112-24 *passim;* 32:194-95,
    197, 202-3; quoted, 14:271-77; 26:114,
    119; fac. diary entries, 26: opp. 97
Bigler, Jenny, 10:378, 379
Bigler, John, 3:153, 154-55; 6:7; 7:6;
    8:343, 359; 9:44, 45; 10:82; 11:173;
    15:49, 179, 274, 280, 368-69; 16:285,
    337, 343-44, 346; 17:182, 198, 265-66;
    19:166, 182; 23:245, 356; 24:169-70;
    29:230-31, 233-34, 242; 34:43, 252,
    257-58; 35:212, 214; 38:17, 49-50, 198
Bigley, John and Caroline (Smith),
    28:292
Bigler (Tahoe), Lake, 4:10; 7:7, 8, 14;
    9:307; 12:324; 17:76, 77-78
Big Meadows (Bridgeport), 26:242-43,
    244, 248
Big Rock Irrigation District, 40:212
" 'Big Silver, The,' California's Greatest
    Silver Mine," by Dwight L. Clarke,
    32:1-41; phot., 32: opp. 1
Big trees (*Sequoia gigantea*), 4:7, 14-15;
    11:172-73, 327-28; 18:343; 27:260;
    28:185-86; 33:245; bks. on, rev.,
    3:300-301; 9:185-86; *see also* Calaveras
    Grove
Big Trees, by Fry and White, rev.,
    9:185-86
Big Trees of the Giant Forest, by
    Stewart, rev., 9:185-86
Big Valley, Lake Co., 32:364, 368
Bill (Yokayo Indian), 26:210-15 *passim*
Billiards, 22:261; 38:329; 39:295
Billings (Benicia, 1849), 29:16
Billings, Dr. (Acapulco, 1860), 11:11
Billings, Frederick, 7:110; 11:10; 15:10,
    13-14, 175, 182, 267, 274; 16:198-200;
    17:172; 25:103-4; *see also* Halleck,
    Peachy & Billings
Billings, George E., 31:295

Billings, Josh, 18:369
Billings, T., 15:179
Billings, Thomas, 9:142, 155
Billings (ship), 31:295
Bills, H. C., 15:281
"Billy the Cooper," *see* Thorne, William
Bimetallic League, 28:48, 49
Bindach (berdach, bundosh, berdash),
    22:197, 214; 23:135
Bingham (S.F., 1849), 22:69
Bingham (Marysville, 1873), 10:370
Bingham, Charles Edward, 28:294, 295
Bingham, Mrs. Charles Edward, *see*
    Thorne, Emily
Bingham, Hiram, 35:195
Bingham, William St. Maur, 22:34
Binney, Charles, 30:258
"Biographical Note on Lafayette
    Maynard," from *Alta California,* 16:77
"Biographical Traces of Consul John
    Parrott," by Frank A. Knapp, Jr.,
    34:111-24
Birch, G. F., 8:6, 8
Birch, James E., 9:179; 26:128; 36:118,
    128, 129; 37:372-73
Birch, Mrs. James E. (Julia Chase),
    37:373
Birch, William, 20:305; 21:41-42, 51, 64,
    264-66; *see also* Birch's Minstrels
Birch's Minstrels, 10:181, 200
Birch *v.* Woods, 8:347
Birchville, 3:143, 156, 161; 28:236, 240
Bird, Bernard, 16:338
Birds, 2:286; 5:358; 8:19, 146; 12:305;
    28:230; blackbirds, 5:53; 8:146; 12:195;
    23:358; 28:218; booby, 30:244;
    buzzards, 5:137; 7:361; cardinals,
    7:361; 28:230; crows, 7:361; doves,
    7:361; falcon, 12:305; finches, 28:218,
    230; grouse, 5:71, 81; 33:363; hawks,
    2:286; 8:146; 12:305; humming birds,
    5:71; 8:19, 146; 23:318; larks, 12:305;
    28:214; linnets, 7:361; 12:305; magpies,
    7:364; 8:146; nightingale, 28:230;
    owls, 8:166; 12:305; parrot, 4:199;
    partridges, 2:286; 3:23; 7:361; 8:146;
    pigeons, 5:83; 12:305; 20:41-42;
    30:244; 35:155; ravens, 5:137; road
    runner, 8:221; sparrows, 7:361; 8:146;
    32:257, 258; thrushes, 7:361; vultures,
    5:137, 138; 12:305; woodcock, 5:64;
    woodpeckers, 12:305; bks. on, rev.,
    3:298-99, 300; *see also* Condor; Quail;
    Water birds
Birdsall, George, 15:281

Birdsall, J. S., 18:206
Birdsall, Louis Aiken, 16:342-43
Birdsall, Sophie, *see* Latham, Mrs.
  Milton S.
Birdseye, J. C., 31:229
Birds of California, by Dawson, rev.,
  3:298
Birgham (A.) & Co., 30:262
Birmann, Martin, 9:398-99
Birmingham Emigrating Co., 8:81-82
Birnie, Robert, 28:99, 107
Birnie, Rogers, 4:36
"Birthdays of Urban Communities,"
  see "Determination of the ..."
Biscaccianti, Elisa, 4:59-61; 10:185, 201,
  393, 19:229; 20:300-301; 21:51, 71,
  162; 29:114
Bishop (Calaveras Co., 1855), 22:79
Bishop (Contra Costa Co., 1851), 34:4
Bishop (Santa Barbara Co., 1850s),
  18:171
Bishop (Yuba Co., 1859), 10:169
Bishop, A. W., 1:17; 24:80
Bishop, Alva Curtis, 23:91
Bishop, Anna (Payne), 4:60; 6:339;
  15:165, 166, 167, 174-80 *passim*,
  184, 274, 276, 371; 16:84; 19:236;
  20:305; 22:31, 272
Bishop, Charles (on *Ruby*, 1795), 10:328
Bishop, Charles (d. 1849), 28:60, 67
Bishop, Ella, *see* Drury, Mrs. Wells
Bishop, Frederick Aubrey, 21:288;
  23:91; 30:377
Bishop, John, 12:327
Bishop, S. A., 9:306, 310
Bishop, Simeon and Helen (Apperson)
  21:288; 23:91
Bishop, Thomas B., 38:261
Bishop, Thomas Benton, 36:45
Bishop, William, 20:44
Bishop, William Wallace, 23:91-92
Bishop's Creek Canyon, 32:199, 201, 203
Bishop's Creek Valley, 26:242-43
Bishop's Rock, 31:155
Bissell, Anna, *see* Haight, Mrs.
  Henry H.
Bissell, Clifford H., 39:81-82, 180, 270,
  359; "The French Language Press in
  California," 39:1-18, 141-73, 219-62,
  311-53
Bissell, G. W. P., 15:74, 373; cor.,
  15:72-73
Bissell, George R., 31:194; letter to,
  31:195-99

Bissonette (fur trader, 1844), 4:309;
  5:395
Bithell, J., 30:258, 266, 366
Bit of Old China, A, by Stoddard, rev.,
  5:88
Bitter Springs, 10:37; 14:68
Biven, Rasey and William, 25:192
Bixby, Mrs. Fred Hathaway (Florence
  Elizabeth Green), obit., 40:365-66
Bixby, Llewellyn, 19:288; obit., 21:92
Bixby, Susanna, *see* Bryant, Mrs.
  Ernest A.
Bjork, Kenneth, *West of the Great
  Divide*, rev., 37:372
Black (Yuba Co., 1856), 9:66
Black (brothers, Yuba Co., 1883), 28:234
Black, A. G. and Mrs., 5:338, 339
Black, Ab., 7:112
Black, Arthur, 2:35
Black, George, 12:173
Black, George A., 35:339
Black, George E., 9:133, 134, 143, 153
Black, Henry Moore, 15:9; 40:350
Black, James, 16:249
Black, Jeremiah Sullivan, 15:5, 6, 15, 16,
  17, 19; 19:163; 21:120; 322; 31:201
Black, John (Mex., 1846), 6:183
Black, John (U.S.N., d. 1849),
  30:41-47 *passim*; 36:307-11 *passim*
Black, John Alexander, 21:305
Black, Joseph, 17:42
Black, Peter, 30:41-46 *passim*;
  36:307-11 *passim*
Black, W. L., 4:321
Black Adder (ship), 30:211
"Black Bart," *see* Boles, Charles E.
Black Bear Mine, 6:345, 346, 353-56
Black Blunders (minstrel show), 20:305
Blackburn, William (1847), 8:75-76;
  12:33; 15:370; 19:131, 135, 138, 142;
  34:296; 40:27
Blackburn, William (1869), 34:20
Black Crook (barge), 22:155-56, 168
Black Crook, The (play), 21:157-58,
  164, 172
Black Diamond, 8:17; 12:33; 30:345
"Black Friday" (1855), 24:179;
  26:194-95
Black Hawk Mine, 27:117
Black Hawk Ranch, 31:89
Black Hawk War, 4:272-73; 17:304, 306;
  39:213
Black Hook, The (play), 21:157
Black Hussars, San Francisco, 38:17

Blackmon, Robert E., 33:284; "Noah Brooks," 33:193-217
Black Point, 25:319, 321, 322
Black Rock Canyon, 18:307, 308, 309
Black Rook, The (play), 21:159
Black's Hotel, Yosemite, 5:337, 339
Black Statue, The (play), 20:305
"Black Steward" (Allen Light), 32:267
Blackwood, William C., 24:223-24
Blacow, John and Sophie (Rathke), 27:383
Blacow, Robert, 27:383
Blagdon, Daniel, 29:258
Blagueur, Le (newsp.), 39:251,253, 312, 314, 346
Blaine, A. C., 7:16
Blair, A. W., 40:311
Blair, J. H., 31:333
Blair, James, 9:397; 12:27; 34:121
Blair, Montgomery, 19:365-66; 21:120
Blaisdell, Mme., 20:248
Blaisdell, H. L., 25:194, 203
Blaisdell, Nathaniel, 21:383; obit., 35:373-74
Blaisdell Brothers, 20:248, 254
Blaisdell & Co., 15:175
Blaive, Dominic, 22:301
Blake, Anson Stiles, 10:91; 26:185; 37:284
    "The California Centennials," 26:97-106; "Distinguished Editorial Service," 37:92; "The Hudson's Bay Co. in San Francisco," 28:97-112, 243-58; "A San Francisco Boyhood," 37:215-28; ed. "Working for Wells Fargo—1860-1863; Letters of Charles T. Blake," 16:30-42, 172-81; foreword, "History of Las Posadas Forest," 35:1-2
    addresses: "California Life in the Mines," 12:180; "The First Emigrant Train to California," 10:413; "Infant Years [of CHS]," 36:175-77; "Life in the California Mines, 1851-52," 10:91; "Life of the Early Day Miners," 8:90; "San Francisco, 1846-48," 6:381-82; "Working for Wells Fargo in 1863," 16:88-89
    obits. of David P. Barrows, 33:371; Templeton Crocker, 28:90; Kimball G. Easton, 4:214; Alfred Ghirardelli, 35:374; Edward F. Haas, 18:189-90; Frederick L.

Lipman, 29:377; Mark L. McDonald, Jr., 12:88
    bk. revs. by, 4:291-92; 9:400-401
    "Meetings of the Society," 5:414-17; 6:102, 197-99, 285-87, 380-81; 7:95-99, 200-201, 289, 410; 8:90-94, 187, 283, 386; 9:90-91, 292, 407-8; 10:91, 206-7, 307, 413; 11:88-91, 188-89, 295, 389-90; 12:84-87, 180, 366-67; 13:88-92, 188-89, 284, 411; 14:86, 87, 186-87; 17:185-86, 285, 356; 18:86-90, 184-85, 286, 376
    reps. of Sec.-Treas., 7:97-98; 8:91-92; 9:91-93; 10:92-94; 11:89-91; 12:85-87; 13:89-92; 14:88-91; 15:90-92; 16:90-92; 17:90-92; 18:86-90
    phot., 37: opp. 208
Blake, Mrs. Anson Stiles (Anita Day Symmes), 35:7
Blake, Mrs. B. M. (Mary K.), 4:211; 24:72
Blake, Charles Morris, 23:262, 273-74, 279; 24:64, 72; 30:262
Blake, Charles Thompson, 2:204, 208; 8:90; 10:91; 12:94, 98; 16:88; 26:185-86; 30:260-61: 37:216; "Working for Wells Fargo, 1860-1863," letters, ed. Anson S. Blake, 16:30-42, 172-81; port., 10: opp. 30
Blake, Mrs. Charles Thompson (Harriet Waters Stiles), 2:204; 16:40, 177, 178
Blake, George C., 3:84; 12:50
Blake, George M., 35:12
Blake, Gosham, 15:76
Blake, J. A., 13:32
Blake, J. B., 21:233
Blake, James, 11:148; 21:368-69
Blake, M. C., 40:206
Blake, Marguerite May, 28:280
Blake, Theodore A., 11:307, 315
Blake, William, 22:20
Blake, William Phipps, 4:67; 11:304, 315; 23:345; 34:197
Blake, Moffitt & Towne, 34:281
Blakemore, Robert M., 29:298, 300, 305-6
Blake's College, 24:64
Blakeslee, Samuel Valentine, 15:41, 43; 24:215-16, 218-19, 220; 26:170, 174
Blakesley (Blakely, 1844), 4:320
Blanc (S.F., 1850), 5:21, 29; *see also* White
Blanc, Pignon (or Pimo), 13:358, 382
Blancarte, José María, 12:319, 321

Blanchard (S.F. peninsula, 1850),
    5:375-76; 6:37
Blanchard (Yuba Co., 1859), 10:189
Blanchard, N. W., 1:18
Blanchard, William, 12:225; 23:332;
    35:198(?)
Blanchard, William K., 20:44
Blanchet, Fr. (S.F., 1849), 5:43
Blanchet, Augustin Magloire
    Alexander, 29:142-43
Blanchet, Francis Norbert, 29:142
Blanchot (Paris, 1849), 5:21
Blanck, E. L., 32:27, 29-30, 34, 37, 41
Blanco, Gov. (of Sonora, 1850s), 18:6,
    12-15 *passim*
Blanco, Miguel, *see* White, Michael
Blanco, Rafael, 12:117
Blanco, Cape, 2:125; 3:225, 226;
    10:329; 25:112, 255
Blanco de San Sebastian, Cabo, 7:367,
    369, 393; 8:55; 9:206, 207, 217; 10:329;
    25:263
Blanco Villaseñor, Sarmiento, 37:195
Bland, Adam, 13:321, 332, 333
Bland, Henry Meade, *Stevenson's
    California*, rev., 3:291-96
Blandeau (S.F., 1849), 5:20
Blanding, Gordon, 25:231
Blanding, Lena, 25:233
Blanding, Louis, 15:164
Blandville, Comte de, 21:325
Blangy, de (S.F., 1850), 5:30
Blankstein, M. S., 14:398
Blanquie, Raoul H., 24:286; addresses:
    "French Activities in California Prior
    to Statehood," 25:372-73; "Jean
    François Galaup de Lapérouse,"
    26:371-73; "The French in
    California," 30:84; obit. of Pierre A.
    Bergerot, 39:74-75
Blaschke, Edward L., 12:209
Blasco, Pablo, 3:367
Blasdel, Henry Goode, 18:210-12, 213,
    216; 37:197
Bledsoe, A. J., 19:67-68; 28:47, 49
Bledsoe, Albert T., 17:304
Bledsoe, M. C., 3:46
Bledsoe, Moses O., 17:303-4
Blethen, James H., 17:81
Bligh, Capt. (of *Providence*, 1792),
    2:309
Blinn, Gustavus, 11:152
Blinn, L. W., 31:294
Bliss (1858), *see* Peck & Bliss
Bliss, Duane, 17:79; 19:95; 22:191

Bliss, Hope, 22:191
Bliss, Josephine, 9:345, 346, 354, 368,
    370, 378; 10:258, 283-84
Bliss, Leslie Edgar, selection of "The
    Twenty Rarest and Most Important
    Works Dealing with the History of
    California," 10:79-83
Bliss, Phyllis F., 23:189
Bliss, Simeon M., 8:201, 202, 210, 337;
    9:54, 151, 154, 157, 163, 259, 261, 266,
    287, 345, 346, 347, 353, 356, 364-74
    passim; 10:54-61 *passim*, 168, 172, 188,
    189, 251, 258, 279, 283, 284, 364, 367,
    370
Bliss, Mrs. Simeon M. (Jennie Phillips),
    9:287; (Maggie Phillips McCubbin),
    9:287
Bliss, Mrs. Walter D. (Edith Pillsbury),
    25:233; obit., 10:414
Bliss, Will M., 19:95
Bliss brothers (Oregon Bar), 8:355
Bliven, Ralph, 30:297, 300; 31:56, 62
Block, Eugene B., *Great Train
    Robberies of the West*, rev.,
    38:169-71; obit. of Mrs. Amanda
    Schlesinger, 40:274-75
Block, Maurice, address, "Architectural
    Restoration of 'Lucky' Baldwin's
    'Queen Anne' Cottage," 32:376-78
Block (A. J.) & Co., 30:360
Blodget (Marysville Buttes, 1860),
    10:252
Blok, T., *Brief Geographical-Statistical
    Description of California*, extract,
    12:189-90
Blom, Johan Reubold, 15:184
Blood, Elnora, 30:285
Blood, William Francis and Nellie
    (Moody), 30:285
Blood, William Henry and Ethelinda
    (Burgess), 30:285
Blood Creek (Tomki Creek), 27:220
"Bloody Bill," 9:139
Bloody Canyon, Mono Co., 26:236
Bloody Run, Nevada Co., canyon,
    28:234; ditch, 3:144
Bloomer, Amelia Jenks, 31:86
Bloomer, John Godfrey and Emeline
    Augusta (Atwill), 28:285
Bloomers, *see* Dress
Bloomfield (Marysville, 1850), 14:399
Bloomfield, John J., 21:305
Bloomfield, William, 15:239
Bloomfield company, 28:233, 240;

see also North Bloomfield Gravel
    Mining Co.
Bloomfield Deflecting Nozzle, 29:206
Bloor, Mrs. (Marysville, 1858), 9:263
Bloor, George W., 8:358; 9:266,
    287; 10:53
Blossom (S.F., 1855), 15:278
Blossom Rock, San Francisco Bay,
    23:281; 30:2
"Blowing up the Wind," by Edward
    C. Kemble, 14:81
Bluck, Col. (Black or Buck?, Siskiyou,
    1855), 17:176
Blue, George Verne, 18:384; "Report
    of Capt. La Place . . . 1839,"
    18:315-28
Blue and Gold, 33:313
Blue Bar, 9:148, 177
Blue Canyon, 13:16; 18:358
Blue Goose Mining Co., 30:246
Blue Lakes: gap, 32:370; toll road,
    32:364
Blue Lakes Water Co., 26:196
Blue Law Gospel, 32:124, 131, 136-37,
    138
Blue Mountain (Table Mtn.), 6:243;
    illus., opp. 243
Blue Springs, 32:202
Blue Tent, Nevada Co., 23:384
Blue Tent, Siskiyou Co., 21:127
Blue Wing Hotel, Sonoma, 16:305, 316
Blum, Hermann, 28:141
Blum, Isidor, 28:141
Blume, Frederick Gustavus, 14:130;
    26:20
Blume, Mrs. Frederick Gustavus (María
    Antonia Cáceres de Dawson), 14:130
Blummer, Charles, 38:323-24
Bluxom (Marysville, 1859), 10:57
Bluxome, Isaac, Jr., 8:367; port., 6:
    opp. 3
Bly, Edwin P., trans. of M. G. Vallejo's
    letters, 29:149-51, 152-53
Blyth, Charles R., obit., 38:360-61
Blythe, J. F., 32:55
Blythe, Thomas H., estate, 38:55-56
Blythe (place), 36:219
Boalt Trust, 25:88
Boardman, George Chauncey, 26:265
Boardman, W. F., 12:175; 31:328
Boardman, William H., 23:330
Board of Fire Underwriters, 26:263
Board of Manufacturers and Employers,
    35:60

Board of Marine Underwriters,
    26:353-56 *passim*
Board of Wagon Roads, 7:17
Board Ranch, 33:299
Boarman, Charles Sylvester, 27:383
Boarman, Edith Alvord, 27:382
Bobb, Charles V., 32:37, 40-41
Bocanegra (Mex. min. of for. affairs),
    18:143
Bochsa, Robert Nicholas Charles,
    15:175; 16:84; 22:31, 36
Bocker, Henry, 17:240
Bocqueraz, Leon, 16:192, 273, 280-81;
    17: No. 4, Pt. 2, p. 2; 36:33-34
Boddy, E. Manchester, 26:286
Bode, George C., 11:127
Bode, William, drawing by, 27: opp. 19
Bodega, 4:158, 168; 6:259; 12:189, 247-50
    passim, 255-59 *passim*, 268, 271-75
    passim; 13:35; 16:143; 17:62, 63; 18:67,
    69, 160, 310, 322, 338; 22:341, 345;
    23:39; 24:332; 25:360; 26:171; 28:102;
    33:64; *see also* Bodega Bay
Bodega Bay, 2:301-4, 335; 3:173, 174;
    8:323-24, 327; 9:242; 10:318, 319, 331,
    334, (map) opp. 337, 337-45; 11:310;
    12:189, 190, 191, 209, 221-30 *passim*,
    236, 240, 244, 245, 250, 251, 254, 256;
    16: No. 1, Pt. 2, pp. 6, 13, (map) opp.
    49, No. 2, p. 108; 17:63-64, 244;
    18:174, 293, 294, 315, 327, 328; 25:349,
    360; 28:100, 107, 108, 110; 36:309
Bodega y Quadra (or Cuadra), Juan
    Francisco de la, 2:257, 269, 275, 281-92
    passim, 332-33, 339; 3:218, 219; 9:205,
    207-8, 221, 224, 225, 240, 241, 242;
    10:313-21 *passim*, 337; 14:112, 113;
    15:59; 31:114; 40:110, 115, 116-17,
    238; maps of explorations, 9: opp. 201;
    10: opp. 313, opp. 337
Boden, Charles R., "San Francisco's
    Cisterns," 15:311-23; address, "The
    Broderick-Terry Duel," 15:382-83;
    obits. of A. B. C. Dohrmann, 16:95;
    Prentis C. Hale, 16:95-96; Michael M.
    O'Shaughnessy, 13:415-16
Boden, Hamilton J., 21:291, 305
Bodfish (New York of the Pacific,
    1850), 12:30
Bodfish, C. N., 12:30; 14:217
Bodie, 3:398; 4:64-80; 7:92, 114, 119;
    15:381; 23:383; 26:237, 242; 33:189;
    illus., 4:65
Bodie Mining Co., 6:68, 75-76
"Bodie, the Last of the Old-Time

Mining Camps," by Grant H. Smith, 3:398; 4:64-80
Bodie Rancho, 26:241
Bodin, Walter, 20:143
Bodinier, J. V., 19:29, 41, 42
Bodley, Thomas, 13:32; 30:329
Body, Waterman S., 4:67; 7:114; 26:237, 245
Body Mining District, 26:237; *see also* Bodie
Böhme (d. Fort Laramie, 1855), 12:290
Bogardus, Mrs. (Yuba Co., 1857), 9:157
Bogardus, Edgar, 24:168
Bogardus' Race Track, 9:149, 153, 155, 177
Bogardus' Rancho, 8:199, 348
Bogart, Capt. (Colorado R., 1857), 22:169, 171
Bogart, J. C., 10:377, 381
Bogatyre (ship), 26:15, 16
Boggs, Albert G., 16:133
Boggs, Mrs. Angus Gordon (Mae Hélène Bacon), quoted, 13:260-61
Boggs, Biddle, 21:300-301, 305, 326; *v.* Merced Mining Co., 10:264
Boggs, John, 27:199
Boggs, Lilburn Williams, 3:176; 5:394-95, 396; 6:151, 152; 10:23; 14:144; 16:133; 17:232; 24:26; 28:324; 29:325; 36:242
Boggs, William Montgomery, 1:136; 16:133; 24:58
Boggs family, 16:133; 24:67
Boggs *et al. v.* Dr. Gellar, 10:360
Bogue, David, 11:66
Bohemian Club, 4:208-9; 19:101, 104-6, 111; 20:132; 21:328-29; 30:153, 155; 32:237, 255, 260; 36:200; 38:2, 153, 155
Bohemian Girl (opera), 10:172, 195
Bohm, S. H., 17:81
Bohme, Frederick G., 35:283; "The Portuguese in California," 35:233-52
Bohmer, Hermine, 28:293
Bohn, Henry G., 32:74, 77, 78
Boileau, Alexander, 11:180
Boileau, J., 22:323, 325, 347
Boillon (S.F., 1849), 5:20
Bois de Latour (S.F., 1849), 5:27
Boise, Capt. (Colorado R., 1875), 22:174
Boisvant, Louis, 22:196, 219; 23:31, 125
Bojorques, Bartolo, 16:249; 17:258; 20:271
Bojorquez, Pedro, 30:217
Bolado, Dulce, *see* Davis, Mrs. Francis H.

Bolado, Joaquín, 13:35
Boland, Edward R., 30:378
Boland, Stuart Morton, 26:93
Bolaños, Francisco de, 3:5, 21, 387-97; 6:315, 317; 7:21, 71, 257, 272, 274, 300, 363, 371, 379, 385-92 *passim*; 8:33-34, 37, 43-45, 55-69; 19:220; 20:319, 325; 23:220; 36:228-30
Bolcof, José Antonio, 27:104
Boleo Mine, 1:36
Boles, Charles E. ("Black Bart"), 10:304; 12:178; 15:192; 17:115
Boles (or Bowles), Joseph, 14:313; 15:240
Boley, Archie and Victor, 10:57
Bolina (ship), 15:225; 17:55
Bolinas Bay, 10:338, 342; 19:319, 321; 27:293
Boling, John, 5:330-31; 21:359-62
Bolivar (ship), 8:106; 14:332, 341, 343, 346; 18:70; 23:322
Bollene, Estelle, 10:377-81 *passim*
Bollinger, George, 8:358
Bollon, José María, 35:236
Bolt, Joseph Earle, 29:90
Bolton, Herbert Eugene, 5:324; 7:24, 61; 10:319; 12:177; 16:271, 272, 273, 275; 19:187-88; 23:372-73; 24:7, 8-9, 190; 25:193, 195, 202, 372; 29:143; 34:194; 36:31, 33, 238; "Francis Drake's Plate of Brass," 16: No. 2, Pt. 2, pp. 1-16; "In the South San Joaquin ahead of Garcés," 10:211-19; addresses: "The Escalante Expedition to California," 6:103; "Palou, First California Historian," 17:356; *Anza's California Expeditions*, rev., 10:84-85; *Fray Juan Crespi*, rev., 6:376; ed. Palou, *Historical Memoirs of New California*, rev., 6:375; obits. of Herbert I. Priestley, 23:186-87; Mrs. Michael Maloney, 30:86-87; art. on, 32:97-103; phot., 32: opp. 97
Bolton, James Robert, 15:366; 18:242, 250; 21:322, 331; 34:120; *see also* Bolton & Barron
Bolton & Barron, 14:346; 17:83; 18:12; 22:114; land claim, 15:364, 365, 366; 17:83; 23:229, 245; *see also* New Almaden Mine
"Bolton of California," by Lawrence Kinnaird, 32:97-103
Bombardier, Mrs. (El Dorado Co.), 27:86
Bomgarner, George, 8:6

Bona (violinist, 1858), 9:391

"Bonanza Inn," address by Carroll D. Hall, 34:87

Bonanza Inn, by Lewis and Hall, rev., 18:369-71

Bonaparte, Napoleon I, 13:35; 29:26

Bonaventura (Bonadventure, Boveantura, Buenaventura) River (Sacramento and San Joaquin rivs.), 2:346-47, 348; 22:194, 195, 202, 213; 28:121, 122, 243

Bond, Aubury H., 19:370-71

Bond, Charles R., 15:164; 18:46-53 *passim,* 60

Bond, Charles W., 26:355

Bond, E. L., 9:40

Bond, J. Gorham, 15:165

Bond, James B., 16:346

Bond, Nathan Burton, 26:302

Bond, William, 9:57, 58, 89

Bondurant, J. M., 28:340; 33:276

Bonelli, Mrs. Richard (Mona Modini), 31:286

Bonestell (Louis) & (Henry) Williston, 22:30, 36; 30:108, 115, 251-52, 254, 264, 265, 353, 364

Bonfanti, Marietta, 21:163, 164, 165

Bongard, Heinrich Gustav, 18:336, 337, 345

Bonheim, D., 30:366

Bonheur, Stella, 21:159

Boniface, George C., 21:146

Bonilla, José Mariano, 1:170; 6:160; 15:347; 21:320; 22:50; 25:32; 36:11; 40:31

Bonita, Point, 25:331; 27:293, 294

Bonlard, J. M., 9:388

Bonnard, Francis A., 13:299

Bonnell, Allison C., 25:132

Bonnell, E., 15:305

Bonner, Mr. Charles (Rosa Gore), 19:232, 233

Bonner, Ernest C., 4:47

Bonnet, Capt. (of *Lion,* 1847), 12:348; 28:342

Bonnet (S.F., 1850s), 32:110

Bonnet, Ben, 33:363

Bonneville, Benjamin Louis Eulalie de, 3:76; 4:279; 16:49; 22:150; 26:235; 28:201, 225

Bonney, Benjamin F., *Across the Plains by Prairie Schooner,* ed. Lockley, rev., 3:89-90

Bonney, Jarvis and Truman, 3:89

Bonnycastle, John C., 1:217, 223-29

passim, 233, 238, 243-44, 248, 252-54, 258-66; 16:339; 33:123, 253, 259-61, 338, 341, 343

Bonpland (Tahoe), Lake, 4:10

Bonté, John Harmon C., 17:48

Bon Ton Critic, 16:336

Boodwell, Georgie, phot., 38: foll. 8

Book Club of California, 39:71

Booker, Henry, 24:58; 30:51

Booker, S. A., 10:78, 173, 195

Booker, William Lane, 23:339, 344

Bookey (Honey L., 1863), 21:238

Book of [mining] Claims, 23:351

"Book of Remembrance," 27:375; 28:91, 180, 376; 30:88-89, 281-82, 379-80; 31:90-91, 180-81, 282-83, 376-77; 32:88-89, 172-73, 278-79, 373-74; 33:77-78, 180-81, 272-73, 369-70; 34:85-86, 176-78, 276-78, 370-72; 35:79-80, 170-72, 278-80, 369-71; 36:83-85, 178-80, 278-80, 371-73; 37:85, 180, 276, 379; 38:85, 175, 277, 359; 39:73, 174, 267, 354-55; 40:83, 177, 271, 364

"Booksellers of Old San Francisco," address by Robert E. Cowan, 20:282

Book trade, 30:97-115, 249-67, 353-67; 32:112; 35:6; 36:345; *see also* names of firms

Boon, W. W., 33:363

Boone County, Mo., emigrants from, 24:237-38, 241, 242, 257

Boonville, 33:361-62, 366

Boote, George, 40:45

Booth, Miss (Marysville, 1860), 10:251

Booth, Edwin, 3:36; 6:339; 7:284; 15:163, 169, 278, 281; 16:184, 285; 17:320; 20:129, 300, 304, 307; 21:61, 67, 74, 243, 248; 23:370; 35:141

Booth, Frank, 35:265

Booth, H. J., 27:170

Booth, Henry J., 9:395; 25:43

Booth, J. B., 9:26

Booth, John Wilkes, 7:284

Booth, Junius Brutus, 3:36; 4:211; 7:284; 20:300

Booth, Junius Brutus, Jr., 7:283, 284, 285; 9:283; 10:69, 389; 16:84, 341; 20:296, 297, 300, 304; 21:41, 45, 51, 53, 55, 59, 60-61, 67

Booth, Mrs. Junius Brutus, Jr., *see* Land, Agnes

Booth, Lucius A., 4:245-46; 5:178

Booth, Newton, 4:227; 5:95; 10:190,

251; 17:205; 19:252; 23:121; 34:102-3, 250, 254; 35:338
Booth, Mrs. Newton, *see* Glover, Mrs. J. T.
Booth, William L., 34:27, 30
Booth & Co., 10:190; 23:121
"Boot Jack" (d. Sacramento, 1853), 36:146
Booze, E. G., 17:305
Borax, 17:99, 110-12, 116-17, 210, 216; 18:195, 205, 214; 32:363, 365; 33:189
Borax Lake, Lake Co., 32:365
Borax Lake, San Bernardino Co., *see* Searles Lake
Borde (purser of *Warren*, 1848), 2:188
Bordelaise (ship), 8:136
Borden (master of *Bowditch*, 1847), 28:114
Borden (New York Flat, 1855), 8:341, 342
Borden, John W., 27:93
Borden, Joseph, 25:25
Borden (place), 25:25
Bordon (supercargo of *J.R.S.*, 1848), 28:113
Borel, Alfred, 26:84
Borel, Antoine, 25:230, 232; 26:84-85; 30:208; fund honoring, 26:84-85
Borgia, Mrs. De (Yuba Co., 1857), 9:152
Borica, Diego de, 1:164, 165, 175-76, 177; 4:150; 6:163, 165; 15:60-61; 17:121, 122, 246, 249; 36:5; 38:274
Boring, Samuel N., 3:159-60
Borland, James, 18:361-62
Borlase, William Copeland, 33:372
Bornheimer (Marysville, 1858), 9:264
Boroman, H. W., 40:223, 224, 225
Boronda, Anastasia, 14:130
Borosolvay (place), 17:117
Borrego Valley, 10:214, 216
Borthwick, John David, 6:217-18; 22:74-76, 255-73 *passim*; 30: 259, 357; 37:79; 38:38
Boruck, Marcus D., 10:26, 45, 68, 285; 15:277; 25:336-37, 344
Boscana, Gerónimo, 19:208-9, 215
Bosche, Mrs. John, 25:87
Boschulte, Theodore, 26:57
Bosio, G. B., port. of Lapérouse, 20: opp. 47
Bosquet, Thomas, 22:62
Bosqui, Edward, 3:40; 30:138, 139; art. on, 21:321-32; children of, 21:332;

phot., 21: opp. 321, *see also* Bosqui & Co.
Bosqui, Mrs. Edward (Helen Van Allen), 21:326; 24:266
Bosqui, Edward Lawrence, 21:330
Bosqui, Helen, 21:332; 22:96
Bosqui, Kenneth, 21: 322
Bosqui (Edward) & Co., 1:12, 20; 28:6; 21:327
Bosqui Engraving and Printing Co., 21:327
Boss (Philippines, 1898), 31:60, 62
Boss, Andrew C., bk. rev. by, 39:362-64
Bossagige, Léon, *see* Bossange, Léopold
Bossange, Léopold, 5:13, 21, 26, 42, 346
Bosserons (or Bosseront; Fr. consul, 1842), 11:203, 212, 213
Boston, Joseph, 33:65, 68
Boston (sloop of war, 1831), 20:194
Boston (schr., 1849), 18:331
Boston (cruiser, 1940s), 27:185
Boston and California Joint Stock Mining and Trading Co., 2:82; 20:44; 26:169
Boston and Newton Joint Stock Association, 22:119-46
"Boston Hide Droghers along California Shores," by Adele Ogden, 8:289-305
Boston House, San Diego, 31:37
Boston Ravine, 6:222, 225-36 *passim*, 332; *see also* Grass Valley
Boston Rubber Shoe Co., 31:185
Boston Symphony Orchestra, 25:245, 246-47
Bostwick, Frank F., 30:205
Bostwick, Henry R., 30:198, 205
Bosworth, John H., 17:174
Bosworth, Solomon Dewey, 6:340
"Botanist on the Road to Yerba Buena, by Alice B. Maloney, 24:321-25
Botany and botanists, 4:14; 5:262-69 *passim*; 12:292, 306; 14:75; 18:104, 335-46; 23:373; 29:2; 31:286; in Shasta region, 4:124, 126, 131; 24:326-29; 32:249; plants introd. by missionaries, 4:361-72; bk. on *Flora* rev., 4:88; *see also* Behr, Hans H.; Brackenridge; Coulter, Thomas; Douglas, David; Eastwood, Alice; Haenke; Jeffrey, John; Kellogg, Albert; Menzies; Nuttall, Thomas
Botello, Narciso, 4:159; 13:219, 220, 221; 16:360; 18:167, 178; 33:347

Botta, Paolo Emilio, 8:132, 146, 150, 222, 239, 245, 250, 324, 327
Bottle Hill, 30:111
Botts (S.F., 1855), 16:283
Botts, Bettie, 35:14
Botts, Charles Tyler, 9:243; 10:63, 153, 156, 158-59; 19:7, 230, 236; 28:361; 30:129; 35: 111; fac. sig., 10: opp. 159
Botts, Mrs. Charles Tyler, 35:13
Botts, William, 19:231
Bouchacourt, C., 30:329
Bouchard, Capt. and Mrs. (S.F., 1851), 6:56
Bouchard, Hypolite de, 1:168, 176, 194-95; 8:186; 11:82; 13:206-7; 14:15; 15:139; 16:102, 188; 29:309-10; 36:7
Boucher (Marysville, 1856), 3:160
Bouchet, Louis, 13:211, 335
Boucicault, Dion, 10:65, 69, 389; 21:51-52, 53, 171, 173
Boudin (Marysville, 1851), 15:49
Boudinot, F., 10:196
Boudrye (or Bouerye), F. F., 32:109
Bouet, Juan (Jean), 13:325
Boulbon, *see* Raousset de Boulbon
Boulet, Paul, 39:316
Boullenois, Louis-Marie-Gustave de, 22:304
Boullet, Mrs. E. O. H., 29:294
Boulton (Nevada Co., 1852), 20:43
"Bound for the Land of Canaan, Ho!," Diary of Levi Stowell, ed. Marco G. Thorne, 27:33-50, 157-64, 259-66, 361-70; 28:57-68
Boundaries, county, bk. on, rev., 2:366-67
Boundaries of California, 20:106, 107; eastern, 4:11, 290; 19:13; 10:154-57; 15:376; 18:205-9; 39:291; northern, 8:104; 11:311; 19:13, 368-72; 20:106-7; 24:301; 28:372-73; 31:125; southern, 5:321-27, 337; 8:104; 9:3-15; 10:235-38; 11:162; 16:305; 19:2, 3, 13, 178, 217-18; 20:106-7; maps showing, 5: opp. 321; 9: opp. 6, opp. 12; surveys of, 4:11; 9:3-15; 15:179; 18:205-9; 22:19
"Boundary Line between California and Oregon, The," by Francis S. Foote, 19:368-72
Bourdas, M. A., 8:217, 316
"Bourdon burial," 35:258
Bouret (S.F., 1849), 5:21
Bourland, William, 28:337

Bourn, William Bowers, 36:205, 207, 210, 293, 295, 300
Bourn, Mrs. William Bowers (Sarah Chase), 36:207-10 *passim*, 293, 299, 300
Bourn, William Bowers, II, 9:96; 25:230, 232, 246, 249; 36:205, 207, 208, 212, 293-300 *passim*; family of, 27:254
Bournie, Dr. (Sacramento, 1857), 9:170
Boussole (ship), 15:213, 216; 20:51, 52; 26:371
Boutwell, Edward B., 14:357
Bouvet, Lucien, 36:74-75
Bouvette, Juan and Loreta (Cota), 13:331
Bouzet, E. de, 11:206-7; 12:54-55, 60, 161
Bovee, James S., 6:14-15, 16; 27:153
Bowden, Joseph, 28:290
Bowdone, J., 21:238
Bowditch (ship), 28:114
Bowen (on *California*, 1849), 13:387; 27:259-66 *passim*
Bowen (Grass Valley, 1850), 6:224
Bowen, Asa M., 26:62
Bowen, Isaac, 15:39; 16:260
Bowen, John, 4:275; 6:59
Bowen, Thomas G., 23:290
Bowen, William Alvin, obit., 17:94
Bowen, William Ezra and Minnie (Gray), 31:381
Bowen, William J., 17:42, 45; 31:330-33 *passim*
Bowen v. Aubrey, 10:251
Bower, William, 28:337
Bowers, Lemuel S. ("Sandy"), 12:327; 23:91-92
Bowers, Mrs. Lemuel S. (Eilly Orrum), 15:381
Bowers, Stephen, 19:59-64 *passim*, 72; 27:318
Bowie, Capt. (San Pedro, 1863), 16:67
Bowie, A. J., 29:198-99
Bowie, Augustus Jesse, 4:202; 9:112; 11:10; 16:345; 19:231; 28:34
Bowie, Charles, 8:342
Bowie, E. J., 16:283
Bowie, George W., 9:112, 113, 116, 157, 178; 15:168; 40:344, 350
Bowie, H., 11:127
Bowie, Hyde Ray, 13:32
Bowie, Hamilton, 9:26; 13:32; 15:180, 181, 274; 16:183; 37:140
Bowie, Haskins, 13:32
Bowie, Henry P., 27:320

Bowie, Mrs. Henry P., *see* Howard, Mrs. William D. M. (Agnes Poett)

Bowker, Lawrence, 39:265-66

Bowland, E., 14:398

Bowlen, Frederick John, 15:311; address on San Francisco disaster of 1906, 21:184; obit., 24:283

Bowles, Joseph, *see* Boles

Bowles, Philip Ernest, obit., 5:102

Bowles, Samuel, 16:181

Bowling, John, 4:13; 28:331-34 *passim*

Bowlsby, L. J., 9:180

Bowman (Monterey, 1835), 16:327

Bowman, Andrew W., 18:118, 135

Bowman, Alexander, 26:72

Bowman, Denis Evarts, 25:380

Bowman, Feble, 9:349, 357, 360, 373-74

Bowman, J. H., 27:195

Bowman, Jacob N., 25:379; 30:284; 31:380; 33:380; "Cornerstone of the State Capitol," 33:329-35; "Determination of the Birthdays of Urban Communities," 27:51-62, 104; 31:325-33; "Driving the Last Spike at Promontory, 1869," 36:97-106, 263-74; "The Lost Toma de Razón," 21:311-20; "New Haven and the Two Alvarados," 12:173-75; "The Original Constitution of California, 1849," 28:193-97; "The Peraltas and Their Houses," 30:217-31; "Preservation of the State Archives," 28:143-50; "The Question of Sainsevain's Signature," 28:361-62; "The Seal of the California Supreme Court," 33:73-75; "The Spanish Anchorage in San Francisco Bay, 25:319-24; "The Third Map of Yerba Buena," 26:267-68; "Weights and Measures of Provincial California," 30:315-38; address, "The Passing of California Historical Traditions," 31:79; bk. rev. by, 39:368-71

Bowman, John H., 11:9

Bowman, Mrs. Samuel Millard, 24:262

Bowman Dam, *see* Dams

Bowman Lake and reservoir, 29:199, 207

Bowsher, A. L., 36:97, 105

Bowstead, James, 24:166

Box and Cox (play), 23:355, 370; 30:355

Box Canyon, 25:302; 34:193-94

Boxing, 15:182; 20:135, 291

Box S Ranch, 27:117, 118

Boyce, John, 10:356, 357, 362

Boyd (Oregon trail, 1844), 4:320

Boyd, Maj. (S.F., 1851), 28:35

Boyd (Timbuctoo, 1858), 9:375

Boyd (or Boyce), George W., 14:278

Boyd, James T., 17:171; 37:155

Boyd, John and Anne (Dean), 28:292

Boyers, William, 33:257

"Boyhood Experiences . . . in the Yuba Diggings," address by Charles A. Ramm, 11:88

Boyle, Andrew A., 13:342-43

Boyle, Edward F., 9:397

Boyle, Emmet D., 2:208

Boyle, Pat, 8:200

Boyle, William G., 35:341, 344

Boynton (Yuba Co., 1860), 10:255

Boynton, Albert Eugene, 36:253

Boynton, Joseph, 2:115

Boynton, Ray, 38:2, 3

Boys' College (Benicia), 24:64

Boys' High School, San Fancisco, 35:139

Boys of the Sierra; or The Young Gold Hunters, by Hendrik Conscience, 37:312-13

"Boy's Voyage to San Francisco, 1865-66, A," from the Diary of William B. B. Ingalls, ed. F. Bourn Hayne, 36:205-12, 293-306

Bozio, Orlando, 39:239, 253

Brace, F. Richard, 24:379

Brace, Philander, 8:373; 15:158-61 *passim*, 282; 24:173-74

Brackenridge, William Dunlop, 24:321-25; Journal of, 24:326-36; port., 24: opp. 321

Brackett, John Ely, 10:23

Brackett, Joshua G., 23:65-66

Bracy (Yuba Co., 1858), 9:353; 10:55, 171, 363

Bradbury, A. W., 35:30, 31, 32

Bradbury, Eugene, 2:121

Bradbury, John (botanist, 1811), 18:341-42

Bradbury, John, Capt., (1880s), 21:329

Bradbury, John D., 20:44

Braden, E. B., 32:10

Braden, Ida Belle (Hollenbeck), 25:285

Braden Copper Co., 31:296

Bradfield's sawmill, 34:222

Bradford, Mrs. (Sacramento, 1858), 9:257

Bradford, Miss (Sacramento, 1861), 10:281

Bradford, Capt. (Colorado R., 1870), 22:173
Bradford (S.F., 1879), 21:251
Bradford, Abram Clarke, 9:104
Bradford, C. H., 9:110
Bradford, John, *Historical &c. Notes on Kentucky*, ed. Stipp, rev., 11:386-87
Bradford, John O., 31:213, 217
Bradford, John S., 6:150; 14:376; 30:55, 64, 131, 146
Bradford, N. D., 9:137, 174
Bradford, Thomas, 19:146
Bradley (Georgetown, 1850), 30:103
Bradley, Maj. (San Joaquin Co., 1857), 21:325
Bradley, A. D., 21:251
Bradley, Bennett Trice, 10:62; 11:8, 9
Bradley (or Fegan), Catherine, 9:351
Bradley, Cornelius B., 4:49
Bradley, Frederick Worthen, 23:94; obit., 12:371
Bradley, Mrs. Frederick Worthen (Mary Elizabeth Parks), 23:94
Bradley, Harold W., 25:285
Bradley, Henry Sewall, 12:371; 23:94
Bradley, Henry W., 34:295; 35:55
Bradley, John D., 23:94
Bradley, Lewis Rice, 28:379; 35:336-37
Bradley, Thomas Westly, 29:276; 30:9, 13
Bradley and Rulofson, 34:295-96, 299; 35:48, 55, 56, 57
Bradshaw (Placerville, 1852), 30:111
Bradshaw (lawsuit, S.F., 1860s), 21:118
Bradshaw, J. A., 14:396
Bradshaw, John, 8:332-34; 23:203, 215-16, 305-6, 315, 330, 332; 35:198
Bradshaw, N., 6:374
Bradshaw, Samuel C., 16:336
Bradshaw, William D., 12:16
Bradshaw's Ferry, 12:10, 16
Bradway, Charles, 33:363
Brady, A. B., 12:72
Brady, Henry, 21:305
Brady, James D., 13:331
Brady, James H., 24:343, 346, 353, 354, 358, 364
Brady, John, 21:305
Brady, Lavinia R., 15:195
Brady, William, 9:369, 373, 375; lawsuits, 9:360, 368, 373; 10:167, 168, 178, 273
Bragdon (riv. str.), *see J. Bragdon*
Bragg, Braxton, 27:216, 217; 30:165

Bragg & Co., 9:358
Brainard (Sacramento, 1860), 10:283
Braislin, William C., library of, 6:193-94
Braisted (San Juan del Sur, 1852), 36:143, 144
Braly, Mrs. James C. (Lizzie Whisman), 16:136-37, 141
Braly, James M., 7:113; 26:237
Braly, John Hyde, 16:141
Braly, John W., 26:169
Braly, Mount, 7:114
Brambila, Fernando, 15:214
Brambilla, Elvira, 21:68-69, 159
Branch, Francis Ziba, 2:36; 4:127, 132, 138; 18:163, 171, 175-76, 259
Branchi, Alexander M., 18:166-67, 178
Branch Turnpike Co., 8:347
Branciforte, Villa de, 1:25-31 *passim*; 15:188; 18:294, 310; 27:104; 40:12, 13
Brand, L. C., 31:16
Brand, Miriam, 29:190
Brand, William Watson, 13:32
Brandegee, Mrs. Townshend Stith (Mary Katharine Layne Curran), 32:180, 182, 183
Brander, William, 16:324, 330
Branding, of cattle and horses, 8:104; 14:9-10; 20:345; 26:244; 38:260, 263
Brandt, John, 10:76
Brandy City, 9:148, 149, 165, 177; 10:256
Brandy Gulch, 9:78; 11:238, 239
Brandywine (ship), 19:43, 44; 30:19
Branham, G. S., 9:145, 151
Branham, Isaac, 14:152; 27:107; 28:63; lawsuit, 38:51
Brannan, Mrs., 27:320-21
Brannan, John, 22:379; 25:118
Brannan, Samuel, 6:12; 8:172; 9:90; 10:395; 11:18, 136, 161, 179; 14:272, 276-82 *passim*, 388; 15: opp. 40, 370; 16:76, 130, 137, 139, 142; 17:83; 18:36, 37, 46, 50-60 *passim*; 19:152, 231; 21:332; 25:5, 110, 118, 223; 26:121, 123, 124, 182, 329-30; 27:129; 30:99, 161; 32:195, 196; 33:65; 34:211; 37:211; 38:42; 40:125
on *Brooklyn*, 3:34; 10:298; 11:129-30; 15:244; 17:295; 25:127; 27:229-38 *passim*; Mormon, 4:154; 10:298; 11:129, 132; 14:176, 277; 15:244; 16:130, 139, 140; 25:127; 26:165, 166, 329; 27:129
press of, 3:101; 11:130, 389; 17:296; 26:165; printer and newsp. pub.,

5:407; 10:16, 299-301; 11:129, 130, 132, 143-44; 14:277; 17:300; 26:330
complaint against RR, 4:246; 21:328; con. w. Vig. Com., 3:39; 16:344-45; 18:371; 29:161, 162-63; 34:247
art. on, 10:298-301; bk. on, rev., 4:392-94
Brannan City (proj.), 10:385, 395
Brannan County, 14:405
Brannan House, San Francisco, 19:229, 236
Brannan St. drawbridge, San Francisco, 16:283, 340, 342; 17:169
Branner, John Casper, 30:215
Branquart, Victor, 39:246
Bransom, Benjamin, 28:337
Brant, John P., 6:10
Brashear, Minnie M., and Robert M. Rodney, eds. *Art, Humor and Humanity of Mark Twain*, rev., 38:368-70
Brastow, S. D., 2:92, 122
Bravo, J., 3:335
Bray, Absalom Francis, address, "Early California Cases," 32:174
Bray, Edmund, 8:168, 170, 171, 172
Bray, John G., 26:264
Bray, Walter, 10:393
Bray and Bros., 29:176
Brayle, Mrs. (Yuba Co., 1857), 9:157
Brayton, Al, 33:363
Brayton, Albert Paulding, 20:9
Brayton, Ed, 33:363
Brayton, Isaac H., 10:198; 20:9; 21:33; 27:301; 35:305
Brayton Hall, Oakland, 20:2, 5, 9
Brazoria, 14:202
Breck, Henry C., 32:190
Breckenridge, Thomas E., 18:174
Breckinridge, John Cabell, 9:104; 10:252, 257, 268; 11:17, 18; 17:314, 317, 318-19; 22:228
Bree, Tommy, 4:62
Breed, Arthur H., 28:14
Breed, D. C., 11:127
Breeder and Sportsman (weekly), 30:154
Breen, Edward J., 33:352, 356
Breen, Isabella, 33:353, 356
Breen, James Frederick, 33:352, 356
Breen, Mrs. James Frederick (Catherine McMahon), 33:352, 353
Breen, John, 33:351-52, 355, 372
Breen, Patrick, 1:296; 8:384; 21:288; 32:89; 33:349-59

Breen, Mrs. Patrick (Margaret Bulger), 33:349-58 *passim*
Breen, Patrick, Jr., 33:352
Breen, Mrs. Patrick, Jr. (Amelia Anderson), 33:352, 356
Breen, Peter, 33:353
Breen, Simon Preston, 33:353, 356
Breen, Mrs. Simon Preston (Marie Constance Palmsay), 33:353
Breen, William and Mary (Zanetta), 33:352
"Breens of San Juan Bautista, The," by John S. Enright, 33:349-59
Breeze, William Francis, 4:45; 31:300
Breeze, Mrs. William Francis (Evelyn Norwood), 31:300; 37:217
Bremer, Anne, 38:2
Brenham, Charles J., 15:266; 16:67, 68; 17:84; 22:112, 113; 32:185; *see also* Sanders & Brenham
Brennan, Charles J., 15:317, 320, 321, 323; phot., opp. 316
Brennan, Michael, 6:332-35; 12:72; 19:28
Brennan, Thomas, 11:9
Brennen, John H. and Ann (Sharp), 28:294
Brent, Joseph Lancaster, 13:39, 315, 330, 336; 29:234, 237; 40: foll. 294
Brent, Thomas L., 28:202-4
Bret and Stetson, 14:399
"Bret Harte Discovery, A," by Boutwell Dunlap, 4:207-9
"*Bret Harte Legend, The*," by Stewart, rev., 7:287-88
Bretnor, Mrs. Reginald (Helen Harding), 27:187
Breton (S.F., 1851), 6:56
Bretonne, La (mining co.), 22:303, 310
Brett, John, 10:44-45, 65, 67
Brett, Otis, 10:45, 66
Bretz, Aaron, 19:60-61, 64, 68, 69; 27:316; 28:47, 53; phot., 19: opp. 59
Breuer, Henry Joseph, 37:29
Breuil, Edmond, 35:338
Breven, Herman, 15:369
Brew, Chartres, 6:28, 29, 30
Brewer, A. L., 27:255
Brewer, Charles, 35:196, 199
Brewer, David Josiah, 36:44, 46, 51
Brewer, Mrs. Josiah (Emilia Ann Field), 36:42, 46
Brewer, W. A., 1:18
Brewer, William Henry, 4:16-22 *passim*, 55; 7:121, 122; 23:109; 24:269-70; 26:234; 29:204; 34:220;

36:13-14; letter from, 7:122-31;
Up and down California, ed.,
Farquhar, rev., 9:401
Brewer, Mount, 4:17, 18, 20, 55
Breweries: Marysville, 14:399; 15:46;
Yreka, 28:213, 229
Brewerton, George Douglas, 10:38-39,
298; 29:35, 38
Brewster (Sacramento, 1858), 9:250
Brewster, Charles O., 14:388
Brewster, George, 14:316
Brewster, I., 14:303-4
Brewster, John A., 7:13, 14, 16, 17;
9:42, 45
Brewster, R. E., 2:244
Brewster, S. T., 14:378, 379, 396; 15:28
Brewton (Sacramento, 1857), 9:170
Brewton, Ada, 9:170, 245
Breyfogle (Death Valley, 1866),
18:211-12
Breymand (of Fr. mining co., 1849),
22:297
Bric-a-Brac Club, Sacramento, 19:106
Brickell (Colfax, 1861), 4:250
Bricks and brickmaking, 2:136; 13:330;
14:20; 15:279; 23:377; 38:337; *see also*
Adobe bricks
Bridalveil Fall, Yosemite, 1:276-77
Bride, Laura, *see* Powers, Laura Bride
Bridewell, F. Albert, 25:380
Bridge (Papeete, 1841) and sister,
14:323
Bridge (Yuba Co., 1859), 10:56
Bridge, Norman, 31:18, 21, 29
Bridge, Samuel J., 29:253, 254
Bridge (Puente) Creek, 1:148; 29:35
Bridgeport, 26:235, 242-43, 245, 248;
Valley, 235, 244
Bridger, James, 4:342; 6:118; 16:141;
22:150; 26:324, 325; bk. on, rev.,
290-91
Bridges (San Joaquin R., 1850), 11:261
Bridges, Appleton, 36:153
Bridges, Francis W., 22:192
Bridges:
over Alder Cr., 4:223;
American R., 9:260; 10:280, 293;
11:230; 19:146; 25:223
Bear R., 11:232, 246; 19:146-47
Colorado R., 27:116
Deer Cr., 19; 146-47
Feather R., 10:42, 43, 47, 64, 66, 69,
74, 361, 362; 29:205
Fraser R., 19:148
Klamath R., 19:146

Mission Cr., 17:169
Mokelumne R., 25:382
Napa Co., 16:142
Oregon Cr. (covered), 28:237,
239-40, 242
Sacramento R., 9:284
San Francisco Bay, 27:339; *see also*
Golden Gate Bridge; San Francisco-
Oakland Bay Bridge
Stanislaus R., 19:146
Sutter Slough, 23:349
Trinity R., 19:146
Tuolumne R., 19:146
Yuba R., 8:203, 209, 212, 338, 344,
355-60 *passim*; 9:254; 10:77, 181,
182, 254, 255, 279, 396; 15:53;
covered, 28:237-38, 242; 39:107-8
"Brief Sketch of the Life of Edward
Cleveland Kemble, A," 14:80
Brier, James Welsh, 13:314, 317; 18:198
Brier, Mrs. James Welsh (Juliet Wells),
18:201
Brier, John W., 18:215
Brier, William Wallace, 10:198; 15:
opp. 40, 43, 44, 57
Brierly, A. A., 29:90
Brierly, Benjamin, 15:182, 186; 27:231,
307, 309; 31:5; 32:133
Brigand, The (play), 21:45
Briggs (Sacramento, 1852), 36:141,
144-47 *passim*
Briggs, Alfred, 10:62, 70
Briggs, Francis, 18:174
Briggs, George Gregg, 10:178, 18:22,
363; 25:34, 172, 175; *see also* Briggs'
Ranch
Briggs, Henry, 8:36-37, 40, 42; map by,
opp. 37
Briggs, Joseph W., 28:302, 303, 318;
see also Briggs' Ranch
Briggs, LeRoy H., 24:286
Briggs, Martin Clock, 15:186; 27:307;
31:1-11; 40:329, 333; family of, 31:9;
phot., 31: opp. 1
Briggs, Mrs. Martin Clock (Ellen
Green), 31:4
Briggs, Robert M., 9:115, 116, 248, 249,
256, 259, 260, 268, 281, 283; 10:257,
268
Briggs, Samuel M., 9:133, 138, 140, 143;
lawsuit, 9:134
Briggs, "Scotty," 34:317-18
Briggs' Ranch and orchard, 9:350;
10:172, 194; 18:22, 363; 24:265; 28:318
Bright, Judge (Marysville, 1851), 15:29

Bright, Sam, 30:245-46

Brighton, 14:269, 282; 16:127, 138, 142; 19:139, 143; 26:110; *see also* Natoma

Brill, Abe D., 8:201; 9:248, 250, 273; 11:53-54, 57

Brillante (ship), 11:206, 207; 12:54, 55, 56, 60, 161, 162, 339

"Brilliant California Novelist, Gertrude Atherton, A," by Henry J. Forman, 40:1-10

Brincken, William, 15:240

Brinsmade, A. A., 1:267; 14:330; 25:115, 336, 343

Brinsmade, A. P., 28:34

Brinsmade, Peter Allan, 25:115, 343

Briones, Antonio, 13:208

Briones, Gregorio, 16:249; 19:321

Briones, Juana, *see* Miranda, Mrs. Apolinario

Briot, Dr. (S.F., 1849), 5:17, 20, 27, 176, 347, 351-71 *passim*, 373; 6:37, 42, 44, 56; 39:9

Brisa (ship), 22:169

Brisard, Mme. (1860s), 9:170, 171

Bristol, Corydon, 13:10, 32, 33

Bristol, R. D., 29:225

Briston, Charles, 26:204

Bristow, Dr. (Placer Co., 1850s), 2:205

Bristow, Elijah, 19:116, 135

Bristow, James H., 9:27, 29

Bristow, William, 9:142, 144, 155

Britannia (ship), 13:250

British: comment on California, 22:254-74 *passim*; 32:81-86, 269-75; 33:23-28; holders of Mex. bonds, 18:136-46; proposals for colonization of Calif. by, 18:135-47; *see also* Great Britain

"British-American Relations in Connection with the Acquisition of California," address by E. D. Adams, 2:258

British Blonde Burlesque Troupe, 21:165

British Columbia, 19:148; 21:374; camels in, 9:313; letter from, 11:151; *see also* Fraser River

"British Comment—As of 1849-1851," by S. Laird Swagert, 32:81-86, 269-75; 33:23-38

"British Vice Consul in California and the Events of 1846, The," by Ernest A. Wiltsee, 10:99-128

Brito, Pedro, 14:211

Brittain (Marysville, 1861), 10:284

Brittan, John W., 9:109; 15:280, 364, 372; 16:282

Britton, Joseph, 19:150; 25:8; *see also* Britton & Rey

Britton & Rey, 4:11, 13; 20:276, 277; 22:34-35; *Map of the State of California*, 34:212-14

Brizard, Alexander, 21:190; 39:57

Brizard, Henry Francis, obit., 21:189-90

Brizevin (on *Jacques-Laffitte*, 1849), 23:67

Broadhurst, Stephen, 6:60

Broadwater, Thomas, 15:34

Broadway, Harry, 30:222, 228

Brobeck, William Irvin, obit., 6:288

Brock, Capt. (of *Quito*, 1849), 29:1, 15

Brockhaus, Friedrich Arnold, 31:364

Brocklebank, M. T., 10:70, 282, 379

Brockman, Israel, 24:58; 29:324

Brockman, Mose, 7:116

Brockway, Squire (Mokelumne Hill, 1854), 30:246

Brockway, S. W., 9:100

Brode, Charles, 26:188; 33:274

Brode, Mrs. Charles (Clara Alexander), 33:274

Brode, Hilda, *see* Lawler, Mrs. Oscar

Broderick (New York Flat, 1855), 8:341

Broderick, David Colbrith, 10:53, 59, 167, 168, 206, 293; 17:321; 20:306, 309; 27:369; 32:295; 38:197-98, 216-17
    accusations against, 37:144-49; bust of, 10:259, 270; candidate for Senate, 9:25, 285; 15:270; 19:166-67, 261, 268; 32:146-48; 38:208; debates and feud w. Gwin, 19:166-67, 264-65, 268; 32:145, 146, 313-25
    Democratic leader, 3:155; 6:7; 8:364; 9:45, 47, 177, 285; 11:14, 15; 15:204; 17:179, 181, 312-13; 19:268-69, 353; 20:301; 21:30-31; 32:151-56 *passim*
    duel and death, 3:42; 9:270, 285; 10:174, 175, 197-98; 11:4; 14:377; 15:382-83; 17:314, 321; 19:347-48; 20:310; 21:39, 47; 27:100; 32:223; 38:212-15, 217; 40:203-4; estate and will (forged), 40:203-14; eulogy by Wilkes, 38:199-215
    fireman, 15:311; 23:70, 71; friend of Maguire, 15:311; 23:70, 71; meetings and speeches, 10:166, 170, 191, 193; 38:211-12; resolutions censuring, 10:44, 66, 272, 287
    U.S. Senator, 9:53, 75, 77, 272, 285; 19:167, 268, 276, 345; 20:309;

21:30-31, 42; 37:144; 38:209-11
ports., 10:175; 38:196

Broderick, W. J., 19:61, 72

Broderick, Mount, 1:281

"Broderick-Terry Duel, The," address
by Charles R. Boden, 15:382-83

Brodhead, Richard, 19:180-81

Brodigan, Teddy, 7:113-14

Brodt, Helen (Tanner), 22:370

Broemmel, George Martin, 23:89, 189

Broemmel, J. C. Berthold, 23:189

Bromley, Washington Lafayette,
34:245, 246

Bromwell, Louis L., 27:343, 349

Bronco Pegasus, A, by Lummis, rev.,
8:85-86

Bronk, George M., 15:29

Bronson, William, *The Earth Shook,
the Sky Burned,* rev., 38:373-74

Brontes (ship), 37:206-7, 209

Bronze Horse (play), 38:19

Brooke, Mildred Crew, *see* Hoover,
Mildred

Brooke, J. M., 23:336, 337, 339, 342

Brookes, Samuel Marsden, 30:137;
36:193-204; 37:21; phot., 36: opp. 193

Brookes, Mrs. Samuel Marsden (Julia
Beldon Jones), 36:195, 198

Brookes family, 36:193-98

Brookline (ship), 8:290-93; 16:222;
23:193-98 *passim*, 301, 302, 304, 330,
331; 33:376; illus., 23: opp. 193

Brooklyn, Alameda Co., 10:72

Brooklyn (ship), 3:34, 114; 10:298;
14:80; 15:244; 16:139; 17:295, 300;
25:127; 26:165; 37:229-40; illus., 37:
opp. 225

Brooklyn and Fruitvale Horse Railroad,
27:72; phot., opp. 72

Brooklyn Tannery, 33:69

Brooks (Cruces, 1849), 27:36

Brooks (on *London,* 1849), 7:210, 216,
398

Brooks (Camptonville, 1855), 8:344, 345

Brooks (Brandy City, 1857), 9:153, 155

Brooks (Auburn, 1860), 29:112, 120

Brooks (Death Valley, 1861), 18:206,
207, 209

Brooks, Corp. (Del Norte Co., 1862),
26:3

Brooks, Mrs. (S.F., 1865), 36:296

Brooks, Mrs. B. L., 19:231

Brooks, Benjamin, 14:77

Brooks, Charles Wolcott, 23:342-46
passim; 29:253

Brooks, Elisha, *A Pioneer Mother of
California,* rev., 2:84

Brooks, George J., 29:253

Brooks, J. Tyrwhitt (pseud. Henry
Vizetelly), 4:182; 11:65-68; 13:175;
33:126

Brooks, James and Oceana (Fisher),
28:293

Brooks, James Marion, 20:270

Brooks, Joel R., 28:337

Brooks, Noah, 5:200; 6:69-76; 10:270,
294; 15:8; 16:203-4, 207, 311-12;
28:8-9; 30:130, 137, 145; 33:193-217;
34:57, 58; phot., 33: opp. 193

Brooks, Mrs. Noah (Caroline Augusta
Fellows), 33:194, 204

Brooks, Norman C., 23:345

Brooks, Samuel, 30:137

Brooks, Samuel Houston, 9:247, 273

Brooks, William H. J., 14:74-75, 77

Brooks (Chas. W.) & Co., 29:254

Brooks Islands, 23:345, 346, 347

Brooks's Mill, 9:162

Brooms and broom making, 10:291;
28:237

Brophy, John, 9:345; 10:77; 15:28, 29

Brosnan, C. M., 10:255, 267, 295; 15:366;
16:82; 26:175, 183, 263, 266

Brotchie, William, 28:102, 255

Brother Jonathan (ship), 12:12; 15:164,
169, 172, 178; 16:66; 17:315; 19:144,
154; 25:103; 26:9, 359-60; 32:361;
36:134

Brotherston (James) and Co., 6:254-64
passim

Brotherton, Capt. (of *Ferdinand,* 1849),
29:257

Broughton (Sacramento, 1862), 10:372

Broughton, William Robert, 2:275, 282,
285, 287, 290, 292; 10:321, 328

Brouillet, John B. A., 29:143

Brower & Dryer, 5:140

Browett, Daniel, 14:278-80

Brown, Capt. (Calif. Bat., 1846), 19:132

Brown (via Mazatlán, 1849), 21:305

Brown, Capt. (of *Samuel M. Fox,* 1849),
34:26, 27

Brown (brothers, from Washington,
1849), 28:57

Brown, "Major" (from Natchez, 1850),
8:356

Brown, Mr. and Mrs. (from Texas,
1850), 23:161

Brown (from N.Y., 1854), 8:203

Brown (or Bevin; duelist, 1854), 15:174

Brown, Capt. (of *Defender*, 1855), 16:184, 282

Brown, Judge (S.F., 1855), 15:364

Brown (mate on *Bald Eagle*, 1861), 32:212

Brown, Capt. (S.F., 1862), 9:331

Brown, Dr. (Santa Barbara, ca. 1910), 36:73

Brown, Abram, 28:337

Brown, A. R., 9:160

Brown, Alan K., 39:180; "Salt for the Scraping: . . . San Francisco Bay Salt Industry," 39:117-20

Brown, Alexander ("the Greek"), 9:374; 10:41, 63

Brown, Alice M., 31:292

Brown, Andrew, 31:93

Brown, Annie Florence, 26:91

Brown, Arthur (architect), 38:2

Brown, Arthur (engineer), 35:263

Brown, Benjamin F. and Mary Campbell (McIntyre), 31:292

Brown, Beriah, 20:156, 165

Brown, Blanche, 33:364, 367

Brown, Bliss, 19:383; "The Old Limekilns of Marin Co.," 19:317-22

Brown, Bolton Coit, 4:47-48, 54, 55

Brown, Mrs. Bolton Coit (Lucy Fletcher), 4:47

Brown, Mrs. C., 30:258

Brown, Carrie Benedict, 34:374

Brown, Charles (1830s), 2:53; 17:253; 31:301

Brown, Mrs. Charles (Rosalía de Haro), 14:130

Brown, Charles (S.F., 1855), 15:371

Brown, Charles (Yuba Co., 1856), 9:66

Brown, Charles (Anderson Valley, 1862), 33:363-66 *passim*

Brown, D. Mackenzie, 26:285; ed. and trans. "A Petition from Alpheus B. Thompson to Governor Victoria," 26:249-52

Brown, David, 13:338; 15:270

Brown, Deuteronomy, 6:169-80

Brown, Earl, 29:200

Brown, Edward, 31:292

Brown, Elam, 30:1, 4-5, 9; fac. sig., 10: opp. 159

Brown, Erasmus, 30:8

Brown, Everett J., obit., 26:90-91

Brown, Mrs. Everett J. (Winifred Osborne), 26:91

Brown, Ezekiel, 15:281

Brown, Fanny, 21:65, 142

Brown, Gertrude K. (Mrs. Frank E.), 34:92; "Initial Monuments for California's Base and Meridian Lines," 34:1-17

Brown, Gustav, 40:293

Brown, Harry, 10:395

Brown, Harvey S., 21:120; 27:147

Brown, Henry S., 9:26; 16:79

Brown, Hugh G., 25:380

Brown, I. E., 8:356

Brown, J. P., 8:358; 9:60, 61, 74, 132, 134, 141, 145, 152(?), 160, 166, 169, 346(?), 369; phot., 9: opp. 64

Brown, J. T. and Elizabeth (Fraice) and children, 33:363, 364

Brown, Jacob B., 9:27, 29; 16:79

Brown, Capt. James (Mormon Bat., 1847), 14:272

Brown, James (nr. Lassen's, 1849), 30:60, 62

Brown, James S., 14:269, 273-74, 276; 26:110-24 *passim*, 132

Brown, Jim (San Bernardino Co., ca. 1900), 27:119

Brown, John (San Pascual, 1846), 21:342, 344; 22:49

Brown, John ("Juan Flaco," 1846), 3:115; 12:165; 13:302; 17:329; 25:130; 29:334-35

Brown, John (Marysville, 1861), 10:357, 384, 385

Brown, John (S.F., 1862), 9:319

Brown, John (San Bernardino Co., 1890s), 27:122

Brown, John ("Pottawatomie"), 10:188, 201; 14:348

Brown, Mrs. John ("Pottawatomie"), 17:89; 20:255; 23:287

Brown, John Henry, 3:34; 5:129; 10:354; 11:68, 132, 137; 13:379; 15:65; 17:296-99 *passim*, 301; 19:135; 27:44, 50, 265; *Reminiscences . . . of San Francisco*, rev., 12:364-65

Brown, John R., 4:250

Brown, John W. and Mathilda (Delger), 26:90

Brown, Jonathan, 14:180

Brown, K. B., 15:381

Brown, Karl F., 27:186

Brown, Kenneth Marsh and Olive (Dudley), 29:381

Brown, M. S., 15:280, 364

Brown, Madie D., 29:189, 331; 36:284; "Gen. M. G. Vallejo and H. H. Bancroft," 29:149-59; "The Vineyards

of Gen. M. G. Vallejo," 36:241-50; trans. Thomas Savage letter to M. G. Vallejo, 29:160

Brown, Margelina, 30:4

Brown, Martha, 17:239

Brown, Martin, 5:125

Brown, Mary Campbell, *see* Hooper, Mrs. John Albert

Brown, N. A., 14: opp. 209, 401

Brown, Orlando, 26:347

Brown, Oscar M., 40:349

Brown, P. F., 37:199

Brown, Perc S., 25:285

Brown, R. W., 32:354

Brown, Ralph and Millie (Prather), 33:364-67 *passim*

Brown, Sam, 6:342-43

Brown, Seth, 36:253

Brown, Mrs. Stella (Ingrim), 18:94

Brown, T. M., 34:271

Brown, Thomas, 23:276

Brown, Thomas Marsh and Barbara Abigail (d'Arcy), 29:381

Brown, Thomas P., 20:288

Brown, W. A., 30:115

Brown, W. H. (Yuba Co., 1851), 15:49

Brown, W. H. (actor, Marysville, 1859), 10:77

Brown, W. R.(?), 27:193

Brown, William (d. 1846), 20:210

Brown & Fields, 9:160

Brown & Parker, 27:44, 50

Brown House, San Francisco, *see* Brown's Hotel

Browne, Bothwell, 33:41

Browne, Charles Farrar, 21:144-45; 23:109

Browne, G. R. A., 32:375

Browne, James H., 13:32

Browne, John Ross, 6:153; 8:195, 370; 10:44, 68, 304; 21:57, 108; 24:90; 26:72, 75; 28:193-97 *passim*; 29:207, 246; 30:141, 166; 32:226; 35:51; 36:12-13; 38:115-16; bk. on, rev., 8:280; port., 28: opp. 193

Browne, L. A., 26:247

Browne, Ross E., 29:200, 207, 208

Browne, Spencer Cochrane, 20:190; 26:75; 30:74; obit., 24:90-91

Brownell, Allen, 20:46

Browning, Robert L., 21:297, 304-5; 22:70-71

Browning Club, San Diego, 35:354

Brown's Express, 34:344

Brown's Hotel, San Francisco, 3:34; 17:298, 301

Brown's Pass, 12:9

Brown's Valley, 6:219; 15:52

Brownsville, 8:340, 356; 9:52; 10:172

Bruce, Capt. (Colorado R., 1872), 22:173

Bruce, H. W., 15:374, 376

Bruce, John, address, "Gaudy Century," 28:88-89

Bruce, Samuel C., 10:293

Bruce, W. W., 37:208, 210

Bruff, Joseph Goldsborough, 27:363, 366, 367, 369; 28:58, 65, 67; 30:58-62, 158; 32: 200, 202; 38:275; art. on route of, 39:263-66; map, foll. 264; phot. of rock ment. by, 39: foll. 264

"Bruff's Route in Eastern California," by Georgia Willis Read, 39:263-66

Bruheim, Adolph ("Jim"), 10:353-54; 12:296; 14:211

Bruhn, Daniel, 20:346

Bruillon (S.F., 1855), 16:283

Bruja (ship), 22:160

Brumagim, Jacob H., 9:72

Brumagim, John W., 9:72; 11:127

Brumagim, Mark (& Co.), 9:54, 72, 76, 362; 10:54; 14:395, 398, 401; 15:52; store, illus., 9: opp. 62

Brumagim *v.* Bradshaw, 21:118

Brun, Samuel J., 39:226, 244

Brundage (Placerville, 1853), 11:54

Brunel, Georges, 39:316

Bruner, Christian, 19:126-27, 140-41

Bruner, Joseph A., 26:173

Brunesville, Col., (on *Republic*, 1855), 15:282

Bruns (Yuba Co., 1857), 9:138, 139

Brunson, J., 27:36, 37, 47, 160

Brush (Grass Valley, 1862), 19:147

Brush, George Jarvis, 7:121

Bruton, Esther, 38:4

Brutus (ship), 1:208; 19:145, 155; 22:65; 26:165

Bryan, Abner and Lydia (Adams née Swain), 28:379-80

Bryan, Mrs. Carleton Felton (Kathryn Maxwell), 25:190

Bryan, Charles H., 8:342, 349; 9:44-45; 15:35, 369

Bryan, Joseph Turner and Elvira (Ellis), 23:189

Bryan, Mary, 28:380

Bryan, W. P., 20:13

Bryan, William Jennings, 19:62; 28:50-52; 36:70

Bryant (Sacramento and Marysville, 1858-59), 9:248, 364; 10:61, 171, 176
Bryant, Alexis, 15:375; 16:84
Bryant, Andrew Jackson, 10:193; 31:44; 37:198
Bryant, Berryman, "Reminiscences of California, 1849-1852," 11:35-39
Bryant, Mrs. Berryman (Henrietta Frances Reeve), 11:39
Bryant, Dan, 21:159
Bryant, Dolores (Waldorf), 18:384; 20:96; "Baltimore Fire Laddie, George H. Hossefross," 23:69-77; "Gentleman from Vermont, Royal H. Waller," 22:110-18; "Loaded Words," 23:147-48; "Charles P. Kimball, San Francisco's 'Noisy Carrier'," 18:329-34; "No. 77 Long Wharf," 21:75-79; obit. of Mrs. Desiré Fricot, 22:91-92
Bryant, Edmund G., 9:316-17; 27:95
Bryant, Edwin, 5:395; 10:352; 13:152, 154; 15:330-31; 16:58; 20:344; 22:130, 133, 148; 24:45; 25:129; 28:267, 324; 29:312, 336, 341; 30:53, 233; 36:11-12, 58-59, 61
Bryant, Mrs. Ernest A. (Susanna Bixby), obit., 25:375
Bryant, Herman Carl, 18:384
Bryant, Mrs. Herman Carl, *see* Bryant, Dolores (Waldorf)
Bryant, Jerry, 20:304
Bryant, John, 8:289; 23:193; *see also* Bryant, Sturgis & Co.
Bryant, John J., 7:396
Bryant, Robert, 33:301, 307
Bryant, W. C., 15:280
Bryant, W. S., 21:238
Bryant, William, 6:152; 24:26
Bryant House, San Francisco, 7:396
Bryant, Sturgis & Co., 8:105, 289-97; 19:56; 23:193-218 *passim*, 301-34 *passim*
Bryarly, Wakeman, 29:297, 302, 306
Bryce, Reuben P. and Ellen F. (Lyon), 28:293
Bryson, James, 28:337
Bryson, William, 26:11
Buache, Philippe, 1:192; 3:218; 9:201
Bubbs, John, 4:20
Bucareli y Ursúa, Antonio María, 40:237-48; fac. p. of Instructions, 40: opp. 238
Bucareli Sound, 9:227, 240
Buccleugh's (Yuba Co., 1856), 9:52

Bucha (Indian) trail, 30:168
Buchanan (Sutter's Fort, 1845), 5:125; 26:110
Buchanan, A. Russell, 31:286; "James A. McDougall," 15:199-212; ed., "H. H. Haight on National Politics, May 1861," 31:193-204
Buchanan, Mrs. Ada, 10:378-79
Buchanan, Franklin, 15:183, 185
Buchanan, James, 6:31; 19:276; Sec. State, 2:246; 5:323; 9:4, 80; 10:137, 147; 11:200; 16:321; 18:219; 19:47, 53; 29:30; Pres. candidate, 9:66, 78, 104, 106; Pres., 9:111, 112, 249, 271, 274, 376, 397; 10:66, 191, 194; 11:11-18 *passim;* 19:264, 268, 276, 277; 31:195-96, 200, 201; 34:49; Larkin's reports to, 1:189-90; 5:301-4; 6:186-87, 271-74, 368; 7:83-84; 9:81-85; letters and instructions, 2:247-48; 5:297-301; 11:201; 14:147; 16:321; 18:217; 19:46, 47, 51, 52
Buchanan, John C., 6:134
Buchanan, McKean (purser, 1846), 20:213, 232
Buchanan, McKean (actor, 1855), 10:362, 370; 16:84, 182-83
Buchanan, Maria, 14:389
Buchanan, Minna C., 9:246, 273
Buchanan, Robert Bloomer, 9:273; 14:222, 229, 377-83 *passim*, 389, 403, 405; 15:28-33 *passim*, 39, 41, 53, 57; 16:260; 26:383
Buchanan, Robert C., 26:1
Buchanan, Virginia, 10:370-71
Buchanan, William C., 27:352
Buchanan-Breckinridge clubs, 9:64, 65
Buchser, Frank, port. of J. A. Sutter, 14: opp. 28
Buck, Frank Henry and Annie Elizabeth (Stevenson), 21:379
Buck, Frank Henry [Jr.], obit., 21:379
Buck, Mrs. Frank Henry [Jr.], (1, Zayda Zabriskie), 21:379; (2, Eva Benson), 21:379; 22:94
Buck, Franklin Augustus, 10:202, 413; 30:251, 259, 261, 361
Buck, Samuel M., 10:62, 70
Buckbee, Edna Bryan, 23:189; obit. of C. H. Segerstrom, 25:376-77
Buckel, Cloe Annette, art. on, 19:74-76; port., 19: opp. 74
Buckelew, Benjamin Rush, 5:407; 6:43, 45-46; 15:169, 370; 39:12-13
Buckelew, W. C., 9:173

Buckeye, Calaveras Co. (?), 19:145
Buckeye, Yuba Co., 9:52, 69, 70
Buckeye (flour) Mill, Marysville, 27:194, 195
Buckeye Ranch and sawmill, Yuba Co., 10:171, 194; 33:299
Buckingham, Charles E., 9:26; 15:77, 178, 276, 281
Buckingham, John A., 10:295; 29:251
Buckkeugh (Yuba Co., 1855), 8:340; *see also* Buccleugh's
Buckler (Mariposa Co., 1850), 12:75
Buckley (Yuba Co., 1859), 10:58
Buckley (Aurora, 1863), 7:116
Buckley (RR conductor, 1879), 18:368; 23:119
Buckley, Dr. (L.A., 1904), 31:23
Buckley, Christopher A., 5:94; 35:144
Buckley, Edward J. ("Ned"), 4:62; 21:172, 265
Buckley, Edward P., 9:26
Buckley, John P., 26:232
Buckley, Thomas, 26:9, 11
Buckley & Co. (Yuba Co., 1857), 9:140
Buckmaster, Miss L. A., 10:246-55 *passim*, 260, 272, 278, 279, 287
Bucknall, George James, 2:67; 8:284
Bucknall, Mrs. George James (Mary Eliza Davis), 2:3, 4, 5, 53, 63, 67; 6:40; 8:187; obit., 8:284-85; phot., 8: opp. 284
Bucknell, Hannah, 28:293
Buckner, Leona (Kreyenhagen), 22:287-88
Buckner, Mrs. Simon Bolivar (Adele Blanc), 26:381
Bucks Creek hydroelectric plant, 29:203
Bucksport & Elk River Railroad, 38:65, 68
Buckwheat, 12:192
Budd, James, 28:49
Budd, John, 13:396
Buddhism, 34:303-5
Buddington (pilot, S.F., 1855), 16:282
Buddington, Capt. (Colorado R., 1862), 22:170
Budworth, James H., 21:166
Bueckel, Edward, 10:297
Buel, David E., 9:247, 250, 251, 269
Buel, Frederick, 15:185; 26:171; 29:112; 32:122-23, 128-29
Buelna, Antonio, 15:121-22, 225, 341, 354-55; 16:217
Buena Vista County, 34:265-66
Buena Vista Lake, Hills, Indian village,

Kern Co., 10:213-19 *passim*; 11:103, 248, 250, 253-56 *passim*, 265; phot., 10: opp. 216
Buenavista Valley, San Diego Co., 25:302; 30:51
Buenos Aires (ship), 22:353
Buentello Elizondo, José, 37:201
Bués brothers (Trinity Co., 1850), 5:240-41
"Buffalo Bill" (William F. Cody), 21:244
Buffaloes and buffalo hunting, 2:26; 4:136; 22:129-30, 134, 136; 6:316; 24:43-44, 45, 238, 366; 32:263-66 *passim*
Buffalo Ranch, 33:300
Buffington, Collier, 31:125
Buffington, John M., 9:104, 106
Buffum, Edward Gould, 9:29; 12:27; 13:56, 76; 15:270; 23:53; 24:343-44; 30:105; 40:132
Buffum, William N., 2:122
Bugbee, Samuel Charles, 25:5
Bugbee (S. C.) & Son, 24:262
"Buggy Ride in 1854 in Alameda County, A," address by Ezra Decoto, 18:184-85
Buhne, Hans Henry, 19:376
Builders Insurance Co., 26:355; 27:165, 168, 270
Buildings, prefabricated, 8:265; 23:102; 27:172; 29:145; 34:66; 38:41, 42, 43; *see also* Houses, prefabricated
"Building the Larkin House," by Robert J. Parker, 16:321-35
"Building the Railroad down the San Joaquin in 1871," from reminiscences of Clarence M. Wooster, 18:22-31
Buldakoff (ship), 6:259; 12:194
Buler (Negro, Yuba Co., 1857), 9:144, 146
Bulger, Edward, 6:50; 8:371; 15:158
Bulger, Margaret, *see* Breen, Mrs. Patrick
Bulkhead bill, 29:108, 109; 36:329; 38:26, 333
Bulkley, Charles S., 33:2, 5, 7, 10, 11, 148-52 *passim*; 35:291, 294, 303
Bull, James A., 30:92
Bull, Ole, 6:340; 15:166-67, 169; 19:229
Bull-and-bear fights, 8:152-53, 232; 12:281; 13:322; 24:269; *see also* Bullfights
Bullard's Bar, 8:193, 203, 204, 205, 212,

338, 343, 345, 350; 9:57, 138, 144, 158, 161, 162, 163, 347
Bullard's Bar Guards, 8:205, 213
Bulletin, San Francisco, 8:362, 365-66; 12:11; 13:82; 14:354; 16:182, 339; 17:81-85 *passim*, 168-82 *passim*, 310; 20:309-10, 329, 334, 336-37; 21:23-37, 324; 23:147-48, 338-44 *passim*; 26:228-29, 354; 27:340; 28:135; 30:135-39 *passim*, 195, 200; 32:221, 224; 34:348; 37:139-43 *passim*; quoted, 6:5, 11, 16, 24, 28; 15:12-18 *passim*; 16:345, 346-47; 17:81-84 *passim*, 169-74 *passim*, 177-82 *passim*; 23:339-41 *passim*; 26:136, 137; 31:238; 32:147, 149, 150, 253, 299; 37:143-69
Bulletin, Le (monthly), 39:318-19, 346
Bulletin, Sonoma, 23:259-60, 24:58
Bullfights, 8:229-30; 13:322, 347, 352; 20:293; *see also* Bull-and-bear fights
Bull Head (Indian, 1870), 6:346-47
Bull in China Shop (play), 10:246, 260
Bullion Mine, 4:68
Bullock, Thomas S., 40:249
Bulmore, Laurence E., address, "Life at New Almaden," 26:373-74
Bulwer-Lytton, Baron Edward George Earle, 10:75
Bulwer-Lytton, Sir Edward Robert, 11:151
"Bummer" (dog), 2:242-43; 24:264
Bumpass, Kendall Vanhook, 22:370
Bumpass Hell, Lassen Park, 22:370
Bunch of Grapes (saloon), San Francisco, 15:184
Bumstead, Edward Dorgriffin, 13:32
Bunker (nr. Mormon I., 1849), 29:259
Bunker, John, 2:113, 116, 117, 122
Bunker Hill & Sullivan Mine, Idaho, 32:27
Bunker Hill Co., Nevada Co., 11:236
Bunker Hill mining claim, Bodie, 4:68
Bunker Hill Quartz Mill, Amador Co., 31:290
Bunnell, Barker, 29:13
Bunnell, Lafayette Houghton, 1:274; 4:12, 13, 15, 203; 5:330, 336-37; 28:333; 30:274
Bunster, Charlie and Ira, 33:381
Bunte, Heinrich, 12:290
Bunting, W. C., 22:250
Burbank, Caleb, 9:249, 251, 259, 269; 10:274, 289
Burch, Frederick P., 2:128, 129, 137

Burch, John Chilton, 4:238, 239, 262, 270; 10: opp. 48, 62, 168, 192; 11:11, 16, 25; 28:62; 32:148; 38:352
Burch, William S., 27:34, 36, 362
Burchfield (Aurora, 1864), 9:198, 200
Burck, C., 2:136
Burdell, Galen, 25:111, 257, 325, 330
Burdell, John, 18:267-68
Burdge, B., Jr., 22:250
Burdick, James, 10:44-48 *passim*, 61, 62, 65, 70
Burditt, Henry, 35:196, 200
Burdue, Thomas, *see* Berdue
Burgdorff, Ferdinand, 37:29
Burger *v.* Cole, 10:356
Burgess, Cool, 21:169
Burgess, Ethelinda, 30:285
Burgess, George H., 30:137
Burgess, Sherwood D., 30:90; "The Forgotten Redwoods of the East Bay," 30:1-14
Burgess, Thomas H., 21:355; 26:44, 47, 62; 29:269; 30:51
Burgess, W. F., *see* Burgess, Gilbert & Still
Burgess, W. T., 8:358
Burgess, William H., 16:337; 30:243-44
Burgess, Gilbert & Still, 28:1, 2, 14, 35, 378; 30:105, 106, 110, 114, 252-53, 264, 353
Burgoyne, William Moser, 25:223
Burgoyne & Co., 15:186
Burgoyne's Building, San Francisco, 15:267
Burheim, James, 18:296
Burials at sea, 1:216, 222, 224; 13:9-10; 20:210; 37:235
Burk, Lew, 13:258
Burke (d. S.F., 1854), 15:178
Burke, Alexander, 26:215
Burke, Alfred Imlay, 31:185
Burke, Edmund, 37:207
Burke, Isaac C., 27:221
Burke, Jackson, address, "Private Presses of California," 28:184
Burke, James H., 26:211, 215
Burke, James W., 8:293; 14:332; 18:69, 71, 164
Burke, John and Barbara (Forbes), 31:185
Burke, John H., 17:77, 80
Burke, M. J., 27:151, 152
Burke, Martin, 21:98, 103, 104
Burke, Mary Ann, 28:292
Burke, Robert E., 31:287; 36:113

Burke, T. W., 19:60, 61, 67, 68, 72; 27:316, 317
Burkhead, William N., 9:26
Burling, W. B., 11:296
Burling, William, 19:232
Burlingame, Joel, 15:29, 42
Burlingame (place), 17:245, 251, 254, 255, 257
Burlingame Treaty, 34:315
Burnell, Mrs. Archibald (Edna Hazel Frisby), 29:326
Burnell, Mrs. Martin (Bertha Ophelia Frisby), 29:326
Burnell, R., 10:272, 287, 372, 374, 375
Burnett, Ellsworth, 4:274-76
Burnett, Henry, 6:361
Burnett, John M., 1:16; 24:80
Burnett, L., 10:254
Burnett, Peter Hardeman, 3:81; 4:352; 5:355; 8:181; 9:116, 390; 10:73, 76, 138, 139, 144-45, 148, 163, 199; 12:31; 13:380; 14:161; 16:53-55, 75; 17:234; 18:301; 19:4, 7, 331; 20:112; 22:365; 23:160, 164; 24:27-28; 25:287; 26:329, 330, 331-32; 28:59, 64, 67, 68, 326, 329; 30:57; 31:44, 148; 35:317; 36:343-44; 40:123-36; phot., 40: opp. 123
Burnett, Sarah Elizabeth, 29:381
Burnett, Thomas Tiffin, 29:381
Burnett, Wellington Cleveland, 8:342, 359, 360; 9:46, 107, 350, 351, 381
Burnett's ferry, 39:44, 48
Burney, Mr. and Mrs. (Sacramento, 1860), 29:109, 114, 118
Burney, James, 1:272; 5:330; 28:326-27, 330
Burnham, George M. (?), 12:313, 314
Burnham, John, 26:302
Burnham, Richard F., 26:170, 172
Burnham, S. B., 15:280, 364
"Burning of the *Golden Gate* in July 1862," by André Chavanne, ed. and trans. Desiré Fricot, 19:27-42
Burns (S.F., 1854), 31:243
Burns (S.F., 1855), 17:82; 37:160
Burns, Capt. (S.F., late 1850s), 19:229
Burns, Miss (Sacramento, 1858), 9:245, 246, 250
Burns, Aaron M., 26:175
Burns, Alex, 15:54
Burns, Daniel M., 38:354, 355, 356
Burns, James ("Jimmy-from-Town"), 12:320; 15:38, 180, 269
Burns, James Franklin, 13:335; 32:331
Burns, John, 27:219

Burns, John H., 10:381, 393
Burns, Mary Jane, 33:352
Burns, Robert E., 23:384
Burns, Thomas P., 26:268; 32:89; "History of a Montgomery Street Lot," 11:69-72; "The Oldest Street in San Francisco," 13:235-39; obit., 14:191
Burns, Tom, 3:56, 57
Burns, W., 9:162; 10:174
Burns, Walter, 9:53, 64, 65, 71; 10:56(?), 180(?), 183
Burns, William (Monterey, 1855), 29:20, 21
Burns, William (filibuster, 1865), 37:210
Burns' Diggings, 28:332
Burnside, Ambrose, 16:202-3, 309; 22:356, 357
Burr, Capt. (Colorado R., 1861), 22:169, 170
Burr, Ephraim Willard, 16:284; 19:150; 26:229, 265; 31:300, 382
Burr, H. T., 13:296
Burr, John Atlantic, 37:235
Burr, Sarah (Sloat), 37:235
Burr (C.C.) & Co., 31:185
Burr, Mattoon & Co., 31:382
Burrass, Charles D., 12:169; 19:132, 138; 21:3; 25:145-46; 29:337-39 *passim*
Burrell, Clara, 28:304, 316, 319
Burrell, Eliza, *see* Sykes, Mrs. Zenas
Burrell, Henry, 30:225, 228, 230
Burrell, James Birney, 28:298, 299, 303, 316, 319, 321, 322; 29:39-58 *passim*, 56, 58, 174, 176
Burrell, Mrs. James Birney (Mary L. Campbell), 28:319
Burrell, Lyman John, 28:297-317 *passim*; 29:39-59 *passim*, 173-79 *passim*; port., 29: opp. 177
Burrell, Mrs. Lyman John (Clarissa Wright), 28:297-322; 29:39-59 *passim*, 173-79
Burrell, Martha, 28:316, 319
Burrell family, 28:297-98, 319
Burrell (place), 28:317
"Burrell Letters, The," ed. Reginald R. Stuart, 28:297-322; 29:39-59, 173-79
Burriel, Andrés Marcos, 1:52; 9:202
Burrill (Marysville, 1851), 15:45
Burrill, Mrs. (S.F., 1854), 15:266
Burrill, George Thompson, 13:318, 323, 325
Burris, David, 29:321
Burritt, Samuel L., 19:321(?), 38:42

Burro, Arroyo, 18:267
Burroughs (overland, 1850), 24:243
Burroughs (in mines) 1853), 33:298, 299
Burroughs, Charles D., *see* Burrass
Burroughs, John, 4:296
Burrowes, George, 27:153-54; 29:107, 117; Classical School, 39:292
Burrows (from Ore., 1841), 24:321
Burrows, Ogden Hoffman, 26:72
Burson (Yuba City, 1858), 9:266
Burson, L. M., 11:9
Burs, Scott, lawsuits, 8:352; 9:165
Bursk (lawsuit, Marysville, 1859), 10:180, 181
Burt (overland, 1849), 22:127
Burt, Capt. (Colorado R., 1864), 22:170
Burt, William, 13:258
Burtchaell, Mrs. Clarence, 25:380
Burthey, Louis, 5:14, 349
Burtnett, Almira, *see* Hopkins, Mrs. Casper T.
Burton (Plumas Co., 1851), 18:303
Burton, Edward F., 9:46, 115, 116; 10:62
Burton, Henry Stanton, 1:212, 217, 223-24, 229, 231, 248, 252; 12: opp. 318; 18:177; 22:60-61; 33:250-51, 261, 341-45; 34:22; 35:14
Burton, Mrs. Henry Stanton (Amparo Rúiz), 21:329, 332; 35:14, 17
Burton, J. W., 38:309
Burton, John, 14:17, 19; 15:224-25
Burton, Lewis T., 2:36, 45; 18:164, 176, 277
Burton, Mrs. Lewis T. (María Antonia Carrillo), 18:176
Burton, William, 15:240
Burton's News Depot, 30:258
Bush (Sonora, 1860), 34:294
Bush, Lt. (on *Olga*, 1865), 33:6
Bush (S.F., 1867), 11:127
Bush, Alice Edna, 27:186
Bush, Edward and Mary Ellen (Pedlar), 27:186
Bush, G., 17:84
Bush, J. C., 34:158
Bush, Norton, 36:201
Bushnell, Prof. ("electro-biologist," 1861), 39:299
Bushnell, Horace, 36:350
Bush Street Ladies' Gymnasium and Seminary, 39:290
Bush Street Theatre, San Francisco, 21:255, 259; 35:142; 37:227

"Business Letters of Alfred Robinson," ed. Adele Ogden, 23:301-34
Busse, Fritz, 40:359
Bustamante, Anastacio, 12:344; 13:102, 136-38, 147, 304; 14:264; 16:366, 368; 17:54, 55, 57, 59, 162
Bustamante, Carlos María, 24:291-92, 308; 25:60, 76, 363
Bustamente y Guerra, José de, 3:215-16, 218-19, 233-34, 237; 40:118
Buster, Frank, 33:363
Buster, Mike, 33:363
Bustillos family, 19:298
Busto, Pedro de, 3:364-65; 19:242
Buston, George, 29:22
Buswell, Alexander, 21:237; 29:110
Butler, Mr. and Mrs. (boardinghouse, S.F., 1856), 14:76; 19:236
Butler (Sacramento, 1858), 9:258
Butler, A. B., 25:32, 172
Butler, Andrew P., 19:18, 164-65, 266
Butler, Anthony J., 10:197; 32:154, 159; 40:205, 206, 210
Butler, Benjamin Franklin, 15:305; 30:252, 256, 265; 33:372
Butler, Charles, 13:31
Butler, Chester Gregson, 19:113; 20:96
Butler, E., 11:34
Butler, G. W., 9:61, 65; lawsuit, 9:130
Butler, Grace Helen, 32:375
Butler, M. F., 15:280; 39:200
Butler, Richard, 24:169, 170
Butler, Mrs. Thomas Bennet (Eliza Jane Gregson), 19:113, 129, 141
Butler, Warren C., 34:345
Butman, Frederick A., 10:293; 24:264, 265, 266; painting by, 37: opp. 129
Butman, John G., 13:20
Butron, Manuel, ranchos of, 4:90, 91; 19:158; 29:337; *see also* Ranchos: Natividad
Butte, Mont., 15:324, 326, 327
Butte City, Calif., 11:322
Butte Creek, 11:115-16, 119; 22:323, 335; 23:132
Butte Democrat, Oroville, 34:49
Butte Mining and Exploring Co., 18:199
Butter, 3:57; 14:21, 201, 202; 20:260; 34:118; *see also* Dairying
Butte Record, 18:199; 20:161; quoted, 29:197
Butterfield, Charles P., 26:204
Butterfield, Harry Morton, 27:122; addresses: "Pioneer Builders of California's Horticulture," 28:373;

"Pioneer Horticulture in California,"
19:375
Butterfield, John, 2:215-16, 219
Butterfield Overland Mail, 2:211-22;
13:344; 14:162; 15:99, 189, 190;
19:356; 20:81; 21:372; 25:287, 307;
31:40; 34:198, 199; 36:128; 38:28, 330
"Butterfield's Overland Mail," by
LeRoy R. Hafen, 2:211-22
Butterflies, 1:211; 12:305; 32:249-50,
258, 262
Butterworth, Samuel Fowler, 15:8, 14,
16; 29:198
Button, Fred L., address, "Oakland
Sixty Years Ago," 4:210-11
Buttons: found at Monterey, 25:218;
phoenix (of Henry Christophe),
26:350; 33:87
Butts, W. R., 9:42
Butts (William) and Wheeler, 13:336;
see also Wheeler, John O.
Butz, P., 8:358
Byington, Lewis Francis, address,

"Early Mining Days in Sierra
County," 3:302
Bylaws, California Historical Society,
1:1-7; amendments, 4:404-5; 5:101;
9:91; 10:207; 17:20 (present bylaws
not included)
Byllesby hydroelectric interests, 30:342
Bynum, Shashell, 9:46, 107
Byrd, Thomas Jefferson, 8:208
Byrne, Edna, *see* Carleton, Mrs.
Frederic W.
Byrne, Henry H., 6:7; 15:186, 257; 16:84
Byrne, J. W., 25:230, 232
Byrne, James K., 10:249, 262, 358
Byrne, L. M., 15:170
Byrne, Mary (Tanner), letters of,
17:41-47 *passim*
Byrne, Napoleon Bonaparte, 17:41-49
Byrne, Peter, 17:45
Byrne family, 17:41, 45, 48
Byrnes, William, 26:246
"Byrnes of Berkeley, The," from letters
of Mary Tanner Byrne, comp. Mary
T. Carleton, 17:41-49

C

Caamano, Jacinto, 2:282(?); 10:313,
314, 317
Caballeria y Collell, Juan, 12:121
Caballero, Feliz, 8:329-30; 14:236, 238,
254, 257
Caballero, José, 14:235, 236, 239, 247,
253-54
Cabaniss, George Henry, 6:69; 33:372
Cabaniss, George Henry, Jr., 31:377;
obit. of Ethel R. Shorb, 38:361-63
Cabaniss, Thomas Thompson, 6:69, 71
Cabazon (place), 12:9
Cabetius (S.F., 1950s), 32:110
Cabeza de Vaca, Alvar Núñez, 1:42;
3:290, 307; 6:299, 304, 310
Cabinet de Lecture Français, Le,
30:108, 257
Cable Canyon, 12:112
Cable car, 14:191; 19:140-51
Cables: transatlantic (*see* Atlantic
cable); transpacific 30:194
Cabo, as used by Cabrillo, 7:24
Cabortes, Juan, 4:168

Cabot, Juan, 10:29; 23:6, 7, 13
Cabot, Pedro, 23:7
Cabot, Sebastian, 3:391; 7:135; maps by,
3:312, 313, 372, 378
Cabrera Bueno, José González, *see*
Gonzáles Cabrera Bueno
Cabrie (antelope), 22:323, 330, 335,
338, 339, 342, 343; 23:36
Cabrillo, Juan Rodríguez, 1:47, 49, 51,
157; 2:259; 3:262, 265, 313-14, 387-89;
4:3, 154; 6:311-12, 315, 318, 327;
7:20-77, 144, 148, 183, 254; 8:51, 69;
11:44-46, 317; 12:20; 13:195; 20:191,
234, 315; 21:374; 22:34; 25:309, 310;
27:289-90; 35:234; 36:220-24
"Cabrillo and California," address by
Max Savelle, 21:374
Cacafuego (ship), 16: No. 1, Pt. 2, p. 4
Cáceres, Francisco, 14:121-22, 130;
family of, 14:130
Cachalot (ship), 5:28; 14:132, 133
Cache Creek, 22:338; 23:291, 293, 296;
25:221; 32:366, 367

Cache (or Indian) Valley, 18:303, 313
Cactuses, 2:321; 3:222; 12:15; 18:105, 117; 21:207; 25:298
Cadborough (ship), 8:98; 28:252
Cadell (on *London*, 1849), 7:208, 217, 219, 223, 225
Cadell, Dolores, comp. "Some California Dates of 1859," 38:25-30
Cadets and Sons of Temperance, 15:180
Cadman, Paul Fletcher, 24:379
Cadmus (ship), 26:176, 183
Cady ("Irish Curley"), 13:258
Caen, Herb, *Hills of San Francisco*, rev., 38:271-72
Caesar (ship), 12:304
Cahalan, Christopher W., 10:62, 70
Cahill, Mrs. John Edward (Margaret Kennedy), 25:94
Cahuenga: campaign of (1847), 14:325, 344-45; 15:229-30; 16:57; 18:159; 20:149; capitulation of, 1:147, 171; 12:150, 334; 13:135-36, 303, 318; 18:176; 22:41, 64, 367; 30:53
Cahuenga Pass, 34:21; battle at (1831), 13:212-13
Cain (Yuba Co., 1857), 9:130, 131
Caine, Philip P., 10:61
Caire, Delphine Adelaide, 25:380; obit., 29:81-83
Caire, Jeanne, obit. of Delphine A. Caire, 29:81-83
Caire, Justinian, 25:380; 29:81
Caire, Mrs. Justinian (Maria-Cristina Sara Molfino), 29:81
Cajiers (Cajius, etc.) Creek, *see* Raft River
Cajon Pass, 10:215, 218; 12:7, 111, 112, 116; 27:116-17, 121; 29:33-35
Calafia, Queen, *see* California: name
Calaveras, 7:12; *see also* Calaveritas
Calaveras Chronicle, Mokelumne Hill, 1:102; 39:4
Calaveras County, 22:68, 92; 30:246; county seat, 11:176-83; mining in, 22:67-83 *passim*
Calaveras Grove, 4:8, 14, 15, 26; 9:312, 332-34; 11:173, 327-28; 14:78; 22:92; 27:379; illus., 9: opp. 299, opp. 312
Calaveras River, 13:72-73; 23:60; 27:157
Calaveritas, 7:12; 22:68
Caldeira, William, 16:192, 273, 280-81; 17: No. 4, Pt. 2, pp. 1, 2; 36:28, 33-34
Caldera (ship), 33:167; 35:304-5
Calderon (Santa Barbara, 1851), 18:267
Calderón y Henríquez, Pedro,

"Memorial," ed. and trans. Henry R. Wagner, 23:219-25; map, 23: opp. 219
Caldwell (Sacramento R., 1849), 20:32
Caldwell, Augustine B., 8:359
Caldwell, C. G., 15:76
Caldwell, J. McHenry, 32:141
Caldwell, John Isaiah, 9:243, 269, 369, 370, 377, 393; 10:42, 51, 52, 53, 62
Caldwell, William, 10:70
Caldwell's Upper Store (Nevada City), 8:359; 11:236
Caleb Curtis (ship), 25:258
Caledonia Colony, 25:174
Calef, John Haskell, 11:127
Calendar, ecclesiastical, 37:299-300
Calevala (ship), 26:15; 39:306
Calexico, 34:158, 160
Calgrove, John, 14:180
Calhoun, Andrew, 14:181
Calhoun, James C., 16:83
Calhoun, John Caldwell, 10:134, 142, 222, 226; 19:1-2, 15-16; 20:369; 31:199
"Caliban" (pseud.), 6:9-10
Calico (place), 27:116, 121
Califa (Indian, 1839), 17:149
"California" (pseud.), 24:30-37
California: boundaries, *see* Boundaries British reports on (1849-51), 32:81-86, 269-74
capitals, 15:267, 269; Benicia, 11:163; 17:261, 263-67 *passim*; Los Angeles, 12:36; 13:215, 217, 222, 231-32, 301; Monterey, 12:36-37; 13:198; Sacramento, 5:285-86; 11:163; 15:268; 17:234, 261-67 *passim*; 32:216; San Jose, 9:268; 11:163; 14:152-54; 17:234, 260; 23:375; Vallejo, 11:163; 17:234, 261-68 *passim*; prop. removal to Oakland, 5:256, 258, 282; to San Jose, 5:285-86; temporary, at S.F., 10:374-81 *passim*; New York of the Pacific (prop.), 12:30-31
capitols: at Benicia, 17: (phot.) opp. 260, 261, 263, 264, 268; offered at New York of the Pacific, 12:30; at Sacramento, 9; (illus.) 247, 249, 268, 274-75; 10:282, 295; 24:180; 28:94; 32:216; 33:329-35; 38:337; 39:177; at Vallejo, 17:234
conditions in 1844, 17:21-27; in 1850-51; 31:143-45, 253-59, 307-11; 32:81-86
description in early '50s, 15:234-36
extent before Conquest, 8:259-60; in

1846, 25:289-91; before 1849,
24:20-22; *see also* Boundaries
name, 1:41, 46-56; 3:309, 311, 318, 337,
346, 380, 389; 6:167-68, 325; 9:188;
11:320; 19:219-24; 24:313; 28:23-30;
prop. change to Moctezuma, 16:217
rural society, 24:193-228
16th-cent. ideas and plans for, 8:26-33
visual knowledge of to 1700, 36:213-40
California: island, 1:40-41, 47; 3:311,
337, 346; 8:27, 36, 37; 19:220, 221;
28:23; kingdom, 8:26-32 *passim*
California (Boston ship), 4:164; 5:132;
8:105, 293-300 *passim;* 12:151; 18:59,
70; 23:196-201 *passim,* 217, 309-16
passim, 330, 331, 332; 27:105
California (schr., formerly *Clarion* and
Kaniu), 14:247, 252, 253, 256, 257, 264,
265, 341; 16:358, 362, 364, 368; 17:22,
57-61 *passim,* 153; 18:174, 311;
19:193-96, 211-13, 214; 35:200
California (str., formerly *Algoa*),
31:296
California (P.M.S.S.), 2:119, 201; 6:286;
8:275; 13:249-50, 251, 358, 381, 386-97
passim, 401, 403; 15:166; 16:68, 304-5,
339; 17:177; 20:120; 22: 111; 23:51, 57;
24:24; 26:100, 102, 168; 27:10, 34-43
passim, 47-50 *passim,* 264, 362; 28:57,
64, 290-91; 29:4, 7; 31:142; 33:324, 344;
35:12, 112, 113; 39:51; illus., 13: opp.
247
California, Gulf of, 3:318-37; 11:365-82;
20:223; 25:357; 27:206; 28:121
California, Mar de la, 8:26, 27, 30, 32
California, Puerto (or Boca) de, 3:388,
389, 392
California, Punta (or Cabo) de, 1:49,
50, 52; 3:20; 7:59, 229, 296, 305; 8:26,
30, 32
California Academy of Sciences, 1:17;
11:308, 313; 18:384; 21:309, 329;
23:343; 28:141; 31:337, 342; 32:180-83
passim, 247-51 *passim,* 254, 257, 260;
art. on, 21:363-71; phot., 21; opp. 363
"California Academy of Sciences and
the Early History of Science in the
West," by Robert C. Miller,
21:363-71, 374
"California and Australia Gold Rushes as
Seen by Amos S. Pittman," ed.
Theressa Gay, 30:15-37
California and Hawaiian Sugar Refining
Corp., 27:200
"California and the Civil War: A

Bibliographical Essay," by Benjamin
F. Gilbert, 40:289-307
California and the Nation, 1850-1869,
by Ellison, rev., 6:377-79
"California and the Nation: A Tally of
Two Histories," by John W.
Caughey, 40:193-202
California and Utah Camel Association,
8:353; 9:316
"California: A Possible Derivation of
the Name," by A. E. Sokol, 28:23-30
California-Arizona Stage Lines, 22:162
California Art Union, 15:276; 30:136-37;
33:311, 317; 36:199, 203
California as I Saw It, by McCollum,
ed. Morgan, rev., 40:74-76
California as It Is and as It May Be, by
Wierzbicki, rev., 12:364-65
California Associated Raisin Co.,
25:170
"California Associations with
Washington, D.C.," address by
Jack H. Ralston, 23:80-81
California Baptist Education Society,
27:10
California Battalion, Civil War, 40:298
California Battalion of Mounted
Riflemen, 12:167; 13:47, 52, 123, 124,
151, 304; 17:79, 123, 230, 278, 282,
300, 339, 346, 348, 350; 18:74, 75, 169,
172, 173-74; 19:118, 132, 140, 141, 142,
186; 21:3, 14, 341, 343, 356, 357; 22:52,
54, 55, 64, 66, 367, 368; 23:294;
25:125-28 *passim;* 26:56; 29:30, 273-75,
333-43 *passim;* 30:49-53 *passim,* 169;
33:108, 111, 112, 121; cartoon, 18:
foll. 72
"California Bibliographies," comp. by
Willard O. Waters, 3:245-58
California Botanical Club, 32:184
California Brass Band, 16:83
"California Centennials," by Anson S.
Blake, 26:97-106
California Central Railroad, 4:226; 38:25
*California China Mail and Flying
Dragon,* San Francisco, 21:327-28
California Chinese Chatter, ed. Dressler,
rev., 6:281-82
California Christian Advocate, 31:2-4, 7
California Chronicle, San Francisco,
1:57; 7:280; 8:361-62; 9:24; 15:165;
20:336; 30:252; 37:149-51
California Chronik, San Francisco,
19:193

California College of Arts and Crafts, 15:302, 303

California College of Pharmacy, 23:191; 30:67; 32:250-53, 256, 257, 261

"California Constitutional Convention of 1849," addresses by Thomas W. Norris, 24:376; 28:372-73

California Copy, by Weeks, rev., 8:82-83

"California Copyrights, 1851-1856," by Edith M. Coulter, 22:27-40

California Cotton Mills, 30:285; 31:298

California Council of Progress, 36:254

California County Boundaries, by Coy, rev., 2:366-67

California Courier, 39:11-12

California Democrat, San Francisco, 15:172, 282; 16:282; 28:135

California Dime Museum, Pomona, 37:177

California Division of Beaches and Parks, 26:129, 130, 135, 160

California Dorée, La (ship), 13:378

California Dragoons, 18:72-84

"California, 1846-1860: Politics," by Earl S. Pomeroy, 32:291-302

"California Emigrant Letters," comp. by Walker D. Wyman, 24:17-46, 117-38, 235-60, 343-64

California Exchange, San Francisco, 22:260; Bldg., 17:177

California Exchange Saloon, Marysville, 15:46

California Express, Marysville, 8:358; 9:62, 65, 134, 245, 266, 287, 349, 379-85 *passim*, 389, 390; 10:177, 192, 199, 265, 266; 14:407; 15:40, 56, 154; 20:165; 33:203; 34:49-50

California Farmer, 12:21; 19:250; 30:114, 362, 363

California Farmers Insurance Co., 26:355

California Fishing Co., 29:318

"California for Hungarian Readers: Letters of János Xánthus," ed. Henry M. Madden, 28:125-42

"California French Filibusters in Sonora," by Helen B. Metcalf, 18:3-21

California Fusileers, San Francisco, 38:17-18

California Genealogical Society, 1:107-9

"California Gold Discovery: Centennial Papers," 26:107-62

"California Gold Rush Padre: ... the

'Padre of Paradise Flat,' " ed. John B. McGloin, 40:49-67

California Guards, 2:119-20; 10:198; 15:164, 168, 174, 178, 179, 182, 277, 370, 375; 16:200; 23:340; 27:106, 111; *see also* First California Guard

California Historical Society:
collections, 25:85-86; 33:372-76
Committee for Determination of Location of San Francisco's First Dwelling, 11:73-78
fellows, 38:73; 39:70-71
history, 1:9-22, 107-10; 19:89; 21:95, 183; 24:79; 28:364-66; 36:175-77
publications (1874-93), 1:20-22
quarters, 17:74; 19:89; 21:371; phot., 17: opp. 74; 39: opp. 65
services, 15:387-88
see also Awards of Merit; Bylaws; Exhibitions; Meetings of the Society; Wagner Memorial Award

"California Historical Society, 1852-1922," by Henry R. Wagner, 1:9-22

California Historic-Genealogical Register, 1:108

California Historic-Genealogical Society, 1:108-9

"California History and Our Own Society," address by Henry R. Wagner, 19:89

"California History from Adobe Bricks," address by George W. Hendry, 15:89-90

California History Nugget, Oct. 1928, rev., 7:409

California Home Insurance Co., 26:355; 27:270

California Home Journal, 3:269; 10:295

California Hospital Association, 31:14-15

California Hospital Hotel, Los Angeles, 31:14

California Hotel, San Francisco, 20:132, 137

California House, Benicia, 6:148, 151; 20:153

California House, Yuba Co., 9:52, 69

California in 1851, by Clapp, rev., 12:176-77; *see also Shirley Letters*

California Immigrant Union, 24:108; 25:101; 27:169-71, 346

"California in 1844 as Hartnell Saw It," by Lauro de Rojas, 17:21-27

"California in History," by John D. Hicks, 24:7-16, as address, 184

"California in Retrospect," address by David P. Barrows, 29:374-75

California Institute (library), San Francisco, 38:299

California Institute of Technology, 36:78

California Insurance Co., 26:361, 362; 27:67, 167-73 *passim*, 268, 270, 342, 343-44, 348-49; *see also* California Mutual Marine Insurance Co.

California in the Kitchen, ... a Check List ... 1870(?)-1932, by Glozer and Glozer, rev., 40:258-59

"California in the Eighties," from letters of Anna Seward, 16:291-303; 17:28-40

"California Journal of Archibald Menzies, The," address by W. L. Jepson, 8:386

California Lancers, *see* Lanceros de Los Angeles

California Land Commission and Commissioners, 13:320; 15:171, 270; 16:182, 285; 17:173; 18:273

California League of Independent Bankers, 37:267-75 *passim*, 347-58 *passim*

California Legislature, American period: first, 11:160; 19:14-15; 20:107; 23:364, 375; 26:105; 28:63-64; 29:75-76; in 1850s and '60s: 8:194, 211, 354; 9:71, 243-60 *passim*, 268-85, 380, 383, 393; 10:40-53 *passim*, 61-75 *passim*, 271-83 *passim*, 286-96 *passim*, 372-78 *passim*, 387-91 *passim*; 14:152-54; 17:260-68; 30:132, 133, 146-47; 32:216; in 1873-74, 17:205, 206; in 1893, 19:59-73 *passim*

California Legislature, Mexican period, 1:27, 29, 30; 8:103; 13:119-20; 20:239; 27:335, 337; *see also* Juntas

"California Letters of Edward Hotchkiss, The," ed. Helen Throop Pratt, 12:91-110

"California Letters of James Carr, The," ed. Carl I. Wheat, 11:157-75

California Letters of William Gill, ed. Clark, rev. 3:200-201

"California Life in the Mines," address by Anson S. Blake, 12:180

California Light Horse Guard, San Francisco, 38:17

California Lumber Co., 15:177

California Magazine, see Hutchings' Illustrated California Magazine

California Mail Bag, 28:13, 17, 18

California Market, San Francisco, 5:85-86

"California Martyr's Bones, A," by Clarence Cullimore, 33:13-21

"California Material in the Archives of Spain," address by Henry R. Wagner, 2:258-60

California Medical College, 30:67

California Merchants' and Miners' Almanac, 17:181

California Mining and Trading Co., 22:121, 147

California Minstrels, 21:169, 171, 242

California Mutual Marine Insurance Co., 25:100; 26:262-64, 355; *see also* California Insurance Co.

Californian, Bakersfield, 32:5

Californian, Monterey and San Francisco, 3:114, 193; 6:143-44, 145, 149, 153; 7:277; 10:16, 24, 26, 138, 299; 11:130-33 *passim*; 12:168; 13:56, 60, 76, 267; 15:180; 17:296, 300, 301; 18:79; 19:330-31; 20:215; 22:51, 65; 25:128-29; 26:83, 164; 28:115; 35:104, 106, 108, 201; fac., 35: opp. 193

Californian (weekly), 5:409-10

"Californian and His History, The," address by Herbert I. Priestley, 10:206

California National Guard, 10:309; 29:247, 375; 34:157-71, 326; 35:29-35; 38:20, 21, 22; *see also* Militia

"California National Guard and the Mexican Border, 1914-16," by James J. Hudson, 34:157-71

California Native Cavalry (1864), 27:222

"California Never Was an Independent Republic," by George Tays, 15:242-43

Californian ... Magazine, 21:50; 28:9-10, 13

"California Newspaper Centennial," address by Neal Van Sooy, 26:83-84

California Northern Railroad, 10:386, 395

"Californians against the Emperor," by Robert R. Miller, 37:193-214

California, Oregon and Mexico Steamship Co., 16:67-68

California-Oregon Power Co., 30:339-43

"California-Oregon Trail, The," address by William G. Paden, 18:85

California; or, The Heathen Chinee (play), 34:360-61

California Outlaw: Tiburcio Vasquez, comp. Greenwood, incl. account by Beers, rev., 40:260-63

California Pacific Eastern Extension Co., 25:344

California Pacific International Exposition, San Diego, 36:161-62

California Pacific Railroad Co., 9:259; 25:344; 27:195-96, 202

California Packers, 35:121

California Park Commission, 26:107, 108, 129, 130

California Pharmaceutical Society, 32:250-53 *passim*

"California Phases of the Pony Express," address by Raymond W. Settle, 34:87

California Pilgrimage, by Kip, rev., 1:197-98

"California Place Names," address by Erwin G. Gudde, 28:184-85

California Place Names, by Gudde, rev., 39:364-66

California Police Gazette, 10:175

California poppy (*Eschscholtzia californica*), 4:154-55; 12:207; 18:338

California Positive and Negative Electric Cough and Consumption Cure, 31:26

California Practice Act, 9:71

"California Preparations to Meet the Walla Walla Invasion, 1846," by John A. Hussey and George W. Ames, Jr., 21:9-21

"California Prior to Conquest: A Frenchman's Views," ed. William F. Shepard, 37:63-77

California Public Balance, San Francisco, 28:36

California Publishing Co., 28:10

California Raisin Growers' Association, 25:173

"California Rancho [Buri Buri] under Three Flags, A," by Frank M. Stanger, 17:245-59

California Rand Silver Mine, art. on, 32:1-41

California Rangers, 8:83-84

"California Recollections of Caspar T. Hopkins," 25:97-120, 255-66, 325-46; 26:63-75, 175-83, 253-66, 351-63; 27:65-73, 165-74, 267-74, 339-51

"California Redwood Pioneers," address by Rodney S. Ellsworth, 17:185

"California Regiment, Colonel Baker, and Ball's Bluff," by Paul Fatout, 31:229-40

California [Bear Flag] Republic, 1:83, 88, 171, 182; 10:10-11; 24:57, 63; 25:123; 31:207, 211

California's Architectural Frontier: Style and Tradition in the Nineteenth Century, by Kirker, rev., 40:168-70

"California's Bantam Cock: The Journals of Charles E. DeLong," ed. Carl I. Wheat, 8:193-213, 337-63; 9:50-80, 129-81, 243-87, 345-97; 10:40-78, 165-201, 245-97, 355-95; 11:47-64

"California's Biggest Nugget," by John B. Farish, 3:259-61

California School of Arts and Crafts, 15:302, 303

California School of Design, 30:139; 36:199-200; 37:25-26

California School of Fine Arts, 38:1-2, 4, 7-8

California School of Mechanical Arts, 19:153

"California's Day Book," by John A. Hussey, 25:121-31

"California's First Legislature," address by Herbert C. Jones, 29:75-76

"California's First Pianos," by E. D. Holden, 13:34-37

"California's First Tabloid Newspapers," by Boutwell Dunlap, 3:268-69

"California Sidelights on the Presidential Election of 1864," by William F. Zornow, 34:49-64

California Silk Culture Assoc., 31:335-42 *passim*

California Silk Manufacturing Co., 31:340

"California's Influence upon the Constitution of Argentina," by V. Aubrey Neasham, 16:43-47

California Society of Montmartre Boulevard (cartoon), 39: opp. 1

California Society of Natural History, 10:44

"California Society, Sons of the American Revolution," by William W. Winn, 29:289-95

"California Soldiers in the Civil War," by Leo P. Kibby, 40:343-51
"California Soldiers in the Philippines," from correspondence of Howard Middleton, ed. Harold F. Taggart, 30:289-304; 31:49-67, 163-73
California Songster, 30:251-52
California Southern Railway, 27:121
California's Pioneer Circus, ed. Dressler, rev., 6:98-99
"California's Place in the Tapestry of History," address by Charles C. White, 26:280-81
California Springs, Texas, 18:108, 134
California's Redwood Wonderland, by Thornbury, rev., 3:203
"California's Role in the Nomination of Franklin D. Roosevelt," by Russell M. Posner, 39:121-39
California Stage Co., 7:13; 8:347; 9:173, 179, 181, 185; 13:261; 14:160; 17:168
California Star, San Francisco, 3:34; 7:277, 280; 10:16, 138, 298-301; 11:129-37 (incl. fac.), 143-44; 13:56, 76; 14:80, 277; 17:300; 20:118; 21:372; 26:83, 99, 165; 32:195; 37:236, 317; cited, 6:149; 10:17-18, 23, 25; 30:233, 234
California Star and Californian, 7:278; 10:138
California Star Oil Co., 17:115
California State Agricultural Society, 9:385; 10:196; 20:261-63; 27:10, 253; 36:245-46; *see also* State Fair
California State Archives, 28:143-50; 36:111
California State Geological Survey, 4:15-23; 7:121-31, 410; 9:401; 38:165
California State Grange, 27:174
California State Historical Association, 7:409
California State Horticultural Soc., 336
California State Journal, 14:157
California State Library, 10:53, 76, 278; 17:265; 18:49; 19:67, 246-49; 38:297-98
California State Medical Society, 4:182, 188, 191-94 *passim*; 28:374
California State Park Commission, 25:193, 194, 200-203 *passim*
California State prison, 9:180; 10:52; *see also* San Quentin
California State Seal, 10:163; 15:302; 22:81; 33:73

California Statesman, Sacramento, 15:273
California State Swamp Commission, 28:93
California State Telegraph Co., 29:346-53 *passim*; 33:10
California State Tide Land Commission, 21:121-22
California Steam Navigation Co., 8:211; 9:55, 72, 277, 394; 10:73, 193, 293; 15:168, 171, 365; 16:65-67 *passim*, 177, 285, 341; 17:182; 24:88, 262; 27:67, 171, 271; 32:223
California Theatre, San Francisco, 21:161-76 *passim*, 243-47 *passim*, 252, 259-64 *passim*, 274; 37:226
"California, Training Ground for Spanish Naval Heroes," by Donald C. Cutter, 40:109-22
California Transportation Co., 29:190-91
California Trona Co., 17:116-17
"California Unveiled," by Trény, trans. Desiré Fricot, 23:41-68
California Volunteers (1862), 10:372, 387, 388, 390, 393; 26:1-11 *passim*; 29:235-36; 31:42; 33:376
"California Voyages, 1539-1541," ed. and trans. Henry R. Wagner, 3:307-97
California Watch Co., 34:327
California Weekly, 38:252
California Wesleyan College, 29:59; 31:2-3; 33:73; 36:349; *see also* University of the Pacific
California Wharf and Warehouse Co., 27:199
California Wine Association, 36:110
California Wire Cloth Co., 19:156
California Wire Works, 19:153, 156
Californie, La (semi-monthly), 20:70; 22:310; 39:6
Californie Dorée, La (ship), 13:378
Californien, Le, San Francisco, 5:27; 6:44; 23:61; 39:10-11, 346
Californienne, La (company), 22:289, 296-309 *passim*; 23:45-46, 48, 59, 61-67, 68; 33:126
"Californiennes, Les," 39:148
Californios, *see* Mexican Californians; Spanish Californians
Californischer Staats-Kalender, 11:224
Calistoga, 4:393; 16:130; 20:6; 32:364; 36:295
Calkin, Kate Florence, 27:283

Calkin, Milo, 15:280; 27:284; 27:284; 30:93

Calkin, Mrs. Milo B., 30:93

Call (S.F., 1855), 16:79

Call, Anson, 22:15, 17

Call, George W., 12:200-206 *passim*

Call, San Francisco, 1:102, 296-97; 11:190; 20:334; 28:136; 30:195, 196, 197, 201, 202; cited, 34:55-56, 59; 36:38-39; 36:51-59 *passim*

Callahan, Mrs. D. E., 10:247, 250

Callahan, Isaac, 18:166; 33:343, 344

Callaghan Block, Shasta City, 30:36

Callao (place), 20:206, 209

Callao (ship), 23:51

Callbreath (of Victoria, 1862), 9:313, 329

Callender, Franklin D., 14:356; 15:84

Callingham, W. J., 19:107

Callot, *see* Tallot

Calloway, Thomas, 13:256

Callville, Nev., 22:13, 15-19 *passim,* 25, 151

Calmes, Mrs. Waller (Martha Cooper), 6:152

Calpella, 27:220

Calthrope, Lord, 28:56

Calvary Cemetery, San Francisco, 23:75

Calvary Presbyterian Church, San Francisco, 10:279, 293; 15:167, 270, 305; 17:84; 27:149-56; 32:134; 39:303

Calvé, Emma, 35:142

Calvin, David, 9:157, 178

Calvin, Dawson, 13:256

Calvin, James and Adaline (Carson), 1:150

Calzada, José Antonio, 23:373

Calzada, Juan, 24:317

Camacho, Sebastián, 25:149, 166

Camanche (riv. str.), 9:72; 22:368; 30:159

Camanche (monitor), 25:41-42; 33:236

Camaralzaman (play), 10:200

Camargo Company, 23:259, 261-76

Camarillo, Juan Roberto, 23:190; obit., 24:91-92

Camarillo (place), 38:278

Camasa (Cosumnes) River, 22:329; 23:35

Cambon, Pedro Benito, 14:102, 106

Cambuston, Henri, 3:181-82; 8:120; 11:205-11 *passim,* 352, 353; 12:41, 44, 46, 129, 135, 136, 333; 13:78, 160, 174; 16:374, 375; 30:98

Camels, 4:26; 6:347; 10:94, 282, 295; 11:234, 383; 13:343; 16:341; 18:205-9; 30:360; 38:338, 339; arts. on, 9:299-335; bibliog., 9:336-44; bk. on, rev., 9:182-84

"Camels in California," by Arthur A. Gray, 9:299-317

"Camels in the Sketches of Edward Vischer," by Francis P. Farquhar, 9:332-35

Cameo (ship), 19:376

Camerer, Clotilde, 29:284

Camerer, Eugene, drawing by, 11: opp. 364

Camero, Manuel, 13:200

Cameron (lawsuit, Marysville, 1858), 9:363, 364

Cameron (Sacramento, 1859), 10:42

Cameron (S.F., 1860), 29:118

Cameron, Miss (S.F., 1864), 24:263

Cameron, Donaldina, 11:85; 27:20

Cameron, Duncan, 26:204

Cameron, George Toland, 25:232; obit., 34:375-76

Cameron, J. D., 34:293, 294

Cameron, J. M., 26:171

Cameron, Jessie (Anderson), 33:372

Cameron, John (1813), *see* Gilroy, John

Cameron, John (Yuba Co., 1859), 10:169

Cameron, John (d. Ft. Bragg, 1862), 27:226-27

Cameron, William R., 36:92; "Rancho Santa Margarita of San Luis Obispo," 36:1-20

Cameron (D. E.) *v.* J. A. Sutter, 14:378-79

Cameron House, Santa Clara, 36:211

Camilla (ship), 21:321

"Camille," *see* Glover, Mrs. J. T.

Camille (play), 15:281; 20:140-41; 21:42, 143; 33:45; 39:307; *see also* Dame aux camélias

Camillo Rancho, *see* Ranchos: Olompali

Caminetti Law, 10:262

Cammett, John, 9:27, 29

Camp, Charles Lewis, 3:96; 12:187; 13:88; 32:105-6; 36:92, 176

"Col. Philip Leget Edwards," 3:73-83; "Kit Carson in California," 1:111-51; "Our Founder, Henry R. Wagner, Is Dead," 36:79-82; "William Alexander Trubody and the Overland Pioneers of 1847," 16:122-43

ed. "The Chronicles of George C. Yount," 2:3-66; "The Frémont Episode," 3:270-89; "An Irishman in the Gold Rush," 7:205-27, 395-408; 8:17-25, 167-82, 262-77; "James Clyman, His Diaries and Reminiscences," 4:104-41, 272-83, 307-60; 5:44-84, 109-38, 255-82, 378-401; 6:58-68; "The Journal of a 'Crazy Man,' . . . Albert Ferdinand Morris," 15:103-38, 224-41

foreword to "A Frenchman in the Gold Rush," 5:3-4; introd. to "The Journal of Benjamin Dore, 2:87-89; note to "Sutter Writes of the Gold Discovery," 11:43

account of luncheon meeting, 13:88

address: 31:280; "Beaver and Sea Otter," 6:102; on history of California Missions, 11:295; "Gold Days in California, Australia, and South Africa," 28:277-78; "Mormons in California," 9:90; "Prince Paul of Württemberg's Journeys in America," 16:380-81

bk. revs. by, 2:252-56, 364-67; 3:89-94, 201-3, 297-301; 4:91-94, 290-91; 5:315-16, 403-5, 408-9; 6:95-96, 375, 376; 7:88-90, 194-95; 8:81-84, 89, 185-86, 381, 383-84; 9:184-85, 401; 10:84; 11:86; 13:410; 19:280-81

check lists by, 9:288, 403; 10:86-90, 202-4, 302-6, 408-12; 11:82-85, 289-94, 383-85; 12:77-81, 178-79, 358-63; 13:86, 185, 281, 407

reps. of Publication Com., 5:99-100; 6:106

obits., of George E. Dane, 20:381-82; C. Hart Merriam, 21:284-86; Henry R. Wagner, 36:79-82

Camp, Edgar Whittlesey, 20:384; "Hugh C. Murray, California's Youngest Chief Justice," 20:365-73

Camp & Eggert, 15:367

Campa Cos, Miguel, 9:202-42 *passim*

Camp Alert, 10:375, 379, 389

Camp Anderson, 11:106, 107

Camp Babbitt, 20:163; 40:305

Campbell (from Sydney, 1850), 5:141, 143, 144

Campbell, Judge (Mokelumne Hill, 1852), 30:240, 246

Campbell (Yuba Co., 1852, '55, '57), 3:150; 8:344, 345; 9:143

Campbell, Capt. (Marysville, 1859), 10:59, 174, 189

Campbell (Yuba Co., 1859-'62), 10:56, 259, 285, 381

Campbell, Judge (Marysville, 1859), 10:179

Campbell (policeman, Marysville, 1859), 10:177

Campbell (Mt. Shasta, 1862), 7:126, 129

Campbell (musician, S.F., 1864), 24:263

Campbell, Albert H., 2:217

Campbell, Alexander, 10:295, 381; 14:354-55, 360; 15:280; 17:81, 175; 37:209

Campbell, Bartley, 21:173, 174, 175; 34:363

Campbell, Charles, 26:170

Campbell, D., 33:363

Campbell, David, 6:18

Campbell, J. M., 6:227

Campbell, James (La Mesa, 1847), 21:351; 33:105

Campbell, James (d. S.F., 1854), 15:174

Campbell, James H., 4:256

Campbell, Dr. John (1849), 34:28-30, 36

Campbell, John, rev. of Baer, *Architecture of the California Missions*, 38:273-74

Campbell, John Archibald, 19:366

Campbell, John B., 36:274

Campbell, Mary L., 28:319

Campbell, Patrick, 33:105

Campbell, Peter, 16:339

Campbell, Reuben P., 33:341-42

Campbell, Richard, 18:347-54; 20:341, 346

Campbell, Robert (w. Ashley, 1825), 18:351-52

Campbell, Robert (Cisco, 1875), 18:364, 366

Campbell, S. W., 24:286

Campbell, Thomas R., 13:296

Campbell, Thompson, 15:280; 16:184; 34:52

Campbell, W. L., 11:9

Campbell, William, 12:115

Campbell, William Jackson, 28:334-37 *passim*

Campbell, William Wallace, 4:36; 36:151

Campbell, Poole & Co., 28:335; ranch and ferry, 336, 337

Campbell *v.* Campbell, 10:179

Campbellites, *see* Disciples of Christ

Camp Bidwell, 19:369

Camp Colorado, 22:157
Camp Downey, 29:235-36
Camp Drum, 9:308
Campe, J. E., 19:72
Camp Far West, 6:235; 9:271; 10:169, 192, 348; 11:111-12, 117, 121-22, 244; 13:17; 14:222; 35:15
Camp Gaston, 26:11; 27:222
Camp Grant, 21:107; 30:171
Camphene works, 33:68
Camp Independence, 22:2, 3
Campi's restaurant, San Francisco, 35:141
Camp Joseph H. Pendleton, 22:176
Camp Kearny (1847), 1:233
Camplido, Carlos, 15:40
Camp Lincoln, 26:1, 7-11; illus., opp. 1, opp. 8
Camp Mackall, 27:215
Camp meetings, 2:136; 10:359; 27:301, 309; 38:173
Camp Merritt, 30:289; 31:50, 51
Camp Nome Lackee, 30:161
Camp Norris, 28:340
Campo (place), 35:346
Campora, Count and Countess of, 5:36; 32:117-18
Campos, María Antonia, 13:200-202
Campo Seco, 11:166; 15:171; 16:282; 38:309
Camp Otay, 34:159, 160
Camp Riley, 9:6
Camp Sumner, 26:2
Camptonville, 3:148, 150; 8:199, 203, 204, 205, 209, 338-45 *passim*, 349, 352, 358; 9:52-66 *passim*, 70, 73, 76, 78, 129-30, 137, 139, 140, 144-69 *passim*, 177, 263, 265, 266, 352-53, 384; 10:56, 171, 256, 359; 11:59; 29:203
Camp Union, 10:372, 387
Camp Warren (town), 30:261; 38:309
Camp Wright, Mendocino Co., 27:221-24
Camp Wright, San Diego Co., 27:227; 40:314, 315, 316
Camp Wright, San Francisco, 27:227; 40:315, 316
Camulos, *see* Ranchos: Camulos
Canackus (Kanakas?) Co., 35:208
Canada Hill, 2:206
"Canada Jack" (Jean Baptiste), 26:62
Canadians in Calif., 5:146, 147, 166, 167, 229-34; *see also* French Canadians; "Fur Brigade to the Bonaventura"; Laframboise, Michel; Trappers

Canaga, Mrs. B. E., 24:94
Canal Gulch, 30:260
Canals: across Isthmus of Darien (prop.), 17:83; across Isthmus of Panama (*see* Panama Canal); across Nicaragua (prop.), 31:256, 260; 33:26
Canals and ditches, 3:144, 148-52 *passim*, 259; 6:215, 245; 9:69, 74-75, 136, 141, 142, 150, 165, 174, 282; 11:228, 233, 237-38, 242, 245, 330, 333; 13:28; 17:84; 27:262; 28:234; 29:193-200 *passim*, 205; 35:77, 78
Canavan, P. H. and Mrs., 19:237
Canby, Edward Richard Sprigg, 11:103, 120-21; 15:286; 16:304; 19:22, 237; 21:190; 28:163; 33:344, 345; 34:128, 132, 133, 134, 138, 139; 35:12-17 *passim*, 20; 38:375; bk. on, rev., 39:85-88; orders to Derby, 11:105-6, 247-49; Derby's reps. to, 11:106-20, 249-63; Lyon's rep. to, 24:52-54
Cancan, Le, San Francisco, 39:149
Candia, Demetrio, 2:156
Candinmarruh (ship), *see Kantin Maru*
Cané, Vicente, 36:10
Canfield, Ellen, 28:292
Canfield, William D., 24:60-61
Cañizares, José de, 9:210; 13:157, 158, 180; 14:105, 192; 25:320; 30:2; Diary of the Portolá Expedition, ed. and trans. Virginia E. Thickens and Margaret Mollins, 31:109-24, 261-70, 343-54; maps of San Francisco Bay, 13:180 (reprod. opp. 180); 14: (reprod. opp. 111), 192
Cann (Le Hâvre, 1851), 31:313-14
Canning and preserving, 35:121, 123, 265-66
Cannon, Frank E., 10:54, 61
Cannon, George Q., 18:215
Cannon, James G., 9:66, 79, 130, 144-45, 149, 153, 158, 287; 10:56, 170
Cannon, Mrs. James G. (Ann Eliza Phillips), 9:287
Cannon, Marion, 19:59-70 *passim*; 27:313-16 *passim*; 28:47, 48
Cannon, Mrs. Marion (née Holland), 16:303
Cannonade mining claim, 11:333
Cannons:
  American, 2:350; 8:369; 40:272; at San Juan Bautista, 18:75; Santa Barbara, 18:164, 165-66, 177; Frémont's, 26:235; *see also* Howitzers

Mexican: at Los Angeles, 12:165; San Diego, 14:237; Sonoma, 2:362; 15:64, 65, 69; 17:164, 278

Russian: bought by Sutter, 11:350; at Fort Ross, 12:190; at San Pascual, 26:24, 28-29, 34, 36, 37, 50, 54

Spanish: at Monterey, 15:115; in Panama, 20:19; San Francisco, 2:360; 3:84; 15:58-69 (phot. opp. 58); 17:179; San Pedro, 13:205; Sonoma, 2:362; 15:64, 65, 69; 17:164, 278

Canoas, Pueblo de las, 7:22, 23-24, 47, 54, 55, 74

Canoe (Cow) River, 22:102, 209, 216, 217; 23:134

Canoes, 2:315, 326; 3:6, 7, 18, 229; 7:349, 351; 9:222, 234

Cañon City, 16:337

Cantelow, William, 20:44

Cantenat (San Jose, 1854), 30:262

Cantero (ship), 2:87-88, 90-122; 11:158

Cantil Blanco, 15:59; *see also* Fort Point

Canton, China, 23:304, 306, 308, 313, 314, 318

Canton Chinese Theater, Sacramento, 23:104

Cantor (Indian, 1820s), 29:310

Cantua, Manuel, 16:355; 29:268, 327

Cantua, Vicente, 13:278; 15:119; 23:9

"Can We Insure a Future for the Past?" by Stephen W. Jacobs, 38:97-100

Canyon Creek, 29:195, 197; 33:55, 56

Canyonville, 16:307

Capacity (ship), 22:5, 7, 168

Capcapelic (Indian, 1845), 21:5

Capen, James Winchell, 27:229-36 *passim*, 306, 309

Caperon, Paulin, 23:180; 33:169-74

Caperton, John, 34:246

Cape Verdeans, *see* Portuguese

Capitana (flagship), Alvarado's, *see* Santiago; Becerra's *(Concepción)*, 1:39; Cermeño's, 3:4; *see also* San Agustín; Loaysa's, *see Victoria*; Vizcaíno's, *see San Diego*

Capitán Indian Reservation, 34:204

Capitol Hotel, Sacramento, 19:65

Capp, Charles S., 27:171

Capp, Charles Singer, 22:32, 38

Capps, Edwin M., 36:65

Capron, M. and Mme. (from Paris, 1850), 22:305

Capron, Elisha Smith, quoted, 22:271

Capron, John G., 31:155

"Capt. Andrés Castillero, Diplomat," by George Tays, 14:230-68

"Captain Buckskin," *see* Yount, George

Capt. Sutter (ship), 22:70

"Captivity of Olive Oatman, The," by William B. Rice, 21:97-106

Capuchino, Rancho del, 28:132-33

Carabuza (or Carabalza) *v.* Cornish, 10:186, 187

Carasa, Juan de, 6:307

Carbajal, Pedro, 4:145

Carberry, Thomas ("Irish Tom"), 7:116

Carbonel, Esteban, 8:34, 36

Carcene, Armand, 15:172

Carden, H. B. P., 14:225

Cárdenas, Lázaro de, 7:20, 61-62, 76

Cárdenas, Pedro D., 25:72, 74, 150, 158, 166, 356, 362-63

Carder, William, 7:116

Cardinell, Charles, "Adventures on the Plains," 1:57-71

Cardinet (from Paris, 1850), 22:306

Cardon (cactus), 3:311, 322, 354

Cardona, Nicolas de, 1:36; 8:34, 36

Cardozo (John) & Co., 35:235

Cardwell, James, 22:178; 23:121

Careri, Giovanni Francisco Gemelli, 36:239

Carey (Tuolumne Co.), 11:166

Carey, Edward, 15:179

Carey, James C., 15:281

Carey, John T., 26:203

Carib (ship), 22:170

Caribbean (ship), 23:336

Carl, Charles, 30:356, 365

Carl & Flint, 29:115, 124

Carle, Abel, 39:316

Carle, Hippolyte J., 39:244, 246, 247

Carle, Louis, 39:316-19

Carle (H. J.) and Sons, 39:315

Carleton, Capt. (of *William Penn*, 1855), 16:83

Carleton, Charles, 2:121

Carleton, Charles Erskine, 31:331, 333

Carleton, Frederic W., 17:44, 45

Carleton, Mrs. Frederic W. (Edna Byrne), 17:41, 44, 45, 48

Carleton, G. W., 28:10, 11

Carleton, H. W., 19:232

Carleton, James Henry, 12:3; 24:276; 29:229, 230, 236, 239, 240, 242; 34:137, 140; 40:314, 318, 319, 320, 344, 348, 349; letter from, 29:229-30

Carleton, Mary Tennent, comp. "The

Byrnes of Berkeley," from letters of Mary T. Byrne, 17:41-49
Carlile, Thomas, 37:10-13
Carlin, James W., 30:153
Carlin, William P., 27:219, 221
Carling, Hugh, 9:313
Carlisle, George, 8:201-7 *passim*
Carlisle, Henry Coffin, 24:286
Carlisle, Robert, 2:115
Carlos Pacheco (ship), 22:352
Carlos III of Spain, 31:109, 111
Carlsen, Emil, 37:29; painting by, 37: foll. 24
Carlson, W. H., 19:60-61, 67-68
Carlson and Currier, 31:340
"Carleton, Carrie" (Elizabeth C. Wright), 28:5-6
Carlton, Frank D., 28:4, 12
Carlton, G. E., 30:243
Carlton, H. P., 16:284
Carlyle, Mrs. (Sacramento, 1858), 9:372
Carmagan, James (or Joseph), 22:348
Carman, W., 17:176
Carmany, John H., 28:9; 30:140
Carmel, 35:239
Carmel Valley, 1:233
Carmel (ship), 31:295
Carmelita (ship), 22:10, 169
Carmelites, 7:311; 36:228
Carmel Mission, *see* Missions: San Carlos Borromeo
Carmelo, Rio del, 3:222; 7:356-57; 8:56
Carmen, Arroyo, 31:354
Carmichael (in mines, 1854), 3:153
Carmichael, Lawrence, 15:239
Carnahan, H. L., 40:223
Carnes (d. Sacramento, 1848), 20:36-37
Carnes, Henry, 29:231-33, 235, 244
Carnicer, Baltasar, 23:4
Carolan, Evelyn, 27:190
Carolan, Francis J., obit., 2:371
Carolan, James and Emily (Berger), 27:190
Carolan, Peter, 27:190
Carolina (str., 1850), 3:93; 8:268; 11:300; 15:179; 27:362; 30:39
Carolina (steam tug, 1855), 16:82
Caroline (ship, 1836), *see Sarah and Caroline*
Caroline (brig, 1849), 5:9, 226
Caroline (str., 1851), 28:40
Caroline (str., 1883), 29:191
Caroline E. Foote (ship), 9:310, 313, 328-31; 39:306

Caroni, Signor and Signora (acrobats, 1855), 16:284
Carosso, Vincent P., 36:114
Carpenter (sheriff, L.A., ca. 1860), 24:273
Carpenter, B., 26:297
Carpenter, Benjamin, 5:125
Carpenter, F. M., 24:273(?); 29:237
Carpenter, Harvey C., 9:50, 59, 61, 62, 66, 68, 130-45 *passim*, 159, 173; 10:183, 285, 374; lawsuit, 9:145
Carpenter, Mrs. Harvey C. (Mary Munger [or Smith]), 9:136-37, 267; 10:285, 374
Carpenter, J. E., address, "Centennial Plans," 26:277
Carpenter, Jonathan, 32:155
Carpenter, Lemuel J., 5:109; 13:215, 230; 15:231
Carpenter, Mary A., 10:272, 287
Carpenter, R. B., 30:70
Carpenteur (trapper, 1832), 22:329, 348
Carpentier, Edward R., 16:285(?); 17:83, 176; 34:258(?)
Carpentier, Horace Walpole, 4:210; 16:285(?); 24:172, 174, 176, 180; 26:210, 211, 215; 29:346-52 *passim*; 30:1; 31:325, 326, 327; 34:258(?)
Carpentier and Clark, 33:352
Carpinteria, 3:169; 10:302; 18:164, 165
Carpon, H., 7:11
Carquinez Strait, 6:148-49; 15:178; 23:364; 27:197, 199
Carr (Yuba Co., 1850s), 9:52; 10:285; 11:57
Carr (Potter Ravine, 1853), 33:298; *see also* Garr
Carr, Lt. (Sacramento, 1858), 9:371
Carr, Mrs. Byron Thorpe (Mary Sewall Buck), address, "Romantic Tales of '49," 10:413
Carr, Charles Hardy, 26:381
Carr, Deborah Anna, 27:194
Carr, Ezra S., 24:107; 28:186
Carr, Harry, 20:142
Carr, Helen S., "The Authorship of the So-Called 'Gordon Manuscript,'" 8:374-77
Carr, Horace and Ellen, 20:257
Carr, Hugh, 11:57(?); lawsuit, 10:183, 184
Carr, James, 30:112; 32:295-96; "California Letters," ed. Carl I. Wheat, 11:157-75; drawings by, 11: opp. 157

Carr, Jesse Douglass, 7:412; 9:112; 23:315

Carr, Mrs. Jesse Douglass, (Elizabeth Wood), 7:412

Carr, John, 15:283

Carr, Matthew D., 8:358

Carr, Mrs. Matthew D., 9:285; *see also* Laird, Mrs. Luther

Carr, William (Colorado R., 1850), 22:2

Carr, William (San Jose, 1850), 11:161

Carr, William (exiled, 1856), 6:50; 8:371

Carr, William B., 5:179-80; 7:18, 19; 15:76

Carr, William Jarvis, 11:157; 36:253

Carranco, Lorenzo Joseph, 5:196; 8:375-76

Carrasco, Archipielago de, 10:323

Carravahal (Carvalho?; guide, 1849), 18:350, 351

Carredda, Joseph, 37:303, 304

Carrera, Antonio, *see* Correa

Carrese (actor, 1858), 9:275

Carretas (carriages), 6:250-51; 12:12; 13:314

Carrey, Edmond, 39:230, 231

Carriage Makers' Association, 35:66

Carrie (Joseph A.) & (James E.) Damon, 30:356, 365

Carrier, Mrs. Craig (Marguerite), 22:94

Carrier Dove (ship), 29:113-14

Carrigan (Kerrigan?), Dick, 8:205

Carrigan, Peter, *see* Kerrigan

Carriger, Nicholas, 16:355; 19:127, 141; 29:321, 325, 327; quoted, 2:65-66

Carrillo, Anastasio, 13:208; 14:239; 18:165, 177, 256, 257-58, 275; 27:335, 336, 337

Carrillo, Antonia, 18:71

Carrillo, Carlos Antonio de Jesús, 1:170; 10:82; 13:208, 222; 14:232, 237-40 *passim*, 245, 251, 256, 260-64 *passim*; 16:352, 357-64 *passim*; 17:50, 60; 18:174, 175, 176, 255-58 *passim*, 348, 353; 23:218; 27:286, 335-36, 337; 29:312; 33:343; 34:21; rancho of, 30:52

Carrillo, Domingo, 13:208; 16:222, 230; 27:334, 335, 337

Carrillo, Mrs. Domingo (Concepción Pico), 27:337

Carrillo, Francisca, *see* Thompson, Mrs. Alpheus B.

Carrillo, Francisca Benicia, *see* Vallejo, Mrs. Mariano Guadalupe

Carrillo, Guillermo, 18:258

Carrillo, Joaquín (father of Mrs. M. G. Vallejo), 16:222, 249; 29:310

Carrillo, Joaquín (s. of Domingo), 18:256, 275, 278

Carrillo, Joaquín (lt. col. militia, 1861), 29:247

Carrillo, Mrs. Joaquín (María Ignacia López), 29:319

Carrillo, José (s. of Carlos Antonio), 18:257, 275

Carrillo, José (lt. of Lanceros, 1861), 29:235, 247

Carrillo, José Antonio Ezequiel, 3:121; 5:195; 8:248; 9:81; 10:151; 11:342, 347, 348; 12:135; 13:135-36, 207-12 *passim*, 215, 222, 223, 231, 310, 313, 321, 326; 14:238, 256, 261, 262, 263; 16:57, 225, 236, 358-64 *passim*; 17:50, 52, 53, 233; 18:164, 165, 176; 22:61, 64; 26:32-33; 29:335; 30:53; 33:279; fac. sig., 10: opp. 159

Carrillo, Josefa, *see* Fitch, Mrs. Henry D.

Carrillo, José Raimundo, 13:198, 208; 18:71; 27:337

Carrillo, Mrs. José Raimundo (Tomasa Ignacia Lugo), 27:337

Carrillo, José Ramón, letter from, 1:184-85

Carrillo, Julio, 13:336; 16:249; 17:226, 229; 24:59-60; 29:322; 36:242

Carrillo, Leo, 24:268, 270

Carrillo, Luis, 18:258

Carrillo, María Antonia, 18:176

Carrillo, María Antonia Victoria, *see* Ortega, Mrs. José Francisco de

Carrillo, María de la Luz, 27:107; 29:311-12

Carrillo, María Josefa, 1:170; 18:175

Carrillo, Mariano, 20:237, 238

Carrillo, Pedro C., 13:114; 15:165, 370; 18:256-57, 275; 40:31

Carrillo, Mrs. Pedro C. (Josefa Bandini), 23:217

Carrillo, Raimundo, 12:135; 14:8; 18:71, 163-64, 176, 256, 258, 276; 23:373; *see also* Carrillo, José Raimundo

Carrillo, Ramón, 16:249; 17:147, 148; 21:350; 29:236, 247, 267, 312; *see also* Carrillo, José Ramón

Carrillo, Ygnacia, 20:237

Carrillo de Pacheco, Ramona, *see* Wilson, Mrs. John

Carrillo family, 13:208; 18:255-58; 27:337; 29:310, 319

Carrington, Henry, 9:26
Carrisa Plain, 1:153, 156
Carrizito Cañon, 26:26, 53
Carrizo Canyon, Corridor, 34:193-208 *passim;* 36:120-25 *passim,* 129; map, 34: opp. 200
Carrizo Creek, Spring, Station, Wash, 1:145; 21:217, 300; 25:297, 298, 307; 34:193, 196, 197; 36:117, 118, 123, 127; map, 36: opp. 200
Carrol, Frank, 21:293-94, 306
Carroll, A. W. de la Cour, 4:49
Carroll, Jo P., phot., 32: opp. 1
Carroll, John, 22:34
Carroll, Nicholas, 9:42
Carroll, Mrs. Richard T. (Mary Ann Murphy), 24:89; obit., 13:191-92
Carroll, Thomas, 30:219, 222, 228, 229
Carroll, W., *see* Wiegand, Conrad
Carroll, William, 16:338
Carrolton, 9:75
Carry the News to Mary (play), 20:2
Carson (Grass Valley, 1850), 6:225, 226
Carson, Adaline, 1:150
Carson, Alexander, 22:339, 345, 346; 23:24; 24:232
Carson, Christopher ("Kit"), 3:106, 270; 4:5, 157; 10:38, 298; 12:3; 13:150, 305; 16:49, 142; 18:349; 19:298; 22:51; 23:91; 25:140-41; 29:30; 36:57; w. Frémont (1843-44), 9:187; 10:37; 16:54; (1845-46), 3:270, 273; 4:9, 10; 6:90; 10:38; 12:56; 15:62; 17:224; 29:136; w. Kearny (1846), 8:252; 17:344; 18:74, 167; 21:199-203 *passim,* 207, 214-24 *passim,* 337, 345, 355; 24:95; 25:295; 26:23, 24, 47-48; under Mason (1847-48), 1:246, 251; 3:122-23; 29:30-35; arts. on, 1:111-51; 29:29-38; autobiog., dict. to Peters, rev., 5:408-9; bk. on, by Vestal, rev., 7:194-95; port., 1: opp. 104
Carson, Mrs. Christopher (María Josefa Jaramilla), 1:150
Carson, George, 13:335
Carson, Hamilton, 1:150
Carson, James H., 3:91; 10:409; 22:82
Carson, John, 38:66, 69
Carson, Lindsay, 1:150; 16:306; 24:54
Carson, Moses B., 1:135, 150; 13:215, 230; 15:134; 20:151, 153; 21:13; 22:341, 345; 23:19, 39; 24:54
Carson, William, 38:59-69 *passim*
Carson, William McKendree and Mary Isabelle (Mitchell), 29:285

Carson Canyon, 6:126; 7:7; 16:338; illus., 6: opp. 122; 9: opp. 332
Carson City, 12:325; 15:381; 17:76-77; 20:250
Carson Hill, 11:165, 324, 326; 22:73-77 *passim*
Carson Pass, 1:124; 6:363; 7:7, 9; 32:196
Carson River, 3:67, 69, 200; 4:10; 6:125-26, 362; 12:325; 24:120, 121; 32:198, 203; 34:215
Carson's Creek, 7:401; 8:263; 20:100; 27:160, 161
Carson Valley, 4:11; 6:363; 7:8, 9, 12, 13, 16; 12:325; 21:228-33 *passim,* 238; 30:239, 376; 32:196; 34:215, 220; 38:334-35; illus., 9: opp. 312
Carswell, Miss Helen, 28:294
Carswell, Mrs. Helen M., 14:74, 76
Carswell & Co., 30:366
"Carta de Flores, La," ed. Douglas S. Watson, trans. Thomas W. Temple II, 12:147-54
Cartago, Inyo Co., 17:115
Carter (San Bernardino, 1852), 14:181
Carter, Abiel, 20:28, 44
Carter, Alfred W., 25:227
Carter, Annetta, 29:378
Carter, B. H., 31:339
Carter, Charles, son of, 15:185
Carter, Charles D., 9:26; 15:271
Carter, Cassius, 35:353, 355
Carter, Charles Franklin, 8:131; trans. "Duhaut-Cilly's Account of California in ... 1827-28," 8:131-66, 214-50, 306-36
Carter, Fred, 31:157
Carter, George, 19:116, 136
Carter, Capt. Henry (of *William Little,* 1831), 23:301, 330
Carter, Lt. Henry (1863), 40:319
Carter, Isaac W., 10:406
Carter, J. B., 3:116, 118; 17:337-38
Carter, J. O., 25:226
Carter, Jesse Washington, 27:381
Carter, John Denton, 20:384; "George Kenyon Fitch, Pioneer California Journalist," 20:329-40; "Thomas Sim King, Vigilante Editor," 21:23-38
Carter, Joseph O., 12:142-46 *passim;* 14:318, 342, 343
Carter, Nathaniel C., 31:20-21
Carter, Solomon, 7:113
Carter, William Alexander, 31:189
Carter and Shurtleff, 5:183
"Carterhia" (Sierra Madre), 31:21

Carth, Thomas, 24:117

Carthagina (ship), 8:265, 268

"Carthay Center," by Mary E. Curry, 5:198

Cartography, *see* Maps

Cartoons: Civil War, 40; foll. 294; of Derbec, 39: opp. 144; French, 39: opp. 1; Korea, 30: opp. 193; of Tom Maguire, 21: opp. 239; of Theodore Roosevelt, 38: opp. 244; of William H. Russell, 18: foll. 72; seeing the elephant, 39: foll. 29

Cartwright, Mrs. (Santa Clara Co., 1853), 29:40

Cartwright, Charles, 13:295

Cartwright, Fred, 13:295

Cartwright, George W., 39:21

Cartwright, John W., Sr. and Jr., 13:296

Cartwright, Sylvester, 34:67

Caruso, Enrico, 21:183; 25:235; 33:40-41

Carvalho, Charles, 15:177; 23:108, 111

Carvalho, Solomon Nuñez, 35:236

Carvalho family, 35:235, 241

Carvil (Spanish Bar, 1851), 2:138

Cary, Annie Louise, 21:245, 258; 33:223

Cary, William M., 7:18-19

Casad, Michael R., 9:364, 391

"Casa Grande," Richardson's, 3:32, 34; 13:238; 14:125, 344; 17:299

"Casa Grande," Vallejo's, 29:149, 151; 36:242

Casa Montezuma (or Casa Blanca), 21:211, 223

Casa Nevada, La, Yosemite, 5:339

Casarín, Manuel Jimeno, *see* Jimeno Casarín

Casas, Bartolomé de las, 8:29-30

Casas, Laurent, 39:248

Casassa, Charles H., 30:69

Cascade Range, pass over (phot.), 22: opp. 209

Cascarones, 12:282; 20:225; 28:38

Casco (ship), 3:292, 296

Casco House, Sacramento, 9:376, 397; 10:40, 46, 47, 174, 190, 247, 250, 274, 275

Case, Bascom, 2:188-94 *passim*

Case, Charles L., 15:164

Case, Charles S., 22:39

Casebolt's Carriage Factory, San Francisco, 5:86

Casena, María Isobel de, 29:132

Casey, Mrs. (S.F., 1855), 15:368

Casey, E. W., 26:247

Casey, James, 18:23

Casey, James P., 3:41; 4:192; 6:3, 7; 8:365-71 *passim*; 13:82; 14:351, 352, 354; 15:80-81, 366; 16:80, 182, 283, 336, 341; 17:83, 310; 18:276; 20:261, 306; 21:23, 25-26; 24:173-74; 32:221, 224; 37:142, 169; port., 8: opp. 368

Casey, John J., 15:319, 322-23

Casey, Michael, 35:67, 68, 147, 150

Casey, Silas, 19:22

Cash, James, 29:338

Cashier (Cassia, Casua, Casus, etc.) Creek, *see* Raft River

Cashman, William F., 33:319

Cason, Minnie, 9:87

Caspar (place), 21:383

Cass, Lewis, 19:173, 174, 334; 22:315

Casselli, Agustín, 30:222, 228

Casserly, Eugene, 6:45-46; 10:285, 286, 355; 27:67, 166; 30:132, 133, 146-47; 39:13

Casserly, John B., 25:232

Cassill, F. M., 37:200

Castaic Lake, 10:212, 214, 215, 218

Castañares, José María, 12:150-51; 14:258, 259, 261

Castañares, Manuel, 12:129, 147-54; 13:44; 17:60-61, 155; 24:294

Castañeda, Carlos E., ed. *Nuevos Documentos . . . Historia de Mexico,* Vols. II, III, rev., 9:401-2

Castañeda, Juan, 14:235-36; 16:359; 17:52-53

Castañeda, Pedro de, 3:264-65, 384; 6:303

Castaveja, Juan, 38:259

Castellanos, Francisco de, 6:309

Castelli, Abbé (Fr. mining co. official), 22:299

Castellon, Juan de, 3:311, 315, 316-18; 19:240-44

Castera, John, 39:344

Castigliano (or Castiglione), *see* Castillo, Domingo de

Castilla, Luis de, 3:394; 6:313, 315, 317, 321, 322

Castilla, Ramonda, 30:98

Castillero, Andrés, 4:84; 5:191-95; 11:343; 12:35, 134; 13:58-59, 77, 106; 14:158, 346; 15:3-4, 6, 7, 14, 19, 347, 356, 363; 16:356-59 *passim*, 361, 362, 365, 368; 17:52, 162; 21:318; 26:374; 28:267; art. on, 14:230-68; claim of, *see* New Almaden; lawsuit, 10:191

Castillero, Luis, 15:341

Castillo (Lower Calif., 1840), 15:105-6,
113
Castillo, Domingo del, 1:45, 47; 3:312,
384, 385, 386; map, 3:381; 7:150; 11:45
Castillo, Felipe, 25:293, 294, 295
Castillo Bueno, Juan del, 7:377
Castillo Negrete, Luis de, 12:318-19
15:347-48, 356, 358; 27:206
Castillo Negrete, Manuel, 15:130
"Castine," *see* Brooks, Noah
Castle, Anne, 32:191
Castle, C. H., 28:51, 52
Castle, George Parmelee, obit., 12:88
Castle, J. B., 40:44-45
Castle, William, 4:209
Castle Dome, Yosemite, 22:157
Castleman, Riva, "Cleaning up the
Waterfront: 1847," 35:367-68
Castle Rock, 3:50
Castleton, Kate, 35:141
Castor, Thomas F., 28:213, 221, 230
Castran, Pedro, 4:145
Castree, D. B., 9:26
Castree & Byrne, 15:170
Castro, Ángel, 4:83; 15:119
Castro, Antonio, 16:246
Castro, Carlos, 8:115
Castro, Estevan, 9:107
Castro, Francisco María, 8:243; 9:190;
16:111, 113; 30:220; 36:241
Castro, Guillermo, 33:350
Castro, Henri, 18:132
Castro, Joaquín (Santa Rosa, 1836),
16:246
Castro, Joaquín (Santa Cruz Mts., 1848),
13:79
Castro, Joaquín de (San José, 1778),
14:6
Castro, Joaquín Ysidro, 15:277
Castro, John Elliot de, *see* Elliot de
Castro
Castro, José, 1:80, 91, 92, 126-27, 133-38
passim, 183, 189-90, 234; 3:110-14
passim, 180-90 *passim*, 271, 275, 276,
280-89 *passim*; 4:81-87 *passim*, 383;
5:134, 195, 302, 303; 6:182, 189, 190,
191, 272-80 *passim*, 369, 370; 7:79-85
passim; 8:71, 72, 75; 9:81-85 *passim*;
10:35, 100-106 *passim*; 11:75, 206, 220,
343, 347, 356; 12:35-44 *passim*, 48, 52,
53, 128-33 *passim*, 137, 147-53 *passim*,
161-65 *passim*, 238, 336, 355-56;
13:45-48 *passim*, 99, 100-101, 109-20
passim, 123, 132, 138, 145-56, 229, 231,
236, 328; 14:124, 148, 230-34 *passim*,

237-41 *passim*, 245, 255; 15:3, 4, 62,
119-31 *passim*, 225-31 *passim*, 241,
339-55 *passim*; 16:102, 106, 107, 217,
221-22, 241, 248, 348-53 *passim*, 359,
363, 364; 17:51, 54-58 *passim*, 69, 136,
139, 140, 152, 156-64 *passim*, 220,
272-83 *passim*, 326, 346; 18:69-70, 72,
76, 78, 80, 157-60 *passim*, 172, 178,
20:225, 239; 21:3, 11, 216; 22:52;
23:327, 374; 25:122-28 *passim*, 293;
27:146, 353; 29:135, 151, 158, 261, 263,
267-73 *passim*; 30:98; 32:265; 33:351;
34:119; 36:11; cor., 2:69-71, 354-55;
3:182-83, 185-86, 276-77; 4:83-85, 375,
382; 5:188-89; 6:80-83, 278-79, 366-68;
7:81-82; 8:71, 72, 75; 10: (fac.), opp.
99, 104-6, 119, 122; 11:352-53;
13:116-19; procs., 1:93-95, 178; 3:279;
4:384-85; 10:123; (reprod.) 12: opp.
125; 13:117-18; 15:354; port., 14: opp.
230
Castro, Mrs. José (Modesta), 1:258;
3:181
Castro, José Tiburcio, 12:128, 134;
16:223-24
Castro, Juan, 16:43
Castro, Macario, 1:165
Castro, Manuel A., 9:103
Castro, Manuel de Jesús, 1:77; 3:284;
4:81; 5:195; 6:87, 277; 11:206, 352-53;
12:135, 147; 13:47, 51, 100, 105-11
passim; 18:163, 164, 176; 25:18, 145;
29:336; cor., 3:273-74, 277, 278-79;
4:375-83, 385-87; 5:186-88, 189-90,
192-93, 296-97, 308-10; port., 14: opp.
230
Castro, María de los Angeles, *see* Majors,
Mrs. Joseph L.
Castro, Simeón, 28:262; 29:25
Castro, Mrs. Simeón (María Antonia
Pico), 20:264
Castro, Vicente, 38:259-61, 263-64
Castro, Victor, 11:142; 16:246; 17:42,
45; 30:56, 322; 31:330; 37:194
Castro family, 38:259, 263
Castro Valley, 30:9
Castroville, Tex., 18:102, 132
Caswell (from Victoria, 1860), 29:114
Caswell, Mrs. George W. (Daisy F.
Badger), obit., 23:90
Caswell, H., 9:394
Caswell, Sam, 3:152
Catala, Magín de, 14:14; 23:374; 38:102,
105-6
Catalán, Francisco, 37:199

Catalina (ship), 8:106; 14:264; 16:361; 19:206, 210, 214, 216; 23:215, 318, 320, 330, 331, 332

Catalina Island, *see* Santa Catalina I.

Caterpillar Tractor Co., 31:89

Catez, Charles H., 9:26

Cathcart, James F., 13:32; 21:65; 241

Cathedral of the Blessed Sacrament, Sacramento, 39:199, 206

Cathedrals, The (play), 20:143

Catherine (ship), 12:225

Catholic Book Store, San Jose, 30:367

Catlin, Amos Parmalee, 1:18; 9:107, 114; 27:93; 33:373

Catlin, Mrs. Amos Parmalee (Ruth Donaldson), 27:93

Catlin, George, 6:118; 16:52-53

Catlin, John, 27:93

Catoira, Gomez Hernandez, 7:231, 232

Cator, Thomas Vincent, 19:60-73 *passim;* 27:311-18; 28:47-55; port., 28: opp. 47

Cator, Mrs. Thomas Vincent (Ethel Chapman), 27:312, 314; 28:50, 54; Edith V. (Chapman) Houghton, 28:54

Cattermole, George, 8:337, 349-50

Cattick, Joseph W., 29:237

Cattle, 2:184, 267, 289, 290, 291, 295, 308, 310, 322; 3:77, 120-21; 4:25; 5:130-35 *passim,* 217, 249, 273, 274, 367; 8:102, 111, 156; 10:377; 12:282-87 *passim;* 13:202, 203, 204, 339, 349; 14:5, 6, 9-10, 13, 199-203 *passim,* 222; 16:368; 17:42; 19:197, 203-10 *passim;* 21:1, 3, 196, 207, 209, 220, 338, 341, 349; 22:319; 23:259, 297; 27:210; 29:49, 53; 34:22; 35:159; 38:260-64 *passim*

business, 5:170, 274; 8:265, 274; 13:327; 18:11; 19:384; 29:20, 304; 32:259; 34:22, 23; drives, 3:77; 5:249; 8:98; 10:39; 12:274; 18:11; 19:197; 30:53

at missions and presidios, 1:165, 169; 2:41-42, 279-86 *passim,* 295, 322, 337; 5:217; 8:319; 12:283; 16:118, 119; 17:246, 247, 336; 18:320; 19:207, 210; 23:252

raised by Russians, 12:189, 193, 242, 251, 260, 262

rustling, 15:173; 21:207; 27:210; 31:311; 39:291

slaughter, 5:130; 8:111, 237; 12:290, 293; 13:204; 22:319; *see also* Matanzas

see also Beef; Branding: Dairying; Hides and tallow; Livestock

Caughey, John Walton, 20:95; 24:11; 36:115; fellow CHS, 38:73; "California and the Nation . . .," 40:193-202; ed. George F. Kent journal, "Life in California in 1849," 20:26-46

Cauwet, Pierre, 39:6, 219

Cavalier, W., 35:321

Cavalier, William St. Cyr, 16:276-77; 24:267, 369; 26:186; obit., 24:374-75

Cavaller, José, 1:161-62; 23:374

Cavallier, Jean Baptiste Edmond, 16:82; 22:23(?)

"Cavemania" (prop. state), 31:126

Caven, J. B. ("Bur"), 8:203, 212

Cavendish, Thomas, 2:159; 7:185, 257, 302, 309

Caverley, John P., 21:306

Cavert & Co. (Sacramento, 1851), 23:171-72

Caviar, 12:293-94

Cavière (S.F., 1850s), 32:110-11

Cavillia, C., 27:36

Cavis, Joseph M., 10:377, 390; 26:239, 247

Cawley, Daniel M., 13:261

"Caxton" (pseud.), *see* Rhodes, William H.

Cayota [Stage] Line, 14:402

Cayucos (fishing boats), 1:55; 29:318; 30:311

Cayuelas, Francisco, 1:169

Cayuga (ship), 13:390; 27:44

Cayute Creek, *see* Coyote Creek

Cayvan, Georgia, 35:142

Cazadora (ship), 37:247, 264

Caziare, Louis V. and Hettie (Ritchie), 19:233

Cazneau, Thomas Nugent, 15:143-45; 26:256, 352-53

Cazotte, Charles de, 31:321; 37:206

Cea, Francisco de, 3:21

Ceballas (or Cevallos), Ciriaco, 3:237; 40:118

Cebrian, Carmen, *see* Bernal, Mrs. José C.

Cebrian, John C., "Presentation of the Serra Birthplace," 11:280-88; obit., 14:190-91

Cebrian, Mrs. John C. (Maria J. de Laveaga), 14:190

Cecil, T. M., 18:81

Cedar Bar, 6:218

Cedar Cottage, Yosemite, 5:337-38; phot., 5: opp. 340

Cedros Island, 1:42; 2:49, 140, 158, 316, 351, 352, 356, 362, 367; 3:351-55; 6:325; 7:42, 58, 72, 170, 191, 240, 243, 311, 315, 331-35, 372; 8:60-61; on maps, 7:333, 335

Celebration of the Fourth of July ... Los Angeles ... 1847," by H. H. F. Toye, 1:238-39

Celebrations: address on (S.F.), 4:400; Arbor Day (Yerba Buena I.), 32:234-35; Atlantic cable (Marysville), 9:360, 367, 389; Bunker Hill (S.F.), 15:366; Chinese New Year's (S.F.), 15:272; inaug. of gov. (Sacramento), 9:244, 270; New Year's (in mines), 20:40-41; St. Patrick's Day (S.F.), 10:377, 390; 15:275; 24:49; Victory of Allies in Crimea (S.F.), 16:341; 17:84-85; 27:212; Washington's Birthday (Folsom), 4:223; 9:181; (S.F.), 15:272; 37:360; at sea, 1:230; *see also* Admission Day; Christmas; Festivals; Fourth of July; Thanksgiving

"Celebrations in San Francisco," address by Charles B. Turrill, 4:400

Celeste, Mme. (Mrs. Henry Elliott), 21:152

Celeste, Mme. (Mrs. McKinley), 9:248, 273-74

"Celestial Drama in the Golden Hills," by Lois F. Rodecape, 23:97-116

Celestial Valley (town), 8:343, 348, 359; 9:51, 53

Celestin (S.F., 1850), 5:345

Celis, Eulogio de, 8:106; 12:335; 13:34-35, 313, 339; 14:342; 16:247; 17:154, 327-30; 18:177; 19:202-3, 207, 209, 215; 21:357; 27:109; 33:249

Cels, E., 31:141-42, 147

Cemeteries in San Francisco, 23:75, *see also* Laurel Hill Cemetery; Yerba Buena Cemetery

Cendrars, Blaise, *L'Or*, 9:398-99

Cenizas (San Martin) Island, 3:18

Cenizo, Fr. (w. Fages, 1781), 33:16

Censuses, 10:233; 24:140; 25:311; of 1768, 3:225; of 1828, 5:217; 1860-70, 25:311-18; 38:29; 39:295; 1890, 25:311; 1900, 25:311; *see also* Population

"Census of California Spanish Imprints, 1833-1845," by George L. Harding, 12:125-36

Centennial (riv. str.), 35:125

Centennial Movement (play), 34:361

"Centennial of the Pacific Coast Survey," address by Erwin G. Gudde, 29:185-86

"Centennial Plans," address by J. E. Carpenter, 26:277

Center, A., 30:290, 297, 299-300, 304; 31:49, 61, 65, 166, 172

Center, John, 6:13; 15:365; 33:375

Centerville, El Dorado Co., 22:384

Centerville, Fresno Co., 25:18, 20, 175

Centerville Butte, 39:263

Centerville Canal and Irrigation Co., 11:245; 25:20-21

Centerville Racecourse, 10:198, 283, 296

Centipedes, 17:29

Central America (ship), 9:179; 21:302, 308; 31:274; 34:336-38; 36:139; *see also George Law*

Central California Colony, 25:22-32 *passim*, 169, 172

Central Hill Mining Co., 11:330

Central Hotel, San Francisco, 16:130

Central Milling Co., 30:285

Central Pacific Railroad, 2:210; 3:398; 4:93, 219; 5:105; 10:407; 15:98; 18:355-68; 26:360; 27:11, 196, 271, 339; 30:136; 32:368; 39:177; building of, 4:255-70 *passim*; 5:178-83; 7:100; 13:17; 18:149; 37:130, 132; inception, 4:240-51; in San Joaquin Valley, 18:23-31; timetable (fac.), 24: opp. 365

Central Park, San Jose, 10:358

Central Theater, San Francisco, 33:42

Central Valley Project, 24:12; 30:311-12

Centre Diggings, 26:292, 295

Century Club of California, 25:16; 31:250

"Century of Mills College, A," address by Lynn T. White, Jr., 31:85-88

Cercle Français, San Francisco, 20:131

Cérès (ship), 5:5-21, 26, 27, 30, 38, 40, 42, 176, 177, 228; 32:106

Cerf, Marcel E., obit., 14:286-87

Cerf, Mrs. Marcel E. (Katherine Agnew Martin), 14:286

Cermeño, Sebastian Rodríguez, 7:256, 363, 388, 392; 8:51; 11:309, 312; 20:315-28; 21:82; 27:290, 294; 31:100-108 *passim*; "Relation," trans. H. R. Wagner, 3:10-24; art. on by Wagner, 3:3-24; fac. p. of MS, 3:24

Ceron, Alvaro de, *see* Saavedra Ceron

Ceron, Jorge, 3:311, 339; 6:298
Cerro Gordo (mining camp), 17:101, 109, 110, 115, 208, 214, 215
Cerros Island, *see* Cedros Island
Cerruti, Enrique, 29:152-56 *passim,* 160, 327-28; phot., 29: opp. 153
Cervantes, A. L., 37:200
Cervantes, Andrés, 16:222
Cervantes, Cruz, land-grant case, 30:331
César (ship), 37:319
Céspedes, *see* García de Céspedes
Chabolla, Luis, 15:18
Chabolla, Pedro, 13:60-61, 78
Chabot Observatory, 30:285
Chadbourne, J., 29:253-54
Chadburn (Nevada Co., d. 1853), 11:233
Chadwick, E. C. M., 10:293
Chaffey, Ben, 26:280
Chaffey, George, 26:280; 28:380
Chagres, 8:4-13 *passim;* 13:4, 390; 29:3, 6; 20:16; 29:3, 10; 39:101
"Chagres River Route to California in 1851, The," by Georgia W. Read, 8:3-16
Chaigneau, Alfred, 39:169, 223-32 *passim*
Chaigneau, Emile, 15:46-47
Chalfant, Pleasant A., 9:193, 195
Chalfant, Willie Arthur, 9:193, 195; 25:242; *Death Valley,* rev., 9:186; *Outposts of Civilization,* rev., 7:91-92; *The Story of Inyo,* rev., 2:178-79
Challenge (Amer. clipper, 1852), 10:294; 23:99
Challenge (Brit. ship, 1854), 18:16-17; 35:321
Challenger (clipper), 16:337
Cham, cartoon by, 39: opp. 1
Chamberlain, C. M., 9:29; 15:176
Chamberlain, John, 15:123; 16:56
Chamberlain, Levi, 14:321
Chamberlain, Selah, 25:232
Chamberlain, Mrs. Selah (Edith McDonald), obit., 35:83-84
Chamberlin, E. Kirby, 30:146
Chambers, David, 26:193; 15:372
Chambers, H., 9:62, 157, 359
Chambers, Thomas J. A. and Caroline (Wilson), 28:294
Chambers, Mrs. William Ely (Hazel Nesbitt), 28:378
Chambray (S.F., 1850), 5:36
Chamisso, Adelbert von, 11:83; 12:207-8; 16:86; 18:338, 345
Chamon, Eugène, 39:159

Chamon, Jean Baptiste Julien, 39:159, 164
Champaigne, François, 22:197, 201, 207, 219; 23:21, 34, 136, 139
Champion (ship), 35:199
Champlain, Miss (S.F., 1862), 10:378
Chan Ah Kin, 23:104
Chana, Claude, 14:203, 208, 211, 217
Chandler (on *Glencoe,* 1849), 11:157
Chandler, Capt. (Sacramento, 1849), 24:121
Chandler (C.P.R.R., ca. 1880), 23:120
Chandler, Jabez, 13:32
Chandler, Joseph N., 29:237
Chandler, Mrs. Logan (Helen Baily), 27:93
Chandler, Sarah Elizabeth, 31:377; 33:373
Chandler's Diggings, 9:380
Chandlerville, 9:380
Chandlerville quartz diggings, 9:350, 380
Chaney, Everett H., 25:190
Chaney, Ralph W., 25:193-94, 198, 201-3, 213; address, "Prehistoric California," 9:407-8
Chanfrau, Francis S., 20:297; 21:243
"Changes in the Popular Concept of 'California,' by Lynn T. White, Jr., 19:219-24
Chanks, H., 15:305
Channel Islands, 2:48-49, 329-30; 3:6, 17-18, 227; 7:23, 48-54 *passim,* 57, 58, 73, 74, 76, 169, 172, 191, 349-54, 371, 387-88, 389; 8:58, 156, 164, 232; Indians of, 3:6, 17, 18, 70, 227-30; 7:23, 48-52 *passim,* 76, 349, 351-52, 354, 370, 371; 25:353, 363-64; sea otter hunting on, 12:226, 232; on map, 7: opp. 46, 350, 353; *see also* names of islands
Chaparral, 23:373
Chaparral Hill, 11:240
Chapel, George, 15:240
Chapin (Dry Creek, 1850), 30:239
Chapin, Dr. (San Jose, 1883), 24:223
Chapin, Elizabeth R., 28:294
Chapin, William Wallace, address, "Forty Years after the 1915 Exposition," 35:75
Chapin's Sheep Ranch, 12:7
Chapline, J. L., 13:32
Chapman (Napa, 1851), 2:136
Chapman, Miss (actress, 1864), 21:65
Chapman, A. F., 21:238

Chapman, Albert Pickett, 7:14;
　20:38-39, 42-44
Chapman, Caroline, 7:285; 20:298;
　21:41
Chapman, Charles Edward, 3:256;
　*History of California: The Spanish
　Period*, 1:46, 47; rev., 1:194-97
Chapman, Cristina (Alviso), 38:183;
　trans. "Early Days at Mission Santa
　Clara," 38:101-11
Chapman, Edith, 28:54
Chapman, Ethel, *see* Cator, Mrs.
　Thomas Vincent
Chapman, George and Mary Ross
　(Parks), 7:283
Chapman, Isaac M., 4:45
Chapman, Joseph, 13:206-7
Chapman, Mrs. Joseph (Guadalupe
　Ortega), 13:207
Chapman, Joseph S., 15:185
Chapman, Sarah (Mrs. William B.
　Hamilton), 7:283, 284
Chapman, W. H., 9:362; 10:200;
　lawsuit, 10:168, 170, 180, 187
Chapman, William B., 7:283, 284;
　15:173, 179; 16:84, 285; 20:298,
　300-301; 21:41
Chapman, Mrs. William B. (Phoebe
　Taylor), 7:284
Chapman, William S., 25:18, 21-22,
　25-29; 27:171
Chapman (ship), *see I. F. Chapman;
　J. M. Chapman*
Chapman Family, 7:282-85, 406;
　20:297-98, 304; 21:41
Chapman's Pass, 7:13
Chapo (Indian, 1850), 24:52
Chappel (or Chappell), Jay B., 33:5,
　7, 12, 153, 163-64, 167; 35:295, 296,
　299, 300, 303; phot., 33: opp. 1
Chappel, Scott R., 23:121; 33:5, 7, 12,
　149
Chappell, J. N., 34:53
Chappell, Maxine, 26:285; "Early
　History of Mono County," 26:233-48
Chappellet (metallurgist, 1867), 18:155
Chappellet, Felix, 17:47-48; 39:163
Chappellet, Mrs. Felix (Milvia Frick),
　39:163
"Chapter in the Early Life of Thomas
　Oliver Larkin, A," by Robert J.
　Parker, 16:3-29, 144-71; as address,
　16:187
"Characters of the Champagne Period

in San Francisco," address by Evelyn
　Wells, 18:185
Charague (Indian, 1846), 25:294
Charbonneau, Jean Baptiste, 21:201, 222
Charbonneau, Toussaint, 4:126, 127
Charbonnel (S.F., 1849), 5:21
Charcoal Flat, 33:193
Chard, William George, 15:127, 241;
　22:366; 28:260; 30:54
Charity Valley, 7:12
Charivari, Le (Fr. pub., 1850), 22:314
Charivaris, 9:66, 165
Charlefoux (trapper, 1837), 10:31;
　14:252
Charles (opera singer, 1860), 10:265
Charles (ship), 28:198; 33:261
"Charles Christian Nahl," by Eugen
　Neuhaus, 15:295-305
Charles Cooper (ship), 2:116; 11:158
Charles Coulson Rich, by Evans, rev.,
　16:85
"Charles Fernald to Hannah Hobbs,"
　ed. Cameron Rogers, 34:41-48
Charles Quint (ship), 37:318
Charles the Second (play), 9:369; 15:48
Charleston (ship), 25:39-53
"*Charleston*, The, an Industrial
　Milestone," by Ruth Teiser, 25:39-53
Charlestown Mining Co., 29:297-306
　passim
Charles Twelfth (play), 15:48
Charlevoix, *see* Charlefoux
Charley (Indian, 1830s-1904),
　26:210-15 *passim*
Charley's Ranch, 6:242-43; 9:69; 33:295
Charley's Restaurant, Marysville, 14:394
Charlton, Richard, 23:218
Charmer (ship), 15:279
Charon (ship), 12:226
Charpentier (from France, 1850),
　22:307
Charpentier (or Carpenteur), C.,
　22:323, 329, 348
Charter Oak, Tulare Co., 28:334
Charter Oak Hall, San Francisco, 25:33
Charto, El (ship), 27:48
Chas (Charles?), Harry, 8:342
Chase, Arthur, 35:296
Chase, Benjamin T., 15:372
Chase, Charles, 35:105
Chase, Franklin, 23:262
Chase, George, 36:211
Chase, Mrs. George, 36:207, 211
Chase, George M., 10:68; 25:344
Chase, Harold Stuart, 22:288

Chase, John, 13:32
Chase, Lew A., 29:190
Chase, Moses, 4:211; 30:285
Chase, Pearl, 26:93-94; 29:185
Chase, Rufus, 30:17
Chase, S. U., 5:125
Chase, Salmon Portland, 19:363-64;
    34:53, 54, 55
Chase, Samuel H., 10:275; 11:9
Chase, Sarah, *see* Bourn, Mrs. William B.
Chase, Stephen Henry and Elizabeth P.
    (Dunlap), 28:293
Chase (ship), 8:181, 262
Chaste, Chasty, Chestet (Shasta), 24:233
Chaste River, *see* Shasta River
Chateau Briant, Le (ship), 13:375, 382
Chateauneff, Sheriff (Santa Barbara Co.,
    1859), 18:260
Châtelier, Pierre François Henri, 22:304
Chatfield, Charles N. ("Nels"), 28:239,
    242
Chatfield, Solon, 28:239
Chatham (ship), 2:265, 275, 276, 282,
    291, 292, 299, 300, 308, 310, 311, 316,
    318, 331, 335; 10:325; 15:60
Chat Noir, Le (weekly), 39:315, 346
Chaume, Thion de la, 22:297
Chauncey (S.F., 1867), 11:127
Chauncey, Henry, 13:245
Chautauqua Circle, Sierra Madre, 31:22
Chauvel Restaurant, Nevada City,
    11:232
Chauviteau, Hector, 35:321; 39:10, 142
Chauviteau, J. J., 5:12, 27, 28, 38, 42,
    343, 346; 22:297; 28:34
Chauviteau's Building, 15:186
Chavanne, André, 6:333-35, 356-57;
    12:72; 29:203, 208; "The Burning of
    the *Golden Gate* in July 1862," ed.
    and trans. Desiré Fricot, 19:27-42;
    port., 19: opp. 27
Chavanne, Louis, 19:27
Chaves, Francisco de, 3:21
Chaves, Pedro de, 3:21
Chávez, Antonio, 12:319-20, 321;
    21:315(?)
Chavez, Cleovaro, 17:101, 110, 116
Chávez, José Antonio (N. Mex., 1830),
    10:27, 28; 20:342
Chávez, José Antonio (Monterey Co.,
    1846), 5:189, 190; 21:315(?); 25:145
Chavira y Lerma, Josepha, 20:237
Chavis (Chavez?), Antonio, 21:315
Chedie, G. W., 21:238
Chee Kung Tong, 27:21, 28

Cheese, 3:57; 5:375; 11:136; 14:168, 201;
    20:261-66 *passim*; 25:34; 29:53; *see
    also* Dairying
Cheeseman, B. F., 13:258; 14:401
Cheeseman, Morton, 13:258; 14:401
Cheesman, David W., 9:116; 11:127;
    27:97, 101, 103
Cheever, Miss (S.F., 1875), 37:217
Cheever, George N., 13:296
Cheever, H. C., 37:217
Cheever, Henry, *see* Chever
Cheever, Henry A., 33:373
Cheever, John, 13:296
Chellis, John H., 10:374, 387; 30:134-35;
    34:62
Chelsy Smith (ship), 2:136
Chemin, Léon, 39:149-152, 154, 159, 238
Chenery, Richard, 4:225; 9:42
Chenery, Richmond, 10:293
Cheney, John Vance, 1:18; 24:80; 35:355
Cheney, O. P., 13:32
Cheney, Zachariah, 14:177, 182
Chen Shu Tang, 30:149
Cherington, Reed B., address, "The
    Present Condition of the Missions,"
    4:401-2
Cherokee, Butte Co., 29:196-97
Cherokee, Nevada Co., 10:349; 28:236
Cherokee (ship), 4:191; 11:125
Cherokee Bar, 8:342, 347, 359
Cherokee Siphon, 29:196-97
Cherries, 12:193, 205, 206, 258; 15:364;
    25:26
Cherry, John W., 10:62, 70
Cherry Hill Gap, 29:194-95; phot., 29:
    opp. 200
Cherry Springs, Tex., 18:106-7
Chesapeake (ship), 26:340; 31:255
Cheshire (ship), 6:205-12, 214
Chesley, Mrs. (Sacramento, 1859),
    10:42, 176
Chetco Point, 10:329
Chevalier (San Juan de los Lagos, 1849),
    23:269
Chevalier, Dr. (S.F. and mining region,
    1849-50), 5:25; 13:374, 383-84
Chevalier, J. B., 22:23; *see also* Cavallier
Chever (or Cheever), Edward English,
    1:16-17; 24:80; 27:263
Chever (or Cheever), Henry, 14:212;
    26:124
Chevers, William H., 16:345; 19:236
Chevral, A. B., 39:240
"Cheyenne" (pseud.), 24:243-45
Chiarini, Virginia, 10:288

Chicago fire of 1871, effect of, 27:168, 270

Chicago Park, 38:137

Chichizola, Augustino, 31:283; 33:375

Chichizola (Antonio) & Son, 31:283

Chickering, Allen Lawrence, 17: No. 4, Pt. 2, pp. 1, 24; 25:284; 30:93; 31:303; 34:92; 36:21, 31
  "An Arboreal Archive," 34:19-20; "Further Notes on the Drake Plate," 18:251-53; "Samuel Norris: Litigious Pioneer," 25:219-28; "Some Notes with regard to Drake's Plate of Brass," 16:275-81
  trans. Edmond Leuba, "Bandits, Borax and Bears," 17:99-117; *idem*, "A Frenchman in the Panamints," 17:208-18
  introds. to "Drake in California," 36:21; "Hall McAllister to 'Mannie'," 36:21; foreword to "The Old Occidental," 32:57
  address, "Newest Light on 'Drake's Plate'," 18:85
  obits. of Annie M. Alexander, 29:378; Wallace M. Alexander, 18:379-81; Mrs. Wallace M. Alexander, 34:184-85; Paul Bancroft, 36:181-82; Mrs. Ernest A. Bryant, 25:375; Mrs. Selah Chamberlain, Sr., 35:83-84; Everette L. DeGolyer, 36:86; Henry F. Dutton, 32:375; Raymond C. Force, 31:89; Morton R. Gibbons, Sr., 28:374-75; Lowell E. Hardy, 30:189; Mrs. Lowell E. Hardy, 36:281; John Howell, 35:180-82; Norman B. Livermore, 33:81-82; Duncan McDuffie, 30:280-81; Mrs. Duncan McDuffie, 34:182-83; Parker S. Maddux, 32:374-75; Garret W. McEnerney, 21:283; Armand T. Mercier, 36:375-77; C. O. G. Miller, 31:176-77; Harry E. Miller, 18:190; Mrs. Randolph H. Miner, 36:182-83; Margaret J. Moffitt, 36:183-84; Warren Olney, Jr., 18:190-91; Samuel Pond, 33:182; Mrs. Henry S. Pritchett, 35:376; Bernard Ransome, 25:187; Stuart L. Rawlings, 19:381-82; Lloyd M. Robbins, 34:373-74; Alfred Sutro, 24:89-90
  obit., 37:86-88; phot., 37: opp. 1

Chickering, Martha A., 27:185; "The Founding of a Mojave Desert Community," 27:113-22

Chickering, William Henry, obit., 24:92

Chico, Mariano, 11:76; 12:131, 137; 14:231, 261, 338, 351; 15:338, 350-51; 16:246-51; 23:324, 327, 328, 333

Chico (place), 36:313; 38:335; *see also* Ranchos: Arroyo Chico

Chihuahua, Mex., 1:112; 18:231, 234-37, 247; 34:135, 166

Child, Cornelia Josephine, *see* Smith, Mrs. Stephen Sears

Child, Mrs. George R. (Sara Batchelder Treat), 21:123

Childers, Morris R., 5:125

Children of Cypress, The (play), 10:376, 389

Children of the Abbey (novel), 10:357, 367

Children's American Church Missionary Society, 34:320

Children's Hospital, San Francisco, 19:153

Childs, "General" (S.F., 1854), 15:178; *see also* Chiles

Childs, Ebenezer L., 6:183, 187-88; 16:4, 170, 171, 263, 264, 270; 18:51, 53, 54, 61, 62; 29:166; letters to, 16:264-69; 37:13-15

Childs, Mrs. Elmer E. (Anna L. Reier), obit., 19:85

Childs, John L., 31:132-35 *passim*

Childs, John S., 12:323

Childs, Mark A., 21:351-54 *passim*; 22:43, 44, 48-58 *passim*; 33:105-6, 111

Childs, Ozro William, 13:319

Child's Ford, 11:108

Child's store, Los Angeles, 3:165

Chile, 17:198-200, 204; 19:326; 22:241-42; 25:264; 30:19-20; *see also* Chileans; Valparaiso

Chileans, 1:102; 2:105; 6:238; 7:220, 221; 8:353, 359; 9:76; 11:324; 14:210; 16:79; 17:4; 19:326-27; 22:241, 268; 23:55, 56; 24:125, 354; 27:45, 263, 264, 266, 359; 29:168, 169; 35:38; 37:138; 40:2

"Chilean War," 8:353; 17:4

Chile (or Chilean) Bar, 8:201, 210

Chile Exploration Co., 31:296

Chiles, "Maj. Gen." (Colusa Co., 1855), 17:176-77, 178-79; *see also* Childs

Chiles, Joseph Ballinger, 2:62-63; 4:8; 6:60, 61, 144; 16:53-54, 56, 59, 133, 135; 18:173; 20:148; 22:366; 26:187;

29:320; 32:197-99, 203, 207; 35:1; 38:327
Chiles, Wallace, 26:187
Chiles Valley, 2:63
Chili (ship), 13:248; 33:340
Chili Junction, 21:307
Chilton, Robert H., 24:242
Chilwell (Yosemite, 1868), 4:27
Chimnabada (Pudding Creek), 30:163
Chimney Hill, Yuba Co., 10:168, 192
Chimney Rock, 3:50, 51; 4:330; 6;113, 115; 16:141; 22:131, 148; 24:43-45
China, 4:284;
  books on, 28:4-5
  emigrants from, 10:300; 12:109; 14:202-7; 15:165-72 *passim*, 175, 269; 19:329-30; 22:269; 23:97-98, 99; 24:202-26; 27:257; 28;128, 343-46 *passim*; 31:276; 32:209, 213-14; 34:159, 314, 315; 37:335; 39:289, 300-301
  envoy to, 30:141-45
  houses from, 7:404; 8:169-73 *passim*; 11:179; 26:75; 38:41
  investments in, 28:357-58, 359
  laundry sent to, 37:134
  return of Chinese to, 15:172, 279; 16:337, 347
  Russian relations with, 30:193-202
  trade with, 13:276; 25:167; 30:193, 194, 196; 32:222, 304
China (ship), 11:50; 23:112; 30:200
China Mail, Hong Kong, 32:211; letters printed in, 32:212-22, 303-11
China Ranch, 14:67
Chinard, Gilbert, 21:288; 22:383; "When the French Came to California," 22:289-314
Chinatowns, 4:71, 72; 5:88; 6:281; 18:361; 20:129, 132-34; 22:267, 269; 23:100, 102, 108; 25:176; 27:20-31 *passim*, 256; 28:128; 34:71, 302-4; 35:131, 132; 37:335-39; 38:34; bk. on, rev., 39:367-68; map (S.F.), 27:256
Chinatown San Francisco, by Palmer and Walls, rev., 39:367-68
Chincha Islands, 26:74, 75
Chinese, 2:120; 3:252; 8:19, 25, 167, 175; 9:50, 51, 255; 10:300; 11:232, 233, 332; 13:12, 333; 15:172, 176, 269, 285; 16:33; 17:179-80; 20:372; 23:97-115; 24:158; 26:347; 28:214, 229, 295; 30:143; 31:22; 32:303-8; 36:147; 37;79-84, 129-36, 334-39; 38:33-34

art objects and china, 11:360; 26:144, 161, 339; 31:99-108; 36:344
celebrations and festivals, 3:40; 6:40; 12:103; 15:272; 22:270; 23:106, 109
companies and societies, 15:177, 276; 21:372; 23:99, 103; 27;19-31, 258; 32:304, 305; 34:307
dress, 3:40, 70; 23:98, 99; 27:19; 34:71
feeling against, 5:287, 288; 23:100; 24:204-26 *passim*; 27:169, 170; 32:303-4; 34:307-15 *passim*, 363; 35:42; 37:221-22, 339; 38:331; 39:289
fictional discovery of America by, 14:47-58
food and restaurants, 16:299, 341; 23:111; 27:258; 32:304; 37:79-83, 129-32, 320
funerals, 8:267; 16:342
gamblers, 8: (illus.) opp. 348; 15:186; 22:269; 27:31
harvest hands, 16:299
highbinders, 15:276; 27:19-31; 37:35
houses, 11:179; 22:255; 26:71, 75; 34:308, 311
immigration, *see* China, emigrants from
laborers, 15:202; 16:299; 17:46, 47; 18:24, 368; 21:248; 23:98; 24:194, 199, 202-27, 360; 25:176; 27:170; 28:128, 343; 30:143, 144; 32:222, 304, 306-7; 34:308, 309, 311, 315; 35:42; 36:267
laundries, 6:281; 15:53, 54; 22:257, 269; 32:306
lawsuits, 6:282; 9:148, 149, 150, 158, 159
measures to exclude, 9:257, 258, 282-83; 14:202-27; 15:380; 24:109, 222; 27:257; 28:343; 34:316
miners' licenses and taxes, 8:337, 338, 340-55 *passim*, 9:50-54 *passim*; 10:376, 389; 11:59; 16:341, 343; 17:179-80; 23:100; 24:178-79; receipt, illus., 8: opp. 344
in the mines, 3:70, 202; 8:193, 206, (illus.) opp. 348, 356-57; 10:71; 11:230, 336; 22:272; 24:178; 28:234, 237, 238; 32:305; 33:198-99; 34:310; 35:42, 43, 215-16, 228
opium, 3:304; 37:336
religion, 5:88; 15:163; 27:27; 32:135, 137, 304; 34:303-5; 38:34
riots and tong wars, 3:203; 6:281-82; 23:103; 27:19, 20-21; 35:215-16
San Francisco, 1:198; 3:40-41; 6:40;

8:267; 12:97, 102, 103, 109; 15:163, 174, 176, 177, 186, 267, 269, 272, 276, 277; 16:83, 341, 343; 22:255, 265, 269-70, 274; 23:99-112; 24:360; 27:19-31 *passim*, 367; 30:143, 149; 34:71; 35:130, 131

stereotypes, 34:357-67

women, 15:174, 267, 277; 23:98-99; 26:347; 27:19; 28:345; 32:305-6; 34:303, 307, 315; 35:228; 36:147; 37:132

bks. on, rev., 5:88; 6:281

see also Chinatowns; Chinese theater; Foreign Miners' Tax

"Chinese and Japanese Immigration to the Pacific Coast," by Hart H. North, 28:343-50

Chinese Camp (or Diggings), 11:336; 18:100; 21:308; 22:70; 35:207, 215-16

Chinese Dummy, A (play), 34:367

"Chinese Highbinder Societies in California," by Hart H. North, 27:19-31

"Chinese in California, as Reported by Henryk Sienkiewicz," ed. and trans. Charles Morley, 34:301-16

Chinese Invasion, The (play), 34:367

Chinese language, printed works in, 1:41; 21:327; 27:256; 28:128; 30:255

Chinese Mission, San Francisco, 15:163; 32:130

Chinese Must Go, The (play), 34:363

Chinese Question, The (play), 34:362

Chinese Six Companies, 23:99; 24:219; 28:343; 32:304-5, 312; 37:131

"Chinese Stereotype in American Melodrama," by Stuart W. Hyde, 34:357-67

Chinese theater and theatrical troupes, 34:305-6; in Auburn, 9:369; Sacramento, 23:104; San Andreas, 23:106; San Francisco, 16:340; 20:129, 132-34; 21:51; 22:266, 270; 27:258; 34:305-6; art. on, 23:97-116; illus., 23: opp. 97

Chingery, Jacob and Mary, 14:223; *see also* Gingery

Ching-Wang and His Laundry (play), 34:367

Chinn, James Weeks and Elizabeth (Jessup), 28:380

Chinn, Virginia, 28:380

Chino, meaning of, 13:233

Chino, battle of, 13:125, 302; 18:71; 21:223

Chinquapin, 18:339; 33:60

"Chinquopin" (pseud.), 22:30, 39

Chipley, Col. (L.A., 1870), 32:334, 337, 347

Chipman, William Farragut, obit., 18:94-95

Chipman, Mrs. William Farragut (Bernice Harrell), 32:9

Chipman, William Worthington, 33:373

Chipman (W. F.) & (L. C.) Woodman, 38:314

Chipps Island, 35:123

Chips's Flat, 6:335; 11:240

Chirikof, Alexei, 23:219, 225

Chirikoff (ship), 12:191, 193, 225, 228, 229; 16:108

Chismore, George, 2:245

Chistiakov, L. A., 12:191, 237

"Chivalry" Democrats, *see* Democratic Party

Chivereau, 22:205, 209, 210, 328, 330, 339, 343; 23:31

Chivington, J. M., 34:138

Choate, Daniel L., 17:75, 77, 78

Chocolate, Arroyo, 31:353

Chocuay, site of Petaluma, 16:111

Choice, H. B., 25:174

Cholera, 2:50-51, 120; 3:93; 4:173, 190, 205, 283; 6:39; 8:274; 9:358; 10:406; 11:162, 190; 12:102, 103, 104; 13:79; 14:399; 15:371; 16:83, 182, 284; 18:131, 231-32, 241; 20:333; 21:291; 22:121-28 *passim*; 23:370; 24:118, 119, 238, 240, 246; 26:177; 27:35, 47, 232; 28:67; 29:10, 211, 213, 302; 34:34; 39:49

Chollar, William, 6:229

Chollar-Potosi Mine, 6:229

"Cholos," 11:200, 206; 12:147, 149; 13:227-28; 18:68, 71; 20:38

Choquet de Islas, Diego, 40:116

Choris, Louis (Ludovick), 11:83; 12:207, 233; 18:345; drawing by, 14: opp. 99

Chorpenning, George, 7:19; 12:323

Chow Choo (play), 23:108

Chowdon (Chondon?; Yuba Co., 1857), 9:151

Chrisman (Chino, 1851), 14:69, 70

Christ, Frederick, 32:265, 266

Christensen, Gotthilf Wilhelm Becher, *see* Norris, Samuel

Christenson, Edwin, 31:295, 296, 303

Christian (from Utica, 1849), 27:162

Christian, Capt. (Colorado R., 1872),
    22:174
Christian, Charles, 9:165
Christian, John, 15:240
*Christian Advocate, see California
    Christian Advocate*
Christian Church, 27:124
Christian Hill, Yuba Co., 10:286, 297
Christian Science, 26:282; 31:24, 30
Christie, Henry, 14:182
Christine (place), 33:365-66
Christman, Enos Lewis, 10:87
Christmas: San Francisco (1854),
    15:268; Sausalito (1846), 20:220; nr.
    Warner Hot Springs (1776), 20:235
Christmas Gift lode, 18:201, 204
Christy (S.F., 1862), 10:379
Christy, George, 9:385; *see also* Christy's
    Minstrels
Christy, Samuel Benedict and Sarah
    Adele (Field), 36:46, 51
Christy, Stephen Field, 36:46, 51
Christy's Minstrels, 9:354, 370, 385;
    15:179-80, 184; 21:46
Chronicle, San Francisco, 11:190; 21:28;
    30:195; 34:375; 38:241; cited, 30:195,
    197, 202, 203, 204; 31:303, 304; 32:237,
    243, 248; 38:237, 243
Chronicle, Vallejo, 8:285
Chronicle, Virginia City, 11:190
"Chronicles of George C. Yount, The,"
    ed. Charles L. Camp, 2:3-66
Chronique de Calaveras, La,
    Mokelumne Hill, 35:316; 39:4
"Chronology of Protestant Beginnings
    in California," by Clifford M. Drury,
    26:163-74
"Chronology of the Life of Pierson
    Barton Reading," comp. Gertrude A.
    Steger, 22:365-71
Chronometers, 7:214; 37:289-310 *passim*
Chrysopolis (ship), 10:279, 285, 357,
    374, 375, 380; 23:338; 32:223; 38:335
Chrysopolis Camp, 26:242-43
Chrysopylae (Golden Gate), 25:124
Chuckawalla (place), 12:10, 14-15
Chula Vista, 34:160
Chums (play), 21:256
Church, Edward B., 30:69
Church, Edward W., 9:72; 15:272
Church, Mrs. L. T. (Grace M.), 24:379
Church, Moses James, 25:19-24, 28, 35,
    36, 169
Church & Clark, Sacramento, 19:252
Church & Mix, Yreka, 28:229

Church Divinity School of the Pacific,
    22:93; 33:382
Churchill, John, 12:327
Churchill, Winston, letters to, 39:309-10
Churchman, James, 9:40; 15:204, 367
Churchman, T., 19:127, 128, 141
Churches:
    Benicia, 20:166; 26:168; 27:302
    Berkeley, 37:51-61
    Coloma, 26:169; 32:124
    Columbia, 30:51, 53, 55, 127, 131
    Crescent City, 32:164, 165
    Los Angeles, 19:185
    Marysville, 10:76, 176, 178, 185, 198;
        15:41-45, 57; 31:5; 33:292
    mining region, 32:50-56, 123-29
    Mokelumne Hill, 32:52
    Monterey, 26:174
    Napa, 27:306, 308
    Nevada City, 6:246; 32:51, 54, 125,
        129, 130
    Oakland, 15:171; 17:45; 26:361; 27:350
    Oregon, 4:356; 5:58, 61, 68, 69; 20:22,
        24, 25; 21:6, 7
    Placerville, 32:51, 54, 55, 124
    Sacramento, 9:40, 102, 254, (illus.)
        opp. 258, 279, 280, 371, 394;
        10:64-65, 288, 292; 12:92; 26:169-72
        passim, 231, 361; 27:304, 309
    San Francisco, 1:198; 3:34, 36, 37, 43;
        6:284; 7:400; 10:279, 290, 293, 295;
        12:95-106 *passim*; 14:74-79; 15:163-
        74 *passim*, 180, 183, 185, 186, 266,
        268, 270, 305, 365, 366, 373, 376;
        16:130, 344; 17:84, 173; 18:180;
        19:153, 192, 299-307; 20:13, 15, 22,
        24, 166-67; 22:35, 111; 23:157, 176,
        235, 246; 24:263; 25:334, 341;
        26:165-72 *passim*, 361; 27:10, 13,
        123-29 *passim*, 149-56, 230, 301, 306,
        307, 309, 350, 365, 370; 28:33, 291;
        30:185; 32:122, 126, 134; 34:65, 233,
        235; 38:334; 39:303
    San Jose, 14:157; 26:167-72 *passim*;
        27:130, 230, 231
    Santa Clara, 27:131, 308
    Santa Cruz, 26:167
    Santa Rosa, 27:306
    Sonoma, 27:306, 308
    Sonora, 32:51, 53, 55, 125, 126-27
    Stockton, 20:166
    Weberville, 26:174
    see also Missions; names of churches
Church of the Advent, San Francisco,
    26:361

Church Temperance Colony, 25:169
Chutes Theater, San Francisco, 33:39, 41, 44
Chuttusgelis (Soledad), 23:2
Cibola, 1:45; 3:262, 263, 264; 6:299-301, 307, 308, 312-13, 316, 319
Cider, *see* Apples
Cimber (ship), 39:300
Cincinnati Hill Mine, 6:230
Cinder Cone, Lassen Park, 18:302, 313
Cinderella (opera), 10:173
Cinnabar, 6:249; 26:373-74; *see also* Quicksilver
Cinquantin (San Jose, 1848), 13:271
Ciprés, Marcelino, 36:352
Cipriani (Angel's Camp, 1859), 11:327
Cipriani, Leonetto, 35:318
Cipriano (S.F. Bay, 1827), 8:239
Cipriano (Indian, 1827), 16:219; *see also* Cypriano
Circuses, 6:30-31, 238; 18:359-60
    Dr. Bassett's, 10:280, 293
    Bennett's National, 9:140, 175
    Lee & Marshall's National, 9:54, 175; 10:357, 368; 15:167, 184; 16:80, 81, 84
    New National, 9:385
    Olympic, 3:35; 9:385
    Risley's Vatican, 9:152, 177; 16:183, 284, 285
    Rowe's, 3:35; 6:13; 9:175, 385; 10:368; 16:130-31; 20:293, 294; 26:230
    bk. on, rev., 6:98-99
    United States, 10:293
Cisco, 5:178; 18:149-56 *passim*, 364-68
Cisneros, Elenora de, 25:236
Cisterns, in San Francisco, 15:185, 311-23, 372; 17:175-76, 177; 22:256
"Citadin" (pseud.), 39:160
Citizens' Alliance, 27:314
Citizen Saloon, Oregon Hill, 8:199, 207, 337, 349
Citizens of Crescent City (militia), 34:269
Citizen's Reform Ticket (Know Nothing), 9:27, 29, 32, 33
Citizen's Steam Navigation Co., 15:168
City Bakery, Marysville, 14:398
City College, San Francisco (1863), 35:291
City Drugstore, Marysville, 14:395-96; 15:54
City Fire Insurance Co., 26:256
City Front Federation, San Francisco, 35:64, 67, 148-49, 152

City Guard, Los Angeles, 29:234, 237, 239, 246
City Guard, Sacramento, 10:198, 295; 24:172-76 *passim*
City Guard, San Francisco, 15:164, 168, 171, 178, 181, 184, 373; 16:345; 38:17, 21-22
City Hospital, San Francisco, 6:41
City Hotel, Marysville, 14:215
City Hotel, Sacramento, 24:357; 30:157
City Hotel, San Francisco, 3:34; 7:105; 11:132; 13:379; 19:236; 20:293; illus., 30: opp. 97
City Hotel, San Jose, 14:153
City Hotel, Sonora, 10:45, 68
City of Lakeport (ship), 32:365-66
"City of New York of the Pacific, The," by Ernest A. Wiltsee, 12:25-34
City of Para (ship), 31:49
City of Paris (dept. store, S.F.), 31:297
City of Pekin (ship), 17:36-39 *passim*; 30:151
City of Puebla (ship), 30:289-94; 31:61-62
City of San Francisco v. Kelsey Hazen, 15:276
City of the Golden Gate, The, by Williams, rev., 1:199
City of the Rocks, 32:199, 203
City of Tokio (ship), 17:36; 18:369
City Tract Society, San Francisco, 15:183
Civic Center, San Francisco, phot., 24: opp. 1
Civil fund, California, 19:175-77
Civilian (ship), 5:142
Civil War, 3:167-68; 4:287; 6:5, 32-34; 8:194, 195; 9:270, 317; 10:280, 293, 295, 357, 379, 384, 388, 389, 393; 11:62; 12:3; 15:9, 17, 285; 16:195, 196, 200-208, 307-20; 17:237, 314, 318-20; 18:286; 19:74-75, 146; 20:14, 24, 81, 194-95, 259; 21:52, 66, 67, 82, 112, 132-33; 22:26; 27:178-80, 268-69; 28:155-56; 31:6-7, 275; 32:216, 217; 39:86, 87; 40:101; in Calif. politics, 34:49-64 *passim;* Confed. sympathizers, 20:154-70; 26:18; 27:149-56; 28:165-73; 34:125-26; defense of S.F. during, 33:229-40; San Jose *Mercury* and the, 22:223-34, 355-64; Starr King's oratory, 33:220-27
C. K. McClatchy (ship), 23:94

Claim jumping, 3:130-31, 145-46; 8:203; 9:153

Clamor Público, El, Los Angeles, 13:337; 22:30; 39:322-23

Clapin, Joseph, 21:222

Clapp (S.F., 1865), 20:257

Clapp, Curtis, 14:341

Clapp (or Clappe), Fayette, 1:300; 4:178-79

Clapp (or Clappe), Louisa Amelia Knapp Smith (Mrs. Fayette), 14:389; 30:111, 252; 32:125, 140; 33:373; 38:37; *Shirley Letters*, rev., 1:299-301; 12:176-77

Clapp & Underwood, 30:355

Clapper, Edward, 18:307-8, 309, 314

Clar, John, 30:338

Clara (ship), 8:106; 18:178; *see also Clarita*

Clara, Punta (Pt. Delgada), 10:330

Clara Belle (ship), 22:172, 173; 33:2, 6, 10, 148, 149, 166-67; 35:302, 303, 304

Claremont Colleges, 36:78, 149

Clarence, Miss (Marysville, 1851), 15:48

Clarence King, by Wilkins, rev., 38:164-65

Clarendon House, Sacramento, 9:243, 268; illus., 9: opp. 258

Clarey, Capt. (of *Edalina*, 1849), 13:6

Clarion (ship), 14:317, 341; 23:216

Clarissa Perkins (ship), 27:366

Clarita (ship), 4:164; 8:106; 14:326, 341, 345; 19:197, 200, 214

Clark, Capt. (L.A., 1846), 3:118

Clark (Irishman, S.F., 1850), 8:264

Clark (Mormon, S.F., 1851), 14:73

Clark (policeman, S.F., 1855), 16:337

Clark, Miss (S.F., 1860), 29:122, 125

Clark, A. C., 13:335

Clark, A. H., 18:201

Clark, Albert H., 16:285

Clark, Alson, 5:198

Clark, Ann, *see* Hart, Mrs. Jerome A.

Clark, Asa, 10:279, 292

Clark, Mrs. Baylies C. (Gertrude Voorhies), 31:93

Clark, C. F., 26:128

Clark, Cortin, 35:300

Clark, Edward Stephens, 1:107, 108, 110

Clark, Edward Strong, 19:383

Clark, Eva Turner, ed. *California Letters of William Gill*, 3:200-201

Clark, F. B., 13:296

Clark, G. E., 13:258

Clark, G. P., 6:336

Clark, Galen W., 3:26; 4:15, 24, 28; 5:332, 337-40; 15:379; 30:275; 33:245

Clark, George, 14:181

Clark, George T., ed. "Letters of Leland Stanford to Mark Hopkins," 5:178-83; addresses: "Letters of Leland Stanford," 5:205; "Some California Politics about 1860," 9:90-91; *Leland Stanford*, rev., 10:407

Clark, H. Q., 9:79

Clark, Henry B., 4:45

Clark, Irene, 20:384

Clark, J. E., 29:291

Clark, J. M., 30:367

Clark, James E., 37:210, 211

Clark, Jerry, 19:237

Clark, John, 35:297-98

Clark, John A., 15:181, 277

Clark, John Goddard, 2:3; 22:37; 25:190

Clark, Jonas G., 26:264

Clark, Jonathan, 34:272

Clark, Joseph (né Machado), 35:238

Clark, Joseph C., 20:209-10

Clark, L. B., 9:268

Clark, Lorenzo, 2:121

Clark, M. L., 25:306

Clark, Meriwether Lewis, 33:340

Clark, M. S., 26:204

Clark, Moses, 13:32

Clark, Nellie, 30:382

Clark, Miss O. J., 10:63

Clark, Orange, 2:3-4; 20:16, 24; 22:32, 37; 25:190; 26:71, 75

Clark, Mrs. P. B., 10:274, 290

Clark, Paul Odell, 33:380; "Stephen Sears Smith, Hardwood Lumber Dealer of San Francisco," 33:321-28; 34:65-82

Clark, Reuben, 33:333; 38:33

Clark, Robert C., 9:107; 10:278; 11:9

Clark, Samuel, 26:204

Clark, Smyth, 15:178, 271

Clark, Sterling Benjamin Franklin, *How Many Miles from St. Jo?*, ed. Mighels, rev., 9:88-89

Clark, Susie C., 31:19

Clark, Ted K., 28:378

Clark, Thomas D., *Frontier America*, rev., 38:370-71

Clark, Gen. William (1827), 2:228; 16:52-53 letter to, 2:233-36

Clark, William (w. Clyman, (1844), 4:321

Clark, William (Marysville, 1851), 15:54

Clark, William Andrews, Jr., 21:282

Clark, William H. (S.F., 1853), 27:251

Clark, William H. (Marysville, 1855), 9:56

Clark, William R. P., 25:190

Clark, William Squire, 5:406; 11:133-34; 19:231; 21:311; 22:383, 384; 35:375; *see also* Leese *v.* Clark

Clark (ship), 27:293

Clark, Mount, 4:21, 22, 23, 36, 55

Clarke (Yuba Co., 1857), 9:135

Clarke, Calvin Rutter, 23:296

Clarke, Dwight Lancelot, 32:93-94; " 'The Big Silver,' California's Greatest Silver Mine," 32:1-41; bk. rev. by, 40:77-79

Clarke, E. W., 13:32

Clarke, George, 29:40, 41, 42

Clarke, Henry, 29:40

Clarke, J., 15:280

Clarke, J. A., 9:244-48 *passim*, 269, 368, 369, 372, 392; 10:52

Clarke, J. T., 28:298, 316; 29:40, 41, 54, 56

Clarke, Mrs. J. T. (Mary Ann Graves), 19:139; 28:298; 29:40, 41, 53-54

Clarke, James M., "Antonio Melendrez," 12:318-22

Clarke, Jeremiah, 27:135

Clarke, John H., 36:154

Clarke, John Hopkins, 19:20

Clarke, Lavenia, *see* McMahan, Mrs. Samuel Green

Clarke, Newman S., 10:198; 19:229; 23:344; 27:219

Clarke, Nicholas, 24:75

Clarke, Robert F., 29:41

Clarke, Samuel W., Jr., 33:352

Clarke *et al. v.* Haggerty *et al.*, 10:55

Clarkson, H. C., 16:79

Clark's Point, San Francisco, 3:33; 15:65; 17:301; 22:257, 269, 384; 25:125

Clark's Station, *see* Wawona

Clary (S.F., 1855), 16:82

Clary, William W., 19:383; obit of John I. Perkins, 21:191

Classen Chemical Co., 31:298

Classon, Robert and Eva (Schneider), 28:292

Claughley (S.F., 1855), 17:179

Claughley, George and Henry, 21:77

Claughley, Thomas, 21:76, 77, 78

Claughley, Mrs. Thomas (Rowena Granice), 21:75-78

Clavigero, Francisco Javier, 8:374-76; 19:221; 40:199

Clawson, Marion, 24:188; "What It Means to Be a Californian," 24:139-61

Clay, Alvira, 10:256, 267

Clay, Clement Comer, 19:345

Clay, George Franklin, 10:384, 394

Clay, Hattie, 10:170, 193

Clay, Henry, 10:222, 224, 225, 229, 230, 231; 11:16, 19; 19:15, 16-17, 18, 350, 351; 23:298; 37:367

Clay, John, 9:178; 10:267; *see also* Clay's Ranch

Clay, L., 26:297

Clay, Thomas, 29:23, 28

Clay, Willard, 10:382, 394

Clayes, O. M., 30:135

Claymore, Antoine, 4:139

Claymore, Basil, 4:139

Claypool, Capt. (of *Greyhound*, 1849), 20:46

Clay's Ranch, 9:157, 159, 166, 352, 353; 10:170, 359

Clay Street Reading Room, San Francisco, 38:314

Clayton (Philippines, 1898), 30:295

Clayton, Charles, 27:170-71

Clayton, Hal, 9:65(?); 10:167, 192

Clayton, J. E., 4:15

Clayton, John M., 9:5-9 *passim*, 12

Clayton, William (1848), *Latter-Day Saints' Emigrants' Guide*, 3:52, 63; 8:82; 32:199, 200

Clayton, William (San Diego, 1902), 35:357

Clayton Compromise, 10:134-36

Clayton's Oyster Saloon, San Francisco, 28:39

Clayton's Ranch, Yuba Co., 9:52

Cleal, J. G., 24:176

Clear Creek Ditch, 9:136, 141, 142, 150, 165, 174

Clear Lake, El Dorado Co., 7:7, 9; *see also* Red Lake

Cleary, Alfred J., 15:319; address, "Panama Pacific Exposition," 14:86-87

Cleary, C. W., 36:253, 255-56; 39:32

Cleaveland, D. (lawsuit, 1857), 9:141, 142, 143

Cleaveland, Henry W., 33:373; 38:32

Cleeman, Walter, 37:360-61

Clegg, Charles Myron, coauth. Beebe, *San Francisco's Golden Era:* . . .

San Francisco before the Fire, rev., 40:77-79

Cleland, Robert Glass, 6:136; 8:381; 16:288; 27:186-87; address, "Valley of Dry Bones," 29:375-76; *From Wilderness to Empire . . .*, rev. 38:167-69; *History of California: The American Period*, rev., 1:302-3

Clear Lake region (Lake Co.), 11:266-73; 15:232; 16:305; 17:116, 149, 231; 20:234; 23:31, 297; 24:49-56; 27:107; 29:312; 32:363-71

Clemence, Stella, 3:25

Clemens, Cyril, address, "Mark Twain in the West," 7:410

Clemens, Samuel Langhorne, 1:299; 3:297; 4:74, 211; 5:202; 7:117, 410; 10:409; 12:84, 359; 15:381; 17:78; 18:280; 19:373; 20:185; 21:50, 57-62 *passim*, 74, 145, 147-48, 176; 26:233-38 *passim*; 30:362; 34:362; 36:365-70 *passim*; addresses on, 7:410; 29:77-80; arts. on, 34:317-22; 36:35-40; bk. on, rev., 3:196-99; coauth. *Sketches of the Sixties*, rev., 5:409-12

Clement, Ada, 25:236

Clement, Basil, *see* Claymore, Basil

Clement, Evelyn (Atkinson), 24:94

Clement, H. N., 24:214-15, 379; 27:346

Clement, Mrs. H. Newell (Genevieve Arcularius), 33:188-89

Clement, Randolph R., 24:379-80

Clementine (ship), 15:341, 347, 350, 352-53, 358; 23:318, 320, 327, 332, 334

Clements, Mrs. (Sacramento, 1858), 9:251

Clements, J. B., 18:259

Clements, James B., 21:306

Clements, John, 17:179

Clements, Q. A., 9:317

Clements, Z., 13:32

Clemons, Mary, *see* Maguire, Mrs. Thomas

Clendenen, Clarence C., 34:190; "Dan Showalter—California Secessionist," 40:309-25; "The Expedition That Never Sailed: A Mystery of the Civil War," 34:149-56

Cleopatra (riv. str.), 9:54, 55, 72

Cleopatra (play), 20:134

Clergeon, Dr. (S.F., 1850), 5:350-51; 6:43, 47, 57

Cleveland, David, 31:40-41

Cleveland, Miss E. A., 25:31

Cleveland, Grover, 7:412; 37:171-79 *passim*

Cleveland, W. H., 31:47

Cleveland Forbes (ship), 23:189

Clevenger, Irma, 20:192

Clevenger Cañon, 26:28, 53

Cliff House, San Francisco, 21:168

Clifford, Capt. (San Blas, 1840), 15:129, 238

Clifford, Alfred, 13:31

Clifford, Henry Hoblitzelle, 30:92

Clifford, Pinckney, 13:338; 15:270

Clifford, Utie, 21:65

Clifford, Walter C., 20:192

Clift (Placerville, 1858), 7:19

Clift, Frederick C., 9:188; 10:99; 16:255, 288; obit., 15:289

Clift, Robert, 29:242, 248; 33:119-20, 123

Clift Hotel, San Francisco, 15:289

Clifton Colony, 25:175

Clinch, Downey C., 24:94

Cline, Walter Branks, 31:176; obit., 11:296

Cline, Mrs. Walter Branks (Clara Emily Smith), 11:296

Cline, William H., 20:140

Clinton (place), 15:174

Clinton (ship), 16:337

Clinton House, San Jose, 14:156

Clio (ship), 8:331

Clipper Flouring Mills, 15:271

Clipper Gap, 2:203; 26:360; 30:344

Clipper ships, 8:384; 10:294; 15:172, 277, 279, 282, 366, 367, 375; 16:81, 182, 337, 347; 17:75; 20:31, 46; 22:353; 26:74, 226-27; 27:137, 198, 292-93; 30:170, 211, 244; 33:327; address on, 30:276-77; *see also* Bald Eagle; Flying Cloud; Great Republic; N. B. Palmer; Sea Nymph; Sea Witch; Westward Ho, etc.

Clockmaker's Hat, The, 10:75

Clocks and watches, 16:79; 19:208; 26:43; 27:1-8; 36:70; 37:103-4, 289-310 *passim*

Clogenson, Eugénie, 33:169-74 *passim*

Closa, Ubach and Valentin, 8:384

Clot, A., 39:318

Clothier, Isaac H., 31:337

Clothing, *see* Dress

Cloud, James H., 22:52, 56, 65; 33:338-39

Cloud Creek, Cloud Mine, 4:38

Clouds Rest, Yosemite, 1:279

Clough, Abner P., 18:22; 20:181-84

Clough, Barney, 9:161, 264, 346, 365; 10:363; lawsuit, 9:66
Clough, J. P., 29:107
Clough, Joseph, 27:32
Clough, William, 4:41
Clover, 4:363; 5:266
Cloverdale, 32:364
Club House (saloon), Marysville, 9:373
Clubs, in San Francisco, 19:226; *see also* names of clubs
Cluff, Will S., Jr., 33:380; ed. "John Swett's Diary . . . 1853," 33:289-308
Clyde (ship), 34:97, 105
Clyman, James, 16:133; 17:161; 23:293-94; 28:266; 36:58; "Dairies and Reminiscences," ed. Charles L. Camp, 4:105-41, 272-83, 307-60; 5:44-84, 109-38, 255-82, 378-401; 6:58-68; fac. p. of diary, 5:opp. 109; port., 4: opp. 105
Clyman, Mrs. James (Hannah Mecombs), 6:59, 60, 62-63
Clyman, John, 4:272
Clyman, Lancaster, 4:272; 5:47; 19:128, 141
Clyman, Lydia Alcinda, *see* Tallman, Mrs. Beverly L.
Clyman family, 6:63
Clyne, S. E., 34:158
Clyne & Brown, 14:207
C. M. Weber (ship), 22:76, 77; 29:39, 55-56
Coad, Henry, 10:63; 16:285
Coad, Samuel, 33:373
Coal, 10:300; 13:58, 60, 61, 62, 401, 402, 403; 16:337; 17:168, 175; 22:350; 23:343; 31:39; 33:344; 38:25, 158; imported, 16:282, 346; 22:349, 350; 31:315; mining and shipping, 12:33; 30:345; in Ore., 28:221, 231; used in making steel, 30:344-48 *passim*
Coan, Ernie, 29:91
Coarse Gold, 25:18; 28:334, 335, 336
Coast Manufactory and Supply Co., 28:372; 31:177
Coast Pilot, 11:307, 311, 315, 316
Coast Rangers, 34:269
Coates, Anna, 27:186
Coates, George I., 27:186
Coates, James, 19:124, 140; 25:220
Coates, Susan D., 33:167
Coats (Santa Barbara, 1859), 18:260
Coats, H., 29:112
Cobb, Mrs. (Sacramento, 1858), 9:371
Cobb, Henry A., 10:390; 15:377; 17:83; 23:339, 340, 344; 30:358; 38:20; 39:142; 40: opp. 206
Cobb, James C., 14:163
Cobb, Sinton & Bond, 40:206, opp. 206
Cobb Valley, 23:375
Coblentz, Edmond David, 19:95; 35:266; address, "A Roving Reporter," 35:169
Coblentz, Mrs. Edmond David, *see* Schweitzer, Mrs. Melville
Coburn, Joe, 21:263
Coburn, Loren, 16:380; 20:264, 265
Cochan (ship), 22:163, 166, 167
Coche (San Juan Bautista, 1850), 5:371
Cochran, Mrs. Roswell, 30:289
Cochran, Thomas, 5:125
"Cock-Eye," *see* Fury, William
Cock fighting and "carrera del gallo," 6:231; 8:230; 9:267; 10:277-78, 372; 24:65
Cocks, Henry, 29:27-28
Cocopah (ship), 22:11, 17, 23, 24, 152, 167
Cocopah No. 2 (ship), 22:18, 25, 152, 153, 155, 161, 167
Cocos Island, 15:270; 26:218
Coddington, Robert, 10:361
Codman, John, 31:27
Codornices Creek, Berkeley, 17:42-47 *passim*; 30:219, 231
Cody, B. F., 9:266
Cody, Francis, 26:204
Cody, William Frederick ("Buffalo Bill"), 21:244
Coe, B. D., 18:65
Coe, L. W., 36:269
Coes, George H., 9:385; 10:181, 200; 20:305; 21:64
Coeur de Lion (ship), 15:375
Coffee, Andrew Jackson, 33:373
Coffee, 13:8; 16:346
Coffey, James Vincent, 1:15-18 *passim*
Coffill, Mrs. William C. (née Segerstrom), 28:378
Coffin, A. G., 29:254
Coffin, Alexander, 9:40, 103
Coffin, Charles G., 29:1, 4
Coffin, Henry, 29:1, 4, 14-16
Coffin, Ivory, 33:105
Coffin, J., 30:260
Coffine, Frederick J., 26:203
Coffing, Edwina B. (Stuart), 27:381
Coffroth, James Wood, 6:14, 17; 9:40, 42, 107; 10:60, 78, 173, 195, 266, 355, 367; 15:376; 35:77-78; bk. on, rev., 5:311-12

Coggins (Sacramento, 1859), 10:78
Coghill, J. H., 6:11
Coghlan, Nathan Coombs, 36:48
Coghlan, Rose, 21:256
Cogswell, Henry Daniel, 18:288
Cogswell, J. P., 15:376
Cogswell, James Lafayette, 18:288;
    29:289, 290, 291; phot., 29: opp. 289
Cogswell, William, 31:21
Cohen, Alfred Andrew, 15:273-74, 279,
    368, 371-72, 377; 16:84, 340-42, 347;
    17:168-82 passim; 21:34; 26:359; 27:93
Cohen, Frederick A., 15:371-72, 21:34
Cohen, Louis, 15:164
Cohn (North San Juan, 1858), 30:361
Cohn, Elkan, 37:277
Cohn, Fritz Ludwig, 19:383, ed. and
    trans. Henry Cohn, "St. Louis
    [California] and Poker Flat in the
    Fifties and Sixties," 19:289-98
Cohn, Henry (Heiman),
    Jugenderrinerung, trans. and ed. Fritz
    L. Cohn, 19:289-98; family of, 19:289
Cohn, Louis, 15:364
Cohn family, 19:289
Coins and coinage, 6:237; 15:177; 19:260;
    27:365, 369-70; 28:130; 29:93;
    octagonal $50 gold pieces, 6:237;
    24:183; Utah coins from Calif. gold,
    15: (illus.) opp. 244, 244-46; Mexican,
    26:349-50; 27:132
Coit (S.F., 1850), 23:163
Coit, Benjamin Billings, 14:75; 15:281
Coit, Howard, 19:233
Coit, Mrs. Howard (Lillie Hitchcock),
    12:366; 15:384; 19:229, 233
Cojo Anchorage, 7:49, 75; 8:245
Coke, Henry J., 28:56
Coker, Richard, 36:210
Colbey (Yuba Co., 1856), 9:52
Colbirth, Peliah, 2:121
Colborn & Sands, 17:183
Colburn, Charles, 15:76
Colburn, Mrs. Frederick H. (Frona
    Eunice Wait Smith), addresses,
    "Peter Lassen and His Mountain,"
    7:201; "The Wives of the 'Big Four,'"
    12:84; The Kingship of Mt. Lassen,
    rev., 3:94
Colburn, G. D., 20:43
Colby, Amasa Drake, 17:44
Colby, John, 13:296
Colby, Gilbert W. and Carrie Amelia
    (Smith), 25:190
Colby, S. B., 14:215, 220

Colby, Walter S., 20:44
Colby, William Edward, 4:50, 52, 55;
    25:190; 32:34; 38:251-52; address,
    "Half a Century of Conservation,"
    21:183; obit. of Joseph N. LeConte,
    29:187
Colcord, Roswell Keyes,
    "Reminiscences of Life in Territorial
    Nevada," 7:112-20
Cold Springs, 6:238; 7:7, 9; library
    association, 38:307
Coldwell, Colbert, 19:95; obit. of Milton
    E. Eisner, 39:77-79
Cole, Capt. (Yuba Co., 1851), 15:49
Cole, Mrs. (S.F., 1851), 28:40
Cole (Yuba Co., 1856), 9:57, 66
Cole, Mme. (Yuba Co., 1857), 9:162
Cole, Cornelius, 4:244, 245; 9:104, 106;
    26:308; 33:209; bk. on, rev., 8:382-83
Cole, Mrs. Cornelius (Olive Colegrove),
    8:382
Cole, George H. T., 13:31
Cole, Horace, 21:114
Cole, Richard Beverly, 4:191-94 passim,
    198, 201; 7:95; 15:88
Cole, Thomas, 16:172
Cole & Stevens, 8:338, 355
Colegio de San José, Hartnell's, 23:348
Coleman, Mrs. (Sacramento, 1858),
    9:371, 372
Coleman, A., 22:250
Coleman, B. C., 22:250-51
Coleman, B. F., 22:251
Coleman, Edith B., 25:233
Coleman, Evan J., 19:233
Coleman, H. R., 29:225
Coleman, J. B., 31:128
Coleman, Michael, 19:135
Coleman, Murray N., 32:31-32
Coleman, William, 10:62
Coleman, William Tell, 6:36; 8:367;
    14:352-53; 15:76, 253-54; 16:182;
    18:283, 371-73; 19:233; 20:294; 26:196;
    27:350; 32:149-50, 200; 35:126; 37:221
Cole's California Exchange, San
    Francisco, 28:38
Colfax, Schuyler, 4:256; 16:81; 37:131
Colfax (place), 4:266; 13:15, 17;
    18:355-60 passim, 367
Colgan, James A., 33:343
Colgate, H. C., 27:280
Colgate Power House, 29:202-3
Colibri, Le (San Francisco), 35:313;
    39:150
Collbran, H., 30:198, 205

Collbran-Bostwick Development Co., 30:205

"Collections of the Society," address by George L. Harding, 25:85-86

Colleen Bawn (play), 10:362; 21:51, 53

College Homestead Association, 31:328

College of California, 1:14, 21; 4:210; 16:336-37; 27:351; 31:328, 329; *see also* University of California

College of Notre Dame, 14:157; 30:249; 37:43

"College of Physicians and Surgeons of California," by Loren B. Taber and Vivian A. Prindle, 30:67-71

College of St. Augustine, 23:279; 30:262

College of St. Ferdinand of the Propagation of the Faith, 40:55; *see also* San Fernando

College of the Pacific, *see* University of the Pacific

Colleges: bill to appropriate public lands for, 19:345-47; Alemany's claim for lands for support of Catholic, 17:178; *see also* names of colleges

Colley, F. A., 29:225-26, 359

Colliard, Aimé, 5:42, 346

Collier, Charles, 36:66

Collier, James, 5:22; 9:10; 16:185; 21:300, 303-4; 25:345

Collier, James I., 15:76

Collier, Julia (Caswell), obit. of Mrs. George Caswell, 23:90

Collier, Louis A., 11:179-81

Collier, Randolph, 31:131-32, 134-35

Collignon (Monterey, 1786), 18:335, 345

Collingwood (ship), 1:138; 3:88, 106, 108, 112; 9:83; 10:118; 14:327, 345; 17:282; 18:75; 29:274

Collins, Capt. (Colorado R., 1859), 22:169

Collins, Asa W., 20:280

Collins, Claude J., 34:340

Collins, Isabel (Porter), 28:379

Collins, J. B., 26:2

Collins, James, 10:370

Collins, John (Yuba Co., 1858), 9:262, 367, 368, 369; 10:56, 61, 165, 166, 172, 173, 174, 180, 187, 189, 254, 256, 368

Collins, John (actor, S.F., 1859), 21:46

Collins, John Anderson, 17:77, 80; 20:31, 45; 26:340

Collins, Mrs. John Anderson (Elizabeth), 17:77, 80

Collins, Joseph W., 28:206, 207, 352; letter from, 28:351

Collins, Mrs. Joseph W., 28:206, 207, 208

Collins, Julia (Gould), 15:371; 20:305

Collins, Mary, 9:149

Collins, N., 16:184; 17:81

Collins, O .B., 4:61

Collins, Perry McDonough, 33:1-2, 10, 11

Collins, Peter, 10:56

Collins, Roger, 9:367, 368, 369; 10:170

Collins, S. B., 10:186, 187

Collooney (*Collony, Colony, Colooney;* ship), 23:280; 30:238

Colm, W. W., 32:9, 37, 41

Colma, 31:298

Colman, Ronald, 28:286

Colnett, James, 10:337-38, 339; 18:337, 345; 20:80

Coloma, 3:128; 8:201, 210; 12:66; 13:58, 169-70, 296; 15:96; 17:232; 19:124-26, 133; 22:29, 38, 150; 23:166-70; 24:358, 363; 26:169, 297; 27:229, 230, 281-82; 30:26, 36, 111, 259, 362; 32:124; 38:318; archaeolog. excavations, 26:107-62; name, 26:158; illus., 6: opp. 205; 8: foll. 202; 26; foll. 126, opp. 128; map, 26: foll. 130

Coloma Grays, 10:198

Coloma Mill Co., 30:36

Colombat, Henry, 39:313

Colon (ship), 37:208-10

"Col. E. D. Baker," by Milton H. Shutes, 17:303-24

Colonel Fremont (ship), 20:102

"Colonel Philip Leget Edwards," by Charles L. Camp, 3:73-83

Col. Staunton (ship), 29:211

Colorado (Colorado R. str., 1855), 22:7, 10, 11, 15, 21, 22, 23, 167; phot., 22: opp. 14

Colorado (Colorado R. str., 1865), 22:15, 22, 153, 154, 155, 158, 164, 165, 167

Colorado (P.M.S.S., 1865), 26:359, 363; 27:267; 28:4; 29:219; 36:206

Colorado (barge, 1870s), 22:156

Colorado (sloop), 1875), 22:174

Colorado, Territory of (prop.), 10:74

Colorado City, 22:11, 12, 23; *see also* Yuma, Ariz.

Colorado Desert, 10:27, 85, 214

Colorado River, 1:70, 114; 3:167, 250; 5:213, 214; 9:303-4, 306; 11:291, 385; 12:7, 13, 14, 16-17; 14:347; 15:105-11, 132, 201; 18:350; 21:97, 102, 104, 215, 216; 25:294, 295, 296, 306, 307; 27:206; 28:255; 34:136; boundary of Calif.,

9:3, 4, 6, 11-13; 18:206; 19:217-18;
Derby's survey of, 11:365-82; mining
on, 2:18, 163, 167, 169; 3:16-17, 163,
169-70; 12:11-12, 17; seen by Spanish
explorers, 3:324-25, 384, 385-86; 8:27;
10:85; 36:218-20, 232-35; steam
navigation on, 22:1-25, 151-74;
trappers on, 1:112-18 *passim*; 2:16,
18-19, 231, 233, 235; 15:105,
108-11, 133; 28:121, 225; on maps, 2:
opp. 236; 3:372, 381, 383; 9: opp .11,
opp. 12; 11: opp. 365, 380; 12: opp. 3;
21: opp. 213
Colorado River Railroad Co., 27:339
Colorado Steam Navigation Co., 22:11,
15, 18, 19, 23, 153-65 *passim*
Colt, Col. (Yuba Co., 1856), 9:66
Colt (Sacramento, 1861), 10:282
Colt, E. W., 8:358
Colter, John, 4:126
Colton, David Douty, 10:197, 356;
14:286; 15:255; 26:292-97 *passim*, 300,
306-7; 40:204, 208, 211
Colton, G. Q., 23:164
Colton, Isaac W., 40:211, 212
Colton, John, 26:297
Colton, John B., 18:197
Colton, Walter, 3:113-14; 4:92; 6:143-47
passim, 153; 10:16, 126-27, 151, 299;
11:130-33, 389; 12:129, 168, 171, 343;
13:52, 56, 76; 15:236; 17:296, 301;
18:35, 52, 61-62, 79; 19:300; 20:215,
233; 22:51; 23:371; 25:127, 129-30;
26:164, 167; 28:289; 29:25; 30:105;
35:201; 36:341; 40:15-16, 20, 21, 22;
art. on, 35:97-117; port., 35: opp. 97
Colton (place), 12:117
Colton Hall, Monterey, 6:153; 10:150,
161; 11:133; 17:233; 23:359, 371; 35:97,
109-10, 113, 114; 40:21; phot., 35: opp.
112; 40: opp. 16
Columbia, 5:311; 10:413; 11:332-33, 335;
15:143, 166, 272; 24:382; 28:276-77;
30:115, 259; 35:40, 77-78; 38:37, 308,
309, 318; churches in, 32:51, 55, 127-35
passim, 139; letters from, 15:144-45;
35:209-13, 219-20; newspapers, 24:269;
34:343; State park, 24:191-92, 267-70,
282, 374-75; 28:276-77
Columbia (ship, 1787, 1792), 10:328;
11:29
Columbia (N.W. Co. schr., 1813, 1815),
1:176; 35:236
Columbia (H. B. Co. bark, 1840),

8:98-100; 14:205; 28:97, 98, 249, 250,
262; 30:3
Columbia (brig, 1844), 5:46, 47
Columbia (P.M.S.S., 1854), 2:134;
15:368, 374, 377; 16:339; 20:22; 27:218;
32:165, 168, 360, 361
Columbia (bark, 1885), 22:349
Columbia & Stanislaus River Water Co.,
11:333, 335; 35:77, 78
Columbia Barracks, 28:201-7 *passim*
Columbia College, Eugene, Ore., 32:240
Columbia Fusileers, 37:366
"Columbia—'Gem of the Southern
Mines,' " by Elizabeth G. Potter,
24:267-70
Columbia Hill, Nevada Co., 9:51, 69;
10:348; 29:201
Columbian Insurance Co., 26:256
Columbia Park Boys' Club, 34:182
Columbia River, 2:299; 5:58-59;
11:289-303 *passim;* 17:23, 134, 135;
18:320, 321, 322, 339; 20:22-23;
discovered and named, 11:29; H.B.
Co. and N.W. Co. on, 8:97-101 *passim;*
18:318-22 *passim*, 327; 22:97-103
passim; 28:118, 120; Indians, 21:1-7;
Spanish explorers at, 2:299; 9:235;
10:318, 319, 321, 326, 327
Columbia Steel Co., 12:33; 30:345-51
Columbia Theater, San Francisco,
25:235; 33:40, 46
Columbus (U.S. ship, 1846), 1:233;
4:303; 12:343, 346; 22:50, 53; 26:166;
28:342; 33:253
Columbus (str., 1850), 2:118; 8:266, 268;
29:376
Columbus Buggy Co., 28:380
Columbus House, Strawberry Valley,
8:360; 10:359
Colusa, 6:156; 10:248, 252-53, 258-59,
274, 284, 359; 16:65; 25:340
Colusa (riv. str.), 25:327, 328
Colusa County, ranchos in, 30:54
Colusa County Bank, 29:92
Colville, Andrew, 28:243-44
Colville, Samuel, 22:35; 23:373
Colville mines, 11:374, 377
Colvocoressis, George Musalas, 24:321
"Comanche George," *see* Lawrence,
Marion
Comanche Springs, 18:116, 135
Comano, Lt. (Jacinto Caamano?, 1792),
2:282
Combe, Andrew, 30:365
Combe, George, 30:365

Combination Gold and Silver Mining
    Co., 18:202
Combs, Mrs. Allen, 26:136
Combs, Cas, 13:258
Combs (or Coombs), Frederick S.,
    21:306
Combs, S. Leslie, 17:31, 33, 35
Comet (clipper, 1850s), 10:294
Comet (schr., 1889, 1900s), 31:158, 294
Comète (ship), 8:132, 244-45; 18:347
Comets, 9:67, 80, 145, 146, 148, 176-77,
    358, 360, 362; 10:286, 297
Comley-Barton Opera Troupe, 19:99
Commerce and trade (1820s and '30s),
    14:21-22; 16:237 (*see also* Hides and
    tallow); (1846-47), 12:347-48; 22:319;
    (1848-49), 13:273, 276, 355-56, 358,
    364, 367-68, 376; (1850s), 17:183, 185
    trade (proj.) w. Asia (1825),
    25:150-66
    trade w. China, 13:276; 25:167; 30:193,
    194, 196; 32:222, 304; w. Indians,
    13:273; at Monterey, 13:273, 258; w.
    New England, 8:289-305; 13:248; w.
    Northwest, 13:248 (*see also* Hudson's
    Bay Co.); w. Philippines, 2:140;
    13:247, 248; 25:150, 151, 167 (*see also*
    Philippine Islands); w. Russians,
    12:194; 14:22; 30:200; w. Sandwich
    Islands, 14:22; 35:348; bet. S.F. and
    Colorado R. (*see* "Steam Navigation
    …"); bet. Santa Fe and L.A., 10:27-39;
    w. South America, 13:248, 276; at
    Yerba Buena (1848-49), 13:273,
    355-56, 367-68, 376
Commercial Advertiser, San Francisco,
    15:175, 177
Commercial Book and Job Steam
    Printing Co., San Francisco, 30:358
Commerciale, La (company), 22:303,
    310
Commercial Hotel, San Francisco, 6:36
Commercial Insurance Co., 27:270
Commercial National Bank, Los
    Angeles, 37:270
Commerford, Henry, 30:41-44 *passim*;
    36:307
Committee of 100 (1872), 27:65, 73,
    271-72, 339-40
Committee of 100 (1901), 35:150
Committee of Safety, San Francisco
    (1877), 18:372; 37:221-22
Commodore (ship), 33:167
"Commodore Edmund B. Kennedy …

versus Governor Nicolás Gutiérrez,"
    by George Tays, 12:137-46
Communism, 36:48; 39:223
Comonfort, Ignacio, 16:82; 19:275
Compagnie de la Seine et du
    Sacramento, La, 22:299-300
Compagnie des Gardes Mobiles, La,
    20:71
Compagnie Française et Américaine
    de San-Francisco, La, 22:300, 301-2
Compagnie Générale pour
    l'Emigration et la Colonization, La,
    20:298
Compagnie La Californienne, *see*
    Californienne
Compagnie Transatlantique, La,
    Comptoir des Deux-Mondes, 22:303
Compañía Cosmopolitana, 16:237;
    24:293
Compañía Restauradora de la Mina de
    la Arizona, 18:11-14
"Compound Interest: Alvinza Hayward
    Pays a Debt," from reminiscences of
    Clarence M. Wooster, 20:181-85
Compton (brothers; Rough and Ready,
    1850s), 6:235
Compton, Mrs. Henry C. (Henria
    Packer), 31:381; obit., 38:177-78
Compton, Henry Truman, 25:192
Compton, Mary Murdock, 31:381
Compton (place), 31:294
Comstock, Arnold M., 13:32; 26:71, 75,
    175, 176
Comstock, Mrs. Arnold M. (Sarah T.),
    26:71
Comstock, Henry Thomas Paige, 2:206;
    6:341; 12:327, 329, 330
Comstock, James, 6:70
Comstock, Peter, 8:199-200
Comstock, W. B., 17:174
Comstock Lode, 2:260; 4:64, 66; 10:260,
    291; 11:190; 12:328-30; 16:88; 31:185;
    35:128; 37:218-20; *see also* Virginia
    City; Washoe
Conable, Edgar Wallace, 31:26
Conant, Roger, *Mercer's Bells—The
    Journal of a Reporter*, rev., 40:255-56
Conaway, Carvel, 6:229
Concepción, *see* Antonio de la
    Concepción; Francisco de la
    Concepción
Concepción (ship), 6:298
Conception, Point, 7:25, 48, 49, 55, 74,
    389; 8:57, 156; 27:337; 36:222-23
Concord coaches, 13:260-61; 14:161

Concorde, La, Los Angeles, 39:346
Concordia-Verein, Dutch Flat, 38:319
Conde, *see* García Conde
Condee, George M., 10:62
Condemned Bar, Yuba Co., 8:338, 355; 15:31
"Condemned Bar [Placer Co.] in 1849," from the Journal of Erastus Saurin Holden, ed. E. D. Holden, 12:312-17
"Conditions in Califorina in 1848," letter from Chester Smith Lyman, 13:176-79
Condit-Smith, Mrs. J. (Sarah Swearingen), 36:44, 45, 49, 52
Condon, C. M., 34:159
Condor, California, 7:31; called "griffin," 19:220-21, 223
Condor (ship), 11:219
Confederación (ship), 6:150; 11:141
Confederate activities and sympathy, 9:194, 198; 10:282, 296; 13:167; 20:154-70; 21:221; 22:358-61; 23:296; 24:275-77; 28:167; 29:229-49 *passim;* 33:229-38 *passim,* 365; 34:45-46, 48, 125-43, 149-54, 347; 40:291-94
"Confederate Minority in California, The," by Benjamin F. Gilbert, 20:154-70
Confer (Stockton, 1892), 34:354
Confidence (Fr .bark), 16:337
Confidence (riv. str.), 3:93; 6:240; 9:55; 10:72
Confidence Engine Co. No. 1, Sacramento, 9:252, 277; 10:275, 285, 290; 15:369
Congdon, C. N., 7:11-12
Congdon, Sophie Mandell, 14:74, 79
Congregational churches, 1:198; 3:37; 6:227, 284, 337, 341; 9:102, 280; 10:278, 292; 12:92; 15:41, 166, 168, 183, 185, 365, 376; 22:35; 23:370; 24:263; 32:51, 54, 124, 129, 130; illus., 9: opp .258
Congregation Emanu-El, San Francisco, 15:167, 174; 36:298, 306; 38:34; phot., 38: foll. 40
Congregation Sherith Israel, San Francisco, 15:170, 173
Congress (ship, 1838), 14:320
Congress (U.S .frigate, 1846), 1:143, 241; 2:167-72 *passim;* 3:111-15 *passim,* 187, 188; 5:302; 6:145, 146, 185, 189, 273, 277; 7:82; 8:77; 10:120, 121; 12:41, 48, 52, 56, 58, 166, 168, 351; 13:115; 14:328, 345; 17:277, 282, 284, 329, 339, 340; 18:61, 62; 20:216, 226, 233; 21:338, 341, 344, 350, 356, 357; 22:50, 51, 55,
56, 58, 66; 25:126-31 *passim;* 26:24, 48, 49, 164; 29:275; 33:104, 105, 108, 251; 35:102-4
Conies, 16: No. 1, Pt. 2, pp. 30, 44; 36:29
Conland, William, 3:118
Conley, S., 31:333
Conlin, Lawrence and Thomas, 33:12; 35:303
Conmy, Ellen, 29:91
Conmy, John J. and Maria (Cherry), 21:383; 29:91
Conmy, Peter Thomas, address, "The Vigilance Committee of 1851," 30:185, 275-76
Conmy, Thomas Cherry, 21:383
Conn, W. A., 11:8-9
Connecticut Insurance Co., 26:256
Connell, S., 15:172
Connelly, John, 21:44, 46
Connelly, M. S., 15:181
Conner (nr. Weber Cr., 1848), 2:190
Conner, Edward, 20:335
Conner, John W., 22:37(?); 30:102, 114
Conner & Forrest, 30:150
Conner (James) Type Foundry, 34:347
Conness, John, 5:338; 10:53, 75, 78, 193, 197, 271, 272, 282, 286, 287, 355, 356, 357, 367, 369; 11:9, 21, 63; 13:31; 20:367; 22:230, 231; 24:276; 25:94; 28:171; 32:147, 151, 159; 33:208, 235; 34:53, 55, 57-59, 63-64
Conness, Mount, 4:22, 36, 42, 55; 25:94
Connolley, Stephen and Frances, 17:42
Connolly, David W., 10:62
Connolly, Thomas A., 22:94
Connor, John, 30:254, 264
Connor, P. O., 10:189
Connor, Patrick Edward, 9:258; 10:390; 18:182, 286; 27:218; 40:349
Connor, Perry, 23:297
Conover, Simpson, 29:22, 27
Conquest of California, 1:14, 21, 140-48, 240-41; 13:301-5; 14:148-49; 19:120, 132-33, 175; 20:193-220 *passim;* 21:193-94, 216, 220, 333-57; 22:41-66; arts. on, 8:251-61; 17:123-40, 271-84, 325-50; 18:72-84; 25:121-31; docs. on, 1:72-95, 178-91, 286-95; 286-95; 2:69-74, 162-72, 246-51, 350-62; 3:84-88, 109-25, 178-90; 7:82-85; 8:71-77, 251-61; 9:81-86; 11:205, 209; 12:37-48 *passim,* 52-60 *passim,* 163-69, 334-46 *passim;* 13:109-36, 145-46; *see also* Bear Flag revolt; California Battalion

Conrad, Barnaby, *San Francisco: Profile with Pictures*, rev., 39:182

Conrad, Ephraim Francis and Mary (Bryan), 28:380

Conrad, J. C., 33:363

Conroy & O'Connor, 36:103

Consag, *see* Konscak

Conscience, Hendrick, 37:312-13

Considine, William, 9:314

Consolidated Amador Mine, 20:181

Consolidated Tobacco Co., 40:103

Consolidated Virginia and California mines, 37:219, 220

Consolidated Virginia Mine ("Big Bonanza"), 16:88; 27:346; 28:281; 37:219, 220

"Constance," *see* Winman, Gertrude

Constantine (ship), 12:199, 273; 17:68

Constitution (ship), 2:352; 3:108; 6:350-51; 17:125; 21:155; 26:222, 223, 226, 230; 32:361

Constitutional Convention (1849), 1:209, 270; 6:152-55; 10:131, 145-46, 150-63, 220; 13:380; 14:150; 16:197-98; 17:233; 19:4-14; 20:100-107; 22:81; 23:61, 352, 356; 27:16, 261; 28:196, 372-73; 35:13; fac. sigs. of delegates, 10: opp. 159

Constitutional Democrat, Ukiah, 20:165

Constitutional Union Party, 9:119; 22:228, 358

Constitution of California (1824), 27:333

Constitution of California (1849), 10:81, 151-64, 222, 302, 408; 16:43-47, 198; 19:350; 20:110; 26:101; 28:193-97, 361-62 (*see also* Constitutional Convention); ratification of, 10:163; 12:29; 23:356

Constitution of California (1879), 5:203; 27:343; 35:126, 143; 37:218, 223; 38:233

Consulate, U.S., in California, 37:1-17; *see also* Larkin, Thomas O.

Conte Bianco (fishing boat), 35:240

Continental (ship), 22:10, 22-23, 154; 40:256

Continental Mexican Petroleum Corporation, 30:214

Continent's End, ed. Sterling, rev., 5:90-92

"Continuation of the Annals of San Francisco," comp. by Dorothy H. Huggins, 15:88, 163-86, 266-82, 364-77; 16:79-84, 182-84, 282-85, 336-47; 17:81-85, 168-85

Contra Costa, 1:28; 13:107; 15:62; 27:210; 29:82; 31:326-27

Contra Costa (ship), 38:26

Contra Costa Academy, 17:49

Contra Costa County, 9: 189; 31:330

Contra Costa Steam Navigation Co., 10:72

Contract and Finance Co., 4:261; 37:130

Contracts: for carrying mail (1846), 10: (fac.) opp. 353, 353-54; for transportation across plains (1852), 11: (fac.) 34, opp. 34

Contreras, Felipe de, 2:155

Contreras, Fred, 30:222, 226

"Contribution of Dr. Herbert E. Bolton to the Study of the History of the West, The," address by William G. Paden, 19:187-88

"Contribution towards a Bibliography of the Camel, A," by William S. Lewis, 9:336-44

Convent of Notre Dame, Marysville, 9:372

Conversion, Punta de la, 8:57, 164

Convoy (ship), 26:249-50, 251; 28:123

Conway (clerk, 1858), 9:253, 352

Conway, Edmond, 33:2, 10, 12

Conway, George Robert Graham, obit., 30:278-80

Conway, Isaiah, 36:321

Conway, J. R., 13:318

Conway, John, 5:339-40

Cook, Dr. (from Louisiana, 1849), 18:115

Cook, Capt. (of *Gen. Pierce*, 1855), 16:282

Cook, Judge (Prairie City, 1855), 9:38

Cook (brothers; S.F., 1876), 4:68

Cook, A. G., 7:14

Cook, Carroll, 21:184; 30:69; 35:259

Cook, Charles E., 18:261

Cook, Charles F., 26:320

Cook, Charles W., 14:164; 17:176; 21:323-24; 25:109; *see also* Palmer, Cook & Co.

Cook, David, 24:58

Cook, E., 29:107

Cook, Eli, 6:12

Cook, Elisha, 15:280, 364

Cook, Ernest E., 16:132

Cook, Mrs. Finlay, address, "Memories of Ina Coolbrith," 11:188

Cook, Grove C., 5:76, 77-78, 132, 255; 15:19; 18:33, 36; 21:1, 2, 9, 15-16

Cook, H. C., 34:128

Cook, H. D., 32:354
Cook, Henry, lawsuit, 10:180
Cook, James, 3:215; 9:204-6 *passim;* 10:321, 328; 18:335; observatory of, illus., 37: opp. 304
Cook, James F., 20:314
Cook, Martin E., 24:49
Cook, May, 29:92
Cook, Theodocia, 38:342, 343
Cook, Walter, 25:12-13
Cook, William, 10:166, 284
Cook, William G., 12:115
Cook, Folger, & Co., 16:284
Cook *v.* King, 9:357
Cooke, C. W., 20:115
Cooke, George W., 29:225
Cooke, Rev. J., 26:171
Cooke, James, 21:150
Cooke, John, 3:204
Cooke, Philip St. George, 1:60, 68; 13:304; 18:130; 21:198, 212, 221, 222, 333, 342, 353, 355, 356; 22:42, 47, 48, 49, 52, 54, 58, 59, 148; 25:302; 29:36; 33:108-10, 113-14, 266-67
Cooke, Viola R., 30:82
Cooke, William, 28:380
Cooke, Mrs. William (Lucy Rutledge), 28:380-81; 30:82
Cooke, William B., 16:82; 29:126; 30:108; *see also* Cooke & LeCount; Cooke, Kenny & Co.
Cooke (William B.) & Co., 30:102, 114, 251, 253, 353
Cooke & LeCount, 22:34; 28:43; 30:102, 105, 107-14 *passim*
Cooke, Baker & Co., 22:243, 251; 30:100
Cook, Kenny & Co., 30:108, 250-53 *passim*
Coolbrith, Ina Donna, 3:293; 4:95, 211; 5:90, 91; 7:78; 9:392; 10:87; 11:188; 12:79; 13:335, 348, 354; 28:7; 32:235, 237; 33:373; 36:110
Cooley, Judge (Santa Barbara, 1863), 18:272
Cooley, Charles, 27:304
Coolidge, H. W., 9:390; 10:251
Coolidge, Joseph, 29:251
Coolot, A., 29:104, 108, 111, 124; 30:366
Coombs, Asa, 9:348-51 *passim*
Coombs, Frank L., 10:76; address, "Historic, Reminiscent, and Otherwise," 7:289
Coombs, John J., 9.27
Coombs, Levi, 16:134
Coombs, Nathan, 11:9; 18:158, 173

Coombs, R., 9:68, 136, 137
Coombs, Samuel W., 33:381
Coombs, Thomas M., 9:137, 139, 144-48 *passim,* 158, 170; *see also* Link *v.* Coombs
Coombsville, 29:329
Coon (Sutter's Fort, 1844), 17:158
Coon, Henry Perrin, 21:34, 331; 24:264; 26:257-58; 29:103, 112, 121; 33:234
Coon, Robert S., 26:108, 130, 135, 158
Coonan, Clarence, obit. of Charles P. Cutten, 22:379-80
Cooney, John, 17:83, 176
Cooney, Patrick J., 39:123
Cooney, Percival J., 29:240
Coon Hollow, 8:201, 210; 11:58
Coons, Edith F., 32:1-2, 12, 16, 20-21, 25, 33, 41
Coons' Ranch, 18:121-22, 135
Cooper (2d off. on *Avon,* 1833), 14:314
Cooper (via Mex., 1850), 1:60
Cooper (medium, Marysville, 1857), 9:169
Cooper (S.F., 1860), 29:119
Cooper, Ana María de Guadalupe, 12:135
Cooper, C. M. N., 14:217
Cooper, Charles H., 15:240
Cooper, Charles P., 15:53
Cooper, David, 1:60
Cooper, Edward T., 14:299, 313
Cooper, Elias Samuel, 4:150, 179, 180, 187-88, 193-94, 197, 200, 201, 205, 206; 5:93
Cooper, Elizabeth, 6:152
Cooper, Emma, 36:314-15, 319, 323
Cooper, Ethel, 21:192; 26:94
Cooper, F., 29:40
Cooper, Fernando M., 2:49; 4:153, 180
Cooper, Frances, 6:151-52; 20:150-51, 152
Cooper, Frederic Taber, comp. *Rider's California,* rev., 4:397-98
Cooper, George Vincent, drawing by, 14: opp. 269
Cooper, Henry, 15:121
Cooper, James A., 21:192
Cooper, James Graham, 4:16; 21:368
Cooper, Jesse C., 15:277
Cooper, John Bautista Rogers, 2:37, 49; 8:29, 301; 9:190; 10:414; 12:236, 238, 261, 297; 14:127, 128, 346; 15:225, 339; 16:4, 143, 248, 265, 270, 322, 355; 17:57, 142, 145, 236; 19:127, 128, 129, 134, 141, 194, 212, 214; 20:341-42; 23:213,

218, 313, 330, 331, 332; 26:249, 250; 29:27, 157, 166; 30:98; 34:117-18, 123; 37:2
Cooper, Mrs. John Bautista Rogers (Encarnación Vallejo), 17:142, 145
Cooper, John I., 9:316-17
Cooper, Juan Bautista Guillermo, 12:135
Cooper, Katherine (Wakeman), 30:159
Cooper, L. F., 19:370
Cooper, Laura, 10:359
Cooper, Luther, 11:75; 16:325
Cooper, Martha, 6:152
Cooper, Oscar, 26:94
Cooper, Rose, 16:283
Cooper, Samuel E., 22:61
Cooper, Sarah Brown (Ingersoll), 21:373; 28:9; 31:252
Cooper, Stephen, 2:64-65; 6:148-49, 151-52; 9:76-77; 20:150-53 *passim*
Cooper, Susan, 6:152; 20:150-51, 152
Cooper, Thomas Benton, 6:157
Cooper Medical School, 4:206; College, 30:67
Coos Bay, 25:255, 263
Coos Bay Times, Marshfield, Ore., 18:384
Copco One Dam, 30:340
Cope, Walter B., 6:288
Cope, Warner Walton, 9:155; 10:49, 52, 61, 283, 373(?); 11:6
Cope, William, 21:353; 22:45; 33:105
Copeland (in mines, 1849), 27:160
Copeland, Capt. (Santa Barbara, 1860s), 18:272
Copiapo (ship), 21:307
Copper and copper mining, 1:117, 143, 144; 2:18; 16:42; 17:138; 21:202, 203, 222; 31:127, 129
Copper City, 22:369
"Copperheads," 20:160, 167, 258; 21:129; 22:358; 34:52, 57-58, 60
Coppin, George, 21:65
Coppinger (or Copinger), John, 15:115, 135, 224, 228; 17:253; 28:260
Copsey, Arthur, 32:376
Coptic (ship), 30:200
Copyrights, *see* "California Copyrights..."
Coquelin, Benoît Constant, 20:138
Cora, Charles, 8:369-71; 13:82; 14:351, 354; 15:81, 204-5; 16:344-47 *passim;* 17:81, 83, 175, 176; 20:306; 24:174; 37:155-65 *passim;* defended by Baker, 3:42; 10:190; 15:205; 17:310; hanged,

3:41; 8:371; 17:310; 20:260; 21:26; 24:173; port., 8:368
Cora, Mrs. Charles (Arabella Ryan), 8:370; 16:347; 17:81
Coral, Robert, 10:184
Corbaley, R. C., 29:225
Corbán, *see* Gómez de Corbán
Corby (dancer, S.F., 1855), 15:279
Corbyn, Sheridan, 21:67, 160, 162, 167, 179
Corbyn & Bigger, Melodeon, Sacramento, 9:276
Corcoran, John M., 1:18
Corcoran, Katharine, *see* Herne, Mrs. James A.
Cordelling, 4:111; 8:18, 19; 15:110
Corder, Arthur E., obit., 37:376-77
Corder, Thomas W., 37:376-77
Cordero, Antonio, 3:313; 19:243
Cordero, José, 15:214
Cordero, Mariana S., 27:94
Cordero, Thomas, 28:265
Cordes, Frederick Carl, 39:180; "Letters of A. Rotchev, ... Fort Ross, ... Report of the Russian-American Company for the Year 1850-51," trans., 39:97-115; obit. of Hans Barkan, 356-57
Cordona, Nicolas and Tomás de, 1:36
Cordova, Alberto, 15:61
Cordua, Theodor, 5:305; 10:353; 11:110, 121; 14:204-6 *passim*, 217, 221, 226, 227, 383, 390; 15:54, 55; 16:56-57, 131, 138; 18:342-43; 28:264-65; "Memoirs," ed. and trans. Erwin G. Gudde, 12:279-311; port., 12: opp. 279
Cordua's Bar, 12:303
Cordua's Ranch, 9:75; 14:198-204, 207, 227, 383; 15:52; *see also* New Mecklenburg; Marysville
Corea (ship), 30:200
Corey, Frank, 9:385
Corey, J. M., 7:113; 26:237
Corey, Mount, 7:113
Coriolanus (play), 21:149
Corliss, Willson, 18:262, 263, 264
Corn, 1:166; 5:47, 131, 135, 217; 8:237, 319; 14:7, 11, 20; 18:335; 22:319; 32:355
Cornbloom, Charles, 37:198
Cornelison, Wiley, 21:237
Cornelius, Br., 21:372; address, "William Keith," 21:278
Cornelius Cole, by Phillips, rev., 8:382-83

Cornelius' ferry, 28:330

Cornell, Capt. (of *W. L. Marcy*, 1854), 15:185

Cornell, W., 8:341; 10:172

Cornell Watch Co., 34:327

Corner (Yuba Co., 1857), 9:139

"Cornerstone of the State Capitol," by J. N. Bowman, 33:329-35

Corn Exchange Insurance Co., 26:256

Corney, Peter, 1:176, 195

Cornish (lawsuits, Marysville, 1859), 10:185, 186, 187

Cornishmen, 26:374

Cornoyer, Joseph, 22:206, 217, 218, 220; 23:31, 35, 127, 138

Cornwall (dentist, 1857), 9:161, 162

Cornwall, George N., 16:134

Cornwall, Pierre Barlow, 6:61; 9:256, 261; 12:33, 34; 14:375, 376; 15:76, 370; 24:72; 25:11

Cornwall, William A., 15:275

Cornwell, Henry, 40:34

Coronado, Francisco, 18:262-63

Coronado, Francisco Vásquez de, 1:45; 3:263-67 *passim*, 384; 6:300, 301, 315, 316, 318, 322, 328; 7:20; 13:86

Coronado (place), 17:35; 20:140; 31:149

Coronado, Hotel del, 31:156; 35:269, 351-52; 36:71, 154

Coronados (islands), 7:46, 345; 8:217; 31:350, 352, 354

Coronado trail, 25:372

Coronation (ship), 15:182

Coronel, Antonio Francisco, 13:50, 55, 217, 318, 326-27, 383; 21:331; 25:293-94, 298-300, 304; 26:23, 56; 29:234, 246, 247; 32:339

Coronel, Hernando de los Rios, 7:264-65

Coronel, Ignacio, 13:217, 223, 312, 318; 29:246

Coronel, Manuel, 29:235

Coronel, María Antonia, 26:57

Corporations, regulation of, 10:273, 288; 19:10-11

Corral Flat, 30:241-42

Corral Hollow, 17:168

Correa, Antonio, 3:389; 7:20, 55, 70

Correa & Bahnsen, 15:277

"Corrections and Addenda ... Vigilance Committee ... 1856," by Thomas L. Rayner, 8:364-73

Correo Mercado (ship), 14:258; 15:359, 360

Corrigan, J. P., 9:26

Corrister, W. D., 20:305, 314

Corsair (ship), 17:294

Corsair ,The (play), 9:255,280

Corse, Capt. (Sacramento, 1856), 24:172, 174

Corser, Charles H., 9:26, 109; 15:281, 364; 17:84, 85

Corte Madera, 12:298; 14:201; 15:279

Corte Madera Creek, 17: No. 1, Pt. 2, p. 12

Cortés, Hernando, 1:36-52 *passim;* 3:262, 307-14 *passim*, 320, 336, 368, 374; 6:294-99 *passim*, 301-10 *passim*, 318-21 *passim;* 7:71, 135, 139, 192, 309; 19:240-43 *passim;* 26:311; 30:279

Cortés, Juan, letters to, 37:249-63

Cortes (ship), 15:88, 164, 166, 170, 171, 181, 182, 266, 271, 275, 364; 16:84, 184, 338; 17:81, 172, 179; 23:103; 29:102, 111

Cortes, Sea of, *see* California, Gulf of

Cortes Bank, 31:154-58 *passim*

Cortina, Francisco, 25:362

Cort Theater, San Francisco, 25:235, 238, 241, 242, 245

Corvallis, Ore., 28:207

Corvalom, Christoval, 27:63

Corwin, Eli S., 34:318-19

Corwin, Frances M., 14:176, 177, 182

Corwin, James, 26:171

Corwin (ship), 20:194

Corwine, Amos B., 11:11

Cory, Miss (Yuba Co., 1857), 9:142

Cory, Benjamin, 2:182, 188, 191, 195

Cory, Clarence Linus, 4:48; 35:272

Corys, Sargent, 14:278, 279

Corzell, Lewis, 14:211

Cosby, John Dabney, 9:46, 107

Cosgrave, George, 20:191, 288; "A Diplomatic Incident on the Little Mariposa," 21:358-62; "James McHall Jones," 20:97-116; trans. Friedrich Gerstäcker, "The French Revolution," 17:3-17; obit., 24:375-76

Cosgrove, James, 9:356

Cosío, José María, 14:257

Cosmopolitan Bathhouse, Yosemite, 5:339

Cosmopolitan Hotel ,Los Angeles, 13:339

Cosmopolitan Hotel, San Francisco, 2:205; 19:229; 30:209; 35:120

Coso, 10:381, 393; 18:208; mines nr., 10:261, 393; 18:200, 204, 206, 208

Coso (prop. county), 26:243

Coso Gold and Silver Mining Co.,
18:200
Cospar (in mines, 1848), 2:193, 194, 196
Cossit (Downieville, 1858), 9:357
Cossley-Batt, Jill L., *The Last of the
California Rangers*, rev., 8:83-84
Costa, L., 22:68
Costansó, Miguel, 1:158-59; 3:225, 227;
4:143; 10:80-83 *passim*; 13:185, 196,
198; 19:77; 31:110; 36:2, 218;
40:122, 198
Coster, John H., 11:127
"Costs of the Modoc War," by Richard
H. Dillon, 28:161-64, 286
Costume, *see* Dress
Cosumnes River, 1:150; 13:74, 75, 170,
174; 22:329; 23:35, 130; 32:196; 34:2
Cot, Antonio José, 23:210, 217, 322, 332
Cota, Mrs. Francisco, 27:109
Cota, Guillermo, 12:232; 13:205, 207, 211
Cota, Leonardo, 13:126, 327, 349;
17:329; 26:33, 42
Cota, Loreta, 13:331
Cota, Manuel, 12:133
Cota, Pablo, 13:198
Cota, Rafaela, *see* Temple, Mrs. John
Cota, Roque, 13:202
Cota, Simon, 23:6
Cota, Valentin, 12:133
Cota family (Gaviota, 1864), 18:263,
264
Cotham (M. C.) & Co., San Francisco,
3:268, 269
Cottage Sawmill, 9:52, 70
Cotter, Richard, 4:18-22 *passim*, 54
Cotter, Richard M., 33:12, 149, 153-57
passim, 163-64, 167
Cottle, Benjamin H., 22:223, 224
Cotton, Arthur, 30:91
Cotton, Ben, 21:163-64, 169, 173
Cotton, Edwin, 30:91
Cotton, Hamilton, 39:133
Cotton, Mrs. J. S., letters to, 27:225, 226
Cotton, Lutie, 30:91
Cotton, 1:167; 5:205-6; 6:159-65; 12:157;
16:15; 18:226, 298; 21:212, 329; 22:13,
18, 25, 319; 27:144
"Cotton and Gold," address by James
A. B. Scherer, 5:205-6
Cottonwood Creek (Poso Creek?),
11:254
Cotton Wood Post Office, 28:352
Cottro (Indian, 1836), 16:249
Couch, Jesse, 13:257
Coughtin (Coughlin?), Patrick, 24:53

Coulp (Marysville, 1850s), 9:173
Coult, Theodore A., 10:181, 200, 361,
372, 387
Coulter, Edith Margaret, 20:288;
25:195; fellow CHS, 38:74;
"California Copyrights, 1851-1856,"
22:27-40; obit. of Lucy Ward
Stebbins, 34:180-81
Coulter, George W., 4:24; 5:337
Coulter, S. T., 30:263
Coulter, Thomas, 2:227; 18:335, 341
Coulter, W., 38:214
Coulter, William A., 25:196; 37:30
Coulter and Murphy's Hotel, Yosemite,
see Cedar Cottage
Coulterville, 22:182
Council Bluffs, 2:30; 4:112, 119, 128
Council of Federated Trades, *see* San
Francisco Labor Council
Counterfeits and counterfeiting, 1:252;
15:377; 16:83; 17:180
Count of Monte Cristo (play), 16:301
Country Road-Blocking System, 29:362,
363
Counts, Calvin, 33:363
County boundaries, 9:259; bk. on, rev.
2:366-67
Courcelle, de, *see* Naudet
Courier, John W., 2:122
Courier, Crescent City, 32:163
Courier, San Francisco, 7:281
Courier, Shasta, 21:383; 29:91
Courier (ship), 2:235; 8:331; 18:70;
bk. on, rev., 38:371
Courier and Enquirer, New York,
25:334
Courner, I. W., 22:37
Courrier de Californie, Le, San
Francisco, 39:159-60, 346
Courrier de Cherbourg, Le (ship),
31:140, 311-16
Courrier de l'Europe, Le (weekly),
39:142, 149, 346
Courrier de Los Angeles, Le, 39:327-28,
346
Courrier des Amériques, Le, San
Francisco, 39:159, 347
Courrier de San Francisco, Le, 32:115;
39:165-66, 169, 222, 225, 315, 346, 347
Courrier du Pacifique, Le, San
Francisco, 39:313, 315, 319, 347, 348
Courrier Français, Le (weekly),
39:343, 347
Courrier Français des Etats-Unis, Le,
39:225; *see also Courrier du Pacifique*

Courtaine, Henry, 4:61; 21:42-43, 53, 70, 152, 265; 39:301

Courtaine, Mrs. Henry (Emma Grattan), 21:42, 43

Court House Bluff (or Rock), 6:114; 22:131

Courts, in Mexican period, 1:33; *see also* Alcalde

Courts, in American period, 9:172; 16:79; 19:261; 20:104
  admiralty, 35:110
  Circuit, 15:369; 16:285; 19:261
  County, 9:71, 172, 268, 357, 361-74 *passim;* 15:180; 17:172; 20:104
  District, 9:131, 172, 264, 269, 348, 356-57, 358, 372, 380; 10:53, 54, 55, 356; 15:180, 183, 274, 277, 278, 364, 368, 369, 377; 16:79, 80, 81; 17:170-71, 175, 176, 180, 182; 20:104
  Justices', 9:64, 66, 71-72, 129-52 *passim,* 155, 160, 161, 165-68 *passim,* 172, 349, 356, 363, 373, 375; 15:270; 20:104
  Mayors', 9:172; 15:369; 16:285; 17:81, 82, 83
  Probate, 9:172
  Recorders', 9:172, 261, 346, 350, 357, 360, 367, 370, 374, 375
  of Sessions, 9:172, 286, 287, 348, 349, 363, 373, 379, 390; 10:41, 57, 63, 364; 15:275, 369; 17:175, 176, 177
  Sheriffs', 9:149, 151, 346, 347
  Superior, 9:172, 348; 15:364, 368, 370; 16:368; 17:84, 85, 175, 177, 180, 182; 20:366, 367; 26:91
  Calif. Supreme, 8:354, 355; 9:172, 269, 362, 366, 389, 390; 10:70, 273, 356; 15:267, 268, 274, 276, 370; 16:80; 17:170, 171, 180; 20:104, 365-73; 26:209-15 *passim;* 33:73-75; phot. of seal, 33: opp. 73
  U.S. District, 13:339; 15:182, 266, 277, 368, 369; 16:79, 80; 17:176; 19:265; 20:110; 21:120; 22:28-29; 25:324; 26:210; 27:134
  U.S. Supreme, 15:274, 368; 16:79, 182; 19:261; 21:120

Coutant, J. L., 22:251

Couts, Cave Johnson, 1:236; 12:77; 21:304; 22:19; 25:307; 33:109, 342

Couts, Mrs. Cave Johnson, *see* Bandini, Isidora

Coutts, Mrs. Gordon (Alice), 37:30

Coutts, Peter (Paulin Caperon), 23:180; 33:169-74

Covarrubias, José María, 9:104; 10:117; 11:9, 342; 13:109, 217, 231; 16:364; 17:233; 19:7; 21:311-13, 322; 27:108-10; 29:231, 232, 244, 246; fac. sig., 10: opp. 159

Covell, A. T., 25:33, 34

Covelo, 27:221, 222-23

"Covered Wagon in Court, The," 33:175-78

Covillard (S.F., 1850), 6:38, 42

Covillaud, Charles, 9:75, 77; 10:269, 367, 383; 12:280, 299; 14:203-15 *passim,* 219, 221, 383, 389, 405-6; 15:24, 29, 42, 51, 53, 280; phot., 15: opp. 21

Covillaud, Mrs. Charles (Mary Murphy), 9:77; 12:280, 299; 14:206, 220-21; port., 14: opp. 195

Covillaud, Fajard & Co., 14:207, 214

Covillaud House, Marysville, 14:379, 393-94

Covington (Sacramento, 1861), 10:277

Covington, Elam, 20:112

Cowan, Robert Ernest, 1:108, 110; 3:247-48, 252; 11:65, 68; 12:125, 126; 14:87; 15:196; 28:364-65
  "Alexander S. Taylor," 12:18-24; "Auction Sales of Californiana," 1:96-99; 2:77-80; 3:191-95; 6:192-94; 7:405; 8:278-79; "Bibliographical Note: *Laws for the Better Government of California,*" 2:75-76; "The Leidesdorff-Folsom Estate," 7:105-11; "Meetings of the Society," 4:400; "Norton I," 2:237-45; "Recent Auction Prices," 8:78-79
  forewords: to "Bancroft's Guide to the Colorado Mines," 12:3-4; to "Documentary," 2:161-62; introd. to "Journal of John McHenry Hollingsworth," ed. H. R. Wagner, 1:207-8
  contrib. to "The Twenty Rarest and Most Important Works . . . History of California," 10:79, 82
  addresses: "Alexander S. Taylor, First Bibliographer of California," 10:91; "The Bibliography of California," 3:101; "Booksellers of Old San Francisco," 20:282; "The Discovery of Gold in California," 5:95-96; "Some Forgotten Characters of Old San Francisco," 13:88; "Some Romantic Realities in the History of California," 8:90

obits. of John L. Hitchcock, 5:104-5;
James D. Phelan, 9:294-95
bk. revs. by, 1:99-102, 197-99, 302-3;
2:81-84; 3:200-201, 290-91; 4:89-91;
5:88-89, 311-12, 405-7; 6:281-82;
7:86-87, 407; 8:183-85, 379-80,
382-83; 18:371-73
rep. of Publication Com., 3:95-96
The Pioneers of California, rev., 8:186
obit., 21:282-83
Cowboy (ship), 12:141
Cow Creek, *see* Canoe River
Cowden, Henry, 21:306
Cowden, J. S., 26:306
Cowell, Mrs. Effie, 9:143, 149, 150, 158;
10:256, 267, 365
Cowell, Mary (Mrs. James S.
Slingerland), 9:147, 151, 152, 170;
10:256, 267, 288, 359
Cowen, William, 3:149-50
Cowie, Thomas, 1:135; 12:56; 17:240;
20:224; 24:58, 71; 25:124; 29:266-67,
270
Cowles, Cornelia S., *see* French, Mrs.
Erasmus Darwin
Cowles, Josiah E., 3:105, 106, 107
Cowles, Samuel, 9:29; 27:153; 33:265
Cowlitz (ship), 8:98; 17:142; 28:99,
100-107 *passim*, 243, 248, 252
Cowsby, A. E., 9:140
Cox, Alexander J., 16:133; 24:58
Cox, Cornelius C., 21:303-4
Cox, Henderson, 14:278-80
Cox, Isaac, 20:80, 152; 21:127-40; 30:358
Cox, John, 21:337, 345; 25:296, 306;
26:49
Cox, Joseph, 28:337
Cox, Leander, 14:217
Cox, M. B., 26:182-83
Cox, R. M., 15:280, 364
Cox, Thomas, 9:104
Cox, William George, 6:22-23
Cox's Bar, 21:127
Coy, Capt. (filibuster, 1855), 17:172
Coy, Owen Cochran, 1:164; 7:409;
8:381; bk. revs. by, 2:178-79, 366-67;
6:377-79; ed. *Pictorial History of
California*, rev., 5:89-90
Coyle, Peter, 21:306
Coyote Canyon, 10:214, 216
Coyote Creek, 22:71, 73, 74, 81
Coyote Diggings, Calaveras Co., 22:74
Coyote Flat, 22:76
Coyote Hill, 29:193
Coyote Ravine, 11:236

Coyote-hole diggings, 6:245-46; 8:359;
11:236; illus., 6: opp. 245
Coyote Holes, Kern Co., 17:105, 106,
108, 116
Coyote mining claim, Butte Co., 33:295
Coyote mining claim, Kern Co., 32:14,
29-36 *passim*
Coyotes, 2:43; 6:215, 247; 8:147; 11:114;
12:208, 305; 13:68; 17:28; 18:74;
19:118, 119; 27:194; 28:218; 29:256,
258
Coyote Valley, 24:55, 56
Coyoteville, 8:359; 11:236
Coytier, L., 28:46
Coytisa (Indian, 1819), 3:26
Crabb, Henry A., 9:41, 47, 144, 176;
19:274, 279; 21:32
Crabb, Horace and Daisy Anna (Davis),
2:67
Crabb, Jeremiah, 21:342; 22:49
Crabtree, Lotta, 4:60-61; 6:341; 8:84;
9:77, 176; 10:291, 376, 390; 14:411;
17:353; 20:307; 21:61, 77-78; 31:378;
bk. on, rev., 8:84
Crackbon, Joseph, 13:31
Crackborn, Charles, 10:284
Cracklin, Charles, 6:233
Cracklin, Tom, 6:227, 228, 332, 347
Cracklin's Hotel, Grass Valley, 6:232
Craddock, Mrs. J. H. (Nancy Trego),
10:252, 259
Craddock, John, 13:258
Cradles (mining), 5:221-22, 223; 6:216,
244, 245; 12:314-15; 13:161-62;
23:350; 26:123-24; 39:103
Craft (Yosemite, 1856), 1:274
Craft, Marcella, 25:236
Crafts, Farish, & Co., 9:346, 347
Craggs Flat, 11:240
Craig (S.F., 1852), 34:34
Craig (Auburn, 1870s), 18:361
Craig, Elisabeth, 25:380
Craig, Evelyn, *see* Pattiani, Evelyn Craig
Craig, Hugh, 22:192; 31:341
Craig, John, 18:356
Craig, William (1840s), 25:142, 144
Craig, William (1940s), 26:349
Craine, Jeremiah V., 22:38; 30:265
Craine, William, 38:34
Cram, Rogers, & Co. Weaverville
Express, 28:226, 231
Cramer, B. H., 13:32
Cramer, James W., 13:32
Cramer, John, 13:32
Cramer & Co., 8:341, 345, 353; 9:50

Crampton, Charlotte, 21:148-49, 151
Crampton, Gregory, address, "Gold
 Rushes and Their Significance,"
 19:375
Crandall (Yuba Co., 1856), 9:60
Crandall, "Grandma" (Auburn, 1870s),
 18:361
Crandall (San Diego, 1935), 36:162
Crandall, Dwight, 9:46; 32:152
Crandall, J. R., 9:113, 116
Crandall, Jared B., 7:17, 19; 13:256;
 14:160; *see also* Hall & Crandall
Crane (Indian, 1845), 1:129
Crane, Addison Moses, 10:377, 387, 390
Crane, Charles H., 28:216, 221; 34:34
Crane, Clarkson, trans., Bernard de
 Russailh, *Last Adventure*, 39:3; rev.,
 10:205
Crane, Erwin J., 25:95
Crane, George Whitfield, 4:234; 9:254,
 269, 282; 29:23, 27
Crane, Mrs. George Whitfield, *see*
 Sánchez, Mrs. José María
Crane, James E., 30:263
Crane, James M., 21:229-33, 237; 22:30,
 38; 28:34
Crane, John, 15:177; 25:344
Crane, L. T., 8:356; 10:189
Crane, Lauren E., 24:367
Crane, Richard Taller, 40:153
Crane, Mrs. Talmage Burton (Ethel
 Hastings), 23:190
Crane, William Henry, 35:142
Crane (James M.) & (F.W.) Rice,
 6:45; 7:281
Cranfors, *see* Granfors
Crapo, William, 4:34-35
Crarey, Capt. (S.F., 1849), 22:69
Crary, Mrs. (Sacramento, 1861), 10:278
Cravath, Ruth, 38:4
Craven, C., 8:203
Craven, J. Bur, 8:203
Craven, Nettie, 25:88
Craven, Tunis Augustus Macdonough,
 30:235; "Naval Conquest in the
 Pacific," Journal of, ed. John H.
 Kemble, 20:193-234; port., 20:
 opp. 193
Cravens, Robert O., 2:205; 10:76
Craw, S. B., 24:243
Crawford, Mr. and Mrs. (S.F., 1850),
 7:396, 397, 398, 404
Crawford, George, 21:351; 33:105
Crawford, George W., 10:148, 164
Crawford, Hilary H., 27:284-85

Crawford, J., 9:180
Crawford, Martin Jenkins, 19:365
Crawford, Moses, 9:347
Crawford & Co., 31:158
Crawford's Claim (play), 34:364
Crawley, L. J., 31:333
Crawley, Stephen, 17:84
Creaner, Charles M., 15:161; 29:20,
 21, 26
Creation, The (oratorio), 15:276
Creatures of Impulse (play), 21:171
Credit association, San Francisco
 (1855), 16:336
Cree, William J., 21:306
Creed, Wigginton, 30:346-49 *passim;*
 31:300
Creed, Mrs. Wigginton (Isabel
 Hooper), 31:300, 340
Creel, George, 39:125
Cregan, Jerry, 18:357-58
Creigh, J. D., 17:116
Creighton, Edward, 29:346-47, 350-54
 passim
Creighton, John Hayes, 21:192
Creighton, Samuel, 28:290
Crellin, Mrs. Anita M., 26:381
Cremone Theater, San Francisco, 20:135
Cremony, John Clare, 12:3, 28:3; 40:349
Crenshaw, George H., 10:50, 62, 70
Crescent City, Del Norte Co., 15:369;
 23:369, 376; 26:1-11 *passim*, 201, 203,
 360; 28:228-29; 29:111; 30:263;
 32:161-70, 190; 34:269-70; 38:319;
 church, 32:164-65
 lighthouse, 35:325-34; newspaper,
 32:162-63; phot., 35: opp. 328
Crescent City, Stanislaus Co., 11:358-62;
 23:369
Crescent City (ship), 13:3, 28, 390;
 23:53; 29:3; 33:324
Crescent City and Yreka Plank and
 Turnpike Co., 32:163
Crescent City Bay, 10:334
"Crescent City on the Tuolumne," by
 Helen T. Pratt, 11:358-62
Crescent Rifles, 34:269
Crescent Social Club, Crescent City,
 32:168
Crespi, Juan, 1:158-60; 9:203-4;
 10:211-12; 11:279; 13:180, 196-98;
 15:329-30; 19:287; 28:19; 31:113-17,
 121, 124, 261-62, 270, 350, 354; 36:1-2;
 37:292, 298; biog. of, rev., 6:376
Crespo, Manuel, 4:152-53; 15:347-48;
 16:355

Cressey, Capt. (of *Sea Gull*, 1850), 2:123
Cressy, Josiah Perkins, 15:367; 20:277
Cressy, T. R., 27:236
Creswell, Harry Thornton, 6:288
Cretigny, Louise, 29:225-26
Cricket (ship), 32:338
Crigler, John, 24:128, 136
Crim, Samuel, 33:375
Crimean War, 15:184, 267, 372, 375,
    377; 16:84, 337, 341; 17:84-85; 27:212;
    32:163; 38:338
Crimes and Career of Tiburcio Vasquez,
    rev., 7:195
Crins, John, 22:78
Crisman, Joel, 4:310, 321
Crisman, S., 4:310
Crist (overland, 1849), 22:129, 131
Crites, Angus K., 32:9
Critic, San Francisco, 21:153
Crittenden (Yuba Co., 1855), 8:340
Crittenden, Alexander Parker, 7:118;
    14:367; 19:256; 32:148, 158; 38:49
Crittenden, John Jordan, 10:290; 11:18,
    19; 15:6; 19:345, 361; 31:196-97
Crittenden, R. D., 10:273, 275, 288;
    11:8, 9
Crocker, Benjamin R. and Rosanna,
    28:294
Crocker, Charles, 4:219, 245, 246, 247,
    258, 261, 268; 5:178; 9:36; 10:273, 288;
    15:76; 18:24; 19:234, 238; 21:328, 369;
    24:367; 26:181; 27:170, 171; 31:337;
    37:130; 38:311, 352
Crocker, Charles Frederick, 11:88;
    27:319; 34:340
Crocker, Mrs. Charles Frederick, 34:340
Crocker, Charles Henry, 25:230, 232
Crocker, Charles Templeton, *see*
    Crocker, Templeton
Crocker, Edwin Bryant, 2:204; 5:178,
    179, 181; 9:175; 15:76; *California
    Digest*, 9:141, 175; 22:39, 40
Crocker, Everett F., 2:92, 101, 113, 121;
    "lines" composed by, 2:99-100, 111-12
Crocker, Helen, *see* Russell, Mrs. Henry
    Potter
Crocker, Henry Robinson and May
    (Hall), 23:96
Crocker, Templeton: active in
    reorganization of CHS, 1:19; 19:89,
    94; 21:95, 183; art. on, 28:364-66;
    36:175; collection of, 1:72, 79-90,
    182-83, 190-92, 210, 291; 2:69, 71,
    162-72, 246-50, 351-52, 354, 357-62;
    3:84-88, 188, 252, 284-85, 286-87;

4:83-85; 5:193-95, 308; 6:83-87, 181,
    265, 268-71, 274-80, 368-72; 7:81;
    19:79-81, 89, 376-80 *passim;* 21:95,
    185-88 *passim;* 25:250; obit., 28:90
Crocker, William Henry, 25:230, 232,
    235, 249, 250; 36:68; obit., 16:383-84
Crocker, Mrs. William Henry (Ethel
    W. Sperry), 16:383; 20:136; obit.,
    13:287
Crocker (H. S.) & Co., 27:270; 30:130,
    147
Crocker Art Gallery, 39:198
Crocker National Bank, 31:303, 305
Crockett (L.A., 1854), 13:319
Crockett, Joseph Bryant, 4:234, 237;
    14:364-67 *passim*, 371, 373; 15:70,
    146, 273; 38:300; cor., 14:365;
    15:72-75; 40: foll. 206
Crockett (place), 27:197; 35:150; phot.,
    27: opp. 197, opp. 200
Crockett & Co., 14:401
"Crofton" (Contra Costa Co.), 29:100
Croix, Charles François de, 31:110, 122
Croix, Teodoro de, 13:199; 14:7;
    27:63, 64
Croke, James, 10:388
Crónica, La, San Francisco, 16:80
Cronise, Titus Fey, 1:208; 3:27-28;
    24:106; 39:117, 119
Cronkhite, J. W., 31:331
Cronyn, George W., *'49, a Novel of
    Gold*, rev., 5:312-15
Crook, George, 26:1-2, 10; 38:153
Crooks, Stephen, 26:119
Cropper, T. B., 15:275
Crosby, Elisha Oscar, 13:251, 254, 392;
    14:163, 164, 212, 405; 20:103; 23:369,
    370; 32:126; 33:373; 34:184; 38:49;
    art. on, 27:133-40; fac. sig., 10: opp.
    159
Crosby, J. C., 34:126, 131
Crosby, John D., 10:74
Crosette, George H., 9:44-45; 15:369;
    18:199
Cross (Yuba Co., 1857), 9:159, 162, 163
Cross, Mrs. (Marysville, 1858), 9:354
Cross, August, 22:251
Cross, Ira Brown, 30:364; address,
    "Early Banking in California," 23:380
Cross, Osborne, 16:339
Cross, Ralph Herbert, 25:94; 34:286;
    address, "Early Inns of California,"
    20:83
Cross, Sharon, 2:112, 121
Cross & Co., 6:354-55; 27:173

Cross *v.* Harrison, 8:261
Crossett, J. L., 25:108, 109
Cross-filing in elections, 31:287; art. on, 38:349-57; 39:19-34
Cross, Hobson & Co., 23:58; 24:24; 30:99
Crossing the Plains, by Ackley, rev., 8:86
Crosthwaite, Philip, 26:40-41, 51, 59
Crosthwaite, Mrs. Philip (María López), 26:41
Crothers, Robert A., 30:195
Crotty, Homer Daniel, address, "Sketches of Mariposa in the Fifties," 33:276-77; obits. of Florence Green Bixby, 40:365-66; Frederick W. Williamson, 21:286-87
Crouch, Cyrus, 15:45
Crouch, H. B., 36:201
Crow (Railroad Hill, 1857), 9:165
Crow, Thomas, 9:351, 383
Crowald (S.F., 1851), 30:109
Crowan (S.F., 1850), 8:274
Crowe (S.F. and Sacramento, 1859), 10:41
Crowe, Mary Ann, 27:285
Crowe, John C., 27:285
Crowell, E. A., 9:19
Crowell, Eugene, 8:340(?), 356
Crowell, John M., 8:340(?), 346, 356; 9:130, 132, 133, 149, 157, 172, 177; 10:77, 367
Crowell, Zenas, 26:358, 362
Crowell & Co. *v.* M. McKinty, 9:53
Crowley (S.F., 1864), 24:263
Crowley, Patrick, 27:21, 26; 29:82
Crowninshield, Jacob, 24:24
Crown Princess (ship), 29:10
Crown Zellerbach Co., 36:112
Crowold (S.F., 1851), 30:109
Crozier, R. G., 9:30
Cruces, 8:4, 13-14; 27:35, 47; 34:34
Crumpton, Hezekiah John, 2:206
Crumpton, Washington B., 2:206
Crusader (brig, 1833), 14:342; 23:312
Crusader (str., 1861), 20:194
Crutcher, William M., 2:205
Cruthers (Benicia, 1853), 27:308
Crutsinger (Yuba Co., 1855), 8:346
Cruz, Antonio F., 21:320
Cruz, José de la, 2:341-43
Cruzado, Antonio, 23:371
Cruzador (ship), 23:332
Cryer, George E., 36:258; 37:273
Crystal, Helen (Dormody), 26:381
Crystal, Quartz Mill, 11:324
Crysup (Benicia, 1853), 27:308

Cuadra, *see* Bodega y Quadra
Cuba, 20:24; Senate bill re, 9:67, 80; 10:66; 19:177-78; 32:322
Cubas, Ignacio de, 25:60, 362
Cubberley, Elwood Patterson, 4:49
Cuberly, Mr. and Mrs. (S.F., 1855), 15:375
Cubillas (Guaymas, 1850), 11:369
Cucamonga, 3:165-66, 169; 12:7; 17:216; 27:113, 118; *see also* Ranchos: Cucamonga
Cuddy (Placerville, 1863), 16:177
Cuesta, Ramón de la, 4:158
Cuesta grade, 38:262
Cueva, Pedro de la, 14:13
Cuevas, Mariano, 1:37; 30:279
Cull, Laurence F. and Mary (MacCormick), 9:294
Cull, Ursula, 9:294
Cullen (S.F., 1867), 11:127
Cullen, B., lawsuit, 10:180
Cullen, Charles B., 13:318
Cullen, G. P., 10:359, 368
Cullen, Michael, 15:177
Cullimore, Clarence, 33:92-93; "A California Martyr's Bones," 33:13-21; 36:15; drawing by, 36: opp. 1
Cullimore, Mrs. Clarence (Rosemary Thelen), trans. letter of Manuel Toussaint, 33:18-19
Cullum, Mrs. G. W., *see* Halleck, Mrs. Henry W.
"Cully-Bool," Mendocino Co., 30:164
Culmer, Frederick A., 26:380; " 'General' John Wilson, Signer of the Deseret Petition," 26:321-48
Culp, James D., 40:103
"Cultural Diggings at Crescent City in the 'Fifties," by Frances T. McBeth, 32:161-70
Culver, Myron, 13:3
Cumberland (ship), 18:5
Cumberland College, Sonoma, 36:349
Cum Chon, 14: opp. 209
Cumming, George and Marion (Baine), 19:286
Cumming, Joseph Moore, obit., 19:286
Cumming, Mrs. Joseph Moore (Virginia Kerr), 19:286
Cummings (S.F., 1864), 24:265
Cummings (d. ca. 1874), 18:359
Cummings, Gordon Parker, 38:32
Cummings, Rev. H., niece of, 17:83
Cummings, Richard, 4:313, 316

Cummins, Thomas, 12:138; 14:320, 336, 337, 346
Cumuchí (Indian, 1838), 16:360
Cuneo, Clorinda Agnes, 21:92-93
Cuneo, Joseph, 21:92-93
Cuneo, Rinaldo, 38:2
Cunliff, William, 26:204
Cunningham (Feather R., 1861), 10:362
Cunningham, Charles, 12:12-13, 17
Cunningham, Charles Edward, 29:298-305 *passim*
Cunningham, George Farley, 29:298, 302, 305
Cunningham, James, 28:360; 29:148
Cunningham, James, Jr., 29:298, 305
Cunningham, Joseph, 28:360
Cunningham, Lewis, 10:165, 189, 394; 14:213, 398, 401; 15:24, 29, 43, 52
Cunningham, N. C., 9:42
Cunningham, Robert B., 23:343; 38:332
Cunningham, William, 23:311, 331
Cunningham, William H., 2:235; 8:331; *The Log of the Courier*, rev., 38:371
Cunningham and Brumagim, 14:395, 398, 401
Curiel, Bernardo, 15:356
Curio, Juan de, 6:311
Curl, William H., 29:122
Curle, R. M., 30:265
Curle Bros., 30:109, 258, 265, 266
Curlew (ship), 22:174
Curran, Mrs. (ca. 1884), 32:254
Curran, Homer F., 27:239
Curran Theater, San Francisco, 27:239; *see also* Cort Theater
Curren, Bridget, 10:56
Currey, John, 9:42, 381; 10:78, 192, 195, 197; 11:22; 19:265-66; 23:295; 26:209, 210, 263, 266; 32:159
Currie, Anne H., 36:379; "Bidwell Rancheria," 36:313-25
Currier, Ezekiel, 2:121
Currier, John C., 36:105, 270
Currier & Ives, 30:355-56
Curry, Charles Forrest, 39:21, 22
Curry, Mary (Mrs. Donald B. Tressider), 22:96
Curry, Mary (Estell), "Carthay Center," 5:198; "Meetings of the Society," 6:380, 381-82
Curry County, Ore., 31:125-38 *passim*
Curse of Cain, The (play), 21:257
Curtin, John Barry, 39:21
Curtis (overland, 1849), 21:300

Curtis (Monterey, 1851), 31:313
Curtis (Napa, 1851), 2:136
Curtis, Dr. (Sacramento, 1853), 36:146
Curtis, Benjamin Robbins, 15:6, 15
Curtis, D. B., 9:269
Curtis, Elizabeth, 32:191; 36:73
Curtis, Greenleaf, 26:10
Curtis, J. C. (or J. S.), 9:42, 107
Curtis, J. W., 9:391; 10:177, 199
Curtis, James E., 26:7, 9
Curtis, James F., 6:15; 15:164; 34:245-46; 40:349
Curtis, Jotham, 10:350
Curtis, M., 13:3
Curtis, M. B., 17:48; 27:345
Curtis, Mrs. M. B. (Albina De Mer), 17:48
Curtis, Michael, 17:42
Curtis, N. Greene, 9:36, 397; 10:296; 29:340; 33:331
Curtis, Samuel T., 11:9, 21
Curtis, William, 20:115
Curtis and Shoemake Colony, 25:175
Curtisville, 13:383; 20:115
Cushing, Caleb, 15:252; 17:21; 21:120
Cushing, Charles Stuart, address, "Society of California Pioneers," 6:197-98; obit. of William F. Chipman, 18:94-95; obit., 25:89-90
Cushing, Daniel, 21:383
Cushing, G. H., 15:76
Cushing, Henry, 21:383
Cushing, I. H., 26:204
Cushing, J., 13:31
Cushing, James B., 14: opp. 209, 378, 394, 398, 399; 15:21, 23, 24, 28, opp. 40
Cushing, John, 11:171
Cushing, Mrs. John (Grace Isabel Beaver), 23:94
Cushing, John M., 21:383; 25:89
Cushing, Mrs. John M. (Ann Kennedy), 25:89
Cushing, Oscar K., 21:383; 25:89
Cushing, Robert, 8:365-66; 15:366; 16:80, 283, 336-37, 341
Cushing, Samuel A., 12:138; 14:316
Cushing, Simon, 15:76
Cushing's (Yuba Co., 1858), 9:367
Cushman, Charles A., 2:122
Cushman, Charles D., 15:275, 367
Cushman, Pauline, 40:307
Cusick, James, 15:77
Customhouse, Monterey, *see* Monterey
Customhouse, San Francisco, 13:376; 20:31; 25:345; 32:146; buildings,

3:32-33, 84; 8:267, 270; 15:270; 16:184;
17:181, 298; 22:267; 24:47-48, 70;
25:344-45; clerks, 13:299; 14:75, 76;
25:333-37 *passim*, 343, 344, 345; 26:72,
73; 30:257; law establishing, 19:165,
183
Custom House Block, San Francisco,
26:40
Customs, collectors of, 5:19; 8:100, 151;
14:346; 18:35, 65; 25:332, 337, 344, 345
Customs duties and regulations:
Mexican, 8:100, 109, 151, 291, 292,
303-4, 332; 12:151, 281; 14:327-28;
17:24, 59; 18:66; 22:319; 23:315-16,
322, 323, 324
United States, 10:25-26, 129, 143, 160;
12:142, 143; 13:376; 14:329-30;
15:269; 18:35; 22:319; 24:319-20
Custot, Octave, 8:120; 17:68
Cuteye Foster's Bar, *see* Brandy City
Cutler, Charles T., 16:183
Cutler, Charlotte Louise, *see* McAllister,
Mrs. Matthew Hall
Cutler, Fletcher Arnold, address, "The
Settlement of California," 4:399-400
Cutler, Nathan, 10:62
Cutler, Nathaniel T., 2:128
Cutler, Rufus Putnam, 10:295; 15:182;
25:341; 29:251; 34:233
Cutler, Thomas, 39:58
Cutrell, William E., 1:238; 33:254
Cutten, Charles Pryde, addresses:
"Story of the Last Expedition of
Dr. Josiah Gregg," 6:197;
"Adventures . . . in the Discovery of
Humboldt Bay," 19:375-76; account
of luncheon meeting, 8:387; bk. revs.
by, 7:408; 8:281-82; obit., 22:379-80

Cutten, David Page and Kate
(McGrath), 22:379
Cutter (Marysville, 1859), 10:166
Cutter, Donald C., 26:136; "California,
Training Ground for Spanish Naval
Heroes," 40:109-22; bk. rev. by,
40:71-73
Cutter, James H., 17:239
Cutts, A. W., 14:217, 399
Cutts, James Madison and Mrs., 11:16
Cuyamaca Club, San Diego, 35:345, 356
Cuyamaca Mountains, 26:27, 34, 53, 59;
34:194-205 *passim*; 36:119-29 *passim*
Cuyamaca Rancho State Park, 34:193,
200, 201
Cuyamaca Water Co., 34:158
Cuyama Valley, 26:57; 34:200, 201;
36:120-31 *passim*
Cuyler, M., 11:305, 306
Cuyler's Harbor, 36:223
Cyane (ship), 1:138, 231; 2:165, 168;
3:108-13 *passim*, 124; 5:297, 301; 6:277,
365-69 *passim*; 7:82, 84; 9:82; 12:37,
43, 48, 351; 17:125, 130, 149, 271, 272,
282; 19:142, 143; 20:213, 215, 232;
21:344, 350, 351, 352, 356; 22:49, 66;
25:125, 127; 26:221; 27:179; 29:157,
275; 31:210, 216; 33:233-34, 252
Cybele (ship), 31:35; 38:41
Cyclone (ship), 33:327
Cypress Point, 7:25, 26, 51, 57, 75
Cyprey, Baron Alleye de, 11:196-204
passim, 222; letter to, 11:341-46
Cypriano (Indian), 28:330, 331; *see also*
Cipriano
Cyrano de Bergerac (play), 20:138
Czapkay, Lajos J., 28:131-32, 142; 38:34

D

Dadd's Gulch, 9:57, 58, 60, 61, 65, 130,
135-40 *passim*, 143, 144, 158, 160,
161, 177
Daedalus (ship), 2:275, 282, 290, 291,
309, 310, 311, 316, 321, 331, 337; 10:325
Daegener, William, 21:96; 23:188; 25:87
Dagelet, Lepaute, 3:224
Daggett, Capt. (of *Oscar*, 1838), 14:320
Daggett (Marysville, 1852), 9:395

Daggett, John, 6:345, 353-56; 10:62, 70;
11:9; 31:137
Daggett, Rollin Mallory, 36:367, 370
Daggett's Pass, 7:8, 9; 34:215
Dague (Natividad, 1846), 29:339
Dague, Théophile, 12:61, 171, 331;
affidavit, 12:332-33
Daguerreotypes, 6:110, 111; 8:203;
9:138; 10:200; 14:157; 15:54, 305;

23:267; 28:33; 34:291-95 *passim*, 298, 344

Dahl, Count Bejarn F., 37:53, 55

Dahlberg, Harry W., 29:381

Dahlman, Charles, 21:76

Daing, Dr. (S.F., 1849), 5:17, 22-23, 26, 34, 38; 6:52

Dairying, 12:287; 20:260-71; in 1849, 12:316; in 1850s, 5:375, 377; 8:21; 15:54, 376; 20:260-63; 29:53, 173, 177; 30:239, 245; in 1870s, 25:34; 33:171; in 1905-9, 19:76; Portuguese engaged in, 35:241, 242, 243; Swiss, 30:307, 310, 311, 312

Dakin, Susanna Bryant (Mrs. Richard Y.), 25:380; obit. of Mrs. Oscar Lawler, 33:274-75; bk. rev. by, 38:379-81

Dale (ship), 2:251; 12:351; 13:272, 396; 18:375; 20:193-234 *passim;* 22:50; 24:48; 33:251, 253, 268

Dale & Co., 30:366

Daley, Charles F., 13:340-41

Daley, Thomas, 9:265

Dalgonar (ship), 22:353

Dall, John H., 35:50, 55

Dall, William Healey, 33:12, 166, 167; 35:292, 304

Dall, William L., 17:77, 80; 22:171

Dallam, Richard B., 10:291

Dallas, George Mifflin, 21:223

Dalles, The, Oregon, 22:195, 213, 216

Dalrymple map, 25:320

Dalton, Alfred P., 27:187

Dalton, Alfred P., Jr., and Hannah (Newmark), 27:187

Dalton, Dennis, 27:187

Dalton, Edward F., 27:187

Dalton, Henry (Sacramento R., d. "1820s"), 27:187

Dalton, Henry (1843), 1:250, 258; 5:408; 13:230; 17:176; 28:257

Dalton, Mrs. Henry (María de Guadalupe Zamorano), 1:258; 28:257

Dalton, Henry F., 5:407

Dalton, John E., 27:187

Daly, Henry F., 20:300

Daly, John, 7:116

Daly, John Augustin, 21:160, 174-75; 34:360

Daly, Richard H., 28:340

Daly, William, *see* Daylor

Dame, Timothy, 9:360, 362, 364, 369-74 *passim*, 389; 10:55; 14:166, 169

Dame aux camélias, La (play), 15:281; 20:131; *see also* Camille

Dame blanche, La (opera), 15:278

Dameron, James P., 29:290-92; phot., 29: opp. 289

"Dame Shirley," *see* Clapp, Louisa

Damewood, "Boston," 29:247

"Damndest Finest Ruins, The," by Lawrence W. Harris, 35:161-64

Damon, James E., 30:356, 365

Damon, John F., 17:181

Damon, Luke, 21:306

Damon, Samuel Chenery, 16:209; 19:300; 26:169; 34:319; *A Journey to Lower Oregon and Upper California, 1848-49*, rev., 7:195-96

Damon and Pythias (play), 10:386; 20:295

Dams: 3:149; 6:223, 238; 29:197-99, 361-62; 35:208; Alta, 28:236; Birdsall, 28:236; Bowman, 29:197, 198-99, (phot.) opp. 201; Brush, 28:236; at Cahuenga, 13:205; Deer Cr., 6:245; English, 28:233-39 *passim;* 29:197, 198, (phot.) foll. 200, 207; Eureka Lake Co., 28:234; Faucherie, 29:199, (phot.) foll. 200, 206; Feather R., 6:243; French, 29:197-98, (phot.) foll. 200; Jacksonville, 35:208; Klamath R., 30:340, 341, 343; Milton, 28:233, 236; 29:194; 207; in San Mateo Co., 31:301; Shasta, 36:379; Spaulding, 29:205; Tuolumne R., 35:208; wing, 6:218-19; 13:16; Yuba R., 6:215-16; 14:209; 18:154; 28:233-40 *passim*

Dana, James Dwight, 4:17; 24:321, 323

Dana, John F., 9:288

Dana, Julian, address on John A. Sutter, 14:186

Dana, Richard Henry, Jr., 8:294; 10:3; 11:77-78; 14:21-22; 100, 125, 346, 410; 15:378; 16:66; 17:292; 18:342; 23:360-61; 26:225; 32:327; 35:99; 38:27

Dana, William A., 9:26, 29

Dana, William Goodwin, 1:170, 263; 2:45-46; 9:288; 14:127; 18:163, 175, 258, 259; 23:208, 217, 218; 33:344; ranch, *see* Ranchos: Nipomo

Dana, Mrs. William Goodwin (María Josefa Carrillo), 1:170; 18:175

Dana (Joseph) & Co., 11:34, opp. 34

Dana, Mount, 4:17, 42, 55

Danaïde (ship), 8:118-19; 11:196; 12:49; 37:63, 64, 65, 72

Danberger, Maj. (Death Valley, 1850s), 21:327

Dance of Death, The, by William H. Rulofson, 35:48, 50, 52, 55, 56

Dances and dancing: fandango, 8:312; in saloons, 14:392; *see also* Indians: dances of

Dancing Feather (pilot boat), 15:185

Dane (on *Westward Ho*, 1853), 28:322

Dane, George Ezra, trans. Francisco Palou, "The Founding of the Presidio and Mission of . . . St. Francis," 14:102-10; address, "New Strikes in Old Diggings," 10:413; introd. to installment of "French Consulate in California," ed. Nasatir, 13:56-62; account of luncheon meeting, 14:186; bk. revs. by, 11:386-87; 12:176-77, 364-65; 18:373-74; obit., 20:381-82

Danes in California, 25:169-70; 30:305; *see also* Lassen, Peter; Norris, Samuel; Sherreback, Peter

Daney, Eugene, 35:345(?); 36:157

Dangers of Working Girls, The (play), 33:42

Danicheffs, The (play), 21:245

Daniel (Indian, 1836), 16:246

Daniel, Brother, 25:189; "The Old Franciscan Library at Mission San Juan Bautista," 25:133-38

Daniel, Pancho, 13:340-42

Daniel (ship), 22:353

Daniell, John, 8:41

Daniels (Indian, 1851), 36:315

Daniels, Charles, 8:202, 343

Daniels, Samuel Houston, obit., 5:102-3

Daniels, Seneca, 13:32

Daniel Webster (bark, 1850), 2:105

Daniel Webster (str., 1852), 8:16

Danites, The (play), 34:362, 364

Dannals, Charles W., 8:343

Dannals, Mrs. Charles W., 8:347

Dansas, Capt. (of *Olympe*, 1849), 13:382

"Dan Showalter—California Secessionist," by Clarence C. Clendenen, 40:309-25

Dantí, Antonio, 2:268; 14:112; 37:245, 259

Danube (ship), 13:210; 19:215

Daphne (ship), 14:298-99

Dardi, V., 37:350

Dargie, William Edward, 30:195; 35:163

Dargie, Mrs. William Edward (Herminia Peralta), 30:222, 227, 228, 230

Daridge (Davidge?; S.F., 1856), 15:255

Darien, Isthmus of, 6:306; 17:83

Darling, A. W., 32:239

Darling, George, 6:222, 225

Darling, J., 22:251

Darling, William, 19:230

Darlington (S.F., 1854), 15:183

Darlingtonia californica, 24:323, 327, 338, 340; phot., opp. 339

Darly, Nathan, 15:239

Darmont (playwright, 1891), 20:137

Darneille, E. M., 9:133, 135, 141, 143, 148, 153-65 *passim*, 173, 267; 10:57; lawsuit, 9:133, 134

Darr (Sierra Co., 1858), 19:293

Darra (ship), 22:351, 352

Darrow, Clarence, 39:85; 40:157, 158, 215

Dart, George, 28:354, 358

Dart, John Paul, letters of, ed. Howard Mitchum, 35:205-31

Dart, Mrs. John Paul (Edith McTarnahan), 35:205

Dart (ship), 8:106

Darwin, Charles Robert, 16:286; 32:251, 253-54; 36:347-48

Darwin (place), 17:214, 218; 18:200, 215; 33:265

Darwin, Mount, 4:47, 55

Dashaway Association, 10:57, 77, 276, 377, 379; 38:329

Dashaway Hall, San Francisco, 10:77, 377, 378; 36:294

Dashing Wave (ship), 15:367

"Dates of Palou's Death and Lasuén's Birth Determined," by Maynard Geiger, 28:19-22

Daughter's Vow, The (play), 15:271

Dauvray, Helen ("Little Nell"), 21:173

Davenport, Alfred, 4:320

Davenport, Eleanor Mack, obit., 20:382

Davenport, F. M., 8:342, 359, 360

Davenport, Fanny Lily Gypsy, 20:130

Davenport, Jean Margaret (Mrs. Lander), 10:75, 369; 15:273, 281, 366; 21:51, 52

Davenport, John Pope, 35:238

Davenport, Timothy Woodbridge, 17:319

Davenport, William F. and Elizabeth (Hewitt), 20:382

David, Edouard, 15:49, 53

David, Felicien, 15:164

David, Mrs. Harold, comp., "Some California Dates of 1859," 38:25-30

David, Jules, 15:262; port., 6: opp. 3
David Crockett (ship), 29:117; 33:327
Davidge, William H., 34:235, 237
David Paddock, 26:217-19, 223, 224, 230
David Scannell (yacht), 15:369
Davidson (nr. Hangtown, 1850), 26:297
Davidson (S.F., 1860), 11:10
Davidson, Benjamin, 23:339, 344; 31:42, 313, 314, 322; *see also* Davidson (B.) & Co.
Davidson, E. B., 30:359, 366
Davidson, G. Aubrey, 35:363-64; 36:69, 70, 75
Davidson, George, 1:55; 6:91, 92; 7:24, 70; 21:368; 23:122; 25:336; 26:200; 27:291, 292; 31:302, 337; 36:21; active in CHS, 1:14-21 *passim;* 11:299; 24:79; art. on, 11:299-320; list of writings, 11:314-20; U.S. Coast and Geodetic Surv., 4:42; 6:91; 7:61; 11:301-9, 313; 29:185, 186; 30:39-40, 42, 46; phot., 11: opp. 299
Davidson, Mrs. George (Ellinor Fauntleroy), 11:305
Davidson, George R., 9:26; 15:367; 16:84; 25:336, 343
Davidson, Jesse, 24:58
Davidson, John Wynn, 1:141, 238-41 *passim,* 246, 251, 254, 256, 259, 304; 13:304, 305; 21:204, 222, 224, 333; 22:46; 24:52, 53, 276, 277; 26:23, 40; 29:31, 37, 239, 242, 248; 33:112-17 *passim,* 249, 255, 267, 269, 339, 341, 343
Davidson, Peter (San Jose, 1847), 14:19
Davidson, Peter (Lucerne Valley, 1897), 27:117, 122
Davidson, Winifred, 20:287; 31:39; "The First White Children Born in California," 20:235-40
Davidson (B.) & Co. (bank), 15:272, 374; *see also* Davidson, Benjamin
Davidson's (Auburn, 1858), 9:368
Davie, John Leslie, 32:239
Davies, David, address, "History of the Sutro Tunnel," 20:83
Davies, Donald, 13:414
Davies, Jessie, 3:96
Davies, Phoebe (Mrs. Joseph R. Grismer), 35:142
Davies, William, obit., 13:414
Dávila, González; *see* González Davila
Dávila, José, 4:145-46
Davis, Col. (Santa Clara, 1850), 11:162
Davis (Placerville, 1853), 30:311
Davis (Camptonville, 1856), 9:60

Davis, Mr. and Mrs. (Nevada City, 1862), 10:385
Davis, Dr. (Philippines, 1898), 30:300
Davis, A. C., 12:138
Davis, Alfred E., 5:86; 21:327
Davis, Andrew McFarland, 1:14; 24:80
Davis, B. K., 26:239
Davis, Baalam, 9:162
Davis, Benjamin F., 29:229, 40:349
Davis, Charles, 33:363
Davis, D. A., 20:115
Davis, Daisy Anna, 2:67
Davis, Daniel C., 14:271; 33:120-22
Davis, David, 15:16
Davis, David A., 6:152
Davis, E. L., 10:41(?), 62
Davis, Edwin F., obit. of Charles F. Lambert, 38:280
Davis, Elizabeth Ann, 2:67
Davis, Erwin, 23:230, 232, 245; 29:118; 33:312
Davis, Mrs. Francis H. (Dulce Bolado), 13:35; 24:372
Davis, Frank, 8:199, 206, 207, 337-53 *passim;* 9:50, 51, 53, 54, 58, 147, 148, 262, 267, 284
Davis, George, 28:233, 241
Davis, George B., 33:297, 298, 299, 303
Davis, George H., 22:33
Davis, George R., 4:49, 50, 55
Davis, Girardus P. (or T.), 21:306
Davis, H. P., 27:93
Davis, Henry, 29:102, 106, 107, 108
Davis, Henry L., 19:150
Davis, Horace, 1:13-19 *passim,* 108; 10:414; 19:230; 38:300
Davis, Mrs. Howard (Caroline Bosqui), 21:332
Davis, Howell, 10:248-49
Davis, Isaac, 9:40; 10:296; 24:166
Davis, Isaac Elphinstone, 22:287
Davis, Jacob Z., 15:76
Davis, Jay A., 23:300
Davis, Jefferson, 9:301, 302, 337, 338, 341; 10:226, 231, 297; 11:118; 19:17-18, 178, 270, 345, 361, 363, 364; 22:200; 28:200, 216, 227, 229; 34:46, 129, 130, 131, 141; 36:317
Davis, Jerome, 1:138
Davis, John, 33:12, 149
Davis, John Calvert, 2:4, 67; 8:284; 14:209
Davis, Mrs. John Calvert (Elizabeth Ann Yount), 2:4, 63, 67; 8:284

Davis, John Calvert George Frederick and Margarethe (Claus), 2:67
Davis, John Francis, obit., 9:189
Davis, Joseph H., 5:125
Davis, L. A., 28:358
Davis, Lavinia, 29:285
Davis, Lily, 25:374
Davis, Louis W., 4:39, 55
Davis, Luther, 22:384
Davis, Mary Eliza, *see* Bucknall, Mrs. George J.
Davis, Milton F., 4:45
Davis, Morgan, 11:170; 38:308
Davis, N. H., 9:269
Davis, Nat, 28:93
Davis, Paul H., 24:380
Davis, Peter, 14:163, 164
Davis, Peter J., 30:61, 63
Davis, Phoebe, *see* Davies, Phoebe
Davis, Richard DeWarrene, 17:179; 30:93
Davis, Robert G., 31:47
Davis, S., 13:32
Davis, Sam, 2:260, 261; 20:131-36 *passim*, 142
Davis, Shelden, 6:349
Davis, Spencer, 14:223
Davis, Stephen, 20:166
Davis, Stephen and Elizabeth (Stace), 28:292
Davis, Susie Frances, 2:67
Davis, W. S., 21:235
Davis, Warren Johnson, 30:93
Davis, William, 12:223, 224, 225
Davis, William Hawley, 20:95; "Emerson the Lecturer in California," 20:1-11
Davis, William Heath [Sr.], 14:127, 128; 23:208, 217
Davis, Mrs. William Heath [Sr.] (née Holmes), 14:127
Davis, William Heath [Jr.], 1:170; 3:30; 4:154, 172, 173; 5:407; 8:124-25; 11:135, 143; 12:140, 281; 13:51-52, 230; 14:22, 125, 127, 128, 202, 324-26, 337, 342-45 *passim*; 15:236; 16:76; 17:54, 141, 292, 295, 297; 25:374; 27:105, 319; 28:198; 30:51, 226, 321; 33:342, 344; 34:119, 121; 38:39, 41, 42; art. on, 31:33-48; *Seventy-five Years in California*, rev., 8:183-85
Davis, Mrs. William Heath [Jr.] (María de Jesús Estudillo), 25:374; 31:33, 38, 45, 46
Davis, William Lyle, 29:145

Davis, William Newell, Jr., 21:288; 31:189; 36:111; "State of Jefferson," 31:125-38; "The Territory of Nataqua," 21:225-38; as address, 21:184
Davis (J. M.) & Co., lawsuit, 9:66
Davis & Ray, 22:38; 30:367
Davison, H., 14:177, 182; 15:174
Davison, H. B., 30:261, 267
Davison, John P. J., 29:291
Davison, Warren, 29:381
Davison, Warren W., 29:381
Davy, J. Burtt, 32:258
Dawes (S.F., 1849), 27:366
Dawley, Isaac N., 9:381
Dawn and the Dons, by Ford, rev., 6:195-96
Dawson, Ernest, 26:378
Dawson, Emma Frances, obit. by Helen Throop Purdy, 5:87
Dawson, Hartwell, 35:206, 210, 216
Dawson, Henry, 35:206, 210, 216
Dawson, James, 14:130; 17:145
Dawson, Mrs. James (Antonia Cáceres), 14:130
Dawson, Leo, 40:218
Dawson, Nicholas, 14:18-19; 18:33-34; *Narrative*, rev., 12:176-77
Dawson, P. W., 35:210, 212
Dawson, William L., *The Birds of California*, rev., 3:298
Dawson House, Sacramento, 9:255-59 *passim*, 280; 10:64; illus., 9: opp. 258
Day, Clinton, 25:93
Day, David G., 27:364-65; 28:61, 64
Day, Francis, 5:309, 310
Day, Hannibal, 10:192; 11:106-12 *passim*, 117, 121, 122, 123
Day, Henry C., 15:165, 168
Day, J. M., 9:113
Day, John (Ore., 1814), 24:232
Day, John (Calif., 1849), 11:118, 123
Day, John S., 1:216-17, 223, 224
Day, Roger S., 16:32, 39, 42
Day, Sherman, 4:11; 7:7-9, 17, 18, 19; 9:46; 14:163-64; 15:269; 25:93
Day, Thomas, 21:159
Day, W. C., 4:35
Day after the Fair (play), 23:101
Day after the Wedding (play), 15:48
"Day Journal of Milton S. Latham, The," ed. Edgar E. Robinson, 11:3-28
Daylor, William (Cosumnes R., 1844), 2:195; 13:75-76, 79; mill of, 2:185;

13:74, 75, 159, 174; 34:22; ranch of, 1:149; 13:79

Daylor, William, letter from Jamestown (1849), 24:345

Daynes, Mrs. Grace J., 30:382

Days, Antonia, 25:169

Days of '49, by Young, rev., 5:312-15

Dayton, Dello G., 37:380; 38:88; "Polished Boot and Bran New Suit," 37:359-68; 3:17-23

Dayton, Nev., 32:197, 203

Dayton, Ohio, company from, 22:131

D. C. Hawkins (ship), 17:80

Dead Heart, The (play), 10:360, 369

Deadman (lawsuit, 1861), 10:275, 356

Deadman's Cut, Nevada Co., 3:145; 11:233

Dead Man's Island, 3:118; 13:303; 16:66; illus., 13: opp. 301; *see also* Anniversary Island

Dead Men's Point, *see* Muertos, Punta de los

Dead Shot, The (play), 15:48

Deadwood (mining camp), 16:39

"Dead wood" (mining term), 3:136-39 *passim*

Deady, Matthew Paul, 21:128, 158; 25:257, 263

Deaf and Dumb Asylum, 36:297, 306

Deakin, Alfred, 26:280

Deal, David, 32:55, 132; 33:373

Deal, Mrs. David, 32:55, 126-27

Deal, William Grove, 15:45; 26:169

Dealing, O. W., 9:309

Deamer, William White, 37:60-61

Dean, Anne, 28:292

Dean, Daniel, 8:202, 205, 340; 9:57, 135, 137, 143, 145, 261, 348; 11:55, 57

Dean, James S., 33:329

Dean, Julia, *see* Hayne, Julia (Dean)

Deane, Dorothy (Newell), *Sierra Railway*, rev., 40:249-50

De Angelis, Johnny, 4:62; 21:166

De Angelis, Thomas Jefferson, 4:62, 63, 302

Deans, William C., 27:222

Dearborn, Capt. (*City of Pekin*, 1887), 17:38, 39

Deardoff (lawsuit, Marysville, 1859), 10:186

Deardorff, William G. C. R., 26:298

"Dear Yesterdays in San Buena Ventura," address by Myrtle S. Francis, 13:188-89

Deaths, ordinance for registry of, 15:268

Death Valley, 2:178; 13:314; 17:356; 19:186; art. on, 18:195-216; bks. about, 7:89-90; 9:186; 11:294; 16:185; 18:180, 283; 19:78, 373; 20:81, 374; 21:80

Death Valley, by Lee, rev., 9:186

Death Valley in '49, by Manly, ed. Quaife, rev., 7:89-90

Death Valley, the Facts, by Chalfant, rev., 9:186

Deaves, E., 20:305

Debating societies, *see* Lyceums; Ugly Club

De Blois, Capt. (Colorado R. 1863), 22:170

De Boom, Cornelius, 27:142

Debs, Eugene Victor, 40:215

De Camp, John, 35:329

Decatur (ship), 15:376

Deception Creek, 22:323, 335; 23:132; *see also* Butte Creek

Dechamp, A., 22:328, 336, 347, 348; 23:24

Dechanet (S.F., 1849), 5:30-31, 354-55, 373; 6:56

Dechezelles, A., 39:314

Decker, Malcolm, 23:94

Decker, Peter, 10:247; 14:401

Decker & Hite, 10:193

Decker & Jewett; Decker, Jewett & Co.; Decker, Jewett & Paxton; Decker-Jewett Bank, 9:72; 10:191, 370; 14:401

Declaration of Rights, California Constitution, and sigs., 10: opp. 159

Decoto, Ezra, address, "A Buggy Ride in 1854 in Alameda County," 18:184-85

De Courcelle, *see* Naudet

De Courcey, Henry A., 15:174; 39:4

Deep Creek, Mono Co., 26:235

Deep Sea Derby, 26:226-27

Deer, 1:113, 114; 2:284; 3:360; 5:112, 114, 128, 137, 138, 264, 265; 8:241; 10:213; 12:290, 293, 305; 13:20, 29, 68-69; 14:103-4; 20:40, 41; 22:200, 205-12 *passim*, 325, 330-43 *passim*; 23:29-33 *passim*, 38, 124, 128-35 *passim*, 141, 297; *see also* Animals, wild

Deer Creek, Nevada Co., 3:129; 6:245-46; 13:27; 19:146-47; 29:195; 30:125, 126; 33:55

Deer Creek, Tehama Co., 18:296-300

passim, 311; 20:10; 22:212, 217; 23:133

Deer Creek, Tulare Co., *see* Moore's Creek

Deer Creek and Coyote Water Co., 11:237

Deer Creek Dry Diggings, 8:359; 11:236; 30:125, 126; *see also* Nevada City

Deer Creek House, 8:201

Deer Creek Mining Co., 11:237

Deering, Alexander, 4:24

Deering, Charles Jameson, obit., 12:88

Deering, Frank Prentiss, 25:230, 232; obit. of John B. Farish, 8:388; obit., 18:188-89

Deering, James S. H., 20:115

Deetkin & Chappellet, 18:155

Defenbaugh, James, 9:245

Defender (riv. str.)., 16:183, 184, 282, 285, 341; *see also Goliah*

Defiance (riv. str.), 10:285, 297, 364, 371

De Ford, Miriam Allen, 33:188, 284; "Palo Alto's 'Mysterious Frenchman,'" 33:169-74

De Forest, Charles N., 9:96

De Fremery, James, 26:232, 381; 31:337

De Fremery, Leon, 26:381

Degnan, John, 30:284

Degnan, Laurence V., 30:284

De Golyer, Everette Lee, 33:189-90; obit., 36:86

De Groot, Henry, 12:11; 26:233; his map of Nevada, 34:212-13

De Haga, J., 10:265

Dehon, J. T. 15:176, 179

Deidesheimer, Philip, 2:206

Deighan, J. P., 9:170, 181, 243-46 *passim*, 250, 251, 252, 258, 261, 371, 372, 394

Deighton, Elizabeth, 28:293

Deirup, Harry, 36:321

De Lachapelle, *see* Lachapelle

Delafield, Richard, 9:302

Delafond (S.F., 1850), 6:38

Delafont, L., 16:341

Delatie, George, 2:122

Delamarre, *see* Lamarre, de

Delaney, Charles McC., 16:341

Delaney, John, 21:306

Delaney, Pat, 4:27

Delano, Alonzo, 13:185, 186; 15:301, 378; 18:312; 22:30, 38; 30:191, 258, 260, 265, 266, 358; 34:359, 360;

38:38, 115, 352; Delano & Co., 6:334; 12:65

De Latour, Mrs. Georges (Fernande Romer), 21:192

Delavan, James C., 6:332, 334; 10:83 (?); 12:65-71 *passim*

Delaware (ship), 22:171

"Delayed Discovery of San Francisco Bay, The," by H. F. Raup, 27:289-96

Delehanty, William M., 21:169

Deleissèques, Olivier, 8:120; 11:205, 206, 209; 12:41, 44, 46, 333; 13:365, 381

Delemater, Theodore, 8:346

Delgada, Punta, 10:330; *see also* Arena, Point

Delgado, Carl, 36:322

Delger, Frederick, 26:90

De Lisle, Joseph Nicolas, 1:192; 9:201, 202

Dellenbaugh, Frederick S., 7:88; art. on, 14:347-49

Del Mar, Alexander, 27:345-47

Delmas, Delphin Michael, 35:259-60; 38:49

Delmas, Mrs. Delphin Michael, *see* Hoge, Pauline

Delmira, 14:345; 17:296

Delmonico's restaurant, San Francisco, 3:38

Del Monte, 7:117; *see also* Hotel Del Monte

Del Norte (ship), 26:9

Del Norte County, 19:370; 31:126, 127; 34:270, 271; military posts, 26:1-11

Del Norte Investigator, 32:163

De Long, Charles Egbert, 4:269; 15:333; 30:359; "California's Bantam Cock," Journals of, ed. Carl I. Wheat, 8:193-213, 337-63; 9:50-80, 129-81, 243-87, 345-97; 10:40-78, 165-201, 245-97, 355-95; 11:47-64; defendant in lawsuits, 9:62, 145; phot., 8: opp. 193; 10: opp. 245, opp. 378; fac. pp. of journal, 10: opp. 355

De Long, Mrs. Charles Egbert, *see* Vineyard, Elida

De Long, Francis, 9:277

De Long, James Reid, 8:193, 203-6, 212, 342, 348, 352; 10:253, 265, 385, 395; cor., 11:53-64

De Long, John, 10:43

De Long family, 8:198; 9:150, 156

Del Poyo, Macias, 6:310

Del Real, *see* Real

Delta, Visalia, 10:309; 20:162, 164
Del Valle, Antonio, 14:235; 15:341, 356
Del Valle, Ignacio, 13:231, 313, 318, 327,
  349; 14:235; 15:341, 347, 348; 16:360,
  366, 367; 31:287
Del Valle, Joaquín, 15:349
Del Valle, Lucretia, *see* Grady, Mrs.
  Henry F.
Del Valle, Luis, 18:16-17; 27:207;
  35:320-22
Del Valle, Reginaldo Francisco, 13:327;
  31:287; 32:185; 33:375
De Massey, Ernest, *see* Massey,
  Ernest de
Dement, William C., 4:350
Demming, Andrew, 18:206-7
Democrat, Mariposa, art. from,
  1:273-85
Democrat, Nevada City, 30:360
Democrat, Stockton, 20:162
Democratic Party, 3:39, 153-55, 168;
  5:94, 286-87, 311; 6:7; 8:194, 204, 206,
  344, 358-61 *passim*, 364-65; 9:24-29
  passim; 34, 35, 36, 39, 43-48 *passim*,
  62-65 *passim*, 71, 72-73, 94, 103-16
  passim, 114, 115, 116, 150-51, 157, 158,
  173, 177, 178, 261, 269-74 *passim*, 285,
  347-56 *passim*, 377-87 *passim*, 391,
  394-95; 10:25, 26, 29, 40, 41, 61, 72,
  75-78 *passim*, 166-73 *passim*, 191-200
  passim, 249-69 *passim*, 277, 281, 287,
  290, 295, 355-59 *passim*, 367, 368, 369,
  383; 11:3-28 *passim*, 173; 15:5, 28-30,
  33, 174, 202, 204-5, 280, 281, 371, 374;
  16:80, 81, 82; 17:44-45, 179, 309-15
  passim; 19:59-73 *passim*, 147, 167,
  173-74; 256, 261, 264-69 *passim*, 276,
  347, 351-54, 360, 364; 20:109, 158, 160,
  270, 333-37 *passim*, 366; 21:25, 30-32,
  131, 132, 133, 379; 22:223, 227-32
  passim, 358; 24:169, 170, 171; 27:316,
  317, 356; 28:47-53 *passim*, 58, 59, 60,
  153-54; 30:128-29, 130; 31:193, 194,
  196, 200; 32:145-59 *passim*, 295, 299,
  301, 315, 317, 320-23 *passim*; 35:225;
  37:171, 173, 174; 38:204-5, 239, 244,
  349-57 *passim*; 39:300
Northern wing ("Tammany"), 3:155;
  6:5; 8:364; 9:25, 45, 119, 177, 271,
  285; 10:386
Southern wing ("Chivalry"), 3:155,
  168; 8:364; 9:25, 119, 177, 285, 379;
  10:356, 367; 31:194; 32:223
see also Democratic Party conventions;
  Democrats

Democratic Party conventions: city,
  9:25; 15:171, 172; county, 8:204;
  9:53, 63, 71, 384-85; 10:59, 60, 77, 78,
  253, 254, 266, 283, 356, 357, 383, 385;
  15:29, 377; 16:80, 81; national (1932),
  39:132; state, 3:83, 153-55; 6:7; 8:204;
  9:25, 26, 43-44, 53, 54, 72-73, 104, 115;
  10:254, 283, 266, 355-56, 367; 15:166,
  167, 279, 366, 368, 369; 16:345-46;
  31:195, 196, 200; 38:357
Democratic Press, San Francisco,
  20:156, 165
Democratic Standard, Sacramento,
  30:129
Democratic State Central Committee,
  10:19, 266, 281, 295, 356, 357
Democratic State Journal, Sacramento,
  9:39, 248, 250, 274; 15:164
Democrats:
  "Anti-Electionists," 9:25-29 *passim*;
    15:166, 167, 174
  "Anti-Lecomptonites," 8:194; 9:243,
    271-72, 274, 379, 381-87 *passim*,
    394-95; 10:40, 41, 61, 62, 63, 66,
    72, 75-78 *passim*, 173, 191-97 *passim*,
    259; 15:205; 21:31; 31:194; 32:322
  "Bone and Sinew," 9:25, 27, 29;
    15:172
  Breckinridge, 9:64, 65; 10:252, 253,
    265, 283, 356, 357, 367, 383
  Broderick ("Tammany"), 9:119, 177
  "Chivalry," 9:119, 177, 285; 10:367;
    31:194; 32:223
  Douglas, 9:379; 10:367; 31:194
  "Electionists," 9:25, 26, 29; 15:166,
    167
  Lecomptonites, 9:271-72, 273, 278,
    285, 353, 384-85, 387, 391; 10:40, 51,
    60, 62, 63, 66, 71-77 *passim*, 173, 179,
    191, 192, 195, 261; 11:22; 15:205;
    21:31; 31:194
  "Mudsills," 9:347, 379, 385, 387
  "Rosewater," 8:364; 9:25, 26-27, 29
  see also Democratic Party
De Mofras, Eugène, *see* Duflot de
  Mofras
Demorande, Rey, 22:301
De Mott, John, 8:347; & Co., 8:361;
  9:173
Dempfill, Capt. (Benicia, 1863), 9:308
Dempster, Clancy J., 21:37
Den, Nicholas Augustus, 2:255; 4:157,
  164; 6:4; 18:71, 259, 276; 36:10; port.,
  4: opp. 158
Den, Richard Somerset, 2:199; 4:157,

163-66, 177; 17:24; 18:68, 71, 267; 33:103, 106; port., 4: opp. 158

Denervaud, Calixte and Maybelle Elizabeth (Neall), 31:286

Denervaud, Marie, *see* Dun, Marie

Denger, Catherine, 21:384

Denham, James, 15:180

Denhardt, Robert Moorman, 20:384; "Driving Livestock East from California Prior to 1850," 20:341-47

Denhardt, Thornton T., 33:284-85

Denin, Kate, 15:163; 21:152, 251, 256

Denin, Susan, 15:88

Denio, W. F., 15:280

Denison, Capt. (from Ohio, 1850), 24:243

Denison, Charles W., 31:238

Denison, Ella (Strong), 36:149-50

Denit, Daniel, 14:278

Denkichi (Japanese, S.F., 1851), 23:336

Denman, Frank Hardenbergh, 22:288

Denman, James, 16:283

Denman, William, 38:354; 39:22, 131

Denman Grammar School, San Francisco, 27:280

Dennett, Lewis L., 38:251

Denney (overland, 1850), 3:49, 51

Dennis, Ed M., 13:296

Dennis, Thomas, 18:261

Dennis, W. E., 15:364

Dennis, William, 15:175; 17:172

Dennis Martin Creek, 31:301

Dennison (Marysville, 1851), 15:54

Dennison (S.F., 1854), 15:181

Dennison, Ammi P., 20:44

Dennison, Samuel, 27:264, 266; 28:59, 66; *see also* Dennison's Exchange

Dennison (or Denison), Thomas, 33:6, 7, 12, 161, 167; 35:302, 304; phot., 33: opp. 1

Dennison's Exchange, San Francisco, 3:39; 23:70; 27:264, 266, 365

Denny, Mrs. and Miss (Sacramento, 1859), 10:42

Denny, G. J., 24:266; painting by, 12: opp. 217

Denny, M. E., 11:176

Densmore, Dr. (Long Beach, ca. 1900), 31:16

Dent (Mormon Bat., 1847), 22:52

Dent, Capt. (Knight's Ferry, 1859), 10:198

Dent, Miss (Stockton., 1859), 10:44

Dent, George W., 10:44, 62, 67; 11:8, 9

Dent, Mrs. George W., 10:45

Dent, Lewis, 10:153; fac. sig., 10: opp. 159

Dentists and dentistry, 14:396-97; 15:54; 17:181; 18:65, 68-69, 76, 288; College, 30:67

Denton, Samuel H., 25:223

Dent's Crossing, 28:330

Denver, Arthur St. Clair, 10:62, 387; 11:8, 9; 27:282

Denver, Frank (Sacramento, 1855), 9:36; 11:11 (?)

Denver, Frank (Farallone Is., 1855), 11:11 (?); 16:339

Denver, James William, 3:153-54; 10:75, 167, 191, 257, 268, 274; 11:6, 8, 21, 23, 173; 14:346; 15:167, 204, 205, 206; 16:84, 184; 19:261; 24:274; 30:161; 32:148-49, 158, 224; 34:150, 153

Denz, John B., 24:35

De Peyster, Nicholas, 22:251; 23:254, 255; 27:251

Depot Hill, 9:64, 77

Depot Hill Ditch and Mining Co., 9:78

Depouey, Henri, 39:150

Depp, John, 24:55

Deppe, Ferdinand, 23:319, 333

Depressions (financial): of early 50's, 11:54-55, 58; of 1878, 21:248

De Pue, Edgar J., 25:232

De Quille, Dan (pseud.), *see* Wright, William

De Quine (Death Valley, 1850), 18:198

Derbec, Etienne, 16:344; 22:300, 310; 32:112-15 *passim*, 301; 35:131, 343 (?); 39:15-16, 141-43, 152, 161, 164-70 *passim*, 232, 238; 40:296; cartoon, 39: opp. 144; letter of, 22:310-11

Derbec Blue Gravel Mining Co., 39:170

Derby, Emma C., "Diary of . . . European Tour . . . 1867," 31:219-28, 355-74; 32:65-80

Derby, George H., 30:108; 31:220

Derby, Mrs. George H. (Cecilia Bancroft), 31:220, 222, 369, 371

Derby, George Horatio, 9:193, 194, 197, 200; 12:367; 13:402; 15:374; 19:229, 230; 22:3, 7, 168; 24:59-62 *passim*, 72, 275; 30:252, 354, 358; 38:115; "Topographical Reports," ed. Francis P. Farquhar, 11:99-123, 247-65, 365-82; maps by, 11: opp. 99, opp. 102, opp. 247, opp. 365, 380

Derby, Howard W., 26:163

Derby, J. C., 31:221, 222
Derby, Orin, 15:366, 367
Derby, Roger Alden, 28:224
Derby (George H.) & Co., 30:107-8; 31:220
Derby & Jackson, 30:365
Derby (ship), 12:221
Derham, B., 9:26
Derickson, Ben, 28:238, 242
De Ro, Charles, 19:232
Deroches (S.F., 1854), 14:74
Derrick, Henry, 16:80
Derrick, S. R., 22:251
Derrickson, S. L., 22:251
De Russy, René E., 33:230, 231, 234
"Descent on California in 1683, The," Henry R. Wagner, 26:309-19
Deschamp, A., 23:24
Deschutes River, 23:144
Descubierta (ship), 3:217-18, 232-34, 236; 15:214
Deseret, Mormon state, 22:12; 26:327; petition, 329-32
Desert (Rosamond) Lake, 17:105, 209
Desert Springs, Kern Co., 17:208, 209
Desert Voices, a Descriptive Bibliography, by Edwards, rev., 38:77-80
Deshayes, Léon, *see* Barra
Deshler, James, 27:215; 30:161
Desiertas, Islas, *see* Coronados
Desmarais, Léon, 18:17
De Smet, Pierre-Jean, 23:290; 29:140, 145
Des Pointes, Adm. (1854), 15:176, 179, 180
Destruction Island, 10:325
"Determination of the Birthdays of Urban Communities," by J. N. Bowman, 27:51-62, 104; 31:325-33
Detreville (Stockton, 1892), 34:351, 354
Detweiler, Jacob, *Autobiography*, rev., 2:83-84
"Deuteronomy Brown," by Charles B. Turrill, 6:169-80
Deutsch, Lenna A., ed. *Mercer's Belles*, rev., 40:255-56
Deutsch, Mrs. Michael (Ida Lilienfeld), 34:377
Deutsch, Monroe Emanuel, 9:293; 24:380; obit., 34:377
Deuxchands Hotel, San Francisco, 14:140
De Vancij, Gaspard, *see* Vancij
De Veer, Daisy Williamson, *The*

Story of Rancho San Antonio, rev., 4:93
D'Evani, L., 9:177; 15:367; 16:183, 283
"Development of Transportation Routes in the Clear Lake Area," by Fredrick J. Simoons, 32:363-71
Devere, William, *see* Divier, William
Devil's Cellar (Yosemite Valley), 23:368
Devil's Gate, 3:53; 4:136; 6:113, 117; 22:136, 149
Devil's Postpile National Monument, 4:52
Devil's River, 18:105, 110, 112, 133
Devine, P. J., 10:270
Devine, Preston, 26:381-82
De Vire, *see* Divier
Devoe (Gila R., 1849), 1:70
Devoe, Benjamin O., 23:74
Devoe, James B., 13:297; 20:335; 23:163; 30:132
De Voll, H. H., 31:48
De Voto, Bernard, 24:17
De Vries, Marion, 28:51
Dewell, Benjamin, 17:240; 24:58
Dewey, George, 7:383; 30:296; 31:62, 66
Dewey, John, 37:44
Dewey, Squire P., 19:231; 38:298; lawsuit, 16:343
Dewey, Mrs. Squire P., (Mary E.), 19:229
Dewey & Co., 31:337
De Witt, Frederic M., 3:95; obits. of Ilo R. Aikin, 9:189; Mrs. John C. Hays, 3:399; reps. of Exhibit Com., 4:99-101, 212-13, 303; 5:100, 206-7, 418; 6:106; 7:99; 8:93; obit., 23:90-91
De Witt, Susan, 30:66
De Witt, Kittle & Co., 29:106
De Wolf (S.F., 1855), 16:282
Dexter (S.F., 1855), 15:375
Dexter, Asa, 21:383
Dexter, Henry Cushing, 21:383
Dexter, P. B., 19:152; 25:6
Deyerle, Charles P., 33:344; 34:27, 30, 32; letter from, 34:24-25
De Young Charles, 21:144, 153; 35:144; 37:223-24
De Young, Gustavus, 21:153
De Young, Michel Henry, 19:64; 30:195; 34:375; 37:224; 38:354; 40:42
De Young, Mrs. Michel Henry (Katherine Deane), 35:163
De Young family, 35:162

De Young (M. H.) Memorial Museum, 31:377

Dezaux, P., 39:159

D'Heureuse (Whitney surv., 1860s), 4:15

Dhualle (ship), 23:211, 212, 218

Dia, José, 31:333

Diablo, Mount, 12:26; 27:157

Diamond (worked for Sutter, 1848), 14:278

Diamond (ship), 18:311; 28:251

Diamond Springs 8:201, 210; 9:39; 26:122; 30:36; 32:141; hotel, 6:239; letter from, 24:260

Diana (brig, 1835), 12:140, 142, 144; 14:317-18, 341-42; 33:376

Diana (Russian frigate, 1855), 16:83

Diana (Confed. ship, 1863), 6:33

"Diana, The," gambling house, San Francisco, 21:40

"Diary of a Trip from Ione to Nevada in 1859, The," by Susan M. Hall, 17:75-80

"Diary of a 'Used-up' Miner, Jacob Henry Bachman, The," ed. Jeanne S. Van Nostrand, 22:67-83

"Diary of Emma C. Derby ... European Tour ... 1867," 31:219-28, 355-74; 32:65-80

Diary of Johann August Sutter, The, ed. Watson, rev., 11:386-87

Diary of Philip Leget Edwards, The, rev., 12:176-77

Dias, Cristobal, 13:155, 157

Días, Juan and Mrs., 37:201

Diaz, Benito, 24:47; land claim, 19:357

Diaz, François (or Francisco), 5:372

Díaz, Juan M., 33:13, 15, 16, 19

Díaz, Manuel, 3:182, 275-88 *passim*; 4:81-82, 378-80; 10:100, 103-4; 13:78; 35:103, 105, 107, 110

Díaz, Melchor, 6:300-301; 36:220

Díaz de la Vega, Benito, 37:111, 117, 119, 242-48 *passim*

Díaz de la Vega, Rómulo, 21:210, 223; 23:262, 263, 267, 268

Díaz del Castillo, Bernal, 1:38, 41, 49; 3:311, 312; 6:304

Dibble, A. B., 9:42, 103, 106, 354

Dibble, A. P., 22:17

Dibblee, Albert, 20:192; 22:24, 383; 25:90; 36:110

Dibblee, Benjamin Harrison, 20:192; obit., 25:90-91

Dibblee, Harrison, Jr., 22:383

Dick (Yokayo Indian), 26:210-15 *passim*

Dickenson (Marysville, 1858), 9:346

Dickenson (or Dickinson), Gallant Duncan, 35:108, 116

Dickenson Gulch, 35:116

Dickerson, Charles A., 20:44

Dickerson, T. L., 15:325-28

Dickey, H. W. K., 20:114

Dickey, J. H., 9:366, 367; 10:177

Dickey, William, 16:58; 36:314

Dickie, George William, 25:44, 49-51

Dickie, James, 25:44

Dickinson (Ft. Vancouver, 1850), 2:128

Dickinson, Charles, 15:275

Dickinson, D., 13:32

Dickinson, Daniel Stevens, 19:267

Dickinson, H. W., 22:147

Dickinson, J., 13:32

Dickinson, William B., 10:62; 11:6, 7, 9, 21

Dickinson's (Dickenson's?) Ferry, 12:6

Dickinson's gambling house, Stockton, 18:267

Dickinson Type Foundry, 34:346

Dickman, Charles, 37:30

Dickman, William, 15:305

Dickmann, Mrs. Richard C. (Grace Baash), 33:381

"Dicksburgh," 12:76

Dick's Creek, 11:252

Dickson, Edward Augustus, 22:288

Dickson, Z. L., 13:32

Dickson, De Wolf & Co., 16:282

Dictionary of the American Indian, by Stoutenburgh, Jr., rev., 39:274

"Did the Chinese Discover America?" by Douglas S. Watson, 14:47-58

Did You Ever Send Your Wife to the Mission Dolores? (play), 28:36

Dido (ship), 16:79

Die, *see* Dye, Job Francis

Diego, Francisco García, *see* García Diego y Moreno

Diehl, Israel S., 6:74; 32:132-33

Dietrich, Mrs. Francis Joseph (Henrietta Flora Mann), 31:276

Dietz, David, 23:226

Diffendorf (Sacramento, 1861), 10:280

Diggs, Annie, 19:63, 66, 72; 27:315

Digraw (Sacramento, 1849), 29:257

Dill, William, 5:330; 28:331, 334

Dillaway, Joseph B., 20:44

Dille, Elbert R., 31:7

Dillingham, John, 31:152
Dillon, Charles, 10:376, 389; 21:54
Dillon, Edward, 27:217, 220-21
Dillon, Guillaume Patrice, *see* Dillon,
    Patrick
Dillon, Henry C., 19:62, 72
Dillon, John (Double Springs, 1849),
    11:177-78
Dillon, John (San Jose, 1850), 13:256,
    257
Dillon, Nathan and Zilpha (Van
    Leuren), 27:189
Dillon, Patrick (Guillaume Patrice),
    5:229, 344, 349; 6:42, 47, 157; 12:157;
    13:380, 385; 15:370; 16:83; 17:85, 169,
    174; 18:11, 16, 17; 27:144, 203, 207-14
    passim, 369; 29:161; 31:140, 147, 148,
    314, 317, 320; 32:113-14; 33:130;
    39:141, 145, 150, 324; art. on,
    35:309-24; letter to, 31:143-45
Dillon, Mrs. Patrick, 15:183; 35:323
Dillon, Richard Hugh, 28:188; 37:188;
    40:160; "Costs of the Modoc War,"
    28:161-64, 386; "Rejoice Ye Thieves
    and Harlots!," editorials of James
    King of William, 37:137-69; bk. revs.
    by, 38:373-74; 39:367-68; ed. Harris,
    The Gila Trail, rev., 40:160-62
Dillon, Sydney D., 36:97, 105, 273, 274
Dillon and Gross, Stockton, 10:67
Dime House, San Francisco, 22:265
Dimmick, Kimball Hale, 19:7; 29:234,
    235, 242, 245; fac. sig., 10: opp. 159
Dimond, Charles, 31:233
Dimond, Denis S., Jr., 30:222, 228
Dimond, Edwin Rudolph, 25:232; obit.,
    12:371-72
Dimond, Mrs. Edwin Rudolph (Harriet
    Newton), 12:371; obit., 13:288
Dimond, F. M., 18:221
Dimond, W. H., 12:371
Dimond: Boys' Club, 30:228; Canyon,
    30:6, 9, 10; Park, 30:227
Dingley, Charles L., 21:96; obit., 21:379
Dingman, D. V., 8:352, 353; 9:50, 69,
    345; *see also* Dingman & Co.;
    Dingman's
Dingman, Jim, 9:348
Dingman, O. H., 10:181; lawsuit *v.*
    Bursk, 10:180
Dingman & Co., lawsuits, 9:130, 131,
    166
Dingman's (Yuba Co., 1854, 1857),
    8:208; 9:130, 138
Dinkelspiel (L.) & Co., 31:297

Di Nola, A., 31:185
Dinsmore (Yuba City, 1858), 9:368
Dinsmore, William B., 2:216
Dionne, Comte de, 22:299
Dionoske (Japanese, S.F., ca. 1851),
    23:336
Diosdado, Antonio, 25:309
Diplomacy (play), 21:246
"Diplomatic Incident on the Little
    Mariposa, A," by George Cosgrave,
    21:358-62
Dippel, Andreas, 25:252
Diputación, see California legislature,
    Mexican period
Disappointment, Cape, 8:99; 9:235;
    10:326, 327; 17:135
"Disbanded Volunteer" (pseud.),
    24:258
Disciples of Christ (Campbellites),
    16:133; 26:170; 27:124
Discovery (ship), 2:265, 280, 282, 284,
    291, 292, 300, 301, 305, 317, 321, 327,
    334, 337; 10:325; 14:111, 112; 15:59, 60
"Discovery of California, The," by
    Henry R. Wagner, 1:36-56
"Discovery of Gold in California, The,"
    address by Robert E. Cowan, 5:95-96
"*Discovery of Gold in California, The,*"
    by Rickard, rev., 7:199
Discovery of the Oregon Trail, The,
    by Stuart, ed. Rollins, rev., 15:191
Diseases: 30:26-27; asthma, 14:78; 31:19;
    catarrh, 33:250, 251, 260; croup,
    11:147-48; *delirium tremens*, 26:320;
    diarrhea, 22:124, 128; 24:352;
    diphtheria, 5:146-49; epidemic of
    1833, 23:20-22, 131; hydrophobia,
    2:59-60; influenza, 20:358; 22:51-52;
    lues, 4:151; malaria, 19:118; measles,
    4:152; 12:13; 21:4; 24:237; 30:292;
    mumps, 30:297; Oroya fever, 17:202,
    359; Panama fever, 24:263; 14:377;
    phthisis, 4:147, 151; pneumonia,
    12:253; remittent fever, 33:252, 258;
    rheumatism, 24:349; scarlatina, 4:152;
    syphilis, 18:68; 23:252; tuberculosis,
    4:147; 8:82-83; 31:13-31 *passim*;
    typhus, 9:238; yellow fever, 39:101;
    see also Cholera; Dysentery; Scurvy;
    Smallpox; Typhoid
Disque (Dutch Flat, 1875), 18:360
"Distinguished Editorial Service," by
    Anson S. Blake, 37:92
"Distressingly Virtuous Isaac [Cox],
    The," by Alice B. Maloney, 21:127-40

Disturnell map, 19:217, 218

Ditches, mining, *see* Canals

Divier, Andrew, 9:144, 169, 347

Divier, William, 6:49; 23:71, 72, 73

Divine, Davis, 14:163-64

Diving bell (1855), 17:84

Division of California (prop.), 10:51, 74, 151; 11:24; 13:346; 28:373; 31:125-26, 136-37, 319-20; 32:162; 38:26; *see also* Nataqua, Klamath, Colorado, Jefferson

Divorces, 23:174; Act concerning, 10:252, 277

Dix (courier, 1846), *see* Dye, Job Francis

Dix, Capt. (of *Cheshire*, 1850), 6:206, 207-8

Dixon (Ft. Ross ranch, 1860s), 12:200

Dixon (Fresno, 1875), 25:27

Dixon, George, 18:337, 345

Dixon, John, 9:50, 64, 65, 77, 167, 178

Dixon, Maynard Lafayette, 37:26, 30-31; 38:2-3, 7

Dixon, W. L., 27:263

Doak, Thomas W., 16:325-26, 330, 332; 29:25

Doan (Colusa, 1860), 10:248

Doane, Charles, 8:369-70; 14:353

Doane, Seth, 14:300-302

Dobbie, Alexander Malcolm, 21:288; 23:260

Dobbie, Lucie Elise Northup, 20:384, 21:288

Dobbin, James Cochran, 31:213, 214, 217

Dobbins, Bill (Indian), 20:355, 356, 364

Dobbins, Marcus ("Mark") D., 8:213; 9:265, 389; 10:181, 199, 200, 360, 361, 367, 369, 372, 387

Dobbins, William M., 8:213; 15:34

Dobbins' Ranch (Yuba Co.), 8:207, 213, 338, 341; 9:52, 62, 63, 78, 158, 161-62, 163, 266; 10:56, 170; 15:34

Dobbs, J., 22:251

Dobie, Charles Caldwell, address, "San Francisco One Hundred Years Ago," 14:186; obit., 22:91

Dobie, Frank, 39:215

Dobson (w. Vancouver, 1792), 2:275, 332

Dobson (Yuba Co., 1856), 9:76

Dockweiler, Henry, 32:339

Dockweiler, Isidore Bernard, 38:357; 39:123, 126, 128

"Dr. C. Annette Buckel, the 'Little Major,' " by Margaret E. Martin, 19:74-76

"Doctor Comes to California, A," Diary of John S. Griffin, ed. George W. Ames, Jr., 21:193-224, 333-57; 22:41-66

"Dr. Edward Turner Bale," by Dean Albertson, 28:259-69

"Dr. John S. Griffin's Mail, 1846-53," ed. Viola L. Warren, 33:97-124, 249-70, 337-47; 34:21-39

Dr. Rabe's Punch (newsp.), 28:36

"Documentary" (Conquest of Calif., 1845-46), 1:72-95, 178-91, 286-95; 2:67-74, 161-72, 246-51, 350-62; 3:84-88, 178-90, 270-89; 4:81-87, 374-91; 5:184-95, 296-310; 6:77-90, 181-91, 265-80, 364-74; 7:79-85; 8:71-77; 9:81-86

Dodd, Charles E., 20:44

Dodero, Nicolás, 14:17; 15:122, 137

Dodge (Columbia, 1854), 35:219

Dodge, F., 12:325, 326; 21:233

Dodge, Grenville Mellen, 36:97, 99, 267, 269, 271

Dodge, Henry, 4:273, 275, 276; 16:49-52 *passim*

Dodge, Henry Lee, 19:237; 22:114; 40:44

Dodge, Mrs. Henry Lee, 19:230

Dodge, Jonathan S., 37:269, 274

Dodge, Sally, *see* Morris, Mrs. Milton

Dodge & Lockwood, 8:341

Dodson, Dr. (Sacramento, 1858), 9:244, 247, 250, 255; 10:42

Dodson, Arthur McKenzie, 13:315

Dodson, C. B., 14:220

Dodson Toll Road, 32:364

Doe (S.F., 1851), 2:137

Doebler, Miss (Marysville, 1858), 9:360, 361, 370, 371

Dog fights, 6:231

Dogs, 2:242-43; 3:340; 24:264; 33:159

Dogtown (Magalia), Butte Co., 10:251

Dogtown, Mono Co., 26:236

Dog Town, San Joaquin Co., 30:91

Doheny, Mrs. Edward Laurence (Carrie Estelle Betzold), 25:190; obit., 38:278-79

Doheny (Edward Laurence) Memorial Library, 25:190

Dohrmann, Andrew Bernard Charles, 23:95; 25:232; obit., 16:95

Dohrmann, Frederick William, 23:95

Dohrmann, Frederick William, Jr., obit., 15:97

Dohrmann, Robert L., 23:95

Dohrmann family, 15:97; 16:95

Doke, Philip, 14:17

Dolan, Patrick, 33:349, 355

Dolbear, C. E., 17:116

Dolbeer, John, 38:59-69 *passim*

Dolbeer & Carson Lumber Co., 36:110; 38:59-69 *passim*

Dolch, Ed, 27:116, 121

Dole, Albion, 2:121

Doll (Sacramento, 1859), 10:52

Dollar, Robert, 26:286; 27:21; 38:178, 179

Dollar, Robert Stanley, 26:286; 31:297; obit., 38:178-79

Dollart (ship), 9:313, 318-31

'Dollart Case, The," by Arthur A. Gray, 9:318-31

Dolliver, Clara, 28:5

Dolly (ship), see *Dhualle*

Dolores (Monterey, 1829), 16:221

Dolores (Indian girl, 1850s), 30:221

Dolores, Isla de los (Destruction I.), 10:325

Dolphins, 1:210; *see also* Porpoises

Dolphus (ship), 32:269

Dominga (ship), 2:93, 94

Domingo (Indian, Santa Barbara, 1853), 29:244

Domingo, Armayo de (Indian, L.A., 1849), 33:346-47

Domingo, Juan, *see* Gönninger, Hans

Domínguez, Demisio, 13:212

Domínguez, Feliciana, 29:247

Domínguez, Francisco, 7:240, 251

Domínguez, Juan José, 13:202, 203; rancho of, *see* Ranchos: San Pedro

Domínguez, Justo, 29:236

Domínguez, Manuel, 13:223; 17:233; 23:314, 317-18; 32:331, 340; fac. sig., 10: opp. 159; rancho of, *see* Ranchos: San Pedro

Domínguez, Mariano, 24:308; 25:60, 73, 362

Domínguez, Pedro, 29:247

Dominguez Hill, 32:330

Domínguez Rancho, 13:325, 349; Battle of, 3:116-18; 13:52, 303; 17:336-38; 21:216, 224; 22:51; 26:33; *see also* Ranchos: San Pedro (L.A. Co.)

Dominicales, Les (Fr. newsp.), 39:149

Dominicans, 8:308, 329, 330; 21:276; 33:353; college, Monterey, 37:43

Dominis, John, 28:123

Don, Lady (Emily Sanders), 21:152, 154

Don, Eugene E., 39:30

Doña Ana (place), 34:126, 137

Don Agustin V. Zamorano, by Harding, rev., 13:409

Donahoo, M. J., 25:35

Donahue, James, 10:389; 14:364; 18:100; 19:237; 25:41, 344; 26:262; 30:344; 37:375

Donahue, James Mervin, 7:292; 10:292, 389

Donahue, James P. and Mariana S. (Cordero), 27:93-94

Donahue, Mary Ellen ("Mamie"), 7:292; 10:389

Donahue, Michael, 10:389; 25:41

Donahue, Peter, 7:292; 10:292, 376, 389; 18:100; 25:41, 42, 43; 26:196; 27:179; 30:344; 32: 336; 33:236; 37:375

Donahue, Mrs. Peter (Annie Downey), 7:292; 10:277, 292, 389; 37:375-76

Donahue, Mrs. Peter (Mary Jane Maguire), 10:292, 389

Donahue, Thomas E., 27:93, 94

Donahue, William E., 33:373

Donahue's Union Iron and Brass Foundry, *see* Union Iron Works

Donaldson, A. C., 27:93

Donaldson, Joseph, 33:295, 296, 297, 307

Donaldson, R., 22:251

Donaldson, Ruth, 27:93

Donaldson, William, 26:237

Don Caesar de Bazan (play), 16:283, 285

Dondero, J. D., 32:376

Don Giovanni (opera), 15:274

Donho (Donahue?; Mokelumne Hill, 1851), 2:138

Doniphan, Alexander William, 11:293; 18:230, 231, 233, 245, 246, 248, 310; 25:301; letter to, 24:28

Donnell, A. C., 27:349

Donnelly (S.F., 1855), 16:342

Donnelly (Sacramento, 1861), 10:279

Donnelly, Florence (Holland), 29:91

Donnelly, Ignatius, 27:314

Donnelly, Owen, 8:205; 9:138-48 *passim*

Donnelly, William, 33:363

Donner, Mrs. A. J., 24:262

Donner, Eliza P., 19:122, 127, 139, 141

Donner, Elitha C., 19:122

Donner, George, 25:127; *see also* Donner family; Donner party

Donner, Georgia A., 19:122, 127, 141

Donner, Leanna, 19:96

Donner, Mary M., 19:122, 139

Donner family, 19:122, 127, 141

Donner Lake, 3:136; 4:171, 278; 5:179, 378; 10:348-52 *passim;* 16:142; 33:350

Donner party, 1:296; 4:291; 5:388, 395; 11:141, 145; 12:291, 299, 352; 14:205, 206, 272-73; 15:100; 16:141; 19:96, 121-23; 22:52; 28:298, 324; 30:233; 33:350; aid sent to, 1:96; 6:241; 10:350-51, 354; 12:291; 14:129, 206; 17:231; 19:121; 29:327; 30:233-34; camps of, 3:137; 4:171, 278; 16:126, 142; 24:73-76; route of, 3:136; 10:346-52; 15:100; 24:73-74; 32:195 (*see also* Hastings Cutoff); bk. on, rev., 40:251-52

"Donner Party and Relief Hill, The," by W. W. Waggoner, 10:347-52

Donner Pass, 1:125; 4:240-42, 247-48, 259, 265-68

Donoghe, W. K. O., 33:12

Donohoe, Joseph Augustin (1826-1895), 1:12-18 *passim;* 17:174, 179; 19:231; 21:327; 30:208

Donohoe, Joseph Augustin (1863-1939), obit. of Albert H. Payson, 9:95-96; obit., 18:189

Donohoe, Mrs. Joseph A. (Noelie Christine Parrott), 18:189; 25:233

Donohoe, Mrs. Nellie, 39:126

Donohoe, Simon, 8:6

Donohoe, Kelly Banking Co., 18:100, 189; 30:208, 210

Donohue, J. Augustine, rev. of Forbes, *Apache, Navaho, and Spaniard,* 40:158-60

Donovan (Marysville, 1858), 9:348

Don Pedro's Bar, 11:170-73 *passim;* 13:174

Don Quixote (ship), 5:191, 307; 11:204, 220; 12:149, 281, 288; 14:303, 315-29 *passim,* 341-45 *passim;* 15:347, 349; 17:298; 23:312, 327, 331, 334; 28:260, 342; 31:33; 35:200; illus., 14; opp. 291

Doodley, Capt. (Colorado R., 1863), 22:170

Doolittle, J., 29:291

Doolittle, R. A., 26:350

Dorcey, Dr. (from N.J., 1850), 5:295

Dore, Benjamin, "Journal of," 2:87-139; phot., 2: opp. 87

Dore, Mrs. Benjamin (Jane Amanda Hall, née Waters), 2:88

Dore, Frank E. and Louise (Vandor), 2:89

Dore, Harry E., 2:87, 88-89; 7:206

Dore, Mrs. Harry E. (Anita Estelle Harrington), 2:89

Dore, John S., 19:62-68 *passim,* 72; 27:313-16 *passim;* 28:47, 49

Dore, Maurice, 19:237

Dorion, Thomas A., 39:5

Doris (ship), 31:295

Dorland, Jr., son of, 22:196, 218

Dorland, T.A.C., 29:224, 359

Dorman, Orrin, 20:304

Dornin, John, 35:257, 261

Dorotea (ship), 23:211, 218

Dorr, Ebenezer, 1:173-77; 10:320; 38:275

Dorr, Nathaniel, 23:313, 332

Dorrey (on *Héros,* 1827), 8:312

Dorsey, Cope, 6:344

Dorsey, Hilliard P., 13:335; 15:174

Dorsey, Richard, 8:206

Dorsey, Samuel P., 6:332, 333, 335, 343

Dorsey, Stephen, 9:138, 146

Dorsey, Susan (Miller), 36:152

Dorst, Joseph Haddox, 4:44

Dosch, Henry E., *Vigilante Days at Virginia City,* ed. Lockley, rev., 3:297

Dosh, Samuel H., 9:46

Dos Palmas, 12:9, 13, 16

Dos Pueblos, 7:74

Dos Rios, 27:221

Dotan's Bar, 16:31

Dottridge's saloon, San Diego, 22:351

Doty (N. R. Dougherty?; 1844), 4:320

Doty, James T., phot., 39: foll. 182

Doty, Samuel, 28:294

Doubet, Abbé (1850), 5:34, 39, 355, 362-63

Doubleday, Ulysses, 21:293, 306

Double Eagle Mining Co., 11:60

Double Springs, 22:77, 82; 27:160, 161; 31:143, 148; art. on, by E. A. Wiltsee, 11:173-83; phot., 11; opp. 179

Dougal, William H., 23:248; art. on, 22:235-52; drawings by, 22: opp. 249; 23: opp. 247; phot., 22: opp. 235

Dougherty, Capt. (Colorado R., 1862-69), 22:170-73 *passim*

Dougherty, Anton, 13:24-25

Dougherty, Bridget, 9:65

Dougherty, Harry, 10:285(?), 358, 359

Dougherty, John (trapper and Indian agt., 1812, 1835), 4:127; 16:50, 53
Dougherty, John (Sierra Co., 1861), 10:272
Dougherty, John (S.F., 1906), 15:316, 322
Dougherty, Lewis Bissell, 10:202
Dougherty, M. C., 30:164
Dougherty, William E., 27:224
Douglas, Capt. (of *Salem*, 1849), 30:17-18
Douglas, Charles D., 27:222
Douglas, David, 4:92, 154; 18:339-41, 346; 24:337; 32:272; 33:60; letter of, 2:223-27
Douglas, George, 7:18, 19
Douglas, I. W., 22:36
Douglas, Sir James, 6:18-29 *passim;* 10:203; 11:150-51, 154; 12:244, 249; 17:63, 141; 22:104-5; 28:98, 100-101, 247, 254-56, 262; 29:149, 158, 337; 36:243; "A Voyage from the Columbia to California in 1840," from Journal of, ed. Herman Leader, 8:97-115; port., 8: opp. 97
Douglas, John, 18:288
Douglas, John W., 26:168, 170, 172; 27:162, 301; 33:292, 301-2; 35:12, 14
Douglas, Mrs. Melvyn (Helen Gahagan), 39:34
Douglas, Robert David, 33:272
Douglas, Lord Sholto, 9:74
Douglas, Stephen Arnold, 2:212; 9:246, 271, 272, 371, 394, 395; 10:21, 140, 141, 177, 185, 199, 221-37 *passim,* 249, 251, 252, 257, 262, 268, 285, 297; 11:4-18 *passim,* 26, 27, 28; 15:200-205 *passim;* 17:304, 309, 317; 19:13-18 *passim,* 173, 174, 257, 259, 268, 270, 276, 344, 347, 351, 352, 353; 22:228; 31:193, 202
Douglas, Mrs. Stephen Arnold (Martha Denny Martin), 11:13, 16
Douglas, Thomas, 3:35; 11:134, 143; *see also* Douglass
Douglas, Thornton G., 26:188
Douglas Democrat, 24:274
Douglas Flat, 22:72, 73, 76, 82
Douglass (Thomas Douglas?; in mines, 1848), 2:187-94 *passim,* 201; 13:177-78
Douglass (Culiacán, 1849), 39:41, 44, 50
Douglass, Mrs. (Marysville, 1858), 9:357
Douglass (Calaveras Co., 1856), 22:79
Douglass, David F., 9:112; 10:74; 14:356, 357; 15:78-79, 146

Douglass, Emma T., *see* Maguire, Mrs. Thomas
Douglass, George, 18:103, 112, 132, 133
Douglass, George A., 10:43, 62, 70, 189
Douglass, George M., 22:159, 174
Douglass, George N., 10:62
Douglass, H. L., 32:354
Douglass, James A., letters from, 24:117-18, 127-28
Douglass, Mace, 34:216
Douglass, William A., 2:244
Dovalle, *see* Ovalle, Gonzalo de
Dove, James G., 15:239
Dow (Negro, 1849), 18:101, 103, 109, 125, 129, 132, 244
Dow, E., 21:235
Dow, E. P., 33:298
Dow, George, 33:12; 35:304
Dow, William, 10:62, 70
Dow, William H., 9:109; 15:280, 364
Dow distillery, San Francisco, 17:169
Dowd, A. T., 4:14; 11:173; 18:343
Dowd, William, 39:56
Dowdell, Capt. (of *Zealandia*), 31:60, 61
Dowell, B. F., 21:135
Dowell, Thomas, 14:178, 181-82
Dowling James, 15:368; 20:304; 21:158
Dowling, William M., 20:192
Downer, F., 17:176
Downey, Annie, *see* Donahue, Mrs. Peter
Downey, Eleanor, *see* Martin, Mrs. Edward J.
Downey, John Gately, 4:166-67; 7:291; 10:78, 254, 260, 277, 280, 286, 292, 295, 355, 358, 360, 361, 367, 375; 11:10, 22; 13:314, 329, 336, 347; 16:200; 22:229, 232, 355; 23:338; 24:274; 26:2; 27:155; 28:166; 29:108, 109, 234, 239, 240, 243, 352; 32:216, 223, 328, 330, 331, 345; 33:334; 38:27, 330, 331, 333; 40:292, 297; art. on, 6:327-31; letters to, 29:229-30, 238-39
Downey, Sheridan, 39:137, 300
Downey (John G.) & (James P.) McFarland, 13:313, 319
Downey Guards, 10:277
Downie, William, 8:353
Downieville, 3:302; 7:13; 8:202, 211, 339; 9:70; 10:61, 73; 11:54, 242; 13:28; 14:209, 402; 15:31; 23:226; 27:193; 28:237, 238; 30:110, 259, 360, 366; 32:134; 33:55-56, 198-99; 38:309; camel assoc., 9:316-17; Chinese in, 6:281-82; 33:198-99; fire, 9:246, 271;

newspapers, 9:173, 315; illus.,
8: opp. 208
Doxey, William, 37:51, 55
Doyle (Placerville, 1854), 11:58
Doyle (Sacramento, 1858), 9:371
Doyle, Miss (S.F., 1864), 24:263
Doyle, Augustus, 30:254
Doyle, Helen (MacKnight), address,
"The Land of Little Rain," 14:410
Doyle, John Thomas, 1:10-15 *passim*,
21; 6:103, 104; 10:391; 17:171-72;
24:79
Doyle, Michael J. and Emma (Bergson),
28:379
Doyle, Mrs. Richard Sullivan, 30:85
Doyle, Robert E., 36:118, 127
Dozier, Rowena, 40:272
Dozier, Erwin Yount, 2:67
Dozier, Thomas Bona, 2:67; obit., 9:94
Dozier, Mrs. Thomas Bona (Maud
Watson), 2:67
Dracut (ship), 14:176
Dragoons, U.S., 25:202-307 *passim;*
26:21-62 *passim;* 28:203, 223, 228, 230,
231; 33:97-115 *passim,* 249-64 *passim;*
Fauntleroy's, 18:73-84; 25:126, 129
Drake, Mrs. (Strawberry Valley, 1862),
10:380
Drake (Ventura Co., 1884), 16:300, 303
Drake, Francis, 15:59; 16:188; 34:88;
36:217; anchorage of, 1:16, 21; 5:413;
6:91-92, 95; 8:40; 10:337; 11:308-12;
16: No. 1, Pt. 2, pp. 6, 13, 19, 23, 27,
31, 32-35, (map) 46; 26:163; 31:99;
33:87-88; 35:182; 36:21-34, 224;
bibliog. of, 16: No. 1, Pt. 2, pp. 49-57;
bks. on, rev., 6:91-95; plants taken to
England by, 18:335; plaque posted by,
16: No. 1, Pt. 2, pp. 1-2, 6, 10-13,
(phot.) foll. 10, 16, 19-23, 30, 31,
44-45; No. 2, pp. 192, 271-81; 17: No.
4, Pt. 2, (phot.) frontis., pp. 1-27,
(phot.) foll. 30; 18:85, 192, 251-52,
374; 20:315; 30:93-94; 36:27-28, 31-34,
172; statue of, 16: (phot.) opp. 279;
voyage of, 3:204-7, 266; 6:91-95;
7:235; 8:38, 70; 16: No. 1, Pt. 2, pp.
2-6, 14-15, 27-46; 18:281; 20:81, 323;
27:289, 290, 291; 30:279; 31:224-26;
ports., 16: No. 1, Pt. 2, opp. 19, opp. 27
Drake, Frank, 8:201
Drake, John, 3:205; 11:310; 36:24, 25
"Drake and California," by Douglas S.
Watson, 16: No. 1, Pt. 2, pp. 19-24
"Drake in California: . . . Evidence and
the Testimony of the Plate of Brass,"
by Francis P. Farquhar and Walter
A. Starr, 36:21-34
Drake's Bay, 7:392; 11:306; 12:224-25,
226, 228; 27:68, 289; 33:7; Cermeño
at, 3:5-6, 8, 12-14, 22; 20:315-28;
27:290; Drake possibly at, 11:308-9,
312-13, 317; 16: No. 1, Pt. 2, pp. 6, 13;
17: No. 4, Pt. 2, pp. 2, 24; 27:291;
excavations at, 20:319-27; 31:99-108;
36:28-29; maps, 16: No. 1, Pt. 2, opp.
49; 20:320; phot. of relics found at,
20: foll. 320; 31: foll. 99
"Drake's Plate of Brass," by Allen L.
Chickering, 17: No. 4, Pt. 2, pp. 1-4
"Drake's Voyage around the World,"
address by Henry R. Wagner, 3:204-7
Dramatic Chronicle, San Francisco,
21:144, 153, 159; 34:348
Dramatic Museum, San Francisco,
15:47; 20:293, 295; 22:266
Drannan, William, 1:150, 151
Draper, Hiram, 2:122
Draper, Robert E., 7:117; 26:241
Draymen's Association, 35:61-68
passim, 145-51 *passim*
Dreadnaught (ship), 22:171
Dreamland Rink, San Francisco, 31:304
Dredgers and dredging, 3:202; 6:244;
15:51-52; 22:167, 309, 373
Dresel, Emil, 31:287; *see also* Küchel
& Dresel
Dress: of early Californians, 2:294-95;
8:247-48; 13:50, 52; 23:317; Calif.
Battalion (1846), 29:340; in 1849,
13:49-50; 20:31; in '50s and '60s,
20:251, 253; 21:41, 54-55, 150; of
Chinese, 3:40; 23:98, 99; 27:19; of
Indians (*see* Indians: appearance and
dress); of mission fathers, 2:42; of
mountain man, 3:75; of soldiers and
sailors, 21:356; 29:273; of Edward
Stokes, 21:355; bloomers, 24:165;
28:40-41, 202, 226; 31:86; hoop skirts,
21:54-55; *see also* Uniforms
Dressler, Albert, 5:405; ed. *California
Chinese Chatter*, rev., 6:281-82; ed.
California's Pioneer Circus, rev.,
6:98-99; ed. *Letters to a Pioneer
Senator*, rev., 4:291-92
Drew, George, 13:296
Drew, John (1827-1862), 10:42, 63;
21:46
Drew, John (1853-1927), 35:142
Drew, Joseph W., 25:115, 120

Drexel, Sather & Church, 9:72; 15:272
Driese, Don N., 30:284
Driggs, R. H., 33:277
Drinking and drunkenness, 5:70; 8:312; 9:52, 153, 216; 10:395; 12:63; 14:154, 319; 17:59, 168, 292, 325; 28:259; 32:218; 33:57; 35:214; among actors, 21:42, 148-49; 39:301; clergy, 2:53; filibusters, 21:32; in Hawaiian Is., 35:194; on ships, 1:212; 5:141, 142; 26:227; 28:315; 30:243; 32:355; 35:101; among soldiers, 1:212, 218, 223, 227, 228, 246-47, 255; 18:77; *see also* Liquor
Driscoll, Capt. (of *Capacity*, 1852), 22:5, 168
Driscoll, Charles, 26:14
Driscoll, Cornelius, 13:258
"Driving Livestock East . . . Prior to 1850," by Robert M. Denhardt, 20:341-47
"Driving the Last Spike at Promontory, 1869," by J. N. Bowman, 36:97-106, 263-74
Drobish, Harry E., 36:110
Dromedary Line, 9:306; 30:360
Drought (1862-63), 3:169
Drown, Ezra, 13:338
Druhe, John Herman, 19:192
Druhe, Rudolph C., 19:192
Drum, John S., 1:19; 31:176; 37:268
Drum, Richard C., 9:308; 15:9; 24:262; 29:248
Drumgoold, John, 9:139, 149, 152, 158
Drummond *v.* Brady and Brady, 10:178
Drunkard, The (play), 15:48
Drury, Aubrey Wheeler, 22:383; 24:84; 29:185; 31:380; "John Albert Hooper," 31:289-305; "Meetings of the Society," 21:278; 22:84-87, 183, 374-75; 23:80-88, 180-81, 380; 24:184-85; Reps. of Sec., 22:85-87; 23:81-83; 24:184-85; 25:82-83; addresses: "Some California Place Names," 15:89; "William Walker, Filibusterer," 35:75; bk. rev. by, 4:397-98; obits. of John D. Galloway, 22:187-88; Joseph D. Grant, 21:93-94; Duncan McDuffie, 30:280-81; James A. B. Scherer, 23:92-93; obit., 39:75-77; phot., 39: opp. 75
Drury, Clifford Merrill, 19:383; 20:95; 26:187; 21:373; "Chronology of Protestant Beginnings in California," 26:163-74; "John White Geary and His Brother," 20:12-25; "Timothy Dwight Hunt and His Wedding Records," 28:289-96; "Walter Colton, Chaplain and Alcade," 35:97-117; introd. to Charles A. Farley, "The Moral Aspect of California," 19:299-307; address, "The Coming of White American Women to the Pacific Coast," 18:376
Drury, Mrs. Clifford Merrill (Miriam Leyrer), 35:92; ed. "The Jeffers-Willey Wedding," 35:11-21
Drury, Newton Bishop, 23:190; 25:201; address, "The National Park Service," 29:184-85
Drury, Wells, 10:87; "Meetings of the Society," 4:210-12; 5:93-95; Rep. of Publicity Com., 4:101-2; address, "How Californians Gave Life and Color to Nevada's Bonanza Boom Times," 2:260-61; bk. rev. by, 3:196-99; *An Editor on the Comstock Lode*, rev., 15:381; obit., 11:190
Drury, Mrs. Wells (Ella Bishop), 21:288; 23:190; obit., 23: 91-92
Dry Creek, Amador, Sacramento and San Joaquin cos., 2:185, 195; 30:239; 31:143
Dry Creek, El Dorado Co., 2:189; 3:127
Dry Creek, Tehama Co., 30:160
Dry Creek, Yuba Co., 8:341, 358; 9:52-53
Dryden, David A., 15:42; 32:131
Dryden, William G., 13:315, 336, 339; 24:273; 29:234, 236-37, 240
Dry Diggings, 4:181, 8:210; 13:159, 165, 168, 169, 170, 174; 24:259, 346, 352, 353; 31:143
Dryer (S.F., 1850), 5:140
Drysdale, Amy (Horn), 30:115
Dry Slough Co., 10:274
Drytown, 2:137; 15:172; 17:75, 78; 24:130
Duane, Charles P. ("Dutch Charley"), 6:48-50; 8:366, 371-72; 9:75; 15:88, 163, 175, 186, 313; 16:81, 342; 17:177; 23:71
Duane, John, 6:36; 15:313
Duarte, Francisco, 16:249
Duarte, José, 26:41
Dube (Jacob Dublin?; d. S.F., 1854), 15:163
Du Bois, V., 30:293; 31:50
Du Bois, William E., 15:246

Du Bony, Capt. (of *Victoire*, 1849), 13:382

Dubosc, Pierre, 8:123

Dubosq, Theodore, 27:369-70

Dubrenil (Dubreuil?; S.F., 1850s), 6:56

Du Brodt, Capt. (of *Fanny*, 1849), 23:259, 274, 275, 276

Dubruille, Baptiste, 22:206, 220; 23:125, 132, 139

Duchene, John, 18:303-4, 313

Duchess of Clarence (ship), 31:185

Ducks, wild, *see* Water birds

Duckwall (W. J.) party (1853), 34:216

Duckworth, Walter, 8:113

Duclos, Angelina, 34:244, 248-249

Duclos, Louis E., 14:142

Ducommun, Charles, 13:316, 319, 326, 336, 345; 30:262, 363

Dudhope (ship), 22:353

Dudley, Charles C., 2:205; 10:70

Dudley, Ezra C. and Sarah Elizabeth (Burnett), 29:381

Dudley, Robert, 8:39-41

Dudley, William L., 9:381

Dudley, William R., 4:49; 23:14

Dudoit, Jules, 14:329, 342

Due, John F., coauth. *The Electric Interurban Railways in America*, rev., 39:374-75

Duels and dueling, 2:166, 170; 10:177; 19:9-10; 20:82, 309; 21:34, 39; 22:260; 25:337, 345-46; 28:42; 32:217; 39:301 in Amador Co. (1861), 40:301
Bale-Salvador Vallejo, 4:153; Barbour-Field (not fought), 9:380; Bixby-Spitts, 7:384; Broderick-Smith, 20:314; 38:207-8; 40:207-8, 213; Broderick-Terry, 9:270, 285; 10:197; 15:382-83; 18:181; 20:310; 21:39; 32:23; 38:212-15; 40:203; Brown(or Bevin)-Dorsey, 15:174; Coffroth-McKibben, 10:60, 78; Denver-Gilbert, 14:346; 32:224; Derbec-La Chapelle, 16:344; 39:142; Draper-Eichelroth, 7:117; 26:241-42; Dube-Essler, 15:163; Ferguson-Johnston, 9:378, 387-8; 10:268; Folsom-Russell, 7:107; Graham-Lemon, 22:260; Graham-Walker, 25:343; Gwin-McCorkle, 19:25; Houser-Turner, 9:265, 286, 395; Lippincott-Tevis, 8:212; Kelley-McAllister (not fought), 11:126-27; McQuaid-Smith (not fought), 10:47, 71; Magruder-Osborn, 13:323-24;

Piercy-Showalter, 39:297; 40:312-13; Rust-Stidger, 10:395; 14:407; Smith-Truett (not fought), 16:183; Teed-Wilber, 9:250; Washburn-Washington, 38:214-15

Duff, Howard C., 25:190

Duff River (Pudding Creek), 30:163

Duffie, James, 15:163

Duffie, Mary Anne, 28:293

Dufford, Jacob, 9:286

Duffy, Philip G., 25:94

Duflot de Mofras, Eugene, 8:116-29 *passim*; 11:196-97, 203; 12:267, 273; 13:43, 44, 53; 16:378; 17:142; 18:140, 316; 20:344; 23:44-45; 28:105; 29:315; 30:3, 329; 33:126; 34:114; 39:118, 40:98

DuFour, Clarence John, 12:187; "The Russian Withdrawal from California," 12:240-76; address, "Gen. John A. Sutter," 6:198-99

Dugan, Richard, 28:358

Duhaut-Cilly, Auguste Bernard, 8:117; 12:209, 230; 13:210; 15:330; 25:321; "Voyage," trans. Charles F. Carter, 8:131-66, 214-50, 306-36; illus. from bk., 8: opp. 154, opp. 226, opp. 325

Duis, Lutze, 9:139

Duke, John Marve, 31:377; 33:373

Duke of Sacramento, The (play), 22:32, 38

Duke's Motto, The (play), 21:165

Dulanto, Andrés, 25:134, 135, 136

Dumars, Jo, 9:258

Dumas, Alexandre, 14:132-42; 23:287; 27:240, 242

Dumas, Alexandre *fils*, 30:355; "History of the Lottery of the Golden Ingots," 33:130-40

"Dumas's *Gil Blas en Californie*," by George R. Stewart, Jr., 14:132-42

Dumb Belle (play), 20:295

Dumetz, Francisco, 12:121, 123-24; 20:237

Dumke, Glenn Schroeder, 29:381-82; 38:183; "History in Your Own Backyard . . . ," 38:131-40; bk. rev. by, 39:272-74

Dummer, Samuel R., 13:321

Dumont d'Urville, J. S. C., 12:156, 159

Dun (Yuba Co., 1857), *see* Dunn

Dun (or Dunn, Lucy, 9:358, 360, 361, 371, 375

Dun, Marie Denervaud (Mrs. Harry

W.), 31:286; "Hannah Lloyd Neal,"
31:241-52
Dunbar (of Mountain House, 1851),
33:56
Dunbar (Timbuctoo, 1858), 9:364, 376;
10:51
Dunbar, Edward E., 19:275; 27:47;
38:314
Dunbar, Elizabeth, *see* Jewett, Mrs.
William Smith
Dunbar, John R., ed. "Some Letters of
George Sterling," 40:137-55
Dunbar, S. G., 22:251
Duncan (from Ore., 1845), 5:125
Duncan, Arthur L., 11:92-93; obit.,
9:293
Duncan, David, 22:32, 37
Duncan, James M., 3:122; 17:340, 343;
26:24, 28
Duncan, Joseph Charles, 3:268-69;
10:282, 295; 21:34
Duncan, Robert and Mrs., 25:190
Duncan, Stafford, 38:2
Duncan, Thomas, 22:137-38, 149
Duncan, William L., 33:373
Duncan's Art-Union, 15:183
Duncan Sisters, 4:61
Duncombe, Charles, 10:42-49 *passim*, 62,
63-64, 69
Dunham, Albert, 2:58; 33:116, 118
Dunham, William H., 13:32
Dunlap, A., 29:292, 294
Dunlap, Boutwell, 2:20; 3:252; 7:280;
"A Bret Harte Discovery," 4:207-9;
"California's First Tabloid
Newspapers," 3:268-69; "The Family
of George C. Yount," 2:67-68; "Some
Facts Concerning Leland Stanford
... in Placer County," 2:203-10;
obit. of Thomas B. Dozier, 9:94; obit.,
10:95
Dunlap, Elizabeth P., 28:293
Dunlap, H. W., 10:62; 11:9
Dunlap, Joseph S., 15:368; 20:304
Dunlap, Presley, 15:273
Dunlap, Thomas, 16:84
Dunleavy, James G. T., 2:182
Dunn (or Dun, Yuba Co., 1857),
9:134, 143, 158; & Co., 9:145, 149
Dunn (Sacramento, 1859), 10:167, 176,
184
Dunn, Ann, 21:78
Dunn, Francis J., 10:385, 395
Dunn, Isabella, *see* Kimball, Mrs.
Charles P.

Dunn, James, 18:332
Dunn, James A., 9:161, 180, 258
Dunn, Jane, 32:375
Dunn (or Dunne), John, 18:267-68, 277
Dunn, John H., 15:165
Dunn, Julia (Payne), 10:48, 176, 190
Dunn (or Dunne), Patrick H., 18:259,
267, 270, 277
Dunn, Thomas, 16:138
Dunne, E. F., 37:198
Dunne, Peter Masten, 29:145; 31:382;
address, "Background of the
California Missions," 25:86; obit.,
36:87-88
Dunne, William H., 26:38, 44, 46, 47,
60, 61
Dunnell's San Diego Hotel, 31:45
Dunning, Alice, 21:165, 171, 173
Dunphy, Thomas, 24:173
Dunphy (place), 32:197
Dupee, William H., 12:29, 31
Dupetit-Thouars, Abel, 8:117, 125,
129; 12:156; 15:213
Dupont, Charles, 5:373; 6:39
Du Pont, Samuel Francis, 1:138; 2:168;
13:237; 19:133; 25:127; 29:157, 275,
278; 31:210
Duport, Jr. (on *Jacques-Lafitte*, 1849),
23:67
Dupre, F., 10:168
Dupuy, Edouard Joseph, 39:242-45
passim
Dupuy, Foulkes & Co., 8:266, 270, 275
Duquesnay, C., 39:219, 220
Duran (or Doran), Sra., rancho of,
18:120
Durán, Narciso, 2:255, 256, 345-46;
3:27-28; 6:258; 8:238; 14:22, 233, 249;
16:109, 115-17, 219, 221, 372; 23:374;
25:121; 30:2; 36:291; 37:97-128,
241-65, 304
Durand, Rosalie, 10:196
Durand, St. Vrain, 5:125; 18:174
Durand, W. F., 29:203
Durango, Mex., 18:232, 249; 21:321
Durant, Henry, 4:210; 16:336; 21:368;
27;269, 351; 35:291
Durant, Thomas Clark, 36:263, 266-72
Durant-Brayton College School, 35:291
Durbin, John Price, 32:120, 121
Durbrow, William, 29:197-98
Duret, Marie, 21:42
Durham, "Elizzie," 20:255
Durivage, John E., 21:291, 292, 303;
26:337; 28:34; 36:120, 122-32 *passim*

Durkee, C. W., 13:257; 14:385, 402
Durkee, John L., 15:85, 180, 258, 282; 23:74; 24:176, 180
Durkin, Margaret, 15:372
Durst, Cyrus, 9:132
Durst, D. P., 10:272, 280
Dusty Bar, 22:76
Dusy, Frank, 4:37, 38, 41
Dutch, 8:50, 54; *see also* Netherlands
"Dutch Bill," *see* Winkley, P. William
"Dutch Charley," *see* Duane, Charles P.
Dutch Charley's dance hall, San Francisco, 16:81
Dutch Corners, *see* Newman
Dutch Flat, 4:240, 241, 242, 247, 259, 260, 265, 266, 268, 300; 18:360-61; 23:121; 28:235; 38:34, 319
"Dutch George," *see* Lehman, George
Dutchman's Ranch, 9:151, 177
"Dutch Sam," 10:272
Du Théâtre au champ d'honneur (play), 20:143
Dutton (trapper), 2:29-30
Dutton, David Dewey, 18:292-94
Dutton, Henry and Mary (Talbot), 32:375
Dutton, Henry Foster, obit., 32:375
Dutton, Mrs. Henry Foster (1, Jane Dunn; 2, Violet Phillips), 32:375
Dutton, John and Mrs. (née Roman), 29:91
Dutton, Mrs. Samuel Edwards (Annie King), 12:372
Dutton, Warren, 29:91
Dutton, William Jay, 32:375
Duval, Capt. (of *Fanny*, ca. 1840), 11:199

Duval (overland, 1849), 40:161, 162
Duvall, A. J., 27:263
Duvall, Robert Carson, 10:125; 17:338; 26:49, 55, 62; "Extracts from the Log of the U.S. Frigate *Savannah*," kept by, 3:105-25; port., 3: opp. 105
De Vrees Creek, *see* Islais Creek
Duxbury Point, 27:293
Dwight, W. W., 14: opp. 209, 396
Dwinelle, John Whipple, 1:10, 12; 10:303; 18:94; 22:88, 89; 24:217, 219-20; 28:33, 116; 33:373; 34:349
Dwinelle, Justin, 31:231
Dwinelle, Samuel H., 17:314; 19:285
Dwyer, J. P., 10:76
Dwyer, Thomas, 22:94
Dwyer, William P., 22:94
Dyaert, Fr. (Marysville, 1858), 9:372, 376
Dye, Clarkson, 30:36
Dye, Job Francis, 2:362; 6:270; 8:74; 13:105; 14:333; 15:64, 121-22, 233; 16:323, 329; 18:56, 81-82; 22:366; 29:135; 30:54; 32:264, 265, 267
Dyer, Barlow, 26:308
Dyer, Harry, 35:295
Dyer, J. P., 9:72, 277
Dyer, Jones, 14:177
Dyer, Joseph T., 33:6-7, 12, 157-64 *passim*
Dyer, Josephine, 28:293
Dysentery, 4:143, 151, 189; 6:220, 221, 225; 20:36; 21:341-42, 345; 22:53, 242, 243-44; 26-297, 341; 28:301; 30:23; 39:46

E

Eagan, Richard, 21:329
Eagar, Arabella, 11:142
Eagar, John, 35:116; 37:237
Eagar, Mrs. Lucy, 37:235, 237
Eagar, Mary (Mrs. Milton Little), 11:142; 30:98; 35:109, 110, 116
Eagar, Thomas, 30:8
Eagle Bakery, Marysville, 14:398
Eagle Canyon, 8:343, 359
Eagle Hotel, Los Angeles, 13:319

Eagle Hotel, Marysville, 14:394
Eagle Hotel, Placerville, 8:201
Eagle Ranch Pass, 7:7, 8
Eagle Saloon, San Francisco, 15:174; 18:38
Eagle Theatre, Sacramento, 20:37, 46, 312; 29:186
Eagleville, 9:353, 385; 10:171, 194, 359
Eagon, John A., 10:44, 46, 61, 70, 280; 11:8-9

Eames, Alfred W., 24:380

Eames, Charles, 13:297

Eames, Emma, 25:235

Eames, William J., 17:269

E. A. Rawlins (ship), 22:166, 170

Earl (Red Bluff, 1859), 10:167, 169, 180

Earl, John O., 12:329; 19:232

Earl, Lake, 26:8

Earle, David and Mary Louise (Rowland), 28:292

Earlie, Maggie, 9:264, 345

"Earliest Crossings of the Deserts of Utah and Nevada ... Jedediah S. Smith," by C. Hart Merriam, 2:228-36

Early, Jacob M., 4:272

"Early Associations between California and Australia," address by E. R. Wyeth, 26:279-80

"Early Automobiling Days in California," address by Edwin S. Moore, 32:378-79

"Early Banking in California," address by Ira B. Cross, 23:380

"Early Botanical Explorers on the Pacific Coast," by Alice Eastwood, 18:335-46

"Early California Cases," address by A. F. Bray, 32:174

"Early California Lithographs," address by John Howell, 15:192-93

Early California ... Post Office Cancellations, by Lyon and Wiltsee, rev., 8:385

"*Early Cartography of the Pacific*," by Wroth, rev., 24:77-78

'Early Day Politicians and Political Bosses," address by Daniel Q. Troy, 5:94-95

Early Days at ... San Juan Bautista, by Mylar, rev., 8:383-84

"Early Day Shipping," address by J. B. Warner, 5:415

"Early Days in Yosemite," ed. Ansel F. Hall, 1:271-85

"Early Days of Methodism in California," address by Andrew J. Hanson, 5:416-17

"Early Days on the Mountain Division," reminiscences of Clarence M. Wooster, 23:117-22

"Early Day Transportation ... in the West," address by Aubrey Neasham and John A. Hussey, 35:75

"Early Engineering Center in

California," by J. W. Johnson, 29:193-209

"Early History of Cotton Cultivation in California," by E. Philpott Mumford, 6:159-66

"Early History of Mono County," by Maxine Chappell, 26:233-48

"Early History of Stanford University," address by Donald B. Tresidder, 23:180-81

Early History of the Fraser River Mines, The, by Howay, rev., 5:402-3

"Early Inns of California," address by Ralph H. Cross, 20:83

"Early Mapping of the American West," address by Carl I. Wheat, 35:75

"Early Military Posts of Del Norte County," by Fred B. Rogers, 26:1-11

"Early Military Posts of Mendocino County," by Fred B. Rogers, 27:215-28; as address, 27:378

"Early Mining Days in Sierra County," address by Lewis F. Byington, 3:302

Early Nevada, by Fletcher, rev., 9:184-85

"Early 19th Century California (?) Copper Medallion, An," by Robert F. Heizer, 26:349-50

"Early Outposts of the Fur-Trade Empire," address by Joel E. Ferris, 33:82-85

"Early Relations of California with British Columbia," address by Frederic W. Howay, 21:374

"Early San Francisco Theatres and Theatrical Folks," address by James Madison, 4:301-2

"Early Theaters of San Francisco," address by James Madison, 14:411

"Early Trails of the Clear Lake Region," address by Benjamin C. Jones, 32:376

"Early Years in Yosemite," by Carl P. Russell, 5:328-41

"Early Years of William Francis Herrick, The," by Amy R. Russell, 26:217-32

Earnshaw, John, *Thomas Muir ...* rev., 38:274-75

Earp, Wyatt, Berry Stapp, 10:410; 36:219

Earthquakes, 15:320-21; 17:29; 20:252; 23:251; 31:276; (in 1808), 23:251; (1812), 2:253; 13:205; (1827), 8:148,

248-49; (1829), 33:42; (1839), 33:42;
(1840), 23:251; 26:12; (1845), 5:263;
(1847), 1:246; 13:307; (1853),
35:213; (1854), 15:179, 266; (1855),
13:338-39; 15:371, 374, 376; (1857),
9:157; 13:339; (1860), 10:247, 261;
38:332; (1865), 6:356; 10:304; 27:172;
(1868), 5:404; 6:356; 10:304; 23:243,
246, 255; 27:172; (1872), 9: opp. 196;
(1885), 17:29; (1906) *see* San
Francisco earthquake and fire;
(1925), 29:91
Earth Shook, the Sky Burned, The, by
Bronson, rev., 38:373-74
"Eastbound Route of Jedediah S.
Smith," by Fred N. Fletcher, 2:344-49
Easterbrook (overland, 1849), 22:125,
126, 129
Easterby, Anthony Young, 25:19, 21,
171-72
Easterby Colony (or Rancho), 25:19,
21, 171-172
"Eastern End of the Pony Express,
The," address by Waddell Smith,
29:73-75
Eastern Oregon Land Co., 31:303-4
Eastham, Henry, 13:32
Eastin, James W., 11:141; 16:137, 141
Eastin, Thomas, 16:137
Eastin, W. B., 29:291-92
East Lake (ship), 32:366
Eastland, Joseph Green, 2:244;
18:99-135 *passim,* 229-50 *passim;*
33:373
Eastland, Thomas Butler, 18:99-100,
130-31; 30:93; 33:373; journal and
letters, 18:101-29, 229-45
Eastland, Mrs. Thomas Butler
(Josephine Green), 18:99
Eastling, Mrs. Harvey V., 27:94
"East Looks West: The Manila
Galleon," address by Lauro A. de
Rojas, 15:382
East Lynne (play), 21:56
Eastman (Sacramento, 1853), 11:55, 57
Eastman, August, 30:55
Eastman, Harrison, 20:28, 37, 44;
34:347
Eastman, J. C., 10:271-75 *passim,* 278,
283
Eastman & Loomis, 27: opp. 97
Easton, Ansel Ives, 17:254, 255, 257;
34:337, 340
Easton, Mrs. Ansel Ives (Adeline
Mills), 34:337, 340

Easton, Asahel S., 9:42
Easton, David, 28:340
Easton, Giles Alexander, 20:192;
26:190; 27:254, 255; 37:58-59
Easton, J. S., 15:179
Easton, James H., 29:237
Easton, Kimball Gushee, 26:190; obit.,
4:214
Easton, Mrs. Kimball Gushee
(Katherine Olden), 4:214
Easton, Langdon B., 33:262
Easton, Robert Eastman, 20:192;
26:190; 27:255; 31:304
Easton, Stanley Alexander, 20:192
Easton, "Tony," 30:208
Easton, Wendell, 25:32-34
Eastwood, Alice, 3:9; 4:56; 18:384;
21:370; 22:193; 24:322; 32:247, 256,
258; "Account . . . of the Plants in
the Brackenridge Journal," 24:337-42;
"Early Botanical Explorers on the
Pacific Coast," 18:335-46; ed.
"Archibald Menzies' Journal of the
Vancouver Expedition," 2:265-340;
addresses: "History of Golden Gate
Park," 8:187; "Some Early Botanical
Explorers of California," 18:376; bk.
rev. by, 4:88; address on, 32:180-85
Eastwood, Stewart C., 26:382
Eaton, Albert, 2:115-21 *passim*
Eaton, Benjamin S., 13:335; 21:195;
31:19
Eaton, Ira A., 14:401
Eaton, J. L., 15:28
Eaton, James, 5:289
Eaton, Joseph B., 15:62; 18:53, 54
Eaton and Babb, 14:401; 15:31
Eaton (J. B.) and Co., 8:297, 299, 300
Eayrs, George Washington, 12:223;
13:205
Ebbert, George Wood, 4:283
Ebbets (or Ebbetts), Edward A., 9:26
Ebbets (or Ebbetts), John, 23:331
Ebbets (or Ebbetts), John, Jr., 22:346
Ebbetts, J., 12:138
Ebbetts, John, 4:11; 34:209-27 *passim*
Ebbetts Pass, 4:11; 34:212, 217-27 *passim*
Eberstadt, Edward Emory, "The
Journal of Riley Root," 10:396-405;
ed. Sawyer, *Way Sketches,* rev.,
5:404-5; obit., 37:375
Echeandía, José María, 2:235; 6:258;
8:161-64, 291; 11:74; 12:140, 236-37,
242; 13:211, 213-14; 14:124; 16:217-32
passim; 18:176, 348, 349; 23:7, 194,

204, 215-16, 331; 24:293; 25:346;
27:333, 336; 30:316; 33:279; 36:121;
37:262

Echo de l'Ouest, L', San Francisco,
39:226, 248-49, 253-59 *passim*, 311-15
passim, 347

Echo de Notre-Dame des Victoires, L',
39:246-47, 346

Echo du Pacifique, L', San Francisco,
16:344; 20:165; 30:256-57; 32:112-16
passim, 301; 35:318; 39:4, 16, 141-43,
149, 151, 160-61, 164, 166, 226, 315,
347

Echoes of the Past, by Bidwell, ed.
Quaife, rev., 8:87-88

Eckart & Johnson, 10:246

Ecker, George O., 9:26

Eckfeldt, J. M., 19:146

Eckfeldt, Jacob R., 15:246

E Clampus (or Clampsus) Vitus, 3:202;
5:404; 9:59-62 *passim*, 73, 74; 13:353;
23:73; 31:177

Eckles (Marysville, 1859), 10:176

Eckman, John S., 8:351, 362; *see also*
Fall, Eckman & Co.

Eckman, Julius, 15:167, 170

Eclipse (riv. str.), 11:230; 15:183

Eclipse (ship), 12:220

Eclipse (yacht), 15:278

Eclipses: (1860), 10:252; 29:118;
(moon, 1855), 16:283

Eco del Pacífico, El, San Francisco,
39:16, 143, 164

Ecuador (ship), 39:144

Edalina (ship), 13:6-7, 12, 26

Eddie, Thomas, 4:113, 120, 127, 139

Eddington, John, 33:363

Eddy (Nevada Co., 1852), 3:144

Eddy, Mrs. (Yreka, 1856), 6:74

Eddy (Yuba Co., 1858-61), 9:352; 10:55,
57, 171, 358, 359

Eddy, Mrs. (Yuba Co., 1858), 9:352,
357; 10:359

Eddy, Ellery W., 26:9, 11

Eddy, George 13:31

Eddy, James E., 13:31

Eddy, Mary Morse (Baker), 31:24, 30

Eddy, Ripley A., 8:363; 14:398, 402-3;
15:54; 30:103, 110; *see also* Eddy &
Brother

Eddy, William H., 10:349; 19:121,
138-39

Eddy, Mrs. William H. (1, Eleanor; 2,
F. Alfred; 3, A. M. Pardoe), 19:139

Eddy, William M., 28:382

Eddy, William Matson, 11:126, 134;
13:296; 22:34; 30:329, 330

Eddy & Brother, Marysville, 30:258, 266

Eddy, Mount,, 24:323, 325

Ede, William, 34:337

Eden, Richard, 3:263

Eden (ship), 27:293

"Eden to Eldorado," address by Lucy
Lockwood Hazard, 8:187

Eden Valley, 27:221

Edgar (brothers; Berkeley, 1872),
31:329

Edgar, William, 9:347, 348, 374; 10:44,
266

Edgar, William F., 13:330, 352

Edgar's Hall, Greenville, 10:170

Edgerly and Wickman, 9:319

Edgerton, Henry A., 10:272, 273, 274,
287, 288, 289, 296, 355-56, 357, 368,
381; 11:9; 36:44

Edgerton, Mrs. Henry A., 36:44

Edgington, William, 6:63

Edhelyertha, *see* Sandels Edhelyertha

Edith (play), 21:143

Edith (ship), 10:145; 27:45

Editor on the Comstock Lode, An, by
Drury, rev., 15:381

Edmiston, Robert, 25:21

Edmonson (Marysville, 1851), 15:49

Edmonston, Benjamin Brooke, 30:93

Edmunds, B. F., 28:335, 336, 337

Edmunds, Emily Ann, 32:193

Edmundson, William, 30:36

Edna (ship), 31:297

Edouard (ship), 5:20, 141

Edouart, Alexander, 27:217, 226; 29:129,
261, 333; 30:49, 165-71 *passim*;
paintings by, 29: foll. 336; 30: foll. 56

Edouin, Willie, 21:154, 157

Education:
American period, 15:268; 19:76;
27:269; 28:34-35; 32:127-30, 165-69;
36:348-51; bill to grant land for,
19:18; *see also* Schools
Spanish-Mexican period, 14:14,
23-24, 75; 16:103-7; *see also*
Schools
of women, 31:85-88; *see also* Schools:
for young ladies; Mills College;
Young Ladies' Seminary

Edward, H. F., 32:214, 222

Edward (ship), 14:305-7

"Edward Bosqui, Printer," by Henry
R. Wagner, 21:321-32

"Edward D. Baker," address by
Walter McGovern, 13:188
Edward Everett (ship), 2:82; 12:32;
13:185; 20:27, 44; 23:370
"Edward O. C. Ord on Frontier
Defense," ed. Robert W. Johannsen,
35:23-27
Edwards, Dr. (S.F., 1850), 12:100
Edwards, Dr. (Mariposa, 1852), 28:335
Edwards, Anderson, 30:147
Edwards, Charles, 35:329, 332
Edwards, Edward, 28:337
Edwards, Elza Ivan, 27:94; *Desert
Voices*, rev., 38:77-80
Edwards, Emily, 16:338
Edwards, Henry, 21:160, 252
Edwards, Mrs. Hugh, 32:168
Edwards, John (Camptonville, 1854),
8:199
Edwards, Lt. John (Tehama Co., ca.
1857), 27:215
Edwards, L. B., 5:343
Edwards, LeRoy Mallory, 37:272
Edwards, Moses R., 33:55-56
Edwards, Philip Leget, 15:202, 211,
270; art. on, 3:73-83; *Diary*, rev.,
12:176-77; fac. title p., 3:80; port..,
3: opp. 73
Edwards, Robert, 20:294
Edwards, T., 27:38, 48, 366, 367, 370
Edwards, Thomas, 3:74
Edwards, Uriah, 9:269
Edwards, W. H., 30:69
Edwards, Sanford & Co.'s express,
28:226
"Edward Vischer," address by Erwin
G. Gudde, 16:286
"Edward Vischer's First Visit to
California," ed. and trans. Erwin G.
Gudde, 19:193-216
Edwin, Sophie, 6:10; 9:275; 10:65, 77,
376, 389; 21:59, 63, 69, 148, 157
Edwin Forrest Theatre, *see* Forrest
Theatre
Eel River, 22:103; 23:29, 40; 25:118
Eel River & Eureka Railroad, 38:68
Eells, Cushing, 4:279
Egbert (Colfax, 1861), 4:250
Eggers, George H., 25:35
Eggers, Herman C., 25:35
Eggert, Capt. (Colorado R., 1872),
22:174
Eggleston, Benjamin Thomas, 23:226
Eggleston, C. V., 40:218-24 *passim*
Eggleston, George W., 26:167

Eggs, 3:57; 17:174; 24:65; 38:336;
39:153; *see also Cascarones*
Egidy, Emmy von, 9:398-99
Egyptian Hall, San Francisco, 21:255
Ehmann, Edwin W., 23:190
Ehrenberg, Herman, 5:232; 12:4, 16;
15:284; 22:164
Ehrenberg, Ariz., 12:4, 16, 17; 22:151,
155-64 *passim*
Ehrenfels, Camille (Johnston), 26:286;
address on William Keith, 28:88
Ehrlich, Theodore, 19:288
Ehrman, Sidney Hellman, obit., 9:293
Ehrman, Sidney Myer, 6:375; 9:293;
fellow of CHS, 38:73; address on
earlier California historical societies,
21:183; obits. of Charles J. Deering,
12:88; Alfred I. Esberg, 35:84-85;
William L. Gerstle, 26:281-82;
Timothy Hopkins, 15:97-98; Robert
B.Motherwell II, 22:285; Julian H.
Newbauer, 11:191; Mrs. Joseph Sloss,
21:381; Marcus C. Sloss, 37:182-83
Eich, John, 9:358, 359, 360, 369, 388
Eichelroth, Lillian, *see* Fricot, Mrs.
Desiré
Eichelroth, W. H., 7:117; 26:241
Eichelroth, William E., 9:267; 22:92
Eichler, Lou, 14:225
Eichler, R., 36:368
Eicholtz, L. H., 36:105
Eigenbrodt, Charles S., 25:115
Eigenmann, C. H., 31:157
"1883 Flood on the Middle Yuba River,
The," by Doris Foley and S. Griswold
Morley, 28:233-42
"1849 Letter from California, An,"
from Joseph Ledlie Moody, 13:84-85
Eilerman, B., 9:374(?), 10:200
Eilers, Marguerita, 10:186
Eisen, Francis Theodore, 25:29-30
Eisen, Gustavus Augustus, 4:38, 43;
21:369; 32:183
Eisner, Milton Daniel, obit., 39:77-79
Eisner, Milton S. and Lena (Reinstein),
39:77
Ela, James M., 25:106-9 *passim*
El Buchon, 1:158, 160
El Capitan, Yosemite, 1:272, 276, 277,
278
El Cerrito (Albany Hill), 30:220; 31:330
El Cerrito Creek, 30:219, 220
Eld, Henry, 24:321, 324, 332-33
Elder (Sonoma and Lake cos., 1870s),
20:269

Elder, George, 15:76
Elder, Paul, Jr., 23:95
Elder Creek, 30:160, 162
El Dorado, El Dorado Co., *see* Mud Springs
El Dorado, Nev., 22:9, 162
El Dorado (saloon), Los Angeles, 13:321
El Dorado (saloon), Marysville, 14:392; 15:40, 45-46, 50
El Dorado (gambling house), San Francisco, 8:273; 16:130; 27:368; 33:57
El Dorado (barge), 22:156, 168
Eldorado (riv. str.), 8:19
Eldorado, L' (company), 22:302
El Dorado Canyon, Placer Co., 2:204-5
El Dorado Canyon, Colorado R., 3:163, 167, 168, 169; 12:12; 22:14-17 *passim*, 151, 163
El Dorado County, 7:6, 11, 17, 18, 19; 20:158; early homes in, 27:280-82
El Dorado Ditch Co., 16:30, 31
'Eldorado Gothic: Gold Rush Architects and Architecture," by Harold Kirker, 38:31-46
El Dorado Hotel, Foster's Bar, 8:199, 348, 352, 362; 9:157, 161, 164
El Dorado Mining Co., 15:52
El Dorado News Depot, Stockton, 30:110
Eldredge, Albert S., 33:373
Eldredge, Zoeth Skinner, 1:110; 30:39
Eldridge, Benjamin and Eliza (Rainey), 32:90
Eldridge, James, 15:4, 19
Eldridge, Thomas A., 30:17, 35
Election frauds, 15:173, 174, 281; 16:307, 340
Elections:
    under Mex. regime, 1:26; 27:333-38
    under U.S.: in 1850s, 6:220; 8:360, 365; 9:106-11, 115-16, 178-79; 15:173; 37:331-32; direct primary, 5:285; presidential (1856), 9:66, 78, 100, 104, 106; (1860), 27:101, 103; (1864), 22:232-33; 34:49-64; to ratify State Constitution, 12:29; on statehood for Calif., 3:127
Electra (ship), 22:163, 167
Electric Interurban Railways in America, The, by Hilton and Due, rev. 39:374-75
Electric lighting and power, 34:350; 35:272; 37:228; *see also* Hydroelectric

Eleonore, *see* Leonore, Mme.
Elephant, 38:336; seeing the, 8:82; 10:405; 12:95; 22:149, 243; 24:35, 37; 27:363; 32:291; 34:22, 72; illus., 39: foll. 344
Elet, J. A., 29:142, 144, 146
Elevator, Occidental Hotel, San Francisco, 32:59-60
Eleven Mile House (nr. Marysville), 9:154
Elha (Sutter's Fort, 1848), 26:119
Elias, Jacob, 13:335
Elias, Solomon Philip, *Stories of Stanislaus*, rev., 3:90-92
Elijah (Indian, 1844), 29:322-23
"Elisha Oscar Crosby," by Charles A. Barker, 27:133-40
Eliza, Francisco de, 10:314, 317-40 *passim*
Eliza (ship), 6:257, 260, 261; 23:303, 305, 331
Elizabeth (brig, 1848), 18:177
Elizabeth (storeship, 1850), 8:265
Elizabeth (schr., Colorado R., 1857), 22:169
Elizabeth Lake, 17:102-3
Elizabeth Pass, 28:186
Eliza City, 5:34; 7:206, 403; 8:25, 167-82; 10:366; 14:216-17, 218, 384, 389, 399, 402; 15:41
Elizalde, Juan, 28:265
Elk, 1:114; 2:54, 58, 236; 5:113, 127, 130, 136, 153; 7:361; 12:208, 290, 305; 13:20, 21; 14:103, 139, 142; 16:134; 22:209, 211, 216, 325-44 *passim*; 23:19, 24-27 *passim*, 31-38 *passim*, 123-37 *passim*
Elk Camp, 26:4
Elkins, Felton Broomall Ashley, 19:288; obit., 23:185
Elkins, Mrs. Frances (Adler), 26:94
Elkins, Meyer, 40:233, 234, 235; phot., opp. 215
Elkins, Nathan, 40:233, 234, 235
Elkins, Mrs. William L., Jr. (Katherine Felton), 10:206; 19:288; 23:185; obit., 14.95
Elk Mountain, 23:142
Elk River Mill & Lumber Co., 38:66
Elleman (Marysville, 1858), 9:374
Ellen Craig (ship), 16:337
Ellen Foster (ship), 15:375
Ellery, Epes, 30:254, 255, 354-55, 356, 365; 33:373
Ellery, Nathaniel, 39:21, 22

Ellery & Doyle, 30:254, 255
Ellett, Charles, 15:29-30
Ellig, John, 5:125
Ellington, James, 13:338
Elliot, George H., 15:65-66, 68; 19:233
Elliot, Mrs. George H. (Nellie Ritchie), 19:233
Elliot, George W., 20:114
Elliot, John B., 39:127
Elliot, Thomas, 27:227
Elliot de Castro, John, 12:231, 232-33; 35:236
Elliott, Lt. (U.S.N., 1849), 1:270
Elliott (S.F., 1853), 33:292, 301, 302, 307
Elliott, Miss (m. George Hudson, 1853), 28:294
Elliott, Dr. (Sacramento, 1858), 9:251
Elliott, Capt. (of *Azalene*, 1889), 31:155
Elliott, Caroline A., 28:294
Elliott, Edward G., 27:36, 47
Elliott, Gardner, 26:232
Elliott, Mrs. Henry, 21:152
Elliott, J. H., 31:28
Elliott, S. G., map by, 10:347-48
Elliott, Thomas, 33:307
Elliott, Thomas B., 31:19
Elliott, Thompson Coit, 22:191
Elliott, W. T. C. ("Rough"), 21:235, 238
Elliott, Washington, 24:263; 26:71; 29:125, 127; 36:298(?)
Elliott, William B., 17:240; 19:131, 135, 142; 24:58
Elliott, Mrs. William B. (Elizabeth Patton), 19:131, 135, 142
Ellis (Indian, 1840s), 21:2, 6
Ellis, (S.F., 1849), 27:260
Ellis, Alfred James, 15:370; 16:81; 17:174, 179, 301; 19:4; fac. sig., 10: opp. 159
Ellis, Arthur McDonald, 5:408; 13:353; obits. of Grant Jackson, 4:215; Maurice H. Newmark, 9:94-95; Charles B. Turrill, 6:202; obit., 11:191
Ellis, Asa, 8:342, 343; 9:52
Ellis, C. J., 17:179
Ellis, Charles S., 9:385; 10:166
Ellis, Elvira, 23:189
Ellis, Frederick W., 16:132
Ellis, George M., rev. of Harris, *The Gila Trail: The Texas Argonauts and the California Gold Rush*, 40:160-61
Ellis, Henry, 9:201

Ellis, Moses, 29:253-54
Ellis, R. B., 10:62, 69, 70; 11:9
Ellis, Rensselaer, 13:3
Ellis, S. C., 11:127
Ellis, Sam N. L. (or L.N.), 4:51; 28:186
Ellis, Samuel, 33:316
Ellis, William, 38:219
Ellis, William Turner, 28:233, 235, 240
Ellis & Brother, Santa Rosa, 30:363
Ellis & Co., San Francisco, 15:172
Ellis (Hyman and Nathan) Co., Ukiah, 33:375
Ellison, Mrs. John F. (Minnie Cason), ed., *Judge John F. Ellison*, rev., 9:87-88
Ellison, Joseph, "The Struggle for Civil Government in California," 10:3-26, 129-64, 220-44; *Californa and the Nation, 1850-1869*, rev., 6:377-79
Ellison, Robert S., 21:383
Ellison, William Henry, 19:95; 32:264; ed. "Memoirs of Hon. William M. Gwin," 19:1-26, 157-84, 256-77, 344-67; ed. William A. Streeter, "Recollections of Historical Events in California, 1842-1878," 18:64-71, 157-79, 254-78
Ellison *v.* Noyes, 9:362
Ellsworth, Anson M. and Josephine (Phillips), 9:287
Ellsworth, Rodney Sydes, address, "California Redwood Pioneers," 17:185; *Giant Sequoia*, rev., 3:300-301
Elmar, Patrick, lawsuit, 9:140, 145
Elmira (ship), *see Delmira*, 14:345
El Monte, 3:169; 12:7, 12; 13:321, 332; 20:157, 168; 29:240; 32:328
Eloesser, Leo, 22:94, 383; obit. of Howard Christian Naffziger, 40:273-74
El Paso, Tex., 34:126, 128, 139
El Paso del Norte (Juarez), 1:59; 9:13; 18:121, 122, 125-27, 229, 245; 34:126; 40:163
El Pueblo, Los Angeles, by Hill, rev., 7:93-94
"El Reposo" (sanitarium), 31:20
El Rio, 16:297, 303
Elsey, Charles, 24:189
Elsey, Fred Tilden, obit., 17:191
Elstner, H. R., 29:349-50
Elstner, Milton Rains, 7:118; 18:282
El Tucho (place), 29:23, 27-28

Elvira Harbeck (ship), 15:277, 280; 19:230; 25:336
Elwell (Camptonville, 1857), 9:137, 262, 266; 10:55
Elwell, David A., 9:350, 360, 380
Elwell, Robert J., 23:208, 212, 217
Elwell, Mrs. Robert J. (Vicenta Sánchez), 23:217
Elwell, W., 10:254
Elwood, Isaac, 29:350-56 *passim*
Ely, A., 9:42
Ely, Benjamin E. S., 9:149, 150, 151, 170, 177, 254, 257, 259, 269, 281, 349, 353; 10:54, 76
Ely, Charles Arthur, 33:373; 38:166
Ely, I., 21:227
Ely, Justin, Jr., 21:306
Elysian Valley, 18:303
Emanuela (ship), 22:170
Embarcadero, on Sacramento R., 24:25
Embarcadero, San Francisco, 26:267, 268
Embuscade (ship), 17:168, 169; 35:323
Emeline (ship), 25:330-32
Emerald Pool, Yosemite, 1:281, 282
Emeric, Joseph, 33:373
Emerson, Capt. (San Jose, 1850), 11:162
Emerson (Mokelumne Hill, 1851), 30:242
Emerson, David L., 20:2
Emerson, Edwin, 33:93
Emerson, Mark L., address, "Shell Mounds and Caves around San Francisco Bay," 13:284
Emerson, Ralph, 29:242
Emerson, Ralph Waldo, 4:28, 296; 33:225; 37:40; arts. on, 20:1-11; 33:241-48
Emerson, William ("Billy"), 12:80; 20:2; 21:166, 172; 35:142; *see also* Emerson Minstrels
"Emerson and California," by John Q. Anderson, 33:241-48
Emerson Minstrels, 20:2; 21:166-69 *passim*, 172, 173, 175; 34:352
"Emerson the Lecturer in California," by William H. Davis, 20:1-11
Emery, Capt. (Colorado R., 1866), 22:171
Emery, George Washington, 35:329, 332
Emery, James H., 2:122
Emery & Co., Murphy's, 11:330
Emick, Isaac R., 14:177

Emigrant Gap, 23:117, 119, 120
Emigrant Road Commission, 7:4-6; 15:267
"Emigrant's Dream, The," by Ernest A. Wiltsee, 15:324-48
Emigrant Spring, 18:200, 201; 32:202
Emigrant train (railroad), 16:292-96; 18:363-64
Emigration, 10:4-6; 12:354; 24:17-46, 117; of 1844, 4:277-78, 280; from Calif., 15:175, 268; 17:184; 29:165; 33:26; from British Isles, 7:205; 32:273; 33:23-26 *passim*; from N.M., 10:34; from Switzerland, 30:305-8; *see also* Immigration; Overland journeys
Emilie (ship), 15:371
Emma (lake str.), 32:365
Emma Adelia (schr.), 18:373
Emma Louisa Morgan (ship), 27:293
Emmanuel, E., 22:83
Emmert, Paul, 22:36; 33:29-30
Emmet Guard, 10:390
Emmett, Daniel Decatur, 20:244, 258
Emmons, George Foster, 22:347; 24:321-22, 332; 36:307
Emmons, Thornton, 36:379; coauth. "More on the Ewing Mutiny," 36:307-11
Emory (Marysville, 1853), 22:35
Emory, C. C., 13:31
Emory, Frederick, 15:88
Emory, S., 13:31
Emory, William Hemsley, 1:142-45 *passim*; 2:217, 232; 9:4-15 *passim*; 13:151, 152, 154, 304; 17:343; 19:3; 21:194, 215, 216, 221, 345, 354; 22:46, 49, 64; 25:293, 294, 300, 303, 306; 26:23, 27, 42-49 *passim*; 33:266, 267; 34:197
Emory's Crossing, 8:338, 340, 344, 348, 355; 9:51; 28:234, 237, 239, 241-42
Emparan, Mrs. Ricardo de (Luisa Vallejo), 1:184, 293; 17:237, 239; coauth. *History of . . . Sonoma*, rev., 2:364-65; fac. wedding invitation, 17: opp. 225
Empire City, 11:361-62; 23:369, 376
Empire City (ship), 8:7; 12:312; 20:15, 17; 24:67; 34:337
Empire County Argus, 30:111
Empire Guards, 37:362
Empire Mine, 15:290
Empire Ranch (hotel), 3:147, 159,

160-61; 8:199, 208-9; 9:63, 70, 351, 355; 10:192, 370; 11:155
Empire Sawmill, 9:66
Empire Stage Line, 14:385, 402
Employers' and Manufacturers' Association, 35:65-68, 145-49, 152
Emric, Joseph, 16:341
Emslie, James J., 21:293, 306
Enchanted Beauty, The (play), 21:56
Enchantress, The (play), 21:182
Encinal (Oakland), 31:326
Encinal de San Antonio, 15:173
Encinal National Bank, Alameda, 34:330
Encinal Tanning Co., 33:72
Encino, *see* Ranchos: Encino
"Endearing San Francisco Quartet," 9:175
Endicott, William H., 3:153-54
Endyear's Bar, 13:28
Engaño, Cabo (or Punta), 3:312, 313, 372, 376, 380; 7:22, 55, 72
Engelson, Lester G., "Proposals for the Colonization of California by England ... 1837-1846," 18:136-48
Engelhardt, Zephyrin, 5:324; 23:3, 6, 251; 30:321; *Mission Dolores* (extract), rev., 7:409; *Santa Barbara Mission*, rev., 2:252-56
Engers, Capt. (of *Johanna and Oluffa*, 1849), 25:100
England, Thomas, 38:34
England, *see* Great Britain
Englander (Marysville, 1858), 9:357
Engle, Clair, 36:323
Engle, Wiliam A., 40:218, 230
Engler, George, 14:399, 407; 15:46
Engler, Jacob, 19:292
English, B. F., 32:376
English, James L., 3:83; 9:36, 116; 15:276
English, William, 19:60; 27:316
English, William Hayden, 9:272; 11:14, 15, 26, 27
English Bar, 8:338, 355; 9:164
English Comic Opera Company, 21:173
English Dam, *see* Dams
"English Jim," *see* Stuart, James
English Mountain, 28:233
English Opera Troupe, *see* Lyster's
Engs, Mrs. Edward W. (Eleanita Rawlings), 19:382
Ennis, Scott, 33:12
Ennis, William H., 35:292-307 *passim;*

Journal, ed. Harold F. Taggart, 33:1-12, 147-68
Ennis, Mrs. William H. (Susan D. Coates), 33:167
Enquirer, Oakland, 8:285
Enright, John Shea, 33:380; "The Breens of San Juan Bautista," 33:349-59
Enright & Murphy, 33:375
Enríquez, Martin, 7:235-38 *passim*, 252
Enriquita quicksilver mine, 14:159; 30:170
Ensenada, Lower Calif., 12:318-19; 21:329-330; 27:203, 205; 31:354
Ensign, Eliza and father, 37:234
Ensign, George H., 9:259, 283; 15:276(?)
Ensworth, A. S., 10:62
Enterprise, Virginia City, see *Territorial Enterprise*
Enterprise (ship, 1801), 12:217
Enterprise (riv. str., 1854), 15:168
Enterprise (H.B.M. ship, 1854), 15:175
Enterprise (schr., Colorado R., 1870), 22:173
Enterprise (Matson str., 20th cent.), 30:212
Enterprise Canal, 25:22
Enterprise Colony, 25:174
Entewa (California romance), 22:32, 33; 30:110
Epadon, L' (ship), 35:313
Eperson (d. Ham's Fork, 1847), 16:128
Epic of the Overland, The, by Fulton, rev., 4:299-300
Epigram, The, San Francisco, 10:64
Episcopal church, *see* Protestant Episcopal church
Epperson (Marysville Buttes, 1862), 10:382
Epperson Toll Road, 32:364-65
Eppinger & Co., 27:199
Epstein, Henry, 35:273, 346
Epworth League, 35:68
Equal Rights Expositor, Visalia, 20:160-64 *passim*
Erie (ship), 2:163; 3:108, 113; 7:82; 17:125; 22:51, 65; 26:221; 28:342; 34:119
Erkson, Alexander Combs, 29:56
Erkson, Mrs. Alexander Combs (Caroline Millard), 24:41, 56, 177, 179
Ermatinger, Edward, 22:100-105 *passim*
Ermatinger, Emil (Francis?), 19:197, 214
Ermatinger, Francis (Frank), 17:68,

145; 19:310; 22:100, 101; 28:243, 245, 249, 254
Ernández, Attilano, 37:204
Ernani (opera), 15:183
Ernst, Will R., 24:380-81
Eroclydon (ship), 16:282
Erwin (Galena Hill, 1854), 8:205
Erwin, Joseph, 38:309
Erwin, Richard ("Dick"), 10:172
Erwin, S. M., 6:113; 10:398
Erythea (botanical journal), 32:258-59
Esberg, Alfred Isaac, 25:230, 232; obit., 35:84-85
Esberg, Edith, 21:381
Esberg, Mendel and Matilda (Hirschfeld), 18:286; 21:381; 35:84
Esberg, Milton Herman, 35:84; obit., 18:286-87
Escalante, Silvestre Vélez de, 6:103; 10:27; 22:194
"Escalante Expedition to California, The," address by Herbert E. Bolton, 6:103
Escambia (ship), 27:293
Escamilla, Joaquín de los Santos, 1:95, 178; 35:103
Esche, Otto, 9:310-11, 313, 318-31
Esche Brothers & Co., 30:258
Eschscholtz, Johann Friedrich von, 4:154-55; 12:207-9; 18:338
Eschscholtzia, see California poppy
Escobar, Agustín, 11:209-10
Escobar, Marcelino, 21:320
Escoceses, Los (political party), 8:223
Escondido Spring, Tex., 18:115, 135
Escott, Lucy, 10:265; 21:51; 29:119; 38:338
Esdon, Alexander, 32:90
Esdon, Erskine E., 32:90; 33:373
Eshleman, John Morton, 39:28
Esmeralda (ship), 22:14-19 *passim*, 23, 24, 25, 167
Esmeralda County, Nev., 26:236, 238, 240-42
Esmeralda Lode, 26:237
Esmeralda mining district, 10:261; 39:291
Esmeralda Star (later *Union*), 9:193, 194, 198-99; 23:260
Esparza (Gov. Baja Calif., 1860), 13:328; 38:339
Espérance, L' (company), 22:296-97
Esperanza Consolidated Oil Co., 30:212
Esperanza Sanatorium, 31:20
Espí, José de la Cruz, 23:4

Espindola, Manuel, 29:323
Espinosa (L.A., 1838), 13:222
Espinosa (S.F., 1854), 15:179, 183; 16:283
Espinosa, Estevan, 16:221
Espinosa, Hipólito (or Apolito), 12:117, 120; *see also* Hipólito
Espinosa, Martín de, 3:310, 363-67; 19:242
Espinosa, Prudencio, 4:378, 379, 380
Espinosa, Rodrigo de, 2:140; 7:27, 146, 151, 172, 173, 182, 192, 253; (log, 1565), 7: (fac.) 152-68, (trans.) 169-71
Espinosa, Salvador, 23:9
Espinosa, Trinidad, 15:122
Espinosa de los Monteros, Juan José, 24:292, 308; 25:60, 166, 362
Espinosa y Tello, José, 3:215, 218, 237; 40:118
Espirito Santo (fishing boat), 35:240
Espiritu Santo Island, 3:318, 336, 346; *see also* Perlas
Esquimaux, 35:307
Essex Mine, 6:353
Essig, Edward Oliver, 10:302; 12:187; 31:340; 39:98, 113; "The Russian Settlement at Ross," 12:191-209; address, "Some Russian Influences on the History of California," 8:90-91
Essler (S.F., 1854), 15:163
Estabrook, Ethan, 28:97
Estanislao (Indian, 1829), 3:91; 14:22; 16:219
Estavan, Lawrence, address, "Highlights of San Francisco Opera History," 18:376
Este, Thomas, 9:259
Estee, Morris M., 28:49
Estell (Sacramento, 1858), *see* Estill
Estelle (Mrs. Simon), 5:21, 26
Esténega, Tomás Eleuterio, 8:142-48 *passim;* 19:207, 215
Esterbrook (overland, 1849), 22:129-30
Esterbrook, William W., 2:122
Estero Bay, 11:247, 250
Estevan, C. G., 33:347
Esther (ship), 6:257, 260
Estill (or Estell), James Madison, 9:248, 253, 273, 284, 371; 17:263; 21:33; 29:158-59; 32:147-57 *passim*
Estrada, Adelaida, 29:27
Estrada, Carolina, 24:381
Estrada, Joaquín, 1:170; 36:10-15
Estrada, José Antonio, 24:333
Estrada, Josefa, 13:35

Estrada, José Mariano, 1:170; 14:22; 16:217, 218, 219; 18:175; 23:205, 216

Estrada, José Ramón, 1:170; 12:238; 16:248, 348, 352; 18:175; 29:27, 318

Estrada, Julian, 1:170; 18:163, 175

Estrada, Nicanor, 14:234, 237, 252-57 *passim*, 267; 16:240

Estrada, Patricio, 15:347, 348, 356

Estrada, Pedro, 1:170; 13:34

Estrella, 11:250, 251, 264

Estudillo, Dolores, *see* Bandini, Mrs. Juan

Estudillo, José Antonio, 14:231; 15:339; 19:209, 216; 26:22; 31:33

Estudillo, José Guadalupe, 31:47

Estudillo, José Joaquín, 4:385, 386; 10:73; 11:76, 142; 23:216; 31:45; letter from, 13:107-8

Estudillo, José María, 3:25-26; 12:122, 224; 14:9, 12, 26; 28:258; 31:34; 37:106

Estudillo, Marcelina, 23:216

Estudillo, María Antonia, *see* Pedrorena, Mrs. Miguel

Estudillo, María de Jesús, *see* Davis, Mrs. William Heath

Estudillo home, San Diego, 4:396

Estudillo House, San Leandro, 10:73; 31:283

"Etc.," Harte's section of *Overland Monthly*, 28:8, 9

Etchison, James, 2:291-92

Ethiopian Minstrels, 17:172

Ethiopian Serenaders, 15:46

Ethno-Historical Society, 1:10

Etholin, Adolphus, 12:237, 249, 269; 17:64

Etienne, Mrs. E. J. (Ida Precht), 32:248; quoted, 261-62

Etiwanda, 26:280; 27:113, 120

Etna (riv. str.), 25:223

Etna Mills, 6:345, 346

Etoile des Pauvres et des Souffrants, L' (monthly), 39:223-25, 347-48

Eubanks, Brantley M., 28:379; obit., of Joseph J. Geary, 38:180

Eucalyptus, 16:143; 18:338; 27:280; 32:245, 246, 247, 256; 35:185

Euchre Diggings, 20:39-42

Eugene, Ore., newspaper, 32:231

Euphemia (ship), 14:326, 330, 342, 345, 346; 31:33; 33:340-41; 38:40

Euphrasia (ship), 38:166

Eureka, Humboldt Co., 2:124; 5:145, 248; 22:384; 30:359-60; 34:266; 38:59-69 *passim;* newspaper, 19:68; 27:318

Eureka (proj. town), on Napa R., 17:234

Eureka, Nevada Co., 11:238, 240, 242; 29:194, 195; *see also* Graniteville

Eureka (ship, 1849), 38:165-67

Eureka (ship, 1884), 16:302

Eureka Engine Co., Marysville, 9:354, 385-86; 10:250, 258, 264, 285

Eureka Flour Mills, San Francisco, 16:347

Eureka: From Cleveland by Ship to California, 1849-50, by Fletcher, rev., 38:165-67

Eureka Lake, 29:197-98

Eureka Lake & Yuba Canal Co., 29:193-96, 199, 205

Eureka Light Horse Guard, San Francisco, 15:174, 373; 37:363, 364, 367

Eureka Lodging House, San Francisco, 2:242

Eureka Mills, 11:243

Eureka Mine, Amador Co., 20:184

Eureka Mine, Nevada Co., 19:28

Eureka Quartz Mining Co., 15:52

Eureka South, *see* Graniteville

Eureka Theater, San Francisco, 21:56, 62, 64, 145, 146

Europa (frigate, 1836), 14:342; 15:347; 23:327, 334

Europa (ship, 1858), 29:105; 30:356

Eurydice (ship), 15:176, 183, 374

Eusebio (Indian, 1846), 6:185

Eustace (ship), 30:382; 33:376

Evans (Yuba Co., 1859), 10:168, 169

Evans, Albert S., 20:266, 267; 35:238

Evans, Alfred, 2:139

Evans, Benjamin C., 22:128, 147

Evans, Chris, 8:281-82

Evans, David, 38:63, 68

Evans, Elliot A. P., 23:189; 33:380; "William S. and William D. Jewett," 33:309-20; ed. "Some Letters of William S. Jewett, California Artist," 23:149-77, 227-46; address, "William Dunbar Jewett," 32:174; obit. of Mrs. Charles H. Janin, 35:183

Evans, George, 4:60; 10:201

Evans, George H. (M.D.), 23:287

Evans, George H. (mining eng.), 29:208

Evans, George S., 11:7, 8; 24:278; 40:299, 349

Evans, George T., 25:341

Evans, George W. B., 33:276-77

Evans, Henry J., 39:55-56

Evans (Hepzebah) *v.* John H. Drumgold, 9:158

Evans, Hugh, 16:51-52

Evans, Israel, 6:60-61; 14:273, 276, 278; 26:112-13, 122; 32:195

Evans, J., 13:32

Evans, James, 8:358

Evans, John Henry, *Charles Coulson Rich*, rev., 16:85

Evans, Luther Harris, 29:284

Evans, Morris, 32:130, 135

Evans, Nelson, 2:139

Evans, Oliver Perry, 22:383; 33:373; 35:178

Evans, Mrs. Oliver Perry (Nora M. Ryan), 35:179

Evans, P. J., 16:182

Evans, Perry, 22:383-84; obit., 35:178-79

Evans, Richard S., 7:61

Evans, Robert, 26:234-35

Evans, West, 36:103

Evans, William (d. 1851), 14:176

Evans, William (S.F., 1854), 15:169

Evans, Mrs. William (Hannah), 14:175, 182; 37:237

Evans *v.* Ford, 9:352

Evarts, William Maxwell, 21:120

Eveleth, Dwight, 14:182

Everding (John) & Co., 31:331

Everest, George, 21:65

Everett, Amelia, 37:284; "The Ship *Brooklyn*," 38:220-40

Everett, C. E., 28:335, 337

Everett, Elisha, 14:271

Everett, J. P., 15:181

Everett, John C., 17:333-34

Everett, John H., 8:300; 12:146; 23:200, 319-20, 333

Everett, Orlando, 2:128

Everhart, Lazarus, 1:92; 4:309, 310; 5:125; 27:352

Everitt, Henry, 8:199, 209

Everline (ship), 14:315

Eversfield, Charles, 33:104-5, 106

Evershed, Thomas E., 21:312, 313, 314, 315

Everts, Frank D., 19:296

Eviction (play), 21:256

Evodio, José, 15:356

Evoy, Mrs. B. M., 31:333

Evrard, James, 20:296

Ewald, John, 37:211

Ewalt, John, 16:81, 84

Ewer, Ferdinand Cartwright, 1:299; 9:180; 10:290; 16:81, 336; 17:177; 20:332; 23:175, 229, 245, 337; 25:337, 345; 28:34; 29:2, 3; 30:252; 36:343, 346; 38:300; art. on, 13:291-300; 14:74-79; port., 13: opp. 291

Ewer, Mrs. Ferdinand Cartwright (Sophia Mandell Congdon), 14:74, 79

Ewer, Peter Folger, 13:291-96 *passim*, 299-300; drawing by, 13: opp. 297

Ewer, Warren B., 31:336-42 *passim*

Ewer family, 13:291; 14:75-77

Ewing, Judge (from Texas, 1849), 18:129, 135, 229, 230, 238

Ewing, Calvin, 28:49

Ewing Thomas, 9:8, 9, 12, 13, 14; 19:20; 26:323; letters to, 14:368-69; 26:324, 325-26, 333

Ewing family (Sonoma Co.), 11:11

Ewing (ship), 10:411; 11:300, 302; 25:110, 255, 260-63, 266; 29:186; 30:39-47; 36:307-11

Examiner, San Francisco, 10:268; 11:190; 30:195, 199, 203-4; 31:303; 32:237, 260-61

Excelsior, *see* Meadow Lake City

Excelsior Co., 18:154

Excelsior Mine, 35:341

Excelsior Printing Office, 31:381

Exchange (ship), 15:170, 171, 172, 175

Exchange Hotel, San Francisco, *see* American Exchange Hotel

Exchange Hotel, Slate Range Bar, 8:342

Excrement, medicinal use of, 19:123, 139; human, as fertilizer, 37:81

Exhibitions, California Historical Society, 3:95; 4:99-101, 212-13, 303, 403; 5:98, 100, 206-7, 418; 6:106; 7:99; 8:93

Expédition Française pour les Mines d'Or de Sacramento, 22:292

"Expedition That Never Sailed, The: A Mystery of the Civil War," by Clarence C. Clendenen, 34:149-56

"Exploration of the Sierra Nevada," by Francis P. Farquhar, 4:3-58

Explorer (ship), 22:8, 9, 167; illus., 22: opp. 1

Explorers, The: The History of San Diego, by Pourade, rev., 40:353-55

"Exploring California, 1860-1873," address by Francis P. Farquhar, 7:410

Expounder (ship), 33:376

Express, Marysville, *see California Express*

Express (ship), 19:213
Express Building, San Francisco, 25:5
Express companies, 6:332; 8:203, 212, 385; 9:173, 407; 13:259; 14:403; 15:328; 17:81; 28:226; Bowers', 6:246; Everts', 19:296, 297; Freeman's, 14:403; Gregory's, 13:88; 16:30, 378; 22:224; Hawes', 11:30-32, (frank, illus.) opp. 30, 31; Hawley's, 14:403; Monson's, 14:403; Palmer's, 14:403; Rumrill's, 8:202, 211; Todd's, 13:259; Tracy's and King's, 16:177, 181; *see also* Adams & Co.; Langton's Pioneer Express; Pacific Express; Wells Fargo & Co.
Express Hotel, Marysville, 8:211
"Extracts from the Log of the U.S. Frigate *Savannah*, Kept by Robert Carson Duvall," 3:105-25
Eymerlin (sailor, 1845), 11:223, 340, 345, 348

Eymont, Capt. (of *Chateau Briant*, 1849), 13:382
Eyre, Edward Engle (1823-1899), 9:270; 23:287; 24:277; 27:5; 32:185; 40:315, 349
Eyre, Edward Engle (b. 1890), 23:287; 32:185
Eyre, Edward Lilburn, 13:192; 23:287
Eyre, Mrs. Edward Lilburn (Florence Atherton), 23:287; 32:185; obit., 13:192
Eyre, Gerald, 21:257
Eyre, M. D., 9:26
Eyre, Robert, 25:232
Eyre (Edward L.) & Co., 27:284
Eytinge, Rose, 21:243, 251
"Ezel" (pseud.), 24:23
Ezeta, Bruno de, *see* Hezeta
Ezeta, Entrada de (Columbia R.), 10:326, 327

F

F., V. J., *see* Fourgeaud, Victor J.
Fabens (San Bernardino, 1852), 14:181
Fabian, Bentham, 24:106
"Facétie" (pseud.), 39:160
"Fact *vs.* Fancy in California History," address by Carl I. Wheat, 7:289
Fagen, Pierce B., 2:205
Fages, Pedro, 1:155, 158, 161, 162, 169; 3:6, 100; 4:4, 143; 10:211-19; 11:29, 274, 277; 13:196, 198, 202-3; 14:7, 9; 15:213, 216-17, 219; 17:120, 122; 26:372; 30:2; 33:15-16, 373; 36:2-5 *passim*, 129; route, 10: (map) opp. 211; 34:193-208; 36:120-21, 126
"Fages' Crossing of the Cuyamacas," by Hero E. Rensch, 34:193-208
Faget, T. B., 17:85
Fagg, Robert A., 30:361
Fagg & Feast, 22:39
Fagoaga, Francisco, 24:291; 25:149, 356, 362
Faint Heart Never Won Fair Lady (play), 16:283, 339; 28:37
Fair, Harry Heasley, obit., 40:84-85
Fair, James Graham, 8:384; 17:236;

18:151, 153, 155; 19:234; 23:383-84; fac. letter, 17: opp. 224
Fair, Mrs. William D. (Laura Hunt Stone Grayson), 7:118; 19:256
Fairbanks, G. V., 8:358; 10:167, 189; lawsuit, 10:180
Fairbanks, Nathaniel, 14:180
Fairbrother (Calaveras Co., 1850), 22:72-75 *passim*
Fairchild (comedian, 1851), 15:44, 45, 48
Fairchild, David, 11:9, 23; 13:3, 6, 15, 24, 26
Fairchild, Ephraim, 11:141; 16:136, 138
Fairchild, James G., 31:135
Fairchild, John, 20:308
Fairchild, Mrs. John B., *see* Oatman, Olive
Fairchild, Joseph D., 12:323
Fairchild, Lucius, 11:84; 38:38
Fairchild, Mahlon Dickerson, "The First Ore from 'Washoe,' " 12:323-30; "Reminiscences of a 'Forty-Niner,' " 13:3-33; "A Trip to the Colorado Mines in 1862," 12:11-17

Fairchild, O. L. C., 12:323
Fairchild, Theodore Tracy, 12:11
Fairfax, Charles S., 9:54, 72, 104, 106,
    251, 259, 269, 276, 380, 397; 10:44, 395;
    11:10, 122; 12:200; 15:29, 33, 368
Fairfield, 17:268
Fair Haven Oil Co., 16:284
Fair House, Marysville, *see* Pavilion
Fair Oaks Ranch, 31:19
Fairs and exhibitions: church,
    32:126-27, 140; Indian, 24:231; Ladies'
    Christian Commission, 23:237, 246;
    24:261-66; Mechanics', 17:316; 20:266;
    36:245; Northern Dist., Marysville,
    10:194, 360, 369; 36:245; State
    Agricultural Soc., 10:196, 198
Fairweather, Thomas, 28:234
Fairy Minstrels, 9:59, 61, 73
Fairy Saloon, Oregon Hill, 8:199, 207
Fajard, Eugene, 14:207
Fake, Capt. (Colorado R., 1865), 22:170
Falamante, José D., 29:236
Falcon (ship), 13:389, 390, 397; 18:375;
    20:13, 99, 330; 27:34, 35, 47; 29:8
Falcon, Cabo, 9:235, 241
Falconer, Eric A., 24:189; addresses,
    "General E. O. C. Ord," 22:374-75;
    "The Presidio of San Francisco,"
    24:184
Fales, Fernando, 9:277
Falkenau, Louis, 30:382
Falkenberg, Emelia Antonia von, 31:382
Falkner, Capt. (Colorado R., 1861),
    22:169
Fall, Mrs. (Marysville, 1861), 10:280
Fall (L.A., 1871), 32:337
Fall, John C., 8:350, 351, 362; 9:73, 157,
    164, 385; 10:42, 47, 64, 66, 172-73, 181,
    251, 258, 262, 265, 269, 361-62; 14:400,
    401; 15:28, 33, 51; family of, 10:269;
    see also Fall, Eckman, & Co.
Fall, Eckman & Co., 8:350, 351, 362;
    9:51, 57, 58; lawsuit, 9:62
Fall, Hanson & Co., 10:361
Fallon (lawsuit, S.F., 1850), 34:241-42
Fallon, James, 24:268
Fallon, Malachi, 24:364
Fallon, Thomas, 14:148, 205; 25:126;
    28:339; 29:273; cor., 8:72-74, 75-76
Fallon, William O., 1:73, 134; 4:307;
    6:140, 273; 7:79; 17:220-22, 240;
    19:122, 139; 24:58; 29:264
Fallon Hotel, Columbia, 24:268
Fallon, Hudson & Co. (lawsuit, Yuba
    Co., 1858), 9:370

Fall River, 22:208, 216; 23:137
Fall River Valley, 22:208; newspaper,
    31:190
Falls, Richard J., 1:255; 26:43
Falls of Clyde Mining Co., 26:243
Falmouth (ship), 22:22, 168
Fama (ship), 14:129, 346; 17:293;
    28:243, 254
"Family of George C. Yount, The," by
    Boutwell Dunlap, 2:67-68
Family Jars (play), 15:48
"Famous Voyage of Sir Francis Drake,
    The," from Richard Hakluyt, *The
    Principall Navigations, Voiages and
    Discoveries of the English Nation,*
    3:205; 11:311; 16: No. 1, Pt. 2, pp. 16,
    22, 23, 27-30, 52; 36:22-23; *see also*
    Hakluyt, Richard
Fanchon (play), 21:149
Fandango Pass, 30:57, 58
Fannie Frisbie (ship), 22:170
Fannie (or *Fanny*) *Hare* (ship), 22:172,
    173, 174
Fanning, H. F., 16:138
Fanning, Howard, 33:363
Fanny (whaler, 1831), 10:99; 11:199
Fanny (bark, 1849), 23:259, 274-76
    passim; 25:327
Fanny (str., 1861), 31:232
Fanny Major (ship), 16:337; 22:169;
    34:254
Farallon Islands, 8:136, 139, 233; 11:291,
    301; 16:339; 17:174; 27:290, 291;
    38:336; mentioned by Spanish
    explorers, 3:5, 12, 14-15; 8:55, 56;
    9:204, 236; seal and sea-otter hunters
    at, 8:289; 12:194, 196, 221, 224-31
    passim; 23:193, 210, 217
Far East, Russian aggression in,
    30:193-206
Fargo, Frank F., 16:79
Fargo, William George, 2:216; 14:162
Farish, Adam Thomas, 8:388; 10:198;
    15:23, 24, 28, 43, 51, 55
Farish, Mrs. Adam Thomas (Mary
    Wren Prather), 8:388
Farish, John Bolton, "California's
    Biggest Nugget," 3:259-61, 302; obit.,
    8:388
Farish, Mrs. John Bolton (Etta Louise
    Paddock), 8:388
Farish, Mrs. L. B., 15:52, 54
Farish, William A., 3:259-60; 8:388
Farish (A. T.) & Co., 3:260

Farley, Charles Andrews, 19:299, 300; 26:171, 174; 29:251; "Thanksgiving Sermon," 19:300-307

Farley, George S., 9:132, 143, 153, 154, 156, 160-65 *passim*, 173, 265; 9:346; 10:167, 170, 374

Farley, James A., 39:121, 123, 128, 132, 133

Farley, James T., 9:46, 48-49, 102, 112

Farley, John, 16:80

Farley, Minard H., 18:199-200

Farmer, Zach, 36:161

Farmers' Alliance, 19:59-73 *passim*; 27:313-17 *passim*; 28:48

Farmers & Merchants National Bank, Los Angeles, 32:12; 36:328

Farmers' and Teamsters' Co., lawsuit, 25:223

Farmer's Hall, San Francisco, 15:271

Farnham (on *Panama*, 1849), 27:364

Farnham, Thomas Jefferson, 4:90; 14:321, 344; 15:103, 125-31, 138, 236, 239-40

Farnham, Mrs. Thomas Jefferson (Eliza Woodson Burhans), 22:266, 278; 23:358; 27:261, 265; 29:57, 58; 30:257-58

Farnhurst, Henry, 15:372, 373

Farnsworth, Alphonso M., 14:176-77

Farquhar, Francis Peloubet, 2:3, 5; 7:92; 8:89; 9:186-87, 336, 401; 36:93; "Camels in the Sketches of Edward Vischer," 9:332-35; "Exploration in the Sierra Nevada," 4:3-58; "A Footnote on the Name California," 6:167-68; coauth. "Drake in California," 36:21-34; ed. "The Topographical Reports of Lt. George H. Derby," 11:99-123, 247-65, 365-82; "The Whitney Survey on Mt. Shasta, 1862," 7:121-31; addresses: "Exploring California, 1860-73," 7:410; "Phoenixiana," 12:365; "The Pioneers of the Sierra," 3:97; "Literature of the Yosemite, the Big Trees, and the Sierra," 28:185-86; bk. revs. by, 6:91-92; 7:286-87; 9:182-84; 38:164-65; obits. of Mrs. George J. Bucknall, 8:284-85; John W. Mailliard, Jr., 34:178-80; George W. Stewart, 10:309-10; *Place Names of the High Sierra*, rev., 5:315-16; ed., Brewer, *Up and Down California*, rev., 9:401; phot., 39: opp. 80, opp. 360; 40: opp. 366

Farquhar, Robert David and Marion (Jones), 2:68

Farquharson, David, 24:166

Farragut, David Glasgow, 14:356, 357; 15:158; 20:195; 24:63, 174

Farrand, Max, 1:18

Farrell, James, 17:83

Farrell, John, 30:254

Farrell, Millard B., 31:229

Farrell, William B., 26:14

Farren, Robert, 15:181

Farren, Timothy, 9:264

Farrington, Herman S., 2:121, 137

Farrington, Nath., 2:122, 137

Farrington, Rosanna, 6:227

Farrish (S.F., 1855), 15:375

Farron, Thomas J., 21:243

Farron, William, 10:171

"Farthest West" (pseud.), 16:209-15; 29:3

Farwell (S.F., 1855), 15:375

Farwell, Edward Augustus, 14:205

Farwell, John M., 36:120, 123

Farwell, S. B., 15:169; 16:339

Farwell, Willard Brigham, 9:26, 29; 15:270, 273; fac. sig., 17: opp. 200

"Far-Western Wing of the Rebellion, 1861-1865, The," by W. H. Watford, 34:125-48

Fashion (riv. str.), 9:72

Fashion Restaurant, Sacramento, 10:286; 32:148

Fast Folks; or, The Early Days of California (play), 34:359

Father, Come Home (play), 20:2

Father Rhine House, Sacramento, 9:283

Fatjo, Paula, 26:286-87

Fatout, Paul, 31:286; "The California Regiment, Colonel Baker, and Ball's Bluff," 31:229-40

Faucett (S.F., 1852), 8:276

Faucherie, B., 29:195

Faucherie Lake, 29:206; Dam, *see* Dams

Faucon, Edward H., 12:146; 23:321, 322, 333

Faulkner, William, 13:297; 25:266

Faulkner (William) Foundry Co., 34:355

Fauntleroy, Daingerfield, 3:111-12, 187; 17:278, 282, 338, 339; 18:72-84 *passim*; 20:216, 233; 21:12, 14-15, 19; 25:126, 129; 29:273, 334

Fauntleroy, E. H., 11:306

Fauntleroy, R. H., 11:303, 305

Fauntleroy (ship), *see* R. H. Fauntleroy

Faure, Victor J., 36:244, 245, 250
Faust in Black (play), 20:2
Faustus (play), 21:176
Faveau y Quesada, Antonio, 31:110
Favel, J., 22:197, 200, 203, 209, 217, 221;
 23:20, 38, 136
Favores Celestiales, by Kino, 36:234
Favorita, La (ship), 15:216; 18:315
Favorite (brig, 1825), 14:305
Favre, Jules, 22:297
Fawcett, George, 22:30-31, 32, 34
Fay, Caleb T., 27:369; 29:290, 291, 292
Fay, Carl, 32:58, 62
Fay, Herbert R., 34:158, 159, 160
Fay, John, 12:183
Fay, Luke, obit., 12:183
Fay, Mrs. Luke (Eugenie Gariaud),
 12:183; 19:82
Fay, Maud, 25:94, 236
Fay, Paul Burgess, Jr., 25:94
Fay et Cie., 30:257
Fayerweather, A. H., 12:138
Faymonville, Bernard, 25:27, 169
Faymonville, William, 25:29
Fayolle (Hermosillo, 1852), 18:15
Fayolle, Amedée, 6:48, 49
Fazio (play), 21:146
Fearon, Arthur D., 23:190
Feast (Weaverville, 1856), 22:39
Feast, William, 26:242, 247
Feather River, 3:202; 6:240-43; 8:23-25;
 10:189; 11:109-19 *passim;* 12:284, 285,
 307; 14:196-200 *passim,* 205, 206,
 210-17 *passim,* 383-85, 389, 390, 403;
 15:22; 17:348; 19:314; 22:331-44
 passim; 23:59-60, 131, 349, 365, 369;
 24:331; 28:235; bridges over, 10:42,
 43, 47, 64, 66, 69, 74, 361, 362; mining
 on, 3:202; 6:243, (illus.) opp. 243;
 13:170-74 *passim;* 15:52; 17:84;
 23:59-60; 27:193; 28:302; map, 14:
 opp. 224
Feather River in '49 and the Fifties, The,
 by Mansfield, rev., 3:202-3
Feather River Tannery, 33:67
Fechter, Charles Albert, 21:171
Fechtig, B.Y., 32:161-62
Federation Hall, San Francisco, 30:67-68
Federation of Improvement Clubs
 (S.F., 1901), 35:150
Fedora (play), 20:130, 137
Fegan, Catherine, 9:351
Fegan, J. J., 9:350
Felch, Alpheus, 15:169; 16:347; 17:172,
 173, 178, 183

Felch, Mrs. John (Letitia Jane Joiner),
 31:190
Felch, Walton C., 22:124, 147
Felicita (Indian girl, 1846), 26:52
"Felix" (pseud.), 6:5, 7, 11
Félix, Diego, 8:110
Félix (or Féliz), Domingo (d., L.A.,
 1836), 13:218, 219, 220
Félix, Mrs. Domingo (María del Rosario
 Villa), 13:218-21; 23:324
Félix, Fernando, 16:249; 24:53; 26:209
Félix, Vicente, 13:202-3
Féliz (or Félix), Domingo (San Mateo
 rancho, 1844), 16:285; 17:169
Féliz, José Francisco, 13:221
Féliz, Mrs. Leonardo (Barbara Sánchez),
 17:255
Feliz, Rafael, 13:107
Féliz, Reyes, 13:329; 16:259-60
Féliz, Rosita, 16:259, 260
Felker, Capt. (Colorado R., 1865),
 22:171, 172
Fellom, Matthew, 14:17
Fellows (S.F., 1853), 33:301
Fellows, Caroline Augusta, 33:194, 204
Fellows, Thomas, 37:200
Fellows of California Historical Society,
 38:73-74; 39:70-71; phot., 39: opp. 72
Felt, J. J., 26:264
Felton, Charles Norton, 8:340, 345, 349,
 350, 356, 360; 9:53, 54; 14:95; 19:59,
 67, 288; 23:185
Felton, Mrs. Charles Norton (Charlotte
 Ashley), 14:95
Felton, Charles Norton, Jr., 14:95
Felton, Mrs. Charles Norton, Jr., (Cora
 Smedberg), 10:206; obit., 20:383
Felton, John Brooks, 12:72; 14:75;
 19:231, 236; 21:120, 328
Felton, Katherine, *see* Elkins, Mrs.
 William L., Jr.
Fences, 5:259, 273; 11:134; 15:177;
 32:94; 27:70-71; *see also* "No fence
 law"
Fenderich, Charles, 14:78
Fendrick (Eliza City, 1850), 8:179
Fenenga, Franklin, 26:108, 130, 136,
 186-87; "Artifacts from Excavation of
 Sutter's Sawmill," 26:160-62
Fenian Brotherhood, 10:390
Fenimore Cooper (ship), 23:336-37
Fennell, Martin, 6:36
Fennell, Michael, 15:364; 33:330, 331
Fenner, Channing G., 16:81
Fennimore, Arthur R., 26:188

Fennimore, James, *see* Finney, James
Fensinton (on *Westward Ho*, 1853), 28:322
Fenton, Miss (Yuba Co., 1856), 9:67
Fenton, Frank Leo, address, "Rise of the San Francisco Theater," 18:286
Fenton, H. G., 26:94
Fenton, Henry, 35:350
Fenton, Herschel, 4:61
Fenton expedition, 11:309-10
Ferary (Yuba R., 1850), 12:301
Ferdinand (whaler, 1846), 12:169
Ferdinand (schr., 1849), 29:257
Ferdon, William, 35:161
Ferguson (of Bear Flag party), 24:58, 72
Ferguson, Capt. (Strawberry Valley, 1859), 10:171, 255
Ferguson (S.F., 1862), 10:375
Ferguson, Charles D., 32:127
Ferguson, George, 17:253
Ferguson, Hamlet, 18:241-42
Ferguson, Jesse, 2:18; 13:210; 15:109, 112-13, 134
Ferguson, John W., 25:22, 29
Ferguson, Milton James, 10:76
Ferguson, Paris Jasper, 15:54
Ferguson, R. D., 9:249, 251, 252, 257, 260, 261, 269-76 *passim*, 283, 394; 10:375(?)
Ferguson, W. F. (W. T.?), 13:32
Ferguson, William I., 9:46, 47, 358, 378, 387-88; 10:268; 17:313; 24:170; 25:337, 344; port., 9: opp. 358
Ferguson, William T., 9:107, 112
Ferguson's Landing, 17:115
Fergusson, David, 40:318, 349
Fergusson, Harvey, obit. of Spencer C. Browne, 24:90-91
Fern, Miss (Sacramento, 1859), 10:48
Fern, Fanny (Sara P. Parton), 9:60
Fernal, Edward, 8:201
Fernald, Beatrice, 34:92
Fernald, Charles S., 29:231; 34:41-43; letters to Hannah Hobbs, ed. Cameron Rogers, 34:41-48
Fernald, Mrs. Charles S. (Hannah Hobbs), 34:43
Fernández, Agustín, 15:140, 141, 142; 116:110
Fernández, Alonso ("the Tarifeño"), 7:137; 148, 188; *see also* Hernández, Lorenzo
Férnandez, Bartolomé, see Hernández Barreda, Lorenzo
Fernández, Gregorio, 1:164
Fernández, José, 12:135, 235

Fernández, José Zenon, 14:23
Fernández, Sabas, 16:250, 352; 17:147-48
Fernández de Hijar, Juan, 6:322
Fernández de Ladrillero, Juan, 3:387-89; 6:317, 319; 7:230; "Declaration," trans. Henry R. Wagner, 3:390-97
Fernández del Campo, José, 16:219
Fernández de Navarette, Martín, *see* Navarrette
Fernández de San Vicente, Augustín, 15:140-42; 16:110; 24:290, 294
Fernández Pérez, José, 15:60
Ferndale (ship), 31:151
Ferrari, Louis, 37:354
Ferrell, William C., 31:34, 39
Ferrer (or Ferrelo), Bartolomé, 7:20, 51, 54-55, 70, 76; 22:34; 27:289, 290, 291, 294; 35:234; 36:220, 223
Ferrer, Manuel, 4:208; 17:82
Ferrier, Walter H., 11:366, 375, 377, 382
Ferrière (ship), 22:303
Ferries: across American R., 13:25; Carquinez Straits, 6:148-49; 20:152; Colorado R., 22:1-2, 20; Feather R., 14:403; Gordon's, 12:6, 7; Heath and Emory's, 12:6; Kern R., 11:256; Kings R., 11:258, 259; 28:334, 336, 337; Sacramento R., 23:375; S.F. Bay, 5:14; 10:72; Stanislaus R., 22:83; Yuba R., 10:195-96; 14:403
Ferris, Charles, 21:363, 365
Ferris, Hiram, 26:300
Ferris, Hiram Gano, 26:188; art. on, 289-307; phot., 26: opp. 289
Ferris, J. M., 26:299
Ferris, Joel Edward, 26:188, 380; "Hiram Gano Ferris of Illinois and California," 26:289-307; address, "Early Outposts of the Fur-Trade Empire," 33:82-85
Ferris, John A., 28:3
Ferris, John F., 9:51, 59, 137, 139
Ferris, John Milton, 26:290
Ferris, Leonard W., 9:107
Ferris, M. O., 26:297
Ferris, Stephen, 26:290
Ferris, Warren Angus, *Life in the Rocky Mountains*, ed. Phillips, rev., 19:280-81; ed. Auerbach, rev., 19:281
Ferris, William, 26:204
Ferry, Hypolite, 23:47; *Description de la Nouvelle Californie (1850)*, 14:136-40 *passim*; 19:221-22; 22:298,

309; 27:240, 241, 242; 33:126; map from, 13: opp. 61

Ferry Bar, 8:343, 359

Fessenden, Miss (S.F., 1860), 29:122

Festival Hall, San Francisco, 1915, 25:245

Festivals and carnivals: Carnes tolendas (Monterey, 1847), 20:225; Corpus Christi (Monterey, 1770), 11:275, 278; (Los Angeles, 1851), 14:70-71; Dias Ocho (Chile, 1849), 22:243; Espirito Santo, 35:244; Indian, 12:308; *Mai Fest* (S.F., 1855), 15:278; St. Anthony (Mission San Luis Rey, 1826), 8:229-32; St. John (Santa Barbara, 1827), 8:329; St. John the Baptist (Monterey, 1770), 11:278; St. Peter (Monterey, 1770), 11:278; *see also* Celebrations

Feutel, Henry, 18:154

Fichaux (S.F., 1849), 5:21

Ficklin, Benjamin F., 19:262; 29:355

Fidalgo, Salvador, 3:233; 10:323; 40:121, 238

Fiddes, Mrs. (S.F., 1854), 15:179

Fiddletown, 24:167, 169; 38:34

Fidèle Messager, Le (newsp.), 39:5

Fiebre de las riquezas, La (novel), 27:237-48

Field (S.F., 1850), 12:98, 109

Field, Charles Kellogg, 16:86; 32:237

Field, Cyrus West, 19:263; 36:42

Field, David Dudley, 9:174; 36:47, 51

Field, Edward (S.F., 1853), 34:258; lawsuit, 34:258-59, 333-34

Field, Edward (Nantucket, 1868), 21:328

Field, Emilia, *see* Ashburner, Mrs. William

Field, Eugene, 31:29

Field, Hiram, 2:127, 128

Field, Robert, 30:290, 294, 301-2; 31:64, 163, 164, 166, 172

Field, Stephen Johnson, 1:9; 5:95; 9:71, 75, 116, 137, 148, 154, 162, 174, 266, 269, 276, 380, 389, 390, 397; 10:47, 53, 199, 251, 264, 295; 11:22; 14:218-24, 229, 376, 378-82, 386, 391-97 *passim*, 401, 405, 406; 15:9, 21-22, opp. 40, 43; 19:261; 20:365; 21:124, 183, 332; 24:186; 32:148, 149, 151, 155, 158, 296; 33:324; 34:66-68; 38:47; art. on, 36:41-55; bk. on, rev., 10:85; ports., 10: opp. 3; 14: opp. 375

Field, Mrs. Stephen Johnson (Sue Virginia Swearingen), 36:41-52 *passim*

Field family, 36:41-42, 45-47

Fields (Dadd's Gulch, 1857), 9:160

Fifer (or Pfeifer), Augustus, 38:327

Fifer, M. William, 6:21, 22, 25, 28

Fifield, Levi, 14:278; 26:113, 121, 122, 127

Figaro, San Francisco, 21:154

" 'Fighting Joe' Hooker," by Milton H. Shutes, 16:304-20

Figs, 1:169; 2:273, 321; 12:282; 21:369; 23:319; 25:26; 29:173

Figuer, Juan, 1:162

Figueroa, Francisco, 13:209; 14:258; 16:353, 354, 355; 17:327-30 *passim*

Figueroa, José, 1:29; 3:30; 4:152-53; 10:30; 81:206; 11:74-75, 78, 389; 12:126, 130, 139, 238, 243-44; 13:217, 235-36; 14:124, 231, 341, 343; 16:231-45 *passim*; 23:9, 39, 310-11, 324, 332; 24:293; 27:59-60; 29:310, 311, 330; 33:280; 36:242; 38:105

Figueroa, Manuel, 13:202

Figueroa, Santos de, 25:310

Fikes (Yuba Co., 1856), 9:61

Filcher, J. S., 18:361

Filibusters, 9:144, 176; 12:4; 15:88; 18:3-21; 19:274; 21:31-33; 27:145-46; 35:218, 220; *see also* Raousset de Boulbon; Walker, William

Filipinos, 24:159; 30:298-304 *passim*; 31:50, 54, 65, 66, 67, 163-72 *passim*

Filkins, Charles E., 9:163, 365; 10:251, 356, 364, 391; 10:251, 364

Fillmore, Jerome A., 18:355, 360-61; 22:179-80; 23:117, 121

Fillmore, Millard, 9:66, 77, 78, 100, 102, 105, 106; 10:238; 19:174, 265, 267

Filoza, Miguel, 28:262

Finance, Adolphe de, 5:17, 22-23, 26, 42, 346; 6:39, 44

Finance, J. B. de, 6:44, 57; 30:102, 256; 32:108, 109; 39:13

Financial Center Bldg., San Francisco, 31:297

Finch, Caleb, 17:310-11

Finch, Cullen and Mrs. (née Jones), 36:198

Finch, John N., 29:291

Finch, W. C. B., 35:193

Finch, W. R., 18:199

Finch, William, 8:207; 9:353

Finchly, Miss (Sacramento, 1858), 9:249

"Finding Facts about the Stanfords,"

by Caroline Wenzel, 19:245-55; as address, 19:282

Findla, James, 16:136-41 *passim;* 26:264

Findlay, Miss (Yuba Co., 1859), 10:169

Findlay, Henry, ranch of, 9:370, 394; 10:169

Findlay, William, 9:394

Findley, Thomas, 9:116, 170, 181, 253(?), 397; 10:286, 297

Fine, Beatrice, 25:236

Fine, J. H., 16:136

Fine Arts Society, San Diego, 36:161

Fine Gold, 28:335-36; 38:219

Fink, Colin Garfield, 17: No. 4, Pt. 2, pp. 3, 5, 27-28; 20:323; coauth. "Report on the Plate of Brass," 17: No. 4, Pt. 2, pp. 7-26

Fink's Springs, 16:296, 302

Finlay, N., 22:196, 201, 218

Finlayson, Mrs. Roderick (Sarah Work), 22:104, 105, 107, 218

Finley (Sonoma, 1851), 24:49

Finley (or Findlay; Slate Range Bar, 1857), 9:157, 178; 10:171

Finley, Dozier, obit., 40:272-73

Finley, J. W., 15:179

Finley, Joco, 33:84

Finley, Newton Gleves and Rowena (Dozier), 40:272

Finley, Samuel F., 26:8

Finley's Camp, 13:18

Finly (Finley?; Sonoma, 1846), 4:376

Finnell, John, 16:132-33

Finney, Charles Grandison, 16:299

Finney (or Fennimore), James, 12:327, 330

Finney, Seldon J., 20:270

Firebaugh's Ferry, 12:6; 25:2; 38:29

Fire companies: of Benicia, 10:285; Columbia, 24:268; Marysville, 9:263, 264, 285, 354, 361, 366, 385, 386, 390, 391; 10:54, 57, 165, 174, 178, 179, 182, 186, 254-68 *passim,* 285, 365, 380, 381, 382; 15:369; Sacramento, 9:252, 277, 377, 397; 10:275, 285, 290; 15:369; 20:370; San Francisco (*see* San Francisco Fire Dept.); San Jose, 14:167; Stockton, 10:45, 68; Timbuctoo, 10:251, 253, 258, 265, illus. opp. 252

Fire-fighting equipment, 14:168; 24:268-69; illus., 10: opp. 252; *see also* San Francisco Fire Dept.

Firefly (or *Fire-fly;* bay str.), 14:161; 17:264

Fireman's Fund Insurance Co., 22:147; 26:355; 27:168, 270; 36:184

Firemen's Charitable Fund, 15:167, 169, 175; 16:183

Firemen's Journal, 10:68; 15:277

Fires: in Angels Camp, 15:368; Auburn, 15:364; Bidwell, 15:169; Campo Seco, 15:171; Columbia, 15:166; French Corral, 15:172; Grass Valley, 16:83; Jamestown, 16:84; Marysville, 15:54-55, 168; Mokelumne Hill, 15:171; Oakland, 15:367; Nevada City, 11:238; 15:272; Sacramento, 15:166, 173, 279, 297; 17:262; 23:166, 172, 177; 27:303-4; St. Louis, 15:171; San Francisco: (1849) 2:202; 5:25; 15:311; 16:127; 20:293; 22:69; 23:70-71; (1850) 2:115, 118, 120; 5:247; 6:213; 7:401-2; 8:173, 175, 176, 272-73; 12:96, 101, 108, 110; 15:311-12; 18:4; 20:293; 21:75, 311, 321, 331; 22:246, 251; 23:164, 176, 369, 376-77; 34:69; 37:328-29, 362; (1851) 2:132; 12:108, 110; 20:293, 295-96; 22:77, 113, 267, 275; 23:171, 377; 24:70; 28:41-42; 37:328-29, 362; (1852) 23:172, 173, 177; (1854) 15:166; (1855) 15:271, 272, 279, 366-72 *passim,* 376; 16:79, 338; 17:176; (1863), 26:16-17; (1906) *see* San Francisco earthquake and fire; (1920s) 15:321, 323; Scott's Bar, 16:84; Stockton, 12:108; 15:272; 22:76; Weaverville, 16:82

Fires: brush and grass, 2:185; 5:122, 135, 154; 13:74, 265, 268-69; 23:34; 39:304; forest, 5:153, 176, 239-40; 38:225-26

Fire train, 18:365

Fireworks (1792), 2:288

Firk (1846), sketches by, 18: foll. 72

Firks, Henry, 15:54

First, Walter, 18:270

First Baptist Church, Sacramento, 26:171; 27:304, 309

First Baptist Church, San Francisco, 12:96; 26:169; 27:10, 123-30 *passim,* 306, 307, 309, 365, 370; 28:291; 30:185

First Baptist Church, San Jose, 27:130, 230

First Calaveras Guard, 37:363

First California Guard, San Francisco, 9:270; 10:373; 16:82; 34:231-32; 37:359-67 *passim;* 38:17, 19-21; badge, 37: opp. 352; *see also* California Guards

"First Californian . . . at the Court of the Tenno, The," address by Payson J. Treat, 14:86

First California Regiment (in Philippines), 31:167, 168

First California Volunteer Rifle Battalion, 37:363

First Church of Christ, Congregational, Sacramento, 9:102; 10:278, 292; 26:170; illus., 9: opp. 258

First Congregational Church, Mokelumne Hill, 30:245

First Congregational Church, San Francisco, 12:372; 15:166, 168, 365, 376; 26:169; 28:291

"First Crescent City Lighthouse, The," by Esther R. Smith, 35:325-34

"First Emigrant Train to California, The," address by Anson S. Blake, 10:413

First Federal Trust Co., 31:304

First Forty-niner, The, by Scherer, rev., 4:392-94

First Light Dragoons, San Francisco, 15:164, 366; 16:82; 37:363

"First Mail Contract in California, The," by Douglas S. Watson, 10:353-54

"First Mention of George Washington in California History, The," by Douglas S. Watson, 11:29

First Methodist Church, San Francisco, 16:130; 26:168, 170-71

First Methodist Church, Santa Cruz, 26:167

First National Bank, San Diego, 35:360-62; 36:76

First National Bank, San Francisco, 31:303-5

First National Gold Bank, 30:285

"First Native-Born California Physician, The," by George D. Lyman, 4:284-89

First New York Volunteers, *see* New York Volunteers

"First Ore from 'Washoe,' " from reminiscences of Mahlon D. Fairchild, 12:323-30

First Presbyterian Church, Benicia, 26:168

First Presbyterian Church, San Francisco, 12:105-6; 20:22; 22:111, 114; 26:168; 27:350; 28:291; 32:126

"First Printing in California, The," address by John Howell, 10:206

"First Steamship Pioneers," 26:102

"First Steam Vessel to Navigate San Francisco Bay, The," by John H. Kemble, 14:143-46

"First Transcontinental Railroad, The," address by Charles B. Turrill, 3:398

First Unitarian Church, San Francisco, 10:295; 15:169; 19:153, 299; 20: opp. 1, 2-6 *passim;* 25:341; 26:71, 171, 361; 29:251-54; 31:248-49; 38:34; phot., 38: foll. 40

"First Utah Coins Minted from California Gold, The," by Reva H. Stanley, 15:244-46

"First White Children Born in California, The," by Winifred Davidson, 20:235-40

Fischer (Murphy's, 1850), 17:7, 8

Fischer, Agnes, 32:175

Fischer, F., 12:209

Fischer, J. H., 30:293

Fish, "Father" (Argus Pass, 1849), 18:203

Fish, Hamilton, 19:170, 362

Fish, Isaac B., 32:52, 123, 128, 130, 134, 135, 136

Fish, Ross A., 15:370, 371; 31:229

Fish, Sidney, obit., 29:85-86

Fish & Williams (lawsuit, S.F., 1854), 15:183

Fisher (Negro, 1846), 25:299

Fisher (Galena Hill, 1854), 8:207

Fisher (S.F., 1860), 29:118

Fisher, Alexina, *see* Baker, Mrs. John Lewis

Fisher, Alvin, 29:5, 6, 15, 16, 17, 169, 171, 172, 255-59

Fisher, Benjamin, 2:117, 118, 121

Fisher, Ezra, 26:168-69

Fisher, Henry F., 33:2, 12, 148, 149-50

Fisher, L. P., 15:376; advertising agency, 34:146

Fisher, Oceana, 28:293

Fisher, Ralph T., 23:190

Fisher, Samuel, letter to, 29:16-18, 167

Fisher, Walter M., 15:104

Fisher, William, 4:81; 27:107

Fisher, William Archibald, 25:174

Fisher House, San Francisco, 9:328

"Fisherman's Peak," 4:33-34

Fishes, 2:315, 320; 7:307, 308, 332, 348; 8:135-36; 11:115, 122; 20:359; 12:305; 26:218; 32:260; 35:240; 38:260; *see also* Fishing, commercial; Salmon; Sardines

Fishing, commercial, 16:341; 31:153-59; 35:239-40; 37:81-82, 129

Fiske, Eugene R., 25:114-15, 120
Fiske, George (of Sanger), 4:41
Fiske, George (Yosemite photog.),
  5:332
Fiske, Henry M., 9:46, 47, 48, 107
Fisk's (James) French Opera Bouffe
  Troupe, 21:167
Fitch, Dr. (Yuba Co., 1855), 8:343, 345,
  350, 352
Fitch, Augustus, 26:169
Fitch, George Kenyon, 12:312;
  13:297-99; 26:228; 30:133, 139, 148;
  32:224; art. on, 20:329-40; phot., 20:
  opp. 329
Fitch, Mrs. George Kenyon (Clara V.
  Duvall), 20:336
Fitch, George L., 1:16; 24:80
Fitch, George S., 12:71
Fitch, Henry Delano, 8:106; 14:321,
  324, 342, 344; 17:143, 145; 19:200, 214;
  22:57-58, 66; 24:54, 71; 25:130; 26:22;
  40:24; papers, 30:317
Fitch, Mrs. Henry Delano (Josefa
  Carrillo), 17:142, 145; 30:335; 36:243
Fitch, Thomas, 10:359(?), 374(?);
  11:48, 49; 36:367, 368; & Co., 36:366,
  367, 368
Fitch, William, 20:186
Fitch (Henry S.) & Co., 30:109
Fitch, Rutherford, & Co., 33:68
Fitzgerald (on *Cérès*, 1849), 5:38
Fitzgerald (Alaska, 1867), 35:298
Fitzgerald, Alexander, 21:159
Fitzgerald, Con, 15:182
Fitzgerald, Edward H., 34:30
Fitzgerald, John, 18:368; 22:179; 23:117,
  120
Fitz Gerald, Maurice Fitz Stevens,
  address, "Personal Experiences . . .
  of the Modoc War," 15:286; obit.,
  21:190-91
Fitzgerald, Oscar Penn, 32:122;
  40:329-38 *passim*
Fitzgerald, William F., 37:176
Fitzhugh, William MacPherson, obit.,
  8:189
Fitzpatrick (Valparaiso, 1849-50), 7:221
Fitzpatrick (S.F., 1850), 8:265, 266, 268
Fitzpatrick (S.F., 1860), 29:112
Fitzpatrick, Benjamin, 19:264
Fitzpatrick, J. E., 10:297
Fitzpatrick, Thomas, 1:120, 140; 3:270;
  4:107, 120, 127, 128, 135, 138, 140, 337,
  338; 10:203; 16:49; 19:314, 315;
  21:82, 199, 222; 23:290

Fitzsimmons (Placer Co., 1859), 10:59
Flack, Robert, 36:162-63
Flaco, Juan, *see* Brown, John
Flag, United States: first made in Calif.,
  6:152; raised at Los Angeles, 17:124;
  at Monterey, 3:111, 112; 7:84; 9:82;
  10:11; 14:148; 15:58, 63, 243; 17:271,
  281; 25:193-218; at San Diego, 25:127;
  at San Jose, 8:72-73; 14:148, 170;
  25:126; at San Juan Bautista, 13:52;
  25:126; at Santa Barbara, 30:51; at
  Sonoma, 3:84; over Sutter's Ft.,
  25:126; at Yerba Buena, 2:356-62;
  3:33, 84, 188; 8:71, 74; 15:306-10;
  17:295, 299; 24:48
Flagg, James, 11:158
Flags that have flown over California,
  15:96, 190; art. on, by Philip B.
  Bekeart, rev., 8:186; address on, by
  Phil T. Hanna 16:187-88; Mexican
  and Spanish, 15:61, 141-42; 31:212;
  see also Bear Flag; Flag, United States
Flaherty, Barney, *see* Williams, Barney
Flaherty, Michel, 33:346
Flanders, Alvan, 10:280; 27:346, 347
Flannagan, Moses, 6:7; 40:210
Flannigan (S.F., 1885), 16:82
Flashner and Hammell, 13:319
Flattery, John, 8:352; 9:262, 367, 368,
  374; 10:58, 170, 185, 252
Flattery, Cape, 10:323
Flax, 5:211; 12:193; 22:319
"Flea in California History and
  Literature, The," by Douglas S.
  Watson, 15:329-37
Fleas, 1:215; 5:129; 6:37; 8:343; 11:116;
  12:96, 100, 102, 104; 15:218; 16:301;
  22:256-57; 24:359; 27:363, 364, 368;
  28:57-58; 29:256; 30:157; 33:296, 299;
  35:17; art. on, 15:329-37
Fleming, Charles, 21:306
Fleming, J. J., 31:331
Fleming, Sandford, 22:94; 27:92; ed.
  "Selected Letters of Osgood Church
  Wheeler," 27:9-18, 123-31, 229-36,
  301-9
Fleming's Point, 31:331
Fletcher (Murphys, 1850), 17:10; 22:73
Fletcher (1855), letter to, 26:204-5
Fletcher, Annie, 24:172
Fletcher, Artemus, 27:349
Fletcher, C. A., 9:318, 321, 324
Fletcher, Eliza, *see* Roman, Mrs. Anton
Fletcher, Francis, 3:205; 10:337; 11:311,
  312; 16: No. 1, Pt. 2, pp. 1, 2, 6-32

passim; No. 3, pp. 273, 276, 279, 280; 17: No. 4, Pt. 2, pp. 7, 8; 26:163; 27:291; 36:22, 23, 24; *see also World Encompassed*

Fletcher, Fred N., 20:192; "Eastbound Route of Jedediah S. Smith," 2:344-49; reply to, 3:25-59; *Early Nevada,* rev., 9:184-85

Fletcher, Robert Samuel, *Eureka . . . Ship to California,* rev., 38:165-67

Fletcher, Stephen, 24:172, 379

Fletes, Ignacio, 8:143, 219, 222, 223, 224

Fleury, Mrs. Désiré, 19:236

Flickinger, Joseph H., 34:105

Fling, Guy Freeman, 16:133

Flinker, O. W., 13:32

Flinn, Eliza Jane, 8:337, 340, 350; 9:60

Flinn, Silas, 9:57, 64

Flinn, William, 9:60

Flint (Feather R., 1849), 11:113

Flint, A. R., 29:109

Flint, Addison C., 11:360(?); 25:264-65

Flint, Augustus P., 29:115

Flint, Benjamin, 9:288

Flint, Edward Putnam, 32:357, 358, 359

Flint, Isaac A., 5:265, 270

Flint, James Putnam, 33:381

Flint, Putnam, 30:245

Flint, Thomas, 19:288

Flint, Thomas, Jr., 38:355, 356, 357

Flint, W. F., 6:243

Flint, Wilson, 9:27, 29, 39, 47, 48, 315-16; 15:164; 16:81

Flint, Peabody & Co., 33:381

Flogging, 3:146, 14:222, 224; 15:31; 28:42, 43; 32:134

Flood, James Clair, 8:359; 16:340; 19:234, 238; 39:301

Flood, James Leary, 21:329, 332; 22:176

Flood, John (from Pittsburgh, 1849), 13:84

Flood, John (S.F., 1855), 17:84

Flood, Michael, 30:356

Flood, Renée, 39:321

Floods: American and Sacramento rivs., 2:209; 8:277; 10:279, 293, 352, 364-67 *passim,* 371, 373, 374, 381, 387-88, 392; 11:338; 23:232-33, 357, 358, 365-67; 33:30; 39:306-7; Feather and Yuba rivs., 3:146; 11:54-55; 28:233-42; Los Angeles, 13:205-6, 209, 346-47

Flora (ship), 37:113

Flora of San Francisco, A, by Howell, Raven, and Rubtzoff, rev., 37:371

Florcken, Herbert G., 14:416; ed. "The

Law and Order View of the San Francisco Vigilance Committee of 1856" from correspondence of Gov. J. Neely Johnson, 14:350-74; 15:70-87, 143-62, 247-65

Florence, William Jermyn and Malvina (Pray), 21:44

Florence, Los Angeles Co., 3:342

Florence (ship), 22:171

Florence Hotel, San Diego, 35:269

Florence Saloon, Marysville, 14:392

Flores, Amando, 29:245

Flores, Antonio (1602), 7:298, 300, 343, 369, 377, 390

Flores, Antonio (1851), 15:40

Flores, Gumesindo, 10:33; 15:125; 18:164, 176; 28:261, 262, 263

Flores, José María, 1:145, 243; 3:115, 124, 125; 4:165; 8:258; 10:123, 126, 128; 11:342; 12:57, 61, 147, 149, 165, 335; 13:45-53 *passim,* 102, 112, 125, 132, 133, 134, 146, 225, 302, 303, 304; 17:327-34 *passim,* 345; 18:174, 176, 178; 21:215, 220, 223, 333, 339, 348, 349, 354; 22:41, 43, 50; 25:130, 131, 293, 298; 26:31, 32; 29:335, 336, 342; 28:257; 30:52, 53; art. on, 12:147-49; cor., 1:290-91; 12:150-54; fac., 12:148

Flores, Mrs. José María (María Dolores Zamorano), 1:236, 239, 241, 244, 247, 257-58; 12:149

Flores, Juan, 13:340-42

Flores, Pablo, 17:115

Flores Ranch (nr. San Gabriel), 31:20

Florian, Father, see Schwenninger, Martin

Florida (ship, 1528), 7:135

Florida (ship, 1851), 28:38

Flour, 2:105; 12:293; 13:276; 14:168, 202; 16:141; 21:379; 27:194-202 *passim;* 35:348; exported, 16:283; 17:183; 30:197; imported, 16:140; 23:277; 27:194; warehouses, 27:199

Flour mills, *see* Grist- and Flour mills

Flournoy, Thomas C., 9:44, 45

Flower, Enola, 29:284-85

Flower, G. A., 26:204

Flower, Samuel, 9:26, 29; 15:172; 20:112

Flower Festival Society, Los Angeles, 31:25

Floyd, Richard S., 32:376

Floyd (ship), 22:7, 169

Floyd-Jones, DeLancey, 26:1

Flügge, Charles William, 6:183-84;

12:283, 285; 14:198-200, 205, 324;
16:57; 21:348, 357; 27:108, 110, 300;
33:67; 38:327; rancho, *see* Ranchos:
Boga

Flumes, *see* Aqueducts

Fly (ship), 8:106; 21:353

Flyaway (ship), 23:192

Flying Cloud (clipper), 8:384; 10:294;
13:251; 15:364, 367, 369; 20:277;
26:226, 227; 28:293, 314, 320; 29:106

Flying Cloud (sloop), 12:31

Flying Cloud (yacht), 15:278, 369

Flying Dart (ship), 22:10, 169

Flying Fish (ship), 17:182; 26:226-27;
29:39; 32:222

Flying Mist (ship), 23:108

Flynn (S.F., 1854), 15:163

Flynn, H. C., 37:200

Fog, Maurice, 39:343

Fogg, Hiram, 2:115

Fogg, T., 10:75

Foggin, Frederick, 27:50

Fogus, Shelton C., 19:249-50; 39:197

Foley (S.F., 1854), 15:165

Foley, Dan, 8:207, 342, 345

Foley, Doris, 28:284; coauth. "The 1883
Flood on the Middle Yuba River,"
28:233-42

Foley, F., 15:371

Foley, Thomas M. 23:95

Foley, William E., 23:95

Foley, William H., 20:293

Folger, E. P., 16:284

Folger, Francis B., 17:177; 27: opp. 97

Folger, Herbert, 1:108

Folger, R. M., 9:35

Folkes, James, 35:210, 216

Folks, Giles A., 26:204

Folleen, Augustus, 21:306

Follet, Mme. (née Petit), 22:305

Follett, William T., 14:178, 181

Folsom, Gustavus Decatur, 7:110;
10:374

Folsom, Joseph Libbey, 2:75, 76, 188;
4:89; 7:107-11; 8:269, 270; 9:276;
10:132, 293; 11:141, 142; 12:295-96,
301; 13:281; 14:329-30, 346; 15:163,
172, 366, 372-76 *passim*; 16:139, 285,
341; 18:36; 19:133, 229, 231; 21:311-14
passim; 26:125, 337; 27:251; 28:34;
33:341, 342, 373; 38:41; prom. note
(fac.), 7: opp. 110; port., 7:107;
see also Leidesdorff-Folsom estate

Folsom family, 7:110; 15:374

Folsom (place), 3:27, 4:224; 7:109;

8:210; 9:181; 10:43, 280, 293; 11:230,
246; 16:31, 32; 19:290, 291; 23:354,
370; 25:286; 32:218-19; letters from,
16:32-42; railroad, 11:230, 321; *see also*
Negro Bar

Foltz, R. M., 14: opp. 209, 398; 15:29

Fonda, William T., 8:199, 201, 210;
10:386; 15:54

Fong Wing, 27:21

Font, Pedro, 1:162-63; 4:4; 10:216;
15:59; 20:235-36, 239; 23:1, 372-73;
30:2; 35:26; 36:4

Fonte, Bartholomew de, 9:201-2; 11:310;
36:217

Food:
in Alaska (1866), 35:293
bear meat, 5:260
of Chinese, *see* Chinese: food and
restaurants
clams, 22:249; 23:277
at Coloma, 26:112, 114
cookbook, 30:258
at Fine Gold (1907), 38:219
flapjacks, 3:133; 6:221
at Fort Jones (1853), 28:215
of Indians, *see* Indians: foods of
at McAllister party, 11:128
Mexican, 12:12; 29:14
of miners, 3:70; 5:173, 225; 19:125
of missionaries, 8:312
mule meat, 1:120; 17:344; 26:47, 50
in Nicaragua, 36:140
on overland journey, 18:292
on Portolá exped., 31:115
of railroad workers, 37:132
reptiles, 5:173
at Bay of St. Catherine, 2:95, 96, 97
at San Blas, 29:14
in San Francisco (1849), 2:114, 115;
22:69; 23:277; 27:362; (1850-51),
12:104, 105, 107; 22:265; (1884),
16:300-301; (1899-1902), 32:57, 62
at San Juan del Sur, 36:143
on shipboard, 1:215, 216-17, 224, 229;
2:91, 94; 7:212, 214; 20:230;
22:337-38; 30:17, 19, 20, 293;
32:310; 33:7
of soldiers (1846-47), 21:341;
26:47-51 *passim*; 29:341; at military
ball (1850), 2:129; in Philippines
(1898), 30:300; 31:49, 50, 53-54,
58, 65
of Spanish Californians, 8:312; 24:22
turtle soup, 28:39

at M. G. Vallejo's (1842), 17:142-43, 144

in Visalia (1870s), 18:29

in Yerba Buena (ca. 1845), 17:297

"Food Habits of Nineteenth-Century California Chinese," by Robert F. G. Spier, 37:79-84, 129-36

Fool of the Family, The (play), 10:365, 371

Fool's Revenge, The (play), 10:254, 266

Foot, Solomon, 19:270, 345; 22:116

Foote, Arthur Burling and Jeannette Stanwood (Hooper), 31:302

Foote, Francis Seeley, 19:288; 22:888; "The Boundary Line between California and Oregon," 19:368-72; "A Note on the Southern Boundary of California," 19:217-18

Foote, Franklin, 29:21-22

Foote, Henry Stuart, 8:370; 9:39, 47, 111; 10:221, 224, 225-31 *passim;* 14:364, 371, 372, 373; 15:73, 202; 19:20; 35:226, 230

Foote, Henry Stuart, Jr., 16:336

Foote, Mrs. Henry Stuart, Jr. (née Badger), 23:90

Foote, Henry W., 35:354

Foote, William W., 19:60, 61, 67

Foote's Crossing, 28:234

"Footnote on the Name California, A," by Francis P. Farquhar, 6:167-68

Forbes, Alexander, 10:5; 13:59, 61, 77; 14:158, 334, 346; 17:128; 18:138-39, 140, 143; 25:321; 30:320; 40:199

Forbes, Andrew B., 4:225; 11:127; 17:179; 19:232, 238

Forbes, B. C., 9:154, 165, 178; 30:349

Forbes, B. F., 8:358

Forbes, Cleveland, 13:386-90, 397; 27:50

Forbes, Diego (James), 21:320

Forbes, Edwin Alexander, 34:160

Forbes, Eli B., 33:251

Forbes, Helen, 38:2-3

Forbes, Jack D., 40:255; bk. rev. by, 40:253-55; *Apache, Navaho,* and *Spaniard,* rev., 40:158-60. .

Forbes, James Alexander, 2:182; 3:88, 113; 5:302; 6:80, 135, 188, 190, 271; 8:112, 125; 10:99-128; 12:39, 50, 59; 13:59, 61, 77, 78, 121; 14:17, 19, 163, 164; 16:57; 17:137, 142, 157, 167, 279; 18:139, 145; 21:320(?); 24:333-34; 27:107; 28:103, 110, 243, 252-53; 29:14, 58

Forbes, Mrs. James Alexander (Ana María Galindo), 10:99; 11:71-72

Forbes, John M., 31:287

Forbes, John Murray, 20:1, 6; 33:244

Forbes, Robert, 26:204

Forbes, Robert Bennet, 31:287

Forbes, Mrs. W. C., 10:356, 367

Forbes, W. J. ("Semblens"), 15:381

Forbes, William, 15:240

Forbes (A. B.) & (W. F.) Babcock, 17:181

Forbes-Robertson, Johnston, 35:141

Forbes, Suñol & Co., 13:78

Forbestown, 8:342, 346, 358; 9:52, 69, 352; 10:171, 359; 33:299

Forbush, Benjamin, 6:152

Force, Raymond Charles, obit., 31:89

Force, W. H., 22:251

Forbes' Diggings, illus., 6: opp. 252

Ford (Camptonville, 1850s), 9:172; lawsuit, 9:352

Ford (S.F., 1867), 11:127

Ford, Charles, 9:40

Ford, Henry Chapman, 23:14; "Some Detached Notes . . . on the Missions of California," 3:238-44; etchings by, 16: opp. 348; 23: opp. 1

Ford, Henry Lambert, 30:171, 172

Ford, Henry Lewis, 1:135, 137; 15:230, 370; 17:240, 276; 18:81, 82; 19:132, 142; 21:14, 15; 24:58; 25:123; 27:216, 225, 226, 378; 31:209, 215; art. on, 29:129-38, 261-78, 333-44; 30:49-66, 157-75; ranches of, 30:53, 56, 158; port., 29: opp. 132

Ford, Mrs. Henry Lewis (Susan Anne Wilson), 30:60, 61, 157, 160, 167, 172

Ford, Jerome B., 21:383

Ford, Dr. John S. (1849), 18:130

Ford, Col. John S. (1864), 40:319

Ford, Lemuel, 16:50-51

Ford, Martine (Yugera; Martina Higuera?), 30:171

Ford, Nathaniel, 4:277-78, 309, 312, 315, 320, 326

Ford, Noah Eastman, *see* Ford, Henry Lewis

Ford, Richard Heman, 30:171

Ford, Tirey Lafayette, 19:67; *Dawn and the Dons,* rev., 6:195-96; obit., 7:290

Ford, William, 15:29

Ford family, 29:130

Ford (ship), 22:11

Ford's Bar, 30:104

Fordyce Valley, 18:149, 150, 151;
29:200
Fore, Pauline, 34:281
Foreigners: treatment by Spanish
Californians, 15:118-31 *passim*,
136-37, 224-31 *passim*, 237-41 *passim*;
17:54-58 *passim*, 63-64, 139, 140,
151-63 *passim*, 220, 272-76 *passim*, 281;
24:309; by Americans, 32:297-301,
303-12 *passim; see also* Chinese,
feeling against; Foreign Miners' Tax
Foreign Miners' tax, 5:227; 8:193, 337,
338, 353-57 *passim*; 9:54, 72; 11:59,
323, 331; 12:98; 14:133-34; 15:267;
16:183, 341, 343; 17:3-6, 179; 19:325,
327, 330; 21:358; 24:178-79; 30:36-37;
31:144, 145; 35:39-43 *passim*, 316;
receipt (fac.), 8: opp. 344; in
British Columbia, 6:19
Foreman, David N., 22:73, 82, 83
Forest, Antoine, 28:157, 159
Forest (ship), 12:28
Forest City, 9:368, 392; 11:152-53;
28:239, 240
Forester (ship), 12:229
Forest Hill, 2:206, 208; 16:31
Forest Hill Divide, 2:203-8 *passim*; 16:30
Forey, John C. and Annie (Bartlett),
28:293
"Forgery of the Broderick Will, The,"
by David A. Williams, 40:203-14
"Forgotten Exploration in Search of a
Route across the Sierra," by Stewart
Mitchell, 34:209-28
Forgotten Frontiers, by Thomas, rev.,
11:387-88
"Forgotten Mother of the Sierra:
Letters of Julia Tyler Shinn,"
38:157-63, 219-28
"Forgotten Redwoods of the East
Bay," by Sherwood D. Burgess,
30:1-14
"Forgotten Voyages," address by
James A. B. Scherer, 18:85-86
Fork House, 7:14
Fork Lake, *see* Tulare Lake
Fork of the Roads, San Bernardino Co.,
17:208
Forman, Anna, 40:320
Forman, Charles, 10:393
Forman, Ferris, 9:260, 284, 397; 10:70,
278, 292, 381; 15:79-80, 83, 249-51;
19:347; 24:121; 25:224; 29:241-42;
38:315; 40:349
Forman, Henry James, "A Brilliant

California Novelist, Gertrude
Atherton," 40:1-10
Formhals, Suzanne, 29:92
Formosa (ship), 38:27
Forney, John Wien, 11:15, 25, 27
Forrest (Shasta, 1849), 3:90
Forrest, Edwin, 21:54, 149, 151-52, 164
Forrest, Mrs. Edwin (Catherine Norton
Sinclair), 20:304
Forrest, French, 15:130; 34:123;
37:64-65
Forrest, James O., 30:103, 114
Forrester Island, 9:241
Forrest Theatre and Melodeon,
Sacramento, 4:60; 6:13; 9:271, 273,
279, 394; 10:289; 20:314; 21:43;
39:304; illus., 9: opp. 258
Forsman, James S., 26:7
Forster (Wood's Creek, 1852),
11:164-68 *passim*, 174
Forster, J. H., 9:10, 11
Forster, John, 13:101, 229, 257, 260,
340; 20:346; 21:329, 332, 346-49
passim, 356; 22:175-76
Forster, Marcos, 22:175
Forsyth, John, 19:275; cor., 37:5-6, 7-8
Forsyth (or Forsythe), R. E., 9:363;
10:189
Forsythe, William, 25:35
Fort, first in Los Angeles, 1847, 13:304;
21:353; 22:44
Fort, "Frémont's" (nr. San Pascual),
26:31, 52
Fort Alcatraz, 20:167, 169; 22:360;
23:300; 33:229-39 *passim*
Fort Atkinson, 4:138, 139
Fort Baker, 20:350, 363
Fort Bliss, 34:125, 126, 140
Fort Boise, 4:349; 5:57; 10:400
Fort Bragg, 25:94; 27:216-19; 30:165,
166, 169, 170; phot., 27: opp. 218
Fort Bridger, 3:55; 4:342; 6:118; 22:139,
150; 26:324, 325, 331; 30:57
Fort Churchill, 11:62; 36:35
Fort Colville, 22:100, 101, 105, 107,
197, 214
Fort Craig, 34:131, 133, 138, 139
Fort Crook, 26:1
Fort Dick, 26:7, 11
Forte, La (ship), 15:176, 179, 180, 373
Fort Fillmore, 34:126-31 *passim*
Fort Gaston, 20:363
Fort George, 2:126; 8:98; 18:327; 20:22;
22:98; 24:231, 232
Fort Hall, 4:278, 280, 345; 5:55; 16:55,

126, 128; 18:292, 299; 19:131, 135; 22:144, 150; 24:123; 32:197, 199; road via, 24:73; 32:201
Forthcamp, J. D., 25:169
Fort Hill, Los Angeles, 21:353; 22:44; 25:131; 33:257; *see also* Fort Moore
Fort Hope, 6:19; 11:154, 155
Fort Humboldt, 26:2; 27:222
Fortification of San Francisco harbor, 2:359-62; 3:84-86; 15:172; 19:179-80, 262, 264, 269; 33:229-40
Fort Inge, 18:102, 133
Fort John, 22:132, 148
Fort Jones, 6:71; 26:1, 9, 202; 28:199, 202, 228; letters from, 28:210-23, 351, 354-56
Fort Jones (town), 6:71; 28:228
Fort Kearney, 6:114; 22:128, 148; 24:39-43, 45
Fort Kiowa, 4:119, 120
Fort Langley, 11:153, 155
Fort Laramie, 4:331-32; 6: 115; 8:81; 10:400; 11:53; 22:132, 137, 148; illus., 6: opp. 114
Fort Leavenworth, 22:148
Fort McKibben, 12:319; 27:205
Fort Mahan, 23:289
Fort Mason, S.F., 15:58, 66; 25:319, 322, 323; 39:177
Fort Miller, 1:198; 5:335; 13:330; 28:337
Fort Mohave, 2:206; 9:306, 307, 308; 12:10; 18:206; 22:9, 10, 11, 22, 25; 27:116; 29:229; see also Mohave
Fort Montgomery, 11:137; 15:62, 65, 68
Fort Moore, 1:238-39; 3:97; 13:304-5; 22:59, 60; 33:257
"Fort Moore and the Battle of San Pasqual," address by Orra E. Monnette, 3:97
Fort Nez Perce (Walla Walla), 22:101, 196, 197, 213, 214; 28:120, 122
Fort Nisqually, 22:103
Fort Osage, 23:298
Fort Platte, 4:331-32; 22:148
Fort Point, 1:137, 289; 2:275, 359-60; 15:59, 62, 66, 180; 19:357-59; 25:124, 319-23 *passim*; 27:293, 294; 28:94; 33:229-33 *passim*, 237; reef, 19:282
Fort Reading, 18:302, 312; 22:368; 28:216, 221, 228, 352-53
Fort Riley, 34:139
Fort Robidoux, 2:8
Fort Rosecrans, 33:115; 34:158
Fort Ross, 3:173; 8:90, 318, 323-27; 12:189-216 *passim*, 242-76 *passim*;

14:324; 16:99, 100, 108-9, 118, 188, 232-36 *passim*, 352, 360-61, 367, 377; 17:62-68 *passim*, 142, 244; 18:174, 293, 338; 19:319; 23:23, 39; 28:110, 257; 30:3, 321, 324; 32:44; 33:62, 63; 39:98-99, 110; 40:98-99; illus., 8: opp. 326; 12: opp. 191, opp. 199, 202, 204, opp. 217, 227, opp. 237, 241, opp. 249, 276; 39: opp. 97, opp. 112
Fort Sacramento, 17:229, 275; 21:10, 14, 17; 22:221; *see also* New Helvetia; Sutter's Fort
Fort Sanderson (Côte Sans Dessein), 2:6
Fort Seward, 20:353-58 *passim*, 363
Fort Simpson, 11:307; 22:97, 103, 104, 107; 28:111
Fort Street Congregational Church, Honolulu, 34:318-20
Fort Sumter, 10:280, 293; 29:232; 31:201; 34:51; 39:295
Fort Sutter, *see* Sutter's Fort
Fort Tejon, 1:198; 9:304-7, 317; 12:6; 13:341; 17:198; 28:125-26, 131; 29:229; 38:330
Fort Ter-Waw, 26:1-5, 10; illus., opp. 1
Fort Umpqua, 25:120, 256, 264
Fortunas, Cabo de, *see* Arena, Point
Fortune, La (company), 22:300-301, 310; 31:140, 146, 311-16 *passim*
Fortuni, Buenaventura, 8:240-42; 16:119; 37:97-118 *passim*, 253, 259, 262
Fortunio (play), 21:176
Fort Vancouver, H.B. Co. post, 1:118, 120; 2:127; 5:44, 59; 8:97, 98, 125; 18:318-19, 321, 327, 340; 19:311; 22:98-103 *passim*, 107, 213; 23:142, 28:103, 104, 105, 119-22 *passim*, 226, 244, 251, 257; 33:83
Fort Vancouver, U.S. military post, 2:127-30, 16:339; 28:199, 200, 208, 225, 357
Fort Victoria, 22:99, 104, 105
Fort Waters, 10:401
Fort Weller, 27:219-21
Fort Yale, 6:19-28, 30; 11:153; 13:151, 154, 155
'49: A Novel of Gold, by Cronyn, rev., 5:312-15
Forty-Niners, The (play), 34:363
Fort Yukon, 33:6
Fort Yuma, 9:306, 307; 12:17; 16:295-96; 18:206; 20:157; 21:98, 107, 108, 111; 22:1-11 *passim*, 18-24 *passim*, 151-57

passim, 161-67 passim; 34:136, 137;
38:148; 40:315
"Forty Years after the 1915 Exposition,"
address by William W. Chapin, 35:75
Forward (ship), 16:81
Forward Ho (ship), 30:211
Fosdick, Jay, 19:121-22
Fosdick, Mrs. Jay (Sarah Graves),
19:121-22, 139
Foss, Phillip O., *Politics and Grass: . . .
Grazing on the Public Domain*, rev.,
40:73-74
Fossatt, Charles, 15:4, 6, 8, 15
Fossils, 11:332
Foster (San Jose, 1848), 2:182
Foster, Mrs. (L.A., 1851), 14:71, 72
Foster (Sacramento, 1853), 36:145, 146
Foster (sou. Calif., 1853), 35:210
Foster, Lt. (Ft. Tejon, 1862),
10:375, 376
Foster, Abbie (Kelley), 34:44
Foster, Arthur W., 25:380
Foster, C. W., 30:260
Foster, Edwin J., 24:94
Foster, G. W. (or J. W.), 13:31
Foster, George (Natividad, 1846),
19:132, 138; 21:3; 25:145, 146
Foster, George (Grass Valley, 1850s),
6:332, 333
Foster, Joseph E., 12:169; 19:132; 21:3;
25:145; 29:337, 338, 339
Foster, Stephen Clark, 2:18; 10:151;
13:305, 307-8, 326, 329, 334, 338,
348, 350; 33:343, 347; fac. sig., 10:
opp. 159
Foster, Theodore, 13:319, 320
Foster, Theron, 10:258
Foster, Thomas, 13:335, 338
Foster, Timothy, 13:335
Foster, William ("Portuguese Joe"),
9:262, 357
Foster, William McFadden, 12:280, 299;
14:206-11 passim; 19:121, 122, 138;
27:194
Foster, Mrs. William McFadden (Sarah
A. C. Murphy), 12:299; 14:206;
19:138
Foster House, Marysville, 14:393
Foster's Bar, 8:201-11 passim, 336, 338,
340, 348, 350, 352; 9:52, 53, 57, 60,
63-66 passim, 76, 130, 134-41 passim,
148-58 passim, 164-69 passim, 262,
266, 347, 352, 353; 10:56, 170, 256,
359, 394; 12:299; 14:402; 15:34; 19:138;

30:266; letters from, 11:54-57, 59-60;
illus., 11: opp. 47
Foster's Bar Bridge, 10:181-82
Foster's Bar Turnpike Co., 9:159
Fotheringhame, Frances M., 28:293
Foulkes (Foulk, Vaulks, Voulks; S.F.,
1850), 8:263, 265, 275
Foulks, Miss (Yuba Co., 1856), 9:59
Foulweather, Cabo, 10:328
"Foundations of California Rural
Society," by Paul S. Taylor,
24:193-228
"Founding of a Mojave Desert
Community," by Martha A.
Chickering, 27:113-22
"Founding of the Presidio and Mission
of . . . St. Francis, The," by
Francisco Palou, trans. George E.
Dane, 14:102-10
Fountain Head, San Francisco, 22:263;
27:307; 28:39; *see also* Winn, M. L.
Four Creeks, 28:325, 330, 334, 337
"Four Early Sketches of Monterey
Scenes," by Henry R. Wagner,
15:213-15
Fourcade (nr. Santa Cruz, 1850),
5:363-65
Fourcade, Albert Richard, 13:271, 272,
279
Fourcade, John R., 13:271, 272, 279
Four-Fingered Jack, *see* García,
Bernardino
Fourgeaud, Victor John, 4:170-75
passim, 182, 194, 200; 10:299; 11:127,
129, 134; 12:29; 16:138; 21:372;
24:355; arts. on, 11:138-49; 20:117-25;
letters from, 20:119-20; 24:29-30
Fourgeaud family, 11:127, 138, 139,
146, 149
"Four Interesting Pioneer
Personalities," address by Louis
Taber, 17:186
Four Months among the Gold-Finders,
by J. T. Brooks (Henry Vizetelly),
11:65-68; 13:76
Fournier, Claudius, 22:304
Fourri, François le, 2:36
Fourth Crossing, 22:68, 79-80, 82
Fourth of July celebrations:
Alviso (1853), 29:42; Benicia (1849),
6:152; Camptonville (1856, 1857),
9:62, 75, 151; Camp Wright (1865),
27:222; Columbia (1853), 35:212;
Los Angeles (1847), 1:238-39; 22:60;
nr. Marysville (1860), 10:251; Napa

(1871), 6:64; Napa Valley (1847),
2:64-65; San Diego (1851), 31:37;
San Francisco (1836-41), 3:31, 40;
15:369; 16:250; 17:292; (1849),
27:263; (1850s) 2:118-19; 11:361;
12:97; 15:369; 22:247; 24:47, 48;
37:364-66; (1860s) 29:116; 39:300;
(1876) 29:291-92; (1890) 27:312;
San Jose (1850), 20:110; on shipboard,
13:9; Smartsvile (1860), 10:251;
Sonoma (1846), 29:271; Sonora
(1856), 35:231; Yreka (1853), 28:217,
219, 230
Foute, Robert Chester, 36:45
Fouts, A., 9:140
Fowler (killed, 1846), 1:135; 12:56;
20:224; 25:124; 29:26-67, 270
Fowler, Capt. (of *Dancing Feather*,
1854), 15:185
Fowler, A., 9:36
Fowler, C. B., 9:149; 10:285, 360
Fowler, D. T., 28:48, 50
Fowler, Edwin W., 36:327-30 *passim*
Fowler, Frederick Hall, 4:51-52
Fowler, Harlan D., 26:382
Fowler, Henry, 16:134; 17:155, 240;
28:266
Fowler, Jacob, 18:351
Fowler, James E., 33:64
Fowler, John (on *Brooklyn*, 1846),
37:234
Fowler, John (S.F., 1850s), 26:254-58
passim
Fowler, John T., 17:44
Fowler, Stephen, 33:64
Fowler, Thomas, 18:26, 27; 25:22
Fowler, Capt. W. (of *Diamond*, 1843),
28:251
Fowler, W. H. C., 27:349
Fowler, William, 17:155; 28:266
Fowler, William, Jr., 16:123, 140
Fowler (place), 25:174
Fowler and Frye, 30:157
Fowler Switch Canal Co., 25:174
Fox (S.F., 1849), 34:26
Fox (S.F., 1885), 16:79
Fox, George, address, "Santa Clara in
the Past," 3:208-9
Fox, James, 9:369
Fox, John S., address, "The Mexican
Background of Mining Exploitation
in California," 18:184
Fox, P. V., 33:276
Fox & O'Connor, 8:369; 16:345

Fox (George L.) Comic Pantomime
Company, 21:167
Foxen, Benjamin, 13:306; 29:343
Foxen, William Domingo, *see* Foxen,
Benjamin
Foy (or Foye), Bill, 8:199, 200; 9:262;
10:167; *see also* Foye, William H.
Foy, John E., 9:276
Foy, Samuel C., 13:335
Foye, William H., 8:358; 9:152, 169;
see also Foy, Bill
Foy, Nugent & Co., 9:276
Fra Diavolo (opera), 15:184
"Fragments of a Stoneware Jar Found
at Drake's Bay," by Kamer Aga-Oglu,
31:106-8
Fraice, Elizabeth, *see* Brown, Mrs. J. T.
Fraits, Mrs. George, *see* Gregson,
Adelia J.
Frame (Mt. Shasta, 1862), 7:125, 129
Frampton, Mr. and Mrs. (Yuba Co.,
1856), 9:61, 153
"Franc" (pseud.), 39:160
Français, Le (weekly), Los Angeles,
39:339-42 *passim*, 348
Français, Le (tri-weekly), San
Francisco, 39:149
France, Jules de, 5:20, 27-28, 38, 348;
6:44; 39:3, 9-10, 13, 15, 149
France: gold rush from, 18:9; 20:70-72;
22:289-314; 23:51; 31:139, 311-14;
33:125-42; 35:309, 314-15 (*see also
Massey, Ernest de*); intervention of,
in Mex., 12:208; 19:177; policy of, on
Pacific Coast, 8:116-29 *passim*; 18:315,
316, 324-25; 25:373; 33:125 (*see also*
French Consulate; Lombard); pubs.
about Calif. printed in, 14:132-40;
20:70; 22:289-314; 23: (illus.) opp.
40, 41-67; 33:126, 129-41; 39:6
France, La (company), 22:301
France, La (newsp.), San Francisco,
39:239-40, 242, 348
France d'Aujourdhui, La, 39:316, 348
Francesca (ship), 14:344
Francesca da Rimini (play), 35:142
Franceses, Arroyo de los, *see* French
Camp Creek
Frances Lake (Emerald Pool), 1:281,
282
Frances River (Kaweah River), 11:257
Francfort, Georges, 39:222, 223
Franchère (mining region, 1850s),
30:126, 361
Franchlieu, Marquis de, 5:14, 233

Francia, Gonzalo de, 7:267

Francis, Francis, 3:131

Francis, Henry L., 14: opp. 209

Francis, Jewitt, 26:204

Francis, Myrtle (Shepherd), address, "Dear Yesterdays in San Buena Ventura," 13:188-89

Francis, Mrs. Samuel Ward (Harriet Hannah McAllister), 11:126

Francis (ship), 27:293

Francis and Stewart, 23:354; 24:49

Francisca, *see* Benicia

Franciscans, 8:308, 328, 330; 26:309; 30:235; 36:335, 352; 37:292-93; trail used by, 29:57; *see also* Missions

Francisco (Mexican; San Diego Co., 1846), 21:355

Francisco (Indian, Kings R., 1852), 28:336

Francisco (Indian, Ft. Yuma, 1856), 21:98, 103, 111

Francisco, Domingo, 3:24

Francisco de la Concepción, Fr., 3:14

"Francisco de Ulloa Returned," by Henry R. Wagner, 19:240-44

"Francisco Palou's Boundary Marker," by George W. Hendry, 5:321-27

Francis de Poe (ship), 6:210, 211, 212

Francis Drake and Other Early Explorers, by Robertson, rev., 6:91-92

"Francis Drake's Plate of Brass," by Herbert E. Bolton, 16: No. 1, Pt. 2, pp. 1-16

Franck, Frederick C., 19:67

Franco-Californien, Le, San Francisco, 39:169, 223-32 *passim,* 238-39, 247-48, 256, 257, 312-15 *passim,* 348

François (Indian, 1843), 18:296

Francolino (Mexican, 1855), 15:376

Franconia Landing, San Francisco, 21:116

Frank, the Baker, 9:165

Frank, G., 8:340

Frank, George, 17:84

Frank, Otto H., 9:320, 329

Frankenburger, L. C., 28:335, 337

Franklin (Yosemite, 1856), 1:274

Franklin, Lady (Hermit Valley, 1862), 9:334

Franklin, Dwight, 27:381

Franklin, Gertrude, 28:33

Franklin, J. J., 11:9

Franklin, Sir John, 15:175, 181

Franklin, Stephen, 28:33

Franklin, William E., "Peter H. Burnett and the Provisional Government Movement," 40:123-36

Franklin, Sonoma Co., 30:263

Franklin, Tex., *see* El Paso

Franklin (ship), 8:290, 331-34 *passim;* 23:203, 215-16; 35:198

Franklin Adams (ship), 2:113; 22:169

Franklin Library Association, Spanish Flat, 38:307

Franklin Literary Depot, Columbia, 30:259

Frank Norris: A Bibliography, by Lohf and Sheehy, rev., 39:366-67

"Frank Norris," address by Franklin D. Walker, 26:277-79

Frank's Building, San Francisco, 37:196

Frantre, Edward, 26:204

Frantz, Harry W., 24:188; "When I Think Back to San Francisco" (poem), 24:163-64

Franzika (ship), 2:237

Frascati, The, San Francisco, 22:267

Fraser, David M., 17:265

Fraser, James (S.F., 1849), letter from, 34:26-27

Fraser, James (Sonoranian Camp, 1849), 13:384

Fraser River gold rush, 5:402; 6:18-30; 9:265, 267, 287, 346, 365, 378, 391; 10:303; 15:324; 19:148; 30:286; art. on, 11:150-56; bk. on, rev., 5:402-3

"Fray Benito de la Sierra's Account of the Hezeta Expedition," ed. Henry R. Wagner, trans. A. J. Baker, 9:201:42

"Fray Francisco Palou," address by Gerald J. Geary, 17:356

Fray Juan Crespi, by Bolton, rev., 6:376

"Fray Junípero Serra," address by Augustine Hobrecht, 11:188-89

Frazee, C., 13:32

Frazee, Isabelle, 35:354

Frazer (Monterey, 1835), 16:327

Frazer (S.F., 1849), 27:262, 264

Frazer, Abner, 5:125

Frazer, Alexander, 11:366

Frazer, George W., 15:239

Frazer, William, 5:116, 125

Frazier, James, *see* Fraser, James

Freaner, E. B., 9:198, 200; 24:277

Freaner, U. B., 32:161, 162, 163

Freanor, George, 9:104

Freanor, James L. ("Mustang"), 13:6

"Frederic Hall," by Kenneth M.
    Johnson, 38:47-58
"Frederick S. Dellenbaugh," by
    R. L. Underhill, 14:347-49
Fredericks, Miss (Marysville, 1858),
    9:354
Fredericks, C. C., 15:171, 182; 16:80
Fredericks, Jack, 18:31
Fredet (Big Bar, 1850), 5:227, 235, 246
Fredonia (ship), 36:310
Fredricks, Jessica, 25:252
Freed, R. M., 33:12
Freedom's Phalanx, 9:35, 39, 44-45;
    15:280
Freelon, Thomas W., 15:176, 180, 183,
    248, 262, 375; 16:283, 319, 337, 339,
    341; 17:172-78 *passim*; 21:27; 38:312
Freeman (on *London*, 1849), 7:207,
    217, 219, 223, 225, 398
Freeman, Rev. Mr. (El Monte, 1853),
    13:332
Freeman, Capt. (Colorado R., 1858,
    1869), 22:169, 172
Freeman, Miss (S.F., 1864), 24:263
Freeman, James, 36:376
Freeman, John M., 14:403
Freeman, Leslie J., 19:96, 185; address,
    "Alameda County, Past and Present,"
    25:373-74
Freeman, St. George, 31:21
Freeman, Thomas, 8:209; 9:353, 355;
    28:237-39, 242
Freeman, W. F., 28:202
Freeman, William H., 27:94
Freeman *v.* Bellegarde, 21:116
Freeman Hotel, Auburn, 31:76
Freeman's Crossing, 8:209; 10:171, 194;
    28:237, 238, 242
Freemasons, 2:66, 119, 243; 3:90, 164;
    4:195; 5:103; 6:71, 152; 8:238, 358;
    9:145, 152, 166, 176, 180; 10:250-60
    passim, 263, 266, 273, 275, 279, 282,
    292, 362, 365, 386; 11:102; 12:80, 82;
    13:30, 334-36, 341; 14:78, 84; 15:172,
    373; 17:180, 181; 18:299, 312; 19:289;
    24:59-60, 67, 72, 166-72 *passim*, 180,
    275; 26:292, 294, 297; 27:34, 262, 362;
    28:60-67 *passim*; 29:115, 245; 30:69,
    382; 33:73-75, 331-33; 35:356; 38:336;
    burials by, 15:275; 16:345; 18:309;
    26:297; 28:65; cornerstone of Capitol
    laid by, 10:282, 295; 33:331-33; in
    Mex., 8:223; bldg. at Shasta, illus.,
    18: opp. 304

Freer, Henry A. and Mary A. (Tolle),
    28:292
Freestone (place), 19:129
Free Trade (ship), 33:327
Freight and freighting, 11:232; 14:402;
    17:23; 18:23; 20:38, 39; 22:18, 157-58;
    23:354; 27:193-94; 30:239; 35:43-44;
    see also Pack trains
Freischutz, Der (opera), 15:167
Frémont, John Charles, 1:96, 151,
    247-48; 5:328; 6:15, 285-86, 368; 7:4;
    8:184; 9:7, 8; 10:76; 12:75; 14:19;
    15:8; 16:125-26, 141, 201; 17:315;
    18:344, 369; 20:123; 21:325; 22:30,
    147, 215, 233, 355-56; 23:260, 292;
    24:68, 70; 31:215; 35:15, 223; 38:337,
    338
  1842 exped., 1:119; 1843-44 exped.,
    1:119-24; 2:232; 4:9-10; 10:36,
    37; 12:289; 16:54; 26:235, 246;
    36:359-63; 1845-46 exped.,
    1:125-39; 4:9-10; 19:50, 51, 52, 57;
    21:23, 322-36 *passim*; 33:247, 249
  in Calif. 1846-47, 1:81, 82, 83, 92,
    83, 92, 126-39, 146-47, 148, 171-72,
    182, 236, 237, 289; 2:69-73 *passim*,
    356, 359, 360, 362; 3:112, 113, 125,
    186, 188, 189; 5:269-72; 6:140, 141,
    142; 10:10, 101-11 *passim*, 114, 121,
    200; 11:353, 354; 12:37, 43, 48,
    56-61 *passim*, 166-67, 170, 171, 290,
    299, 331-37 *passim*, 340, 346; 13:47,
    100, 104-12 *passim*, 133, 135, 136,
    301-6 *passim*; 15:62-64, 68; 16:100,
    211, 215; 17:136, 139, 140, 161, 163,
    220-31 *passim*, 325, 339, 340, 345,
    348; 18:72, 74, 161-65 *passim*, 169,
    174, 298-99; 19:120, 131, 132, 133;
    21:3, 10, 21, 199, 344, 346, 351-56
    passim; 22:41-56 *passim*; 23:363;
    24:57, 71; 25:121-29 *passim*, 145,
    146; 26:53; 28:342; 29:135-36,
    261-65 *passim*, 270-75 *passim*, 322,
    333-43 *passim*; 33:108, 112-17
    passim; 35:107; 36:11; *see also*
    "Frémont Episode" documents
  court-martial, 8:251, 253-57;
    13:150-54; 25:304; 32:197
  Kit Carson w., 1:119-39; 4:9; 29:30
  difficulty w. Kearny and Mason,
    1:247-48; 8:251-61; 10:18;
    12:344-45; 18:178; 21:194; 22:46,
    55, 64, 66; 25:304
  flag of, 31:215

Gov. of Calif., 8:253; 10:15, 18;
12:344; 16:196; 21:199; 22:45, 50
pres. candidate, 9:66, 78, 100, 104,
106; 19:174; 21:325; 22:232;
34:56-60 *passim*
Senator, 10:164; 16:198; 19:14, 19, 20,
21, 26, 182, 183, 263; 28:64,68
see also California Battalion;
Ranchos: Las Mariposas
Frémont, Mrs. John Charles (Jessie
Benton), 1:246; 2:371; 6:183; 7:88;
13:4, 150, 151; 15:99-100; 16:305;
18:369; 19:3; 21:326; 29:30; 33:225;
35:15; 36:363; address on, 21:278;
letter to, 5:190
Fremont (place), 8:23; 11:117; 14:212,
218; 23:349, 365, 369; 26:169; 27:128
Fremont (ship), 15:164; 28:372
Fremont Association, 18:109, 112, 115,
134
"Frémont Episode" documents,
3:270-89; 4:81-87, 374-91; 5:184-95,
296-310; 6:77-90, 181-91, 265-80,
364-74; 7:79-85; 8:71-77; 9:81-86;
10:100-110
Fremont Hotel, San Francisco, 7:398
Fremont Older (ship), 22:191
"Frémont's Cannon," by Carl P. Russell,
36:359-63
"Frémont's Fort," 26:31, 52
*Frémont's Fourth Expedition: . . . the
Disaster of 1848-1849*, ed. Hafen and
Hafen, rev., 40:165-68
*Frémont, the West's Greatest
Adventurer*, by Nevins, rev., 7:88-89
Fremstad, Olive, 33:41
French (Rancheria, d. 1855), 15:376
French, Miss (S.F., 1862), 8:197;
10:378, 379
French, Capt. (San Pedro, 1863),
16:67
French, Gen. (S.F., 1867), 11:127
French, Addison, 26:59
French, Albert H., 10:182, 199, 200,
246, 260, 358, 360, 369
French, Alfred, 9:46
French, Alfred C., 26:59
French, C. W., 35:365-66
French, Erasmus Darwin, 10:247, 261;
17:218; 18:197-200 *passim*; 26:38-39,
55, 58-59, 60-61; 33:98, 102, 264-66
French, Mrs. Erasmus Darwin
(Cornelius S. Cowles), 26:58;
33:265-66

French, Parker H., 1:57, 59, 60; 9:38;
17:178; 21:321, 330; 38:49, 51, 88
French, William (Monterey, 1836),
8:299; 12:138, 146; 14:317, 342;
23:327, 334; 26:249
French, William (S.F., 1855), 16:81
French (Samuel) & Company, 9:173;
21:246, 247
in California, 5:7-43, 139-77, 219-54,
342-77; 6:37-57, 222, 223, 229;
8:116-29, 135-66, 214-50, 306-35,
347, 349; 10:77; 11:323, 326; 12:104;
13:344-45; 14:132-34, 209-10, 213,
395, 398; 17:3-17, 168; 18:4-5,
10-11, 316, 347; 19:27-28, 340, 343;
20:71-72, 77-78; 22:61, 255, 264-68
passim, 273-74, 309; 23:51-52, 55;
24:360; 25:372-73; 29:208; 30:84;
32:105-18; 33:127; 35:128, 219-20,
309-24; 39:1-18; *see also* Bernhardt;
Chana; Chauviteau; Chavanne;
Covillaud, French Consulate;
Leuba; Lombard, Saint-Amant;
Sicard
in the Pacific, 7:233, 252; 12:155-56;
15:269; *see also* Duhaut-Cilly;
Duflot de Mofras;
Dupetit-Thouars; Lapérouse;
Laplace
in Sonora, 11:388; 18:4-19; 25:319-20;
see also Raousset-Boulbon
"French Activities in California Prior
to Statehood," address by
Raoul H. Blanquie, 25:372-73
French and Spanish Book Store,
30:102, 256
French Bar, Amador Co., 31:148
French Bar, Yuba Co., 8:338, 355
French Benevolent Society,
Los Angeles, 12:157; 27:144
French bookstores, 6:57; 30:102, 256,
257
French Café, Panamint, 17:211
French Camp, 2:184, 195; 13:72, 79,
160; 19:313; 22:70, 102, 343; 23:40,
128; 31:148
French Camp Creek, 13:374; 23:38
French Canadians, 5:196, 229-34
passim; 8:120, 128; *see also*
Canadians; Trappers
French Charley's restaurant, Berkeley,
35:254, 257
"French Consulate in California, The,
1843-1856," ed. Abraham P. Nasatir,
11:195-223, 339-57; 12:35-64, 155-72,

331-57; 13:56-79, 159-75, 262-80,
   355-85
French Corral, 3:45, 140-47, 156, 161;
   6:232; 9:61, 70, 74-75; 15:172; 28:236,
   237, 240, 241; 29:193, 199; 30:266
French Creek, 31:148
French Crossing, 23:133, 145
French Dam, *see* Dams
French Dry Goods Store, Sonoma,
   24:61
French Guard, 10:390
French Gulch, Calaveras Co., 22:79
French Gulch, Shasta Co., 6:70
French Hill, 31:148
French Hospital, San Francisco, 38:26;
   39:238, 258; *see also* Société
   Française
French Hotel, Panama, 29:7
French House, Oak Valley, 8:347
"French Imperialists in California,"
   by Rufus K. Wyllys, 8:116-29
"French in California, The," address
   by Rauol H. Blanquie, 30:84
French in Sonora, The, by Wyllys, rev.,
   11:388
French Lake, 29:197-98
French language:
   books, 14:132-42; 22:309; 30:256, 265
   broadside, 11:40-41 (incl. fac.)
   newspapers: in Calif., 5:27; 6:44-45,
      57; 32:107; 35:316; 39:1-18, 141-73,
      219-62, 311-53; in France, 20:70;
      22:290-96, 299, 308, 310; 28:129;
      33:126
   pamphlets, 22:289, 298, 309-10;
      23:41-68
"French Language Press in California,
   The," by Clifford H. Bissell, 39:1-18,
   141-73, 219-62, 311-53
"Frenchman in the Gold Rush, A,"
   Journal of Ernest de Massey, trans.
   Marguerite E. Wilbur, 5:3-43,
   139-77, 219-54, 342-77; 6:37-57
"Frenchman in the Panamints, A,"
   by Edmond Leuba, trans.
   Allen L. Chickering, 17:208-18
Frenchman's Bar, 8:355; 9:61, 74, 75
French Mutual Benefit Society, *see*
   Société Française de Bienfaisance
   Mutuelle
"French Pessimist in California, A,"
   ed. and trans. Abraham P. Nasatir,
   31:139-48, 253-60, 307-24
"French Pete" (Grass Valley, 1850s),
   6:342

French Peter's store, Long Bar, 9:353
"French Revolution, The," by
   Friedrich Gerstäcker, trans.
   George Cosgrave, 17:3-17
French Spy, The (play), 21:60
French Theater, San Francisco, 4:48;
   22:266; 28:36-37; 32:109
Frenchtown, 10:54, 57, 77
French Travellers in the U.S., by
   Monaghan, rev., 13:184
"French War," 5:229; 17:4-17
Frenzeny, Paul, 21:324
Fresno, 18:25-26, 30; 20:141; 25:19,
   31, 294; newspapers, 21:96; 25:29;
   see also Fresno County
Fresno Canal and Irrigation Co.,
   25:21-24, 28, 34, 169, 171, 173, 175
Fresno City, 12:6
Fresno Colony, 25:171
Fresno County, 25:17-38, 169-77
Fresno River, 38:325, 326, 339
Fresno Station, 25:19
Fresno Slough, 11:260-61, 262
Fretz (Ralph S.) & (William C.)
   Ralston, 16:341; 21:327
Freund (Sonora, 1860), 34:294
Frey (Murphy's, 1850), 17:8
Frey, John, 22:372
Frey Brothers' Valley View Flouring
   Mills, 25:175
Friant (place), 38:220
Frick, Dominique, 25:190-91;
   39:154-63 *passim*
Frick, Harry E., 25:190-91
Frick, Milvia, 39:163
Frick, Shirley, 29:285
Fricot, Desiré, 22:92, 289; ed. and
   trans. André Chavanne,
   "The Burning of the *Golden Gate*
   in July 1862," 19:27-42; trans.
   "California Unveiled," by Trény,
   23:41-68; obit., 19:380-81
Fricot, Mrs. Desiré (Lillian
   Eichelroth), obit., 22:91-92
Fricot, Jules, 19:27-28
Friedel, Henry, 21:327, 332
Friedlander, Isaac, 11:127; 25:18, 25;
   27:171, 172, 173; 33:373
Friedlander, Mrs. Isaac, 11:127
Friedlander, T. Cary, 27:202
Friedman, Joseph S., 15:54, 57; 33:373
Friend, Dr. (Carson's Creek, 1849),
   27:160
Friend, Honolulu, 13:176-78;
   16:209-15; 19:300; 37:231

Friendship (ship), 11:367
Frignet, Ernest, 22:255, 269
Frink, George W., 19:236; 26:74
Frink, L., 9:36
Frink's Ranch (San Timoteo), 12:7, 8
Frisbee, Capt. (R.B.?; Sacramento,
    1858), 9:371; *see also* Frisbie, John B.
Frisbie, John B., 1:226, 228, 229;
    9:371(?); 11:142; 17:235; 25:327,
    340; 27:202; 29:155, 156, 158-59;
    34:25-26; 36:243; 37:361
Frisbie, Mrs. John B., *see* Vallejo,
    Epifania
Frisbie, Levi C., 11:142; 17:235
Frisbie, Mrs. Levi C., *see* Vallejo,
    Adelayda Rosario
Frisby, Adela Isidora, *see* Gantner,
    Mrs. John O.
Frisby, Alpha, 13:32
Frisby, William Edward Rose and
    María Ynez Telisilla (Vallejo),
    25:375; 29:326
Frisby family, 29:326
Frisius (M.) and Co., 9:310-11, 312
Fritz (Death Valley, 1861), 18:206
Fritz, Emanuel, 25:213; 26:130, 159;
    30:223,230
Fritz, Emil, 40:317
Fritz, Henry, 21:264
Froebel, Julius, 13:347; 15:272
Frohman, Charles, 21:262
Frohman, Daniel, 21:261
Frohman, Gustave, 21:262
Frolic (ship), 3:108; 17:125
*From '49 to '83 in California and
    Nevada*, by Marye, rev., 2:365
"From Market Street . . . to Ignatian
    Heights," address by
    John B. McGloin, 35:75
"From Quill and Pen to Typewriter,"
    address by Howard Willoughby,
    32:174
*From Wilderness to Empire:
    A History of California*, by Cleland,
    rev., 38:167-69
Frondoso, Cabo (Point Adams), 9:235;
    10:327
Frontier, the, 32:43; American:
    38:370-71; Spanish northern, 32:43-48
Frontier America, by Clark, rev.,
    38:370-71
Frost (Angel I., 1854), 15:165
Frost, Edward, 29:201
Frou-Frou (play), 20:131, 137
Fruit and fruit growing, 1:166; 2:273,

278, 321; 3:223, 224; 5:374; 8:112, 115;
    9:286, 350; 11:322; 12:173, 282; 13:8;
    14:7, 10, 168; 17:41-42; 18:363-64;
    19:288; 22:319; 23:190; 25:31; 27:119;
    28:263; 29:173, 175, 177; 32:257;
    grown by Russians, 12:190, 193, 200,
    205-6, 258, 259; irrigated, 25:26-32
    passim, 170, 172, 175; 27:113, 119;
    see also names of specific fruits
Fruitvale, Alameda Co., 27:71-73, 382
Fruit Vale Estate, Fresno Co., 25:172-73
Fry (L.A., 1894), 28:48
Fry, Donald Hume, 29:101, 190, 366
Fry, Mrs. Donald Hume (Sara Cone
    Bancroft), 29:97, 101, 190, 217, 227,
    360, 363, 366
Fry, Elizabeth Red, *see* Ralston,
    Mrs. William C.
Fry, Jacob, 2:207
Fry, James B., 2:207
Fry, John D., 2:207; 11:12, 26
Fry, Walter, and John R. White,
    Big Trees, rev., 9:185-86
Frye (Sacramento, 1849), 30:157
Fryer, Annie R., *see* Threlkeld,
    Mrs. Melville
Fryer, Charles Edmund, 25:285
Fryer, John, 21:376, 384
Fryer and Hubbard, 38:314
Frytown, 2:207
Fuca, Juan de, 7:275; 9:201-2; 11:310;
    36:216-17
Fuchs (Murphy's, 1850), 17:6-10 *passim*
Fuente, Juan de la, 37:200, 204-5
Fuentes, Andrés, 10:37
Fukuzawa, Yukichi, 23:346
Fulcher, Clinton J., 39:33
Fuller (d. 1849), 21:295, 306
Fuller, J. E., 13:32
Fuller, Joel W., 16:183
Fuller, John Casimiro (Jack), 3:32;
    10:91; 14:121, 122, 128-30; 17:293-97
    passim; 32:235
Fuller, Mrs. John Casimiro
    (Concepción Ávila), 14:128, 129;
    17:293
Fuller, María Concepción, 14:129;
    32:235
Fuller, Mary A., 30:130
Fuller, Mortimer, 9:64, 349, 351, 353,
    374, 379, 382-83; 10:50, 53, 54, 62, 75,
    367
Fuller, Orlando, 9:358, 382
Fuller, William and Ellen (Canfield),
    28:292

Fuller, William M., 14:175, 177
Fuller & Sanders' Band, 24:263
Fullerton, Samuel, 33:68
Fullmer, Charles C., 23:190
Fulton, Robert L., *The Epic of the Overland*, rev., 4:299-300
Fulweiler, J. M., 18:361
Fulwider, John, 20:363
Fumos, Baía de los (San Pedro Bay), 7:47, 73
Funchal (ship), 23:217
Funerals and funeral processions:
    E. D. Baker, 17:320-21; D. C.
    Broderick, 3:42; 10:198; Chinese,
    16:342; Henry Clay, 37:367; J. L.
    Folsom, 15:372, 373; A. S. Hallidie,
    19:153-54; W. D. M. Howard,
    27:111-12; Indian, 15:108-9; James
    King of William, 14:354; 20:260, 307;
    N. Lothian, 15:267; in L.A. (1857),
    13:341-42; Negro (S.F., 1855), 16:346;
    W. H. Richardson, 16:345; 34:232;
    at San Juan del Sur, 36:144; sermon
    by O. C. Wheeler, 12:97; suicide
    (Sacramento, 1849), 23:355; Green
    Wildes, 10:277, 291; Joshua Wilson,
    15:45
"Fur Brigade to the Bonaventura,"
    ed. Alice B. Maloney, 22:193-222,
    323-48; 23:19-40, 123-46

Furlong, Harold Sproul, 25:380-81
Furlong, Mrs. Herbert W. (Martha Rice), 30:382
Furlong, Matthew and Clarissa Durant (Langley), 30:382
Furnace Creek, 18:198, 200, 207, 211-15 *passim*
Furnace Creek Ranch, 18:214
Furniture, M. C. Vallejo's, 17:142; Salvador Vallejo's, 29:324
"Further Letters of Archibald Gillespie," ed. Richard R. Stenberg, 18:217-28
"Further Notes on the Drake Plate," by Allen L. Chickering, 18:251-53
Fur trade, 2:12; 4:5, 105, 110-41, 279-82, 290-91; 6:102; 8:97; 10:315, 400; 12:141, 191, 194, 217-39, 294; 13:205; 14:83, 86; 15:133; 16:49, 108; 17:87, 244; 18:292, 309, 319, 327, 328, 347-52 *passim;* 19:280-81; 24:231-33; 33:82-84; *see also* Hudson's Bay Co.; Trappers
Furuseth, Andrew, 35:64, 148, 151-52
Fury, William ("Cock-Eye"), 15:168, 177; 16:84, 285, 339-40
Fu Sang, 1:192; 14:47-56
Fuster, Vicente, 6:163-64, 166; 20:235-40 *passim;* 23:371; fac. sig. 20: opp. 235

G

G., M. M. (pseud.), 24:39
Gabb, William More, 4:16, 21
Gabb, Mount, 4:21
Gabbert, Mrs. Harry G. (Florence Doyle), 28:379
Gabel, Henry F., 33:381
Gabilan Peak, 3:271; 4:81-82; 10:102-4; 17:163; 29:262
Gable, Gilbert E., 31:125-31 *passim*
Gabriel, Seymour and Anna (Neuberg), 27:94
Gabriel, Walter Adolph, 27:94
Gabrilowitsch, Ossip, 25:236
Gadsden, James, 24:105
Gadsden Treaty, 19:178; 34:150
Gadski, Johanna, 25:251
Gaffey, John, 19:67, 69; 27:318; 28:47

Gaffney, Michael, 15:281, 364
Gagarin, Princess Helena de, 3:176, 177; 12:197-98; 29:314; 39:99
Gage, Mr. and Mrs. (Yreka, 1856), 6:74
Gage, G. T., 36:100, 271
Gage, Henry Tifft, 5:286-87; 28:53, 189; 35:151-52; 38:355-57
Gage, Lyman Judson, 35:355; 36:155
Gage, Stephen T., 22:96; 23:95
Gaguin (northern mines, 1850), 5:237-43 *passim*
Gahagan, Helen (Mrs. Melvyn Douglas), 39:34
Gaidamack (ship), 26:15
Gaieté Group, The, 21:167
Gaieties, The, San Francisco, 21:77
Gaiety Girls, 33:41

Gaillard, Henri, 22:302-3; 23:64, 66
Gaines, Edmund Pendleton, 18:109, 134
Gaines, Ruth, 39:263, 266
Gairdner, Meredith, 22:103
Gaither (Marysville, 1860), 10:259
Galapagos Islands, 15:279; 25:102, 109; 26:218
Galatea (ship), 16:347
Galbraith, Edith C., "Malaspina's Voyage around the World," 3:215-37
Galbraith, Isaac, 2:46-48
Galbraith, J. D., 9:252, 269
Gale, Dr. (Yuba R., 1849), 14:207
Gale, George L., 9:246
Gale, Joseph, 18:349; 19:197-98, 214; 23:291
Gale, William Alden, 6:263; 8:289-94, 301, 304; 16:265, 268, 270; 23:193-212 *passim*, 302-32 *passim*
Galena Hill, 8:199, 203, 204, 207, 211; 9:52, 64, 67, 129, 145, 151, 157, 158, 161, 168, 353
Galena House, 8:203, 211; 9:70
Galen's Hospice, 33:245
Galera, Cabo de, *see* Conception, Point
Galerie Beaux Arts, San Francisco, 38:2-3
"Galgos, Los" (greyhounds), 26:25, 33
Gali, Francisco, 1:194; 2:141-42; 7:240-53 *passim;* 27:290-91; 36:226
Galiano, Dionisio, *see* Alcalá Galiano
Galilee (ship), 22:353
Galindo (San Jose, 1853), 13:30-31
Galindo, Ana María, *see* Forbes, Mrs. James A.
Galindo, Eusebio, 17:250
Galindo, José Antonio, 14:121-22, 131; 23:372
Galindo, José Leandro, 38:101, 103, 106-11 *passim*
Galindo, Mrs. José Leandro (Rosa Linares), 38:109
Galindo, Juan Crisóstomo, 10:99; 38:107, 111
Galindo, Nasario, 38:100-101; MS, 38:101-11
Galindo, Nicolás and María Teresa (Pinto), 38:111
Galindo (ship), 22:235-40, 247-48, 250
Gallagher (Butte Co., 1851), 15:39
Gallagher (lawsuit, Yuba Co., 1857), 9:130
Gallagher, Edith (McTarnahan), 35:205
Gallagher, James, 17:172-73

Gallagher, Joseph A., 10:377; 34:336
Gallagher, María, 34:336
Gallagher, Martin, 6:18-19, 50; 8:371
Gallagher, P. A., 10:271, 280, 283, 374, 379, 388, 390; 11:9
Gallagher, William, 18:303
Gallais, Alexandre, 11:348-49
"Gallant Militia Man, The" (poem), 37:364-65
Gallarreta, Pedro de, 27:63
Gallatin, Albert (1824), 9:16; map of Indian tribes, 2:232, 347-48, 349; 3:29; 34:266
Gallatin, Albert (Sacramento, 1877), 39:198, 205
Gallego, Hernan, 7:228, 231; acct. of Mendaña exped., 7:229-30
Galler, John, 18:203
Gallino, Luis, 30: opp. 224, 229
Gallon, James, 22:251
Galloway, James and Emily Meyers (Hoover), 22:187
Galloway, Mrs. James E., 10:280, 361
Galloway, John Debo, 21:89, 288; address, "Some Engineering Works on the Comstock," 19:187; obit., 22:187-88
Galt, 17:75; 18:22-23
Galton, Blanche, 21:172
Galton, Susan, 21:170
Gálvez, José de, 2:176; 4:142-43; 9:202-3; 11:274-79; 13:199; 14:4; 17:118; 23:219; 25:76, 78, 359, 365; 27:63, 64; 30:323; 31:109-12
Galucci, Alfred D. and Mary (McLennon), *James E. Birch*, rev., 37:372-73
Galvin (lawsuit, Marysville, 1859), 10:187
Galvin, E. R., 15:270
Gambia (ship), 23:345; 28:378
Gamble, Alex, 7:116-17
Gamble, James (Port Orford, 1851), 25:120
Gamble, James (of telegraph co., 1869), 24:365-67; 29:355
Gamble, John M., 37:31
Gamble, Mary, 24:378; "To Europe via Promontory in 1869," recollections of, 24:365-68
Gamble, William, 7:14, 17
Gamble, William A., 9:359
Gambling, 5:14, 36, 142-44; 6:129, 219-20; 7:395; 8:272, 311; 9:140; 12:92; 13:275; 15:49, 50, 57; 18:267;

19:292-93, 299; 20:30-31, 37, 123, 225, 369; 21:39-40; 22:260-62, 268, 273; 23:157; 24:24, 105, 357, 361, 364; 26:66, 296; 27:31, 42, 363, 369; 31:254; 32:110-11, 115-18; 33:57; 34:253; 35:206, 210; 37:155-56, 325-27; 38:381; bk. on, rev., 7:408; legislation on, 9:256
Ganahl, Frank, 10:359, 369
Ganargwa Mining Co., 12:11; 13:3-6, 26, 28
Gandara, Manuel M., 18:13, 15
Gandon, Adolphe, drawing by, 17: opp. 3
Gandonnière, A., 39:147, 149, 150
Ganée, Pierre, 39:329, 335, 342
Ganges (ship), 29:105
Gannett, Henry, 4:53
Gannon, Robert I., 29:139
Gantner, John Oscar, 25:375; 31:72; 33:373
Gantner, Mrs. John Oscar (Adela Isidora Frisby), 29:326; obit., 25:375
Gantner, Vallejo, 25:375; 29:329, 331
Gantner Brothers, 32:260-61
Gantt, John, 12:288; 15:229, 237; 18:158-59, 172, 173; 22:366; 29:134; "Three Letters of," ed. Alice B. Maloney, 20:147-53; art. on, 16:48-60
Ganz, Rudolph, 25:236
Garbato, Drusilla, 16:337, 344; 17:82
Garbato, Luigi, 16:344; 17:82
Garber, John, 6:349; 10:248-49, 262
Garceau, Mrs. Alexander (Gertrude Hyde), obit., 16:190-91
Garcés, Francisco, 3:226; 4:4; 10:27, 211-18 *passim;* 22:2; 33:13-21; 34:194-95; map showing 1776 route, 10: opp. 211; port., 33: opp. 16
García (Monterey, 1829), 16:221
Garcia, Capt. (Colorado R., 1862), 22:170
García, Anastasio, 16:346; 17:82; 18:268, 277; 29:22, 23-24, 27
García, Mrs. Anastasio, 29:23
García, Antonio, 12:117
García, Bernardino, 13:330; 16:258, 260; 17:256; 27:265; 29:267, 277
García, Mrs. Bernardino (Ilaria Sánchez), 17:256; 27:262
García, David, 12:118
García, Diego, 23:1-4
García, Felipe Santiago, 13:202
García, Francisco (Monterey, 1841), 30:98

García, Francisco ("El Royador"), 18:268, 270, 277
Garcia, Mrs. Frank H., 20:383
García, Gabriel, 26:36, 41
García, Gerónima, 38:106
García, Inocente, 21:320; 36:11
García, José María, 27:335, 338
García, Rafael, 16:249; 19:320-21, 322
García, Reyes, 15:356; 38:106
García Conde, Alejo, 24:292; 25:149, 363
García, Conde, Diego, 24:292; 25:363
García Conde, Pedro, 5:321; 9:4, 5, 11, 12, 13; 39:39, 50
García de Céspedes, Andrés, 8:44-45
García Diego y Moreno, Francisco, 2:255; 16:241; 17:153; 19:201; 29:147; 40:67
Garcia River, 23:38
Garden Valley, 9:61, 154, 157-58
Gardes Mobiles, 20:71; 22:312
Gardet (S.F., 1850), 5:42
Gardiner, Capt. (Yuba Co., 1854), 8:199; 9:165
Gardiner, Howard C., 13:32
Gardiner, James J., 16:81, 84
Gardiner, John, 10:170
Gardiner, John William Tudor, 8:199(?); 9:165(?); 27:225; 28:213
Gardiner & Kirk, 30:258, 265
Gardipie, Baptiste, 22:196, 204, 220, 340; 23:129, 133, 135
Gardner (Nevada City, 1851), 3:133
Gardner (S.F., 1855), 16:337
Gardner, Erle Stanley, 40:157
Gardner, Francis M., 13:7, 9, 32
Gardner, Frank, 29:1, 5, 7
Gardner, J. H., 15:270
Gardner, James T., 22:251
Gardner, James Terry, 4:16-23 *passim,* 55; 9:401
Gardner, James V. P., 2:216
Gardner, John, 15:39
Gardner, John S., 4:116
Gardner, Samuel, 9:26
Gardner, William, 13:258
Gardner, William H., 33:230, 232
Gardner, Mount, 4:20, 47, 55
Garfias, Manuel, 13:318, 322, 327; 18:161; 26:32-33
Garfielde, S., 30:146
Garharst (Nevada City, 1860), 10:247
Garibaldi (ship), 33:327
Garland, Judge (Sacramento, 1858), 6:13

Garlic, 35:123

Garner, John Nance, 39:122-29 *passim*

Garner, William Rufus, 3:194; 11:259, 265; 13:54; 15:119-20, 236, 241; 16:323, 329; 27:107; 29:26; 30:98, 321; 35:111; *Letters from California*, 1846, rev., 4:90-91

Garnett, Mrs. (S.F., 1850s), 19:229

Garnett, John, 8:211

Garnett, Porter, 37:217

Garnier (filibuster, 1854), 18:13, 15

Garoutte, Mary Eudora, 10:307; 22:191; address, "A Summer with Our Neighbor Authors," 13:411

Garr (Carr?), Judge (Yuba Co., 1853), 33:292

Garra (Indian, 1846), 21:356

Garretson, D. F., 35:357

Garrett, Lula May, "San Francisco in 1851, as Described by Eyewitnessess," 22:253-80

Garrett, Thomas, 30:195

Garrett House, San Francisco, 19:229

Garrison, Cornelius Kingsland, 9:26, 30, 31, 32; 14:164; 15:167, 174, 180, 185, 266, 271, 281, 364, 370, 371, 376; 16:283, 341, 346; 17:85; 22:10

Garrison, John H., 28:337

Garrison, Samuel J., 20:160-64 *passim*; 23:300

Garrison, W. L., 17:179

Garrison, William R., 40:212

Garrison & Fretz, 19:155

Garrison (C. K.) *v.* (Elias L.) Baird, (Charles) Hopkins *et al.*, 15:266

Garsey's (Camptonville, 1854), 8:199, 200

Garst, Elias, 15:24

Garter, Ephraim, 9:253; 10:51, 62

Gartz, Kate (Crane), 40:139, 147, 153

Garvey (Sacramento, 1858), 9:248

Garvey, Bruce, 10:178, 181

Garvin, William, 2:128

Garwood, George M., 9:26; 15:179, 280

Garwood, Joseph F., 15:24

Gary, George L., address, "Western Rendezvous of the Fur Trappers," 32:174

Gary, Lew, 33:363

Gas: companies, 18:100 (*see also* San Francisco Gas Co.); lights, 17:177; 28:42, 46; rates, 15:370, 373

Gashwiler, Mrs. (later Mrs. George C. Yount), 2:66; 20:153

Gashwiler, John W., 6:354-55

Gaskill, De Witt Clinton, 30:286

Gaskill, R. C., 10:375, 377

Gasper (S.F., 1861), 39:292

Gasquet, Louis, 5:302; 11:203-8, 212-23, 339-57; 12:35-64, 161-62, 172; 13:59, 121-22; 17:137-38, 167; 29:149

Gass, John H., 27:305

Gast, A. A., 24:189

Gast, Ross H., 24:189

Gastaldi, Giacomo, 7:66, 234, 249, 250, 252

Gaston, Frank, 9:145, 155

Gates, Capt. (Colorado R., 1858), 22:169

Gates, Dan Virgil, 24:175; 28:175

Gates, E. M., 9:317

Gates, Horatio Sylvester, 23:339, 344

Gates, Uriel, 8:204(?), 343(?), 358; lawsuit, 9:132

Gates, Warren S., 23:226

Gatherer (ship), 22:353

Gatliff, W. H., 28:353

Gattens (or Gettens), Daniel, 8:213; 9:78, 169, 256, 262, 267, 373; lawsuit, 9:66

Gattens (or Gettens), John, 9:347, 349; 10:56, 57

Gatton (consul at Mazatlán), 20:16

Gaucheron, T., 29:235

"Gaudy Century," address by John Bruce, 28:88-89

Gaulne, Oscar de, 5:28-29, 39, 42, 229, 232, 247, 343

Gaulois, Le (weekly), 39:233, 330-34 *passim*, 348

Gauthier, Mirandol and Pioda, 6:45

Gautier, Mme. (Yosemite, 1856), 1:274, 282

Gautier, Abel Frédéric, 12:159; 23:339, 344; 27:148; 32:113; 35:323; letter from, 28:156-57

Gavigan, William J., 5:95

Gaviota Pass, 18:262, 263, 264, 276; 29:343

Gay, Arthur O., 13:296

Gay, John, 30:24, 25, 30, 35

Gay, Theobald, 39:240

Gay, Theressa, 30:90; ed. "The California and Australia Gold Rushes, as Seen by Amos S. Pittman," 30:15-37

Gaylor, Charles, 21:160

Gaylord (lawsuit, Marysville, 1859), 10:179

Gaynor, John P., 31:300

Gazette, Anaheim, 28:379; 31:287; 32:341

Gazette, Nevada City, 10:394

Gazette, Santa Barbara, 16:84

Gazette, Stockton, 34:349

Gazette, Victoria, 30:364

Gazette Française de l'Ouest Américain, 39:320-21, 348

Gazette Républicaine, La, San Francisco, 6:45; 32:106, 107; 39:11-12, 348

Gear, John, 8:202, 211; 9:76

Geary (lawsuit, S.F., 1850), 34:241-42

Geary, Alfred, 40:28

Geary, Edward Ratchford, 20:15, 23, 25; letter from, 20:15-23

Geary, Mrs. Edward Ratchford, 20:17, 18, 20

Geary, Gerald J., addresses, "Fray Francisco Palou," 17:356; "Santa Clara's Hundred Years," 30:377-78

Geary, John and Katherine (Kelly), 38:180

Geary, John White, 3:37, 40; 5:94; 17:186; 18:37; 20:12-15, 21, 23, 45; 27:232, 362, 368-69; 28:58, 64, 67, 116; 32:295, 301; 33:373; 34:241 (?), 333; 38:20

Geary, Mrs. John White (1, Margaret Ann Logan), 20:13; (2, Mary Church Henderson), 20:15

Geary, Joseph J., obit., 38:180

Geary, S. R., 28:67

Geary, Thomas, 28:48, 49

Geary, William Logan, 20:13, 24

Geddes, Paul, *see* Green, Talbot H.

Geddes family, 18:41-42

Gedge, John Harry Priestly and Zarela Margarita (Vallejo), 29:326

Gee Hop, 36:147

Geese: domestic, 16:133; wild, *see* Water birds

Geiger, Maynard, 28:92; "Dates of Palou's Death and Lasuén's Birth Determined," 28:19-22; *Life and Times of Fray Junípero Serra*, rev., 39:359-62; phot., 39: opp. 360

Geiger, Vincent E., 20:334; 24:170; 29:297; 30:133

Geiger, William, 18:292, 309

Gejnolea, Capt. (Colorado R., 1856), 22:169

Geldern, Otto von, 36:247

Geller, William M., 10:43, 251; lawsuit, 10:360

Gelston, Roland, 16:182

Gelston & Co., 11:141; 20:30, 35; 28:115

Gelteuchine, Capt. (of *Calevala*), 26:15

Geltz, S. V., 36:264

Gem (riv. str.), 9:72; 10:356, 367

Gemeling, John Georgius, 10:80

Gem Saloon, Marysville, 9:361; 10:246; 14:394

General Arthur (ship), 31:230-31

"General E. O. C. Ord," address by Eric A. Falconer, 22:374-75

General Grant National Park, 4:15, 44; 10:310

General Jesup (brig), 22:22, 170, 171

General Jesup (str.), 11:291; 22:6-11 *passim*, 21, 167

"General John A. Sutter," address by Clarence J. DuFour, 6:198-99

" 'General' John Wilson, Signer of the Deseret Petition," by Frederic A. Culmer, 26:321-48

"Gen. M. G. Vallejo and H. H. Bancroft," by Madie D. Brown, 29:149-59

General Morgan (ship), 19:376; 22:169, 379; 25:118

General Paterson (brig, 1850), 2:127

General Patterson (schr., 1853), 22:6-7, 168, 169

"General Persifor F. Smith," address by L. H. Bash, 6:286-87

General Petroleum Co., 30:212-15

General Pierce (ship), 16:282

"General Vallejo, the Man of Vision," address by Emmet Seawell, 5:415-16

General Viel (ship), 22:6, 7, 168

General Wool (ship), 25:332

General Worth (ship), 3:92-93; 14:406; 25:332(?)

General Zaragosa (ship), 22:162

"Genesis of the Pacific Mail Steamship Co., The," by John H. Kemble, 13:240-54, 386-406

Genoa, Nev., 7:9, 16, 19; 12:323-27 *passim*; 17:76, 77, 78; 18:305; 21:228-30, 232; 30:376; 32:196; *see also* Mormon Station

Gentleman from Idaho, A (play), 34:364

"Gentleman from Vermont: Royal H. Waller," by Dolores Waldorf, 22:110-18

Geographical Society of the Pacific, 11:308, 311

"Geological History of San Francisco

Bay," address by George D.
Louderback, 23:380

George, Henry, 10:89; 15:6; 18:156,
281; 19:156; 24:15, 97-115; 25:95;
30:117-23; 33:210, 216; 37:44; 38:306;
phot., 24: opp. 97

George, James, 9:26; 15:164; 16:80, 84

George, Richard, 24:100

George, S. R., 15:84

George, Samuel Gregg, 18:201-4 *passim*,
215; 37:198; phot., 18: opp. 195

George, W. A., letters from, 24:121,
348-50, 357, 358

George (ship), 16:284

George and Henry (ship), 13:34;
18:65-66, 67; 33:64; 37:13

George A. Pope (ship), 23:94

"George Christopher Lovdal, San
Diego's First Harbor Master," by
Myrtle L. Rosenthal, 31:149-59

"George Davidson, Geographer," by
Henry R. Wagner, 11:299-320

George Emery (ship), 22:22, 168

George E. Wright (ship), 33:2, 6-7, 10,
148-49

"George Kenyon Fitch, Pioneer
California Journalist," by John D.
Carter, 20:329-40

George Law (ship), 9:161, 179; 20:260;
27:327; 34:336; *see also Central
America*

George Ryan (ship), 31:36

Georges (ship), 5:11-12, 30; 6:44

George's (or Gorgy's) Ranch, *see*
Tschernikh, George

George S. Wright (ship), 33:2, 6, 7,
10, 148, 166

Georgetown, 7:7; 8:201, 210; 12:94;
20:38; 30:103-11 *passim*, 260, 266;
37:312; Indians at, illus., 38: opp. 145

George Washington (ship), 21:288

Georgia (ship), 8:9, 10; 35:291

Georgia Minstrels, 21:242-43

Georgiana (brig, 1849), 30:100

Georgiana (str., 1861), 31:231

Georgina (riv. str.), 17:84, 168

Gerald, E. F., 23:121

Gerard (French miner, 1850), 5:348,
377

Gerbe d'Or, La (company), 22:309

Gerberding, Albert, 20:270

Gerberding, Christian Otto, 16:81, 182;
20:336-37; 21:24, 30, 34; 26:229, 232;
32:224; 37:139-40

Gerbode, Mrs. Frank L. A. (Martha B.
Alexander), 18:380

Gercke (S.F., ca. 1854), 15:181;
see also Gerke

Gerhard, Frederick G. and Augusta,
22:288

Gerhard, George, 22:288

Gerichten, Charles, 19:297

Gerke, Henry, 11:141; 16:128, 136, 137,
139; 18:302, 313; 19:231; 30:66;
see also Gercke

Gerkins, Jacob F., 39:213

Gerlough, L. S., 23:191

German, Antonio, 29:25

German Benevolent Society of San
Francisco, 9:311; 15:166, 176, 371

German Coffee Saloon, San Francisco,
22:69

German Evangelical Church, 38:26

Germania Concert Band, 15:171; 16:282

Germania Society, San Francisco,
15:271; 16:84

German Land Association, 25:19

German Pioneers in Early California,
by Gudde, rev., 7:93-94

Germans, 7:93; 9:270, 311; 11:149, 331;
17:4-8 *passim*; 20:68-69, 77; 22:128,
262, 265; 23:243; 25:19, 169; 35:128-29;
40:63; in Texas, 18:102, 132-33;
see also Behr; Cohn; Cordua; Flügge;
Gottig; Lienhard; Vischer

German Savings & Loan Society, 27:170,
173-74

German Society, San Francisco, 28:35

German Theatre, San Francisco, 21:66,
261

Gerónimo (Indian, 1826), 23:6

Geroult, Ad., 11:199-200, 203

Gerry, Samuel Russell, 4:194

Gerstäcker, Friedrich Wilhelm
Christian, 3:32, 35; 12:298, 301; 22:181,
257, 277; "The French Revolution,"
trans. George Cosgrave, 17:3-17

Gerster, Etelka, 35:142

Gerstle, Lewis, 26:281; 35:307

Gerstle, Mark Lewis, 25:249

Gerstle, William Lewis, 38:4; obit.,
26:281-82

Gerstung, Henrick and Hermine
(Bohmer), 28:293

Gervais, Joseph, 5:234(?); 23:146

Geschwind, John and Joseph, 33:363

Gessner, Corp. (William?), 36:62, 66

Gest, James, 7:14

Getzler, F. W., 9:389; 10:259

Geysers, 12:107

Geysers, The (resort), 16:250; 21:152; 33:318

Ghent, William James, obit. of Francis R. Hagner, 20:94; *Road to Oregon*, rev., 8:89

Ghio, the "Swiss Warbler," 10:374, 388

Ghirardelli, Alfred, obit., 35:374

Ghirardelli, Domingo, 16:341; 30:374; 35:374

Ghirardelli, Louis and Johanna L., 35:374

Giacome (Indian or Mexican, 1844), 10:37

Giacome, Rancho de, 29:323

Ghiselin, George H., 17:203, 205

Giannini, Amadeo Peter, 30:218; 36:68, 76; 37:267-75, 347-58

Giannini, Mrs. Amadeo Peter (Clorinda A. Cuneo), obit., 21:92-93

Giannini, Mario, 37:269, 350

Giant Forest, 4:15, 30, 41, 43

Giant Sequoia, The, by Ellsworth, rev., 3:300-301

Gibb, Daniel, 11:10; 15:269

Gibbons (Llano del Rio, 1917), 40:227

Gibbons, Alexander S., 31:3-4; 32:55, 132

Gibbons, Edward, 15:281; 31:325

Gibbons, Henry, 4:187, 190-91, 198; 15:276; 16:183, 283; 17:176; 21:363, 365; 28:374, 375; 33:381; office of, illus., 4: opp. 190

Gibbons, Henry, Jr., 4:191; 28:374; 37:89

Gibbons, Henry III, obit. of Henry Walter Gibbons, 37:89-90

Gibbons, Henry Walter, obit., 37:89-90

Gibbons, Mrs. Henry Walter (Hazel Nonan), 37:89

Gibbons, Morton Raymond, obit., 28:374-75; phot., opp. 289

Gibbons, Mrs. Morton Raymond (Mary Stubbs), 28:375

Gibbons, Walter, 15:372

Gibbons, William P., 15:372; 16:183; 17:176; 30:1, 11; 31:337, 339

Gibbs (S.F., 1849), 34:22

Gibbs (on *Golden Age*, 1866), 36:302

Gibbs, Alfred, 24:59

Gibbs, George, 18:180; 29:276

Gibbs, John, 17:240; 24:58, 72

Gibbs, William T., 30:111, 115, 260

Gibson, Capt. (Bodega Bay, 1790), 2:301; 10:338

Gibson, A., 10:200

Gibson, F. W., 32:331

Gibson, Fanny, 21:169

Gibson, Horatio Gates, 10:198; 17: opp. 200; 19:229; 27:216-17, 218, 225; 30:165, 166; 33:373

Gibson, Hugh S., 4:53

Gibson, James, 1:177

Gibson, Jane, 22:379

Gibson, M. M., 29:93

Gibson, Marion, 5:125

Gibson, P., 24:168

Gibson, Reed, 4:114, 115

Gibson, Samuel, 3:122; 17:240, 340, 342-43; 21:336; 24:58; 26:21, 24; 29:266-67, 271; 30:51, 53-54

Gibson, Mrs. Thomas E. (Ursula Cull), obit., 9:294

Gibson, William, 30:39-47 *passim;* 36:307-10 *passim*

Gibson and Hodges, Los Angeles, 13:319

Gibson's Island, 2:301, 302

Gibsonville, 11:228, 238, 240, 242

Gibsonville Blues, 29:236

Giddings and Woods, 31:40

Gideon, Jacob, 22:79

Giese, Mrs. Richard S. (Lulu Gabel), 33:381

Giesler, Jerry (through Pete Martin), *The Jerry Giesler Story*, rev., 40:157-58

Giffen, Mrs. Guy James (Helen Smith), 21:288; 22:287; address, "The Adobe Houses of California," 22:183; obit. of William C. Latham, 24:186

Gifford, Charles F., 14:398

Gifford, Edward Winslow, letter to, 31:103

Gifford, Fannie, 10:361

Gifford, Henry B., 34:258, 333

Gift, William Wirt, 24:174

Gift, George W., 22:30, 35; 29:237, 240, 247-48

"Gift of Fray Junípero Serra's Birthplace to the City of San Francisco," 11:79-81

Gihon, John Hancock, 20:299; 23:100; 28:64; 30:108, 252, 256, 265

Gihon & Butler, 30:252, 256, 265

Gihon, Johnson & Butler, 30:256

Gihon, Manuel, 3:235-36

Gila (ship), 22:152, 153, 155, 162-63, 167

Gilam (Sacramento, 1858), 9:253

Gilard, M. Louis, 14:142

Gila River, 1:112, 117, 147, 149; 2:9, 10, 16-19; 3:386; 9:3, 4, 6, 10-14 *passim;* 10:27; 11:365, 377, 388; 15:111, 201, 374; 19:217; 21:101, 108-11 *passim,* 203-16 *passim,* 223, 298-99; 22:1, 3, 5, 9, 12, 19, 20; 25:293, 294; 34:31; 40:161; maps showing, 9: opp. 11, 12; 10: opp. 27; 15: opp. 213

Gila Trail, The: The Texas Argonauts and the California Gold Rush, by Harris, ed. Dillon, rev., 40:160-62

Gilb, Corinne Lathrop, rev. of Robinson, *Lawyers of Los Angeles,* 39:85

Gilbeau, P., 22:198, 217, 220; 23:125, 136

Gilbert, Benjamin Franklin, 25:191; 26:93; 33:284; "California and the Civil War, a Bibliographical Essay," 40:289-307; "The Confederate Minority in California," 20:154-70; "The Mythical Johnston Conspiracy," 28:165-73; "San Francisco Harbor Defense during the Civil War," 33:229-40; "Welcome to the Czar's Fleet," 26:13-19; address, "Navies in the Pacific, 1861-65," 27:178-80; bk. rev. by, 38:167-69

Gilbert, Edward, 1:216; 2:117(?); 7:278, 281; 10:152, 153, 163, 238, 241; 14:329-30, 345-46; 19:14; 20:102; 26:347; 32:221, 224; 37:316; 40:132; fac. sig., 10: opp. 159

Gilbert, Ferdinand, 4:62; 10:294; 21:178

Gilbert, Grove Karl, 4:42, 48, 51, 53, 56

Gilbert, Hammond Barnes, 26:93

Gilbert, Sir Humphrey, 3:204, 266; 7:235, 252

Gilbert, Isaac N., 4:320, 353

Gilbert, James A., *see* Burgess, Gilbert & Still

Gilbert, John L., 19:63, 65, 66, 72; 27:315

Gilbert, William Schwenk, 21:171

Gilbert (F.) and Baldwin's "Great Dragon Troupe," 21:178

Gilbert (E.) & Co., 7:280

Gilbert's Melodeon, San Francisco, 4:62; 10:281, 294, 376, 390

Gil Blas en Californie, Un, by Dumas, art. on, 14:132-42

Gilchrist (of Sacramento police), 15:275

Gilchrist, David V., 26:304

Gilchrist, Edward, 3:187; 17:327-34 *passim;* 29:336; 33:103, 106, 112, 113; 35:103-4

Gilchrist, John G., 30:365

Gilcrest, Samuel Fleming, 22:192

Gildea, William Brown, 3:89; 4:163; 19:119, 138

Gildemeester, John Paul Henry, 23:344

Gildersleeve, C. C., 28:240

Gildersleeve, John, 14:223

"Gilding the Sunflower . . . Oscar Wilde's Visit to San Francisco," by Lois F. Rodecape, 19:97-112

Gile, Joseph, 23:206, 209

Giles, J. B., 9:388

Giles (George) & Co., 8:358

Giles, James & Co., 9:268, 345, 346, 358, 363

Giles, Rosena A., obit. of May Hazel Southern, 22:381-82

Gilham, Mitchell, 19:128, 141

Gili, Bartolomé, 1:164; 23:3, 4, 16

Gilkey's Express, 39:57

Gilky, L. B., 13:31

Gill, Irving, 36:71-72

Gill, William, *California Letters,* rev., 3:200-201

Gill, Mrs. William (Harriet Tarleton), 3:201

Gillam, Josephus, 11:179

Gilland, John, 39:320

Gillem, Alvan C., 28:163

Gillespie, Archibald Hamilton, 1:92, 128-29, 132, 133, 146, 240, 291; 2:73; 3:115-22 *passim,* 271; 5:271, 297-301 *passim,* 304-7 *passim;* 6:79, 81, 82, 89, 181-88, 265-73 *passim,* 364-73 *passim;* 9:84, 86, 106-11 *passim,* 114, 121; 11:135; 12:37, 40, 43, 48, 57, 58, 147, 165, 166, 168, 336-37, 340; 13:301, 302, 303; 15:62, 63; 16:211, 213, 321, 334; 17:228; 18:174, 288, 298-99; 19:131-32; 20:233; 21:224, 335-39 *passim,* 345-51 *passim,* 355; 22:46, 51; 25:121, 129, 130, 131, 293; 26:21-39 *passim,* 54, 58; 27:110; 28:342; 29:157, 262, 270-75 *passim,* 334, 335; 30:51; 33:105, 106, 112; 40: arts. on, 17:123-40, 271-84, 325-50; 18:217-28; 19:43-58; cor. and reps., 5:297; 6:87-88, 189-91, 266-68, 370-71; 8:76-77; 17:125-40, 271-84, 325-47; 18:217-28; 19:43-44, 53; 26:21; bk. on, rev., 40:162-65

Gillespie, Charles V., 6:11; 7:106;

11:135; 19:231; 25:132; 26:329-30, 339, 347; 27:321; 28:290

Gillespie, Mrs. Charles V. (Sarah Beutner), 26:335, 339; 27:321

Gillespie, Eugene F., 11:109, 121; 14:212, 221

Gillespie, George, 19:63, 72; 27:315; 28:54

Gillespie, J. M., 9:180

Gillespie, John, 4:320

"Gillespie and the Conquest of California," ed. George W. Ames, Jr., 17:123-40, 271-84, 325-50

Gillett (S.F., 1850), 23:358

Gillett, James Norris, 26:91; 35:29-30, 33; 39:19, 20

Gillette, E. A., 9:103

Gilliam, Albert M., 37:16

Gilliam, Cornelius, 4:277, 318, 327-28, 339, 352

Gilliam, Harold and Ann, *San Francisco, City at the Golden Gate*, rev., 40:359-60

Gilliam, Jonathan P., 37:7-9, 16

Gilligan, Biddy, 22:267

Gilligan & Stevens, 9:265

Gillingham, William, 18:362-63

Gilliland, Mrs. Drew L. (Adeline B. Latham), 9:378

Gillis, Lt. (Mazatlán, 1846), 2:167, 170, 171, 172

Gillis (Sacramento, 1860), 11:10

Gillis, G., 18:211-12

Gillis, Hudson B., 39:58

Gillis, James L., 10:76, 411

Gillis, James N., 3:196, 199

Gillis, Mabel Ray, 10:76; 11:188; 19:282

Gillis, Stephen Edward, 15:381; bk. on, rev., 3:96-99

Gillis, William, 27:6

Gillis, William Robert, 9:289; *Memories of Mark Twain and Steve Gillis*, rev., 3:196-99

Gilman (lawsuit, Marysville, 1859), 10:188

Gilman, Charles, 27:362, 368; 28:60; 29:169, 171, 257, 258; 34:242

Gilman, Daniel Coit, 24:323; 27:341, 351; 30:140

Gilman, Henry, 9:55

Gilmer, Jeremy Francis, 25:371

Gillmore, Collins, 31:155

Gilmore, F. R., 25:48

Gilroy, John (John Cameron), 4:82; 14:11-12, 197; 23:375; 29:20, 25

Gilroy, Nicodemus, 29:25

Gilroy (place), 11:39

Gilson, Emma (Burke), 31:185

Gilstrap, W. H., 19:72; 27:318

Gil y Taboada, Luis, 8:149; 16:109; 36:8

Giménez, Col. (Guaymas, 1854), 18:12-13

Gingery (Chingery? worked for Sutter, 1847), 16:138; 25:220; 26:110, 111

Gingg, Emil, 27:1

Giovanari, P. A., 36:244

Gipsy (ship), 16:68

Giraud, Mme., 20:128

Gird, Richard, 27:117, 121

Gisippus (play), 16:341

Gitchell, John R., 9:72; 10:358

Giulietta (schr.), 6:31

Giulitta (clipper), 27:137

Glacier Point Mountain House, 5:339

Glaciers, 1:284; 4:27, 28, 31, 42, 51; 7:130

Gladding, J. F., 9:99

Gladding, McBean Co., 23:384; 35:349

Gladwin, Mrs. (S.F., 1864), 24:262

Gladwin, William H., 25:107

Glanton, John J., 22:1

Glascock, William H., 17:44-45

Glaser, W. B., 24:265

Glasford, Charles C. D., 13:32

Glasgow (ship), 11:381

Glass, Hugh, 2:24-33; 4:116, 119, 129

Glasscock, Carl Burgess, *Bandits of the Southern Pacific*, rev., 8:281-82

Glasscock, H. A., 9:195

Glasscock, James, 10:360

Glassford, Robert, 16:134

Glaucus (ship), 22:353

Glazier, Simon W., 9:73

Glazier (Isaac) & Co., 9:56, 58, 73

Gleason (Timbuctoo, 1858), 9:364

Gleason, James H., 14:329-38 *passim*, 345; 18:46

Gleason, Joseph M., address, "Peninsula Explorations," 3:99-100

Gleason, Matt, 36:164

Gleason, Morton D., 25:194

Gledhill, Mrs. William Edwin (Andriette Bowen), 31:190, 381

Gleeson (Richard T.) Library, 33:354

Glen, R. G., 29:231

Glen, Thomas, 15:281

Glen, William, 8:267, 268

Glencoe (ship), 2:93, 94, 98; 11:157-59

Glendale, 31:16

Glen Ellen, 13:37
Gleney, Capt. (from New Haven),
  12:98
Glenn, Alexander and Virginia
  (Chinn), 28:380
Glenn, Elizabeth, 28:380
Glenn, Hugh James, 7:290; 24:228
Glenn, M. M., 9:195
Glidden (S.F., 1867), 11:127
Gliddon, George R., 14:333, 346
"Glimpse of San Francisco in the '50's,
  A," letters of Murray Morrison,
  13:80-83
Globe, Le (company), 22:303
Globe (newsp.), San Francisco, 10:295;
  15:72; 21:34; 34:335
Globe Theatre, San Francisco, 23:110,
  111
Glosen, I., 13:336, 353
Glover, Aquila, 10:351, 352
Glover, Aseneth, 26:168; 28:292
Glover, J. T., 10:49, 51, 60, 165, 166, 170,
  190, 288
Glover, Mrs. J. T. (Octavine C. Payne),
  10:48, 51-61 *passim*, 69, 165, 167,
  177-90 *passim*, 246, 247, 250, 254, 271,
  276, 278, 286
Glover, William, 5:406; 33:65;
  37:237-38
Glover and Baker, 34:347
Glozer, Liselotte F. and William K.,
  *California in the Kitchen: ...
  California Imprints in the Field of
  Gastronomy from 1870(?)-1932,*
  rev., 40:258-59
Gluyas, Mary, 29:103, 110, 113, 116, 125
Gluyas, Reeve, 29:107-26 *passim*
Glynn, James, 14:342
Goad, Frank, 10:273
Goad, William Frank and May (Cook),
  29:92
Goald, Samuel, 14:181
Goat Island, 5:7, 178; 8:382; 14:129;
  17:293; 25:264; 27:73, 260, 271, 274;
  see also Yerba Buena Island
Goats, 2:41, 42, 295; 12:193; 14:5, 6, 9,
  129; 16:119; 17:293; 23:252; 38:263
Goble, Silas, 26:234-35
Goble, Thomas, 35:295
God, John (Indian, 1827), 2:14, 15
Godchaux, Prosper, 10:73; 31:283
Goddard, Miss (actress, 1855), 16:84,
  183
Goddard, Elnathan B., 21:114; house of,
  17:44

Goddard, George Henry, 4:11; 7:8-9;
  22:33; 34:209, 212-19 *passim*, 222, 223,
  228
Goddard, Mount, 4:11, 21, 39, 47, 51, 55
Godden, Thomas B., 29:20, 25
Godden, Mrs. Thomas B., *see* Ortega,
  Encarnación
Godeau, Alexis G., 39:256
Godeau, Jules, 39:227, 243, 256-59,
  312-14; phot., 39: foll. 232
Godeffroy, Sillem, & Co., 15:177
Godenski (ballet), 16:340
Godey, Alexis, 1:122-23, 131, 138;
  3:122, 270; 4:376; 10:37; 17:341;
  21:322, 331, 332, 355; 26:34, 44, 47,
  56-57, 62; 29:25, 275
Godfrey (Yuba Co., 1857), 9:143, 156
Godfrey, Si, 10:171
Godwin, Capt. (Colorado R., 1864),
  22:170
Godwin (William) & Co., Sacramento,
  3:268-69
Gönninger, Hans ("Juan Domingo" or
  Johann Groningen), 13:210-11, 344;
  19:204-5, 215; 25:124-25
Görlitz (Yuba R., 1850), 12:301
Goethe, Charles Matthias, 21:383-84
Goetzmann, William H., *Army
  Explorations in the American West,
  1803-1863,* rev., 39:83
Goff (S.F., 1861), 10:285
Goff, Daniel, 15:240
Goff, David, Marion and Samuel, 4:321
Goff, Walter, 35:148
Goin, "Big Jake," 13:258
Gold: amt. taken from diggings, 13:162,
  167, 171-75 *passim*, 177, 179, 271, 373;
  23:58; deposits nr. L.A. (1849), 29:14;
  overexploitation of, 31:253-56; price
  of, 2:199; shipments, 13:226; 15:88,
  164-86 *passim*, 366, 375; 16:31, 33, 84,
  338; 17:184; 23:53; to Eng. 33:84;
  sought by Spanish explorers, 6:294,
  295-301 *passim*, 308-9; as stimulus,
  6:200; *see also* Gold coins; Gold
  discoveries; Gold dust; Gold mining;
  Gold regions
Gold (play), 34:366-67
"Gold and Ghost Towns," address by
  John W. Winkley, 27:85-87
Gold and Sunshine, by Ayers, rev.,
  1:101-2
Goldberg, M., 34:354
Gold Bluff Co., 3:151

Gold Bluffs, 3:203; 12:4; 20:45; 25:118-19; 26:7, 340; 31:244, 255, 311

Gold Canyon, Sierra Co., 11:240

Gold Canyon, Nev., 12:325, 326, 327; 34:215, 227

Gold coins and coinage, 6:237; 15:173; 16:35, 36, 184; 17:184; 19:260; 24:183; 34:70; Utah, from Calif. gold, 15:244-46; 24:183

"Gold Days in California, Australia, and South Africa," address by Charles L. Camp, 28:277-78

Gold discoveries:
before 1848, 1:167; 2:35-36, 49; 3:89; 4:91; 7:199; 8:120; 10:86; 12:295; 13:58, 224-26; 14:210; 17:24; 19:203, 215; 22:320
in 1848, 1:148; 2:83; 4:89; 5:95-96; 6:247; 11:42-43; 12:295, 357; 13:56, 62, 63, 170; 14:82, 150, 273-79; 16:127, 142; 17:232; 19:125, 133-34, 140; 22:141, 150; Bigler's acct. of, 14:273-76; news of, 10:298-301; 11:129-37; 12:357; 13:56-57; 19:326-31 *passim*, 336; effects of, 12:295-97; 14:202-3; 19:331; in England, 32:270-75; in France, 33:125-42; Emerson's comments on, 33:241-43, 246
outside Calif.: Arizona, 12:4, 11; Australia, 19:328; 32:273; New Zealand, 19:335

Gold dust and nuggets, 1:266; 2:198; 4:175; 5:19, 38; 6:62, 236, 237; 7:403; 11:166, 167; 12:295; 13:168-72 *passim*, 177, 179; 15:165, 182, 185, 377; 16:129, 184; 20:119; 23:51, 53, 58, 60; 24:128, 183, 344; 26:347; 29:5, 9; 33:50; 35:216; 39:110-11; assaying and buying, 9:140; 16:31-40 (*see also* Assay offices); biggest nugget in Calif., 3:259-61; found nr. Auburn, 31:274; on Yuba R., 31:274; refinery in S.F., 28:131, 137; sent to Eng., 23:58; 32:84; taken from Calif. by Mormons, 15:244, 245; 22:138; 24:183; by Russians, 39:110; taken to France, 23:51; 31:311

Golden Age (ship), 8:372; 13:82; 15:178, 267, 272, 275, 279, 375; 16:83, 184; 17:168; 19:296; 20:260; 26:175, 183; 29:218-19, 381; 32:209; 33:204; 36:300-301

Golden City (ship), 21:156

"Golden Crucible, The," address by Blake Ross, 9:188

Golden Eagle Hotel, Sacramento, 3:154; 9:251, 254, 255, 276; 10:250, 261, 372, 373, 374; 35:336

Golden Era (weekly, 1850s), 5:410; 7:283; 30:251, 260-66 *passim*

Golden Era (1880s), 32:234

Golden Era (str.), 27:327

Golden Farmer (play), 38:19

Golden Fleece (ship), 15:180

Golden Gate, 13:10; 15:61; 25:124; delayed discovery of, 27:289-94 *passim*; legend of origin, 2:62; name, 3:173; 25:124

Golden Gate (str., 1851-62), 6:356-57; 15:164, 165, 168, 183, 273, 277, 278, 281, 366, 375; 16:79; 17:182, 320; 19:296; 26:74, 75; 27:327; 28:125, 127; 29:102; 34:34, 232, 334; 35:217; 38:27; arts. on, 19:27-42; 32:349-61

Golden Gate (pilot boat, 1855), 15:280

Golden Gate (bark, 1865), 33:2, 6, 7, 11, 149, 151; 34:334-35; 35:291, 292

Golden Gate and Miners' Union Iron Works, San Francisco, 33:375

Golden Gate Bridge, 15:379; 23:185; 25:124

Golden Gate Hotel, San Francisco, 15:166

Golden Gate International Exposition, 32:184

Golden Gate Nursery, 33:375

Golden Gate Park, 8:187; 32:183-84; 37:217-18

Golden Gulch, The (play), 34:364

Golden Hinde (ship), 6:93; 16: No. 1, Pt. 2, pp. 1-6 *passim*, 13, 14, 19, 23, 35; 17: No. 4, Pt. 2, p. 1; 27:290, 294

Golden ingots, society and lottery, *see* Lingots d'Or

Golden Rock Water Co., 32:359

Golden State (newsp.), Stockton, 19:63, 68

Golden State (ship), 6:352, 353

Golden West (ship), 15:177

Goldfellen, Ann, 28:292

Goldfield Consolidated Mining Co., 32:31

Gold Flat, 3:135, 137

Gold Hill, Nevada Co., 6:228-29; 11:244; 12:65; 30:261

Gold Hill, Nev., 12:327, 328, 329; 17:76-77, 80; 23:260; 38:25; newspaper, 11:48, 190

Gold Hill Co. (Grass Valley), 11:243, 244-45

Goldhunter (bark, of Bangor, 1850), 2:126

Goldhunter (ship, of Fall River), 2:103

Gold Hunter (str., 1850), 2:114; 8:182, 262; 31:37

Goldie, James, 23:216-17, 331-32

Gold Lake, 6:127; 11:242; 33:200, 201; Lassen's search for, 39:263-66; map of route, 39: foll. 264; *see also* Gold Lake hoax

Gold Lake hoax, 8:176; 13:17, 28; 26:104; 31:255; 33:201; 39:263

Gold mining:
  coyoteing, 6:245; 11:54, 236
  "crevicing," 6:215, 243, 248
  dredging, 3:202; 6:244, (illus.) opp. 244; 15:51-52
  dry washing, 13:165
  hydraulic, 9:174, 175, 177, 179, 384; 11:166, 227-42 *passim*, (illus.) 231; 12:11; 18:360; 28:233-41 *passim*; 29:193-209; 33:56
  w. knives, 11:243; 13:164
  placer, 2:186-87, 191-93; 3:126-27, 130, 151-53, 161-62; 4:66; 5:221-22, 244; 6:215-19, 223-24, 238, 243-48 *passim*; 11:255, 322; 12:66; 13:15, 17, 75, 161-62, 171, 373-74; 15:51; 22: (illus.) opp. 300; 23:52-57 *passim*, (illus.) opp. 60, opp. 167, 167-70, 350, 353; 24:258-60; 26:104, 123-24; 27:298-99; 35:208, 209
  quartz, 3:150, 163; 4:67; 6:228-30, 243-44; 7:114-18 *passim*; 11:227, 228, 236, (illus.) 241, 243, 244, 324, 337; 12:65-76 *passim*, 327, 328, 329; 15:52; 18:149, 154; 24:254-55; 26:298-301 *passim*, 307; 35:41, 43, 223, 227
  shafts and tunnels, 3:129, 135, 140; 6:225, 229, 231, 245, 332; 7:118; 9:133; 11:229, 233, (illus.) 235, 237-42 *passim*, (illus.) 241, 323, (illus.) 325, 326, 333
  sluicing, 3:161-62, 259; 6:245-46; 13:28; *see also* Aqueducts

Gold Mountain, Nevada Co., 15:52

"Gold Mountain, Big City, Chinese Map," by William Hoy, 27:256-58

Gold regions:
  northern, 3:93, 129-36, 140-53, 200, 259-60; 5:219-36, 242-46; 6:223-31 *passim*, 243-46, 332, 334; 9:133, 380, 392; 1:228-45; 12:65, 71; 13:27-28, 275, 377, 384-85; 18:154; 19:28; 26:298-307 *passim*; 29:193-209; 33:51-56, 295-300; map, 5:218; Bear R., 11:110, 112; 13:17-19, 170, 174; Feather R., 3:202; 6: (illus.) opp. 243, 243; 11:110; 13:171, 173, 369; 23:59-60; 24:127, 257; 27:299; Klamath R., 3:93; 5:236, 245; Scott Valley area, 28:213, 229; Trinity R., 5:38, 146, 177, 219-36; 23:59; Yuba R., 3:93; 5:38, 293-95; 6:215, 218-19, 244; 8:193, 208-13 *passim*, 353-63 *passim*; 9:177, 285, 380, 384; 12:301, 303; 13:171, 174, 175; 14:203-11 *passim*; 15:51-52; 23:57, 349, 350; 29:193-207 *passim*; 31:273; 33:51-55 *passim*; *see also* Gold Bluffs
  central, 2:131; 3:126-29, 140; 6:238; 11:42, 228; 13:75, 263, 374; 20:39-43 *passim*, 184; 24:23, 25-26, 28, 126-33 *passim*, 252-60 *passim*, 349, 363; 25:105; 30:24, 26-27; American R., 2:186-94; 6:248; 11:230; 12:66-67, 71, 314, 315; 13:14-16, 26-27, 169-70, 174, 175; 14: (illus.) opp. 269, 273-78; 23:52, 54, 58-59, 60, 167-70; 26:294-97; 27:297-99; 29:167; 34:71-72; bet. American and Cosumnes rivs., 13:159-70 *passim*; 23:52
  southern, 2:138, 195, 198; 11:165-75, 228, 243, 322-26, 329-37; 13:271-72, 383; 16:83; 17:115; 18:201, 202; 19:28; 21:325-26; 28:113, 114, 277; 32:1, 19, 23; 35:208, 209, 214, 216, 221-27 *passim*; Calaveras R., 23:60; 25:158-61; Kern R., 15:271-75 *passim*; Mariposa and Merced rivs., 12:73-76; 13:358; 23:60, 367, 368, 376; San Gabriel Canyon, 13:336; nr. San Luis Obispo, 1:167; Stanislaus R., 2:195; 13:173, 373; 20:119; 23:60; 24:30, 344-45; Tuolumne R., 2:198; 11:170-75 *passim*; 23:60; 24:131; Woods Creek, 11:166-69; 13:383; 23:60; 24:125
  east of Sierra Nevada, 4:66-78; 5:336; 7:113-19;
  in High Sierra, 4:25-26, 38, 39
  outside Calif.: Australia and So. Africa 28:277-78; Colorado R., 3:163, 167, 169; 12:4, 11; 22:10-11, 14; map, 12: opp. 3; Fraser R., 5:402; 6:19-30; 15:325; Idaho,

15:324; Montana, 15:324-28 *passim;*
Oregon, 15:324; Queen Charlotte
I., 22:104
statistics (1858), 11:228, 337
Gold Run, 6:246; 13:27; 26:170; 30:125
Gold rush:
in Calif., 1:253-55, 258-67; 2:137-38,
182-200; 3:93, 202; 6:214-37;
10:403-5; 12:64, 296, 313-17;
13:272-77 *passim,* 356-77 *passim;*
19:375; 20:38-42; 22:70-80;
24:23-30, 125-33; 33:24-25
overland, 1:59-71; 3:46-72, 200;
5:289-92, 404; 6:61-63, 376; 7:89;
8:81-82, 185; 9:88, 291; 13:84;
19:324, 325, 342; 2:122-50; 24:18-19,
30-46, 117-25, 133-38, 235-52
via Cape Horn, 2:87-114; 3:92-93;
6:205-12; 7:197; 19:324; 22:119,
235-36, 237-43
via Panama, 9:196-97; 12:312; 13:4-5,
389-95, 398-403; 19:144, 324, 343;
20:330; 27:35-38; 29:3-11; 39:101-2;
see also Panama crossing
Colorado R., 12:11-17, 323
Nevada, 12:324-30
from: Australia, 19:328-29, 336
China, 19:329-30; 28:343; *see also*
China; Chinese
France, 5:4-43, 219-54; 20:70-72;
22:289-314; 33:125-42
Germany, 20:69
Great Britain, 19:332; 32:85, 86;
20:65-66
Hawaii, 19:327-28
Ireland, *see* Kerr, Thomas
Mexico, 13:277, 363; 19:324-26
Norway, 20:67-68
Oregon, 19:330-31, 342
South America, 19:326-27
books and plays based on, 14:132-42;
27:237-48; 34:356-67 *passim*
doctors in, 4:177-91, 194-97, 202,
203-5
"movies," 33:29-38
"Gold Rushes and Their Significance,"
address by Gregory Crampton, 19:375
"Gold Rush: Extracts from the Diary
of C. S. Lyman," ed. Frederick J.
Teggart, 2:181-202
"Gold Rush Movies," by John F.
McDermott, 33:29-38
"Gold Rush Steamers," address by
Ernest A. Wiltsee, 17:285
Gold Springs, 11:331-32

Goldstein, A. S., and Helena
(Alexander), 34:181, 182
Goldstein, Lutie D., obit., 34:181-82
Gold vs. Grain, by Kelley, rev.,
39:181
Gold-washing machines, 2:186, 187;
6:219; 13:161-62; 23:45-46; 24:258,
343; 30:21; 39:105; drawing of, 22:
opp. 300
Goliah (ship), 14:72; 15:178, 269, 270,
271; 16:83; 31:42; 32:352-53, 354, 360
Gollan, Gordon, 30:92
Goller, John, 13:314, 319, 336
Goll's Diggings, 26:297
Golovnin, Vasilii M., 12:199, 212
Golovnin (ship), 18:347; 33:63
Gómara, Francisco López de, 1:38,
49, 50; 3:262-66 *passim;* "Chronica de
los Barbarojas," 1:38; his *Conquista
de Mejico,* 1:37, 46; 3:308; 6:303;
Historia General de las Indias, 1:49,
50; 6:303; 7:59-60, 64, 65, 68
Gómez, Alonzo, 2:141-43, 156; 7:241,
245
Gómez, Francisco, 1:158
Gómez, José Joaquín, 3:282; 8:114-15;
10:104; 12:267, 332; 19:132; 26:250-52;
29:336; rancho of, 29:336, 337, 338
Gómez, Manuel, 23:252
Gómez, Rafael, 15:338; 16:234
Gómez, Santiago, 15:356
Gómez, Vicente, 23:13
Gómez de Corbán, Toribio, 7:262-63,
297, 299, 300, 307, 327, 331, 349, 357,
359, 376; 8:45
Gómez Pedraza, Manuel, 25:74, 78
Gómez Renfigo, Francisco, 16: No. 1,
Pt. 2, p. 4
Gompertz, Helen Marion, *see* LeConte,
Mrs. Joseph N.
Gondola, The (gambling house),
Sacramento, 24:357
Gondolier, The (play), 16:285
Goñi, Matías, 26:314, 318; 27:310;
29:139
Goñi, Pedro, 29:139-40
Gonzales (Marysvile, 1858), 9:372, 375
Gonzales, Agapita, 9:267
Gonzales, Francisco, 36:234
Gonzales, Juan, 15:122
Gonzales, Juan José, 16:285
Gonzales (Leandro) *v.* José Antonio
de la Guerra, 18:255
Gonzales, Manuel (Indian), 14:6
Gonzales, Ygnacio Elías, 14:254

González, Macedonio, 13:101
González, Manuel María,
	15:347-48, 356
González, Miguel, 8:151-52, 248;
	16:218; 23:216
González, Rafael, 16:353; 23:331;
	30:98; 33:279
González Cabrera Bueno, José, 8:34;
	31:115, 119
González Dávila, Gil, 6:296, 306
González de Ibarra, Francisco,
	23:208, 217
González de Ibarra, Manuel, 24:292,
	308; 25:60, 362
González (or Gonzales) Rubio, José
	María de Jesús, 12:196; 16:369-70;
	18:257, 276; 23:9; 29:144, 147;
	32:122; 37:98
Good, Joe, 12:11
Goodall, Capt. (of *City of Pueblo,*
	1898), 30:292
Goodall, Nelson & Perkins, 16:68
Goodall, Perkins & Co., 35:148
Goodchild, A. C., 3:7-8
Goodchild family, 38:264-65
Goode, Herbert and Robert, 25:175
Goodell, Nathaniel D., 38:33, 36
Goodenow, Mrs. (Yuba Co., 1854),
	8:207; *see also* Goodwin, Miss
Goodfellow, George E., 11:291
Goodfellow, Henry, 9:51, 58, 69, 347
Goodfellow, William S. and Alice,
	16:384
Good Hope (ship), 29:103, 105-6
Goodhue (S.F., 1849), 27:44
Goodhue, Bertram Grosvenor, 36:67, 71
Goodman, Arthur J. and Minna C.
	(Buchanan), 9:273
Goodman, J. H., 17:174
Goodman, Joseph T., 3:197; 12:84;
	15:381; 21:141, 142; 25:35;
	36:367, 370
Goodman, L. C., 11:9
Goodman, Louis Earl, 33:175-78; obit.
	of Robert L. McWilliams, 34:378
Goodman, Morris L., 13:335
Goodman Castle (riv. str.),
	10:280, 293
Goodrich, Levi, 38:33, 42
Goodrum, Capt. (Colorado R., 1866),
	22:171, 172
Goodsell, Thomas, 3:118
Goodspeed, George, 18:28-29
Good Templars, International Order
	of, 30:247

Goodwin, Capt. (of *Huntress,* 1849)
	and Mrs., 2:202
Goodwin, Miss (Yuba Co., 1854),
	8:209, 213
Goodwin, Capt. (Colorado R., 1872),
	22:173
Goodwin, Andrew, 15:38-39
Goodwin, Cardinal L., address,
	"California's Communication with
	the East," 3:97
Goodwin, Charles Carroll, 9:384;
	15:381
Goodwin, Charles H., 21:240, 256-57,
	264-65
Goodwin, E. C., 9:42, 352(?)
Goodwin, H., 36:294, 305
Goodwin, Henry Leavitt, 16:338;
	17:177
Goodwin, Isaac, 14:177, 182
Goodwin, Mrs. J. W. (Alice Prescott),
	18:384
Goodwin, Jesse O., 9:65, 78, 107, 112,
	116, 154, 178, 352, 358, 384; 10:72,
	189, 198, 251, 252, 358, 359, 367, 384;
	14:379-82 *passim,* 390, 392, 397; 15:21,
	28, 35, 43, 49; port., 9:355
Goodwin, Mrs. Jesse O. (Mary E.
	Wadsworth), 9:384; 14:397
Goodwin, Madison, 26:204
Goodwin, Nathaniel Carll, 21:266
Goodwin, Ozias, 23:325, 332
Goodyear, Andrew, 8:211; 20:344-45
Goodyear, Miles, 8:211; 20:344-46
Goodyear, Watson Andrews, 4:32-34
Goodyear Rubber Co., 30:289
Goodyear's Bar, 8:211; 9:70; 17:311;
	30:266
Goodyear's Hill, 8:202
Goold, Edmond Louis, 19:230, 236;
	21:120
Goose Creek, Utah, 32:199, 203, 206;
	illus., 6: op. 116, opp. 118
Goose Lake, 22:101, 213; 28:228
Goose Valley, 26:52
Gorda, Point, 9:208; 10:330
Gorder, C. von, 36:99
Gordon (S.F., 1850), 7:399-400
Gordon, Capt. (Nevada Co., 1850s),
	6:338
Gordon (S.F., 1855), 15:374
Gordon (on Mt. Shasta, 1856), 6:74
Gordon, Miss (Yuba Co., 1859),
	10:170
Gordon, Alexander (Marin Co., 1862),
	10:376, 390

Gordon, Alexander (Fresno Co., 1880s), 25:174
Gordon, C. C., 19:233
Gordon, George, 10:67; 16:182; 19:231-32; 27:71; 28:42; 33:373
Gordon, Hattie Hodge, see Mann, Mrs. Stephen Hodge
Gordon, Helen M. (Nellie), 19:233
Gordon, J. (Yuba Co., 1859), 10:194
Gordon, J. P., 32:170
Gordon, James E., 1:16; 24:80
Gordon, John, 18:375
Gordon, Capt. John (of *America*), 5:255; 17:130
Gordon, Mary van, 30:4
Gordon, S. B., 9:269
Gordon, William ("Uncle Billy"), 5:126, 128, 138, 274, 275; 7:289; 16:133; 23:293, 297, 365, 375; 29:134
Gordon, Fr. William, 8:374-77
Gordon & Steen, 8:276; 15:88, 183, 273
Gordon-Cummings, Constance Frederica, 28:186
"Gordon Manuscript, The," 8:374-77
Gordon's Ferry, 12:6, 7
Gordon's Ranch, 23:365; *see also* Ranchos: Quesesosi
Gore, G. W., 35:201
Gore, Rosa, 19:232, 233
Gore Island, 3:324, 325
Gorgona, 8:13; 13:4-5; 20:18; 29:10
Gorgy's Ranch, *see* Tschernikh
Gorham, Ambrose, 15:184
Gorham, Charles M., 8:361
Gorham, George C., 5:95; 8:361; 9:173, 380; 10:54, 58, 59, 64, 198, 284, 285, 294, 296, 384; 15:43; 33:215
Gorham, Harry M., 31:185
Gorham, William R., 15:168, 181; 17:83, 179
Gorie, Albert H., 25:94
Goris, Jan Albert, 37:380; 38:183; trans. "A Belgian in the Gold Rush," 37:311-46; 38:141-55
Gorley, Hugh A., 40:317, 318
Gorman, John, 16:323, 324, 328, 329
Gorman, Michael, 9:355-61 *passim*, 376; 10:44, 166
Gorman, "Paddy," 22:14, 159
Gorman (place), 12:6
Gorrill, William Henry, obits. of Charles S. Cushing, 25:89-90; Perry Evans, 35:178-79
Goshen, 18:27-31
Gospel Pioneering, by Pond, rev., 1:198

Goss, Helen Rocca, 32:383; "An Ill-Starred Voyage, the S.S. *Golden Gate*," 32:349-61
Gosselin (from Le Havre, 1849), 5:27
Gossmann, L., 31:26
Gottig (or Göttig), Lawrence, 12:184; 27:170, 173-74; 31:337
Goucher, George G., 19:67, 68, 69; 28:47
Goudland, Het, by Hendrick Conscience, 37:312-13
Gougenheim, Adelaide and Josephine, 10:63, 358, 368; 16:184, 285; 21:46, 53
Gough, Charles H., 9:26; 16:342
Gough, John Bartholomew, 20:2, 6, 10, 11
Gouin, Capt. (of *Aurélie*, 1851), 29:81
Gould, Capt. (of *Mary Frances*, 1848), 14:333
Gould (S.F., 1862), 10:378, 379
Gould, Frank Horace, 19:72, 73
Gould, Mrs. George Jay (Edith M. Kingdon), 35:142
Gould, James G., 9:26
Gould, John(?), 9:355, 372
Gould, Julia, 15:165, 167
Gould, L. A., 25:22
Gould, W. B., 26:70, 74-75
Gould, Will D., 13:352
Gould & Curry mine, 11:61; 12:329; 17:76-77, 79
Goulding, James E., 27:113-22
Gourley, Anna, 10:263
Goustiaux, Auguste, 39:226
Gove, A. J., 8:203, 212
Gove, A. S., 9:46
Government Farm, Del Norte Co., 26:3
Government in California, by Barrows, rev., 5:203-4
Government of California: prestatehood, 1:23-35; 10:11-26, 129-50; 14:8; 16:197-98; 17:58-59; 19:4 5; 25:267-78; State, 5:203-4; *see also* Constitution
Governor (ship), 27:293
Governor Dana (ship), 8:179, 181, 182, 202, 211; 9:55, 169; 10:170, 358, 372; 12:30; 14:224, 384, 385, 388, 406; 15:43
Governor's Mansion, Sacramento, 39:198, 205
Governor Winslow (ship), 14:295
Gowen, Albert N., 2:112, 121

Goycoechea, Felipe, 2:316, 322, 326; 10:338-45 *passim;* 38:172

Goytino, Jean-Pierre, 39:332, 336-37

Grabhorn Press, 1:386-87; 39:71

Grace, Thomas, 19:254

Grace Cathedral, San Francisco, 10:290; 23:246; 26:170

Grace Episcopal Church, Sacramento, 9:371, 394; 10:42, 64-65, 288; 26:170, 361; illus., 9: opp. 258

Grace Episcopal Church, San Francisco, 4:199; 10:290; 12: 99, 106; 14:74-79 *passim;* 23:235, 246; 26:170, 171-72; 32:122; 38:334

Grachett, Mrs. (Nevada Co., 1862), 10:385

"Grade-School Grizzly," by Bertha F. Herrick, 25:178-81

Grady, E., 15:182

Grady, Edward T., 32:6-9, 16, 17, 27, 28, 36, 37

Grady, Henry Francis, 31:287

Grady, Mrs. Henry Francis (Lucretia del Valle), 31:287; 32:185

Grady, James J., 33:68

Graff, E. C., 29:225, 226

Graggy, Jacob, 9:53, 70

Graggy Mill ,Yuba Co., 9:53, 70

Graham, Col. (S.F., 1850s), 19:229

Graham (Yuba Co., 1857), 9:149

Graham, Mrs. (Del Norte Co., 1862), 26:4

Graham, A. Clason, 21:306

Graham, A. J., 9:269

Graham, A. Spencer, 21:306

Graham, Adelaide, 29:187

Graham, Mrs. Alex E. (Florence Nickerson), 31:220

Graham, Campbell, 15:172

Graham, Isaac, 4:90; 5:133-34, 358; 10:5; 12:261; 13:229-30; 14:230, 234, 258, 318, 343; 15:115-29 *passim,* 134, 135, 137, 138, 227, 230, 233, 239, 241, 339; 16:143, 349, 354; 17:54; 18:160, 174, 295, 310; 20:224-25, 234, 264; 21:328; 27:162, 164, 260; 28:260; 29:26, 28, 132, 135; 32:264-65, 266; 33:64; 37:63; lawsuit, 18:35; 25:129; 104-6; port., 15: opp. 103; *see also* "Graham affair"

Graham, Mrs. Isaac, *see* Bennett, Catherine

Graham, James, 26:204

Graham, Joseph M., 18:365

Graham, Lawrence Pike, 17:264; 33:340, 346

Graham, Mary S., 14: opp. 209

Graham, Montrose Charles, 21:306

Graham, W. G., 9:180

Graham, W. H., 9:260; 22:260; 25:336, 343

"Graham affair," 8:118, 119; 15:104, 115-31, 134, 137-38, 227, 233-34; 18:139; 34:123; 37:64

Graham & Steward, 33:65-66

Graham House, San Francisco, 8:273

Graham's Pass, 39:298

Graham's Ranch, Yuba Co., 10:169, 192

Graham's Store, on Bear R., 9:357, 358

"Grains of Gold," address by Frank H. Probert, 7:200

Grajera, Antonio, 2:332-39 *passim*

Gramboss (Grambis, Grambs, Grambss, Grampas), Frederick, 9:391, 395, 397; 15:45, 46, 47

Granada, Marcelino, 11:178

Grancsay, S. V., 17: No. 4, Pt. 2, p. 10

Grand English Opera Co., 21:172

Grand Hotel, San Francisco, 19:225

Grand Opera House, Los Angeles, 20:138

Grand Opera House, San Francisco, 20:132, 137; 21:240, 241, 244, 250, 251; 25:235; 33:39-40; 37:226

Grand-Perret (organization), 5:161, 176-77, 237

Grande, Juan, 7:394

Grandsaigne, Capt. de (of *Argo,* 1845), 11:341, 345

"Gran Estrago del Mar," 26:12

Granfors, John, 10:184, 185, 186

Granger (S.F., 1851), 14:72

Granger, Lewis C., 13:314, 335

Granger, Ralph, 35:359

Grangers, 20:269, 271; 25:30; 27:171, 174, 199

Grangeville, 18:29

Granice, Celeste, 17:240

Granice, George (né Claughley), 21:77

Granice, H. H., 17:239

Granice, Henry (né Claughley), 21:77

Granice, Rowena, 21:75-79 *passim*

Granite Creek, 8:201, 210

Granite Pass, 32:199, 203

Granite State and California Mining and Trading Co., 22:121, 147

Graniteville, 10:348, 349; 28:234; 29:194

Grannis, George W., 7:110-11; 16:206; 19:232, 237

Grant (overland, 1849), 21:306

Grant, Col. (Nicolaus, 1850), 14:406
Grant (Downieville, 1858), 30:366
Grant, A. G., 13:31
Grant, A. S., 9:103
Grant, Adam, 21:93; 30:207-10
Grant, Mrs. Adam (Emma F.
    Gummer), 21:93; 30:208-9
Grant, Annie, 15:300
Grant, Blanche C., ed., *Kit Carson's
    Own Story*, rev., 5:408-9
Grant, Daniel G., Jr., 26:94
Grant, Gilbert A., 9:26; 10:62; 15:281;
    27: opp. 97
Grant, James A., 22:368; 30:159
Grant, Joseph Donohoe, 25:230, 232;
    "Reminiscences," 30:207-15, 339-51;
    obit., 21:93-94
Grant, Mrs. K. P., 17:32, 40
Grant, Lewis T. and Mary E. (Myrick),
    28:294
Grant, Reginald F., 39:317, 318
Grant, Ulysses Simpson, 3:203;
    4:287-88; 11:49, 50; 13:38-39, 42, 238;
    16:202, 309, 315; 18:369; 19:75, 229;
    20:158; 22:357; 30:209
Grant, Ulysses Simpson, Jr., 35:359,
    365; 38:355
Grant, William, 11:164
Grant's Creek, 12:8
Grant's Pass, 31:126
"Granville Orchard," 29:100, 363
Grapes and vineyards, 1:166, 169, 241;
    2:55, 65, 273; 5:211; 8:112; 12:193, 208,
    259, 282; 13:83, 206, 207, 210, 211, 214,
    315, 342, 349; 14:7, 10; 15:235; 16:118;
    17:41-42, 144, 237; 18:106, 120, 121,
    298; 19:203, 208; 21:328, 329; 23:242;
    25:27-36 *passim*, 170-75 *passim*;
    27:119, 285, 379; 29:173, 175; 30:309,
    312; 36:8; art. on, 36:241-50; phot., 8:
    opp. 241; *see also* Wine and wine
    making
Grape Shot (ship), 15:366
Grapevine Canyon, 10:214, 215, 218;
    12:6
Graphic, Oakdale, 21:383; 30:191
Graphite, 17:216
Grass, Fred, 10:362
Grassat (from Paris, 1849-50), 22:304;
    23:67
Grasshoppers, 15:171; 20:359; as food,
    1:154
Grass Valley, Nevada Co., 1:198; 3:201;
    6:222-36, 243-44, 332-41, 353; 10:249,
    297, 385; 11:60, 232, 243-44; 12:65, 71;

15:52, 182, 290; 16:83; 18:355-56,
    359; 19:28, 147-48, 354; 22:34; 26:170;
    30:259, 260, 266, 361; 32:130, 132;
    38:309; churches, 32:52-53, 124-30
    passim; newspaper, 9:382; theater,
    21:179
Grass Valley, Plumas Co., 29:300, 305
Grattan, C., 4:183
Grattan, Emma, 21:42
Grau, E. A., 27:285
Grau, Maurice, 20:134
Gravelly Ford, 32:197
Gravelly Valley, 32:364
Gravel Range Lodge, F. and A.M.,
    9:166
Graves, Augustus Bostwick, 29:291
Graves, Charles L., 21:142, 160
Graves, Franklin Ward and Elizabeth,
    19:139
Graves, Hiram Throop, 19:146; 29:291
Graves, Jackson Alpheus, 9:178; *My
    Seventy Years in California*, rev.,
    7:90
Graves, James, 22:236, 251
Graves, Mary Ann, 19:121, 139; *see also*
    Clarke, Mrs. J. T.
Graves, Robert, 35:134
Graves, Samuel, 29:291-92
Graves, Sarah, 19:121-22, 139
Graves, W. A., 26:110
Graves, William B., 26:227; 28:315, 321;
    29:39
Graves family, 19:121, 139
Gray (dep. surv., San Bernardino Mt.,
    1852), 34:11
Gray (S.F., 1855), 16:342
Gray, Mr. and Mrs. (née Spencer,
    1857), 9:165
Gray (San Diego, 1889), 31:157
Gray, Andrew Belcher, 9:4, 5, 6, 10-12;
    15:164; 31:33-38 *passim*, 42, 45, 381;
    maps by, 9: opp. 6, 11
Gray, Andrew F. V., 3:123; 17:344;
    21:355; 22:44, 64; 26:49, 62
Gray, Arthur Amos, 9:183, 336; 27:139;
    "Camels in California," 9:299-317;
    "The Dollart Case," 9:318-31
Gray, Asa, 24:324; 32:251, 255
Gray, George D., 38:65
Gray, Frederic T., 10:295; 25:341;
    29:251
Gray, Giles H., 26:232
Gray, Henry Martin, 4:187, 192-96
    passim; 16:283

Gray, Mrs. Horace (Katharine Meeker), 23:287
Gray, James (or John), 16:83, 285, 339
Gray, Jeremiah, 7:281
Gray, John (S.F., 1855), 9:42
Gray, John B., 15:19
Gray, Dr. John B., 10:363; 14:396
Gray, Michael, 8:202, 206, 211, 337, 338, 341, 343; 9:54, 73, 137, 139, 158, 262, 263, 345, 378; 10:47, 359
Gray, Minnie, 31:381
Gray, Nathaniel, 27:32; 30:256
Gray, Nicolas, 19:129, 141
Gray, Percy, 37:31
Gray, Robert, 2:290, 306; 10:317, 321; 11:29; 13:240
Gray, Samuel Cotton, 30:262, 363; 33:375
Gray, Thomas, 9:246, 249, 269, 272, 274; 16:80, 84
Gray, W. C., 7:14
Gray, William H., 4:279
"Gray Eagle," *see* Baker, Edward D.
Gray Eagle Bar, 19:145
"Gray Eagle of Liberty," see Nye, James W.
Gray's Harbor, 10:319, 321, 323, 333
Grays Harbor (ship), 31:295
Grayson, Andrew Jackson, 21:327; 27:233
Gray's Opera House, San Francisco, 21:170
Graysonville, 28:330
Great Britain: alleged attempts to acquire Calif., 2:258; 11:33, 196-98, 201-2; 12:39, 50; 17:21; 18:136, 139-40, 145-46, 147, 325; 19:46, 50; emigration to Calif. from, 20:65-67, 74-75; govt. express through Mex., 17:125-26, 129-30; interest in Hawaiian Is., 17:131-34 *passim;* in Pacific N.W., 17:135, 306; 18:319, 322, 329; relations with Mex., 17:21-22, 27; *see also* "British Comment"; "British Vice Consul"; Hudson's Bay Co.
"Great Express Extra of the California Star, The," by Douglas S. Watson, 11:129-37
Greathouse, George, 13:258
Greathouse, Ridgley, 20:159; 33:234; 40:300
Great Republic (clipper), 26:357-58; 29:106
Great Republic (str.), 37:216
Great Salt Lake, 4:282; 6:117, 119;

14:271, 281; 32:196, 199; first circumnavigation of, 4:140; 5:387; Frémont and Carson at, 1:119
"Great Scandal of 1851, The," address by John A. Hussey, 17:285
Great Sierra Consolidated Silver Mining Co., 4:40
Great Train Robberies of the West, by Block, rev., 38:169-71
Great Western Insurance Co., 26:256
Great Western Power Co., 29:204
Greaves, Mrs. Thomas T. (Jessie A. Hooper), 31:299, 301, 302
Gredelue (S.F., 1854), 15:179
"Greek George," 9:315; 13:344; 17:109
Greeley (Fresno R., 1850), 28:325
Greeley, Horace, 9:91; 10:172, 173, 194-95; 17:312; 21:276; 27:103; 30:128; 31:236; 38:27
Greeley, R. F., 37:199
Greely, Fred Henry, 8:211; 9:77; address, "Pioneers and Pioneer Native Sons of Marysville," 8:187
Greely, Justus, 8:211; 9:77; 27:195, 197
Greely, Fitton & Co., 14:337
Green (w. Micheltorena, 1845), 18:159
Green (on *London*, 1850), 7:397
Green (supervisor, S.F., 1855), 16:84
Green (waterman, S.F., 1855), 15:367
Green, Capt. (Colorado R., 1869), 22:172, 173
Green, Adam Treadwell and Harriett, 40:365
Green, Alfred Augustus, 9:26; 27:109; 28:292
Green, Mrs. Alfred Augustus (Dolores Leyorcita), 28:292
Green, C. R., 25:337
Green, Carry, 9:173
Green, Charles, 21:242
Green, Mrs. Charles Edward (Mary E. Eldridge), obit., 15:97
Green, Duff, letters to, 16:71-75
Green, Mrs. Duff (Lucretia Maria Edwards), 16:73
Green, Mrs. Duff, Jr. (Rebecca Pickens), 15:383-84
Green, E., 26:247
Green, Edward L., 26:214-15
Green, Ellen, 31:4
Green, Ephraim, 14:276, 278
Green, Floride, address, "Mrs. Lillie Hitchcock Coit," 12:366-67; obit. of Annie (King) Dutton, 12:372; obit., 15:383-84

Green, Franklin Theodore and M. Georgia (Rooker), 28:379
Green, Frederick P., 20:32, 46
Green, George, 35:185
Green, George W., 23:209
Green, H. A., 24:58
Green, Harvey, 14:177
Green, Henry (S.F., 1850), 8:266, 267
Green, Henry (Tenn., 1853), 18:40, 41
Green, James, 17:172-73
Green, John (on *Brookline*, 1829), 23:206, 209
Green, John (stage driver, 1850s), 9:163; 13:258
Green, John (Mormon, 1852), 14:181
Green, Jonathan, 26:164
Green, Joseph de Puissay, 30:100
Green, Julia, 28:292
Green, Michael, 33:257
Green, Talbot H. (Paul Geddes), 5:308; 16:5; 17:285; 23:289; 25:132; 27:106, 107; 28:59, 66, 113, 114, 116; 35:105; art. on, 18:32-63
Green, Mrs. Talbot H. (Sarah Armstrong), 18:36-37, 43-49 *passim*, 55, 59, 60, 61; 19:137; *see also* Montgomery, Mrs. Allen
Green, Talbot H., Jr., *see* Wallis, Talbot H.
Green, Theodore and Maria (Le Vere), 28:379
Green, Gen. Thomas (Rose's Bar, 1849), 23:351, 370
Green, Thomas (N.Y., 1850), 36:242-43
Green, Thomas D., 15:266; 16:282
Green, Thomas Jefferson, 24:105
Green, William (Tepic, 1840), 15:240
Green, William (Mormon I., 1848), 26:122
Green, Will Semple, 6:140, 156, 157
Green & Hodden, 5:38
Greenbank, John, 6:348, 357-59
Greenbaum, Joseph, 37:31-32
Greenbaum, Will J., 25:234, 242, 247, 251
Greenberg, Morris and Stuart N., 22:288
Green Bushes (play), 16:184
Greene, Miss (1898), 30:294; 31:50
Greene, A. Crawford, 30:92
Greene, Clay M., 20:289; 34:362, 363, 367; address, "Reminiscences of Early San Francisco," 4:211-12
Greene, Edward Lee, 32:254; 37:51-61
Greene, George W. (S.F., 1855), 17:177

Greene, George W. (civil eng., 1858), 7:19
Greene, Hugh W., 18:52, 62
Greene, James C., 30:92
Greene, Lewis F., 33:12, 161, 164; 35:306
Greene, Mrs. M. L., 25:194
Greene, William G., 9:109; 15:178, 281, 364
Greenhithe Point, 11:374, 375, 382
Greenhorn Cutoff, *see* Lassen Cutoff
Greenhorn Mountain, 28:277
"Greenhorn War," 26:306
Greenhow, Robert, 1:9; 15:172
Greenhow, Mrs. Robert (Rose O'Neill), 11:14; 15:172
"Greenland" (Furnace Creek Ranch), 18:214
Green Oaks Ranch, San Mateo Co., 20:265-67, 271, 273, 288
Greenough, Mrs. (S.F., 1850s), 19:229, 232, 236
Greenough, Thomas H., 29:291
Green River, 1:123, 2:38; 4:140; 5:140; 6:117-18
Green Springs, illus., 21: opp. 289
Green Valley (Rescue), El Dorado Co., 27:281
Green Valley, San Diego Co., 34:201, 202; 36:119, 125-32 *passim*
Green Valley, Sonoma Co., 19:127, 128, 129
Greenville, 8:213, 352; 9:50, 69; *see also* Oregon Hill
Greenville House, 10:256
Greenwood (from Conn., 1850), 30:26
Greenwood (Lassen Co., 1855), 18:303, 313
Greenwood, Britain, 2:63; 5:268, 399; 19:135
Greenwood, Caleb, 3:89; 5:378, 399; 19:116, 131, 135-36; 24:73; 28:286; 32:197
Greenwood, E., 13:31
Greenwood, John, 5:399; 19:135, 138
Greenwood, Robert, comp., *The California Outlaw: Tiburcio Vasquez*, rev., 40:260-63
Greenwood, Sam, 5:399; 19:135
Greenwood Diggings, 30:26
Greenwood Valley, 6:247
Greeves (Hangtown, 1854), 11:58
Gregara, Antonio, *see* Grajera, Antonio
Gregg, A. J., 28:49
Gregg, Josiah, 6:197; 10:202, 203; 12:78;

18:245, 248, 249; 19:376; 20:280; 25:118

Gregg, Robert H., 4:169

Gregg, Stephen, 18:201

Gregoire, Louis, 32:112-13; 39:229

Gregory, Andrew Jr., 10:62

Gregory, Durell S., 10:62

Gregory, Edith, comp., "History of Las Posadas Forest," from memoirs of John M. Morris, 35:1-9, 155-60

Gregory, F. H., 31:213

Gregory, Henry, 17:174

Gregory, Joseph W., 13:88, 258-59

Gregory, T., 13:32

Gregory, Warren, 4:49

Gregory, William, 9:286

Gregory, Cabo, 10:329

"Gregory's Express," address by Ernest A. Wiltsee, 13:88

Gregson, Adelia J., 19:130, 141

Gregson, Ann E., 19:119, 127, 143

Gregson, Eliza Jane, 19:113, 129, 141

Gregson, James, 1:98; 19:113, 115-34 *passim*; 26:122; phot., 19: opp. 113

Gregson, Mrs. James (Eliza Marshall), 7:106; 14:143-44; 26:122; 28:296; "Memory," 19:114-30; phot., 19: opp. 113

Gregson, John N., 19:129, 141

Gregson, Mary Ellen, 19:126, 140

Gregson, William F., 19:128

Gregson family, 19:130, 141

"Gregson Memoirs, The," 19:113-43

Greis, John, 8:346; 9:140, 145, 162; lawsuit, 9:145

Grenell, Levi O., 27:230-31, 236

Grenier (from France, 1850), 22:301

Grennan, Tom, 9:267, 371; 10:55

Grenville, Point, 9:227

"Grésely," *see* Pepiquignot

Grétry (ship), 6:38; 22:298, 304-5

Grey, Capt. (Colorado R., 1856), 22:169

Grey, Charles, 9:262

Grey, Cyrus, 14:72

Grey, Mike, *see* Gray, Michael

Grey Eagle (ship), 23:261, 279

Grey Eagle City, 37:312

Greyhound (ship), 20:31, 46

Gridiron, The, 22:11, 22

Gridley, Reul Colt, 40:303

Grieman, Thomas, 8:349

Grier, Thomas P., 8:343, 345; 9:157

Griff, Juan, *see* Griffin, John Strother

Griffin (Marysville, 1850), 14:394

Griffin, Alice, 25:285

Griffin, Allen, 26:94; obit. of Sidney Fish, 29:85-86

Griffin, Bulkley Southworth, 34:92-93

Griffin, Charles Francis, address, "Sixteenth (Center) Street, San Francisco," 7:410; obit., 30:87-88

Griffin, Christine, 34:37

Griffin, Eliza, 33:339; 34:37, 38

Griffin, Francis Marion and Margaret (Malloy), 30:87

Griffin, Frank W., 25:230, 232

Griffin, Mrs. Frank W., 25:233

Griffin, George Butler, 7:268; 30:335

Griffin, John Smith, 18:309

Griffin, John Strother, 1:145, 146, 238, 240, 241, 245, 258; 4:167, 168, 192; 12:31; 17:343; 18:168, 178; 20:192; 25:303, 305, 307; 26:23, 36-41 *passim*, 45; 32:328; 33:373; art. on, 33:97-124, 249-70, 337-47; 34:21-39; Diary, ed. George W. Ames, Jr., 21:193-224, 333:57; 22:41-66; rev., 24:95-96; phot., 22: opp. 41

Griffin, Mrs. John Strother (Louisa Hayes), 21:195; 34:38

Griffin, Mary, 34:37

Griffin, Mrs. Miles, 25:87

Griffin, Samuel P., 3:118

Griffin (ship), 28:378

Griffing, Frederick, 27:172

Griffing *v*. Gibb & Frazer, 34:237

Griffins, 19:220, 221

Griffin Yeatman (ship), 22:120, 122

Griffiss, Wilmot, 35:362; 36:74-75

Griffith (fluist, 1851), 15:45

Griffith (San Joaquin Co., 1855), 15:270

Griffith, Calvin Chesterfield, 23:294; 24:58, 71; 17:240

Griffiith, Humphrey, 9:65, 72, 381, 394; 10:44, 45, 62, 87, 254, 255, 266; 15:76

Griffith, James A., 23:294

Griffiith, M. and Miss, 11:127

Griffiith, Margaret, 32:190-91

Griffith Gaunt (play), 21:160

Griffon (ship), 14:259, 343

Griggs (Sacramento, 1852), 36:140, 141, 144, 146

Griggs, E. E., 23:287; 30:258, 366

Griggs, Edward H., 37:41

Grigsby, Achilles Fine, 16:131, 141, 142; children of, 16:131, 132

Grigsby, E. D., 16:142

Grigsby, Granville, 24:55-56

Grigsby, John, 1:75; 6:137, 139-40, 144;
 13:54; 15:65; 16:131; 17:161, 220-22,
 224, 230, 240; 19:131, 142; 24:58;
 25:125; 29:263, 264, 265, 271, 335, 336,
 339; 30:53; 31:217; ranch of, 16:131
Grigsby, John Sylvester, 16:142
Grigsby, John Worth, 16:131, 142
Grigsby, Lura Jane, *see* Trubody, Mrs.
 William Alexander
Grigsby, Robert F., 16:132
Grigsby, Samuel H., 16:132, 133
Grigsby, Terrell, 16:131-32
Grigsby-Ide party, 24:71; *see also*
 Grigsby, John; Ide, William B.
Grijalva, Hernando de, 1:39; 6:298;
 20:222, 233-34
Grim, Henry G., 15:177
Grimes, Andrew Jackson, 28:239
Grimes, Eliab, 1:235; 6:270; 8:299;
 12:138, 345; 14:324, 326, 344, 345;
 16:138; 17:231; 25:222, 223; 26:249;
 27:106, 112
Grimes, Hiram, 14:326, 345; 25:222;
 26:216
Grimes, Hiram T., 28:382
Grimm, Henry, 34:363
Grimsley, Thornton, 4:280
Grimwood, A. D., 11:127
Gringo, Harry, *see* Wise, Henry A.
Grinnell, Henry, 21:98, 108
Grinnell, Joseph, 3:248, 253;
 *Bibliography of California
 Ornithology*, rev., 3:298-99; coauth.
 Animal Life in the Yosemite, rev.,
 3:299-300
Grippin, Reuben, 13:3
Grismer, Joseph R. and Phoebe
 (Davies), 35:142
Grist- and flour mills, 1:175-76; 2:55,
 59-60, 64, 65; 3:32; 5:273; 8:114;
 11:42; 12:194; 293; 13:207, 330;
 14:22, 128, 269, 273, 278-82 *passim;*
 15:271; 16:4, 127, 132, 138, 142-43,
 232; 17:183, 252, 295; 18:22, 65-70
 passim, 259; 19:124, 133, 139, 143;
 25:96, 175; 27:193-202; 28:266;
 33:365-66; 34:148; 35:123, 348;
 37:232
Griswold, Georgiana, 4:208
Griswold, H. H., 26:126-27
Griswold, Harriet (Booth), 33:373
Griswold, Theodore, 16:138
Grith, Lt. (Civil War), 31:237, 240
Grivas, Theodore, "Alcalde Rule . . .
Local Government in Spanish and
 Mexican California," 40:11-32
Grivel, Elior, Comte de, 5:344-45,
 349, 352; 6:37, 39, 56
Grivel, Ernest, Comte de, 5:344, 345,
 349, 352; 6:37, 39, 56
Grizzly Bear, 23:362, 373
Grizzly bears, 2:26-27, 33-34, 43,
 58; 4:13, 119, 122-23, 152; 5:138;
 6:247; 12:292, 304-5; 13:22-23;
 14:139; 15:178; 17:47, 49, 113-14,
 117; 18:81, 296; 20:41, 354; 22:78-79,
 209, 210, 212, 245, 324, 325; 23:294;
 24:329; 25:178-81; 28:211, 228;
 29:47, 52, 173, 299; 30:25; 32:220,
 265-66; 33:114; 35:207, 220; 36:3,
 11; 40:257; *see also* Bears
Grizzly Damming Co., 35:208
Gronberg, Andrew, 33:12
Groningen, John, *see* Gönninger, Hans
Groom, Robert W., 9:250, 258, 269;
 11:9
Gropius, panorama by, 10:196
Grosch (or Grosh), Edgar (or
 Ethan) Allen, 6:341; 12:328;
 23:267, 280
Grosch (or Grosh), Hosea Ballou,
 6:341; 12:328; 23:267, 280
Groscup (miner, 1850), 26:297
Groslui, C., 22:217, 220; 23:21, 137,
 138, 139; son of, 22:195, 196
Gross, A., 39:160
Gross, E. W., 19:233
Gross, Elizabeth, 28:380
Gross, Mrs. George E. (Ethel Gage),
 23:95
Grosse, Marion A., 32:191
Grossman, John, 33:363
Grotjan, Mrs. Louisa, 24:263
Grout, Newton, 26:136, 152, 158
Grove, Mrs. (Sonora, 1853), 32:127
Grove, Lt. (on *Sitka,* 1854), 15:180
Grove, Edward, 36:63
Grove, Samuel C. and Fannie A.
 (Allen), 28:294
Grovenor, Jack, 9:262
Grover, E. Whitney, 5:335
Grover, L. Chace, 25:191
Grover, Stephen F., 5:332-35
Grover & Baker, 24:263
Groves, Dr. (d. Chihuahua, 1849),
 18:231
Groves, I. N., 8:343, 359; 9:65, 131,
 132, 139, 160, 162, 166, 266, 360,

361; 10:46, 54, 167; Lawsuit, 10:167, 183

Groves, Joseph, 8:342, 343, 348; 9:58, 59, 130, 147, 262

Grow, G. B., 35:358

Groza, Manuel, 9:348, 354

Grub, Thomas R., 6:363

Gruber, Ann, 13:32

Grub Gulch, 3:94

Grubler, Solomon Henri, 32:162

Grunsky, Carl Ewald, 11:265; address, "Reminiscences of Sacramento," 11:88

Grunsky, Charles and Clotilde (Camerer), 29:284

Grunsky, Clotilde, *see* Taylor, Clotilde (Grunsky)

Guachama (or Guachinga), 12:115, 121, 122

Guadalajara, Mex., 16:82; 17:126, 128; 23:270

Guadaloupe (ship), 15:173

Guadalupe Hidalgo, *see* Treaty of . . .

Guadalupe quicksilver mine, 11:361, 362; 14:159

Guadalupe River, Lower Calif., 5:325; 31:354

Guadalupe River and slough, 14:4-5, 7, 9, 12, 22; 19:158; 23:363; 27:301; 28:63; 34:229

Gualala River, 23:24

Guanajuato, Mexico, 17:128

Guano, 26:74, 75

Guapos ("braves"), 16:249; 29:311; *see also* Indians: Satayomi

Guapot, Alexis, 6:55

Guatemala, 6:309-12 *passim*; 27:137, 138; prop. union w., 15:140

Guaymas, 11:369-70, 381; 13:140, 146; 18:5, 6, 17; 21:328; 22:162; 23:333; 27:211; 34:136, 150, 151, 152; letters from, 13:125-58, 131-32, 140-42; 18:7; harbor (1539), 3:321-22; (1850-51), 11:368-69, 381

Gudde, Erwin Gustav, 19:288; 30:91; 36:307; "Mutiny on the Ewing," 30:39-47; "The Source of the Sutter Myth," 9:398-99; ed. and trans. "Edward Vischer's First Visit to California," 19:193-216; "The Memoirs of Theodor Cordua," 12:279-311; addresses: "California Place Names," 28:184-85; "Centennial of the Pacific Coast Survey," 29:185-86; "Edward

Vischer," 16:286; *California Place Names*, rev., 39:364-66; *German Pioneers in Early California*, rev. 7:93-94; ed. *Sutter, Neu-Helvetien*, rev., 14:185-86

Guelin (Humboldt Co., 1850), 5:148

Guerin, Pat, 9:164, 262, 362

Guerra, Bautista, 2:36

Guerra, Ana María de la, *see* Robinson, Mrs. Alfred

Guerra, Antonio María de la, 18:169-70, 255; 29:232, 233, 243, 244-45

Guerra, Francisco de la, 18:71, 169, 254

Guerra, Mrs. Francisco de la (María Asunción Sepúlveda), 18:68

Guerra, Joaquín de la, 18:170, 179, 255

Guerra, José Antonio de la, 15:341, 354, 355; 17:161; 18:170-71, 254; 30:98

Guerra, Juan de la, 15:213-14, 215

Guerra, María Angustias de la, *see* Ord, Mrs. James L.

Guerra, María Teresa de la, 18:170, 179

Guerra, Miguel de la, 18:255

Guerra, Pablo de la, 1:9; 9:46; 10:254, 271, 286, 372; 11:8-9; 13:112, 327, 339; 14:327, 345, 375; 17:164, 233-34; 18:65-66, 69-70, 166, 169, 254-55, 261, 271; 19:7; 20:112; 21:322; 23:344; 24:72; 28:196; 32:159; fac. sig., 10: opp. 159; port., 18: opp. 157

Guerra, Santiago de la, 18:169

Guerra, de la, family, 18:168-71, 254-55

Guerra y Noriega, José de la, 1:168; 4:396; 6:259; 8:157, 164; 10:286; 12:232; 14:233, 247, 248, 249; 15:141; 16:356, 365, 367, 372; 17:55; 18:68, 69, 71, 161, 168-70; 22:288; 23:199, 218, 252; 27:333; 36:289; lawsuit, 18:255

Guerra y Noriega, Mrs. José de la (Antonia Carrillo), 18:71

Guerrero, Juan, 13:108

Guerrero, Pedro, 15:356

Guerrero y Palomares, Francisco, 1:190-91; 4:380-90 *passim*; 5:308, 309-10; 11:72; 12:248, 272; 13:104-5; 17:67, 144, 163; 28:243, 254, 267; 35:314; letter, 10:102

Guest, John, 3:123; 26:47, 49

Guffroy, Louis J., 14:142

Gugenhayen, Martin, 29:121
Guggenhime, Richard E., 25:191
Guiberson, Dr. (Ventura, 1883),
   16:298, 303
Guiberson, Gordon Greene, 30:92;
   31:283-84
Guiberson, Mary Greene, collection of
   lithographs, 31:283-84
Guiberson, S. A., Jr., 30:92
Guiberson, Mrs. S. A., Jr. (Ethel
   Lavinia Heanan), 30:92
Guidebooks: French, 39:2; overland,
   3:46, 52, 63, 73, 81-82; 4:82; 8:82;
   10:82, 83; 22:33, 136, 149; 32:193-207;
   Pike's Peak gold rush, 27:182; to
   the Sierra Nevada, 4:37-38; Yosemite,
   4:16
Guilbeau (nr. French Camp, 1833),
   23:125
Guild, A. H., 9:99
Guild, H. M., 11:177-78, 180
Guilez, José, 37:116, 118, 241-42,
   248, 251-52, 254
Guilfoil, Mrs. James (Beatrice Oreña),
   22:288
Guilfoyle, Merlin J., 31:280
"Guillaume Patrice Dillon," by A. P.
   Nasatir, 35:309-24
Guillen, Clemente, 3:340; 8:376
Guillocheuse-Parret (S.F., 1849),
   5:21
Guillon, Gabriel, 39:148
Guilmoto, J. Louis, 14:142
Guinn, James Miller, 38:133-34
Guiou (Guion?; Auburn, 1850s),
   9:393
Guipuzcoana (ship), *see Joven
   Guipuzcoana*
Guirado, F. L., 13:330
Guirado, Rafael, 4:159; 13:220, 222,
   327
Guitar, O., 24:242-43
Guitaries, *see* Gutiérrez (1850)
Guizelman, John, 9:156, 159
Guller, J., 9:156
Gulliver, Charles, 17:256
Gulnac, Juan P., 18:82
Gulnac, William, 2:198; 14:17, 19;
   18:173; 29:132
Gulnac, Mrs. William (María Isabel
   de Caseña), 29:132
Gummer, Emma F., 30:208-9
Gummer, Joseph Channing and Sarah
   (Davis), 30:208-9
Gump, Abraham Livingston, 37:22

Gump, Richard, obit. of Charles
   S. James, 38:360
Gump's (S. & G.), 37:22
Gunn (San Jose, 1853), 13:29
Gunn, G. W., 16:183
Gunn, Lewis Carstairs, 9:104, 116;
   30:260; 32:129-30; 35:201; coauth.
   Records of a California Family,
   rev., 8:87
Gunn, Mrs. Lewis Carstairs (Elizabeth
   LeBreton), 32:126-27; 35:77; coauth.
   Records of a California Family,
   rev., 8:87
Gunn, William, 29:121
Gunnison, Parker and Cowles,
   25:342
Gunnison, (John W.) expedition, book
   on, rev., 38:80-83
Guns: 29:270; carbines, 13:51; 26:35,
   37, 57; muskets, 13:51; 17:278;
   25:290; pistols, 33:117, 118-19,
   Frémont's rfle, 29:274; at San Juan
   Bautista, 17:282; *see also* Cannons;
   Howitzers
Gunsight Lead, 18:197-204 *passim*,
   212, 215; 26:58
Gunst, Abraham, 37:277
Gunst, Morgan Arthur, obit.,
   37:277-78
Gunst, Moses A. and Ophelia (Cohn),
   37:277
Gunter, Melado, *et al. v.* Geary and
   Fallon, 34:241-42
Gunther, Fred, 32:28
Gunton, Mrs. Howard M., 29:285
Gushee, F. A., 13:31
Gushee, Horace, 20:192, 265, 273;
   26:190
Gushee & Curtis, 20:263
Gustave, Le (ship), 31:141-42, 147
Guthrie, Alfred B., quoted, 32:263
Guthrie, C. L., 22:192
Gutiérrez (Eliza City, 1850), 7:403,
   404; 8:17, 25, 168-81 *passim*, 264
Gutiérrez, "Young" (Eliza City, 1850),
   7:404; 8:17, 22, 167, 179, 264, 265
Gutiérrez, Diego, map by, 1:49;
   3:265; 7:71
Gutierrez, F., 30:137
Gutiérrez, José de Jesús María,
   16:119, 235, 237; 23:20-21, 39
Gutiérrez, Juan, 3:21, 24
Gutiérrez, Manuel, 13:211
Gutiérrez, Nicolás, 12:131, 137-46,
   147; 13:136-37; 14:230-31, 234-45,

239, 259; 15:115, 338-63; 16:248, 251, 348-49, 356; 19:322; 23:324, 327, 333, 384

Gutiérrez, Pablo, 11:121, 19:136; 26:132

Gutiérrez, Romualdo, 23:373

Gutiérrez, Sancho, 7:63

Gutiérrez, Sebastián, 7:267

Gutiérrez de la Concha, Juan, 40:118

Guy (N.Y. Vol., 1847), 33:257

Guy, Abel, 12:72; 15:280; 19:29-30, 41, 42

Guy Mannering (play), 16:283

Guys, Edouard, 5:25, 41, 344; 12:159; 13:280, 378; 35:311, 312

Guzmán, Diego de, 1:45; 3:319, 364, 368; 6:300, 307

Guzmán, José María, *Breve Noticia*, 10:83; trans. Mary Y. Roberson, 5:209-17; fac. table, 5:217; fac. title p., 5: opp. 209

Guzmán, Nuño de, 1:37, 38, 39, 44, 45, 46; 3:364; 6:297-300 *passim*, 307, 320, 323

Gwin, Ella, 19:233

Gwin, James, 19:23, 24

Gwin, William McKendree, 2:211, 214; 3:155; 4:202, 238-39; 8:364; 9:25, 177, 197, 263, 272, 285; 10:53, 61, 66, 75, 147, 151, 155-59 *passim*, 164, 167, 192, 193, 222, 225, 229, 238, 255, 277, 291; 11:3, 4, 6, 11-21 *passim*, 28; 12:20; 13:38-41; 15:146, 173, 199-200, 203, 270, 275, 280; 16:184, 198, 305; 17:82, 181, 261, 312, 316, 317; 18:347; 19:230, 232; 20:96, 97, 100-106 *passim*, 110-11, 114, 158; 21:31, 276, 324; 22:361; 27:261-62, 266; 28:64, 68, 373; 29:165; 30:161; 31:214, 217; 32:145-59 *passim*, 295, 313-25 *passim*; 35:318; 38:208-17 *passim*; "Memoirs," ed. W. H. Ellison, 19:1-26, 157-84, 256-77, 344-67; fac. sig., 10: opp. 159; port., 19: opp. 1

Gwin, Mrs. William McKendree, (Mary Bell), 11:13, 17; 19:230, 232, 238

Gwin, William McKendree, Jr., 40:291, 306

Gwin mine, 4:197, 202; 21:190; 25:383

Gwinn, Harrison, 10:62; 11:9

Gyger, Théodore, 39:342, 343

H

Haan, Matthew J., 11:136

Haas, Edward Francis, obit., 18:189-90

Haas, Mrs. Edward Francis (Carolyn Mabel Thompson), obit., 36:374-75

Haas, John L. and Mary (Reid), 28:293

Haas, Louise (Falkenau), 30:382

Haas, Robert Bartlett, 34:381; "William Herman Rulofson, Pioneer Daguerreotypist," 34:289-300; 35:47-58

Haas & Rosenfield, 29:105

Haas, Baruch Co., 35:350

Haase, A. E., rev. of Newhall, *The Newhall Ranch*, 37:369-71

Hacher, Capt. (Paris, 1849), 22:292

Hacket (or Haggert; S.F., 1855), 17:82-83

Hackett, George H., lawsuit, 9:366, 367

Hackett, James Henry, 21:51; 29:102

Hackett (John K.) and (Charles D.) Judah, 4:219; 28:360

Hackfeld and Co., 40:44, 45

Haddin (d. S.F., 1855), 15:376

Haden, John M., 34:36

Hadenfeldt, Charles, 27:8

Hadji Ali, *see* Ali, Hadji

Hadley, Henry, 25:233-34, 238-45 *passim*

Haenke, Tadeo, 3:215-23 *passim*, 233; 18:366; 24:337

Haenszel, Allen L., 36:284

Haenszel, Arda M., 36:284; "The Visual Knowledge of California to 1700," 36:213-40

Haet, Thomas, 15:371

Hafen, LeRoy R., "Butterfield's Overland Mail," 2:211-22; coed. *Frémont's Fourth Expedition . . .*, rev., 40:165-68; bk. rev. by, 37:369

California Historical Society Quarterly

Haga, Juan de, 21:51, 68; 29:119
Hagadorn, Wesley, 31:19
Hagan (on *New World*, 1855), 15:274
Hagemeister, L. A., 12:191, 193, 234-35
Hagenmeyer, George, 30:163
Hager, Alice, 23:287; 24:84
Hager, Anna Marie and Everett
    Gordon, comp. *The Historical
    Society of Southern California
    Topical Index*, rev., 40:259-60
Hager, Edith, 24:84
Hager, Ethel, 23:95, 287
Hager, John Sharpstein, 9:26; 11:127;
    15:364, 369; 16:282, 340, 343;
    17:169-70, 173, 177, 178, 180; 19:156;
    23:95, 287-88; 27:272-73, 339; 31:47;
    37:162; 40:207, 209, 210
Hager, Mrs. John Sharpstein
    (Elizabeth Lucas Hicks), 23:95
Haggerty & Co., lawsuit, 10:55
Haggerty Gulch Creek, 19:317
Haggin, James Ben Ali, 17:175, 191;
    19:28, 232, 233, 238; 25:224-25;
    27:5; *see also* Haggin & Tevis;
    Lux *v.* Haggin
Haggin & Tevis, 5:86; 17:191; 25:224
Hagner, Francis Randall, obit., 20:94
Hague, James Duncan, 4:19; 29:194
Hahn, Herman F., 32:191
Hahn, William, painting by, 37:
    opp. 240
Hahnemann, Samuel C. F., 32:243
Hahnemann Hospital College, San
    Francisco, 30:67
Haight, Andrew J., 28:382
Haight, Fletcher Mathews, 22:28;
    31:194
Haight, Henry Huntly, 1:10; 9:26;
    15:175-76, 202, 272; 20:66-67; 25:101;
    26:193, 378; 27:156; 31:194, 199;
    letter, 31:195-99
Haight, Mrs. Henry Huntly (Anna
    Bissell), 13:81; 19:229
Haight, Raymond LeRoy, 22:94;
    26:378
Haight, Samuel W., 18:45, 56; 34:26
Haine, Arthur, 38:148
Haine, Jean Joseph François, "A
    Belgian in the Gold Rush," trans.
    Goris, 37:311-46; 38:141-55
Haines, A., 36:63
Haines, Alice J., 23:286; 24:84
Haines, Francis, 25:189; "Tom Hill—
    Delaware Scout," 25:139-48
Haines, J. W., 9:36; 31:6

Haines, James W., 36:99, 268
Haines, Perry, 31:51, 54, 63, 65
Haines, Robert Dudley, 25:381
Haines, William, 4:26
Hairon, Capt. (of *Le Courrier de
    Cherbourg*), 31:311
Hait, Jacob, 21:350-51; 33:105
Haiwacott, Elizabeth Frances, 28:294
Hakluyt, Richard, *Divers Voyages*,
    3:370; 8:38; *Principall Navigations*,
    1:43; 3:309, 313, 314, 318, 324, 357,
    384; 6:304; *see also* "Famous
    Voyage"
Haldeman, P. M., 9:269, 283
Hale, Edward Everett, 1:53; 6:167
Hale, Frank, 6:231-33, 237
Hale, Henry M., 16:346
Hale, Horatio Emmons, 28:105;
    37:14-15
Hale, J. G. (or J. D.), 32:124
Hale, James E., 2:205; 9:369, 393;
    10:383; 18:361
Hale, Marshall, 16:96
Hale, Prentis Cobb, obit., 16:95-96
Hale, Reuben Brooks, 16:96
Hale, Richard Lunt, *The Log of a
    Forty-Niner*, ed. Russ, rev.,
    3:92-93
Hale, Stanley, 36:74
Hale, Titus, 25:381
Hale, William (from Haverhill, 1849),
    6:214
Hale, William (Klamath Co., 1855),
    26:204
Hale, William (Mendocino Co.,
    1862), 33:364
Hale & Emory, 22:35
Hale & Norcross mine, 11:64
Hale Creek, *see* Ten Mile River
Haley, John J., 10:67
Haley, Robert (L.A., 1850), 13:333
Haley, Robert (S.F., 1858), 6:17, 18;
    9:29
Haley & Thompson, 15:182
Half Dome, Yosemite, 1:279-81
Halfhill, A. P., 31:158
Half Moon Hotel, San Jose, 14:19
Halfway House, Los Angeles Co.,
    32:328
Halfway House, San Mateo Co.,
    5:376-77
Half Way House, Yuba Co., 15:
    opp. 40
Halgerson, Henry, 31:331, 333
Haliday, Thomas J., 11:7, 9

Hall (from Oahu, 1840), 14:321
Hall, Lt. (S.F., 1848), 16:343
Hall (Calaveras Co., 1850), 22:71, 72, 73
Hall (or Hale), Miss (Yuba Co., 1856), 9:63
Hall (Dobbins Ranch, 1857), 9:158-59, 162, 163, 259
Hall (Yuba Co., 1857, '58, '59), 9:140, 142, 143; 10:169, 171; lawsuit, 10:252
Hall, Capt. (Colorado R., 1870), 22:173
Hall, A. H., 7:11
Hall, Ansel Franklin, 4:54; ed. "Early Days in Yosemite," 1:271-85; address, "Yosemite Pioneers," 4:210
Hall, B., 27:362
Hall, Basil and Lizzie (Winner), 37:235
Hall, C. John, 13:296
Hall, Carroll Douglas, 24:188-89, 336; addresses, "Bonanza Inn," 34:87; "Some Footnotes to Sutter's Fort," 30:375-76; coauth. *Bonanza Inn*, rev., 18:369-71
Hall, Edward C., 29:234
Hall, Edward F., Jr., 29:253-54
Hall, Edwin, 28:300, 302, 309
Hall, Elbridge Gerry, 25:111, 119, 257; 27:111; 30:253
Hall, Frederic, 14:24; 38:47-58; family of, 38:54; lawsuit, 38:52
Hall, Mrs. Frederic (Imogene Nicholls), 38:54
Hall, Frederick Chauncey and Lucy (Allen), 17:75
Hall, G. D., 10:70
Hall, H. C., 8:337, 353
Hall, H. T., 4:250
Hall, Henry M., 15:270
Hall, Isaac M., 11:360
Hall, J. T., 6:371
Hall, Jesse S., 9:325-28, 330
Hall, Capt. John (1822), 25:320-21, 324
Hall, John (ret. to Ohio, 1851), 28:303, 307
Hall, John Linville, *Around the Horn in '49*, 10:82; rev., 7:197-98
Hall, Lottie, 19:232
Hall, Lovick Pierce, 20:160-64; 23:300
Hall, Mrs. Mark M. (Elizabeth Field Christy), 36:46
Hall, Mira, 30:284
Hall, Nellie, 10:279
Hall, Nelson, 12:138; 35:200

Hall, O. C., 9:103, 113, 115
Hall, O. S., 2:130
Hall, Rhodolphus, 20:243-58
Hall, Mrs. Rhodolphus (Kate C.), 20:248-57 *passim;* letter from, 252-53
Hall, Robert, 2:130
Hall, Samuel C. and Mary A., 15:172, 173, 175
Hall, Susan Mitchell, "Dairy of a Trip from Ione to Nevada in 1859," 17:75-80
Hall, Thomas J. (or H.), Jr., 21:291, 306
Hall, W. L., lawsuit, 9:132
Hall, Warren F., 13:256, 258; 14:160; 36:123; *see also* Hall & Crandall
Hall, Willard P., 13:152; 22:47-48, 64; 33:110, **267**
Hall, William (on *Cantero*, 1849), 2:122
Hall, William (on *Ewing*, 1849), 30:41-44 *passim;* 36:307-11 *passim*
Hall, William (San Jose, 1850), 13:256; *see also* Hall & Crandall
Hall, William (ex-Mormon, 1851), 22:30, 33
Hall, William Hammond, 33:373
Hall, Winslow G., 35:47
Hall & Co., 9:65
Hall & Crandall, 13:256-60 *passim;* 14:160; 28:226
Hall & Hayward's Grand Farewell Concert, 1865, fac. program, 20: opp. 243
Hall Brothers' "Miner's Rest," 30:158
Halleck, Henry Wager, 1:9; 6:153; 7:110-11; 8:259; 10:131, 135, 154-62 *passim*, 291; 11:10, 103, 120; 13:320; 14:359, 367; 15:9-12 *passim*, 376; 16:307, 312, 313-4; 17: opp. 168, 173-74, 320; 19:6, 157, 158, 182, 232; 21:183, 311, 312, 313; 22:52, 65; 28:193, 373; 33:108, 109, 110, 114, 206, 269, 337, 338, 341; 34:31, 134; 40:307; art. on, 16:195-208; fac. sig., 10: opp. 159; port., 16: opp. 195
Halleck, Mrs. Henry Wager (Elizabeth Hamilton), 7:111; 16:200, 207
Halleck, Peachy and Billings, 7:108, 110, 111; 15:6, 9, 10, 368; 16: 89, 198-99, 200
Halleck, Peachy, Billings & Park, 17:172
Halley, William, 30:322

Hallidie, Andrew Smith, 14:191; 27:350; 28:114; 29:381; 31:301; 33:373; 35:259; arts. on, 19:144-56; 25:1-16; port., 19: op. 144

Hallidie, Mrs. Andrew Smith (Martha Elizabeth Woods), 19:148-49

Hallie (lake str.), 32:366

"Hall McAllister to 'Mannie,' " 34:231-37

Halloran, Helen Le Vere (Green), 28:379

Hall's Valley, Santa Clara Co., 38:52; ranch in, 21:93

Halo Chamo (or Halo Chemuck), 12:351; 20:33, 34, 46

Halphen, E., 31:333

Halpin, Pat, 26:35

Halstead (S.F., 1898), 30:300

Halstead, James S., 22:23

Halstead, Peter, 19:265-66

Halsted, James L., 11:9

Ham, R. S., 13:384

Ham, Zacharias, 2:36

Haman, John O., 19:288

Hamann *v.* Henry Cook, 10:180

Hambaugh, J. M., 31:31

Hambleton, J. D., 11:127

Hamblin, Jacob, 22:13

Hamblin, Maria L., 28:293

Hamblin, Thomas, 20:297

Hambly, Thomas C., 22:114; 34:210

Hambrook, Richard E., 24:286-87

Hamel, William, 26:95

Hamelin, Rear Admiral (1846), 11:207, 348; 12:160; *see also* Legoarant de Tromelin

Hamell, William, 16:284

Hamett, Mary, 15:177, 178

Hamilton (Monterey, 1849), 28:193, 362

Hamilton (San Diego Co., 1861), 40:316

Hamilton, Alexander, 16:191, 200; 40:3, 4-5

Hamilton, C., 22:251

Hamilton, Caroline, 7:284, 285

Hamilton, Charles, 35:354

Hamilton, Ebenezer, 9:395; 10:76, 366; 15:43, 53, 56, 57

Hamilton, Edward ("Ned"), 35:163

Hamilton, Elizabeth, *see* Halleck, Mrs. Henry W.

Hamilton, H. W., 10:398

Hamilton, Henry, 29:235; 39:4

Hamilton, J. W., 29:235

Hamilton, Jo, 2:206; 18:361, 363

Hamilton, Laurentine, 27:269, 350

Hamilton, Mary, 14:177

Hamilton, Newton, 18:303-4, 313

Hamilton, R., 22:251

Hamilton, Richard, 30:8, 10

Hamilton, William (Contra Costa Co., 1852), 30:8-9

Hamilton, William (Grass Valley, 1859), 6:342

Hamilton, William Bishop, 7:283, 284; 16:285, 344; 21:66

Hamilton, Mrs. William Bishop Sarah Chapman), 7:283, 284; *see also* Chapman Family

Hamilton, William C., 29:225

Hamilton, William H., 7:284

Hamilton, Mrs. William H. (Mabel McDonald), 35:83

Hamilton, William Stephen, 4:109; 10:204

Hamilton Church, Oakland, 26:361; 27:341, 350

Hamilton City, Butte Co., 7:14; 14: opp. 209; 23:369; 33:296

Hamilton City, Nev., 21:163

Hamilton Hall, Sacramento, 10:64

Hamlet (or Hamblet), Eli, 27:38, 48, 157, 158, 161

Hamlet (play), 10:376; 16:183

Hamley, George W., 30:52

Hamlin, Mrs. (S.F., 1853), 28:316, 322; 29:39

Hamlin, Chauncey J., 4:50

Hamlin, Hannibal, 19:165, 345, 363

Hamlin, J. E., 30:360, 366; store (illus.), 30: opp. 257

Hamlin, Thomas T., 9:269

Hamm, S. F., 10:62

Hamme, M. von, 21:163

Hammon, Miss (Yuba Co., 1854), 8:208, 337, 340; 9:58, 73

Hammon, Wendell P., 3:202

Hammond, Abram Adams, 34:249, 254

Hammond, Charles Mifflin, 38:236

Hammond, Chauncey, 35:357

Hammond, Daniel, 13:4, 20, 21

Hammond, David D., 13:31

Hammond, Francis A., 14:61, 71, 73

Hammond, George Peter, 25:372; 32:90; 36:171; fellow of CHS, 38:73-74; address "The Bancroft Library," 26:85-88; bk. revs. by 11:387-88; 39:271-72

Hammond, J. B., 11:9

Hammond, John Hays, 14:183;
  obit., 15:290-91
Hammond, Mrs. John Hays,
  (Natalie Harris), 15:291
Hammond, Richard Pindell, 10:254, 255,
  267; 12:26-27; 13:299; 15:211, 290;
  16:83, 183-84; 19:176. 256; 25:337,
  344; 26:72; letter, 34:36
Hammond, Robert, "Historical Aspects
  of Tobacco Culture in California,"
  40:97-107
Hammond, Samuel A., 31:152
Hammond, Thomas C., 1:140, 141, 240,
  241; 3:122; 17:341, 343; 21:209, 223,
  335, 336; 25:292, 296, 305; 26:29, 30,
  31, 36, 38, 44, 55; 33:339-40
Hammond, William, 4:192
Hammond, William Hall, 30:82
Hammond (John) & Co., 34:330
Hampshire Mills, 8:341, 347, 357; 9:52
Hampton, Col. (Kings R., 1850),
  11:258, 259
Hampton, Crittenden, 34:298
Hana (Hawaiian, 1850), 28:292
Hanbury, John B., 31:154
Hanchett, William, 32:94;
  "The Question of Religion and the
  Taming of California, 1849-1854,"
  32:49-56, 119-44
Hancock, Allan, 13:352
Hancock, George, 34:37, 38
Hancock, Henry, 9:269; 10:49, 62, 70,
  72; 13:306, 322, 351
Hancock, John H., 12:70
Hancock, Winfield Scott, 7:291; 9:306
Hand, Charles S., 6:152
Hand, E. B., 14:396; 15:29
Handbook for Californiacs, by Mott,
  rev., 5:403
Handley, William James, 15:352-53, 362
Hand organ (at Mission Santa Barbara),
  23:361
Hanford, Capt. (Murphy's, 1850s),
  11:329
Hanford, H., 22:35
Hanforth (Marysville, 1859), 10:180
Hang Far Low (restaurant),
  San Francisco, 27:258
Hang Heong Low (restaurant),
  San Francisco, 23:111; 37:131
Hangings:
  Casey and Cora, 3:41; 4:192; 6:7;
  8:371; 15:81; Griffith, 15:270;
  Jenkins 3:40; Judas (effigy),
  23:269; Sheldon, 15:271; Sheppard,

15:168; Stanner, 18:265; Stuart,
  2:136; 6:49
  at Drytown, 15:172; Empire Ranch,
  3:148; Iowa Hill, 15:271; Jackson,
  15:376; Los Angeles, 15:270; Rough
  and Ready, 6:234; Sacramento,
  6:51; San Antonio, 27:210;
  Tequila, Mex., 23:270-71
Hangtown, 3:72; 6:128-29; 20:42;
  28:380; 30:377; 32:196, 203; 37:138;
  letters from, 11:53-54; 26:294-95;
  illus., 6: opp. 6:128; *see also* Placerville
Hanify (J. R.) & Co., 31:295
Hanks, Ebenezer, 22:13
Hanks, H. G., 18:197-98
Hanks, Henry G., 2:178; 30:382
Hanks, Julian, 2:182, 186-87; fac. sig.,
  10: opp. 159
Hanley (lawsuit, S.F., 1860s), 21:118-19
Hanlock (lawsuit, S.F., 1855), 17:180
Hanlon Brothers (acrobats), 10:382,
  394; 21:262, 274
Hanly (Bullard's Bar, 1854), 8:205
Hann, T. R., 15:173, 181
Hanna (Marysville, 1858), 9:367
Hanna, John, 29:253, 254
Hanna, Marcus Alonzo, 31:378
Hanna, Phil Townsend, address and
  film, "Historical Flags of California,"
  16:187-88; *Libros Californianos*, rev.,
  38:83-84
Hanna, William P., 39:58
Hannager, Capt. (L.A. Co., 1854),
  13:336
Hannah (Hanna?; partner of Gantt),
  16:58
Hannah (Amer. brig., 1846), 3:280,
  285; 5:306
Hannah (Brit. clipper, 1854), 32:354
"Hannah Lloyd Neal," by
  Marie D. Dun, 31:241-52
Hannibal, William, 29:56
Hannigan, Josephine, 31:303
Hannum, Anna Paschal, ed. Pancoast,
  Quaker Forty-niner, rev., 9:291
Hansel Springs, 32:202
Hansen, Christian, 19:211, 216
Hansen, H. W., 15:302
Hansen, Mrs. James, 25:32
Hansen, Walter E., 24:190-91
Hansen, Woodrow James, *The Search
  for Authority in California*, rev.,
  40:253-55
"Hans Herman Behr," by
  Robert T. Legge, 32:243-62

Hanshew, T. W., 34:363-64
Hanson, Lt. (1792), *see* Anson George
Hanson, Andrew J., address, "Early Days of Methodism in California," 5:416-17
Hanson, George M., 14:403; 15:42, 57; 20:362, 363; 26:5, 7; 27:222; 33:293(?), 363; 36:318
Hanson, J. K., 29:107
Hanson, James H., 10:43, 44, 253
Hanson, V., 33:153, 161-64 *passim*
Hanson's Drug and Book Store, Auburn, 30:361
Hansonville, 9:69; 10:257, 268, 358
Happy Hollow, 30:209
Happy Valley, San Francisco, 2:135, 137; 19:237; 20:29, 45; 23:276; 25:104, 116; 28:32, 57; 29:148; 33:325; 34:68-69, 71; illus., 20: opp. 26
Haraszthy De Mokcsa, Agoston, 17:237, 238; 19:186; 21:373; 28:130, 131, 137, 141; 36:244, 248
Haraszthy, Arpad, 17:237; 28:130, 141-42; 36:244, 247-48
Haraszthy, Mrs. Arpad, *see* Vallejo, Jovita
Haraszthy, Attila, 17:237; 36:244
Haraszthy, Mrs. Attila, *see* Vallejo, Natalia
Harbin, James M., 24:71; 25:221; 28:267
Harbin, Matthew, 24:56, 71
Harbinger (ship), 8:328; 16:119; 23:333
Harbison, John S., 24:271
Harbison Grocery Co., 35:346-47, 358
Harcourt, Thomas Arundel, 35:47, 51
Harcourt, Mrs. Thomas Arundel (Fannie Anne Rulofson), 34:295, 299; 35:47-48
Hardcastle, Edmund La Fayette, 9:5-6, 10, 13, 14, 15
Harden (Honey Lake, 1857), 21:229
Hardestill, S. V., 10:383, 394
Hardie, James Allen, 1:249; 11:142; 33:341-42
Hardin, James Allen, 18:314
Harding, Annie, 24:172
Harding, George Laban, 10:303; 14:416; 18:192; 35:201; "Census of California Spanish Imprints, 1833-1845," 12:125-36; addresses: "Agustin Vicente Zamorano," 13:411; "The Collections of the Society," 25:85-86; bk. rev. by, 13:183-84; obits. of Edward E. Eberstadt,

37:375; Guy C. Miller, 34:183-84; Caroline Wenzel, 38:176-77; *Don Agustin V. Zamorano*, rev., 13:409
Harding, Helen, 27:187
Harding, Samuel C., 15:186, 282
Harding, Thomas, 33:12, 149
Harding Mine, 18:314
Hardy, Alfred, 13:340, 341; brothers of, 13:340
Hardy, Benjamin J., 31:245
Hardy, Charles, 35:346; 36:155
Hardy, F. L., 35:311
Hardy, Grahame, 25:191
Hardy, J. P., 9:36
Hardy, James H., 7:117-18; 9:381; 10:42, 380, 381, 393; 11:6; 40:295
Hardy, Lowell Edwin, 23:286; 24:84; obit., 30:189
Hardy, Mrs. Lowell Edwin (Florence Mayhew), obit., 36:281
Hardy, Lowell J., 22:288; 30:189
Hardy, Rex, Jr., 27:187
Hardy, Robert W. H., 11:367, 369, 382; 22:160
Hardy, Thomas M., 5:275; 6:374; 16:138; 19:117, 118, 119, 131, 137; 29:134, 135, 263, 276
Hardy, William B., bookstore of, 25:191; 30:363
Hardy, William H., 2:206; 22:16, 17
Hardyville, Ariz., 2:206; 22:15, 16, 17, 151, 155, 157, 165
Hare, Charles, 26:15; 33:373
Hares, *see* Rabbits and Hares
Harg & Kennedy, 29:109
Hargis, Donald E., 32:383; 38:282; "The Issues in the Broderick-Gwin Debates of 1859," 32:313-25; "Straight Toward His Heart . . . Eulogy of David C. Broderick," 38:197-217
Hargis, L. D., 20:166
Hargrave, William, 5:127, 272; 6:60, 140; 17:155, 224, 240; 24:58; 28:266; 29:134
Hargraves, Edward Hammond, 26:279; 28:277; 30:15, 28, 37; 32:273
Harker, Mary Margaret, 17:359; " 'Honest Harry' Meiggs," 17:195-207
Harkness, Harvey W., 31:337; 32:257
Harkness, W. H., 36:268
Harlan (San Jose, 1850), 34:242
Harlan, Jacob Wright, 27:370; 30:5

Harlan, Mrs. Jacob Wright
  (Ann Eliza), 27:370
Harlan, Joel, 30:5
Harley Steamship Co., 31:296
Harlin, James M., 24:26
Harlow, John, 2:127
Harlowe, Capt. (of *Telegraph*), 15:278
Harmon, Albion K. P., 15:76
Harmon, Charles, 35:6
Harmon, D. B., 8:358
Harmon, Ednah, 24:94
Harmon, John, 35:156
Harmon, John B., 15:75; 26:266
Harmon, John H., 29:355
Harmon, Mrs. S. H., 24:262
Harmon, Sarah Melissa, *see*
  Morris, Mrs. John M.
Harmon, Silas S., 24:95; 32:53, 125,
  129-32 *passim*, 135, 144
Harmon, Mrs. Silas S., 32:128
Harmon and Springer, 22:29
Harmount (Monterey, 1850), 29:27
Harney, William Selby, 11:20; 18:109,
  130, 134
Harney Lake, 22:202, 214
Haro, Diego de, 3:363, 364, 366
Haro, Francisco de (to Calif., 1819),
  3:32; 11:74-75; 13:236; 14:100, 130-31,
  186; 16:339; 17:250-51, 255; heirs,
  16:339; 21:120; letters, 14: opp. 121,
  121-22
Haro, Mrs. Francisco de (Emiliana or
  Josefa Sánchez), 14:130; 17:255
Haro, Francisco de (1827-1846),
  1:136; 12:56; 14:131; 25:124; 29:270
Haro, Gonzalo López de, *see*
  López de Haro
Haro, Josefa de, 16:339
Haro, Ramón de (1827-1846), 1:136;
  12:56; 14:131; 25:124; 29:270
Haro, Ramón de (1867), 21:120
Haro, Rosalía de, 14:130
Harold, Yates, 13:32
Harpending (lawsuits, Yuba Co., 1857),
  9:158, 167
Harpending, Asbury, 20:159; 21:373;
  26:18; 27:179; 28:167; 33:234, 373;
  35:340; 40:300
Harper, James, 4:321
Harper, Sam, 17:209, 215-16
Harper, William, 29:167
Harran, James C., 15:179
Harrass (mate on *Victoria*, 1850), 8:17,
  18, 167
Harrell, Alfred, 32:5-41 *passim*

Harriet* (ship), 4:153; 28:259
Harriet Blanchard (ship), 14:343;
  22:346; 35:199
Harrigan, "Buck," 9:258; 10:277
Harrigan, Edward, 4:61, 62
Harriman, Edward Henry, 30:341
Harriman, Job, 40:215-36
Harriman, Oliver, 25:192
Harriman, William D., 10:390
Harrington, Daniel, 16:80
Harrington, J. J., 33:166, 168; 35:307
Harrington, John, 10:390
Harrington, Joseph, 10:295; 25:341;
  29:251
Harrington, William, 34:295, 298, 299
Harrington, William D., 15:169
Harrington, William Pierce, 14:401
Harrington, Mrs. William Pierce
  (Sally Tennent), 10:264
Harriott, Fred, 21:249
Harriott, Mrs. Fred, *see* Morris, Clara
Harris (San Bernardino, 1852), 14:181
Harris (Yuba Co., 1858), 9:367, 368,
  374; 10:41, 42
Harris, Miss (Yuba Co., 1861), 10:285
Harris, Capt. (to Hawaii, 1900), 35:248
Harris, A., 5:338
Harris, A. H., 22:33
Harris, Abraham W. and Hannah
  (Bucknell), 28:293
Harris, Arnold, 13:243, 244, 247, 252
Harris, Benjamin Butler, *The Gila
  Trail: The Texas Argonauts and the
  California Gold Rush*, rev., 40:160-62
Harris, C. W., 37:198
Harris, Mrs. E., 10:375, 379-80
Harris, Elias B., 12:330; 17:77, 79
Harris, Mrs. Elias B.
  (Anna Isabella Stevens), 17:79
Harris, Fanny, 10:378, 379
Harris, Frank, 15:380
Harris, G. F., 34:272
Harris, J. H., 9:103
Harris, James O., 9:245, 248, 269, 271
Harris, John D., 14: opp. 209, 394
Harris, Josiah A., 20:329, 330, 331, 335
Harris, L. C., 9:109
Harris, Lawrence Wilkinson, 31:305;
  36:68; address by, 35:161-69
Harris, Moses ("Black"), 4:124, 278-83,
  307, 319, 326, 340; 5:82
Harris, N. B., 29:196
Harris, Natalie, 15:291
Harris, P. Y., 9:77
Harris, Stephen C., 28:59, 66

Harris, Stephen Randall, 4:187, 195;
15:370
Harris, T. J., 14:394
Harris, Thomas S., 18:215
Harris, Townsend, 23:337; 32:212, 222;
38:200
Harris, W., 4:23
Harris, W. D., 15:179
Harris, William Torrey, 37:40, 42
Harrison (lawsuit, 1850s), 8:261
Harrison, A. S., 11:301-3
Harrison, A. T., drawing by, 15: opp.
364
Harrison, Benjamin and Caroline
Lavinia (Scott), 20:135
Harrison, Edward H., 28:45, 290
Harrison, George R., 17: No. 4, Pt. 2,
pp. 3, 20-24 *passim*
Harrison, John (London, 1729),
37:290-92, 309; port. 37: opp. 289
Harrison, John (S.F., 1856), 8:369, 370
Harrison, Joseph, 30:115
Harrison, Napoleon B., 3:109; 18:52, 62
Harrison, Ralph C., 1:12-13, 16-17;
36:45
Harrison, W. A. (or W. H.; d. 1849),
21:306
Harrison, William Henry, 17:305
Harrison, William R., 22:368
Harrison's News Depot, Columbia,
38:318
Harry Hastings (ship), 29:106
Hart, Capt. (Mormon Bat., 1848),
14:281
Hart, A. S., 10:62
Hart, Albert, 19:156
Hart, Bob, 21:169, 173
Hart, Ed, 11:358, 360
Hart, James, 12:328
Hart, James David, 15:292; "*Dale
Lowell Morgan*," 40:367-70,
*American Images of Spanish
California*, rev., 40:250-51; bk rev. by,
18:280-81; obit. of Joseph Henry
Jackson, 34:279-80; phot., 40: opp. 368
Hart, Jerome, 33:257
Hart, Jerome Alfred, 19:111; 35:163, 375
Hart, Mrs. Jerome Alfred (Ann Clark),
obit., 35:375
Hart, Julien, obit., 15:292
Hart, Robert D., 9:19
Hart, Simeon, 34:126, 127, 128, 131
Hart, William H. H., 38:353
Hart, Joyce & Sullivan, 19:228
Hart *v.* Burnett, 21:117-18

Hart's Ranch, 28:327
Harte, Francis Bret, 1:103; 4:95, 101,
211, 212-13, 406; 8:187; 12:177, 361;
17:315-16; 18:181, 280, 281; 21:50, 80,
163, 277; 22:281; 28:6-9 *passim*, 17;
30:138, 141, 151, 152, 360; 32:231, 233,
238; 33:210, 211-12; 34:359-62 *passim*;
38:115, 119, 126, 308-9; art. on,
4:207-9; bks. on, rev., 5:199-203,
409-12; 7:287-88
Harte, Mrs. Francis Bret (Anna
Griswold), 1:301; 4:208; 5:199, 201
Harte, Geoffrey Bret, ed. *Letters of
Bret Harte*, rev., 5:199-203
Hartford, A. K., 2:122
Hartford (ship), 8:275
Hartford Insurance Co., 26:258
Hartford Union Mining and Trading
Co., bk. on, rev., 7:197-98
Hartley (Sacramento Co., 1862), 10:373
Hartley, Henry, 18:153-54, 155-56, 366
Hartley, Henry Hare, 10: opp. 48;
12:30; 23:295
Hartley, Samuel, 25:32
Hartley, T. J., 11:181
Hartmann, Emil A., 27:3
Hartnell, Anna, 29:26
Hartnell, William Edward Petty,
3:278, 288; 6:254-59 *passim*, 263, 264;
8:105, 114, 290; 10:81, 103, 104, 112;
12:43, 230, 243; 15:236, 286-87, 333;
16:106, 368; 17:22, 53; 18:143, 144,
169, 170, 179; 23:9, 218, 258, 348;
27:107; 28:114, 193, 362; 29:132, 313;
30:98; 35:105, 106, 107, 110; letter,
17:22-27; *see also* Hartnell's Ranch;
McCulloch, Hartnell and Co.
Hartnell, Mrs. William Edward Petty
(María Teresa de la Guerra), 18:170,
179
Hartnell (place), 11:321-22
"Hartnell School at Alisal, 1836, The,"
address by Henry R. Wagner,
15:286-87
Hartnell's Ranch (Monterey Co.),
3:271, 284; 4:81; 13:58; 15:286-87,
333; *see also* Ranchos: El Alisal or
Patrocino
Hartnell's Ranch (Sacramento Co.),
11:321; 34:22, 24
Hartshorne, Mrs. (Marysville, 1860),
10:246
Hartshorne, Benjamin Minturn, 11:127;
22:6, 20

Hartshorne, Mrs. Benjamin Minturn (Julia Norton), 11:127
Hartson adobe, Napa Co., 16:134
Hartweg, Theodor, 12:292; 18:342-43
Hartwell, W. H., 27:201
Hartwell, William H., 10:189, 386
Hartz, A., 21:163
Harvard Club of San Francisco, 33:376
Harvey, Charles, 18:23
Harvey, D. H., 10:200
Harvey, Genevieve, introd. to Susan M. Hall, "Diary of a Trip from Ione to Nevada in 1859," 17:75
Harvey, John Downey, 7:291; 10:292; 23:191
Harvey, Obed, 10:272, 278, 287, 372, 377, 378, 379; 17:75; 18:23
Harvey, Mrs. Obed, *see* Hall, Susan M.
Harvey, Walter H., 10:292, 358; 23:191; 28:330, 335-38 *passim*
Harvey, Mrs. Walter H., *see* Martin, Mrs. Edward J.
Harville, John W., 11:9
HasBrouck, Joseph, 29:99, 361
Hasbrouk, Josiah, 33:373
Haselden, R. B., 16:275-76; 18:151; "Is the Drake Plate of Brass Genuine?," 16:271-74
Hasey, A. G., 21:227, 235
Hasey, S. L., 10:394
Haskell (lawsuit, Marysville, 1859), 10:57
Haskell, D. H., 4:270
Haskell, Daniel C., 24:322
Haskell, Daniel Hale, 15:169, 371; 16:31; 17:170, 172; 22:35; 36:129
Haskell, Henry, 15:370
Haskell, Jacob W., 2:124, 127-30 *passim*
Haskell, John M., 15:364
Haskell, Leonidas, 10:197
Haskins (Marysville, 1858), 9:346, 350, 378
Haskins, A. B., 13:31
Haskins, J. W., 26:242, 243
Haskins, L. W., 13:31
Haskins, Patrick, 15:174
Haskins, R. A., 15:29
Haskins, S. H., 22:251
Haskins, Samuel Moody, 21:384
Hastings (Marysville, 1858), 9:361; 10:183
Hastings, Mrs. (Sacramento, 1858), 9:244
Hastings (Stockton, 1869), 34:349

Hastings, Benjamin F., 13:32
Hastings, Daniel N., 30:262
Hastings, Hubbard, 15:375
Hastings, J., 28:34
Hastings, Mrs. John Russel (Katherine Bagg), 23:95
Hastings, Lansford W., 2:76; 3:275; 4:87, 105, 108; 5:124, 264, 271, 276, 378, 383, 390; 6:58-59, 132-33; 7:106; 10:6-7, 153, 155, 304; 11:136; 12:184; 17:154, 158, 161; 19:135; 20:157; 21:82; 23:370; 24:73; 26:110, 124; 28:324, 373; 29:335, 336, 339; 30:53; 34:142, 148; 40:321; fac. sig., 10: opp. 159
Hastings, Mrs. Lansford W. (Charlotte Catherine Toler), 35:11, 15, 21
Hastings, Robert P., 34:190; "Rufus Allen Lockwood," 34:97-110, 239-63, 333-40
Hastings, Samuel A., 21:366
Hastings, Samuel J., 8:300
Hastings, Serranus Clinton, 9:40; 20:109, 366, 368; 23:190, 295; 24:216, 219; 26:209-15 *passim*; 32:376; 33:74; 34:241, 250, 252
Hastings & Co., 30:114
Hastings (E. P.) & Co., 15:76
Hastings College of the Law, 25:87; 26:211; 35:178-79
Hastings Cutoff, 5:383-87; 6:362; 10:348; 24:73; 27:180; 32:199-201; art. on, 36:57-62
Hastler, E. J., 15:164
Hasty, Capt. (Colorado R., 1853), 22:168
Haswell (Sacramento, 1858), 9:371
Haswell, D. C., 9:359
Haswell, E. C., 10:55
Hatch, Mrs. (Sacramento, 1858), 9:371; 10:53
Hatch (Dep. Surv., Mendocino Co., 1860), 27:215
Hatch (Santa Barbara, 1860), 18:166
Hatch (Inyo Co., 1860s, later S.F.), 9:198, 200
Hatch, A. D., 13:31
Hatch, Francis L., 9:152, 154, 177, 251, 264, 348, 349, 350, 358, 359, 363, 369; 10:42, 63, 168, 171, 252, 359, 362, 368, 369, 393
Hatch, Francis M., 25:226
Hatch, Frederick Winslow, 9:36, 110
Hatch, Ira, 22:13
Hatch, J., 30:262

Hatch, John, 10:52
Hatch, Miss L. H., 25:31
Hatch, Orrin, 14:278
Hat Creek, 22:101, 103, 216; 33:136
Hatfield, George, 36:110
Hatfield's Store, 8:341, 344, 346, 356; 9:57
Hathaway, Barnaby W., 10:372, 374; 13:31; 27: opp. 97, 103; letter to, 27:98-101
Hathaway, C. (S.F., 1855), 15:367
Hathaway, Charles W., 9:109; 15:280, 364; 26:264; 29:253
Hathaway, E. D., 13:31
Hathaway, Edmund V., 13:31
Hathaway, Mrs. Edmund V., 36:296, 299, 305-6
Hathaway (C. W.) & Co., 29:254
Hathwell, C. A., 10:76
Hatter (S.F., 1849), 28:292
Hattie Fickett (ship), 22:25
Hauck, Herman J., 30:377
Haug, Julius and Alma, 25:252
Haun, Andrew Jackson, 9:273; 10:167, 189; 14:377
Haun, David L., 10:253, 255, 256, 367; 14:377; 32:216, 223
Haun, Henry Peter, 8:342, 359; 9:54, 72, 178, 273, 381; 10:247, 250; 11:11, 25; 14: opp. 209, 377, 379-81, 399; 15:22, 28, 29, 33, 38, opp. 40; 38:28; *see also* Haun House
Haun House, Marysville, 9:154, 162, 169, 178, 261, 263, 264, 268, 346, 348, 374, 396; *see also* St. Nicholas Hotel
Haus, J. T., 15:276
Hauser, Caspur (Kaspar?), 8:347
Hauser, George, 32:331
Haveland, William S., 16:183
Haven, Charles D., 27:350
Haven, Joshua P., 7:6; 9:26, 32; 10:198; 23:339, 340, 344; 25:104, 116-17, 331; 26:179-82 *passim*, 257, 352
Haven (or Havens), Langdon A., 21:304, 306; 22:69
Haven, Richard S., 26:257, 258, 352-53
Havens, H. W., 9:269
Haverly, Christopher ("Col. Jack H."), 21:175, 182, 242, 245, 270
Haverly's California Theatre, 19:107
Haverly's Minstrels, 21:242; 37:227
Haviland, Anna, 21:378
Haviland, Mark, 21:237
Hawaiian Agricultural Co., 25:226

Hawaiian Commercial & Sugar Co., 40:34-36, 41-48 *passim*
Hawaiian Evangelical Association, 34:319
Hawaiian Gazette, 39:162
Hawaiian Islands, 4:92; 8:132-34; 12:88; 14:209, 315, 319, 321, 326, 337, 338, 339; 17:131-35; 18:70, 141, 182, 278, 315, 341, 347, 379; 19:47; 20:372; 23:197, 199, 200, 215, 218, 314, 322, 330-34; 28:99, 102, 103, 198, 250-57 *passim*, 289; 33:103; 34:318-19; and gold rush, 19:327-28, 334-35; newspapers, 35:193, 195, 200; resolution on annexation, 5:288; sugar from, 40:32-48; trade via, 8:298-99, 304; *see also* Sandwich Islands
Hawaiian Reformed Catholic Church, 34:318, 319
Hawaiians, 14:326; 28:292; *see also* Kanakas; Sandwich Islanders
Hawes, Horace, 10:83; 16:81, 84, 342; 19:4; 22:192; 23:160; 34:241
Hawes, Joseph, 11:31-32
"Hawes & Co.'s San Francisco and New York Express," by Ernest A. Wiltsee, 11:30-32; illus., 11: opp. 30
Hawk, Nathan, 16:142
Hawkins (San Jose, 1853), 14:157
Hawkins, H. Z., 14:394; 15:29
Hawkins, Hiram R., 9:115, 368, 369, 375, 392; 10:183
Hawkins, James, 33:364
Hawkins, Sir John (1569), 16: No. 1, Pt. 2, pp. 3, 5; 30:278-79
Hawkins, John (1863), 26:247
Hawkins' Bar, 11:170-75 *passim*; 38:307-8; 39:47-48, 51; letters from, 11:172-73, 174-75
Hawks, William W., 9:26, 29, 46, 102; 15:278
Hawley, Asa H., 11:9
Hawley, Belle (Chapman), 7:282, 283
Hawley, John, 35:361; 36:75-76
Hawley, T. R., 14:403
Hawley, William, 14:401
Haworth James (?), 10:363
Haworth, William, 12:15
Hawson, Henry, 39:31
Hawson amendment, 38:351
Hawthorne, Hildegarde, 22:192
Hawthorne, J. C., 9:46
Hay, R. J., 34:158

Hay, 2:290; 6:224-25; 8:334, 347;
  12:294, 295, 296, 302; 14:200-203
  passim, 402; 23:255, 354; 26:63, 244;
  27:194; 29:304; 33:300, 303; hay press,
  16:131
Haycock, George, 7:14
Hayden, Albert, 25:95
Hayden, Brace, 25:95
Hayden, C. C., 9:36; 20:44
Hayden, Ferdinand Vandiveer, 32:182
Hayden, Jonathan, 9:145; lawsuit,
  9:135, 136, 140
Haydon, Charles H. and Eliza
  (Holmes), 28:293
Haydon, S. C., 30:262, 362-63, 367
Hayes (or Hays; from Ore., 1845),
  5:125
Hayes, Mrs. (Sacramento, 1858),
  9:377; 10:48
Hayes, Benjamin, 12:120, 122, 320;
  13:315, 318, 322, 327, 330, 338, 351;
  18:134, 255, 275; 21:195; 26:51; 34:38;
  36:120, 123, 125; *Pioneer Notes*, ed.
  Wolcott, rev., 8:280-81
Hayes, Catherine ("Kate"), 4:60, 208;
  6:339; 10:68, 86; 15:166; 19:229, 236;
  38:19
Hayes, Henry, 11:9
Hayes, Jacob, 14:72, 182
Hayes, James, 5:125(?); 25:145; 29:337,
  338
Hayes, Jay Orley, 38:356, 357; 39:20
Hayes, Katherine (Mrs. Thomas P.
  Roark), 29:382
Hayes, Louisa, 21:195; 34:38
Hayes, Michael, 10:377; 16:342
Hayes, Rutherford Birchard, 19:251
Hayes, Thomas, 10:297; 15:364, 365;
  16:80, 81; 17:169, 255; 33:301, 303,
  308, 373; 38:214; 40:313
Hayes, William, 6:11
Hayes & Bailey, 28:40
Hayes Park, San Francisco, 10:285,
  297, 374, 377, 388, 390
Hayes railroad bill, 9:259, 260, 284
Hayes Valley, San Francisco, 10:297;
  18:333; 33:308
Hayes Valley Hose Co., No. 3, 18:333
Hayford, William B., 18:356, 364
Hayfork Valley, 20:357-58, 364
Hayman, Albert, 21:263
Hayne, Mrs. Arthur, *see* Hayne, Julia
  (Dean)
Hayne, Duncan and Agnes (Howard),
  27:319

Hayne, Francis Bourn, 36:284-85; ed.
  "A Boy's Voyage to San Francisco,
  1865-66," 36:205-12, 293-306
Hayne, Julia (Dean), 6:10-11; 9:163,
  179; 10:274-75, 283, 289; 20:307;
  21:41-42, 52-53, 55, 57, 64; 25:6
Haynes, Lt. (overland, 1849), 26:328
Haynes, Lt. (Clear Lake, 1850), 24:52
Haynes, Asa, 18:196
Haynes, John P., 11:9; 32:170
Haynes, John R., 36:253, 255, 259
Haynes, Nahum, 21:366
Haynes, T. J., 17:177
Hays (stage driver, 1850s), 13:258
Hays (North San Juan, 1858), 9:366
Hays, J., 8:345; lawsuit, 8:347
Hays, Mrs. John Caperton
  (Anna McMullin), 27:382; obit., 3:399
Hays, John Coffee, 3:399; 7:396; 8:366,
  367; 15:290; 16: 184; 17:44, 47;
  18:105-9 *passim*, 123, 130, 131; 19:168,
  256; 22:113, 267; 23:164, 171; 30:165,
  331, 332; 31:333, 382; 33:373; 34:14-16,
  17; port., 18: opp. 99
Hays, Mrs. John Coffee
  (Susan Calvert), 18:131
Hays, Kate, 10:46
Hays, R. T., 8:195
Hays, Mrs. R. T. (Jenny Vineyard),
  8:195; 9:356; 10:42, 43, 63
Hays, Robert, 15:177
Hays, William, 15:38
Hayward, Alvinza, 12:33; 31:290;
  art on, 20:181-85
Hayward, James A., 36:328
Hayward, Thomas, 13:32
Hayward, William, 20:244, 248-49, 254,
  255
Hayward, newspaper in, 24:62, 72
Haywood (Nevada Co., 1850s), 6:338
Haywood, Benjamin, 15:164
Haywood, Philip H., 3:121
Hazard, Lucy Lockwood, address,
  "Eden to Eldorado," 8:187
Hazelrigg, Arthur, 21:128
Hazelton, D., 20:44
Hazelton, George W., 30:264
Hazelton, John E., 13:31
Hazelton, William B., 25:20
Hazen, Kelsey, 15:276
Hazleton (on *Cheshire*, 1850), 6:206,
  213
Hazzard, Louise, 36:182
Heacock, E. H., 10:283, 375
Head, Addison E., 19:233

Head, Samuel C., 29:20
Head Building, San Francisco, 25:241
Healdsburg, 19:130; 30:363
Healey, John P., 20:111
Health Insurance (1930), 28:374
Health resorts, 8:83; 31:19-23 *passim;* 39:273
Health Seekers of Southern California, by Baur, rev., 39:272-74
Healy (lawsuit, 1861), 10:356
Healy, Misses (San Diego, ca. 1900), 35:352
Healy, Frank W., 25:234-35, 242
Healy, Lucien B., 9:113, 116; 30:325
Healy, Mrs. Lucien B. (Sarah Elizabeth Ide Cooper), 29:262
Healy, Patrick Joseph, 21:311; 29:157, 159
Heanan, Charles Oris, 30:92
Heanan, Mrs. Charles Oris (Mary Owner), 30:92; 31:284
Heanan, Ethel Lavinia, 30:92
Hearst, Mrs. George (Phoebe Apperson), 2:343; 25:229; 31:340; plans for Univ. of Calif., 25:12
Hearst, William Randolph, 12:201; 15:283, 284; 20:132, 139; 28:230; 30:195; 39:121-27 *passim,* 131, 134, 137
Hearst Ranch (San Luis Obispo Co.), *see* Ranchos: Piedra Blanca
Heart, Miss (S.F., 1865), 36:210
Hearts of Oak (play), 21:256
Heath, Charles H., 9:136, 173
Heath, Harold, 17:243
Heath, Kate, 19:104
Heath, R. W., 32:354
Heath, Richard W., 16:304
Heath, Russell, 9:269; 29:21, 26
Heath, W. H., 13:32
Heath and Emory's Ferry, 12:6
Heatherington, J., 13:32
Heath's Gallery, 10:178, 200, 248
Heaven, Louise (Palmer), 28:3, 6
Hebard, (Hebbard, Hibbard; Calaveras Co., 1850), 22:71-73
Hebbard (Marysville, 1859), 10:184
Hebe (ship), 6:257, 259
Hebrew Benevolent societies:
    Los Angeles, 13:333; 39:175;
    Marysville, 10:182, 200
Hebrew Young Men's Literary Assoc., San Francisco, 38:306
Heceta, Bruno de, *see* Hezeta
Hecht, Sarah, 26:282
Heckle, Miss (Marysville, 1858), 9:372

Hecla (ship), 22:353, 354
Heco, Joseph, 23:336
Hecox, Adna A., 2:182; 26:165, 166, 167; 27:162, 164
Hector (ship), 5:42, 139-46 *passim,* 342, 343; 32:105
Hedding Elijah, 5:76-79 *passim,* 255; 21:2-9 *passim;* 29:322-23
Hedge, Nelson, 13:257
Hedges, Mary, 28:289
Hedley, King, 21:251
Heebner, Mrs. Ernest (Metha McMahan), 23:300
"Hee Li," 14:56-58
Heenan, John Carmel, 21:58-59; 32:218, 223
Heenan, Mrs. John Carmel, *see* Menken, Ada Isaacs
Hegg, Roy E., 36:157
Heimann, Jacob, 19:291-92
Heintzelman, Mrs. (Sacramento, 1861), 10:280
Heintzleman, H. P. 9:46; 27:216; 30:162
Heintzleman, Samuel Peter, 11:376, 377, 382; 13:381; 20:259, 271; 21:107-9, 112; 22:2, 3, 4, 20
Heinzelwood, *see* Henchelwood
Heiser, Charles L., quoted, 32:295, 296
Heiskell, Lucy B., 19:96
Heiskell, Tyler Davis, 19:96
Heitman & Hoelscher, 33:67
Heitzeberg, Paul, 39:151, 220, 221
Heizer, Robert Fleming, 20:81, 188, 191, 375, 384; 21:80-82; 22:194; 26:108, 130, 186; 27:132; 32:285; "Alexander S. Taylor's Map of California Indian Tribes, 1864," 20:171-80; "An Early 19th Century California(?) Copper Medallion," 26:349-50; "Archaeological Evidence of Cermeño's California Visit," 20:315-28; coauth. "Archaeological Exploration of Sixteenth-Century Indian Mounds at Drake's Bay," 31:99-108; "Archaeological Investigation of Sutter Sawmill Site," 26:134-59; "Walla Walla Indian Expeditions to the Sacramento Valley," 21:1-7; ed. "Techniques and Implements of the American Whale-Fishery, from an Early Japanese Account," trans. Hitoshi Watanabe, 32:225-29; addresses, "Archaeological Evidence of . . .

Cermeño's California Visit," 21:82; "Some Anthropological Perspectives on California History," 33:85-88

Helbing, August, 27:171

Helen, Lake, Lassen Co., 22:370

Helena, Mont., 15:324, 326, 328

Helena (bark, 1841), 12:254, 255, 274, 275

Helena (str., 1900s), 31:295

Helena Augusta (bark), 22:119; 25:108

Helen Hensley (riv. str.), 15:161; 24:94

Helen Mine, 32:359

"Helios" (pseud.), *see* Muybridge, Eadweard J.

Heller, Carrie, 35:126

Heller, Elizabeth, 31:287

Heller, Emanuel S., 1:19; 25:230, 232, 241, 249-50; 31:176, 287; obit., 5:103-4

Heller, Mrs. Emanuel S. (Clara Hellman), 5:104

Heller, Mat, 36:69

Heller, Moses and Amelia (Nickelsburg), 5:103

Heller, Sig, 35:126, 257

Hellespont (ship), 35:198

Hellman, Mrs. Anthony C. (Belle J. Hoge), 10:295

Hellman, Christian, 11:245

Hellman, Herman W., 13:345, 346

Hellman, Isaias M., 13:346

Hellman, Isaias William, 13:224, 335, 345, 346; 21:329; 25:15; 32:331, 333; 35:358; 36:328

Hellman, Isaias William, Jr., 25:232

Hell-roarin' Forty-niners, The, by Ritchie, rev., 7:407

Hell's Hill, 10:171, 194

Helm, William, 4:41

Helper, Hinton Rowan, 22:256-76 *passim;* 24:106

Helps, Sir Arthur, 31:219, 220

Helvetia, Alameda Co., 4:211

Helvetia and Lafayette Co., 6:229

Helvetian (ship), 15:375

Helvetius (ship), 14:315

Hembkey, Conrad, 21:343

Hemerle, John, 22:61-62, 63

Hemme, Valentine W., 29:235

Hemp, 2:278; 5:211; 12:193; 13:204; 14:10, 319; 17:23; 22:319

Hempstead, Charles H., 16:184, 344

Henarie, Mr. and Mrs. (Sacramento, 1858), 9:255, 258, 371

Henarie, Daniel Van B. and Mary A. Hosley, 28:294

Henchelwood (Colorado R., 1851), 11:377; 22:20

Hendee, D. H., 34:299

Hendel, Charles, 19:294, 297

Hendel & Co., 11:241

Hendershott, Henry B., 11:123

Henderson, A. J., 29:237

Henderson, Andrew J., 6:276, 280, 370, 372; 17:226, 229-30; 19:139; 22:43, 64; 33:106, 123

Henderson, B. F., 14:403; 15:21

Henderson, Ernest Norton, 37:39

Henderson, Mary (Mrs. William McPherson), 35:354

Henderson, Mrs. Robert Burns (Jennie A. Crocker), 27:254

Henderson, William T., 18:201

Hending (S.F., 1854), 15:175

Hendley, A. C., 29:253, 254

Hendley, John, 24:58

Hendren (on *London,* 1849), 7:213, 217, 219, 223, 397; 8:182, 264, 266-69 *passim,* 276

Hendricks, Mrs. (S.F., 1864), 24:265

Hendrickson, W., 19:61, 71

Hendry, George W., 10:303; 30:229; "Francisco Palou's Boundary Marker," 5:321-27; coauth. "The Plant Content of Adobe Bricks," 4:361-73; address, "California History from Adobe Bricks," 15:89-90

Hendry, James, 33:105

Hendy (Joshua) Iron Works, 32:32

Hendy Woods, 33:362; phot., 33: opp. 360

Henecy, John, 35:332

Heney, Francis Joseph, 32:231

Heney, Mrs. Francis Joseph (née McMullin), 27:382

Hengler, Thomas M., 21:169

Henick, Mrs. (N.Y., 1860), 11:11

Henley, Justice (Sacramento, 1858), 9:258

Henley, Thomas J., 15:165, 171; 18:306; 19:256; 26:202, 326; 27:215, 216, 219; 28:59; 30:160-61, 164-66, 173

Henly, Mrs. (S.F., 1862), 10:379

Henly, Bart, 10:379

Hennecart (S.F., 1850), 14:133

Hennell, Frederick, 26:232

Henness Pass, 4:241, 247, 259; 7:14; 10:348, 350; 28:233, 236-37

Hennessy, James, 16:80, 283

Henning, A. E., 25:195

Henriques, David, 15:179

Henríquez (weaver, 1792), 6:162-63
Henry, Mrs. (Yuba Co., 1861), 10:359
Henry, Miss (Marysville, 1862), 10:380
Henry (Fresno, 1871), 18:30, 31
Henry, Alexander, 24:231-32
Henry, Andrew, 2:26-27; 4:117, 119,
126, 127
Henry, Benjamin D., 30:243, 245
Henry, Brice M., 11:9; 23:18
Henry, C., 10:200; 20:305
Henry, Charles A., 25:169, 171
Henry, Clara Augusta, 36:88
Henry, H. H., 30:358
Henry, William, 24:232
Henry, William P., 26:204
Henry Astor (ship), 29:1, 16, 171
Henry Astor Company, 29:171, 172, 259
Henry Brigham (ship), 39:302
"Henry Douglas Bacon," by
Milton H. Shutes, 26:193-200
"Henry George and the California
Background of *Progress and
Poverty*," by Charles A. Barker,
24:97-115
"Henry George's Oxford Speech," by
Elwood P. Lawrence, 30:117-23
Henry Kelsey (ship), 14:176
Henry Lee (ship), 7:197, 198
Henry M. Stephens (ship), 23:189
Henry R. Wagner Memorial Award,
38:358; 39:62-63; 40:366; phot., 38:
opp. 358; 40: opp. 366
"Henry Wager Halleck, Lincoln's
Chief of Staff," by Milton H. Shutes,
16:195-208
Henry Ware (ship), 18:375
Henshaw, Frederick William, 2:204;
26:214
Henshaw, George, 8:274
Henshaw, Henry Wetherbee, 7:23, 61
Henshaw, Joshua S., 13:405
Henshaw, Tyler, 2:204
Hensley, M. M., 16:58
Hensley, Samuel J., 3:116, 118; 6:12, 61,
141; 11:11, 14, 25, 26; 14:163, 164;
15:269; 16:66, 337; 17:180, 275, 327,
337, 340, 344; 18:297; 21:341, 346-47,
356; 22:366-67; 25:132; 26:23; 32:197,
199
Hensley, Merrill & King, 37:139
Hensley, Reading & Co., 22:367; 37:139
Henslier, James, 15:376
Hentch and Berton, 12:72
Hentrich, Mrs. Lewis, 31:337
Henverin, Michael, 33:330

Hepburn, A. M., 9:395
Hepburn, H. P., 18:38; 22:35, 37, 38
Hepburn, Hiatt O., 34:257
Hepburn, James, 20:108-9
Herald, Cleveland, 20:329-38 *passim*
Herald, Crescent City, 32:161-63
Herald, Marysville, 9:380; 10:394, 395;
14:225, 386-91 *passim*, 398, 407;
15:55; 16:258; quoted, 15:21-53
passim, 56; facs., 14: opp. 209;
15: opp. 40
Herald, New York, 10:298-301
Herald, San Bernardino, 9:194, 198;
23:260; 24:275
Herald, San Diego, 9:197, 200; 24:275;
31:36, 39, 46; quoted, 12:322
Herald, San Francisco, 9:276, 382;
12:20; 13:299; 15:32, 174; 20:306, 335,
336; 21:25, 31; 22:361; 28:135; 29:22,
176-77; 31:236, 238; 32:223, 296,
349-61 *passim*; 34:209, 211; 37:138,
151-53; quoted, 12:321
Herald, Sonora, 1:98; 5:311; 7:277; 35:77
Herald-Courier, San Francisco, 28:36
Herald—New Era, Benicia, 8:285
"Herald of the Gold Rush—
Sam Brannan," by Douglas S. Watson,
10:298-301
Herald of the Morning, Sacramento,
9:170, 181
Herald of the Morning (ship), 15:279
Herald of Truth, 27:9, 17
Hérard, F., 31:317
Herbert, Albert, 29:303
Herbert, Noblet, ". . . to Mrs. John
Augustine Washington," ed.
John A. Washington, 29:297-307
Herbert, Philemon Thomas, 6:9, 32, 33;
14:368, 371; 15:167, 204; 19:261;
21:33; 29:177; 34:126, 127, 130;
38:214-15
Herblay, Émilie de, 25:225, 226, 227
Herbs, 2:152; medicinal use of, 4:149;
15:381; 19:127; 23:204
Hercules (tug), 8:371
Herd, Henry, 16:323, 328
Hereford, Frank, 9:112; 24:170
Hereford, Robert S., 13:319
Hereford, Rockwell, rev. of Kelley,
Gold vs. Grain, 39:181
Heren, James, 24:260
Hergesheimer, Edwin, 23:122
Herman, William, *see* Rulofson,
William Herman
Herman (ship), 9:313; 33:234

Herman-Au, C. E., drawing by, 26: opp. 128; map, 26: opp. 130

Hermance, L., 27:305

Hermann, Alice, 19:230

Hermann, Estelle, 19:230

Hermann, Louisa Clemence, *see* McAllister, Mrs. Hall

Hermann, Lucien, 9:27, 28, 29, 32; 15:173, 275; 19:231-32

Hermann, Samuel, 15:370; 17:174; 19:230

Hermann, Mrs. Samuel (Marie Elizabeth Eugénie de Buys), 34:233

Hermann, William, 40:209

"Hermann Wenzel and His Air Clock," by William Barclay Stephens, 27:1-8

Hermione (ship), 16:283

Hermitage House, San Diego, 31:45

Hermit Valley, 9:333-34; 34:220; illus., 9: opp. 306

Hermosa Mexicana (ship), 14:12; 37:247, 264

Hermosillo, Nicolás, 26:32-33

Hermosillo (ship), 18:6

Hernandez (Yuba Co., 1857), 9:169

Hernández, Alonso, *see* Fernández, Alonso; Hernández Barreda

Hernández, Gonzalo, 3:21; 7:394

Hernández, Pablo, 10:37

Hernandez, Agua de, *see* Resting Springs

Hernández (Maximiliano) & Co., 13:78

Hernández Barreda, Lorenzo (or Alonso), 6:311; 7:20, 55, 70, 76

Hernandez Catoira, Gomez, *see* Catoira

Hernani (play), 20:131

Herne, James A., 4:61; 21:172, 182, 241, 255, 256, 266

Herne, Mrs. James A. (Katharine Corcoran), 21:255, 256, 266

Héroïne (ship), 11:206, 223, 340, 344

Herold, Rudolph, 15:166; 19:236; 22:39; 25:252; 26:71

Heron, A. R., 36:253

Heron, Matilda Agnes, 6:10; 10:75; 20:304; 21:143-44

Heron, Mrs. W. Cochran, 7:105

Héros (ship), 8:132, 134-41, 145, 149, 150, 156, 157, 164-65, 214, 221-22, 224, 232-34, 238, 244-50 *passim*, 330, 331, 333; 12:209

Heroult, Siskiyou Co., 30:344

Herre, W. F., 30:357; 39:151

Herrera, Antonio de, 3:309, 314, 323; 6:305; 7:55-58, 60, 63; 36:24; map by, 7: opp. 186

Herrera, Jesús, 37:201, 204

Herrera, José Joaquín, 1:190; 6:77, 269, 271, 370; 10:111; 18:144, 222, 223

Herrera, José María (Monterey, 1824), 8:151, 163; 12:236-37; 15:341, 350-51, 356, 358; 16:217-19

Herrera, José María (L.A., 1836), 4:159; 13:220

Herreshoff, Constance, 36:153

Herrick (alias Spencer), 10:177

Herrick, Anson, 23:191

Herrick, Bertha F., "Grade-School Grizzly," 25:178-81

Herrick, Byrd, 32:376

Herrick, Mrs. Edwin, 19:232, 238

Herrick, Edwin M., 23:191

Herrick, Ephraim Swan Trow, 26:220, 222, 226-28; 28:322

Herrick, James, 2:205; 7:14

Herrick, Stephen S., 1:110

Herrick, William Francis, 16:84; 20:335; 25:178; 28:322; 29:39, 55; art. on, 26:217-32; port., 26: opp. 217

Herrick, Mrs. William Francis (Lucy Fiennes Kendall), 25:178; 26:228

Herricks' milk ranch (S.F., 1855), 15:376

Herring (Yuba Co., 1857), 9:168

Herron, Walter, 27:352

Herron, William F., 36:48

Herschfeld, H., 16:338

Herschler, J. Barton, 19:320

Hersey, Stephen, 16:4

Hersum, Z. K., 29:291

Hertz (Sacramento, 1850), 12:93

Hertz, Alfred, 25:236, 239-41, 244-46, 248

Herzog, Charles, 31:135

Hescock, David, 21:235

Heslep, Augustus M., 6:9; 26:182

Heslep, Joseph, 15:270

Hesperia Land and Water Co., 27:113

Hesperman (Santa Barbara, 1848), 18:266

Hess, J., 6:10

Hess, Thomas, 8:199, 209, 338, 341, 344, 346, 348; 9:70, 353; 10:171; 28:237

Hesse, Frederick G., 35:255, 272

Hesser, W. C., lawsuit, 9:367; 10:54

Hess's Crossing, *see* Hess, Thomas

Hester, Craven P., 15:278; 29:247; 34:248; 38:49

Hester, Robert A., 29:237, 247

Hester School District, 38:350

Heston, Thomas M., 11:9

Hetch Hetchy Valley, 4:7, 12, 28; 10:204; 11:390; 38:249-58; bk. on, rev., 5:316-17

Hetherington, Joseph, 8:373; 15:158-69, 161; 21:365-66; 24:173-74

Heustis, A. J., 26:171

Hewell (Sacramento, 1859), 10:60

Hewes, David, 10:392; 36:98-99, 106, 272

Hewes, Mrs. David (Anna Maria Lathrop), 10:379, 392

Hewes, Frederick, 21:299, 306; 22:69

Hewett, Adam, 5:125

Hewit, Henry Stewart, 21:107-8, 112; 34:25

Hewitt, Capt. (Colorado R., 1864), 22:170

Hewitt, Andrew, 10:366, 383

Hewitt, Eldridge E., 32:335-36, 341, 346

Hewlett, Mrs. Frederick (Cleora M. Whitney), obit., 10:95-96

Hewlett, Henry, 25:285

Hewlett, Palmer Baker, 1:232

Heydenfeldt, Solomon, 11:8; 15:269; 19:230, 236; 20:261, 272, 366-67, 371; 21:120; 32:145, 148, 157; 34:252

Heyman, Henry, 10:286

Heyman, Katherine Ruth, 10:63

Heyman, Max L., Jr., *Prudent Soldier . . . Major-General E. R. S. Canby*, rev., 39:85-88

Heyneman (mining region, 1859), 11:229, 333

Heyneman, George, 36:77, 157-64 *passim*

Heyneman, Mrs. George (Alice Wangenheim), 35:119, 273, 351; 36:77, 156, 157

Heyneman, Lionel and Lucy (Simon), 35:269

Heyneman (Leonard D.), (Morris) Pick & Co., 10:291

Heywood, Benjamin, 16:82

Heywood's Building, Sacramento, 10:271

Hezeta, Bruno de, 9:201-42, 321, 325, 326; 16: No. 1, Pt. 2, p. 15; 40:110, 114-15, 116, 238

Hezeta, Vicente de, 40:115

"H. H. Haight on National Politics, May 1861," ed. A. Russell Buchanan, 31:193-204

Hiawatha (play), 9:254

Hibben, Thomas N., 29:107(?); 30:365

Hibben & Caswell, 29:107-12 *passim*, 120

Hibben & Co., 30:256

Hibberd, Isaac N., address, "The Sailing Ships' Part in the Development of California," 12:366

Hibernia Savings and Loan Society, 38:26

Hibernicon (panorama show), 21:151

Hibler, George, 5:125

Hichborn, Franklin, 36:252, 253, 254, 258, 259; 37:273, 274, 352; 38:368; 39:82; "The Party, the Machine, and the Vote," 38:349-57; 39:19-34

Hickey, Patrick J., 26:247

Hicklin family, 31:377

Hickman, David H., 24:238

Hickman, James, 2:7

Hickman, Richard, 18:204

Hickman, Richard Owen, *Overland Journey to California*, ed. White, rev., 8:185-86

Hickok (San Jose, 1848), *see* Hecox, Adna A.

Hickok, James Butler (Wild Bill), 10:409; 11:290; 12:178

Hicks, E. H., 7:113; 26:237

Hicks, John Donald, 21:384; 24:93; 31:237, 240; 36:177; "California in History," 24:7-16; as address, 24:184; "History in California," 36:107-16; address, "The Roaring Seventies," 22:84; bk. rev. by, 38:370-71

Hicks, Richard, 6:20, 26-27

Hicks, W. F., 9:263, 345, 354, 370, 385; 10:281, 362, 368

Hicks, William, 20:149; rancho of, 20:100

Hicks, Judd & Co., 31:169

Hidaka Keizaburo Tameyoshi, 23:342

Hidalgo (ship), 22:14, 170

Hidalgo de Montemayor, Gonzalo, 3:310, 363, 366; 19:242-43

Hidalgo y Costilla, Miguel, 18:235, 247; 27:132

Hides and tallow, 2:43; 3:30-31, 169; 5:130, 258; 8:98, 105, 108, 111, 143, 237, 238-49 *passim*, 318, 320, 331; 10:3; 12:194, 290-91, 347, 357; 14:12, 21, 126, 200, 201, 319, 320, 325; 15:114, 118, 226-27, 286; 17:23, 25, 252, 339; 19:204-7 *passim*; 22:319; 23:193-218, 301-34, 372; 28:101, 102, 103, 109,

244-50 *passim;* 37:69, 115-16; arts. on, 6:254-64; 8:209-305 *passim;* 33:59-69

"Hides and Tallow: McCulloch, Hartnell and Co.," by Adele Ogden, 6:254-64

Hiffert, Carrie, 9:388-89; 10:42, 48, 70-71

Higaller, *see* Ali, Hadji

Higbee, James T., 2:203

Higbie (A.) & Co., 30:255

Higby, William, 10:381; 33:206

Higgins (on *Arabian*, 1849), 28:292

Higgins (brothers; Nevada Co., 1850), 13:27

Higgins (Placerville, 1854), 11:58

Higgins, Capt. (Colorado R., 1861), 22:169

Higgins, Charles S., 25:43

Higgins, David, 15:377; 24:170-71

Higgins, Edward (U.S.N., 1846), 25:125, 196

Higgins, Edward (Benicia, 1847), 6:152

Higgins, Elliot, 22:251

Higgins, F. Hal, 26:94

Higgins, George, 30:21, 35

Higgins, George H., 20:272

Higgins, James, 1:116

Higgins, John, 15:123, 240

Higgins, Silas, 14:180

Higgins, William Longinus, 16:81

Higgins' store, West Berkeley, 31:330

Highbinder societies, 27:19-31

Highflyer (ship), 16:182

"High grading," 32:18-20

Highland Springs—Pieta Toll Road, 32:364

Highlanders, *see* Wallace Guards

"Highlights of San Francisco Opera History," address by Lawrence Estavan, 18:376

Hight, D., *see* Hite, Dennis

Hight, Mrs. C. E. (Grace Slover), 30:284-85

Hight, George V. and Nancy, 14:393

Highton, Henry Edward, 27:67

Higley, Horace A., 9:116; 17:42

Higuera, Dolores, 26:35

Higuera, Francisco, 26:36, 37, 42

Higuera, Joaquín, 13:202-3, 207

Higuera, José Manuel, 14:6

Higuera, Leonardo, 26:32

Higuera, Nicolás, 16:241, 351

Hihn, F. A., 38:343

Hijar, José María, 11:342, 347, 353;

12:37, 150, 153; 13:217; 16:237-39; *see also* Hijar-Padrés colony

Hijar, Juan F., *see* Fernández de Hijar

Hijar-Padrés colony, 13:35, 217, 318; 16:100, 236-38; 18:179; 24:293; 29:26; 36:9

Hi Jolly, *see* Ali, Hadji

"Hilachas, Las," 26:33

Hildebrand, Joel Henry, 17: No. 4, Pt. 2, p. 3; "A Word Concerning Professor Colin G. Fink," 17: No. 4, Pt. 2, p. 27

Hildebrant (Marysville, 1858), 9:346, 347

Hildreth (RR supt., 1871), 18:31

Hildreth, George and Thaddeus, 24:269

Hildreth Diggings, 24:269; *see also* Columbia

Hiler, Hilaire, 38:3

Hilgard, Eugene Waldemar, 20:270; 31:337, 339; 33:60; 38:220

Hill (Sacramento, 1856), 20:367

Hill, Albert A., 10:62, 70

Hill, Barton, 21:245, 248

Hill, Mrs. Chelton (Adaline Blood), 30:285

Hill, C. Wilson, 9:386

Hill, Daniel Antonio, 2:255; 4:157; 12:18-19; 18:161-62, 164, 174-75; 23:196, 208, 217

Hill, Mrs. Daniel Antonio (Rafaela Olivera de Ortega), 12:19; 18:174; 23:217

Hill, E. K., 8:356

Hill, H. Stanton, obit. of Edwin V. Van Amringe, 36:184-85

Hill, Henry, fac. sig., 10: opp. 159

Hill, Hiram Morgan, 13:192

Hill, J. B., 32:52-53

Hill, James, 13:32

Hill, James Madison, 13:32

Hill, John H., 10:271, 273, 275, 288, 372

Hill, Joseph John, 10:88; *History of Warner's Ranch*, rev., 7:86-87

Hill, Laurance Landreth, *El Pueblo, Los Angeles*, rev., 7:93-94; *La Reina, Los Angeles*, rev., 8:88

Hill, R. D., 9:256, 269

Hill, Roy, 25:285; 27:185; "Mexican Insurgent Provisional Coinage," 27:132

Hill, Samuel, 15:76

Hill, Sarah Althea, 9:270

Hill, Thomas (artist), 3:398; 24:265, 266; 30:139; 37:22-23, 32

Hill, Tom (Indian), 25:139-48; 29:337-38, 339
Hill, W. H., 32:9
Hill, Werner, 24:37
Hill, William, 21:228, 235
Hill, William H., 9:255, 269, 355, 386
Hill, William Henry, 9:371, 394; 10:64, 296
Hill & Stillman, 15:170
Hilland (Hillard?; on *Westward Ho*, 1853), 28:322
Hillegass, G. W., 39:247
Hiller, Dr. (Virginia City, 1875), 11:64
Hiller, Baron Fritz von, 38:343-47
Hillhouse, J., 4:310
Hillman, James H., 31:151
Hillman, Rhuben, 2:122
Hillman & Co., 30:363
Hillman's Hotel, San Francisco, 15:272; Temperance House, 16:342; 22:263
Hill's Bar, Fraser R., 6:20, 21, 24, 25-30
Hill's Ferry, 35:125, 137, 138
Hillyear, Capt. (Colorado R., 1864), 22:170
Hillyer, Curtis J., 2:205
Hillyer, E. W., 2:205
Hillyer family, 29:102, 105
Hilsee, Agnes W. (or T.), *see* Winn, Mrs. Adolphus G.
Hilsee, Joseph Warren, 13:92; 28:94
Hilsee, Katharine, 13:92
Hilton, George W., coauth. *The Electric Interurban Railways in America*, rev., 39:374-75
Himes, George H., 19:77
Hinchman, *see* Banning & Hinchman
Hinckley, Rev. Mr. (Del Norte Co., 1863), 26:9
Hinckley, Askins (or Atkins), 9:268, 350, 357, 360, 361
Hinckley, J. C., 27:97, 99, 101
Hinckley, Lillian, 35:305
Hinckley, Lyman F. (T.?), 21:306
Hinckley, Sarah ("Sallie"), 21:157
Hinckley, Theodore Charles, 37:188; "Pomona's Call to Fame," 37:171-79
Hinckley, Thomas D., 14:316, 342; 35:196
Hinckley, William Crawley, 29:253, 254
Hinckley, William Sturgis, 1:92; 3:33; 5:308; 8:299; 11:71, 135; 12:138, 146; 14:124-27, 230, 315-22 *passim*, 330, 332, 341-42; 15:339, 341, 349, 353, 358; 17:169, 172, 294, 295, 301; 18:67, 70;
23:302, 312, 319, 327, 330-34 *passim;* 28:253, 257, 265, 266; 29:132, 271; 30:98; 35:196, 199-200
Hinckley, Mrs. William Sturgis (Susana Martínez), 11:135, 142; 14:342; 17:295
Hinds, Ralph M., 23:191
Hinds, Richard Brinsley, 18:344
Hinds, Thomas W., 23:191
Hines, Benjamin S., 10:62, 70
Hines, William, 22:251
Hing Chuen Yuen (Chinese theater), 23:111-12
Hinkle, George, 23:383; "Samurai in San Francisco: The Japanese Embassy of 1860," 23:335-47
Hinkle, George Bell, 23:383
Hinman, Alanson, 4:326
Hinman, H. D., 17:76, 79
Hinrichsen, Kenneth C., 28:379
Hinton, John, 36:120, 123-24, 125
Hinton, W. M., 39:151
Hioh (Indian, 1579), 16: No. 1, Pt. 2, pp. 7-13, 29, 39
Hipólito, 12:114, 117, 119-21
Hippolyte (Santa Clara Co., 1850), rancho of, 5:357
"Hiram Gano Ferris of Illinois and California," by Joel E. Ferris, 26:289-307
Hirsch, George, 26:204
Hiscox, T. S., 13:31
Hispanic Society of America, 11:286
"Historical Aspects of Tobacco Culture in California," by Robert Hammond, 40:97-107
"Historical Flags of California," address and film by Phil T. Hanna, 16:187-88
Historical Memoirs of New California, by Palou, ed. Bolton, rev., 6:375
Historical Sketch of Los Angeles County, California, 13:350-51
Historical Society of Southern California Topical Index ... 1884-1957, comp. by Hager and Hager, rev., 40:259-60
Historical Society of the State of California, 1:9; 16:200
"Historical Writings on the California Chinese," address by William Hoy, 20:282
"Historic Columbia," address by Joseph R. Knowland, 28:276-77
"Historic Mt. St. Helena," by Honoria Tuomey, 3:171-77

"Historic, Reminiscent, and
Otherwise," address by
Frank L. Coombs, 7:289

"Historic Spots Marked by the Native
Sons of the Golden West," address
by Joseph R. Knowland, 2:368-69

History Company, 29:359-60

"History in California," by
John D. Hicks, 36:107-16

"History in Your Own Backyard:
Digging History Out of Journalism,"
by Glenn S. Dumke, 38:131-40

"History of a Montgomery Street Lot,"
by Thomas P. Burns, 11:69-72

History of California Newspapers, by
Kemble, rev., 7:286

*History of California: The American
Period,* by Cleland, rev., 1:302-3

*History of California: The Spanish
Period,* by Chapman, rev., 1:194-97

"History of Golden Gate Park," address
by Alice Eastwood, 8:137

"History of Las Posadas Forest," from
memoirs of John M. Morris, comp.
Edith Gregory, 35:1-9, 155-60

"History of San Quentin Prison,"
address by Leo L. Stanley, 13:88

"History of the Book Trade in
California, 1849-1859," by
Hugh S. C. Baker, 30:97-115, 249-67,
353-67

*History of the Mission, Presidio and
Pueblo of Sonoma,* by Tuomey and
Emparan, rev., 2:364-65

"History of the Oil Industry in
California," address by
Edmond O'Neill, 8:386

*History of the San Francisco
Committee of Vigilance of 1851,* by
Williams, rev., 1:99-101

"History of the Sutro Tunnel," address
by David Davies, 20:83

History of Warner's Ranch, by Hill,
rev., 7:86-87

Hitchcock (overland guide, 1844),
4:333, 346

Hitchcock (Sutter's Ft., 1846),
22:221

Hitchcock, Charles McPhail, 9:100,
101; 34:32, 36

Hitchcock, Mrs. Charles McPhail
(Martha Taliafero), 19:229, 230, 232

Hitchcock, Ethan Allen, 10:410;
20:259; 28:199, 204, 205, 215, 216,
224, 225, 340; 30:249; 38:300

Hitchcock, George B., 5:104; 30:113;
see also Marvin & Hitchcock

Hitchcock, John L., obit., 5:104-5

Hitchcock, Lillie, *see*
Coit, Mrs. Howard

Hitchcock, R. B., 3:116, 117; 17:338

Hitchens, James, 9:250, 252, 268, 372-73;
10:177, 182, 183, 189, 246, 247, 281;
18:199-200, 206, 209, 216

Hitchens' Spring, 18:200, 209

Hite (Yosemite, 1856), 5:337

Hite, Dennis, 33:298, 299, 303

Hite, Levi, 9:109; 10:170, 193, 251

Hitt, William W., 24:38, 45, 117

Hittell, Mrs. Emily C., 31:342

Hittell, Franklin, 24:372

Hittell, Mrs. Franklin, 24:372; 30:114

Hittell, John Shertzer, 1:208; 8:362;
13:349; 15:172; 18:280; 22:36, 38-39;
24:106, 107, 112, 372; 26:131, 133;
27:169; 28:2-3; 29:227; 30:103, 137,
149, 252, 254, 255, 356; 31:208; 36:355;
38:300, 301

Hittell, Theodore Henry, 1:15, 17, 22;
2:247, 251, 350-51; 4:53; 6:217-18;
24:80; 31:342; 32:264; 33:373; 36:355

Hittell, Mrs. Theodore Henry
(Elise Christine Wiehe), 31:335, 336,
337, 342

Hixson, Jasper Morris, 19:288

Hixson, Morris C., 19:288

Hi-ye the Usurper (play), 23:104

Hizaliturri, Pedro, 37:204

H.M.S. Pinafore (operetta), 35:142

Hoadley, George E., 17:172

Hoadley (Miles) map, 25:321

Hoar, Edward, 34:42

Hobart, Edgar, 1:107, 110

Hobart, J. A., 9:268; 31:333

Hobart, J. H., 31:325

Hobart, Walter, 20:181, 184

Hobbs (Yuba Co., 1857), 9:155

Hobbs, Caleb S., 22:14, 23

Hobbs, Hannah, 34:43; letters to,
33:44-48

Hobbs, M., 25:252

Hobrecht, Augustine, 31:280; addresses:
"The Architecture of the Santa
Barbara Mission," 5:414-15;
"Fray Junípero Serra," 11:189

Hobson (Warm Springs, 1861), 10:358

Hobson, Cross, 8:271, 272

Hobson, George, 37:13

Hobson, Hadley, 23:383

Hobson, Joseph, fac. sig., 10: opp. 159

Hoburg, William Helmer, 26:94
Hochgesangt, Ch., 22:297; 23:66; & Co., 23:62
Hock Farm, 1:134; 6:240-41; 8:24, 168-74 *passim*, 181, 199; 10:177, 199; 11:112-13; 12:301; 19:118, 137; 20:120; 26:131; 29:300; 33:292, 317; illus., 6: opp. 239, opp. 240
Hodden (S.F., 1850), 5:38
Hodgdon (Sacramento, 1858), 9:245; 10:48
Hodge (Yuba Co., 1856), 9:65, 156, 162
Hodge, Mrs. (Youngs Hill, 1860), 10:256
Hodge, A. C., 30:112
Hodge, Frederick Webb, 32:97-98
Hodge, H. C., 30:266
Hodge, John G., 29:254; 30:264; *see also* Hodge & Wood; Le Count & Strong
Hodge (John G.) & (Frank S.) Wood, 29:103, 124-25, 253, 254
Hodge (Orrin W.) *v.* Jonathan Hayden, 9:135, 136, 140
Hodges (Feather R., 1851), 27:193
Hodges, Alpheus P., 13:310, 319(?), 335
Hodges, Frank, 11:165, 171
Hodges, Orlando J., recollections: "Prospecting on the Pacific Coast, 1848-1864," ed. William F. Zornow, 33:49-58
Hodges, Thomas J., *see* Bell, Tom
Hodgkins, W., 13:32
Hodson, Georgia, 10:196, 265
Hoehn, Charles, 22:94
Hoelscher (Marysville, 1858), 33:67
Hoepkin, Albert, 15:277
Hoeppner, Andrew, 13:35, 36, 37; 17:166, 297
Hoey, Michael, 3:118
Hoff, Miss (S.F., 1862), 10:378, 379
Hoff, John J., 9:109; 15:281; 40:205, 209
Hoff, William C., 15:370
Hoffman (w. Kotzebue, 1824), 12:208
Hoffman, Abe, "A Look at Llano: Experiment in Economic Socialism," 40:215-36
Hoffman, Alice Colden, 25:285
Hoffman, D. B., 4:169
Hoffman, Ogden, Jr., 9:318, 320; 10:72; 14:75; 15:6-7, 164, 169, 368; 16:285; 19:165, 230, 236, 266; 20:111-12, 269; 22:28; 27:136, 139; 31:150; 34:257; 35:321

Hoffman, Victor, 16:347; 38:34
Hoffman, William, 29:118, 120
Hoffman, Col. William, 38:25
Hoffmann, Charles F., 4:16-23 *passim*, 32, 55; 7:121, 126, 127; 9:401
Hoffmann, Joseph Casimir, 25:236
Hoffmann, Mount, 4:23, 28, 36
Hofmann, Joseph A., 28:12
Hogan, John, 15:267; 16:83
Hogan, Mrs. John (Hattie Clay), 10:170
Hogan, John C., 36:93; coauth. "The Last Will and Testament of Stephen J. Field," 36:41-55
Hogan, Michael and Mary Ann, 25:340
Hogarth *et al. v.* McAllis *et al.*, 10:273
Hog Canyon, 11:243
Hoge, Frances (Mrs. Tyler), 10:295, 374, 377
Hoge, Joseph P., 10:266, 269, 279, 281-82, 295, 367, 374, 376, 380, 393; 20:156
Hoge, Josephine, 10:295, 374, 377
Hoge, Mary, 10:281, 374, 377, 378, 379
Hoge, Pauline, 10:258, 269, 276-82 *passim*, 295, 377, 379
Hoge & Wilson, 40: foll. 206
Hogeboom, Lawrence V., 29:291
Hogg (1855), 4:15
Hogg, Thomas Egenton, 27:179
Hogg, Will, 31:63
Hogs, *see* Swine
Hogthorp, Capt. (Colorado R., 1873), 22:174
Hogue, A. H., 4:51
Hohfeld, Edward, 22:94
Holbrook (S.F., 1855), 16:79
Holbrook, Charles, 6:349; 27:5; 37:181
Holbrook, Mrs. Charles (Susan Hurd), 37:181
Holbrook, J. C., 14:78
Holbrook, James E., 24:287
Holbrook, Mary Hurd, 22:93
Holbrook, Olive, *see* Palmer, Mrs. Silas H.
Holbrook, Samuel F., 22:277
Holbrook, Washington, 37:237
Holbrook, William A., 23:206
Holbrook, Merrill & Stetson, 6:349
Holcomb, Breed and Bancroft, 28:14
Holcombe & Doyle (Holcombe Bros.), 33:68
Holcomb Valley, 24:275; 27:122
Hold, Larkin, 9:146

Holdaway, Shadrach, 14:269, 270, 271, 278-79, 280

Holdaway family, 14:269-70

Holden, E. D., "California's First Pianos," 13:34-37; ed. "Condemned Bar in 1849," 12:312-17

Holden, Edward Singleton, 1:13; 2:263; 21:183; 24:79; 35:256, 259, 260

Holden, Erastus Saurin, 4:24, 234; 7:10; "Condemned Bar in 1849," excerpt from Journal, ed. E. D. Holden, 12:312-17

Holden, Mrs. Erastus Saurin (1, Jane Dana), 12:312; (2, Mary Maria Lyon), 12:313

Holden, William, 10:62, 375, 377, 388

Holden's Station, 9:333-34

Holder, Charles Frederick, 31:17, 29

Holder, Warren J., 34:169

Holding, D. M., 13:31-32

Holdman, Dr. (on *Golden Gate*, 1853), 34:35

Holdredge, H. G., 30:137

Holeman, Jacob H., 26:347

Holenleek, Mrs. (Mormon, 1852), 14:177

Holinski, Alexandre J. J., 22:253-54, 255, 262-72 *passim*

Holladay, Ben, 12:323; 15:328; 33:206; 38:52

Holladay, Edmund Burke, 2:204; 23:287

Holladay, Samuel W., 2:204; 9:248, 249, 260; 27:346; 31:302; 33:373

Holladay and Brenham, 16:67, 68

Holladay Hill, 31:302

Holland, Dr. (on *Golden Age*, 1866), 36:302

Holland, Alexander, 2:216

Holland, B. E., 15:181

Holland, Edward, 6:36

Holland, F. S., 6:152

Holland, Franklin W., 29:91

Holland, Frank Sargent and Alice (Conmy), 29:91

Holland, Nathaniel, 16:81, 84

Holland, Mrs. Nathaniel, 36:208, 212

Holland, Robert and Isabel, 16:298, 303

Holland (A.) *et al. v.* City of San Francisco, 17:182

Holland Colony, 25:173

Holle, Rebecca, 28:294

Holley, M. W., 22:251

Holliday, W. B., 29:226

Holliday, Mrs. W. B. (Louise Cretigny), 29:225-26

Holliday, W. J., 25:191

Holliday, William, 24:168

Hollingsworth (Paris, 1867), 31:223

Hollingsworth, John McHenry, 13:207; 20:114-15; 26:40, 59; 27:110; 29:31, 35, 37; 33:254, 260-61, 337-38, 341-43, 373; 34:22; Journal, ed. H. R. Wagner, 1:207-70; drawing by, 1:203; fac. sig., 10: opp. 159

Hollis (Marysville, 1859), 30:128

Hollis, B. F., 9:391

Hollister, John James and Lottie Steffens), 25:285; 27:287

Hollister, William Welles, 24:207-11, 217, 219; 25:36, 285; 27:70-71, 73, 287; 31:286

Holman, Alfred, 1:19; 30:195; obit., 10:96

Holman, Francis A., 17:176

Holman, G. C., 9:269; 10:62

Holman, Mrs. Zena G., 24:381

Holmes (via Mex., 1850), 1:60

Holmes, Capt. (Colorado R., 1856), 22:169

Holmes, Ahira, 16:284

Holmes, Eliza, 28:293

Holmes, Ellis H., 14:75; 16:283

Holmes, F., 40:211

Holmes, H. T., 33:333

Holmes, Harold Charles, 6:192-93; 31:284; obits. of Mrs. Ebenezer Jamieson, 13:92; William W. Winn, 39:177-78

Holmes, Henry, 25:229

Holmes, Mrs. Horace T. (Viola Zarelda Frisby), 29:326

Holmes, Isaac Edward, 34:246-48

Holmes, John, 9:160; lawsuit, 9:130, 166

Holmes, John Andrew Christian, 23:205, 206, 216, 302, 330

Holmes, Jonathan, 14:278, 280

Holmes, L. A., 1:283

Holmes, Oliver Wendell, 31:239

Holmes, Rachel (Hobson), *see* Larkin, Mrs. Thomas Oliver

Holmes, Samuel A., 25:24

Holohan, James B., 39:21

Holt, Col. and Mrs. (S.F., 1850s), 19:236

Holt (Tuolumne Co., 1852), 11:165

Holt, Emerson, 22:286

Holt, George, 6:235

Holt, J. F., 11:152
Holt, Samuel, 6:235
Holt, Thomas H., 9:27
Holt Manufacturing Co., 31:89
Holton, E. D., 31:19
Holton, Isaac, 26:290
Holway, Mary (Gordon), *Art of the Old World in New Spain and the Mission Days of Alta California,* rev., 2:173-77
Holy Cross Cemetery, 32:261
Homan, M., 22:251
Homeier, Louis, 25:236; 28:382
Homeier, Max and Katherine, 28:382
Home Journal, New York, 28:216, 230
Homem, André, 11:44; map by, 11:44-46, reprod. opp. 44
Homem, Diego (Diogo) de, 11:44; maps by, 3:312-13, 382-86 *passim;* fac., 3:383
Homem, Lopo, 11:44-45
Home Mutual Insurance Co., 26:355; 27:270, 332
Home of Rest Sanatorium, 31:15
Homer ("Nova Scotia"; S.F., 1850), 8:269, 272
Homer mining district, 4:39
Homesteading, 19:178; 24:112, 113, 177; 32:322; bills and laws, 19:178-79, 256, 258; 24:193; 26:211; 38:331-32; *see also* Lands: public; Squatters
Homfrey, de (S.F., 1850), 5:39-40
Honcut City, 9:69; 10:194
Honcut Creek, 8:340, 356; 9:52; 10:172-73, 194; 14:196, 205, 206, 375, 389
Honcut House, Yuba Co., 10:56, 172, 194
Honcut Ranch, *see* Ranchos: Honcut
Hondius, Jodocus, 36:26; broadside, 36:25-27
" 'Honest Harry' Meiggs," by Mary M. Harker, 17:195-207
Honey Lake and Valley, 7:13, 16, 17; 9:165, 180; 10:74; 12:326; 18:303-9 *passim;* 21:225-38 *passim;* 29:100, 381; 39:264
Honey Lake Irrigation Co., 29:100
Honey Lake Valley Land and Water Co., 29:359, 361-62
Honeyman, Francis, 34:326
Honey Moon (play), 9:245
Hong Kong, 15:372; 26:363; 32:216
Honolulu (ship), 14:333, 337, 342; 23:358; 28:289

Hood, William, 4:250
Hood *v.* Fish & Williams, 15:183
Hoogs, Octavian, 6:44-45; 26:229; 32:107; 39:11-12
Hook, George W., 9:46
Hooke (Hawkins Bar, 1853), 11:170
Hooker, Charles Gay and May (Osgood), 29:92
Hooker, Joseph, 10:198; 11:365-66; 16:195; 19:3; 24:59, 62; 33:206, 216; art. on, 16:304-20; phot., 16: opp. 304
Hooker, Osgood, 29:91-92
Hooker, Sir William J., 18:339
Hooker & Co., 15:76
Hooker Guards, 38:22
Hooley, Richard M., 20:305; 21:41, 42, 172-75 *passim,* 182, 265
Hooley Comedy Company, 21:172, 173-74, 250, 254
Hoopa Valley, 20:349, 351, 363
Hooper (Manila, 1898), 31:59
Hooper, Albert Campbell, 31:295, 299, 302; 37:217
Hooper, Alice Maud, 31:302
Hooper, Arthur Appleton, 31:300
Hooper, Arthur Willard, 31:299, 303; foreword to "John Albert Hooper," 31:289
Hooper, Mrs. Arthur Willard (Josephine Hannigan), 31:303
Hooper, C. A., 12:33
Hooper, Charles Appleton, 31:291, 298-300, 340-41
Hooper, E., 11:127
Hooper, Franklin Perry, 31:291, 294, 298, 300, 303
Hooper, George F., 31:36, 37, 38; 32:191
Hooper, George Williams, 31:298, 300
Hooper, Isabel (Mrs. Wigginton Creed), 31:300, 340, 341
Hooper, Isabel (Mrs. William E. Norwood), 31:300
Hooper, J. E., 22:251
Hooper, Jeannette Stanwood, 31:302
Hooper, Jessie Appleton, 31:302; *see also* Greaves, Mrs. Thomas T.
Hooper, John, 31:289-91, 300
Hooper, Mrs. John (Martha Stanwood Perry), 31:290, 300
Hooper, John Albert, 25:285, 286; art. on, 31:289-305; phot., 31: opp. 289

Hooper, Mrs. John Albert, 31:292, 299, 300, 302

Hooper, Joseph G. and Mary (Pardow), 32:191

Hooper, Mary McIntyre, 31:302; 37:217

Hooper, R. H., 13:296

Hooper, Samuel, 19:48-49, 53, 56; 23:201, 215

Hooper, Thomas T., 2:128

Hooper, William B. (Ariz., 1860s), 22:151-52, 157

Hooper, William B. (S.F., 1887), 17:36, 40; 32:57

Hooper, William H. (from Cincinnati, 1850), 22:384

Hooper, William H. (S.F., 1851), 28:116

Hooper, William Horace, 31:290, 291, 300

Hooper family, 31:299, 302-3

Hooper Lumber Co., 31:294, 303

Hoose, James H., 37:42-43

Hoover, Daniel, 15:185

Hoover, Herbert, 2:68; 24:11; 28:280; 34:331; 36:113

Hoover, Mrs. I. J., 32:167-68

Hoover, Mildred Crew (Brooke), address, "Recent Visits to Old Ranchos," 16:380; obit. of Mrs. James P. Smith, 17:191-92; obit., 19:287

Hoover, Theodore Jesse, 22:94-95; obit., 35:179-80

Hoover, Mrs. Theodore Jesse, *see* Hoover, Mildred Crew (Brooke)

Hoover Dam, 36:219

Hoover-Young Commission, 30:343

Hope, Ada, 21:172

Hope, Alexander W., 13:329; 29:234, 246; 34:21, 30, 38

Hope, Jacob H., 31:20

Hope, Thomas R., 15:173

Hope (schr. 1848), 18:177

Hope (bark, 1849), 4:195; 23:149-56 *passim*, 162; 33:316, 319

Hope Company, 23:150-51; 158-65 *passim*

Hope Ranch, Santa Barbara, 31:298

Hope Valley, 7:7, 8, 9, 12; 12:325; 34:220

Hopewell (ship), 21:224; 25:303

Hopkins (on *Glencoe*, 1849-50), 11:157

Hopkins, Judge (S.F., 1850), 26:339

Hopkins (Yuba Co., 1856), 9:65, 67, 135, 141, 168

Hopkins, Caspar Thomas, 24:108-12 *passim;* "California Recollections," 25:97-120, 255-66, 325-46; 26:63-75, 175-83, 253-66, 351-63; 27:65-73, 165-74, 267-74, 339-51; 28:169; phot., 26: opp. 63; family of, 27:342

Hopkins, Mrs. Caspar Thomas (Almira Burtnett), 26:71, 176, 260, 353, 359, 360; 27:72, 73, 267, 342

Hopkins, Charles, 14:164; 15:169, 266

Hopkins, Edward Whiting, obit., 5:105-6

Hopkins, Frank, 15:76

Hopkins, George W., 14:394

Hopkins, James, 8:205, 341

Hopkins, Joseph, 9:109; 15:281, 364

Hopkins, L. B., 7:118

Hopkins, Mark, 4:219, 245-46, 260, 261; 5:105; 9:36; 15:76, 97, 98; 18:24; 26:181; 38:311, 352; letters from Stanford, 1867-69, 5:178-83

Hopkins, Mrs. Mark (Mary Frances Sherwood), 19:234, 238; 36:200

Hopkins, Mortimer, 20:271

Hopkins, Myra, 25:103; 27:347-48, 351

Hopkins, R. R., 14:61, 69, 178

Hopkins, Robert, 16:306; 24:58

Hopkins, Rufus C., 21:312

Hopkins, Sarah (Winnemucca), 38:153-54

Hopkins, Sheldon U., 25:332-34, 337, 344

Hopkins, Sterling A., 6:11; 9:270; 15:86, 146, 148-50, 156-57; 21:27-28, 36; 24:174; illus., 6: opp. 3; 15: opp. 143

Hopkins, Thomas, 22:114

Hopkins, Timothy, 5:178; 32:191; obit., 15:97-98

Hopkins, W. H., 10:365

Hopkins, William, 26:171

Hopkins Creek, 29:304

Hoppe, Jacob D., 2:205; 10:152, 155; 12:351; 20:46; 26:332-33; 28:195-96; 29:56; 34:22

Hopper, Charles, 16:126, 133-40 *passim*, 143; 18:33

Hopper, David, 16:136

Hopper, Mrs. De Wolf (Edna Wallace), 21:266

Hopper, James Marie, 40:149, 155

Hopper, John, 19:127

Hopper, Thomas, 16:135-36; 19:127

Hopper, William, 22:62
Hopper family, 16:136
Hops, 17:176
Hop Sing Tong, 27:27
Hoquiam Lumber & Shingle Co.,
　31:295
Horan, Michel, 2:122
Horcasitas (ship), 10:317
Horizon (play), 34:360
Horn, B. C., 15:276
Horn, Benjamin, 19:232
Horn, Eph, 15:368; 20:304, 305
Horn, George, 22:37
Horn, Thomas Lodowick, 15:276
Horn, Cape, 1:223; 2:101; 4:153;
　18:375; 19:324; 20:26, 203-5; 22:240;
　28:315-16; 30:19
Horn, Cape, on American R., 18:355,
　357, 367
Hornby, Robert A., 25:286
Horner, I. N., 14:164
Horner, John Miers, 12:173; 14:175,
　176, 177, 182; 30:12; 33:302; 37:236
Horner, Joseph, 14:176
Horner, William Yates, 14:176
Hornet (ship), 15:364
Horning, Walter, 25:233
Hornswoggle Ravine, 8:349
Horrible Club, Virginia City, 9:312
Horsemanship, 1:225-26; 2:267, 279;
　6:249; 8:153; 19:205; 25:290
"Horse Marines: California, 1846,"
　by George W. Ames, Jr., 18:72-84
Horse racing, 7:395; 9:147-56 *passim*,
　159, 265, 286, 354; 10:176, 198, 251,
　264, 296, 360, 361, 414; 13:215, 322-23;
　14:155; 15:48-49, 170, 185, 227, 276,
　367, 374; 17:255; 21:123; 27:222, 223;
　31:331; *see also* Race horses; Race
　tracks
Horses, 1:116, 117, 134, 165; 2:41-42,
　184, 277, 279, 283, 295, 321, 322;
　5:217, 249, 273, 274, 367; 8:113, 156,
　237, 334, 342; 12:167, 193, 249, 251,
　260, 262, 274, 283, 286-87; 13:202,
　204, 257-58; 14:5, 6, 9, 199, 320;
　15:177; 16:118, 119, 242; 17:43, 176,
　331; 18:72, 77, 78, 159, 256, 271;
　19:120, 185, 196, 199, 203-11 *passim*;
　21:1, 3, 6, 196, 198, 215, 216, 220, 333,
　342, 356; 22:52, 270, 274, 341, 344;
　23:21, 252, 253, 259, 263, 330, 332,
　357-65 *passim*; 23:153, 330; 24:230;
　28:41, 46; 29:255, 338; 33:344, 345;
　38:142-43, 261, 266-68; breaking of,
38:266, 267, 341-42; trade in,
　10:27-39; 20:341-46 *passim*; wild,
　2:200; 5:127, 130; 6:249; 12:286;
　19:203; 20:346; 21:337; *see also*
　Horsemanship; Horse racing; Horse
　thieves; Race horses; Race tracks
Horse Shoe Bar, 19:146
Horseshoe Bend (on Mid. Yuba),
　28:234, 241
"Horseshoe Bill," 6:16-17
Horsethief Canyon, 12:123
"Horsethief Jack," 39:298
Horse thieves, 1:115, 117, 122, 250;
　3:273; 4:313, 314, 315; 5:77-78, 134;
　8:120; 10:29-38 *passim*, 398; 11:356;
　16:57, 245, 246, 360; 18:78; 20:343;
　21:1, 12; 22:200, 333, 344; 23:36, 38,
　123-29 *passim*, 138
Horsetown, 20:255
Horshoe Bend (nr. S.F.), 6:16, 18
Hort, Samuel, 29:254
Hortensia (ship), 31:35
Horton, Capt. (of *Honolulu*), 23:358
Horton, Alonzo Erastus, 31:39
Hosford, C. O., 26:167-68; 28:290, 292
Hosford, Mrs. C. O. (Aseneth
　Glover), 26:168; 28:292
Hoskin deflector, 29:206-7
Hosley, Mrs. Mary A., 28:294
Hosmer, Alvin, 13:3, 28
Hosmer, Charles, 17:177
Hosmer, H. B., 9:26, 29
"Hospice, The," 22:251; 23:247-58
" 'Hospice, The,' or 'Mission San
　Mateo,' " by Frank M. Stanger,
　23:247-58
Hospitals: first in Calif., 4:144; 33:103;
　in mining camps, 4:180-81; 6:243;
　24:354; in Marysville, 14:396;
　Sacramento, 4:189-90; 24:355; San
　Francisco, 4:189-90, 206; 6:41;
　15:280; 16:283, 337; 19:153; 23:148;
　29:170-71 (*see also* Marine Hospital);
　Vernon, 4:204; Yuba County, 10:393
Hossefross, George H., 8:366; 15:170,
　311; 23:69-77
Hostetter (S.F., 1870), 14:395
Hotaling, Anson Parsons, 30:344
Hotaling, Richard, 32:237
Hotchkis, Finlay Montgomery and
　Katherine (Preston), 23:95
Hotchkis, Preston, 23:95
Hotchkis, Mrs. Preston (Katharine
　Bixby), 40:365, 366

Hotchkiss, Charles F., 12:94, 96; 22:242, 243

Hotchkiss, Edward, 23:370; 24:383; 33:373; "California Letters," ed. Helen Throop Pratt, 12:91-110; port., 12: opp. 91

Hotchkiss, George, 12:92

Hotchkiss, Leonard, 12:93-94, 100, 104; 22:243, 251

Hotel d'Afrique (minstrel show), 20:305

Hotel de Bordeaux, San Jose, 14:156

Hotel de France, Marysville, 14:395; 15:49

Hotel de France, Sonora, 11:169

Hotel del Coronado, 31:156

Hotel Del Monte, 20:137

Hotel de Redwood, 38:344

Hotel des Deux Mondes, San Francisco, 5:345, 346, 349; 6:37

Hotel Deuxchands, San Francisco, 14:140

Hotel de Ville, San Francisco, 34:42

Hotel Du Nord, Marysville, 10:285

Hotel Mondelet, San Francisco, 5:349

Hotel Richelieu, San Francisco, 6:51, 56, 57

Hotels: in Marysville, 24:348; in the mountains, 20:251, 254; in San Francisco, 22:263-64; *see also* names of hotels

Hot-ponds, 39:118

Hot springs: nr. Alturas, 22:207; Matilija, 17:32, 40; nr. Mission San Miguel, 15:235; in Nev., 32:203, 206; in Ore., 22:205, 215; nr. Sonoma, 13:37; *see also* Geysers; Mud springs; Warm Springs

Houck, James, 5:125

Hough, J. A., 22:122-23, 125, 147

Houghtaling, Edward, 9:64, 65, 77, 144; lawsuits, 9: 166, 167

Houghton, Edith V. (Chapman), 28:54

Houghton, H., 9:36; 10:63

Houghton, James F., 26:240; 30:134-35

Houghton, Sherman O., 10:267; 19:139

Houghton, Mrs. Sherman O. (1, Mary M. Donner; 2, Eliza P. Donner), 19:139

Houlding, E. W., 26:163

"Hounds," 1:100; 3:39; 19:4, 167, 168, 184; 27:106, 263, 264, 266, 358-61 *passim*, 368; 28:152; 29:161-65,

168-70; 30:208, 209; 32:294, 297; 34:231

Houqua (ship), 14:127

"Hour's Walk through Yerba Buena, An," by Douglas S. Watson, 17:291-302

House, Gilbert, 13:258

House, Oaks R., 12:29

Housely, F. James, 25:251

House of David, 2:240-41

Houser, Duncan H., 9:265, 266, 286

Houses, prefabricated, 8:326-27; 13:357; 30:24; 31:35; iron or zinc, 7:398-404 *passim*; 8:25, 170, 263, 265, 270, 275; 13:357; 14:215; 25:259, 266; 29:15; 32:269-70; 38:39, 41; 39:110; from Belgium, 32:269-70; from China, 7:404; 8:169-73 *passim*; 11:179; 26:75; 38:41; from England, 38:41; from France, 22:303, 309, 314; from Honolulu, 30:209; from the U.S., 8:173, 175; 11:158; 27:14; 30:159; 31:35, 36; 38:41-42

Houston, Alexander H., 5:179; 26:260, 266

Houston, John S., 13:32

Houston, Sam, 9:263, 285; 19:272-73, 344, 345

Hoution (S.F., 1860), 29:118-19

Howard (Auburn, 1850s), 9:393

Howard, Mr. and Mrs. (Timbuctoo, 1858), 9:375

Howard, Abraham, 27:255, 328, 329

Howard, Agnes, 27:319

Howard, Charles B., 35:29-34

Howard, Claude, 34:166

Howard, D. N., 14:164

Howard, Edward H., 17:179

Howard, Edward Whiting, 27:105, 254-55, 319

Howard, Fannie, 16:183; 21:63

Howard, Charles Webb, 19:230, 231; 21:380; 31:377

Howard, Frederick, 27:249

Howard, Frederick Paxson, obit., 21:380

Howard, Mrs. Frederick Paxson, 24:183, 373

Howard, George Henry, 26:264; 27:107-8, 109-10, 252, 254, 319-32 *passim*; 32:376

Howard, Mrs. George Henry, *see* Howard, Mrs. William Davis Merry

Howard, George Henry, Jr., 27:254, 255

Howard, J. L., 9:36; 13:32
Howard, James, 10:267
Howard, James B., 15:53, 57
Howard, Jean, *see*
　McDuffie, Mrs. Duncan
Howard, John Galen, 22:187; 35:182
Howard, John L. and Anna
　(Finlayson), 34:182
Howard, John Kenneth, 27:319
Howard, Joseph Henry Poett, 27:319
Howard, Oliver D., 16:315, 318; 32:234
Howard, Robert, 38:4
Howard, Sidney Coe, obit., 18:287
Howard, Virginia, 21:64; 39:307
Howard, Volney E., 6:12; 14:355, 364,
　366-68; 15:70, 73, 76-79, 147, 374;
　16:183; 19:236; 24:180; 32:334, 337,
　347
Howard, William A., 11:307; 28:35
Howard, William Davis Merry, 2:182;
　4:164-65; 5:406; 6:79-80; 7:106; 8:75,
　297, 301; 10:301; 11:71-72, 135-36,
　142: 14:143, 163, 346; 16:76, 139;
　17:294, 331, 334; 18:36, 44-56 *passim*,
　59; 19:231, 237;22:30; 23:254; 26:337;
　28:292, 294-95; 30:289; 33:345-46;
　36:110; 38:20, 41; 40:132; art. on,
　27:105-12, 249-55, 319-32; port.,
　27: opp. 319
Howard, Mrs. William Davis Merry
　(Agnes Poett), 27:249-53 *passim*, 319;
　28:292; letters to, 27:320-32; port.,
　27: opp. 326
Howard, Mrs. William Davis Merry
　(Mary Warren), 1:235, 249, 253;
　14:321; 17:326; 27:105, 110, 112
Howard, William H., 2:122; 24:166, 168
Howard, William Henry (s. of Edward
　W.), 27:319, 320
Howard, William Henry (s. of
　W. D. M.), 27:249, 250, 252, 254, 255,
　322-31 *passim*
Howard, Mrs. William Henry
　(Anna Dwight), 27.254
Howard, William James, bk. on, rev.,
　8:83-84
Howard family, 27:319, 320
Howard & Green, 18:36, 50; 27:106-7
Howard Benevolent Society,
　Sacramento, 10:290, 292
Howard Cattle Co., 27:255
Howard's Fireproof Building,
　San Francisco, 21:76
Howard Street Presbyterian Church,

San Francisco, 25:334, 341; 26:168,
　361; 27:307; 31:11
Howay, Frederic William, 8:89; 10:303;
　19:384; 22:193; ed. "To the Fraser
　Fraser River: The Diary and Letters
　of Cyrus Olin Phillips," 11:150-56;
　addresses, "Early Relations of
　California with British Columbia,"
　21:374; "Outline Sketch of the
　Maritime Fur Trade," 14:86; *Early
　History of the Fraser River Mines*,
　rev., 5:402-3; obit., 22:380-81
"How Californians Gave Life and Color
　to Nevada's Bonanza Boom Times,"
　address by Wells Drury, 2:260-61
Howe, Agnes E., 17:31, 32, 40
Howe, C. L., 29:252
Howe, Con, 29:121
Howe, Delos J., 40:306
Howe, Fanny, 10:277, 291; 29:113
Howe, George, 25:325, 333-34, 341
Howe, J. B., 23:341; 38:332
Howe, J. F., 28:195
Howe, Julia (Ward), 11:125; 34:232;
　37:40
Howe, Louis, 39:121, 122
Howe, Mary, 10:277, 291
Howe, Octavius Thorndike,
　Argonauts of '49, rev., 2:81-83
Howe, Robert, 10:50, 62, 70; 11:9
Howell, B. H., 15:280
Howell, Charles S., 9:269
Howell, Ed, ranch of, 11:272
Howell, Franklin Davenport, 26:287
Howell, Isaac, 24:56, 71
Howell, John Gilson, 5:409; 8:94, 183,
　185; addresses: "Early California
　Lithographs," 15:192-93; "The First
　Printing in California," 10:206;
　"Robert Louis Stevenson," 6:380;
　obits. of George D. Lyman,
　28:281-82; Helen (Throop) Pratt,
　24:87-88; obit., 35:180-82
Howell, John Gilson and Anne
　(Belshaw), 35.181
Howell, John Thomas, 24:322, 339;
　33:93; coauth. *Flora of San Francisco*,
　rev., 37:371
Howell, Warren Richardson, 18:288;
　21:191; obit. of Mrs. Jerome A. Hart,
　35:375; "The Plath Sale," 38:365-67
Howell Mountain, 24:56, 71; 35:1, 2,
　7-9, 156-60 *passim*
Howes, Capt. (Colorado R., 1866),
　22:171

Howison, George Holmes, 36:350-51; 37:39, 45-46

Howison, Samuel, 20:114-15

Howitzers, 1:144; at Clear Lake, 24:52; on Colorado R., 22:9; Frémont's, 18:164; 25:292, 304; 26:235, 246-47; 36:359-63; Kearny's, 13:133; 21:204, 205, 209; 25:292, 297, 302, 304; 26:34, 36, 51, 58; 33:113; illus., 25: opp. 289; *see also* Cannons

Howland (on Golden Gate, 1853), 32:359

Howland, Gardiner Greene, 13:245; *see also* Howland & Aspinwall

Howland, Robert, 7:117

Howland, T. G., 13:31

Howland & Aspinwall, 1:57; 13:244-46, 251; 18:218; 23:176; 29:4, 5

Howland, Angell and King, 7:117

Howland Flat, 11:238, 240

How Many Miles from St. Jo?, by Clark, ed. Mighels, rev., 9:88-89

"How Revolutions Against Mexican Control Held California for the United States," address by George Tays, 14:283

Howser, Fred N., 26:287

Howson, Frank, 21:159

Howson, John, 19:99

Howson's English and Italian Opera Troupe, 21:152, 154, 157

Hoxie, Capt. (of *Phoenix*), 15:366

Hoxie, H. M., 36:101

Hoy, William, 27:284; "Gold Mountain Big City, Chinese Map," 27:257-58; address, "Historical Writings on the California Chinese," 20:282

Hoyer, Cornelius, 12:139

Hoyle, M. F., 7:195

Hoyt, Charles, 11:122

Hoyt, Franklyn, 32:383; "The Los Angeles & San Pedro: First Railroad South of the Tehachapis," 32:327-48

Hoyt, Helen P. (Mrs. S. T.), 35:283; "The Sandwich Island Story of California's First Printing Press," 35:193-204

Hoyt, John C., 17:84; 26:351

Hoyt, William D., Jr., 24:378

Hubbard (or Hulbard; S.F., 1850), 38:314

Hubbard (Timbuctoo, 1859), 10:168

Hubbard, Adolphus Skinner 1:9, 16-19 *passim,* 107, 108; 6:200

Hubbard, C. G., 10:181, 185, 200, 251

Hubbard, Charles M., 13:296

Hubbard, Gardner, 23:284

Hubbard, George C., 7:278

Hubbard, Harry D., 19:77, 96

Hubbard, I. M., 29:346

Hubbard, J. C., 9:26

Hubbard, Joseph, 15:280

Hubbard, Dr. L. (Marysville, 1860), 10:252

Hubbard, Lorenzo, 10:266; 11:148; 16:339; 22:40; 37:201

Hubbard, Samuel, 18:384; obit., 23:284-85

Hubbard, Mrs. Samuel (Josephine Wolfsberger), 23:285

Hubbard, Theodore Worthington, 1:19, 108; 19:89; 23:285; reps. of Sec.-Treas., 3:96-98; 4:96-98; 5:98-99; obit. of Bethuel M. Newcomb, 3:210; obit., 6:200

Hubbs, Paul K., 11:173; 16:336; 29:2, 259-60

Huber, Francis Henry, 38:327

Huber, Johann, 12:302

Huber, Joseph, 29:237; 31:17

Huber, Walter Leroy, 4:51, 55; 10:304; 23:384; address, "One Hundred Years of Engineering in California," 34:87

Huberdeault, M. G., 8:14

Huc, E. R. M., 9:303, 339

Huckin, C., 10:70

Huddart, R. Townsend, 12:99, 101

Huden, George, 33:364

Hudner, Charles, 21:288

Hudson, Capt. (of *Oregon*, 1853), 2:83; 24:65

Hudson, David (came 1845), 17:240; 19:131, 135, 142; 24:58

Hudson, David (came 1849), 21:299, 306-7, 308; 22:71, 78

Hudson, George and Mrs. (née Elliott), 28:294

Hudson, Grace Carpenter (Mrs. John W.), 37:26, 32-33

Hudson, James J., 34:190; 35:92; "California National Guard and the Mexican Border, 1914-16," 34:157-71; "The McCloud River Affair of 1909," 35:29-35

Hudson, Julia, 9:265, 286

Hudson, Martin, 6:60

Hudson, Millard F., 1:110

Hudson, Phineas, 25:259

Hudson, Thomas, 17:82

Hudson, Wilford, 14:277-78; 26:121-22; 32:195

Hudson, William, 19:131, 135, 142

Hudson, William H., 2:83(?); 19:29, 32; 24:65(?)

Hudson, William K., 9:178(?), 360, 389; lawsuit, 351, 357

Hudson & Co., 9:349; lawsuit, 370

Hudson (W. K.) *v.* Catherine Fagan, 9:351, 357

Hudson's Bay Company, 2:130, 131; 3:77; 4:320; 5:46, 55, 59, 62, 63, 113; 6:18, 80; 8:128; 9:201; 11:150-51, 196; 12:80, 248-56 *passim*, 269, 274, 276, 294; 13:12, 16, 241, 251; 14:126; 17:23, 63, 65, 66, 68, 133-38 *passim*, 145, 293; 18:173, 319, 322, 323; 19:46, 214; 21:2, 6; 24:217, 229, 232, 233, 332; 25:256, 264; 28:113, 201, 202-3, 217, 225; 30:63, 83

    arts. on, 22:97-109, 193-222, 323-48; 23:19-40, 123-46; 28:97-112, 117-24, 243-58

    ships, 4:170; 5:60, 304; 8:98-100; 13:240, 248; 28:98, 99, 103, 105, 243, 247-52 *passim*

    trappers, 1:114; 4:5; 8:120-21, 128; 9:395; 18:328; 19:308-15; 22:366; 24:332; 28:97-98, 111, 117-24, 243, 245, 251

    see also Douglas, James; Fort Vancouver; Rae, William G.; Simpson, George; Work, John

"Hudson's Bay Co. in San Francisco, The," by Anson S. Blake, 28:97-112, 243-58

Hudspeth (San Jose, 1850), 14:155

Hudspeth, B. F., 19:96

Hudspeth, Benjamin, 19:96

Hudspeth, James M., 5:378; 19:96

Hudspeth, William David, 19:96

Hudspeth's Cut-Off, 24:245

Hübner, Henriette, 28:131

Hückstädt, Otto, 12:303

Hueneme (place), 17:31, 40

Hueneme (ship), 31:155

Huerne, Prosper, 38:35

"Huero, El" (Dolores Higuera), 26:35

Huerta, Victoriano, 34:157, 160-61

Hueter, E. L., 25:232

Huff, Lizzie, 10:379

Huff & Co., 11:244

Huffman, Robert E., 34:381, "Newspaper Art in Stockton, 1850-1892," 34:341-56

Hugenin, Daniel C., 21:20

Hugg, Benjamin P., 8:204-5, 212, 343, 348, 349; 9:154, 166; 10:77, 171, 367; 11:9; 28:235

Huggenberger (Sutter's gardener), 8:170

Huggins, Amos Williamson, obit., 14:414

Huggins, Dorothy Harriet, 1:96; 14:414; 19:89, 288; 22:194; 24:84; 36:175-76; 39:71; "Women in War-Time, San Francisco, 1864," 24:261-66; comp. "Continuation of the Annals of San Francisco," 16:79-84, 182-84, 282-85, 336-47; 17:81-85, 168-85; ed. Thomas B. and Joseph B. Eastland, "To California through Texas and Mexico," 18:99-135, 229-50; ed. "San Francisco Society," 19:225-28; "Meetings of the Society," 18:85-86; rep. of Sec.-Treas., 6:104-6

Huggins, Mrs. Edward (Letitia Work), 22:100, 107

Huggins, Henry, 22:193

Huggins, Joseph, 22:288; 24:93

Huggins, Joseph W., 22:288

"Hugh C. Murray, California's Youngest Chief Justice," by Edgar W. Camp, 20:365-73

Hugues or (Huguée), Capt. (of *Medicis*, 1845), 11:341

Hughes ("pedestrian"; S.F., 1854), 15:165

Hughes (San Rafael, 1859), 6:31

Hughes (Pico Canyon, 1869), 17:115

Hughes, Charles James, 16:341; 17:85

Hughes, E., 8:358

Hughes, F. J., 10:260

Hughes, Herman, 30:114

Hughes, J. A., 32:9, 20, 28, 41

Hughes, John H., 13:321; 29:234

Hughes, Thomas E., 25:171, 176

Hughes and Pioche, 5:13, 346

Hughes Lake, 10:212, 215, 218

Hugues, Aimé, 5:13, 346

Huichica (place), 17:146, 147, 148, 156; 29:315, 317

Hui Shen, 14:47-56

Hulbert, Eri B., 36:133-34; letters, 36:134-40

Hulbert, Mrs. Eri B., (Mary Louisa Walker), 36:133; letters to, 36:134-45; phot., 36: opp. 136

Hulbert, Rev. Eri B., 36:147

Hulbert Mill Co., 31:295

"Hulbert-Walker Letters, The: To California via Nicaragua in 1852," ed. Elizabeth W. Martin, 36:133-47

Hulburt (Timbuctoo, 1859), 10:167

Hull (S.F. and Marysville, 1851), 15:49

Hull, Clinton T., 1:110

Hull, Joseph B., 5:132; 10:17; 17:231; 20:217, 233

Hull, William E., 27:218-19

Hull (P. P.) and Co., 22:30

Hullings, Dr. (Placerville, 1850s), 4:180-81

Hulsa, Paul, 21:235

"Human History of Yosemite, The," address by Carl P. Russell, 5:206

Humboldt (S.F., 1851), 6:56

Humboldt, Alexander von, 30:319, 327

Humboldt (ship), 11:300; 22:7, 169; 23:51; 30:40

Humboldt, District of the, 26:4, 9; 27:226

Humboldt Base Line, 34:3, 14-16

Humboldt Bay, 2:124-25; 5:248; 7:394; 11:291, 302, 303, 314, 317; 18:5; 23:166, 176; 25:110; discovery of, 6:197; 11:299, 317; 19:375-76; 22:367, 379; 25:118; lumbering nr., 22:384; 38:60-69 *passim;* map, 7:368

Humboldt City, 2:124; 5:145, 248; 23:165

Humboldt County, 20:349, 354, 360, 362; 31:130; 34:268, 271-72; bk. on, rev., 3:203; Indians in, 39:291; Swiss in, 30:309, 310

Humboldt House, Marysville, 15:50

Humboldt Lake, 5:378-79, 382

Humboldt Lumber Manufacturers' Association, 38:68

Humboldt Lumber Manufacturing Co., 38:60

Humboldt River and Sink, 3:61-66 *passim,* 138, 139, 200, 201, 271; 4:8; 5:379-83 *passim;* 6:123-24, 362; 7:5; 8:82; 22:213; 24:121, 123; 26:336; 28:119, 121, 123; 32:197, 198, 199, 203, 207; *see also* Mary's River; Ogden's River

Humbug, *see* North Bloomfield

Humbug Creek, 9:77; 10:350

Humbug Ditch, 9:64, 77, 139

Humbug Valley, 7:14

Hume (Yuba Co., 1856), 9:61

"Humor of the Mines," address by Leon O. Whitsell, 11:295

Humphrey, Isaac, 13:174; 19:125, 134

Humphrey, James, 26:123

Humphrey, Norris, 4:320

Humphreys, Andrew A., 18:347

Humphreys, Charles, 28:97

Humphreys, Clement, map by, 21: opp. 113

Humphreys, William Penn, 27:45

Hunchback, The (play), 10:356

Hundley, P. O., 11:9

Hungarians in California, 28:125-42; *see also* Haraszthy

Hungerford, Dr. (Sacramento, 1849), 11:37

Hungerford, Daniel E., 37:197, 208, 210, 211

Hunnewell, James, 23:301, 330; 35:193-99 *passim;* cor., 35:196-97

Hunsaker, Clay, 9:77

Hunsaker, Daniel, 12:183

Hunsaker, Nicholas, 9:77

Hunsaker, William Jefferson, 6:35; obit., 12:183-84

Hunsaker, Mrs. William Jefferson (Florence Virginia McFarland), 12:184

Hunsaker, Willis, 9:77

Hunt, Mrs. (Marysville, 1859), 10:170

Hunt (Oroville, 1861), 10:281

Hunt, B. C., 13:32

Hunt, B. T., 7:18, 19

Hunt, G. W., 3:90

Hunt, Mrs. George W. (Alice Warner), 5:289, 292

Hunt, Hattie, 9:244-55 *passim,* 261, 264

Hunt, Henry, 26:204

Hunt, J. W. L., 9:110

Hunt, James, 4:320

Hunt, Jefferson, 1:238; 18:196; 21:98; 22:11, 13

Hunt, Jeptha T., 3:90

Hunt, John, 37:58

Hunt John H., 2:90, 99, 122; 14:406; 15:49(?)

Hunt, John S., 3:90

Hunt, Jonathan, 26:178, 179, 255, 259, 357, 358; 27:165, 166-67; 29:98, 105

Hunt, Lewis C., 26:2

Hunt, P. K., 10:375

Hunt, Patrick, 9:26, 27; 17:177

Hunt, Rockwell Dennis, 26:287; 27:191; 31:93; "Martin C. Briggs, 'Methodist Trumpeter,' " 31:1-11; coauth. *A Short History of California,* rev., 8:380-81

Hunt, Thomas Sterry, 21:321, 330
Hunt, Timothy Dwight, 6:284; 12:95;
    15:43; 16:336; 19:328; 22:35;
    26:167-74 *passim*; 27:18, 49, 307;
    30:46, 102; 32:133, 136, 165; 35:14;
    art. on, 28:289-96
Hunt, Mrs. Timothy Dwight
    (Mary Hedges), 28:289
Hunt, Tobert, 24:121
Hunt, Wilson Price, 4:141; 5:57;
    15:191; 22:345; 27:182
Hunt family, bk. on, rev., 3:90
Hunter, Benjamin F., 3:123; 6:268-69,
    274, 276-77; 10:109; 17:274; 26:49
Hunter, Edward (L.A., 1856), 29:234
Hunter, Edward (S.F., 1893), 39:226
Hunter, Jesse D., 13:330; 22:54, 62;
    33:111, 116-23 *passim*
Hunter, Mrs. Jesse D., 22:56
Hunter, Lewis B., 4:168
Hunter, R. S., 34:135-36
Hunter, Robert E., 5:376-77
Hunter, Robert M. T., 11:13, 26, 28;
    19:171, 270, 345, 361
Hunter, William L., 4:34, 49, 54
Hunter's Hot Springs, Ore., 22:205, 215
Hunter's Point, 17:181
Hunting, commercial, 7:399, 400;
    13:20-21; 20:36; 21:238; 22:265-66
Huntington, Archer, 11:285-87
Huntington, Collis Potter, 4:219,
    245-46, 260-61, 263, 268, 300; 5:178-83;
    7:17; 13:4, 20, 21; 15:76; 26:181;
    31:327; 38:311, 352
Huntington, Henry Edwards, 1:72, 96;
    11:83; obit., 6:200-202
Huntington, Thomas, 22:169
Huntington & Hammond, 13:20-21
Huntington Beach, 31:294
Huntington (Henry E.) Library, 1:74,
    192; 5:196-97, 209; 6:201; 38:361
Huntly, Sir Henry Vere, 12:65, 70;
    15:179; 22:264; rep., 12:73-76
Huntress (ship), 2:202; 33:268, 337
Hurd, Susan, 37:181
Hurdy-gurdy girl, 10:256, 267
"Hurdy-gurdy wheels," 29:200
Hurlburt, H. L., 33:373
Hurst (Sacramento, 1858), 9:261
Hurt, Peyton, "The Rise and Fall of
    the 'Know Nothings' in California,"
    9:16-49, 99-128
Hurtado de Mendoza, Diego, 1:38, 44,
    46; 6:297, 307, 320, 324, 368
Hus, M. P., 39:244

Husband, Bruce, 38:315
Huse, Charles E., 18:271-72, 278;
    34:241-42, 260
Huserne, Mme. (S.F., 1851), 32:118
Huss (1860), 29:110
Hussey, Capt. (Colorado R., 1859),
    22:169
Hussey, Frank, 10:393; 21:55
Hussey, John Adam, 19:95; 20:344;
    25:189; 29:89; 31:286; "California's
    Day Book," 25:121-31; "Identification
    of the Author of 'The Farthest West'
    Letters," 16:209-15; "Kit Carson at
    Cajón—Not Tejón," 29:29-38; "New
    Light on the Original Bear Flag,"
    31:205-17; "New Light Upon
    Talbot H. Green," 18:32-63; "The
    Old State House at Benicia,"
    17:260-70; "The Origin of the
    Gillespie Mission," 19:43-58; coauth.
    "California Preparation to Meet the
    Walla Walla Invasion, 1846,"
    21:9-21; addresses: "Early Day
    Transportation . . . in the West,"
    35:75; "The Great Scandal of 1851,"
    17:285; bk. revs. by, 38:374-76; 39:85
Hussey, Mrs. S. A., 30:243
Hussey, S. S., 20:43
Hussey, Thomas, 13:8, 32
Hussey, Bond & Hale, 16:346
Hutching, Edwin E., 24:287
Hutchings, Daniel F., 27:342, 349
Hutchings, Gertrude ("Cosie"), 30:284
Hutchings, James Mason, 1:273;
    4:12-13, 23-24, 35; 5:336, 338; 9:137,
    173; 15:379; 20:276; 22:35-39; 23:376;
    28:3; 30:275, 357; 32:193, 194;
    see also Hutchings & Rosenfield
Hutchings, Mrs. James Mason
    (Emily Ann Edmunds), 32:193
Hutchings & Rosenfield, 11:226; 30:357
Hutchings House, Yosemite, 5:338
*Hutchings' Illustrated California
    Magazine*, 9:135, 137, 138, 173, 174;
    15:301; 20:276, 26:217, 218; 30:357;
    34:215
Hutchings' "Table of Distances,"
    9:69-70
Hutchins, Capt. (of *New World*),
    27:306
Hutchins, E. Pierce, 35:338, 343
Hutchinson, Capt. (of *Tyro*, 1820s),
    14:295, 299
Hutchinson (owner of *Lucy Long*,
    1850s), 25:327, 328, 329

Hutchinson, A., 13:31
Hutchinson, C. J., 16:183
Hutchinson, E. L., 28:53
Hutchinson, F., *see* Simmons, Hutchinson & Co.
Hutchinson, H. M., 35:305, 307
Hutchinson, H. T., lawsuit, 10:178, 183, 186
Hutchinson, James Sloane, 4:48-50, 54, 55, 304
Hutchinson, John J., 30:266
Hutchinson, Joseph, 25:40
Hutchinson, Joseph Kellogg, obit., 4:304
Hutchinson, William A., 21:307
Hutchinson Vocalists, 26:225, 230
Hutson, Wilford, 32:195
Hutton, A. W., 13:352
Hutton, James D., 11:163
Hutton, O., 18:206
Hutton, William Rich, 1:255, 268; 21:276; 25:198; 30:99, 113; drawings by, 25: opp. 193; 26: foll. 126
Hyacinth Farm, 30:329
Hyatt, Caleb, 9:26; 16:81
Hyatt, Elisha, 14:178-82 *passim*
Hyatt, Jacob, 11:155
Hyatt, John, 14:181, 182
Hyatt, Sam, 17:75, 78
Hyde (lawsuit, 1861), 10:188, 356, 386; 10:188, 356, 386
Hyde, Columbus, 13:3
Hyde, Frederick A., 25:286
Hyde, George (S.F., 1847), 5:406; 11:72, 142; 16:190-91; 27:352; 30:329

Hyde, Mrs. George (Ellen McCoy), 16:190-91
Hyde, George (L.A., 1923), 40:139, 153
Hyde, Gertrude, 16:190-91
Hyde, Henry C., 26:71
Hyde, James L., 9:32; 15:184, 186, 276, 281
Hyde, Margaret, 39:293
Hyde, Orson, 17:78; 21:228
Hyde, R. E., 2:205
Hyde, S. S., 25:20
Hyde, Stuart W., 34:381; "The Chinese Stereotype in American Melodrama," 34:357-67
Hyde, W. C., 17:179
Hyde, W. F. and Mrs., 26:71, 74, 75, 179, 361
Hyde, W. H., 33:4-5, 7-8, 12
Hyde, William, 26:71
Hydraulic Ditch Co., 11:166
Hydraulic mining, *see* Gold mining; Flumes and fluming
Hydraulic Press, North San Juan, 9:181; 10:394; 21:332; 29:194-96, 205; 30:126-28
Hydroelectric power, 29:202, 203; 30:339-44
Hyenne, Ed, 11:344-45
Hyer (camel driver, 1861), 18:206
Hyer, John G., 11:113
Hyer, Tom, 8:366
Hyland (Marysville, 1859), 10:180
Hylton, T. A., 3:176; 12:197, 198
Hyman brothers (Hyman W., Henry W., Michael, Morris and Joseph), 27:383

I

Iaccheri, G., 39:227
Iaeger, *see* Jaeger
Iamkuk (Indian, 1833), 23:38
Iardella, L. A., 28:64, 68
Ibáñez, Florencio, 23:4-5, 13
Ibarra, Antonio, 26:41
Ibarra, Francisco Gonzáles de, *see* González de Ibarra
Ibarra, Gil, 16:360
Ibarra, José María, 26:31
Ibarra, Juan María, 16:222
Ibarra, Manuel, *see* Gonzáles de Ibarra, Manuel

Icaza, Isidro, 24:292; 25:76, 149, 363
Icazbalceta, García, 36:173-74
Ice, commerce in, 12:98; 13:339-40; 15:54; 16:339; 38:332
Ice cream (in 1850s), 11:333; 14:394; 28:39; 30:259
Idaho, 15:324, 325
Idaho (ship), 22:162, 166, 168, 173, 174
Idaho-Maryland Mine, 19:28
Idaho Mine, Virginia City, 6:343
Ide, Simeon, 11:82
Ide, William Brown, 17:161; 18:297-98, 311; 29:262; 30:53-54, 55, 63, 329-30;

in Bear Flag revolt, 1:74-91 *passim*,
134-35, 137, 179, 180, 190, 286; 3:180;
4:286; 6:137-41 *passim*, 369; 7:80, 84;
9:81-85 *passim*; 10:10-11; 16:212;
17:221, 222, 224, 275; 24:57-58; 25:123;
29:264, 266, 268, 272; 31:209; cor.,
1:82-85; 3:179; pledge, 1:89-90; procs.,
1:72, 74-79, 97, 181-82; 10:101, 112,
115; fac., 1: foll. 74
Ide, Mrs. William Brown
(Susan G. Haskell), 21:9
"Identification of the Author of
'The Farthest West' Letters," by
John A. Hussey, 16:209-15
I. F. Chapman (ship), 33:327
Iglesias, José M., 17:239
Ike, Little (Indian), 26:201, 206
Ike, Mrs. Mary (Indian), 26:201, 206
Ikelheimer and Bros., 30:69
Iken, Valentine, 17:84
Ilarequi, *see* Salazar Ilarequi
Illilouette Falls, 1:282
Illinois (ship), 8:9; 20:248; 27:327
Illinois Association, 38:132
Illinoistown, 4:242, 266; 13:15, 17, 19,
24; 26:305
"Ill-Starred Voyage, An: The
S.S. *Golden Gate*, January 1854,"
by Helen R. Goss, 32:349-61
*Illustrated Flora of the Pacific States,
An*, by Abrams, rev., 4:88
Illustrated London News, 32:81, 83, 84,
269, 270
Illustrious Stranger, The (play), 10:200
Ilmen (ship), 12:231, 232, 233
Imas, Hiram A., 10:62
Imbrie (Augustus C. Imbrey?), 11:166
Imhuff *v.* Haskell, 10:57
Immigration Association of California,
16:285
Immigration into Calif., 19:323-43;
20:65-69; before gold rush, 5:125;
10:34, 36; 12:115-16, 288, 290, 340,
341, 352; 14:147; 17:56, 58, 150-56
passim, 161; 19:131; in gold rush,
13:272, 275, 277; 19:323-38; 20:65-73
(*see also* Gold rush); in 1853-55,
15:175, 268; 17:184; in 1860-70,
19:341; in 1870-1945, 24:139-48;
28:343-50; laws concerning,
15:169-70; 34:316; planned, 10:5-6;
15:374; 24:108; 27:169-71, 346; from
Mexico, 13:356; from Ore., 5:125;
13:356; from the Orient, 28:343-50;

30:204; 34:307, 315 (*see also* Chinese);
from Switzerland, 30:308; *see also*
Emigration
Impartial Californien, L', 39:240-41,
244
Impeachments, 9:111; 10:380-81;
15:163, 166
Imperial (ship), 39:298
Imperial Valley, 10:214, 216, 217;
16:296; 25:297; 34:157, 158; 33:190
"Important Letter, An: Aaron Leggett
to William L. Marcy," 11:33-34
"Impressions of ... Senator Phelan,"
address by Clay Miller, 32:175
Inauguration of Governor: in 1854.
38:17; in 1858, 9:244, 247, 270; in
1860, 11:8, 10, 22; in 1862, 10:387;
in 1887, 5:288
Inca (ship), 6:257
In Camp and Cabin, by Steele, ed.
Quaife, rev., 8:87-88
Ince, Annette, 9:245, 271; 21:42, 64, 172
Inconstant (ship), *see* Natalia
Indépendant, L' (weekly), 39:159,
170-71, 246, 348
Independence, Mo., 3:90, 200; 16:124;
22:122, 131; 24:18, 30-38 *passim*;
letters and newsp. arts. from, 4:280;
24:30
Independence (frigate, 1846), 1:231;
2:351; 12:345, 351; 16:83, 182; 17:168;
18:62; 20:221, 233; 22:50; 33:232-33,
251
Independence (str., 1853), 6:357-59;
35:211
Independence Flat, 22:78, 83
Independence Gold Mining Co., Ltd.,
35:338, 343
Independence Mine, 3:259; 15:343
Independence of California from
Mexico, 11:33; 12:37-38; 16:349;
17:271, 279, 280; proc., 12: opp. 125
Independence Rock, 3:53; 4:138;
6:116-17; 8:81; 11:82; 22:149, 23:298
Independent, San Andreas, 34:343
Independent, Stockton, 26:244; 34:341,
343, 347-54
Independent (ship), *see* Independence
(str.)
Independent City Guard, San Francisco,
38:17; *see also* City Guard
Independent National Guard, San
Francisco, 10:198; 16:285, 344; 34:324,
325; 38:17, 21; *see also* Nationals

Independent Opposition [steamship]
Line, 15:88, 165, 169, 176, 178
Independent Order of Odd Fellows,
2:119; 4:195; 8:341, 358; 9:60; 10:54,
76, 250, 252, 359; 13:338; 20:13, 269;
28:60, 67; 30:247; 31:190; 32:169-70;
38:305, 308, 311; Hall, Marysville,
10:252, 265, 293-94
Independent Party (1892), 27:316
Independent Presbyterian Church,
San Jose, 26:170
Independent Unpaid Axe Co., 23:76
Independent Water Co., San Francisco,
17:181
Index, Sacramento, 20:333
Index (ship), 8:106; 14:209
Indiana (ship), 31:59
Indian affairs, Supts. of, 15:165; 27:215,
219
Indian agencies, agents, and
commissioners, 3:26, 147; 8:363;
17:231; 18:306; 19:165, 183; 21:369;
22:368, 369; 26:2, 3, 5, 201-7, 323-26,
347; 27:224; 28:162-63, 326, 328;
30:166; 36:314; 38:154
Indiana Ranch, 8:213, 346, 360; 9:52,
72, 129, 149, 152, 158; 10:57, 170, 172
Indian Bar, 1:299
Indian Bar Co., 11:174
Indian Diggings, 15:375; 24:167, 180
Indian Diggings Hotel, 24:168, 169
Indian Hill, 9:64, 165, 180
Indianola Colony, 25:172
Indian Run, 12:8
Indians, 3:226-30; 5:150-52; 8:312-18;
11:215, 389; 12:164, 306-11; 14:13;
16:236; 19:199-200; 20:171-78;
22:207-13 *passim*, 320-21, 329, 337,
341; 23:1, 2, 29-40 *passim*, 124-45
passim; 26:325, 326; 36:335-36;
38:142-45
appearance and dress, 2:293, 294,
302-3, 324; 3:12-13, 16, 228, 229,
306, 327, 345; 5:149-50, 151, 172;
6:161-62, 346; 7:46, 48, 49, 308-9,
348, 356; 8:243, 313-14; 10:331,
335; 12:306; 14:109-10, 119; 15:108,
133, 222; 19:131, 199; 20:316;
22:320; 36:222; 38:150-51
attacks and uprisings, 2:155, 157,
253; 3:23, 147, 340; 4:113; 5:196,
387; 6:116, 122, 234, 235; 7:46;
8:242, 311; 9:227-28; 10:37, 38, 262;
11:10, 86, 120, 266-73; 12:111, 123,
169, 326; 14:13, 22, 108-10, 118-19;
15:234; 16:118, 219, 250, 338;
20:237; 21:97, 208, 223; 22:1; 23:371,
375; 24:308, 343-44; 36:318; 38:148,
150, 330, 334; 39:298, 303, 306
baskets made by, 2:315, 326, (phot.)
opp. 341, 341, 343; 3:16, 228, 242-43,
244; 5:149; 6:248; 8:189, 314;
19:199; 20:360, 361; 26:122, 123
battles with, 16:219, 236, 245, 250,
341, 360; 17:149; 19:131; 20:234;
22:198, 214; 38:336; *see also*
Modoc War
beliefs of, 2:59-62; 7:351; 8:60-62,
315-16; 12:307; 15:108; 36:336
boats, 2:58, 315, 326, 340; 3:6, 7, 13,
16, 18, 229, 354; 7:349, 351; 10:331;
11:311; 14:113; 20:316; 22:328,
344
burials, cremation, etc., 2:320, 325;
3:328; 6:115; 7:56; 12:13, 307;
15:108-9, 112; 20:224; 22:210, 216;
38:152
dances, 2:284; 6:235, 241; 7:56; 8:60;
12:307; 17:148
dwellings, 1:130; 2:152-53, 273,
295, 318, 319, 325; 3:13, 22, 227,
242, 327; 5:147; 6:240, (illus.)
opp. 240; 7:47, 351; 8:24, 174, 314;
10:213, 219; 12:13; 14:119-20;
15:111, 218, 330; 19:199; 22:213;
24:51; 36:318; 38:144-45
employment of, 8:311; 35:108-9;
see also Indians: slaves and servants
expeditions against, 10:262; 12:122;
14:22; 16:219, 250, 355; 17:149;
20:259; 24:49, 51-55; 26:2; 38:330,
334, 335
foods, 1:154; 2:56, 149, 154, 293, 319,
325; 3:14, 16, 18, 19, 23, 244, 327;
5:147, 165, 168, 172; 6:240, 248;
7:47, 49, 56, 351; 8:243; 10:331;
11:104, 109; 12:293, 308; 13:16,
73; 14:13, 104, 109; 15:108, 134;
20:224, 317, 318, 359, 360; 22:320,
335, 336, 344, 345; 24:231, 329;
25:144; 26:234, 246; 34:197, 199;
36:335; 38:145-46
horse and cattle thieves, 1:122, 273;
3:62, 226, 273; 5:77-78; 12:111;
13:24; 14:23; 16:57, 245, 246, 360;
18:302; 21:1, 12; 22:334; 23:36, 38,
125, 126, 129, 138, 368; 24:239;
25:294; 38:331
languages of, 2:55; 5:152; 12:306-7;
17:245; 36:334, 335; 38:154

legislation concerning, 11:15, 26-27; 19:19, 165, 183, 258-59
medicines and medicine men, 4:149; 6:240-41; 36:335
in the mines, 12:301; 13:66, 172, 173; 28:325
mistreatment of, 2:199, 369; 8:148, 214-17, 242; 20:224, 362; 38:147, 331
mounds made by, 13:284; 17:245; 20:319-23; 30:230; 31:99-108
music, 36:336
pictures of, 6: opp. 240; 14: opp. 99; 15: opp. 213, foll. 214; 39: foll. 180
population, 2:56; 3:225, 227; 8:308-9; 11:263; 12:3, 118; 16:119, 242; 33:86
rancherias or villages, 1:120, 130; 2:16, 55; 3:21, 22, 23, 242-43; 5:148-49; 6:240; 7:47, 48, 49; 8:174; 10:342; 11:113, 119, 248, 259, 262, 269; 12:8, 9, 284, 307; 14:106, 196, 198; 15:329; 20:317, 318, 324; 21:110; 22:344; 23:31; 26:209-15; 28:333; 34:199, 202, 203-4; 36:313-25
reservations, 20:349, 362, 363; 26:1, 5, 6, 11; 27:215-24 *passim*; 28:329; 34:203, 204; 36:313, 316, 317; 38:147
salt journey, 20:360-61
sickness among, 2:50-51, 253, 254; 11:110, 113; 12:13; 16:109, 360; 23:131-32, 145; 24:331, 336; 33:85
slaves and servants, 5:32; 12:309; 16:246; 19:198; 20:349, 362; 24:231; *see also* Indians: employment of
surround hunt, 22:327, 343
temescales, *see* Sweat houses
trails, 12:112; 29:57; 30:168; 34:193, 194-95, 203
treaties, 6:115; 16:236; 19:183; 28:327, 328; 36:314-17
weapons, 1:155; 2:294, 295; 7:307; 8:314-15; 20:359, 360; 24:21; 33:86-87
as witnesses, 9:67, 79
women, 2:55, 56, 324; 5:150; 6:248; 7:351; 8:158, 311, 314, 315; 10:331; 14:109-10; 15: (illus.) foll. 214; 38:145, 151, 153-54
see also Indian tribes and groups
Indians:
Bidwell's, 36:313-23
seen by Drake, 16: No. 1, Pt. 2, pp. 6-9, 27-30, 34-35; 20:325
Frémont's encounters w., 1:1 2, 129-33; 6:89-90; 17:273; 19:131

Lassen's, 18:296, 297, 306
Livermore's, 5:130
Mission, 1:24, 26, 115, 161, 162, 166, 169; 2:54, 253-54, 273, 279, 283, 284, 318, 320, 341; 3:7, 225, 227, 230, 239-44 *passim*; 5:32; 6:161; 8:159, 160, 216, 228-31, 242-43, 308-9, 316-18, 329, 330; 10:33; 11:257; 12:122, 164, 283, 309, 311; 14:4, 13, 22, 108, 119-20; 15:114, 217-23; 16:109, 115, 118-19, 236, 242; 18:319-20; 20:23; 22:321, 343; 23:3-13 *passim*, 20, 36, 40, 374; 34:204; 36:335; 38:144
Savage's, 28:325
Sutter's, 8:170, 171; 12:309; 15:226-27, 230; 18:296; 19:118-19; 26:110, 111, 112, 118-23 *passim*
at Bodega and Tomales bays, 2:302-4; 10:331, 343, 344; 12:221; 16:108
on Calif. coast, 2:148-57 *passim*; 7:46-49 *passim*, 347-56 *passim*, 361, 371, 389; *see also* Indians; Santa Barbara Channel
nr. Clear Lake, 11:266-73; 15:232; 16:305; 17:149; 24:49-56; 29:312
on Colorado and Gila rivs., 1:70, 114, 116-17, 167, 384; 5:214; 11:373-78 *passim*; 15:105, 108-12 *passim*, 132-33; 21:97, 102-4; 36:233
at Drake's Bay, 3:8, 12-13, 14, 22, 23; 20:316-17, 318, 325; *see also* Indians: seen by Drake
on Feather and Yuba rivs., 11:109, 110, 113, 119; 12:284, 307; 14:196, 198, 211; 22:327-28, 343, 344; 23:131-32; 24:331
at Fort Ross, 12:196
in Humboldt and Trinity cos., 5:147-69 *passim*, 172, 175, 229
Klamath R., 11:389; 26:201-7
Los Angeles Co., 5:408; 13:195, 197, 204, 206, 222
Lower Calif., 3: 327-35 *passim*, 340-57 *passim*; 5:196; 6:161-62; 7:44, 45, 307, 308-9, 323, 339-45 *passim*; 8:308; 11:86; 20:178; 24:296; 26:313-18 *passim*; 31:109-24, 261-70, 343-54; 36:233
in Mendocino Co., 20:349, 360, 362; 27:215-27 *passim*; 30:164-68 *passim*
Monterey, 1:175-76; 2:293-94; 3:227; 7:361; illus., 15: foll. 214; 39: foll. 180

Napa Valley, 2:55-62
Nevada, 6:340, 346
Northwest Coast, 9:227-29, 240;
    10:323-27
Pit R., 1:118; 18:302; 22:216; 24:231;
    27:223
Rogue R., 25:112-14; 26:1; 28:199,
    213, 223-24, 231; 31:274
Sacramento R., 11:115, 119-20;
    12:307, 309
Salmon R., 5:242, 244
nr. San Diego, 7:46, 347-48, 387
San Francisco Bay region, 1:115;
    2:271, 273; 14:108-10
San Joaquin Valley, 10:213, 217-18,
    219; 14:22, 106
San Luis Obispo Co., 1:153-57,
    162; 3:6, 7, 15-16, 17; 20:318;
    23:350
San Rafael, 2:58, 59
Santa Barbara Channel, 2:315, 319,
    320, 324-26; 3:6, 17, 18-19, 226,
    227-30; 7:23, 46-51 *passim*, 56,
    74, 351-52, 354, 371; 20:318, 324
Smith R., 26:4, 5, 8
nr. Sonoma, 16:112, 113, 118, 119,
    242; 17:147-51 *passim;* 29:315-18
    passim
Trinidad Bay, 2:297; 9:217-23;
    10:335-36
Tulare Valley, 4:374; 11:253-65
    passim
Indians of Los Angeles County, by
    Reid, rev., 5:408
Indian Springs, Nevada Co., 10:348,
    349, 351
Indian Springs, Yuba Co., 9:51, 69
Indian tribes and groups:
    Achistoy, 16:249
    Achomawi, 22:210, 211, 216
    Aloquiomi, 16:119
    Ansactoy, 16:249
    Apache, 1:60, 139, 144; 2:16; 11:388;
        12:3; 18:5-6; 21:97, 101-2, 199,
        202-10 *passim*, 222, 223; 34:126,
        128, 129, 137; 38:144, 148, 153;
        39:298
    Arapahoe, 16:50, 51, 52; 32:265,
        266; 38:152
    Arikara, 4:112-19, 279; 16:50, 51
    Aspasniac, 3:227
    Atenomac, 16:119
    Blackfoot, 4:141; 16:50; 22:198
    Bolbones, 20:174

Cahuilla (or Coahuilla), 3:242;
    12:13, 118; 20:175
Cainamero, 16:245, 246, 249, 356;
    17:148, 151; 38:104
Camillares, 34:199, 202
Canijolmano, 2:55; 16:119
Canoma, 16:119
Carquin (or Karkin), 16:119; 20:174
Caymus, 2:55-62; 16:119, 133
Cayuse, 4:351, 353; 5:58, 76-80
    passim; 21:1-7 *passim;* 22:198, 199;
    23:135; 24:230, 231, 232; 25:143-44
Chemoco, 16:119
Cheyenne, 6:115; 16:50, 52; 38:152
Chichimecos, 3:13
Chichoyomi, 16:119
Chiliyomi, 17:150
Chilula, 5:161-62
Chinook, 24:230
Chocuyem, 16:119
Chorsuptoy, 16:249
Chowchilla, 1:272; 20:175; 28:324,
    331-32, 333
Chumash, 7:23, 24, 70; 20:315, 327;
    36:221-22, 228
Clatsop, 24:230
Clustinomayomi, 17:150
Cocopa, 11:375-77, 378; 20:176;
    21:104, 106; 22:11
Colusa, 20:174
Comanche, 24:46; 25:140; 38:152
Coyayomi, 16:119
Crow, 3:90; 4:122, 124-31; 6:116
Cupeño, 25:299, 303
Delaware, 1:129; 15:62; 17:69, 273;
    see also Hill, Tom
Diegueño, 25:298, 307; 26:27, 30-31,
    42, 52
Digger, 2:136; 6:235; 10:37; 16:133;
    19:118-19; 30:165; 38:152
Eslenes, 3:227
Guapos, *see* Indians: Satayomi
Guilitoy, 16:249; 20:174
Hayomi, 17:150
Hock, 6:240-41; 8:24, 170, 171, 174;
    11:110, 113; 14:196; illus., 6:
    opp. 240
Holiyomi, 17:150
Hol-o-lu-pai, 36:315
Hopi, 2:19-23; 10:411
Huilca, 16:119
Hupa (or Hoopa), 5:162-69 *passim*,
    172; 20:173; 26:40
Huymen, 16:119
Iowa, 6:113; 10:398

Karoc, 2:355; 24:229
Kaw, 4:311-16; 22:125
Kawia, 11:257, 258, 265; 20:175
Kiowa, 38:152
Klamath, 1:120, 128-29; 6:89-90;
    17:273; 19:131; 20:173; 22:216;
    24:231; 26:4; 28:199, 222, 231;
    31:293
Kodiak, *see* Aleuts
Kon-kau, 36:315
Lacatiut, 16:119
Laguna, 2:16
Lassik, 20:362, 363
Libantiloyomi, 16:111
Liguaitoy, 16:249
Linayto, 16:119
Loaquiomi, 16:119
Locnoma, 16:119
Luckno, 12:310-11
Lutamin Klamath, 24:229
Maidu, 22:217, 327-28, 343, 344;
    36:315
Makah, 10:323
Malaca, 16:119
Maricopa, 2:8, 11, 17; 21:108-11
    passim, 212, 213, 223
Mayacoma Indians, 2:55; 3:171;
    16:119; 20:173; 32:365
Me-choop-da, 36:313-23
Migueleño, 1:166
Mill Creek, 4:94
Mimal, 14:211
Miwok, 2:54
Miwok, Coast, 10:345; 20:316-28
    passim; 31:99, 100; 33:88
Moco, *see* Indians: Hopi
Modoc, 10:202; 15:286; 20:173;
    21:190; 22:216; 24:229, 231; 26:201,
    292, 293; 28:161-64, 286; 39:86, 87
Mohave, 1:114, 116; 2:11-12; 12:112,
    122, 123; 19:311, 312; 20:175;
    21:97, 98, 102-6 *passim*
Moquelumne (or Mokelumne),
    13:73, 159; 16:347, 360; 20:174;
    27:140
Moqui, 11:388
Mono, 1:273; 5:336; 10:409; 26:234,
    246
Mottiyomi, 17:150
Muticolmo, 16:119
Napa, 2:55; 20:174
Napajo, 16:119, 250, 348, 351
Navaho, 1:112; 2:12, 13, 21; 10:87;
    11:388; 12:3; 21:197, 198, 200, 210;
    39:86, 87

Neuch-teus, 28:331-32
Nez Percé, 4:349, 351; 5:77; 21:1-7
    passim; 22:198; 24:231; 25:141-44
    passim
Noches Colteches, 10:218
Nomlaki, 20:173
Notonto, 3:91:11:248, 259-60, 264
Nutchu, 1:272
Okechumne, 2:54
Oleomi, 16:119
Olhones, 14:13; 29:57
Osage, 35:4-5
Oustomah, 10:348
Paiute, 2:38-39, 229, 230-31, 234;
    5:335, 336; 6:343; 12:111, 326;
    18:306, 307, 314; 20:175; 22:98;
    24:21; 26:234; 38:330
Papago, 2:10-11
Paque, 16:119
Paquenjilayomi, 17:150
Patwin, 22:335, 336, 344
Pawnee, 5:395, 396; 10:399; 16:50,
    51, 52, 125; 22:128; 24:42, 46,
    239
Petaluma, 16:119
Picuris, 2:14-15
Pima, 1:61-68 *passim*, 149; 2:7-8, 17;
    21:111, 211-13, 217, 223, 298; 22:52
Polnomanoc, 16:119
Pomo, 2:55; 10:337; 11:266-73;
    20:172, 316; 23:31-32, 33, 40;
    24:49-56; 26:209-15; 30:163
Pomo, Coast, 20:316; 23:26, 27, 39
Potawatomi, 22:124; 24:239
Putah, 16:119
Qu-Lah-Na-Poh, 11:269
Runsien, 3:227
Sac, 10:398; 24:239
Salson, 14:108
Sanpeet, 2:228, 234
Satayomi (Satiyomi, Sotoyome),
    16:119, 236, 245, 246, 249, 250,
    351, 355-56; 17:149; 29:311, 312,
    315, 317
Scioyomi, 17:150
Seri, 11:370
Shasta, 20:173; 22:211; 24:229-33
    passim, 326-27, 329
Shoshone, 6:118, 343; 18:195; 22:139
Sioux, 1:16; 4:112, 113, 117, 118;
    6:115; 10:399; 16:125; 24:46
Snake, 3:55-56; 5:387; 6:122; 22:139,
    195-202 *passim*
Soneto, 16:119
Sonoma, 16:112

Soquel, 20:175

Suisun, 16:112, 119, 244, 250; 17:148; 29:311, 312, 316

Su-nu, 36:315

Supuyomi, 17:150

Tache, 11:253, 262, 264-65

Tamal, 16:119

Taos, 2:13-14

Télumne (Telamni, Telomni, Tulamni), 10:219; 11:254, 265; 20:176

Tillamook, 24:230

Tin-Taché (Ton Taché), 11:253, 254, 264

Tinte Taché, 11:253, 262

Tlayacma, 16:119

Tmuracan, 3:227

Tolen, 16:119

Topayto, 16:119

To-to, 36:315

Tulare (Tulareños), 1:166; 3:91; 4:374; 28:323-41

Tuliyomi, 17:150

Tuolumne, 20:174

Ukiah, *see* Indians: Yokayo

Ululato, 16:119

Umpqua, 24:233

Ute, 5:387; 6:113; 11:356; 20:173; 27:114-15; 29:32, 33

Utinomanoc, 16:119

Vaysh, 3:227

Wailaki, 20:173, 349-61, 362, 363

Walla Walla, 4:354; 5:76-80; 12:168, 169; 17:230; 18:81; 21:1-21 *passim;* 22:199, 324, 343; 23:125; 24:230, 232; 25:129-30, 144-47 *passim;* 29:322-23, 334, 337, 339; 33:86

Wappo, 2:55-62

Wapumni, 26:110

Wasco, 24:230, 231

Washo, 7:11; 20:173

Wim-mul-che, 2:236, 345, 348; 3:25-26; 4:5

Wintun, 2:55; 20:362

Xabe-napo, 11:266, 269

Xolo-napo, 11:266

Yahano, 25:297, 307; *see also* Indians: Diegueño

Yahi, 4:94

Yaqui, 8:224

Yatchachumne, 20:174

Yohaiyak, 24:52

Yokayo, 20:173; 26:209-15; 36:313

Yokuts, 4:301; 10:219, 304, 309, 409; 11:248, 253, 264, 265; 20:171; *see also* Indians: Notonto; Tache; Tulare

Yolo, 16:245; 29:311, 312

Yoloitoy (or Yolotoy), 16:250, 355; 29:312

Yosemite, 1:199-200, 272-73; 4:24; 5:328-36 *passim;* 10:302; 20:276; 23:376; 28:331-33

Yreka, 20:173

Yuba(or Yubu), 12:284; 14:198

Yuki, 20:173

Yuma, 2:11, 14, 376; 12:85; 15:109; 20:176, 259; 21:98-104 *passim,* 110, 299; 22:1, 4, 20; 25:294; 33:15-16, 20; 34:195, 196; 36:120, 218-20

Yurok, 5:147-55 *passim,* 169; 20:327; 26:206; 36:336

Zaclom, 16:119

Zuñi, 2:15

Indian Uprising in Lower California, by Taraval, ed. Wilbur, rev., 11:86

Indian Valley, Alpine Co., 7:11

Indian Valley, Lake Co., 32:364, 370

Indian Valley, Plumas Co., 18:303, 313; 29:39, 55; 38:379

Indian Valley, Sierra Co., 6:215, 216; 9:63, 64, 76, 153

Indian war debt, 19:258-59

Indian Wells, 17:110, 212, 213, 215-16; 18:201, 203

Indigent sick, of San Francisco, 16:183, 283

Indio, 31:16-17, 24

Indo-China, stoneware from, 31:103, 104

Industrial Indemnity Co., 36:112

Industrial Legion, 28:48-49

Industrial Relations in the San Francisco Bay Area, 1900 to 1918, by Knight, rev., 39:362-64

Industrial School, San Francisco, 10·373, 388; 36:297, 306; 38:27

Industrial Union, 27:314

Industrial Workers of the World, 40:144

Inebriates, bill to estab. home for, 10:277, 291

Ingalls, Eleaser Stillman, 33:373

Ingalls, John, 17:187

Ingalls, Rufus, 2:128, 129; 21:199, 201, 222; 33:107, 268, 307, 337, 340

Ingalls, William Bowers Bourn, 36:205-12, 293-306; phot., 36: opp. 304

Inge, Samuel W., 11:6-8, 21; 19:256; 35:321

Ingersoll, Chester, 16:136, 138; 17:351

Ingoldsby, John, 15:168

Ingomar (play), 10:52

Ingram, Daniel, 33:364

Ingram, Diana Elizabeth, *see* Prather, Mrs. William

Ingram, E., 31:331

Ingram, R. Henry, 20:158

Iniestra, Ignacio, 12:152-53; 13:44; 14:235

"Inigo," *see* Webb, Charles Henry

"Initial Monuments for California's Base and Meridian Lines," by Gertrude K. Brown, 34:1-17

Inman, J. M. ("Jack"), 36:258

Innocenti (artist), 37:38

Ino (ship), 12:69

Inquirer, Marysville, 6:11-12; 8:361; 9:133, 156

"Inquiry into the Significance of the Raising of the American Flag at Yerba Buena, An," by Douglas S. Watson, 15:306-10

Insane Asylum, State: at Marysville (prop.), 10:49, 50, 52, 71; at Stockton, 8:353; 9:257, 258; 10:43, 44, 45, 65, 67; 20:252; 23:376

Insects, 12:206, 305; 26:234; 29:173; 32:257; collection of, 12:207, 208, 209, 305; 17:359; 29:14; 32:249-61 *passim;* bedbugs, 9:157; grasshoppers, 1:154; 12:305; 35:215; lice, 1:212; 12:305; locusts, 38:110; termites, 15:272; *see also* Fleas; Mosquitoes

Inskeep, E. W., 15:35

Inskeep, Mrs. Mary E., 28:293

"Instructions of Viceroy Bucareli to Ensign Juan Pérez, The," trans. Manuel P. Servín, 40:237-48

Insua, Juan, 31:331

Insurance and insurance companies, 16:74-75; 26:178-82 *passim*, 254-66 *passim*, 351-58 *passim;* 27:66, 67-68, 165-68, 270, 344, 349-50; 28:297; 35:244, 268; *see also* names of companies

Interest on money: in 1840s, 8:109; 17:23; 20:29; 23:158; in 1850s, 9:73; 10:63; 17:254; 28:213; 30:24; in 1920s, 31:298; 39:107

International, L' (tri-weekly), 39:219-20, 348

"International Boundary Survey from San Diego to the Gila River, The," by Lewis B. Lesley, 9:3-15

International Company of Mexico, 21:330

International Hotel, San Francisco, 6:15; 10:44, 67, 197, 293; 16:81, 183, 284; 17:180; 19:229; 21:167; 23:338

"In the Mountains of Mendocino," by Kent, rev., 5:92

"In the South San Joaquin ahead of Garcés," by Herbert E. Bolton, 10:211-19

"Introduction and Supplement to 'A History of California Newspapers,'" by Douglas C. McMutrie, 7:277-81

Invader (yacht), 30:214

I. N. Van Nuys (ship), 25:287

Inverness, 10:342; Ridge, 339, 343

Inverness Park, 19:317, 321

Invincible (clipper), 10:294

Invincible (schr.), 11:365-82; 22:3, 7, 20, 165, 168

Invisible Prince (play), 9:249, 275; 10:178, 200

Inyo County, 26:239, 243; bk. on, rev., 2:178-79

Inyo Independent, 9:193, 195; fac. page, 9: opp. 196

Inyo Register, 9:195

Ione (place), 11:322; 17:75, 79

I.O.O.F., *see* Independent Order of Odd Fellows

Iowa (ship), 13:381; 20:259

Iowa and Sac Indian Mission, 6:113; 10:398

Iowa Hill, 2:204-5; 15:271; 16:31; 17:174; 28:380; 30:260-61, 367; 32:133, 143

"Ira J. Willis Guide to the Gold Mines, The," ed. Irene D. Paden, 32:193-208

Iredale, A. S., 29:292; 32:169

Irish, John P., 28:48, 50; 32:235, 238

Irish, 21:220; 22:183; 24:49, 71; 25:315; 28:13; 29:93; 34:70; 35:129; *see also* "Irishman in the Gold Rush"

Irish Ambassador, The (play), 10:63

Irish American Co., 6:230

"Irish Leaders in Early California," address by Thomas F. Prendergast, 22:183

"Irishman in the Gold Rush, An: The Journal of Thomas Kerr," ed. Charles L. Camp, 7:205-27, 395-404; 8:17-25, 167-82, 262-77

Irish Mother, The (play), 21:148

Irish Tiger, The (play), 9:135, 136, 173

Iron and steel, 5:269; 27:179; 30:344-51; 35:365-66; foundries, 17:117; 18:22, 149; *see also* Union Iron Works

Iroquois (ship), 31:158

Iroquois Club, 5:95

Irrigation, 8:228; 37:81; 38:280; in Fresno Co., 25:17, 20-34 *passim,* 169-76 *passim;* in Los Angeles, 13:201; Mojave Desert, 26:280; 27:113-20 *passim;* Nevada Co., 28:233; 29:197-99; in San Jose, 14:5, 7

Irvin, John, 15:240

Irvine, Robert, 22:81

Irvine, Samuel Glasgow, 20:15, 19, 24

Irving, Robert M., 26:204

Irving House, San Francisco, 22:69, 81; 27:250

Irving Institute, 30:69

Irwin (Young's Hill, 1854), 8:203

Irwin, Benoni, 2:244

Irwin, Charles F., 33:373

Irwin, James, 34:169

Irwin, John L. C., 39:29-30

Irwin, Richard, 10:274, 278, 283, 289, 355-56, 367, 390

Irwin, Selden M. and Mrs., 21:63

Irwin, Wallace, 3:44

Irwin, Capt. William, 18:244, 250

Irwin, Gov. William, 29:289; 30:134, 147

Irwin, Mrs. William G., 25:233

Irwin (William G.) & Co., 40:38

Isaac (on *London,* 1849), 7:213

Isaac, J., 29:107

Isaacs, B., 16:338

Isaacs, J. D., 35:263

Isaacs, Solomon, 16:338

Isaac Todd (ship), 23:375

Isabel (brig, 1850), 5:147

Isabel (schr., 1865), 22:17, 154, 170-74 *passim*

Isabella (schr., 1810, 1839), 12:223, 224, 225; 14:128

Isabella (transport, 1846), 1:208; 33:261, 262

Isabella (brig, 1850), 7:226

Isbell, James C., 2:184; 4:169, 183; 13:73, 79

Ish, T. A., 26:170

Isham, J. B. G., 16:342; 32:350-61 *passim*

Ishi (Indian), 4:94

"Is History Becoming Less Interesting?," address by Lynn T. White, Jr., 23:380

Isidor (Negro, 1850), 6:223

Isidoro (Indian, 1846), 29:268

Isis Theater, San Diego, 20:140

Isla, Juan de la, 2:259; 7:235-36, 246, 252

Islais Creek, 21:113, 116-17, 122

Islares, Martin de, 6:311

Islas Desiertas, *see* Coronados

Isleta, 21:197, 221

Isnard, Joseph, 5:349-50; 6:43, 52-55; 39:13

Isnard and Cann, 31:313-14

Isoms, Ira, 28:337

Issler, Anne (Roller), address, "Stevenson and Silverado," 23:180

"Issues in the Broderick-Gwin Debates of 1859," by Donald E. Hargis, 32:313-25

"Is the Drake Plate of Brass Genuine?" by R. B. Haselden, 16:271-74

Isthmus (ship), 13:390; 29:105; 32:353

Italian Opera Troupe, 15:181, 183, 267, 274, 278

Italians, 2:197; 8:345, 349; 20:72, 78-79; 24:360; 35:29-35; 38:332, 336, 338, 340

"Italian-Swiss in California," by H. F. Raup, 30:305-14

Itrovide (ship), 12:300

Iturbi, Juan de, 1:36; 8:34, 36

Iturbide, Agustín, 14:15; 15:140; 24:292

Iturrigaray, José de, 33:373

Ivers (sou. Calif., 1870), 32:345

Iverson, Alfred, 19:270, 345

Iverson, Chris, 25:286

Ives, Joseph Christmas, 18:205-6; 22:8, 9, 10, 165

Ives, W. H., 32:121, 139

Ivey, Cyrus, 14:176-77, 182

Ivey, Everett D., 24:189

Ivy Social Club, San Francisco, 19:107-8

Iwakura (Sacramento, 1872), 11:50

Iwanow (S.F., 1850), 39:110

I.W.W., 40:144

J

J. A. Bayard (ship), 22:170
Jack, "Captain" (Indian), 15:286; 28:161
Jack, Ola, 26:203
Jackass and Tiger Co., 35:224
Jackass Hill, 3:196, 199
Jack Hays (riv. str), 14:384, 385; 30:158
Jackling, Mrs. Daniel C. (Virginia Joliffe), 36:183
Jacks, David, 29:20, 25-26; 38:174
Jacks, Mrs. David (María Cristina Romie), 29:25
Jacks, Margaret Anna, 38:74, 76
Jacks, Noel H., address, "True Tales of Early California Days," 15:193
Jacks Family Emigrating Co., 24:242
Jackson (mid. on Erie, 1846), 3:113
Jackson (S.F., 1849), 28:57
Jackson (Mariposa Co., 1850), 12:75
Jackson (in mines, 1850), 11:160
Jackson, Capt. (Portland, 1850), 2:126
Jackson (Mormon, 1852), 14:182
Jackson (Yuba Co., 1855), 8:341
Jackson, Miss (Sacramento, 1859), 10:59
Jackson, Mrs. (Sacramento, 1859), 10:48, 53
Jackson (nr. Kern L., 1861), 18:204
Jackson, Mrs. Alden A. M., 37:237
Jackson, Alexander M., 34:127-28
Jackson, Andrew, 10:8; 11:19, 20; 14:147; 19:1, 167, 168; 37:3, 4
Jackson, Andrew R., 9:371, 394; 10:50, 62, 66, 378, 379, 381
Jackson, Mrs. Charles M. (Harriot West), obit., 27:379
Jackson, David E., 2:35; 10:4, 28; 20:342; 28:119
Jackson, Mrs. Edward (Margaret Work), 22:103, 107
Jackson, Fred, 35:345, 353, 360
Jackson, Grant, 3:46; obit., 4:215
Jackson, Harry, 21:157
Jackson, John H. P., 4:320
Jackson, John R., 4:320
Jackson, Joseph Henry, 24:287; 30:353; 36:110, 114; obit., 34:279-80
Jackson, Thomas, 10:256

Jackson, Thomas Jonathan ("Stonewall"), 28:229
Jackson, W. Turrentine, 33:93-94; 39:81; "Mazatlán to the Estanislao: ... Lewis Richard Price's Journey to California in 1849," 39:35-51
Jackson, Wesley, 30:260, 367
Jackson, William and Mary C. (Francis), 4:215
Jackson, William A., map by, 13: opp. 378
Jackson (place), 2:137; 11:179-80, 181, 322; 15:376; 16:338; 30:260, 362; 32:128; newspapers, 20:164, 183, 185
Jackson County, Ore., 31:125
Jackson Creek, 31:148
Jackson Forks, 28:233
Jackson Ranch, 28:234
Jacksonville, Tuolumne Co., 38:37
Jacksonville, Ore., 28:199, 232; 31:274; letters from, 28:223-24, 351-54, 274
Jacksonville Extension Co., 35:208
Jack's Restaurant, San Francisco, 24:286
Jacob, Eugène and Jules, 22:304
Jacob, Richard Taylor, 4:376; 6:151; 22:44, 64; 29:335, 336
Jacobi, A. L., 33:61
Jacobi, Arnold, 13:335
Jacobs, Capt. (S.F., 1849), 36:309
Jacobs (S.F., 1856), 21:41
Jacobs, Cyrus, 24:34
Jacobs, E., 18:26, 27
Jacobs, E. J., 2:133
Jacobs, Gaskell S., 29:382
Jacobs (or Jacobsen), J. H., 31:331, 333
Jacobs, Sam, 18:366; 22:178; 23:118
Jacobs, Stephen W., 38:183-84; "Can We Insure a Future for the Past," 38:97-100
Jacobsen, H. J. T., 19:60-69 *passim*; 27:316; phot., 19: opp. 59
Jacobson (artist, 1864), 24:265
Jacobson, Pauline, 21:40, 73, 144
Jacqua, E. J., 36:149
Jacques Laffitte (ship), 22:297, 302, 303-4; 23:65-67
Jaeger (or Iaeger), Lewis (or Louis) John Frederick, 22:2, 20

Jaime, Antonio, 23:4, 5, 6, 13; 25:135
J. A. McClellan (ship), 39:302
James (Marysville, 1858), 9:358; *see also* Giles, James & Co.
James (Death Valley, 1861), 18:206
James, Alfred, 12:323
James, Charles Sexton, obit., 38:360
James, George F., 8:370; 16:336; 17:81
James, George Wharton, 23:13, 15
James, J. B., 9:388
James, John W., 16:340
James, Lewis F., 21:241
James, Marquis and Bessie (Rowland), 36:112
James, W. E., 4:35
James, William, 36:356; 37:40, 41, 42
"James A. McDougall," by A. Russell Buchanan, 15:199-212
James Blair (riv. str.), 9:376, 397; 10:246, 271
James Bridger, by Alter, rev., 4:290-91
"James Clyman, His Diaries and Reminiscences," ed. Charles L. Camp, 4:105-41, 272-83, 307-60; 5:44-84, 109-38, 255-82, 378-401; 6:58-68
James E. Birch, by Galucci and Galucci, rev., 37:372-73
James L. Day (ship), 25:111
"James McHall Jones," by George Cosgrave, 20:97-116; as address, 20:283
James M. Ryerson (ship), 19:376
Jameson, J. M. ("Jack"), 32:2-41 *passim*
Jameson, John McKnight, 2:21
Jamestown, 5:404; 13:373, 383; 15:272; 16:84; 20:100-101, 114; 22:344; 24:344; 35:216
James Wilson Marshall, by Bekeart, rev., 4:89
Jamesworth, Charles, 27:67
Jamieson, Mrs. Ebenezer (Katharine Hillsee), obit., 13:92
Jamison, Albert E., 18:307, 314
Jamison, Stephen and Anna (Smith), 28:294
Janauschek, Fanny, 21:173, 174
Janes, Henry B., 9:103, 106, 113
Janes, Horace P., 17:171, 172; 19:232; 27:264(?); 33:373; 37:155
Janes, T. M., 17:169
Janes, Doyle, Barber & Boyd, 17:171, 172; 37:155
Janeway, Mrs. G. Harold (Mary Louise Davis), 30:93

Janin, Charles Henry, 35:183
Janin, Mrs. Charles Henry (Erwina Dunbar Smith), obit., 35:183
Janin, Louis, 6:354
Janion, R. C., *see* Starkey, Janion & Co.
Janson (or Jansen), Charles J., 6:49; 12:106; 15:34, 37
Janson, Bond & Co., 26:355
Janssens, Victor Eugène Auguste, 14:252; 18:172, 179; 36:9
Janveter, Robert, 33:364
Japan, 8:50; 11:50, 51, 52; 18:85-86, 93; 30:195-204 *passim*; 38:338; embassy from (S.F., 1860), 18:93; 23:335-47; 29:109; 38:332; emigration from, 19:330; 28:343-50; treaty with, 15:163; 18:86; *see also* Japanese
Japanese, 3:255; 5:288, 8:50; 11:50-51; 12:107; 18:85-86; 19:330; 23:335-47; 24:158-59; 27:280; 28:38, 343-50; 29:107, 109, 120; 30:198-204 *passim*; 38:332, 338; acrobatic and theatrical troupes, 21:154-56, 178
Jaqua, E. J., 36:149
Jaramillo, Juan, 3:265
Jaramillo, Juan José, 12:117
Jaramillo, María Josefa, 1:150
Jarboe, John R., 1:13, 15-18
Jarnagin (or Jarnigan), John M., 15:88
Jarrett (Yuba Co., 1857), 9:157; 10:386
Jarrett (Henry C.) and (Harry) Palmer Troupe, 18:355, 370; 21:246
Jarrett and Rice Co., 21:260
Jarves, James Jackson, 18:166, 178; 32:106
Jarvis, Charles, 11:157-74 *passim*
Jarvis, Edward, 11:157, 164-69 *passim*, 173
Jarvis, Edward (nephew), 11:157, 165-71 *passim*
Jarvis, Frank, 11:157, 168
Jarvis, James, 11:157, 164, 168
Jarvis, Leonard FitzEdward, 11:157-70 *passim*, 174, 175
Jarvis, Peter, 13:32
Jaso, Juan de, 3:311, 339; 6:298
Jason (ship), 31:207
Java (ship), 22:296-97; 35:313
Jayhawkers, 9:186; 18:180, 196-201 *passim*, 207, 208, 210, 215; 19:186
Jayhawker Well (or Spring), 18:200, 201, 208, 209, 210, 213; phot., 8: opp. 208
Jayme, Antonio, 25:135

Jayme (or Jaume), Luis, 20:236; 23:371
Jayne, Anselin H., 22:251
Jayne, C. F., 22:251
J. B. Ford (ship), 22:154, 170-74 *passim*
J. Bragdon (riv. str.), 8:201, 210; 9:72; 10:376; 15:266, 367
"Jean de Nivelle" (pseud.), 39:160
"Jean de Paris," *see* Véron, Pierre
Jeanette's Wedding (operetta), 15:180
"Jean François Galaup de Lapérouse," address by Raoul H. Blanquie, 26:371-73
"Jean François Galaup de Lapérouse, a Check List," comp. by Edward W. Allen, 20:47-64
Jean-Georges, Louis, 14:142
Jeanne d' Arc (play), 20:134
"Jean Tout Court" (pseud.), 39:160
Jecker-Torre and Co., 18:11
"Jedediah Smith's Route across the Sierra," by C. Hart Merriam, 3:25-29
J. E. Donald (ship), 7:211, 212, 213
Jee, Arthur W. (?), 13:296
Jeffers, Lottie, *see* Westcott, Mrs. George C.
Jeffers, Martha, *see* "The Jeffers-Willey Wedding"
Jefferson, Joseph, 21:52, 72
Jefferson, Mary Ann, *see* Paty, Mrs. John
Jefferson, T. H., 32:199-200
Jefferson, Thomas, 10:3; 11:29; 29:185
Jefferson (place), 13:28
Jefferson, State of (prop.), 31:125-38
Jefferson, Territory of (Colo.), 31:136, 138
Jefferson Davis (ship), 15:167-68, 271; 16:82
Jefferson House, Yuba Co., 8:341, 358
"Jeffers-Willey Wedding ... 1849, The," ed. Miriam Drury, 35:11-21
Jeffrey, J., 32:165, 168
Jeffrey, John, 18:343, 346; 28:201, 205, 217, 225-26; 32:165, 168, 249
Jeffrey, John Heatley and Nellie (Hamilton), 35:332
Jeffries, Mrs. (Marysville, 1857), 9:163
Jeffries, Horace, 10:247
Jefts, James M., 14:394
Jeghers, A. J., 11:127

"Jehan Du Bief," *see* Lusinchi, Augustin
Jenkins, Mr. and Mrs. (Stanislaus Co., 1850), 11:360
Jenkins, David, 23:192
Jenkins, George, 10:394
Jenkins, John (stage driver, 1850), 13:256-57
Jenkins, John (S.F., 1851), 3:40; 22:113, 260; 24:48, 70; 28:42; 34:236
Jenkins, Olaf P., 17: No. 4, Pt. 2, p. 3
Jenkins, Richard, 9:347, 369, 373, 374
Jenkins, Robert S., 22:251
Jenkins, T. F., 11:9
Jenney, Ralph, 36:64, 161
"Jennie of the Green," 6:337-38
Jennings (Philippines, 1898), 30:290, 292-93, 295, 300; 31:59-65 *passim*
Jennings, George, 31:300
Jennings, H. N., 18:206
Jennings, H. V., 9:381
Jennings, John (Sacramento, 1856), 9:103
Jennings, John (S.F., 1881), 21:257
Jennings, Thomas, 7:405; 31:300
Jennings, William, 22:17, 24
Jenny (ship), 2:276, 299; 10:328
Jenny Lind (ship), 13:258; 29:20, 25
Jenny Lind theaters, San Francisco, 3:35-36; 7:284; 10:205, 381, 389, 393; 14:411; 20:294-301 *passim;* 21:53; 22:113, 260, 266; 28:36, 37, 45; 33:43; 38:19; illus., 20: opp. 289
Jensen, A. C., 24:287-88
Jensen, Elmer D., 21:383
Jensen, Holger and Helen (Webster), 34:332
Jensen, James M., 40:251; bk. rev. by, 40:250-51
Jensen, William, 30:208
Jepson, Willis Linn, 18:344; 23:373; 32:258; 35:2; address, "California Journal of Archibald Menzies," 8:386; 9:91
"Jeptha H. Wade in California," by William F. Zornow, 29:345-56
"Jérémie" (pseud.), 39:160
Jernegan, W. L., 12:324
Jerome (Philippines, 1898), 39:49
Jerome, Edward B., 17:320
Jerome, Mrs. Thomas (née Baker), 17:322
Jerome, Timothy, 9:372
Jerry Bryant (yacht), 15:369, 370

Jerry Giesler Story, The, by Giesler, rev., 40:157-58

Jersey Flat, 13:28

Jess, George H., 24:288

"Jessie Benton Frémont," address by James A. B. Scherer, 21:278

Jessup, Armeda, *see* Pratt, Mrs. Leonidas

Jessup, Elizabeth, 28:340

Jessup, John Bright, 34:104; *see also* Lockwood, Rufus Allen

Jessup, Jonathan Trumbell, *see* Lockwood, Rufus A.

Jessup, Richard M., 15:164, 255, 262; 16:81; 17:174

Jessup, William H., 16:283

Jessup family, 34:98-99, 104

Jess Valley, 24:288

"Jesuit Arrival in San Francisco in 1849, The," by John B. McGloin, 29:139-47

Jesuits, 1:12; 4:361; 5:196-97; 6:103-4; 8:238, 374-77; 16:86, 185; 20:222-23, 234; 29:139-47; 32:122, 139; 36:87-88, 341; in Lower Calif., 26:309, 310

Jesup, Thomas Sidney, 33:266, 267

Jesurun, Edward, obit., 11:388

Jesús, Felipe de, 23:6

Jesús, María Vásquez del Mercado, 23:8

Jesús María Creek, 25:222; 27:87

Jesús María land grant, *see* Ranchos: Rio de Jesús María

Jewell (Dry Creek, 1850), 30:239

Jewell, Edward S. and Mary (Markham), 33:190

Jewell, George C., 20:271

Jewell, Sam, 30:263

Jewess, The (play), 9:245, 271

Jewett, Mrs. Clinton, 27:187

Jewett, Isaac T., 23:159, 173-74, 227

Jewett, John H., 10:166, 184, 191, 281, 358, 370; 14:216, 400-401; 15:21, 33, 36; *see also* Decker & Jewett

Jewett, Seward and Alvira (Clay), 10:267

Jewett, William Cornell and Mrs., 23:163, 176

Jewett, William Dunbar, 23:149; 33:312-15; 35:183

Jewett, Mrs. William Dunbar (Myriem Pemberton), 33:314

Jewett, William Smith, 16:346; 23:287; 24:261, 265-66; 33:309-13; "Some Letters of," ed. Elliott Evans,

23:149-77, 227-46; phot., 23: opp. 149; drawings by, 23: opp. 156, opp. 167, opp. 227

Jewett, Mrs. William Smith (Elizabeth Dunbar), 33:312, 313, 318, 319; 35:183

Jewish synagogues and temples, 15:167, 170, 173, 174; 36:298, 306; 38:34; phot., 38: foll. 40

Jews, 10:377; 14:404; 15:170, 176; 22:254, 267, 268-69, 272; 29:175, 242; *see also* Hebrew

Jillson, Mrs. Carlos ("Caddie" Young), 9:172

Jiménez, Francisco, 9:13

Jiménez, Fortún, 20:234

Jimeno, Manuela, 33:268, 338, 340, 341

Jimeno Casarín, Mrs. Manuel (María Angustias de la Guerra), *see* Ord, Mrs. James L.

"Jimmy-from-Town," *see* Burns, James

Jinkerton, Andrew, 15:39

Jirokichi, "Techniques and Implements of the American Whale-Fishery," 32:225-28

J. M. Chapman (ship), 20:159; 26:18; 27:179; 33:234; 40:301

Joachimssen (Stockton, 1850s), 30:258

Joaquín (Portuguese, 1879), 35:235

"Joaquin Miller," address by Juanita Miller, 10:307

"Joaquin Miller Foundation, The," by William W. Winn, 32:231-41

"Joaquin Miller's 'Real Name,' " by William W. Winn, 33:143-46

Jobson, David, 15:29; 23:103; 38:314

Job's Saloon, San Francisco, 23:338, 340

Jocelyn, Pember J., 10:181, 200

Jocelyn, Stephen Perry, 32:94; "The Old Occidental [Hotel]," 32:57-64

Jocko (pantomime), 15:183

Jode, Gerard de, map pub. by, 7: opp. 69

Johanna and Oluffa (ship), 25:100

Johannsen, Robert W., 35:92; ed. "Edward O. C. Ord on Frontier Defense," 35:23-27

John (on *Susan Drew*, 1847), 1:227-28

John Adams (ship), 14:357; 15:161

John A. Hooper (ship), 31:296

"John Albert Hooper," based on research by Aubrey Drury, 31:289-305

John Allyne (ship), 20:34, 46; 30:172
"John Augustus Sutter's European
   Background," by James P. Zollinger,
   14:28-46
John Begg (ship), 6:255, 257, 260;
   8:290; 18:179
John Benson (ship), 13:389
"John C. Frémont," address by James
   D. Phelan, 6:285-86
John Day country, Ore., 15:324, 374
John Day River, 2:195, 198(?), 199,
   213
"John Gantt, 'Borderer,'" by Alice
   B. Maloney, 16:48-60
"John G. Downey as One of the
   'Kings,'" by Julia H. Macleod,
   36:327-31
John Gilpin (ship), 26:227
John L. Stephens (ship), 15:88, 165,
   173, 181, 186, 274, 279, 282; 16:81,
   342; 21:42; 26:199; 27:327; 37:199
John Marsh, Pioneer, by Lyman, rev.,
   9:400-401
John Martenal (ship), 2:123
"John Muir: Some Personal
   Recollections," by Augustin S.
   Macdonald, 17:18-20
John Muir Trail, 4:49, 52
John N. Gossler (ship), 15:171
"John Paul," *see* Webb, Charles Henry
John Rickson (ship), 7:218
Johns, Thomas D., 15:179, 370,
   375; 17: opp. 200; 31:34, 39, 45
Johns, Tremenhere, 21:144
Johns, William, 22:95
Johnson (San Diego, 1847), 22:57
Johnson (S.F. to Oahu, 1849), 14:337
Johnson (Iowa Hill, 1855), 15:271
Johnson (S.F., 1855), 15:375
Johnson (d. L.A., 1855), 15:270
Johnson (Yuba Co., 1855-59), 8:352;
   9:136, 139, 140, 346, 373, 376;
   10:42, 54
Johnson (S.F., 1858), 6:15, 16
Johnson, Dr. (bought bks., 1860),
   29:118, 119
Johnson, Dr. (Marysville, 1861), 10:363
Johnson(constable, San Bernardino,
   1861), 39:299
Johnson, A. D., 22:159
Johnson, A. H., 4:33, 34, 35, 54
Johnson, A. M., 7:18-19
Johnson, A. W., 14:402
Johnson, Adelaida, 1:258
Johnson, Amasa P., Jr., 36:156-57

Johnson, Andrew H., 26:204
Johnson, Anita, *see* Mellus, Mrs. Henry
Johnson, Asa, 22:231
Johnson, B. F. ("Quartz"), 5:328
Johnson, Belle, 29:294
Johnson, Cave, 27:34
Johnson, Charles, 11:127
Johnson, Charles B., 15:370
Johnson, Charles Russell, 25:94; 27:218
Johnson, D. G., 18:292
Johnson, David W., 3:118
Johnson, Edith, 10:219
Johnson, Edward, 27:217, 220-21
Johnson, Francis, 14:321, 343; 28:97
Johnson, Frank Tenney, 5:198
Johnson, G. W., 26:227; 28:315-17;
   29:39
Johnson, Gardiner, 26:188; obit. of
   Orla St. Clair, 40:178-79
Johnson, George Alonzo, 22:4, 6-10
   passim, 16, 18, 159
Johnson, George B., 19:72
Johnson, George C., 19:232
Johnson, Grove Lawrence, 38:236
Johnson, Gus, 37:347
Johnson, Henry, 2:122
Johnson, Hiram Warren, 25:186-87,
   381; 27:183; 30:191; 31:378; 34:158,
   162; 36:110, 251-52, 254, 259, 261;
   37:273, 352; 38:229-47, 349, 351, 356;
   phot., 38: opp. 229
Johnson, Mrs. Hiram Warren, Jr.
   (née Bowles), 5:102
Johnson, J. B., 15:281, 364
Johnson, J. H., 4:14
Johnson, J. W., 29:284; "Early
   Engineering Center in California,"
   29:193-209
Johnson, James (Ariz., early 1840s),
   21:207, 223
Johnson, James (to Ore., 1844), 4:321
Johnson, James (L.A., 1846), 1:249;
   3:118; 17:339
Johnson, James A., 10:50, 62; 11:9
Johnson, James G., 13:333
Johnson, John, 9:139, 169
Johnson, John Franklin, 37:270-74
   passim, 348
Johnson, John Neely, 3:155; 7:10, 17;
   8:358, 360, 367; 9:42-48 *passim*, 170,
   181, 250, 260, 261, 375; 15:168, 264,
   265, 377; 16:82, 337; 17:77, 80, 182;
   21:27, 98; 24:169, 170; 29:176, 247;
   38:17; art. based on cor. of,
   14:350-74; 15:70-87, 143-62, 247-65;

family of, 15: 265; ports., 9: opp. 99; 14: opp. 350
Johnson, Mrs. Karl E., 25:381
Johnson, Kenneth M., 26:382; 38:88; "Frederic Hall," 38:47-58
Johnson, Mrs. ("Irish") Mary (Marysville, 1861), 10:360
Johnson, Mary (S.F., 1876), 29:294
Johnson, Nelson, 8:207; 9:168
Johnson, Otis Russell, 25:94
Johnson, Overton, 4:283; 11:291
Johnson, P. C., 11:9, 21, 22
Johnson, R. P., 7:5; 9:36
Johnson, R. W., 19:20, 21
Johnson, Reverdy, 15:6; 17:316
Johnson, Robert, 16:321
Johnson, Robert Underwood, 4:43; 38:251-58 *passim*
Johnson, S. L., 11:127
Johnson, Sargent, 38:3
Johnson, T. B., 22:251
Johnson, T. P., 16:79
Johnson, T. R., 30:108, 256; *see also* Gihon, Johnson, and Butler
Johnson, W. H., 22:33
Johnson, W. R., 7:115
Johnson, W. S., 38:314
Johnson, Willard D., 4:42, 51, 55
Johnson, William, 1:139; *see also* Johnson's Rancho
Johnson, William H., 14:223
Johnson, William J., *see* Johnston
Johnson, William Neely, 9:26, 140, 174, 245, 259, 261; 10:76; 14:352, 369-71; 15:265; 16:83-84; 34:211
Johnson & Carey, 11:166
Johnson (George A.) Co., 22:6-19 *passim*, 23, 24
Johnson (H.) & Co., 15:372
Johnson Cutoff, 7:5, 7
"Johnson-Hughes Incident of 1916," address by George E. Mowry, 25:85-86; 26:79
Johnson Lode, 5:328
Johnson's Crossing, 23:349
Johnson's Pass, 7:8, 9
Johnson's Rancho, 5:276; 6:134; 10:347-50, 352; 11:101, 105, 109-11, 121; 13:171; 14:205, 212, 214, 222, 224, 384; 19:116, 136; 23:353; 29:298
Johnston (Sacramento, 1849), 13:85
Johnston (Mojave Desert, 1874), 17:215
Johnston, Dr. (Lt., U.S.A., 1898), 30:303; 31:50, 52, 56, 58
Johnston, A. L., 26:188

Johnston, Abraham Robinson, 1:140-45 *passim*, 240; 3:122; 17:341, 343; 21:194, 204, 215, 220, 221, 222, 336; 25:295-96, 300-303, 306; 26:23, 29, 35, 40, 43, 44, 52, 55, 57; 34:195, 197, 199
Johnston, Adam, 26:327, 347; 28:326, 327, 331, 334
Johnston, Albert Sidney, 7:291; 19:271; 21:276; 22:9, 18; 26:260-61, 353; 28:165-73; 29:229, 240, 243, 248; 31:75; 33:229, 230, 338; 34:38, 155; 40:291, 343, 347
Johnston, Mrs. Albert Sidney (Eliza Griffin), 21:195; 31:75; 33:339; 34:37, 38
Johnston, George C., 26:262
Johnston, George Pen, 9:27, 29, 387, 388; 10:257, 268; 15:270, 278; 16:83; 19:231, 236; 25:337
Johnston, Hancock, 34:38
Johnston, J., 8:360
Johnston, J. S., 9:55
Johnston, Joseph Eggleston, 18:116, 124
Johnston, William B. (S.F., 1860), 23:344
Johnston, William B. and Janet (Newlands), 22:95
Johnston (or Johnson), William J., 14:269, 273; 26:112-17 *passim*, 122, 128
Johnston, William Preston, 28:166
Johnstone, Lt. (w .Vancouver, 1792), 2:275-78 *passim*, 302, 303, 333, 334
Johnstone, Mrs. Bruce (Elsie Leale), 29:190
John Stuart (ship), 15:177; 25:331; 29:108-9
"John Swett's Diary . . . 1853," ed. Will S. Cluff, Jr., 33:289-308
"John Work of the Hudson's Bay Co.," by Alice B. Maloney, 22:97-109
John T. Wright (ship), 10:285; 32:223
"John White Geary and His Brother Edward," by Clifford M. Drury, 20:12-25
"John W. Mackay," address by Grant H. Smith, 16:88
Joice, Erastus Volney, 28:57, 59, 65, 66, 116
Joice, William, 36:47, 51
Joiner, Letitia Jane, 31:190
Jolliffe, *see* Moffitt, Mrs. Herbert C.
Jolliffe, William Howard, family of, 36:183-84
Jones (ferry, Kings R., 1850), 11:258

Jones (S.F., 1850), 6:43
Jones, Rev. Mr. (Young's Hill, 1857),
 9:145, 147
Jones, Miss (Ohio Flat, 1858), 9:352
Jones (sheriff, Marysville, 1861),
 10:365
Jones, Capt. (Colorado R., 1873),
 22:174
Jones, Alice, 2:68
Jones, Anna (Hamrick), 27:188
Jones, Avonia, 10:57, 74-75, 77; 21:46
Jones, Benjamin C., address, "Early
 Trails of the Clear Lake Region,"
 32:376
Jones, Bertrand, 8:346, 352
Jones, Mrs. C. W., 10:290
Jones, Cullen, 30:382
Jones, D. (Dr. W. W. ?), 27:366
Jones, Dana H., 25:381
Jones, David Rhys, 33:375; address,
 "What the Indians Remember of
 ... Jedediah Smith," 11:389
Jones, Edgar A., 31:341
Jones, Edward, 14:364, 367, 368, 371,
 373; 16:340, 347; 17:169-82 *passim*;
 21:323-25
Jones, Elbert P., 2:116; 3:34; 4:170, 175;
 5:406; 11:130-32, 134; 17:296, 298,
 300
Jones, Mrs. Elbert P. (Sarah Kittleman),
 11:132; 17:298
Jones, Everett, 31:301
Jones, Franklin L., 9:26, 27
Jones, Georgina Frances, 2:68
Jones, H. H., 13:31
Jones, Hal, 36:69
Jones, Henry B., 35:256
Jones, Henry Z., 30:222
Jones, Herbert C., 36:252, 253, 255, 258;
 address, "California's First
 Legislature," 29:75-76; introd. to
 "The Party, the Machine, and the
 Vote," 38:349-51
Jones, Isaac, 36:257
Jones, J. T., 15:171
Jones, J. W., 30:262, 363
Jones, Jack, 33:364
Jones, James McHall, 10:152, 156, 158;
 19:7, 8-9, 165, 265; 22:28; 26:333;
 28:193, 361, 373; 31:177; art. on,
 20:97-116; fac. sig., 10: opp. 159; port.,
 20: opp. 97
Jones, Jenny, 10:376
Jones, Jerry, 22:341, 345; 23:23

Jones, John (San Mateo Co., 1840s),
 17:253
Jones, John (Brandy City, 1857), 9:165,
 166, 180
Jones, John Coffin, Jr., 8:106, 299;
 12:138, 139, 141; 14:317-18, 341, 343;
 16:4; 22:346; 23:203, 215, 305, 319,
 331, 332; 26:249, 251; 28:258; 34:113,
 118-19
Jones, John M., 13:339
Jones, John Percival, 2:68; 15:381;
 17:210, 213, 218; 27:346; 31:185;
 38:166
Jones, Mrs. John Percival (Georgina
 Frances Sullivan), 2:3, 4, 68; 35:159
Jones, John S., 26:204
Jones, John Wesley, 6:109-10; 26:147;
 33:30; "Pantoscope of California,"
 6:109-29, 238-53; sketches from
 daguerreotypes, 6: opp. 9-opp. 128
 passim, opp. 238-opp. 252 *passim*; 26:
 foll. 126
Jones, Joseph B., 9:189
Jones, Julia Beldon, *see* Brookes, Mrs.
 Samuel Marsden
Jones, Mrs. Laura A., 25:335
Jones, Lydia Coffin, *see* Winslow, Mrs.
 Charles Frederick
Jones, Madison Ralph, obit., 9:189-90
Jones, Margaret Louisa (Axton),
 27:189
Jones, Marion, 2:68
Jones, Mary, 10:359
Jones, Nathaniel, 30:5
Jones, Roger, 28:213, 228; 33:266, 267,
 338
Jones, T. L., 8:358
Jones, T. W., 30:262
Jones, Thomas, 15:239
Jones, Thomas ap Catesby, 6:151;
 8:296; 10:8, 132, 202; 11:196-97;
 13:34, 43, 228-29, 272, 396, 397, 400;
 15:20, 227, 228, 285; 17:146-49 *passim*,
 261; 19:4, 200, 201, 214; 20:31, 45;
 23:290; 25:196; 27:18, 43, 50; 28:249,
 256; 29:315; 30:40, 43-47; 32:293;
 33:50; 34:115-16, 121; 35:112;
 36:308-11 *passim*
Jones, W., 11:127
Jones, W. P., 17:177
Jones, Walter E., 8:358
Jones, Walter Parker, 12:188
Jones, Webster A., 25:381
Jones, William Carey, 12:174; 13:154;

17:257; 19:182; 30:324, 329; 34:254-55; 35:15

Jones, William Carey [Jr.], 1:14, 15, 17, 21; 24:79, 80; 37:51; obit., 2:371

Jones, William D., 37:8

Jones, Wilson, 13:324

Jones, Zachariah ("Buffalo"), 2:182; 14:19-20; 27:162, 260; 29:57; sawmill, 27:260; 29:57

Jones (David), Wooll & Sutherland, 25:7; 30:382

Jones (G. W. C.) *v.* Samuel Norris, 25:225

Jones' Bar, 10:348

Jones' Camp, 2:187

Jones's Creek (Los Gatos), 29:43

Jones' Hotel, Sacramento, 15:273

Jones' Hotel, San Francisco, 22:263, 264; *see also* Portsmouth House

"Jones' Pantoscope of California: A 'Lecture' by J. Wesley Jones," 6:109-29, 238-53

Joon, Joaquin, *see* Young, Ewing

Jordan (Spanish Bar, 1851), 2:138

Jordan, David Starr, 1:19; 4:49, 55; 10:87; 13:187; 25:178; 28:186; 31:30; 32:260; 35:239; 37:41

Jordan, Emily, 21:64-65

Jordan, William H., 27:223

Jore, Léonce, 19:384

Jorgensen, Christian, 30:284; 37:33

Jornada del Muerto, 20:345; 21:213; 32:43; 34:126

Jornal Português, Oakland, 35:244

Jorres, Gustave, 35:359

José (hanged, Jackson, 1855), 15:376

"José Huero," (Joseph Chapman), 13:206-7

José Jesús (Indian, 1851), 28:330

"José Viejo" (Santa Barbara, 1846), 18:164

Joseph (ship), *see Saint Joseph*

Joseph, Mount, 2:236

"Joseph de Moraga Commissioned Lieutenant," ed. and trans. Pablo Avila, 27:63-64

Josephine ("Little Cricket"), 9:374

Josephine (bark, 1849), 22:367

Josephine (brig., 1864-72), 22:154, 159, 170-74 *passim*; 37:210

Josephine (ship, wrecked), 27:293

Josephine County, Ore., 31:126-38 *passim*

Josephine Mine, 21:325-26

Joset, Joseph, 29:141, 142, 146

Josselyn, Charles, 31:301

"Jota Jota" (J. J. Warner), 13:214

" 'Jottings' on Civil War California," by Andrew Wilson, ed. John H. Kemble, 32:209-24, 303-12

Jouan, Aguste, 17:174

Joughin, Eleanor, 28:188

Joullin, Amedée, 37:33

Jourdain (S.F., 1849), 5:20

Jourdain, Emile, 12:157

Jourdain, Etienne, 5:27, 355, 373; 6:56; 13:274, 279, 380

Jourdain Hotel, San Jose, 5:27, 355

Jourdan *v.* Phelps, 9:358

Journal, Hayward, 24:62, 72

Journal, Salinas, 29:89

Journal (German), San Francisco, 15:272

Journal, Stockton, 34:342, 343

Journal d'Hygiène et de Santé, Le, 39:247, 348; fac. cover, 39: foll. 232

Journal du Lundi, Le, 39:219, 348

Journal des Pichets, 39:5

Journal du Stock Mineur, Le, 39:160

"Journal of a 'Crazy Man,' The: . . . Albert Ferdinand Morris," ed. Charles L. Camp, 15:103-38, 224-41

"Journal of Benjamin Dore, The," ed. Charles L. Camp, 2:87-139

"Journal of Captain John Paty, 1807-1868," 14:291-346

Journal of Commerce, San Francisco, 15:179; 18:331; 20:332, 338; 27:174; 28:36

"Journal of David Jackson Staples, The," ed. Harold F. Taggart, 22:119-50

"Journal of George Russell Adams," ed. Harold F. Taggart, 35:291-307

"Journal of John McHenry Hollingsworth," ed. Henry R. Wagner, 1:207-70

"Journal of John Wood, The," Henry R. Wagner, 6:360-63

Journal of *José Longinos Martínez: . . . Naturalist of the Botanical Expedition in . . . California . . . 1791-1792*, trans. and ed. Simpson, rev., 40:263-65

"Journal of Madison Berryman Moorman, The," address by Irene D. Paden, 27:180-81

"Journal of Riley Root, The," by Edward Eberstadt, 10:396-405

Journal of the Birmingham Emigrating

Co., A, by Loomis, ed. Ledyard, rev., 8:81-82
"Journal of William Dunlop Brackenridge," 24:326-36
"Journal of William H. Ennis," ed. Harold F. Taggart, 33:1-12, 147-68
Journey through the Rocky Mountains . . ., by Jacob H. Schiel, rev., 38:80-83
Journey to Lower Oregon and Upper California, A, by Damon, rev., 7:195-96
Jous's & Co., Timbuctoo, 9:357
Joven Guipuzcoana (ship), 8:106; 15:126, 128, 238; 17:54; 18:179; 19:216; 26:61; 28:260
Joven Tartar (ship), 18:71
Joy, Capt. (of *Henry Astor*, 1849), 29:16
Joy, Hartford, 16:36, 56
Joyce (or Joice; S.F., 1851), 19:228
Joyce, E. V., *see* Joice, Erastus V.
Joyce, John, wife and daughters, 37:237
Joyce, John F., 27:34-45 *passim*, 362, 365, 368, 370; 28:57, 59, 63, 65
Joyce, Matthew, 15:281
J. R. Mora (ship), 17:172
J. Ross Browne, by Rock, rev., 8:280
J. R. S. (ship), 19:326; 28:113, 114
J. S. Cabot (ship), 22:169
Juan (w. Dr. LeConte, 1851), 21:109-10
Juana Basilia (Indian, ca. 1822), 2:341, 343
Juan Antonio (Indian, 1863), 12:8, 118
"Juan Cojo," *see* Gönninger, Hans
Juan de Dios (Indian, 1826), 23:6
Juan de Fuca, Strait of, 9:202, 207; 10:313, 314, 315, 321, 323, 324; 15:214, 215
Juan Fernandez, island of, 3:93
"Juan Flaco," *see* Brown, John
Juan Francisco, Port (Tomales Bay), 2:335; 10:334, 342
Juanita claim, 32:4-5, 11, 13
Juan José (ship), 8:106
"Juan Largo," *see* Warner, Jonathan T.
Juan Perez Sound, 9:204
Juan Rodriguez, Isla de, 7:51, 52
Juárez, Benito Pablo, 34:150; 37:193, 194, 199, 202, 211, 212
Juárez, Cayetano, 13:36; 16:133, 134,

249, 356; 17:225; 26:209-10; 28:264; 29:319
Juárez, José, 28:324-26
Juárez, Marcos, 16:249
Juarez, Mex., *see* El Paso del Norte
Jubaville (Marysville), 14:219, 220
Judah, Mrs. and children (Isthmus of Panama, 1851), 20:18
Judah, Charles D., 4:219; 15:281; 28:360; 29:148
Judah, Edward, 4:250
Judah, H. R., 4:219, 263
Judah, Henry M., 4:219; 40:349
Judah, Mrs. Marietta (Starfield), 9:279; 10:77, 389; 16:184, 283; 21:45, 53, 157
Judah, Theodore Dehone, 3:398; 4:300; 5:178; 7:8; 9:42; 10:293, 306; 11:11, 25; 21:80; 24:167, 180; 32:223; 38:28, 352; art. on, 4:219-71; phot., 4: opp. 219
Judah, Mrs. Theodore Dehone (Anna Ferona Pierce), 4:220, 221, 227, 241, 244, 245, 263, 264
Judd, Gerrit P., 17:132; 29:2; 35:196
Judd, John, 6:335
Judd, Lucy, 10:258
Judge John F. Ellison, ed. Ellison, rev., 9:87-88
" 'Judge' Robert Thompson," by Augusta B. Warren, 30:237-48
Judges, 20:14, 104, 110-11, 366; 26:343-44; 27:209; *see also* Alcades; Courts; Field, Stephen J.; Jones, James McHall; Murray, Hugh C.
"Judio, El," *see* Sánchez, José María
Judith (opera), 15:174, 178
Judkins, Alvin B., 31:381
Judkins, Mary Elizabeth, 31:381
Juignet, P., 20:128; 39:232, 262
Juilliard, Charles F. and Sarah (Chilton), 35:83
Jules, Victor, 32:117
Julia (later *Julia Ann*; schr., 1841), 7:105; 14:343; 17:293; 22:51-58 *passim*; 30:51, 52; 33:252
Julia (schr., 1856), 15:85; 24:180
Julia Ann (str., 1880s), 32:366
Julian (Fr. Canadian, d. 1846), 22:366-67
Julian, Courtney C., 38:132, 133
Julian, J. M., 20:332
Julian Petroleum Corporation, 38:132-33
Julien, Paul, 21:144

"Julius Wangenheim, an
    Autobiography," 35:119-44, 253-74,
    345-66; 36:63-78, 149-64
Jump, Edward, 2:243; 14:412
Jumuba, 29:34
Juncosa, Domingo, 1:161; 10:216-17
Junction House (nr. Camptonville),
    8:209; 9:51, 155-59 *passim*
Junction P.O., 12:29, 31, 32
Junius (ship), 6:257, 260
Junks, Chinese, 37:82
Juno (*Unona;* ship), 1:90; 3:84, 108;
    6:271; 7:84; 9:83; 12:39, 50, 191,
    207; 16:108; 18:144
Juntas, 1:31; in 1824, 20:239; in
    1825-27, 24:289-320; 25:57-78,
    149-68, 267-78, 347-67; 30:325; in
    1836, 1:30; in 1840, 10:8; in 1846,
    4:286; 5:193-95; 6:86, 189, 269-70;
    17:279
Jurupa, *see* Ranchos: Jurupa
Jury, first in California, 18:35; 25:129;
    35:104-6
Jussieu, Antoine Laurent de,
    18:335, 344
Justh & Co., lithographs by, 14:
    opp. 224
Justices of the peace, 1:31-32; 9:71;
    15:270; *see also* Courts, Justices
Juventa (ship), 22:171, 172, 173

K

Kabler, Nicholas, 9:269
Kadiak (ship), 12:191, 194, 228, 240;
    16:108
Käseberg, *see* Keseberg
Kahler, Carl, 20:137
Kahn, Edgar Myron, 19:192; 25:93;
    "Andrew S. Hallidie as Writer and
    Speaker," 25:1-16; "Andrew Smith
    Hallidie," 19:144-56; comp. "Some
    California Dates of 1859," 38:25-30;
    bk. revs. by, 39:182; 40:359-60; obits.
    of Frederick Baruch, 18:188; Marcus
    M. Baruh, 21:189; Anna W. Beaver,
    17:93; Morgan A. Gunst, 37:277-78;
    Mabel Thompson Haas, 36:374-75;
    Mrs. William H. Powers, 26:89-90;
    Walter Rothchild, 17:95-96; Weston
    H. Settlemier, 26:282; Paul A.
    Sinsheimer, 35:377-78; Joseph Sloss,
    18:363; Richard Sprague, 18:95;
    Lawrence Strassburger, 15:384-85
Kahn, Julius, 30:70
Kahn, Otto, 25:235
Kahuku Ranch, 25:225-27
Kahului (place), 40:36-37, 39
Kains, A. C., 25:232
Kalakaua, King, 40:34, 39
Kalalina Bay, 9:240
Kalifornia Kiddie Kollege, 24:15
Kalisher & Wartenberg, 33:66
Kalloch, Isaac M., 35:144; 37:224
Kalloch, Isaac S., 8:83; 19:110; 35:114;
    37:223-24
Kallock, Amariah, 27:229, 230, 236
Kaloa (ship), 29:221
Kalthoff, G. H., 25:252
Kamamalu (ship), *see Diana* (brig)
Kamchadell (ship), 16:83
Kamchatka, 23:221, 222
Kamehameha II, 8:132-34
Kamehameha III, 14:321, 326, 338, 343;
    18:315; 35:194, 196
Kamehameha V, 38:338
Kamer, Joseph, 15:46
Kamer Aga-Oglu, coauth.
    "Archaeological Exploration...
    at Drake's Bay," 31:99-108
Kamp, (Portland, 1850), 2:126
Kanaka Bar, 8:338, 355
Kanaka Flats, 7:13
Kanakas, 2:47, 48, 271; 5:407; 8:355;
    14:145, 303, 326; 16:138, 284;
    17:131; 19:194-95, 328; 24:227;
    28:292; 39:109
Kanawyer, Poly A., 4:41
Kane, Miss (Sacramento, 1858),
    9:259, 261
Kane, Elias K., 6:155; 35:14, 17
Kane, Mrs. Elias K., 35:14, 17, 19
Kane, Genevieve, 33:41
Kane, James, 9:317
Kane, Paul, 21:3, 6; port. of Yellow
    Serpent, 21: opp. 1

Kaniu (ship), *see Clarion*

Kanota, Louis, 22:200-222 *passim;* 23:27-28, 38, 128, 139

Kanrin Maru (ship), 18:86; 23:335-41 *passim*, 346; 38:332

Kansas, 11:15, 26; question of admission into Union, 9:246, 249, 254, 264, 271-72, 274, 278-79, 286, 358, 381, 388; 10:66, 191; 11:22, 26; 31:193-94; "English compromise," 9:272

Kansas-Nebraska bill, 9:73, 278; 19:259-60, 276, 352, 353, 354, 355; 31:193, 195, 199, 200

Kaplan, Walter F., obit. of Joel W. Kaufmann, 24:187

Karabahal, Rosalc, 28:292

Kardos, Emil, 27:94-95

Karnes, Henry, 18:277

Karoc Indian Stories, by Olden, rev., 2:365

Karr (in mines, 1848), 30:54-55

Karr, Richard, store of, 29:42, 56

Kasch, Charles, 25:286; 26:284-85; "Klamath County, California," 34:265-73, as address, 34:87; "The Yokayo Ranchería," 26:209-15

Kashaw, Israel, 21:307

Kashevaroff, Λ. P., 12:191-200 *passim*

Kasson, C. S., 15-21, 23, 53

Kasten, Henry, 31:333

Kasten, M. K., 25:172

Kate Heath (ship), 25:258, 266

Katharine and Petruchio (play), 16:283

Katie Lloyd (ship), 22:163, 167

Katsui Rintaro, 23:335, 338-40, 344

Kauffman, Edward 22:35

Kaufmann, Gordon B., 25:381

Kaufmann, Joel W., obit., 24:187

Kaufmann, William, 24:187

Kauhane, Samuel, 25:227

Kavanaugh, Hubert H., 20:166; 40:294, 329, 335, 336, 337

Kavanaugh, Mrs. John (Esther Jewell), 33:190

Kaweah Co-operative Commonwealth Colony, 4:41

Kaweah River, 4:41; 11:257, 265

Kay, Thomas Belcher, 19:329; 26:260

Kays, John C., 14:332

Kean, Mr. and Mrs. Charles, 21:65, 74, 150, 164

Kearn (Marysville, 1851), 15:49

Kearney, Denis, 2:241; 5:95; 8:83;

15:381; 21:248; 24:220, 225; 35:143; 37:221, 222, 339

Kearney, M. Theodore, 25:27, 28, 172-73, 174

Kearny, John, 21:307

Kearny, Philip, 16:186, 318; 24:59; 28:213, 229

Kearny, Stephen Watts, 1:139-47 *passim*, 233, 234-35; 3:122, 124, 125; 4:273; 10:23; 12:334-35, 351, 356; 13:47, 79, 150, 304; 16:125, 141; 17:340-41, 349; 18:61, 167, 178, 265; 21:333-37, 341, 344, 345, 356; 22:42-52 *passim*, 59, 66, 148, 175; 25:291-307 *passim*, 371; 26:23-31 *passim*, 54-55; 29:36; 30:53; 33:97, 101, 107, 110, 120, 249, 266-67, 339, 340; capture of Los Angeles, 12:336; 13:303; 18:233; 30:52; difficulty with Mason, 1:248; difficulties with Stockton and Frémont 8:251-61; 10:15; 12:344-45; 13:150-53; 16:196; 17:231; 21:194; 22:45, 46, 50, 64; as gov. of Calif., 10:18-20, 22, 123, 137, 354; 12:336, 343-46; 18:178; 22:45, 53, 65; 30:108, 109; 34:259; march to Calif., 21:193, 194-224; 24:95-96; 25:130, 291-303; 30:97-98; guns, 2:41; 13:133 (*see also* Howitzers); instructions to, 2:351; 8:251; 10:13, 15, 19, 22; 14:149; 25:122; 32:293; at San Pasqual, 1:240-41; 4:291; 13:47, 303; 17:342-45 *passim*, 347, 349; 18:74, 178; 21:336; 25:291; 26:34-39, 43-51 *passim*, 55, 61; 30:51; port., 8· opp 251

Kearny, Mrs. Stephen Watts(Mary Radford), 26:59; 33:339

Kearny, Thomas, "The Mexican War and the Conquest of California," 8:251-61

Kearny, Woolly, 6:50, 8:372

Kearny (prop. town), 14:212, 376, 405

Kearsarge Pass, 4:14; mines nr., 4:25-26

Keating, George, 17:82

Keating, John, 16:346; 17:82; 29:23

Keating, William J., 15:76

Keaton, Sam ("One Eyed") and Mrs. 10:166

Keefer, Abraham, 25:224

Keefer, H., 30:362

Keeler (Camptonville, 1856), 9:52, 63

Keeler, Charles Augustus, 4:53
Keeler, J. E., 4:35
Keeler, Jack, 9:140
Keeler, Ralph, 15:381
Keeler's Ferry, 34:222
Keelikolani, Princess Ruth,
  40:39, 46
Keemle, Charles, 4:127, 128, 139
Keenan, Alexander Stanislaus,
  obit., 37:375-76
Keenan, Mrs. Alexander Stanislaus
  (Laura M. Maguire), 37:375-76
Keenan, Ralph T., 24:288
Keene, Benjamin Franklin, 9:44,
  45; 21:276
Keene, Florence R., 13:189, 412;
  33:90
Keene, Laura, 15:165, 169; 16:84;
  20:304
Keeney, James Ward, 23:384
Keeney, L. G., 20:185
Keeney, Mrs. Charles, 24:262
Keeney (or Kinney), "Put,"
  20:183, 184
Keeney, W. F., 20:185
Kegel, Otto, 25:252
Kehler, T. B., 9:349, 356
Kehoe, William, 31:155
Kehrlein, Mrs. Oliver, comp.,
  "Some California Dates of 1859,"
  38:25-30
Keiger (alias Davis; Marysville,
  1862), 10:383
Keiger, John, 15:30
Keiser (lawsuit, Marysville, 1859),
  10:178
Keith, W. H., Jr., 29:225
Keith, William (L.A., 1833), 13:216
Keith, William (artist, 1859),
  4:28, 29, 53; 17:18, 19; 21:278;
  28:6, 88; 29:224; 30:137-38; 36:201;
  37:24-25, 33-34; 38:7
Keithahn, Edward L., 39:97, 114
Kellam, Thomas H., 26:171;
  27:127, 131
Kelleher, John, 10:248, 251
Keller (S.F., 1849), 27:45
Keller, Albert W., 22:170
Keller, George, 10:82
Keller, Henry, 38:172
Keller, James H., 9:26, 27
Keller, John, 9:345, 377; 10:178,
  188; 15:29
Keller, Matthew (Mateo), 13:315,

329, 336, 342, 351; 21:329; 32:328,
  330; 38:172
Keller and Co., 35:55
Keller v. Hyde, 10:188, 356, 386
Kellersberger, Julius, 30:230, 231;
  31:325, 326, 330, 332
Kellett, Henry, 11:300, 306
Kelley, Capt. (S.F., 1854), 15:164
Kelley (or Kelly; Yuba Co., 1856),
  9:67, 143, 144
Kelley (clairvoyant, 1858), 9:361
Kelley (C.P.R.R., 1875), 18:360;
  23:118, 120
Kelley, "General" (S.F., 1893),
  28:48
Kelley, A. J., 15:169
Kelley, Douglas Ottinger and
  Annie A. (Fletcher), 24:172
Kelley, Hall Jackson, 3:77; 37:16
Kelley (or Kelly), John H.,
  24:58
Kelley, M. H., 6:36
Kelley, Robert L., *Gold vs. Grain*,
  rev., 39:181
Kelley, William H., 21:383
Kellinger (Copper City, 1862), 22:369
Kellogg (Marysville, 1858), 9:362-65
  passim, 370; 10:177
Kellogg (Sonoma Co., 1875), 20:269
Kellogg, Albert, 4:28; 18:343; 21:327,
  332, 363, 365, 368; 32:249, 254, 258
Kellogg, Clara Louise, 21:245
Kellogg, E. A., 26:356, 358
Kellogg, E. B., 30:337
Kellogg, Florentine Erwin, 4:154;
  28:266
Kellogg, John, 40:350
Kellogg, Louise, 29:378
Kellogg, Martin, 1:14, 18, 21; 6:337;
  20:2; 24:79; 25:178
Kellogg, Vernon Lyman, 4:49
Kelly (singer, Yuba Co., 1850), 8:347;
  14:393
Kelly (Ft. Yale, B.C., 1858), 6:28
Kelly (S.F., 1882), 21:261
Kelly, Edward, 23:209
Kelly, Edwin, 21:167
Kelly, Eugene, 30:208
Kelly, Hugh, 15:182
Kelly, James, 1:123
Kelly, John, 2:128
Kelly, John W., 32:1-30 *passim*, 34, 37,
  38; phot., 32: opp. 1
Kelly, Mrs. John W. (Ida M.), 32:16,
  17, 20, 25-26, 41

Kelly, Margaret P., coauth. "The Plant Content of Adobe Bricks," 4:361-73
Kelly, Niva, 21:111
Kelly, Robert, 21:111
Kelly, Mrs. W. F. (née Wickson), 24:94-95
Kelly, William, 14:152-53
Kelly, William B., 2:128
Kelly & Co. *v.* the Ridge Co., 10:384, 385
Kelly (Eugene) & Co., 30:208
Kelly mine, see California Rand Silver Mine
Kelp: in 1587, 2:148; in 1602, 7:42, 331; 8:59, 218; in 1793, 2:331; in 1827, 23:222
Kelsey (S.F., 1854), 15:170
Kelsey (S.F., 1860), 29:121
Kelsey, America, 19:119, 137
Kelsey, Andrew, 11:266-73; 17:155, 220, 240; 24:49, 51-54 *passim*, 58, 71, 72; 28:265; 29:134
Kelsey, Benjamin, 5:127, 136, 137; 17:155, 240; 23:291; 24:54, 58, 72; 29:263
Kelsey, David, 17:155, 240; 28:265
Kelsey, David B., 20:44
Kelsey, H., 19:72
Kelsey, Herbert, 35:142
Kelsey, John, 17:44
Kelsey, Nancy, 12:176; 16:87
Kelsey, Samuel, 1:73; 6:140; 17:155, 220, 221, 222, 240; 24:54, 58; 28:265; 29:134, 263-64, 266
Kelsey (place), 8:201, 210
Kelsey, Smith & Risley, 28:40
Kelseyville, 11:266-73; 32:364
Kemball, Gilbridge G., 6:368
Kemble, Edward Cleveland, 7:278; 8:362; 11:129, 130, 132; 12:125; 13:76; 14:74; 15:182; 17:295-96, 300; 20:335, 338; 26:123; 35:201; "Blowing up the Wind," 14:81; art. on, 14:80; hist. of Calif. newspapers, 7:278-81; 12:125; 39:2; reprint, rev., 7:286; writings quoted, 6:140-41; 10:299; 12:126; 21:29; 26:337(?); 29:337, 339-42 *passim;* 30:49-51
Kemble, Ella, 21:172
Kemble, Gouverneur, 11:11
Kemble, John Haskell, 19:96; 20:287; 24:189; 27:319; 32:285; "The First Steam Vessel to Navigate San Francisco Bay," 14:143-46; "The Genesis of the Pacific Mail Steamship Company," 13:240-54, 386-406; "The 'Senator,'... Pioneer Steamship," 16:61-70; ed. "Andrew Wilson's 'Jottings' on Civil War California," 32:209-24, 303-12; ed. "Naval Conquest in the Pacific: The Journal of Lieutenant Tunis M. Craven . . . 1846-49," 20:193-234; bk. revs. by, 38:272-73; 40:263-65
Kemp (w. Derby, 1849), 11:107, 111
Kemp, E., 5:140-45 *passim,* 342
Kempton (lawsuit, 1859), 10:177, 186
Kempton, Jennie, 24:263
Kempton's (Robinson's) Crossing, 9:54, 73
Kendall (Aurora, ca. 1860), 7:118
Kendall (police capt., S.F., late 1870s?), 35:130
Kendall, Alonzo, 33:364
Kendall, Joseph, 25:178
Kendall, Lucy, *see* Herrick, Mrs. William Francis
Kendall, Mary A., 31:176
Kendall, William Smith and Catherine, 29:286
Kendall, William Smith, Jr., and Joanna Jefferson (Jacobs), 29:286
Kendall (E. A.) & (W. R.) Spencer's Book and Music Emporium, 30:361, 367
Kendall, Benson & Co., 37:230
Kendall's Band, 15:181; 16:82
Kenderdine, Thaddeus S., 27:381
Kendrick, John, 10:318; 11:29
Kendrick, Juan, 10:318
Kendrick, Louise, 26:71, 72
Kenebeck (Lassen Co., 1855), 18:303
Keney, Adolph and Agnes (McDermott), 24:94
Kenitzer, Henry, 15:192
Kenna, Robert E., 7:413
Kennan, George, 33:2, 6, 11, 12
Kennebec Bar, 14:217
Kennebec Co., 8:25; 14:217
Kennebec House, New York of the Pacific, 12:30
Kennebec Mining Co., 33:375
Kennedy (S.F., 1849), 27:263, 363; 28:57, 64
Kennedy (Marysville, 1858), 9:354
Kennedy, Mrs. (Sacramento, 1858), 9:251-61 *passim,* 267, 274, 371, 372, 376, 377; 10:46, 48, 275, 285, 286, 356, 357, 361, 372

Kennedy, Ann (Mrs. J. M. Cushing), 25:89
Kennedy, Annie Ellicott, *see* Bidwell, Mrs. John
Kennedy, Edmund Pendleton, 14:230; 15:357, 358; art. on, 12:137-46
Kennedy, Elijah R., 17:316; 40:289-90
Kennedy, Ella, 10:258, 272, 274, 286, 361, 373, 375, 376
Kennedy, Gerald Driscoll, 24:381
Kennedy, Mrs. Gerald Driscoll (Helen Weber), 24:381
Kennedy, Guy, 36:320
Kennedy, H., 40:321
Kennedy, Hugh, 14:398; 15:29, 45
Kennedy, James (Stanislaus Co., 1850), 11:360
Kennedy, James (Sacramento, 1861), 10:272
Kennedy, James F., 10:78
Kennedy, Joseph B., 21:339, 342; 26:56
Kennedy, Julia, 9:249, 254-67 *passim*, 274, 346-59 *passim*, 369-77 *passim*; 10:46-60 *passim*, 258, 271-78 *passim*, 361, 373, 375, 376
Kennedy, Lawton R., 14:146; 23:286, 382
Kennedy, Mrs. Lawton R. (Freda), 20:384; 22:287
Kennedy, Thomas, 13:84
Kennedy, Wall, 16:134
Kennicott, Robert, 33:2, 5, 7, 152-64 *passim*; 35:291, 292
Kennovan, James, 15:268; 38:25
Kenny, George L., 29:98, 102-3, 123, 125, 218, 225; 30:108, 354; 31:219; *see also* Bancroft (H. H.) & Co.; Cooke, Kenny & Co.
Kenny, J. B., 36:264
Kenny, Robert Walker, 36:110
Kenny, Samuel, 15:178
Kenny & Alexander, 29:123, 125
Kent (Eliza City, 1850), 8:169-70
Kent (Sacramento to Marysville, 1859), 10:41
Kent, Adeline, 38:4
Kent, Arthur H., 24:288
Kent, Charles (Nevada Co., 1854), 3:154
Kent, Charles (Gila R., ca. 1844), 21:207, 223
Kent, Edward, 20:30
Kent, Edward A. and Abba (Ward), 28:293
Kent, Frank, 26:189

Kent, George F., Journal: "Life in California in 1849," ed. John W. Caughey, 20:26-46
Kent, John Horace, 16:81, 84
Kent, S., 13:31
Kent, William, 36:254, 260; "In the Mountains of Mendocino," rev., 5:92
Kent, Mrs. William (Elizabeth Thacher), 23:95
Kent, William H., 21:383
Kent (ship), 14:128; 17:295; 18:276; 23:323, **333**
Kentucky Ranch, 9:52, 53, 69
Kenway & Robertson, 28:198
Kenyon (Marysville, 1860), 10:256
Kenyon, Daniel, 13:3
Kenyon, M., 13:32
Kenzie, Mr. and Mrs. (Sacramento, 1859), 10:47, 48, 51, 379
Keoka (ship), 22:171; 37:210
Keough, Thomas, 4:20
Keppel, Capt. (of *Meander*, 1851), 11:381
Keppel, Mark, 36:252
Kern, Lt. (U.S.N., 1860), 23:339
Kern, Benjamin S., 1:96
Kern, Edward Meyer, 1:72, 96, 296; 3:270, 271, 272; 4:10; 10:353, 354; 16:214; 17:225-29 *passim*; 19:119, 120, 138; 21:10-21 *passim*; 22:221; 25:126-30 *passim*
Kern, Richard H., 38:82
Kern (place), 18:27, 28
Kern County, oil fields, 30:211; 32:9, 27
Kern County Museum, 38:75
Kernes (Marysville, 1860), 10:260-61
Kern River, 4:10; 11:255; diggings, 15:271-75 *passim*; 18:277; 19:145; 25:1, 2-3; 31:243, 244; oil fields, 30:211; 32:9; power co., 10:393
Kerns, Thomas J., 19:59-73 *passim*; 27:316, 317; 28:47
Kerr, George, 34:342-43; & Co., 30:133
Kerr, James Andrew, 7:206
Kerr, John, 7:206
Kerr, Orpheus C. (Robert Henry Newell), 21:59, 60
Kerr, Thomas, Journal: "An Irishman in the Gold Rush," ed. Charles L. Camp, 7:205-27, 395-404; 8:17-25, 167-82, 262-77; sketches by, 8:18-24 *passim*
Kerr, Mrs. Thomas (Margaret), 7:206
Kerr, Thomas Henry, 7:206
Kerr, Virginia, 19:286

Kerrigan, Peter, 8:205; 9:355; 10:361, 374; 10:169
Kerrison, Harry, 15:267
Kerry, Corp. (Clear Lake, 1850), 24:53
Kerving (or Kerwing), Mrs., *see* Kewen, Mrs. Edward J. C.
Keseberg, Lewis (or Louis), 11:141, 145; 12:291-92; 16:129, 138; 19:122, 123, 139; 20:124; 30:233, 234
Keser, L., 14:398
Kessenick, Burt, rev. of Brashear and Rodney, eds. *Art, Humor and Humanity of Mark Twain*, 38:368-70
Kessler, Peter, 8:193, 199-200, 205, 209
Kessler, Richard Theodore, 31:71; 33:373
Ketch, Dan, *see* Denkichi
Ketcham, Lewis N., 10:62
Ketcham, Thomas E., 20:363
Ketchum, Emily, *see* Bancroft, Mrs. Hubert Howe
Ketchum, Frank, 33:6, 157, 159-60, 163, 168; 35:295, 304
Ketchum, W. Scott, 29:249
Kettel, Thomas Prentice, 30:233
Kettele, J. G., 17:179
Kettenshaw Valley, 20:352-53, 363
"Kettle-drum," 19:227-28
Kettleman Hills, 30:215
Kewen, Achilles, 15:182, 371
Kewen, Edward J. C., 5:95; 9:26; 10:267, 296; 13:80, 336; 15:174, 371; 16:183-84; 20:167; 23:357, 371; 26:21-22, 51; 30:251, 263; 32:327; 40:295
Kewen, Mrs. Edward J. C. (Fannic White), 10:267; 13:80; 28:63, 64
Kewen, Perry, 5:95
Keyele (S.F. to Oahu, 1849), 14:337
Keyes (S.F., 1852), 20:313
Keyes, Erasmus Darwin, 15:266, 373; 16:82, 339; 27:216; 30:161-62
Keyes, Mrs. Sarah, 5:399
Keyes, Theodore R., 18:282
Keyes & Co., 15:181
Keys, George, 17:174
Keyser, Charles, 10:77
Keyser, Philip W., 9:248, 249, 273; 10:44; 14:392, 398; 18:250
Keyser, Sebastian, 5:276; 6:134; 11:121
Keystone House; Ranch, 8:341, 358; 9:52, 63, 65, 66, 70, 129, 130, 131, 144, 148, 149, 158, 159, 162, 266
Khlebnikof, Kiryll, 12:192-96 *passim*, 205, 213, 229, 236, 237, 238, 273; 16:232; 30:321, 336; 33:63
Kiakhta (ship), 12:194; 18:347; 33:63
Kibbe (Sacramento, 1861), 10:275, 283
Kibbe, Mrs. (née Affleche; Sacramento, 1861), 10:280, 283, 286
Kibbe, William C., 9:254, 258, 279-80, 283, 353, 354, 358, 359, 361; 10:290; 11:173; 14:361, 367; 15:70, 146, 264; 22:37; 24:173; 29:231-32, 236, 239, 241; 30:166; 34:153; cor., 14:359-60; 15:71, 85-86, 143-61, 247-49, 252-60, 262, 263; 29:232-33, 235, 236
Kibbe, Mrs. William C. (Emma Leonard), 9:280
Kibby, Leo P., 40:253; "California Soldiers in the Civil War," 40:343-51; bk. rev. by, 40:251-53
Kibling petition for pardon (1861), 10:286
Kiburz, *see* Kyburz
Kidder, John F., 18:356
Kiel, Jarvis, 5:340
Kientz, Christian, 8:199, 201, 208
Kiernan, Edward, bk. rev. by, 39:371-74
Kierski and Brother, 30:359; 34:348
Kilburn, Charles L., 24:121
Kilburn, Ralph L., 28:265-67
Kilday, Edward, 21:267
Killinger, John, 33:52
Kimball, Charles Proctor, 13:185; 22:112; 30:108, 115, 251-52, 253, 354, 365; arts. on, 18:329-34; 21:75-78; phot., 18: opp. 329
Kimball, Mrs. Charles Proctor (Isabella Dunn), 18:332; 21:76, 78
Kimball, George, 14:176
Kimball, Hazen, 6:61; 14:176
Kimball, Heber Chase, 6:119; 15:245; 26:190, 326
Kimball, James Stephen, 18:333
Kimball, Oliver, 12:137, 221
Kimball, Proctor, 18:332-33
Kimball, Rebecca, 18:333, 334
Kimball, Sarah Louise, 1:107-8; obit. of Henry B. Phillips, 3:399-400
Kimball, William, 10:281, 390
Kimball family, 14:176
Kimeshaw Lakes, 29:196
Kim-Ka (pantomime), 16:340
Kimmel, Joseph Houston, 28:294
Kimura Settsu-no-kami, 23:335, 339-40, 344
Kincaid, Mrs. (Marysville, 1861), 10:361

Kincaid (Willow Springs, 1874), 17:216
Kincaid, C., 13:85
Kincaid, Mrs. Lemuel (Ana Vallejo),
    29:326
Kincannan, Capt. (Marysville, 1851),
    15:45
Kindall, T., 22:251
King (S.F., Dec. 1849), 28:62
King (Marysville, 1850), 14:394
King, A. J., 29:234, 240
King, Ada, 10:196
King, Andrew J., 13:326, 350
King, Annie, 12:372
King, Charles James, 1:17; 24:80
King, Clarence, 1:284; 4:16-25 *passim*,
    29, 32-33, 34, 42, 53, 54, 55; 7:121;
    9:401; 38:114-27 *passim*; biog. of,
    rev., 38:164-65
King, Edward, 9:57, 58, 73, 148, 165;
    10:188
King, Edward A., 14:182; 18:165, 166,
    177
King, Ervin T., 7:117
King, G. W., 30:112, 259
King, George A., 9:160
King, George H., 8:337, 349, 350, 352,
    362; 9:50, 51, 57, 59, 60, 129-46 *passim*,
    259, 263, 268; 10:55, 59, 61, 167, 188,
    367; lawsuit, 9:62; phot., 9: opp. 142
King, Mrs. George H. (Julia Lyman),
    8:362; 9:57, 59, 79, 145, 162, 176;
    10:55, 167; phot., 9: opp. 142
King, Capt. Henry (came 1846;
    d. 1849), 1:239; 21:23; 29:336; 37:138
King, Henry (on *Sylph*, 1849), 13:32
King, Henry (L.A., 1857), 29:237
King, Henry L., 27:366
King, Homer (d. 1876), 9:268; 10:70;
    11:9
King, Homer (S.F., 1901), 36:45
King, James (east on *California*, 1849),
    27:362, 368
King, James, of William, 1:17; 11:187;
    17:174, 178; 21:23-26 *passim*, 33, 324;
    22:248, 252; 22:229; 28:116; 37:137-43;
    w. Adams & Co., 15:273; 21:24;
    37:139; banker, 21:24; 22:248, 252;
    37:139; ed. of *Bulletin*, 8:365, 366;
    16:182, 345, 346-47; 17:81-85 *passim*,
    169-73 *passim*, 177-78; 21:23, 26, 324;
    22:40; 28:71; 29:176; 37:140-69;
    shooting and death of, 3:41; 4:157,
    167, 191-93, 201; 6:3, 7; 7:95; 13:82;
    17:310; 18:276; 20:306, 336; 21:26;
    29:175; 32:221; trial and hanging of

Casey, 14:351-54; 20:260 (*see also*
    Vigilance Committee, S.F., 1856);
    ports., 37: opp. 144
King, Mrs. James, of William
    (Charlotte Libbey), 12:372; 29:94
King, James L., 40:211
King, John (L.A., 1862), 12:12; 32:328,
    333, 338, 347
King, John (Colorado R., 1865), 22:17
King, Lyman M., 39:28
King, Maria, 10:361
King, May Ann (Flinn), 10:383
King, Robert, 15:127
King, Samuel D., 21:312; 30:330, 332;
    34:17; reports to, 34:4-13, 17
King, Thomas Butler, 10:147; 13:402;
    17:85; 19:3, 4; 20:71; 24:254; 25:120,
    332, 334, 337, 340, 345, 347; 26:332,
    333; 27:172, 261; 28:58, 64; 34:243;
    35:314, 317-18; 40:131
King, Thomas Sim, 6:9, 11, 12, 16;
    14:354; 20:336; 23:147; 26:229; 38:25;
    art. on, 21:23-38; port., 21: opp. 23
King, Thomas Starr, 4:208; 5:198;
    6:341; 10:278, 282, 284, 292, 295, 296,
    303, 360, 376; 17:312, 321; 20:3;
    24:105, 278; 25:8, 334, 341; 29:110,
    377; 32:298-99; 33:306; 34:53-54;
    36:348-49; 39:307; 40:291; arts. on,
    29: 251-54; 33:219-27; letters of, to
    Hannah L. Neall, 31:247-49
King, Mrs. Thomas Starr, 24:265
King, William (Klamath Co., 1855),
    26:204
King, William (Marysville, 1858),
    9:357; 10:180, 259
King, William Freeman and Elnora
    (Blood), 30:285
King, William S., 33:344; 34:32; 35:14
"King boys" (L.A., 1855), 15:270
King v. Woodson *et al.*, 10:58
King, Mount, 4:20, 47, 55
Kingcome, John, 33:235-36
Kingdon, Edith, 35:142
King Ho, 23:109
Kingman, Tracy, 9:143, 170, 243-47
    passim
Kingsburg, W. H., 38:61
Kingsburg (place), 25:175; 30:305;
    Colony, 25:175
Kingsbury, Alice, 6:341; 21:149, 152
Kingsbury, D. D., 16:79
Kingsbury, Julius Jesse Backus,
    11:104-6, 121; 34:23

Kingsbury, Kenneth Raleigh, obit.,
    17:94-95
Kingsbury and Centerville Canal, 25:22
Kings County, oil operations in, 31:298
Kingship of Mt. Lassen, The, by
    Colburn, rev., 3:94
Kingsland (actor, 1859), 10:77
Kingsland, Ambrose C., 21:290, 303
Kingsland, Daniel C., 21:290
Kingsley, Nelson, 22:278
"King's Orphan," *see* Sandels
    Edhelyertha, G.M. Waseurtz af
Kings River, 1:126; 4:4, 5, 9, 20, 21, 22,
    28, 29, 30, 37, 41, 47; 11:247, 258-59,
    264, 265; 28:334-37 *passim; see also*
    Wimmel-che River
Kings River and Fresno Canal Co.,
    25:22, 173
Kings River Canyon, 1:126; 4:12, 13, 14,
    20, 26-31 *passim*
Kinkaid, Judge (San Jose, 1850), 34:240
Kinkaid, Charles L. and Elizabeth
    (Abbot), 27:189
Kinkaid, James E. and Ellen (Dillon),
    27:189
Kinkaid, Menna, 27:188
Kinkead, John H., 11:51
Kinlock, George, 16:325, 330; 25:197
Kinlock, George David, 14:209, 212, 227
Kinlock, Georgiana, 10:63
Kinman (San Bernardino, 1860), 24:277
Kinman, Seth, 39:298
Kinnaird, Lawrence, 32:190; "Bolton
    of California," 32:97-103; address,
    "Admission Day," 24:376; bk. rev.
    by, 39:359-62
Kinney, Abbot, 20:139; 31:18, 20, 29
Kinney, "Put," *see* Keeney
Kino, Eusebio Francisco, 3:291; 5:197;
    6:103; 8:80; 11:294, 383; 14:3, 84;
    15:283; 19:221; 25:364; 26:309-19
    passim; 27:310; 29:139, 143; 36:217-18,
    233-35
Kinoshita, T. H., 28:186
Kinsey, Henry, 9:348, 359-60, 362
Kinton, S. B., 13:32
Kinton, T. S., 13:31
Kintze, *see* Kientz
Kinville, Joseph, 8:342-43, 350, 358
Kinyon, Marcus L., 2:216
Kinzer, G. W. and Mrs., 25:332, 333,
    341
Kip, William Ingraham, 10:290;
    14:74-79 *passim;* 15:180, 185; 16:346;
    17:320; 19:232; 23:229; 24:278;

25:345; 28:10, 231; 29:2, 377; 30:260,
    262; 31:5, 236; 32:125, 350-56 *passim,*
    360, 361; 33:190, 311, 317, 381; 34:233;
    36:41, 294; 37:51-61 *passim;*
    A California Pilgrimage, rev. 1:197-98
"Kipling's San Francisco Debut," by
    Irving McKee, 30:151-55
Kirby, C. K., 25:174
Kirby, Mrs. J. H., *see* Stark, Mrs. James
Kirby, Jones, & Co., 33:65
Kirkaldie, George, 10:258
Kirk & Co., 30:366; *see also*
    Gardiner & Kirk
Kirk Bros., 30:266
Kirkbride, Walter Harold, 18:384;
    obit., 24:91
Kirker, Harold, 38:88; "Eldorado
    Gothic, . . ." 38:31-46; *California's
    Architectural Frontier: . . .
    Nineteenth Century,* rev., 40:168-70
Kirkpatrick, J. M., 3:93
Kirkpatrick, J. S., 15:29
Kirkpatrick, M., 10: opp. 48, 62; 11:8, 9
Kirk survey, 21:229
Kirwin, Mrs. (Marysville, 1861),
    10:279
Kit Carson (ship), 16:81
Kit Carson, by Vestal, rev., 7:194-95
"Kit Carson at Cajón—Not Tejón," by
    John A. Hussey, 29:29-38
"Kit Carson in California," by
    Charles L. Camp, 1:111-51
Kit Carson Pass, *see* Carson Pass
Kit Carson's Own Story, ed. Grant,
    rev., 5:408-9
Kitt (or Kitts, Yuba Co., 1856), 9:57
Kittle, Nicholas G., 19:232; 29:106, 112
Kittle, Mrs. Nicholas G. (née Scott),
    19:232; 29:107, 112
Kittleman, George, 14:177
Kittleman, Sarah, 11:132; 17:298
Kittredge, Abbott E., 24:263
Kitts, Joseph, 18:307, 314
Kitty Kelly (ship), 32:366
Kiyoyuki, Morita Okataro, 23:342
"Klamath" (variations in spelling),
    34:266
Klamath, State of (prop.), 10:74
Klamath Bluffs, 26:11
Klamath County, 30:382; 34:265-73;
    39:53-59 *passim*
"Klamath County, California," by
    Charles Kasch, 34:265-73
Klamath Flats, *see* Yreka
Klamath Glen, 26:4

Klamath Lakes, 17:273; 22:213; 28:212; 30:340

Klamath Mounted Rangers, 34:269

Klamath News, 39:55

Klamath Reservation, 26:1-11 *passim*

Klamath Rifles, 34:269

Klamath River, 5:145; 19:146; 22:103; 23:138, 293; 25:110, 111, 118; 26:1-11 *passim;* 39:55; mining on, 3:93; 5:236, 245; used for power, 30:339-43 *passim*

Klauber, A., 35:269, 273, 346, 347; 36:163

Klauber, A. E., 28:189

Klauber, Edgar, 35:345; 36:163

Klauber, Hugo, 35:346, 358; 36:77, 163

Klauber, Laura, *see* Wangenheim, Mrs. Julius

Klauber, Laurence M., 28:189

Klauber, Melville, 35:127, 261, 272-73, 345-47, 350, 358-59, 363; 36:63, 156, 163

Klauber family, 36:163

Klauber (A.) & (S.) Levi, 35:272-73, 345-46

Klauber-Wangenheim Co., 35:346, 358; 36:163

Klein, Ada, 20:288

Klein, Charles, 18:292

Klick, John, 9:137, 141

Klinkofstrom, Martin, 19:232; 26:14; 39:111

Klipstein, Henry W., Jr., 32:39, 40

Klondike, gold rush to, 30:378

Klotz (John and Frederick) Woodyard, San Francisco, 33:375

Klotz, Rudolph, 22:370

Knapp, C. H., 22:251

Knapp, Frank A., Jr., 34:190; "Biographical Traces of Consul John Parrott," 34:111-24

Knapp, J. R., 38:314

Knapp Grocery Store, 24:268

Kneass, Dallas A., 29:291

Kneedler, Joseph M., 21:309

Kneeland, Samuel, 28:186

Kneiss, Gilbert H., 29:382; bk. revs. by, 38:169-71; 39:374-75

Knickerbocker Engine Co. No. 5, Sacramento, 9:377

Knight (in mines, 1848), 14:278

Knight (Marysville, 1858), 9:366, 376; 10:253

Knight (lawsuit, S.F., 1880s), 21:121

Knight, Alfred, 31:190

Knight, Atkins, 2:107

Knight, George, 22:251

Knight, George A., 12:183

Knight, Henry, 15:240

Knight, Robert, *Industrial Relations in the San Francisco Bay Area, 1900 to 1918*, rev., 39:362-64

Knight, Samuel (Honey Lake, 1855), 18:303

Knight, Samuel (S.F., 1861), 21:192; 22:92; son, 16:172; 22:92; grandson, 1:19; 21:192; obit., 21:192

Knight, Mrs. Samuel (Mary Hurd Holbrook), 21:192; 22:93

Knight, Steven, 26:215

Knight, Thomas, 17:240; 19:131, 135, 136, 142; 23:294; 24:58

Knight, William, 5:123, 126; 6:137, 144-45, 152, 374; 10:68; 13:224; 15:229; 17:220, 221, 224, 240; 18:158, 164, 172; 24:58; 29:134, 262, 264

Knight, William Henry, 29:100, 121, 123, 219; 31:190

Knight's Ferry, 10:45, 68; Dragoons, 10:198; newspaper, 3:91

Knight's Landing, 13:224; 16:65; 18:172; 23:365, 375; 29:134

Knights of the Columbian Star, 20:154-56; 40:293

Knights of the Golden Circle, 20:154, 156; 22:359, 362; 34:153; 40:292, 293

Knights Valley Rancho, 20:269

Knilberling (Marysville, 1861), 10:362

Knipe, Capt. (Colorado R., 1863-67), 22:170, 171, 172

Knjas (ship), 39:110

Knopf, S. A., 31:26

Knowland, Joseph Russell, 24:267, 270; 25:194, 195, 200-204 *passim;* 26:130, 134, 186; 32:239; "Report of the President," 32:174-76; 34:87-89; addresses: "Coming Centennial Celebrations," 24:282; "Historic Columbia," 28:276-77; "Historic Spots Marked by the Native Sons of the Golden West," 2:368-69; "Progress . . . in Preserving Our Historic Landmarks," 21:82-83; introd. to "California Gold Discovery: Centennial Papers," 26:107-8; introd. to Neasham, "Raising of the Flag at Monterey . . . 1846," 25:193; obits. of George T. Cameron, 34:375-76; William S. Cavalier, 24:374-75; Arthur E. Corder, 37:376-77; R. Stanley Dollar, 38:178-79; Wells Drury, 11:190; Alfred Holman, 10:96; Frank A.

Leach, 8:285-86; phot., 39: opp. 80, opp. 360
Knowles, Frank, 4:34
Knowles, Josiah Nickerson, 33:373
Knowles, Richard and Sarah, 14:72, 182
Know Nothing Party, 3:155; 8:194, 212, 341-45 *passim*, 357-61 *passim*; 9:54, 57, 65, 72, 73, 157, 181, 270, 275; 11:59, 60; 15:173, 182, 276, 280, 366, 374, 376-77; 16:79, 339; 17:172; 20:368; 22:115; 26:5; 27:144, 208-10, 211; 28:73, 154-55; 32:145-46; 35:223, 225, 226; art. on, 9:16-49, 99-128; *see also* American Party
Knox, Franklin, 9:113-14
Knox, George, 11:126
Knox, Israel W., 15:376; 17:76, 77, 79
Knox, John T., 9:36
Knox, Martin, 10:189
Knox, W. T., 33:333
Knox, William F., 24:166
Knox, William L., 20:44
Knox and Boyle mine, 35:341
Knox (R. F.) & Co., 16:284
Knoxdale Institute, 8:356
Knudson, S., 24:121-22
Knudson, Thomas, 27:226
Koch, Mrs. Edward C. (Margaret Rau), 33:94
Kodiac (ship), 38:332
König, William, 19:120, 138
Kohl, C. Frederick, 25:249
Kohl, J. G., 11:304
Kohl, William, 35:305
Kohler, Charles, 27:170
Kohler, F. H., 16:01, 84
Kohler, Frederick D., 6:49; 15:311; 23:70-71; 27:369; 38:204
Kohlmoos Hotel, Alameda, 27:1
Konscak, Ferdinand, bk. on, rev., 2:365-66
Korbel Brothers, 21:249-50
Korea, 30:193-206 *passim;* cartoon (1904), 30: opp. 193
Korsinski, Mme. Von Gulpen, 15:46; 20:294, 295
Koshland, Mrs. Marcus Simon (Corinne Schweitzer), 25:233
Koster, Frederick J., 25:286; obit., 38:180
Kostromitinoff, Peter [Pyotr], 5:78; 12:199, 238, 245-75 *passim;* 15:184; 16:232, 233; 17:64-68 *passim;* 23:23, 39; 28:102, 110; ranch of, 12:193, 258
Kostromitinoff, Peter S., 23:344

Kotchenreiter, G., 37:38
Kotzebue, Otto von, 11:83; 12:207-8; 14:18; 18:338, 345; 25:320; 30:320
Koue (S.F. or San Jose, 1850), 11:162
Krahe, William, 27:3
Krakatoa Island, 16:303
Kraker (S.F., 1874), 35:342
Krand, Pierre, 22:304
Kreisler, Fritz, 25:236
Kremlin Hotel, San Francisco, 19:230
Kremp, Capt. (Colorado R., 1858), 22:169
Kress, George H., 18:288
Krmpotic, M. D., *Life and Works of the Rev. Ferdinand Konscak*, rev., 2:365-66
Kroeber, Alfred Louis, 7:23; 21:82; 26:234
Kroh, Henry, 26:171
Kroh, Mary Matilda, 28:294
Kruder, Henry, 28:337
Kruse, E. & E. T., 31:295
Krusenstern, Captain A. J., von, 12:207
Kuchel, Theodore B., 31:287
Küchel, Charles C., 28:379; 31:287
Küchel, Conrad, 28:379
Küchel & Dresel, 15:192-93; 20:276-77; 22:38; 28:379; 31:287; lithographs, 3: opp. 45; 9: opp. 62, opp. 68, opp. 358
Küner, Georg Albrecht Ferdinand, 33:73-74
Küstel's *Nevada and California Processes . . . ,* 28:4
Kungle, Charles H., 10:77, 282, 296; 11:91, 23
Kuntze, John C., 16:138; 26:112, 113
Kunzel, Fred, 36:162
Kunzen, Mr. and Mrs. (Cordua ranch, 1845), 12:290; 14:211
Kuprianof, Ivan, 12:191, 199, 209, 243-44, 245, 250, 268; 17:63-65
Kuro Siwo, 23:336, 343
Kurtz, D. B., 10:74
Kurtz (W. W.) and Co., 30:251, 354, 364
Kuskoff, Ivan Alexander, 3:174; 12:191-95, 204, 225-42 *passim;* 16:108
Kuskoff (place), 3:176
Kutner Colony, 25:174
Kutusov (ship), 12:233
Kutz, Joseph, 10:372
Kuykendall, John J., 4:13; 5:330; 28:331
Kyburz, Samuel E., 11:43; 25:220
Kyle, J. B., 9:265, 266; 10:285
Kyne, Peter Bernard, 31:296; 36:74

L

L., D. J., 24:253

Labadie, A. Peter, 8:208, 213, 360; 9:54, 61, 69, 72, 134, 135, 138, 145, 149, 150, 152, 156, 159; 10:170

Labadie, Ed S., 39:223

Labadie, F. S., 8:208, 213

La Barge, Joseph, 4:140

La Barge Creek, 4:140; 5:391

Labatt, Abraham C., 15:280

Labatt, H. S., 15:281

Labatt, Henry J., 9:390; 10:377, 390

Labatt, S. K., 29:234, 245

Labaudt, Lucien, 38:3-4

Labonne, Eugene, 33:8, 12, 148

Labor, 21:67, 248; 24:193-227; 27:313, 314; Japanese, 28:343, 344, 347; "white collar," 31:26-27; *see also* Chinese: laborers; Strikes; Teamsters; Unions, Wages

Laborie, Antoine, 13:345

Labourdère, Joseph, 13:65, 165

La Brea: pits, 13:197, 210, 309, 351; 15:235; Rancho, *see* Ranchos: Brea

Lachapelle, Alfred de, 6:46; 7:198; 16:344; 18:20; 30:254, 264; 39:15, 142, 144, 146, 166, 259; *see also* La Chapelle, Bertrand

La Chapelle, Bertrand de, 5:249, 250, 251; 6:46, 47; *see also* Lachapelle, Alfred

Lachapelle, Olivier de, 6:46; 18:6, 13; 39:144, 145

"Lachryma Montis," 4:284, 287; 17:235, 237, 239; 24:63; 29:151-60 *passim;* 36:246; vineyard, 36:242-48 *passim;* 37:195

La Cieneguilla, Lower Calif., 31:116, 263-64

Lackawanna (ship), 23:346

Lacor, Roger, 39:345

Lacoste, Auguste, 22:298; 23:45, 46; 33:126

Lacy, Edward S., 28:380; 29:113; 32:164-65; 34:233

Ladd (left Calif. 1836), 23:319

Ladd (Bridgeport, 1863), 26:243

Ladd, George, 2:205

Ladd, Mrs. George (Elizabeth Peterson Mitchell), 2:205-6

Ladd, Harvey C., 9:198; 24:277; 40:100

Ladd, Samuel, 37:230

Ladd, W. Frank, 29:254

Ladd, William Sargent and Caroline Ames (Elliott), 28:294, 295

Ladies Beware ("comedietta"), 16:184

Ladies' Christian Commission Fair, 23:237, 246; 24:261-66; 26:38-39, 40

Ladies Home Journal, San Francisco, 31:337

Ladies' Protection and Relief Association, 15:370; 20:382; 25:189

Ladies' Silk Culture Society of California, 31:336-40 *passim*

Ladrillero, *see* Fernández de Ladrillero

Lady Adams (ship), 33:261

Lady Adams Building, Sacramento, 39:199; phot., 39: foll. 200

Lady Adams Company, 39:290

Lady Blackwood (ship), 25:320-21

Lady Drinkwater (launch), 16:143

Lady Killer of San Francisco, (burlesque), 15:270

Lady of Lyons, The (play), 10:52, 75; 15:48

Laet, Jean de, map by, 36:218

Lafayette, Calif., 30:5, 6, 9, 10

Lafayette, Ore., 2:132

Lafayette Hotel, Los Angeles, 13:339

Lafayette Park, San Francisco, 31:302

Laferte (La Fort, Lefort, Lafont), Michel, 22:217, 220, 330; 23:38, 127, 130

Laferty (Yuba Co., 1856), 9:53

Lafevre's restaurant, Santa Barbara, 18:259

Lafler (or Laffler; Mex., 1849), 23:263

Lafler, Henry A., 40:149, 150, 155; phot., 38: foll. 8

Lafond, Gabriel, 1849 cor., 23:52-53

Lafonso, Elmer, 36:320-21

Lafonso, Holai, phot., 36: opp. 320

Laforge, J. B., 9:42

Lafragua, José María, 13:101, 128, 141, 146

Laframboise, Michel, 3:77; 8:101-2; 22:102, 103, 217, 323-48 *passim;* 23:19, 22, 23, 24, 28, 29, 30, 39, 138-43 *passim,* 146; 25:264; 28:111, 124, 249, 251, 255

Lafuente, José, 16:80

Lagasse, Pierre, *see* Legace, Pierre

Laglaise (S.F., 1854), 15:174, 178, 179, 183; 32:110
Lagoda (ship), 8:294; 23:315, 320, 325, 332; 35:193, 197-203 *passim*
La Grandière, M. de, 15:176
LaGrange, Oscar Hugh, 26:308
La Grange (place), 3:91
Laguna Salada, San Francisco, 17:301
Lagunita (Indian Wells), 17:216
Lahiff, Henry, 26:107
La Honda, 38:346
Laine, J. R., 38:67, 69, 70
Laird (Sonoma Co., 1875), 20:269
Laird, D. W., 36:100
Laird, Luther, 8:358; 9:285
Laird, Mrs. Luther, 9:263, 264, 267, 268, 274, 285, 345-61 *passim*, 365, 370, 372; 10:42, 48, 380
Lajeunesse, Basil, 1:129; 4:376; 6:89; 15:121
Lake, Delos, 8:366; 11:10; 15:270, 276, 282, 364; 19:237; 34:249
Lake, Kate B., 27:20
Lake County, 32:363-71
Lake House, Sacramento Co., 9:252, 277; 10:277
Lake House, nr. San Francisco, 15:181, 282
Lakeman, J. M., 6:353
Lake Mining District, 26:245
Lakeport, 32:366
Lakeville, 16:112, 244
Lake Vineyard Land and Water Association, 27:342
La Langle, Viscount de, 3:223, 224; 15:215, 220
Lalor, E., 10:368
Laman, D. B., 9:165, 166, 346
Lamanon (1786), 3:224
Lamar, Alexander, 31:23
Lamar, Joseph B., 10: opp. 48, 52, 62, 66, 70; 11:9
Lamarck, Jean Baptiste Pierre Antoine de Monnet, Chevalier de, 18:335, 344
Lamarque, B. L., 6:222-23; 19:28
Lamarre, de (actor, 1850), 5:141, 143, 167; 14:133
Lamb, Capt. (Colorado R., 1867), 22:172
Lamb, George A., 2:128
Lamb, John, 2:7
Lamb, W. Kaye, 28:99, 111-12, 244
Lambayecana (ship), 26:125
Lambdin, George, 10:266
Lambdon (Sutter's Fort, 1847), 16:138

Lambeer, John (lawsuit, 1855), 16:343
Lambert, Andrés (Andrew) and Juana (Jane), 1:177
Lambert, Aylmer Bourke, 18:336, 340, 345
Lambert, Charles E., obit., 38:280
Lambert, Mrs. Charles E. (Rebecca Porkitt), 38:280
Lambert, Mrs. Charles F., 23:95
Lambert, Daniel, 26:260
Lambert, Edward A., 21:294, 307; 22:71(?)
Lambert, George J., 26:259-60, 262
Lambert, James, 26:260
Lambert, John, 11:9
Lambert, John Booth, 21:291, 307
Lambert, John Robert, 21:307; 22:71 (?)
Lambert, John S., 21:307
Lambert, Joseph, 21:307
Lambertye (S.F., 1850), 5:37
Lambroscini, Eleanor, 33:94
La Mesa, 13:47, 112, 117, 119, 123; battle of, 1:146, 148; 3:125; 12:335; 13:47, 51, 303; 17:124, 345, 349; 21:351, 357; 22:51; 33:105-6, 252
Lamfist (or Lemfist), Abram, 2:120, 121
Lamoisse (owner of *Georges*, 1850), 5:30
Lamolère, de (S.F., 1849), 5:21, 27, 40-41, 348; 6:38, 56
Lamon, James C., 4:23; 5:338; 15:379; 30:275
Lamon, R. B., 1:283
Lamon, Ward Hill, 15:15; 19:363
Lamont, George A., 23:299
Lamont, Jennie, 21:65
La Montagnie, J. de, 27:98
Lamott, Mrs. (Sacramento, 1858), 9:371; 10:42, 43, 48, 65
La Motte, A. D., 29:92
La Motte, Alfred Victor and Suzanne (Formhals), 29:92
La Motte, François, 11:223, 340, 345, 348
La Motte, Victor J., 29:92
Lamproie (ship), 11:219
Lampson, Nathaniel, 30:8
Lampson, Robin, address, "Writing an Epic of the California Gold Rush," 14:283
Lamson, James, journal and drawings, 24:83; 33:373
Lamson, Joseph Sterry, 23:191

Lancaster, Clay, *Architectural Follies in America*, rev., 40:357-59
Lancaster, John A., 10:394
Lancaster (ship), 26:16, 356; 33:233, 237; 27:179
Lancers, 9:244, 270; *see also* Lanceros; National Lancers
Lances, 12:169; 13:50-51, 100, 213; 25:290; 26:25, 33-37 *passim*
"Lances at San Pascual," by Arthur Woodward, 25:289-308; 26:21-62
Lancey, Thomas Crosby, 13:396; 20:231; 29:333; 33:253
Lanctot, Benoni, 28:4
Land (Fraser R., 1858), 11:151, 153
Land, Agnes, 10:69, 369; 21:51, 53, 63, 65
Land, Isabel, 10:69, 389
Landaeta, Martín de, 2:267, 268, 270, 307; 14:111, 117
Land cases, claims, titles: 8:261; 14:7; 15:5-8, 366, 367, 368; 16:197, 198; 17:174, 178, 247-52 *passim;* 19:18-23 *passim,* 157-66 *passim,* 171, 172, 182, 183, 357-58; 20:108-9, 260; 21:118-22 *passim,* 226, 311-20; 23:10-11; 24:177-78; 25:221-25; 26:70; 27:107-10, 133-40 *passim;* 30:324, 329-30, 331; 30:310; 34:240, 251, 257
  Alamos y Agua Caliente, 21:320
  J. S. Alemany: for college, 17:178; for Indians, 17:182
  Alamos y Agua Caliente, 21:320
  Angel Island, 27:108
  Boga, 27:108
  Buri Buri, 16:183, 285; 17:249-57 *passim*
  Campo de los Franceses, 15:277
  Camulos, 21:320
  Cañada de Capay, 25:221-22
  Cañada de Raymundo, 15:266
  Carmel, 25:221
  Ciénega de Gabilán, 21:315
  Los Coches, 20:108-9
  Corte Madera del Norte, 16:285
  Guilicos, 27:108
  Gulnac, 16:82, 182; 17:174
  Jimeno, 27:107
  Larkin's children's, 6:270
  Loma del Espiritu Santo, 21:320
  Lup-Yomi, 27:107-8, 109
  Mare Island, 19:163, 171, 357; 25:320
  Las Mariposas, 15:275, 368; 30:331; 34:254-57, 262-63
  Mission Dolores, 27:109
  Mission La Purísima, 27:109
  Mission San Buenaventura, 18:178
  Mission San Gabriel, 27:135
  Missions San José, San Juan Bautista, San Luis Obispo, San Miguel, Santa Clara, 17:178
  Mission Soledad, 23:10-11
  Natividad, 15:134
  New Almaden, 15:5-8; 16:202; 17:316; 20:108; 30:338
  New Helvetia, 25:221
  Omochumne, 25:221, 223-25
  Panoche Grande, 15:380; 19:367
  Del Paso, 25:220, 223-25
  Petaluma, 15:280; 16:235
  Posito de las Animas, 16:347
  Posolmi, 16:347
  Potrero, 16:339; 21:18-22 *passim*
  Potrero de los Cerritos, 16:285
  Potrero de Santa Clara, 16:285; 27:107
  Pueblo of San Francisco, 21:123-25
  Pulgas, 15:266; 17:247, 249
  Punta de Quintin, 15:370
  Las Putas, 27:108
  Refugio, 21:320
  Rinconada del Arroyo de San Francisquito, 27:135
  Rincón de la Ballena, 21:316
  Rincón de las Salinas y Potrero Viejo, 16:80; 27:107
  Rincon de San Francisquito, 16:285; 27:134
  Rio de Jesús María, 25:221
  Rio de los Americanos, 15:366
  Roblar de la Miseria, 27:108
  San Antonio o El Pescadero, 16:285
  San Cayetano, Garden of, 17:178
  San Francisco de las Llagas, 16:282
  San Francisquito, 17:176
  San Mateo, 27:251-52
  San Pablo, 15:277; 30:219, 220, 222
  San Pedro y Buri Buri, 16:285
  Scherrebeck's, 16:339
  Soscol, 15:280
  Sutter's for Moquelumne Indians, 16:347, 392
  tax titles, 15:183
  Los Ulpinos, 16:285
  Yerba Buena, Island of, 15:280; 17:174
  see also Bolton and Barron; Homesteading; Lands: public; Limantour; Ranchos
Land Commissions, *see* California Land

Commission; U.S. Board of Land Commissioners
Lander, Edward, 4:234
Lander, James H., 13:335; 24:275; 32:344; quoted, 328-31 *passim*, 345, 348
Lander, John M., 2:90, 110, 113, 116, 118, 121
Lander, William C., 2:117, 121
Lander's Bar, 9:355, 386; 10:173
Landes, Charles, 9:329-30
Land grant colleges, 19:345-47; 32:314
Land grants, 1:169-70; 4:90; 6:270; 8:104, 109, 310; 12:284; 13:203; 15:368; 16:196-97; 17:174, 252; 19:18-19, 158-59; 21:124, 311-20; 24:113, 177, 299-301; 25:60-64 *passim*; alcalde grants, 8:104; 16:343; 28:67-68, 266; 34:259; measurement of, 30:315, 324-29 *passim*, 334, 338; railroad, 4:227, 238, 255; 24:109; *see also* Land cases; Ranchos
Landgridge (lawsuit, Marysville, 1859), 10:181
Landigan's, at Timbuctoo, 10:255
Landis (Auburn, ca. 1875), 18:361
Landis, Benjamin, 15:42
Landis House, Yuba Co., 10:58
Landis *v.* Paine and wife, 9:265, 356-57, 362
"Landmarking Pilgrimage through the '49 Mining District, The," address by H. C. Peterson, 3:97
"Land of Little Rain, The," address by Helen M. Doyle, 14:410
Land of Sunshine, 31:18
Landon, Hank, 8:343, 348, 350
Landrum, George, 15:370
Lands: Henry George's ideas about, 24:112-14; mineral, 24:113; Mission, 17:178; 19:159; 22:62; 23:10-11; 24:309; 25:60 (*see also* Ranchos, Mission); offered by Mex. govt. for colonization, 25:60-64; in payment of debt, 17:21-22; Pre-emption Act, 24:193; public: 1:25; 8:104; 15:169, 272; 19:18, 19, 21, 158, 164-65, 169, 178-79, 183, 345-47; 24:113, 176-78, 299; 28:299; pueblo and town, 1:25; 8:310; 13:202; 14:7-8, 20-21; 15:169, 176, 276; 16:343; 19:158, 159; 20:113; 21:121-25 *passim*; 24:113-14; 25:321, 322; 30:323; 35:110; 38:51; tide, 21:121-22; 22:113-25; *see also* Real Estate

Lane, Charles D., 20:181-82, 184
Lane, Franklin Knight, 6:288; 36:70; 38:254, 357
Lane, Harriet, 11:12, 13, 16, 17, 25
Lane, James A., 27:221
Lane, Joseph, 4:238; 11:13, 14, 26, 28; 16:84; 17:314, 317; 19:358; 28:199, 200, 224-25, 231-32, 351, 358
Lane, LaFayette, 21:130
Lane, Levi Cooper, 4:191, 198, 205-6; 5:93
Lane, Riley, 9:358, 365, 391; 10:55
Lane, T. A., 26:247
Lane, Crawford & Co., 32:220, 224
Lane's Crossing (or Station), 3:166, 168, 169
Lang, C. E., 22:39
Lang, Victor, 15:268
Langdon, C. W., 2:204
Langdon, Samuel, 23:376
Langle, Vicomte de (1786), 3:223-24; 15:215, 220
Langlet, S., 5:24
Langley, C., 34:345
Langley, Clarissa Durant, 30:382
Langley, Samuel P., 4:35, 38
Langley, Mount, 4:19, 33, 35, 54
Langlois (San Jose, 1850), 5:25, 26, 30, 373
Langlois (Fr. consular agt., S.F., 1849), 13:380; 35:311
Langlois, Anthony, 5:43; 32:122
Langlois, B. Louis, 14:142
Langlois, Jean François, 33:128
Langlois, William, 15:240
Langrishe and Glenn Troupe, 21:172
Langsdorff, George Heinrich von, 7:196; 12:207, 227; 25:320; *Narrative of the Rezanov Voyage*, ed. Russell, rev., 7:196-97
Langton, A. T., 30:110, 360; *see also* Langton & Co.
Langton, Samuel W., 8:338, 339, 353; 9:317; 13:32; *see also* Langton's Pioneer Express
Langton, Mrs. Samuel W., 8:353
Langton, Thomas, 8:353
Langton & Co., 30:258, 259, 266
Langton's Pioneer Express, 8:338, 339, 353; 9: (illus.) opp. 62, 76; 11:60, 234; 16:79
Langtry, Lillie, 16:301; 19:108; 35:141
Langworthy, T., 15:45
Lanning, Charles J., 31:36-37
La Nord, Louis de, 37:210

Lans, G. A., 26:227; 28:321, 322

Lansdowne, Marquis of, 23:121-22

"Lansford W. Hastings," address by
Leon O. Whitsell, 21:82

Lansing, Christopher, 10:44, 46, 51, 62;
11:8-9

Lansing, J., 9:394

Lanson, Georges, guidebook by, 39:2

Lansquenet (card game), 8:207

"Lanterns at Monterey: Serra's
Description of the Founding of
Monterey," by Thomas W.
Temple II, 11:274-79

Lanzoni, Alessandro, 15:183

La Paz, Ariz., 12:16-17; 22:13, 16, 18,
151, 161, 162

La Paz, Lower Calif., 1:208; 3:308;
18:177; 20:222; 22:155, 162; 26:309;
29:139; 31:111, 115

La Paz, bay or port of, 1:39, 40, 41, 48,
50, 51; 3:319, 334, 335, 339, 368;
6:298; 7:259-60; 26:309, 312, 313;
27:310

Lapérouse, Jean François de Galaup de,
1:176; 3:215, 223, 224; 8:116-17;
15:213, 215, 330; 18:335, 344-45;
37:305; "A Visit to Monterey in
1796," 15:216-23; check list, 20:47-64;
port., 20: opp. 47

Lapham, Roger Dearborn, 22:383;
24:1, 3, 162

Laplace, Cyrille Pierre-Théodore,
8:116-17, 125, 129; 12:156, 159;
18:315-28

La Playa, San Diego, 31:343, 344, 345

La Porte (Rabbit Creek), 9:52, 69, 70;
19:291, 296, 298; 29:304; 30:362, 367;
38:309

La Purísima Concepción Mission, *see*
Missions: La Purísima Concepción

Lara, Francisco Dorio, 26:41-42

Lara, José de, 13:200, 201, 202

Lara, Juan, 33:121

Lara, Romualdo, 16:239-40

Larcher, Ed, 39:228, 229, 232, 233

Larco, Nicholas, 16:341; 29:82

Larios, Justo, 15:4

Larison, G. B., 9:288

Larisson, Jack, 4:116

La Rivière, Boursier de, 35:316, 317,
318, 322

Larkin, Alice Sistare, 16:321

Larkin, Caroline, 17:236

Larkin, Francisco R., 18:62; 27:299, 300

Larkin, Frederick H., 18:54, 62; 27:299

Larkin, Henry, 11:51

Larkin, Lew, 34:93

Larkin, Sophia, 15:176

Larkin, Thomas Oliver, 4:234; 8:297-303
passim; 11:75; 12:48, 60, 140, 142, 146,
345; 13:232, 278, 395; 14:128, 163,
318, 328, 329, 343; 15:116, 124, 125-26,
225, 236, 266, 302; 16:139, 187; 17:151,
157, 167, 231, 236, 280; 18:32, 34-38
passim, 68, 228; 20:16, 18, 21; 25:145,
196-97, 199, 205; 27:49; 28:195, 259,
260, 261, 266, 267; 29:25, 132, 151;
30:3, 98, 234, 321; 32:83; 33:67, 115;
34:113-19 *passim,* 255; 35:106, 110, 200
    land owned or claimed by, 4:90;
        16:340; 17:178, 232; 20:152; 27:107,
        108, 298, 299, 300
    marriage, 2:50
    partner of Semple, 6:147, 149; 13:267;
        16:340; 17:232, 301-2; 20:152;
        24:63; 27:62
    U.S. Consul, 2:49, 168, 171, 356;
        3:109, 272; 4:165, 375, 378, 391;
        5:132; 6:265, 280, 369; 7:106; 10:121;
        12:39, 40, 129, 135; 16:210, 211,
        215; 17:137, 138, 139, 227, 228, 279;
        18:144, 217, 310; 19:45-48 *passim,*
        51, 52, 55; 21:2, 5; 23:202; 25:125;
        28:253, 293; 29:135, 156, 157, 158,
        336; 37:1-2, 13-15; consular cor.,
        1:90-92, 178-81, 183, 189-90, 286-89,
        292-95; 2:71-74; 3:178-84, 186, 187,
        273-89; 4:81-83, 85-87, 376-77;
        5:77-80, 124, 184, 191, 255, 297-308;
        6:77-80, 87-89, 182-84, 186-91, 266,
        269-74, 364-66, 368, 372-73; 7:79-80,
        83-85; 8:76-77; 9:81-85; 10:100,
        103, 104; 14:147; 22:315; 23:293-94
    letters: to Atherton, 28:113-15, 342;
        29:166; to Childs, 16:264-69; to his
        sons, 27:297-300
    "My Itinerary," ed. Parker, 16:11-29,
        144-70
    arts. on, 16:3-29, 144-71, 263-70,
        321-25
    fac. sig., 10: opp. 159; port., 16: opp. 3

Larkin, Mrs. Thomas Oliver
    (Rachel Hobson Holmes), 6:364;
    16:4, 322; 28:260, 261, 262

Larkin, William, 16:9-10, 153

Larkin, William F. (?), 15:163

Larkin family, 16:3; 27:299, 300

Larkin House, Monterey, 16:321-35;
    phot., opp. 321

Larkin's children, 27:299; ranch of, 30:53
"Larkin to Atherton," ed. A. T. Leonard, Jr., 28:113-15, 342
Larkyns, Henry, 35:50
Larned (on *George and Henry*, 1843), 18:66
Larocque, Joseph Sebastian, 22:196, 197, 199, 205, 219; 23:22, 23, 25, 28, 38, 123, 124, 125, 134
Larrainzar, Manuel, 21:358, 359, 362
Larson, Hans, 26:204
Larue, James B., 10:72
Lascroux, Rene (?), 39:258, 259, 260, 313
Las Cruces, Santa Barbara Co., 18:262
Las Flores, *see* Mission asistencias; Ranchos: Santa Margarita y Las Flores
Laspeyre, Thomas, 10: opp. 48, 53, 62; 11:7-9; 20:166; 40:311, 312
Las Plumas hydroelectric plant, *see* Big Bend plant
Las Posadas Forest, 35:1-9, 155-60
Lasquisimes, Rio, *see* Stanislaus R.
Lassator, James Ruler, 25:307; 34:199, 200, 202, 207; 36:117-29 *passim*, 132
Lassator, Mrs. James Ruler, 34:199
Lassen, Alexander Charters and May C., 3:94
Lassen, Peter, 1:127, 128, 132; 3:94; 5:305; 6:88, 164; 7:201; 10:74; 11:109, 110, 115, 116, 119, 121; 12:326-27; 16:137; 21:10, 225-29 *passim*, 235-36; 22:366; 26:333, 343; 30:54, 62, 63; art. on, 18:291-314; port., 18: opp. 291; phot. of grave, 18: opp. 304; rancho of, 6:164; 17:272, 273; 28:262; 30:63; 39:263; *see also* Ranchos: Bosquejo
Lassen County, 18:304; 31:130; *see also* Honey Lake
Lassen Cutoff, route, trail, 11:110; 18:300-302, 312; 24:246; 28:298, 318; 30:60, 62; 31:342; 32:203; 39:263
Lassen Peak, 3:94; 18:301, 312; 22:370; eruption of, 18:302
Lassik (Indian, d. 1863), 20:353-54, 361, 362, 363
Lassiter, Mrs. (Marysville, 1861), 10:356
Lassiter, James H., 10:178, 258, 275, 358, 359
Last Adventure: San Francisco in 1851, by Benard de Russailh, rev., 10:205

Last of the California Rangers, The, by Cossley-Batt, rev., 8:83-84
Last of the Mill Creeks, The, by Moak, rev., 4:94
Last of the Vaqueros, by Rojas, rev., 40:69-71
"Las Trancas," 29:319, 326, 328
"Last Spanish Exploration of the Northwest Coast, The," by Henry R. Wagner, 10:313-45
"Last Will and Testament of Stephen J. Field, The," by John C. Hogan and Ewald W. Schnitzer, 36:41-55
"Last Will of Pedro de Alvarado, The," by Henry R. Wagner, 25:309-10
Lasuén, Fermín Francisco de, 1:165, 169; 2:338-39; 3:224; 5:414; 6:160, 162, 166; 8:108; 15:213, 217, 220; 17:122; 20:238; 23:1-3, 12, 371-75 *passim*; 26:372-73; 28:19-22; 31:116; 33:278; 34:204, 230; 36:336
Las Vegas, 22:9, 12, 13, 15, 25
Lasvignes, L., 10:360
Laswell & Co. *v.* Fallon, Hudson & Co., 9:370
Lataillade, Cesáreo, 12:135; 13:121, 380-81; 18:170, 179, 266; 19:207, 215
Latazi (Indian, 1845), 21:5
Latham, Dana, 26:94
Latham, J. K. S., 11:10, 25
Latham, James H., 32:150
Latham, Milton Slocum, 2:209-10; 5:179; 9:397; 10: opp. 48, 60, 78, 166, 167, 168, 192, 195, 207, 246, 260, 282, 283, 295, 296, 383-84; 14:76; 15:173, 202, 203, 204, 208, 211, 275, 368; 16:80, 82, 83; 17:319, 320; 19:230, 238, 269, 347, 355; 21:25; 22:231, 361; 24:274; 25:344, 345; 27:5; 31:235; 33:231, 233, 373; 34:154; 36:42; 38:27, 329, 330, 333, 334; 39:291; "Day Journal," ed. E. E. Robinson, 11:3-28; art. on, 32:145-59; phot., 11: opp. 3
Latham, Mrs. Milton Slocum (1, Sophie Birdsall), 2:210; 11:10, 24; 19:232, 238; 32:157; (2, Mary W. McMullin), 27:382
Latham, William B., Jr., 9:345, 378; 24:186; family of, 9:378
Latham, Mrs. William B., Jr. (Phoebe Bell Carpenter), 9:378
Latham, William C., 15:167
Latham, William Carpenter, 9:378; obit. 24:186

Latham (Edith and Milton)
Foundation, 35:183
Lathrop, Mrs. (m. to Higgins, 1849),
28:292
Lathrop (Mormon Tavern, 1849), 20:39
Lathrop, Anna, 10:392
Lathrop, Benjamin B., 16:184
Lathrop, Eli C., 8:202, 204; 15:76
Lathrop, George, 18:307, 314; 21:227-28,
235
Lathrop, Jane, *see* Stanford, Mrs. Leland
Lathrop, H. B., 9:40; 29:196
Lathrop, R. P., 37:350
Lathrop, Solomon, 31:342
Lathrop (place), 18:23, 27, 28
Latimer, Mr. and Mrs. B. F., 15:166,
268, 271
Latimer, Mary, 9:248, 274, 367
Latona, Mrs. Cruz, 9:374, 375
Latour, Dr. (from France, 1850), 22:301
Latter-day Saints, Church of Jesus
Christ, of, *see* Mormons
Lattimer (S.F., 1855), 16:183
Lattimer (Marysville, 1858), 9:362
Lattimer, David, 22:77, 83
Lattimer, James, 9:362(?); 13:258
Lattin, A. J., 9:358
Laub, Charles H., 34:36
Lauck, J. B., 35:30, 32
Lauder, Eugen, 18:212-13
Laugenour, Margaret (Cross), 25:94
Laughlin, Mrs. (S.F., 1855), 15:370
Laughlin, Ada (Edwards), 26:188
Laughlin, Richard, 2:18, 37; 13:210,
230, 325
Laundry and laundries, 3:32; 14:129;
17:196, 294; 23:161, 162; 26:333;
27:368; sent to Orient, 3:32; 17:196
Laura (ship), 22:171, 172, 173
Laura Bevan (ship), 20:275, 278
Laura Virginia (ship), 19:376; 22:379;
25:118
Lauray, Julian, 39:320
Laurel Hill Cemetery, San Francisco,
4:199-202; 10:293; 18:334, 343;
19:154; 22:26; 24:278; *see also* Lone
Mountain
Laurel Hill Mining District, 26:245
Laurencel, Henry de, 15:4, 19
Laurenul (Laurencel?), Capt. (of *La
Pacifique*, 1848), 13:273
Laurie, Annie (pseud.), 20:142-43
Lausanne (ship), 12:244-45; 17:63-64;
18:292-93, 310
Lauterwasser, F. P., 9:320

Lavalard, Louis C., 14:142
Lavalle, L., 22:218
La Viña Sanatorium, 31:29
Law, George, steamship line of,
28:360
Law, William C., 20:159
Law, *see* Courts; Judges; Mining law
Law and Order faction, San
Francisco, 9:62, 75, 106, 258, 259, 283;
10:50, 73; art. on, 14:350-74;
15:70-87, 143-62, 247-65; *see also*
Vigilance Committee, San Francisco
"Law and Order View of the San
Francisco Vigilance Committee of
1856, The," from correspondence
of Gov. J. Neely Johnson, ed.
Herbert G. Florcken, 14:350-74;
15:70-87, 143-62, 247-65
Lawler (Yuba Co., 1860), 10:253
Lawler, F. W., 27:312
Lawler, Oscar, 33:274-75; 39:215
Lawler, Mrs. Oscar (Hilda Brode),
26:188; obit., 33:274-75
Lawler, William, 15:177; 33:274
Lawler family, 33:275
Lawless (Marysville, 1857), lawsuit,
9:132
Lawley Toll Road, 32:369
Law Library, *see* San Francisco Law
Library
Lawlor, Frank, 21:248; 24:263
Lawlor, Mrs. R. C., 25:190
Lawrence (Calaveras Co., 1850),
22:72-73
Lawrence, Miss (1856), *see* May, Hattie
Lawrence (Philippines, 1898), 31:50
Lawrence, A. C., 11:7-9; 38:331
Lawrence, Eleanor Frances, "Mexican
Trade between Santa Fe and Los
Angeles," 10:27-39
Lawrence, Elwood P., 30:191; "Henry
George's Oxford Speech," 30:117-23
Lawrence, Hannah, 11:11, 17
Lawrence, James, 1:116
Lawrence, Mrs. James H., *see* Lawrence,
Mary Viola (Tingley)
Lawrence, Joseph E., 7:278; 13:298;
20:334-35
Lawrence, Marion ("Comanche
George"), 18:303-4, 313; 21:235
Lawrence, Mary Viola (Tingley),
1:301; 4:207; 5:412; 10:392; 28:6, 7
Lawrence (ship), 12:31; 14:214, 215,
219, 224, 384, 385, 401
Lawrence's Station, 14:168

Laws, Robert, Jr., 26:130
Laws: for better govt. of Calif. (1848),
    2:75-76; 10:81, 82; of Burgos
    (1512-1513), 40:76-77; of the
    Indies, 7:138; 33:280; Mex., estab.
    metric system (1857), 30:325, 326,
    335; of Town of S.F. (1847), 2:75;
    see also Sunday laws
*Laws for the Better Government of
    California* (1848), 2:75-76; 10:81, 82
Laws of Burgos of 1512-1513, The, trans.
    by Simpson, rev., 40:76-77
Laws of the Town of San Francisco
    (1847), 2:75
Lawson (Yuba Co., 1859), 10:168, 169,
    251
Lawson, Albert, 26:204
Lawson, Andrew Cowper, 32:37
Lawson, Emilie, 28:7
Lawson, James S., 11:301-7, 314
Lawson, John, 25:232
Lawson, P. S., 22:251
Lawson, Peter, *see* Lassen, Peter
Lawson, Sam, 33:364
Lawson, Thomas, 33:118, 267, 399;
    letter from, 34:37-38
Lawton (Vernon, 1849), 23:349
Lawton (Field's sec'y., 1899), 36:44
Lawton, Alfred, 14:378; 15:21
Lawton, Harry, *Willie Boy: A Desert
    Manhunt,* rev., 39:371-74
Lawton, Irving, 13:31
Lawton, Orlando, 13:31
Lawyers of Los Angeles, by Robinson,
    rev., 39:85
Layne, Joseph Gregg, "Annals of Los
    Angeles," 13:195-234, 301-54; obit.
    of William J. Hunsaker, 12:183-84
Layton, Charles, 17:82; 29:23, 28
Layton, Christopher, 14:278; 28:292
Layton, Robert, 21:307; 22:69
Lazard, Solomon, 29:236-37, 247
Lazard Frères, San Francisco, 27:170
Lázaro (Indian, 1846), 26:27
"Lazarus" (dog), 2:242-43; 24:264
Lazier (Lassen Co., 1855), 18:303, 313
Lea, Luke, 28:339, 340
Leach, Frank Aleamon, obit.,
    8:285-86
Leach, L. B. (pseud.), 7:10
Leach, Lewis, 25:29; 28:339
Leach, Maria, 14:74; 15:164, 175;
    25:335, 343
Leach, R. L., 20:44
Leach, Stephen W., 4:207-9; 10:390;

14:74; 15:164, 166, 174-80 *passim,*
    271; 31:249
Leach, Mrs. Stephen W. (Georgiana
    Griswold), 4:208
Lead, 5:268
Leader, Herman A., ed. "A Voyage
    from the Columbia to California in
    1840," 8:97-115
Leader, San Francisco and Oakland,
    15:174
Leahy, Daniel, 19:120, 124, 137
Leahy, Mrs. Daniel, 19:119-23 *passim*
Leahy, "Libby" and Mary Anne, 19:121
Leake, Charles A., 15:167
Leake, Chauncey, 21:368
Leake, Paul R., 33:316
Leake, W. S. ("Sam"), 19:67, 68, 73;
    28:47
Leal, Andrés, 7:394
Leale, John, 27:285; *Recollections of
    a Tule Sailor,* rev., 18:373-74
Leale, Marion, 27:285; obit., 35:85-86
Leale, William G. and Lily (Banks),
    29:190
Leaming, Christopher, 17:115
Leang Shang, 23:104
Lear, Robert R., 13:296
Leary, John, 25:103
Lease (Colusa, 1861), 10:359
Lease, Mary, 27:315
Leather, *see* Hide and tallow trade;
    Tanning
"Leather A Dragoons," 29:273
Leather-jacket soldiers, 11:278; 13:196,
    208; 20:240; 31:114; 34:205
Leathers, John B., 2:122
Leavenworth, Henry, 4:117, 119, 138
Leavenworth, Thaddeus M., 3:39;
    7:106; 16:343; 19:4, 123, 139; 20:121,
    125; 26:165-66, 167; 27:266; 28:289,
    296; 29:161, 164, 168, 170; 34:259
Leavitt, Mrs., boardinghouse of
    (Sacramento, 1850s), 26:181
Leavitt, Francis Hale, "Steam
    Navigation on the Colorado River,"
    22:1-25, 151-74
Leavitt, Hiram L., 34:223
Leavitt, John, 9:243, 244, 394; 10:56,
    179, 180, 183
Leavitt, Michael Bennett, 21:164, 180,
    260
Lebarge, Michael, 33:6, 12, 168; 35:295,
    304
LeBras, François, 35:314
LeBreton, Albert J., 1:14; 24:79

Lecointe, Capt. (of *Héroïne*, 1845), 11:340, 344

Lecompton constitution, 9:271-72, 278, 279, 285; 10:66; 11:26; 31:194, 200; 32:314, 320-23 *passim*

"Lecomptonites," *see* Democrats

Lecomte (Sacramento, 1849), 30:23

LeConte, John, 26:200; 27:351

LeConte, John Lawrence, 21:107-10 *passim*, 112; 31:35, 45

LeConte, Joseph, 1:15; 4:27, 30-32, 42, 46, 48; 10:89; 23:288; 25:13-14, 101; 29:187; 37:45-46

LeConte, Joseph Nisbet, 4:18, 30, 31, 39, 47-55 *passim*; 23:288; obit., 29:187

LeConte, Mrs. Joseph Nisbet (1, Helen Marion Gompertz), 4:48, 55; 29:187; (2, Adelaide Graham), 29:187

Lecoq, Mathurin, 12:35, 354

LeCount, Josiah J., 30:107, 114, 252, 254, 353, 354; *see also* Cooke & LeCount; LeCount and Strong

LeCount & Strong, San Francisco, 17:79; 22:37; 30:107, 250-54 *passim*, 262, 353; bldg. (illus.), 30: opp. 353

Ledger, see Amador Weekly Ledger

Ledlie, J. C., 9:394

Leduc, Mme. (Marysville, 1851), 15:47

Ledyard, Edgar M., ed. Loomis, *Journal of the Birmingham Emigrating Co.*, rev., 8:81-82

Lee, Dr. (San Jose, 1849), 2:201

Lee (S.F., 1855), 15:268

Lee, Augustus, 21:307; 22:71-78 *passim*

Lee, Barton B., 4:321

Lee, Bourke, *Death Valley*, rev., 9:186

Lee, Cornelius R. V., 29:235

Lee, Daniel, 3:74, 76, 77

Lee, Edward, 30:230

Lee, H., 9:42

Lee, H. C., 10:368

Lee, Harvey, 9:243, 249-50, 252, 257, 269, 275, 362, 363, 390; 10:43, 199, 282

Lee, Jason, 3:74-79 *passim*; 5:69; 11:290; 16:86; 30:25, 36

Lee, Jennie, 21:170

Lee, John Doyle, 17:188, 274

Lee, John H., 13:151, 152, 154

Lee, Richard B., 17:177

Lee, Robert E., 10:201; 16:312, 317, 318

Lee, Robert P., Jr., 13:32

Lee, S. S., 15:184

Lee, Samuel Yorke at, 27:34, 46

Lee, Theodore, 3:123; 26:49

Lee, Thomas Jefferson, 30:332, 333, 338

Lee Ah Kroon, 23:104

Lee and Bennett's Circus, 9:175

Lee and Marshall's Circus, 9:54, 175; 10:357, 368; 15:167, 184; 16:80-81, 84; 34:345

Leech, John, 33:364

Lee Kan, 23:111

Leek Springs, 32:207

Leermakers, John A., 19:383-84

Leery, William, 13:175

Lees (S.F., 1854), 15:175

Lees, Isaiah W., 27:19, 20; library of, 3:254; 23:91

Leese, Jacob Primer, 1:91-97 *passim*, 137, 179, 189, 286; 2:69; 3:31; 4:169, 170; 5:305; 8:128; 9:277; 11:69, 70, 73-78, 136; 12:247, 248, 266, 272, 337; 13:216, 236-37; 14:100, 121-27 *passim*, 144, 342; 15:19, 370; 16:100, 249-50; 17:58, 67, 69, 141-45 *passim*, 147, 155, 159-60, 292, 294, 299, 318, 321; 18:67, 70; 19:133; 21:317; 23:291, 333; 24:381; 26:20, 267; 27:50, 108-9; 28:100-101, 108, 257, 264-69 *passim*; 29:318; 30:322; cor., 2:72-74; 6:77-79; 11:75; 14:126; prisoner of Bear Flag party, 1:91-97 *passim*, 137, 179, 189, 286; 2:69; 6:272, 273; 7:79; 10:105; 13:107-8, 166, 175; 15:230; 17:220-22, 224, 228-29, 275; 19:118, 132; 24:57; 25:123; 29:264-65, 321; 30:322; *see also* Leese v. Clark

Leese, Mrs. Jacob Primer (Rosalía Vallejo), 4:169; 11:69; 14:125, 126; 17:142, 145, 227, 294; 24:381

Leese, Jacob Richard, 14:127; 24:381

Leese, Mrs. Jacob Richard (Caroline Estrada), 24:381

Leese, Rosalía, 3:31; 4:169; 11:73, 74; 14:126; 17:299

Leese v. Clark, 21:311-17 *passim*; 30:329

Leet, Samuel T., 11:8, 9

Leete, Benjamin F., 4:245, 300

Lee Took, 23:111

Leevining, 26:236

Lefever, Josiah, 10:62

Lefever, Myron, 9:358, 360

Lefranc (d. Hermosillo, 1854), 18:15

Legace, Josette, *see* Work, Mrs. John

Legace, Pierre, 22:100, 104, 217; 23:125, 139

Legal Tender (ship), 22:172

Legar, Miguel de, 7:299, 327, 334, 377

Legaspi, *see* López de Legaspi

Le Gay, C., 11:127

Leger (Mokelumne Hill, 1859), 11:322

Legge, Robert, 25:381

Legge, Robert T., 25:381; "Hans Herman Behr," 32:243-62; "Note on J. P. Leonard, M.D., Gold-Rush Visitor," 31:161-62; ed. "Medical Observations of J. P. Leonard . . . 1849," 29:211-16

Leggett, Aaron, 11:33-34

Leggett, Dan, 9:61

Legoarant de Tromelin, Rear Admiral (S.F., 1849), 13:280, 378-79; 33:126; 35:311; *see also* Hamelin

Le Grand, Capt. (of *Cachalot*, 1850), 5:28; 14:133

Leguere, Pierre, 13:65

Leheuze (Monterey, 1851), 31:317

Lehman, Androuche, 10:288; *see also* Lehman Family

Lehman, George, 13:331-32

Lehman, Martin, 20:138

Lehman Family, 20:298

Leicht, *see* Von Leicht

Leidener (Yuba Co., 1858), 9:352

Leidesdorff, William Alexander, 2:359; 4:375; 5:405-7; 7:105-6, 108; 11:132, 142; 13:172-73, 262; 15:64, 366; 16:210, 212, 214; 17:230, 293, 298, 301; 27:112; 29:158; 30:1, 5; 37:2, 16; 31:206; 33:374; cor. during Amer. occupation, 1:91-92, 178-81, 182-83, 190-91; 2:356-57; 3:288-89; 4:391; 5:304-5, 307-8; 6:79-80, 182, 365-66; estate, 7:105-11; 16:182; 20:123; 27:106; steam schr. of, 14:143-46; port., 7: opp. 105

Leidesdorff-Folsom estate, 9:276; 16:84; 17: opp. 168, 182, 293; art. on, by Robert E. Cowan, 7:105-11

Leisdesdorff Hotel, San Francisco, 16:130

Leidig, George F., 5:338-39

Leidig's Hotel, Yosemite, 1:278; 5:339

Leighton (Auburn, 1850s), 9:393

Leighton, William H., 10:395

Leighton, Mrs. William H., 10:364, 365, 371, 378, 379, 386, 389, 392; 21:53-54, 55

Lein, Rebecca, 28:294

Leke (Tuolumne Co., 1854), 35:212, 215, 220

Lelaidier (Fr. shipowner), 31:316, 317

Leland (bookseller, S.F., 1853), 30:254

Leland, Abbie M., *see* Miller, Mrs. Joaquin

Leland, Henry, 9:391; 10:59, 77, 174, 176, 177, 199, 247, 285

Leland, John, 14:140

Leland, Richard, 28:123

Leland, Mrs. S. A., 19:230, 236

Leland, William W., 14:386; 25:266

Leland Stanford, by Clark, rev., 10:407

Leland Stanford Junior University, *see* Stanford University

Lelia Byrd (ship), 13:204

Lellan, Charles H., *see* McLellan, Charles H.

Lema (stream), 16:111

Lemaitre, Joseph, 5:20

Leman, Mark, 15:268

Leman, Walter M., 9:275; 10:77, 389, 393; 21:57-58, 69-70, 148; 28:13

Lemar, Alexander, 31:23-24

Lembert, John Baptist, 4:40-41

Lemcke, Mary (Dunbar), obit. of Mrs. Henry C. Compton, 38:177-78

Leming (Colusa, 1861), 10:360

Lemman, Capt. (Colorado R., 1865, 1869), 22:171, 172

Lemmon, John G., 4:53

Lemon, David, 36:101-2, 105, 271, 272

Lemon, Frank, 31:233

Lemon, George Frank, 22:260; 25:343

Lemon, James McK., 26:71, 75

Lemon, Manuel, 7:11

Lemon, Otis E., 36:102

Lemon (ship), 10:32

Lemos, Pedro, 38:1

Lendrum, John H., 27:215; 33:229

Lengfeld, Lewis, 25:94

Lennan, Jacob, 15:376

Lenoir (from Ore., 1845), 5:125

Lenoir, Dr. (overland, 1849), 24:236, 354

Lenore (ship), *see* Leonore

Lenox, T. (or J.), 11:42; 19:123, 133, 139

Lenox, Mrs. T. (or J.), 19:122, 123, 124

Lent, John A., 15:366; 16:81

Lent, William M., 9:26

Lenzen, Edna (Kreyenhagen), 29:285

Leo, Brother, 12:183; address, "Some Phases of California Literature," 8:283

Leon, Andrés, 16:221

Leon, Francis, 21:167

Leon, José, 15:372

Leon, Wilhelm, 10:57

Leon, Mex., 17:127

Leonard, Alexander Thomas, Jr., 25:288; 27:380; "The New Bell at Santa Clara Mission," 8:378; "Rambles in California: A Question of Authorship," 30:233-35; "San Francisco's 176th Birthday," 31:279-82; "Meetings of the Society," 6:103-4; 30:377-78; ed. "Larkin to His Sons," 27:297-300; obits. of Mrs. Frank H. Andrews, 19:191-92; George H. Barron, 21:378-79; Frederick J. Bowlen, 24:283; Juan R. Camarillo, 24:91-92; Mrs. Edward L. Eyre, 13:192; Tirey L. Ford, 7:290; Charles F. Griffin, 30:87-88; Lillie B. Matson, 10:96; Andrew J. Molera, 10:414; Webster K. Nolan, 31:178; Henry A. Van C. Torchiana, 19:87

Leonard, Charles, 29:103

Leonard, Ephraim W., 11:127; 29:7

Leonard, Hiram A., 19:229; 28:221

Leonard, John Preston, 31:161-62; "Medical Observations of . . . 1849," ed. Robert T. Legge, 29:211-16

Leonard, Mark, 6:71-76 *passim*

Leonard, Willard, 15:43

Leonard, Zenas, 1:271; 4:6-7, 127, 128; 5:328; 10:81, 83; 28:185; 32:266-67

Leonard *v.* Darlington, 15:183

Leonardi, Francesco, 15:183

Leong Ah Ghue, 23:104

Leonidas (ship), 14:346; 15:356; 16:364

Leonor (ship, 1830s), 12:140; 15:351; 23:305, 318, 324, 331, 333; 29:151; 30:98, 113

Leonore (or Eleonore), Mme. (S.F., 1851), 28:36; 32:109

Leonore (ship, 1849), 4:204; 20:44

Léotaud (S.F., 1853), 39:146

Leplat, P. L. J., 14:142

LePlongeon, Auguste, 14:213, 398

Leppien, Fred and Elizabeth (Deighton), 28:293

Lepreux (S.F., 1850s), 32:115-16

Lerman, J. J. (John J. Lermen?), 12:201

Lermen, John J., 26:382

Lerner, Tina, 25:236

Leroux, Antoine, 22:48

Leroux, Jules, 39:223-24, 225

Leroux, Pierre, 39:225

Leroy (East Bay, 1841), 8:120; 30:3, 4

Leroy (Sonora, 1850), 17:7

Leroy, A. V. H., 17:182

Leroy, C. W., 22:251

Leroy, Jean-Aristide, 22:304, 308

Leroy, R., 8:110

Lersner, Maurice, 16:82

Lesley, Lewis Burt, "The International Boundary Survey from San Diego to the Gila River," 9:3-15; ed. Stacey, *Uncle Sam's Camels*, rev., 9:182-84

Leslie, Harry, 21:161

Lessack, Miss (S.F., 1861), 10:281, 379

Lester (Yuba Co., 1857), 9:130

" 'Let California Come In,' " by William H. Seward, 24:116

Letcher, William H., 26:345

"Letter from the Mines, A," by C. Berry, 5:293-95

Letters from California, 1846, by Garner, rev., 4:90-91

"Letters of an Artist in the Gold Rush," ed. Frank M. Stanger, 22:235-52

"Letters of A. Rotchev, Last Commandant at Fort Ross, and . . . Report of the Russian American Company . . . 1850-51," trans. by Frederick C. Cordes, 39:97-115

Letters of Bret Harte, The, ed. Harte, rev., 5:199-203

"Letters of Leland Stanford to Mark Hopkins," ed. George T. Clark, 5:178-83; as address, 5:205

"Letters of Narciso Durán," trans. Francis Price, 37:97-128, 241-65

Letters to a Pioneer Senator, ed. Dressler, rev., 4:291-92

Leuba, Edmond, 39:7; "Bandits, Borax and Bears: A Trip to Searles Lake in 1874," trans. Allen L. Chickering, 17:99-117; "A Frenchman in the Panamints," trans. Allen L. Chickering, 17:208-18

Levant (ship), 2:169; 3:108-13 *passim;* 5:255; 7:82, 84; 9:82; 12:47; 17:125, 228, 282; 18:73; 25:125, 127; 34:119

Levanter (ship), 16:83, 285, 339

Levati, Frank, 35:33

L'Evèque, Capt. de (of *Artemise*, 1854), 15:171

Lever, Edward A., 37:196, 205, 211

Leveridge, Asa, 15:377

Leverson, Montague R., 27:346-47

Levi, Gene, 20:135

Levi, Michel, 35:119

Levi, S., 35:345, 346; *see also* Klauber & Levi

Levick (San Bernardino, 1856), 29:242

Levin, J. & C., 15:54

Levine, Rachel, 40:5

Levinsky (peddler, Amador Co.),
20:183

Levinthal (Yuba Co., 1857), 9:139

Levison (Sacramento, 1857), 9:161

Levison, Jacob Bertha, 25:232, 246;
address, "Recollections of the San
Francisco Disaster of 1906,"
21:183-84

Lévy, Daniel, *Les Français en Californie*,
39:2, 4, 15-16

Lévy, I. O., obit. of Sam Behrendt, 20:93

Levy, Julius, 15:275; 16:84, 336, 338

Lewekamp, John, 26:204

Lewelling, Henderson, 27:382

Lewelling, J., 27:73

Lewelling (A.) & Co., 27:73

Lewis, Capt. (of *Everline*, 1834), 14:315

Lewis (Yokayo Indian), 26:210-15
passim

Lewis, A., 9:58, 61, 62, 63

Lewis, Charles Lux, 23:191

Lewis, Charles W., 20:261; 40:350

Lewis, David, 21:101

Lewis, Edward J., 9:243, 248, 249, 253,
260, 267, 269, 357, 362; 10:49, 71;
11:9

Lewis, Mrs. Frank (Martha Jane Reed),
2:63-64

Lewis, Gus, 9:52, 57, 58, 67, 137, 140-44
passim, 148, 149, 151, 155, 156, 157,
262, 265, 346, 352, 353; 10:55

Lewis, H. B., 13:11

Lewis, Harriet, 20.293

Lewis, Henry H., 1:231

Lewis, J. H., 9:170; 31:6

Lewis, J. R., 33:7, 12, 148

Lewis, James, 9:157, 178, 374

Lewis, Miss Jeffreys, 21:172, 257

Lewis, John A., 9:42; 13:320

Lewis, John Roome and Frances M.
(Fotheringhame), 28:293

Lewis, Joseph E. N., 29:302, 306

Lewis, Lucy (Wright), 29:179; letter
to, 29:176-78

Lewis, M. B., 3:26; 28:334

Lewis, Mary Jane (Fulkerson), 29:285

Lewis, Miranda Wilmarth (Sheldon),
23:191

Lewis, Nat, 3:164-65; 12:11

Lewis, Oscar Joseph, fellow of CHS,
39:70; foreword to Civil War
Commemorative issue, 40: opp. 289;

obit. of Albert M. Bender, 20:92-93;
*The War and the Far West,
1861-1865*, rev., 40:351-53; coauth.
Bonanza Inn, rev., 18:369-71; phot.,
39: opp. 72

Lewis, Philip B., 14:64, 72-73

Lewis, Thomas, 15:240

Lewis, W. H., 37:198

Lewis, William, 16:183

Lewis, William E., 20:115

Lewis, William J., 12:174; 14:163;
21:117, 118, 119; 30:329

Lewis, William S., 9:182; "Contribution
towards a Bibliography of the Camel,"
9:336-44

Lewis, William T., 10:378, 379, 387, 390

Lewis (ship), 27:293; 36:135, 139

Lewis & Murray, 9:143, 144, 151, 255

Lewis *v.* Gordon & Steen, 15:183

Lewitzow Lelkendorf (ship), 19:290

Lexington (place), 29:57

Lexington (ship), 1:232, 234; 2:251,
350; 16:196; 20:222, 233; 22:50, 65;
28:113, 114; 30:18, 35; 33:113, 251

Lexington House, Plumas Co., 9:52, 69,
70; 33:299, 300

Leya, Emile, 15:46-47

Leyba, Alejo, 18:268

Leyba, Pancho, 18:260

Leyba, Santiago, 21:320

Leyorcita, Dolores, 28:292

Leyssègues (or Leyssèques), Olivier de,
see Deleissèques

Leyton, *see* Seyton

L'Héritier (S.F., 1853), 32:301; 39:147

Libbey, Elliot, 5:255; 6:80; 18:70; 31:216

Libbey, William, 2:115

Libby, Daniel B., 33:166, 167, 168;
35:295-96

Libertad (ship), 15:167-70 *passim*, 175

Liberty Bank of America, 37:355, 356

Liberty Bank of San Francisco,
37:270-71

Liberty Cap, Yosemite, 1:281

Liberty Colony, 25:175

Liberty Loans, 36:74-75

Liberty (Ye) Playhouse, Oakland,
20:139; 33:44-45

Liberty ships, 21:373

Librarians' Association of Central
California, 19:152; 25:4, 12

Libraries: 15:167; 38:295-319;
circulating, 30:354, 359, 362, 363;
38:295; Crescent City, 32:169; 38:319;
Doheny, 25:190; private, 4:284;

12:20; 20:108, 113; 29:151; 30:98, 101, 315, 359; public, 38:295-320; public school, 15:169; *see also* Bancroft Library; Mercantile Library; San Francisco Public Library

Libros Californianos . . ., by Phil T. Hanna, rev., 38:83-84

Lichau, Edward, 22:79, 83

Lichau, L. and Mary, 22:83

Lichtenstein, Franz, *see* Lightstone, Frank

Lick, James, 1:15; 11:312; 17:186; 21:368, 369; 25:6, 11; 28:298; 29:56; 32:257-58; 38:28, 41,305

Lick House, 19:225; Block, 28:12

Lick Observatory, 11:312; 18:181, 183; 21:368

Liddle (Liddell, Little; S.F., 1850), 8:182, 262-76 *passim*

Lieber, Francis, 27:341, 351

Liebert, A., 6:46; 32:108-9

Liederkrantz Society, Marysville, 9:360, 367, 375-76; 10:188

Lienhard, Heinrich, 11:42-43; 18:181; 21:80; 36:59, 62; 38:42

Lies, Eugene, 10:44, opp. 48, 62, 67, 70; 18:255

Life and Adventures of . . . Joaquin Murrieta, by Paz, trans. Belle, rev., 5:203

"Life and Death of Klamath County, The," address by Charles Kasch, 34:87

Life and Letters of John Muir, The, by Badè, rev., 4:292-98

Life and Times of Fray Junípero Serra, The, by Geiger, rev., 39:359-62

Life and Voyages of Wm. M. Phillipson, The, rev., 5:403-4

Life and Works of the Rev. Ferdinand Konscak, by Krmpotic, rev., 2:365-66

"Life at New Almaden," address by Laurence E. Bulmore, 26:373-74

Life in California before the Conquest, by Robinson, ed. Russell, rev., 4:298-99

"Life in California in 1849 . . . Journal of George F. Kent," ed. John W. Caughey, 20:26-46

"Life in the California Mines, 1851-52," address by Anson S. Blake, 10:91

Life in the Rocky Mountains, by Ferris, ed. Phillips, rev., 19:280-81; ed. Auerbach, rev., 19:281

"Life of Ferdinand C. Ewer, The," by Henry R. Wagner, 13:291-300; 14:74-79

"Life of the Early Day Miners," address by Anson S. Blake, 8:90

Light, Allen B., 32:267

Light Dragoons, San Francisco, 15:164

Lighters and lighterage, *see* Barges and barging

Lighthouses, 16:339; 19:359; 27:71; 35:325-34

Lightner, "Bony," 23:120

Lightner, C. W., 10:62

Lightstone, Frank (Franz Lichtenstein), 5:125; 14:19, 149

Ligue Henri IV (society), 39:238-39, 241

Li Hung-chang, 30:141

Lilac (Indian, 1836), 16:249

Liliencrantz, Henry Tod, 38:282, 367; "Recollections of a California Cattleman . . . ," 38:259-68, 341-47

Lilienthal, Ernest R., 29:286

Lilienthal, Samuel, 29:285-86

Lilienthal, Theodore Max, 38:87; "A Note on Gottardo Piazzoni," 38:7-8

Lillard, John H., 18:199-200, 206

Lilley, W. B., 18:201

"Lillie, Miss" (Lizzi Swindlehurst), 21:152

Lima, Peru, 20:206-8; 23:303, 306-10 *passim*, 312, 326-31 *passim*

Limantour, José Yves, 5:27; 12:349; 13:129; 17:169, 172, 174; 19:163; 21:315, 321-22, 331; 26:253-54; land claims, 1:32; 5:27; 15:6, 19, 277; 16:342, 344; 17:172, 174; 19:163, 357; 21:315, 322, 331; 25:321, 322, 324; 26:253-54

Limantour Estero, 31:99-108 *passim*

Limback, Mrs. (Sausalito, 1892), 36:28

Limekilns, 19:317-22; 33:62; phot., 19: opp. 317; plan, 19: opp. 320

Lime Point, 19:264, 269; 27:294; 32:318-19, 323; 33:231

Linares, Joseph Ramón, 20:236

Linares, María Gertrudis, 20:236

Linares, María Juliana, 20:236

Linares, Rosa, 38:109

Linares, Salvador Ygnacio, 20:235-36, 239, 240

Linares, Ygnacio and Gertrudis (Rivas), 20:235-39 *passim*

Linck, Wenceslao, 31:115, 116, 269

Lincoln (Wood's Cr., 1852), 11:168
Lincoln, A. L., 22:1
Lincoln, Abraham, 4:105, 255, 272,
   288; 6:352; 9:317; 10:257, 258, 267,
   268, 371; 15:3-20, 190, 200, 201, 207;
   16:89, 200-206, 307-17 *passim;* 17:237,
   303-24 *passim;* 19:362-66; 20:160-68
   passim, 255; 21:66, 191; 22:26, 183,
   225, 227, 228, 232, 233, 357, 362;
   23:296; 26:195-200 *passim,* 211;
   27:87-88, 89, 98, 100; 31:196, 197,
   201-4 *passim,* 231, 232, 275, 292;
   33:195, 207-8; 34:51-58 *passim;*
   39:294; 40:290, 295, 296, opp. 302
Lincoln, Ashbrook, 30:284; 38:282;
   "The San Francisco Bay-Area Press
   Views Russian Aggression in the Far
   East, 1903- 1905," 30:193-206;
   "My dear Governor: Letters . . .
   Theodore Roosevelt and Hiram
   Johnson," 38:229-47
Lincoln, Granville H., 16:140
Lincoln, Jerome, 26:264; 27:173
Lincoln, Robert Todd, 31:44, 47
Lincoln, Seth S., 16:140
Lincoln & Snyder, 17:84
Lincoln (ship), 11:307
Lincoln Grammar School, San
   Francisco, 25:192; 34:328; 37:224-26;
   40: opp. 302
"Lincoln's California Contacts," address
   by Milton H. Shutes, 22:183
"Lincoln's Chief-of-Staff, Henry
   Wager Halleck," address by
   Milton H. Shutes, 16:89
Lind, Jenny, 33:243, 247
Lind, John E. and Theresa
   (McNamara), 35:332
Lind, John Y., 29:108
Lind, William, 26:204
Linda (place), 14:205, 213, 216, 217,
   218, 395, 403; 15:39-40
Linda (riv. str.), 14:213, 214, 224, 384;
   15:52
Linda Steam Dredging Co., 15:52
Lindberg (Wood's Creek, 1853), 40:99
Linden, Harry, 35:336, 342, 343
Lindenberger, Thomas E., 36:305
Lindenberger, W. H., 23:297
Lindgren, Raymond E., rev. of Bjork,
   West of the Great Divide, 37:372
Lindley, Charles, 9:263-64, 266, 286,
   365, 381; 10:63, 170, 183, 187, 268,
   295, 367; 15:29; 16:257; 22:36; 30:251,
   263, 353

Lindley, Curtis H., 38:230
Lindley, Walter, 4:166
Lindsay, Thomas, 12:115
Lindsey, John, 38:319
Lindsey, Tipton, 4:43; 25:22
Linen, James, 28:6
Linforth, James, 22:24
Lingard, Alice and Dickie, 21:173
Lingard, William Horace, 21:165, 171
Lingard, Mrs. William Horace, *see*
   Dunning, Alice
Lingenfelter, J. W., 31:231, 233
Lingots d'Or (society and lottery),
   20:71; 22:311-12, 314; 35:309, 315;
   39:172; art. on, 33:125-42; illus.
   22: opp. 312
Link, Xavier, 9:66, 136, 137, 139, 143,
   146, 152, 154, 156, 161, 173, 345, 360,
   372, 374, 378
Link v. Coombs, 9:68, 136, 137, 139,
   145, 146
Linn, James S., 16:136, 138
Linnaeus, Carolus (Carl Linné),
   18:335, 344
Linthicum, J. F., 10:177, 252, 265
Lion, Le (ship), 12:348; 28:342
Lion, California (panther or puma),
   2:58; 11:114
"*Lion of the Vigilantes, The,*" by
   Scherer, rev., 18:371-73
Lipman, Edward Crossley, 29:92
Lipman, Frederick Lockwood, 29:92;
   obit., 29:377
Lipman, Joshua, 13:32
Li Po Tai, 35:130
Lippincott, Benjamin S., 15:280; 16:81,
   84; 20:101, 114; fac. sig., 10: opp. 159
Lippincott, Charles E., 8:199, 203, 204,
   205, 208, 212; 9:46, 50; 10:275
Lippincott, William (1855), 15:366
Lippincott, William (1938), 17:243
Lippitt, Francis J., 16:82, 282; 17:182;
   19:237; 26:4, 332; 27:226; 29:161;
   40:349; fac. sig., 10: opp. 159
Lipscomb, Samuel A., 21:291, 307
Lipscomb, William A. (or H.), 21:294,
   307
Lipsis, Elias, 4:61
Liquor: aguardiente, 14:129, 130;
   blackberry cordial, 16:296; brandy,
   13:166, 274; 14:10; 22:319; 23:277,
   278; 32:335; 37:110; milk punch,
   11:18-19; whiskey, 16:133; prices on
   ship, 32:309; saloons, 6:245; 15:184;
   22:262-63; traffic, 5:23; 11:209; 17:59;

22:262-63; 23:22; 31:314; 35:350-51;
see also Drinking and drunkenness;
Prohibition; Temperance; Wine
Lisa, Manuel, 4:126, 127
Lisbon House, San Francisco, 35:235
Lisle's Bridge, 25:223
Lissner, Meyer, 26:85; 38:230
Litayre (ship), 12:222
"Literature of Yosemite, the Big Trees,
and the Sierra," address by
Francis P. Farquhar, 28:185-86
Lithographs, 15:54, 99, 192-93, 301,
302, 305; 22:33-39 *passim;* 34:350;
Marysville, 15:54; reprod., 9: opp. 62,
opp. 68, opp. 358; 30: opp. 257;
flag raising at Monterey, 25:196;
Nevada City, reprod., 9: opp. 68;
Sacramento, 31:283-84; reprod.,
9: opp. 258; San Francisco,
11: 363-64; 21:332; 31:284; Stockton,
31:283-84
Little, Mrs. (Sacramento, 1858), 9:250
Little, Edell F., 29:286
Little, Henry S., 8:262; *see also* Liddle
Little, John T., 23:166, 170, 176; 30:36
Little, Milton, 2:63; 35:105, 107, 110;
38:314
Little, Mrs. Milton, *see* Eagar, Mary
Little, W. C., 38:22
Little, William C., 12:138
Little, William H., 13:340-41
"Little All Right" (acrobat), 21:154,
156
Little & Co., 22:37
Little Bummer (place), 6:71, 76
Little Camass River, 22:328
"Little Cricket" (Josephine), 9:374
Little Grass Valley, 29:300, 305
"Little Ike" (Indian, 1890), 26:201, 206
Little Klamath, *see* Yreka
Little Mariposa Creek, 21:358-62
passim
Little Miss Nobody (play), 34:364
"Little Nell" (Helen Dauvray), 21:173
"Little Pete" (Chinese), 27:23-24
Little River, 9:221
Little Truckee River, 5:378; 7:9; 10:347,
348
Littlefield, John, 13:258
Littlefield, John W., 13:296
Littlejohn, David, 15:120-21; 30:98
Little Sitka, see Sitka (steam launch)
Live Oak Bar, 19:134
Live Oak Park, San Jose, 10:358
Livermore (horticulturist, 1883), 24:223

Livermore, Horatio Gates, 33:81
Livermore, Horatio Putnam, 24:223(?);
29:254; 33:81; 37:228
Livermore, María Josefa, 38:183
Livermore, Norman Banks, obit.,
33:81-82
Livermore, Mrs. Norman Banks
(Caroline Sealy), 33:82
Livermore, Robert, 2:183, 196; 5:130;
14:12; 21:316; 33:350; 34:6; 38:110,
183; 39:43, 50
Livermore (place), 23:294, 364
Liverpool and London Fire and Life
Insurance Co., 25:100; 26:179, 181
Livestock, 2:41-42; 4:37; 5:217; 8:98,
102, 319; 12:193, 199, 242-43, 246,
249; 14:5, 6, 9, 21, 23; 16:119, 242;
19:210; 20:341-46; 21:1; 22:13; 23:250,
252; *see also* Beef; Cattle; Dairying;
Goats; Horses; Mules; Oxen; Sheep;
Swine
Live Woman in the Mines, A (play),
34:359
Live Yankee (ship), 17:174
Livingston, Laurence, 25:286
Livingston, W. R., 7:70
Livingston-Little, Dallas E., rev. of
Foss, *Politics and Grass: . . . Grazing
on the Public Domain*, 40:73-74
Livingstone & Co., Foster's Bar, 9:130
Lizardi and Company, 17:21; 18:137
Lizzie Homer (riv. str.), 33:6, 149;
35:306
L. J. Rose of Sunnyslope, by Rose, rev.,
38:379-81
Llagas Creek, 14:104
Llano del Rio: colony, 40:215-36;
Company (of Calif.), 40:217;
(of Nev.), 40:224
Llebaria, John F., 15:44
Llewellyn Iron Works, Torrance,
30:347
Lloyd, David, 22:163
Lloyd, Elizabeth, 31:241-45 *passim*
Lloyd, Hannah, *see* Neall, Mrs. James
Lloyd, Isaac, 31:241
Lloyd, James T., 30:258
Lloyd, Peter H., 31:280
"Loaded Words," by Dolores W.
Bryant, 23:147-48
Loan of a Lover, The (play), 16:283
Loaysa, García Joffre de, 6:309, 310,
311; 7:133, 135, 180
Lob, Richard, 8:343
Lobar, Juan, 2:36

Lobato, Miguel García, 16:222
Lobb, William, 4:14; 18:343; 32:249
Lobenstine, William C., 20:69
Lobo, Santiago, 26:41
Lobos, Farallon de, 8:57
"Local History in the United States,"
   address by Frederic L. Paxson, 20:282
Locan, Mrs. Franz (Rosa Gore),
   19:232, 233
"Location of the Donner Family Camp,"
   by P. M. Weddell, 24:73-76
Lochead, James K., 20:192
Lockaby, J., 13:32
Locke (on *California*, 1849), 27:36,
   38, 39, 45, 157, 158, 161
Locke, Charles E., 19:98, 105, 108
Locke, Dean Jewett, 18:22-23
Locke, E. R., 15:29
Locke, James O., 23:205, 211, 216
Locke, William J., 36:253
Lockeford, 18:23
Lockhart, Benjamin, 13:32
Lockley, Fred, *To Oregon by Ox-Team
   in '47*, rev., 3:90; ed. Bonney, *Across
   the Plains by Prairie Schooner*, rev.,
   3:89-90; Dosch, *Vigilante Days at
   Virginia City*, rev., 3:297
Lockwood, J. L. ("Ante"), 8:346, 352,
   361; 9:51, 66, 78, 130, 131, 149, 150,
   152; 10:58, 368
Lockwood, Rufus Albert Joseph,
   34:104, 336
Lockwood, Rufus Allen (Jonathan
   Trumball Jessup), 10:191; 16:285;
   20:109; 21:322, 331; art. on 34:97-110,
   239-63, 333-40; port., 34: opp. 336
Lockwood, Mrs. Rufus Allen
   (Harriet Hill), 34:101-5 *passim*,
   336, 338-39; phot., 34: opp. 97
Lockwood, W. G., 9:180
Lockwood family, 34:98-105 *passim*,
   336, 338; phot., 34: opp. 97
Locofocos, 15:28; 26:322, 334, 346
Locomotives, 40:250; "Arrow," 18:30;
   Baldwin, 4:239; 31:293; 40:250;
   logging, 38:65; "Sacramento," 4:223,
   (illus.) opp. 268; "San Gabriel,"
   32:332; "Sequoia," 31:293;
   "Theodore D. Judah," 4:258
Loder, George, 15:164, 369; 16:182,
   283; 17:82; 20:305; 25:342
Lodge, Michael, 16:325, 331; mill of,
   27:162
Lodge, Robert, 36:99

Loehr, Ferdinand von, 15:172; 30:254,
   264
Loeser, Lucien, 10:301; 26:125
Loewy, Baronn & Co., 30:256
Loewy Bros. & Birgham, 29:108; 30:262,
   265, 267, 363, 367
Lofton, J. K., 10:367
Lofton, Squire, 10:183, 200
Log of a Forty-niner, The, Hale, ed.
   Russ, rev., 3:92-93
Log of the Courier, The, by
   Cunningham, rev., 38:371
Logan (San Pedro, 1820s), 6:262
Logan, Pvt. (d. L.A., 1847), 33:256
Logan, James, 8:201
Logan, Jonathan, 11:8-9
Logan, Robert, 9:68, 159, 168, 267;
   10:170, 171, 256
Logan, Thomas Muldrup, 4:194; 26:347
Logging: donkeys, 38:64; engines,
   38:64-65; *see also* Lumber
Lohe, H., 15:368
Lohf, Kenneth A., coauth. *Frank
   Norris: A Bibliography*, rev.,
   39:366-67
Lohse, Charles S., 30:286
Loing, F., 31:333
Loiseau, Adolph, 39:167, 169
Lok, Michael, 8:38; 9:201
Lola Montez (play), 21:60
Loma, Point, 7:347, 387; 8:217-18,
   220-21; 23:205; 31:120; 32:352;
   33:115; 34:159
Loma Alta, *see* Telegraph Hill
Lomas (to Mazatlán, 1849), 14:333
Lombard, Jules Barthélemy, 12:157,
   158, 159; 27:141, 143; 31:139-40,
   323-24; 35:317; letters, 31:141-46,
   147, 253-59, 307-22
Lombardi, I (opera), 15:278
Lombardi Opera Co., 25:231, 241-42
Londeau, Maurice, 25:293; 26:45
London, Jack, 4:100; 10:408; 18:374;
   29:92; 30:199; 39:309-10; 40:137;
   phot., 39: opp. 309; 40: opp. 137
London, James, 2:291-92
London (ship), 7:206-27 *passim*, 396-97;
   8:276
London and San Francisco Bank, 11:5
Lone Mountain Cemetery, 4:182;
   10:266, 279, 293; 11:146, 149; 15:165,
   172, 209, 373; 16:345; 17:314, 321;
   18:343; 21:364; 34:232; *see also*
   Laurel Hill Cemetery
Lone Pine Mining District, 17:115

Lone Tree, San Joaquin Co., 12:6
Long, Dr. (Sutter's Ft., 1847), 16:137
Long (Marysville, 1851), 15:33
Long, Mrs. (Sacramento, 1858), 9:258, 261; 10:176
Long (Chimney Hill, 1859), 10:168
Long, C. W., 38:60
Long, Claude, 29:81
Long, David and Selina (Patch), 16:131
Long, John F., 21:232
Long, John P., 9:77
Long, Lawrence, 6:259
Long, Robert W., 19:384
Long, Sarah R., 29:294
Long, W. H. (pseud. W. H. Ives), 32:121, 139
Long, William S., 9:104; 15:377; 24:170
Long Bar (nr. Foster's Bar), 8:342, 349, 358; 9:158, 347, 353; 10:170
Long Bar (nr. Parks' Bar), 8:359; 9:70, 351, 355, 356; 10:168, 173, 249, 254, 255, 284, 358; 14:402
Long Bar (Trinity mines), 5:220-21, 230
Long Beach, 13:302; 31:294
"Long Drive on the Hastings Cut-off, The," by Henry J. Webb, 36:57-62
Long Lake, Plumas Co., 11:242
Longley, Howard, 4:49
Long's Bar, Butte Co., 30:54; 33:295
Longshoremen, 35:63-64
Longtain, André, 22:196, 198, 203, 208, 217, 221; 23:35, 125, 140-41
Long tom, 3:130; 6:223-24, 238; 11:237
Long Tom Saloon, Sonora, 10:45
Long Valley, Mendocino Co., 27:218; 32:364, 376
Long Wharf, San Francisco, 2:117, 135; 6:251; 18:10-11, 329, 331, 332, 333; 21:75-79; 22:113, 254-55, 259; illus., 21: opp. 75
Loo Choo (ship), 1:208, 218; 18:177; 19:56; 22:65; 24:48, 70; 25:130
Loofbourrow, David Thomas, 9:269
"Look at Llano, A: Experiment in Economic Socialism," by Abe Hoffman, 40:215-36
Look Out (ship), 15:375
Loomis, Augustus Ward, 27:149-50; 28:4-5; 29:11, 116; 32:304, 311; 37:133
Loomis, Barney, 22:78
Loomis, George, 14:95
Loomis, Leander V., *Journal of the Birmingham Emigrating Co.*, ed. Ledyard, rev., 8:81-82
López, Ana Gertrudis, 13:200

López, Baldomero, 37:245
López, Benito, 13:329
López, Bernardino, 23:360-61, 363
López, Bonifacio, 26:30
López, Claudio, 13:210, 211, 326
López, Cristóbal, 26:49
López, Diego, 7:394
Lopez, Esteban, 7:377, 390
López, Francisca, 20:238
López, Francisco (San Diego, 1769), 26:32
López, Francisco (nr. San Fernando, 1842), 7:199; 12:295; 13:58, 224-25
López, Gregorio, 37:201
López, Juan, 21:320
López, María, 26:41
López, María Ignacia, 29:319
López, María Josefa, 26:32, 41
López, Pedro, 13:224
López de Cárdenas, Garci, 7:20
López de Contreras, Pedro, 8:43
López de Gómara, Francisco, *see* Gómara
López, de Haro, Gonzalo, 40:117, 118, 238; map by, 19:221
López, de Legaspi, Miguel, 2:140; 7:62, 142, 144-47, 150, 172, 175, 181, 183, 235, 236, 237; 15:382
López de Villalobos, Ruy, 3:388, 394; 6:314, 322; 7:136, 137, 138, 181, 183, 184
López de Zúñiga, Diego, 3:387, 389; 6:311, 315-17, 319, 330; instructions to, 324-29
López, Portilla, Juan Nepomuseno, letter to, 15:358-59
Lord (on *Cantero*, 1849-50), 2:122
Lord, Miss (Benicia, 1852), 27:303
Lord, Bracket, 22:147
Lord, Charles, 21:240
Lord, Charles L., 27:68
Lord, Joseph M. (?), 12:30
Lord, Nathaniel, 14:406
Lord, Philip B., 39:264-66; map by, 39: foll. 264
Lord, Robert Waterston, 18:375
Lord, William, pack train of, 39:57-58
Lord (D. S.) & Co., 30:107, 264; & Webb, 30:254, 264; *see also* Negbaur & Lord
Lord Dufferin (ship), 15:164
"Lore and Lure of California, The," address by William G. Paden, 25:185-86

Lore and the Lure of the Yosemite, The,
by Wilson, rev., 1:199-200
Lore of the California Vaquero, by
Rojas, rev., 38:371-73
Lorenzana, Francisco Antonio, 1:45, 47
Lorenzana, Jacinto, 27:335-36, 338
Loreto, 5:196; 13:156; 26:310; 31:112;
37:293
Loring, A. F., 15:171
Loring, Samuel, 17:177
Loring, William Wing, 30:56; 34:128
Loriot (ship), 12:138-41 *passim;* 14:343;
16:239; 23:318, 320, 332
Lorrimer, H., 22:251
Lorton, William B., 18:196, 215
Los Amigos Rancho, 27:285
Los Angeles, 1:198; 10:406; 12:147, 149,
157, 232, 349; 13:47, 52, 100; 15:270;
16:226, 230, 231; 17:231, 280, 333;
18:70, 71, 157-64 *passim,* 178, 277;
22:30; 30:262; 33:112, 118, 118-23
passim; 34:39
    American attacks and occupation,
    1:139, 146-47, 235-57 *passim;* 3:115-
    18, 124-25; 12:53, 57-61 *passim,*
    163-68 *passim,* 335, 340; 13:113, 123,
    125, 301-4; 14:328; 17:123, 124, 284,
    325-53, 365; 22:41-47, 59-63; 33:113,
    249-64
    Bernhardt at, 20:139-43 *passim*
    camels in, 9:305-7; 13:343
    capital, 12:36, 38; 13:100, 112, 215,
    217, 222, 228, 231-32, 301
    Carson at, 1:115-16, 147, 148, 149
    censuses, 12:117; 13:321
    churches, 13:317, 321, 332-33
    in 1826-1828, 8:165, 246-47; 13:209-11
    in 1835-1838, 14:232, 233, 234, 240;
    15:242; 16:239, 359, 360
    in 1840-1844, 8:108; 12:116, 117, 282;
    14:324; 19:201-3
    in 1850s, 13:83, 310-11; 14:69, 70-72
    in 1862-1864, 3:164-65, 169; 12:7,
    12-13; 22:13
    in 1880s, 16:296-97
    founding of, 13:198-200
    French in, 12:157, 158
    garrison (1847-49), 33:249-69, 337-46
    government, 13:209, 317-18
    hotels, 13:208, 313, 319, 321, 339
    military companies, 29:232-42
    Mormons in, 14:70-72; 33:108
    name change (prop.), 16:217
    newspapers, 13:319-20, 336-37, 347;
    20:186; 22:30, 361; 23:198; 26:286;
    29:245; 32:327, 344; 33:198; 39:289
    Pío Pico at, 13:112, 113, 201
    population, 13:211, 221, 310
    pueblo, 1:25-32 *passim;* 8:108, 165,
    246-47; 12:282; 13:209; 40:12, 13
    railroads, 10:393; 13:325; 21:384;
    32:327-48
    Stevenson's Regt. at, 1:249-57 *passim;*
    13:305, 306-7
    trade w. Santa Fe, 10:27-39
    vigilance committee, 13:218-21
    Ewing Young at, 1:115-16
    articles on history, 13:195-234,
    301-54; on railroads, 32:327-48
    letters and orders from, 12:147, (fac.)
    148, 149; 19:201-6; 22:55-56; 33:112,
    118, 120, 123
    bks. on, rev., 7:93; 8:88, 379-80;
    40:355-56
    views of: (1853) 8: opp. 88; (1857)
    13: opp. 195; (1929) 8: opp. 88
Los Angeles (ship, formerly *Ohio,*
1853), 31:41
Los Angeles (ship, 1870), 31:41; 32:338
Los Angeles & San Pedro Railroad,
13:325; 32:327-48
"Los Angeles & San Pedro, The: First
Railroad South of the Tehachapis,"
by Franklin Hoyt, 32:327-48
Los Angeles Cable Co., 10:393
Los Angeles City Guard, 29:234, 237,
239, 246
Los Angeles County, 1:303; health rush,
31:13-31; railroads, 32:327-48; bk. on
Indians, rev., 5:408
"Los Angeles County in the Health
Rush, 1870-1900," by John E. Baur,
31:13-31
Los Angeles County Medical
Association, 33:100
*Los Angeles from Mission to Modern
City,* by Nadeau, rev., 40:355-56
Los Angeles Gas & Electric Corp.,
31:176
Los Angeles in the Sunny Seventies, by
Archd. Ludwig Salvator, trans.
Wilbur, rev., 8:379-80
Los Angeles Library Association, 38:312
Los Angeles military companies:
Greys, 29:237, 240-41; Guards,
29:232, 234, 246; Lanceros, 29:236,
247; Mounted Rifles, 29:229-30,
237-40 *passim;* Rangers, 29:234
Los Angeles Mutual Dairymen, 35:243

Los Angeles River, 1:148; 13:196-99
    passim, 205-6, 209, 347
Los Angeles State and County
    Arboretum, 32:376-78
Los Angeles Terminal Railroad, 32:344
Los Angeles Young People's Socialist
    League, 40:218
Los Gatos, 16:285; 29:43
Los Nietos, 32:328; *see also* Ranchos:
    Los Nietos
Lossing, Benson J., 6:109-11
Lost Bride, The (novel), 10:356
Lost Cannon Creek, 34:223
"Lost Cement Mines," 26:237-38, 245
"Lost Toma de Razon, The," by J. N.
    Bowman, 21:311-20
"Lost Wagons" (pools), 18:210-11
Los Verdugos, 30:52
Lothian, Napier, 15:267; 20:305
Lott, Charles F., 10:189
Lott, Peter F., 16:343
Lotteries and raffles, 14:399; 15:50, 170,
    175, 176, 183, 276, 369; 34:353; 35:343;
    see also Lingots d'Or; Metropolitan
    Homestead Association
Lottheimer (S.F., 1855), 16:283
Lottie Carson (ship), 38:68
Lotty, Mlle. (S.F., 1906), 33:42
Lot Whitcomb (ship), 15:171
Loud, John, 15:29
Loud, Mrs. Oliver Stuart (Catherine
    MacLean), 32:191
Louderback, Davis, Jr., and Frances
    Caroline (Smith), 36:88
Louderback, George Davis, 26:12;
    address, "Geological History of San
    Francisco Bay," 23:380; obit., 36:88-90
Louderback, Mrs. George Davis (Clara
    Augusta Henry), 36:88
Louderback, Sophia, 28:293
Louis, Mr. and Mrs. (Murphys, 1850),
    17:6-12
Louis, the Iroquois, *see* Shanagorati,
    Louis
Louisa (bark, 1831), 8:183; 14:343;
    31:33
Louisa (brig, 1849), 35:184
Louisa Jacoba Johanna (ship), 15:172
Louise (ship), 4:154
Louis XI (play), 35:142
Louisiana (Amer. bark), 15:372; 23:261,
    279
Louisiana (Fr. ship), 22:307
"Louis Sloss, Jr., Collection of

California Paintings," by Jean Martin,
    37:19-38
Loutrel, B., 30:254, 264
Louzade, James, 15:240
Lovdal, George Christopher, 31:149-59;
    phot., 31: opp. 147
Lovdal, Mrs. George Christopher,
    31:150-51; phot., 31: opp. 147
Love, Harry, 11:386; 13:329-30; 16:257,
    260-61; 28:338
Love, John, 33:339-40; 34:22
Love, John S., 10:169, 367, 382
Love, W. G., 30:99
Love (play), 10:275
Love and Revenge (play), 23:108
Love Chase, The (play), 9:163; 10:283
Lovegrove, George H., 30:359, 366
Lovejoy, Asa Lawrence, 18:301
Lovejoy, John K., 9:42; 16:339
Loveland, H., 3:118
Loveland, L. F., 20:115
Lovell, Capt. (L.A., 1851), 13:320; 34:30
Lovell, P. H., 12:323
Lovell, S. W., 11:9
Lovett, Charles J., 26:257
Lovett, Hobart McKinley, 25:191
Lovett, Joseph, 34:359
Lovett, William Edward, 25:191
Lovey, Marion, 23:120
Loviot, Fanny, 22:268, 279
Low, C. Adolph, 19:233; 29:253, 254
Low, Charles L., 29:253
Low, Charles P., 33:325-26; 34:74
Low, Frederick F., 9:55; 10:269; 15:9,
    11-12, 17; 16:305; 17:314; 19:3, 230,
    236; 20:266; 22:232; 29:244, 245;
    30:130, 135, 141; 33:234; 34:52, 56;
    37:195; 40:297, 303
Low, Mrs. Frederick F., 11:127
Low, Garrett W., 20:186
Lowder, Samuel, 2:113, 121
Lowe, Mount, 31:20
Lower Bar, 31:143, 148
Lower California, 1:40; 3:254; 6:161-62;
    15:374; 20:213, 222, 226, 234;
    21:329-30; 22:56, 57, 58, 61, 163;
    27:205, 206, 353, 354; 30:54; 36:235;
    boundary, 5:321-27; discovery and
    naming of, 1:36-56; explorations
    along coast, 3:18-20, 312-13, 337-62;
    5:196-97; 6:298; 7:41-46, 71-73, 305-45,
    380-87; govt. of, 25:271, 272, 276,
    354-56; land expeds. in, 15:105-13,
    132; 26:309-19; 31:109, 111-24, 261-70,

343-54; map, 7: opp. 42; Walker's
expeds. to, 12:318-22; 27:203-6 *passim*
Lower Hotel, Yosemite, 5:337, 338, 339
Lower Lake, 24:51; 32:365-66, 368, 369
Lower Soda Springs, 24:336
Lowery, John (Marysville, 1859, 1862),
10:187, 380
Low *et al. v.* Spring and Healy, 10:356
Lowie, Robert Heinrich, address,
"Relations of California Indians to
Other Western Tribes," 12:84-85
Lowrie (Marysville, 1858), 9:348;
see also Lowery
Lowrie, W. J., 40:45
Lowry (Marysville, 1862), 10:380
Lowry, Anthony W., 33:257
Lowry, Mrs. D. A., 6:74
Lowry, Samuel, 26:211
Lowry, T. J., 21:368
Loy, Horace, 14:278; 26:122
Loy, William Edward, 1:110
Loyer, Fernand, 39:2
Loyola, Martín Ignacio de, 2:143-51
passim, 156-57
Lubbock, Sir John, 31:220
Lubey, William, 20:308
Lucas (on *Westward Ho*, 1853), 28:322
Lucas, A. J., 8:358
Lucas, James H., 23:95
Lucas, John (Tepie, 1840), 15:240
Lucas, John (Mt. Whitney, 1873),
4:33-34
Lucas, Maria, 28:293
Lucas, Rodney M., 2:128, 129, 137
Lucas, Mrs. William Palmer (Virginia
Cumming), 19:286
Lucas, Turner & Co., 7:291; 15:166, 179,
272; 16:83, 284; 24:174, 179
Lucatt, Edward, 20:45
Luce (Tuolumne R., 1850), 35:208
Luce (on *Westward Ho*, 1853), 28:322
Luce, Moses A., 31:154
Lucerne Valley, 27:113, 117-22 *passim*
Lucero (Marysville, 1858), 9:363
Lucket (d. Cruces, 1849), 27:35
Luckett, A. W., 33:346
Lucout, Cabo, 10:328
Lucretia Borgia (play), 10:55, 77;
16:339
Lucrezia Borgia (opera), 10:253, 265;
15:165
Lucy Long (riv. str.), 25:327, 328
Ludlow, Fitz-Hugh, 33:225
Ludlow (ship), 31:294
Ludlum & Clark, San Francisco, 24:262

Ludwig Salvator, Archd., 13:354; *Los
Angeles in the Sunny Seventies*, trans.
Wilbur, rev., 8:379-80
Luego (Lugo?), Antonio, 28:325
Luelling, *see* Lewelling
Lütke, Feodor P., 12:213, 220; 18:336;
30:336
Luff, Frank, 26:215
Lufkin, John O., 2:128
Lugari (ship), 23:192
Lugo, Antonio María, 12:111-19
passim; 13:207, 215, 331, 348; 14:240;
25:287; 33:249-50
Lugo, Felipe, 13:220, 348, 349
Lugo, Francisco Salvador, 13:203;
28:189; 29:309
Lugo, José, 16:366
Lugo, José del Carmen, 10:89; 12:111,
114, 117-19, 122; 13:308, 348
Lugo, José María, 13:348; 25:287; 29:32,
33, 34
Lugo, María Antonia, 16:102; 29:309
Lugo, María de Jesús, 13:215; 28:189
Lugo, Seferino, 14:6
Lugo, Pedro de, 3:20-24
Lugo, Tomasa Ignacia, 27:337
Lugo, Vicente, 12:118-19; 13:310, 313,
327, 348, 349
Luhrs (of Red Bluff), 16:137
Luis, Fr. (Sonoma, 1876), 29:328
Luke, William, 6:348
Lukens, Theodore P., 4:49; 38:250-51,
255
Lull, L. L., 1:77
Lull, Louis R., 1:10; 9:26; 10:62, 70;
13:225, 299; 15:370; 16:79, 83
Lumber and lumbering, 4:407; 5:18, 47,
259, 358; 8:120, 326-27; 10:389; 11:36,
119, 159-60; 12:100, 101, 192; 13:357,
366; 14:320; 16:140, 323-24, 327-32
passim; 17:23, 195-96, 237-38, 254;
18:66; 20:181; 21:383; 22:155; 23:55,
157, 191, 308; 24:357; 25:106, 152;
26:112, 113, 120, 123-26 *passim*, 236,
244-45; 27:65-66, 67, 264-68 *passim*,
274; 28:99, 107, 113, 267; 29:5, 8, 10,
15, 17, 57, 170; 30:1-11, 230; 31:35,
287, 289-305 *passim*; 32:191; 33:326-28;
34:66, 74-80 *passim*; 35:29, 30, 147,
160; 37:73, 233; 38:59-71; *see also*
Sawmills
Lummis, Charles Fletcher, 5:91;
8:375-76; 11:283-84; 13:150; 40:195;
Bronco Pegasus, rev., 8:85-86; ed.

Spanish Songs of Old California, rev., 2:363-64

Luna, Domingo, 8:329-30

Lund, Mrs. Gustav J., 25:191

Lundy, Eli B., 14:222

Lundy (place), 4:39; 26:245

Lung Quong Toy Dramatic Company, 23:112

Luning, Nicholas, 26:262; 27:344

Lush, Hiram, 13:3

Lusinchi, Augustin, 39:227, 243, 247-56 *passim*, 312-16 *passim*, 320

Lusitania Hotel, San Francisco, 35:235

Lusk (Yuba Co., 1857), 9:164

Lusk (A.) & Co., 24:215

"Lust for Riches," by Luis Monguió, 27:237-48

"Lutèce" (pseud.), 39:160

Luther, John B., 13:31

Luther and Price, 16:323-34, 329

Luther's Pass, 7:8, 9

Lux, Charles, 17:254, 255, 257; 23:191; lawsuit, 17:257

Lux, Frederick, 34:53

Lux College, 23:191

Lux *v.* Haggin, 10:262; 24:194

Luzenilla, Francisco de, 26:312

Lyceum Co., 35:142

Lyceum Gazette, San Francisco, 28:134, 142

Lyceum of Free Culture, San Francisco, 2:242

Lyceums, 9:57, 73; 32:129-30, 137, 168-69

Lyceum Theater, San Francisco, 21:43, 45, 46, 51, 167; 23:109; 28:133-34

Lycomia (ship), 33:291

Lyden family, 9:77

Lydia Thompson Burlesque Company, 21:165

Lydik, Ed, 28:239-40

Lye, Mary, 15:39

Lyell, Mount, 4:22, 27, 28, 36, 42, 51, 55

Lyman, Amasa, 14:61, 64, 67, 70-73 *passim*, 178-82 *passim*; 22:12, 13, 14, 23; 26:326-30 *passim*; 30:57

Lyman, Chester Smith, 5:353; 12:93; 13:176; 14:19, 151; 17:254; 23:254; 26:166-67; 28:289; 29:113; 33:374; 39:118, 120; extracts from his Diary, ed. F. J. Teggart, 2:181-202; letters, 13:176-79; *Around the Horn to . . . California*, ed. Teggart, rev., 4:91-92

Lyman, Dean Briggs, 8:362; 9:68, 160, 262, 373, 374; 10:188; 22:287; 28:281; phot., 9: opp. 160

Lyman, Edward Dean, 9:79

Lyman, Elizabeth, *see* Potter, Mrs. David

Lyman, George B., 9:67, 79, 158, 160

Lyman, George Dunlap, 9:79; 12:364; 16:288; 30:82; 35:181; "The First Native-Born California Physician," 4:284-89; "The Scalpel under Three Flags in California," 4:142-206; "Victor J. Fourgeaud, M.D.," 11:138-49; address, "The Sponge, James King of William, His Surgeons and the Vigilantes," 7:95-96; bk. revs. by, 5:89-90; 7:195-96; 8:84; *John Marsh, Pioneer*, rev., 9:400-401; *Saga of the Comstock Lode*, rev., 13:183-84; obits. of Joseph K. Hutchinson, 4:304; George H. B. Wright, 22:93; obit., 28:281-82

Lyman, Jonathan Huntington, 10:35; 12:115

Lyman, Julia, *see* King, Mrs. George H.

Lyman, Richard M., Jr., and Mrs., 33:381

Lyman, Theodore Benedict, 34:233

Lyn, Miss (Yuba Co., 1859), 10:169

Lynch, Bert C., 27:188

Lynch, Ellen, 40:213

Lynch, James, 29:36

Lynch, Jeremiah, 19:67; 27:317

Lynch, John, 16:80, 283

Lynch, Joseph, 18:303, 304, 313; 21:227, 228, 235

Lynch, Joseph Peter, 18:265-66

Lynch, Patrick, 8:344; 9:168, 366

Lynch, Philip, 10:62, 70

Lynching and lynch law, 6:234; 13:219; 15:31, 172, 270-71, 375-76; 18:260-61, 266; 23:324; 27:210, 356, 358, 361; 28:75, 151-53, 159; 29:162, 303; 31:311; 33:53, 56; 34:70; *see also* Hangings; Vigilance Committee

Lynde, Isaac, 34:129-30

Lynde, John D., 13:32

Lyon, Caleb, 22:69, 81; 35:11, 13

Lyon, Ellen F., 28:293

Lyon, Harvey B., 28:382

Lyon, Mary Maria, 12:313

Lyon, Nathaniel, 24:51-54; 27:224; 30:58; 31:36, 46

Lyon, Robert, 26:246

Lyon, W. Parker, 9:289; 10:99; coauth. *Early California . . . Post Office Cancellations*, rev., 8:385
Lyon, Worthington S., 28:382
Lyons (overland, 1850), 24:241
Lyons, Aaron, 29:22, 25
Lyons, H., 9:66
Lyons, Henry Augustus, 11:127; 20:113, 366-67, 371; 28:64; 32:376
Lyons, Joseph, 9:142, 162, 369
Lyons, Michael, 9:168, 169

Lyons, Moses, 35:270
Lyons, Peter, 15:121, 233
Lyons, William H., 9:258
Lyons (E.G.) Co., 31:185
Lyons Station, 17:102, 115
Lyster, Fred, 10:196; 21:249, 256
Lyster, William S., 10:265; 21:51; *see also* Lyster's English Opera Co.
Lyster's English Opera Co., 10:201, 253, 265; 21:47, 51
Lytle, Andrew, 29:242

M

M. M. (1849), newspaper arts. by, 24:45-46, 132-34, 136-37, 353-54
Mabry, Harry Cooper, 28:285
McAdie, Alexander George, 4:36, 53
McAdoo, William Gibbs, 36:69, 75; 39:121-37 *passim*; phot., 39: opp. 128
McAlister, William, 26:299
McAllep, William J., 22:173
McAllis (lawsuit, Marysville, 1861), 10:273
McAllis, John, 10:367
McAllister, A. C., 10:375, 376, 390
McAllister, Benjamin Cutler, 11:126, 127; 34:232-37 *passim*
McAllister, Mrs. Benjamin Cutler (Julia Bedlow Parkman), 11:127-28; 34:235, 237; phot., 11. opp. 124
McAllister, Eva, *see* Pritchett, Mrs. Henry S.
McAllister, Francis Marion, 11:126; 34:233-36 *passim*
McAllister, Hall, 2:241; 9:318; 11:124-28 *passim*; 13:402; 16:305; 19:3-4, 230; 23:246; 22:30; 27:67, 266; 29:162-65 *passim*, 257; 33:374; 35:376; 36:309; letter, 34:231-37; phot., 11: opp. 124
McAllister, Mrs. Hall (Louisa Clemence Hermann), 11:127; 19:230; 34:233; 35:376
McAllister, Harriet Hannah, 11:126; 34:235, 237
McAllister, James, 34:20
McAllister, Julian, 11:126; 33:232; 34:234; phot., 11: opp. 124
McAllister, Matthew Hall, 11:124-27

passim; 15:6, 7, 275, 368, 369, 377; 16:183, 282, 285, 336, 338, 339, 341, 345; 19:261; 23:344; 27:109; 34:232, 233-44
McAllister, Mrs. Matthew Hall (Charlotte Louise Cutler), 11:125; 34:232-37 *passim*; phot., 34: opp. 232
McAllister, Matthew Hall (s. of Cutler), 11:127, 128; 22:177
McAllister, Robert, 15:240
McAllister, Samuel Ward, 11:124, 125, 127; 34:232, 236
McAllister family, 11:124-28; 34:231-37; 35:376
McAllisters & Bergin, 34:236
McAlpin, Blanton, 9:27
Macao, 2:142, 143, 145; 7:248; 25:151, 167
McArthur, Lewis Ankeny, 29:185; address, "Peter Skene Ogden," 22:375; *Oregon Geographic Names*, rev., 7:286-87; obit., 31:178-79
MacArthur, Mildred (Yorba), *Anaheim, "The Mother Colony,"* rev., 39:88
Macarthur, Walter, 35:151-52
McArthur, William Pope, 11:300-302; 25:110, 118, 260-62; 29:185-86; 30:39-40, 43, 46; 31:179
McAtee, Patrick, 4:63
Macauley, John P., 16:283
McBean, Atholl, 23:384
McBean, Mrs. Atholl (Margaret Newhall), 21:384
McBee, John C., 28:337
McBeth, Charles P., 26:4

McBeth, Frances Turner (Mrs. Willis V.), 29:286; 32:190; "Cultural Diggings at Crescent City in the 'Fifties,' " 32:161-70

Macbeth, 9:257; "Burlesque," 20:305

McBride, W. B., 13:85

McBryde, F. W., 30:333-34

MacBurney (of Stevenson's Regt.), 1:222

McCabe, Judge (1855), 15:274

McCabe (Yuba Co., 1856), 9:62

McCabe, Edward D., 10:76

McCabe, John H., 21:158

McCafferty (Yuba Co., 1859), 10:170

McCahill, Barney, 10:49

McCahill, Thomas, 9:26

McCall, Capt. (Mono Co., 1853), 34:216

McCall, John, 20:167-68; 40:295

McCall, R. H., 15:29

McCall, Robert, 9:40

McCalla, T., 27:263

McCallum, John G., 9:46, 103, 107, 112

McCann (S.F., 1854), 15:165

McCann, Ferdinand J., 14:398; 15:24, 29, 53

McCarney, John, 16:79

McCarslin, Andrew, 2:121

McCarthy, J. Harvey, 5:198

McCarthy, Timothy, 6:36; 21:40, 70

McCarty, Jane, 9:267

McCarty, John Templeton, 9:348, 363, 367, 379; 10:57, 170, 172, 173; 14: opp. 209, 390, 391, 392, 406; 15:21-22, 28

McCartysville (Los Gatos), 16:285

McCarver, Morton Matthew, 4:355; 10:152, 155, 156, 157; 16:53; 20:103, 105; 23:370

McCauley, Mr. and Mrs. (Warm Springs, 1861), 10:358

McCauley (Yosemite, 1871), 5:339

McCauley, John F., 9:257, 260, 273, 284

McCeney, Julius C., 11:127

McChesney, J. B., 4:29

McChristian, Mrs. (Mary Ellen Gregson), 19:126, 140

McChristian, Patrick, 13:175; 17:240; 19:131, 135, 142; 24:58, 72; 30:321

McClanahan (Grass Valley, 1850s), 6:337

McClanahan, C. W., 15:43

McClatchy, Mrs. Carlos Kelly (Phebe Rideout Briggs), 23:95

McClatchy, Charles Kenny, 21:240; 23:94, 95

McClatchy, Eleanor, 19:282; 23:94

McClatchy, James, 23:95-96; 24:98, 276; 28:166, 167, 169; 33:209, 210

McClatchy newspapers, 39:129

McClay Negro Testimony Bill, 22:225

McClellan, George Brinton, 9:302; 16:202, 309; 20:258; 22:232, 233, 356-57

McClelland (lawsuit, Yuba Co., 1858), 9:268, 346

McClelland, Samuel, 18:206-7

McClelland (ship), 22:368, 369

McClellen, Michael T., letter of, 24:25-27

McClenachan, Robert, 6:38; 15:170

McClennan, Isaac, 20:38, 44

McClinton, J. G., 9:199-200

McCloskey, Calvin, 10:227, 358

McCloskey, "Country," 20:291

McCloskey, James J., 34:360

McClosky, James, 16:184

McCloud, Alfonso (Alonzo?), 15:166

McCloud River, 22:103; 35:29-35 *passim*

"McCloud River Affair of 1909, The," by James J. Hudson, 35:29-35

McCloud River Lumber Co., 35:29-34

McClure (Iowa Hill and S.F., 1854), 15:271

McClure, David, 37:53, 55-56, 60

McClure, J. H. H., 22:251

McClure, L. A., 2:207

McClure, Margaret M., 2:207-8; letter, 2:208-10

McClure, Nathaniel F., 4:45, 48

McClure, Samuel, 9:147

McClure, Stuart L., 30:93

McClure, William, 2:207

McClure's Bank, Dutch Flat, 18:361

McClurg, James B., 14:321, 344

McCollam, Thomas W., 33:374

McCollum, William, *California as I Saw It*, ed. Morgan, rev., 40:74-76

McComas, Francis, 37:26, 34

McComb, Elenor, 14:175

McCombe, John, 32:169

McCombe (Gilbert) & Co., 16:284

McCombs, *see* Mecombs

McConnel (Marysville, 1858), 9:358

McConnell, James E., 24:267, 270

McConnell, John R., 10:248, 249, 358,

368, 369; 11:173; 15:366; 22:230; 24:276

McConnell, Samuel, 9:72

McConnell, William, 9:244

McCorkle, Joseph W., 9:150, 177, 351, 372, 383; 10:44, 60, 61, 165, 167, 255, 267, 355; 14: opp. 209, 398; 15:270; 19:25; 30:146; 32:146-55 *passim*

McCorkle, Gentry P., 40:222, 230, 231, 235

McCormac, Alice Bay, *see* Maloney, Alice Bay

McCormack (or McCormick), Hugh, 18:205

McCormick, Lt. (Sausalito, 1849), 27:261

McCormick (Yuba Co., 1857), 9:130

McCormick, John, 15:376

McCosma, *see* Cosumnes River

McCoun, W. H., 9:46

McCourtnay (Marysville, 1858), 9:265, 348

McCown, Theodore D., 25:200-203 *passim;* introd. note to Aubrey Neasham, "Raising of the Flag at Monterey . . . 1846," 25:193-94

McCoy, Austin, 3:157-58

McCoy, Clark, 3:153, 156-57

McCoy, James, 36:120, 124

McCoy, W. W., 9:250, 269

McCracken, Isabel, 19:192

McCracken, John, 12:96

McCrady River, 28:228

McCray, E. P., 33:355

McCrea (S.F., 1855), 15:275; *see also* McRae

McCready, Irene, 16:283

McCreary, Charles and Mrs., 19:106

McCreery, Andrew, 25:10

McCreery, Mrs. Andrew B. (Belle Swearingen), 36:44, 45

McCrellish, Alec. 6:19

McCrellish, Frederick, 20:165; 27:271, 274; 28:12

McCubbins, Thomas, 8:346, 347, 352

McCue, Jim, 3:156; stage line, 8:345, 360

McCulloch, Hugh, 6:255-64 *passim;* 8:105, 290

McCulloch, Michael, 15:177

McCulloch, Hartnell and Co., 8:105, 290, 296; 12:230; 18:179; art. on, 6:254-64

McCullough (Sacramento, 1858), 9:257

McCullough, John, 6:341; 21:152, 161-73 *passim,* 241-48 *passim;* 35:142

McCullough, Saditha, 34:373

McCurdy, Mrs. Alice B., 23:298, 299

McCurdy, Samuel, 15:270

McCusker, Peter, 21:307

McCutchen (or McCutcheon), William, 10:348, 350; 19:138

McDaniels (Marysville, 1858), 9:367

McDermit, Charles, 11:9

McDermott, Agnes, 24:94

McDermott, D. A., 7:280

McDermott, John Francis, 20:191; 33:93; "Two Fourgeaud Letters," 20:117-25; "Gold Rush Movies [panoramas]," 33:29-38

McDermott, Patrick, 24:94

McDiarmid, Finley, 32:201-2

McDonald, A., 22:251

McDonald, Alexander C., 24:58

McDonald, Alexander D., 15:28, 53; 24:348

McDonald, Archibald, 9:114

Macdonald, Augustin Sylvester, 3:248; "John Muir: Some Personal Recollections," 17:18-20; "The Sea Otter Returns to the California Coast," 17:243-44

MacDonald (or McDonald), Benjamin, 6:152

McDonald, Calvin B., 9:173

McDonald, Charles E. S., 15:375

McDonald, D. L., 35:83

McDonald, Edith, *see* Chamberlain, Mrs. Selah

McDonald, Estelle, 10:55, 77

McDonald, Finan, 22:100, 213; 24:233

McDonald, George, 24:169

McDonald, J. Wade, 31:154

McDonald, Jack, 7:116

McDonald, James, 15:180, 268; 17:83; 35:83

McDonald, James B., 10:169, 252, 256, 259, 265, 271, 278, 281, 285, 286, 357-63 *passim*

McDonald, Mrs. James B. (Ellen Trego), 10:257, 259, 264-65, 275, 362, 365

McDonald, James M. (Sacramento Co., 1859), 10:62; 11:8, 9

McDonald, James M. (S.F., 1861), 9:312

McDonald, James M. (S.F., 1892), 36:201

McDonald, James R., 27:97, 99, 101

McDonald, Juilliard, 35:83

MacDonald, L. M., 37:271

McDonald, Mark L. and Ralphine (North), 35:83

McDonald, Mark L., Jr., 35:83; obit., 12:88

McDonald, Mrs. Mark L., Jr. (Isabelle Juilliard), 35:83

McDonald, Mary Ann, 28:293

McDonald, R. H., 24:173; 26:262

McDonald, R. J., 15:375

McDonald, William, 27:352; 28:290

McDonald (J. C.) & Co., 9:181

McDonald & Levy, 22:37

McDonald's Mill, 10:256

McDonald v. Abbott, 10:276; v. Hall & Patton, 10:252

McDonough, A. N., 22:159, 172-74

McDonough, James, 8:6, 8

McDonough, John E., 21:42

McDonough, Thomas, 4:34

Macdonough Theater, Oakland, 33:44

M'Dougal, David, 26:359

McDougal, Elijah, 23:358

McDougal (or McDougall), George, 12:26, 32; 19:131, 135, 136, 142; 27:352

McDougal, John, 9:27; 10:50, 73, 77, 197; 12:32; 14:355; 15:28, 280; 16:183; 19:7, 176; 20:333, 366; 22:113; 23:160, 370; 24:202; 28:59, 64, 66, 67, 195, 327, 331; 29:27, 244, 245; 31:148, 235; fac. sig., 10: opp. 159

McDougall, Frederick A., 29:21-22, 26

McDougall, Mrs. Frederick A. (María Antonia Pacheco), 29:26

McDougall, James A., 4:252, 253, 256; 8:370; 9:355; 10:70, 255, 267, 271-79 *passim*, 282, 290, 292; 11:6, 7, 8, 21; 15:6, 167, 182; 16:82; 17:304, 310, 320, 321; 19:259-60; 25:5; 31:235; 32:147, 148, 157; 33:206-7, 215; 34:250; 39:294-95; art. on, 15:199-212; port., 15: opp. 199

Macdougall, W. J., 21:147

McDougall, William, 15:76

McDougall (G.) & Co., 13:381

McDowall, David, 9:99

McDowell, Henry Burden, 33:374

McDowell, Irvin, 11:127; 13:38-39; 15:66; 16:205; 20:158, 165; 26:9, 363; 28:171; 33:237; 37:197; 40:307, 343

McDowell, Mrs. Irvin (Helen Burden), 11:127

McDowell, James, 8:210; 19:137

McDowell, Mrs. James (Margaret Pyles), 8:210; 19:119, 137

McDowell, John A., 33:355

McDowell, Robert, 3:137, 139-47 *passim*, 151

McDowell Hill, 13:26

McDuffee (McDuffe, McDuffy), Andrew Jackson, 18:45; 27:107

McDuffie, Duncan, 4:49-50, 55; 25:381-82; obit., 30:280-81

McDuffie, Mrs. Duncan (Jean Howard), 30:281; obit., 34:182-83

McDuffie, James Y., 30:166, 168; 37:166-68

Mace (Marysville, 1861), 10:281

Macedonian (ship), 26:221

McElderry, Dr. (Modoc Co., 1873), 28:163

McElroy, John, 13:320

McElroy, Robert, 16:182

McElroy, Robert McNutt, 8:251

McElvoy, Katy, 10:283

McElwain, Edward F., 16:339

McEnerney, Garret William, 37:347-48; obit., 21:283

McEvitz, Barney, 9:141, 150, 165; lawsuit, 9:141, 142, 143

McEvoy, J., 15:372, 373

McEwen, Arthur, 15:381

Macey, Obed, *see* Macy, Obed

Macey, Roland H., *see* Macy, Rowland Hussey

McFadden, James, 31:293-94

McFadden, John (Santa Ana), 31:293-94

McFadden, John (Stockton), 39:303

McFarlan, Andrew, 9:328-29

MacFarland, James P., 4:166; 36:328

McFarland, Thomas Bard, 9:113, 116; 10:247, 261, 262, 365

McFarland, Mrs. Thomas Bard, 10:365

McGainey, J., 15:173

McGarrahan, William, land claim of, 19:359, 367

McGarry, Edward, 40:349

McGeary, Jo, 8:342

McGee, Bart, 17:218

McGee, James, 17:44

McGee, John B., 9:46

McGee, Joseph W., 10:166, 179, 184-85, 200, 385

McGee, Thomas L., 31:154

McGehee, William J., 14:175-76

McGeorge, Thomas, 9:26, 27

McGettigan, Mrs. Charles D.

(Francisca Vallejo), 4:289; 5:416; 29:330; address, "Mariano Guadalupe Vallejo," 9:90; obit. of Mrs. John O. Gantner, 25:375

McGill, James, 33:257

McGillivray, Montrose, 28:107

McGillo, Don, *see* Pedrorena, Miguel de

McGillycuddy, Valentine T., 4:124

McGilvary, Evander Bradley, 37:39

McGilveray (Sutter's Fort, 1847), 22:221

McGimsey, J. A., 33:364

McGimsey, "Port," 33:364

McGinniss, Miss (Sacramento, 1861), 10:283

McGinnis, Felix S., 20:192; obit., 24:186-87

McGlashan, Charles Fayette, 23:191; 24:75

McGlashan (John) & Co., 30:256, 365

McGloin, John Bernard, 29:189; 31:279-80; "The Jesuit Arrival in San Francisco in 1849," 29:139-47; ed. "A California Gold Rush Padre . . . the 'Padre of Paradise Flat,'" 40:49-67; addresses: "Archbishop Joseph Sadoc Alemany," 29:376-77; "From Market Street . . . to Ignatian Heights," 35:75; obit. of Peter M. Dunne, 36:87-88

McGlone, William, 15:240; 29:338

McGlynn, Daniel C., 33:72

McGlynn, John A., 28:59, 66; 40:205-13 *passim*; letter to, 40: foll. 206

McGlynn, M., 28:49

McGovern, Walter, address, "Edward D. Baker," 13:188

McGowan, Mrs. (Marysville, 1858), 9:348; 10:178

MacGowan, Alexander B., 27:223

McGowan, Edward ("Ned"), 4:157, 191, 192, 201; 7:95; 8:366-67; 9:250, 276; 15:155; 17:178, 179; 18:259, 276; 30:358; 37:141-42; art. on, 6:3-36; port., 6:8

McGowan, James, 19:62, 67-68, 69, 73; 28:47

McGowan, Capt. John (of *Polk*, early 1850s), 6:5, 16

McGowan, John (S.F., 1854), 15:164

McGowan, John E., 6:36

McGowan, Lee, 10:357

"McGowan's War," 6:20-29

McGown, Andrew J., 21:307; 22:71

McGrath, Hugh and Jane (Gibson), 22:379

McGrath, Margaret, 28:293

McGrath, Thomas H., 22:147

McGraw, E. W., 27:346-47

McGraw, Nellie, 38:224

MacGregor, John A., 25:232

McGrew (Sacramento, 1855), 9:38

McGroarty, John Steven, 31:18

McGuire (Marysville, 1858), 9:368, 369, 373; 10:59

McGuire, James, 2:121

McGuire, Thomas L., 20:38, 42, 44

McGuire and Place *v.* Pacific Mail Co., 34:232

Machado, Agustín, 13:207, 349

Machado, Antonio, 23:359, 360; ranch of, 23:359-60; *see also* Ranchos: Ballona

Machado, F., 13:327

Machado (Clark), Joseph, 35:238

Machado, Manuel, 13:207

Machado, Rafael, 26:29-32 *passim*, 41, 54

McHale *et al. v.* Whitcomb *et al.*, 9:64

McHardy, Alex, 9:161, 162

McHardy, George W., 8:346; 9:64, 65, 77, 133, 134, 138-53 *passim*, 160, 164, 165, 347, 365; 10:56; lawsuits, 8:352; 9:64, 65, 132, 141, 144, 365, 366

McHardy, Mrs. George W., 8:347; 9:64, 77, 153, 165

McHardy, P., 8:347

McHenry, John, 28:34; 39:303

Machin, Tim N., 30:135

McIlhany, Edward Washington, 29:298, 300, 306

McIlrath (Philippines, 1898), 30:290

M'Ilvaine, William, drawing by, 26: foll. 126

McIntire, Edward Buckman, 31:93-94

McIntire, John A., 4:227

MacIntosh, Edward Manuel, 12:197, 269; 17:63, 145

McIntosh, Charles, 18:158, 173; 29:339

McIntosh, Charles K., obit. of Frank B. Anderson, 14:413-14

McIntosh, R., 17:176

McIntyre, Misses (Warm Springs and S.F., 1861), 10:358, 379

McIntyre, Mary Campbell, 31:292

McIntyre, William, 18:199, 200

McIntyre, William L. and Mrs., 13:13

McIsaac, Capt. (Colorado R., 1870), 22:173

McK. (S.F., 1849), letters from, 24:29, 343, 356-57

Mack, Effie Mona, address, "One Hundred Years of Nevada History," 30:376-77

Mack, John W., 21:163, 169

Mack, W. B., 15:76

Mackintosh (Brit. consul, Mex., 1845), 18:145

McKain, Walter C., Jr., 25:379-80; coauth. "Santa Barbara County between Two Social Orders," 25:311-18

Mackall, William W., 27:216

McKay, Maj. (San Quentin, 1858), 9:253

Mackay, Ann, 28:293

McKay, Baptiste, 23:144

McKay, Jean Baptiste Desportes, 8:113; 12:269; 17:68; 19:308; 28:97

Mackay, John W., 2:206; 15:381; 16:88; 25:46; 38:381

Mackay, Mrs. John W. (Marie Louise Antoinette Bryant née Hungerford), 27:95

McKay, Joseph W., 5:80

McKay, Michael, 16:342

McKay, Thomas (1825, 1830s), 3:76, 79, 81; 24:230, 233

McKay, Thomas (Marysville, 1849), 14:206, 211

McKay, William, 24:230-31

McKean, William Wister, 2:251; 20:197, 198, 204, 214, 220, 232, 234

McKee, Col. (S.F., 1861), 27:153

McKee, Albert B. and Alice Maud (Hooper), 31:302

McKee, David, 29:102

McKee, Ernest, 4:50

McKee, Irving, 30:191; "Kipling's San Francisco Debut," 30:151-55

McKee, J. O., 38:33

McKee, John, 16:182; 29:102, 105, 106, 108, 122

McKee, John D., 25:229, 230, 232, 246, 254

McKee, R. (Robert?), 17:177

McKee, Redick, 3:26; 27:224; 28:328, 333; 36:314

McKee, Mrs. S. B., 36:45

McKee, William H., 3:182; 26:320; 28:266

McKeebe & Co. (lawsuit, 1859), 10:174

McKeeby, Lemuel Clarke, "Memoirs of," 3:45-72, 126-70

McKeeby, Mrs. Lemuel Clarke (Caroline Augusta Sampson), 3:156, 160-61

McKeeby's Diggings, 3:45, 147, 148, 151

McKehn, W. J., 40:223

McKell, David McC., 26:189

McKelvy, W., 9:66, 148

McKenna (on *London*, 1850), 7:397

McKennon (on *Westward Ho*, 1852), 26:227; 28:322

McKenzie (San Diego, 1916), 35:363

McKenzie, Donald, 5:57

McKenzie, F. S., 9:42, 45

McKenzie, John, 16:340

McKenzie, John Washington, 9:26, 29; 15:178, 180, 182; 16:79(?)

McKenzie, Robert (hanged, 1851), 22:113, 114; 25:331, 340; 28:43

Mackenzie, Rev. Robert (1882), 19:110-11

Mackenzie, Robert C., 27:95

McKenzie, Webster A., 26:189

McKeon, Peter, 8:340, 356; 9:141, 147, 151, 157, 266; 10:180

McKeon, Thomas, 21:63

McKewen (Santa Barbara, 1859), 18:260

McKibben, David, 13:84

McKibben, James, 12:319

McKibben, Joseph C., 9:104, 106, 272, 365, 381, 388, 391; 10:60, 75, 77, 165, 166, 167, 190-97 *passim*, 278, 292, 296, 355, 356; 13:84; 16:345(?)); 32:155, 156, 159; 38:214

McKibben, S. C., 16:345

McKibben, William, 9:108; 10:293; 15:281, 374

Mackie, Peter, 25:112

Mackie, W. W., 30:324

McKiernan, Charles ("Mountain Charley"), 29:42, 44, 57-58

McKillicon's mine, 28:234

McKim (riv. str.), 16:73; 17:181; 20:30; 25:338, 339; 27:128

McKinlay, James, 8:106; 13:230, 238; 14:324, 326, 344; 20:149, 152; 29:20, 26; 36:11

McKinlay, Mrs. James (Carmen Amesti), 29:26

McKinley (clawed by bear, Napa Co.), 16:133

McKinley, Celeste, *see* Celeste, Mme.
McKinley, J., 4:310
McKinley, Pres. William and Ida (Saxton), 31:302
McKinney (Marysville, 1859), 10:176, 178, 246
McKinney, D. W., 4:250
McKinney, James, 32:2
McKinney's Humbug, 22:75, 76, 82
McKinster, William H., 13:3
McKinstry, Elisha W., 19:134
McKinstry, George, Jr., 1:96, 97; 4:163, 168-69, 177; 7:106; 10:352; 12:300-301; 14:144, 145; 16:138; 19:119, 134, 138, 140; 25:220; 26:110, 123
McKinstry, Justus, 1:9; fac. sig., 12: opp. 318
McKinstry, Laura Livingston, obit., 13:414-15
Mackintosh, Charles, 18:158, 173
Mackintosh, James, 14:316
Mackintosh, Stephen Davis, 12:138; 14:316; 35:200
McKinty, M., 11:56; lawsuit, 9:53
McKissack, William M. D., 33:107
McKissick (or McKizack; Ore., 1846), 5:395, 398
McKittrick, Myrtle (Mason), 29:380; "Salvador Vallejo," 29:309-31
McKnight, Robert, 1:112, 117, 143; 21:202, 222
McKorkell, William, 4:208; 22:38; 28:38
McKorkle (harpist, 1855), 17:82
McKosky, Mary, 31:210
McKune, John H., 16:80; 33:374
Macky, Constance L., 38:2
Macky, E. Spencer, 38:2
McLain, George P., 20:138
McLane (S.F., 1849), 27:361
McLane, Allan, 11:11
McLane, D., company of, 6:361-63
McLane, Frederick, 33:234
McLane, James, 15:275
McLane, Louis: Sec. of State (1833), 37:3-5; min. to Great Britain (1845), 19:55
McLane, Louis [Jr.] Calif., (1846), 11:11; 13:135, 136, 153, 154; 15:373; 16:40; 17:77, 79-80, 169, 179; 18:73, 78, 81; 19:232; 22:41, 46, 64; 29:335, 339-40; 30:52, 53; 37:217
McLane, Lucy Neely, *A Piney Paradise*, rev., 38:173-74

McLane, Robert Milligan, 19:165
McLane, Sadie, 37:217
McLaren, John (Marysville, 1859), *v.* H. T. Hutchinson, 10:178, 183, 186
McLaren, John (S.F., 1870s), 3:42; 8:187; 37:218
McLaughlin, Mrs. Alfred (Emma Moffat), 19:384; obit. of Monroe E. Deutsch, 34:377
McLaughlin (or McLoughlin), C. F., 22:323; 23:142, 143
McLaughlin, Charles, 5:179-80, 181; 16:284; 26:266
McLaughlin, David, 25:287
McLaughlin, John A., 16:340, 342
McLaughlin, Patrick, 12:330
McLaughlin, William, 2:121
McLaughlin brothers (1890s), 27:30
McLaughlin *v.* Brady, 9:373
Maclay, Charles, 11:51; 31:3; 40:333
Maclay, William J., 31:3-4
McLean (Stockton, 1850s), 30:258
McLean (S.F. supervisor, 1855), 16:182
McLean, Charles, 38:60, 61
McLean, E. E., 33:101, 115
McLean, Edward, 26:254-58 *passim*
McLean, Frances, 28:294
McLean, Hector H., 14:60, 175
McLean, Mrs. Hector H. (Elenor McComb), 14:175
MacLean, John Douglas and Winnie Sarah (Morris), 32:191
McLean, John T., 27: opp. 97
McLean, Nathaniel H., 3:26
McLean, W. F., 23:72
McLean & Fowler, 26:254-59, 262
McLean, Jeffry & Co., 22:81
McLean's Ferry, 22:70, 73, 81
McLean's Spring, 18:200, 208, 210, 213
McLellan (S.F., 1862), 10:379
McLellan, Charles H., 26:71, 72, 74, 175
McLellan, Mrs. Charles H. (Louise Kendrick), 26:71, 72
McLellan, George B., 20:258
McLellan (Jim) Gold & Silver Mining Co., 33:375
McLelland, Miss (Marysville, 1860), 10:251
M'Lenan, J. (V.?), drawing by, 32:290
McLeneghan, Samuel, 9:308-10, 312
McLennan, Donald, 10:291
McLeod (in mines, 1849), 13:12, 14, 15
McLeod, Mrs. (Sacramento, 1856), 6:74
McLeod, C. C., 15:28, 32
McLeod, Alexander Roderick, 1:118;

19:313; 22:98, 213, 344, 348; 23:35, 40, 125, 137; 28:119-20, 124

McLeod, John, 25:264; letter to, 19:309-10

MacLeod, Julia (Hamilton), 36:379; "John G. Downey as One of the 'Kings,' " 36:327-31

McLoud (Death Valley, 1861), 18:206

McLoughlin, Eloisa, *see* Rae, Mrs. William G.

McLoughlin, Mrs. Frank, 36:45

McLoughlin, John, 1:118; 2:223; 3:76-77, 81; 5:44, 71, 76, 82, 304; 8:97, 107; 16:88; 17:63, 138, 142, 294; 18:327; 21:2, 82, 372; 22:103, 107, 213, 343; 23:142-43; 24:230; 25:140, 142; 28:98, 99, 105-12 *passim*, 117, 120, 243-58 *passim*; 29:149; 30:321; 34:266, cor., 98-104 *passim*

McLoughlin, H. M., 29:234

Maclure, Mount, 4:22, 28, 42

McMahan, Calvin Clarke, 23:300

McMahan, James Byrd, 23:293, 299

McMahan, James Edwin, 23:300

McMahan, Nelson, 23:290, 292, 298, 299

McMahan, Samuel Green, 5:115-16, 125; 17:161; art. on, 23:289-300

McMahan, Mrs. Samuel Green (Lavenia Ellen Clarke Yount), 23:295-96

McMahan family, 23:289, 300

McMahan-Clyman party, 23:293

McMahon (S.F., 1854), 15:163

McMahon, Bert, 40:218

McMahon, Catherine, 33:352, 353

McMahon, James, 33:352

McMahon, Jeremiah, 29:21, 22, 26

McMahon, Mrs. Thomas Morgan (Isabella Breen), 33:353, 356

McManus, James, 29:240

McMasters, J. C., 12:31

McMeans, Selden A., 9:38-39, 99, 102; 11:173; 16:183

McMenomy, J. H., 5:85-86

McMenomy, James, 9:347

McMenomy, Roger, 9:150

McMenomy's ranch, 10:170

McMickle, Grove C., 15:175

MacMillan, H. R., 25:191

McMillan, Robert, 4:195

McMillen, W. W., 28:334

McMinn, James B., 9:109; 15:280, 281, 370

MacMonnies, Frederick and Alice (Jones), 2:68

MacMullen, Jerry, 22:354; "Windjammer Days in San Diego," 22:349-54; bk. rev. by, 38:377-78

McMullin (S.F., 1867), 11:127

McMullin, Anna, 3:399; 27:382

McMullin, Elizabeth, 27:382

McMullin, John, 3:399; 27:382

McMullin, Mrs. John (Elizabeth Fleming Morgan), 3:399; 27:382

McMurray, G., 9:60, 177(?)

McMurtre, L. C., 21:235

McMurtrie, Douglas Crawford, 7:286; "An Introduction and Supplement to 'A History of California Newspapers,' " 7:277-81; *Pacific Typographical Society*, rev., 7:408

McMurtrie, William Birch, 24:373

McMurty (S.F., 1860), 38:339

McNab, Gavin, 5:95; 19:61, 71, 72; 27:316

McNab and Smith, 35:62

McNabb, Capt. (filibuster, 1855), 17:172

McNabb, James Henry, 30:130

McNair, John E., 24:58

McNair, John G., 15:271

McNair, William, 22:30

MacNamara, Eugene, 6:271-72; 10:117, 118; 12:50; 13:59; 18:144; 19:46

McNamara, Nicholas and Margaret (Driscol), 35:332

McNamara, Theresa, 35:332

McNamara, James B .and John J., 40:215-16

McNaub, John, 37:354

McNaull, William, 18:304, 313

McNay, Frank 31:31

McNear, Seward B., 27:200

McNear (G. W.) & Co., 27:199-200

McNee, Duncan, 35:157

McNeil, Samuel, 21:303

McNeill, J. A., 9:46

McNeilly, John, 21:349, 352; 22:43, 49; 33:111

McNess (Marysville, 1858), 9:361; 10:281

McNevin, Catharine, 16:83

McNevin, Edmund, 27:343

McNichol, Donald, 33:12

McNulty, Bertrand and Mrs., 11:127

McNulty, C. A., 9:27

McNulty, Marion, 34:246

McNulty, P., 9:68

McNulty's Hall, Sacramento, 20:277

McNutt (Marysville, 1858), 9:268, 355

McNutt, Mrs. Maxwell (Florence McDonald), 35:83
Macomb, Montgomery M., 4:36
Macomber, Charles, 25:226-27
Macondray, Frederick W., 15:185, 266; 19:230; 34:211
Macondray, William A., 15:266
Macondray (F. W.) & Co., 8:176, 369; 14:371; 25:258, 265-66; 29:253; 30:299
McPherson, A. W., 11:26
McPherson, Alex., 27:226; 30:166
McPherson, James B., 19:237
McPherson, Murdoch M., 15:285, 380
McPike, Henry H., 39:126, 127, 135
McPlum, William, 9:319
McQuaid (Yuba Co., 1855-61), 8:346, 350; 9:64, 65, 68, 131, 132, 136-55 *passim*, 166, 167, 168, 353, 359, 373; 10:49, 168, 171, 181, 252, 281, 359, 365
McQuaid, Isaac Clark, *see* McQuaid (Yuba Co.); McQuaid, J. C.
McQuaid, J. C., 9:60; 10:181, 200; *see also* McQuaid (Yuba Co.)
McQuaid, John A., 8:360-61; 10:55, 63, 254, 294, 359, 367, 368, 369; *see also* McQuaid (Yuba Co.)
McQueen, Molly, 10:168
McQuinn, J., 10:365
McRae, Arch., 2:249
McRae, Bert, 31:155
McRae, Collins, 33:8, 12, 149, 151
McRae, James A., 31:154-57 *passim*
MacRee, Samuel, 33:262-63
McReynolds, Frank, 34:169
McRuer, Donald C., 26:264, 265, 355; 27:172, 346; 29:253, 254; 31:292
MacSheey, Lt. Col. (1850), 22:299
McTarnahan, Edith, 35:205
Mactavish (or McTavish), Dugald (or Dougald), 5:304, 305; 17:138; 28:253, 258
McVea, James, 13:32
McVeigh (S.F., 1854), 15:181
McVeigh, Lois H., "Meetings of the Society," 16:89, 187-88, 286, 380-81; 17:89-90, 186; 18:85
MacVicar, Barbara (McClung), 40:327; "Southern and Northern Methodism in Civil War California," 40:327-42
McVickers, Henry, 16:326-27, 332
McWhorter, M., 19:65
McWilliams, Carey, 31:25
McWilliams, John, 30:112

McWilliams, Robert L., 26:382-83; obit., 34:378
MacWillie, M. H., 34:129
Macy, Capt. (of *Galindo*, 1849), 22:238, 239
Macy (purser on *Golden Gate*, 1854), 32:359
Macy (or Macey), Charles B., 13:31; 29:7
Macy, Obed, 13:315, 319, 335
Macy, Rowland Hussey, 13:31; 14: opp. 209; 22:281
Madame X (play), 20:141
Madary, M. R., 4:49
Madden, Henry Miller, 28:188; ed. "California for Hungarian Readers: Letters of János Xánthus," 28:125-42
Maddern, Minnie, 14:411
Maddox (or Madox), Richard, 11:309, 310, 311; 36:25
Maddox, William A. T., 12:59, 170, 171, 331, 332, 333; 18:35; 22:55, 66
Maddux, David, 9:110
Maddux, Parker Simmons, 25:95; obit., 32:374-75
Maddux, Mrs. Parker Simmons (1, Edith Marion Walker; 2, Grace Helen Butler), 32:375
Madigan, Mrs. (L.A., 1869), 32:331
Madigan, Thomas F., obit., 16:191
Madison, Frank Delino, 25:95
Madison, James (Marysville, 1859), 10:183
Madison, James (S.F., 1925), "Some Shadows of the San Francisco Stage," 4:59-63; addresses: "Early San Francisco Theatres and Theatrical Folks," 4:301-2; "Early Theaters of San Francisco," 14:411; bks. rev. by, 5:203; 6:98-99
Madison, Marshall P., 25:94-95
Mad River, 9:221; 20:352-53
Madsen, Martin C., obit., 27:183-84
Maeder, Fred, 4:61
Mafra, Ginés de, 6:309, 311
Magagnotto, Peter, 9:395; 40:62
Magdalena Bay, 3:343, 388; 7:311, 315; 8:63, 64; maps, 7: 316, 317
Magee, David, bk. rev. by, 38:83-84
Magee, Mrs. Richard, 25:286
Magee, S. R., 16:302
Magee, Thomas, 23:122
Magee, Thomas L. and family, 16:293, 297, 302; 17:35
Magee, William, 22:368, 369

Magee, William A., 23:122; obit. of
  Frederick P. Howard, 21:380
Magellan, Fernando, 6:293, 294; 7:132,
  133-34, 179-80, 187
Magenta flume, 11:242; 29:194-96;
  phot., 29: opp. 200
Maginnis, J. D., 31:134
Magne, L., 22:304
Magnet (ship), 14:298
Magnolia (whaler, 1846), 3:118, 119
Magnolia (ship, 1850), 12:92-97 *passim*,
  103, 109; 29:170
Magnolia (hotel), Sacramento, 32:148,
  152-53, 154
Magnolia Saloon, Marysville, 14:392
Magoffin, James W., 34:126
Magoffin, Susan Shelby, 25:305-6
Magruder, John Bankhead, 11:367;
  13:320-21, 323-24; 31:36, 46
Magruder, Lloyd, 8:360; 9:266, 287,
  365, 381; 10:253
Magruder, Theophilis Richard,
  35:326-29, 331
Maguey, as food, 34:199
Maguire, Mrs. (S.F., 1850s), 19:236-37
Maguire, Capt. (of *Plover*, 1854),
  15:181
Maguire, Judge (Santa Barbara, 1854),
  18:264
Maguire, Misses (S.F., 1862), 10:379
Maguire, James, 20:292
Maguire, James G., 5:95, 287; 27:316;
  28:51, 53; 38:355, 357
Maguire, James Thomas, 21:239-40,
  263-67 *passim*
Maguire, John, 20:308; 21:47
Maguire, Joseph, 4:209
Maguire, Laura, 37:375-76
Maguire, Mary Jane, 10:292, 389
Maguire, Thomas, 3:35-36; 6:15; 10:74,
  200; 15:189, 368; 16:183; 19:229;
  20:2; 23:108; 28:37; art. on,
  20:289-314; 21:39-74, 141-82, 239-75;
  cartoon, 21: opp. 239; phot.,
  21: opp. 39
Maguire, Mrs. Thomas (Emma
  Theresa Douglass), 20:290, 292;
  21:42, 46, 50, 52, 62, 165-66
Maguire, Mrs. Thomas (Mary
  Clemons), 21:239, 266, 269
Maguire, "Tom, Jr.," *see*
  Maguire, James Thomas
Maguire's Academy of Music, San
  Francisco, 21:62-69 *passim*, 148-59
  passim, 178; phot., 21: opp. 141

Maguire's New Theater, San Francisco,
  21:171-76 *passim*, 241, 242, 243, 272;
  see also Alhambra Theatre
Maguire's Opera House, San Francisco,
  3:36; 7:283; 10:376, 389, 393; 20:2,
  308-9; 21:41-67 *passim*, 145-63 *passim*,
  167-72 *passim*, 241, 243, 264; 23:108,
  341; 28:133; 33:43; 36:209; 38:322;
  phot., 21: opp. 141
  28:133; 33:43; 36:209; 38:322; phot.,
  21: opp. 141
Maguire's Opera House, Virginia City,
  21:56-60, 141-42, 176
Mahan, Dennis Hart, 28:359; letter,
  28:356-57
Mahan, Stephen, 23:226
Mahen, Dennis, 18:356, 357
Maher (Feather R., 1860), 10:253
Maher, Patrick, 26:204
Maher, Zacheus J., 29:139, 145
Maher *v.* C. and J. Riley, 10:273, 280,
  288
Mahon, B. F., 21:312, 314
Mahoney, David, 10:357, 358; 32:147,
  152, 153
Mahoney, Denis, 21:307
Mahoney, John J., 31:185
Mahood (or Mayhood), James, 33:2, 6
Maier, Henry Carl, obit., 39:355
Maier, Herbert, 25:200-201
Mail, Stockton, 34:351, 352, 354
Mailhebuau, Camille, 39:226
Mailland, William, 25:307
Mailliard, Adolphe, 11:125
Mailliard, John Ward, 33:374; 34:179
Mailliard, Mrs. John Ward (Lizzie
  Page), 34:179
Mailliard, John Ward, Jr., obit.,
  34:179-80
Mailliard, Joseph, 34:179
Mailliard, William S., 34:179
Mails, *see* Pacific Mail Steamship Co.;
  Postal service
Main, Charles, 26:264
Main & Winchester, 16:310; 29:253;
  33:68
Maine Mining Co., 15:30
Marin Street House, Oregon City,
  2:130
Mainwaring, Constance, 38:163
Maison, N. E., 29:224-25
Maisons en Californie (company),
  22:314
Maitorena, José Joaquín, 13:209(?);
  27:333

Maitoreno (Monterey, 1822), 13:209
Maître des Forges, Le (play), 20:131
Majestic Theater, San Francisco, 33:41
Majidi, El (ship), 27:180; *see also*
    Shenandoah
M. A. Jones (ship), 15:169
Major, Daniel G., 19:369-70, 371
"Major James D. Savage and the
    Tulareños," by Annie R. Mitchell,
    28:323-41
Majors, Ergo A., address, "Pony
    Express History," 32:174
Majors, Greene, address, "The Pony
    Express," 3:97
Majors, Huling 21:62-63
Majors, Joseph L., 11:75; 15:224-28
    passim, 233; 18:295, 310
Majors, Mrs. Joseph L. (María de los
    Angeles Castro), 15:137, 227, 233
Majors, Juan José Crisótomo, *see*
    Majors, Joseph L.
Majors, O. Cort, 25:380
Major Tompkins (ship), 15:274
"Making of Cosmopolitan California,
    The," by Doris M. Wright,
    19:323-43; 20:65-79
Makins, Mrs., restaurant of, Berkeley,
    35:254
Makins, James N., 11:9; 29:292
Malaby, Zachary T., 39:126
Malaga Colony, 25:172
Malakoff tunnel, 29:201, 207
Malarín, Juan, 15:342; 26:286; 35:105,
    107
Malarín, Mariano, 10:62, 70; 11:9, 21
Malaspina, Alejandro, 7:313; 10:313-14,
    321; 15:213, 214, 380; 16:87; 18:336,
    345; 40:118; art. on, 3:215-37; bk. on,
    rev., 40:71-73, sketches by artist on
    exp., 15: opp. 213, foll. 214;
    39: foll. 180
Malaspina in California, by Cutter, rev.,
    40:71-73
"Malaspina's Voyage around the
    World," by Edith C. Galbraith,
    3:215-37
Maldonado, Gabriel, 7:261
Maldonado, José, 10:317
Maldonado, José María, 16:355
Maldonado, Lorenzo Ferrer, 11:310;
    36:217, 238
Maldonado, Rodrigo, 3:311
Malek Adhel (ship), 3:121; 14:329,
    331, 342, 345; 22:49, 64, 65
Maleton, Edward, 20:288

Malheur Lake, 22:202, 214
Malibu, The, by Robinson and Powell,
    rev., 38:171-73
Mallard, Joseph S., 13:314
Mallett, Alfred, 33:374
Mallett, J. H., 6:9
Mallett, John Holland, 25:380
Mallett's (hotel or boarding house),
    San Francisco, 8:269, 270
Mallon, J. H., 11:49
Mallory, Henry C., 21:307; 22:70
Mallory, Stephen R., 19:170, 345
Malo, José Ramón, 27:109
Malone, Frank, 9:354; 10:49, 272
Maloney, Alice Bay (McCormac),
    18:384; 21:140; 22:191; 24:285-86;
    "A Botanist on the Road to Yerba
    Buena," 24:321-25; "The
    Distressingly Virtuous Isaac [Cox],"
    21:127-40; "John Gantt, 'Borderer,' "
    16:48-60; "John Work of the
    Hudson's Bay Company," 22:97-109;
    "Peter Skene Ogden's Trapping
    Expedition to the Gulf of California,
    1829-30," 19:308-16; "The Richard
    Campbell Party of 1827," 18:347-54;
    "Shasta Was Shatasla in 1814,"
    24:229-34; ed. "Fur Brigade to the
    Bonaventura," 22:193-222, 323-48;
    23:19-40, 123-46; ed. "Some Oatman
    Documents," 21:107-12; "Three
    Letters of John Gantt," 20:147-53;
    obit., 30:86-87
Maloney, J. R., 15:85, 86
Maloney, Michael C., 18:384; 30:86
Maloney, Mrs. Michael C., *see*
    Maloney, Alice Bay (McCormac)
Malony, Capt. (of *Libertad*, 1854),
    15:169
Maloon, Henry, 30:225, 228, 229, 230
Malsbary, Mrs. Inez, 30:285
Malter, George, 25:172
Mameluke Hill, 8:201, 210
Mammoth City, 4:39; 26:245
Mammoth Grove, 9:332-34
Mammoth Grove Hotel, 9:333; illus.,
    9: opp. 299
Mammoth Pass, mining nr., 4:39
Man, Charles, 32:193
Manayunk (place), 15:176
Manchester, J. B., 9:318-19; 34:257
Manchester, Peter B., 16:80, 83
Manchuria, 30:193-206 *passim*
Mancillas, Pedro, 37:199
Mancisidor, Juan Ignacio, 6:263; 23:217

Mandeville, Alicia, 10:51, 75, 371

Mandeville, James W., 9:46, 72, 116, 273; 10:170, 193; 11:4; bk. on, rev., 4:291-92

Mandeville, Jenny, 10:389

Mandeville Island, 17:47

Man from Denver, A (play), 34:364

Manganese, 31:127

Mangum, Willie Person, 19:20

Manhattan Gold Dredging Co., 26:282

Manhead (Indian, 1830s), 25:140

Manila (ship), 31:295

Manila, P.I., 30:296-304

Manila galleons, 1:157, 158; 2:140-60; 3:3, 4-5, 10-12, 313; 7:239-43, 302, 356, 359, 366; 8:34, 44-50; 9:208; 15:382; 23:219-24 *passim;* 25:167; 27:289; 31:109; 36:226, 227, 239

"Manilas" (gang), 29:27

Manje, Juan M., 36:233

Manjer, Daniel, 30:24, 26

Mankins, J. B., 21:227

Manley (w. Vancouver, 1793), 2:319

Manly, William Lewis, 13:314; 18:196, 198, 201-4, 214-15; *Death Valley in '49,* ed. Quaife, rev., 7:89-90

Mann, Hattie Maie, 31:276

Mann, Henrietta Flora, 31:276

Mann, Henry N. and Louise (Scheffer), 29:382

Mann, Houston, 1:283; 4:13; 5:337

Mann, Ira, Jr., 31:271, 275, 276

Mann, Mrs. Ira, Jr. (Mary Bacon), 31:271

Mann, Julia Inez, 31:276

Mann, Milton, 1:283; 4:13, 15; 5:337

Mann, Stephen Hodge, 31:271-77; phot., 31: opp. 272

Mann, Mrs. Stephen Hodge (Hattie Hodge Gordon), 31:275-76, 277

Mannasse, Moses, 26:42, 60

Mann Brothers trail (Yosemite), 1:283; 4:13; 5:337

Manning, Agnes M., 25:192

Manning James and John, 5:49

Man of Destiny, The (play), 21:63

Manrique, Miguel, 9:205, 209-10

Manrow, J. Poole, 6:9; 15:164

Mansfield (Marysville, 1862), 10:386

Mansfield, Charles T., 14:175

Mansfield, George C., *The Feather River in '49 and the Fifties,* rev., 3:202-3

Mansfield, Joseph, 15:270, 274

Mansfield, Joseph King Fenno, 28:216, 229-30

Mansfield, Mrs. Walter D., 1:108

Mansion House, San Jose, 11:159; 14:156; 22:246

Mansions on Rails, by Beebe, rev., 38:382-83

Manso, Lucas F., 14:235

Manson, Donald Jan, 28:123

Manson, John S., 29:253, 254, 402

Manson, Marsden, 38:250, 252-53

Mantz, William H., 8:361; 9:173

Manuel (New Mexican, 1846), 18:174

Manuel (Indian, 1880s), 38:259-60

Manuel (ship), 22:169

Manuela (ship), 22:169, 170

Man with the Iron Mask, The (play), 9:263, 285

Manypenny, G. W., 27:216; 30:161

Manzanillo, Mex., 3:316; 36:301-2

Manzanita, 5:263, 265; 12:293; 15:185; 20:39-40; 32:183

Manzanita Hill, 28:240

Mapes, D. S., 22:251

Mapleson, J. Henry, 21:156

Maple Springs House, 8:213; *see also* White Maple Springs

Maple Springs Mill, 9:72

"Map of Cabrillo's Discoveries, A," by Henry R. Wagner, 11:44-46

Maps: Agnese's (1540-64), 3:265, 312, 325, 374-79; Alarcón's exped., 1:45; Anson's, 31:119; Antonio de la Ascención's, 8:33-37 *passim;* in Arch. des Indies, 3:368; 8:33-37 *passim;* Arrowsmith's (1790), 19:221; Ayala exped. (1775), 25:320; MS in Ayer coll., 3:265; 7:68

Bancroft's, of Colorado mines, 12:4; Beechey's, 25:320; 26:268; Behring's expeds., 23:219; by Bellin, 9:206-7, 217, 240; Blagrave's 7:185, 186; by Bodega and Mourelle, 9:207; from Briggs, 8:36-37, 40, 42; Britton & Rey's (1857), 34:212

Cabot's, 3:312, 313, 372, 378; 7:63; Cabrillo's exped., 3:262, 265; 7:62, 183, 185; 11:44-46; Calderón y Henríquez', 23:220; lists of Calif., 3:257-58; early, showing name "California," 1:49-50, 51; 3:265; Calif. voyages, 3:368-83; Cañizares', 13:180; 14:192; 25:320; Castillo's, 1:45, 47, 49, 51; 3:312, 361, 380-86 *passim;* ancient Chinese, 14:52-53; Coronado exped., 3:265

Dalrymple's, 25:320; Daniell's, 8:41; Degroot's of Nevada, 34:212; Disturnell's, 19:217, 218; showing Drake's voyage, 3:206, 266; Dudley's, 8:36, 40; Elliott's of Central Calif., 10:347; Emory's, 21:221
Fernández de Navarrette atlas, 8:33-34; Freire's, 7:184; Gallatin's (1836, 1838), 3:29; Gastaldi's, 3:265; 7:66, 183; in Gilbert's *Discourse*, 3:266-67; from Gómara, 7:64-65; Gray's, 9:6, 11; Diego Gutiérrez' (1562), 1:49; 3:265, 389; 7:71; Sancho Gutiérrez', 7:63
in Herrera's *Descr. Indias Occident*, 7:63; 8:40; of Hezeta's discoveries, 9:207-8; Holt's (1866), 34:212-13; André Homem's, 11:44-46; Diego de Homem's, 3:312-13, 382, 385, 386; insurance (of S.F.), 26:263
Laet's, 36:218; López de Haro's (1788), 19:221; Martínez y Zayas', 10:319; Martyr's, 7:184; Mason's of mines on American R., 26:124; Mercator's (1569), 1:49; 3:266; 6:294; 7:184; Molyneux globe, 7:62, 185; Mourelle's, 40:111; from Nordenskiöld, 3:374; Northwest Coast, 3:262, 265-67
Ortelius', 3:265, 266, 267; 4:3; 6:294; 7:69, 183, 184, 186, 266-67; Pantoja's, 5:322, 323; 9:3, 4; Plancius', 7:185-86; of S.F. Bay, 25:320-21; of San Mateo Rancho, 27:252; Alonso de Santa Cruz's, 3:370; illus. early Spanish voyages, 3:369-83
Taylor's of Indian tribes, 20:171-80; Tramezini's, 8:38; Ulloa's exped., 3:311-16 *passim*, 380; Vizcaíno's voyage, 7:301-68 *passim*; 8:33-41 *passim*; Wilkes', 3:29; 25:321; of Yerba Buena, 26:267, 268; Zaltieri's, 3:267; 7:250; Nicolas Zamorano's, 3:386
Maps, charts and plans (reprod.):
by Agnese, 3:375, 377, 379; Alcalá Galiano's explorations (1792), 40: foll. 112; American R., South Fork, 26:149; (gold mines), 26: opp. 124; Anza's route along Santa Barbara Channel, 10: opp. 211; MS in Arch. de Indias, 8:35; from Ayer Coll., 7: opp. 68
Bancroft's 1868 Map of Calif. (sec.), 5:218, of Colorado Mines, 12: opp.

3; by Bodega and Mourelle, 9: opp. 201; Bodega Bay, Vol. 16, No. 1, Pt. 2, opp. p. 49; boundaries bet. Calif. and Mex., 5: opp. 321; 9: opp. 11, opp. 12; by Briggs, 8: opp. 37; loc. of Buena Vista village, 10: opp. 216
by Cabot, 3:373; showing Cabrillo's discoveries, 11: opp. 44; by Calderón y Henríquez, 23: opp. 219; Calif. Indian tribes, 20: opp. 171; Camp Lincoln, 26: opp. 8; by Cañizares, of Puerto de San Francisco (1776), 14: opp. 111; (1781), 13:181; by Castillo, 3:381; Central Sierra surveys, 7: opp. 3; east coast of China (ancient), 14:53; Clear Lake area, 32:367; Coloma in 1857, 26: opp. 130; colony system, Fresno, 25: opp. 17; junc. of Colorado and Gila rivs., 9: opp. 11, opp. 12; 17: opp. 217; lower Colorado R., 11: opp. 365, 380; Colorado Mines, 12: opp. 3; Colton's, 31:192
Daniell's (1637), 8: opp. 41; Derby's, of Lower Colorado R., 11: opp. 365; of Sacramento Valley, opp. 99; of Tulares Valley, opp. 247; route of Donner party, 10:346; Drake's Bay, Vol. 16, No. 1, Pt. 2, opp. p. 49; 20:320; 31:100; showing where Drake's plate was found, Vol. 16, No. 1, Pt. 2, opp. p. 64; secs. of Dudley's (1647), 8:39
Fages' route through San Joaquin Valley (1772), 10: opp. 211; his trail over Cuyamacas (1782), 34: opp. 200; Feather and Yuba rivs., 14: opp. 224; Fraser R. mining reg., 11: opp. 155; Fresno colony system, 25: opp. 17
Garcés' route (1776), 10: opp. 211; Gastaldi (ca. 1553), 7:67; from López de Gómara (1552), 7:65; from Herrera (1601), 7: opp. 186; by André Homem (1559), 11: opp. 44; sec. by Diego Homem (1568), 3:383; Humphrey's of S.F. Co., 21: opp. 113; Jackson's of Mining District of Calif. (1849), 13: opp. 378
Kearny's route (from Emory), 21: opp. 193, opp. 202, opp. 213; Larkin's travels, 16: opp. 144; route

of Lassen and Bruff, Gold L. trip of 1850, 39: foll. 264; by P. B. Lord showing route to Gold L., 39: foll. 264; Lower Calif., by U.S. Navy Hydrographic Off., 7: opp. 42

Martínez y Zayas': of Bodega and Tomales bays, 10: opp. 377; of N.W. Coast, 10: opp. 313; of Trinidad Bay, 9:219

Mason's of Gold Mines, So. Fork American R., 26: opp. 124; Mission Soledad, 23: opp. 12; part of Monterey (1879), 25: opp. 205; showing Monterey Bay, from Ferry's *Description de la nouvelle Californie*, 13: opp. 61; Monterey Custom House, 25:207; Spanish explorations and discoveries on N.W. Coast, 9: opp. 201; 40: foll. 112

Ortelius' (1564), 7: opp. 69; Overland route from Wadsworth's *Guide*, 3: opp. 45; routes to and from Panamints, 17: opp. 208; Pantoja's of port of San Diego (1782), 9: opp. 3; houses of Peraltas, 30: opp. 224, opp. 225; Portolá's route (1769), 10: opp. 211; from Ramusio (1566), 7:67; Riley's route through mining dists., 11: opp. 102; Rivera exped. (1769), 31:117

Sacramento and vicinity (1855), 39: opp. 193; Sacramento Valley (1849), 11: opp. 99; Sacramento Valley Railroad, 4: opp. 222; San Francisco Bay: by Cañizares, 13: opp. 80; from Hypolite Ferry, 13: opp. 61; San Francisco Co. (northern part), 21: opp. 113; San Juan Ridge and vicinity, 29: opp. 193; San Mateo Rancho, 27:252; Santa Barbara Channel, 10: opp. 211; by Alonso de Santa Cruz, 3:371; Santa Cruz Mtns., early trails, 29:51; cross sec .of sawmill, 26: opp. 157; Central Sierra, 7: opp. 3; crossing the Sierra bet. Lake Tahoe and Yosemite N. P., 34: opp. 209; Jedediah Smith's route (1826), 2: opp. 236; Spanish-Mex. influence in Calif., 32:45; Old Spanish Trail, 10: opp. 27; illus. early Spanish voyages, 3:369-83

passim; Stanislaus mining region (1850), 11: opp. 359; Sutter's sawmill, 26:138, cross sec. of tailrace, 145

Taylor's of Calif. Indian tribes, 20: opp. 171; Tomales Bay, Vol. 16, No. 1, Pt. 2, opp. p. 49; Trinidad Bay, 9:219; Tuolumne mining region (1850), 11: opp. 359; Upper Calif., by U. S. Navy Hydrographic Off., 7: opp. 46; illus. Vizcaíno's voyage, 7:301-68 *passim*

Whipple's of Colorado-Gila R. junction, 9: opp. 12, of mouth of Gila R., 19:217; Yerba Buena (1839), 26:267; (1847), 17: opp. 291; discovery of Yosemite, 5:329; northeastern Yuba Co., 8: opp. 199; by Zaltieri (1566), 7: opp. 250

Maraquita (ship), 23:313, 332
Maraschi, Father (1859), 10:197
Marble (S.F., 1854), 15:163
Marble Heart, The (play), 10:42, 65
Marble quarry, 24:269
Marcelo, Manuel, 17:146
Marchena, Juan de, 7:376
Marchessault, Damien, 13:345; 29:239; 39:324
Marcy, Randolph B., 2:217; 4:141; 34:212
Marcy, Samuel, 1:231
Marcy, William George, 1:217; 223-24, 228; 35:97, 111
Marcy, William Learned, 8:259; 10:13, 137, 138, 147; 11:33-34; 15:251-52; 21:358-62; 32:293
Marden, Horace, 7:118
Marden, W. H., 25:175
Mare Island, 20:154; 23:343-44; 32:358; 34:87; 36:296; land claim, 19:163, 171, 357; 25:320; naming of, 6:148; Navy Yard, 6:151, 335-36; 14:356; 16:67; 19:163, 171-72; 20:233; 24:63; 26:16; 31:294; 33:229-33, 236; 40:299, 302, 306
"Mare Island Century," address by Russell F. O'Hara, 34:87
Marhoffer, Jacob, 35:332-33
María Antonia (ship), 14:123
María Ester (ship), 14:344; 23:205, 206, 216, 217; 37:254-55, 259
Marianita, La (ship), 31:313
Mariano, Juan Lobo, 26:37

"Mariano Guadalupe Vallejo and
    Sonoma," by George Tays,
    16:99-121, 216-55, 348-72; 17:50-73,
    141-67, 219-42
Marian Watson (ship), 5:140
Maricopa oil field, 32:9
Marin County, 20:270; address on,
    29:373-74; dairying in, 20:260-65
    passim; 30:309, 310
Marine (ship), 34:337
Marine Hospital, State, 15:88, 169,
    186, 276; 34:252
Marine Hospital, United States,
    14:356; 25:190
Marine Hotel, San Francisco, 5:343,
    345-46
Mariners' Benevolent Association,
    31:151
Marino, José Matías, 27:108
Marion (S.F., 1855), 15:282, 364
Marion (ship), 33:112
Marion Rifles, San Francisco, 9:244,
    251, 270; 10:198; 15:164, 174,
    176-77, 373; 16:83, 285; 17:168;
    23:71; 25:336, 343, 344; 37:362-67
    passim; 38:18, 19, 21
Marion Watson (ship), 5:140
Mariposa, 1:273; 28:325, 326, 330, 332,
    335; 30:115; 33:276-77; 38:308;
    newspapers, 1:273; 4:13
Mariposa (ship), 13:177; 20:137;
    30:292
Mariposa and Yosemite Water Co.,
    1:275
Mariposa Battalion, 1:272, 277; 4:12,
    13, 185, 203, 210; 5:328-31; 8:84;
    28:84, 327-34 *passim,* 338
Mariposa Commercial and Mining
    Co., 25:88
Mariposa Company, 12:76
Mariposa County, 21:359-61; 28:334;
    gold specimen from, 32:273
Mariposa Creek, 21:358, 359
Mariposa Estate (Frémont's), 7:411;
    17:83-84; 19:19, 144; 21:325-26;
    25:1; 26:346; 34:335-36; *see also*
    Land cases; Ranchos: Las Mariposas
Mariposa Grove, 4:14, 15, 24; 12:73,
    74
Mariposa Mine, 12:74-76; 33:276, 277;
    34:256, 335-36, 339
Mariposa River, 4:13; 12:73, 74; 28:325
Mariposa Road, phot. of opening
    festival, 5: opp. 340

Market Street Mission Railroad, San
    Francisco, 17:172; 38:336
Market Street Railway, 15:167, 168,
    175; 23:230, 245
Markham, Charles Edwin Anston,
    27:280
Markham, Clements R., 29:274
Markham, Henry Harrison, 5:286-87;
    19:64
Markham, Pauline, 4:61
Mark Hopkins Institute of Art,
    15:302, 316; 33:314, 317
Markle, John W., 24:74-75
Markley, William J., 9:269
Markov, Aleksandr, 12:238
Marks, Bernard, 25:26-27, 29, 30
Marks, G. S., 13:32
Marks & Witowski, 30:266
Mark Twain, *see* Clemens, Samuel L.
"Mark Twain and the Mark Twain
    Papers," address by Dixon Wecter,
    29:77-80
"Mark Twain at the Sanitary Ball—
    and Elsewhere?" by William C.
    Miller, 36:35-40
"Mark Twain in the West," address
    by Cyril Clemens, 7:410
Marlette, Seneca Hunt, 4:11; 7:6, 7-8;
    9:44, 45; 11:173; 15:285; 17:76-79
    passim; 34:217-18
Marlette-Day Survey, 7:7-8, 17-19
Marley (on *London,* 1850), 7:397
Marlowe, Julia, 35:142
Marney, Maj. (in mines, 1849), 24:126
Marot, Georges-Emile *fils,* 22:304
Marple, William, 30:137
Marque, Emile, 39:167, 169, 227,
    231, 233
Marqués, Gabriel, 3:364-65
Marqués, Gerónimo, 7:341; 8:27-28
Marques, Punta de (Chetco Point),
    10:329
Marquínez, Marcelino, 4:149; 37:117
Marriage by Moonlight (play), 21:256
Marriages: Chinese, 15:277; records
    kept by T. Dwight Hunt, 28:289-96;
    see also Weddings
Marriner, Mrs. R. K., 4:208; 24:263
Marriott, Frederick, 2:67; 12:76;
    20:165; 21:327; 36:99
Marriott & Wheeler, 15:175; 16:82
Marroquín Francisco, 25:309
Marryat, Francis Samuel, 15:334-35;
    16:84; 22:254-73 *passim,* 276; 38:32,
    40

Marryat, Frederick, 14:136-37, 140, 141

Mars, Amaury, 39:9, 12, 236, 342-43

Marsden, Joseph, 22:178

Marsh, Charles, 4:246, 250, 262, 264; 5:178

Marsh, Erasmus, 9:159

Marsh, G. F., 4:36

Marsh, George P., 9:301-2, 341

Marsh, Mrs. George W. (née De Long), 11:52

Marsh, James and Mary A. (Ranny), 28:293

Marsh, John, 4:158-62, 170; 5:305; 6:266; 9:77; 10:7, 31; 12:29; 13:175, 221-22, 230; 16:56-58; 17:54, 56, 152; 18:33, 34, 58, 297; 20:148-52; 22:315-22; 23:290-99 *passim;* 30:98; 34:8; 37:6-7; bk. on rev., 9:400-401

Marsh, Robert G., 21:64

Marshal, C. P., 15:376

Marshall, Capt. (of *Virago,* 1854), 15:181

Marshall, A. A., 14:396

Marshall, Anna Hughes, 14:114, 129, 135, 138

Marshall, Benjamin F., 9:248-49, 250, 256, 258, 259, 269; 11:181

Marshall, Edward Colston, 9:39, 40, 47; 10:267; 30:174

Marshall, Eliza, *see* Gregson, Mrs. James

Marshall, Henry, 19:114, 127-41 *passim;* 29:338

Marshall, Mrs. Henry (Mary Jane Coterril), 19:130

Marshall, J. R., 10:357, 368; 21:155, 178; *see also* Lee and Marshall's Circus

Marshall, Mrs. Jacob (Elvira Whiteside), 9:261, 284

Marshall, James Wilson, 2:206; 4:105; 5:96, 125; 10:299; 12:295; 13:164; 14:273-79 *passim;* 17:174; 19:124, 125, 133-34; 21:83; 23:261; 26:107-28 *passim,* 134, 139, 148, 159; 27:281; 28:339; 30:36; 32:194, 195; 35:331; quoted, 29:270; bk. on, rev., 4:89; drawings by, 21: opp. 111, opp. 116

Marshall, Capt. John (of *California*), 13:388, 391-97 *passim;* 27:45, 48-49

Marshall, John and Anna (Hughes), 19:114, 127, 135

Marshall, Lucy (Agar), 36:285; "Samuel Marsden Brookes," 36:193-203

Marshall, Martha L., *A Pronouncing Dictionary of California Names,* rev., 5:88-89

Marshall, Mary Ann, *see* Ames, Mrs. Thaddeus M.

Marshall, P. B., 14:321

Marshall, R. B., 36:256

Marshall, Robert B., 4:50

Marshall, Mrs. Samuel Baxter, *see* Marshall, Lucy (Agar)

Marshall, William, 21:220, 224, 334, 356; 25:303, 308; 26:24, 27, 39

Marshall family, 19:113-43 *passim*

Marshall & Wildes, 23:215, 217

Marshall County (prop.), 38:333

Marshall's Melodeon, *see* Melodeon, Sacramento

Marsh's Juvenile Comedians, 10:250, 262-63

Marston, Anna Lee (Gunn), ed. Gunn, *Records of a California Family,* rev., 8:87

Marston, George White, 35:354-55, 357, 361, 363; 36:63-64, 67, 69, 155, 162

Marston, Sylvanus B., 2:90, 95, 115-18 *passim,* 121, 132, 135, 137

Marston, Ward, 3:116, 118; 10:101, 124-26; 14:149; 17:335, 337-38

Marston, William, 33:12

Martha (opera), 15:179

Martha (ship), 7:212; 22:383

Martha Gould (ship), 11:159

Marti, Benedict and Anna Barbara (Weber), 28:293

Marti, Werner H., bk. revs. by, 40:162-65, 351-53

Martiarena, José Manuel, 23:4, 374

Martin (w. Kearny, 1846), 21:200

Martin (Death Valley, 1849), 18:214

Martin (Sacramento, 1850), 30:103

Martin, Mme. (San Jose, 1850), 5:356; 14:156

Martin (Yuba Co., 1857), 9:157

Martin, Mrs. (Yuba Co., 1857), 9:155

Martin ("the Wizard," 1859, 1867), 10:45, 68; 21:157

Martin, Mrs. (S.F. and Santa Cruz, 1900), 38:342-47

Martin, Anne Henrietta, 33:374

Martin, Auguste Louis, 12:352, 353, 354; 13:58

Martin, Camilo and Mary (Hyde), 16:191

Martin, Dennis, 16:380

Martin, Diego de, 7:146, 148-50, 172-73, 182

Martin, Edna, *see* Parratt, Edna Martin

Martin, Edward J., 7:291; 10:292

Martin, Mrs. Edward J. (Eleanor Downey), 10:292; 23:191; 28:338; obit., 7:291-92

Martin, Edwin S., 33:94

Martin, Elizabeth (Wyant), ed. "The Hulbert-Walker Letters ...," 36:133-47

Martin, Ephraim, 32:195

Martin, Fernando, 8:219; 16:227; 37:262

Martin, Genevieve, *see* Martin, Jean

Martin, George Curtis, 22:192

Martin, Granville, 36:125-26

Martin, Green C., 9:42

Martin, Irving, obit. of Mrs. Charles M. Jackson, 27:379

Martin, J. Ross, 36:201

Martin, J. West, 26:200

Martin, James P., 27:218

Martin, Jean (Mrs. Frederick H.), 37:91; "Louis Sloss, Jr., Collection of California Paintings," 37:19-38

Martin, Jesse B., 14:276, 278; 26:119, 122; 32:195

Martin, John, 16:285; 22:341, 345; 23:23

Martin, Juan, 1:166

Martin, Julian, 24:26-27

Martin, Katherine, 38:342, 343

Martin, Miss L. J., 37:41

Martin, Leonidas ("Leo"), 10:395; 14:398

Martin, Margaret Elizabeth, 19:95; "Dr. C. Annette Buckel, the 'Little Major,'" 19:74-76

Martin, Mrs. Mary, 30:289

Martin, Milton, 35:158

Martin, Noble, 5:284

Martin, Pete, *The Jerry Giesler Story*, rev., 40:157-58

Martin, Robert S., 15:177

Martin, Mrs. Rosanna, 28:294

Martin, Thomas S., 1:126, 132-36 *passim*; 18:262, 264, 277; 29:136, 235

Martin, Walter S., 25:232; 31:303

Martin, William, 27:345

Martin, William H., 9:26; 27:169, 171

Martin, William Jennings, 16:55, 56

Martin & Co., 8:199, 201

"Martin C. Briggs, 'Methodist Trumpeter,'" by Rockwell D. Hunt, 31:1-11

Martinetti, Paul, 21:178

Martinetti-Ravel Troupe, 10:273, 281, 288; 16:340; 21:52, 72, 154, 157-58, 179

Martínez (dragoon, 1846), 25:293

Martínez, Agustín, 21:320

Martínez, Enrico, 7:267, 273-74

Martínez, Esteban José, 9:204; 15:216; 40:238

Martínez, Francisco, 29:237

Martínez, Ignacio, 4:163; 5:134; 8:140-41, 148, 214, 234, 238; 11:135; 12:194, 236; 13:235; 14:123; 15:330; 16:115, 219-21, 225; 17:291, 292, 295; 23:210, 217, 372

Martínez, José (1789), 40:238

Martínez, José (1839), 17:149

Martínez, Juana, 31:45

Martínez, Juan Ignacio, 12:117; 29:31

Martínez, Luis Antonio, 1:167-68; 16:222-23; 36:6-8

Martínez, Manuel, 10:32

Martínez, Margarita Aceves de, 38:106-7

Martínez, María, 16:80

Martínez, María Antonia, *see* Richardson, Mrs. William A.

Martínez, Pedro Adriano, 37:127; letter to, 37:116-17

Martínez, Santiago, 10:36; 12:113-21 *passim*

Martínez, Sixto, 12:117

Martínez, Susana, *see* Hinckley, Mrs. William Sturgis

Martinez, Contra Costa Co., 23:364; 24:64, 286; 25:328; 27:303; 30:6, 10

Martinez, Riverside Co., 12:9, 13

Martínez y Orozco, Xavier Tizoc, 38:7; phot., 38: opp. 8

Martínez y Zayas, Juan, 9:204; 10:313-36 *passim*, 340; maps by, 9: opp. 219; 10: opp. 313, opp. 337

Martin House, Yuba Co., 8:341, 358

Martin's Fork (of Mary's R.), 32:206

Martin's Ranch, 8:200, 209; 9:163

Martinsville, 8:209

Martin White (ship), 15:278

Mártires, Arroyos de los, Lower Calif., 31:261, 262, 269, 347

Martires, Ensenada de los, 10:325

Martires, Punta de los (Pt. Grenville), 9:227

Marvin (Yuba Co., 1854), 8:201

Marvin, A. S., *see* Marvin and
   Hitchcock
Marvin, J. B., 1:98
Marvin, John Gage, 1:9; 5:328;
   11:361-62; 23:376; 28:329, 330, 338
Marvin & Hitchcock, 5:104; 26:228, 231;
   30:101, 105-6, 110-13 *passim*, 147,
   250-53 *passim*, 260, 261, 353; 38:304
Marwedel, Emma, 11:85
Marx, Capt. (Klamath R., 1850), 3:93
Mary (ship), 14:346
Mary Ann (ship), 14:329, 330, 342,
   346
Marye, George Thomas, 2:365;
   17:174
Marye, George Thomas, Jr., 11:49;
   *From 49' to '83 in California and
   Nevada*, rev., 2:365
Mary Ellen (ship), 22:170
Mary Frances (ship), 13:176; 14:333,
   342, 346; 34:26
Maryland (ship), 14:343
Mary Mitchell (ship), 7:216, 217, 220,
   221
Mary Phebe (ship), 11:381
Mary's River, 3:61, 271; 5:379, 383;
   6:124; 16:126; 24:120, 121, 123;
   26:336; 32:197, 201, 206, 207; *see
   also* Humboldt River
Mary Stuart (play), 21:174
Marysville, Calif., 3:146, 160; 4:221;
   5:34; 6:242; 7:15, 16; 8:175, 178,
   180, 187, 194, 202-7 *passim*, 211, 337,
   340-47 *passim*, 351, 357, 361; 9:33-34,
   51-58 *passim*, 75-78 *passim*, 154, 158,
   162-63, 169, 173, 179, 259, 261-68
   passim, 284, 345-97 *passim*; 10:41-42,
   46, 49, 53-61 *passim*, 72, 165-88
   passim, 194-200 *passim*, 246-70 *passim*,
   353-72 *passim*, 381-86 *passim*, 394;
   11:61; 12:280, 299, 304; 15:168, 273;
   17:311, 316; 19:292, 294; 21:69;
   30:103, 110, 126, 127-28, 258-59;
   24:348; 26:181, 194, 195; 28:235;
   31:5-6; 32:296; 33:67, 202-4; 35:315,
   316; 37:201; 38:22, 310-11
   art. on, 14:195-229, 375-407; 15:21-57
   Bath House, 14:398
   churches, 10:176, 198, 199; 15:41-44,
      164; 15:164
   Courthouse (illus.), 9: opp. 358
   newspapers, 6:11-12; 8:358, 361;
      9:62, 65, 133, 134, 156, 245, 266,
      287, 378-83 *passim*, 390; 10:177,
      192, 199, 265, 266, 296, 394, 395;
   14: (fac.) opp. 209, 225, 386-89
      passim, 398, 407; 15:21-56 *passim*,
      (fac. adv.) opp. 40, 273; 20:165;
      21:332; 30:128-30; 33:203-4; 34:60,
      61
   railroads, 9:259, 284; 11:230; 27:202
   schools, 9:372, 395; 10:251, 260, 264,
      287; 14:399; 15:53
   theaters, 8:213, 363; 15:47-48;
      21:69-70
   illus., 9: opp. 62, opp. 68, opp. 358
Marysville (Corvallis), Ore., 28:207
Marysville Bookstore, 14:398;
   30:258-59; illus., 9: opp. 62; 30: opp.
   257; *see also* Amy, G. & O.; Eddy,
   Ripley A.
Marysville Brewery, 14:399
Marysville Buttes, *see* Sutter Buttes
Marysville Choral Harmonic Society,
   9:373
Marysville Gymnasium, 10:178, 179,
   182, 186, 199, 260
Marysville Hebrew Benevolent Society,
   10:182, 200
Marysville Jockey Club, 15:49
Marysville Library Association,
   38:310-11
Marysville Hotel and Brewery,
   15:46-47
Marysville Mining Co., 9:268, 345
Marysville Park, *see* "Park, The"
Marysville Rifles, 10:181, 182, 249,
   262, 280-86 *passim*, 294, 355, 365,
   369, 387; 38:22
Marysville Young Ladies' Seminary,
   10:251, 264
Mary Taylor (ship), 25:120
Masakiyo, Yanagawa, 23:346
Mascarel, Joseph, 13:345; 39:324, 341
Mason (overland, 1849), 24:119, 120
Mason, Biddy, 13:333
Mason, E., 26:5
Mason, Dr. Edgar, 32:167, 168, 169
Mason, Edgar, Jr., 32:163
Mason, J. Rupert, 25:95
Mason, James Murray, 19:18, 171,
   177, 345, 348, 361; 28:216, 230
Mason, John Young, 10:13, 19;
   13:243-47 *passim*; 31:212-15 *passim*
Mason, M., 21:235
Mason, Paul, 28:194, 195, 197
Mason, Redfern, 25:239, 244-45
Mason, Richard Barnes, 1:147, 247-57
   passim; 2:75, 76, 188, 200; 5:406;
   10:22-32 *passim*, 137, 138, 144, 145,

301; 11:260, 265; 12:157, 332;
13:56-57, 60, 66, 76, 153, 175, 271,
272, 279, 306, 307; 14:275-76; 16:58,
196, 321; 17:231, 232-33; 19:140,
157, 182; 20:151, 153; 22:51, 54, 55,
65, 66, 292; 26:60, 118, 122, 124-25;
29:30-32, 34-35; 30:54; 33:112-14,
126, 254-55, 259, 264, 269, 337, 341,
343, 345; 35:108; 40:15, 24, 124; maps,
26: foll. 124, 149
Mason, William, 8:6, 8, 15
Mason (ship), 30:20
Masonic Hall Book and Stationery
  Store, 30:265
Masonic order, *see* Freemasons
Masonic Record, 15:166
Masonic Temple, San Francisco, 4:196
Mason Opera House, Los Angeles,
  20:140
Mason Valley, 34:193, 199; 36:119-26
  passim
Masquerades (1851), 28:38
Mass (Oregon City, 1850), 2:130
Massachusetts (U.S.S.), 15:373; 16:80
Massachusetts (whaler), 29:1, 15
Massachusetts & California Co., 33:376
Massachusetts Co., 11:243
Massachusetts Hill, 6:229-36 *passim*;
  12:65, 71
Masseau, A., 22:221; 23:24
Massett, Stephen C., 3:35; 4:302;
  12:28; 14:387, 388, 389, 404, 411;
  15:28-29, 35, 37, 46-47, 50; 16:340,
  344; 20:293; 22:31, 38; 28:38, 56;
  35:51
Massey, A. A., 30:262, 267, 363
Massey, Atkins, 34:325
Massey, Ernest de, 14:154-55, 157;
  15:333-34; 30:102, 107, 114, 256, 357,
  39:3, 9-10, 13-14, 144; Journal, trans.
  Marguerite E. Wilbur, 5:3-43, 138-77,
  219-54, 342-77; 6:37-57; App. to
  Journal, trans. Blanche C. Wagner,
  32:105-18; fac. of handwriting, 5:
  opp. 3
Massey, Ormand de, 6:54
Massey, Thomas, 27:316; phot., 19:
  opp. 59
Massey & Cantenat, 30:262
Massey, Veron, and Co., 5:21
Masson (from France, 1850), 22:304
Masson, Paul, 33:374
Masten, Nathaniel Keese and Emilia
  Antonia (von Falkenberg), 31:382
Masters, Frederick J., 27:30

Masterson (Aurora, 1860s), 7:116
Mastick & Belcher, 9:396
Mastick Station, Alameda, 26:266
Mata, José María, 14:235-36
Matanzas, 3:169; 6:242, 260; 12:290-91,
  293; 14:201; 23:199, 318, 360; 25:289
Matelot Gulch, 24:268
Mather, George, 15:39
Mather, James G., 34:20
Mather, Stephen Tyng, 4:40, 50
Mathews (S.F., 1855), 15:270
Mathews, Arthur F., 37:34
Mathews (or Matthews), Chepa, 29:265
Mathews, Richard, 28:336-37
Mathews, William A., 9:26, 31; 15:276
Mathias de Santa Cathalina, Fr., 13:155
Mathieson, J. Muir, 37:34
Mathurin, Louis, 8:120
Mathy, Ernest L. and Mrs., 27:188
Matilija Hot Springs, 17:32, 40
Matlock (Greenville, 1855), 8:352
Matson, Mrs. William (Lillie B.),
  obit., 10:96
Mattei, Andrew and Eleanor
  (Joughin), 28:188
Matterre, Dr. (Guaymas, 1852), 18:6,
  7, 20
Matteson, Edward E., 11:240; 29:200,
  206
Matthes, François Émile, 1:284; 4:51,
  57; 30:284
Mattheson, R. N., 27:97, 99, 101
Matthews (in mines, 1848), 2:192
Matthews, Alexander, 15:164
Matthews, Charles, 9:100, 101
Matthews, Edward, 20:34, 38
Matthews, Henry, 6:152
Matthews, William B., 10:62
Matthews, William P., 10:76
Matthewson, R. C., 6:46; 39:14
Matthew Vassar (ship), 2:135; 16:80
Mattole Farm (Ind. reserv.), 30:164
Mattole River, 23:28; 30:164
Matute, Juan Bautista, 10:315-45
  passim; 40:121
Maubailly, Pierre-Marie, 39:226, 243,
  250-51, 254, 313, 315
Maubé, Arnaud, 12:332-33; 13:65,
  75, 167
Mauldin, Henry, 34:93
Maupin and Boggs, 24:67
Maurelle, *see* Mourelle
Maurice, A., 14:394; 15:33
Maurie's, nr. Sucker Flat, 10:169

Maury, Miss (S.F., 1864), 24:263
Maury, William L., 13:387; 20:217, 233
Maxfield's Know Nothing Hall, 8:344
Maximilian I (Archd. Ferdinand),
    13:38, 40-41; 38:52-53; *see also*
    "Californians against the Emperor"
Maxson, W. B., 11:9
Maxwell, Mrs. and Miss (S.F., 1867),
    11:127
Maxwell, Lucien, 1:129, 131, 139, 149
Maxwell, Lucy, 25:191
Maxwell, Richard T., 4:168; 19:230;
    33:106
May, Capt. (overland, 1850), 3:46-47
May, Dr. (S.F., 1850), 11:361
May, Mrs. (Yuba Co., 1857), 9:143
May, Charles, 9:159, 160
May, E. C., 27:95
May, Ernest R., 30:191; "Benjamin
    Parke Avery," 30:125-49
May, Hattie (or Hatty), 9:64, 66, 73,
    77, 145, 163, 176, 345, 352; 10:276,
    279, 281
May, I. S., 9:57, 62, 67, 73, 129-35
    passim, 142-54 *passim*, 161, 163
May, John, lawsuit, 9:63
May, John H., 26:2, 10
May, W. B., 9:42
May, William, 22:79
May, William B. and Mary E.
    (Innskeep), 28:293
Maybeck, Bernard Ralph, 38:306
Maybell, Stephen, 21:272
Maybury (overland, 1849), 21:307
Mayer (in mines, 1849), 30:19
Mayer (S.F., 1850), 7:398
Mayer, Samuel D., 30:69
Mayer, Mrs. Samuel D., 31:337
Mayfield, 7:412; 14:166, 168; 18:49;
    27:134, 135, 138-39; 33:171, 173
Mayflower (ship), 14:309-13 *passim*
May Flower (ship), 12:31
Mayhew, Florence, 36:281
Mayhew, George Henry, 36:281
Mayhew, Horace Allen and Mrs.,
    36:281
Mayhew, William, 13:258
Mayhood, *see* Mahood, James
May Lundy Mine, 4:39
Maynard, John, 15:240
Maynrad, John C., 9:27; 15:164, 272,
    367; 19:233
Maynard, Mrs. John C. (Ella Gwin),
    19:233
Maynard, Lafayette, 16:62; 17:76, 79;

33:374; art. on, 16:71-76; obit.,
    16:77-78; phot., 16: opp. 71
Maynard, Stephen and Susie Frances
    (Davis), 2:67
Mayne, Charles, 10:389; 11:127
Mayne, R. C., 6:23-26
Mayo, Edward, 2:91, 121
Mayo, Frank, 10:395; 21:53, 59, 63,
    165, 266
Mayo, Jesse, 24:270
Mayock, Robert Stoney and Mrs.
    (née Rutherford), 27:285
Mayock, Sally Ann, 27:285-86
Mayock, Stonewall Jackson and Ellen
    Alicia (Starbird), 27:285
Mayorga, Julian, 8:376
Mazagran (ship), 14:133, 134
Mazatlán, Mex., 2:159; 3:106, 108;
    5:39, 306, 307; 6:77, 189; 8:222-24;
    14:327, 333, 335-36; 17:23, 129, 130,
    131; 18:35, 52, 218, 241-42, 250;
    19:195, 211; 20:21, 212; 23:274-75,
    302, 324, 327; 26:312; 27:40; 34:123,
    151; 35:105; 37:64; 39:49; Gillespie's
    letters from, 17:125-30; U.S.
    consulate at, 34:111-20 *passim*
Mazatlan (ship), 31:297
Mazatlán Islas de, 7:302, 372-73, 375;
    8:64; on map, 7:303
Mazatlán company, Monterey, 27:338
Maze, Montgomery, 37:200
Mazeppa (play), 21:59-60, 65
Mazeppa (ship), 35:291
Mazerat, Pierre, 22:303
Mazón, Donaciano, 37:197, 204
Mea, Mme., 20:136
Meacham, George W., 27:370
Mead (Sacramento, 1859), 10:61
Mead, James D., 12:115
Mead, Lewis Risdon, 33:374
Mead, Orlando, 16:138
Mead, Warren B. and Sara P. (Sears),
    28:294
Mead, William H., 29:291-92
Mead, Lake, 22:19
Meade & Co., 25:32
"Meadow Lake City and a Winter
    at Cisco in the Sixties," Clarence M.
    Wooster, 18:149-56
Meadow Lake City and mining
    district, 6:344; 18:22, 149-56, 366
Meadow Valley, 16:78; 17:78
Meadows, Don, bk. rev. by, 40:265-66
Meadows, James, 15:240; 21:9; 22:221;
    29:20, 26; 30:54

Meagher, Michael, 6:36
Meakin, Frederick, 35:354
Meander (ship), 11:381
Meaner (Weaver?; Yuba Co., 1857),
  9:140
Means, A., 9:40; 15:376
Means, H .H., 9:42
Mears, Eliot Grinnell, 18:288
Measures, *see* Weights and measures
Meaubert, Adolph, 21:66
Mebius, Christian F., 9:320
Mecartea, Austin, 33:375
Mechanics' Fair, San Francisco,
  17:316; 20:266; 36:245
Mechanics' Institute, San Francisco,
  15:268, 273; 16:184, 337; 17:176;
  19:149-52 *passim*, 286; 20:2; 25:4-12;
  28:141; 35:135; 38:304-5; 39:289
Mechanics' Lyceum, Fort Vancouver,
  2:128
Mechanics' Own (mining co.), 23:163
Me-choop-da ranchería, 36:313-25;
  sweathouse, illus., 36: opp. 320
Mecombs, Hannah, *see* Clyman, Mrs.
  James
Mecombs, Isaac, 6:59-60; 16:133
Mecombs, Lambert, 6:59-61
Mecombs family, 6:59-60
Mecum (nr. Placerville, 1850), 26:297
Meda (ship), 15:282
Médanos, Point, 25:319; *see also*
  Black Point
Medary, Samuel, 11:15
Medea (play), 21:143, 174
Medical Gazette, 28:9
"Medical Observations of J. P.
  Leonard . . . 1849," ed. Robert T.
  Legge, 29:211-16
Medicine and surgery:
  in Mex. and Span. periods, 4:142-76,
  284; 10:86, 404; 15:379; 18:68-69,
  70, 71; in Amer. period, 4:177-206,
  287-89; 6:377; 17:176; 18:76, 81, 168,
  178, 282, 384; 19:75-76, 119, 123, 126,
  127, 138, 139, 141, 374; 21:339-44
  passim, 352-56 *passim*; 22:37, 42-63
  passim; 23:191; 24:23, 354; 28:374-75;
  29:170-71, 211-16; 31:13-31 *passim;*
  37:216-17; education for, 4:177, 179,
  188-200 *passim*, 205, 206; 5:93;
  30:67-71; herbs used by Indians,
  23:204; in Honolulu, 35:196; in
  Marysville, 14:395-96; in the mines,
  4:178-84; 6:221, 222, 225, 243;
  10:404; 24:23; *see also* Hospitals

Médicis, Le (ship), 11:341; 19:27, 380
Medico-Chirurgical Association, 4:182,
  188
Medill, W., 26:323-24
Medina, F. P., 24:265
Medley, Samuel G., 8:86
Medway Colony, 25:174
Meek, Jason S., 8:198
Meek, John, 12:146; 13:353; 14:342;
  23:331
Meek, Joseph Lafayette, 4:6,
  155-56 (?), 279, 291; 19:312, 314;
  25:140
Meek, Stephen Hall, 4:6, 281;
  19:135, 312
Meek, Thomas, 12:138, 226; 23:331
Meek, William B., 8:198, 208; 15:285
Meeker, David, 9:36
Meeks, Joseph, *see* Meek, Joseph L.
Meeks, Washington, 9:36
Meeks, William Newton, 26:71, 75;
  33:374
Meetings of the Society, 3:95-101,
  204-9, 302-3, 398; 4:95-102, 210-12,
  301-2, 399-402; 5:93-100, 205-6,
  414-17; 6:102-6, 197-99, 285-87,
  380-82; 7:95-99; 200-201, 289, 410;
  8:90-94, 187, 283, 386-87; 9:90-93,
  188, 292, 407-8; 10:91-94, 206-7, 307,
  413; 11:88-91, 188-89, 295, 389-90;
  12:84-87, 180, 366-67; 13:88, 188-89,
  284, 411; 14:86-87, 186-87, 283, 410-11;
  15:89-92, 192-93, 286-87, 382-83;
  16:89-92, 187-88, 286, 380-81;
  17:89-92, 185-86, 285, 356; 18:85-90,
  184-85, 286, 376, 19:89 94, 187 88,
  282, 375-76; 20:83-88, 282-83, 376-77;
  21:82-88, 183-84, 225-38, 278, 363-71,
  374; 22:84-87, 183, 374-75; 23:80-88,
  180-81, 380; 24:184-85, 282, 376;
  25:85-86, 185-87, 372-74; 26:83-88,
  371-76; 27:75, 85-89, 178-83, 280-82,
  376-78; 28:86, 88-89, 184-86, 276-78,
  372-73; 29:73-80, 184-86, 373-77;
  30:84-86, 274-78, 375-79; 31:83-88
Méfret, Georges, 39:240
Méfret, Xavier, 39:224, 239-40, 242
Megalia (Dogtown), 10:251
Megunsticook (ship), 16:346
Mehner, William, 8:358
Meiggs, Henry, 1:9; 13:299; 15:177,
  269, 271, 275; 16:337; 17:172, 359;
  19:230, 236; 20:335; 21:383; 23:179;
  25:335, 341-42; 30:1, 5, 7, 163;
  33:327; art. on, 17:195-207; fac.

resolution congratulating, 17: opp. 200; phot., 17: opp. 195

Meiggs, John G., 9:26, 29; 15:177, 182; 16:337; 17:197; 25:342

Meiggs, Mount, 17:201

Meiggs' Wharf, 15:370; 16:347; 17:196; 19:237; 25:342; 26:7

Meighan, Clement W., and Robert F. Heizer, 31:189; "Archaeological Exploration of Sixteenth-Century Indian Mounds at Drake's Bay," 31:99-108

Meigs, Montgomery Cunningham, 28:162; 31:44, 47

Meihl, Mrs. (Yuba Co., 1857), 9:139

Meihl, Charles, 9:356

Mein, Charles, 7:292

Mein, William Wallace, 20:384

Mejicas, Louise, 16:285

Melado (Melhado(?)); S.F., 1850), 34:241-42

Melaney v. Gaylord and Stoddard, 10:179

Melbius, C. F., 27:174

Meléndez, Sebastian, 7:298-300, 377, 385-90 *passim*

Meléndez Valdés, Salvador, 10:338

Melendrez, Antonio, 12:318-22

Melendy, John M., and Nellie (Clark), 30:382

Melendy, H. Brett, 38:88; "Two Men and a Mill . . .," 38:59-71

Melendy, Howard Burton, 30:382; 39:81; "Orleans Bar," 39:53-59

Melendy, Mrs. John M. (Nellie Clark), 30:382

Mellon, John, 22:156, 159-61, 165, 166

Mellus, Francis, 8:295, 297, 301-2; 9:95; 13:347; 18:36, 67, 70

Mellus, Mrs. Francis (Adelaida Johnson), 1:258

Mellus, George, 34:244

Mellus, Henry, 1:235, 249; 5:304-5; 6:80; 8:295, 297, 301, 302; 9:95; 11:71-72, 75, 135, 136, 142; 13:54, 218, 347; 14:332, 346; 17:139-40, 253, 294, 335; 18:36, 47, 50, 52-53, 60; 19:49; 23:201-2, 215, 254; 27:106, 110, 250, 251; 38:334, 340

Mellus, Mrs. Henry (Anita Johnson), 1:249, 258

Mellus & Howard, 3:37; 14:202, 346; 18:36, 70; 19:321; 27:106, 251; 28:113, 253-54; 34:26

Melodeon, Marysville, 9:265, 280

Melodeon, Sacramento, 9:251, 256; 10:272, 274, 279, 281, 361

Melodeon, San Francisco, 21:43

Melone, R., 24:237

Melones, 22:77, 83

Meloney, Aaron R., 9:273, 381, 397; 10:51, 74

Melons, 4:365, 369; 5:131, 275; 11:37; 12:193; 27:260; 28:237; 29:173

"Melpomene on the Half Shell," by Donald C. Biggs, 33:39-47

Melquiond, Cyr, 39:246

Melrose (place), 38:160-61

Melton, F. C., 31:20

Melville, Emelie, 19:97, 98; 21:243; 35:142; address, "Memories of the Past," 7:200-201

Melville, John, 16:341; 17:82

Melvin, Adoma L., 13:296

"Memoirs of Hon. William M. Gwin," ed. William H. Ellison, 19:1-26, 157-84, 256-77, 344-67

"Memoirs of Lemuel Clarke McKeeby," 3:45-72, 126-70

"Memoirs of Theodor Cordua," ed. and trans. Erwin G. Gudde, 12:279-311

"Memorial of Pedro Calderón y Henríquez," ed. and trans. Henry R. Wagner, 23:219-25

"Memories of Ina Coolbrith," address by Mrs. Finlay Cook, 11:188

Memories of Mark Twain and Steve Gillis, by Gillis, rev., 3:196-99

"Memories of the Past," address by Emelie Melville, 7:200-201

Ménard, François, 21:336; 26:45

Mendaña, Alvaro de, 7:228-32

Mendelsohn, H., 19:291-92, 297

Mendenhall, E. T., 13:12, 15, 17

Mendenhall, Elvira Ellen, 13:12

Mendenhall, William M., 30:4

Mendheim, H., 30:357

Mendocino, Cape, 3:5, 6, 11-12, 20, 220; 7:26, 302, 359, 366, 378, 392; 8:55; 9:208, 217, 237; 10:330, 335; 18:319; 23:222; 25:112; 27:291; 30:162, 164; on map, 7:368

Mendocino City, 30:164, 165

Mendocino County, bk. on, rev., 5:92; early settlers in, *see* "Anderson Valley"; Indians in, *see* Indians; lumbering in, *see* Lumber

Mendocino Indian Reservation, 27:216, 219; 30:164-68 *passim*, 170

"Mendocino War," 30:167

Mendota, 11:260

Mendoza, Antonio de, 3:262-64, 370, 387-97 *passim*; 6:299-303, 307-31 *passim*; 7:20, 22-23, 55, 59, 136-39, 141, 296, 366

Mendoza, Diego de, 8:44, 45, 50

Mendoza, Francisco and Linda, 19:216

Mendoza, Juan de, 2:155

Mendoza, Mariano José, 6:163

Mendoza (place), 18:150

Mendoza y Luna, Juan de, 8:44-49 *passim*, 69

Menéndez, José Antonio, 23:318, 332

Menéndez, Salvador, 15:60

Menges, M., 22:251

Mengis (S.F., 1854), 15:166, 167, 175

Menken, Adah Isaacs, 20:243; 21:58-60, 141-42, 145, 164

Menken, Alexander Isaac, 21:58, 59

Meno, Antonio de, 3:309, 311, 363-65; 19:242

Mensch, Fred, 19:371

Mentor (ship), 12:230

"Men Who Met the Yankees in 1846, The," by Helen V. Shubert, 13:43-55

Menzies, Archibald, 8:386; 9:223; 10:338; 11:383; 14:117; 15:60; 18:336-37; 24:337; Journal, ed. Alice Eastwood, 2:265-340; *Journal of Vancouver's Voyage*, ed. Newcombe, rev., 2:256-57

Menzies, Robert H., 21:288; address, "Various Phases of Marin County History," 29:373-74

Menzies, Thomas, 21:288; 29:373

Mercado, Father, *see* Vásquez del Mercado, Jesús María

Mercantile Library, Sacramento, 30:103; 38:298

Mercantile Library, San Francisco, 7:278; 12:20, 22, 23; 15:164, 183, 268, 270; 17:176, 179, 182; 28:134-35, 141, 142; 29:260; 30:249, 358; 31:244; 38: opp. 295, 300-303, 312, 334; illus., 38: opp. 295

Mercantile Life Insurance Co., 31:298

Mercantile Trust Co., 32:375; *see also* American Trust Co.

Mercator, Gerard, maps by, 1:49; 3:266; 6:294; 7:184

Merced, 18:25

Merced, Laguna de, 30:338

Merced Banner, Snelling, 20:164, 165

Merced County, assessor's field book, 33:376

Merced Mining Co., 21:326; 34:335-36; lawsuit, 10:264

Merced River, 4:4; 20:101, 114; 23:259, 368, 369; 28:324, 331-32, 335

Mercedes (ship), 30:99

Mercer, Asa, 40:256

Mercer, Walter, 30:247

Mercer, William F., 19:320-21

Mercer's Bells: The Journal of a Reporter, by Conant, rev., 40:255-56

Merchant (Yuba Co., 1857), 9:146

Merchant, Frederick George, 15:167; 28:294

Merchant, Mrs. Frederick George (Theresa Leonora Perabeau), 28:294

Merchantman (ship), 22:171, 172, 173

Merchants' Drayage and Warehouse Co., 35:67, 146

Merchants' Exchange, San Francisco, 10:374; 15:270, 271, 275, 280; 27:69, 200; 31:298; 38:297; buildings, 26:73, 75; phot., 15: opp. 163

Merchants Fire Insurance Co., 26:254, 258; 27:270

Merchants Hotel, Marysville, 3:160; 8:340, 341, 356; 9:267; 10:61, 167, 185-89 *passim*, 246, 250, 261, 273, 364, 371; 33:292

Merchants Mutual Marine Insurance Co., 26:351, 355; 27:66

Merchants' National Bank, San Diego, 35:358-61; 36:76

Mercier, Armand Theodore, obit., 36:375-77

Mercier, Mme. R. J., 39:311

Mercure, Henry, 1:149

Mercury, San Jose, 22:223-34, 355-64; 29:91

Mercury (Am. ship, 1807), 12:222, 223, 224; 13:205

Mercury (Brit. ship, 1851), 8:275

Mercury mines and mining, *see* Quicksilver mines

Meredith, Charles T., 16:298, 303

Meredith, Henry, 6:343; 9:42

Meredith, William M., 19:17, 26

Meridian lines, monuments for, 34:1-16 *passim*

Merkel, Mrs. Frederika W. Amalia, 28:293

Merkel, Louisa Philippina, 28:294

Mermaid (ship), 29:272

Merola, Gaetano, 25:250

Meroney, Charles S., 32:26, 30, 32, 39-40

Merriam, Clinton Hart, 2:344; 4:5, 24, 53, 57; 10:302; "Earliest Crossing of the Deserts of Utah and Nevada: Route of Jedediah S. Smith in 1826," 2:228-36; "Jedediah Smith's Route across the Sierra in 1827," 3:25-29; address, "A Regrettable Chapter in California History," 2:369; obit., 21:284-86

Merriam, Frank Finley, 36:110, 257, 260; 37:274, 348

Merrifield, Daniel, 15:169

Merrihew, James, Jr., 13:31

Merril, Frances E., 28:292

Merrill (Sacramento, 1849), 37:139

Merrill (Marysville, 1854), 8:201

Merrill, Judge (Marysville, 1859), 10:183-87 *passim*

Merrill, Andrew, 26:204

Merrill, Annis, 16:80

Merrill, Don and Daisy, 37:217

Merrill, Emma Jane, 28:292

Merrill, H. D., 14:278

Merrill, J. M., 9:26; 15:276, 277, 282

Merrill, Jesse, 9:153, 156

Merrill, John, 2:139

Merrill, John C., 29:252, 254; 31:292

Merrill, Mrs. John F., 13:288

Merrill, John H., 16:130; 27:362, 369

Merrill, L. S., 3:65

Merrill, Nathaniel, 30:55

Merrill, R. R., 10:174

Merrill House, San Francisco, 11:142

Merrimac (ship), 20:233; 38:61

Merriman, E. R., 19:64, 73

Merriman & Tucker, 10:180

Merrithew, Capt. (of *Acadia*, 1857), 22:169

Merritt, Emma, 31:297

Merritt, Ezekiel, 1:73, 75, 80, 134; 3:119; 6:137, 139-40, 273, 374; 7:79; 13:107-8; 15:237; 17:219-24 *passim*, 240, 274, 275, 340; 18:297, 311; 24:57; 25:122-23; 28:265; 29:134, 262-67 *passim*, 275; 29:334, 335

Merritt, Frank, 6:36

Merritt, Harry, 30:222

Merritt, Isaac, 26:265

Merritt, Josiah, 29:20-21, 25

Merritt, Ralph P., 4:50

Merritt, Samuel, 15:164; 25:100; 26:262, 264, 265; 27:173, 197

Merritt, Samuel A., 10: opp. 48, 62, 273, 278, 288, 290, 377; 11:9; 32:148, 158

Merritt, Wesley, 30:290, 298, 304

Merritt, Lake, 4:211; 30:10

Merrow, Capt. (of *Magnolia*, 1851), 12:109

Merry, William Lawrence, 25:285

Merryhoff, Baron, 23:319

Merryman, J. H., 21:34

Merryman, James, 6:16

Mertens, Karl Heinrich, 18:336, 337, 345

Mervine, William, 1:289; 2:73, 165, 167, 168; 3:105, 109-18 *passim*, 180, 187; 5:301; 7:84; 8:258; 9:82; 10:101, 124-27 *passim*; 11:210; 12:41-45 *passim*, 58, 166, 168; 13:303; 17:131, 137, 138, 228, 282, 334-40 *passim*; 18:35, 73-84 *passim*; 20:216, 233; 21:12, 14-15, 19, 223; 22:51; 25:125, 197; 29:333, 334, 335; cor., 6:368-70; 11:208-9; 12:41-42; 18:76; orders to Marston, 10:124

Mesa, Antonio and Ana Gertrudis (López), 13:200, 201, 202

Mesa, José Antonio, 12:25, 29

Mesa, José Miguel, 12:25

Mesa, Juan Prado, 15:61; 16:353, 369; 17:52, 143-44, 149; 29:157

Mesa, Luis, 21:320

Mesa, Mrs. Rafael (María Antonia), 27:135

Mesa, Valerio de, 14:6

Mesa, battle of the, *see* La Mesa

Mesa Grande, 26:27, 34, 53

Mescal, 21:220; 31:119, 263, 267

Mescal Land and Water Co., 40:217

Mesick, Richard S., 9:65, 78, 107, 113-14, 116, 364-65; 10:251, 285, 357-59, 362, 364, 385; 15:35

Mesmer, Joseph, 13:345

Mesnager, Georges, 39:331

Mesquite, 1:68; 18:116, 118; 25:292-303 *passim*, 306

Messager, Le, San Francisco, 16:344; 30:264; 39:145-47, 349

Messenger of Destiny: . . . Archibald H. Gillespie, by Marti, rev., 40:162-65

Messer, Nathaniel T., Jr., 30:302

Messerve, Theodore, 34:348

Messmaker, Capt. (of *Cérès*, 1849), 5:6-7, 20, 26, 28, 141

Metal & Thermit Corp., 27:94-95
Metamora (play), 21:54
Metate, 15:105
Metcalf, Helen Broughall (Mrs. Stephen), "The California French Filibusters in Sonora," 18:3-21, 96
Metcalf, Homer, 26:135
Metcalf (or Metcalfe), Peter, 34:243; lawsuit *v.* Argenti, 34:244-49
Metcalf, Victor H., 26:90; 28:345; 38:356
Meteor (ship), 16:81
Methodist Book Concern, 30:255; 32:128
Methodist Episcopal Church, 3:36; 5:416-17; 6:227, 283, 284; 15:41-42, 57; 16:130; 26:163-74 *passim;* 27:304; 32:51-55 *passim,* 124-31 *passim;* 35:68; 40:327-39; *see also* Methodists
Methodist Episcopal Church South, 10:359; 20:165-66; 27:304, 308; 29:55; 32:51, 120-21, 128, 132, 134, 139; 40:327
Methodist Missionary Society, 32:120
Methodists, 2:136; 15:41-42; 16:140; 18:319, 327; 21:6, 7; 24:60, 263; 26:163-74 *passim;* 27:124; 28:291; 29:55; 31:1-11; 32:120-21, 122, 128, 129, 132; *see also* Methodist Episcopal Church
"Methodist Trumpeter," *see* Briggs, Martin
Metric system, Mex. law establishing, 30:325, 326, 335
Metropolitan (ship), 15:282
Metropolitan Homestead Association, San Francisco, 15:367-70 *passim*
Metropolitan Hotel, San Francisco, 10:50, 72, 276, 281, 285, 357, 373; 11:10; 22:82
Metropolitan Insurance Co., 26:256, 258
Metropolitan Minstrels, 20:314
Metropolitan Opera Co., 33:39
Metropolitan Saloon, Coloma, 38:318
Metropolitan Theatre, Sacramento, 10:51, 74-75, 277; 21:160
Metropolitan Theatre, San Francisco, 7:283; 10:371, 376, 381, 388, 389, 393, 394; 14:411; 15:163-84 *passim,* 266-81 *passim,* 366, 367, 371, 375; 16:84, 183, 283, 285, 344; 20:2, 304, 305, 307; 21:41, 42, 52-56 *passim,* 62-68 *passim,* 145, 146, 152, 163-68 *passim,* 178, 180; 23:73, 112; 33:43
Metropolitan Troupe, 9:144, 176

Mettler, Edwin M., 34:169
Metzger, Alfred, 25:236, 242
Metzger, William, 22:159, 173-74
Meuse (ship), 5:8, 9; 20:71; 22:292
Mewhirter, A. L., 25:382
Mexicana (ship), 10:315-33 *passim,* 341
"Mexican Background of Mining Exploitation in California, The," address by John S. Fox, 18:184
Mexican Californians, 15:109; 25:289-91, 312-18 *passim;* 32:298; *see also* Spanish Californians
"Mexican Frank," 3:259-60
"Mexican Insurgent Provisional Coinage," by Roy Hill, 27:132
Mexican Mine, Nev., 11:61; 12:327; 17:77
Mexicano (ship), 37:112, 116, 118
Mexican period in California, *see* Mexico: Calif. under rule of
Mexicans in California, 5:372-73; 13:165, 383; 17:15; 24:158; 28:76; 37:193-95, 201; on farms, 25:314; in gold region, 11:243, 324, 331; 12:73; 21:358-62; 24:344, 345; 35:37-46; in gold rush, 19:324-26, 333; 27:162, 163 *(see also* Sonorans); patriotic clubs of, 37:193-94, 201; in San Francisco, 5:354; 22:271, 360; in Stockton, 23:367; soldiers, 11:220-21; *see also* Cholos
"Mexicans in the California Mines, 1848-53," by Richard H. Morefield, 35:37-46
Mexican Steam Navigation Co., 17:80
"Mexican Trade between Santa Fe and Los Angeles," by Eleanor Lawrence, 10:27-39
Mexican War, 1:207; 2:161, 246-51; 3:88, 109, 110, 113, 253; 5:311; 10:111; 12:37, 49; 13:116; 14:327; 16:78, 196, 304; 17:306-7; 19:118, 162, 175, 331; 20:12, 196, 209, 345, 365; 21:23, 193, 304; 23:259, 262, 270, 280, 294, 351, 359; art. on, 8:251-61; Battle of Sacramento, 18:230, 231, 233, 246-47; veterans, 34:39, in Civil War, 31:230; *see also* Conquest of California
"Mexican War and the Conquest of California, The," by Thomas Kearny, 8:251-61
Mexico: boundary bet. U.S. and, 5:321-24 *passim;* 9:3-15; 19:2, 13, 178,

217-18; 34:125; maps showing, 5: opp. 321; 9: opp. 6, opp. 12; Calif. Natl. Guard on border, 34:157-71; Calif. under rule of, 1:26-34; 167-72; 4:151-76; 11:33-34, 199, 221, 339, 342, 343; 17:248-52; 27:333-36; 33:279; Confederate scheme to march through, 34:149-54; debt of, to British bondholders, 11:33; 17:21-22; 18:136-47 *passim;* exclusion of foreigners from Calif. by, 11:199; Gillespie's letters from, 17:124-30; 18:219-28; journeys through (1848-49); 1:59-62; 18:121-22, 125-27, 229-42; 21:293-98, 321; 23:261-74; lands offered to foreigners, 37:202-3; under Maximilian, 13:38-41 *passim;* 37:193, 212; moves for independence of Calif. from, 11:33; 12:37, 48-49; 15:242-43; 23:326-28 *(see also* Alvarado revolution; Bear Flag revolt); races and casts of, 13:232-33; relations bet. England, France and, 11:33, 195-99 *passim;* 17:21-22, 125; 18:136-47 *(see also* French Consulate); bet. U.S. and, 11:202, 344; 12:37; 19:3 *(see also* Mexican War); schemes for colonization of, 13:39-41; 18:143; 37:202-8; *see also* Mexicans; Sonora

Mexico, War with, *see* Conquest of California; Mexican War

Meyer, Capt. (of *Falmouth*, 1855), 22:22, 168

Meyer (S.F., 1866), 36:297, 299, 300

Meyer, Anton J., 25:219

Meyer, Carl, 12:65; 15:287, 332-33; 18:181

Meyer, Daniel, 35:358-59

Meyer, Eugene and Harriet (Newmark), 22:95; 35:184-85

Meyer, Frederick, 15:302-3

Meyer, J. Henry, 26:84-85

Meyer, Marcus R., 19:99

Meyer, Rosalie, *see* Stern, Mrs. Sigmund

Meyer, Rosa W., 28:294

Meyer, Samuel, 13:335

Meyer, William, 31:340

Meyers, William H., 18:375; 20:231

Meyerwitz (or Meyerowitz), Isadore, 18:303, 304, 313; 21:227, 235

Meyneris, T., 22:251

Mezes, S. M., 17:258

Mezzara, Pietro, 10:270; 40: opp. 302

Mezzara, Mrs. Pietro, phot. and note, 40: opp. 302

Mhoon, John Bell and Charlotte (Miller), 40:85

Michael, M. F., 35:148-49

Michaelis, Adrian, 24:381

Michaelis, Otto E., 4:35

Michaels, Charles Frederick, obit., 23:185-86

Michaels, Henry, 23:185

Michelsen, M., 30:360

Micheltorena, Manuel, 1:31, 33; 4:155; 6:135, 187; 8:296; 11:70-71, 200, 204, 206, 220, 221, 345; 12:129, 135-36, 147, 149-50, 287-88; 13:44-46, 49, 52, 105, 227-32 *passim;* 14:23, 325, 344; 15:228, 229-30, 285, 366; 16:56-57; 17:61, 62, 145-60 *passim,* 174, 294; 18:66, 68, 144, 157-60, 170-76 *passim,* 257, 296, 297; 19:201, 211-13; 20:147, 149, 151; 21:120, 315, 331; 22:366; 25:223; 27:60, 107-8; 28:108, 264, 266; 29:132, 134-35, 321; 32:265; 34:114-15; 36:11

Michigan Bar, 24:170

Michigan Bluff, 2:203-6, 208; 13:26; 16:30-31; 19:146; 30:261; 32:133

Mickle (E.) & Co., 28:40

Mickles, Philo D., 12:65

Middle Bar, 31:143, 148

Middle English Dam, *see* Dams

Middlesex & California Joint Stock Co., 33:376

Middleton, Miss (S.F., 1860), 29:119

Middleton, Edna, 30:290; letters to, 30:298-99; 31:168-69

Middleton, Howard, 30:289-304; 31:49-67, 163-73; phot., 31: opp. 56

Middleton, Mrs. Howard (Mrs. Mary Martin), 30:289

Middleton, John, 6:15; 15:175, 370; 19:230; 27:153; 30:289

Middleton, John (Jr.?) and Ida (Parks), 30:289

Middleton, John H., 19:233

Middleton, John W., 15:19

Middleton, Maggie, 19:233

Middleton, Samuel P., 11:127; 27:153; 29:115

Middletown, Lake Co., 32:364

Middletown, San Diego Co., 31:34

Middle Yuba Canal, 9:69; 11:233, 237; 29:205

Midway Island, 23:345-46

Miel, Charles L., 11:127(?); 39:162-63

Mier, Servando Teresa de, 24:291-92;
25:76, 149, 363
Mier, Mex., 21:293, 301; 23:351, 370
Mier y Teran, José Maríe, 14:237
"Mifflin," letters from (1849),
24:129-30, 258-59, 352
Mighels, Ella Sterling (Clark)
Cummins, 19:251, 253; ed. Clark,
How Many Miles from St. Jo.?, rev.,
9:88-89
Mighels, Henry Rust, 15:381; 30:128
Mighels, Philip Verill, 31:340
Mighels, Mrs. Philip Verill, 31:340;
see also Mighels, Ella Sterling
(Clark) Cummins
Miguel (Mokelumne Hill, ca. 1852),
30:241
Miguel, José de, 2:326
Mikado (operetta), 35:142
Milatovich, A., 34:42
Milbank, Mrs. Morris (Margaret
Willey), 25:191
Miles, Lt. (Philippines, 1898), 31:164
Miles, Emma, 21:157
Miles, S. M., 14:393, 395; 15:23-29
passim, 33, 39, 44, 47, 53; phot., 15:
opp. 21
Miles, Sara, coauth. "Santa Barbara
County between Two Social
Orders," 25:311-18
Miles, William, 1:57
Milford Land and Lumber Co.,
38:63, 67
Milhan, Pvt. (L.A., 1847), 33:257
Military companies, private, 10:181,
190, 200, 372, 387, 371379 68 *passim*;
38:17-23 *passim; see also* Militia;
names of companies
"Military Units in Southern California,
1853-1862," by J. M. Scammell,
29:229-49
Militia:
Mexican period, 13:44-45; 16:352,
366; 17:155
American period, 2:357, 358, 362;
3:84, 85; 9:283; 10:372, 390; 15:53,
76; 16:345; 27:339; 29:229-49
passim; 37:359-68; 38:17-23; *see
also* Calif. Battalion; Calif. National
Guard; Military companies, private
Milk, *see* dairying
Milk Ranch, Yuba Co., 8:213, 340;
see also Stroud's
Millar, Mrs. Rollo R. (née Hall),
38:47, 57

Millard, Caroline, *see* Erkson, Mrs.
Alexander
Millard, Walter, 4:13; 23:376
Millbrae, 17:245, 252
Mille, E .K., 31:126
Miller (Death Valley, 1850), 18:198
Miller, Capt. (Colorado R., 1867),
22:172
Miller, Miss (Yuba Co., 1859), 10:169
Miller, Adolf, 36:70
Miller, A. G., 8:358
Miller, Albert (Marysville, 1851),
15:24, 26, 31, 56
Miller, Albert (S.F., 1855), 15:376;
18:190; 26:232, 355-56, 358; 31:176
Miller, Mrs. Albert (Mary A.
Kendall), 31:176
Miller, Albert S., 11:103, 121; 34:23, 24
Miller, Arthur, 8:344; 9:50, 54, 154, 161,
178, 266, 348; 10:189
Miller, B., 9:26
Miller, Charles H., 9:40
Miller, Charles J., 37:201
Miller, Christian Otto Gerberding,
1:19; 36:176; obits. of Walter B.
Cline, 11:296; George Tourny,
12:184; obit., 31:176-77; phot., 31:
opp. 176
Miller, Mrs. Christian Otto Gerberding
(E. Havemeyer Tucker), 31:177
Miller, Mrs. Christian Otto
Gerberding (Janet McAlpin Watt),
31:177; obit., 37:278-79
Miller, Cincinnatus Heine (or Hiner),
see Miller, Joaquin
Miller, Clay, address, "Impressions of
. . . Senator Phelan," 32:175; obit.
of Frederick J. Koster, 38:180
Miller, Edward Oliver, 39:21
Miller, Estelle, 4:18
Miller, Frank, 35:329
Miller, Genevieve, 24:96
Miller, George, 18:212-16 *passim*
Miller, George W., 24:58
Miller, Guy C., 27:134, 138, 139; obit.,
34:183-84
Miller, H. A., 25:5
Miller, Herschel B. M., 19:62
Miller, H. H., 10:385
Miller, H. M. A., 27:197
Miller, Harry East, obit., 18:190
Miller, Mrs. Harry East (Myrah
Gray Prather), 18:190
Miller, Henry (artist, 1856), 36:13

Miller, Henry (Heinrich Alfred
 Kreiser), 17:255; 21:190; 25:23; 29:89
Miller, Hulings and Margaret (Witt),
 33:144-45
Miller, Huram, 31:377
Miller, J., 22:251
Miller, J. Frank, 26:72; 29:116
Miller, James (Marin Co., 1846),
 9:253, 277-78; 13:192
Miller, James (on *Sylph*, 1849), 13:32
Miller, James M., 19:129, 141
Miller, James P., 9:363; *see also* Miller
 v. Noyes
Miller, Joaquin, 3:297; 11:83; 15:284;
 16:378; 18:281; 19:103; 28:10; 34:362,
 364; 35:48; 40:137; arts. on, 32:231-41;
 33:143-46
Miller, Mrs. Joaquin (Abbie M.
 Leland), 32:233-34, 236, 239
Miller, John F., 9:42
Miller, John Franklin, 33:374
Miller, Juanita, 13:286; 32:235, 236,
 238-39; 33:144-45; address, "Joaquin
 Miller," 10:307
Miller, Lizzie E., 31:14
Miller, Lois, 28:241, 242
Miller, Lucille V., obit. of Mrs.
 Edward L. Doheny, 38:278-79
Miller, May Merrill (Mrs. Justin),
 18:288
Miller, Morris S., 28:352-53, 358
Miller, Newton C., 10:271, 281; 28:234,
 237, 241
Miller, Robert Cunningham, "The
 California Academy of Sciences and
 the Early History of Science in the
 West," 21:363-71; as address, 21:374
Miller, Robert Ryal, 37:284;
 "Californians against the Emperor,"
 37:193-214
Miller, Robert Watt, 25:247; 37:279
Miller, S. A., 25:29, 35
Miller, W. J., 17:84
Miller, W. P., 15:53
Miller, William, 15:181; 17:26, 131
Miller, William C., 36:93; "Mark
 Twain at the Sanitary Ball—and
 Elsewhere?" 36:35-40
Miller, William D., 30:49
Miller & Lux, 21:190; 25:22-23; 29:89;
 33:189
Miller (James P.), *v.* S. E. Noyes, 9:360,
 363, 364, 365, 370
Millerites, 18:112-13, 135
Milleri, Stanislaus, 21:159

Miller's Steam Wagon, 9:374, 396
Millerton, 4:26; 12:6; 25:18, 19
Milleson, M., map and drawing by,
 14: opp. 224
Milligan (Sacramento, 1858), 9:243
Milligan, J. H., 13:32
Millikan, Robert Andrews, 36:78
Milliken, Ellen, 29:93
Milliken, George, Henry and Philip,
 11:158
Milliken, Ralph LeRoy, 20:384
Millington, C., 31:333
Millionaire's Daughter, The (play),
 21:256
"Million Dollar Ranch," San Joaquin
 Co., 30:91
"Millions for a Cent.," trans. Douglas
 S. Watson, 11:40-41
Mills (Feather R. mines, 1849), 19:134
Mills (Yuba Co., 1858), 9:366
Mills, Alexander, 7:206, 207, 212, 213,
 217, 219, 223, 224, 395-403 *passim*;
 8:17-21 *passim*, 167-81 *passim*, 262,
 264, 274
Mills, Anna, 4:36
Mills, Catherine, 9:149
Mills, Mrs. Charles F. (Clare Nichols),
 33:381-82
Mills, Cyrus Taggert, 24:179; 31:86, 87
Mills, Mrs. Cyrus Taggert (Susan
 Tolman), 24:179; 31:86-88
Mills, Darius Ogden, 5:180; 12:33;
 16:183; 17:254-55, 257; 25:46;
 30:349; 31:290, 337; 36:350; phot. of
 residence, 38: opp. 212
Mills, Edgar, 15:76; 36:267-69
Mills, John A., 17:179
Mills, John W,. 15:30
Mills, Luther, 30:8
Mills, Thomas, 39:299
Mills (D. O.) and Ansel Easton *v.*
 Charles Lux *et al.*, 17:257
Mills and milling, *see* Grist- and
 flour mills; Sawmills
Millsap, Walter, 40:231, 232
Mills College, 10:410; 24:179, 378;
 25:190; 27:72-73; 31:86-88; 34:331;
 36:349
Mill Valley, 18:100
Milner (Marysville, 1858), 9:374
Milo (ship), 26:356, 359; 33:238
Miltiades (ship), 22:352
Milton, Maxwell Claypool, obit.,
 26:377-78
Milton (place), 29:194, 199

Milton Badger (ship), 33:2, 149, 151
Milton Dam, *see* Dams
Milton Mining and Water Co., 28:233, 236, 240, 241; 29:193, 198, 199
"Milton S. Latham," address by Edgar E. Robinson, 10:206-7
"M[ilton] S. Latham and the Senatorial Controversy of 1857," by William F. Thompson, Jr., 32:145-59
Minal (place), 11:43
Minarets, The, 4:55; mining region, 4:39
"Mine Littéraire, La," 39:149
Miner (Santa Barbara, 1857), 18:271
Miner, Morris, 14:61, 67
Miner, Mrs. Randolph Huntington (Tulita Wilcox), obit., 36:182-83
Miner, Richard S., 8:361
Miner, Bodie, 11:190
Miner, The, San Francisco (1866), 25:191
Mineral King mining excitement, 4:38
Mineral springs, 24:71; 32:365-66, 370; 36:295, 305; *see also* Bartlett Springs; Napa Springs
Miners' "convention," 35:336
Miners' Exchange and Savings Bank, 15:272, 273, 274; *see also* Wright, A. S.
Miners' Own Book, The, illus. from, 11:225, 231, 235, 239, 241, 325, 334
Miner's Ranch, 15:39
Miner's Rest (tavern), 30:158
Miners' Ten Commandments, The, 36:343
Minerva (ship), 25:258
Mines, Flavel Scott, 12:95, 99, 107; 20:16, 18, 22, 24, 25, 27, 161, 176; 25:108, 117; 26:169-70, 172; 28:34, 291; 33:317
Mines: foreign investors in western, 35:335-44; laws relating to, 6:228; 9:172; 31:310 *(see also* Foreign Miners' Tax); Mexicans in, 35:37-44 *(see also* Mexicans); *see also* Gold mining; Gold regions; Quicksilver mines; Silver; names of individual mines
Minetti, Giulio, 25:248
Mineur, Le, 39:149, 156, 160, 349
Mingins, G. J., 24:266
Ming porcelain and stoneware at Drake's Bay, 31:99-108 *passim*
Minguet (Marysville, 1850), 14:395

Mining and Scientific Press, 10:309; 29:196-204 *passim;* 31:337
"Mining Bureau of the Pacific Coast, The," by Clark C. Spence, 35:335-44
Mining law, 8:354-55; 9:71; 10:404; 23:350-51; 28:4
Minnesota, Sierra Co., 11:240
Minns, George W., 14:75
Minns Evening Normal School, San Francisco, 37:44
Minor, Colville J., 33:252-53
Minor, George, 3:111, 119, 120; 17:340; 35:105
Minor, George W., 13:296
Minor, Robert D., 3:112, 118
Minstrel Guards, 20:307
Minstrel shows, 3:161; 8:340, 346; 9:60, 175; 10:187, 200; 15:46, 166, 371, 375; 17:172; 20:2, 298, 304-9 *passim*, 314; 21:41, 46, 51, 64, 163-75 *passim*, 242, 243, 250, 270; 29:114; 35:142
Mint (riv. str.), 2:201; 11:360; 13:296; 28:63, 68
Mint Canyon, 32:12, 30, 38
Minto, John, 4:352
Mints, *see* Coins and coinage; United States Mint
Minturn, Dr. (Colorado R., 1850), 22:20
Minturn, Charles, 10:72; 28:360; 29:148
Minturn, Edward, 28:360
Minturn Slough, 22:22
Mintzner, William, 25:230, 232
Miramontes, Candelario, 3:30, 32
Miramontes, Ignacio, 16:360
Miranda, Alejo, 15:59
Miranda, Apolinario, 27:59; 28:105
Miranda, Mrs. Apolinario (Juana Briones), 17:292-93; 25:190; 26:268; 27:60; 30:325
Miranda, Juan, 16:249; 22:342, 346; 28:264
Miranda, Presentación, 17:292
Miranda Viña, Joaquín, 37:201
Mirandol, A., 14:134
Mirandol, H. J., 6:45; 32:107; 39:12
Miro, G., 37:38
Mirrielees, Edith R., 29:191
Mirror, San Francisco, 33:194, 198, 213
Mirror Lake, Yosemite, 1:279-80
Mischief (yacht), 15:278
Mischief Making (play), 10:47
Misemon, Peter, 10:284

Mission asistencias and chapels: Las
Flores, 22:176; Pauma, 3:244; 21:345,
356; San Antonio de Pala, 3:243-44;
6:160; San Pedro y San Pablo,
23:250; San Salvador Chapel at
Agua Mansa, 3:241-42; Santa
Margarita, 1:166-67; 36: (illus.),
opp. 1, 7, 14, 15-16; Santa Ysabel,
26:25, 26, 27, 53; on map, 34: opp. 200
Mission Bay, San Francisco, 21:113-21
passim; 27:339
Mission Creek, San Francisco, 21:115
Mission Dolores, by Engelhardt
[extract], rev., 7:409
Mission grape, 36:242, 249
Mission Inn, Riverside, 35:270
"Mission of Nuestra Señora de la
Soledad," by Frances R. Smith,
23:1-18
"Mission, Presidio, and Pueblo," by
Mary Floyd Williams, 1:23-35
Missions, California, 1:23-26 *passim,*
29, 160-61, 169, 196; 2:295-96, 337,
368; 3:223-44 *passim;* 4:361-71, 401-2;
5:217; 6:159-63, 255-64 *passim;*
8:308-9, 319; 12:164, 283; 13:106;
17:24; 20:223; 24:297; 25:58; 30:84-86;
32:46; bks. on, rev., 2:173-77;
4:394-96; *see also* names of individual
missions; Indians, Mission;
Secularization
Dolores, *see* Missions: San Francisco
de Asís
Nuestra Señora de la Soledad,
1:258; 4:363, 367-71 *passim,* 402;
5:217; 6:256; 8:309, 319; 15:114;
23:1-18, 348, 374; 36:9; illus., 23:
opp. 1, opp. 11, opp. 12, opp. 14
La Purísima Concepción, Imperial
Co., 33:14-16
La Purísima Concepción, Santa
Barbara Co., 4:402; 5:217; 6:256;
8:108, 309, 319; 18:175; 23:10, 209,
372; 27:109; 28:381; 33:278
"Saint Matthews," *see* Missions: "San
Mateo"
San Antonio de Padua, 4:362, 366,
367, 371, 402; 5:217; 6:256; 8:309,
319; 11:84; 13:155; 15:285; 23:2, 3,
8, 9, 10, 255
San Buenaventura, 2:321, 323, 327-28,
341, 343; 5:217; 16:297; 18:178;
illus., 16: opp. 291
San Carlos Borromeo, 1:21; 2:283-89;
3:223, 224, 227; 4:90, 147, 148;

5:217; 6:256; 8:151-52, 309, 319;
12:139; 13:155, 156; 15:213-18
passim; 17:120; 20:223, 237; 23:7,
12, 374; 37:298; illus., 15: opp. 213
San Diego de Alcalá, 1:20; 2:334;
3:223; 5:217; 6:159; 8:219, 308, 309,
319; 13:156, 196; 14:4; 20:235-39;
25:21, 25, 30, 47, 52; 32:46;
34:193-208 *passim;* baptismal
records, 20: (phot.) opp. 235,
236-38
San Fernando Rey de España, 1:114,
259; 3:238-40; 4:363, 366, 369;
5:217; 8:309, 319; 12:123, 295;
13:58, 173, 203, 205, 212, 224, 226;
15:115, 116; 17:102; 23:194, 208,
209, 217; 27:33
San Francisco de Asís, 2:272-74;
5:31-33, 217; 6:37, 251, 256; 7:395,
409; 8:142-43, 309, 319; 10:279, 293;
12:106, 196; 13:235; 14:99, 100-101,
104-5, 108, 112, 117-20, 123; 15:364;
16:103, 109-11, 115, 117, 180, 343;
7:172, 245-50 *passim,* 299; 19:197;
23:10, 210, 248-55 *passim,* 362,
372-73; 24:335; 27:57-58, 109, 253;
30:219; 31:280; 36:209; 38:105;
illus., 14: opp. 105
San Francisco Solano, 2:364; 4:284,
364, 366, 368; 5:217; 8:239, 240-43,
309, 319; 12:201, 243; 14:126; 16:99,
100, 112-19, 235-46 *passim,* 351,
368-69, 241; 19:198; 22:330, 340,
341; 23:19-23 *passim,* 211; 24:57;
29:310-11, 313; 32:46; 36:241-42
San Gabriel Arcángel, 1:114, 116,
250, 254, 255; 2:41-45, 337, 345;
3:240-41; 5:217; 6:159, 160, 162,
256, 261; 8:248, 309, 319, 329;
10:216, 217; 12:111, 115, 122, 123,
124, 283; 13:199-213 *passim,* 223;
14:123; 15:374, 376; 18:348;
19:207-8, 215; 23:194, 207, 208, 209,
216, 217, 248, 253, 312, 360, 371,
372; 27:135; 33:112, 113; 34:195, 196
San José, 2:182-83, 196; 4:363-69
passim; 5:130, 217, 352; 6:256;
8:108, 112, 238, 309, 319; 12:147,
173, 196; 13:66, 72; 14:13, 21, 22,
261; 16:219, 233; 17:178; 22:321;
23:195, 210, 375; 24:333; 27:162;
30:2; 33:302, 304, 350; 34:229-30;
37:97-128, 241-65; 38:102; 39:43;
illus., 14: opp. 147
San Juan Bautista, 4:149, 364-71

passim; 5:131, 217, 369-70; 6:256;
8:115, 309, 319, 383-84; 11:291, 295;
12:48; 13:78; 16:115; 17:178, 277;
20:215; 23:362; 25:133-38; 36:324-
25; 37:305-6, 308
San Juan Capistrano, 2:176, 330;
4:401; 5:217; 6:163; 8:309, 319;
13:205, 260, 340; 19:208-9, 215;
21:329, 347, 348, 356; 22:41, 43, 47,
64, 175; 23:194, 207, 208, 325, 360,
371
San Luis Obispo de Tolosa, 1:160-70
passim; 3:7; 5:217; 6:160, 162;
8:108, 309, 319; 10:210, 216, 217;
15:235; 16:222; 17:178, 250; 20:343;
36:2-20 *passim*
"San Mateo," 22:244, 245, 251; art. on,
23:247-258; illus., 23: opp. 247
San Miguel Arcángel, 1:165-66, 169;
4:150; 5:217; 8:309, 319; 10:29;
15:235; 17:178; 18:265; 23:10;
33:62, 268, 337; 36:5, 8
San Rafael Arcángel, 1:115, 135;
5:217; 8:239, 242, 309; 9:253, 277;
12:196, 208, 243; 16:109-10, 111,
114, 115, 117, 241; 17:53; 19:200,
214; 23:10, 176; 29:91, 313; 38:104-5
Santa Barbara, 1:20, 21; 2:316-27;
5:217, 414; 8:158-61, 164, 309, 318,
319, 328-29; 12:19, 77; 18:176, 177,
276, 319-20; 19:201; 23:212, 361-62,
372; 27:337; 33:62; 37:98, 302-3;
bk. on, rev., 2:252-56
Santa Clara, 1:20; 2:277-80, 307;
3:208-9; 5:217, 374, 379; 6:250,
250; 8:108, 256 57, 309, 319, 370;
12:35, 196, 208; 13:58, 107, 270;
14:10, 13-14, 20-23, 261; 15:60, 230,
231; 16:233, 234; 17:120, 178;
20:108; 22:246; 23:195, 210, 250;
24:47-48, 334; 27:162; 30:219, 228;
37:303-4; 38:101-11; illus., 6: opp.
250
Santa Cruz, 2:291; 5:133, 217, 360;
8:148, 149-50, 309, 319; 12:233, 361;
15:122, 227, 233, 235; 26:12; 27:104
Santa Ynez, 5:217; 8:309, 319; 23:209,
363, 373
Soledad, *see* Missions: Nuestra
Señora de la Soledad
Missions, Lower California and
Arizona, 3:225; 4:361; 5:196; 8:58,
374-77; 37:293
Descanso, 31:354
Guevari, 30:217

La Purísima Concepción, 31:114
San Dionisio, 20:222
San Fernando de Velicatá, 13:156;
31:113; 37:295
San Pedro y San Pablo, 15:132; 33:14,
15
Santa Catalina Virgen y Mártir,
15:106, 112, 132
Santa Gertrudis, 31:265
Santa María, 31:109, 113
"Mission San Jose—de Guadalupe?," by
Robert H. Becker, 34:229-30
Mission Valley, San Diego Co.,
26:24-25, 30
Mission Woolen Factory, 10:291
Mission Woolen Mills, 10:373
Missionaries:
Catholic, 1:168; 2:296; 6:161-62;
8:317, 318, 329-30; 20:223, 234;
24:297; 29:139-47 *passim;* 32:50, 51,
121-22; 37:97-99; in Lower Calif.,
5:196, 197; 29:139-40; *see also*
Missions
Mormon, *see* Mormons
Protestant, 32:49-55 *passim,* 119-38
passim; 34:317-22 *passim*
Mississippi (ship), 15:184
"Mississippian in the Gold Fields, A:
The Letters of John Paul Dart," ed.
Howard Mitcham, 35:205-31
Mississippi Bar, 8:338, 341-42, 355
Missouri and California Overland Mail
and Transportation Co., 7:15
Missouri Bar, 8:338, 355, 412
Missouri Compromise, 10:223, 235;
31:105
Missouri Republican, excerpts from,
24:20-43 *passim,* 46, 121, 130-37
passim
Missouri Statesman, excerpts from,
24:23-27 *passim,* 43-45, 117-18,
122-38 *passim*
Missroon, John Stoney, 1:85-90, 179-80;
2:359-60, 362; 3:84-85; 7:79, 80;
10:113-15, 353; 13:54, 55; 15:58,
64-69 *passim,* 306; 16:212-13;
17:223-24, 226, 229; 21:11, 12, 13, 18,
19; 25:128; 27:107; 29:266
Miss Timidity ("musical eccentricity"),
33:41
Mitcham, Howard, 35:283; ed. "A
Mississippian in the Gold Fields: The
Letters of John Paul Dart," 35:205-31
Mitchell (Colusa, 1861), 10:274
Mitchell, Dr. (Marysville, 1862), 10:375

Mitchell, A. H., 9:269; 10:41, 274
Mitchell, Annie R., 28:377-78; 39:210;
 "Major James D. Savage and the
 Tulareños," 28:323-41
Mitchell, Benjamin, 24:58
Mitchell, Consider Davis and Lavinia
 (Davis), 29:285
Mitchell, D. C., 19:145, 146
Mitchell, David D., 6:115; 7:15
Mitchell, E. J., 9:244, 248-55 *passim*
Mitchell, Edith, 10:395
Mitchell, Elizabeth (Paterson), 2:205-6
Mitchell, George, 13:293
Mitchell, Henry K., 9:266, 287, 347;
 10:184, 185, 187, 248, 280, 364, 382-85
 passim
Mitchell, Holbrook T., 27:381
Mitchell, J. A., 9:275
Mitchell, J. B., 14:394
Mitchell, James (or William; from Ill.,
 1849), 21:307
Mitchell, James (from Pittsburgh,
 1849), 13:84
Mitchell, John H., 14:398; 15:21
Mitchell, L., 14:394
Mitchell, Levi, 28:378
Mitchell, Mrs. Lily F. (von Schmidt),
 34:328
Mitchell, Mary Isabelle, 29:285
Mitchell, Mike, 20:305
Mitchell, S. D., 35:159
Mitchell, Stewart, 25:286; 34:286; "A
 Forgotten Exploration . . . Route
 across the Sierra," 34:209-28
Mitchell, Taylor, 26:215
Mitchell, Thomas, 9:140, 144, 145, 257;
 v. Patrick Elmar, 9:140, 145
Mitchell, William, 25:140
Mitchell (T. S.) & Co., 15:54
Mitchell and Nunes, Marysville, 15:55
Mitchler, N., 15:179
Mittau, Lester J., 25:382
"Mittelwestcoastia" (prop. state),
 31:127
Mitten, Homer H., 27:221
Mitten, Mrs. Homer H. (née Requa),
 27:221; 30:93
Mix (Shasta, 1853), 28:229
Mix, Alfred A., 21:307
Mix, George I., 8:209, 212, 341, 350, 357,
 358, 360; 9:52, 135-39 *passim*, 147,
 164, 165, 168, 263, 347, 348, 374; 10:183
Mix, Mrs. George I., *see* Stafford, Mrs.
 Morris G.
Mix, Gustave Louis, 33:374

Mix, W. A., 9:72
Mix, Warren, 17:181
Mixter, Frank M., 39:32
Mizner, Lansing Bond, 6:150; 11:9
Moak, Sim, *The Last of the Mill Creeks*,
 rev., 4:94
Mock, William, 8:360
Mocker, Marie, 27:2
Mocozamy River, *see* Cosumnes River
Modeste (ship), 3:108; 17:125, 135;
 28:252
Modesto, 3:91; 18:24
Modjeska, Helena, 21:329; 31:29;
 34:301, 314; 35:142
Modoc County, 31:127, 137-38
Modoc Lumber Co., 31:287
Modocs and Their War, The, by
 Murray, rev., 38:374-76
Modoc War, 15:286; 21:190; 26:201;
 39:87; art. on, 28:161-63, 286; bk. on,
 rev., 38:374-76
Möllhausen, Heinrich Baldvin, 16:380
Moerenhout, Jacques Antoine, 11:203-8
 passim, 211, 219, 346, 357; 12:55, 56,
 60-61, 155-59, 331, 332, 333; 13:57-62,
 280, 345, 380, 382; 14:151, 152, 322,
 344; 19:325, 384; 27:141-47, 164;
 28:159; 31:140, 308, 311, 321, 323;
 32:126; 35:107, 311; 39:323-24; cor.
 and reps., 11:207-8; 12:160-72, 334-57;
 13:62-76, 159-74, 262-67, 355-79;
 27:145-47, 203-13, 353-59; 28:69-78,
 151-58; 31:146; drawing by, 12: opp.
 347; house, illus., 12: opp. 155; port.,
 12: opp. 331
Moerenhout, Mme. Philip, 28:159
Moffat, Emma, *see* McLaughlin, Mrs.
 Alfred
Moffat, Henrietta, 19:384
Moffat, Henry, 19:384
Moffat, William J., 15:76
Moffett, S. E., 1:15
Moffitt, Herbert C., 36:184
Moffitt, Mrs. Herbert C. (Margaret
 Jolliffe), obit., 36:183-84
Moffitt, James, 19:150; 34:281
Moffitt, James Kennedy, 4:48, 54;
 31:304, 305; obit., 34:281-82
Moffitt, Mrs. James Kennedy (Pauline
 Fore), 34:281
Mofras, *see* Duflot de Mofras
Mohave, Ariz., 22:13, 151, 157, 163; *see
 also* Fort Mohave
Mohave (ship), 22:11, 24, 153, 155, 161,
 167

Mohave No. 2 (ship), 22:152, 153, 163, 167
Mohawk (ship), 20:194
Mohican (ship), 25:42
Mohongo (ship), 16:68
Mohrig (S.F., 1860s), 36:98
Moise, Henry, 22:38
Mojave (place), 35:269
Mojave Desert, 9:306, 307; 10:27, 87, 213-18 *passim;* 12:10; 17:208, 214-16; 32:1-41 *passim*
Mojave River, 1:117, 121; 10:36; 14:68-69; 27:118
Mokelumne Hill, 2:138; 4:197; 7:16; 9:75, 79; 11:180, 322-23; 13:279; 15:171, 267; 19:145; 25:381; 30:115, 239-48, 260; 32:52, 130, 134-36; 35:315, 317-18; 38:38, 309; newspaper, 35:315; 39:4
Mokelumne River, 1:134, 264; 2:138, 184-85; 7:10; 13:72, 74; 20:38(?), 101; 23:36; 32:196; 34:24, 212, 217
Molasses, 29:5; Indians' fondness for, 23:350
Molera, Andrew John, 11:95; obit., 10:414
Molera, Eusebius Joseph, 10:414; 11:281; 21:371; obit. of Edward R. Taylor, 2:262-63; obit., 11:94-95
Molera, Mrs. Eusebius Joseph (Francisca G. Amelia Cooper), 10:414
Molera, Frances M., 26:320; obit. of Mrs. Henry W. Seale, 7:412
Molère, de la, *see* Lamolère, de
Mollnear (or Molenaor), William D., 21:307
Molitor, Agoston, 28:130, 137, 141
Mollins, Margaret, 31:189; coed. and trans. "Putting a Lid on California: Diary of the Portolá Expedition by José de Cañizares," 31:109-24, 261-70, 343-54
Molthrop, Capt. (S.F., 1850), 12:98
Moluccas, 6:294, 296, 306-11 *passim;* 7:132-36, 140, 141, 142, 147, 235; 18:85
Monadnock (ship), 25:42; 31:62
Monaghan, Frank, *French Travellers in the United States*, rev., 13:184
Monarch (ship), 15:374, 376
Monasseau (S.F., 1855), 39:142
Mondelet, Francis (?), 5:14, 349
Mondran, Frédéric François, Vicomte Cazeaux de, 39:325-29
Monea, Rafael, 13:328

Monell, George I. N., 24:165-66
Monet (Yuba R., 1848), 14:210
Money, William, 4:167; 13:337; 22:29
Money: coins (*see* Gold: coins); greenbacks, 23:236
Money (play), 9:371; 21:57, 163
Monger (Yuba City, 1858), 9:366
Mongès, Abbé, 3:224
Monguió, Luis, 27:284; "Lust for Riches," 27:237-48
Monitor (Catholic newsp.), 20:165
Monk, "Hank," 12:323; 15:381; 21:276
Monk, Thomas K., 29:22, 26, 27
Monks, Richard B., 15:168, 180
Monnette, Orra Eugene, 37:272-73, 350; address, "Fort Moore and the Battle of San Pasqual," 3:97; obit., 15:195
Mono County, history of, 26:233-48; *see also* Bodie
Mono Lake, 7:112-13; 18:208; 26:233-34; gold deposits nr., 4:13; 26:236; mining nr., 10:247, 261
Mono Mine, 4:77-78
Mono Pass, 26:236
Monoville, 7:112-13; 10:261; 26:236-37, 241
Monowai (ship), 20:134, 136; 31:158
Monplaisir, M. and Mme. (S.F., 1854), 15:174, 183; 16:283
Monroe, Charles F. (?), 22:352
Monroe, Harry, 13:323
Monroe, John A., 15:372; 16:345; 22:33
Monroe, Phil, 37:56
Monroe Doctrine, 19:45; 32:101-2
Monroe, Thomas, 16:304
Monrovia, 31:22-23
Monsieur Violet, by Marryat, 14:137, 140, 141
Monson, A. C., 7:11; 11:15, 17
Monson, Burdette H., 9:113, 116
Monson (L. B.) & Co., 14:403; 30:104
Monsoon (ship, 1830s), 8:105, 295; 17:141; 18:70; 23:201
Monsoon (clipper, 1855), 15:375
Montagnie, J. de la, 27:98
Montague, Harry J., 4:61; 21:173
Montague, Samuel S., 4:258-59, 269; 5:178, 183; 18:26
Montague Island, 11:373; 22:159-60
Montalvo, García Ordóñez de, *see* Ordóñez de Montalvo
Montana (ship), 22:155-74 *passim*
Montaño, Juan de, 3:310, 365-66; 19:242
Montano, Manuel, 11:111

Montauk (Old Esmeralda) Mine, 7:114

Montaynard Brothers, 15:47

"Montbar" (pseud.), 21:100

Monteagle, Louis F., 25:232, 249

Monte Cristo, 9:145, 350, 358, 380;
30:362

Monte Cristo Mine, 9:176, 350, 380

Montefalcon, Sierra de (Cabo Falcon),
9:235, 241

Monte Mounted Rifles, 29:240

Montenegro, Eugenio, 29:27

Monte Rangers, 29:234, 240

Monterey, Conde de, *see* Zúñiga y
Acevedo

Monterey, 1:26-32 *passim*, 90, 92, 138,
233, 264, 270; 2:249, 251, 354; 3:106,
109-14; 4:147, 148; 6:142, 145; 8:245;
10:125; 13:100; 14:15, 317, 318;
15:139; 16:102, 105; 17:121, 234, 262;
18:51-52, 338; 19:19, 120; 20:21, 112;
21:14; 22:51, 62; 23:194, 197, 316, 327,
331, 334, 358-59; 25:74, 150-52, 160;
27:144, 338; 29:21-28 *passim*; 30:262;
31:110; 33:67; 36:230; 37:1, 2, 3, 14,
63, 64, 65, 75
   arts. on, 1:173-78; 11:274-79;
      15:213-15, 216-23, 338-63
   letters and procs. from, 1:189-90;
      2:72-73, 352-57; 3:178-88, 274-88;
      4:81-87, 375-80; 5:184, 188-95,
      297-307; 6:77-79, 182-84, 186-91,
      364-66, 368-70, 372-73; 7:79-80,
      82-85; 8:71-72, 76-77; 9:81-85;
      12:35-62, 139-46, 161-72, 347-57;
      13:63-76, 271-75, 358-65, 370-75;
      15:341-55; 16:247; 17:135-40, 228;
      19:196-201; 24:23; 27:145-47;
      35:11-21, 112, 113
   in 1790s, 2:282-95, 311-13; 3:220-24;
      4:141, 146, 150; 18:336; 36:229-30
   in 1820s, 8:150-51; 15:140-42;
      16:216-22; 23:203-5
   in 1830s, 4:153, 154; 12:137-46
      passim; 16:4, 222-23, 247-48,
      348-49; 17:52; 18:321-22
   in 1840-47, 4:155-56;
      5:132-33; 8:100-103, 108, 118;
      12:150, 280-81; 15:115, 117, 118,
      123-26, 225, 227; 16:5, 213; 17:54,
      282; 18:33, 34, 35, 65-66, 76-81
      passim, 342; 29:19; 40:21
   Bouchard at, 1:176; 13:206; 14:15;
      16:102-3, 188
   as capital, 4:144, 145, 152; 13:198;
      14:230-33; 19:202; 22:54; 25:71;
      40:13
   customhouse, 3:110; 8:108; 16:5;
      23:315, 358; 25:125, 193-99 *passim*,
      (flagpole) 204-18
   elections at, 1:26, 28; 35:107; 40:20
   founding, 11:274-79
   French Consulate, *see* "The French
      Consulate in California"; Lombard,
      Jules B.
   Com. Jones's seizure of, 13:228-29;
      15:227; 17:146
   Larkin house, 16:321-32
   newspaper, *see Californian*
   presidio, *see* Presidio of Monterey
   printing at, 12:126-37 *passim*
   project to settle, 8:43-45; 23:20
   pueblo, 1:29, 31, 32
   school at, 16:103-6
   U.S. Flag raised, 1:138; 2:353, 356-57;
      3:109-12; 4:353; 7:82, 84; 9:82;
      10:11; 13:109; 15:58, 243; 16:101;
      17:271, 281; 18:72; 23:358; 25:125,
      193-203
   weather, 16:333-34
   bk. on, rev., 6:195-96; illus., 8: opp.
      154; 11: opp. 195; 12: opp. 347;
      25: opp. 205, 207, opp. 212, 215;
      40: opp. 16
   see also Colton, Walter;
      Constitutional Convention, 1849;
      Monterey Bay

Monterey (schr., 1855), 22:7, 8, 10, 168,
169

Monterey (ship, 1891), 20:135

Monterey Bar (Long's Bar), 30:54

Monterey Bay, 1:173-74; 2:282, 291,
295-96, 311; 3:6, 15, 109-13, 220-21;
7:21, 25, 26, 50-51, 57, 62, 75, 357-59,
361-62, 391; 8:43-54, 56, 100, 154, 244,
290; 9:237-38; 12:41, 139-46, 236;
13:395; 14:4, 230, 321; 15:130, 225-26,
342; 16:102, 213; 20:48, 221; 21:12;
23:203, 211, 303-4; 25:125, 152; 31:110;
36:229, 231, 308, 330, 332; 37:75-76;
illus., 8: opp. 154; map showing, 13:
opp. 61

Monterey Company, 15:356; 16:103,
107, 216-21 *passim*

"Monterey Custom House Flag Pole:
Archaeological Findings," by Richard
K. Beardsley, 25:204-18

Monterey History and Art Association,
28:378; 38:75

"Monterey in 1796," by Henry R. Wagner, 1:173-77
Monterey Library Association, 38:296-97
Monterey River, *see* Salinas River
Monterey Whaling Co., 35:238
Montesclaros, Juan, Marqués de, 8:44-48
Montez, Lola, 6:229, 339-41; 7:285; 8:84; 11:245; 16:337; 20:304, 307; 22:32, 39; 30:108, 333; 32:126; 38:19, 26
Montezuma (place), 2:14, 15; 14:144, 202
Montezuma Hill, 9:61, 75
Montgomery, Allen, 18:36, 37; 29:263
Montgomery, Mrs. Allen (Sarah Armstrong), 18:36-37, 59, 60; 19:119, 120, 121, 137; *see also* Green, Mrs. Talbot H.
Montgomery, Mrs. Edward Geoffrey (Emily Pope), 26:287
Montgomery, G. W., 9:243, 269, 371(?)
Montgomery, George (Nevada Co., 1851), 3:131, 133, 135; 6:229
Montgomery, Arch. George (1879-1952), 31:377
Montgomery, George E., 10:64
Montgomery, John Berrien, 1:79, 81, 92, 179, 180; 2:72, 73; 3:33, 34, 124, 181, 285; 4:303; 5:306; 6:140, 365, 373; 7:79, 80, 83, 84; 8:258; 9:83; 10:11, 101, 105-14 *passim*, 353; 11:137; 14:148; 15:58, 63-65, 69, 306; 16:212, 213; 17:223-30 *passim*, 274, 277, 295; 18:72, 81; 21:11-20 *passim*, 365, 24.40, 71; 25:121-28 *passim*, 130, 196; 26:164; 29:266, 272, 325; 31:207-17 *passim*; address and proc., July 9, 1846, 2:357-58; cor. during Amer. occupation, 1846, 1:80-81, 84-89, 90-91, 182-83, 289; 2:69-71, 356-62; 3:84-86, 187; 5:305-6; 6:265, 267-69, 274-80, 370-73; 8:71-75; 9:85-86; 10:105-6, 108-10; 15:63-65; 17:229, 230; 40:19; bk. on, rev., 38:272-73
Montgomery, Mrs. John Berrien (Mary), 31:215; letter to, 209-10
Montgomery, John Elliott, 31:207; letter from, 209-10
Montgomery, John M., 2:195
Montgomery, Julia Maria, 31:210, 216
Montgomery, R. T., 4:106; 6:64, 65
Montgomery, W., 14:402
Montgomery, Walter, 21:142

Montgomery, Wash., 9:371
Montgomery, William Henry, 31:207, 210,216
Montgomery, Zachariah, 9:245, 246, 248, 271, 345, 363, 365, 370, 377, 381; 10:165, 190, 248, 252-53, 261, 280, 282; 20:165
Montgomery Block, San Francisco, 7:111; 10:295, 393; 16:82, 199; 17:180; 30:247; phot., 7: opp. 111
Montgomery Guard, 10:390
Monticello, 27:20-21
Montieth, George, 28:53
Montmert (S.F., 1850), 6:42
Monumental Mine, 3:259-60
Moo, Dexter, 15:76
Mooar, George, 1:13; 24:79
Moody, Charles, 30:285
Moody, Dwight L., 20:2, 6, 11
Moody, J. A., 13:32
Moody, Joseph Ledlie, 25:337, 344; letter, 13:84-85
Moody, Nellie, 30:285
Moody, R. C., 6:22-25 *passim*, 28
Moody, Ransom Grove, 30:285
Moody, T. F., 9:130, 131, 172
Moody, Volney Delos, 3:7, 285
Moody, Mrs. Volney Delos (Adaline M. Wright), 30:285
Moody's Gulch, 30:285
Moon, Andrew J., 30:1; 31:325, 327
Moon, William C., 18:297, 311; 22:366; 29:136; 30:53, 55, 158; ranch of, 30:53, 54, 56, 158
Mooney (Michigan Bar, 1855), 14.170 71
Mooney (engineer C.P.R.R., 1870s), 18:360; 23:120
Mooney, John, 15:103
Mooney, Lyman, 15:177
Mooney, Pat, 6:225, 226
Mooney, Thomas (Yuba Co., 1851), 3:159, 160; 8:209; 10:362, 367, 370
Mooney, Thomas (S.F., 1862), 10:390; 27:165, 168
Mooney, Thomas J., 36:110
Mooney Flat, 33:201
Moonlight (ship), 23:109
Moonshine Creek, 8:341, 357
Moore, Rev. Mr. (Columbia, 1853), 32:132
Moore (lawsuit, Camptonville, 1857), 9:168
Moore, Mrs. (left S.F., 1866), 36:302
Moore, Benjamin Daviess, 1:140-41,

239, 240; 3:122; 13:305; 17:342-43;
21:198, 201, 216, 218, 221, 335-36;
25:295, 306; 26:29, 34, 36, 40, 44, 58,
60; 33:339-40; family of, 26:60
Moore, Benjamin Franklin, 19:9;
20:102, 105, 115; fac. sig., 10: opp. 159
Moore, C. W., 27:346
Moore, Carrie Augusta, 20:2
Moore, Charles E., 15:34, 36, 56
Moore, Constantine, 22:251
Moore, E. J., 10:197
Moore, Edwin S., address, "Early
Automobiling Days in California,"
32:378-79
Moore, Eli, 20:264; 27:260; mill of,
27:162
Moore, F. (Dutch Flat, 1861), 4:250
Moore, Frank (Grass Valley, 1850s),
6:337-38
Moore, Frank (Sacramento, 1860),
4:240
Moore, Frank M., 23:96
Moore, George, 12:200
Moore, "Gild," 33:364
Moore, H. W., 22:251
Moore, Henry, 29:302, 306
Moore, Inez Macondray, obit. of
Felton B. A. Elkins, 23:185
Moore, Isaiah N., 28:213
Moore, J. J., 17:115
Moore, Jacob B., 1:9; 3:37-38; 9:26, 250;
10:62; 15:179, 182; 20:13, 29, 30, 45
Moore, Jacob G., 18:288
Moore, James (Marysville, 1850),
14:223
Moore, James (Napa Valley, 1850),
29:302, 306
Moore, James A., 28:335, 337
Moore, James Rolph, 32:191
Moore, Jeremiah B., 27:218; 34:323-26
passim
Moore, John, 19:129; 29:302, 306
Moore, John H., 38:49
Moore, John Murray, 23:96
Moore, Joseph (Oahu, 1836), 12:138
Moore, Joseph and Anne (Castle),
32:191
Moore, Joseph Alexander and Mildred
T. (Rolph), 32:191
Moore, Joseph H., 22:115
Moore, Lorraina, 28:378
Moore, Luther B., 9:52, 138, 140, 149,
151, 260, 262, 345, 351; 10:52, 59,
172-77 *passim*, 250, 372(?)
Moore, Maggie, 4:212

Moore, Matthew Joseph, 26:60
Moore, Orlando H., 27:217; 28:169
Moore, Philip, 10:40, opp. 48, 62, 65,
71, 372(?); 11:6, 9, 21; 23:344; 27:250
Moore, Roger, 11:57
Moore, Thomas (Monterey, 1796),
see Muir
Moore, Thomas (Napa Co., 1850),
29:302, 306
Moore, Tredwell, 1:273; 4:11, 13;
5:335; 11:248-49, 253-54, 256, 264;
26:236; 34:209, 215, 217, 219, 226-28;
35:19
Moore, W. S., 18:19-20
Moore, William, 29:234-39 *passim*, 246,
247
Moore, William H., 19:231, 236
Moore, William Whiteside, 30:93
Moore (R. C.) & Co., 20:336
Moore (Walton N.) & Co., 31:297
Moore & Rumrey's, New York Flat,
9:131
Moore Dry Dock Co., 32:191
Moores, W. G., 19:192
Moore's Creek, Napa Co., 35:1, 7, 9,
155, 158, 160; ranch on, 35:2, 7-9,
155-60
Moore's Creek (Deer Creek), Tulare
Co., 11:253-54, 256, 265
Moore's Flat, 13:28; 18:202; 20:254;
29:196; 31:186
Moorhead, Dudley T., 25:286
Moorman, Madison Berryman,
27:180-81; 32:196, 201
Mooser, William, obit. of Nathaniel
Blaisdell, 35:373-74
Mooshake, Frederick and Rebecca
(Lein), 28:294, 295, 296
Moraga, Gabriel, 1:271; 4:4; 10:201;
12:122, 224, 229, 241; 14:197; 16:109;
27:104
Moraga, Joaquín, 30:2, 8-9
Moraga, José Joaquín, 14:5, 7, 12, 99-107
passim, 197; 15:58; 22:223; 27:58,
63-64; 31:280
Moraga, Oliver, 27:64, 336
Moraga, Vincente, 13:215
Moraga Valley, 21:326
"Moral Aspect of California, The, a
Thanksgiving Sermon of 1850," by
Charles A. Farley, 19:299-307
Moral Reform Convention, 16:81
Moran, Capt. (of *Firefly*, 1850), 14:161
Moranda, James, 26:215
Morant, Fanny, 10:75

Morcou, Baron de, 32:117
Mordecai, A., 9:302
More, Alexander, 8:342, 346; 9:54
More, L. B., 10:55; *see also* Moore
More family (Napa Co., 1840s), 35:9
Morea (Sutter's Ft., 1846), 22:221
Morea, Miss (Yuba Co., 1860), 10:256
"More about Railroading in California
    in the Seventies: The Fire Train,"
    from reminiscences of Clarence M.
    Wooster, 22:178-80
Moreau, Adrien, 21:329
Moreau, E., 32:111-14
Morefield, Richard Henry, 35:92;
    "Mexicans in the California Mines,
    1848-53," 35:37-46
Morehead, James G., 25:221
Morehead, Joseph C., 33:260
Morehouse, Charlotte, 31:303
Morelli, Filippo, 21:68
Morelos, Juan de Dios, 4:145-47,
    149-50
Morelos (ship), *see San Carlos*
Morelos y Pavón, José María, 27:132
Morengo (hanged, 1850s), 16:261
Moreno, Carlos, *see* Brown, Charles
Moreno, Felipe, 4:162
Moreno, José (mulatto), 13:201
Moreno, Padre José Matías (d.1781),
    33:13, 15, 16, 19
Moreno (Brown), José Matías, 6:87;
    10:112, 113, 115; 12:319; 13:101-5
    passim, 114-24 *passim*, 130, 131, 132,
    136-41 *passim*, 147; 21:312, 313; 27:108
Moreno, Juan Bautista, 26:31, 32, 33, 36,
    56
Moreno, Luis and Gertrudis (Lesna y
    Urea), 26:56
Moreno, Rafael de Jesús, 12:196; 14:23;
    15:213-14
Moreno, Santiago, 36:19
Moreno, Tomás, 14:253
"More on the Ewing Mutiny," by
    Thornton Emmons and Homer C.
    Votaw, 36:307-11
Morera (pilot of *Golden Hind*), 8:38
Moreton (Yuba Co., 1857), 9:166
Morey, Barton, *see* Mowry, Barton
Morey, N. E., 32:169
Morey, Rinaldo, *see* Mowry, Rinaldo
"More Yerba Buena Days," address by
    Douglas S. Watson, 10:91
Morffew, Thomas, 30:67, 69
Morford, William E., 24:23-24
Morgan (San Blas, 1849), 27:40

Morgan (Marysville, 1861), 10:356
Morgan (Austin, Nev., 1863), 6:347
Morgan, Alfred, 11:165
Morgan, Ben, 37:57
Morgan, Charles H., 17:177
Morgan, Dale Lowell, 40:366-70; bk.
    rev. by, 39:83-85; ed. *California as
    I Saw It*, by McCollum, rev., 40:74-76;
    ed. *The Overland Diary of James A.
    Pritchard*, rev., 38:275-76; phot., 40:
    opp. 366
Morgan, E. L., 15:280
Morgan, Ebeneazer, 35:305
Morgan, George, 19:231
Morgan, George E., 3:111, 112, 119, 120,
    121; 26:49
Morgan, John, 9:137, 174
Morgan, Joseph William, 34:300
Morgan, Martha M., 10:82
Morgan, Mary Jane, *see* Rulofson, Mrs.
    William Herman
Morgan, Matt, theatrical troupe of,
    21:243
Morgan, Michael R., 27:215
Morgan, William, 9:285
Morgan, William O., 25:286
Morgana, Juan de, 3:21, 23-24
Morgan and Muncey mining claim,
    6:347, 350
Morgan, Hathaway & Co., 15:364
Morgan Hill, 13:192
Morgan Valley, 32:370
Morgan *v.* Morgan, 9:359, 360, 368
Morillo, Precipiano, 37:201
Morin, Judge (overland, 1846), 5:395,
    396
Morin, L., 4:310, 317
Morineau, A. de, 18:347, 353
Morita Okataro Kiyoyuki, 23:342
Morley, Charles, 34:381; ed. and trans.
    "The Chinese in California, as
    Reported by Henryk Sienkiewicz,"
    34:301-16
Morley, Grace (McCann), 38:4
Morley, John, 35:358; 36:66
Morley, Sylvanus Griswold, 28:284;
    coauth. "The 1883 Flood on the
    Middle Yuba River," 28:233-42
Mormon Bar, Sacramento Co., *see*
    Mormon I.
Mormon Battalion, 1:249, 252; 5:400;
    6:60-61; 12:351, 356; 13:13, 304, 307,
    330; 15:244-45; 21:193, 198, 222;
    22:47-49, 52-62 *passim*, 141; 23:370;
    25:126, 302; 26:110; 29:248; 32:194-207

passim; 33:99, 108-12 *passim,* 115-22
passim, 250; *see also* Mormons
Mormon Camp, El Dorado Co., 2:189
Mormon Camp, Sacramento Co., *see*
    Mormon Island
Mormon Diggings, 10:301; 11:136;
    13:169; 26:124; 32:194-95; *see also*
    Mormon Island
Mormon Island, 2:186; 3:140; 4:221;
    6:248; 9:88; 13:169, 170, 175; 14:277;
    16:127, 129; 23:58, 354, 370; 26:122,
    124; 30:125; 32:195; 33:351; 34:71-72;
    view, 14: opp. 269, *see also* Mormon
    Diggings
"Mormonism," by Parley P. Pratt,
    broadside, 14: opp. 59
"Mormon Mission to California in 1851,
    A," from Diary of Parley Parker
    Pratt, ed. Reva H. Stanley and
    Charles L. Camp, 14:59-73, 175-82
Mormon Prophet, The (play), 10:255,
    266
Mormons and Mormonism, 1:249; 3:34,
    54, 56-58, 69, 166, 275; 4:87, 282,
    392-93; 5:290, 396; 6:46, 60-61, 117,
    119-22, 126, 362; 9:90, 197; 10:8, 155,
    266, 298-99, 398, 400; 11:129-30, 132,
    355; 12:119, 289, 340, 341, 343, 351, 354,
    356; 13:13, 14, 56, 170, 356; 14:80,
    281; 15:201, 207, 273, 282; 16:85, 130,
    139, 140, 141; 17:36, 295, 296; 18:196,
    198, 200, 202; 19:134, 143, 272, 273,
    274; 21:97, 98, 228, 231; 22:11-13, 15,
    23, 25, 29-30, 32, 52-62 *passim,* 135-41
passim, 146, 150, 162, 163; 24:17, 118,
    123-24, 275; 26:109-17 *passim,* 121-24
passim, 165, 290-91, 324-32 *passim;*
    31:38; 32:196, 204; 33:108; 37:229-38;
    in San Bernardino, 9:197; 14:178-81;
    22:12, 13, 30; 24:275; 29:242-43, 248;
    35:26; service in Los Angeles (1851),
    14:72-73; in San Francisco (1846),
    3:34; (1851), 14:72-73; arts. on,
    14:59-73, 175-82, 269-82; 15:244-46;
    bk. on, rev., 37:369; proclamation,
    14: opp. 59; *see also* Mormon
    Battalion
"Mormons in California," address by
    Charles L. Camp, 9:90
Morman Station, 6:126; 7:7, 9; 9:185;
    34:215; *see also* Genoa
Mormon Tavern, 20:39
Mormon trail, 2:189, 190, 191; 3:47-57;
    24:123; *see also* Mormons
Morning Light (ship), 22:170

Moro, Faustino, 4:152-53
Moro, Tomás, *see* Muir, Thomas
Moro, El, *see* Morro Rock
Morrell, Benjamin, 12:230
Morrell, Hiram C., 28:319
Morrell, Mrs. Hiram C., *see* Burrell,
    Clara
Morrell, John, 30:21
Morrell, Samuel W., 30:361
Morrill, Charles, 22:33
Morrill, Edward, 27:382
Morrill, Joseph C., 33:290, 293, 295, 301,
    302
Morrill, Paul, 9:42
Morris, Albert Ferdinand, "Narrative"
    of, ed. Charles L. Camp, 15:103-38,
    224-41
Morris, Clara, 21:173, 248, 249, 250, 266
Morris, George, 32:191
Morris, George R., 19:321
Morris, John E., 24:382
Morris, John Milton, "History of Las
    Posadas Forest," from memoirs of,
    comp. Edith Gregory, 35:1-9, 155-60
Morris, Mrs. John Milton (Sarah
    Melissa Harmon), 35:2, 6-9, 156
Morris, John W., 24:382
Morris, Joseph, 27:130, 131, 231, 301,
    309
Morris, Louis (S.F., 1855), 16:336
Morris, Louis (L.A., 1856), 30:286
Morris, Milton and Sally (Dodge),
    35:2-5 *passim,* 155, 156; phot., 35: opp.
    1
Morris, Robert, 36:379; "The Mother of
    Alfred Robinson," 36:289-91
Morris, Robert H. and Mrs., 11:15, 26
Morris, Robert M., 26:327-28; 30:57
Morris, Thomas, 33:123
Morris, William, 35:160
Morris, William G., 40:291
Morris, Winnie Sarah, 32:191
Morrish, William Francis, 19:96
Morrison (Sutter's Ft., 1847), 22:221
Morrison (stage driver), *see* Ackley &
    Maurison
Morrison, Alexander Francis, 6:288
Morrison, Mrs. Alexander Francis (May
    Benton Treat), 21:123; 36:151-52;
    obit., 18:381-82
Morrison, George H., 27:194
Morrison, J. H., 39:211
Morrison, J. L., 9:367
Morrison, John, 16:342
Morrison, John C., Jr., 15:50

Morrison, Jonas J., 19:72; 27:315
Morrison, Lewis, 21:246, 251, 256
Morrison, Murray, 19:282, 296;
    32:336-37; "A Glimpse at San
    Francisco in the '50's," 13:80-83;
    family of, 13:80
Morrison, Mrs. Murray (Virginia
    White), 10:296; 13:80, 82
Morrison, R. N., 16:337, 339; 28:34
Morrison, Robert F., 13:80
Morrison, Roderick M., 27:160, 163
Morrison, Thomas and Maggie
    (Middleton), 19:233
Morrison, William, 14:211
Morrison (ship), 5:12
Morris Ravine, 33:295-99, 303, 307
Morristown, 11:240
Morro Redondo, 3:352, 354, 358
Morro Rock, 1:157, 159
Morrow, William W., 36:45
Morse (Sacramento, 1849), 23:349
Morse (Calaveras Co., 1850), 22:71-72,
    75
Morse, Amos C., 3:268-69
Morse, Charles and Mrs. (née Sawyer),
    6:335-36, 350, 353
Morse, Constantine, 22:251
Morse, E. F., 6:213
Morse, E. Malcolm, 28:3
Morse, Edwin Franklin, 9:310; "The
    Story of a Gold Miner"
    (reminiscences), 6:205-37, 332-59;
    port., 6: opp. 332
Morse, Mrs. Edwin Franklin (Abbie
    Robinson), 6:337, 350
Morse, Ephraim W., 31:37
Morse, Frank, 6:335
Morse, George D., 35:50
Morse, H. H., 33:212-13
Morse, Henry D., 6:335, 350
Morse, Henry N., 17:101, 115
Morse, John Alexander, 16:336, 337
Morse, John B., 26:189
Morse, John Frederick, 4:182, 188, 190,
    223; 7:281; 9:36; 10:75; 22:35
Morse, M., 13:31
Morse, P. A., 28:116; 34:242, 251
Morse, Salmi, 21:249-53, 272; 33:374
Morse, Samuel Finley Breese, 34:291
Morse, Samuel Finley Brown, 26:189
Morse (ship), 8:106; 14:320, 342, 344
Mortgage Guarantee Co., 36:158-59
Mortimer, John K., 21:248
Morton, Laura Ann, 14:83
Morton, Lemuel, 14:297, 298

Morton, Thomas H., 15:180
Morton's Drayage Co., 35:67-68, 145-47
Morton's Special Delivery Co., 35:67-68
Mory, *see* Mowry
Moscow (ship), 1:231, 289; 4:391; 6:371;
    8:297; 14:345; 15:58, 62; 22:54; 25:124;
    29:271
Moselle, La (ship), 15:269
Mosely (or Moseley), Sam (1847),
    33:104
Moses (Colorado R., 1850), 22:20
Moses, Bernard, 1:13, 14, 16, 17, 21;
    24:79; 35:256
Moses, H. A., 9:251, 269
Moses, Israel, 34:35, 36
Moses, Phoebe, 26:167
Moses, William S., 6:69, 71-76 *passim;*
    7:125; 29:291-92
Moses Taylor (ship), 21:60; 33:2
Mosk, Sanford Alexander, "Price-Fixing
    in Spanish California," 17:118-22
Mosley (Mosely?), Ben, 10:286
Mosquito Creek, 29:193, 205
Mosquitoes, 2:183-85, 195; 5:126, 128;
    8:5, 18-21, 25, 167; 11:256; 12:32,
    95-96, 305; 13:71; 20:33-34; 23:33-35,
    37, 123-25, 130, 132, 367, 369; 27:298,
    364; 29:14, 300; 30:42
Moss, D. H., letters from, 24:119-20,
    125, 355
Moss, J. Mora, 4:226; 17:46; 19:231;
    25:344; 27:71
Moss, John, 3:167; 12:12
Moss, Samuel, Jr., 7: opp. 110
Moss, Sidney Walter, 4:283
Mota, Raimundo de la, 11:359, 361, 362
"Mother of Alfred Robinson, The,"
    by Robert Morris, 36:289-91
Mother's Trust, The (play), 15:165
Motherwell, Robert Burns II, 22:95;
    obit., 22:285
Moth Island, 17:149; 20:214
Moti (Indian, 1836), 16:249, 355
Mott (Marysville, 1851), 8:211
Mott, Edward M., 36:44
Mott, Gertrude (Mrs. Frank K.), *A
    Handbook for Californiacs*, rev.,
    5:403
Mott, Gordon N., 9:42, 159, 163, 179,
    380; 10:60, 395; 11:63; 14:397; 15:28,
    35
Mott, Valentine, Jr., 15:181
Mott, Talbot & Co., 2:352
Mott-Smith, Mrs. Ernest A. (Anne
    Elizabeth Paty), 14:339; 22:288

Mott-Smith, J., 13:32
Motzko, John J., 24:72
Moulder, Andrew Jackson, 9:104, 106, 108; 15:179, 281; 19:156, 230, 236; 29:107; 33:306
Moulin (from Paris, 1849), 22:304
Moulis, Abbé, 22:301
Moulthrop, C. W., 16:81, 84
Moulthrop, Robert, 8:346
Moulton, D. Stellifer, 2:240-41
Moulton, Joseph, 18:174
Moultrie, J. A., 26:247
Mounds, The, Ventura Co., 16:298, 303
Mount, Charles E., 10:62
Mountain, Thomas, 15:173
"Mountain Bill," 18:163
"Mountain Charley," *see* McKiernan, Charles
Mountain Commercial Co., 35:346
Mountain Cottage Hotel, 8:352, 363
Mountain Democrat, Placerville, 20:162
Mountain Echo, Downieville, 9:173
"Mountain Echoes" (MS serial), 28:317
"Mountaineers, The" (musical troupe), 15:164
Mountaineers, The (play), 15:278
Mountain Herald, Yreka, 23:207; 28:216, 225, 230, 231
Mountain Home, Grass Valley, 11:244
Mountain Home, Santa Clara Co., 29:43-57 *passim*, 173-78
Mountain Home Ranch, San Mateo Co., 31:300-301, 305
Mountain House, Goodyear's Hill, 8:363; 9:392
Mountain Lake Water Co., 10:378, 391; 11:390; 17:175, 177
Mountain [stage] Line, 14:402
Mountain man, dress of, 3:75
Mountain Meadows, 20:345; massacre, 14:60, 65; 19:271-74; 21:231; 29:243, 248; 32:322, 325
Mountain Messenger, Downieville, quoted, 18:306-7
Mountain View Cemetery, Oakland, 24:172; 30:248
Mount Diablo Base Line, 34:3-11
Mounted Coast Riflemen, 34:269
Mount Hope [mining] Co., 6:334; 12:72; 19:28
Mountjoy, Miss (Sacramento, 1858), 9:254
Mount Ophir Mine, 11:243
Mount Shasta City, 7:124
Mount Vernon (ship), 12:30

Mouravieff (or Murav'ev), M. N., 12:191, 235
Mourelle de la Rua, Francisco Antonio, 9:205-8, 221, 226, 227, 228, 240-41; 10:337; 40:109-14, 116; map, 40: foll. 112
Mouser, Silas M., 30:67
Mouton (San Jose, 1851), 35:316
"Moving Mirror of the Overland Trail," James Wilkins', 33:29, 32-38; adv., 33:35
Mowe, George W., 10: opp. 48; 27:168
Mowry, Barton, 14:175, 176, 177, 182
Mowry, George E., 36:114; address, "The Johnson-Hughes Incident of 1916," 25:185-87
Mowry, Rinaldo, 14:72, 73, 175, 176, 182
Mowry, Sylvester, 6:32; 9:307, 317; 18:205-6, 209; 38:339
Moxley, W. A., 24:288
Moya y Contreras, Pedro, 2:141; 7:239-40, 243, 245, 248, 253, 256, 275
Moyes, R. B., 29:195
Mozart Music Hall, San Francisco, 21:163
Moziño (botanist, 1792), 2:257
"Mrs. Lillie Hitchcock Coit," address by Floride Green, 12:366
M. S. Latham (ship), 20:186
Much Ado about Nothing, 15:278
Muck, Karl, 25:245, 246
Muckles, Joseph P., 8:203(?), 358
Mud Lake, 22:202, 214
"Mudsills," *see* Democratic Party
Mud Springs (sou. Calif.), 12:6; 16:296, 302
Mud Springs (later El Dorado), 8:201, 210; 15:377
Müggenborg, J. H. C., 9:318-31
Müller (Minal, 1846), 11:43
Mueller, Baron Ferdinand von, 26:280; 32:246-47
Muerhead, James, 34:159
Muertos, Punta de los, 4:144, 167; 9:6; 31:34
Mugan, William D., 38:66
Mugártegui, Pedro Pablo, 1:162, 164
"Mugbooks," 38:133-35, 138
Muggeridge, Edward James, *see* Muybridge, Eadweard J.
Mugu Lagoon, 7:24, 70
Muir, Andrew Forest, 34:381; "Note on Twain and Rising," 34:317-22
Muir, Henry, 31:331
Muir, John, 1:284; 3:207-8; 4:12, 27-31,

35, 43, 53, 55; 5:338; 15:289; 20:2;
21:183; 23:122; 25:178-79, 190; 33:245,
306; 38:249-56 *passim;* art. on,
17:18-20
Muir, Mrs. John (Louie Wanda
Strentzel), 4:295
Muir, Thomas, 1:175; 10:320; bk. on,
rev., 38:274-75
Muir, William S., 14:278
Mula Mill, 38:62
Mulberry trees, 31:335, 336, 339, 341
Mulder, William, coed. *Among the
Mormons,* rev., 37:369
Muldoon, J. P., 10:266
Muldrew, William, 12:200
Muldrow *v.* Norris, 25:223
Mulege, Lower Calif., 13:101, 114-15,
140, 145, 146
Mule Hill, 26:47-51 *passim,* 58, 61;
33:102; phot., 26: opp. 46
Mules, 1:113, 120, 121, 165, 219; 2:198,
335; 4:33; 5:134, 170, 217, 228; 8:342;
11:324; 12:249, 260, 262, 274; 13:202,
211; 14:5, 6, 334; 16:242; 17:340, 344;
18:149; 20:341-43; 21:196, 200-20
passim, 333, 337-42 *passim;* 22:13;
23:170, 252, 263; 24:121; 26:23, 47-50
passim, 298; 28:204, 212, 218; 33:189,
344-45; 34:22; 36:132; meat, as food,
1:120; 17:344; 26:47, 50
Mulford, C. W., 38:308
Mulford, Prentice, 11:170; 18:281;
21:170; 33:324; 38:307-8
Mulford, Samuel B., 9:346; 10:59;
14: opp. 209, 377, 379, 380, 382;
15:21, 28, 49
Mulholland (Marysville, 1862), 10:375
Mulholland, C., 4:49, 54; 9:195
Mulholland, I. H., 9:195
Mulholland, "Shorty," 27:117-18
Mulholland, William, 19:186; 27:122
Mulkey, Cyrus, 4:33
Mulkey, J. L., 4:320
Mulkins, Andrew, 36:119
Mulkins, John, 34:207; 36:119, 128
Mullaly, Joseph, 13:330; 29:234
Mullaly, Thornwall, 36:74
Mullen, Arthur, 39:133
Mullen *v.* Mullen, 9:266, 357, 358
Mulligan, William ("Billy"), 6:50;
8:366-72 *passim;* 9:26, 31; 14:358;
16:346; 17:81-83, 173, 182; 23:71;
37:157, 159-60
Mullins, Catherine, 33:94
Mullot & Tallot, 5:13, 42, 346

Mulloy, James, 17:83
Mull Ranch, 33:296
Mulnaer (Trinity Co., 1850), 5:228, 235
Muloch, Dinah Maria (?), 4:209
Mulqueen, Miss or Mrs. (d. S.F., 1855),
15:376
Mumford, E. Philpott, "Early History
of Cotton Cultivation in California,"
6:159-66
Mummy, The (minstrel show), 20:305
Muncey, Jack, 6:347
Munch (Marysville, 1858), 9:363, 364
Muncio, Claudia, 25:250
Mundell, J. E., 31:128
Munger, Asahel, 18:309
Munger, Mary, *see*
Carpenter, Mrs. Harvey C.
Municipal government (to 1850), *see*
Alcaldes; Ayuntamiento
Munie, Alexander, 32:110
Munk, Joseph Amasa, *Activities of a
Lifetime,* rev., 3:201-2
Muñoz, Juan Antonio, 15:343, 347-48,
356, 358, 362
Muñoz, Juan Bautista, 31:219
Muñoz, Pedro, 1:166
Munrás, Estevan, 16:217
Munrás, Salvador, 35:107
Munro, Perly, 26:129
Munson, Miss M., 10:246, 260
Munz, Philip R., rev. of Howell *et al.,
A Flora of San Francisco,* 37:371
Muragaki, Awaji-no-kami, 23:342
Murayama Osamoto Atsushi, 23:342
Murchison, Charles F. (George
Osgoodby),
Murden, Lyman P., 20:44
Murderer's Bar, 39:105; address on, by
Wendell T. Robie, 35:75; letters
from, 39:102-3, 106-9
Murdoch, Francis B., 9:116; 22:224
Murdoch, James E., 20:304
Murdock, A. H., 9:42
Murdock, Charles Albert, 5:202; 20:4,
6, 8; 33:374; 38:308-9; address,
"The Real Bret Harte," 4:95
Murdock, John, 14:61, 67, 71, 73, 175-76
Murdock, William, 31:313
Murguia, José Antonio, 1:161; 3:208
Murieta, Joaquín, 5:313; 7:195; 8:83;
10:86; 11:82, 182, 386; 13:327, 329, 330;
15:57, 300; 16:305; 21:362(?); 23:367,
369; 26:383; 28:338; 29:277; Ridge's
Life of, 16:256-62; 22:30, 36;
27:244-46; 30:251, 353; bks. on, rev.,

5:203; 11:386; head of (poster), 11: opp. 386; 15:277

Murillo, Peter, 30:226, 230

Murphey, Edith V. A., 20:384; "Out of the Past, a True Indian Story," told by Lucy Young to, 20:349-64

Murphy (Yuba Co., 1857), 9:152; 10:172, 173, 251, 360

Murphy, Mrs. (Marysville, 1858), 9:358

Murphy, Miss (Sucker Flat, 1860), 10:256

Murphy, Bernard, 16:282; 34:232

Murphy, Bernard D., 24:89

Murphy, Con T., 21:166

Murphy, Daniel, 2:185(?), 190, 198; 14:163; 18:158, 159, 173

Murphy, Daniel C., 36:253; obit. of Charles A. Sullivan, 7:413

Murphy, Daniel T., 30:208, 209

Murphy, Evelyn A., obit., 24:89

Murphy, Harriet, *see* Nye, Mrs. Michael C.

Murphy, J., 11:11, 25

Murphy, J. F., 17:176

Murphy, J. Philip, 24:288

Murphy, James, 13:191; 16:282; 34:232

Murphy, John (1846), 1:292, 293; 2:72, 73; 17:227, 228

Murphy, John (S.F., 1854), 15:163

Murphy, John J., 30:359

Murphy, John L., 4:41

Murphy, John M., 2:185(?), 188; 13:29; 14:149; 16:127(?); 17:277, 278; 18:158, 159, 173

Murphy, Mrs. John M. (Virginia E. Backenstoe), 19:139

Murphy, Joseph, 4:62; 21:51, 163, 173

Murphy, Martin, 13:191; 14:17, 415; 18:173; 24:89; grandchildren of, 13:191-92

Murphy, Martin, Jr., 7:79; 24:89; 25:122; 29:262; 33:350; 36:14; children of, 13:191

Murphy, Mary, *see* Covillaud, Mrs. Charles

Murphy, Mary Ann, 13:191

Murphy, Michael, 26:204

Murphy, Patrick W., 13:191; 20:270; 36:14, 16; 38:262

Murphy, Richard, 13:31

Murphy, S., 29:104, 108

Murphy, Sarah A. C., *see* Foster, Mrs. William M.

Murphy, Thomas R., 15:317, 323

Murphy, Timothy, 5:305; 16:249; 17:164; 23:176; 28:260

Murphy, William G., 14:205

Murphy, Mount, 26:114

Murphy and Mack Minstrels, 21:163

Murphy, Grant & Co., 30:208, 209

Murphy's [Camp], Calaveras Co., 5:229; 11:57, 172, 229, 327, 329-30; 14:132, 141; 17:3-17; 22:70-76 *passim*, 82; 31:287; 38:309

Murphy's, Santa Clara Co., 14:168

Murphy's Minstrels, 21:51

Murray (Yuba Co., 1856), 9:59, 60, 143, 144, 145, 152, 159, 168, 169, 255, 355, 369, 373(?); 10:285; *see also* Lewis & Murray

Murray, Misses (Marysville, 1858), 9:374

Murray, Edward, 11:378, 382; 35:17(?), 20(?)

Murray, Mrs. Edward, 35:19

Murray, Edward F., 32:263-64, 267

Murray, Frank, *see* Sullivan, "Yankee"

Murray, G. W., 15:281

Murray, George, 30:109, 256, 265

Murray, Mrs. George H. (Irma Clevenger), 20:192

Murray, Hugh Campbell, 6:11; 7:109; 9:42-43, 45, 389-90; 15:148, 204, 211, 377; 16:81, 83; 26:334, 345, 348; 34:253; art. on, 20:365-73

Murray, James, 2:122

Murray, John (Marysville, 1851), 15:37

Murray, John (S.F., 1854) and Susan (Bain), 28:294

Murray, John Frederick Alexander, 22:36

Murray, Keith A., *The Modocs and Their War*, rev., 38:374-76

Murray, Michael, 2:188

Murray, R. J., 8:357

Murray, Robert, 1:219, 229, 252, 254, 256, 264; 33:252-69 *passim*, 337-38, 340-41, 344; 34:25, 28, 31

Murray, Thomas, 15:271

Murray, Walter, 1:17; 10:50, 62, 71; 18:177, 270, 277

Muscatel Estate, 25:174

Musgrove, J. D., 16:184

Musical Association of San Francisco, 25:229-54

Musical Hall, San Francisco, 15:163-80 *passim*, 266, 276, 366, 368, 374; 16:81, 84, 182, 337; 17:82, 176, 181; 19:236; 25:335, 342; 38:19

Musser, J. J., 21:232-33
Musso (Napa Co., 1878), 35:7-8, 155
"Mustang," *see* Freanor, James L.
Mustard, 4:363, 365; 8:165, 166, 246;
　12:193; 16:298; 17:336; 22:245-46
Mutiny: on *Ewing*, 30:39-47; on
　Susan Drew, 1:212-15
"Mutiny on the Ewing," by
　Erwin G. Gudde, 30:39-47
Mutual Orchard Co., 27:342
Mutual Savings Bank, 31:304
Muybridge, Eadweard J., 4:188; 35:50
Muybridge, Mrs. Eadweard J. (Flora
　Stone), 35:50
Muygridge, E. J., 30:365; *see also*
　Muybridge
"My Dear Governor: Letters
　Exchanged by Theodore Roosevelt
　and Hiram Johnson," by Ashbrook
　Lincoln, 38:229-47
Myers (Sacramento, 1851), 6:51
Myers, Harriet (Kelley), 25:94
Myers, Harry, 13:84
Myers, William, 30:54, 61
Mygatt, Milton and Helen (Young),
　27:286
"My Itinerary," by Thomas O. Larkin,
　ed. Robert J. Parker, 16:11-29, 144-71
Mylar, Isaac L., *Early Days at . . .
　San Juan Bautista*, rev., 8:383-84
My Partner (play), 34:363
Myrick, Alexander, 29:258

Myrick, David F., 28:285
Myrick, Mary E., 28:294
Myrick, T. S. (?), 10:281, 378
Myrtle, Fred S., 2:67
My Seventy Years in California, by
　Graves, rev., 7:90
"Mysterious Chapter in the Life of
　John A. Sutter, A," ed. Doyce B.
　Nunis, Jr., 38:321-27
"Mythical Johnston Conspiracy, The,"
　by Benjamin F. Gilbert, 28:165-73
Music:
　bands, 1:235, 238; 7:396; 14:392, 393;
　　15:181, 267; 16:82, 267, 282;
　　19:229; 20:244-51 *passim*; 24:263;
　　38:18
　instrumental, 8:171; 9:249, 359;
　　15:45-46, 47, 165, 169, 267; 16:83,
　　283, 337; 17:82; 19:236; 20:243-56
　　passim; 22:31; 25:229-54, 284-85,
　　341; 26:361-62; 28:37-38; 33:341;
　　38:20; *see also* San Francisco
　　Symphony
　military, 38:20
　at Missions, 13:34; 23:361-62; 25:138;
　　30:51; 37:98-99, 101, 250, 256
　vocal, 4:59-61, 207-9; 6:339; 8:147;
　　9:373, 388-89, 393, 395-96; 10:42,
　　68-69, 201; 15:46, 47, 164, 166;
　　16:84, 337; 17:82, 181; 19:236;
　　20:248, 300; 23:5; 25:238; 38:19;
　　see also Minstrels; Operas; Songs

N

Nadeau, Remi A., 13:345; 17:115,
　215-16; *Los Angeles from Mission to
　Modern City*, rev., 40:355-56
Nadeshda (schr., 1870s), *see*
　Alice Haake
Nadezhda (ship, 1806), 12:207
Naffziger, Howard Christian, obit.,
　40:273-74
Naffziger, Mrs. Howard Christian
　(Louise McNear), 40:273
Naffziger, Lizzie (Scott), 40:273
Nagel, Louis, 27: opp. 97
Nagle, Capt. (Colorado R., 1855),
　22:168, 169
Naglee, Henry Morris, 1:212-14, 229,
　248-49; 11:163; 15:164, 273, 280;

16:84, 282, 285, 341, 343; 17:85, 168,
　170, 172, 175, 177, 180; 20:109; 40:307;
　bank of, 23:176
Naglee *v.* Cohen and Palmer, Cook &
　Co., 17:172, 180
Nagy, Sandor, 28:132
Nahl, Arthur, *see* Nahl, Hugo Wilhelm
　Arthur
Nahl, Charles Christian, 9:138, 280,
　385; 11:235, 239; 15:383; 16:343;
　22:30, 39; 30:127, 137, 358; art. on,
　15:295-305; paintings by, 15: opp.
　295; foll. 126; 27: opp. 319
Nahl, Hugo Wilhelm Arthur, 15:296,
　300, 302, 305; 29:120
Nahl, Perham Wilhelm, 15:296, 302-3

Nahl, Virgil, 15:303
Nahl family, 15:295-96, 302-5
Naiad Queen, The (play), 10:250, 262-63; 15:181
Naile, Henry, 15:120, 122, 137
Naileigh, William Hill, 21:238
Naiqueret, Paul, 35:320
Nakahama, Manjiro, 23:336
Names, geographic, *see* Place names
"Naming of the Elector-Designate, Santa Barbara, 1830," ed. and trans. Pablo Avila, 27:333-38
Namur, N., 9:397
Namura, Gohachiro, 23:342
Naniwa kan (ship), 25:49, 50
Nan, the Good for Nothing (play), 9:369
"Nantucket to the Golden Gate in 1849," ed. Helen I. Oehler, 29:1-18, 167-72, 255-60
Napa, 2:136; 6:63; 15:189, 235; 16:131; 18:173; 36:295-96; 38:312; church, 27:308
Napa (ship), 15:178
Napa College, 31:1, 4
Napa County, 22:359; Centennials Committee, 26:280
Napa Creek and River, 23:20; 24:57
"Napa leather," 33:69
Napa [sulphur] Springs, 13:83; 15:72, 158
Napa Valley, 2:54-62, 65; 5:127, 135-36, 273; 6:62-68; 7:289; 12:295, 302; 13:266; 16:122, 131-34, 348; 18:70; 23:294, 296; 30:311; 34:25-26
Napier, M. K. (or W. K.), 8:358; 10:56, 359, 368, 383, 394
Napier (ship), 29:105
Napoleon First (play), 10:246, 259-60
Napoleon III, 13:40-41; 15:366; 17:234; 35:318-19
Naponi (Indian, 1850s), 36:314
Narcisse (play), 21:146; 36:212
Narjot, Ernest Etienne, 15:283; 30:137
Narragansett (ship), 27:179; 33:236
Narrative of Nicholas "Cheyenne" Dawson, rev., 12:176-77
Naruse Genshiro Masanori, 23:342
Narváez, José María, 24:312
Narváez, Pedro, 3:186; 4:375; 11:206; 35:105
Nasatir, Abraham Phineas, 27:185; 31:189; 37:66; 39:6, 146, 147, 150; "Guillaume Patrice Dillon," 35:309-24; ed. and trans. "Alexandre

Dumas fils and the Lottery of the Golden Ingots," 33:125-42; ed. "The French Consulate in California, 1843-1856," 11:195-223, 339-57; 12:35-64, 155-72, 331-57; 13:56-79, 159-75, 262-80, 355-85; ed. and trans. "A French Pessimist in California," 31:139-48, 253-60, 307-24; ed. and trans. "The Second Incumbency of Jacques A. Moerenhout," 27:141-48, 203-14, 353-60; 28:69-79, 151-60; bk. revs. by, 13:184; 40:71-73
Nash, Jacob, 18:199
Nash, James, 15:29
Nash, John H., 6:144; 10:23; 14:278; 28:267; 31:217; 40:24
Nash, John Henry, 21:282; 25:382
Nash, Joseph, 33:374
Nash, William B., 9:368
Nash & Davis, 30:111
Nashville (ship), 20:194
Naslednik Alexander (ship), 7:106; 12:275; 14:143
Nast, Thomas, 34:353
Natalia (ship), 13:35; 16:238; 29:26
Natalie, La (ship), 31:314
Nataqua (prop. territory), 9:180; 10:74; 18:304-5; art. on, 21:225-38
Natchez, 8:340, 356; 9:69; 15:39, 57
Nathan, Paul D., trans. *The San Sabá Papers*, rev., 39:271-72
National, Grass Valley, 9:382
National, San Francisco, 11:10
National, Le (weekly), 39:5, 151, 160-62, 165, 219-21, 321, 349
National Aqueduct, 29:194
National Circus, *see* Lee and Marshall's Circus; Bennett's National Circus
National Democrat, Marysville, 9:287, 351, 380-91 *passim;* 10:189-200 *passim;* 30:130; 33:203; 34:49-50
National Exchange Hotel, Nevada City, 10:384, 394; 33:375
National Guard, California, *see* California National Guard
National Guards, San Francisco, *see* Independent National Guard; Nationals
National Hotel, Camptonville, 9:166, 180
National House, Marysville, 14:394
National Insurance Co., 26:355; 27:67, 168, 270
Nationalists (French immigrants), 5:21
National Lancers, San Francisco,

15:164, 168, 174, 364, 373; 16:83;
37:363, 364, 367
"National Park Service," address by
Newton Drury, 29:184-85
Nationals, The, 34:324-31 *passim;*
see also Independent National Guard,
San Francisco
National Society of Sons of
Revolutionary Sires, 29:289
National Society of Sons of the
American Revolution, 29:290-95
National Theater, Downieville, 38:19
National Theater, Sacramento, 9:252,
270, 277, 377; 10:42, 368; 21:44;
illus., 10: opp. 48
National Theatre, San Francisco,
14:133; 20:293
Native American Party, 9:18; 22:115;
23:74; *see also* Know Nothing Party
Native Sons of the Golden West,
2:368-69; 4:399; 29:94, 381; 39:177
Natividad, 15:116-22 *passim,* 233, 234,
241; *see also* Natividad, Battle of;
Ranchos: Natividad
Natividad, Battle of, 12:58, 332-33;
13:52; 18:169, 173; 19:120, 132, 138,
141; 21:3; 25:145-46; 29:337-39
Natividad Island, 3:313, 350, 376; on
map, 7: opp. 333
Natoma, 14:269, 278, 282; 26:109, 112;
see also Brighton
Natoma Vineyard Co., 31:377
Naturalization, 32:316-17, 322-23
Naud, Edouard, 13:315, 345
Naudet (de Courcelle; S.F., 1850),
5:36, 42, 142, 143, 144, 155-77 *passim*
Nauman, George, 21:104
Nauvoo, 26:291
Nava, Diego de la, 27:310
"Naval Conquest in the Pacific: The
Journal of Lt. Tunis ... Craven ...
1846-49," ed. John H. Kemble,
20:193-234
Navarrete, Bernardo, 12:146; 15:347,
352-53, 356, 358-59
Navarrete, Martín Fernández de, 3:314,
384, 387; 7:60-61; 8:33; 10:319
Navarro, José Antonio and María
Rufina Dorotea (1781), 13:200
Navarro, José Antonio (1836), 15:356
Navarro, Joseph, 12:138
Navarro, Marcelo, 15:356
Navarro (place), 32:366
Navarro River, 23:25; 33:362, 363, 366
Navidad, Puerto de, 3:394; 6:318, 324,

325; 7:22, 41, 54, 55, 58, 137-42 *passim,*
151, 172-76 *passim,* 190, 243, 256, 302,
377; 8:66; on map, 7:301
"Navies in the Pacific, 1861-65," address
by Benjamin F. Gilbert, 27:178-80
Naylor, E. Y., 32:170
Nazarene (ship), 15:370
N. B. Palmer (ship), 33:325-26;
34:72-73, 74
Neafie, A. J., 15:171, 186, 266
Neahr, David, 22:152
Neal (Berkeley, 1850s), 31:333
Neal (Yuba Co., 1857), 9:147, 160
Neal, Alex, Attey, Calvin, George, and
J. (Robert?), 4:310
Neal, Jack, 25:222
Neal, Mrs. Jane Frances, 1:281
Neal, Peter, 4:310
Neal, Samuel, 6:88, 89, 182, 191, 374;
14:206, 210, 226; 18:299
Neale, John H., 21:232, 238
Neall, James and Hannah (Lloyd),
31:241-52, 286; phot., 31: opp. 241
Neall, Maybelle Elizabeth, 31:243, 286
Neall family, 31:241-52 *passim*
Neasham, Vernon Aubrey, 25:284;
26:130, 134, 135, 150; 40:99;
"California's Influence upon the
Constitution of Argentina," 16:43-47;
"The Raising of the Flag at
Monterey ... 1846," 25:193-203;
"Sutter's Sawmill," 26:109-33;
addresses: "Alaska: Historic Links
with California," 30:378-79;
"Early-Day Transportation ... in the
West," 35:75; "Tracing the Coronado
Trail," 25:372; phot., 39: opp. 80
Neblett, Edward, 9:269
Nebraska Colony, 25:175
Ned, "Captain" (Indian), 26:201
"Ned, the Ubiquitous," by
Carl I. Wheat, 6:3-36
Née, Louis, 3:215, 233; 18:336
Need, William, 34:131
Needham, James C., 38:250, 251
Needles (place), 22:162-63
Neelands, Lucia T., *El Toroso,* rev.,
6:99-101
Neer, Mrs. Mary, 30:285
Neff, Jacob Hart, 18:359; 38:356
Negbauer (or Neugebauer), & Co.,
30:107, 109, 112-13, 257, 366; *see also*
Negbauer & Lord
Negbaur & (D.S.) Lord, 30:102, 107
Negley, *see* Naglee

Negrete, Gen. (Durango, 1821), 2:342

Negro Bar, 4:222, 223; *see also* Folsom

Negroes, 1:214; 5:143; 6:217, 223; 7:307, 381; 8:211, 340, 342, 343; 9:140, 144, 167, 286; 11:223, 332; 15:31, 266, 275, 277; 16:346; 17:44, 80, 135; 18:101, 132; 20:298; 21:33, 55, 242; 22:226, 259, 266, 271; 23:155, 270, 351-52; 24:105, 158, 195-98 *passim;* 26:129; 27:114; 28:292, 293; 29:26; 35:215; 36:113; 38:303-4; on Isthmus of Panama, 27:35; 29:10-11; at Los Angeles, 13:316. 200, 201, 202, 312, 316-17, 332-33; legislation to exclude, 9:256, 257, 258, 281-82; 10:151-52; 20:103; testimony in courts, 16:285, 339; 22:225; 32:308, 312

Negro (or Nigger) Slide, 8:211, 338, 355

Negro (or Nigger) Tent, 8:202, 211; 9:172

Neidy, John, 7:118

Neil (Neilsburgh, 1861), 4:250

Neil, Conrad, 14:177

Neil (or Neal), William W. and Sophia (Louderback), 28:293

Neilson, Adelaide, 21:171, 254, 259, 273

Neilson, Mrs. William Delaware, *see* Elkins, Mrs. William L., Jr.

Nekafer, T., 33:153

Neligh, Robert B., 2:191, 194, 195

Nelson (steamship agt., Panama, 1849), 13:391; 29:5

Nelson (d. Mex., 1850), 1:60

Nelson, Mrs. (S.F., 1861), 27:151

Nelson, Capt. (of *Otago*, 1887), 22:352

Nelson, Alfred, 10:178-79, 200

Nelson, Andrew, 18:373; 29:190-91

Nelson, Ariel, 14:222

Nelson, Carry, 10:178, 179, 200

Nelson, Charles, 9:134

Nelson, Cornelius, 15:375

Nelson, Hans C. and Mrs. (née Jones), 27:189

Nelson, Isaac Magnus and Bridget (Murphy), 27:280

Nelson, John, 2:92, 109, 120, 121

Nelson, Nelson Olsen, 31:16-17, 24, 28

Nelson, Sara, 10:178, 179, 200

Nelson, Thomas, 22:251

Nelson, William, 9:5; 13:391, 392

Nelson, William J., 1:60

Nelson Creek, 26:297; 29:299, 304, 305

"Nemo" (pseud. Henri de Pène), 39:160

"Nemo, Sylvain," *see* Bergerot, Pierre Alexandre

"Neptune" (on ships), 1:214; 2:92

Neptune (ship), 6:257, 259, 260

Neptune Hose Co. No. 1, Sacramento, 20:370

Neptune Insurance Co., 26:256, 258

Neptune's Car (ship), 15:277

Nerio (Indian, 1847), 26:110

Nesbett, B. R., *see* Nisbet, Benjamin R.

Nesbitt, James, 20:294

Nesmith, J. F., 6:346, 354-55

Nesmith, James Willis, 5:69-70; 10:254, 266; 16:53-54; 17:314, 323; 28:162, 168

Netherlands, 20:50, 54; emigration from, 20:68, 76; *see also* Dutch

Neuberg, Anna, 27:94

Neugebauer, *see* Negbaur

Neuhaus, Eugen, "Charles Christian Nahl," 15:295-305; address, "Some Pioneer Artists of California," 15:383

Neu-Helvetien, by Sutter, ed. Gudde, rev., 14:185-86

Neumann, A. and Marie (Cordua), 12:298-99

Neumiller, Charles L., 36:253

Neuval, A., 39:153

Neuval, F. N., 39:159-60

Nevada: before 1849, 9:184-85; 1859-64, 7:112-20, 341-44; 8:194; 23:229; 30:376-77; 1870-90, 2:260-61; 7:118; camels in, 6:347; 9:310, 312, 334; Constitutional Convention and Senatorial elections, 11:48-49; taxes, 38:353; Territory, 12:323-24; *see also* Comstock Lode; Nataqua; Virginia City; Washoe

Nevada (riv. str.), 32:223

Nevada (play), 34:364

Nevada Bank, San Francisco, 17:79-80; 25:22

Nevada City, 10:247, 351, 384-85, 394; 11:229; 21:189; 30:112, 259; in 1850s, 3:129-33, 146; 6:246, 341; 8:343, 359; 11:229, 232-40 *passim;* 13:27; 14:385; 30:112; 32:55; 33:55; 38:38; bookstores, 30:112, 260, 266, 360; bridge, 19:146; churches and ministers, 1:198; 30:259; 32:54, 125-32 *passim;* fires, 3:130; 8:359; 11:236; 15:272; newspapers, 10:394; 28:233-42; 29:199-200, 207; 30:360; rain and snow, 10:351; 11:237;

30:126; railroad, 18:355-56, 359;
views of, 6: opp. 246; 9: opp. 68
Nevada City Library Association,
38:308-9
Nevada Colony, 25:35-36
Nevada County, 40:305; hydraulic
mining in, 29:193-209 *passim;* 33:56;
railroad, 18:355-56
Nevada County Bible Society, 32:129
Nevada County Mining Review,
29:208-9
Nevada County Women's Suffrage
Association, 33:376
Nevada Falls, Yosemite, 1:281
Nevada Irrigation District, 28:233;
29:197-99
Nevada Literary Depot, 30:360-61, 367
Nevada Power House, 29:202
Nevada Warehouse & Dock Co.,
27:199
Neve, Felipe de, 1:25, 26; 4:146;
13:198-201, 204; 14:4-7; 15:219;
17:118, 121, 122; 19:158-59; 22:223;
33:278; 34:195, 205; 40:12; Pitic
instructions of, 30:323, 324
Nevett (Nevitt, Novett), Joseph H.,
11:109(?); 27:260, 265, 361-62, 363;
28:62; 34:211(?)
Nevett, Mrs. S. F., boardinghouse of,
10:277, 278, 292
Nevill (or Neville), James H., 8:182
Neville, Amelia Ransome (Mrs.
Thomas J.), 11:127; 30:82; 34:334-35
Nevin, Andrew N. (or M.), 21:307
Nevins, Allan, *Frémont, the West's
Greatest Adventurer,* rev., 7:88-89
Nevins, Thomas Jefferson, 21:363,
364, 366; 33:308
Nevitt, J. H., 34:211; *see also*
Nevett, Joseph H.
New Albion, 16: No. 1, Pt. 2, pp. 1, 2,
9, 11, 16, 19, 24, 30, 44
New Almaden Cavalry, 40:305
New Almaden Co., 14:168, 169; 15:4-15
passim, 19; 16:199-200; *see also*
New Almaden Mine
New Almaden Mine, 5:191, 269;
6:249-50, 368; 10:191; 12:35; 13:58-62
passim, 77-78, 79; 14:157-59, 168, 169,
172, 265-66, 346; 15:268; 16:199-200;
20:121, 125; 28:267; 29:201; 35:43;
36:293; 39:42, 49, 50; art. on, 15:3-20;
address on, 26:373-74; illus., 6: opp.
249; 15: opp. 3

New Archangel (Sitka), 12:217;
39:109-10
Newark (ferry str.), 18:373
Newbauer, Julian H., obit., 11:191
New Bedford Oil and Camphene
Works, 33:68
"New Bell at Santa Clara Mission,
The," by A. T. Leonard, Jr., 8:378
Newbern (ship), 22:154-62 *passim,*
173, 174
Newbery, Capt. (Colorado R., 1867),
22:172
Newburgh, Edward, 19:129, 141
Newburyport (ship), 2:94
Newcastle, 30:261
Newcastle (ship), 16:4, 321
Newcomb, Bethuel Merritt, obit.,
3:210
Newcomb, D., 13:32
Newcomb, George, 11:128
Newcomb, Thomas, 31:152
Newcomb, Rexford, *The Old Mission
Churches and Historic Houses of
California,* rev., 4:394-96
Newcomb, Wesley and family, 13:32
Newcombe, C. F., 2:265; ed. *Menzies'
Journal of Vancouver's Voyage,* rev.,
2:256-57
Newell, Capt. (of *Honolulu*), 14:333,
342
Newell, D. K., 9:114
Newell, Gordon, *Paddlewheel Pirate,*
rev., 38:377-78
Newell, Mrs. Gwendolan, 32:247
Newell, Marshall A., 27:349
Newell, Robert, 5:70
Newell, Robert Henry, 21:59, 60
Newell, Mrs. Robert Henry, *see*
Menken, Adah Isaacs
Newell, Samuel, 39:300
Newell, William L., 7:280-81; 8:361,
362
New England Mining and Trading
Association, 4:203; 20:27
New England Society, San Francisco,
15:267; 38:298
New England Water Co., 24:269
New Era, Benicia, 8:285
New Era (ship), 15:267
"Newest Light on Drake's Plate of
Brass," address by
Allen L. Chickering, 18:85
Newete, J. H., 11:109; *see also*
Nevett, Joseph H.

Newhall, George A., obit., 9:294; 26:232

Newhall, Henry Mayo, 7:292; 10:389; 25:257; 26:196; 27:156

Newhall, Margaret, 21:384

Newhall, Ruth Waldo, *The Newhall Ranch*, rev., 37:369-71

Newhall, oil well and refinery nr., 17:115; 30:210

New Hampshire, 16:150-51

"New Hampshire Minstrel Tours the Coast, A: Rhodolphus Hall and His Letters," by Frank O. Spinney, 20:243-58

"New Haven and the Two Alvarados, Early Towns of Alameda County," by J. N. Bowman, 12:173-75

New Helvetia, 1:292-94; 6:272; 8:120, 123, 127-28; 9:395; 10:9, 299; 11:42, 43, 136, 349; 12:199, 337; 13:43, 58, 62, 170, 172, 262-64, 272, 274, 356, 364, 371, 372; 14:28, 44, 198, 199, 226; 15:4; 16:100, 347; 17:157, 160, 161; 18:296; 20:120, 148, 149; 21:1, 3, 9-17 *passim*, 21; 23:294; 24:22, 331; 25:121, 123, 129; 26:109; 29:133, 134, 135; 30:376; letters from, 5:77-78, 124; 10:109-10; bk. on, rev., 14:185-86; *see also* New Helvetia Diary; Ranchos: Nueva Helvetia; Sutter's Fort

New Helvetia Diary, 14:269, 272, 277-78, 282; 16:212; 17:360; 18:182-83; 19:135-41 *passim*; 25:228; 26:109; 29:135; quoted, 16:137-38; 19:136-42 *passim*; 21:3; 26:109, 110, 121

New Hope (Woodbridge), 36:374

New Idea Theatre, San Francisco, 21:64, 65; 23:110, 112

New Idria quicksilver mine, 14:159

New Jerusalem (El Rio), 16:297, 303

Newlands, Francis G., 22:95; 38:353

"New Light on the Original Bear Flag," by John A. Hussey, 31:205-17

"New Light upon Talbot H. Green," by John A. Hussey, 18:32-63

Newlin, Gurney E., 25:286

Newllano, La., 40:230, 231, 232

Newman, Charles, 7:19

Newman, Juda, 35:124-26, 134

Newman, Mrs. Juda (Carrie Heller), 35:126

Newman, L. W., 16:183

Newman, R. A., 26:136

Newman, Sig, 35:125, 268

Newman, Simon, 35:125, 137, 138, 259, 267

Newman, W. S., 11:58

Newman (place), 35:138, 267-68, 270-72

Newmark, Hannah, 27:187

Newmark, Harriet, 22:95; 35:184-85

Newmark, Harris, 9:94; 13:331, 335; 29:245; 30:262; 32:331, 345; 33:274; 39:175

Newmark, Joseph, 13:333; 22:95; 39:175

Newmark, M. J., 25:95-96; 29:237

Newmark, Marco Ross, 25:286; obit., 39:175-76

Newmark, Maurice Harris, 39:176; obit., 9:94-95

Newmark, Valentine, 27:187-88

New [Neu-, Nova, Nueva] Mecklenburg, 10:353; 12:283-87 *passim*, 290-300 *passim*, 304; 14:200-211 *passim*, 217, 218, 226; *see also* Cordua's Ranch; Nye's Ranch

"New Mexico" (Manuel), 9:370, 372

New Mexico: civil govt., 10:20-21, 224; in Civil War, 34:125-48 *passim*; emigrants from, 12:115-16; Sutter in, 38:321-27; traders from, 10:27-39; 12:113

New National Circus, 9:385

New Orleans, Battle of, 10:41, 62

New Orleans English Opera Troupe, 10:172, 173, 195, 196

New Orleans Minstrels, 21:242

New Orleans Serenaders, 20:298

Newport, 31:293

Newport (ship), 31:293-94

New Retreat restaurant, Marysville, 14:395

News, Gold Hill, Nev., 11:48, 190

News, Iowa Hill, 9:181

News, Los Angeles, quoted, 32:328, 334-41 *passim*; 34:53-60 *passim*; *Semi-Weekly* and *Tri-Weekly*, 13:347

News, Marysville, 9:287, 378, 379, 383

News, Panamint, 18:201, 215

News, San Francisco, 28:36

New San Pedro, 32:345

News Emporium, Marysville, 30:258

News-Letter, Sacramento, 3:268-69

News-Letter, San Francisco, 3:268, 269; 20:165; 21:327

"Newspaper Art in Stockton,

1850-1892," by Robert E. Huffman, 34:341-56

Newspapers, 7:277-81; 20:331-40; 28:135-36; 32:221; art. in, 34:341-55; bks. on, 7:286; 11:294; 16:39; Confederate, 20:160-65; foreign language, 15:175; 28:129, 135; 37:199; 39:221 (*see also* Chinese language; French language); tabloid, 3:268-69; *see also* names of papers

New Star (ship), 14:161

"New Strikes in Old Diggings," address by George E. Dane, 10:413

Newton, Mr. and Mrs. (S.F., 1867), 11:127

Newton, G. W., 28:337

Newton, Harriet, 12:371; 13:288

Newton, Harry, 7:118

Newton, Joel, 26:166

Newty family (fictitious), 38:116-22

New Union Line, 22:14, 15; *see also* Pacific and Colorado Steam Navigation Co.

New World (ship), 2:137; 9:55; 10:170, 193; 11:152; 15:184, 266, 274, 279; 16:63, 64, 183, 184, 282, 285; 17:80; 27:306; 38:377-78

New World Mining and Exploring Co., 18:202

New York, 16:145-46, 153; 26:13-14

New York (ship), 36:205-6

New York & Austin Silver Mining Co., 23:260

New York and California Mutual Benefit Association, 30:17, 19, 35

New York Bar, 6:19

New York Bridge (Yuba R.), 8:344, 360

New York Cheap Bookstore, San Francisco, 30:256

New York Flat, 9:52, 53, 70, 130, 131, 341, 342, 348, 352, 356, 358

New York Guards, San Francisco, 37:362-63

New York Hill Mine, 6:332; 19:28

New York House, New York of the Pacific, 12:29, 30

New York House, Yuba Co., 8:358; 9:52, 70, 131, 353

New York Independent Guards, New York Flat, 8:348, 362

New York in Slices (play), 38:19

New York of the Pacific, 8:17, 167; 12:95-96; 13:367, 381-82; 14:387-88;

15:290; 20:33; 25:344; 30:345; 36:309; art. on, 12:25-34

New York Pilot (ship), 30:238

New York Quicksilver Co., 14:169

New York Ranch, Yuba Co., 8:340, 341, 346, 356, 358; 9:59, 64

New York Store (?), 9:52

New York Volunteers (Stevenson's Regiment), 1:17, 207-70; 2:351; 10:203, 300; 12:352; 13:305, 306-7; 15:276, 331; 16:82, 139, 343; 18:165, 177; 19:125, 140; 20:293; 22:51, 53, 59-62 *passim*; 22:51, 61, 65; 24:48, 58; 25:127, 130-31; 27:160, 163-64; 29:19, 245; 33:113, 114, 123, 250, 262, 263, 264, 337; 34:26; 35:108; uniform (illus.), 1:203

New Zealand, 19:335; 34:70

Ney, James, 7:112

Neylan, John Francis, 36:48; 37:349

Niantic (ship), 11:125; Hotel and Warehouse, 11:125; 22:254; 38:40

Nicaragua, 9:75; 19:275; 33:26; canal across (prop.), 31:256, 260; 33:26; resolutions concerning, 10:44, 65-66; route across, 8:4; 11:30, 31; 17:75; 28:307, 310; 36:139-40; steamships, 15:165, 168, 178, 184; 16:79-84 *passim*, 184, 282, 338, 342; *see also* San Juan del Sur; Walker, William

Nicaragua Accessory Transit Co., 15:168

Nicaragua Steamship Co., 15:165, 178, 184; 16:79-84 *passim*, 184, 282, 338, 342

Nichold's bank, Dutch Flat, 18:361

Nicholls, Imogene, 38:54

Nicholls, John S., 38:54

Nichols (from Mass., 1849), 22:129-30

Nichols, C. M., 36:209

Nichols, E. J., 15:178

Nichols, F. C., 8:358; 9:155(?)

Nichols, Fred, 9:155

Nichols, H. L., 9:394; 10: opp. 48

Nichols, Howard, 12:30

Nichols, John, 15:269

Nichols, John Gregg, 13:314, 317, 321-22, 329-30, 339, 343, 351

Nichols, Jona, 14:388

Nichols, Joseph, 14:177, 182

Nichols, Washington, 24:117

Nichols, William Ford, 33:381-82

Nicholson, Sir F. E. W., 15:181

Nicholson, I. E., 17:46

Nicholson, John, 26:71, 175

Nick, Chief (Indian, 1854), 26:202
Nickel, John R., 29:286
Nickel, 17:107
Nickels, Edward C., 26:226, 267; 29:39, 55; 32:212, 214, 222
Nickerson, Capt. (of *Massachusetts*, 1849), 29:1, 15
Nickerson, Benjamin R., 7:19
Nickerson, Florence, 31:220
Nickols (Yuba Co., 1857), 9:148
Nicochea, José María, 12:321
Nicolas (ship), 14:128; 15:237
Nicolaus, 8:23-24; 9:372, 395; 10:247, 359; 11:108-9, 121; 14:218, 382, 384, 402, 406; 23:145, 353, 369, 370; illus., 8:24
Nicoll (Stockton, 1877), 34:350
Nidever, George, 2:45, 51-52; 4:6; 12:178; 16:58, 185; 18:174, 260-61, 277; 31:287; art. on, 32:263-68
Nidever, Mark, 32:265, 266
Nielsen, Alice, 14:411
Nielsen, H., 9:329
Nieto, Manuel, 13:203
Nieve, Cabo de, *see* Cypress Point
Nigger Alley (Calle de los Negros), Los Angeles, 13:312, 313, 328, 334
Nigger Slide, *see* Negro Slide
Nigger Tent, *see* Negro Tent
Nightingale (ship), 33:11, 166-67; 35:294, 304
Nightingill, A. W., 15:54, 57
Nightingill, Gideon R., 9:63; 10:367; 14:223; 15:57
Night soil, 37:81
Niimi Buzen-no-kami, 23:342, 344
Nikolai (ship), 12:222
Nile (ship), 31:287
Niles, Capt. (of *William Irelan*, 1866), 22:171
Niles, Eben, 9:103
Niles *v.* Harpending, 9:158
Nimocks, Walter A., obit., 7:100
Nina Tilden (ship), 22:14, 15, 19, 23-24, 25, 154, 155, 164, 167
Nine Horse Ditch, 8:213
Ninfa (ship), *see* Morse
Nininger, N., 13:31
Niño, Andrés, 6:306
Ninus (ship), 2:94
Nipissangue, Grand, 24:232
Nipomo, 18:163, 175; *see also* Ranchos: Nipomo
Nisbet, Benjamin R., 17:196, 206; 40:209, 213

Nisbet, James, 8:362; 20:337; 21:27, 30; 25:103; 26:353-54, 359-60; 30:252
Nisbet, Margaret, 26:360
Nisbet, Thomas, 26:360-61
Niswander, J. S., 7:11
Nixon, George, 38:353
Niza, Marcos de, 1:38, 44, 45-46; 3:263, 307; 3:263, 307, 370, 374; 6:300-301, 307, 312; 13:186; 36:218
Noah, M. M., 9:114; 15:271
"Noah Brooks," by Robert E. Blackmon, 33:193-217
Nob Hill, San Francisco, 19:233, 234
Nobili, John, 3:209; 29:139-47 *passim*
Noble, Charles A., 4:49
Noble, H. H., 27:5
Noble, John E., 33:339
Noble, Patrick, 25:46
Noble, Stephen, 26:204
Noble, Susan, 30:66
Noble, William, 26:204
Noble Pass, 7:14, 16; 18:302; 22:369; 30:66
"Noblet Herbert to Mrs. John Augustine Washington," ed. John A. Washington, 29:297-307
Noe, Bart, 9:53
Noe, José de Jesús, 27:109
Noe, Nicolás, 13:205; 37:127
Noel, J. W., 30:263
Noel, William, 30:263
"No fence law," 25:19, 22, 37; 27:70
Noguera, Francisco de, 2:151
Noisy Carrier Book and Stationery Co., 18:332-33; 21:75-76, 78; 30:251-53, 354; *see also* Charles P. Kimball
Nolan, Alta, 27:189
Nolan, P. F., 31:178
Nolan, Webster Kenneth, 29:92; obit., 31:178
Nolan, William H. and Margaret (O'Brien), 29:92; 31:178
Nolan Brothers Shoe Co., 29:92; 31:178
Nolen, John, 36:64
Nolf, L., 39:150
Nombela y Tabares, Julio, 27:237-48
Nome Cult Farm, 27:215; 30:164
Nome Cult Indian Reservation, 27:215, 220, 221; 30:164; *see also* Round Valley Indian Reservation
Nome Cult Valley, 27:215; 30:168
Nome Lackee Indian Reservation, 27:215; 30:160-61, 164; 36:317
Nonan, Hazel, 37:89
Nonesuch (ship), 26:1

Noonday Mine, 4:75

Nooney, Prof. (San Jose, 1850), 11:161-62

Nootka Sound, 3:219; 9:204, 205; 10:314, 317, 318, 320, 337; 15:59; 18:322, 335, 336

Norberto de Santiago, *see* Santiago

Norcom, Casper W., 4:183

Nordhoff, Charles, 37:81, 130-32

Nordhoff (place), 17:28, 31

Norfolk, Sonoma Co., 17:238

Noriega, José, 2:184; 17:225, 229; 39:51

Noriega, José Antonio, *see* Guerra y Noriega

Noriega, María Rosalia, 13:200

Noriega, Matías Antonio de, 23:1, 15

Norman, Albert E., 22:384

Norman, Lucia, *see* Heaven, Louise (Palmer)

Norman, William B., 9:46

Norman (ship), 22:111; 29:1, 4, 7

Norris (bought sheep, 1853), 1:149

Norris (Hawkins Bar, 1853), 11:174, 175

Norris, Benjamin Franklin (Frank), 26:277-78; 33:313; 39:366-67

Norris, Charles, obit., 24:283-84

Norris, Charles H., 25:174

Norris, J. Parker, 22:57, 58, 59, 66

Norris, Mrs. Lucius G. (Esther Sharon), 27:286

Norris, Samuel (G. W. B. Christensen), 1:149(?); 12:26; 13:175; 16:183; 19:140; 26:20; art. on, 25:219-28; lawsuits, 25:220, 223; *v.* Burgoyne and Plume, 25:223; *v.* Denton, 25:223; *v.* Farmers' and Teamsters' Co., 25:223; *v.* Haggin & Tevis, 25:224-25

Norris, Thomas Wayne, 36:110; address, "California Constitutional Convention of 1849," 24:376; 28:372-73; obit. of Fred T. Elsey, 17:191; obit., 31:177

Norris, William, 1:13, 15-18; 26:264; 29:252, 253

Norris Colony, 25:174

Norristown, 25:223

Norst, Cord, 26:236

North, Miss (S.F., 1867), 11:127

North, Hampton, 9:31, 109; 15:168, 269, 280, 281, 369, 371; 16:79, 183; 17:177-78; 37:154, 155

North, Hart H., 27:91; "Chinese and Japanese Immigration to the Pacific Coast," 28:343-50; "Chinese

Highbinder Societies in California," 27:19-31; obits. of William I. Brobeck, 6:288; William H. Thornley, 11:94

North, J. W., 25:34, 171

Northam, E. P., 26:253-54

Northam, Edward F., 25:107

North America (ship), 36:134

North American Aviation, 36:112

North American Party, 9:100

North American Telegraph Association, 29:345-46

North & South Fork Gold Mining Companies, 31:377

North Beach, San Francisco, 17:196; 19:230, 237

North Beach Nursery, 32:184

North Bloomfield, 10:347, 350, 351; 29:198, 201, 204; on map, 29: opp. 193

North Bloomfield Gravel Mining Co., 28:233, 240-41; 29:193, 198-202 *passim*

North Californian, Oroville, 17:84

North Carolina, 16:6-29, 154, 158-70 *passim;* letter from, 16:264-69

North Carolina (ship), 26:13

Northcutt, W. H., 24:240

North Dome, Yosemite, 1:279, 281

Northern California Telegraph Co., 29:346, 348, 350

Northern District Society, 10:360

Northerner (ship), 8:270; 12:104; 38:329

Northern Light (clipper), 8:384

Northern Light (str.), 17:75; 31:235; 32:209, 310, 312; 36:135

"Northernmost Spanish Frontier in California," by H. F. Raup and William B. Pounds, Jr., 32:43-48

Northern Telegraphic Co., 38:25

Northern Yuba Quartz Mining Co., 15:52

Northfork, Madera Co., 38:161, 219, 222-26 *passim*

North Fork Dry Diggings, *see* Auburn

Northgrave, William, 5:125; 26:110

North Honcut House, 10:356

North Pacific Railroad, 10:389

North Palisade, 4:48, 54

Northrop, David Blair, 21:114

Northrup, Albert, 8:199, 201, 210; 11:55, 56

North San Juan, 3:144, 147, 156, 161; 8:193, 199, 200, 201; 9:54, 61, 133, 198; 10:348, 394; 11:232-34; 12:11; 28:237; 29:193, 194; 30:126, 361; 38:308; newspapers, 9:168, 181; 10:394-95;

14:398; 28:238; 30:126-29; illus., 8: opp. 208

North Star (str.), 27:327

North Star Mine, 6:229-30; 15:290; 31:302

North Temescal (Berkeley), 31:330

North Umpqua Ferry, 28:209

Northup, Robinson Gardner, 21:288

North West Company, 8:98; 17:273; 22:97, 98, 99, 346; 24:231-32; 28:117, 118-19, 258; 33:82, 83

Northwestern Pacific Railroad, 17:238; 38:68

Northwest Passage, 6:293, 317; 7:264; 9:201; *see also* Anian, Strait of

Norton, E. F., 15:179, 268

Norton, Edward, 9:26, 27, 29; 14:353; 15:183-84, 271, 273-74, 372; 16:340; 17:182

Norton, Edward Mallory, 25:286

Norton, Elihu, 15:170

Norton, Elizabeth, 21:191

Norton, G. M., 9:26

Norton, Harry and Lizzie M. (Morrell), 28:319

Norton, Henry H., 28:299

Norton, Jared, 33:12

Norton, John C., 2:121

Norton, Joshua Abraham ("Emperor"), 13:87, 88; 14:412; 16:88; 18:181; 21:55, 72; 23:112, 341; 28:285; 35:130; 38:28-29, 330, 333; art. on, 2:237-45; port., 2: before 181

Norton, L. A., 25:286

Norton, Lewis M., 25:286

Norton, "Long," 13:258

Norton, Myron, 9:44, 45; 10:157, 158; 13:335; 15:369; 16:81; 27:266; 29:245, 246; 37:360; 40:131, 132; fac. sig., 10: opp. 159

Norton, Thomas A., 12:146

Norton, William C., 18:361, 363

"Norton I," by Robert E. Cowan, 2:237-45

Nortonville, 12:33; 38:158, 159

Norvick (ship), 26:14, 15; 33:235

Norwegians, 10:86, 302; 20:67-68, 76; 37:372

Norwood, William E., 31:300

Norwood, Evelyn, 31:300; 37:217

Norwood, J., 13:32

Norwood, Romulus, 13:31

Norwood, William E. and Isabel (Hooper), 31:300

Norwood (ship), 31:295

Nosser, J. J. ("Jack"), 32:1-41 *passim*

"Note on Antecedents and Trends in the Domestic Architecture of California, A," by Roland I. Stringham, 25:54-56

"Note on George Nidever," by Virginia Thomson, 32:263-68

"Note on Gottardo Piazzoni, 1872-1945, A," by Theodore W. Lilienthal, 38:7-8

"Note on J. P. Leonard, M.D., Gold-Rush Visitor," by Robert T. Legge, 31:161-62

"Note on the Southern Boundary of California, A," by Francis S. Foote, 19:217-18

"Note on Twain and Rising," by Andrew F. Muir, 34:317-22

Noteware, C. N., 26:247

Noteware, J. H., 26:297

Not Guilty (play), 21:256

Noticias de la Nueva California, see Palou, Francisco

Notowa, 9:131, 151, 172, 177; 10:170; *see also* Ramm's Ranch

Notre Centenaire, ed. Jelanne Biétry Salinger, 39:2-3, 151, 222, 223

Nottingham (Sutter's Ft., 1848), 24:25

Nourse, Floyd H., 28:380

Nourt, Charles, 12:174

Nouveau Monde, Le (mining co.), 11:229; 22:302, 303

Novella, Francisco, 2:342

Novelty Distillery, San Francisco, 16:337-38

Novett, J. H., *see* Nevett

Novo y Colson, Pedro, 3:218, 236

Noxon, Gilbert E., 8:203-7 *passim*, 212, 344, 345; 11:60

Noxon, Mary E. (or W.), 8:206, 208, 212, 340, 343, 344, 348, 352, 353; 9:133-39 *passim*, 145

Noyes, Mr. and Miss (S.F., 1867), 11:127

Noyes, Amos, 11:127(?); 26:356; 29:253, 254

Noyes, Jack, 35:162, 163

Noyes, James P., 27:151

Noyes, L. W., 7:11-12

Noyes, S. E., 9:363; lawsuits, 9:360-65 *passim*, 369, 370

Noyo, 27:219, 226

Noyo River, 23:25; 27:216; 30:162-65 *passim*

Noyse (Noyes?; overland, 1849), 22:139

Nuckles (Muckles?, Nichols?; Yuba Co., 1854), 8:203

Nudd, Lord, & Co., 27:68

Nuestra Señora de Buena Esperanza (ship), 2:145-60

Nuestra Señora de la Merced (ship), *see Mexicano*

Nueva Galicia (ship), *see Santiago*

Nuevo Mundo, El, San Francisco, 37:199

Nuevos Documentos ... Historia de México, ed. Castañeda, Vols. I, II, rev., 9:401-2

Nuez, Joaquín Pascual, 12:122

Nugent, John, 4:219; 6:5; 9:250, 276; 10:255, 266, 267, 274, 275, 277, 290; 13:299; 15:153, 205, 206; 16:345; 20:306, 336; 32:216-17, 223

Nugent, John S., 15:178, 179, 269, 282

Nugent, Thomas, 15:29, 45

Nuit de Noël sous la Terreur, Une (play), 20:141

"No. 8," *see* Winman, Gertrude

"No. 77 Long Wharf," by Dolores W. Bryant, 21:75-79

Nunan, Thomas, 25:243-44

Nunes, Joseph, 34:359, 360

Núñez, Cuaristo, 37:201

Núñez, José Antonio, 18:278

Núñez Cabeza de Vaca, see Cabeza de Vaca

Nuñez Gaona, Puerto de, 10:323

Nunis, Doyce Blackman, Jr., 38:367; ed. "A Mysterious Chapter in the Life of John A. Sutter," 38:321-37; bk. revs. by, 38:171-73; 40:74-76; *Andrew Sublette,* rev., 40:256-57

Nunn, Henry, 33:364

Nunn, Noak, 33:364

Nunn, Sylvester, 33:364

Nutrelle, Jean, 26:46

Nuttall, Robert Kennedy, 4:192

Nuttall, Thomas, 3:74; 18:341-42; 23:319, 325, 333

Nuttall, Zelia, 1:194; 3:205, 206; 6:93, 94; 18:252; "Two Remarkable California Baskets," 2:341-43

Nuttals, Mrs. (Young's Hill, 1855), 8:340

Nutter, David, 19:155

Nutter, Thomas W., 33:293, 295, 297, 303, 305

Nutting (Philippines, 1898), 30:299

Nuttman, James E., 6:17; 15:181(?); 17:177

Nye, Darius, 2:110-11, 118, 122

Nye, Mrs. E. M., 25:175

Nye, Emanuel, 14:211

Nye, Freeman, 2:122

Nye, Gorham H., 8:106; 10:91; 12:138, 140; 14:129, 332, 341, 346; 17:293

Nye, James W., 6:351; 10:78, 360-61, 369, 377, 390; 11:47-49; 21:155; 26:239-41

Nye, Michael C., 12:280, 299; 14:205, 206, 207, 209, 227, 398; 15:49

Nye, Mrs. Michael C. (Harriet F. Murphy Pike), 14:205, 206

Nye & Co., Virginia City, 36:100

Nye Brothers & Co., China, 16:82

Nye, Foster & Co., 14:207

Nye-Marden Colony, 25:175

Nye's Crossing, 28:237

Nye's Ranch (Landing, Post), 9:75; 10:78; 11:121; 14:205-11 *passim,* 214-19 *passim,* 375; 30:126; *see also* Cordua's Ranch

Nymph (ship), 14:342; *see also Morse*

Nystrom, John Linkeus, 15:184

O

Oak, Henry Lebbeus, 1:197; 20:324; 29:160

Oakdale, 21:383; 30:191; 40:249

Oakes, Anthony George, 24:61, 62; 28:46, 284, 285

Oakes, Mrs. Anthony George (Emma), 28:285

Oakes, William H., 22:39

Oakes family, 35:241

Oak Grove House, 8:346, 360; *see also* Abbott House

Oakgrove Tannery, 33:69

Oak Hill Ranch, 9:286

Oakland, 4:210-11; 10:73; 15:171-74

passim, 267, 271, 367; 17:41-49 *passim*;
18:369; 20:9-10; 22:181; 23:260;
30:363; 31:325-30; 38:21, 26, 339;
Bernhardt in, 20:139; birthday of,
31:325-28; book trade, 30:363;
churches, 26:361; 27:341, 350;
Emerson in, 20:5, 9, 10; lumbering nr.,
30:1-14; newspapers, 8:285 (*see also*
Tribune); potential State capital,
9:256, 258, 282; 10:50, 72
Oakland (bay str.), 10:50, 72
Oakland and San Antonio Steam
Navigation Co., 10:72
Oakland and San Francisco Railroad
and Ferry Line, 10:72
Oakland Benevolent Society, 20:2
Oakland Gas Co., 18:100
Oakland Library Association, 38:312
Oakland Light Cavalry, 19:105
"Oakland Sixty Years Ago," address by
Fred L. Button, 4:210-11
Oakley, W. M., 9:388
Oaks, 2:287; 12:190, 194, 293, 317; 13:21;
14:10; 18:336, 339, 342, 344; 20:39;
21:202; 33:59-61; 38:262; pests on,
32:256-57; Vizcaíno's, 36:229, 239
Oak Tree Ranch, Nevada Co., 8:343,
360
Oak Valley (town), 8:338, 344, 347,
353, 356; 9:54, 60, 147, 148, 150, 353;
10:171
Oates, Mrs. James A., 21:173; Comic
Opera Company of, 21:173, 242, 243
Oatman, Harrison B., 21:99
Oatman, I. E., 15:76
Oatman, Lorenzo, 21:97, 99, 100, 107-12
passim
Oatman, Mary Ann, 21:97, 101, 102,
107, 109, 111
Oatman, Olive, 21:107-11 *passim*; art.
on, 21:97-106; port., 21: opp. 97
Oatman, Royce (Roys, Royse), 21:97,
107, 109, 111
Oats, 2:278; 4:368-69; 5:47, 122, 126,
273; 17:183; 20:260; 34:71
Obarr, Alec, 33:364
Oberdeener (Auburn, 1855), 30:260, 361
Obichon, Baptiste, *see* Aubichon,
Baptiste
Obligado (ship), 15:176, 372
Obregon, Balthasar de, 7:233
O'Brien, Agnes N., 5:293
O'Brien, George J., 25:287
O'Brien, J., 16:183
O'Brien, James, 15:240

O'Brien, John, 6:36
O'Brien, Kenneth B., Jr., 30:286
O'Brien, Luke, 10:172, 285
O'Brien, M., 26:8
O'Brien, Martin, 23:95
O'Brien, Mrs. Matthew D. (Elizabeth
Glenn), 28:380
O'Brien, Robert, 25:287; 27:376-78
O'Brien, Thomas, 9:256, 269
O'Brien, William Shoney, 25:172;
33:374
O'Brien's saloon, San Diego, 22:351
Observatory, portable, illus., 37: opp.
304
"Observer" (pseud.), 24:242
Observer, Ventura, 19:63, 72
O'Cain, Joseph, 12:217-24
O'Cain (ship), 12:218-24 *passim*, 227;
19:375
O'Callaghan (Marysville, 1850), 8:179
Ocampo, Francisco, 13:312, 350
O'Carroll, Joseph Ely, 40:138-52
Occident, San Francisco, 20:165
Occidental, Virginia City, 36:365-70
Occidental and Oriental Steamship
Lines, 11:181-82
Occidental Hotel, San Francisco, 19:236;
20:2; 23:246; 30:209; 32:57-64; 33:244;
illus., 17: opp. 36
Occidental Insurance Co., 26:355;
27:168, 270; 32:94
Occidental Market, San Francisco, 5:86
Occidental Warehouse, San Francisco,
27:197
Ocean Bird (ship), 8:22
Ocean House, San Francisco, 10:276;
15:375
Oceanic Quicksilver Mining Co., 16:78
Ocean Pearl (ship), 22:173; 39:291
Ocean Penny Post Co., 15:368
Ocean Queen (ship), 29:219
Oceanside House, San Francisco,
11:127-28
Ocean Telegraph (ship), 29:106
Ocean View, *see* Berkeley
Ocean View House, 31:331
Oceguera, Mariano de, 23:332
Ochiltree, Tom, 6:32, 33, 34
Ochoa, J. E., 37:204
O'Connell (Colorado R., 1853), 22:21
O'Conner (Nevada Co., 1870s), 18:356,
357
O'Connor (S.F., 1855), 15:364
O'Connor, Mrs. (S.F., 1861), 10:276

California Historical Society Quarterly

O'Connor, Basil, 39:123, 137
O'Connor, Charles, 15:6
O'Connor, Joseph, 9:253, 277
O'Connor, M. J., 27:170
O'Connor, M. T., 6:12
O'Connor, Miles P., 11:9
O'Connor, Patrick, 10:189, 254; lawsuits, 10:167, 168, 180, 187, 188
O'Connor, Peter, 8:369; 16:345
O'Connor family (San Diego), 35:352
Ocotillo, 25:298
O. C. Raymond (ship), 29:143
"Octa," *see* Glover, Mrs. J. T.
Octagon House, San Francisco, 34:88
Octavia (ship), 35:198-99
Octoroon, The (play), 10:376; 21:51-52
O'Daugherty, George, 22:224, 230-31, 356, 360
O'Day, Edward Francis, 5:88; address, "Poets and Poetry of San Francisco," 12:180; obit. of Joseph M. Cumming, 19:286; bk. rev. by, 5:311-12
O'Day, Nell, 25:382
Odd Fellows, *see* Independent Order of Odd Fellows
Odell, W. T., 6:71-76
O'Donnell, Mayo Hayes, bk. rev. by, 38:173-74
O'Dwyer, W. W., 15:52, 56
Oehler, Helen Irving (Mrs. J. C.), 29:89; ed. "Nantucket to the Golden Gate in 1849," 29:1-18, 167-72, 255-60
Oettel, Franz, 28:382
O'Fallon, William, *see* Fallon, William O.
O'Farrell, Dan, 10:285
O'Farrell, Jasper, 1:136; 5:407; 6:150; 10:62; 11:9, 21, 134; 12:310-11; 13:175, 237; 17:145, 158, 232, 296; 25:221-22; 26:20, 208; 27:62; 30:326, 329, 330; 36:241
O'Farrell, Pat, 31:331
Off to California, a Tale of the Gold Country, by Conscience, 37:312-13
Ogden, Capt. (or Dr.; Colorado R., 1850), 11:377, 378; 22:20
Ogden, Adele, 12:187; 23:286; "Alfred Robinson, New England Merchant in Mexican California," 23:193-218; "Boston Hide Droghers along California Shores," 8:289-305; "Hides and Tallow: McCulloch, Hartnell and Co.," 6:254-64; "Russian Sea-Otter and Seal Hunting on the California Coast," 12:217-39; ed. "Business Letters of Alfred Robinson," 23:301-34
Ogden, Edmund A., 33:344, 345
Ogden, P. F., 16:183
Ogden, Richard L., 21:382; 34:150
Ogden, Peter Skene, 1:114, 118; 4:5-6, 281; 12:365; 18:328; 22:98, 99, 100, 213, 329, 344; 24:61, 229-33 *passim*; 28:111; arts. on, 19:308-16; 28:117-24; *Traits of American Indian Life*, rev., 12:364-65
Ogden, Utah, 32:202
Ogden's Hole, 19:314, 315
Ogden's (Humboldt) Lake, 5:378-79, 382
Ogden's Landing, 22:6
"Ogden's Report of His 1829-1830 Expedition," ed. John Scaglione, 28:117-24
Ogden's River, 22:195, 213; 32:207; *see also* Humboldt River
Ogg, Clem, 16:85
Ogier, Isaac Stockton Keith, 15:266; 20:112; 21:358; 22:28; report, 21:358-62
Ogilby, R. E., 22:34
Ogle, Charles Henry, 28:213, 221, 230
O'Grady, William H., 15:169, 180; 29:2; 33:302, 308
Oguri Bungo-no-kami, 23:342, 344
O'Hanlon, Robert T., 9:365; 10:189
O'Hara, Henry, 18:201
O'Hara, Russell F., address, "Mare Island Century," 34:87
O'Hare, James, 5:340
Ohio (P.M.S.S.), 8:7-10; 14:72; 23:58; 24:66; 27:366; 31:41(?)
Ohio (U.S.S.), 13:272, 400; 19:4; 20:31, 121; 24:25; 27:12, 13, 18, 43; 29:4; 30:40, 41; 33:49, 268, 337; 35:112
Ohio (U.S. transport?, 1898), 31:59
Ohio Bar, 9:63
Ohio Flat, 9:352; 10:171
Ohio mining claim, 11:233
Ohio Restaurant, Yuba Co., 8:207
Ohleyer, George, 26:95
Ohleyer, Harold R., 26:94-95
Oil (petroleum), 8:386; 11:84; 17:28, 102, 115; 23:190, 239; 30:210-15, 339; 31:298; 32:9
Oil, fish and whale, 15:276; 16:284; 22:257; 29:15; 33:68
Ojai Valley, 17:28-33, 40

Ojima Torimizu, 28:186
O'Keefe, Joseph, 6:335
O'Keeffe, Louise and Kate, 10:374, 377, 379, 388, 390
Okell, Jack, 16:192
Okeson, D., 5:140
Okhotsk (ship), 12:233; 18:347
"Okies," 24:145, 159
Okina (Hawaiian, 1850), 28:292
Olcese, Louis V., 32:17, 18, 27, 41
Olcott, Chauncey, 21:266
Olcott, Egbert, alias Noyes ("Texas") Smith, 4:312
"Old Ames Press, The," ed. Carl I. Wheat, 9:193-200
"Old Block," *see* Delano, Alonzo
"Old Boone," letters signed, 24:38-39, 45, 126, 235-36, 358, 363
"Old California Market, San Francisco," by H. D. B. Soulé, 5:85-86
"Old Cocktail Route, The," address by Daniel Q. Troy, 12:180
"Old Corner," San Francisco, 16:141
Old Corporal, The (play), 36:209, 212
Olden, Sarah Emilia, *Karoc Indian Stories*, rev., 2:365
Olden, Capt. William R. (of *Linda*, 1850), 14:384
Olden, William R. (Anaheim, 1871), 32:341
"Old 'Enterprise' Gang, The," address by Douglas S. Watson, 12:84
Older, Fremont, 15:379; 20:337; 33:40
Older, Mrs. Fremont (Cora Miranda Baggerly), 22:191; 17:352, 356; 38:74
"Oldest Street in San Francisco, The," by Thomas P. Burns, 13:235-39
Oldfield, G. Sharp, 13:32
Oldfield, Otis, 38:2, 4, 7
"Old Franciscan Library at Mission San Juan Bautista, The," by Brother Daniel, 25:133-38
Old Hartford Insurance Co., 26:254
Old Heads and Young Hearts (play), 9:163
"Old Homes of El Dorado [County]," address by Mrs. William H. Voiles, 27:280-82
"Old Ironsides," *see Constitution* (ship)
"Old Limekilns of Marin County, The," by Bliss Brown, 19:317-22
"Old Line," *see* Pacific Mail Steamship Co.
Oldman (S.F., 1855), 15:271

Old Mission, Los Angeles Co., 32:328
Old Mission Churches and Historic Houses of California, by Newcomb, rev., 4:394-96
Old Mountaineer, Quincy, 16:339
"Old Occidental, The," by Stephen P. Jocelyn, 32:57-64
Olds, B. S., 15:24
Olds, Daniel, 19:321
Olds, J. Spencer, 9:100, 101
Olds, Nelson, 19:321
Olds, William B., 9:101; 15:186, 270; law library, 38:315
"Old Spanish California Families," address by George H. Barron, 3:302-3
"Old State House at Benicia, The," by John A. Hussey, 17:260-70
Old Woman Springs, 26:113, 117
Oleander (place), 25:38
Olema Creek, 10:338, 342; 19:317; 33:62
Olga (bark, 1849), 13:26; 14:332, 342
Olga (brig, 1865), 33:2, 6
Oliva, G., 39:153
Oliva, Vicente Pascual, 8:219; 26:26; 37:119
Olivas, Domingo, 21:348, 357
Olivas, Ignacio, 16:224
Olivas, Juan, 13:207
Olivas family, 16:299, 303
Olivebank (ship), 22:353
Oliveira, Emmanuel d', 23:50; letter from, 51-52
Oliver (Olivier), *see* Deleissègues, Olivier
Oliver, Capt. (of *Marion Watson*), 5:140
Oliver, Edwin Letts, 23:96; obit. of Maxwell C. Milton, 26:377-78; obit., 34:374-75
Oliver, George D., 24:75-76
Oliver, John, 7:12
Oliver, Samuel, 3:62
Oliver, William, 23:325, 332
Oliver, William Letts, 6:355
Oliver, Mrs. William Letts (Carrie Benedict Brown), 34:374
Olivera, Manuel d', 35:236
Olivera, María Jesús, 27:109
Olivera, Rosalino (or Rosalío), 16:249
Oliveras, José Ignacio, 13:198
Olives, 1:167; 3:239; 4:363, 365, 369-70; 5:211; 12:206; 15:235; 23:199, 319; 34:22

Olivia (place), *see* Ehrenberg
Olivia (play), 21:256
Olivia (ship), 22:169
Olmstead, J. P., 9:181
Olmsted, Frederick Law, 3:42; 4:24;
    7:411; 30:275; 31:328
Olmsted, John C., 36:67
Olney, Warren, Jr., obit., 18:190-91
Olompali, 16:111; 27:338; 29:268-69;
    30:167; 31:216
Olson, Culbert Levy, 31:125, 126, 131;
    36:110, 113
Olvera, Augustín, 6:87; 9:104; 13:120,
    135-36, 217, 313, 318, 326-27, 330;
    22:64; 25:298; 29:235, 247; 30:53
Olwell, William, 38:330
Olympe (ship), 13:382
Olympia, Wash., 10:176, 178
Olympic Circus, 3:35; 9:385
Olympic Club, San Francisco, 15:301,
    305; 29:115, 118-20, 222; 35:261
Olympic Games, CHS luncheon at
    Squaw Valley, phot., 39: opp. 80
Olympic Theatre, San Francisco, 4:62;
    21:43, 64, 154, 157, 179
Olympus, Mount, 9:204
Omaha Mine, 6:230
O'Meara, James, 8:364; 20:290, 294, 302
O'Meara, John, 9:116; 10:70
Omen Creek, 33:299
Omnibus (play), 15:48
Omnibus Street Railroad Co.,
    San Francisco, 7:292; 10:389
Oñate, Juan de, 8:27, 42; 36:232-33
Onderdont, Andrew, 31:377
O'Neal family and ranch, Madera Co.,
    38:219
Oneale, W. T. (?), 10:251, 279;
    see also O'Neil, William
O'Neall, Charles F., 36:69
"One-eyed Sam of Dutchess," 10:166
One Horse Spring (Indian Run), 12:8
"One Hundred Years in Yosemite,"
    address by Carl P. Russell, 30:185,
    274-75
"One Hundred Years of Engineering
    in California," address by
    Walter L. Huber, 34:87
"One Hundred Years of Nevada
    History," address by Effie Mona
    Mack, 30:376-77
O'Neil, John, 9:170, 244, 253, 269, 349,
    351; 10:41
O'Neil, O. H., 30:322

O'Neil (or O'Neal), William ("Billy";
    Marysville, 1860), 10:250, 257;
    see also Oneale, W. T. (?)
O'Neil, William ("Billy"; comedian,
    1861), 10:364, 371, 393; 21:53, 63
O'Neill, Capt. (of *London*, 1849),
    7:207-27 *passim*, 397, 400
O'Neill, Arthur A., 19:282
O'Neill, Mrs. Arthur A., address,
    "Story of the Wreck of the
    Rio de Janeiro," 19:282
O'Neill, Edmond, 35:255; address,
    "History of the Oil Industry in
    California," 8:386
O'Neill, Eugene, 21:173, 249; 22:192
O'Neill, James, 16:303; 21:173-74, 240,
    244-52 *passim*, 256, 258, 271, 273, 277;
    22:192
O'Neill, Jerome, 22:176
O'Neill, Richard, 21:329, 332; 22:176
O'Niel (O'Neil?), Thomas J., 24:117
Onions, 2:321; 12:267; 33:289, 293-94,
    301
Onion Valley, 29:298, 299-300, 304
On-ka-hy-e (ship), 2:163
Ontario, 26:280; 27:113, 118, 120
Ontiveras (Ontiveros?), Josefa, 1:258
Ontiveros (Ontiveras?), José, 13:202
Onward (riv. str.), 22:153
Opera houses, *see* Grand Opera House;
    Maguire's Opera House
Operas and opera troupes, 10:172, 195,
    201; 15:166, 174, 178-85 *passim*, 274,
    278; 18:376; 19:97, 98, 99; 20:2; 21:47,
    51, 68-69, 152, 161-62, 167-73 *passim*,
    242, 243, 245; 25:235
Ophir, Placer Co., 2:207; 16:30, 31;
    17:78; 28:380; 30:111, 260, 261; 36:145
Ophir and Feather River Mining and
    Canal Co., 17:84
Ophir Mine, Nev., 11:61, 64; 17:77
O'Pingui, *see* Lusinchi, Augustin
Opium, 37:336
Opossum, 12:304
"Opposition Line," *see* Nicaragua
    Accessory Transit Co.
Oramas, Cristóbal, 23:372
Oranges, 3:164; 13:213, 214, 224, 339;
    15:235; 16:297; 19:208; 22:319;
    from Tahiti, 16:81
"Oratory of Thomas Starr King, The,"
    by J. A. Wagner, 33:219-27
Orb (ship), 30:126

Orbit (ship), 38:333

Orchard (w. Vancouver, 1792), 2:275

Orchard, W. C., 17: No. 4, Pt. 2, p. 12

Orcutt, Rice, 23:226

Ord (on *California*, 1849), 27:38

Ord, Edward Otho Cresap, 11:302; 13:308-9, 310; 16:196; 22:374; 26:1, 9; 29:26; 33:260, 341-42; 35:23-24; letters from, 34:22-23; 35:24-25

Ord, James L., 4:158; 18:170, 179, 255, 260, 275; 20:324; 29:26; 33:253, 259, 260, 261, 338, 340-41; 34:22-24

Ord, Mrs. James L., (María de las Augustias de la Guerra), 1:258(?); 6:160, 166; 15:213, 214; 18:170, 255, 275; 33:260, 268, 338-42 *passim;* 34:24; 36:291

Ord, Pacificus, 19:7; 27:38(?); 29:20-26 *passim;* letter to, 34:22-23; fac. sig., 10: opp. 159

Ord, Robert B., 27:38(?); 34:22, 23

Ordaz, Blas, 13:226; 18:257, 275-76

Ordeal by Hunger: The ... Donner Party, by Stewart, rev., 40:251-53

Ordemann, C. C., 32:354

Ordenes, J. M., 14:211

Order of the Star-Spangled Banner, 9:20-21

Order of United Americans, 9:18-20

Orderly Clerk (ship), 12:30

Ordoñez de Montalvo, García, 1:53; 28:23, 29, 30

O'Rear, Benjamin T., 10:77; 11:9

O'Rear, John W., 30:366

Orear, Thomas, 24:117

Oregon, 2:88, 89, 130-32; 3:72-82 *passim;* 7:286-87; 20:15, 247; 21:128-37; 22:98, 214-15; 25:255-66; 29:9; in 1832, 22:195-205; in 1844-46, 4:353-60; 5:44-84, 109-16; 20:25; in 1848-49, 10:396, 401-3; in 1850-51, 2:130-32; 20:22-23; 25:255-66 *passim;* boundaries, 17:306; 19:368-71; British in, 6:90; 17:135; 22:98; emigration (to Calif.), 3:90; 5:83, 109-25; 10:403; 13:241; 18:172; 19:330-31; 20:25; 26:99, 100; immigration, 3:89-90; 4:277-81, 307-60; 8:89; 10:396-402; 13:241; 18:292; 22:316-17, 365-66; Indians from, 21:1-7, 9; 24:229-30; 25:113; Jesuits in, 29:139-47 *passim;* legislature, 21:129-31; mail service to,

13:241, 242-47; mines, 11:171, 324; 16:41; newspapers, 18:384; 32:231; politics, 17:314-15, 306; *see also* Columbia River; Hudson's Bay Co.; Jefferson; Portland, etc.

Oregon (U.S. brig, 1845), 2:163

Oregon (str., 1848), 2:83, 117, 200-201; 3:41; 8:264; 9:5; 10:242; 11:153, 300; 12:102, 312; 13:4, 5, 249, 250, 397-402; 15:171, 272, 290; 16:82; 17:80; 18:241, 250; 20:13, 120, 330, 331; 21:330; 22:10, 154, 171; 23:51; 24:24, 65; 26:2, 100, 105, 194; 27:34, 46, 235, 261, 263, 366, 367; 28:62; 29:7-14 *passim,* 211, 213; 31:1; 35:113, 291, 311-12; 39:38

Oregon (brig, from Sandwich Is., 1850), 2:114

Oregon (str., 1899), 31:167

"Oregon and California Letters of Bradford Ripley Alden, The," 28:199-232, 351-59

Oregon and California Mission Conference (M.E. Church), 26:169, 170

Oregon Bar, Calaveras Co., 31:148

Oregon Bar, El Dorado Co., 30:238

Oregon Bar, Yuba Co., 8:338, 342, 345, 347-49, 355; 9:53

Oregon Camp, 11:39

"Oregon Cavemen," 31:126

Oregon City, Ore., 2:130; 3:90; 5:46; 10:402; 18:292, 301; 21:82; 23:293; 28:206

Oregon Creek, 8:213, 340, 356, 361; 9:51; 28:237-42 *passim,* 392

Oregon Geographic Names, by McArthur, rev., 7:286-87

Oregon Gulch, 31:148; 33:298

Oregon Hill (Greenville), 8:199, 206, 213, 337, 338, 343, 352, 353; 9:50-61 *passim,* 69, 147-52 *passim,* 157, 162, 169, 266, 347; 10:56, 170, 256, 359

Oregon Hill House, 8:343

Oregon House, Yuba Co., 8:340, 350; 9:52, 53, 58-65 *passim,* 69, 70, 266, 347, 352, 353; 10:59, 77, 170

Oregonian, Portland, 21:131; quoted, 21:132-33

Oregon rifle regiment, 2:136

Oregon Sentinel, Jacksonville, 21:130-37 *passim*

Oregon Temperance Society, 3:77

Oregon trail, 4:281, 307-60; 5:55-60, 109-23, 391-401; 8:89; 15:191, 284; 28:220-28; 32:198, 199

Oregon, Victoria and San Diego Steamship Line, 16:66, 67

O'Reilly, Hugh, 11:10

Oreña, Gaspar, 18:170, 179

Orford Head, 10:329, 335

Organs, 37:249-53; pipe, 10:293

Orient, L' (ship), *see Orion*

Oriental (ship), 22:121

Oriental Hotel, San Francisco, 15:171, 280, 369; 16:344; 19:229, 230, 231; 22:264; 28:33, 43, 46; 37:364

Oriental Quartz Mill, 17:80

Oriflamme Canyon, 34:200; 36:120-29 *passim*

"Original Constitution of California of 1849, The," by J. N. Bowman, 28:193-97

"Origin of the Gillespie Mission, The," by John A. Hussey, 19:43-58

O'Riley, Peter, 12:330

Oriole (ship), 20:232; *see also Dale*

Orion (*L'Orient*, whaler, 1822), 8:140; 14:123; 17:292; 23:372

Orion (ship, 1849), 33:376

Orizaba (ship), 13:39; 16:68; 29:217

Orlandini, Domenico, 21:68

Orleans Bar, 26:204, 206, 207; 34:270, 272; art. on, 39:53-59

"Orleans Bar," by Howard B. Melendy, 39:53-59

Orleans Hotel, Auburn, 18:363

Orleans Hotel, Marysville, 10:187

Orleans Hotel, Sacramento, 9:40, 42, 105, 170, 181, 250, 254, 261, 267, 371, 376; 10:40, 44, 46, 48, 271, 274, 275, 279, 283, 355, 356, 372, 373, 374; 11:51; 17:268; 24:174; 32:148, 154; 37:363

Orm (S.F., 1849), 27:366

Ormaechea, José Ignacio, 24:291, 308; 25:60, 149, 362

Orme, William W., 15:16, 17, 19

Ormsby, C. N., 9:104

Ormsby, J. S., 9:269, 280

Ormsby, L. P., 9:36

Ormsby, Waterman L., 2:218, 220; 36:120, 123

Ormsby, William M., 10:249, 262; 12:325; 21:238

Oro (place), 11:162; 18:100, 243, 250

Oro Grande, 27:116, 121

Oroleva, 8:346, 360; 9:52, 69

Orosco, Esteban, 7:390

Oroville, 3:202; 7:17; 10:251, 356, 368, 383; 18:199, 206; 26:181; 30:362; 40:294; lyceum, 38:309; newspapers, 17:84; 34:49

Oroville Guards, 38:22

Orphanages: in San Francisco, 10:276, 291; 15:164, 267, 271; 16:81; 17:181, 183; 28:33; at Vallejo, 30:247, 248

Orpheum Theater, Los Angeles, 20:142-43

Orpheum Theater, Oakland, 20:143

Orpheum Theater, San Francisco, 33:42

Orpheus (opera), 20:2

Orpheus (ship), 21:332; 30:15, 29

Orr, David, 7:14

Orr, J. W., 32: opp. 291

Orr, Nelson M., 26:239

Orrum, Eilly, 15:381

Ortega, Antonio, 16:237, 240, 241

Ortega, Antonio María, 26:54

Ortega, Encarnación, *see* Sánchez, Mrs. José María

Ortega, Francisco de, 8:34, 36; 26:318(?), 319(?)

Ortega, Guadalupe, 13:207

Ortega, Guadalupe Antonio, *see* Ortega, Antonio

Ortega, Ignacio, 20:237; 23:375

Ortega, José, 1:170

Ortega, José Antonio, 25:287

Ortega, José Francisco de, 1:110, 158; 13:198; 20:235, 237-38; 37:297

Ortega, Mrs. José Francisco de (María Antonia Victoria Carrillo), 20:235, 237-38

Ortega, José Francisco María de, 20:235, 237, 238-40

Ortega, José Joaquín, 12:238; 16:223, 224, 363, 364; 21:355; 25:130; 26:24, 26, 52; 29:318

Ortega, José María, 12:232; 20:238

Ortega, Mrs. José María (María Francisca López), 20:238

Ortega, José María Martín, 20:238

Ortega, Juan de Capistrano Antonio María Atenoges, 20:238

Ortega, María Antonia de Jesús, 20:238

Ortega, Martín, 33:279

Ortega, Rafaela Olivera de, *see* Hill, Mrs. Daniel

Ortelius, Abraham, 3:206, 265-67; 4:3; 6:294, 305; 7:69, 183, 184, 234, 250; 11:46; map, 7: opp. 69
Ortiz, (d. Monterey, 1838), 28:259
Ortiz, Vicente, 37:205
Ortiz de Sandoval, Alonso, 7:267
Ortman, W., 9:139-40
Ortman & Serroot, 9:160
Ortman *v.* Deadman *et al.*, 10:275, 356
Orus (ship), 13:386, 390
Osborn, Archibald P. and Martina (Higuera?), 30:171
Osborn (or Osborne), J. Warren, 11:161
Osborn, S. D., 22:147
Osborn & Brannan, 11:161
Osbourne, James A., 22:49
Osbourne, Sam Lloyd, 6:380
Osburn (Osborn, Osborne, Osbourne), William B., 13:323-24; 33:262
Oscar (whaleship, 1838), 14:320
Oscar (bark, ca. 1850), 12:30
Oscar, L' (ship), 1852), 39:172
Osemeiali (Indian, 1836), 16:249
Osgood, Capt. (on *Sylph*, 1849), 13:31
Osgood (ret. East, 1850), 23:163, 164
Osgood, Edward W., 21:302, 307
Osgood, Henry M., 9:269
Osgood, John F., 19:232
Osgood, May, 29:92
Osgood, Pat, 10:44
Osgoodby, George, 37:172-79 *passim*
O'Shaughnessy, Michael Maurice, address, "Water Supply of San Francisco," 11:390; obit., 13:415-16
O'Shaughnessy, William M., 23:190; 24:92
Osio, Antonio María, 8:102-3; 12:225; 14:232-36 *passim*, 251; 16:223-24, 231, 352; 17:160-61; 20:272; 26:41, 55-56, 59; 27:108, 110
Osio, Manuel, 31:111
Oskison, Mrs. John Milton (Hildegard Hawthorne), 22:192
Osley, T. J., 9:103
Osmer & Co., San Francisco, 33:375
Oso Flaco, El, 1:158; 28:380
Osos, Cañada de los, 1:159, 161; 23:374; 36:2
Osoville, 18:22, 149-56 *passim*
Osteopathy, 31:24
Ostrich farm, Coronado, 17:35

O'Sullivan, Curtis D. and Helen (Hooper), 32:191
O'Sullivan, Denis and Elizabeth (Curtis), 32:191, 287; 36:73
O'Sullivan, Hooper, 32:191
Osuna, Gabriela (Peralta), 30:226, 228, 230
Osuna, Juan María, 12:220; 21:347
Osuna, Leandro, 26:35
Oswald, Andrew and Eliza, 15: opp. 40
Oswall, James and Rosale (Karabahal), 28:292
Otago (ship), 22:352
Otay Lake, 34:158
Otay Mesa, 34:159
Oteotanin, Michel, 23:20-23 *passim*
Othello (play), 15:48, 266
Otignon, Mrs. and children (Panama, 1854), 24:69
Otis, Edward, 23:76
Otis, Elwell S., 30:290, 304
Otis, George B., 25:175
Otis, Harrison Gray, 24:225; 35:365; 37:176
Otis, James, 19:230, 232; 29:253
Ott, James J., 6:341
Otter, Capt. (Civil War), 31:235
Otter (ship), 1:173-77; 10:320; 12:217; 38:275
Otter, 12:304; 22:198-202 *passim*, 210, 212, 213, 336; 23:19, 24, 27, 36, 37, 123-28 *passim; see also* Sea otter
Otterson, Martha, 28:292
Ottinger, Douglas, 23:165; 25:110
Ottitiewa, 29:109-10
Oubichon, Baptiste, *see* Aubichon, Baptiste
Ould, Robert, 11:12, 26
Oullehen, Denis J., 18:19-20
Oulton, George, 10:378, 379
Our Gal [fire engine co.], Sacramento, 9:354
Our Sea Saga: The Wood Wind Ships, ed. Sawyer, rev., 8:384
Oury, Granville H., 6:32-35 *passim;* 40:323, 325
Ousley, Henry, 14:224
Ousley's Bar, Yuba Co., 6:244; 8:358; 9:70; 15:51, 52
Outcalt, Peter, 27:349
Outcroppings: ... California Verse, ed. Harte, 28:6-7
"Outdoor Moods of John Muir,"

address by William Frederic Badè, 3:207-8

Outland, Charles, 39:111

"Outline Sketch of the Maritime Fur Trade, An," address by Frederic W. Howay, 14:86

"Out of the Past, a True Indian Story," told by Lucy Young . . . to Edith V. A. Murphey, 20:349-64

Outposts of Civilization, by Chalfant, rev., 7:91-92

Out West, 31:18

Ovalle, Gonzalo de, 6:315, 317, 319, 327, 329; instructions to, 6:330-31

Overland Freight Transfer Co., 34:323, 328, 330

"Overland in 1853: William Warner's Letter to His Mother," 5:289-92

Overland journeys: 8:185-86; 26:292; J. W. Audubon's, 21:289-310; Birmingham Emigrating Co.'s, 8:81-82; Richard Campbell's, 18:350; Charles Cardinell's, 1, 57-71; Kit Carson's, 1, 111-21; James Clyman's, 4:120-25, 129-39, 307-60; 5:55-59; T. B. Eastland's, 18:101-29, 229-41; P. L. Edwards', 3:74-76; James Gregson's, 19:115-16; R. O. Hickman's, 8:185-86; J. W. Jones's, 6:111-29; S. W. Kearny's, 21:193-224; Peter Lassen's, 18:292; L. C. McKeeby's, 3:46-72; D. McLane's, 6:361-62; of Mormons, 14:60-70; New Mexican traders', 10:27-39; P. P. Pratt's, 14:60-70; Robinson and Ogle's, 6:361-62; Riley Root's, 10:396-402; Jedediah Smith's, 2:228-36, 344-49; 3:25-29; J. D. Staples', 22:119-50; W. A. Trubody's, 16:124-27; William Warner's, 5:289-91; I. J. Willis', 32:196-208; William Wolfskill's, 2:37-41; John Wood's, 6:361-63

Overland Journey to California, An, by Hickman, ed. White, rev., 8:185-86

Overland mail, 6:122; 12:323; 14:162; 15:277, 328; 20:250; 36:117-18, 130; *see also* Butterfield Overland Mail; Pony Express; Postal service

Overland Monthly, 4:95; 5:410; 21:332; 28:7-9; 30:139-41, 357; 31:250; 33:211-12

Overland Telegraph Co., 29:349, 353-54

Overman, Charles, 22:156, 159

Overstreet, James T., 34:30

Overton, J. B., 17:175

Overton, J. P., 16:283

Overton, T. C., 10:290

Owen, D., 12:138

Owen, Mrs. Harriet (Kearny), 25:371

Owen, Isaac, 15:42; 26:169-72 *passim*; 31:1, 3; 32:120, 121, 128

Owen, Isaac E., 28:60, 67

Owen, Mrs. J. J., 39:245

Owen, J. R. N., 9:307; 18:206-9 *passim*

Owen, James, 30:7

Owen, James Jerome, 22:223-34, 355-62 *passim*

Owen, John, 27:43, 45; 28:60

Owen, Owen, 22:355, 363

Owen, Robert ("Uncle Bob"), 13:333

Owen, W. B. R., 33:276

Owens (Yuba Co., 1859), 10:59, 177

Owens, Edward, 5:125

Owens, Henry, 5:125

Owens, James, 5:125

Owens, John, 5:125

Owens, P. H., 9:26

Owens, Richard, 1:124-26, 129-32 *passim*, 138; 3:270, 273; 4:10, 376; 22:54, 66; 29:271, 275, 335, 339, 342

Owens, Thomas, 5:125

Owens Lake, 4:10; 18:209

Owens River, 2:178; 26:233; mineral district, 10:261; 26:237; Valley, 2:178; 26:242

Owensville, 26:242, 243

Owhyhee (ship), 28:123; 33:376

Owings, L. S., 34:127

Owless, Ruel, 4:321

Owner, Henry and Mary Ellen (Simpton), 30:92; 31:284

Oxbow Bar, 12:66

Oxen, 1:165; 2:182, 188, 295, 320, 322; 8:25, 112, 113; 12:260, 287, 293; 13:202; 14:5, 6, 7; 15:368; 16:137, 138; 20:181; 21:198, 356; 23:170, 252; 24:134, 241, 343, 344; 27:193

Oxenham, John, 16: No. 1, Pt. 2, pp. 3-4

Oxford (ship), 27:293

Oxnard (ship), 38:41

Oxnard family, 18:95

Oysters, 5:64; 7:308, 348; 8:27; 9:157, 371, 395; 10:49, 186; 11:369; 12:92; 14:394; 15:235; 16:301; 26:218-19; 34:330; *see also* Pearls and pearl fishing

P

Pace, Charles, 26:232

Pacey, E. H., 10:258, 359, 360, 368;
 v. Galvin, 10:187

Pacheco, Dolores, 2:183; 4:374, 383;
 13:107-8; 14:148

Pacheco, Francisco Párez, 16:217, 353;
 26:287; 30:98; 31:259

Pacheco, Ignacio, 16:249

Pacheco, Jordán, 35:236

Pacheco, María Antonia, 29:26

Pacheco, Mariano, 19:201-2, 215

Pacheco, Pablo, 16:241, 249

Pacheco, Petra, 13:278

Pacheco, Romualdo (d. 1831), 1:170;
 11:264; 13:212-13; 16:218; 23:218;
 27:335-36, 336-37; 36:121

Pacheco, Romualdo (b. 1831), 1:170;
 8:197; 10:62, 372, 379; 11:13, 264;
 18:270, 278; 19:201-2, 215; 29:241;
 30:147; 37:194-95, 205

Pacheco, Mrs. Romualdo, *see* Wilson,
 Mrs. [Capt.] John

Pacheco, Salvio, 37:194

Pacheco, Tomás, 12:173; 16:285

Pacheco Pass, 11:103, 105; 12:6; 25:2, 3

Pachula (Indian, 1782), 34:196, 206

Pacific (brig, 1848), 12:18

Pacific (str., 1851-61), 6:17-18; 15:165,
 168, 173, 282, 375; 16:67, 68, 82;
 17:309; 26:68, 74, 175, 176, 177;
 31:37; 36:140

Pacific (str., Collins Line, 1852), 19:144

Pacific, The (weekly), 15:41;
 27:149-50; 30:106; 33:292, 301, 307;
 34:65; quoted, 21:35; 27:149; 32:119,
 122, 126; 34:65

Pacific Agricultural and Colonization
 Co., 25:36

Pacific and Atlantic Rail Road Co.,
 14:163-64; 15:269; 16:200; 17:180;
 26:266; 27:140, 253; *see also*
 San Francisco and San Jose Railroad

Pacific and Colorado Steam Navigation
 Co., 22:15, 17-19

Pacific Atlantic Telegraph Co., 29:346,
 348, 350

Pacific Banner (weekly), 27:10, 17,
 305-6, 309; 30:134; quoted, 123, 130

Pacific Brewery, San Francisco, 15:185

Pacific Chemical Works, 30:382

Pacific Club, San Francisco, 19:236;
 38:307

Pacific Coast Baptist Theological
 Union, 37:44

Pacific Coast Borax Co., 17:116-17

Pacific Coast Bottlers Protective
 Association, 35:147

Pacific Coast Land Bureau, 25:33

Pacific Coast Oil Co., 30:210

Pacific Coast Oyster Co., 34:330

Pacific Coast Railroad, 37:131

Pacific Coast Steamship Co., 31:153

Pacific Company (1849), 13:295, 296

Pacific Electric Railway, 31:21; 36:376

Pacific Emigrant Society, 7:6

Pacific Express Co., 15:273, 372; 19:297;
 26:195, 199; 36:103

Pacific Female College, Oakland, 36:349

Pacific Fur Co., 24:230; 33:82-83

Pacific Gas & Electric Co., 9:176;
 29:199, 202-4; 30:349; 31:176, 300;
 33:81

Pacific Grove, 16:301; 29:25; 38:173-74

Pacific Guards, San Francisco, 15:171

Pacific Hall, San Francisco, phot.,
 25: opp. 1

Pacific Historical Review, March 1932,
 rev., 11:87

Pacific Historical Society, 1:11

Pacific Improvement Co., 29:25-26

Pacific Insurance Co., 17:79; 26:355-58;
 27:165-68, 270

Pacific Library Fund, 15:167

Pacific Light & Power Co., 10:393

Pacific Lighting Corp., 31:176

Pacific Lumber Co., 38:69

Pacific Mail Steamship Co., 7:10; 8:7,
 8, 9; 11:31; 15:164-86 *passim*; 16:68,
 79-84 *passim*, 184, 285, 305, 342;
 17:262, 285, 308; 19:27, 356; 22:166;
 23:246, 345-46; 26:102, 182; 27:34, 172,
 234; 28:372; 32:149, 309-12, 322,
 349-61; 34:232, 235, 337-38; 37:216;
 art. on, 13:240-54, 386-406

Pacific Medical and Surgical Journal,
 11:149; 28:133, 142

Pacific Medical College, 4:191, 197

Pacific Medical Journal, 30:70-71

Pacific Mining Co., 20:45; 26:340

Pacific Museum, San Francisco, 3:36;
 28:133, 142

Pacific News, San Francisco, 1:296;
  10:303; 13:296, 297; 20:338; 25:266;
  quoted, 10:240, 241; 25:260-63
Pacific Ocean Fish and Canning Co.,
  31:154-57
Pacific Oil and Camphene Works,
  16:284; 33:68
Pacific Pioneer Yacht Club, San Diego,
  1:9
Pacific Plank Road, San Francisco,
  15:373
Pacific Police Gazette, 15:165
Pacific railroad, *see* Railroads:
  transcontinental
Pacific Railroad Association, 23:340
Pacific Railroad Convention, 4:233-40;
  38:28
Pacific Republic, 10:6, 258, 268, 271,
  288-89; 13:39; 22:361-62; 23:234;
  28:166-67; *see also* California
  Republic
Pacific Rolling Mill, 25:46. 48
Pacific Rural Press, 2:263; 25:383;
  30:195, 197, 200, 201; 31:337; 32:253
Pacific Saw-Manufacturing Co., 29:381
Pacific School of Osteopathy, 31:24
Pacific School of Religion, 37:43-44
Pacific Service Magazine, Oct. 1929,
  rev., 8:385
Pacific Sheet Steel Corp., 30:349
Pacific Social Science Association,
  27:345-47
Pacific Southwest Trust and Savings
  Bank, Los Angeles, 37:267
Pacific Spectator, 29:191
Pacific Springs, 3:53; 22:137
Pacific Steam Navigation Co., 20:232
Pacific Telegraph bills, 11:14, 26;
  15:170; 29:345; *see also* Telegraph,
  transcontinental
Pacific Telegraph Co., 29:353-54, 355
Pacific Telephone & Telegraph Co.,
  18:384; 19:86; 23:285; 24:89-90
Pacific Theological Seminary, 37:43
Pacific Tract Society, 22:111; 27:10,
  307, 309; 32:142
*Pacific Typographical Society and the
  California Gold Rush of 1849*, by
  McMurtrie, rev., 7:408
Pacific Union Club, 31:292
Pacifique, Le (ship), 13:273
Packano (Indian, 1851), 28:330
Packard, John Quackenbos, 14:400;
  15:38
Packer, George Fox, 31:381

Packer, Henria, *see* Compton, Mrs.
  Henry C.
Packer, Henry Bellington and Mary
  Elizabeth (Judkins), 31:281
Packman, Ana (Bégué), 13:209
Pack trains, 5:170, 173; 6:216-17;
  7:113; 8:355; 9:174, 347; 11:54, 324;
  12:330; 14:402; 17:59, 76, 161; 18:149;
  19:292-98 *passim*; 22:6; 24:119, 121;
  26:236, 244; 27:193; 28:205, 212, 216,
  229; 29:298, 302; 31:40; 32:364;
  33:299; 39:57-58, 291
Packwood, Samuel and William, 4:320
Pactole, Le (company), 22:309
Paddlewheel Pirate, by Newell, rev.,
  38:377-78
Paddock, Nathan C., 2:201
Paden, Irene D. (Mrs. William G.),
  32:285; address, "The Journal of
  Madison Berryman Moorman,"
  27:180-81; ed. "The Ira J. Willis
  Guide to the Gold Mines," 32:193-208
Paden, William Guy, 23:288; 26:246;
  addresses: "The California-Oregon
  Trail," 18:85; "Contribution of
  Dr. Herbert E. Bolton," 19:187-88;
  "Lore and Lure of California,"
  25:185-86
Paderewski, Ignace Jan, 18:369
Padilla, Juan Nepomuceno, 1:135;
  13:36, 339; 17:153, 224, 225; 29:267,
  269, 277
"Padre of Paradise Flat, The," 40:49-67
Padrés, José María, 11:342; 16:224, 225,
  237-40 *passim*; 23:331; *see also*
  Hijar-Padrés colony
Padushkin, Yakov, 12:234
Page, Mrs. (Grass Valley, 1850s), 6:227
Page (brothers, Yuba City, 1851), 8:360
Page, Daniel D., 15:366; 17:172; 26:193,
  195, 199; 32:354; *see also*
  Page, Bacon & Co.
Page, Donald, 29:151-52
Page, Francis W., 15:281, 282, 364;
  17:172; 26:193, 195, 199; 33:374;
  see also Page, Bacon & Co.
Page, Mrs. Francis W., 19:229
Page, Gwynn, 15:273; 34:337
Page, Hugh N. 3:111(?), 187; 5:255;
  11:208
Page, Mrs. James R. (Kate Van Nuys),
  25:287
Page, Joseph M., Jr., 29:225
Page, Julia Ann, 26:193
Page, Nathaniel, 29:253, 254

Page, Robert C., 15:370; 28:294
Page, Mrs. Robert C. (Delia F. Williams), 28:294
Page, T. E., 8:269
Page, Thomas Stokes, 22:96
"Pageant of San Francisco, The," address by Gertrude Atherton, 22:84
Page, Bacon & Co., 15:272-82 *passim,* 364, 365, 370-77 *passim;* 16:31, 32, 282, 285; 17:172; 18:43, 45, 48; 24:166, 179; 26:193-200 *passim;* 30:254; 35:224; 37:139, 151
Pageot, A., 11:206, 209, 211; 12:40; letter from, 12:331-32
Pages, Jules, 37:26, 35
Page's Mill, 9:52, 70
Pahl, P. C. H., 27:119-20, 122
Pahrangat Mining District, 18:210, 212
Paige, Calvin, 26:264
Paige, P. B., 9:70
Paine (d. Angel I., 1854), 15:165
Paine, Lt. (on *Republic,* 1855), 15:282
Paine, Horace J., 25:111, 115, 255, 257, 260
Paine, S. H., 13:32
Paine, Sumner, lawsuit, 9:265, 356-57, 362
Paine, Thomas, 9:42
Painted Rock, San Luis Obispo Co., 1:153, 156
Painter, Frederick J., 4:169
Painter *v.* Adams & Co., 15:279
Paita, Peru, 20:209; 26:219, 220
Pajaros Island, 3:321
Pakenham, Richard, 5:306-7; 11:197; 18:139-40, 141, 145
Pala, *see* Mission asistencias
Palace Hotel, San Francisco, 1:17; 17:239; 18:369-71; 19:100, 225, 234; 20:127; 27:257; 37:215
Palache, James, 37:52, 57-58
Palacio, Francisco, 13:273; 33:341-42
Palacios, Gerónimo Martín de, 7:262, 263, 273, 299-300, 331, 334, 336, 341, 379, 385, 391; 8:44, 51
Palencia, Pedro de, 1:43, 47; 3:309, 363-67
Pali, Dr. (Ventura pioneer), 4:169
Palisades, The, 4:20
Palisade Silver Mine, 16:132
Pallandini, Louis E., 31:281
Pallas (ship), 14:303-4
Pallou, Thomas, 5:363
Palmas, Arroyo (Cajon) de las, Lower Calif., 31:262, 263, 269
Palma Seca (Soda Springs), 12:9

Palmer (d. 1847), 1:223, 224
Palmer (Tehama Co., 1850), 18:302
Palmer (Hawkins' Bar, 1853), 11:170
Palmer (S.F., 1855), 15:277
Palmer, Mr. and Mrs. (Long Bar, 1859), 10:166
Palmer, Alice (Hermann), 19:230
Palmer, Amasa (or John), 22:49
Palmer, Charles T. H., 2:206; 4:214; 8:90; 10:91; 12:93; 16:30, 31, 32, 38, 39; 26:186; 30:103-4, 106, 111, 260, letters to, 16:172-77; *see also* Palmer & Baldwin
Palmer, Edwin C., 11:6, 21
Palmer, Mrs. Harlow (Emily Bancroft), 29:225, 362
Palmer, Harry, 21:246
Palmer, Hiram, 15:42
Palmer, Innis N., 2:129
Palmer, J. A., 7:115, 116, 118
Palmer, J. C., 9:104; 10:247, 261, 385
Palmer, J. W., 4:186
Palmer, Joel, 3:89, 90; 19:135; 21:4, 6; 26:328; 30:57, 60-63
Palmer, John, 31:290
Palmer, Joseph, 4:41
Palmer, Joseph C., 6:14-15; 14:163, 164; 15:157; 16:342; 17:175, 180; 21:322-26; 34:250-51, 335; *see also* Palmer, Cook & Co.
Palmer, M. C., 15:169
Palmer, Minnie, 35:142
Palmer, Phil, coauth. *Chinatown San Francisco,* rev., 39:367-68
Palmer, Rodríguez, 28:34
Palmer, Mrs. Silas Henry (Olive Holbrook), 24:261; 27:5; obit., 37:181
Palmer, T. G., 28:327
Palmer, William A., 31:290
Palmer, William W., 25:119
Palmer (ship), *see N. B. Palmer*
Palmer & Baldwin, 30:260-61
Palmer & Co., 14:403
Palmer, Cook & Co., 15:266, 272, 366; 16:341, 346, 347; 17:82-85 *passim,* 168-80 *passim;* 21:321-26, 331; 25:117-18; 34:250-58 *passim,* 335; 37:143, 146, 152
Palmerston, Henry John Temple, 10:118; 18:146
Palmetto (ship), 33:2, 6, 152
Palms, 3:239; 34:196-98
Palmsay, Marie Constance, 33:353
Palo Alto, 3:100; 27:134, 138; 33:169-73 *passim;* 34:183, 184

"Palo Alto's 'Mysterious Frenchman,' "
  by Miriam A. de Ford, 33:169-74
Paloma, 38:261
Palomares (Cajon Pass, 1842), 10:36
Palomares, Francisco, 13:327
Palomares, Ignacio, 16:360
Palomares, José, 13:209, 327
Palos Colorados, 30:2
Palo Seco Creek, 30:7, 8
Palou, Francisco, 1:162; 4:144; 10:211,
  212; 14:99-101; 17:120, 121, 122, 356;
  19:221; 23:249; 28:19-20, 21; 31:113;
  36:3; 37:292, 295, 299; boundary
  marker of, 5:321-27, (phot.) opp. 326;
  "The Founding of the Presidio and
  Mission of . . . St. Francis," ed.
  G. E. Dane, 14:102-10; "Record of
  Padre Fray Junípero Serra's Death,"
  13:155-58; *Noticias de la Nueva
  California*, 1:12, 20, 375; *Historical
  Memoirs of New California*, ed.
  Bolton, rev., 6:375
Palo Verde, 17:332, 335, 336
Pambrun, Pierre Chrysologue, 22:197,
  214
Pamitas, 34:197, 198
Pamo Valley, *see* Santa Maria Valley
Panama (city), 6:351-52; 7:12; 8:13-14;
  9:5; 13:5, 390, 392, 398-99; 16:184;
  17:309; 20:19-20, 227, 248, 260,
  330-31; 23:51; 24:69; 29:8-10; 34:34;
  letters from, 29:4-11
Panama (str., 1848), 2:139, 201; 8:16,
  265; 9:5, 7; 12:104; 13:4, 249, 250,
  253-54, 397, 402-3; 15:171; 16:84, 305;
  17:175; 18:38; 19:3; 20:257, 275; 22:21;
  23:51, 79; 24:69, 165; 26:8; 27:34, 46,
  218, 219, 260, 293(?), 364; 28:59, 66,
  116; 29:4, 8, 14, 112; 33:376; 39:49
Panama (str., 1855), 17:181
Panama, Isthmus of, *see* Panama
  crossing
Panama-California Exposition,
  San Diego, 36:66-71
Panama Canal, 31:298; 33:27
Panama crossing, 6:351; 8:4-14; 9:5,
  196-97; 11:30-32; 13:241, 390; 20:13;
  17:308-9, 320; 19:324; 20:13, 16-21,
  227, 248, 260, 330; 24:65-69 *passim;*
  27:12; 29:101-2; 32:310; 36:139, 142,
  206, 303; *see also* Gold Rush:
  via Panama
Panama Herald, 9:197; 12:312
Panama-Pacific International
  Exposition, 3:297; 14:86-87; 15:291;

31:298-99; 38:1, 232-33; 39:26;
  address on, by A. J. Cleary, 14:86-87
Panama Railroad, 2:214; 8:4-5, 10;
  10:190; 11:11, 31, 32; 17:308-9, 320;
  20:248, 324; 29:3; 32:310; 36:303
Panama Ranch, 33:189
Panama Star, 20:331
Panamint City, 16:85; 18:201, 203, 205,
  214; newspaper, 18:201, 215
Panamint mining district, 17:107,
  208-18; map, 17: opp. 208
Panamint Mountains, 17:106-7, 115-16,
  210; 18:198-214 *passim*
Panaud, Clement, 12:170-71, 331-33;
  13:276, 280; 17:178
Pancoast, Charles Edward, *A Quaker
  Forty-niner*, ed. Hannum, rev., 9:291
Pandore (ship), 22:298; 23:61
Panics, 1855, 13:80-81; 1873, 34:315
Pannonia (ship), 31:158, 159
Panoramas, 10:165, 174, 189, 196, 250,
  263, 360, 363, 371; 11:229; 20:277;
  21:151; 23:163; 29:118; 33:29-38
Pantheon (saloon), San Francisco,
  35:141
Panther (ship), 15:140
Panto (Indian, 1846), 26:42, 52, 59-60
Pantoja, Juan, 6:299; map by, 9: opp. 3
Pantoja House, San Diego, 31:36-39
  passim, 42
Pantoscope, *see* Jones, John Wesley
Pan-Wache (Indian, 1851), 28:332
Papini, Cecilia, 22:384
Papy, Jasper J., 11:126
"Paradox Town: San Francisco in
  1851," by Julia C. Altrocchi, 28:31-46
Paragon (ship), 28:228-29
Paragon Bay, 28:212, 214, 228
Parburt, George R., 13:9, 32
Parcel, Thomas, 13:32
Pardee, Col. (S.F., 1855), 15:365
Pardee, George Cooper, 24:6; 30:343;
  36:110, 113; 38:356-57; 39:19, 20
Pardee, Mrs. George Cooper
  (Helen N. Penniman), 24:95
Pardee, John, 13:32
Pardeilhan, Henri, 39:320
Pardo, Roberto, 16:360, 366; 17:60;
  27:335, 338
Pardow, Mary, 32:191
Paredes, García de, 3:21, 23
Paredes y Arrillaga, Mariano, 1:190;
  5:306; 6:77, 271-72, 370; 18:144, 145,
  146, 221-27 *passim*
Parepa-Rosa, Mme., 21:161-62; 23:112

Parish, Charles Louis, 25:382
Parish, Henry L., 25:382
Parisot (S.F. and mines, 1849), 5:20-21, 348
Park, F. A., 9:394
Park, Thomas B., 8:297, 301; 11:75;
    18:160, 164; 23:200-201, 215, 319-29
    passim, 333
Park, Trenor W., 8:367; 15:274, 371-72;
    17:169, 171-72, 177, 182; 20:261, 272
"Park, The," Marysville, 9:265, 286,
    348, 350, 366; 10:166, 264, 284
Park & Tyler, 30:265
Parker (Honey Lake, 1855), 18:303
Parker, Dr. (S.F., 1855), 16:79
Parker, Miss (S.F., 1861), 10:281, 282,
    374, 379
Parker, Benjamin, 15:179
Parker, Mrs. Elizabeth Maria, 14:74;
    28:34; *see also* Wills, Elizabeth Maria
    Bonney
Parker, Eustace, 9:248, 249, 250, 255,
    259, 269
Parker, Foxhall A., 2:164, 165
Parker, Henry, 22:79
Parker, James E., 9:195
Parker, James M., 22:34; 30:146
Parker, Jennie, 21:157
Parker, Lizzie (Mrs. Northrop), 10:377
Parker, John (E. Bay, 1840), 30:3, 4
Parker, John (Ukiah Valley, 1851),
    26:210
Parker, Dr. John (Castroville, 1874),
    29:89
Parker, Marvel, 33:374
Parker, Paul P., 23:383; 29:89-90;
    "The Roach-Belcher Feud," 29:19-28;
    "The Tiles from Mission Soledad,"
    23:348; obit. of William Davies,
    13:414
Parker, R. A., 5:147
Parker, Robert, 15:271
Parker, Robert A., 5:406; 11:136;
    13:379; 20:292; 22:252; 27:44; 28:67;
    30:157; *see also* Parker House,
    San Francisco
Parker, Robert J., 17:288; "Building the
    Larkin House," 16:321-35;
    "A Chapter in the Early Life of
    Thomas Oliver Larkin," 16:3-10; as
    address, 16:187; ed. Thomas O.
    Larkin, "My Itinerary," 16:11-29,
    144-71; ed. "Thomas Oliver Larkin
    in 1831," 16:263-70
Parker, Samuel H., 10:50, 62; 11:9;
    25:343

Parker, Samuel Nathaniel, 26:308
Parker, T. H., 17:181
Parker, W. C., 15:376
Parker, W. R., 12:4
Parker, Ward M., 34:258, 333, 334
Parker, William C., 4:175; 12:25-28
    passim, 30-31; 13:381; 15:376(?);
    16:79(?)
Parker, William H., 19:236; 20:294
Parker & Roman, 30:266
Parker Dam, 36:219
Parker House, San Francisco, 2:202;
    3:35; 11:136, 360; 13:379; 16:127;
    20:29, 123, 125, 292-99 *passim,* 310;
    22:244; 27:44, 50, 263, 264, 266, 368;
    38:42
Park Hotel, Santa Barbara, 18:175
Parkinson, George, 18:259
Parkinson, George C., 16:177
Parkman, Julia Bedlow, *see*
    McAllister, Mrs. Cutler
Parks, David, 9:76-77
Parks, David, Jr., 9:77
Parks, Helena, 35:15-16, 19
Parks, Ida, 30:289
Parks, James Franklin, 23:94
Parks, John C., 9:77; 14:394, 405;
    15:21, 29, 43, 44
Parks, Mary Elizabeth, 23:94
Parks, Mary Ross, 7:283
Parks, William H., 9:355, 379;
    10: opp. 48, 62, 372, 379, 394; 11:9;
    13:22; 14:209, 220, 229
Parks and Smith, 14:398
Parks' Bar, 6:218-20; 9:63, 70, 76-77,
    264, 351-52, 355-56, 373; 10:56, 58,
    168, 247-54 *passim;* 13:171; 15:29;
    25:326; 33:202
Parlow, Kathleen, 25:236
Parochial schools, 17:175; 32:127;
    see also San Francisco schools
Parowan, 14:63
Parr, Fred D., 26:189
Parratt, Edna Martin (Mrs. Rogers),
    32:175; 34:88; address, "Returning
    an Historic Call," 34:87; trans. Kino
    document, 24:288; obits. of
    Eleanor (Ashby) Bancroft, 35:372;
    Edwin L. Oliver, 34:374-75
Parrish, Edwin and Julia (Reynolds),
    23:288
Parrish, Joseph, 3:123; 26:49
Parrish, Robert A., Jr., 17:318; 31:231,
    236, 240
Parron, Fernando, 4:143

Parrott, Abby Josephine, 9:96
Parrott, Christine P., 18:189
Parrott, John (d. 1884), 3:285; 5:306, 307; 9:96; 11:127; 15:10, 20, 280, 282; 16:282, 285, 306; 18:189, 250 ;19:231; 26:196; 31:46; art. on, 34:111-24; letters to, 2:247-48; 3:284
Parrott, John (d. 1918), 25:232, 236, 246; 35:304-5
Parrott, Kent, 37:273, 348
Parrott, Tiburcio, 1:12
Parrott, William S., 6:136; 19:46; 34:111-12
Parrott & Co., 7:206; 16:200; 21:288; 34:112, 113, 114, 118
Parrott & Naglee, 16:282, 285
Parrott & Waterman, 33:167
Parrott Building, San Francisco, 17:169; 31:297; 37:131; 38:32, 33
Parrott, Talbot & Co., 34:111-12
Parry, Dr. (Alexander Perry?, 1851), 34:30
Parry, Charles, 18:344
Parry, George, 10:169, 172-80 *passim*
Parsloe, Charles T., Jr., 34:361, 362, 363
Parsons, Edward Lambe, 26:163
Parsons, Edward T., 4:52
Parsons, George Frederick, 35:336, 338, 342
Parsons, Levi, 3:167-68; 16:285; 22:112; 34:258; 36:329
Parsons, Luella Clay, 31:87
Parsons, Samuel, Jr., 35:357
Parsons, William, 15:173
Parthian (ship), 35:198
Parton, Sara P. ("Fanny Fern"), 9:60
Partridge & Brittain, 30:355
"Party, the Machine, and the Vote, The," by Franklin Hichborn, 38:349-57
Partz, Dr. (Mono Co., ca. 1865), 26:243
Pasadena, 31:15, 19-22
Pascal, Dubedat and Co., 39:231
Pascual, Juan, 7:300, 357, 380
Pascul, J. L., 25:12-13
Pasman, Francis, 22:251
Paso de Bartolo, 13:303
Paso del Pino, 14:132, 141
Paso Robles, 11:249, 250, 251, 264
Pasquale (Indian, 1852), 28:337
Passaic (ship), 27:179
Pass Creek Canyon, 32:207
Passe-Partout (weekly), 39:149, 349
"Passing of California Historical

Traditions, The," address by J. N. Bowman, 31:83-85
"Passing of Spanish California, The," by George Tays, 15:139-42
"Passion Play," Salmi Morse's, 21:249-53
Pass of Melfort (ship), 22:353
Pastor's (Tony) Vaudeville Company, 21:243
"Pastry War," 8:118
Patch, Selina, 16:131
Patch, W. Y., 17:179
Patch, Clayton & Co., 33:375
Pate, Benjamin T., 11:9
Patents: Miller's Steam Wagon, 9:374; telegraph, 29:355
Paterna, Antonio, 1:161; 10:217; 13:158; 23:371, 372
Paterson, George Churchill, 20:192
Pathological Society, San Francisco, 4:202
Patience (light opera), 19:97-98, 107
Patigian, Haig, 22:95
Patitoux (Fr. Canadian, 1846), 26:40, 41, 59
Patrick, G. Washington, 34:216
Patrick, George L., 40:319
Patriot, San Bernardino, 9:194, 198; 23:260; 24:275-76
Patriote, Le, San Francisco, 39:150, 151, 152, 349
Patrizi, Ettore, 25:231
Patrizia, Giovanni, 17:214
Patronage, political, 9:285; 19:264-68, 276; 32:146-47, 151-56 *passim;* 38:209
Patronato, 25:272, 278
Pattee, Frank A., 31:18
Pattee, Fred Lewis, 38:114-15
Pattee, Solon, 11:127
Patten, Benjamin Adam, 6:11-12; 17:174
Patterson (Panama, 1849), 27:36
Patterson, A. D., 8:202, 210
Patterson, A. W., 28:6
Patterson, C., 15:376
Patterson, C. P., 15:269; 32:350, 359
Patterson, Carlisle, 6:16
Patterson, Charles, 9:103
Patterson, Elijah, 3:90
Patterson, George, 14:205, 209, 227; 30:3, 4
Patterson, George W. and Clara (Hawley), 35:183-84
Patterson, Henry Hawley, obit., 35:183-84
Patterson, Mrs. Henry Hawley (Sara Morgan), 35:184

Patterson, James, 29:381

Patterson, John A., 28:59, 66, 67

Patterson, R. M., 22:292

Patterson, S. H. N., letter from, 24:245-46

Patterson & Stow, 40: foll. 206

Patti, Adelina, 11:11, 12, 13, 26; 20:133; 35:142

Patti, P., 15:181

Pattiani, Evelyn Craig (Mrs. William L.), 22:192; 31:380-81; "Silk in Piedmont," 31:335-42; obits. of Samuel Hubbard, 23:284-85; Charles F. Michaels, 23:185-86

Pattie, James Ohio, 2:8-13, 16-18, 256; 4:168; 10:4, 81; 13:210; 15:109; 35:236; illus., 15: opp. 110

Pattie, Sylvester, 2:18

Patton (lawsuit, Marysville, 1860), 10:252

Patton, Andrew Gwinn (or Gwynn), 18:33

Patton, D. C., 11:9

Patton, Daniel, 3:175-76, 177

Patton, George Smith, 38:361

Patton, William, 38:34

Patty, Dr. (Camp Wright, 1875), 27:224

Patty, J. H., 21:227

Paty, Ephraim, 14:292, 295, 304, 320

Paty, Henry, 14:292, 293, 303, 313-23 *passim*, 341, 342; 35:195-99 *passim*; *see also* Paty (Henry) & Co.

Paty, John, 12:138, 149, 281, 288; 17:298, 301; 22:288; 28:342; 30:3; 35:196, 200; phot., 14: opp. 310

Paty, Mrs. John (Mary Ann Jefferson), 14:309-10, 325, 337, 338; phot., 14: opp. 310

Paty, William, 12:138; 14:314, 319-20, 324, 333, 337-38

Paty family, 14:292-93, 338-41

Paty (Henry) & Co., 8:299, 341; 12:138

Paty (John and William) & Co., 14:324, 329

Paty (John), McKinley & Co., 14:324, 344

Pauba, *see* Temécula

Paul (Marysville, 1857), 9:137

Paul, Capt. (of *Great Republic*, 1865), 26:357

Paul, A. G., 39:210

Paul, Almarin B., 17:77, 79, 80

Paul, Charles F., 22:33

Paul, John, *see* Webb, Charles Henry

Paul, Rodman Wilson, 29:375; address,

"A Tenderfoot's Adventures in Hunting California History," 20:283

Paul Arniff (play), 21:256

Paulding, John, 18:150-51; 20:183

Pauley, A., 10:367

Paulhaus, Fred, 26:110

Pauline Blanchard (play), 20:137

Pauling and Kendall, 7:118

Paullin, George W., 8:278-79

Paullin, Louisa, 10:268, 393; 16:344

Paullin Family Dramatic Troupe, 10:258, 268

Paulson, J., 8:343

Pauly Ranch, 9:58, 73

Pauma, 3:244; massacre, 21:345, 356

Pauncefort, George, 21:142

Pautah County, 34:265

Pavilion, Marysville, 9:350, 351, 354, 360; 10:172, 252, 283, 360

Pavilion, Sacramento, 10:174, 176, 273, 361; 11:8

Pavis, Juan, *see* Pérez, Juan (1840)

Pawling (Paulding, Pawlding), Joseph, 38:329

"Pawnee" (pseud.), letters from, 24:40-43

Paxson, Frederic Logan, 27:87, 89; 28:86; 38:370; addresses: "The Approach of the Frontiers," 12:367; "Local History in the United States," 20:282; "The Treaty of Guadalupe Hidalgo," 27:87-89

Paxton (Marysville, 1860), 9:72; 10:250

Payeras, Mariano, 6:255; 12:121; 15:141; 16:110-11; 23:4, 6, 362, 372

Payette, Francis, 22:197, 213, 218

Payne, Eliza, 10:190

Payne, George L., 23:189

Payne, Julia, *see* Dunn, Julia (Payne)

Payne, Octavine C., *see* Glover, Mrs. J. T.

Payne, R. K., 5:125

Payne family, 10:190

Payne (Theodore) & Co., 15:163

Payne's [mining] Company, 35:208, 214

Payne's Ranch, Yuba Co., 10:254, 266

Payno, Capt. (Colorado R., 1858), 22:169

Payot, Henri, 30:258, 265, 357, 366; 31:81; 33:374; 39:158; *see also* Vincent & Payot

Payot, Upham & Co., 30:366

Payran, Stephen, 15:39

Payson, Albert Henry, obit., 9:95-96

Payson, Mrs. Albert Henry (Abby Josephine Parrott), 9:96; 18:189
Payson, George, 30:103-4
Payson, Mrs. Henry, 19:229
Payton, R. M., 9:115
Paz, Ireneo, *Life and Adventures of . . . Joaquin Murrieta,* trans. Belle, rev., 5:203
Pazos (Sonoma, 1835), 16:240
Peabody (Yosemite, 1852), 5:332-33
Peabody, E. T., 24:58-59
Peabody, J., 12:138
Peaches, 2:273; 5:266; 12:194, 258, 282; 14:10; 15:173; 17:41; 18:120; 27:119; 29:173, 175, 177
Peachy, Archibald Carey, 7:110; 11:7-10 *passim;* 15:6, 376; 16:198-99; 17: opp. 168; 19:231; *see also* Halleck, Peachy, and Billings
Peacock (ship, 1806), 12:137, 221, 222
Peacock (ship, 1836), 12:137-46 *passim;* 24:321; 28:111
Peale, Rembrandt, port. of Washington, 15:172
Peale, Titian R., 24:321, 333
Pearce, George, 26:29, 31, 54
Pearce, Joseph, 15:240
Pearce, W. Stanley, 24:382
Pearce, William H., 12:138
Pearis, Charles W., 9:269
Pearl (Yuba Co., 1858, 1861), 9:353; 10:363
Pearl, Roger H., 38:183; "The Shiftless Belligerent Pike . . . ," 38:113-29
Pearl (riv. str.), 15:271
Pearley, A., 10:266
Pearls, Island of, *see* Espiritu Santo Island; Perlas, Las
Pearls and pearl fishing, 1:36, 45, 50-51, 54; 6:296-99 *passim,* 306; 7:256-58, 307; 8:27, 31, 34, 261, 307-8; 15:374; 25:152, 168, 349, 351; 26:309, 311
Pears, 1:169; 2:183; 12:193, 205, 206, 258, 282; 17:41; 18:120; 25:31; 27:113, 119, 122; 29:175
Pearson, Edward L., 9:268
Pearson, George F., 23:335; 33:237
Pearson, James G., 9:29
Pearson, John, 35:208
Pearson, Robert H., 12:312; 13:249, 397-401 *passim;* 16:342; 17:80; 18:250; 19:32, 42
Peas, 4:364, 370; 5:266; 8:237; 12:293
Pease, Charles, 33:6, 12, 161; 35:292, 298
Pease, W. C., 6:16; 15:168

Peasley, Thomas, 21:58
Peattie, Donald Culross, 22:384; 24:322; 39:209, 217
Pecher, Edmond, 5:237, 243
Peck, Lt. (w. Frémont, 1845), 3:270
Peck (Yuba Co., 1859), 10:56
Peck (L.A., 1862), 3:165
Peck, A. S., 15:280
Peck, Austin H., Jr., 27:95
Peck, Charles, 38:33
Peck, Charles L., 11:176-78, 182; preëmption notice, 11: opp. 176
Peck, E. S., 14:394; 15:23
Peck, George, 22:31, 33
Peck, Nathan R., 40:333
Peck, Sherman, 12:138; 23:211, 313, 332
Peck, W. Harold, 25:382
Peck & Bliss, 9:248, 249, 251
Peckham, E. P., 9:109; 15:280, 364
Peckham, Robert F., 28:292; 29:25
Peckham, Mrs. Robert F. (Ann Elizabeth Smith), 28:292
Peckinpaugh family, 38:223-24
Pecos River, 18: 114-15; illus., 18: opp. 114
Peden, James A., 15:53
Pedestrian feats, 15:183, 185, 267, 268, 269; 38:25
Pedlar, Micah, Margaret and Mary Ellen, 27:186
Pedrazzini, Clay, 30:305
Pedro II, of Brazil, 6:211; 20:200
Pedrorena, Miguel de, 1:71; 3:119; 8:106; 17:233; 19:209, 215; 21:301, 304; 22:50, 57, 65; 26:22; 28:193, 196; 31:34, 37, 40, 45; 33:117-18, 123; fac. sig., 10: opp. 159
Pedrorena, Mrs. Miguel de (María Antonia Estudillo), 21:304; 34:208
Pedro Valley, 23:250
Pedro y Gil, Rafael de and Josepha (Chavira y Lerma), 20:237
Peebels, Cary, 28:298, 314, 316, 317; 29:39-40, 56
Peeke, C. E. B., 33:190
Peel, Sir Robert, 5:306; 18:146; 32:273; son of, 6:142; 15:235; 22:319
Peeler, James, 15:267
Peer and the Peasant, The, 10:57, 77
Peerless (ship), 22:352
Peevish (H. B. Co., 1833), 22:201, 209, 211, 218, 220, 340
Pefley, Ernest, 36:71
Pegg, Thomas, 6:343
Peg-Leg's mine, 2:9

Peguero, Alonso Esteban, 7:262, 263, 274, 299-300, 318, 327, 331, 336, 343, 347, 349, 377, 386; 8:43

Pegura (or Peguero), Mariano, 16:221

Peirce, Henry Augustus, 8:299; 14:320-21, 342, 343; 23:309, 314, 330; 28:108; 35:193-200 *passim;* letters to, 23:301-2, 308, 313

Peirce & Brewer, 23:333; 28:108, 256

Peirce, Fair & Co., 33:182

Peirson, Misses, Mrs. (Marysville, 1859), 10:42, 46, 55, 165

Peirson, Dr. and Mrs. E. M., 9:365, 366, 372, 376; 10:61, 190; 33:294, 305

Peirson, Oliver H., 9:353; 10:53, 54, 56, 178(?), 190, 262; 13:24; 14:398; 15:50

Peirson, Sarah, 10:55

Peixotto, Sidney I., 4:46

Pelby, Julia, 9:275

Pelican Bay, 28:245; *see also* Trinidad Bay

Pellegrini (S.F., 1873), 21:171

Pellet, Sarah, 8:212; 15:175, 176; 24:165; 32:131

Pellican, see Golden Hinde

Pelly, George, 28:100, 102, 107, 257

Pelly, Sir John Henry, 18:141; 28:107, 254, 257

Pelly & Allan, 28:107, 252

Pelton, John C., 10:288; 16:84; 26:348; 27:10, 236; 28:34

Pelton, Lester Allen, 29:203, 208

Pemberton, J. E., 36:48

Pemberton, Myriem, 33:314

Peña, Agustín de la, 10:317

Peña, Antonio, 16:246

Peña, Cosme, 13:227; 14:231, 249, 255, 258, 261; 15:339; 16:354-55

Peña, Felipe, 16:249; 23:295

Peña, Joaquín, 14:121; 15:61

Peña, José, 29:310

Peña, Tomás de la, 2:277-80 *passim;* 3:208; 9:203

Peñasquitos, Cañada, 26:59

Peñasquitos, Rancho, *see* Ranchos: Santa Margarita de los Peñasquitos

Peña y Peña, Manuel de la, 13:128-29, 143; 14:238

Pendegast, William Wirt, 25:22; 35:50

Pendergast, Joseph, 31:157

Pendleton, E. B., 31:47

Pendleton, George Allan, 1:213; 20:115; 31:38

Pendleton, Joseph H., 22:176

Pène, Henri de, 39:160

"Peninsula Explorations," address by Joseph M. Gleason, 3:99-100

Pennington, John, 8:359

Pennsylvania (ship), 30:293

"Pennsylvanians, The," 9:264, 286, 385

Penny (prison warden, 1862), 10:373

Penny, Moses A., 1:267

Pennypacker, Joseph J. (?), 21:307

Penny Post Co., 16:338; 17:177

Penoche Pass, 11:250

Pensions for teachers, 5:285

Penty, Lester, 9:133

Peoples, John H., 26:329, 347; 30:56-62 *passim*

People's Insurance Co., 26:355; 27:168, 270

People's Line, 16:64

Peoples Park, San Mateo, 36:300

People's parties: in 1850s, 9:106; 16:80, 81; in 1860s, 22:231; in 1890s, 19:59; 27:313; 28:48; *see also* Populists

People's Press, San Francisco, 19:66; 27:318

People's Theater, San Francisco, 15:173, 181, 183

"People's ticket," 9:108, 110-11

Peor es Nada (ship), 18:175

Peoria House, 9:70, 79, 266, 287, 352; 10:170, 366

Pepin (S.F., 1849), 5:20

Pepin, Capt. (of *Thérèse,* 1849), 13:382

Pepiquignot (or Pequinot, "Grésely"; S.F., 1849), 5:20, 176

Pepper, Nelson, 21:359, 360-61

Pepper, Thomas ("Pimiento"), 14:17

Pepper's ranch, 10:170

Peppers, 5:136, 257, 263

Pera, José, 15:40

Perabeau, Theresa Leonora, 28:294

Peralta, Antonia María, *see* Toler, Mrs. William Pinckney

Peralta, Antonio María, 4:211; 7:400; 8:273; 30:2, 218-22 *passim,* opp. 224, 227

Peralta, Francisco, 30:223, 224, 229

Peralta, Gabriel and Francisca (Valenzuela), 14:6; 30:217

Peralta, Hermenegildo Ignacio, 30:218-24 *passim,* opp. 224

Peralta, Mrs. Hermenegildo Ignacio (Rafaela Sánchez), 31:77

Peralta, Herminia, *see* Dargie, Mrs. William

Peralta, Joaquín, 31:77

Peralta, José, 14:121

Peralta, José Domingo, 17:42, 44; 30:218, 219, 220, 224, opp. 225, 226; 31:331, 333
Peralta, José Vicente, 17:225, 226, 229; 30:218, 219, 220, 224, opp. 224, 225
Peralta, Mrs. José Vicente, 25:190
Peralta, Luis María, 4:93; 7:400; 15:278; 17:42, 44; 23:375; 30:2, 4, 217-31 *passim*; 36:349-50
Peralta, Mrs. Luis María (María Loreto Alviso), 30:217, 218
Peralta, María Gertrudis, 30:217
Peralta, María Guadalupe, 30:218, 221, 228
Peralta, Pedro Regaldo, 30:217
Peralta, Rafael, 31:77
Peralta, Sebastian, 14:23; 29:57
Peralta family, 7:400; 17:42; 18:180; 36:349-50; art. on, 30:217-31
Peralta *v.* Peralta, 15:278; 29:247
Peralta Creek, 30:219, 223
Peralta Park, 27:344-45
"Peraltas and Their Houses, The," by J. N. Bowman, 30:217-31
Perasich, Nicholas, 17:211, 218
Perchoir (or Pichoir), Henry, 28:233, 240, 241
Perdriau, Ethel K., port. of Henry L. Ford, 29: opp. 132
Pereda y Arce, Francisco de, 27:310
Pereyra, Gerónimo, 2:143-44
Perez, Eugene Reyes, 25:287
Pérez, José, 13:212, 223
Pérez, José Bernardo de Jesús, 16:241
Pérez, Juan (1770s), 9:203-8 *passim*, 229-34 *passim*, 238; 11:276-79 *passim*; 31:123, 124; 40:237-38, 239, 243, 244, 246
Pérez, Juan (1840), 15:122, 137
Perez, Pedro, 11:276-77, 278, 279
Pérez, Sebastián, 3:21
Pérez de León, I. Evan, 4:152
Pérez Fernández, José, 15:60
Pérez Rosales, Vicente, 22:268
Perham, Franklin Eugene, 26:189
Peril (play), 21:174
Perin, M. R., 4:321
Periodical News Depot, San Francisco, 30:100-101
Peri's (Marysville, 1860), 10:252, 253, 262, 265
Perkey, J. D., 4:320; 5:125
Perkins, Capt. (of *Columbia*, 1844), 5:47
Perkins, A. M., 15:171
Perkins, Asa B., 15:370
Perkins, Dana, 19:67

Perkins, Edward Huntington, 21:191
Perkins, Eli, 4:321
Perkins, Fred B., 1:13, 14; 24:79; 27:346
Perkins, George Clement, 19:8, 67, 156; 27:197; 28:48, 52; 31:337-38; 33:374; 38:38
Perkins, H. K. W., 4:356
Perkins, Henry C., 28:233, 240; 29:200-201, 206
Perkins, James, 15:369-70
Perkins, Joel and John (to Oregon, 1844), 4:321
Perkins, John I., obit., 21:191
Perkins, Mrs. M. Russell, 31:287
Perkins, Richard F., 10:388
Perkins, Rufus, 23:215
Perkins, Samuel J. M., 2:122
Perkins, T. A., 1:107-8
Perkins, Thomas, 13:84
Perkins, William, 14:61, 71
Perkins, William Dana, 10:76
Perkins, Bensley and Co., 17:175
Perkins' New Montgomery Boarding House, San Francisco, 35:157
Perlas, Las, island, 1:48; 3:318, 336, 346, 368
Perley, Duncan W., 11:47, 48; 19:347; 29:20, 26; 38:212, 213
Péron, Capt. (Monterey, 1796), 1:173-77
Peron (S.F., 1850), 5:141, 143
Perot (lawsuit, 1879), 30:333, 337-38
Perote, Mex., 23:273; Castle of, 23:351, 370; 27:382
Perret (to mines, 1849), 5:176; *see also* Grand-Perret
Perret, Mrs. (S.F., 1850), 5:24-25
Perret, Maurice-Edmond, 30:305-14 *passim*
Perrier, George, 6:20, 21, 22, 26-29 *passim*
Perriere, Fanny, 17:77, 178, 179
Perriman, Capt. (of *Dreadnaught*, 1867), 22:171
Perrin, E. B., 25:24, 173
Perrin, E. M., 39:155-56
Perrin, Ervin R., 10:291
Perrin, George and Jeannette, 23:191
Perrin Colonies, 25:173
Perrine, Henry E., 11:358, 361, 362; 17:177
Perring, F., 30:262
Perrin House, Sacramento, 10:291-92
Perrot, Baptiste, 26:45
Perrot, Leopold, 23:54-55

Perry, Dr. (S.F., 1849), 21:308; 22:68(?)
Perry (through Mex., 1850), 21:321
Perry (Mt. Shasta, 1862), 7:126
Perry, Alexander, 33:250, 261, 341
Perry, Dwight R., 13:31
Perry, E. H., 24:362
Perry, E. Wood, Jr., 24:265, 266
Perry, Elijah, 15:240
Perry, Emma, 27:285
Perry, Harry A., 10:360, 369; 39:298
Perry, Mrs. Harry A., *see* Land, Agnes
Perry, Henry G., 11:127
Perry, Irene, 35:141
Perry, J. A., 23:280
Perry, John, Jr., 9:26; 15:164, 179, 272
Perry, Martha Stanwood, 31:290, 300
Perry, Matthew Calbraith, 18:85, 86;
    28:200
Perry, William Hayes, 13:330-31,
    335-36; 31:286
Perry's Great European Panorama,
    10:165
Persey, S., 31:331
Pershbacker, Mrs. (S.F., 1861), 10:276
Pershing, John J., 34:161
Persinger, Louis, 25:236
Person, F., 29:225
"Personal Experiences of the Modoc
    War," address by Maurice
    FitzGerald, 15:286
Personal History and Reminiscences,
    by Root, rev., 4:93-94
"Personal View of the Literature of
    California, The," address by George
    R. Stewart, Jr., 14:410
"Personalities behind San Francisco's
    Street Names," address by Elizabeth
    G. Potter, 19:187
Persons, Ebenezer, 26:110, 113
Peru (S.F., 1849), 5:22-23
Peru, 6:309, 310, 312; 15:140; 17:200-206;
    19:334; 26:75, 218-19; *see also* Lima
Peru (ship), 13:248; 30:289-92
Peruvian (ship), 38:377
Peruvians, 27:38, 48
Peryam, Thomas, 19:320
Pescadero, San Joaquin Co., 2:183, 196,
    200; 21:325
Pescadero, San Mateo Co., 20:264, 268
Pescadero Creek, 29:57; 31:301
Pescadores, bay of, 3:6, 7, 18
Pescatore, Le (ship), 22:300, 303
Peso, value of, 1:196-97
Pestshowroff, Capt. (of *Gaidamack*,
    1863), 26:15

Petaluma, 1:184-85; 14:78; 16:111, 116,
    235, 236, 354; 17:84; 20:260; 30:262,
    310, 311, 362-63, 367; 38:312
Petaluma (str.), 10:276, 373
Petaluma Creek, 23:22
Peter, John Thomas and Elizabeth
    (Peter), 29:285
Peter, Samuel and Anne Elizabeth
    (Lewis), 29:285
"Peter H. Burnett and the Provisional
    Government Movement," by
    William E. Franklin, 40:123-36
"Peter Lassen and His Mountain,"
    address by Mrs. F. H. Colburn, 7:201
"Peter Lassen, . . . Trail-Blazer," by
    Ruby J. Swartzlow, 18:291-314
Peter Pan (play), 35:142
Peters (Timbuctoo, 1859), 10:189
Peters, Charles Rollo, 37:35
Peters, DeWitt Clinton, 1:111, 150
Peters, Harry Twyford, 15:99, 188
Peters, J. D., 35:365
Peters, P. S., 13:31
Peters, Randolph, 23:276, 349
Petersburg, 11:179
Petersburgh (ship), 19:53
"Peter Skene Ogden," address by
    Lewis A. McArthur, 22:375
"Peter Skene Ogden's Trapping
    Expedition to the Gulf of California,
    1829-30," by Alice B. Maloney,
    19:308-16
"Peter Smith Titles," 34:251, 257
Peterson (Yosemite, 1856), 1:275
Peterson (C.P.R.R., 1870s), 18:356-57
Peterson, Fred G., 29:225
Peterson, Harry C., 20:96; address,
    "Landmarking Pilgrimage through
    the '49 Mining District," 3:97
Peterson, William H. (San Pascual,
    1846), 26:45
Peterson, William H. (L.A., 1850s),
    13:335
Peterviue (Amador Co., 1855), 15:376
Pet Hill, 11:155
Peti (Indian, 1836), 16:249
Petit (Trinity mines, 1850), 5:234
Petit, W. H., 9:277
Petit Californien, Le (weekly,
    semi-weekly), 39:167, 225, 227, 234,
    349
Petit Courrier, Le (weekly), 39:245, 349
"Petites Affiches, Les," 39:149
"Petition from Alpheus B. Thompson
    to Governor Victoria, A," ed. and

trans. D. Mackenzie Brown, 26:249-52, 285

Petit Journal, Le (weekly), San Francisco, 39:219, 222-23, 349

Petit-Thouars, Abel du, *see* Dupetit-Thouars

Petra, Majorca, 11:79-81, 280-88; 30:376

Petrel (ship), 11:179

Petroff, Ivan, 4:106; 5:121, 264, 270, 271

Petroleum, 30:210-15, 339; *see also* Oil

Petroliopolis (Lyons Station), 15:102, 115

Petronila, Miss (m. Isaac Thompson), 28:292

Petrov, Capt. (of *Kadiak*, 1808), 12:228

Pettengill, J., 20:44

Pettengill, S. B., 24:225, 226

Pettet, William, 5:406

Pettigrew (Venice I., 1871), 17:46

Pettinos, George F., 10:293; 14:392; 15:46

Pettis, George Henry, 28:170; 40:297

Pettit, A. P., 15:181

Pettitt, Mrs. Ann M. A., 19:230, 236; 28:33

Peyri, Antonio, 6:258; 8:225-31, 291; 19:209, 215; 23:194, 206-7, 216, 371

Peyton, (Philippines, 1898), 31:172

Peyton, Bailie, 9:39, 103, 109, 113, 114; 14:364, 371; 15:72, 73, 146, 280, 281; 16:81, 339; 17:169, 177

Peyton, Bernard, 19:230; 31:47

Peyton, Mrs. Bernard (Estelle Hermann), 19:230

Peytona (bark), 14:386

Peytona (str.), 15:171

Pfeffenhauser, Charles, 19:214

Pfeiffer, Ida, 32:125

Pfister, Edward H. von, *see* Von Pfister

Pfister, Henry Adolph, 39:30

Pflueger, Timothy, 38:3-4

Pflugart, George W., 13:340

Phantom (ship), 5:140

Phare, Le (semi-weekly), San Francisco, 28:135, 142; 39:149-53, 159-60, 322, 349

Phèdre (play), 20:139, 141

Phelan, James, 9:294; 13:85; 29:93

Phelan, Mrs. James (Agnes Kelly), 9:294

Phelan, James Duval, 9:88; 10:307; 13:85; 30:70; 35:149, 150; 36:201; 38:252; address, "John C. Frémont," 6:285-86; obit. of Mrs. Edward Martin, 7:291-92; obit., 9:294-95

Phelan (T. J.) & Co., 17:176

Phelps (lawsuit, Yuba Co., 1858), 9:358

Phelps, Rev. Dr. (Sacramento, 1861), 27:154

Phelps, Bethuel, 2:202; 6:150; 19:322

Phelps, Charles H., 28:10

Phelps, F. S., 19:156

Phelps, Fanny Morgan, 21:65

Phelps, T. J., 15:205, 206

Phelps, Timothy Guy, 10:62; 11:8, 9, 21; 28:50; 33:374

Phelps, Walton, 22:17

Phelps, William Dane, 6:132; 8:118, 295, 297, 305; 14:329, 331, 333, 345; 15:58, 62-63, 68, 69, 226, 236; 18:53; 19:216; 23:201, 215; 29:271

Phelps & Co., Marysville, 30:259

Phenizie, Luther, 13:32

Phifer, *see* Fifer

Phi Gamma Delta, 9:379

Philadelphia (sailing packet), 13:391

Philadelphia (str.), 8:7, 10

Philadelphia Company, 23:276, 349-53 *passim*

Philadelphia Mining Co., 22:14-15

Philadelphia Restaurant, San Francisco, 8:273

Philbrook, Francis D., 2:92, 122

Philharmonic Society, *see* San Francisco Philharmonic Society

Philip, John Van Ness, 31:210, 216

Philippine Islands: soldiers from Calif. in, 20:24; 30:295-303; 31:49-67, 163-73; trade with and routes to and from, 1:157, 158; 2:140-60; 3:3-5, 10-12, 313; 7:132-93, 235-45, 302, 356, 359, 363, 366; 8:44-50; 15:382; 23:219-25; 25:150, 167; 27:289; 31:107-8; *see also* Manila galleons

Philip III, cedula for conquest of Californias, 31:123

Philips, Joe, 10:60

Philips, Oscar, 26:204

Philips, Samuel S., 17:174

Phillips (S.F., 1855), 15:268, 269

Phillips, A. A., 40:205, 209, 210

Phillips, Adelaide, 21:68

Phillips, Caroline ("Callie"), 9:287, 352, 354; 10:366

Phillips, Catherine Coffin (Mrs. Lee A.), 22:94; *Cornelius Cole*, rev., 8:382-83; *Jessie Benton Fremont*, rev., 15:99-100

Phillips, Chauncey Hatch, 37:207

Phillips, Cyrus Olin, "To the Fraser River!," diary and letters, ed. Frederic

W. Howay, 11:150-56; map by, opp.
155

Phillips, Dan, 22:243

Phillips, Frank, 22:243

Phillips, Henry Byron, "Restitution of
Decayed Intelligence, A: More
History of the . . . Society,"
1:107-10; obit., 3:399-400

Phillips (or Philips), John, 14:72, 176,
177, 182

Phillips, John G., 15:76, 83, 84-85, 148

Phillips, Josephine, 9:266, 287, 345, 354;
10:253, 278, 280, 366

Phillips, Mrs. Lee A., *see* Phillips,
Catherine Coffin

Phillips, Paul Chrisler, ed. Ferris, *Life
in the Rocky Mountains*, rev.,
19:280-81

Phillips, Thomas, 9:287; family of, 9:266,
287, 353, 354; 10:366

Phillips, Violet, 32:375

Phillips, William, 9:265, 287, 345-46;
10:185

Phillipson, William M., *Life and
Voyages*, rev., 5:403-4

Philo (place), 33:366

Philosophical Union of the University
of California, 37:45-46

"Philosophy in California to 1906 and
Some of Its Antecedents," by Elmo A.
Robinson, 36:333-57; 37:39-49

Phipps (S.F., 1850), 12:102

Phipps, George, 8:210

Phoenix, Sheriff (Amador Co., 1855),
16:79

Phoenix, John (pseud.), *see* Derby,
George Horatio

Phoenix (dredger), 6:244; 15:51-52;
illus., 6: opp. 244

Phoenix (ship), 15:366

Phoenix, The, Sacramento, 6:4, 8-12

Phoenix Engine Co., Benicia, 10:285

Phoenix Exchange, San Francisco,
8:273; 20:293

Phoenix Hotel, Stockton, 22:76

Phoenixiana, by George Horatio Derby,
11:99, 101

"Phoenixiana," address by Francis P.
Farquhar, 12:367

Phoenix Insurance Co., 26:254, 258,
357-58; 27:167

Phoenix Mine, 31:290

Phoenix Theatre, San Francisco, 20:293

Photographic Art Society of the Pacific
Coast, 35:49, 55

"Photographs of California Missions,"
address by William E. Waste, 34:87

Photography, 9:377; 14:157; 34:289-300;
see also Daguerreotypes

Phrenology, 36:355

Physicians and Surgeons, College of,
30:67-71

Pianos, 6:227; 13:34-37; 17:154, 235;
24:372, 381; 28:38

Piat, R. F., 10:383, 394

Piazzoni, Gottardo, 38:1-3, 7-8; design
for mural, foll. 8

Picayune, San Francisco, 10:241; 28:36;
31:139-40; 39:14, 15, 16

Pichette, Louis, 22:198, 201, 208, 216-17,
220, 329, 335; 23:128, 139

Pichette, Mrs. Louis (Margaret Becier),
25:221

Pickard, Dan, 38:60

Pickard, Herman, 2:105

Pickering, Charles, 4:161; 24:324

Pickering, Loring, 7:278; 13:298-99;
20:334, 335, 336; 25:287; 26:228

Pickering & Bradshaw, 30:111

Pickersgill, Robert W., 8:343, 360; 9:265,
266, 361; 10:58, 77, 179

Pickett, Charles Edward, 10:378, 391;
15:365; 16:183; 21:80, 355; 26:20,
38-39, 132; 36:243

Pickett, George, 40:221, 232

Pickett, J. W., 26:327

Pickett, John T., 34:134, 153

Pickup, George(?), 14:278

Pickwick Hotel, San Francisco, 15:369

Pico, Andrés, 1:171, 172, 240, 259; 3:122,
125; 8:252; 9:257, 269, 282, 283; 10:
opp. 48, 62, 70, 74; 11:9, 342; 12:133,
135; 13:47-48, 52, 99, 132-36, 153, 212,
223, 303, 304, 327, 336, 341-42, 346, 349;
15:285; 16:360, 363-64; 17:178, 340-41,
345; 18:168, 178; 21:322, 337-54 *passim*;
22:41, 43, 44, 64, 175; 25:293; 26:25-46
passim; 27:242, 247; 29:36, 234, 236-37,
239, 241, 335; 30:51, 53; 33:264; 38:26;
40:344; "lady of," 1:239

Pico, Antonio María, 13:58, 78; 15:4, 19;
16:353; 17:233; 27: opp. 97; fac. sig.,
10: opp. 159

Pico, Concepción, 27:337

Pico, Emanuel, 14:155

Pico, Francisco Javier, 23:218

Pico, José Antonio Bernardino, 12:123;
21:345

Pico, José de Jesús, 1:167, 170, 171-72;
6:160, 166; 13:153, 327; 14:258; 16:218,

354; 19:132-33, 142; 25:145; 29:342, 343; 30:52-53
Pico, José Dolores, 3:25, 26
Pico, José María, 13:208
Pico, José Ramón, 27:222
Pico, Mariquita, 26:25
Pico, Miguel and Patricio, 23:218
Pico, Pío de Jesús, 11:220; 12:135; 13:208, 214, 223, 313, 322-23, 349; 14:232, 234, 239, 247, 248; 16:223, 352; 17:60; 21:346, 356; 22:175; against Alvarado, 14:236; 16:360, 363, 364; 17:53; against Micheltorena, 11:204; against Victoria, 13:212; 16:225; gov. of Calif., 1:254, 256; 5:79, 302; 6:186, 189-90, 191, 270, 370; 8:73, 258; 10:99, 100-117 *passim*, 127; 11:206, 342-43, 347, 348, 356; 12:37, 38, 48, 50, 52, 129, 149-53 *passim*; 13:47, 48, 99-149, 214-15, 231-32; 14:147; 16:57, 226, 230; 17:136, 161, 162, 163, 220, 274, 278, 280, 283; 18:167, 176; 19:118, 137; 25:122, 123, 128; 29:135, 333; 33:250; land grants by, 11:71; 12:200; 21:331; 23:254, 255; 27:108, 109, 250; cor., 1:286-89, 290-91; 3:87, 184-86; 5:186-88, 296-97; 6:366-68; 10:114-16, opp. 116; 13:103-49; 33:263; decrees and procs., 1:186-89; 6:83-87; 13:122-24; 23:9-10; speech, 13:304; port., 13: opp. 99
Pico, Salomon, 13:327-28; 18:268, 271, 277
Pico, Santiago de la Cruz, 13:202, 208
Pico, Vicente, 28:179
Pico family, 21:347; 27:337
Pico (ship), 25:259
Pico Canyon, 30:210
Picot de Moras (S.F., 1850), 6:43-44; 39:13
Picpus Fathers, 32:50, 122, 139
Pictorial History of California, ed. Coy, rev., 5:89-90
Pidaucet (from France, 1849), 5:5, 17, 18, 22, 23, 31, 36, 42, 145, 155-61 *passim*, 166, 170-77 *passim*, 219-28 *passim*, 233, 235, 246, 348; 6:56
Piedmont, 4:211; 22:192; 31:335-42 *passim*; 380-81
Piedra Blanca Rancho, *see* Ranchos: Piedra Blanca
Piedra Pintada, La, of Carrizo Plain, 1:153, 156
Piedras Blancas, Point, *see* San Martin, Cape

Pierce (Sonoma, 1850), 24:57
Pierce (Marysville, 1858), 9:376
Pierce (S.F. and Ore., 1850), 12:97, 98
Pierce (Calaveras Co., 1856), 22:79
Pierce, Capt. (Colorado R., 1865-70), 22:171, 172, 173
Pierce, B. F., 2:116
Pierce, Benjamin, 11:306, 307
Pierce, Charles D., 2:121
Pierce, Franklin, 7:4; 9:397; 15:203, 249-51; 19:173, 174, 256, 264, 267; 31:195-96, 200; letter to, 15:80-83
Pierce, H. D., 13:32
Pierce, Horace, 27:304-5
Pierce, J. D., 6:74
Pierce, James, 23:94
Pierce, Mrs. James H. (Marion Thurston), obit., 11:192
Pierce (or Peirce), Joshua H., 22:33
Pierce, Mrs. Nellie, 36:251-52
Pierce, Mrs. Orestes, 36:45
Pierce, Parker H., 15:28
Pierce, R. R., 15:280
Pierce, W. S., 14:396; 15:21, 28, 29
Pierce, William (L.A., 1847), 33:257
Pierce, William (Sacramento Valley, ca. 1851), 22:368
Pierce, Winslow S., 15:182
Pierce *v.* Reeves, 10:168
Pierce, Mount, 34:3, 14
Piercey (Berkeley, 1856), 31:331
Piercy, Charles W., 10:278; 39:297; 40:309-13 *passim*
Piercy, Samuel W., 21:251
Pierpont, James, 32:54, 124
Pierpont, Robert R., 29:159
Pierre's Hole, 22:214
Pierson, Mrs. (S.F., 1850), 12:99
Pierson (Marysville, 1859), 10:178; *see also* Peirson
Pierson, Capt. (Colorado R., 1862-72), 22:170-74 *passim*
Pierson, A. B., 35:163
Pierson, George, 15:52
Pierson, Hiram, 15:186
Pigeon Point, 27:71; 35:238
Pigman, Walter Griffith, 23:178
Pigné-Dupuytren, J. B., 18:17; 35:316; 39:4, 330-32
Pigot, William J., 12:229
"Pike," art. on, 38:113-29
Pike, Austin F., 31:44
Pike, Dan, 9:347
Pike, Harriet (Murphy), *see* Nye, Mrs. Michael C.

Pike, J. M., 33:277

Pike, Naomi L. (Mrs. Mitchell, Mrs. Schenck), 14:205, 227

Pike, Mrs. William M. (Harriet F. Murphy), 14:205

Pike, Zebulon, 12:79

Pike County (ship), 15:167

Pike's Peak gold rush, 27:182

Piland, Wayne R., 35:333

Pilcher, Joshua, 4:117

"Pile Island," San Francisco, 21:75; 22:113

Pilgrim (brig, 1830s), 8:294-95; 9:95; 13:218; 14:346; 23:198, 199, 315, 316, 320, 321, 322, 332, 333; illus., 8: opp. 289

Pilgrim (schr., 1855), 15:269

Pillet, Edmond, 16:83

Pillett (Sutter's Ft., 1846), 22:221

Pillsbury, Edith, *see* Bliss, Mrs. Walter D.

Pillsbury, Evans Searle, 10:414; 18:182; 19:85; 36:45

Pillsbury, Mrs. Evans Searle (Estelle Kendall), 19:85

Pillsbury, Mrs. George Bigelow, 21:192

Pillsbury, Harris, 36:320, 321, 322

Pillsbury, Horace Davis, 10:414; 17:359; obit., 19:85-86

Pillsbury, Mrs. Horace Davis (Elizabeth Taylor), 19:86

Pillsbury, Samuel, 24:266(?); 36:306

Pilot Knob, 36:220

Pilot Peak, 32:202

Pilxin, Capt. (of *Abreck*, 1863), 26:15

Piña, Blas, 20:186

Piña, Lázaro, 13:36; 16:225, 249, 306, 356; 17:63, 64; 18:293, 310

Piña, Máximo, 13:206

Piñadero, *see* Bernal de Piñadero

Pinchot, Gifford, 38:220-21, 249, 253

Pindell, J. M., 32:151-52, 158

Pindray, Charles, Marquis de, 5:15-16, 249-52; 6:46-47; 7:198; 11:388; 18:4-6, 10-11, 13; 35:319; 39:144

Pine, Elizabeth Wecter, bk. rev. by, 39:88-89

Pine (Pinheiro), Frank, 35:235

Pine City, 4:39

Pine Creek, Butte (or Tehama) Co., 22:212; 23:133

Pineda, Antonio, 3:215, 218, 233, 234

Pineda, Arcadio, 3:215, 218, 233, 234

Pine Grove, Amador Co., 18:22; 19:294; 20:181-85 *passim*; Hotel, 20:183

Pine Grove, Sierra Co., 9:61, 69, 70; 11:238, 240; 19:292, 294; mill, 9:52, 70

Pine Grove, Sonoma Co., 38:312

Pine Log, 14:141

Pines, 2:225, 283, 286, 290, 314; 12:190, 223; 16:14; 17:43; 18:328, 335-43 *passim*; 20:39; 26:245; 30:223; 33:60

Pine Street Baptist Church, San Francisco, 27:306-7, 309

Piney Paradise, A, by McLane, rev., 38:173-74

Pink Dominoes (play), 21:246

Pinkham, Benjamin Franklin, 22:30; 30:115

Pinkney, Alex., 4:234

Pinkney, Robert F., 3:111-12, 118; 14:149; 20:217, 219

Pino, Miguel, 11:279

Pinole (food), 20:352; 21:216, 218; 38:104

Piñon nuts, 26:234, 246

Pinos, Bahia de los, 7:25, 26, 51, 57

Pinos, Cabo de (Point Reyes), 7:25, 26, 51, 52, 53, 57, 75, 76

Pinos, Point, 1:174; 3:109; 7:357; 8:56, 100, 154; lighthouse, 29:28

Pinson, D., 13:32

Pinson, Paul, 4:32

Pinto, Rafael, 6:269; 15:127-28; 28:261

Pioche, François Louis Alfred, 5:13, 42, 346; 19:231, 237; 21:329; 36:306

Pioche & Bayerque, 5:42; 7: opp. 110; 22:175, 177; 40:209

Pioda (S.F., 1850), 6:45

Pioda, Louis, 38:342-46

Pioneer, San Jose, quoted, 18:292-93, 310

Pioneer (ship), 35:302

"Pioneer Agricultural Colonies of Fresno County," by Virginia E. Thickens, 25:17-38, 169-77

Pioneer Association, Sacramento, *see* Sacramento Society of California Pioneers

Pioneer Book Store, *see* Marvin & Hitchcock

"Pioneer Builders of California's Horticulture," address by H. M. Butterfield, 28:373

Pioneer Company of Fast Coaches, 24:43

Pioneer Engine Co., Marysville, 10:196, 258

Pioneer Hall, San Francisco, 36:298

"Pioneer Horticulture in California," address by H. M. Butterfield, 19:375

Pioneer Memorial Church, Sacramento, 26:170
Pioneer Mill, 38:60
"Pioneer Miner and the Pack Mule Express, The," address by Ernest A. Wiltsee, 9:407
Pioneer Mother of California, A, by Brooks, rev., 2:84
Pioneer Museum and Art Gallery, Stockton, 27:379
Pioneer Notes, by Hayes, ed. Wolcott, rev., 8:280-81
Pioneer of 1850, A, by Read, rev., 6:376-77
Pioneer, The; or *California Monthly Magazine,* 7:278; 14:74, 75, 76; 25:100-101, 102, 337, 345; 30:252
"Pioneers and Pioneer Native Sons of Marysville," address by Fred H. Greely, 8:137
Pioneers of California, by Cowan, rev., 8:186
"Pioneers of the Sierra," address by Francis P. Farquhar, 3:97
Pioneer Stage Co., 7:17, 19: 20:158
"Pioneers: . . . Three Early California Printing Presses," address by Carl I. Wheat, 11:389
Pioneer Tannery, 33:67
"Pioneer Visitors to Death Valley after the Forty-niners," by Carl I. Wheat, 18:195-216
Pioneer Water Cure Institute, 34:346
"Pio Pico's Correspondence with the Mexican Government," ed. George Tays, 13:99-149
Piopiomoxmox, *see* Yellow Serpent
Piotrowski, Rudolf K., 34:313, 315-16
Pious Fund, 1:10, 14, 21; 4:147; 5:209, 211, 212; 6:103-4; 13:86; 14:235-36, 260; 18:153, 248; 21:283; 22:95; 23:16; 24:307-8, 318; 25:361; 26:310; 27:337; address on, 6:103-4
"Pious Fund of California before the Hague Tribunal, The," address by Jackson H. Ralston, 6:103-4
Pipe lines, for oil, 30:212, 213
Piper, John, 21:142, 176; *see also* Piper's Opera House
Piper, John Henry, 21:176
Piper, N. H., 13:296
Piper, William A., 9:26; 15:367
Piper brothers: N. T. and Samuel, 34:225

Piper's Opera House, Virginia City, 21:142, 165, 176, 242, 270
"Pipes, Jeems," *see* Massett, Stephen
Pipi (Monterey, 1848), 13:65
Pique (S.F., 1864), 24:263
Pique (ship), 15:181, 269
Pirouette (ship), 10:72
"Pisco John," 16:199
Pismo, *see* Ranchos: Pismo
Pitcher, Jonathan, 2:122
Pit Lake, 22:205, 213, 215
Pitman, A. J., 26:345
Pit River, 19:313-14; 22:101, 103, 195, 206-8, 213, 215, 216; 23:136; 28:119, 120, 122
Pittman, Amos Salisbury, "The California and Australia Gold Rushes, as Seen by," ed. Theressa Gay, 30:15-37
Pittman Act, 32:19, 23-24
Pitts, Henry F., 2:185, 361; 3:85; 8:74
Pittsburg, 8:17; 30:345-51 *passim;* 35:265; phot., 12: opp. 25; *see also* New York of the Pacific
Pittsburgh Bar, Yuba Co., 8:338, 345, 349, 355
Pitzer, Jessie S., 9:103; 10:356
Pixley, Frank Morrison, 10:42, opp. 48, 49, 50, 53, 62, 64. 65, 71, 75, 96, 295, 375, 381; 15:29(?), 280, 335; 16:81, 339; 17:169, 315; 30:130
Pixley, Mrs. Frank Morrison, 10:176; 24:68, 266
Pixley, M., 15:29
Pixley, Seymour, 8:363; 10:50, 73
Pixton, Robert, 14:278
Pizarro, Francisco, 6:297, 309
Pizarro (ship), 6:257, 259, 260, 261; 14:343
Place (lawsuit, 1856), 34:232
Place, James, 33:343, 344
Place names, 11:304; 18:200; 22:370; art. on, 32:43-48; addresses on, 15:89; 28:184-85; bks. on, rev., 5:88-89, 315-16, 403; 7:286-87
Place Names in the High Sierra, by Farquhar, rev., 5:315-16
Placer County, 7:14; pioneers, 2:203-10; 8:383
Placer Democrat, Auburn, 20:161; 25:380
Placer Herald, Auburn, 18:361
Placer Hotel, San Francisco, 25:103
Placerito Canyon, 7:199; 10:86
Placer mining, *see* Gold mining

Placer Rifles, 10:198

Placer Times, Sacramento, 7:277, 278; 10:145, 148; 13:297, 298, 299; 15:301; 20:332, 333, 334

Placer Times and Transcript, Sacramento and San Francisco, 9:197; 13:299; 16:79; 17:177; 20:334-39 *passim*

Placerville, Calif., 7:9, 13, 15; 8:210; 13:174; 33:351; in 1850s, 3:72; 6:128-29; 7:5, 13; 9:39; 12:323, 328, 329; 17:75, 78; 30:111, 259; 32:54, 124; in 1860s, 20:255; 22:359; newspaper, 12:323, 329; 20:162; illus., 8: opp. 202; *see also* Dry Diggings; Hangtown

Placerville, Idaho, 16:172-77 *passim*

Placerville, Humboldt, and Salt Lake Telegraph Co., 12:323; 29:346, 348-50, 352

Plaindealer, San Francisco, 26:182

"Plains, The" (gambling house), Sacramento, 24:357

Plainsburg, 18:26

Planche, James R., 9:79

Planel, Louis T., 4:207

Planel, Mme. Louis T., 32:118

Planer, Edward Thomas, Jr., 25:95; address, "Some Observations of California Mission Life," 30:84-86

"Plan of Pitic," 1:25

Plant (ship), 8:293-94; 23:196, 197, 301, 307-10 *passim*, 313, 314, 330, 331

"Plant Content of Adobe Bricks, The," by George W. Hendry and Margaret P. Kelly, 4:361-73

Plante, Charles, 22:197, 198, 200, 203, 208, 217, 221; wife of, 23:136

Planters' Hotel, 8:201

"Plants as Documents of Human History," address by Carl O. Sauer, 22:374-82

Plata piña, 23:311, 313, 331

Plate, A. J., 37:206

Plath, Harry W., 19:192

"Plath Sale, The," by Warren R. Howell, 38:365-67

Platinum, 11:42; 13:63, 64, 65

Platt, P. L., 11:53, 56; 22:31, 33

Platt, Samuel, 9:113

Plattner chlorination process, 18:155

Platt's Music Hall, San Francisco, 10:285, 297; 19:101, 105; 21:145, 174; 24:278

Platt's Pacific Theatre, 21:167

Playing with Fire (play), 21:63

Playter, Charlotte, 19:76

Playter, E. W., 15:376

Plaza, San Francisco, *see* Portsmouth Square

Pleasant, Mary Ellen ("Mammy"), 35:134

Pleasant Grove (hotel), 8:201

Pleasant Neighbor, The (play), 15:48

Pleasants (Camptonville, 1859), 8:203

Pleasants, Joseph E., 12:79; 13:342

Pleasant Valley, Calaveras Co., 11:180

Pleasant Valley, El Dorado Co., 32:196, 207

Pleasant Valley, San Francisco Co., 27:125

Plebeian Daughter, The; or The Father's Vengeance (play), 10:370

Plecker, D. A., 22:37

Pliego, Rodrigo, 8:216-17

Plover (ship), 15:181

Plows and plowing, 2:320; 5:135, 257; 8:111-12; 12:194, 287

Plum, Charles M., 29:254

Plum, N. D., 10:53, 189, 357(?)

Plum, W. D., 10:357

Plumas (riv. str.), 9:72

Plumas City, 8:24, 173; 14:404; illus., 8:24

Plumas County, 15:153; 21:227, 228, 230, 231

Plumb, John H., 21:308; 22:281

Plume, John W. (V?), 25:223

Plummer (Yuba Co., 1857), 9:153

Plummer, Daniel A., 30:7-8

Plummer, Eugene, 13:233

Plummer, Henry, 9:357, 359

Plummer, J. C., 7:19

Plummer, M. D., 20:44

Plums, 12:206; 17:41; 27:119

Plunket, James B., 37:200

Plymouth (ship), *see Don Quixote*

Plymouth Congregational Church, San Francisco, 30:247

Pochahontas (ship), 23:301, 306, 330; 35:198, 199

Podesta, Evelyn (Wells), *see* Wells, Evelyn

Poetry: advertising, 30:365; 38:131; Byron's, 16:161-62; Confederate, 20:162-63; De Long's, 9:68, 170-71; about De Long, 9:275; epitaphs, 2:108, 112; 4:283; of gold rush, 2:99-100, 101, 111-12, 133, 135, 139; 10:399-400; 16:134; 26:114; W. F. Herrick's, 26:230-31; San Francisco, 4:193;

12:180; 14:81; 24:163-64; 35:161-62; (*Brontes* prisoner), 37:208; M. G. Vallejo's, 4:289; 16:229; 29:152; *see also* Songs

"Poets and Poetry of San Francisco," address by Edward F. O'Day, 12:180

Poett, Agnes, *see* Howard, Mrs. William D. M.

Poett, Alfred, 11:127; 23:247; 27:249, 319, 322; maps by, 23:247; 27: opp. 252

Poett, Fred, 30:289-92 *passim*, 297-303 passim; 31:49, 50, 51, 57, 63, 65, 171, 172; phot., 30: opp. 289

Poett, Joseph Henry, 27:249, 251, 252, 326

Poett family, 27:249, 319

Poggi, Francois, 39:313, 314-15

Pohono (Bridalveil Fall), 1:277

Poinsett, Joel Robert, 34:111

Point of Rocks, 3:166, 168

Poison oak, 2:200; 4:149; 24:24; 29:212-13, 216; 30:235; 33:297; 37:314-15; 39:49

Poisons, prepared by Indians, 2:12; 8:314-15

Poker as It Was Played in Deadwood in the Fifties, rev., 7:408

Poker Flat, 19:289-97 *passim*

Polack, Joel S., 15:280

Poland, emigrants and visitors from, 19:340, 373; 34:301, 314

Polhamus, Isaac, 22:152, 159

Polhamus, Isaac, Jr., 22:152, 155, 159, 164-65

Polhemus, C. B., 7:292; 17:177; 25:6

Poli, Manuel A. Rodríguez de, 18:167, 178; 29:231

Police Gazette, 16:256-62 *passim*

"Polished Boot and Bran New Suit," by Dello G. Dayton, 37:359-68; 38:17-23

Politana, 12:114, 117-19, 121

Politics: 1846-49, 10:138-40, 146-64 *passim*; 32:292-94, 297-98
  in 1850s, 10:40, 59-78 *passim*, 166, 190-99 *passim*; 15:199-205; 16:306; 21:25, 30-32, 325; 32:145-59, 296, 299, 313-25; in Yuba Co., 8:204, 206, 212, 213, 340-44 *passim*, 356-60 *passim*; 9:50, 53, 62-66 *passim*, 71, 72-73, 150-58 *passim*, 177, 266; 10:58, 59, 77, 165-73 *passim*, 189-95 *passim*, 199; 15:23-30 *passim*, 33, 273; in San Francisco, 15:171-82 *passim*, 186
  in 1860s, 10:271-82 *passim*, 286-89 *passim*, 295-96; 15:205-10;

19:147-48; 20:154-68 *passim*, 251, 258, 270; 22:223-33 *passim*, 355-62 *passim*; 27:97-103; 31:194-204; 32:299-300; in Yuba Co., 10:283, 284, 286, 287, 290
  in 1870s, 18:363; 20:270, 271
  in 1880s and 1890s, 5:283-88; 19:59-73; 20:270, 271; 27:312-17; 28:47-55
  see also Elections; names of parties

Politics and Grass: . . . Grazing on the Public Domain, by Foss, rev., 40:73-74

Polk, James Knox, 1:147, 207, 302; 3:270; 5:307; 6:77, 78, 135; 8:251; 9:3, 4, 5; 10:8, 20, 25, 111, 121, 133, 137, 140, 141, 147, 301; 11:201, 202; 19:44-54 *passim*; 22:57, 292, 315; 32:293-94; quoted, 8:258-59; 14:149-50; 32:294; proc. of war, 2:246; 3:113

Polk, Leonidas L., 27:314

Polk, Willis, 3:43; 25:285

Polk (ship), 6:16; 15:269

Polka Saloon, San Francisco, 15:369; 16:81, 82; 17:309; 22:268; 32:110-11(?); 35:319

Pollack, R. Starr, 33:12, 149

Pollack Brothers, 33:68

Pollard, Aaron (?), 10:61; 15:376

Pollard, Edward, 13:31

Pollitz, Edward, 40:44-45

Pollock, Edward, 16:285; 25:7; 30:252

Pollock, George Gordon, obit., 29:84-85

Pollock, Lewis, 15:239

Pollock, Robert, 40:349

Poll tax receipt (1854), phot., 8: opp. 344

Polo, Marco, 7:233, 234, 246

Poulshkin, Eugene Paul, 17: No. 4, Pt. 2, pp. 3, 5; 20:323; coauth. "Report on the Plate of Brass," 17: No. 4, Pt. 2, pp. 7-26

Pomaré, Queen, of Tahiti, 12:155, 156, 159; 18:315, 317

Pomeroy (Marin Co., 1858), 9:253

Pomeroy, Earl S., 29:189; 32:383; "California, 1846-1860: Politics," 32:291-302; "The Trial of the Hounds, 1849," 29:161-66

Pomeroy, Mrs. George (Anne Crandall), 25:95

Pomeroy, John Norton, 25:87; 27:346

Pomeroy, Theodore Sedgwick, 32:162-63; 35:329

Pomeroy, Walter, 5:48

Pomier, Henry, 30:108; & Co., 30:257

Pomier, Médard-Camille, 22:303

Pomona College, 36:78, 81; 37:43
"Pomona's Call to Fame," by
     T. C. Hinckley, 37:171-79
Pomponio (Indian, d. 1824), 8:215
Pond, Mrs. (Yuba Co., 1857), 9:145
Pond, C. (lawsuit, Yuba Co., 1857),
     9:141, 142, 143
Pond, Edward B., 19:60; 20:288; 33:182
Pond, J. B., 21:245
Pond, Samuel, 20:288; obit., 33:182
Pond, Mrs. Samuel (Dorothy Ames),
     33:182
Pond, William Chauncey, 18:288;
     30:245; 32:134; *Gospel Pioneering*,
     rev., 1:198
Pons, Theofrede, 30:357, 366
Ponsford (S.F., 1855), 15:277
Ponsford, Keith, introd. to "Early Days
     at Mission Santa Clara," 38:101-2
Pony Express, 1:303; 3:297; 5:313;
     6:352; 8:186; 10:89, 262, 281, 293,
     294, 394; 11:27, 290; 14:408; 15:190,
     196, 285; 19:186, 262; 23:338, 344;
     27:98; 28:286; 29:73-75, 107; 30:86;
     32:174; 38:18, 333-35, 339-40; 39:295
"Pony Express History," address by
     Ergo A. Majors, 32:174
"Pony Peter," 8:206
Poodle Dog restaurant, San Francisco,
     35:141; 39:239
Pool, Thomas, 26:204
Poole, Charles Henry, 15:376
Poole, E. A., 9:277
Poole, Nelson, 38:2
Poole, Thomas B., 20:158-59; 22:359
Poole, William, 15:366
Poole's (or Pool's) Ferry, 28:334, 336,
     337
Poor, Charles H., 33:236
Poorman claims, 28:234, 241
Poorman's Creek, 6:213; 27:193; 29:299,
     304
Poor of New York, The (play), 21:45
Pop (skit), 35:141-42
Pope, Rev. Mr. (Benicia, 1871), 31:87
Pope, Andrew J., 21:380; 26:262, 264;
     27:173
Pope, Charles, 21:63
Pope, Mrs. Charles, *see* Howard,
     Virginia
Pope, Emily, *see* Trumbull, Mrs. Henri;
     Montgomery, Mrs. E. Geoffrey
Pope, F. L., 33:2, 5-6
Pope, George Andrew, 24:88; 26:287;
     obit., 21:380-81

Pope, Mrs. George Andrew (Edith
     Taylor), 21:381; obit., 24:88-89
Pope, John, 30:84
Pope, John Francis, 30:185
Pope, Julian P., *see* Pope, William
Pope, Overton Choules, 1:110
Pope, William, 15:109, 133; 24:56, 71;
     35:1
Pope & Talbot, 21:380, 381; 26:262;
     32:375
Pope of Rome, The (play), 10:43, 65
Pope's Landing, 16:244
Pope Valley, 24:56, 71
Popoff, Admiral (on *Bogatyre*, 1863),
     23:337; 26:14-18; 31:81
Population, 19:323-43; 24:148-52,
     156-57, 314; in 1769, 3:225; in 1820-24,
     24:314; in 1828, 5:217; in 1840-48,
     8:105, 119; 10:16; 17:58; 19:323;
     22:317; 34:120; in 1849, 13:368, 382;
     in 1850, 10:233; in 1860-70, 25:311-18;
     increase (1848-70), 20:73-74; (1854),
     15:175; (1870-1945), 24:140-42, 153;
     Indian (1768-90), 3:225; (1823-30),
     24:314; (1827), 8:308-9; (1840),
     37:73; (1846), 22:317; *see also*
     Censuses
Populists, 19:59-73 *passim;* 27:311,
     315-17; 28:47-55; phot., 19: opp. 59;
     see also People's parties
Porciúncula River, *see* Los Angeles
     River
Porcupine, Los Angeles, 19:63, 72
Porfia, Cabo de la, *see* Pulmo, Cape
Porpoises, 1:215, 224, 230; 2:92; 11:158
Portals West, by Bangs, rev., 40:266
Port Costa, 27:197, 199; 35:150
Port Costa Lumber Co., 31:294
Port Costa Warehouse & Dock Co.,
     27:199
Port Douglas, B. C., 11:152-55 *passim*
Porter, Dr. (Oakland, 1854), 15:173
Porter, Bruce, 3:43; 29:191; 30:94
Porter, Burton B., 30:260
Porter, C. H., 13:31
Porter, Daniel, 13:330
Porter, David, 13:402; 19:230
Porter, David C., 29:234
Porter, David D., 8:10; 13:402; 25:39
Porter, Fitz John, 28:171
Porter, George K. (?), 10:372
Porter, George S., 9:30
Porter, John, 8:204, 205
Porter, John Easton, 26:189-90
Porter, John T., 38:261

Porter, Joseph, 38:20
Porter, Livingstone, 25:192
Porter, Mrs. M. C., 25:233
Porter, Robert, 32:184
Porter, Nathan, 34:53
Porter, Mrs. Warren Reynolds (Mary Easton), 26:189-90
Porter (A. W.) & (H. C.) Hodge, 30:266
Porter & Sawyer, 33:375
Porter Land and Water Co., 3:238
Porterfield, Harvey, 17:240; 24:58, 71; 29:276
Porters' and Packers' and Warehousemen's Union, 35:67
Porterville, 27:188
Port Famine Slough, 22:23
Port Harford, 18:258
Portilla, Pablo de la, 13:212-13; 14:233-53 *passim*, 260, 267; 15:339, 341, 346-48; 16:356-57
Port Isabel, 22:24-25, 152-64 *passim*, 167
Port Jackson, Australia, 1:175, 177; 2:290; 3:234
Portland, Ore., 2:88, 89, 126-27, 130; 16:177-78
Portois, Peter, 31:325-26; 38:34
Portolá, Gaspar de, 1:158-60; 3:100, 291; 4:144; 13:196-97; 15:187, 329; 23:1, 374; 24:91; 27:289, 290, 376-78; 31:111, 113, 121, 353; 36:1-2; 37:293-97; 40:122
"Portolá Discovery Site, The," address by Frank M. Stanger, 27:377
Portola Redwoods State Park, 31:301
Portola Valley, 31:300
Port Orford, Ore., 3:93; 15:171; 25:112; 31:125, 128, 131, 138
Portsmouth (U.S.S.), 1:78, 81, 84-91 *passim*, 182, 289; 2:69, 72, 356-61 *passim*; 3:84, 85, 108, 109, 115; 5:306-7; 6:77, 186, 189, 191, 265, 268, 271, 275-80 *passim*, 364, 365, 369, 371; 7:84; 8:74; 9:82, 85; 10:105, 106, 110, 111; 12:37, 39, 40, 161, 351; 13:106; 15:62, 63, 65, 306; 16:211-14 *passim*; 17:125, 223, 224, 228, 229, 230, 274, 295, 297, 298; 18:51, 52, 62; 19:120, 139; 21:10-13 *passim*, 338, 344, 356, 365; 22:49; 24:48; 25:121, 125, 128; 26:49, 164; 27:206; 29:269; 31:207-13 *passim*; 33:251; 34:119; 35:218; 37:232
Portsmouth House, San Francisco, 3:34; 11:132, 138, 141-42, 143; 15:65; 17:296-98; 19:229; 22:264

Portsmouth Square, San Francisco, 6:213, 251; 7:401-2, 403; 8:262, 273; 10:147, 198, 240, 354; 11:130, 136, 143, 384; 14:333; 15:64, 177, 178, 182, 184, 185; 17:168, 180, 299, 313; 18:37; 19:4, 229; 20:292, 299-300, 303; 22:259-61; 24:48-49, 71; 28:290; 29:162; art. on, 3:30-44
"Portsmouth Square," by Helen Throop Purdy, 3:30-44; as address, 3:101
Portugal, 2:142; possessions of, in New World, 7:132-42 *passim*; 26:374-75; *see also* Portuguese
Portugal, O (magazine), 35:245
Portugalia (magazine), 35:245
Portuguese, 2:142, 143, 194, 196; 7:133-39 *passim*, 147, 241-47 *passim*, 252, 255; 8:349; 9:152; 18:85; 20:72-73; 23:155; publications, 35:244-45; whalers, 35:238; art. on, 35:233-52; *see also* Portugal
Portuguese Bend, 35:238
"Portuguese in California, The," by Frederick G. Bohme, 35:233-52
"Portuguese Joe" (William Foster), 9:262, 357
Portwine (place), 11:240
Posesión, Isla de, *see* San Miguel Island
Posesión, Puerto de la, 7:22, 54, 56
Posey (Yuba Co., 1854), 8:207
Posner, Russell M., 36:285; 37:284; 39:180; "The Bank of Italy and the 1926 Campaign in California," 37:267-75, 347-58; "California's Role in the Nomination of Franklin D. Roosevelt," 39:121-39; "The Progressive Voters League," 1923-26," 36:251-61
Poso Creek, 11:254, 265
Posol (food), 15:220; 38:104
Post, Charles, 18:31
Post, Edward Hotchkiss, 24:382-83
Post, Gabriel B., 15:164, 370; 28:59
Post, Rita (Johns), 22:95
Post, San Francisco, 30:194, 195, 198, 200, 201
Post, Stockton, 25:192
Postal service: 3:37-38, 127, 166; 5:293, 313; 6:122, 145, 224, 246; 7:10, 13, 17, 19; 8:385; 9:308; 10:353-54; 12:98, 99, 323; 13:241-51, 257; 14:127, 162, 399; 15:181, 277, 328; 16:71-72, 338; 17:54, 59, 81, 177, 180, 212-13; 19:262, 356;

20:12-13, 250; 22:53; 24:236, 346-47; 25:128; 27:260, 365; 28:65, 202, 204, 209, 210, 216, 226, 306; 29:116; 33:120; 36:117-19, 123-31 *passim*, 131; fac. 1st mail contract, 10: opp. 353; *see also* Butterfield Overland Mail, Express companies; Pony Express; Post Office

"Post Gold-Rush Era, The," address by Carl I. Wheat, 9:408

Post Office, San Francisco, 3:37-38; 5:94; 10:354; 12:98, 99; 15:165; 16:338; 17:177, 180, 181; 20:12-13, 29-30

Post Office News Depot, Petaluma, 30:362

Post Office Spring (*Ballarat*), 17:210

Poston, Mrs. E. C., school of, 10:251, 264

Potatoes, 2:231; 3:38; 5:47; 7:205; 12:193, 195; 19:127; 20:31; 28:214; Hawaiian, 23:358, 371; *see also* Sweet potatoes

"Potato Patch," 27:292

Pot Hill, 7:221

"Potin, Euphrasie," *see* Dupuy, Edouard Joseph

Potomac (frigate, 1846), 2:250, 251

Potomac (ship, 1854), 15:170

Potosi [mining] Co., 11:60, 61; *see also* Chollar-Potosi

Potrero Nuevo, San Francisco, 4:172; 21:118-20

Potrero Viejo, 21:115, 117; *see also* Ranchos: Rincon de las Salinas y Potrero Viejo

Pottenger Sanatorium, Monrovia, 31:22-23

Potter (Colorado R., 1850), 22:20

Potter (Stockton, 1858), 33:66

Potter (lawsuit, Colusa, 1860), 10:258

Potter, Mrs. David (Elizabeth Lyman), 22:287

Potter, Elizabeth (Gray), "Columbia—'Gem of the Southern Mines,'" 24:267-70; address, "Personalities behind San Francisco's Street Names," 19:187

Potter, George, 20:46

Potter, George C., 15:281

Potter, J. N., 15:181

Potter, Samuel Otway Lewis, 30:290

Potter, Stephen, 13:31

Potter, William (or Thomas?), 27:220

Potter (ship), 22:170

Potter Hotel, Santa Barbara, 18:176

Potter's Bar, 33:293, 295-300

Potter's Ravine, 33:296, 298-99

Potter Valley, 20:167; 27:220; 32:364; 40:295

Potts, John, 4:126

Poulisse (Indian, ca. 1898), phot., 36: opp. 320

Poulsson, P. R., 25:95

Poulterer, Thomas J., 15:279; 19:232

Poultry, 2:42, 322; 8:383; 12:287, 293; 31:31; 36:181

Pounds, William B., Jr., 32:94-95; coauth. "Northernmost Spanish Frontier in California," 32:43-48

Poundstone, Jesse, 19:63, 72; 27:318

Pourade, Richard F., *The Explorers: The History of San Diego*, rev., 40:353-55

Poursuivante (ship), 35:310-11

Poussole (food), *see Posol*

Poverty Bar, 38:309

Poverty Gulch, 39:293

Poverty Hill, 11:240; 23:366, 375-76

Poway Valley, 26:59; 33:266

Powder River, Ore., 16:41

Powell (San Quentin guard, 1854), 15:175

Powell, C. F., 9:44, 45; 15:369

Powell, David, 26:93

Powell, Emmet, 21:308

Powell, H. M. T., 13:310, 350; 33:277; *Santa Fe Trail to California*, ed. Watson, rev., 10:406-7

Powell, John Wesley, 14:347

Powell, Joseph, 9:113, 114, 394; 10:193, 276, 277

Powell, Lawrence Clark, coauth. *The Malibu*, rev., 38:171-73

Powell, Maud, 25:236

Powell, William J., 20:150, 152

Powell Street Academy, San Francisco, 15:267

Powell Street Church, San Francisco, 31:11

Power, Edward, 12:280; 14:229, 393

Power, John A. ("Jack Powers"), 13:327-28; 18:259, 266-70

Power, Robert H., phot., 39: opp. 80

Power, S. T., 30:263

Powers, Aaron H. and Louisa (Sweasey), 29:284

Powers, Laura Bride (Mrs. William H.), 28:378; address, "Robert Louis

Stevenson in California," 20:376-77;
obit., 26:89-90
Powers, O. B., 7:11-12
Powers, R. M., 35:359
Powers, Rolla, 15:185
Powers, Stephen, 30:141, 149
Powers, William, 15:269
Powhatan (ship), 23:335, 337, 338,
342-45 *passim*
Powles, J. D., 18:145
Poynter (Yuba Co., 1854), 8:206
Poynter, J. R., 22:32, 33; 30:110
*Practical Plan for Building the Pacific
Railroad, A,* by Theodore D. Judah,
digest of, 4:229-33
Pracy, G. W. and Mabel (Holliday),
32:286
Prado, Roberto, 17:60
Prager, Samuel, 13:335
Praileur (from France before 1850),
5:25
Prairie Flower, The, character in,
4:283
Prairie House, Sacramento Co., 8:201,
210
Prairie Schooner Lady, by
Harriet S. Ward, rev., 38:378-79
Praslow, J., 18:282
Prat, Pedro, 4:143-45, 167; 21:80;
33:103; 37:295
Prather, Mary Wren, 8:388
Prather, Millie, *see* Brown, Mrs. Ralph
Prather, Myrah Gray (Mrs. Harry E.
Miller), 18:190
Prather, R. C., 30:230
Prather, William and Diana Elizabeth
(Ingram), 33:364, 365, 367
Pratt (on *California*, Oct. 1849), 2:201
Pratt (on *Mary Frances*, 1849), 14:334
Pratt, Addison, 14:73, 279, 282; 18:196,
215
Pratt, E. R., letter from, 24:253-54
Pratt, H., 9:155, 346, 365
Pratt, Helen (Throop) Purdy, 11:73;
"Crescent City on the Tuolumne,"
11:358-62; "Portsmouth Square,"
3:30-44; "Souvenirs of an Interesting
Family," 7:282-85, 406; ed.
"California Letters of Edward
Hotchkiss," 12:91-110; bk. revs. by,
1:299-301; 2:173-77, 363-64; 3:291-96;
4:292-99, 392-96; 5:90-92, 199-203,
312-15, 409-12; 6:96-98, 195-96,
282-84, 376-77; 7:196-97; 8:85-86,
380-81; 9:87; obits. of Ina D.

Coolbrith, 7:78; Emma F. Dawson,
5:87; Edward W. Hopkins, 5:105-6;
Mrs. Albert J. Raisch, 20:286;
obit., 24:87-88
Pratt, Leonidas E., 28:380
Pratt, Mrs. Leonidas E. (Armeda
Jessup), 28:380; 31:337
Pratt, M., 9:141
Pratt, Orson, 4:282; 6:117; 16:141
Pratt, Parley Parker, 15:282; "A
Mormon Mission to California in
1851," from Diary of, ed. Reva H.
Stanley and Charles L. Camp,
14:59-73, 175-82; *Mormonism*
[broadside], opp. 59
Pratt, Mrs. Parley Parker (Elizabeth),
14:61, 72, 177, 181
Pratt, Mrs. Parley Parker (Phebe),
14:61, 72, 176, 177, 181
Pratt, Robert H., 23:117, 121
Pratt, William, 39:265
Pratte, Sylvestre S., 2:10
Pratt House, New York of the Pacific,
12:30
Pray, Amasa and Annie Brewster
(Willey), 35:12
Pray, F. P., 29:225
Pray, Joshua, 2:128
Prayer-book cross, San Francisco,
11:312, 317
Preble (ship), 1:215; 12:98, 351;
14:337, 342; 22:57; 30:18
Precht, Carl, 9:104; 17:176; 32:248,
261-62
Precht, Mrs. Carl (Ida), 32:248, 261
Precht, Ida, *see* Etienne, Mrs. E. J.
Preciado, Francisco, 1:38, 43, 45, 47-48,
147; 3:308-14 *passim*, 320, 322, 323,
332-67 *passim*; 19:240, 244
Precita Creek, San Francisco, 21:117,
118-19
Predpriatie (ship), 12:208
Pre-emption: Act, 24:193, 271; claims,
29:248; notice (fac.), 11: opp. 176
Prefecture system, 1:30-32
"Prehistoric California," address by
Ralph W. Chaney, 9:407-8
Prendergast, John J., 21:239
Prendergast, Thomas F., 19:96; address,
"Irish Leaders in Early California,"
22:183; obit., 24:284
Prendt (S.F., 1854), 15:176
Prentice, Col. (Yuba Co., 1853), 8:363
Prentice, Samuel, 13:210-11

Presbury, William W., 9:356; 10:53, 58, 176, 266, 284

Presbyterian Board of Home Missions, 36:313, 319-21

Presbyterian Churches, 3:37; 10:176, 178, 185, 198, 293, 361, 412; 12:105-6; 15:43-44, 57, 168, 270, 305; 16:344; 20:13, 15, 22, 24, 25, 166-67; 22:111, 114; 24:263; 25:334, 341; 26:163-72 *passim*, 361; 27:15, 124, 149-56, 301, 302, 307, 350; 28:291; 29:55; 32:51, 53, 54, 122-26 *passim*, 129, 130, 134, 164-65; 33:376; bk. on, rev., 6:282-84

Presbyterian Church in California, The, by Wicher, rev., 6:282-84

Presbyterian Hospitality House, 33:376

Presbyterian Women's Missionary Society, 38:224

Prescott (Yuba Co., 1857), 9:154; 10:189

Prescott, Mrs. (Sacramento, 1858), 9:243, 244, 247

Prescott, Alice, 18:384

Prescott, George W., 15:76; 25:43, 44; 27:197

Prescott Mining District, 26:245

"Present Condition of the Missions, The," address by Reed B. Cherington, 4:401-2

"Presentation of the Serra Birthplace," by John C. Cebrian, 11:280-88

"Preservation of the State Archives," by J. N. Bowman, 28:143-50

President (ship), 2:108; 15:181, 374

Presidio (institution), 1:23-35; 5:213-14; 8:310-11; 13:43

Presidio del Norte, 18:116

Presidio of Fronteras, 27:63, 64

Presidio of Monterey, 1:24, 174-75; 2:283-85, 288, 311; 4:144-45, 148, 152; 5:217; 8:122; 12:194; 13:43; 14:102, 230; 16:221, 247, 349; 17:248; 27:208; views, 15: opp. 214; 39: foll. 180

Presidio of San Diego, 2:332-37 *passim*; 5:217; 8:218-19, 224, 332, 333; 12:43; 16:227, 229; 17:248; 20:237

Presidio of San Francisco, 2:270-71; 5:217; 8:140-41; 12:194; 13:43; 14:104-5, 114-16; 15:8, 58-67 *passim*, 196, 306, 308; 16:100, 243, 339; 17:245, 246, 248, 292, 301; 22:253; 23:19-20, 251; 24:184; 25:319-24 *passim*; 30:217

"Presidio of San Francisco, The ," address by Eric A. Falconer, 24:184

Presidio of Santa Barbara, 1:28; 2:316, 323; 5:217; 8:157; 13:43, 202; 16:218; 17:248; 19:201; 33:278, 279

Presidio of Sonoma, 17:248; *see also* Sonoma: military post

Presidio Shoal, 25:321, 323

Presl, Karl Boriwog, 18:336

Press, North San Juan, *see Hydraulic Press*

Presse, La, 39:149

Preston (Min. to Spain, 1860), 11:16-17

Preston (Alaska, 1867), 35:299

Preston, Edgar, 31:301

Preston, F. M., 21:233

Preston, Jasper N., 23:95

Preston, Laura, *see* Heaven, Louise

Preston, O. J., 27:34; 28:59, 65

Preston, William Ballard, 33:338, 339; 34:38; letter to, 34:37-38

Preuss, Charles, 1:120-21; 4:9; drawing by (?), 36: opp. 337

Prevaux, Francis Edward, 16:79; 24:70; 27:229, 230, 231, 236; 32:127, 133-34

Prévé, J. Louis, 14:142

Prévost, Louis, 31:338

Prevost, Mary, 21:41, 42

Prevost, Victor, 35:367-78; painting by, 35: opp. 368

Prévotière, Pierre, 39:343

Price, C., 15:46

Price, Charles R., 2:108

Price, Francis, 37:188; trans. "Letters of Narciso Durán," 37:97-128; 241-65; address, "The Role of the Alcalde in . . . Santa Barbara," 33:278-81

Price, George F., 10:254

Price, Henry, 23:323, 333

Price, James and Mary Anne (Duffie), 28:293

Price, John (Monterey, 1835), 16:326, 331; *see also* Luther and Price

Price, John (Lake Co., 1850), 24:55-56

Price, John M., 15:239

Price, Johnson, 10:62, 275

Price, Lewis Richard, narrative of, 39:35-51

Price, Robert M., 4:49

Price, Rodman M., 3:113, 187; 10:156; 19:7; 25:106, 125; 27:49, 362, 368; 28:59-60; 35:14, 103-4, 106; fac. sig., 10: opp. 159

Price, Sterling, 21:193, 197, 221

Price, Thomas, 24:55-56

Price, William, 27:20, 21; statement,
27:22-31
Price (Samuel) & Co., 17:181
"Price-Fixing in Spanish California,"
by Sanford A. Mosk, 17:118-22
Price Hotel, San Jose, 14:156
Prices, in Calif.:
1781-1803, 2:322; 3:231-32; 17:118-22
in 1835-38, 16:322-32
in 1840-46, 5:130; 8:102, 109; 12:291;
13:48; 14:200; 17:23; 28:100, 102
in 1848-49, 2:192, 198, 199; 4:204;
5:8, 17, 18; 6:62; 10:404; 11:36;
12:29, 313, 317, 357; 13:84-85, 166,
178, 274-75, 276, 355, 361-67 *passim*,
377; 14:20-21, 203; 16:140; 19:126;
20:31-32, 120; 22:243; 23:51-56
passim, 157, 158; 24:25, 343, 346,
348, 355-59 *passim*; 25:104, 107-8;
27:264; 29:5; 30:21
in 1850-53, 5:32, 219, 294, 353; 6:225;
11:54, 159-60, 162, 237; 12:94, 101,
105, 302; 21:363; 23:161, 162, 170,
173; 24:133, 354, 358, 362; 28:211,
230; 39:107
in 1856, 14:157
in 1874, 17:210
in 1884, 16:300-301
on overland journey, 5:291; 6:362-63;
16:140, 141; 24:32-33, 118
in Panama (1849), 29:5
Prices Current and Shipping List, San
Francisco, 13:299; 20:336; 33:68-69
Prichard (Monterey, 1796), 1:177
Prichard, Elsie Griffin (Johnston),
30:75
Pride of the Market, The (play), 9:67,
130, 132, 136; 10:41
Pride of the Sea (ship), 22:170
Priest, Viola M., 28:380-81; 30:82
Priestley, Herbert Ingram, 13:149;
address, "The Californian and His
History," 10:206; obit., 23:186-87
Priestley, W. D., 15:76
"Priests, Pistols, and Polemics," by
Lionel U. Ridout, 37:51-61
Prieto (or Perieto; Indian, 1850), 24:51
Prieto, Antonio, 29:38
Prieto, Guillermo, 17:239
Primavera (ship), 11:204, 220, 342;
14:331, 342; 18:165-66, 177
Prince, Henry, 15:367, 369; 26:1
Prince, Thomas, 30:7-8
Prince, William, 30:7-8, 9
Prince Albert (ship), 28:244, 245, 247

Prince (T. B.) & Co., 30:7, 10
Prince Camaralzaman (play), 21:163
Prince (H. G.) Canning Co., 34:330
Prince Edwards (ship), 22:349
Prince of Wales (ship), 18:345
"Prince Paul of Württemberg's
Journeys in America," address by
Charles L. Camp, 16:380-81
Princesa, La (ship), 10:340; 15:216;
16:105, 106; 37:109, 111, 115, 117, 119
"Principal Actions of the California
Junta de Fomento, 1825-1827," ed.
and trans. Keld J. Reynolds,
24:289-320; 25:57-78, 149-68, 267-78,
347-67
Prindle, Vivian Arthur, 30:91; coauth.
"College of Physicians and Surgeons
of California," 30:67-71
Pringle (in Washington, D.C., 1860),
11:14
Pringle, E. J., 11:127
Pringle, Edward, 19:231, 236
Pringle, William, 11:127
Printers, 30:146; 33:50; *see also*
Printing presses; State printer;
Zamorano
Printing presses, 10:389; 12:79; 20:330,
332; 34:342, 343, 346, 348, 352;
Ames's, 9: (phot.) opp. 193, 193-200;
11:389; 31:36; Brannan's, 3:101;
11:389; 14:80; 17:296; 37:232;
Zamorano's, 3:101, 181, 248; 7:277;
10:206; 12:125-36; 13:53; 16:351,
375; 35:181, 193, 199, 200, 201; in
Sandwich Is., 35:196-201; private,
28:184
Prior, William M., 4:170
Prisons, State, *see* California State
Prison; San Quentin
Pritchard, James Avery, *Overland
Diary*, ed. Morgan, rev., 38:275-76
Pritchett, Mrs. Henry S. (Eva
McAllister), 34:233, 234; obit., 35:376
Privateering, by Confederates, 20:159;
32:309, 312
"Private Presses of California," address
by Jackson Burke, 28:184
Prizefights, *see* Boxing
Probert, Frank H., address, "Grains of
Gold," 7:200
Proclamations:
Castro's, Mar. 13, '46, 4:384-85;
Aug. 9, '46, 10:123
Ide's Bear Flag, 1:72-79, (fac.)
opp. 74; 10:10, 105, 112

Frémont's, Jan. 22, '47, 10:18
Kearney's, Mar. 1, '47, 10:19
Mason's, May 31, '47, 10:22
Montgomery's, July 9, '46, 2:358
Pico's, June 23, '46, 1:186-89
Polk's, May 13, '46, 2:246
Riley's:
    calling Constit. Convention, 10:146;
    for ratification of Constit. (fac.),
    10:131; announcing ratification
    (fac.), 10:154; Thanksgiving
    (fac.), 10:135; resigning authority
    (fac.), 10:162
Sloat's, June 18, '46, 1:291; July 7, '46,
    2:352-54; 3:110-11; 10:11-12, 101;
    draft, July 14, '46, 3:186-87
State of Jefferson, 1941, 31:129
Stockton's, Aug. 17, '46, 10:14
Proctor, Joseph and Mrs., 20:297
Procureur, A. Peter, 27:8
Progrès, Le, Los Angeles (1884-93),
    39:330, 332, 334, 338, 349
Progrès, Le, San Francisco (1868),
    39:220, 349
"Progress . . . in Preserving Our
    Historic Landmarks," address by
    Joseph R. Knowland, 21:82-83
Progressive Party, 38:229-47 *passim*,
    349-50
Progressive Union Mill, San Francisco,
    35:147
Progressive Voters League, 37:273; art.
    on, 36:251-61
"Progressive Voters League, 1923-26,"
    by Russell M. Posner, 36:251-61
Prohibition and Prohibitionists, 5:285;
    9:59; 15:377; 16:80, 84; 27:311; 38:350;
    see also Temperance
Projet d'Association Agricole pour
    la Californie, 22:313
Prolétaire, Le, San Francisco, 39:314,
    349
Promontory, Utah, 24:366, 367; 32:300;
    36:97, 103, 263-72 *passim;* phot.,
    36: opp. 104, opp. 264
*Pronouncing Dictionary of California
    Names, A*, by Marshall, rev., 5:88-89
"Prophet of San Francisco," *see*
    George, Henry
"Proposals for the Colonization of
    California by England . . . 1837-1845,"
    by Lester G. Engelson, 18:136-48
"Prospecting on the Pacific Coast,
    1848-1864," recollections of Orlando

J. Hodges, ed. William F. Zornow,
    33:49-58
Prosper Mill Co., 31:295
Prosser Creek, 24:74
Prostitution, 8:110; 9:253, 254, 261;
    15:267; 16:83; 17:168; 22:268, 270;
    32:126, 305-6; 34:307; 37:154-56, 337;
    38:331
Protestant Episcopal churches, 9:371,
    394; 10:64, 76, 288, 290; 12:95-100
    passim, 106; 14:74-79; 15:185, 373;
    18:180; 20:16, 22, 24; 23:157, 176, 235,
    246; 24:263; 26:163-73 *passim*, 361;
    27:111, 112, 124; 28:33, 223, 231, 291;
    32:53, 119, 122, 125; 34:233, 235;
    37:51-61; illus., 9: opp. 258
Protestant Orphan Asylum, *see*
    Orphanages, San Francisco
Protestants, in early California,
    26:163-74; 28:290-91; 32:49-56
    passim, 119-44 *passim*
Providence (ship), 2:309
Provines, R. R., 27:153
Provost, Mary, 21:41-42
*Prudent Soldier: . . . Major-General
    E. R. S. Canby*, by Heyman, rev.,
    39:85
Prudon (Prudhomme), Leon Victor,
    1:72-73, 79, 91-97 *passim*, 135, 179,
    189, 286; 2:69, 72; 5:195, 249; 6:46-47,
    81-82, 140, 190, 272-73; 7:79; 8:120;
    10:105; 11:136; 12:39, 337; 13:36, 44,
    107-9, 217-21, 315, 345; 14:144, 244-45;
    16:100; 17:57, 59-61, 143, 145, 147,
    150, 155, 220-29 *passim*, 275; 19:118,
    132; 21:13; 24:57; 25:123; 28:265-66;
    29:157, 264, 321; 31:209; 38:172
Pruitt, Mrs. C. W., *see* Seward, Anna
Prunes, 12:205, 206; 25:28, 31; 27:119
Pruzzo, María (de Haro), 29:82
Pryor, Gabriel, 15:240
Pryor, Nathaniel Miguel, 2:18, 37;
    13:210, 230; 14:126; 17:327, 329-31;
    22:59; 25:293
Public Balance, San Francisco, 6:43, 45,
    46; 32:106, 107, 108; 39:12-13; cited,
    6:48
Public domain, *see* Lands, public
Public Education Society of
    San Francisco, 26:282
Public utilities, 30:342-43
Publishing business (1850-59), 30:101,
    102, 251-52
Puccinelli, Dorothy W., 38:3
Pudding Creek, 30:163

Puebla (ship), 30:289, 290-95 *passim*
Pueblo (institution), 1:23-35; 21:124-25; 33:275
Pueblo Valley, 11:136; 27:162; *see also* Santa Clara Valley
Puente (place), 1:148
Puget, Peter, 2:275, 285, 300, 311, 332, 334-35; 10:338
Puget Sound, 11:303
Puget Sound Agricultural Co., 28:100
Puget Sound Association, 28:104, 108
Pugh (Peugh, Pew; in mines, 1849), 27:159-63 *passim*
Pugh (Yuba Co., 1858), 9:359, 360; 10:255
Pugh, George E., 19:352-55, 361
Pujol, Francisco, 4:149
Pujol y Bru, José, 12:320-21; 15:374
Pulliam, Anne R., *see* Wilson, Mrs. ["Gen."] John
Pullman, George M., 2:371
Pullman, James, 8:200-201, 348; 9:57, 165, 266
Pulmo, Cape, called "California," 1:49, 50, 51; 3:389
Pumpelly, Rafael, 23:342, 345, 347
Pumpkin Seed (barge), 22:156
Punch, 32:83-84, 270-73 *passim*
Punta, as used by Cabrillo, 7:24
Pup, The (restaurant), San Francisco, 35:141, 267
Purcell, Charles H., 16:87
Purcell, John, 9:26, 27
Purcell, Mae (Fisher), 19:384; 20:82
Purcell, Michael, 9:64, 77
Purdy (Sonora, 1854), 30:266
Purdy, G., 13:32
Purdy, Helen (Throop), *see* Pratt, Helen (Throop)
Purdy, J. H., 8:362

Purdy, Samuel, 9:44, 45; 15:272, 282, 369, 370; 17:234; 19:176; 27:308
Purísima Concepción, *see* Missions: La Purísima Concepción
Purisima Creek, 15:329-30
Purves, J. M., 22:251
"Pushing the Frontier Westward," address by Mary F. Williams, 9:292
Putah Creek, 11:118; 13:265; 22:339, 345; 23:32, 33, 291, 295, 297; 32:376
Putah Rancho, *see* Ranchos: Las Putas
Putnam, Capt. (of *Susan Drew*, 1846), 1:120, 214
Putnam (Auburn, 1875), 18:362
Putnam, A. J., 22:251
Putnam, Arthur, 38:7
Putnam, Osgood, 25:232
Putnam, R. F., 33:374
Putnam, Royal Porter and Mary Jane (Packard), 27:188-89
Putnam, Ruth, 1:54
Putnam, S. O., 27:171
Putnam, William Porter and Menna (Kinkaid), 27:188-89
Putney, Henry, 13:32
"Putting a Lid on California . . . Diary of the Portolá Expedition by José de Cañizares," ed. and trans. Virginia E. Thickens and Margaret Mollins, 31:109-24, 261-70, 343-54
Putzer, Jozsef, 28:138-42 *passim*
Pygmalion and Galatea (play), 16:301
Pyle, Edward, 2:190
Pyle, John F., 2:190
Pyle, Thomas, 2:184, 190
Pyles, Margaret, *see* McDowell, Mrs. James
Pyramid Lake, Nev., 4:9; 6:343; 7:14; illus., 36: opp. 337
Pyramid Rock (Sentinel Rock), 1:278

Q

Qra-Nas (Indian, 1849), 11:270-71
Q Ranch, 11:322
Quadra, *see* Bodega y Quadra
Quaife, Milo Milton, ed. Bidwell, *Echoes of the Past*, and Steele, *In Camp and Cabin*, rev., 8:87-88; ed. Manly, *Death Valley in '49*, rev., 7:89-90

Quail, 2:286, 317, 336; 5:358; 7:361; 12:14, 293, 305; 13:20; 20:40, 41; 23:297; 29:274
Quaker City Insurance Co., 26:254-56, 258
Quaker Forty-niner, A, by Pancoast, ed. Hannum, rev., 9:291
Qualey, Frank, 10:200

" 'Quand Même,'... California Footnotes to the Biography of Sarah Bernhardt," by Lois F. Rodecape, 20:126-46

Quartz, 11:244; 13:361; 32:273; stamp mills, 1:67; 3:259; 4:67-68; 6:229, 243, 244, 334; 7:114-17 *passim;* 11:227, 228, 236, 243, 244-45, 324, 326; 12:69-75 *passim*, 327-30 *passim;* 15:52; 17:79; 18:22, 149-55 *passim;* 19:28, 146; 21:325; 26:301; (illus.) 11:235; mines, 11:243; 12:65-76; *see also* Gold mining; Silver

Quartz Canyon, 9:63

Quartzburg, 11:229; 28:325

Quayle (McCloud R., 1909), 35:32

Quayle, William, 8:358

Queen, Henry W., 3:111, 118; 17:335; 18:78, 80-81; 21:224

Queen Charlotte Island, 22:104

Queen City (riv. str.), 10:50, 73; 15:175, 176, 182, 184, 266, 279

Queen of Sheba, The (opera), 33:39-40

Queen of Spades, The (play), 10:47, 69

Queen of the East (ship), 30:170

Queen of the Highbinders, The (play), 33:41

Queen of the Pacific (ship), 16:300; 30:276; 31:152

Queen of the Seas (ship), 15:375; 17:174; 30:244

"Queen Victoria" (elephant), 38:336

Querétaro, 33:13-21 *passim*

Quepness, Odilon, 23:6

Quesnelle, A., 22:347; 23:24-25

Quesnell River (Deer Cr.), 22:212, 217; 23:133

"Quest for Pioneers," address by Mrs. Rudolph Altrocchi, 17:89-90

"Question of Religion and the Taming of California, The," by William Hanchett, 32:49-56, 119-44

"Question of Sainsevain's Signature, The," by J. N. Bowman, 28:361-62

Quichote, Le (ship), *see Don Quixote*

Quicksilver, 14:168; used in gold mining, 3:161-62; 6:219, 244; 11:328

Quicksilver mines and mining, 1:167; 3:210; 5:191, 269, 374; 6:160, 249-50, 368; 11:361, 362; 12:35; 13:58-62, 77-79; 14:21, 157-59, 168, 169; 15:235-36, 268; 16:78; 17:79, 138, 279; 20:269; 22:320; 30:170; 31:310, 322; 32:359, 363, 365, 366; 36:293; 39:42; illus., 6: opp. 249; *see also* New Almaden Mine

Quickstep (ship), 11:302

Quigley, Hugh, 28:13

Quigley *v.* McClelland, 9:268, 346

Quijas, José Lorenzo de la Concepción, 2:53; 12:196; 16:236-37, 240-41, 244, 369; 19:198-99, 214

Quimley (San Jose, 1855), 29:53-54

Quimper, Manuel, 40:238

Quinces, 12:193, 258; 18:120; 29:175

Quinn, Anna, 15:169-70; 23:73

Quinn, Isaac N., 10:62; 11:6, 8-9, 21

Quinn, James F., 9:244

Quint, Leander, 7:118; 10:355, 377, 390; 26:239, 247

Quintal, Laurent, 22:196, 199, 219; 23:38, 136

Quintana, Andrés, 4:147-48; 37:117, 242; 38:107

Quintano, Francisco Esteban, 10:35

Quintero, Juan, 16:353

Quintero, Luis, 13:200-202

Quintin, Vincent, 32:108-9

Quinton, Augustus, 9:198

Quiquiriqui vineyard, 36:246-47

Quire, Joseph, 18:364

Quirós, Fernando de, 14:102, 105

Quito (ship), 29:1, 15

Quivey (San Jose, 1853), 13:29

Quivira, 3:262-67; 6:96, 301, 316; 7:264, 296, 305, 366, 369, 378, 392; 8:28, 42

"Quivira, a Mythical California City," by Henry R. Wagner, 3:262-67

Quixano, Manuel, 4:145, 147-48

R

R., W. R., letter from, 24:236-37

Raas, Emile, 39:252-53

Rabbit Creek, 9:52; *see also* La Porte

Rabbit Hole Springs, 18:300

Rabbits and hares, 2:336; 3:360; 5:368; 7:361; 8:166, 220, 221; 11:258; 12:293; 20:41; 21:238; 27:119; drives, 8:220-21; 29:365

Rabbit Springs, 27-117
Rabe, Carl, 4:29, 34, 35
Rabé, William, 4:234; 9:320, 323; 23:340; 27: opp. 97; 28:36
Rabel's Tannery, Sacramento, 10:371, 374, 388
Rabier (mgr. of L'Aurifère), 22:301
Raccoon Strait, 33:235
Race horses:
 Attila, 15:276
 Black Swan, 13:322-23
 Bubbling Water, 10:414
 Cali Damsel, 10:361
 Daniel Webster, 10:176; 15:185
 D. C. Broderick, 15:170
 Fancy, 15:49
 Fred Johnson, 15:374
 Glencoe, 10:361
 Jack, 15:49
 Jim Barton, 10:361
 Joe Wilson, 15:185
 Lady Jane, 15:367
 Lady Mac, 15:185
 Lady Vernon, 15:367
 Limber Jim, 10:176
 Marshal Ney, 15:49
 Morg. Miller, 10:251, 264
 Muggins, 9:155, 159
 Ned McGowan, 15:170
 Peacock, 15:177
 Price McGrath, 15:374
 Rainbow, 10:361
 Red Bird, 10:361
 Rhode Island, 15:170
 Sarco, 13:322-23
 Shot, 10:176, 361
 Sleepy David, 10:49
 Thad Stevens, 21:123
 Tom Maguire, 10:176
 Wake-up-Jake, 15:276
 Wicked Billy, 15:49
 Wild Cat, 15:49
Race tracks, 8:349, 356, 358; 9:385; 15:49, 170, 171, 177, 179, 185, 276, 374; 17:179, 255; 21:119, 123, 168; 27:222; *see also* Horse racing
Racine, Mme. (S.F., 1851), 28:36; 32:109
Rackerby, *see* Hansonville
Rada, Martin de, 7:146, 175, 193
R. Adams (ship), 15:276
Radcliffe, Alden and Elizabeth (Gross), 28:380
Radcliffe, Henry Hayton, 34:342
Radcliffe, Zoe (Green), "Robert Baylor Semple," 6:130-58

Radford, Mary, *see* Kearny, Mrs. Stephen Watts
Radford, Richard C. W., 28:213, 220, 228, 230
Radin, Max, ed. "The Stone and Kelsey 'Massacre' . . . 1849, the Indian Viewpoint," 11:266-73
Radio, 34:160
Rae, William Glen, 5:299, 304; 11:69-71, 135; 17:138, 294; 27:107; 28:98, 99, 106-7, 108, 243-53 *passim*, 257, 258; 33:65; letters, 28:100-104, 247-49, 250-51; port., 28: opp. 97
Rae, Mrs. William Glen (Eloisa McLoughlin), 17:294; 28:105, 107
Rafael, Joseph, 38:7
Raffles, *see* Lotteries and raffles
Rafisch, *see* Rehfisch
Raft River, 32:202, 203, 205
Rahn (Carson's Cr., 1849), 27:160
Railroad construction and maintenance, 4:256-60; 18:23-25; fire trains, 18:365; snow sheds and snow plows, 18:365-68
Railroad Hill, 3:148-51, 153; 8:199, 203, 212; 9:52, 67, 136, 137, 139, 148, 149, 168, 353; 10:171, 256
Railroad House, Sacramento, 10:280
Railroad House, San Francisco, 9:253, 277; 15:182
"Railroading in California in the Seventies," from reminiscences of Clarence M. Wooster, 18:355-68
Railroads: in Alameda Co., 4:211; Benicia and Sacramento Valley, 4:226; Humboldt Co. (logging), 38:65; Napa Valley (prop.), 16:131-32; Nevada Co., 18:355-56; San Joaquin Valley, 18:22-31; to and from San Jose, 7:292; 10:389; 14:163-69 *passim;* 16:200; 18:49; 26:260, 266; 27:140, 253; Sierra Railway, 24:91; 40:249-50; Siskiyou Co. (logging), 35:30; Sonomo Valley, 7:292; 17:238; Ventura Co., 17:33; *see also* names of railroads
Railroads: across Mex., 27:146-47, 204-5, 213-14, 354; in So. Amer. (Meiggs's), 17:198-204
Railroads: transcontinental, 3:398; 4:219, 224, 227-71; 5:178-83; 13:241; 15:54, 190, 202; 17:309, 316; 24:365-68; 26:360; 31:201; 38:351-53
bills in Congress, 2:211, 212; 4:228, 234, 238, 239, 243, 251-56; 7:3;

15:203-4, 206, 208; 19:169, 173-75, 180-81, 256-62 *passim*, 269-71, 344-45, 360; 32:299, 300; 33:246; 39:292

bks. on, 1:303; 3:194, 251; 4:93, 299-300

construction, 4:257-60; 5:178-83

conventions and meetings, 4:224, 233-99, 240, 244-45, 246; 7:4-5; 15:266-67; 34:210-11

costs and financing, 4:225, 230-32, 235-36; 242-46 *passim*, 249, 257, 259; 5:180-81, 183

plays based on, 34:360, 366

resolution in State Legislature, 4:233

routes and surveys, 2:211-12; 4:10-11, 227-37 *passim*, 240-51 *passim*, 252, 259, 265-68, 300; 5:178, 181-82; 7:3, 8, 9; 15:164; 21:136; 22:369; 34:209-28

taxes, 38:353

see also "Big Four"; names of railroads

Railways, street: in Alameda Co., 4:211; Los Angeles Cable, 10:393; San Francisco, 7:292; 9:284; 10:389; 15:167, 168, 175; 17:172; cable, 4:93; 14:191; 19:149-52

Raimond, Reuben Edgar, 22:13, 24

Raimundo, Fr., 3:309, 357, 359, 363-67 *passim;* 19:242

Raimundo, Cañada, 27:189

Rainbow, Cascade of the (Bridalveil Fall), 1:276-77

Rainbow (schr., 1848, formerly *Sitka*), 7:106; 14:145

Rainbow (str., 1861, formerly *McClelland*), 22:369

Raines, Austin J., 37:3-5, 7

Rainfall, 8:111; 10:304-5; 13:205; 16:333-34, 299-300; 26:245, 335, 347; 27:199, 202; 39:290; *see also* Floods

Rains, John, 3:165

Raisch, Mrs. Albert J. (Emma Stealey), obit., 20:286

Raisina Grange, 25:30

"Raising of the Flag at Monterey ... 1846, The," by Aubrey Neasham, 25:193-203

Raisins, 25:30-32

Raisty, Lloyd Bernard, 29:92-93

Rajah (play), 16:301

Raker, John E., 38:254

Ralganal, *see* Benson, William R.

Ralphs, John, 12:117

Ralston, A. J., 11:49

Ralston, A. R., 24:247-48

Ralston, Jackson Harvey, 9:42, 113, 116, 394; 22:95; addresses: "California Associations with Washington, D.C.," 23:80-81; "The Pious Fund ... before the Hague Tribunal,"6:103-4

Ralston, James H., 9:113, 116, 394; 24:166, 180

Ralston, Mrs. James H., (Harriet N. Jackson), 22:95

Ralston, Sam, 19:231

Ralston, William Chapman, 11:64; 12:329; 14:409; 15:191, 378; 16:377; 17:185; 18:24, 369; 19:155, 230; 21:145, 161, 163, 171, 176; 25:10; 26:176, 177, 196, 357; 27:165, 166, 187-88, 270, 339; 29:198; 33:234, 317; 34:327; 35:143; *see also* Fretz & Ralston

Ralston, Mrs. William Chapman (Elizabeth Red Fry), 2:207; 19:230

Ralton, D. E., 10:77

"Rambles in California: A Question of Authorship," by A. T. Leonard, Jr., 30:233-35

Ramey, Earl, 14:288; "The Beginnings of Marysville," 14:195-229, 288, 375-407; 15:21-57

Ramírez, Ángel, 8:304, 331-32; 14:231, 235, 249, 255, 258, 261; 15:339-40; 16:348, 353-55

Ramírez, Francisco P., 13:337; 22:30

Ramirez, José Manuel, 8:359; 9:63, 75-76; 10:42, 198; 12:280; 14:210, 212, 219, 221, 383, 389; 15:22, 29, 43, 45; view of home, 9: opp. 62

Ramírez, José María (alférez, 1828), 8:331; 14:235; 15:347-48; 16:360

Ramírez, José María (artilleryman, 1836), 15:356

Ramírez, Juan, 13:305

Ramírez, María Concepción (Fuller), 32:235

Ramirez Mills, 9:62, 63, 75

Ramm, Charles A., 11:52; address, "Boyhood Experiences ... in the Yuba Diggings," 11:88

Ramm, John, 8:357; 9:69, 172

Ramm's Ranch, 8:211; 9:177; *see also* Notowa

Ramona, by Helen Hunt Jackson, 17:30

"Ramona's marriage place," 4:396

Ramonet, Francisco, 37:205

Rampaging Herd, The: A Bibliography

of ... *the Cattle Industry,* by Adams, rev., 40:170-71
Rampin, Frank, 9:180
Ram's Peak (Wagontire Mtn.), 22:215
Ramsay, G. S., 32:165-67
Ramsdel (ship), *see B. H. Ramsdel*
Ramsdell, A. G., 17:177
Ramsey, Capt. and Mrs. (S.F., 1867), 11:127
Ramsey, Alexander, 19:251
Ramsey & Co., 9:346
Ramusio, Giovanni Battista, 1:38, 43, 47, 49, 51; *Navigationi,* 3:263-64, 308, 318, 384; 6:305, 316; 7:66; map in, 7:67
Rancheria (place), 15:376; 16:79
Ranchos: life on, 5:135-36, 357, 363-69 *passim;* 6:242; 12:285-87, 290-99 *passim;* 15:333; 25:290; 38:109-10
Ranchos and land grants:
  Acalanes, 30:5
  Agua Caliente (San Diego Co.), *see* Rancho San José del Valle; Warner's Ranch
  Agua Caliente (Sonoma Co.), 13:36; 16:306; 21:313
  Aguages (uncl.), 21:330
  Los Alamitos, 40:365
  Los Alamos, 18:170, 171, 254, 271
  Los Alamos y Agua Caliente (Kern Co.), 18:275
  El Alisal, or Patrocino (Hartnell's), 8:114; 13:58; 30:98
  El Alisal (Soberanes' and Butron's), 15:134; 23:348
  Los Alisos, *see* Ranchos: Cañada de los Alisos
  Las Animas, or Sitio de la Brea, or Carnadero, 29:19
  Aptos, 38:259, 260
  Aromitas y Agua Caliente, 29:26
  Arroyo Chico, 6:69; 36:313, 314, 315, 318
  Arroyo de los Pilarcitos, or Miramontes, or San Benito, 16:380
  Arroyo de San Antonio, 22:345
  Arroyo Grande, or San Ramón, 20:267
  Arroyo Seco (Monterey Co.), 29:28
  Asunción, 1:170
  Atascadero, 21:318; 36:14; 38:261
  Ausaymas y San Felipe, 26:287
  La Ballona, or Paso de las Carretas, 13:209; 23:359-60
  Blücher, 29:92
  Boga, 27:108, 298, 299, 300

Bolsa de Chamisal, 20:267
Bosquejo, 16:137; 18:296-304 *passim,* 313; 30:63, 66, 158, 329-30; *see also* Lassen, Peter
La Brea, 13:329, 351; 15:235; 29:23, 28
Buena Esperanza, *see* Ranchos: Encinal y Buena Esperanza
Buena Ventura, 22:366, 369, 370; 29:136
Buri Buri, 16:183, 285, 380; 17:245-59; 22:244, 251; 34:232
El Butano, 16:380
Cahuenga, 30:53; *see also* Cahuenga, capitulation of
El Cajon, or Santa Monica, 21:301, 304; 26:24, 30, 55
La Calera, *see* Ranchos: Las Positas
Calleguas, 24:92
Las Camaritas, 10:290
Campo de los Franceses, 15:277
Camulos, 1:261-62; 17:34; 18:275; 21:320; 32:185
Cañada de Capay, 25:221-22; 30:338
Cañada de Guadalupe, Visitación y Rodeo Viejo, 14:126; 16:380; 21:117
Cañada de la Carpintería, 29:26
Cañada del Chorro, 1:170; 18:172, 176
Cañada de los Alisos, 21:348
Cañada de los Osos, or Pecho y Islay, 1:170; 14:345; 18:172, 176
Cañada de Pala, 38:52
Cañada de Palo Escrito, 29:6
Canada de Pogolomi, 14:130
Cañada del Rincon en el Rio de San Lorenzo de Santa Cruz, 16:337
Cañada de Raimundo, 16:380
Cañada de Verde y Arroyo de la Purísima, 16:380
Capay, 30:53, 54
Los Capitancillos, 38:110
Carmelo (Yolo Co.), 25:221
Carne Humana (or Colijolmanoc), 4:153; 18:70; 28:262-63, 266, 267
Los Carneros, 29:26
Catacula, 35:1
Caymus, 2:53-54, 63, 65; 23:294; 28:262, 268
Los Cerritos, 13:302
Chico, *see* Ranchos: Arroyo Chico
Chimiles, 24:71
Chino, *see* Ranchos: Santa Ana del Chino
Chualar, *see* Ranchos: Santa Rosa de Chualar

La Cienega, 18:178
Cienegitas, 18:177, 275; 27:337
Los Coches, 20:108-9; 34:240
Cordua grant, 15:52; *see also* New
    Mecklenburg; Ranchos: Honcut
Corral de Piedra, 1:170; 20:267-68,
    270
El Corral de Tierra (San Mateo Co.),
    16:380
El Corral de Tierra (uncl.), 21:320
Corralitos (Amesti Ranch), 23:348
Corte de Madera de Novato, 16:285
Cosumnes (Hartnell's Ranch),
    11:321; 34:22, 24
Los Coyotes, 13:350; 21:350; 29:245
Las Cruces, 18:277
Cucamonga, 3:165-66; 12:112; 13:217
Cuyama, 18:179
Cuyumaca, 34:193, 200, 36:128
Dos Pueblos, 4:157; 19:259, 276
Encinal y Buena Esperanza, 29:27
Encino, 13:203, 230
Familia Sagrada, or Bolsa del Potrero
    y Moro Cojo, 10:414
Las Flores, 21:347; 22:48, 175; *see also*
    Ranchos: Santa Margarita y
    Las Flores
La Goleta, 18:175
Guadalupe y Llanitos de los Correos,
    26:286
Guajome, 1:236
Guilicos, 27:108
Honcut, 12:280, 284, 302; 14:200, 226
Huasna, 1:170; 18:175
Huecos, 20:108
Huerhuero, 1:170
Huerta del Rey (Monterey Co.),
    21:320
Huerta del Rey (San Benito Co.),
    13:35
Huichicha, 17:146-49 *passim;* 28:269;
    29:315, 317
Isla de Santa Cruz, 21:318
Isla de Santa Rosa, 18:176, 275
Jacinto, 24:228
La Jota, 2:55, 65; 4:153; 13:12; 35:1,
    159
Juristac, 29:19
Jurupa, 2:8; 12:111, 116-20 *passim;*
    29:34
Laguna (Santa Barbara Co.), 18:176,
    268
Laguna de la Merced, 14:131; 16:380;
    30:338

Laguna de los Palos Colorados, 30:2,
    8-9
Laguna de San Antonio, 20:271;
    29:268
Laguna de Tache, 25:23
Las Llagas, *see* Ranchos: San
    Francisco de las Llagas
Llajome, *see* Ranchos: Yajome
Llano de Tesquesquite, 29:17
Locoallomi, 24:71; 35:1
Lomas de la Purificacion, 18:179
Lomerías Muertas, or Lomerías del
    Espíritu Santo, 29:19
Lupyomi, 27:107-8, 109; 29:318;
    32:376
Las Mariposas, 15:275; 30:331, 332;
    33:276; 34:255; *see also* Land
    cases; Mariposa Estate
Los Médanos (Mesa's), 12:25, 33
Los Meganos (Noriega's and
    Marsh's), 4:160; 22:316
Miramontes, *see* Ranchos: Arroyo
    de los Pilarcitos
El Molino, 19:141
Muñiz, 12:200
Muscupiabe or El Cajon, 12:111-12,
    115
de la Nación (San Diego Co.), 13:260
de la Nación (San Mateo Co.), 17:249
Nacional (Monterey Co.), 13:271,
    278-79; *see also* Ranchos: del Rey
Napa, 21:313; 29:318, 323-25
La Natividad, 3:279; 4:365, 366, 369;
    15:134; 21:3; 29:24, 337, 339
Natomas, *see* Ranchos: Rio de los
    Americanos
Nemshas, 14:208
Nicasio, 16:200
Los Nietos, 13:203, 217
Nipomo, 1:170; 2:45; 10:354; 14:127;
    18:162, 175, 254, 258; 29:343
Nojoqui, 18:176
Novato, 9:277; 22:345
Nueva Flandria, 27:136
Nueva Helvetia, 19:137; 24:331;
    25:221; 29:133; *see also*
    New Helvetia
Nueva (or Neu-) Mecklenburg, *see*
    New Mecklenburg
Ojai, 27:337
Olompali, 25:123; 29:268
Omochumne, 25:221
Paguay, 21:320
Palo Escrito, *see* Ranchos: Cañada
    de Palo Escrito

del Paso, 18:173; 25:220, 223-25
Los Peñasquitos, *see* Ranchos: Santa
  María de los Peñasquitos
El Pescadero (San Joaquin Co.),
  21:325
El Pescadero, or San Antonio
  (San Mateo Co.), 16:285
Petaluma, 4:365, 366, 369, 371;
  15:280; 16:235; 17:155; 19:141;
  30:329; 36:242
Piedra Blanca, 1:170; 13:327
Pilarcitos, *see* Ranchos: Arroyo de los
  Pilarcitos
Pismo, 1:170; 27:135
Pogolomi, *see* Ranchos: Cañada de
  Pogolomi
Portezuela, 13:203
Las Positas (Alameda Co.), 13:67;
  39:43; *see also* Livermore, Robert
Las Positas, or La Calera (Santa
  Barbara Co.), 18:161, 170, 174
Posolmi y Pozitas de las Animas,
  16:347
Potrero de los Cerritos, 16:285
Potrero de San Carlos, 29:24
Potrero de Santa Clara, 16:285; 27:107
Las Pozas, 18:275
Providencia, or La Puente, 12:116;
  13:224; 26:23
Las Pulgas, 15:236, 266, 336, 337;
  16:330, 336-37; 17:247, 249
Pulpunes, 22:316; *see also* Ranchos:
  Los Meganos
Punta de la Concepción, 18:177
Punta del Año Nuevo, 16:380;
  20:264-67; 35:82
Punta de los Reyes, 20:261-64, 272
Las Putas (or Los Putos), 13:278;
  see also Ranchos: Rio de los Putos
Quesesosi, 23:375
Quito, 30:329
de Real Hacienda, *see* Ranchos: del
  Rey (del Presidio de Monterey)
del Rey (del Presidio de Monterey),
  16:303; 17:121; 25:59, 77; *see also*
  Ranchos: Nacional
del Rey (del Presidio de San
  Francisco), 16:380; 17:246-47, 249;
  25:77; *see also* Ranchos: Buri Buri
Rinconada del Arroyo de San
  Francisquito, 26:345; 27:135
Rinconada de los Gatos, 20:286; 29:57
Rincón de la Ballena, 21:16
Rincón de las Salinas y Potrero
  Viejo, 16:80; 21:117; 27:107

Rincón del Diablo, 26:38
Rincón de los Esteros, 38:110
Rincón de San Francisquito, 16:285;
  27:134, 135
Rincón de San Pascual (or Pasqual),
  13:303; 19:215; 21:195; 32:345
Rio de Jesús María, 25:221
Rio los Americanos, 7:105, 109,
  110; 15:366; 17:293(?)
Rio de los Berrendos, 14:346
Rio de los Putos, 23:291, 295; 27:108
Roblar de la Misería, 27:108
Rodeo de las Aguas, or San Antonio,
  18:276
Rodeo Viejo, *see* Ranchos: Cañada
  de Guadalupe
Rosa de Castillo, 13:306
San Agustín, 15:224; 33:64
San Antonio (Nicolas Den's), *see*
  Ranchos: Rodeo de las Aguas, or
  San Antonio
San Antonio (J. J. Gonzales'), *see*
  Ranchos: El Pescadero, or
  San Antonio
San Antonio (A. M. Lugo's), 13:348;
  25:287
San Antonio (Luis Peralta's), 4:93;
  7:400; 15:278; 17:42; 30:1, 217-31
  passim; 31:326; bk. on, rev., 4:93
San Antonio Abad, 26:56
San Bernardino, 12:111, 116-19
  passim, 122; 25:287; 29:32
San Bernardo, 21:336, 345; 26:45, 61;
  33:102
San Bruno, 8:146-47; 27:109
San Buenaventura, *see* Ranchos:
  Buena Ventura
San Carlos, *see* Ranchos: Potrero de
  San Carlos
Sanel, 26:209; *see also* Félix, Fernando
San Emidio, 11:255
San Francisco, 19:215; 30:52; 36:289
San Francisco de las Llagas, 8:115;
  16:282; 34:232
San Francisquito (Los Angeles Co.),
  17:176
San Francisquito (Monterey Co.),
  29:24
San Francisquito (Santa Clara Co.),
  see Ranchos: Rinconada del
  Arroyo de San Francisquito and
  Rincon de San Francisquito
San Gregorio, 16:380
San Isidro (Santa Clara Co.), 23:363,
  375; 29:20

San Joaquín, 13:322
Sanjon (or Zanjon) de los
  Moquelumnes, 17:75
San José de Buenos Aires, 13:208-9
San José de Gracia y Simi, 18:170;
  23:212, 218
San José del Valle, or Agua Caliente,
  7:86, 87; *see also* Agua Caliente;
  Warner's Ranch
San Julian, 18:170, 270
San Justo, 26:287
San Leandro, 25:373
San Luis Gonzaga, 25:2; 26:287
San Marcos, 4:165, 166; 30:49
San Mateo, 21:347; 23:254-56; 27:105,
  250-52; map, 27: opp. 252
San Miguel (Contra Costa Co.),
  13:278
San Miguel (Santa Barbara Co.?),
  18:176, 276
San Miguel, or Los Cerritos
  (Ventura Co.), 16:303
San Miguelito, 18:176; 36:6
San Onofre y Santa Margarita,
  22:175; *see also* Ranchos:
  Santa Margarita y Las Flores
San Pablo, or Cochiyunes, 8:243-44;
  9:190; 15:277; 21:322; 30:56
San Pascual, *see* Ranchos: Rincón de
  San Pascual
San Pedro (L.A. Co.), 13:202, 203;
  see also Domínguez Rancho
San Pedro (San Mateo Co.), 16:285,
  380; 17:255; 23:250, 258
San Pedro y San Pablo (uncl.), 21:320
San Rafael, or La Zanja, 13:203
San Ramón (Alameda and Contra
  Costa cos.), 24:380; 38:10
San Ramón (San Luis Obispo Co.),
  see Ranchos: Arroyo Grande
San Simeon, 1:170; 18:160, 163, 175
Santa Ana, *see* Ranchos: Santa Ana
  del Chino; Santa Ana y Quien Sabe;
  Santiago de Santa Ana
Santa Ana del Chino, 13:125, 215, 302,
  348; 25:131; 27:117, 118; 29:335
Santa Ana y Quien Sabe, 29:26
Santa Anita (Los Angeles Co.),
  1:250; 5:408; 6:99; 31:20
Santa Anita (Huerta del Rey,
  San Benito Co.), 13:35
Santa Clara, *see* Ranchos: Potrero de
  Santa Clara
Santa Clara del (or el) Norte, 18:172;
  33:337

Santa Gertrudis, 13:215
Santa Isabel, *see* Ranchos:
  Santa Ysabel
Santa Manuela, 18:176
Santa Margarita (San Luis Obispo
  Co.), 1:166, 170; 13:100, 110, 112;
  36:187; 38:261-62; art. on, 36:1-20
Santa Margarita y Las Flores (San
  Diego Co.), 13:101, 229, 260;
  21:329, 332, 347, 356; 26:30; art. on,
  22:175-77; phot. of ranch house,
  22: opp. 175
Santa María, *see* Ranchos: Valle de
  Pamo
Santa María de los Peñasquitos,
  21:338, 344
Santa Rosa (San Luis Obispo Co.),
  1:170; 18:163, 175
Santa Rosa (Sonoma Co.), 24:59
Santa Rosa de Chualar, 26:286
Santa Ysabel (San Luis Obispo Co.),
  1:170
Santa Ysabel (San Diego Co.), 1:146;
  21:334, 355; 26:24-28 *passim*, 52
Santiago de Santa Ana, 19:208
San Timoteo, 12:7
San Vicente, 20:108
San Vicente y Santa Monica, 13:313
San Ysidro (modern, Santa Barbara
  Co.), 28:286; 29:380
Los Saucos, 30:53
Sausal, 4:365, 366, 371; 15:134
Sausalito, 14:125; 21:313; 23:372;
  27:271, 274
Secuan (uncl.), 21:320
Sespe, or San Cayetano, 30:52
Simi, *see* Ranchos: San José de Gracia
Sisquoc, 38:261-63
Soledad, 26:33, 44, 55
Soquel Augmentation, 29:57, 58
Soscol (or Suscol), 6:146; 15:280;
  17:153, 159, 160, 231; 29:159
Sotoyome, 1:135, 150; 24:54
Suisun, 15:275; 30:331, 332
El Sur, 10:414; 14:346
Sur Chiquito, 29:24
Tejon, 9:277, 310; 10:388; 11:255;
  13:343; 21:343; 26:54
Tesquesquite, *see* Ranchos: Llano de
  Tesquesquite
Tia Juana (Lower Calif.), 26:38
Tierra Redonda (uncl.), 21:320
Tinaquaic, 13:306; 29:343
Tomales y Baulines, 19:322; 21:380

Topango Malibu Sequit, 13:217, 315; 38:171-73
El Toro, 10:414; 29:27
Trabuco, 13:260
Las Trancas, *see* Ranchos: Yajome
Ulistac, 29:56
Los Ulpinos, 16:285
Valle de Pamo, or Santa María, 21:335, 355; 26:38, 52; 30:51
Valle de San Jose (Alameda Co.), 13:278
Valle de San Luis Gonzaga, 21:320
Vega del Rio del Pájaro, 29:26
Los Vergeles, 19:132, 142; 29:336, 337, 339
La Visitación, 21:117; *see also* Ranchos: Cañada de Guadalupe
Yajome (or Llajome), or Paso de las Trancas, 29:318, 319
Zaca (or Saca), 38:263
Zanjones, 26:286
Zayante (or Sayante), 16:143; 18:295, 310
Ranchos, Mission and ex-Mission: Carmel, 4:90; San Gabriel, 27:135; San Juan Bautista, 17:178; San Juan Capistrano, 13:260; 21:329; 22:175; San Luis Obispo (*see* Ranchos: Santa Margarita); San Miguel, 33:268, 337; Soledad, 1:258; 23:10-11
"Rancho Santa Margarita of San Luis Obispo," by William R. Cameron, 36:1-20, 187
Rand, Miss (S.F., 1861), 10:276
Rand, Caroline, 40:137
Rand, Charles, 8:369; 15:85, 258
Rand, Charles W., 8:369; 15:9; 17:177; writ from Lincoln, 15:7-8
Rand, Frances, *see* Smith, Frances Rand
Rand, Mrs. Lucy (Gage), 28:189
Rand, Olivia, 21:157
Randall (Death Valley, 1850), 18:198
Randall, Capt. (of *Yankee Blade*, 1854), 15:178, 271; 16:347
Randall, A. S., 10:282, 361; *see also* Randall & Co.
Randall, Albert Gallatin, 17:256; *see also* Wainwright, Randall & Co.
Randall, Andrew, 8:373; 15:158, 159; 20:261, 272; 21:363, 364, 365
Randall, Charles H., 26:243, 248
Randall, Eli, 16:138
Randall, Frank, 19:232
Randall, H. M., 31:331
Randall, P. M., 9:116

Randall (A. S.) & Co., 30:130, 366
Rand Divide Mining Co., 32:14
Randle, P. W., 27:218
Randle, Peter Wilkins, 29:289
Randle, Richard Rush, 29:289
Randlett, Horace D., 27:17
Rand mining district, 32:1-41
Randolph, Mrs. B. H., 10:290
Randolph, Edmund, 9:276; 10:166, 167, 191, 260, 271-75 *passim*, 287, 288, 290; 11:9; 15:373, 375; 17:177; 20:167; 28:2, 59, 66, 166-68; 34:243, 246, 248; port., 10: opp. 188
Randolph, Isaac N., 24:57
Randolph, Lee, 38:1, 2
Randolph & Co., 34:328; phot. of store, 34: opp. 329
Randolph Flat, 20:43
Randsburg, 28:189; 32:1-41 *passim*
Raney (Yuba Co., 1857), 9:139
Rankin, Edward, 21:327
Rankin, Ira P., 9:104, 106; 15:282; 21:327
Rankin, Mrs. Ira P., 10:291; 19:229
Rankin, James, 8:196; 9:133
Rankin, Robert, 9:109; 15:280, 364, 372; 16:282
Ranney, Mary A., 28:293
Ransom (Marysville, 1859), 10:179, 247
Ransom, Leander, 30:338; 34:17; report of, 34:4-11
Ransom, Lyman W., 15:24, 28, 31
Ransome, Bernard, 22:95; obit., 25:187
Ransome, Ernest Leslie, 22:95; 27:197
Raoulx, Gaston, *see* Raousset-Boulbon
Raousset-Boulbon, Comte Gaston de, 5:14; 11:388; 13:385; 15:174, 175, 180; 18:7-21; 23:174, 177; 35:319-22; 39:141, 144-45, 331; bk. on, rev., 7:198-99; port., 18: opp. 3
Rapelye (or Rapplyea), Abraham W., 8:341; 9:247; 11:57
Raphael (Indian, 1850s), 36:314, 319
Raphael, Robert H., Jr., 30:286
Raphael Glass Co., 30:286
Rapp, A. H., 39:151, 154
Raschen, Henry, 37:35
Raskin, Charles, 39:233, 332-34 *passim*, 337; port., 39: opp. 312
Raskin, Henri, port., 39: opp. 312
Rasselas (ship), 12:142-45 *passim*; 14:318, 342, 343; 23:333
Rassette, Joseph, 15:368
Rassette House, San Francisco, 10:72; 15:369; 19:229; 22:77, 82, 263-64; 28:33

Ratherchucker, John, 15:76
Rathke, Augusta J. F., 27:283
Rathke, Sophie, 27:383
" 'Rational Amusements in Our Midst,'
  Public Libraries in California,
  1849-1859," by Hugh S. Baker,
  38:295-320
Rats, 12:304; 32:57, 62; trained, 10:361
Rattler, Lew, 4:62
Rattler (yacht), 15:369
Rattlesnake (place), 30:261
Rattlesnake (ship), 15:175
Rattlesnake Bar, 33:54-55
"Rattlesnake Dick," 2:205
Rattlesnake Island, 32:340
Rattlesnakes, 2:12, 27-28, 48-49, 319-20;
  6:217, 233; 8:165, 314; 11:256, 292;
  12:15-16, 208, 305; 15:110; 17:29, 34;
  18:125; 23:204; 31:318
Rau, George J. and Callista (Martin),
  33:94
Raubinger, William, Jr., 35:145
Raup, Hallock Floy, 26:287; 27:380-81;
  32:94-95; "The Delayed Discovery of
  San Francisco Bay," 27:289-96; "The
  Italian-Swiss in California," 30:305-14;
  coauth. "Northernmost Spanish
  Frontier in California," 32:43-48
Ravel, Gabriel, 16:340; *see also*
  Martinetti-Ravel Troupe
Ravel Troupe, 16:340; 21:72; *see also*
  Martinetti-Ravel Troupe
Ravenna, Manuel, 13:340
Ravine Company, 9:144, 147, 150
Rawles, James, 33:364
Rawlings, Capt. (Virginia City, 1876),
  11:51
Rawlings, Lloyd, 19:382
Rawlings, Stuart L., obit., 19:382
Rawlings, Mrs. Stuart L.
  (Eleanor Warner), 19:382
Rawson, C. H., 16:283
Ray (Placerville, 1856), 22:38; 30:367
Ray, Dr. (Galt, 1871), 18:23
Ray, B., 13:32
Ray, G. W., 13:31
Rayburn, F. W., 31:20
Rayburn, Sam, 39:135
Raymond, Israel W., 4:24; 20:383
Raymond, J. A., 9:113, 116
Raymond, John, 21:243
Raymond, Peter, 18:265-66
Raymond, Rossiter Worthington,
  38:124
Raymond, William, 17:108-9

Raymond (schr., 1859), 22:10
Raymond (steam schr., ca. 1908), 31:295
Raymond Lumber Co., 31:295
Rayner, Thomas L., "Corrections and
  Addenda... on the Vigilance
  Committee... 1856," 8:364-73
Raynor, Henry, 21:161
Read (Marysville, 1858), 9:366
Read, Alexander P., 23:191
Read, Clarence, 34:332
Read, Francis, 29:253-54
Read, George Willis, 8:3, 16;
  A Pioneer of 1850, ed. Read, rev.,
  6:376-77
Read, Georgia Willis, 39:270; "Bruff's
  Route in Eastern California,"
  39:263-66; "The Chagres River Route
  to California," 8:3-16; ed. *A Pioneer
  of 1850*, rev., 6:376-77
Read, H. W., 27:131
Read, Isaac, 8:3, 5; journal, ed.
  Georgia W. Read, 8:3, 6-16; port.,
  8: opp. 3
Read, J. A. (John A. Reed?), 13:32
Read, Jay Marion, 23:191
Read, Mrs. John (Ilaria Sánchez),
  17:256; 27:262, 265
Read, Van, 37:169
Reade, Charles, 35:142
Reading, Alice M., 22:370, 371, 382
Reading, Pierson Barton, 1:9; 5:120,
  146; 6:365-66; 10:90; 11:11, 25, 42;
  12:351; 13:135-36, 385; 16:53, 56, 84;
  17:275; 18:56, 312; 19:133, 142; 20:46,
  148, 152; 22:41, 52, 64; 25:145-46;
  26:99, 123; 27:86; 29:134, 271, 335;
  30:51, 53-54; 38:49-50;
  "A Chronology of the Life of,"
  22:365-71; ranch of, 22:368, 369, 370;
  29:135, 136
Reading, Mrs. Pierson Barton (Fannie
  Wallace Washington), 22:369
Reading, Robert, 22:370
Reading family, 22:369-71 *passim*
Reading (town), 22:369; *see also*
  Redding
Reading's Bar, 22:367
Reading's Springs, 18:312; 22:367
Reagan, F. J., 25:95
Real, Antonio Suárez del, 15:227
Real, José María del Refugio Sagrado
  Suárez del, 12:35, 135; 15:4; 30:98
Real Associaçao Benemerita
  Autonomica Micaelense, 35:244

"Real Bret Harte, The," address by
    Charles A. Murdock, 4:95
Real del Castillo, 15:105, 132
Real del Monte Mine, 7:114-18 *passim*
Realejo, Nicaragua, 13:6
Real estate: in 1834: 16:322; in 1848-49,
    13:275, 357, 367; 14:20-21; 16:75;
    20:29, 123; 22:243; 23:56; 24:355, 357;
    27:17; in 1853-54, 15:266; 23:174;
    in 1871: 29:2, 17; in 1916, 31:297;
    beach and water lots, 15:171, 180, 186,
    270, 276; 16:182; 17:173; 34:333;
    see also Lands
Ream, I., 5:289
Reardon (Reardan?), Miss (Marysville,
    1858), 9:345
Reardon (Reardan?), James McC.,
    9:140(?), 359, 360, 361
Reardon, Thomas Birkhead, 9:66, 78,
    141, 155, 266, 347, 356; 10:252, 254,
    255, 266, 273, 285, 356, 395
Reardon, Mrs. Thomas Birkhead,
    10:364
Réau, Cécile, *La société californienne
    de 1850*, rev., 1:102-4
Rebard, L., 16:341
Rebekah, Daughters of, 10:252, 280
Rebellion of Loo Fei, The (play),
    23:108
Reber, Thomas, 22:31
"Recently Discovered Account of the
    Atondo Expedition to California in
    1683, A," by Henry R. Wagner, 8:80
"Recent Visits to Old Ranchos,"
    address by Mrs. Theodore J. Hoover,
    16:380
"Recollections Inspired by a San
    Francisco Directory," address by
    Daniel Q. Troy, 13:188
"Recollections of a California
    Cattleman," from Memoirs of
    H. T. Liliencrantz, 38:259-68, 341-47
Recollections of a Tule Sailor, by
    Leale, rev., 18:373-74
"Recollections of Historical Events in
    California, 1842-1878," by William
    A. Streeter, ed. William H. Ellison,
    18:64-71, 157-79, 254-78
"Recollections of Templeton Crocker,"
    by Henry R. Wagner, 28:364-66
"Recollections of the San Francisco
    Disaster of 1906," address by
    J. B. Levison, 21:183-84
Record, Los Angeles, 11:190
"Record of Padre Fray Junípero

Serra's Death," by Francisco Palou,
    trans. George Tays, 13:155-58
Records of a California Family, by
    Gunn, ed. Marston, rev., 8:87
Redbank Creek, 30:54
Red Bluff, 6:69; 16:65, 180; 20:255;
    26:333; 30:158; 36:281
Red Bluff Hotel, 16:137
Red Cap (Indian, 1855), 26:203, 206
Reddick, Elizabeth, 22:80, 81, 83
Reddick, John B., 22:83
Reddick, William, 22:80, 82, 83
Redding (or Reddings), Mrs.
    (Sacramento, 1858), 9:251
Redding, Benjamin Bernard, 9:110,
    371, 394; 10:53, 75, 191; 27:346; 30:133
Redding, C. A., 25:24-25
Redding, Joseph Deighn, 25:230, 232,
    233, 238, 239, 242, 249
Redding (place), 22:370
Reddy, Pat, 4:73-74; 7:117
Redfield, Oscar F., 10:394
Redington, Alfred, 9:277, 371, 394, 397;
    10: opp. 48, 53, 78, 191, 193
Redington, John H., 12:312-15; 14:395;
    19:232; 29:253-54
Redington, Paul G., 4:52
Redington, Hostetter and Co., 14:395
Red Lake, 6:126, 363; 32:207; illus.,
    6: opp. 124
Redman, R. Augustus, 10:62; 11:8, 9, 21
Redmon, I. W., 20:113
Red Monster and White Warrior
    (ballet), 15:179
Red Mountain, 32:2-3, 31
Red River, *see* Colorado River
Red Rock Canyon, 17:105-7, 115, 209,
    213, 216
Red Rover, The (play), 10:378, 391
Redwood Canyon, 30:8
Redwood City, 27:339
Redwood Creek, 30:10
Redwood House (Oakland Hotel),
    25:95
"Redwood in the History of California,
    The," address by Winfield Scott,
    8:283
Redwood Lumber Association, 27:267,
    274
Redwood Manufacturers' Association,
    12:33
Redwood Peak, 30:7
Redwoods, Coast, 2:125, 225-26; 5:154,
    168; 7:413; 8:283, 327; 9:222;
    11:310-11; 12:205, 209; 15:185, 224,

235, 236; 16:140; 18:336; 23:166;
25:185; 27:260; 28:266; 30:1-14;
31:293, 301; 33:362; 38:59; *see also*
Lumber
Redwoods, giant, *see* Big trees
Redwood Valley, 27:220, 221
Reed (in mines, 1848), 2:190
Reed, Capt. (of *Mercury*, 1851), 8:275
Reed (Yuba Co., 1854), 8:363; *see also*
Reid & Co.
Reed (lawsuit, Yuba Co., 1857), 9:167
Reed (S.F., 1860), 29:111, 113, 117
Reed, B. T., 8:297-303 *passim*
Reed, Charley, 4:61
Reed, D. C., 19:67
Reed, Elliott, 30:112, 262
Reed, Henry, 15:273; 37:139
Reed, Howard S., 24:383
Reed, J. Sewell, 40:298
Reed, James Frazier, 2:64; 5:395;
10:349-51; 24:73; family of 19:139
Reed, Mrs. James Frazier (Margaret
W. Keyes?), 5:399; 19:122, 139
Reed, John (killed 1848), *see*
Reed, William
Reed, John (La Puente, 1859), 26:23
Reed, John A., 13:32(?)
Reed, Joseph, 29:289
Reed, Martha Jane ("Patty"), 2:63-64;
19:139
Reed, Merrill, 31:30
Reed, Rollin, 36:164
Reed, S. B., 36:268-69
Reed, T. L., 9:113
Reed, Thomas K., 19:139
Reed, Thomas Law, 25:175
Reed, Thomas R., 13:32
Reed, Virginia, *see* Backenstoe
Reed, William (Mono mines, 1825,
1860), 26:246
Reed, William (d. 1848), 18:265-66;
33:268, 337; 36:12
Reed, Grimm & Co., 30:107-8
Reedley, 25:175
Reese, Mrs. (on *Uncle Sam*, 1861),
27:154
Reese (brothers; Nevada Co., 1883),
28:234
Reese, Enoch, 22:13
Reese, J. Martin, 6:15, 16; 15:147
Reese, John (Utah, 1853), 22:13
Reese, Col. John (Nevada, late 1850s),
30:377
Reese, Michael, 26:264; 27:341, 342;
29:104, 111

Reese, William, 26:204
Reese River, 28:379; mines, 6:347-50;
10:383, 394; newspaper, 36:367-68
Reeve, William B. and Mary Ann
(McDonald), 28:293
Reeves (lawsuit; Marysville, 1859),
10:168
Reeves, James, 2:108
Reform (str.), 18:373
Reform school, San Francisco, 10:276;
see also Industrial school
Réforme, La, 39:220, 349
Reformed Episcopal Church, 34:320
Refugio (ship), 2:37
Regensberger, Jacob, 9:327; 30:69
Regidores, 14:8, 9
Register, Sacramento, 10:41, 63
Register, San Jose, 22:223
*Reglamento para el Gobierno de la
Provincia de Californias*, 1:12-13, 21,
25; 10:80, 82, 83; 13:199; rev., 8:281
"Regrettable Chapter in California
History, A," address by
C. Hart Merriam, 2:369
Regulators, *see* "Hounds"
Rehan, Ada, 35:142
Rehfisch, Meier, 14:399; 15:29
Rehler, T. B., 8:358
Reid (Stockton, 1853), 10:67
Reid, Felipe, 13:329
Reid, George, 9:346
Reid, Hugo Perfecto, 1:250, 252;
13:215-16, 322, 329; 18:374; 28:361;
30:98-99; *Indians of Los Angeles
County*, rev., 5:408; fac. sig.,
10: opp. 159
Reid, J. M., 9:35
Reid, J. S., 15:366
Reid, Jacob, 5:72
Reid, James, 9:133, 145
Reid, Mrs. James S. (Alberta Bancroft),
29:101, 366
Reid, John W., 25:301
Reid, María Ygnacia, 1:250, 252, 254,
258
Reid, Mary, 28:293
Reid, R. K., 4:183
Reid, Mrs. Robert, *see* Gregson, Ann E.
Reid, Mrs. Whitelaw, 27:254
Reid, William Thomas, 26:196;
35:255-56
Reid (Reed) & Co., Yuba Co., 8:352
Reidshaw, William, 3:156
Reier, Charles, 19:85
Reier, Anna L., 19:85

Reiff, A., Jr., 10:265
Reily, Henry J., 34:168
Reily, James, 34:132-39 *passim*
Reina, Los Angeles, La, by Hill, rev.,
    8:88
"Reine des Fleurs" (San Jose, 1850),
    5:356
Reinhart (on *Brandywine*, 1849), 30:19
Reinhart (Yuba Co., 1856), 9:53;
    see also Reinhart & Bro.
Reinhardt, Mrs. George Frederick
    (Aurelia Henry), 24:383; 31:88
Reinhart, Simon, 9:150
Reinhart & Bro. (Simon, Benjamin and
    Eli), 8:350, 351, 363; 9:58, 130-33
    passim, 156, 346
Reins (Marysville, 1858), 9:376
Reinstein, Jacob Bert, 39:77
Reis, F., 8:337
Reis, Gottlieb Ludwig Gustave and
    Louisa Philippina (Merkel), 28:294
"Rejoice Ye Thieves and Harlots," ed.
    Richard H. Dillon, 37:137-68
"Relations of California Indians to Other
    Western Tribes," address by
    Robert H. Lowie, 12:84-85
Relèvement, Le (semi-monthly),
    39:242, 244-45, 349
Relief (bay str., 1870s), 18:373
Relief (ship, 1845), 2:163
Relief Hill, 10:347-52
Remedios, Los (harbor), 9:240
Remer, John A., 21:241
"Reminiscences of a 'Forty-Niner,' " by
    Mahlon D. Fairchild, 13:3-33
"Reminiscences of California,
    1849-1852," by Berryman Bryant,
    11:35-39
"Reminiscences of Early San
    Francisco," address by
    Clay M. Greene, 4:211-12
"Reminiscences of Joseph D. Grant,"
    30:207-15, 339-51
"Reminiscences of Life in Territorial
    Nevada," by R. K. Colcord, 7:112-20
"Reminscences of Sacramento," address
    by C. E. Grunsky, 11:88
Reminiscences . . . of San Francisco, by
    Brown, rev., 12:364-65
Rémond, A., 7:122
Renardson, Thomas, 14: opp. 209, 394
Renaud, Abbé (from France, 1850),
    22:304
Renckendorff, William, 3:118
Renner, George, 35:67, 145

Rennie, William, 21:308
Renou de Ballon (Paris, 1849), 22:297
Rensch, Hero Eugene, 34:286; "Fages'
    Crossing of the Cuyamacas,"
    34:193-208; "Woods' Shorter
    Mountain Trail to San Diego,"
    36:117-32
Rensch, Mrs. Hero Eugene
    (Ethel Grace Heald), 34:286
Renshaw, J., 8:340
Renshaw, William B., 17:344-45; 21:345,
    356; 25:129; 26:49
Rents: in 1848, 13:263; in 1849, 5:8, 11;
    11:36; 13:357; 20:123; 22:242, 243;
    23:56; 24:26, 355, 357; 27:16, 263, 361,
    368; 30:21; in 1850s, 7:396; 15:168,
    266; 16:344; 24:348, 357; in 1860s,
    23:231, 232
Reporter (newsp.), Napa, 8:285
Reporter (ship), 29:106
"Report of Capt. La Place . . .
    Northwest Coast and California in
    1839," by George V. Blue, 18:315-28
"Report on the First House in Yerba
    Buena," 11:73-78
"Report on the Plate of Brass," by
    Colin G. Fink and E. P. Polushkin,
    17: No. 4, Pt. 2, pp. 7-26
Reptiles: horned toads, 12:305; 17:29;
    lizards, 5:225; 12:305; 17:28; 32:252;
    see also Rattlesnakes; Snakes; Turtles
Republic (str., 1855), 15:282; 22:250
Republic (cargo boat, 1915, formerly
    Walküre), 31:296
Republican (ship), 12:53
Republican (weekly), Shasta, 16:339
Republican Central Committee,
    California, letterhead (1860), fac.,
    27: opp. 97
"Republican Nominating Convention
    of 1860," by Milton H. Shutes,
    27:97-103
Republican Party, 5:286; 8:194; 9:91,
    104-7 *passim*, 111, 115, 116, 355;
    10:168, 257, 258, 272, 286, 287, 355,
    360, 372, 384; 15:205-6, 207; 17:314-15,
    316; 19:59-71 *passim*, 148, 174, 349-50;
    21:325; 22:115, 224, 228-33 *passim*,
    358; 27: opp. 97, 316, 317; 28:47-53
    passim, 154; 30:134-35; 31:194-203
    passim; 32:299, 307, 323; 37:171-78
    passim; 38:230, 238-43 *passim*;
    candidates for gov., 5:286-87; 9:91,
    153, 177-78; nominating conventions,
    8:194; 9:104, 115, 177-78; 10:165, 173,

189, 190; 11:49; 20:270; 27:97-103; 30:129-30
Republic of California, *see* California Republic
Republic of New Granada, *see* Panama
Requa, Amy, *see* Russell, Amy (Requa)
Requa, Isaac Lawrence, 2:206; 23:288; 26:285; 30:93
Requa, Mrs. Isaac Lawrence (Sarah Mower), 36:45
Requa, James, 26:204
Requa, Mark Lawrence, 2:206; 26:285; 30:93; 31:304
Requena, Manuel, 4:159; 13:218-23, 327
Rescue Hose Co. No. 1, Timbuctoo, 10:251, 258; illus., opp. 252
Reservation Valley, 30:160
Reservoirs, in mining operations, 29:193, 197-99, 206
Resolute (ship), 29:39
Resources of California (magazine), 25:326, 340
Restarick, H. B., 35:355
Resting Springs, 10:37; 14:66; 18:206
"Restitution of Decayed Intelligence: More History of the ... Society," by Henry B. Phillips, 1:107-10
Restless (ship), 15:163
Retta (ship), 22:163, 167
Rettel (Carson City, 1860), 29:108
Return of Sit Ping Quai, The (play), 23:106
"Returning an Historic Call," address by Edna Martin Parratt, 34:87
Revalk *v.* Hanlock, 17:180
Réveil, Le, 39:226, 239, 243-44, 350
Revere, Joseph Warren, 2:361; 3:84; 4:286; 6:276, 279; 9:81; 10:354; 13:47, 51, 54; 15:190; 16:100, 101; 17:167, 229-30; 19:133, 144; 21:3, 10-11, 13, 15-17, 20; 25:125; 29:156, 272, 319, 323, 402; 31:207
Revere, W., 28:39
Revere (ship), 33:290, 291
"Rev. Dr. W. A. Scott, a Southern Sympathizer," by John B. Astles, 27:149-56
Revilla, Cristóbal, 9:218, 231
Revilla Gigedo, Juan Vicente, Conde de, 9:205; 10:314, 320, 321, 333; 15:60; 23:1, 2, 15
Revue Californienne, La, 5:27; 39:15, 147, 149, 350
Rey, Capt. (of Cérès, 1849), 5:6-7
Rey, J. J., *see* Britton & Rey

Rey, Leon, 39:226, 231, 235, 236, 249-59 *passim*, 311-13, 315, 319
Rey, Leon M., 39:313
Rey, Georges, 39:313
Rey, Noël, 39:313
Rey, Tamara, 39:321
Rey, Demorande (pharmacist, 1850), 22:301
Reyes, Cristóbal de los, 7:394
Reyes, Francisco, 13:202-3, 207
Reyes, Point, 2:335; 3:5, 220; 7:25, 26, 50-53 *passim*, 57, 75, 76, (on map) 364, 366; 8:55, 56, 69; 10:211; 11:302, 303; 14:324; 17: No. 4, Pt. 2, pp. 3, 24; 26:14; 27:291; 33:234; lighthouse, 27:71; peninsula, 31:104-5
Reynolds, Maj. (S.F., 1855), 17:177
Reynolds, Charles, 21:166
Reynolds, Edward, 15:376
Reynolds, George, 21:166
Reynolds, J. E., 40:263; bk. rev. by, 40:260-63
Reynolds, John, 1:18
Reynolds, Julia, 23:288
Reynolds, Keld J., 24:378; ed. and trans. "Principal Actions of the California Junta de Fomento, 1825-1827," 24:289-320; 25:57-78, 149-68, 267-78, 347-67
Reynolds, Stephen, 35:200
Reynolds, Titus, 37:210
Reynolds, William John, 14:209, 212; 23:350
Reynolds, William P., 29:239, 241
Reynolds Brothers, Marysville, 8:207, 349, 351, 362
Reynolds, Todd, & Co., 30:110
Rezanov, Nikolai Petrovich, 5:412; 6:96-98; 7:95; 12:191, 207, 220, 226, 240; 16:108; bks. on, rev., 6:96-98; 7:196-97
"Rezanov and Concha Argüello," address by Gertrude Atherton, 7:95
Rezanov Voyage to Nueva California, The, ed. Russell, rev. 6:96-98
Rhein, W. W., 34:158
Rhendeshauser (Sierra Co., 1850s), 9:177
Rhett Lake, 28:212, 228
Rheusaw, Hiram, 3:116, 118
R. H. Fauntleroy (ship), 11:303-7
Rhind (on *Ewing*, 1849), 30:41
Rhine (ship), 25:258-59
Rhoades (overland, 1849), 21:308
Rhoades, E. R., 26:247

Rhoades, William P., 31:22
Rhoads, Catherine, 27:187
Rhoads, Daniel, 10:351; 27:187
Rhoads, John B., 10:351; 27:187
Rhoads, Thomas, 27:187
Rhodes (Yuba Co., 1855), 8:349-53 *passim;* 9:50, 51
Rhodes, Augustus Loring, 10:377
Rhodes, Jake, 40:229
Rhodes, William Henry ("Caxton"), 10:252, 255, 265, 266; 16:81; 20:167; 22:39; 23:147; 29:122
Rhodes & Lusk's Shasta Express, 28:226
Rialto (ship), 12:28
Ribero, Juana, 14:395
Ricard, Judge (Death Valley, 1850), 18:198
Ricard (Marysville, 1850), 14:395
Ricardo (Pierre Richards?, 1841), 28:263
Ricard Observatory, 30:377
Rice (Yuba Co., 1854, 1859), 8:207, 346, 347; 9:162; 10:174, 176, 178, 246; lawsuits, 8:346; 9:162; 10:167
Rice, Mrs. (Yuba Co., 1859), 10:178
Rice (Panama, 1860), 11:11
Rice, Daniel W. C., 9:107, 246
Rice, DeWitt C., 14:395; 15:21, 23, 24, 28, 43, 56; 29:254
Rice, F. W., 6:45; 7:281
Rice, George Joseph, 13:210, 319; 18:217; 23:208, 217
Rice, Henry Houghton, 30:247, 382
Rice, Mrs. Henry Houghton (Carrie Batchelder Thompson), 30:246, 247
Rice, Henry Mower, 11:14
Rice, James, 26:345
Rice, Peter, 10:170
Rice, W. M., 28:344, 349
Rice, W. P., 13:32
Rice, Mrs. Warren L. (Bertha M.), 29:382
Rice, William Broadhead, 21:288;" The Captivity of Olive Oatman," 21:97-106
Rice, William G., 9:52
Rice, 38:280; speculation in (1853), 2:238
Rice's Circus, 38:336
Rich, Charles Coulson, 14:61-73 *passim,* 179-82; 15:378; 22:12; bk. on, rev., 16:85
Rich, E. E., 28:99
Rich, Jacob, 13:335

Rich, Juan (John), 1:177
Rich, Thomas, 1:256
Rich, William (1841), 24:321, 323, 333; 30:99
Rich, Maj. William (1848), 1:256; 24:23; 35:18
Richard, Deacon, 18:203
Richard, Pierre, 12:333
"Richard Campbell Party of 1827, The," by Alice B. Maloney, 18:347-54
Richards (Marin Co., 1857), 20:261
Richards (Marysville, 1861), 10:360
Richards, C. E., 13:336
Richards, C. F., 23:191
Richards, Clarissa, *see* Burrell, Mrs. Lyman J.
Richards, Clayton French, 23:191
Richards, J. R., 26:360
Richards, Willard, 6:120-21, 26:326
Richards, Mrs. Willard, 6:120-21
Richardson, Dr. (Manila, 1898), 30:300
Richardson, Edward, 37:229-35 *passim*
Richardson, Elmo R., 38:282-83, "The Struggle for the Valley ...," 38:249-58
Richardson, Friend William, 36:251-61 *passim;* 37:270, 272-73, 347-58 *passim*
Richardson, George Mann, 4:49
Richardson, Israel Bush, 18:109, 110, 134
Richardson, J. S., 13:31
Richardson, Jesse, 15:375
Richardson, Joel, 2:90, 91, 121
Richardson, John H., 22:35
Richardson, Mariana, 13:235, 238-39
Richardson, Mrs. Milton Russell (née Kendall), 29:286
Richardson, W. L., 4:49
Richardson, William A. (b. 1842), 23:12, 13
Richardson, William Antonio, 5:305; 8:140, 141, 235, 239; 11:142; 13:235-39; 14:100, 101, 121-25, 186; 15:330, 370; 16:244, 343; 17:174, 291-92; 19:198; 23:207, 361, 364, 372; 25:321, 322; 27:60; 29:262, 265-66; 28:264-65; 31:35; 32:89, 175; 34:121; capt. of port, S.F., 3:30; 4:169; 13:238; 14:122, 124, 125; 19:214; 23:372; 25:322; 27:60, 265; houses of, 3:31, 32, 34; 4:169; 11:69, 73-78; 13:238; 14:100, 124, 125, 344; 16:249, 343; 17:292, 299; 23:372; maps of Yerba Buena, 3:31, 32; 11:74; 13:235-36; 17:292; 23:372; 26:268; vessels of, 1:137; 3:30, 180; 8:140; 14:123; 16:243-44;

23:372; 25:124; 29:271; family of, 13:238-39; 14:125; 31:46; land grants of, 14:125; 16:339

Richardson, Mrs. William Antonio (María Antonia Martínez), 8:140; 11:142; 13:235, 238; 14:123, 125; 15:330; 17:291, 292; 23:372

Richardson, William H., 8:369; 13:82; 15:204; 16:344-47; 17:81, 83, 310; 19:256; 20:306; 34:232; 35:321; 37:155-56

Richardson and Imbrie, 11:166

Richard III (play), 23:341

Rich Bar, on Middle Fork, Feather R., 29:299, 305

Rich Bar, on N. Fork, Feather R., 1:299, 300-301; 29:305; 32:125

Rich Bar, on Yuba River, 19:28

Richelieu (play), 10:254; 15:278

Richet, A., 39:240, 242

Richfield Oil Co., 17:94

Rich Gulch, 30:243

Richings, Caroline and Peter, 21:64, 68

Richland Tract, Fresno Co., 25:174

Richman, Irving Berdine, 1:23, 40; 3:309, 346

Richmond (ship), 2:99, 105

"Richmond's Golden Anniversary," address by Helen F. Williams, 35:75

Richter, C. Max, 21:368

Richter, George Gustaff, 21:383

Richter, John, 26:236

Richter, M. A., 22:31, 33; 28:34

Rickard, Thomas Arthur, "The Discovery of Gold in California," rev., 7:199

Rickets, "Brother" (San Jose, 1850), 27:231

Rickets (Marysville, 1859), 10:184

Ricketson, Capt. (of *Chase*, 1850), 8:181, 182

Ricketts, John, 16:80

Rickey, Sam, 21:169

Rickman, Cornell, 38:327

Rico, Antonio, 17:159

Rico, Francisco, 5:189-90; 9:81; 12:165; 25:145

Ricord, John, 2:198; 13:78; 17:131-33

Riddell, F. A., 26:136

Riddle, Frank, 28:162

Riddle, Hugh, 24:119

Riddle, Jeff C. Davis, 28:162, 163

Riddle, Spear, 15:270

Rideout, Hannah Jane (Mrs. Minord S.

Thresher), 9:64, 77, 147, 149, 151; phot., 9: opp. 64

Rideout, Norman Dunning, 8:211, 360; 9:74, 76, 77, 142, 178, 287; 23:96

Rideout, Mrs. Norman Dunning (Phebe Abbott), 9:287

Rideout, Samuel, 10:189

Rider (ferry, Kings R., 1849), 11:258

Rider, J. H., 28:325

Rider, Fremont, *Rider's California*, rev., 4:397-98

Ridge, John Rollin, 9:287, 350-51, 372, 382, 384, 389; 10:59, 82, 173, 186, 192, 195, 266-68, 296, 367; 14:389; 15:76; 16:256-62; 22:30, 36; 37:244-46; 28:7; 30:130, 146, 251, 263, 353; bk. by, rev., 7:195

Ridge, Martin B., 40:257; bk. rev. by, 40:256-57

Ridge Co., lawsuits, 10:363, 364, 384, 385, 386

Ridge Telephone Co., 28:234, 241; 29:199, 206

"Ridge's Life of Joaquin Murieta," by Franklin Walker, 16:256-62

Ridgewood Ranch, 28:381

Ridgway, James A. and Catherine (Mullins), 33:94

"Ridinghood," *see* Lawrence, Mary Viola

Ridley, Alonzo, 29:237-40

Ridley, Robert Thomas, 6:141-42; 7:106; 11:137; 12:276; 17:68, 226, 229, 292-98 *passim*; 19:118, 132; 25:124; 27:109; 28:253, 257; 29:271

Ridley, Mrs. Robert Thomas (Presentación Miranda), 17:292

Ridout, Lionel U., 37:91; "Priests, Pistols, and Polemics," 37:51-61

Rieber, Charles Henry, 37:41

Ries, Christopher, 11:243

Riestra, Jesús, 15:356

Riffe, Hannah (Cosgrave), 20:288

Rigden, Duncan L., 26:190

Rigdon, Rufus, 15:76

Rigg, Edwin A., 40:314-18 *passim*, 349, 350

Riggs, Capt. (Sacramento, 1858), 9:250

Riggs, J. R., 4:188

Riley (Mex., 1848), 23:268, 280

Riley (nr. Sacramento, 1864), 9:309

Riley, Bennet, 1:209, 270; 4:118-19, 138; 6:153; 9:7-8; 10:131, 135, 145-51 *passim*, 159-64 *passim*, 231; 11:101, 121; 12:91; 13:363, 380-81; 14:150;

16:139, 197-98, 305; 17:233-34; 19:22,
175-76; 20:100, 114, 121, 125, 259;
21:358, 362; 23:352, 370; 26:101, 328;
29:165; 33:344; 35:14, 17, 114; 40:13,
124, 129-33 *passim*, 136; map, 11: opp.
102; report (1849), 11:102-5;
proclamations (facs.), 10:131, 135,
154
Riley, C. & J., 10:273, 280
Riley, Carmel, 28:93
Riley, Michael and Sarah (Scales), 28:93
Riley, Peter Thomas, 28:93
Riley, Stephen, 27:306, 308
Rincon Hill, San Francisco, 3:203;
17:295; 19:231-33, 238; 30:159, 209;
31:299, 300, 302; 33:234, 237; 36:305;
37:215, 222-23
Rincon House, San Francisco, 26:183
Rincon Place, San Francisco, 26:257,
260, 353-54, 358-59
Rincon Point, 15:176; 17:179; 25:267;
26:268; 33:235; illus., 37: opp. 129
Rincon Rock, 25:258
Rindge, Frederick Hastings and May
(Knight), 38:172-73
Rindge ranch, *see* Ranchos: Topango
Malibu Sequit
Ringgold, Cadwalader, 11:301; 12:267,
274, 275; 17:141; 19:3; 22:235; 23:336;
drawing by, 12:26
Ringgold, J., 12:274, 275
Ringgold (place), 6:361, 363; 30:25, 36
Ringgold Light Artillery, 29:245
Rintaro, Katsui, *see* Katsui
Rio, Juan del, 3:21-24
Rio de Janeiro, 1:218-22, 227; 6:210-11;
13:398; 20:199-203; 23:151-55
Rio de Janeiro (ship), 19:282; 27:293;
30:293
Rio Rico mines, 24:348-50
Rio-Rio, *see* Liholiho
Rios, Petronilo, 30:98
Rios, Santiago, 21:320
Rio Seco mines, 24:357, 358
Ripalda, Jerónimo de, *Catecismo* of,
16:104, 373-75
Ripley, Edward Payson, 9:96
Ripley, Francis L., 20:115
Ripley, Thomas P., 12:29
Ripoll, Antonio, 8:159-61, 164, 318, 328;
16:119
Ripon, 18:23, 24
"Riptides," by Robert O'Brien, quoted,
27:376-78
Rip van Winkle (play), 21:182

Risdon, Mrs. B. H., 27:190
Risdon, David Mattison, 27:190
Risdon, F. Ray, 26:383
Risdon, John N., 22:23
Risdon Iron Works, 25:44
"Rise and Fall of the 'Know Nothings'
in California, The," by Peyton Hurt,
9:16-49, 99-128
"Rise of Modern Art in the Bay Area,
The," by Beatrice J. Ryan, 38:1-5
"Rise of the San Francisco Theater,
The," address by Frank L. Fenton,
18:286
Rising, Judge (Virginia City, 1876),
11:51
Rising, Franklin Samuel, 31:4; 34:317-20
Rising Sun House, Rose Springs, 27:282
Risley (S.F., 1851), 28:40
Risley, H., 35:8
Risley, Richard, 9:153, 177; 15:367;
16:183, 283, 285; troupes of, 8:350;
9:177; 21:154-56; *see also* Risley's
Vatican Circus
Risley's Vatican Circus, 9:152, 177;
16:183, 284, 285
Ristori, Adelaide, 21:172, 174
Ritchie, Archibald A., 15:275, 282;
16:346; 19:232
Ritchie, Mrs. Archibald A., 19:229,
232; 24:262
Ritchie, Hettie, 19:233
Ritchie, Jacob, 9:26
Ritchie, James W., 22:79
Ritchie, Lida, 19:233
Ritchie, Nellie, 19:233
Ritchie, Patsy, 19:232, 233
Ritchie, Robert Welles, *The
Hell-roarin' Forty-niners*, rev.,
7:407; quoted, 9:74
Ritchie, Mrs. William, *see*
Fosdick, Mrs. Jay
Ritman, George L., 31:236-37, 240
Rittenhouse, Euphemia, 28:189
Ritter, Mount, 4:21, 22, 28, 42, 46, 55
Ritter (E. L.) & Co., 15:375
Rivals, The (play), 15:186
Rivas, Domingo, 24:290; 25:367
Rivas, Gertrudis, *see* Linares, Ygnacio
Rivera, Diego, 38:3-4
Rivera, Francisco, 13:44, 53; 17:60
Rivera, Gabriel de, 3:3
Rivera, Juan de, 6:294, 297
Rivera y Moncada, Fernando Javier,
1:158, 163; 3:100; 4:90; 11:275;
13:196-99; 14:102; 15:132; 16:102;

29:309; 31:112-22 *passim*, 261-69, 343-54 *passim;* 33:15; 37:294, 296

Rivero Cordero, Manuel, 31:110

Rivers, J. J., 31:337

Riverside, John (pseud.), *see* Brooks, Noah

Riverside (place), 12:116

Riverside Colony, Fresno Co., 25:175

Riverside Colony, San Bernardino Co., 27:113

Rives, Jean Baptiste, 8:132-34, 140, 144, 157, 165, 220, 224, 231, 232, 238, 245, 250, 322, 335, 336

Rives, Mary (Morton), 3:73, 83

Rix, Alfred, 9:29; 33:374

Rix, Alice, 30:293

Rix, Julian, 37:36

Rixford, Emmet, 4:49; address, "The Beginnings of Medical Education in California," 5:93

Rixford, Emmet H., 27:285

Roach, John and Ann (Mackay), 28:293

Roach, Philip A., 16:81; 29:152, 159; 31:47

Roach, Thomas J., 24:24

Roach, William, 29:19-28

"Roach-Belcher Feud, The," by Paul P. Parker, 29:19-28

Roadarmel, Gordon C., 38:368; 39:358; comp. "Some California Dates of 1860," 38:329-40; "Some California Dates of 1861," 39:289-308

Roads: in Alameda Co., 30:9-10; Alleghany, 28:237; Applegate, 4:281-82; 18:300; Big Oak Flat, 5:341; Blue Lakes, 32:364; Calaveras-Big Trees, 7:13, 14, 16; in Clear Lake area, 32:364-65, 369; in Contra Costa Co., 30:10; Coulterville, 5:341; Donner Pass: 4:240-41, 265; 10:347-48; El Dorado, 7:7, 17-19; 10:51, 74; Emory, 28:239; Ft. Kearney to Calif., 7:15-16; Ft. Smith to Colorado R., 9:388; Henness Pass, 10:348; in Lake Co., 32:364; Mariposa, 5: (phot.) opp. 340, 341; in Mendocino Co., 30:164; Mono Co., 26:243-44; Noble Pass, 7:14, 16; 18:302, 312; to Panamint, 17:210-11, 218; over the Sierra, 4:11, 226, 240-41, 260, 261, 265; 7:3-19; 10:51, 74, 347-48; 15:338; 26:244; Sonora Emigrant, 34:213; toll, 17:218; 32:364-65, 369; Wawona, 3:94; 5:341

legislation, 7:6, 10-11, 15-16; 15:270, 277; 16:338; 19:19

Road to Oregon, The, by Ghent, rev., 8:89

Roane, James M., 10:62, 70

Roanoke (ship), 33:9

Roaring River, 39:293

"Roaring Seventies, The," address by John D. Hicks, 22:84

Roark, Lillian Phipps, 29:382

Roark, Thomas Phipps and Katherine (Hayes), 29:382

Robb, George A., 23:192

Robb, James, 23:192

Robb, John, 23:192

Robb, John S., 4:127; 9:275; 20:124

Robbers, The (play), 10:362, 370

Robberson, John S., 10:48, 62

Robbins, Miss (Oregon Hill, 1855), 8:338

Robbins, Charles Burtis, 37:236-37

Robbins, Georgianna Pacific, 37:235, 236

Robbins, Isaac, 37:236

Robbins, Irving Whitmore, 34:374

Robbins, Jared, 13:261

Robbins, John Roger, 30:99; 33:65; 37:234, 235

Robbins, Lloyd McCullough, obit., 34:373-74

Robbins, Reuel Drinkwater and Saditha (McCullough), 34:373

Robbins, Thomas M., 8:245; 14:341; 16:364; 18:161-62, 164, 174, 277

Robe (Philippines, 1898), 31:59

Robe, Charles F., 30:290

Roberson, Mary Ygnacia, trans. "Guzman's *Breve Noticia*," 5:209-17

"Robert Baylor Semple," by Zoë G. Radcliffe, 6:130-58

Robert Hooper (ship), 28:38

Robert Louis Stevenson (ship), 22:383

"Robert Louis Stevenson," address by John Howell, 6:380

"Robert Louis Stevenson in California," address by Laura B. Powers, 20:376-77

Robert Macaire (play), 20:305

Roberto (Indian, 1844), 20:108-9; 34:240

Roberts, Dr. (Stockton, 1849), 4:183-85

Roberts, Capt. (Colorado R., 1864), 22:170

Roberts, Judge (Marysville, 1858), 9:372

California Historical Society Quarterly

Roberts, Mrs. Amos (Elizabeth Cooper), 6:152
Roberts, David, 15:171
Roberts, Elizabeth (Judson), 26:52
Roberts, George D., 24:212-13
Roberts, James B., 27:153-54
Roberts, Samuel, 19:167; 27:266, 361, 368; 29:163, 169; 34:231
Roberts, Thomas H., 20:44
Roberts, William, 26:165, 167, 169; 28:291
Roberts & Yaney, 30:266
Robertson, Agnes, 10:65
Robertson, James O., 21:238
Robertson, James R., 1:23
Robertson, John, 29:21-22
Robertson, John Wooster, 1:19; 5:413; 20:96; *Francis Drake and Other Early Explorers*, rev., 6:91-92
Robertson, Lorin and Helen (Carswell), 28:294
Robertson, Peter, 21:257, 268; 33:45-46
Robertson, T. W., 9:40
Robertson, William James Roscoe, 22:79, 83
Robidoux, Antoine, 2:8, 10; 4:342; 10:88; 21:223; 24:238(?); 26:49
Robidoux, Joseph, 2:8
Robidoux, Louis, 2:8; 10:5, 37; 13:318; 14:69; 21:215, 223, 336; 24:238(?); 25:295; ranch of, *see* Ranchos: Jurupa
Robidoux, Michel ("Miguel"), 2:8
Robidoux Ranch, 12:116; *see also* Ranchos; Jurupa
Robie, Wendell T., address, "Murderers Bar," 35:75
Robin Hood (ship), 29:106
Robinson (Negro, 1824), 29:26
Robinson (ship owner, 1853), 30:29, 30
Robinson, Mrs. (Buckeye, 1859), 10:171
Robinson, A. Porter, 22:192, 283; 23:79, 193
Robinson, Abbie, 6:337, 350
Robinson, Alexander, 35:163
Robinson, Alfred, 4:155, 167; 8:291-98 *passim*, 304, 305; 12:295; 13:225, 226, 227, 245, 251, 389-90, 400, 409; 16:329; 18:170, 174, 179; 22:192, 283, 287; 23:7-8, 159, 176, 253, 254; 24:84; 25:324; 27:49, 321; 29:166; 30:29(?), 30(?), 99, 321, 322, 323; 33:61, 374; 36:8, 289-91; 37:217; arts.on, 23:193-218, 301-34; *Life in California before the Conquest*, rev., 4:298-99

Robinson, Mrs. Alfred (Ana María de la Guerra), 18:170; 23:199; 36:289
Robinson, Benjamin M., 4:310, 317
Robinson, Carley, 13:257
Robinson, Charles Dorman, 37:36
Robinson, D. C., 22:8, 159, 165
Robinson, David G., 8:205, 213; 9:77; 15: opp. 40, 44-48 *passim*; 20:293-98 *passim*, 304, 313; 23:100; 28:37; *see also* Robinson Family
Robinson, Edgar Eugene, ed. "The Day Journal of Milton S. Latham," 11:3-28; addresses: "Adventures in Manuscript Collecting," 26:84-85; "Milton S. Latham," 10:206-7; obit. of Ray Lyman Wilbur, 28:279-81
Robinson, Edward, 19:117, 136
Robinson, Elmer Edwin, 31:279
Robinson, Elmo A., 36:379-80; "Philosophy in California to 1906 ...," 36:333-57; 37:39-49
Robinson, Frank, 13:84
Robinson, Frederico, 37:201
Robinson, George W., 14:223
Robinson, Henry E., 11:121; 14:212, 405
Robinson, Henry Harrison, 30:131, 146
Robinson, Henry M., 37:267, 348, 351
Robinson, J. B., 9:393
Robinson, J. P., 4:226, 245; 10: opp. 48
Robinson, J. R., 15:274; *see also* Robinson & Co.
Robinson, Mrs. James (Jane Henry Gay), 36:290; port., 36: opp. 289
Robinson, Jesse, 28:351, 358
Robinson, John (Guaymas, 1850), 11:369
Robinson, John (Honey Lake, 1859), 21:238
Robinson, John R., 6:363
Robinson, Josephine, 15: opp. 40, 48; 16:283; *see also* Robinson Family
Robinson, Lester L., 4:226, 245, 265-69 *passim*; 29:198
Robinson, Prescott, 9:36
Robinson, R. P., 4:250
Robinson, Robert, 9:38
Robinson, Robert McClure, 35:92; "San Francisco Teamsters at the Turn of the Century," 35:59-69, 145-53
Robinson, S. S., 4:262
Robinson, Susan, 6:339; 8:213; 9:77, 274, 369, 393; 16:183-84, 283; *see also* Robinson Family
Robinson, T. B., 13:31

Robinson, Thaddeus P., 19:368-69

Robinson, Tod, 10:42

Robinson, W. W., 33:12, 149

Robinson, Walter, 10:179

Robinson, William (Benicia, 1849), 6:150

Robinson, William (Oroville, 1858), 9:393; *see also* Robinson Family

Robinson, William Heppel, 15:31

Robinson, William Wilcox, 39:71, 270; 40:260; "Writing Local History," 39:209-17; bk. revs. by, 40:157-58, 259-60, 355-56; *Lawyers of Los Angeles*, rev., 39:85; coauth. *The Malibu*, rev., 38:171-73; obit. of Joseph Scott, 37:183-84

Robinson & Co. (bank), 15:272, 273, 274

Robinson and Ogle's Co., 6:361-63

Robinson Family (entertainers), 6:339; 9:63, 77, 137, 369, 393

Robinson's Crossing, 9:54, 73

Robinson, Seymour & Co., 4:222; 16:283

Robinson's Ferry, 22:83

Robinson's Landing, 22:11, 23

Robles, Antonio, 14:158

Robles, Secundino, 14:158; 15:4; 16:285; 27:134, 135

Robles, Teodoro, 15:4; 16:285; 27:134, 135

Robles, Paso de, 35:142

Robson, Stuart, 35:142

Rocca, Andrew, 32:349-59 *passim*

Rocco, Salvatore, 35:33-34

Rocha, Antonio, 29:236

Rocha, José Antonio, 13:207, 310, 313, 330; 35:236

Rocha, Juan José, 14:233-35, 239, 257; 16:217(?), 222, 229

Rochelle (ship), 14:337

Rochette, J., 17:177

Rock, Miss (Foster's Bar, 1857), 9:154

Rock, A. D., 37:197

Rock, Francis J., *J. Ross Browne*, rev., 8:280

Rock Creek, Deer Creek and South Yuba Co., 11:237

Rocker, Maj. (overland, 1849), 24:121

Rockers (for gold), *see* Cradles

Rock Island Bar, Yuba Co., 8:347, 361

Rocknell, Hiram, 3:118

Rock Springs, 27:113, 117

Rockwell, John, 11:301-2

Rockwell, John A., 30:323, 336

Rockwell, Porter D., 22:11

Rocky-Bar Mining Co., 6:334; 12:65-76; 19:27; fac. of *Circular*, 12; foll. 76; *see also* Mount Hope Co.

"Rocky Mountain Jack," 26:246

Rocque, G. R., 22:222; 23:31, 136

Rocquebin, J., 22:197, 198, 199, 205, 215-21 *passim*; 23:38, 123, 125, 129, 139, 142

Roda y Arrieta, Manuel de, 23:220

Rode, Joseph, 9:146

Rodecape, Lois Foster (Mrs. DeForest A.), 19:192; "Celestial Drama in the Golden Hills," 23:79-116; "The Chinese Theatre in California," 23:97-116; "Gilding the Sunflower . . . Oscar Wilde's Visit to San Francisco," 19:97-112; " 'Quand Même,' . . . California Footnotes to the Biography of Sarah Bernhardt," 20:126-46; "Tom Maguire, Napoleon of the Stage," 20:289-314; 21:39-74, 141-82, 239-75

Rodeos, 2:41, 43; 12:286; 38:259-60, 263

Roderick, John, 19:214

Rodero, Gaspar, 5:196-97

Rodgers, Edwin A., 11:9, 23

Rodgers, John, 16:182; 23:336

Rodgers, John J. S., 28:344, 349

Rodgers, John Kearny, Jr., 21:308

Rodgers, Robert C., 9:29; 15:376

Rodgers, William P., 10: opp. 48, 61, 70

Rodgers, Meyer & Co., 31:340

Rodgers *v.* Atchison, 10:180

Rodman, Mrs. Willoughby (Arabella Page), 26:287

Rodolph (ship), 20:28, 32, 37, 38, 42, 43, 44-45

Rodney, Robert M., coauth. *Art, Humor and Humanity of Mark Twain*, rev., 38:368-70

Rodolf, Fred W., 19:370-71

Rodríguez ("Navajo," Santa Barbara, 1846), 18:162

Rodríguez, Antonio, 15:356

Rodríguez, Antonio Miranda, 13:201

Rodríguez, Dámaso Antonio, 16:234; 27:335-38; 28:265

Rodríguez, Estaban, 2:140; 7:146, 151, 172-73, 182, 300

Rodríguez, Jacinto, 17:233; 28:261; fac. sig., 10: opp. 159

Rodríguez, Juana, 13:200

Rodríguez, Manuel (San Diego, 1806), 12:220

Rodríguez, Manuel (Santa Cruz, 1855), 27:104
Rodríguez, Pablo and María Rosalía (Noriega), 13:200
Rodríguez, Ramón ("El Venado"), 18:162, 266
Rodríguez, Vincente, 14:333
Rodríguez Cabrillo, *see* Cabrillo
Rodríguez Cermeño, *see* Cermeño
Rodríguez de Poli, *see* Poli
Rodríguez de Villafuerte, 6:297
Roe, Edward Payson, 17:35, 40
Roe, Frederick, J., 6:51
Roeding, Frederick, 25:21, 35-36, 382
Roeding, George C., 25:382
Roeth, George, 31:341
Roether, Charles, 14:205
Roff (Marysville, 1858), 9:267
Rogel, Frances, 15:54
Rogers (Drake's Bay, 1859), 11:306
Rogers (Sweetland's Crossing, 1859), 10:167
Rogers (Trinity Co., 1862), 20:357
Rogers, Cameron, 34:92; ed. "Charles Fernald to Hannah Hobbs," 34:41-48
Rogers, Charles, 20:308; 33:29
Rogers, Daniel, 11:9
Rogers, Earl, 39:85; 40:157-58
Rogers, Franklin R., 36:380; "Washoe's First Literary Journal," 36:365-70
Rogers, Fred Blackburn, 26:93; 28:189; 29:189; 31:215, 216; 38:74-75; "Bear Flag Lieutenant, . . . Henry L. Ford," 29:129-38, 261-78, 333-44; 30:49-66, 157-75; "Early Military Posts of Del Norte County," 26:1-11; "Early Military Posts of Mendocino County," 27:215-28; as address, 27:378; address, "Soldiers of the Overland," 18:286; *Montgomery and the Portsmouth*, rev., 38:272-73
Rogers, George H., 19:156
Rogers, Harrison G., 2:231, 344; 14:196
Rogers, Irving S., 28:286
Rogers, Jacob, 20:307
Rogers, John (Death Valley, 1850), 18:198, 203, 204
Rogers, John (Aurora, 1863), 7:115
Rogers, Katherine, 21:171, 173
Rogers, P. B., 22:251
Rogers, Mrs. R. C. (Lida Ritchie), 19:233
Rogers, Robert T., 22:17, 18, 159
Rogers, W. H., 33:68
Rogers, William M., 6:368

Rogers & Fullerton, 33:68
Rogniat, Baron de, 39:339-40
Rogue River, 23:139; 28:213; 30:340; 31:274; Indian War, 26:1
Rohrer brothers (Morford, Simmons and ?), 22:128, 129, 144
Rojas, Arnold R., *Last of the Vaqueros*, rev., 40:69-71; *Lore of the California Vaquero*, rev., 38:371-73
Rojas, Lauro A. de, "California in 1844 as Hartnell Saw It," 17:21-27; address, "East Looks West: The Manila Galleon," 15:382
Rojo, Manuel Clemente, 13:320
Rojo, Mar (Red Sea), *see* California, Gulf of
Roland, Ernest C., 37:204
Roland's Express, 34:216
Rolant (ship), 13:370, 382
"Role of the Alcalde in . . . Santa Barbara, The," address by Francis Price, 33:278-81
"Role of the Learned Society Today, The," by C. Easton Rothwell, 38:11-16
Rolf, J. W., 18:201-2
Rolfe (Yuba City, 1849), 14:212
Rolingson v. Wetmore, 10:278, 279, 280
Rolland (ship), *see Rolant*
Rolle, Andrew F., 28:286; 31:93; "William Heath Davis and the Founding of American San Diego," 31:33-48
Rollins, Philip Ashton, 27:181-83; ed. Stuart, *Discovery of the Oregon Trail*, rev., 15:191
Rollins, S. M., 22:251
Rollinson, William, 15:179, 186; 27:306, 307, 309
Rolls, William, 9:26
Rolon, Francisco, 3:21
Rolph, George M., 27:200
Rolph, James, Jr., 33:374; 36:110, 260; 38:350; 39:32; address, "San Francisco," 9:188
Rolph, Mildred T., 32:191
Roman, Maj. (from Guaymas, 1855), 15:268
Roman, Anton, 12:23; 22:39; 28:1-18; 29:91; 30:107, 111-12, 137, 259-60, 266, 356, 362; 33:211-12; phot., 28: opp. 1
Roman, Mrs. Anton (Eliza Fletcher), 28:9, 17
Roman, Richard, 16:340, 344; 17:170, 175, 177
Roman & Bro., 30:367

Roman (ship), 15:183; 31:209, 210

Roman Catholic Church and churches, 9:20, 21, 28, 38, 40, 117, 254, 279, 371; 15:44-45, 180; 17:45; in Sacramento, 9:254, 279; 39:199; in San Francisco, 5:43; 15:268, 366; 16:344; 17:181; 21:240; 29:139; 32:261; 39:302; in Ore., 21:7; *see also* Dominicans; Franciscans; Jesuits; Missions; Pious Fund

Roman Catholic orphan asylums, *see* Orphanages

"Romance Period of California History, The," address by William H. Waste, 9:292

Romanio (play), 21:146

"Romantic Tales of '49," address by Mrs. Byron T. Carr, 10:413

Rombeaux, Auguste, 15:168

Rome (ship), 13:381

Romelberg, A., 31:331

Romeo and Juliet, 35:142

Romero, Feodoro, 10:32

Romero, José, 12:122; 25:364

Romero, José Mariano, 12:131; 14:257; 15:347, 348, 356

Romero, Joseph (mulatto, 1778), 14:6

Romero, Pedro José, 13:202

Romero, Vicente, 25:299

Romeu, José Antonio, 4:146

Romie, María Cristina, 29:25

Roncovieri, Alfred, 10:265, 390; 15:174, 178; 32:110

Rondeau, Charles, 22:196, 197, 205, 206, 217, 218, 221; 23:20, 38, 136

Rondeau, Louis, 22:205, 217, 221; 23:20, 38; wife and daughter, 22:196, 198, 201, 217

Roney, Frank, 10:409

Ronstadt, Frederico A., 21:107, 108, 111

Roods, William B., 18:200, 209, 212-14, 216

Rooker, James E., 28:379

Rooker, M. Georgia, 28:379

Rooney, J. F., 31:333

Rooney, Raymonde, 23:94

Roop, Ephraim, 18:304, 313

Roop, Isaac Newton, 10:74; 11:47; 18:304-9 *passim*, 313; 21:225-38 *passim*; 30:66

Roop (Josiah) store, 33:375

Roop, Susan, 30:66

Roos Brothers, San Francisco, 20:131

Roosevelt, Franklin Delano, 39:121-39

Roosevelt, James, 39:33, 129

Roosevelt, Theodore, 3:94; 17:18-19; 24:6; 30:193-206 *passim;* 36:70; 38:229-47, 249-50, 253; cartoons, 38: opp. 229, 244

Roosevelt, Theodore, Jr., 38:230, 232, 234

Root (S.F., 1855), 19:152; 25:6

Root, Henry, *Personal History and Reminiscences*, rev., 4:93-94; obit., 7:100-101

Root, Mrs. Henry W. (Sophie Whipple), address on Bret Harte, 13:411

Root, Ira C., 29:289, 292

Root, K., 5:140

Root, Kingsbury, 13:32

Root, Orson, 23:226

Root, Riley, art. on *Journal of,* 10:396-405; fac. title p., 397

Roothaan, John, 29:141, 142, 144; letter to, 29:144-45

Rootville (Millerton), 25:18

Roper, Daniel, 39:133

Roquefeuille, Camille de, 8:136, 142, 308-9; 25: 320

Rosa (Eliza City, 1850), 7:404; 8:17, 22, 167

Rosa, Carl, 21:162

Rosa, Mrs. Carl, *see* Parepa-Rosa, Mme.

Rosa, José de la, 8:167; 17:220, 225; 23:294; 28:266; messenger from Vallejo to Montgomery, 1:79-81, 89, 90, 179, 180; 2:70; 6:274; 10:106; 29:266; printer, 12:129, 135-36; 16:375

Rosa, Luis de la, 23:261, 266

Rosa, Patti, 4:61

Rosa, Salvador, 4:207; 17:181

Rosa (ship), 16:239; 23:318, 320, 332

Rosamel, Joseph de, 8:118-19, 129; 11:197, 203; 23:67; 37:63-77

Rosamond (ship), 31:294

Rosamond Lake, 17:107

Rosario, Mex., 23:274

Rosario, Rio del, Lower Calif., 31:269, 354

Rosario Strait, 11:303, 304

Rosarito (ship), 22:170

Rosas, Alejandro, 13:200

Rosas, Basilio, 13:200

Rosborough, A. M., art. on, 26:201-7

Rosborough, Alex. J., 26:284; "A. M. Rosborough, Special Indian Agent," 26:201-7

Rosborough, J. B., 26:201-2

Rose (Devil's R., 1849), 18:111
Rose (Placerville, 1850), 26:294, 300, 302, 304
Rose (from Wismar, 1850s), 12:303
Rose (Yosemite, 1852), 1:273; 5:332-35
Rose, Alice, 11:3
Rose, Edward, 4:112, 122, 124, 126-29
Rose, John, 9:386; 11:121; 14:208-9, 212, 217, 223, 403; ranch of, 11:110, 117, 121; 14:212-13, 217; 15:29; phot., 15: opp. 21
Rose, Julius K., 27:108
Rose, Leonard John and Mrs., 38:379-81 *passim*
Rose, Leonard John, Jr., *L. J. Rose of Sunnyslope, 1827-1899*, rev., 38:379-81
Rose, Louis, 33:66
Rose (John) and (William J.) Reynolds, 23:350
Rose (ship), 8:221
Rose Hill Mine, 6:230
Rose Mine, 27:117
Rosenbaum, J. F., 30:266; & Joachimssen, 30:258
Rosenbaum & Van Allen, 30:359; 34:346
Rosenberg, Mrs., *see* Rulofson, Mary Jeanette
Rosenberg Bros., 17:95-96
Rosencourt, Capt. (of *Obligado*, 1854), 15:176
Rosendahl, Frank D., 25:175
Rosenfeld, John, 26:182
Rosenfeld's (John) Sons Co., 27:199
Rosenfield, Anthony, 11:226; 29:105(?); 30:357
Rosenshine, Albert, 37:354
Rosenthal, Adele, 25:236
Rosenthal, Myrtle (Lovdal), 31:189; "George Christopher Lovdal, San Diego's First Harbor Master," 31:149-59
Rosenthal, Toby, port. of Claus Spreckels, 40: opp. 40
Rosentiel, Antoine, 15:276
Rose's Bar, 6:217; 9:285, 355, 386; 14:209; 23:259, 279, 349-53, 370
Rose Standish (ship), 12:99
"Rosewater" Democrats, *see* Democrats
Ross (lawsuit, Marysville, 1859), 10:186
Ross, Albert, 33:330, 333
Ross, Albert E., 39:33
Ross, Blake, 9:290; address, "Golden Crucible," 9:188
Ross, Charles L., 4:172; 11:135, 141, 143;

15:364, 365; 16:139; 26:166; 27:10, 18, 45, 50, 261; 28:113, 115, 290
Ross, D. L., 31:2
Ross, Erskine, 33:274, 275
Ross, Guadalupe, 13:330
Ross, Herbert W., 26:219, 230
Ross, Hiram, 4:273-74
Ross, J. H., 4:61
Ross, John, 28:231
Ross, William George, 9:26, 27; 15:281
Ross, William, 15:376
Ross, Sonoma Co., *see* Fort Ross
Ross and Crockett, 13:319
Rossi, Eleanor, 23:94; 24:84
Rossi, Ernesto, 21:261
Rossiter (or Rossitter), H., 14:392; 20:294
Rotary Club de Mallorca, 11:79-81, 280-88
Rotchev (Rothchef, Rotcheff), Count Alexander Gavriolovich, 3:173, 176; 12:197, 199, 244-48 *passim*, 254, 268, 274, 275, 276; 17:62-68 *passim*; 18:293, 328; 28:102, 110; 29:314; 39:97-100, 114; deed to Sutter, 12:269-70; letters, 39:100-109
Rotchev, Countess Helena de, *see* Gagarin, Princess Helena
Rothchild, Walter, obit., 17:95-96
Rothschild, de (1851), merchandise sold to, 31:312, 313
Rothschild, Baron (1860), 11:11, 14; 15:3
Rothschild, Baruch, 27:8
Rothschild, John, 25:230, 232, 233, 236-37, 242
Rothschild, Samuel, 17:95
Rothschild bank, 22:256
Rothwell, Charles Easton, 38:87-88; "The Role of the Learned Society Today," 38:11-16
Rouche (from Jussey, ca. 1851), 6:55
Rouelle, Jean Baptiste, 14:209-10
Rough and Ready, 6:221-22, 234-35, 245; 10:348; 11:237, 245; 14:385
Rough and Ready Mining Co., 18:201, 204
Rough Diamond (play), 15:48
Roumianzoff harbor, 12:189, 190; *see also* Bodega Bay
"Round House," Los Angeles, 3:164; 13:331-32
Round Tent, Marysville, 14:215-16
Round Tent, Sacramento, 24:357; 38:39

Round Tent (roadhouse), Yuba Co., 10:169, 192

Roundtree, M., 31:331

Round Valley, Mendocino Co., 20:354, 358, 362; 27:215, 220-26 *passim*; 30:164, 168; 36:317; *see also* Nome Cult Indian Reservation

Round Valley Indian Reservation, 20:349, 362; 27:215, 223, 224; 30:164; *see also* Nome Cult Indian Reservation

Roundy, John, 2:92, 102, 109, 122

Rourke, Constance, *Troupers of the Gold Coast*, rev., 8:84

Roushaile, Albert Benard de, *see* Benard de Russailh

Roussel (northern mines, 1850), 5:237

Rousset Sisters, 15:279

Roussillon, Charles, 12:353; 13:160, 167, 174, 372; 18:35; 25:129; lawsuit, 35:104-6; *see also* Graham *v.* Roussillon

"Route of Jedediah S. Smith in 1826, The: Earliest Crossing of the Deserts of Utah and Nevada to Southern California," by C. Hart Merriam, 2:228-36

Routes:
  to California, 8:3-5; 11:30; 19:324; 28:306, 307; by Nicaragua (*see* Nicaragua); overland, 12:288-90, 354-55 (*see also* Overland journeys); by Panama (*see* Panama crossing); by sea (*see* Horn, Cape)
  to Colorado River mines, 12:5-10
  to and from Philippines, *see* Manila galleons

Rover (ship), 12:236; 14:127, 128; 23:332

"Roving Reporter of Fifty-five Years Ago, A," address by Edmond D. Coblentz, 35:75

Rovoir [sic] & Ready, 24:257

Row, E. H. (Edward H. Rowe?), 12:26

Rowan, H., 17:345

Rowan, Stephen Clegg, 3:112; 21:351, 357; 22:58; 25:127; 33:105, 119, 251, 252

Rowdy Creek, 32:168

Rowe, A., 13:32

Rowe, E. A., 14:361, 362, 367; 15:78, 79, 153

Rowe, Edwin A., 9:42

Rowe, George F., 21:243

Rowe, George N., 8:355; 9:129, 159, 163, 166, 179, 257, 261, 264-68 *passim*, 284,

345, 348, 355, 357, 362-69 *passim*, 374, 375, 376; 10:59, 73, 167, 174-80 *passim*, 187, 196, 201, 247, 249, 272, 360, 367, 384; 14:397; 15:28, 29, 33; 30:130

Rowe, Joseph Andrew, 3:35; 6:98-99; 10:368; 20:293, 294; 27:249; *see also* Circuses

Rowe, Mrs. Philip, 25:15

Rowe & Mott, 9:159, 163, 179

Rowell, Chester, 17:39; 25:15

Rowell, Chester Harvey, 27:183; 36:110, 253, 258; 38:228

Rowell, Isaac, 4:194; 15:366; 16:82; 17:176

Rowland, Donald, rev. of Pourade, *The Explorers: The History of San Diego*, 40:353-55

Rowland, John, 10:34, 36; 12:115-16; 13:223, 224, 230, 231, 349; *see also* Workman-Rowland party

Rowland, John D., 14:223

Rowland, Mary Louise, 28:292

Rowland, William, 17:102, 110

Rowland, Walker & Co., 33:375

Roxana (ship), 8:294; 23:198, 309, 311, 331

Roxby, Robert, 26:356

"Royador, El," *see* García, Francisco

Royal, William, 27:346

Royal Chinese Theater, San Francisco, 23:111-12

Royal George (ship), 29:26

Royall, William B., letters from, 24:117, 122-24, 127-29, 258, 346, 352, 354, 364

Royce, Mrs. Josiah (Sarah Eleanor Bayliss), 30:259; 32:200-201, 202; 38:37-38

Royce, Josiah [Jr.], 7:88; 29:157-58; 30:259; 31:203; 32:138; 35:106; 36:346-47; 37:40, 44, 45, 138, 141, 142

Royer, Frank W., 32:40

Roze, Marie, 21:258

Rozenswig, Bernard and Josephine (Dyer), 28:293

Rubery, Alfred, 20:159; 40:300

Rubey, Mary, 1:137

Rubí, Mariano, 23:1-4, 16

Rubidoux, *see* Robidoux

Rubio, Casimiro, 26:41

Rubio, Francisco, 16:224

Rubio, José, 13:342

Rubio, José María de Jesús Gonzales, *see* Gonzales Rubio

Rubio, María Petra, 13:200

Ruby (ship), 10:328

Ruby Range, 32:198

Ruche d'Or, La (company), 22:300, 302-3

Ruche Littéraire, La (weekly), 39:158, 350

Rucker, Daniel H., 11:107; 26:328-29, 347; 30:56, 58, 59; 33:342, 345-46

Ruckle (or Ruckel), Joseph S., 11:159

Rudd, Kit, 10:279

Ruddick, Dick, 26:210-13, 215

Rudolfe, Capt. (Colorado R., 1869), 22:172

Rudyard Reservoir, 29:198

Ruef, Abraham, 33:40; 39:19-20

Rueger, John, 6:148; 14:399; 15:46

Ruelle, Jean Baptiste, 13:174; 14:209-10; 26:123, 132

Rufino, Fr. (w. Unamuno, 1587), 2:156

Rufus (or Rufuss), Ernst, 12:199, 288; 16:57; 33:62, 63, 64

"Rufus Allen Lockwood," by Robert P. Hastings, 34:97-110, 239-63, 333-40

Ruggles, Charles, 29:378

Ruggles, James D., obit. of Sam H. Daniels, 5:102-3

Ruggles Power Press, 34:346

Ruhling (E.) & Co., 36:99, 100

Ruins, prehistoric, in Southwest, 21:204, 205, 211

Ruiz, Agaton, 29:268-69

Ruiz, Amparo, *see* Burton, Mrs. Henry S.

Ruiz, Antonio, 7:375

Ruiz, Carlos, 18:260

Ruiz, Efigenio, 13:203

Ruiz, Francisco María, 6:159, 166

Ruiz, José Manuel, 12:219; 25:364

Ruiz de Peña, Miguel, 8:43

Ruiz Hermanos *v.* Norton *et al.*, 2:238

Rule, John, 9:355

Rulloff (Rulofson), Edward H., 35:53-54

Rulofson, Alfred Currie, 34:295, 299; 35:47

Rulofson, Charles Herman, 34:296, 300; 35:48, 56

Rulofson, Fannie Anne, 34:295, 299; 35:47-48

Rulofson, Mary Jeanette, 34:296; 35:49, 57; phot., 35: opp. 48

Rulofson, Mattie, 35:48, 56

Rulofson, Rodney Morgan, 31:185; 34:299

Rulofson, William Herman, 31:186; art. on, 34:289-300; 35:47-58; phot.

by, 35: opp. 48 and 49; port., 34: opp. 296

Rulofson, Mrs. William Herman (Amelia Violet Currie), 34:292, 295, 296

Rulofson, Mrs. William Herman (Mary Jane Morgan), 31:186; 34:296, 300; 35:48, 54-55, 56; letter to, 35:58

Rulofson, William Howard, 34:292, 295, 299; 35:47

Rulofson family, 34:289-90, 295-300 *passim*

Rulofson's and Cameron's daguerreotype studio, illus., 34: opp. 289

Rumiantzeff (ship), 12:194

Rumsey (Marysville, 1859), 10:47, 168

Rumsey, William, 29:21-22

Rumsey (place), 32:366, 370

Runde, Winfield Scott, 26:190

Rundell, William L., 25:343

Rungan, Levi, 14:180

Runyon, John, 13:3

Rurik (ship), 12:207; 18:338, 345

Ruschenberger, William S. W., 12:138-39

Rush, R. J., 33:2

Rusk, Thomas J., 2:213, 214; 19:177

Russ, Carolyn (Hale), ed. Hale, *The Log of a Forty-niner*, rev., 3:92-93

Russ, Emmanuel (or Imanuel) Charles Christian, 17:186; 38:40

Russ, Jacob, 19:231

Russ, W. P., 18:202

Russailh, Albert Benard de, *see* Benard de Russailh

Russeau, Lt., *see* Rheusaw, Hiram

Russel, Peter, 9:137

Russell (on *Baltic*, 1860), 11:11

Russell, Maj. (U.S. Inf., L.A., 1861), 24:277

Russell, Andrew Campbell, 7:107

Russell, Amy (Requa), 23:288; 26:285; "The Early Years of William Francis Herrick," 26:217-32

Russell, Carl Parcher, 36:380; "Early Years in Yosemite," 5:328-41; "Frémont's Cannon," 36:359-63; foreword to "The Ira J. Willis Guide to the Gold Mines," ed. Irene D. Paden, 32:193-94; addresses: "The Human History of Yosemite," 5:206; "One Hundred Years in Yosemite," 30:185, 274-75; bk. rev. by, 7:91-92

Russell, Charles J. W., 21:368

Russell, Edmund, 28:203, 213, 227
Russell, Eugene, 18:161, 174; 22:50-51
Russell, F. T., letter from, 24:240-41
Russell, Mrs. Henry Potter (Helen Crocker), 16:384; 21:96
Russell, Israel Cook, 4:42
Russell, J. G., 21:169; 24:263
Russell, Mrs. John H., *see* Russell, Amy (Requa)
Russell, Robert W., 29:345, 346, 347
Russell, Theodore, 20:332, 338
Russell, Thomas C.,ed. *Langsdorff's Narrative of the Rezanov Voyage*, rev., 7:196-97; ed. *The Rezanov Voyage to Nueva California*, rev., 6:96-98; ed. Robinson, *Life in California before the Conquest*, rev., 4:298-99; bks. printed by, 1:299-301; 5:412; 6:4
Russell, W. A., 20:160
Russell, William, 6:152; 29:272, 273
Russell, William Henry, 11:130-31; 13:135, 136; 17:230; 21:354, 357; 22:41, 50, 51, 64, 65; 28:324; 29:336; 30:53; cartoon, 18: foll. 72
Russell, William Hepburn, bk. on, rev. 8:186
Russell (ship), 26:218, 230
Russell & Co., 23:213, 301, 304, 308, 313, 318, 330
Russell *v.* Fairbanks, 10:180
Russ Gardens, San Francisco, 10:291; 15:171, 172, 278, 369, 371; 37:364-65
Russ High School, San Diego, 35:356, 358
Russ House, San Francisco, 8:197; 10:379, 391; 17:186; 24:165; 35:270; 38:40
Russia, aggression by, in the Far East, 30:193-205 *passim;* immigration from, 20:68, 76; warships of, on Pacific Coast, 26:13-19; 40:301, 302
Russian American Co., 11:307; 12:191-276 *passim,* 347; 8:98; 14:143; 16:108, 188; 17:23, 244; 18:107; 23:39; 28:101-12 *passim;* 30:378, 379; 39:97, 98, 109-14
Russian-American Telegraph Exploring Expedition, 33:1-12, 147-68
Russian church, Fort Ross, phot., 39: opp. 112
"Russian Colonies in California, a Russian Version," by T. Blok, 12:189-90
Russian Gulch, 12:193

Russian Hill, San Francisco, 19:233; 38:339
Russian Northwest Co., 6:258-59
Russian River and Valley, 12:189, 209; 23:23, 30, 40; 26:209; 32:48, 368
Russians: in California, 3:173-74; 8:323-27; 12:189-276; 16:108; 17:62-68; 19:319; 20:68; 32:44; discoveries by, 9:201, 207; 23:219; fear of encroachment by, 1:193; 9:202; 16:234, 235; 18:325; 23:220, 222; 25:349, 360; Mt. St. Helena ascended by, 2:364; 3:173-77 *passim;* on N.W. coast, 1:192; 9:201, 203, 207; 16:107-8; 18:318, 327; 23:219, 221-22; sea-otter and seal hunting by, 8:135, 233; 12:191, 194, 196, 217-39, 242; 13:205; 17:57, 244; 18:318; 23:210, 217; 25:366; ships of and shipbuilding by, 12:190, 194-95, 242; 14:143; 15:180, 184, 185; 16:108; 18:347; 28:107; *see also* Bodega; Fort Ross; Rezanov
"Russian Sea-Otter and Seal Hunting on the California Coast," by Adele Ogden, 12:217-39
"Russian Settlement at Ross, The," by E. O. Essig, 12:191-209
"Russian Withdrawal from California, The," by Clarence J. DuFour, 12:240-76
Russ Lumber and Mill Co., 31:294
Russum, F. B., 15:277
Russum, Thomas, 6:80; 14:330, 342, 346
Russy, René E. de, 33:230-34 *passim*
Rust, Gen. (Sacramento, 1857), 9:170
Rust, P. C., 9:46, 54, 73; 15:24
Rust, Richard, 8:358; 9:142, 150, 170(?), 250, 261; 10:395; 14:407; 15:56
Rutger (ship), 33:166
Ruth, J., 9:267, 345, 346, 377
Rutherford, Capt. (Colorado R., 1862), 22:170, 171
Rutherford, Frank, 23:367, 368
Rutherford, Thomas, 20:336
Rutherford, Thomas L. and Elizabeth (Yount), 2:67
Rutherford, William and Emma (Perry), 27:285
Rutherford (place), 2:67
Rutherford, Harris & Co., 33:68
Ruth Hall (novel), 9:60
Rutledge, Carolyn, 36:37
Rutledge, John and Nancy (Fulton), 36:374; family of, 36:374

Rutledge, Lucy, 28:380
Rutledge, Peter J., 38:70
Rutter, John, 23:301, 308, 314, 330, 331
Ryan (S.F., 1855), 16:82
Ryan, Mrs. Barney, 9:265
Ryan, Beatrice (Judd), 38:87; "The Rise of Modern Art in the Bay Area," 38:1-5
Ryan, C. H., 29:93
Ryan, Don, 40:148, 152, 155
Ryan, E. Black, 24:171
Ryan, Mrs. Ella W., 28:188
Ryan, George (Angel's Camp, 1861), 30:238
Ryan, George (S.F., 1863), 33:236
Ryan, James T., 10:271, 276; 11:8-9; 19:376; 22:384; 38:61
Ryan, Lawrence, 15:186

Ryan, Mortimer, 26:210, 215
Ryan, Nora M., 35:179
Ryan, R. F. (1853), 22:35, 37
Ryan, Richard F. (1862), 10:377
Ryan, William Redmond, 14:20, 151; 15:331; 16:343; drawing by, 13: opp. 3
Ryder, George W., 9:29; 11:9; 15:280
Ryder, W., 24:58
Rydin, R. Y., 26:383
Rye, 12:189, 192; 32:335
Ryer, Dr. (Stockholm, 1859), 10:44
Ryer, George, 21:51
Ryers, W. M., 33:344
Ryland, Caius Tacitus, 10:358; 14:164, 166; 15:370; 28:317, 322
Ryman, Add, 21:169
Rynda (ship), 26:15
Ryus, William, 1:151

S

Saavedra Ceron, Alvaro de, 6:296, 308-9
Sabatie, P. G., 39:231
Sabatt, Henry J., 22:39
Sabbath, observance of, *see also* Sunday
Sabin (in mines, 1850), 12:98
Sabin, E. L., 36:105
Sabin, Wallace A., 32:238
Sabine (ship), 18:70; 37:237
Sable Harmonizers, 20:295
Sachem (ship), 6:263; 8:289, 290; 23:193, 194, 216, 307, 310
Sacket, J., 22:251
Sackett, Capt. (overland, 1849), 24:121
Sackett, Russell, 13:316
Sackett's Building, Sacramento, 15:275
Sackville-West, Sir Lionel V., 37:172-79 *passim*
Sacramento, 7:17; 12:300; 29:191; in 1849, 11:35-36, 107, 108; 13:12, 13, 20, 84-85, 370-71, 376, 379-80, 381; 20:35-37, 120; 24:355, 356; 27:128; 29:214-15, 257; in 1850s, 2:137; 6:51, 119, 239-40; 8:22, 167, 202, 211, 262, 277; 9:54, 236-60 *passim*, 268-84 *passim*, 371, 394-95; 10:40-53 *passim*, 61-78 *passim*, 165-66, 190-91, 193, 271-83, 286-90 *passim*; 13:25, 260; 15:75, 76, 77, 279; 17:177; 23:104, 166, 227; 24:353, 357, 362; 33:68; in 1860s, 9:309; 10:271-83, 286-90 *passim*,

372-74, 386-87; 30:311; 32:216-18; in 1880s, 19:106
buildings, 9: (illus.) opp. 258; 15:275; 23:354; 39:193-207, (phot.) foll. 200; *see also* name of bldg.
churches, 9:102, (illus.) opp. 258, 394; 10:64, 78, 278, 292; 27:229; 31:11; *see also* name of church
consolidation bill, 9:256, 258, 282
elections and politics, 3:153-55; 6:7; 8:210; 9:32-42 *passim*, 54, 99, 102-4, 109-13, 371, 394; 10:40, 193, 254, 355; 15:167, 168
fires: 15:166, 173, 279, 297; 17:262; 23:166, 172, 177; 27:303-4
floods, 2:209; 4:189-90; 8:277; 10:279, 293, 364-74 *passim*, 381, 387-88, 392; 12:300; 17:261; 23:166, 232-33, 357-58, 366; 30:284; 33:30; 39:306-7
hotels, 8:210; 9:181, 268, 276; 10:75-76; 24:357; 32:148; *see also* names of hotels
lynching, 6:51
map, 39: opp. 193
newspapers, 3:268-69; 4:228; 6:4, 8-14 *passim*; 7:277-81 *passim*; 9:39, 170, 179, 181, 197, 248, 249, 272-75 *passim*, 382; 10:63, 145, 148, 196, 239-42 *passim*; 11:190; 13:297-98, 299; 14:80; 15:8, 164, 202-8 *passim*, 273;

16:339; 17:78, 176-79 *passim,*
300-301; 20:332-39 *passim,* 368;
21:31, 147; 27:219; 30:129, 195-202
passim; 31:5-6; 32:299, 301, 315-21
passim; 33:204-9 *passim,* 329-32
passim; 34:55, 56, 57, 318; 38:75-76;
facs., 6: opp. 3; 38: opp. 321
squatters, 2:119; 8:268; 12:105
theaters, 9:394; *see also* names of
theaters
see also California: capitals, capitol,
Legislature; New Helvetia; Sutter's
Fort
Sacramento, Mex., battle of, 18:233, 246
"Sacramento" (horse), 25:145; 29:338
Sacramento (launch or schr., formerly
Constantine, 1842), 12:199, 247, 251,
274; 14:143; 16:129
Sacramento (str., 1849), 2:202; 19:291,
296; 28:63; 33:57
Sacramento, Le (company), 22:308-9
Sacramento and Yuba Railroad, 10:393
"Sacramento Bill," *see* Colm, W. W.
Sacramento Cadets, 24:173, 175
Sacramento City Cemetery, 23:297
Sacramento City Guard, 10:198, 295;
24:172, 175, 176; 37:362(?); 38:20
Sacramento Civic Repertory Theater,
29:186
Sacramento County, 7:17, 18;
Courthouse, 24:180; *see also* Capitol,
Sacramento
Sacramento Gas Co., 16:184; 17:79
Sacramento Guards, 37:362; *see also*
Sacramento City Guard
Sacramento Hotel, 8:202, 210; 23:369;
24:166
Sacramento Hussars, 10:295; 38:18
Sacramento Jockey Club, 10:198
Sacramento Library Assoc., 19:249;
38:311
Sacramento Mutual Benefit Society,
10:41
Sacramento Philharmonic Society, 9:249
Sacramento Pioneer Association, *see*
Sacramento Society of California
Pioneers
Sacramento, Placer and Nevada
Railroad, 2:205
Sacramento River and Valley, 1:114-15,
120, 121, 131-32; 5:119-21; 6:141, 240;
7:71; 8:17-23; 11:103-23; 14:197, 345;
15:226, 234; 18:296, 298, 311; 20:32-35,
119; 21:1-5, 9, 10; 22:102, 209-13, 265,
323, 329-45 *passim;* 23:19, 32-34, 59, 60,

166, 295, 300, 354; 24:24, 327, 331, 332;
27:128, 298, 306, 307-8; 28:121, 122,
243, 251; boats, 6:141, 240; 10:293, 405;
16:61-66, 79; 18:302, 373; 19:124;
20:30, 34; 21:58; 22:14, 94; 23:354;
27:306; 32:223; floods, 19:120;
23:232-33, 357, 358, 365-67 (*see also*
Floods); mining, 23:59, 60; map, 11:
opp. 99
Sacramento Society of California
Pioneers, 15:372; 23:297, 362, 373;
24:166; 38:311
Sacramento Tannery and Leather
Factory, 33:68
Sacramento Theatre, 9:371; 10:41, 63,
368; 23:104
Sacramento Valley Central Railroad,
4:226
Sacramento Valley Railroad, 4:220-27
passim, 241, 244, 245, 258-59, 265,
267-69; 7:110; 8:362; 9:181, 271;
10:293; 11:230, 321; 15:367, 376; 16:32,
79-80, 184, 283; 17:179; 24:167; 32:218,
223; illus., 4: opp. 268; map, 4: opp.
222
Sacred Heart College, 29:57, 59
Safe Deposit Co. of San Francisco,
10:295
Safford, A. P. K., 2:205; 9:250, 260, 269;
36:100-101, 268, 271
Sagamore (ship), 6:41; 12:103; 22:250;
27:233
Saga of the Comstock Lode, The, by
Lyman, rev., 13:183-84
Sagarra, Eduardo, 16:224
Sage, Rufus B., 20:147, 152
Sager Troupe, 9:141, 145, 251
Saginaw (ship), 10:376, 389; 25:41;
33:233, 240
Saguire (or Salguire), Pablo (de la
Guerra?), 5:306
"Sailing Ships' Part in the Development
of California, The," address by I. N.
Hibberd, 12:366
Saillant (ship), *see Vaillant*
"Sailor Bill," *see* Marshall, William
Sailor Diggings, Ore., 19:369; *see also*
Waldo
Sailors' Union, 35:67
Sainsevain, Jean Louis, 13:336, 345
Sainsevain, Pierre, 12:333, 353; 13:78,
160, 167, 174, 214, 278, 372; 16:337;
17:233; 20:109; 28:193, 361-62; fac.
sig., 10: opp. 159
Saint-Amant, Pierre Charles de, 18:5;

22:253, 255, 262, 266, 268-69, 276; 35:318

St. Andrews Society, San Francisco, 8:275

St. Anne (ship), 30:256

St. Anne's Church, Columbia, 24:268

St. Anne's Valley, San Francisco, 14:129

St. Augustine's, *see* College of St. Augustine

St. Boniface's Church, San Francisco, 32:261

St. Catherine, Bay of, 2:93-98; 11:158-59

St. Catherine's Convent School, 30:262

St. Charles gambling house, Stockton, 18:267

St. Charles Hotel, Benecia, 17:266

St. Charles Hotel, Los Angeles, 3:164

St. Charles Hotel, Marysville, 14:392, 393, 394, 404; 15:47

St. Charles Hotel, Sacramento, 4:244

St. Charles Hotel, San Francisco, 15:272

St. Charles Hotel, Santa Barbara, *see* San Carlos Hotel

St. Clair, Mary, 15:180

St. Clair, Orla, obit., 40:178-79

St. Clair, Pruett, 1:138

St. Clair & Pinkham, 22:30; 30:115

St. Claire, Henri, 27:309

Sainte-Marie, T. P., 18:6, 7

St. Felix, George E., 18:303

St. Francis Church, San Francisco, 40:59

St. Francis Hotel, San Francisco, 11:76; 19:229; 22:264; 26:334, 338, 348; 30:157

St. Francis Xavier Residence, Ore., 29:141, 146

St. George, Point, 10:329

St. George Hotel, Sacramento, 9:397; 10:42, 44, 64, 279, 282, 364; 11:246; 33:333

St. Germain, Baptiste, 2:36

Saint Helena, Mount, 2:364; 3:295; 12:196-98, 209; 18:338; 23:180; art. on, 3:171-77

St. Hill, Thomas N., 26:383

St. Ignatius Church and College, 13:31; 21:240, 250; 27:380; 29:139; 36:298, 306; 37:43; 38:26

St. Isabelle, *see* Ranchos: Santa Ysabel

St. James Church, San Francisco, 36:294

St. John's Episcopal Church, Marysville, 10:54, 55, 76

St. John's Institute, San Juan Bautista, 33:353, 356, 359

St. Joseph, Mo., 6:113, 361; 10:398;

26:292; letters and newsp. arts. from, 24:30-32, 34-38 *passim*

St. Joseph (ship), 6:46; 32:108, 109

St. Joseph, Mount, *see* Lassen Peak

St. Lawrence Mining Co., Downieville, 33:375

St. Losky, Levy & Co., 15:275

St. Louis, Mo., 11:138-40; 22:121; 27:272

St. Louis, Sierra Co., 11:238, 240, 242; 15:171; 19:291-98; phot., 29: opp. 289

St. Louis (U.S. sloop of war, 1840), 15:130-31, 225, 229; 20:194; 34:123; 37:64-65

St. Louis (str., 1859), 4:263; 16:200; 21:61

"Saint Louis and Poker Flat in the Fifties and Sixties," by Henry Cohn, ed. and trans. Fritz L. Cohn, 19:289-98

St. Louis & San Francisco Railroad, 27:272

St. Louis Exchange, Sacramento, 24:355, 357

St. Louis Hotel, Marysville, 9:378; 14:394

St. Louis Library Association, 38:307

St. Louis ranch, *see* Ranchos: San Luis Gonzaga

St. Mark's Episcopal Church, Berkeley, 37:51-61

St. Mary's (sloop of war), 22:30; 24:24; 30:43; 36:310

St. Mary's (str.), 16:78; 17:79

St. Mary's Cathedral, Sacramento, 39:199, 206

St. Mary's Cathedral, San Francisco, 15:268, 366; 16:344; 17:181

St. Mary's College, 37:43

St. Mary's Hall (school, Sonoma), 11:146; 36:243

St. Mary's Hospital, San Francisco, 26:260; 27:380

St. Mary's Library Assoc., San Francisco, 38:306

St. Matthew's Church, San Mateo, 27:254, 255, 320

St. Nicholas Hotel, Marysville, 9:178, 373, 396; 10:173, 178, 246, 253, 257, 259, 264, 271, 284, 356, 359, 369, 380; *see also* Haun House

St. Nicholas Hotel, San Francisco, 15:278

St. Paul (ship), 23:219, 225

St. Paul's Episcopal Church, San Francisco, 26:361

St. Pauls Evangelical Lutheran Church, San Francisco, 19:192
St. Paul's Presbyterian Church, San Francisco, 27:149
St. Peter (ship), 23:225
St. Rose's Church, Sacramento, 9:254, 279
St. Sure, Adolphus Frederic, 23:384
St. Thomas, W. I., 39:100
St. Vallier (ship), 22:163, 166, 167
St. Vincent's Hospital, Los Angeles, 13:333
St. Vrain, Ceran, 2:20
Sajet, Jean, 12:35, 354
Sal, Hermenegildo, 2:268-76 *passim*, 280, 305, 308, 334; 4:147; 14:112, 115-17; 15:59-60; 17:120; 25:319, 320, 322
Salamanca, Secundino de, 10:316
Salaries, federal, in Calif., 32:317-18, 323
Salazar, Alonzo Isidro, 13:203; 25:78, 167
Salazar, Ignacio, 10:35
Salazar, José Antonio, 10:31-32
Salazar, Tomás, 10:36
Salazar Ilarequi, José, 9:4, 11, 13
Salcedo, Felipe de, 2:140; 7:151, 172-73
Salem, Ore., 2:131
Salem (ship, 1849), 30:16-20, 29, 34-35
Salem (ship, early 1900s), 31:295
Sales (Yuba Co., 1855), 8:341
Sales, Alexander, 1:237
Salesorio, Alvert H., 37:197
Salgado, Tomás, 24:292, 308; 25:60, 149, 362
Salinas (ship), 26:258
Salinas, newspapers, 29:89, 90
Salinas River and Valley, 1:159; 8:113; 17:350; 23:1; 36:2; Swiss settlers, 30:309, 310
Salinger, Jehanne Biétry, 20:384; 39:2-3, 312, 320
Salinger Tract, 25:174
Salisbury (ship), 22:351
Sallaberry, J., 39:314, 320-21
Salleman, F., 12:333
Salmeron, *see* Zárate Salmeron
Salmon (S.F., 1850), 5:351
Salmon (S.F., 1854), 21:324
Salmon, Francisco, 37:204
Salmon, James, 25:145
Salmon, 2:58; 5:64; 6:80; 22:318; 27:216; 28:107; 36:379; canning of, 35:265-67
Salmon & Ellis, 30:113; 34:27
Salmon Creek Mill, 38:63
Salmon Falls, 6:248; illus., opp. 248
Salmon Guard, 34:269

Salmon River, 3:201; 5:242-46 *passim*; 26:201; 29:304; 40:51; mining on, 5:242, 245
Salmon Trout River (Carson R.), 3:67; 32:198, 207
Salmon Trout River (Truckee R.), 6:362
Sal si puedes (shrub), 23:362, 373
Salt, Charles, 15:160
Salt, 5:269; 6:259, 261, 262, 347; 7:328; 10:300; 20:263; 22:162-63; 28:100, 102, 109; 35:348-50; 37:373-74; art. on, 39:117-20; journey of Indians, 20:360-61
"Salt for the Scraping: ... San Francisco Salt Industry," by Alan K. Brown, 39:117-20
Salt in California, by William E. Ver Planck, rev., 37:373-74
Salt Lake, *see* Great Salt Lake
Salt Lake City, 3:56-58, 297; 6:119-21; 12:354; 13:84; 17:36; 24:118, 366; 32:194-202 *passim*; letter from, 11:53; illus., 6: opp. 109
Salt Lake Indian Agency, 26:323, 325
Saltonstall, Leverett, 37:10-11
Salt River, 1:112-13; 2:11
Salt Springs, San Bernardino Co., 17:214, 215; gold mine, 14:67
Saltz, H., 25:240
Salud, Cañada de la, 19:287
Salvador (place), 16:79
Salvador (ship), 27:179
"Salvador Vallejo," by Myrtle M. McKittrick, 29:309-31
Salvatierra, Juan María, 6:103, 162; 10:204; 26:310; 36:233
Salvator, Archd. Ludwig Louis, 13:345, 354; 31:13; *Los Angeles in the Sunny Seventies*, rev., 8:379-80
Salvedea, *see* Zalvidea
Samaniego, Lope de, 3:368
Samarang (ship), 19:213
Samelson, Marcia (Wynn), 28:189
Sam Kwok (play), 23:109
Samoset (ship), 27:293
"Sam Patch" (Indian, 1850), 24:51, 55
Sam Patch (play), 9:271
Sample, Col. (Marysville, 1862), 10:380
Sampson (Indian, 1858), 4:14
Sampson, Caroline Augusta, 3:46, 156-61 *passim*
Sampson, E., Jr., 14:161
Sampson, John, 8:359; 9:75; 12:280; 14:210, 212, 219, 383, 389, 405

Sampson, W. H., 15:29
Sam Soule (riv. str.), 9:55
Samuel (Indian, 1840), 21:320
Samuel (S.F., 1850s), 32:108-9
Samuel Churchman (ship), 20:332
"Samuel Green McMahan," by Ellen L.
    Wood, 23:289-300
"Samuel Marsden Brookes," by Lucy A.
    Marshall, 36:193-203
Samuel M. Fox (ship), 34:26-27
"Samuel Norris: Litigious Pioneer," by
    Allen L. Chickering, 25:219-28
Samuel Roberts (ship), 25:111-12, 255,
    259, 261, 264
Samuel Russell (ship), 10:294
Samuels (D.) Lace House, 27:383
"Samurai in San Francisco, the Japanese
    Embassy of 1860," by George Hinkle,
    23:335-47
Sam Yup Tong, 27:23
San Agustín (ship), 3:4, 5, 20, 22, 23;
    7:363, 388; 8:56; 20:316-24 *passim*;
    27:290; 31:100-104 *passim*
San Agustín, Isla de (San Martin I.),
    3:18
San Alejo, 26:59
San Andreas, 23:106; 30:362; 38:309
San Andreas Valley, 17:245, 247
San Andres, Ancon de, 3:324, 325, 326,
    364, 380, 385
San Anselmo, Arroyo de, Lower Calif.,
    31:345
San Antonio (East Oakland), 10:72;
    15:375; 27:210; 30:1, 3, 5, 6
San Antonio, Calaveras Co., 11:182;
    diggings, 11:57, 168
San Antonio, Tex., 18:101
San Antonio (ship, 1542), 7:137
San Antonio (packet, 1768), 4:142-43;
    10:217; 11:276-79; 13:180; 14:102;
    31:110-11, 114, 120, 353, 354; 37:294-98
    passim
San Antonio (ship, 1817), 37:247, 264
San Antonio (str., formerly
    Confidence), 10:72
San Antonio and San Diego Mail Line,
    2:221; 34:198-99; 36:118, 127-28, 129
Sanatoriums, 31:19-23 *passim*; 39:273
San Benitos Islands, 3:312, 361
San Bernabé, Bahia de, 7:305-9; 8:30;
    map, 7:306
San Bernardino, 4:185; 10:35; 11:289;
    18:374; 19:278; 29:242; 34:3; camels at,
    9:305, 310; Confederate feeling in,
    20:157, 168; military companies,

29:242-43; Mormons in, 9:90, 197;
    14:178-81; 22:12, 13, 30; 24:275;
    newspapers and press, 9:194, 197-98;
    23:260; 24:275
San Bernardino Borax Mining Co.,
    17:116, 117
San Bernardino County, 36:284; borax
    in, 17:10-12, 116-17; Confederate
    activity in, 20:156-57; desert
    community in, 27:113-22; Mormons
    in, 14:68-69, 178-81; *see also* Ranchos:
    San Bernardino; San Bernardino
    Valley
San Bernardino Light Dragoons, 29:242
San Bernardino meridian, 18:198-99;
    34:3, 11-13; monument (illus.), 34:
    opp. 1
San Bernardino Peak, 34:3, 11-13
San Bernardino plain (Santa Clara
    Valley), 14:103-4
San Bernardino Valley, 10:214, 215, 217;
    39:299; art. on, 12:111-24
"San Bernardino Valley before the
    Americans Came," by George W.
    Beattie, 12:111-24
San Bernardo, 17:343, 344; 26:44, 48, 50,
    61; *see also* Ranchos: San Bernardo
San Bernardo River and Valley, 26:38,
    59, 62
San Blas, 9:209; 10:315, 318, 320, 322, 336,
    338; 13:399; 14:325, 327, 334;
    15:128-29, 131, 140, 225, 238; 17:25;
    19:211; 20:21; 23:279, 302, 309, 360;
    24:64; 27:40; 29:12, 13-14, 211; 30:238;
    31:110, 111; 36:3; 37:293
San Blaseña (ship), 23:274, 279, 280;
    30:238
Sanborn, Mrs. Elizabeth, 32:141
Sanborn, F. G., 29:99, 225, 361
Sanborn, John B., 33:298, 307
San Bruno, Lower Calif., 26:309
San Bruno Mountain, 17:245, 247
San Buenaventura, 13:188; 16:297, 302;
    17:31, 32; 18:157-59; 30:51; battle of,
    18:275; *see also* Mission San
    Buenaventura; Ventura
San Buenaventura (ship), 3:14; 20:318,
    323
San Carlos (packet, 1768-1780s),
    4:142-43, 303; 6:163; 9:205, 209, 210;
    13:155, 180; 14:102; 23:372; 25:322;
    27:293; 31:110, 111, 120, 353, 354
San Carlos (barkentine, 1820s),
    15:140-41; 16:238; 24:312
San Carlos, Isla de (Forrester I.), 9:241

San Carlos Borromeo (ship), 23:219, 221,225

San Carlos (or St. Charles) Hotel, Santa Barbara, 2:52; 18:164, 262, 272

San Carlos Pass, 34:194-95

San Carpojoro Canyon, 1:159

Sánchez (imprisoned, S.F., 1846), 20:217

Sánchez, Barbara, 17:255

Sánchez, Felipe, 29:237

Sánchez, Francisco (1820s, '30s, and '40s), 1:92; 3:85; 4:385, 387; 10:100, 123-28 *passim*; 12:59, 335; 13:236, 237; 14:129, 149; 15:64, 69; 16:111(?), 353; 17:255; 27:59; 29:157

Sánchez, Francisco (L.A., 1857), 29:236

Sánchez, Francisco Miguel, 2:277-80 *passim*

Sánchez, Guadalupe, 29:237

Sánchez, Ilaria, 17:256; 27:262

Sánchez, Joaquín, 36:6

Sánchez, José Antonio (1830s), 8:242; 12:139, 140, 225; 16:113, 219, 220, 221, 225, 226, 234; 17:149(?), 154, 249-53 *passim*; 36:241; 38:105; ranch of, *see* Ranchos: Buri Buri

Sánchez, José Antonio (L.A., 1861), 29:237, 243

Sánchez, José Bernardo, 2:41, 42-44; 8:248, 329; 12:121-22; 13:210, 223, 234; 23:207, 216

Sánchez, José de la Cruz, 4:385, 386; 16:183; 17:254; 23:253; 27:58, 251-52; ranch of, 22:244, 251; *see also* Ranchos: Buri Buri

Sánchez, José Isidro ("Chino"), 17:254, 255

Sánchez, José María ("El Judío"), 29:19-20, 24

Sánchez, Mrs. José María (Encarnación Ortega), 29:20-27 *passim*

Sánchez, Juan, 18:157, 172; 33:268, 337

Sánchez, Juan Antonio, 29:320

Sánchez, Julia, 17:256

Sánchez, Manuel, 17:255

Sánchez, María, 17:255

Sánchez, Martín, 3:366

Sánchez, Miguel, 2:156

Sánchez, Narciso, 15:356

Sánchez, Nellie Van de Grift, address, "Social Life in Spanish California," 6:380-81; *Spanish Arcadia*, rev., 9:87; coauth. *Short History of California*, rev., 8:380-81

Sánchez, Paula, 17:255

Sánchez, Pedro, 33:121

Sanchez, R. B. and Mrs. (née Crittenden), 7:118

Sánchez, Rafael, 11:209; 35:105

Sánchez, Tomás A., 13:313, 326; 26:35-36, 42; 29:234, 239, 240, 245

Sánchez, Vicenta, 23:217

Sánchez, Vicente, 13:211, 212, 223, 310, 313

Sánchez de Toledo, Francisco, 3:315, 367

Sanchez Hall, Los Angeles, 13:228, 229

Sánchez Ranch, 23:254; *see also* Ranchos: Buri Buri

San Clemente Island, 2:48, 49, 330; 3:6; 7:73, 172, 349, 387, 388; 8:58; 31:155

San Cristobal (ship), 7:137

Sanctotis, Hernando de, 7:256-57, 258, 267

Sandels Edhelyertha, G. M. Waseurtz af, 18:311; 19:194, 214, 215, 216; 29:316; quoted, 18:295-96; 19:215; sketch by, 12: opp. 191

Sanders (Sandeau?, 1846), 26:23

Sanders, Judge (Sacramento, 1851), 3:83

Sanders (S.F., 1865), 36:208

Sanders, A. A., 24:263

Sanders, Allen, 5:125

Sanders, Beverley C., 17:84, 174; 25:337, 344; *see also* Sanders & Brenham

Sanders, C. K., 16:79

Sanders, Emily ("Lady Don"), 21:152, 154

Sanders, George H., 27:173, 174

Sanders, Horace, 17:240; 24:58

Sanders, J. G. Hubert, 15:274, 277, 280, 371; 19:230; 25:335-36, 342, 343

Sanders, Lewis, Jr., 10:78

Sanders, Mary Louise, 20:286

Sanders & Brenham, 15:272; 16:338; 17:84, 169; 37:139

Sanders Colony, 25:175

Sanderson (Stockton, 1859), 10:44

Sanderson, George B., 22:54-55; 33:97, 101, 107-17 *passim*, 249, 251

Sanderson, Winslow F., 24:40, 245

Sand Flat, 10:168, 192

Sandford, C. W., 11:33

Sand Hole, Riverside Co., 12:8-9

San Diego: 31:149; 36:164; in 1776, 14:102; in 1793, 2:331-40; in 1827-28, 8:218-21, 331-34; 16:218; in 1830s, 13:212; 14:232-62 *passim*, 225-31 *passim*; 16:222, 238, 363; in 1840-42, 8:108; 12:227; 19:206-7; in 1840-50, 1:146; 9:6, 9, 13; in 1851-52, 22:3, 4;

in 1880s, 17:35; 22:349-53; 31:149, 186;
in 1890s, 35:269, 273-74, 345-55 *passim;*
in 1900-1920s, 20:140; 35:354-66;
36:63-78, 153-56
Logan Heights, 31:149; Old Town,
9:9; 23:360, 371; 26:24, 47; 31:33-48
passim; 33:115; New Town, 4:144;
8:184; 31:33-45
art gallery, 36:153; chamber of
commerce, 36:63; doctors, 4:143-44,
167-68 (*see also* Griffin, John S.);
first American birth, 22:56; fishing
industry, 31:153-58
Gale and Robinson at, 23:194-99
passim, 205-6, 209, 315-30 *passim*
hide and tallow trade, 8:291, 293,
304-5; 19:206-7, 210; 23:194, 206,
209, 320, 325, 326
mail service, 36:117-22 *passim,* 131
Mexican: fort, 8:218, 333, 334; govt.,
1:26-31 *passim;* legislature, 16:218,
230, 231
newspapers: 9:194, 197, 200; 24:275;
31:36, 39, 46, 151-59 *passim*
parks, 35:357; 36:65-68; public library,
35:356; school, 35:356, 358; trails,
36:117-32; transportation, 16:66-68;
22:2, 3, 4, 6, 10, 155; 31:40, 149;
trappers at, 2:345; 15:109, 133
U.S. forces at (1846-47), 1:142-43,
146; 3:119-24 *passim;* 12:57; 14:271;
15:237; 17:282, 283, 347, 348, 349;
20:226; 21:220, 338-44; 22:48-59, 61;
26:21-25 *passim,* 33, 46-50 *passim,*
291; 33:99-103 *passim;* (1852-1920),
31:35-36; 34:158-60
see also Presidio of San Diego;
Missions: San Diego; San Diego Bay
San Diego (ship), 7:273, 300-382
passim, 389, 390; 20:319; 36:228, 230
San Diego & Arizona Eastern Railroad,
31:149
San Diego Bay and port, 2:331-32, 335;
4:143; 5:214; 7:46, 54, 73, 347-48, 387;
8:58, 69, 217-18, 291, 331-34; 10:335;
12:125; 22:349-54; 23:203, 205, 209;
31:120, 151-53; 32:352-53; 36:228;
maps showing, 7:346; 9: opp. 3 and
opp. 6
San Diego Company, 16:216, 367
San Diego Fishing and Canning Co.,
31:155
San Diego Hill, 11:333
San Diego Lumber Co., 38:68
San Diego River, 23:371; 31:120, 353

San Diego Salt Co., 35:349
San Diego Savings Bank, 35:360-61
San Dieguito (Indian village), 26:30
San Dieguito River, 26:26, 45
San Dimas, Punta de (Cape Sebastian),
10:329, 330
Sandini (outlaw, 1850s), 18:171, 268
Sandl, Mrs. Ruth N. (W.?), 23:192
Sandoval, Cipriano, 13:329
Sandoval, Julián, 36:128
Sand River (Mokelumne R.), 23:36
Sands, Benjamin F., 33:232
Sands, David, 9:355, 356, 369, 386; 17:183
Sands, Preston, 33:232
Sands, William, 33:232
Sandwich Islanders, 1:253; 2:271, 274,
293; 12:224; 19:202; *see also* Kanakas
Sandwich Island Gazette, fac. heading,
35: opp. 193
Sandwich Islands, 1:253; 3:32; 4:91; 5:46;
6:364, 365; 8:334, 336; 11:198; 12:145;
14:69, 313; 15:174, 181, 269, 271, 280;
16:4, 183, 284, 347; 17:23, 131; 18:256;
19:177, 178; 21:356; 25:289; 28:248-56
passim, 317; 29:2, 12; 31:86; 39:110,
111, 154-55; letter from, 12:138;
printing press in, 35:193-204; *see also*
Hawaiian Islands
"Sandwich Island Story of California's
First Printing Press, The," by Helen
P. Hoyt, 35:193-204
San Feliciano Canyon, 7:199
San Felipe, 21:219, 301; 25:298; Valley,
25:302
San Felipe Viejo, *see* Vallecito
San Fernando, 14:234, 240, 244; 21:351,
354; 32:328; "Convenio" at, (1846),
10:100, 102; gold mine nr., 8:120;
19:203; *see also* Missions: San
Fernando Rey
San Fernando, College of (Mexico
City), 28:19, 20; 37:99, 293, 304
San Fernando petroleum and mining
district, 17:115
Sanford, Henry L., 29:20, 22
Sanford, Mrs. Henry L., *see* Sánchez,
Mrs. José María
Sanford, John Bunyan, 39:21
Sanford, Oliver Nason, 31:186
Sanford, W. B., 29:234
San Francisco:
founding, 14:99-110; 27:57-61
Mission, *see* Missions: San Francisco
de Asís
Presidio, *see* Presidio of San Francisco

pueblo, 1:28, 29; 14:100; 16:343;
21:118-25 *passim;* 27:58-60 *passim*
taken by U.S., 2:356-62 *passim;* 3:33,
84, 188; 8:71, 74; 15:306-10; 17:295,
299; 24:48
in 1792, 14:111-20
in 1820s and '30s, 23:195, 314
in 1846-47, 24:47-48; *see also* Yerba
Buena
in 1848-49, 5:8, 9-21; 11:129-37;
14:332; 16:129-30; 17:196; 19:235;
20:29-32, 120, 123, 291-93; 22:69-70,
242, 243-44; 23:276-78; 29:5, 14-17,
161-65, 168-72, 212-14; 27:10-17,
43-45, 361-70; 30:21
in 1850s, 5:22-43; 6:37-45, 213, 251-52;
7:227, 395-404; 12:92, 94-110; 13:82;
14:133, 134; 15:88, 163-86, 266-82,
364-77; 16:78-84, 182-84; 21:363;
22:246-47, 253-76; 23:228, 358;
24:48-49; 26:333-45; 28:31-46,
127-30; 34:66-74
in 1860s, 6:352; 10:291; 19:233; 20:251,
252, 253; 23:228-44; 27:66-71;
29:251-54; 32:219-21
in 1870s, 19:233-34; 29:288-94;
37:215-24, 227
in 1880s, 16:300-301; 27:224-27, 228
bar, 15:164, 182, 186; 26:343-44;
Board of Aldermen, 9:26; 15:164,
166, 172-78 *passim,* 184, 185, 268,
272, 276, 281, 282, 364-73 *passim;*
16:282, 342; 17:81-84 *passim,* 168-82
passim; Board of Assist. Aldermen,
9:26; 15:163-68 *passim,* 176, 185,
272-82 *passim,* 364, 365, 370, 371;
16:82, 340, 342; 17:168, 175, 177;
Board of Education, 15:173; 17:175;
Board of Supervisors, 15:169, 170,
177, 269, 270, 280, 282, 364-72
passim; 16:84, 183, 282-83; 17:176;
21:30; boundaries, 15:176, 183;
21:113
charter, 9:48; 15:278, 282; 19:153;
20:14; 21:121; Common Council,
15:164, 169, 176-84 *passim,* 274,
369, 370; Town Council, 5:405-7;
Consolidation of city and co., 9:48,
110; 15:276, 278; courts, 15:88,
163-85 *passim,* 266-77 *passim,* 282,
364-77 *passim;* 16:80-84 *passim,* 183,
282, 284, 285, 336-43 *passim;* 17:82,
175, 177, 180; 21:120-23 *passim;*
22:267; District bill, 9:260, 284;
elections and politics, 5:41; 7:396,

401; 9:24-33 *passim,* 108-9, 110;
11:137; 15:163-77 *passim,* 184, 186,
279-82 *passim,* 364, 366; 16:79-84
passim, 340; 17:309; 18:37, 38;
22:112; finances, assessments, taxes,
5:406-7; 15:163, 169, 178, 180, 182,
184, 186, 266, 270-78 *passim,* 371,
373, 374; 16:82, 283, 284, 338; 17:83,
170, 176, 179, 182, 196-97; 20:303;
23:228; 28:116; 34:251
government, 1:28, 31; 5:406;
10:143-45; 19:299; 20:14; 21:30;
grand juries, 15:88, 169, 170, 174,
176, 181, 186, 271, 275-76, 281,
282, 365; 17:81, 83, 167, 174, 176,
177; laws and ordinances, 2:75;
15:163-68 *passim,* 175, 185, 272, 276,
282, 367; 16:340, 342; 17:168, 182;
19:299; 21:119, 124; 22:258; 23:238;
lawsuits, 15:182, 186, 276, 282,
366-67, 370; 16:182; message of
Mayor (1855), 15:274; sanitary
reduction works, 34:330; surveys
of, 3:32; 11:134; 13:236; 21:118,
121
buildings, 3:37; 5:12; 14:128; 15:170,
175, 268, 269, 272, 275; 16:129, 130,
139, 182, 183, 184, 344; 17:83;
22:267; 31:297; brick, 3:37; 15:282;
16:129; 19:321; City Hall, 16:342;
20:299-307 *passim;* 22:112, 113,
267; *see also* names of bldgs.;
"El Dorado Gothic"
churches, 23:157-58, 235, 245, 246;
see also names of churches
fires, *see* Fires; San Francisco
earthquake and fire
first: bank, 3:37; brick bldgs., 3:37;
16:129; 19:321; 28:66; bridge, 3:33;
houses, 14:318 (*see also* Yerba
Buena); melodeon, 37:237; post
office, 3:37-38; school, 3:34-35;
4:172; 11:134, 143; 26:348;
27:233, 368; 28:34; other firsts,
3:34-39 *passim;* 4:172; 16:130;
25:334; 28:35; 38:39
hotels, restaurants, saloons, 3:38;
5:349; 6:51, 56, 57; 8:273; 10:276,
290; 11:152; 12:364; 16:130, 140,
307; 17:36, (illus.), opp. 36;
20:292-93; 21:259; 22:262-66
passim; 27:368; 28:46; 33:57;
35:140-42; 37:227, 332-33; *see also*
names of hotels, etc.
newspapers, 7:277-81 *passim;* 10:64;

13:299; 15:175, 272; 16:339; 17:80;
20:28, 165; 21:153; 27:318; 28:36;
*see also Alta California; American;
Californian; California Star;
California Democrat; Call;
Chronicle; Dramatic Chronicle;
Echo du Pacifique; Examiner;
Globe; Herald; Journal of
Commerce; News; News-Letter;
Pacific; Pacific News; Picayune;
Post; Spirit of the Times; Times;
True Standard*
population, 10:405; 11:137; 13:376,
384; 16:338; 22:253; 37:316
real estate, 4:172; 13:275, 367;
14:330-31; 15:171, 179, 180, 183,
186, 266, 270, 276, 279, 282, 367,
368; 16:129, 182; 18:37; 23:56, 157,
174, 228-44 *passim*; 37:315-16;
alcalde grants, 16:343; 28:67-68,
266; beach and water lots, 15:171,
180, 186, 270, 276; 16:182; 17:173;
34:258-59, 333-34; 37:315; city slip
property, 15:276, 282; 16:182; Peter
Smith titles, 34:251, 257; pueblo
lands, 15:169, 176; 16:343; 21:121,
123-24; sales for taxes, 15:272-73;
tide lands, 21:121-22; 22:113-25;
see also Rents; Squatters
schools, 3:34-35; 4:172; 5:407; 6:40;
11:134-35, 143; 14:75; 15:88, 164,
169, 173, 174-75, 183, 275, 384;
16:182, 283, 284; 17:174-75; 20:14;
21:364; 26:348; 27:10, 233, 236;
28:33-34; 33:302, 308; 36:348-49;
37:44; Boy's High, 35:139; for deaf,
dumb, blind, 10:289-90; female
institutes, 17:182; 28:34; 36:348;
Happy Valley No. 2, 16:283;
Lincoln Grammar, 37:224-26;
North Beach No. 5, 15:174-75;
16:284; Powell St. Academy,
15:267; Powell St. No. 3, 15:180;
16:283, 284; private, 4:406; 6:40;
reform, 10:276 (*see also* Industrial
School); Rincon Pt. No. 1, 15:174,
180, 267; 16:283, 284; 33:306;
Roman Catholic, 15:75, 172; 16:284;
17:175; S.F. High, 36:348; 38:29,
338; South Cosmopolitan, 35:21,
127; Spring Valley No. 6, 16:284;
33:308; Union St. No. 4, 10:378;
14:268; 15:182, 268; 16:284
streets and roads, 5:29, 33, 35;
13:235-39; 15:65, 88, 163-66 *passim*,
176, 182, 185, 273, 275; 16:184, 340,
342, 347; 17:173, 176; 19:187;
23:74-75, 230, 238; 27:348;
37:316
Army, 21:117; Battery, 15:65;
17:301; 22:257, 264; Bay View
Turnpike (Barneveld), 21:116;
Brannan, 16:283, 340, 342; 17:169;
21:115; Brenham Place, 17:298;
Broadway, 17:291, 301; 22:257,
269; 23:156; Bush, 22:257, 264;
California, 17:292, 293; 22:256,
264, 266, 267; Center (16th), 21:113;
Clay, 16:339, 340; 17:230, 294-99
passim, 314; 22:256, 259, 266-69
passim; Clement, 24:379; Columbus
(Montgomery Ave.), 21:167;
Commercial, 15:176; 17:173, 309;
22:257, 267, 268; Drumm, 17:173;
Dupont (Grant), 13:237-38; 22:256,
257, 259, 266, 267; Essex, 37:217;
Filbert, 17:293; First, 21:114;
Folsom, 21:113, 114; Front, 22:254,
257; Fundación, Calle de la, 3:31;
11:75; 13:236-37; 17:292, 299;
Grant, 13:235-38; 17:292, 299 (*see
also* Dupont); Halleck, 17:315;
Harris (8th), 21:114; Jackson,
17:301, 310; 22:256, 258, 268; 23:74;
Jones, 11:130; 17:296; Kearny,
15:163, 176, 275; 17:294, 298, 301,
316; 22:259, 268, 269; Kentucky,
21:115; Larkin, 16:5; Leidesdorff,
15:182, 184; 17:291, 293, 294;
McAllister, 11:126; Mason, 16:282;
Mazzini, 21:117; Mellus, 11:136;
Merchant, 17:295; Mission, 6:13;
14:129; 16:283; 17:169; 21:113-14;
22:274; Montgomery, 11:69, 71;
14:126; 17:292-95 *passim*, 310, 315;
22:254-58 *passim*, 267, 268; Natoma,
11:136; Navy (26th), 22:119;
Pacific, 17:301, 312; 22:268, 269;
Pacific Plank Rd., 15:373; Park
(24th), 22:119; Pine, 17:291; Powell,
17:293; Precita, 21:117; Presidio,
16:284; Price (7th), 21:114;
Sacramento, 2:201; 11:69; 17:173,
293, 294; 22:266, 269; Sansome,
17:315; 22:257, 264; Serpentine,
21:117; Steuart, 17:315; Stockton,
16:282; 17:291; 22:248, 258; Third,
21:115; Townsend, 11:135; Vallejo,
16:282; Vernon Place, 37:215;

Washington, 15:182; 17:295, 298; 22:113, 257, 259

theaters, actors, plays, 4:211-12, 301-2; 7:283; 14:73, 133, 175; 15:170; 18:286; 20:127-39, 141, 142-43, 293-309; 21:39-69, 141-76, 240-64; 22:266; 23:106; 28:36; 31:254, 260; 33:41; 34:359; 35:141-42; *see also* names of actors, plays, theaters

transportation, 8:284; 9:284; 15:167, 168, 175; 16:284; 17:172, 178, 180; 19:149-52; 20:292; 22:257-58, 274; 23:230, 245; 37:217, 224, 225; 38:336

water supply, 9:283; 10:391; 14:129; 17:175, 180, 181; 22:253; 23:277; 25:104; 37:224-25; 38:249-58; *see also* Cisterns

see also Bulkhead Bill; Chinese; Customhouse; Hospitals; Orphanages; Portsmouth Square; Prices; Rents; S.F. Fire Dept.; South Park; U.S. Mint; U.S. Post Office; Vigilance Committees; Wharves

San Francisco (ship, 1540), 6:132; 7:267

San Francisco (bark, 1849), 13:20

San Francisco (clipper), 27:292-93

San Francisco (str., 1854), 15:168

"San Francisco," address by James Rolph, Jr., 9:188

San Francisco, Bahia de (Drake's Bay), 11:309; 20:317

San Francisco, Rio de, *see* San Joaquin River

San Francisco Almanac, 26:229, 232

San Francisco & Clear Lake Railroad, 32:368

San Francisco & Colorado River Railroad Co., 26:196

San Francisco and Marysville Railroad, 9:259, 284

San Francisco and Mission Woolen Factory, 10:291

San Francisco and Sacramento Railroad, 4:225

San Francisco & San Joaquin Valley Railway, 9:96

San Francisco and San Jose Railroad, 7:292; 10:389; 14:165-66; 24:262; *see also* Pacific and Atlantic Railroad

San Francisco and Washoe Railroad, 4:265

San Francisco Arguello Boulevard Improvement Club, 31:377

San Francisco Art Association, 21:328, 332; 26:196, 231, 278, 282; 30:138, 139, 148; 33:311; 36:199-202; 37:21-22; 38:1

San Francisco Artists' Union, 36:199

San Francisco Art Union, 28:35

San Francisco Bank, 32:375

San Francisco Baptist Association, 15:164; 27:10, 230, 236

San Francisco Bay, 5:30, 212-13; 11:314-20 *passim*; 14:257; 23:380; 18:142; 25:319-24; in 1776, 14:105-6, 107

in 1792, 14:111, 112-13; in 1845-46, 5:256; 20:214-15; 22:318; in 1820s, 8:140-44 *passim*, 235, 239; 14:123; in 1848-49, 5:6-7, 11-12; 10:403; 13:11, 85, 364-65; 20:291; 23:276; in 1850s, 7:227; 15:176, 369; 20:21; 22:253-54

delayed discovery of, 27:289-96; discovery, 37:297; first ship in, 13:180; 27:293; first steamboat, 14:143-46; fortification of (1860s), 33:29-38; sea-otter and seal hunting in, 12:225-36 *passim;* maps, 13: opp. 61, 181; 14: opp. 111; picture of Indians on, 14: opp. 99; view of, 22: opp. 249

"San Francisco Bay-Area Press Views Russian Aggression in the Far East, 1903-1905," by Ashbrook Lincoln, 30:193-206

San Francisco Bible Society, 15:185; 26:171; 32:123, 129

San Francisco Blues, 9:244, 270; 15:147, 174, 181, 184, 266, 267, 277, 373, 376; 16:82, 345; 17:266; 37:362, 364; 38:17

San Francisco Board of Marine Underwriters, 26:351, 356; 27:79-81, 350

"San Francisco Boyhood, A," by Anson S. Blake, 37:215-28

San Francisco Chamber of Commerce, 17:197; 26:351, 352, 353, 362; 27:68-70, 171; 37:277

San Francisco, City at the Golden Gate, by Gilliam and Gilliam, rev., 40:359-60

San Francisco City College, 35:305

San Francisco Club, 33:376

San Francisco College, 36:348

San Francisco Company, 16:216, 367

San Francisco County Medical Society, 4:188, 190-91

San Francisco Deaf and Dumb Asylum,
10:276, 289, 373; 36:297

San Francisco earthquake and fire of
1906, 3:43; 15:315-18, 321; 20:138-39;
21:183-84, 369-70; 23:374; 24:5-6;
31:295; 33:42-44, 312, 382; 35:161-69;
36:63; 39:182-83

"San Francisco, 1846-48," address by
Anson S. Blake, 6:381-82

San Francisco Female Institute, 17:182;
36:348

San Francisco Fire Dept., 10:381, 393;
15:185, 270, 272, 279, 301, 311-23;
16:343; 17:168, 175-76, 177; 23:69-76
passim

    engines and engine cos.:
        Broderick No. 1, 26:16
        California No. 4, 15:185, 313; 16:285
        Columbian No. 11, 15:185, 271
        Crescent No. 10, 10:369; 15:185
        Deluge, 15:179
        Empire No. 1, 15:185, 311, 372;
            23:71
        Howard No. 3, 10:77, 263, 381, 382;
            15:88, 163, 185, 367, 368; 16:342;
            27:106, 111
        Knickerbocker No. 5, 15:179, 182,
            185
        Manhattan No. 2, 15:172, 179, 180,
            185; 19:192
        Monumental No. 6, 3:37; 15:164,
            166, 174, 180, 185, 313, 372;
            23:71-74; 35:291; 38:305
        Pacific No. 8, 15:167, 185; 16:347
        Pennsylvania No. 12, 15:177, 183,
            185, 313, 367; 16:284-85, 342
        Peterson No. 15, 15:179, 267
        Protection No. 2, 15:311
        Rough Diamond (Young America)
            No. 13, 15:369
        San Francisco, 15:311
        Tiger No. 14, 15:313; 16:342
        Vigilant No. 9, 10:285, 297; 15:185;
            16:79
        Volunteer No. 7, 3:37; 15:185, 364;
            16:338; 17:168, 176
    hook and ladder companies:
        Howard, 2:120
        Lafayette No. 2, 15:183, 185, 305,
            369, 377; 17:178
        St. Francis No. 1, 2:120; 15:183,
            185; 20:294
        Sansome No. 3, 2:120; 15:185;
            38:305-6

    hose company: Hayes Valley No. 3,
        18:333

San Francisco Fire Insurance Co.,
26:265; 27:270

San Francisco Gardeners and Ranchers
Association, 36:110

San Francisco Gas Co., 10:389; 15:370,
373; 16:341; 18:100; 25:344

San Francisco Hall, 15:166, 273, 368;
20:303-8 *passim*; 37:366

"San Francisco Harbor Defense during
the Civil War," by Benjamin F.
Gilbert, 33:229-40

San Francisco House of Refuge, 15:169,
269

San Francisco Hussars, 38:20

"San Francisco in 1851, as Described by
Eyewitnesses," by Lula M. Garrett,
22:253-80

"San Francisco in 1776 and in 1835,"
14:99-101

"San Francisco in 1792," by George
Vancouver, 14:111-20

San Francisco Jockey Club, 15:278

San Francisco Labor Council, 35:60, 64,
150, 152

San Francisco Ladies Orphan Asylum
Society, 22:112, 114

San Francisco Law Library, 15:185, 186,
270; 30:137; 38:315

"San Francisco McAllisters, The,"
by Douglas S. Watson, 11:124-28

San Francisco Medical Journal, 4:174

San Francisco Medical Society, 17:176

San Francisco Minstrels, 9:175, 246,
248, 264, 273, 286, 385; 15:375;
20:305; 21:41, 42, 46, 47, 64; *see also*
Backus Minstrels

San Francisco Mint, *see* United States
Mint

San Francisco Museum of Art, 38:4

San Francisco Musical Association,
25:229-54

San Francisco Normal School and
Teacher's Association, 38:26

San Francisco–Oakland Bay Bridge,
15:379, 381; 22:187; 24:91

"San Francisco One Hundred Years
Ago," address by Charles Caldwell
Dobie, 14:186

San Francisco Opera House company,
21:69

San Francisco Philharmonic Society,
1:9; 15:164, 166; 16:283, 337; 17:82;
25:335, 342; 36:346

San Francisco pilot commissioners, 26:351

San Francisco Police Department, 2:120; 6:12-16 *passim;* 15:88, 163, 165, 176, 180, 181-82, 185, 268, 282; 16:184, 340; 17:168; 37:207

San Francisco Polyclinic, 30:67

San Francisco Press Club, 11:190; 15:182; 20:137

San Francisco: Profile with Pictures, by Conrad, rev., 39:182

San Francisco Public Library, 19:153; 25:14-15, 252; 28:35; phot., 25: opp. 1

San Francisco Remedial Loan Association, 31:298

San Francisco (Verde) River, Ariz., 1:113, 117

San Francisco Sängerbund, 15:164, 166

"San Francisco's Ancient Cannon," by Douglas S. Watson, 15:58-69; as address, 15:90

San Francisco School of Design, 19:101

"San Francisco's Cisterns," by Charles R. Boden, 15:311-23

San Francisco Seamen's Friend Society, 32:119

San Francisco's Golden Era: . . . before the Fire, by Beebe and Clegg, rev., 40:77-79

San Francisco Shipbuilding Co., 31:298

San Francisco's Literary Frontier, by Walker, rev., 18:280-81

" 'San Francisco Society,' from *The Elite Directory* of 1879," ed. Dorothy H. Huggins, 19:225-39

San Francisco Solano, Lower Calif., 31:345, 346, 353

San Francisco Solano Mission, *see* Missions: San Francisco Solano

"San Francisco's Old Spanish Cannon," *see* "San Francisco's Ancient Cannon"

"San Francisco's 176th Birthday," by A. T. Leonard, Jr., 31:279-82

San Francisco Stock Exchange, 31:300

San Francisco Sunday School Union, 15:365

"San Francisco Symphony Orchestra: First Decade," by Leonora W. Armsby, 25:229-54

San Francisco Teachers' Association, 15:169

"San Francisco Teamsters at the Turn of the Century," by Robert M. Robinson, 35:59-69, 145-53

San Francisco Town Journal, 1847-1848, rev., 5:405-7

San Francisco Tract Society, 16:82

San Francisco Turn Gesangverein, 15:166

San Francisco Union Association, 28:35

San Francisco Verein, 38:298

San Francisco Vigilance committees, *see* Vigilance Committee

San Francisco War Memorial Opera House, 25:249-50

San Francisco Woolen Manufacturers, 10:291

San Francisquito, 13:225; 17:24, 176; 19:203

San Gabriel, 32:328; *see also* Mission San Gabriel

San Gabriel, Battle of, 1:146, 148; 3:124-25; 12:335; 13:47, 51-52, 303; 17:124, 344-45, 349; 21:350, 354, 357; 22:51; 33:105-6, 111

San Gabriel (ship), 3:392

San Gabriel Canyon, gold in, 13:336

San Gabriel River, 17:344

Sangalli, Rita, 21:164

Sanger (or Sangers), Capt. (Colorado R., 1855), 22:22, 168

Sanger (place), 25:175

San Gerónimo, Isla de, 8:338, 339

San Gorgonio Pass, 29:242

Sangre de Cristo River, Lower Calif., 15:106, 113

Sanitary Commission, 10:295; 20:265-66; 24:261; 27:11; 29:252; 33:224-25; 40:302-3; ball, 36:35-38; fair, 36:38-39, 40; *see also* Ladies' Christian Commission

San Jacinto (rancheria), 3:242

San Jacinto Valley, 10:214, 215, 217

San Joaquin (riv. str.), 15:51

San Joaquín, Castillo de, 15:60-66 *passim,* 69, 306; 29:271

San Joaquin and Kings River Canal Co., 25:22-23

San Joaquin City, 11:358-59

San Joaquin Engine Co. No. 3, Stockton, 10:45, 68

San Joaquin Guard, 37:362

San Joaquin Pioneer and Historical Museum, 31:276

San Joaquin Republican, Stockton, 20:164-65; 34:342-48

San Joaquin River and Valley, 1:114, 118, 121, 125, 126; 2:35, 44, 183-84, 196-97, 200, 235-36; 3:27, 28, 91; 4:4-9

passim; 8:115; 11:248, 260-62; 13:67-73, 359, 362, 372; 14:22, 106-7; 16:219, 220; 19:312; 21:12, 14, 325; 22:102, 344; 23:60, 127; 24:332-33; 25:2, 17-19; 27:157, 162; 28:121, 333; 34:23; Derby's reconnaissance of, 11:102-5; early visitors to, 10:211-19; Indians, 28:328; jackrabbit drive, 29:365; railroad, 18:22-31; 35:265

San Joaquin Valley Railroad, 35:265

San Joaquin Valley Resources, 10:309

San Jorge, Lower Calif., 6:159; 31:346, 353

San Jorge (ship), 7:137

San Jose, 13:3-34, 148-70; pueblo, 1:16, 24-31 *passim;* 2:279; 4:382; 8:108, 122, 237-38; 12:353; 13:48, 198-99, 209; 14:4-24; 15:224; 17:152, 277, 279; 18:293, 294; 20:236; 30:218; 34:229-30; 40:12, 13; American occupation (1846-50), 2:71; 12:350-51, 353; 14:148-49; 20:216-17; 29:337, 338; in 1848-50, 2:182; 5:18, 26-27, 353-56, 373; 8:72-73; 11:159-63; 12:101; 13:61, 63, 66, 270, 272, 275, 357, 361, 376; 14:20-21, 123, 150-55; 20:123; 22:246; 23:364; 27:370; 28:63, 65; 29:16; 39:41-42, 49; in 1851-55, 6:56; 13:29-30; 14:156-57; 15:269; 20:113; 27:136; 28:65; 30:112, 262; 38:51; in 1860s, 14:165-70; 22:360; archives, 12:126; 14:148; capital and legislature at, 10:164; 11:160, 161; 13:310; 14:152-54; 17:234, 260; 20:110; 23:364, 375; 28:63-64; 38:50-51; churches, 26:165-72 *passim;* 27:130; 34:230; gardens and parks, 10:368; Hall's *History*, 14:24; 38:54; hotels, 5:355; 11:159; 13:279; 14:156; 22:246; insurrections, 15:228, 340, 341; 17:157, 158; newspapers, 14:157, 162; 20:162; 22:223-34, 355-64; 29:91; population, 2:279; 8:238; 14:9, 16-17, 20, 165, 174; prop. site of constitutional convention, 10:138, 139, 148; prop. removal of capital to, 5:285-86; transportation, 13:256-57; 14:160-67; 39:49; Whig party organized at, 20:109; view of, 13: opp. 3

San Jose, Los Angeles Co., 32:328

San Jose (ship), 13:180; 31:110, 123; 37:294

San José, Point, 25:319

San José, Sanjon de, 11:260-61, 262

San Jose Academy, 14:157; 36:349; *see also* University of the Pacific

San José del Cabo, Lower Calif., 8:221; 11:208, 381; 20:213

"San Jose *Mercury* and the Civil War, The," by Benjamin B. Beales, 22:223-34, 355-64

San Jose Normal School, 28:322; 37:44

San Jose Volunteers, 22:360

San Jose Young Men's Library, 38:312

San Jose Zouaves, 40:305

San Juan, Puerto de, 10:323

San Juan (ship), 2:141, 142; 7:146, 235, 239

San Juan Bautista, 1:29, 31; 13:52, 78; 16:239; 18:72-82 *passim;* 21:3, 14; 23:294; 25:126; 29:334, 338, 341; 33:350-53 *passim;* letters from, 2:354-55; 3:183, 184; 4:382-83; *see also* Missions: San Juan Bautista

San Juan Bautista, Lower Calif. 31:351

San Juan Bautista (ship), 7:241-43, 245

San Juan Capistrano, 1:29; 16:227; 17:325; 21:329; *see also* Missions: San Juan Capistrano

San Juan de Dios, 31:116, 123, 124, 261

San Juan de Letran (ship), 7:137, 138, 147

San Juan de los Lagos, Mex., 23:269

San Juan del Sur, Nic., 15:88, 164-73 *passim,* 180-84 *passim,* 266, 269, 271, 277-82 *passim,* 364, 365, 366, 371, 375, 377; 16:79-84 *passim,* 182, 184, 338; 17:75; 33:26; 36:140, 143-45; letter from, 36:139-40

San Juan de Nicaragua, 8:4

San Juan d'Ulloa, Castle of, 16:78; 17:79

San Juan de Ulua, 8:49; 16: No. 1, Pt. 2, p. 5

San Juan Francisco, Puerto de, *see* Tomales Bay

San Juan Pass, 11:103

San Juan Ridge, 10:347, 351; 29:193, 194, 199

San Lazaro (ship), 6:298

San Leandro, 10:50, 73; 15:272; 19:185; 35:241; *see also* Ranchos: San Leandro

San Leandro Creek, 30:219-24 *passim*

San León, Lower Calif., 31:266

San Lucas, Cape, 1:50; 3:308, 337, 368, 380; 6:325; 7:229, 230, 232, 243, 305; 8:30, 31, 32, 64; 11:367-68; 15:355; 22:159-60; 24:64; 28:125, 126; 31:111

San Lucas, Isla de, 7:48, 52, 74, 76

San Lucas, port of, 2:144, 148-57;
3:388, 392, 393; 7:229
San Lucas (ship), 7:146, 148-50, 191
San Luis Obispo, 1:29, 30; 11:249-50;
13:100; 18:163, 258, 265, 270, 277, 278;
newspaper, 32:335; whaling station,
35:238, 239; *see also* Missions: San
Luis Obispo
San Luis Obispo Bay, 11:250; 20:318
San Luis Obispo County, 3:7; 18:268-71
passim; 20: 267-70; Italian-Swiss in,
30:309-11; art. on, 1:152-72
"San Luis Obispo County in Spanish and
Mexican Times," by Helen M.
Ballard, 1:152-72
San Luis Obispo Water Co., 20:269
San Luis Potosí, 16:82; 23:261, 265-68;
38:52
San Marcos, Sierra de (Sierra Nevada),
4:4
San Marcos Pass, 15:285; 29:343;
30:49-51
San Martín (ship), 2:141, 142; 7:137, 239,
244, 245
San Martín, Cape, 7:25, 26, 50, 51, 56,
75-76
San Martín, Islas de, *see* Coronados
San Martín, Sierras de, *see* Santa Lucia
Mountains
San Martin Island, 3:18
San Mateo, 23:247-58; 28:132
San Mateo County, 20:271; 39:303;
40:305
San Mateo County Historical
Association, 22:237
San Miguel, San Luis Obispo Co.,
1:155; *see also* Missions: San Miguel
San Miguel Island, 3:17; 4:154; 7:22,
48, 51, 52, 56, 74, 169, 172, 191, 389;
8:156; 36:223
San Miguel Pass, 11:250-52, 262
San Nicolas Island, 7:169, 172, 191, 389;
8:232-33; 12:232; 18:175
San Pablo, 31:330, 331
San Pablo (ship), 7:146
San Pascual (village), 26:30; *see also*
San Pasqual, Battle of
San Pascual (or Pasqual) Rancho, *see*
Ranchos: Rincon de San Pascual
San Pasqual, Battle of, 1:140-46 *passim,*
240-41, 251; 3:122-23; 4:291; 8:252;
12:335; 13:47, 52, 133, 303, 305;
17:124, 342-47 *passim;* 18:167, 168,
178; 21:335-37, 348, 356; 22:41, 43, 51;
26:94; 30:51, 53; 33:99, 117, 119, 267;

art. on, 25:289-308; 26:21-62; bk. on,
rev., 4:291
San Pedro; San Pedro Bay, 1:235; 3:115,
118, 119; 6:262; 7:47, 73; 8:58,
108, 164, 165, 166; 12:232; 13:125, 128,
195, 204, 205, 223, 303; 14:72, 327-28;
16:66-67, 68; 17:282, 332-40 *passim;*
19:202; 21:224; 22:46; 23:195, 209, 312,
358, 359; 25:128; 26:33; 31:294; 34:38;
illus., 13: opp. 301; railroad, 32:327-48
San Pedro (ship, 1560s), 7:27, 63, 146-51
passim, 185, 239; 31:295; log, 7:152-72
San Pedro (ship, 1594), 3:4; 20:316
San Pedro, Puerto de (Magdalena Bay),
3:388
San Pedro, Puerto de (Monterey Bay),
3:6, 15
San Pedro Lumber Co., 31:294-95
San Pedro y San Pablo (Pedro Valley),
23:250
San Pedro y San Pablo Mission, *see*
Missions: San Pedro y San Pablo
San Pedro y San Pablo River, 3:319,
363, 368, 376, 385
San Prudencio, Lower Calif., 31:348
San Quentin Prison, 9:165, 180, 248,
254-56 *passim,* 273, 277, 284; 10:52,
276, 361, 373; 11:22; 13:88; 15:77, 83,
165, 370; 16:339; 20:141; 29:239; 35:5;
38:27, 337; 37:204; 38:337; 39:293;
40:144; escape attempts, 15:167, 175,
177, 180, 268, 279; 16:285, 336, 339;
38:27; 39:290
San Quintín Bay, Lower Calif.,
12:219-26 *passim,* 237, 238; 31:119, 269,
346
San Rafael, 1:16, 135; 5:34, 39; 10:276;
17:275, 276; 23:252; Indians, 2:58, 59;
newspaper, 29:91; *see also* Missions:
San Rafael
San Rafael, Lower Calif., 31:268, 270,
343
San Ricardo, Arroyo de, 31:264
San Román, Gerónimo de, 7:20, 55
San Roque, Cabo de (Cape
Disappointment), 9:235; 10:326, 327
San Roque, Isla de, 7:326, 327, 383; 8:62
San Sabá Papers, The: ... *Founding of
the San Sabá Mission,* trans. Nathan,
ed. Simpson, rev., 39:271-72
San Salvador, San Bernardino Co.,
12:118, 120; chapel, 3:241-42
San Salvador, Isla de, 7:46, 73, 172
San Salvador (ship), 7:20, 55

San Sebastián (Harper's Well), 10:216;
    34:193-97 *passim*
San Sebastián, Cabo de (Pt. St. George),
    10:329, 330, 334
San Sebastián, Isla de (Santa Cruz I.),
    7:52, 58, 76
San Sebastián, Rio de (Tomales Bay),
    10:337
San Sebastian River (Russian R.), 12:189
Sansevain, *see* Sainsevain
San Simeon, 18:162, 163; 35:238; *see also*
    Ranchos: San Simeon
San Simeon Bay, 11:250
San Simeon Co. (whaling), 35:238
San Simón y Judas, Baia de, 7:343-45
"Sans Souci," San Francisco, 16:183
Santa Agueda (ship), 1:45, 48; 3:309,
    311, 316-61 *passim;* 6:302; 19:240-44
    passim
Santa Ana, Pedro, 9:228
Santa Ana (place), 21:349; 22:47;
    31:293
Santa Ana (ship), 2:140, 159; 7:185, 257,
    302, 309
Santa Anna, Antonio López de, 1:31;
    10:6; 13:101, 129-30; 14:231, 246;
    15:269; 16:81, 83, 283; 17:60, 61, 307;
    18:16, 146, 220; 23:267
Santa Anna Pass, 11:262
Santa Anna y Farias, 16:236, 245
Santa Barbara, 33:278-80; in 1820s,
    23:195, 208, 217; in 1830s, 12:141;
    23:199; in 1840s, 8:108; 11:220; 19:201;
    33:278; in 1870, 25:312, 314
    doctors at, 4:155, 156-58; 17:68, 160
    early settlers, 13:201; 18:168, 175, 176,
        177, 276, 277
    earthquakes, 15:376; 29:91
    govt. and politics: in Mex. period,
        1:26, 29, 31; 11:347; 14:232, 233,
        244; 15:116; 27:333-38; 33:278-80;
        in Amer. period, 18:167; 34:43
    hotels, 2:52; 18:164, 262, 294
    junta at (1846), 6:189; 12:38; 17:279
    letters and procs. from: Alvarado's,
        14:242-43, 244-45, 248-49;
        Robinson's, 23:301-13; others (1850s
        and 1860s), 29:230-31, 232-33;
        34:44-48
    "lost" cannon in, 18:165-66, 177
    Mexican soldiers at, 16:364-65, 367;
        18:164; 33:279; *see also* Presidio of
        Santa Barbara
    military cos. (Amer.), 29:230-33
    Mission, *see* Missions: Santa Barbara

newspaper, 16:84
    port of, 18:168, 175, 178
    Presidio, *see* Presidio of Santa Barbara
    pueblo, 1:29; 33:279
    treatment of foreigners in, 15:123, 238
    U.S. forces at, 1:249, 263; 12:57, 166,
        168; 18:161, 164-65, 174; 19:133;
        21:356; 22:62; 25:128; 30:50-51
Santa Barbara (cutter, 1829), 23:212, 218
Santa Barbara (str., early 1900s), 31:295
Santa Barbara Channel, 7:352; 8:57, 156,
    232; 33:278; *see also* Channel Islands
"Santa Barbara County between Two
    Social Orders," by Walter C. McKain,
    Jr., and Sara Miles, 25:311-18
Santa Barbara County Historical
    Society, 33:278
Santa Barbara Guards, 29:230-31, 233
Santa Barbara Historical Society, 26:249
Santa Barbara Island, 2:329; 8:58;
    (Anacapa I.), 7:352, 388; on map,
    7:350
Santa Barbara Lumber Co., 31:294
Santa Barbara Mission, by Engelhardt,
    rev., 2:252-56
Santa Barbara Mounted Rifles, 29:231-35
    passim
"Santa Barbara's Place in California's
    Background," address by Carl I.
    Wheat, 32:174
Santa Barbara's Royal Rancho, by
    Tompkins, rev., 40:265-66
Santa Catalina, Matías de, 13:155
Santa Catalina Island, 2:49, 329, 330;
    3:6; 7:46, 73, 172, 349-52, 354, 371,
    387; 8:58; 13:204; 23:216; 27:41, 48;
    29:243, 249; on map, 7:350
Santa Catalina Mission, *see* Missions:
    Santa Catalina
Santa Catarina (ship), 3:386
Santa Catharina, Brazil, 2:93-98; 11:158
Santa Clara, 14:162, 168; 17:276; 20:217,
    220; 26:165; 27:130-31; 28:102, 317;
    29:40; 33:65; battle of, 14:149;
    dispatches from, 10:105, 124-26; *see
    also* Missions: Santa Clara
Santa Clara (ship), 8:275
Santa Clara College, 1:10-14 *passim*, 20;
    3:209; 30:249; *see also* University of
    Santa Clara
Santa Clara County, 14:168
Santa Clara Creek, 20:218, 219
Santa Clara Female Seminary, 29:55, 59
"Santa Clara in the Past," address by
    George Fox, 3:208-9

Santa Clara quicksilver mine, 13:78;
31:310, 322; *see also* New Almaden
Mine

Santa Clara Register, 14:157

Santa Clara River, 1:261; Valley, 23:361,
372; 30:52

"Santa Clara's Hundred Years," address
by Gerald J. Geary, 30:377-78

Santa Clara Valley, 5:131; 8:115, 236,
237; 11:136; 14:10, 11, 18, 103-4; 25:2

Santa Cruz, Alonso de, 6:293, 305; 7:174,
175; map by, 3:371

Santa Cruz, 5:133, 360-63, 365; 8:302;
10:139; 12:341, 353, 366; 13:63; 15:125,
224, 227, 235; 18:79; 19:87; 20:256-57;
23:251; 25:129; 26:166, 167; 27:104,
162, 164; 30:3, 4, 5, 8; 33:65; 39:20;
40:12, 13, 27; *see also* Branciforte;
Mission Santa Cruz

Santa Cruz (peninsula of Lower Calif.),
1:39-40, 47-49; 51-52; 6:298; bay and
port of, 1:51; 3:317-19, 322, 332-35,
337, 346, 370, 376; Indians of, 3:327,
331, 335, 346

Santa Cruz (schr., 1846), 11:208; 12:62

Santa Cruz (str., 1859), 22:10, 154, 169

Santa Cruz harbor, 7:25, 51, 75

Santa Cruz Island, 2:49, 329; 3:17, 18;
7:48, 52, 58, 74, 76, 353, 389; 8:156;
14:265; 21:318; 29:81

Santa Cruz Mountains, 4:3; 5:358; 18:79;
27:259-60; 28:299; 29:51, 57

Santa Fe, 1:117; 2:7, 10; 10:27-39 *passim*,
306, 408; 12:113; 13:388; 18:349, 350,
351; 20:341, 342; 34:128, 132, 133, 134,
137

Santa Fe expedition, 11:293; 18:245, 310;
see also Doniphan, Alexander W.

Santa Fe Railway, 12:184; 31:152-53;
32:7

Santa Fe trail, 2:7, 10; 4:308; 10:303;
23:298; 24:17; bk. on, rev., 10:406-7;
see also Spanish trail

Santa Fe Trail to California, by Powell,
ed. Watson, rev., 10:406-7

Santa Gertrudis (ship), 10:315

Santa Guadalupe Mine, 13:78

Santa Inés Mission, *see* Missions: Santa
Ynez

Santa Inez, Rio de, 7:369, 393; 8:28

Santa Lucia Mountains, 1:157; 7:25, 50,
56, 75, 356; 8:57; 36:222-23

Santa Margarita, San Luis Obispo Co.,
33:263; 36:14, 15; *see also* Mission

asistencias and chapels; Ranchos;
Santa Margarita

Santa Margarita formation, 36:14, 20

Santa Margarita River, 36:2, 4

Santa María (Sonoma, 1835), 16:240

Santa María (Indian, 1846), 29:342

Santa María, Vincente de, 2:321, 327

Santa Maria, San Diego Co., 17:340, 341;
21:301; 26:27, 28, 39

Santa Maria Creek and Valley, 26:24, 26,
52

Santa María de Jesús (ship), 2:141, 142

Santa María de la Luz, Cabo de
(Tillamook Head), 10:328

Santa María del Parral (ship), 7:135

Santa Maria Gas Co., 31:304

Santa María Rancho, *see* Ranchos: Valle
de Pamo

Santa Monica, 31:30

Santa Monica (ship), 31:295

Santa Monica Rancho, *see* Ranchos: El
Cajon

Santa Paula (ship), 17:94

Santa Rosa (place), 16:235, 236, 246, 306,
307, 369, 370; 17:50, 237-38, 276;
29:149; 30:363; letter from, 27:307-9;
library assoc., 38:312; newspaper,
21:137-38

Santa Rosa (ship), 1:176

Santa Rosa Island, 3:17; 7:48, 52, 74, 76,
389; 8:156

Santa Rosa Tannery, 33:61

Santa Teresa (place), 28:253; 29:134

Santa Ynez, 16:83; *see also* Missions:
Santa Ynez

Santa Ynez Mountain, 23:362

Santa Ysabel, *see* Mission asistencias and
chapels; Ranchos

Santa Ysabel, Lower Calif., 31:344

Santa Ysabel Valley, 25:298

Santee (place), 26:24

San Telmo, Lower Calif., 31:118, 268,
270

Santiago, Juan José Norberto de, 23:371;
37:127; letters to, 37:118-23, 241-49

Santiago (ship, 1526), 7:135

Santiago (ship, 1540), 6:312; 7:137

Santiago (frigate, 1774), 9:203-42 *passim*

Santiesteban, Antonio, 10:28

Santillan, José Prudencio, land claim of,
15:364-66; 17:83; 18:250; 19:359;
21:322, 331; 23:245; *see also* Bolton
and Barron

Santo Domingo River, Lower Calif.,
31:269, 270

Santos, Antonio, 15:60
Santos, María de los, 13:200
Santos Reyes, Rio de los (Kings R.), 4:4
Santo Tomás, Lower Calif., 22:56, 57, 58; 27:206
Santo Tomás (ship, 1540), 3:316, 317; 6:308
Santo Tomás (ship, 1602), 7:263, 264, 300-59 *passim*, 379-91 *passim*; 8:43; 36:228, 230
Santo Toribio, valley in Lower Calif., 31:343
San Vicente, Lower Calif., 31:353
San Ysidoro, valley of, Lower Calif., 31:264, 265, 269
Sapatarra (Indian), 16:261
Saracen (ship), 26:74
Saragossa Guards, Marysville, 38:22
Sarah (brig, 1849), 23:226
Sarah (schr., 1864), 22:24, 170; 27:68
Sarah and Caroline (ship), 14:317, 318, 342; 15:347, 351; 23:323, 326, 327, 333, 334
Sarah G. Merrill (ship), 35:47
Sarah Sands (ship), 2:107
Saranac (ship), 27:179; 33:236
Saratoga (ship), 2:250, 251
Sardinas, Puerto de, 7:49, 52, 56, 57
Sardines, 7:307; 31:157-58; 36:222
Sardinians, 16:341; 17:85; 38:338
Sardou, Victorien, 21:246-47
Sargeant (Marysville, 1851), 15:29
Sargent, Aaron Augustus, 4:251-52, 253, 256, 268; 9:116; 10:64; 17:320; 24:213, 217, 219; 27:97, 102, 346; 30:141; 38:318
Sargent, Ben F., 34:65
Sargent, D., 27:226
Sargent, David G., 9:138, 140, 145, 148, 155, 166, 167, 174
Sargent, Joshua C., 10:189, 394
Sargent, Grace Tompkins (Mrs. Marston Cleaves), 38:183, 283; ed. "Forgotten Mother of the Sierra," 38:157-63, 219-28
Sargent, Thomas D., 34:256
Sarmiento, José María, 19:212, 216
Sarmiento de Gamboa, Pedro, 3:4, 5, 20; 6:316; 7:228, 232, 253
Sarría, Vincente Francisco, 1:167; 8:151; 9:277; 13:209; 16:109, 114-16; 23:5, 7-8, 374
Sarsfield Guard, San Francisco, 16:336
Sartori, Joseph F., 37:267-68, 348
Sartwell (Marysville, 1851), 15:29

Sartwell, Dugald Stewart, 35:329, 332
Sastise, *see* Shasta
Sasty (Sorty, Sarty) River, 22:103; 23:30, 138; *see also* Klamath River
Satakarass, Pierre, 22:206, 222; 23:38, 125, 134, 139
Sather, Pedar, 9:72; 15:272; 19:232; 37:215
Satinstatesqui (Sonora, 1851), 35:316
Satterlee, John, 9:26; 15:186, 269; 16:285; 21:324; 27: opp. 97; 34:258
Saucelito Water Co., 15:170
Sauer, Carl Ortwin, address, "Plants as Documents of Human History," 22:374
Saunders (Gold Lake, 1849), *see* Stoddard, J. R.
Saunders, Mrs. (Mountain View, 1853), 29:41
Saunders, Col. (Marysville, 1857), 9:355; 10:273
Saunders, C. R., 13:32
Saunders, Charles Francis, *The Southern Sierras of California*, rev., 3:92
Saunders, Elizabeth, 21:63
Saunders, Fred, 35:333
Saunders, George, 27:368
Saunders, John H., 25:344
Saunders, Joseph, 2:99, 113-21 *passim*
Saunders, W. A., 25:26
Saunderson, Edward, 13:31
Sausal Creek, Alameda Co., 27:71-72
Sausalito, 3:30; 13:235, 238; 15:62-63, 170, 181; 17:223, 274; 19:197; 20:220; 23:372
Savage, C. R., 36:97, 105
Savage, Frank M., 31:56
Savage, Hiram N., 36:156
Savage, James D., 1:272; 2:197, 199; 4:12; 5:328-31; 8:84; 21:362; 23:368, 376; art. on, 28:323-41; phot. of trading post, 28: opp. 326
Savage, Morgan, 28:323, 324
Savage, T. B., 22:251
Savage, Thomas, 26:52; 32:267; letter, 29:160
Savage Mine, 11:64
Savannah (ship), 2:168, 169, 354, 356; 3:105-25, 178-79, 184; 7:82; 8:71; 10:124; 12:57, 58, 166, 168; 13:303; 14:149, 327, 345; 15:63; 17:125, 278, 282, 331, 334, 339, 340; 18:72-82 *passim;* 20:31, 215-20 *passim*, 232; 21:12, 14, 21, 224, 350; 22:53; 25:122-26

passim; 26:49; 30:21, 43-45; 34:117, 119; 36:310

Save-the-Redwoods League, 29:185; 33:362

Savelle, Max, address, "Cabrillo and California," 21:374

Savings and Loan Society, San Francisco, 26:229, 232

Savings Union Bank & Trust Co., 32:375

Saw Mill Cottage, Yuba Co., 9:52

Sawmills, 8:356; 9:52; 11:228; 18:295, 297, 311, 314; 23:191; 30:7, 8; 34:222; 37:232; 38:59-71; in Amador Co., 18:22; 20:181, 184; Bale's, 18:70; 28:266, 267; on Bear Cr., 11:119; Branch's, 18:259; Cottage, 52:70; in Grass Valley, 6:336; Hampshire, 8:341, 347, 357; 9:52; Maple Springs, 9:72; in Marin Co., 27:261; in Mendocino Co., 21:383; 27:220, 226; 30:163, 166; in Mono Co., 26:236, 243, 244-45; Moonshine, 8:357; Mud Springs, 15:377; Pine Grove, 9:52, 70; Ramirez', 9:62, 75; in S.F., 15:372; in Santa Cruz Mts., 5:358; 16:143; 18:295; 27:162, 164, 260; 29:57; Stephen Smith's, 13:34-35; 16:143; 18:65-67, 69; Washington, 9:52, 70; Yount's, 2:55; 5:273; *see also* Sutter's sawmill

Sawyer (Napa Co., 1870s), 35:155

Sawyer, A. F., 14:75; 16:283

Sawyer, Charles H., 1:12

Sawyer, E. D., 19:156

Sawyer, Edmund Ogden, Jr., ed. *Our Sea Saga: The Wood Wind Ships,* rev., 8:384

Sawyer, Edwin, 6:353

Sawyer, Frederick A., 11:8-9

Sawyer, J., 34:53

Sawyer, Jesse, 6:335

Sawyer, Lorenzo, 9:26, 29, 42, 174; 10:64; 16:79; 17:169; 19:261; 28:236; 29:202; 32:200; *Way Sketches,* rev., 5:404-5

Sawyer, Otis V., 33:68

Sawyer, Robert W., 22:384

Sawyer, Thomas S., 24:37

Sawyer Documents, 1:189-90; 3:183-84

Sawyer's Bar, 34:269-70; 40:66

Saxony (ship), 34:337

Saxton, J. B., 9:198, 200; 15:164

Saxton, Rufus, 31:43

Sayas, Juan de, *see* Martínez y Zayas

Saylor, Mme. (actress, 1891), 20:136, 141

Sayres (New York Flat, 1855), 8:342

Sayres, Jimmy, 7:115

Sayton (S.F., 1855), 15:280

Saywood (S.F., 1850), 2:116

Sbriglia, Giovanni, 21:68

S. B. Wheeler (riv. str.), 25:327

Scaglione, John, 28:188; ed. "Ogden's Report of His 1829-1830 Expedition," 28:117-24

Scalchi, Sofia, 35:142

Scales Diggings, 11:243

"Scalpel under Three Flags in California, The," by George D. Lyman, 4:142-206

Scammell, J. M., 29.284; "Military Units in Southern California, 1853-1862," 29:229-49

Scammon, Charles Melville, 26:14-16; 33:2, 6, 8, 11, 12, 149-52; 35:239

Scandia (ship), 30:302

Scandinavia, emigration from, 20:67-68, 75-76

Scandinavian Colony, 25:169-70

Scannell, David, 8:367, 369-70; 14:353, 357-58, 360, 413; 15:249, 252-53, 314, 322; 16:80-82, 84, 344, 346, 347; 17:82-84, 172-78 *passim;* 21:27; 23:76; 26:16-17; 37:157, 159-62; phot., 15: opp. 316

Scarpa, George, 17:254-55

Scellen, John D., 9:46

Scenorama, 10:174

Schadt, L., 8:358

Schaefer, Glenn A., obit., 18:382-83

Schaeffer, Frank B., 25:336, 343-44; 37:363

Schaeffer (or Schaffer), John B., 9:26, 27, 109; 11:9; 15:281

Schallenberger, Moses, 1:234; 4:171

Schandorf, Rudolph, 15:277

Scharrenberg, Paul, 35:153

Schedel, George, 33:374

Scheel, Fritz, 25:229

Schegerle, Mrs. Kamerer, 29:119

Schell, Alex. M., 15:269, 270, 271

Schenck, Mrs., *see* Pike, Naomi L.

Schenck, James F., 8:7, 9; 10:376, 389; quoted, 29:274

Scherer, James Augustin Brown, addresses: "Cotton and Gold," 5:205-6; "Forgotten Voyages," 18:85-86; "Jessie Benton Frémont," 21:278; bk. rev. by, 18:369-71; obit., 23:92-93; *The First Forty-Niner,* rev., 4:392-94; *Lion of the Vigilantes,* rev., 18:371-73

Scherrebach, *see* Sherreback

Scheyer, Galka, 38:3
Schiel, Jacob H., *Journey through the Rocky Mountains*, rev., 38:80-83
Schilling, August, 25:86, 249
Schilling (A.) & Co., 23:187; 25:86; 35:146
Schlegel, Gustave, 14:47-56 *passim*
Schleiden, William (or Waldemar), 30:257, 357, 363, 366
Schlesinger, Mrs. Amanda, obit., 40:274
Schlesinger, Bert, 19:67; 40:275
Schlesinger's Literary Depot, 30:362
Schlichtman, Mrs. Emil, 25:95
Schliemann, Heinrich, 12:303
Schliemann, Louis, 12:303
Schloss, Mrs. Aaron, 36:253
Schlosser, Levi, 16:131, 136
Schlosser, Theodore, 16:127, 136, 142
Schmadcke, Richard and Margaret (Bell), 28:294
Schmidt (Yuba Co., 1850s), 12:303
Schmidt, Edward, 30:226-27, 230
Schmidt, Jacob, 11:42; 16:138
Schmidt, John (on *Dollart*, 1862), 9:320
Schmidt, John (Berkeley, 1868), 17:44; 27:345
Schmidt, John C., 30:226
Schmidt, Karl, 12:191, 194, 236, 242
Schmidt, Matt, 40:144
Schmidt, Milton L., 11:8, 9
Schmidt, Winfield, 17:49
Schmidt Tract, Berkeley, 30: opp. 225
Schmiedell, Henry, 14:413; 33:374
Schmulowitz, Nat, 22:95
Schmitz, Eugene E., 33:40
Schneider, Eva, 28:292
Schnell's Japanese colony, 27:280
Schnitzer, Ewald W., 36:93; coauth. "The Last Will and Testament of Stephen J. Field," 36:41-55
Schnitzer, Llano, 40:222
Schoemann, Otto, 27:173
Schofield, John M., 28:161
Scholars' Journal, 16:336
Scholfield, Nathan, 25:115, 119, 120
Scholfield, Socrates, 25:120
Scholl, C. P., 12:302
Scholl (or School), C. R., letters from, 24:124-25, 129
Schoolcraft, Henry A., 11:107, 121; 40:125
Schoolhouse Creek, Berkeley, 31:331
Schooling, William L., 24:126, 356
Schools and teachers, 1:17; 14:75; 32:127-28; in Alameda Co., 4:210, 211;

17:44, 45, 48; 19:76; 31:331; 32:127; 36:349; Benicia, 24:63, 64, 165, 179; 27:67, 303; 29:55, 59; 30:262; 36:349; Brownsville, 8:356; Columbia, 32:128; Crescent City, 32:166-68; Jackson, 32:128; Los Angeles, 13:206, 215, 223, 334; Marysville, 9:372, 395; 10:251, 260, 264, 287; 14:399; 15:53; Monterey Co., 3:181-82; 8:120; 15:286-87; 16:103-6; 35:109-10; Placerville, 15:190; Sacramento, 10:287, 291; 36:349; San Francisco (*see* San Francisco: schools); San Jose, 14:14, 23-24, 157; 35:109; 36:349; San Juan Bautista, 8:384; Santa Clara, 29:55, 59; 36:349; Sonoma, 8:120, 284; 36:349; Ventura Co., 16:291, 298, 300, 336; 17:28-33 *passim*, 40; for young ladies, 10:251, 264, 287; 17:182; 28:34; 29:59; 36:348; 36:349; *see also* Education; Mills College; Young Ladies' Seminary
Schoonmaker, Jean (Howard), *see* McDuffie, Mrs. Duncan
Schorer, John, 9:370, 374
Schoyer, R., 15:374
Schraubstadter, W., 10:390
Schreiber, Charles, 18:174
Schreiber, W. G., 34:158, 169
Schuchardt, William H., 25:382
Schulte, John G. W., 9:27
Schultz (or Schultze; Yuba Co., 1856), 9:52, 59, 67, 132-39 *passim*, 143, 159, 163, 165
Schultz (or Schultze), Mrs. (Yuba Co., 1856), 9:66, 67, 132, 135, 137, 146, 267
Schultz, Mrs. (S.F., 1862), 10:374
Schultz, Carl (painter, 1878), 35:49
Schultz, Dr. Carl (L.A., 1904), 31:24
Schultz, J. S., 26:247
Schultz & Palmer, 25:119
Schultze, John, 9:166
Schulz, Fischer & Mohrig, 36:98
Schumacher, John, 13:319; 32:330
Schumann-Heink, Mme. Ernestine, 25:236
Schurman, Jacob Gould, 37:41
Schussler, Hermann, 19:187; 40:33
Schutz, F. W., 25:190
Schuyler, Daniel, 31:154-55
Schuyler, T., 35:296, 303
Schwabacher, James H., 20:288
Schwartz (Swart or Swat), George, 27:136
Schwartz, John, *see* Swart

Schwartz, Sidney L., 26:190; obit. of Charles R. Blyth, 38:360-61
Schwartz Hotel, St. Louis, Calif., 19:297
Schwarzman, Richard C., bk. rev. by, 40:165-68
Schwegerle, Mme. E., 10:390
Schweitzer, Melville, 6:286-87; 11:184; collection of, 11:184-87
Schweitzer, Mrs. Melville (Lolita Heyneman), 6:286-87; 11:184; 19:95
Schwenninger, Andreas, 40:49
Schwenninger, Martin Francis, 40:49-67
Scoby, Joseph W., 9:244, 369; 10:52, 70
Scofield, D. G., 17:115
Scoggins, James D., 40:229
Scola, Carlo, 15:183
Scollan, John, 18:262, 264
Sconcia, Olivia, 21:68
Scotchler, J. B., 27:66
Scotchman's Creek, 3:140, 141
Scotia (ship), 29:218
Scott (Grass Valley, 1849), 11:244
Scott, Alexander, 29:109
Scott, Alice, 25:49
Scott, Charles E., 28:59, 66
Scott, Charles Lewis, 9:104, 106, 263, 272; 11:11, 12, 25; 29:195; 32:146, 148, 153, 157
Scott, D. B., 7:14; 9:57, 78, 168, 256, 362, 363
Scott, Edward L., 37:13
Scott, George Alexander, 28:190
Scott, Gustave A., 17:82; 24:263; 36:208, 300
Scott, Harvey Whitefield, 21:134, 139
Scott, Henry L., 28:215, 216, 219, 229; 33:255
Scott, Henry T., 25:43, 44; 31:302
Scott, Hugh, 34:164
Scott, Irving Murray, 19:156; 25:42-51 *passim;* 30:344; 31:337
Scott, Irving Murray, Jr., 31:75
Scott, James ("Diego"), 1:170; 8:106; 11:264; 17:26, 145, 253; 18:172, 176; 28:113, 115, 246, 255; 36:11
Scott, John (Sonoma, 1846), 17:240; 24:58
Scott, John (Yuba Co., 1857), 9:153
Scott, Jonathan, 13:315, 318, 330, 335, 338
Scott, Joseph, 21:384; 28:190; obit., 37:183-84
Scott, Mrs. Joseph (Bertha Roth), 21:384

Scott, Levi, 1:119; 4:281, 340; 25:256, 260-63 *passim*
Scott, M. Ainsley, 21:166, 169
Scott, N., 6:374
Scott, N. F., 26:247
Scott, Olivia (Castro), 9:188, 190
Scott, R. J., 21:226, 228, 235
Scott, R. M., 16:208
Scott, William (U.S.M.C., 1847), 33:105
Scott, William (S.F., 1861), 27:152-53
Scott, William Anderson, 1:273; 10:279, 293; 15:164, 167, 267, 270, 365, 376; 16:208, 336, 345; 17:173; 19:232; 20:166-67; 22:39; 29:107, 116-22 *passim*, 126, 377; 31:246; 32:134, 139, 233; 38:301; 39:292-93, 303, 304; art. on, 27:149-56; bks. by, mentioned, 17:173; 22:38; 30:357, 358
Scott, William S., 15:88
Scott, William W., 4:376; 17:220, 240; 19:125, 127, 140; 24:58; 25:126; 26:113, 115, 119, 122, 128
Scott, Gen. Winfield, 11:18, 20, 305; 16:304, 307, 308; 17:307; 19:236; 23:259, 280, 359; 28:200, 204, 216, 221, 222, 225, 230; 38:18, 28
Scott, Winfield (1929), address, "Redwood in the History of California," 8:283
Scott-Siddons, Mary F., 21:241, 243
Scott Bar, Siskiyou Co., 28:1, 4
Scottish Rite Hall, San Francisco, 25:235
Scott's Bar, Yuba Co., 8:342, 348, 359; 16:84(?)
Scott's Bluffs, 3:51; 4:330-31; 6:115; 22:132, 148
Scottsburg, Ore., 25:256, 257, 263
Scott's Valley, Lake Co., 32:364
Scott Valley, Siskiyou Co., 6:70-71; 26:201, 202, 302; *see also* Fort Jones
Scout of the Philippines, The (play), 34:364
Scoville, Henrietta (Linden), 30:225, 228, 230
Scranton, H. L., 12:92, 102, 104
Scranton & Freanor, 13:6
Scranton & Smith, 12:92, 104; 13:6
Screech, Joseph, 4:12
Scribner, T. H., 13:32
"Scrimshawing," 32:229
Scripps, Edward Wyllis, 35:362; 36:72
Scripps, Ellen Browning, 36:78, 149
Scripps College, 21:191; 36:78, 149-50
Scripps Institution of Oceanography, 36:72

Scriver, Charles, 18:174
Scully, W. O. H., 13:85
Scurry, W. R., 34:138
Scurvy, 4:143, 151, 181; 7:359-60, 366-67, 370, 374-75, 376; 9:214, 230, 232; 11:36; 15:167; 19:126, 127, 141; 20:42; 24:134, 345, 352; 25:106; 29:213, 215; 31:353; 33:103, 268, 337; 34:97; 36:214, 230-31, 237
Sea Bird (ship), 6:17; 8:276; 13:325; 14:178; 15:281, 371, 374, 375; 16:337, 341; 29:232; 31:42
Seabough, Samuel, 27:274
Seabury (Brandy City, 1857), 9:165
Seabury, A. M., 29:291
Seabury, C. P., 15:178
Seabury, Gertrude, 29:294
Seabury, Pardon G., 34:258-59, 333, 334
Seabury, Joel H., 9:132, 133, 134, 346(?), 365(?)
Sea Gull (ship), 2:123-27; 25:112
Sea gulls, *see* Water birds
Sea King (ship), *see* Shenandoah
Seale, Henry W., 7:412
Seale, Mrs. Henry W. (née Carr), obit., 7:412
Sea lions, 12:194, 228, 229-30; 13:10; 29:41, 42, 56; *see also* Seals
"Seal of the California Supreme Court, The," by J. N. Bowman, 33:73-75
Seals and seal industry, 3:326; 8:57, 135, 233, 289; 12:217-239; 17:23; 23:24; *see also* Sea lions
Sealy (Sierra Madre, 1880s?), 31:18
Sealy, Caroline, 33:82
Seaman, H. J., 30:361
Seaman, Job M., 21:164
Seaman, Victor Waldron, 22:95
Seaman's Reading Room and Library, San Francisco, 38:306
Seamen's Bethel, San Francisco, 15:366; 16:182
Seamen's Friend Society, 32:119
Sea Nymph (ship), 27:293; 29:109; 39:296
Sea otter, 1:167; 2:37, 45-51 *passim*, 298; 6:102; 8:233, 320; 10:326, 330; 12:191, 194, 217-39, 304; 17:23, 57, 243-44; 23:302-14 *passim*, 318; phot., 17: opp. 243
"Sea Otter Returns to the California Coast, The," by Augustin S. Macdonald, 17:243-44
Searby, William M., 32:250

Search for Authority in California, The, by Hansen, rev., 40:253-55
Searchlight (ship), 22:163, 167
Searchlight, Nev., 3:169
Searle, Dan, 38:76
Searle, John, 16:341; 17:85, 254-55
Searles, Dennis, 17:110-17 *passim*, 210; 18:201; phot., 17: opp. 111; of house, opp. 99
Searles, Edward F., 36:200
Searles, Mrs. Edward F., *see* Hopkins, Mrs. Mark
Searles, John Wemple, 17:110-17 *passim*, 210; phot., 17: opp. 111; of house, opp. 99
Searles, Mrs. John Wemple (Mary Covington), 17:117
Searles Lake, 17:99, 110-12, 116, 209; 28:201, 203, 215
Searls, Niles, 3:160; 10:248, 261, 385; 18:288; 20:82
Searls, Robert M., 18:288
Searles Lake, 17:99, 110-12, 116, 209; 28:201, 203, 215
Sears, Capt. (Colorado R., 1870), 22:173
Sears, Franklin, 5:117, 120, 121, 125; 11:84; 19:141; 30:54
Sears, Harry, 3:161
Sears, John, 17:220, 240; 24:58; 29:335, 336, 339
Sears, Mrs. John, 29:265
Sears, Sarah P., 28:294
Sears, William H., 3:153; 34:51-52, 56
Sears' Diggings, *see* St. Louis, Sierra Co.
Sears Union Water Co., 11:242
Searsville, 31:300
Sea Serpent (ship), 16:182
Seavey, Clyde L., 36:252-53
Seaward, John, 12:217; 14:217, 402
Seawell, Emmet, Address, "General Vallejo, the Man of Vision," 5:415-16
Seawell, Washington, 24:52
Sea Witch (ship), 13:11-12; 20:31, 46; 39:331
Sebastian (Indian, 1774), 34:194
Sebastian, William K., 19:21, 345
Sebastian, Cape, 10:329, 330
Sebastopol, Nevada Co., 3:148, 150-51, 158-60
Secessionists, 10:274, 289, 296, 358, 360, 368, 369; 15:206; 19:360; 20:160; 22:358, 360-61; 31:196, 199; 32:223; 34:57; 39:291, 301; 40:309-25; *see also* Confederate

Second Baptist Church, San Francisco, 15:171, 179, 186, 266

Second Congregational Church, San Francisco, 34:65

"Second Incumbency of Jacques A. Moerenhout, The," ed. and trans. Abraham P. Nasatir, 27:141-48, 203-14, 353-60; 28:69-79, 151-60

Secor, Charles F., 33:236

Secretary (ship), 15:88, 183, 273

Secret Diggings, 11:240

Secret Pass in Ruby Range, 32:198

Secret societies, Confederate, 20:154-56

Secret Springs House, 7:14

Secularization of Missions, 1:27, 28-29, 168-69; 5:361; 12:130; 13:106, 114; 15:114; 16:236-42 *passim;* 18:320; 23:305, 331, 371, 375; 24:290, 293, 307-8; 27:337; 37:66-68, 254

Security Savings Bank, San Diego, 35:361

Security Trust and Savings Bank, Los Angeles, 37:267

Security Trust Co., Bakersfield, 32:5

Seeley, Charles A., 29:291

Seeley, J. W., 26:127

Seely (Camptonville, 1854), 8:203

Seely, David, 12:118-19, 120; 14:61

Seely, Thomas W., 16:66, 67

See Yup Tong, 27:23

Segerstrom, Charles Homer, 28:378; obit., 25:376-77

Segerstrom, Mrs. Charles Homer (Carrie E. Inch), 25:377

Segerstrom, Donald Inch, 25:377; 28:378; address on James Wood Coffroth, 35:77

Segerstrom, Pearl N., 40:256; bk. revs. by, 38:378-79; 40:255-56

Segourney (Nevada Co., 1870s), 18:356

Seguin, Brandt, 15:166

Seguin, Edward, 24:263

Segura, Eduardo, 37:201

Segura, José María, 13:126-28; 17:328-29

Seibert, Charles, 17:106, 107, 209, 213, 214

Selby, T. O., 6:164-65

Selby, Thomas H., 17:177; 19:232; 27:71; 37:215

Selby, Mrs. Thomas H., 27:152, 154, 156

Selby Smelting Works, 32:10, 18-19, 24, 26-27

Selden (or Seldon), Edward A., 33:252

"Selected Letters of Osgood Church

Wheeler," ed. Sandford Fleming, 27:9-18, 123-31, 229-36, 301-9

Selfridge, George, 9:147, 177

Selfridge, Richard, 9:149

Selfridge, Thomas O., 33:233-34; 40:306

Selfridge, W. O., 9:68, 158

Selfridge & Co., 9:135, 160

Seligman, A., 11:50; 27:170

Selina (ship), 21:123

Seliuppert's Saloon, San Francisco, 15:371

Selleck, Silas, 9:99, 102

Selma (place), 25:175

Selover, Abia A., 15:157, 180; 16:345; 17:82, 173-74; 28:64; 37:152, 154

Selover & Sinton, 15:171, 173; 16:182; 17:168, 182; 28:64, 68; 30:258

Selvaggio di California, Il (play), 19:219

Semaine Littéraire, La, 39:149-50, 350

"Semi-Centennial of April 18, 1906, San Francisco," address by Lawrence W. Harris, 35:161-69

Semi-Weekly Observer, Placerville, 12:323, 329

Semple, Charles D., 6:155-56; 9:103; 25:340

Semple, Robert Baylor, 1:73, 75, 97, 138-39; 3:114; 5:264; 10:16, 151, 152, 299; 11:130, 131, 133, 389; 12:129; 13:108, 267, 278; 15:180; 16:5, 340; 17:220-21, 224, 231-34 *passim*, 296-302 *passim;* 18:73, 76, 79, 83; 19:6-7; 20:103, 150, 152, 153, 233; 24:58, 63; 25:124, 128-29, 327, 328, 340; 26:109, 164; 27:44, 61-62; 29:262-65 *passim*, 270, 271; 30:6; 31:211, 216, 217; 35:97, 104, 201; 40:124; art. on, 6:130-58; fac. affidavit, 6: opp. 141; fac. sig., 10: opp. 159; phot., 6: opp. 130

Semple, Mrs. Robert Baylor (later Mrs. Van Winkle), *see* Cooper, Frances

Semple family, 6:130-32

Señan, José Francisco de Paula, 16:111, 114-15

Senasac, Arthur Thomas, 31:287

Senator (ship), 2:137, 201; 3:163; 6:240; 10:381; 12:92; 15:279; 17:176, 177, 266; 18:10; 20:30, 275; 22:259; 24:166, 180, 272; 25:109, 338; 26:328; 27:302; 28:59, 66, 360; 30:157, 172; 31:59, 60; 33:301; 34:71; art. on, 16:61-78; illus., 16: opp. 61

Senator, The (play), 34:367

" 'Senator,' The: The Biography of a

Pioneer Steamship," by John H.
Kemble, 16:61-70
"Senator Benton Lays His Plans," by
Francis M. Wheat, 13:150-54
"Senatorial Election of 1893 in
California, The," by Harold F.
Taggart, 19:59-73
Senator Mine, 15:19
Senators, U.S., direct election of, 5:283
Seneca House, Yuba Co., 10:171, 194
Señora, Rio de la, 7:21, 22
Sentinel Rock, Yosemite, 1:278
Sentinel Rock (Half Dome), 1:278, 279,
280
Seoul (Korea) Mining Co., 30:205
Septin Hill, Amador Co., 38:25
Sepúlveda, Diego, 12:114, 116;
14:233-34; 25:131
Sepúlveda, Dolores, 33:249
Sepúlveda, Encarnación, 21:320
Sepúlveda, Enrique, 19:215
Sepúlveda, Fernando, 13:349
Sepúlveda, Francisco, 13:212, 313, 350
Sepúlveda, José, 13:327, 341
Sepúlveda, José Andrés, 13:322-23, 350
Sepúlveda, Juan (1850s, 1861), 13:327,
330; 29:234, 236, 238, 245
Sepúlveda, Juan (1870s), 20:346
Sepúlveda, Juan María, 29:244
Sepúlveda, Rafael, 13:203
Sepúlveda, Vincenta, 19:208
Sepúlveda, Ygnacio, 13:327, 350, 351
Sequoia, *see* Big trees; Redwoods
Sequoia National Forest, 4:51
Sequoia National Park, 4:15, 44, 45;
10:309-10; 38:162
Sequoyah (Indian), 3:300
Sergas de Esplandian, Las, 1:53-55;
6:167, 296; 19:220; 28:23
Serieuse, La (ship), 20:71; 35:315
Sermans brothers, 6:52
Serra, Antonio and Margarita (Ferrer),
31:281
Serra, Junípero (Miguel José), 1:142,
143, 144-45; 4:142-45 *passim;* 10:295;
13:202; 14:4, 108; 20:236, 238, 239;
23:371; 28:19; 30:316, 318-19, 381;
31:111; 33:278; 37:292-94
birthplace, 30:376; presented to San
Francisco, 11:79-81, 188, 280-88;
14:191; 31:281
death, 13: opp. 154, 155-58
founder of Missions, 1:160, 161, 162;
11:274; 13: opp. 154; 23:372, 374;
31:113; 36:3

letter from Monterey, 11:275-79
Palou's Life of, 13:180; 14:99, 102-10
port., 13: opp. 155
Serrano, Florencio, 35:105
Serrano, Francisco (16th cent.), 7:132,
134, 187
Serrano, Francisco (1799), 13:203
Serrano, José Antonio, 26:31, 42, 58, 60
Serrini, J. R., 4:172
Serroot (Yuba Co., 1857), 9:160
Servín, Manuel P., trans. "The
Instructions of Viceroy Bucareli to
Ensign Juan Pérez," 40:237-48
Sessa, Duquesa de, 5:197
Sessar Cordero, Manuel, 7:390
Sessions, Kate, 32:184; 35:358
Setchell, Dan, 21:148, 151, 164
Settle, Raymond W., address,
"California Phases of the Pony
Express," 34:87
"Settlement of California, The,"
address by Fletcher A. Cutler,
4:399-400
Settlemier, Charles and Augusta
(Carnahan), 26:282
Settlemier, George F., 25:38
Settlemier, Weston H., 25:383; obit.,
26:282
Settlers and Miners Party, 9:44, 115;
15:377; 16:306
Settlers and Miners' Tribune,
Sacramento, 20:333
Settlers' League of California, 15:365,
366, 368, 372
Seven Cities of Cibola, *see* Cibola
Seven Sisters, The (play), 21:53, 151
Seven Sons, The (extravaganza), 10:381,
393
"1781 Cañizares Map of San Francisco
Bay, The," by Douglas S. Watson,
13:180
"17 Years with the Rollins Collection of
Western Americana," address by
Hilda K. Wilgus, 27:181-83
Seventh-day Adventists, 31:15
Seventh New York Volunteers, *see*
New York Volunteers
Seventy-five Years in California, by
Davis, rev., 8:183-85
Severiano (Contra Costa Co., 1851),
34:6
Sevier Lake and River, 28:124
Seward, Anna, "California in the
Eighties," from letters of, 16:291-303;
17:28-40

Seward, Daniel, 2:122

Seward, F. Dwight, 16:291, 292, 297, 302

Seward, Thomas Thompson, 16:338; 33:374

Seward, William Henry, 10:226, 227, 231; 19:251, 266-67, 270, 362-66 *passim;* 26:19; 34:150; "Let California Come In," 24:116

Sewell, Daniel, 34:294-95, 297

Sewell, J. W., 25:27, 29

Sewell, Newton, 9:145; 10:172, 194, 256; 23:356

Sewing machines, 24:265; 36:136, 138; phot., 36: opp. 137

Sexton (Sacramento, 1862), 10:373

Sexton, Daniel, 12:112, 115-16; 26:21, 51

Sexton, Lucy Foster, 14:161

Sexton, Warren T., 10:165, 189

Seybert (Marysville, 1858), 9:358, 359, 370, 372

Seymour (S.F., 1856), 14:353

Seymour, Col. (Salt Lake, 1868), 5:181, 182; *see also* Robinson, Seymour & Co.

Seymour, E. Sanford, 10:82

Seymour, Sir George F., 3:88, 112; 10:101, 116-19, 127-28; 14:327, 345; 17:133, 282

Seymour, H. I., 35:32

Seymour, Jesse, 10:55, 76

Seymour, Samuel, 16:65, 184, 282

Seymour, Simon H., 10:290

Seymour, William, 31:157

Seyton (Nevada Co., 1850s), 6:334; 12:72

Shackleford, Thomas S., 26:333, 340

Shadden, Thomas J., 14:278

Shades, The (gambling house), Sacramento, 24:357

Shadwell (on *London,* 1849), 7:222, 225

Shady Creek, 3:144

Shaeffer (San Diego, 1890s), *see* Shaffer, J. E.

Shaeffer, F. W., 15:24, 28

Shaeffer & Hall, 14: opp. 209

Shafer, Gideon, 23:226

Shafer, Zachariah, 12:29

Shaffer, J. E., 35:348, 349

Shafford, Vera Mae, *see* Sharritt, Mrs. Charles E.

Shafter, Helen, 19:288

Shafter, James McMillan, 10:376-78, 387, 389; 19:288; 20:261, 272

Shafter, Oscar Lovell, 10:260; 11:9; 17:177; 20:261, 272

Shafter, Heydenfeldt and Goold, 21:120

Shafter, Park, and Heydenfelt, 20:261

Shakespeare, ed. of 1632, 30:250

Shaler, William, 13:204; 15:188; 36:6; 40:198

Shales, C. L., 9:317

Shallenberger, F. C., 23:384

Shallenberger, F. G., 23:384

Shanagorati (Shangarette), Louis ("the Iroquois"), 22:327, 328, 347

Shanahan, T. W. H., 19:69; 28:53

Shanghai Theater, San Francisco, 23:104

Shannon, Thomas B., 10:62, 65, 70; 11:9

Shannon, William Edward, 1:213, 223, 224; 10:151, 152; 23:352, 370; 33:259-60; fac. sig., 10: opp. 159

Shannon, Wilson, 29:169, 171

Shannon & Armstrong, 22:40

Shark, 15:282

Shark (ship), 2:163, 166; 3:108; 5:307; 6:189; 17:125; 26:220, 221, 222; 34:119

Sharkey, J. M., 4:194; 16:337

Sharkey, John, 24:58

Sharkey, W., 9:146, 151, 156, 257, 259, 262, 351; 10:47, 57, 59, 168, 170, 184, 251

Sharon, Esther, 27:286

Sharon, Mrs. Frederick W., 25:238

Sharon, Joseph, 29:291

Sharon, William, 2:207; 11:64; 15:381; 22:95; 27:286; 34:245, 246; house of, 19:233-34

Sharon, William E. and Lillian (Mygatt), 27:286

Sharon Mills, 10:340, 341, 356, 358

Sharon Valley, 8:340, 356; 10:58

Sharp, Ann, 28:294

Sharp, C. G., 14:385, 402

Sharp, Eliza M., 28:293

Sharp, George F., 22:33

Sharp, John, 13:257

Sharp, Solomon A., 11:8-9; 16:81, 84

Sharp, Wesley, 12:12

Sharp, William H., 14:74

Sharp (W.) & Co., 30:362

Sharpe, Mrs. Howard G., 17:243

Sharpsteen, Katharine Crittenden, coauth. *El Toroso,* rev., 6:99-101; obit., 22:381

Sharpsteen, William Crittenden, 21:192; 23:179; "Vanished Waters of Southeastern San Francisco," 21:113-26

Sharpstein, John Randolph, 22:381
Sharritt, Mrs. Charles E. (Vera Mae Shafford), 20:288; obit., 22:286
Shasta (Shasta City), 3:90; 5:231; 7:5, 16, 122; 13:257, 260, 261; 18:299; 21:128, 383; 22:367, 368, 381-82; 26:298, 300; 28:1, 211; 30:259, 362, 367; 38:309; 40:60-61; art. on, 24:229-34; letter from, 20:253-56; newspaper, 21:283; 29:91; views of, 18: opp. 304; 30: opp. 104
Shasta (riv. str.), 9:72
Shasta, Mount, 5:117, 257; 10:263; 18:298, 301, 343; 23:293; 24:229, 335; 26:292; 28:210, 211, 245; 30:340; ascent of, 6:69-76; Whitney Survey on, 7:121-31; illus., 24: opp. 229
Shasta Book Store, 28:1
Shasta Butte City, 26:292; letters from, 26:298-301; *see also* Yreka
Shasta County, 21:383; 22:367-71 *passim*, 382; 34:267
Shasta Courier, Redding, 28:225, 226, 230, 231
Shasta House, Sacramento, phot., 39:199, foll. 200
Shasta River and Valley, 6:71; 16:341; 23:138; 24:229, 326; 26:201; 30:340
"Shasta Was Shatasla in 1814," by Alice B. Maloney, 24:229-34
Shattuck, Mrs. (singer, 1860s), 10:358; 24:263
Shattuck, David Olcott, 9:29; 10:357; 15:274, 370; 16:182, 284, 285, 343; 17:180; 34:258
Shattuck, Francis Kittredge, 11:9, 21
Shattuck, Frank W., 15:271; 24:58
Shattuck (D. D.) & (A. C.) Hendley, 29:253, 254
Shaughnessy, Patrick H., 15:315, 318, 322
Shaw, Rev. Dr. (fictitious, 1890), 14:49, 57-58
Shaw, Bethuel P., 2:121
Shaw, E. W., 21:235
Shaw, F. P., 13:31
Shaw, Frank, 7:113
Shaw, H. R., 19:72
Shaw, Henry A. and Margaret (McGrath), 28:293
Shaw, James B., 4:158
Shaw, John, 4:250
Shaw, Laurence L., 31:287
Shaw, Pringle, 22:255, 276
Shaw, Richard G., 27:224

Shaw, Samuel F., 12:138
Shaw, Thomas, 6:143; 17:141, 253; 23:302-6 *passim*, 325, 330, 332; 35:198, 199, 203
Shaw, William J., 1:9; 9:46; 16:80, 84
Shawmut & California Co., 20:28, 36, 37, 42
Shaw's Flat, 11:332, 336; 32:55; 38:308
Shay, John C., *Twenty Years in the Backwoods of California*, rev., 3:93-94
Shea, William, 15:239; 17:54
Shearer, Charles, 22:178
Shearer, George B., 37:201
Shearer, Jacob, 8:360
Shears (S.F., 1854), 15:171
Shedd (Georgetown, 1849), 20:38
Sheehy, Eugene P., coauth. *Frank Norris: A Bibliography*, rev., 39:366-67
Sheep, domestic, 1:69-70, 148-49, 165, 166; 2:42, 267, 280, 290, 291, 295, 308, 310, 322; 3:120; 4:25, 286; 5:217, 258; 8:102, 237, 265, 319; 10:34, 39; 11:369; 12:193, 243, 251, 260, 274, 282, 283; 14:5, 6; 16:67, 118, 119, 242; 17:340; 18:28, 29; 21:220, 322, 329, 338, 341; 23:21, 242, 252, 253, 297; 25:30; 28:66, 98; *see also* Livestock; Wool
Sheep, wild, 22:203, 204, 205, 215
Sheep Ranch Mine, 19:28; 29:208
Sheep Rock, Siskiyou Co., 22:103; 23:137, 146
Sheffield, Charles P., 29:381
Sheldon, "Deacon" (Marysville, 1861), 10:360
Sheldon (L.A., 1888), 37:172
Sheldon, B. A., 15:179; 17:176
Sheldon, Catherine, 25:221
Sheldon, George, 15:271
Sheldon, "Hank", 10:280
Sheldon, Jared, 25:221; 27:187
Sheldon, Mrs. Jared (Catherine Rhoads), 27:187
Sheldon, Lionel A., 36:330
Sheldon, Mark, 17:174
Sheldon, Miranda Wilmarth, 23:191
Sheldon, Nicholas, 23:191
Sheldon, Omar, 31:157
Sheldon, Ross, 8:344; 9:148, 152
Shelikoff, Paul, 8:323-27; 12:191, 209, 242
Shell, Israel, lawsuit, 9:136
Shellmounds, *see* Indians: mounds made by

"Shell Mounds and Caves around San Francisco Bay," address by Mark L. Emerson, 13:284

Shelly and Norris, 25:220

Shelter Cove, 27:218

Shelton (S.F., 1851), 28:35; 38:316

Shelton, C. A., 22:33

Shelton, H. A., 11:9

Shelton, Harry, 10:280

Shelton, William F., 26:204

Shenandoah (ship), 26:356, 359; 27:180; 33:151, 238; 40:301

Shenk, John Wesley, 37:271

Shepard (S.F., 1849), 27:366

Shepard, Cyrus M., 3:74, 76, 77

Shepard, D. M., 14:398

Shepard, Forrest, 2:200; 12:75, 93, 99, 107; 21:321, 330

Shepard, Isaac, 33:374

Shepard, W., 22:251

Shepard, William F., 37:91; ed. "California Prior to Conquest, a Frenchman's Views," 37:63-77

Shepard, William W., 9:250, 269; 10: opp. 48, 62, 70

Shepardson (Calaveras Co., 1851), 22:76

Shepheard, John J., 26:4, 7

Shepheard, Philip W., 17:181

Shepherd, J. Avery, 14:76; 17:182

Shepherd, Mrs. Theodosia, 13:188

Shepherdess (ship), 20:117

Sheppard, William, 21:153

Sheppard, William B., 15:165, 168

Shepperd (Buckeye, 1859), 10:171

Shepperd, Marcus L., 29:242

Sherburn (Yosemite, 1852), 1:273; 5:332-35

Sherburn, John F., 35:32

Sherburne, John S., 33:374

Sherburne v. Yuba Co., 10:380

Sheridan, Capt. (of *Charles Quint*, 1849), 37:318

Sheridan, James E., 9:269, 274; 10:62, 70

Sheridan, William E., 21:252; 35:142

Sherley, J. H., 13:32

Sherlock's Diggings, 35:38

Sherman (S.F., 1861), 30:130

Sherman (S.F., 1866), 37:210

Sherman, Allen Banks, 23:287; introd. to "Sherman Was There," 23:259-60, 288

Sherman, Charles, 23:366

Sherman, Charles W., 15:29

Sherman, Edwin Allen, 9:193, 194; 22:288; 23:259-60; 25:196, 199, 206; 29:239, 248, 289; 31:86; letter, 9:196-200; "Recollections," 23:261-81, 349-77; 24:47-72, 165-80, 271-99; drawing by, 23: opp. 352; phot., 24: opp. 47

Sherman, Isaac, 9:364; 10:57, 58, 59, 166

Sherman, John, 23:358

Sherman, Leander S., 25:286

Sherman, Minna (Eshleman), 25:31

Sherman, Thomas W., 23:358

Sherman, William (S.F., 1854, 1864), 15:179; 24:266

Sherman, William (Promontory, 1869), 36:268

Sherman, William John, 39:122

Sherman, William Tecumseh, 1:14, 151; 4:220; 7:4, 6, 291; 10:23; 13:34; 14:19-20; 15:370; 16:304; 19:251; 21:24, 33; 24:174, 176; 28:296; 33:256, 345, 374; 35:23; 40:20; as banker, 7:291; 17:320; 24:174; in Civil War, 16:195, 309, 315; 21:357; in gold region, 2:188; 17:233; 26:124; 33:269, 337; 34:22; at Monterey, 13:395; 16:196, 321; 23:358-59; 27:49; 29:36; 33:254, 255, 264, 338, 304-41; interest in N.Y. of the Pacific, 8:17; 12:27; 15:290; political candidate, 15:182, 280; 16:81; in San Francisco, 15:182, 280; 19:229; 30:159; as surveyor, 34:22, 24; against Vigilance Com., 9:283; 14:352-69 *passim;* 15:73, 82, 260-62; 21:27; cor., 14:359-60, 362, 367-73 *passim;* 15:260-61; 33:240-41; 40:20; quoted, 6:146-47; 14:352-57 *passim,* 362, 364-66; 15:260-61, 262; 16:201; 24:368; 26:199; 31:21

Sherman, Clay & Co., 25:286

"Sherman Was There," recollections of Edwin A. Sherman, 23:259-81, 349-77; 24:47-72, 165-80, 271-79

Sherrard, Robert B., 9:347

Sherreback (or Scherrebach), Peter T., 17:172; 18:158, 159, 173; land claim of, 16:339

Sherry, Janes & McCrea, 15:275

Sherwin, J. L. C., 9:250, 269

Sherwood, Henry Hamilton, obit., 7:101

Sherwood, James B., 10:173, 196

Sherwood, James W., 21:291, 308

Sherwood, Richard W., 21:308

Sherwood, T. A., 13:32

Sherwood, T. J., 10:358, 367

Sherwood, Walter, 15:172

Sherwood, William K., 15:33

Sherwood, Winfield Scott, 10:157, 160; 14:393; 19:6-7; 23:370; fac. sig., 10: opp. 159

Sherwood Valley, 30:165, 168, 169

Shew, Jacob, 15:370; 27: opp. 97

Shew, William, phot. by, 36: opp. 304

Shiel, Edward, 28:358

Shields, James, 10:282, 284, 296; 19:173, 345; 31:13

Shields, Samuel, 2:36

Shields, W. F., 14:342

Shiels, William, 21:244

Shiels' Opera House, San Francisco, 21:170, 272

"Shiftless Belligerent Pike, The, . . . as Described by Clarence King," by Roger H. Pearl, 38:113-29

Shillaber, Capt. (Colorado R., 1866), 22:171

Shillaber, Theodore, 14:329, 333, 336, 337, 345; 20:108(?)

Shine, A. T., 18:384

Shingles, 2:52, 53; 20:39

Shingle Springs, 3:128; 20:39, 41

Shinn, Beryle W., 16: No. 1, Pt. 2, pp. 1, 2, 14, 20; No. 3, pp. 273, 275, 280; 17: No. 4, Pt. 2, p. 1; 31:100; 36:28, 31, 34

Shinn, Charles Howard, 1:17; 4:51; 24:80; 38:157-58, 160-61, 220, 225

Shinn, Mrs. Charles Howard (Julia Tyler), 38:157-63, 219-28

"Ship *Brooklyn,* The," by Amelia Everett, 37:229-40

Shipbuilding and launching, 1:167; 10:389-90; 12:190, 194-95, 242, 294; 13:207; 14:201, 209; 15:175-76, 183; 16:232, 243; 22:2-25 *passim,* 152-68 *passim;* 25:39-53; 27:65-66, 348; 33:236; 37:82

Shipley, Mrs. Maynard, *see* De Ford, Miriam Allen

Shipley, William Chapman, 30:286

Shipman, Aaron T., 21:308

Shipp, Mrs. E. R. and Anna (Weller), 27:382

Shipping List, San Francisco, 28:36

Ship Rock, illus., 11:372

Ships: Boston, 8:289-305; 12:217-26 *passim,* 229, 230; 22:319; built in Calif. (*see* Shipbuilding); on Colorado R. (*see* "Steam Navigation . . ."); imported from England, 30:236; Japanese, 25:49, 50; in the Pacific (1861-65), 27:178-80; prefabricated,

15:183; 22:5-6, 8, 15, 153; 25:41-42; 33:236; Richardson's, 16:243-44; Russian, 6:25; 12:191, 194, 199, 207, 220, 228-37 *passim,* 240; 16:108; 18:338, 347; 26:13-19; 39:111; in S.F. Bay (1849), 23:56; (1853-54), 15:268; *see also* Clipper ships; Manila galleons; names of ships

Shipwrecks, 6:356-59; 9:179; 12:137; 15:178, 179, 180, 266-74 *passim,* 279; 19:27-42, 282; 21:302, 308; 24:321; 26:9, 14, 360; 27:292-93; 28:111, 259; 31:150, 274; 32:352-53; 33:235; 34:337-38; 39:296; illus., 15: opp. 364

Shires, Henry M., 25:192

Shirkland, Hugh, 9:137, 141, 142, 148, 150, 151, 161, 165, 176, 262, 266, 267

Shirland (alias Stewart), Francis, 23:354; 24:49

Shirley, Dame, *see* Clapp, Louisa A.

Shirley (ship), phot., 22: opp. 349

Shirley Letters, The, by Clapp, rev., 1:299-301

Shirwood (Sherwood?; on *London,* 1849-50), 7:210, 215

Shissler (Michigan Bluff and Idaho), 16:177

Shively, John M., 13:241

Shoaf, Ross, 23:384; 24:191

Shocken, Solomon, 12:201

Shockley, Capt. (of *Roman,* 1846), 31:209, 210

Shockley, Thomas, 11:10

Shoemaker (on *Oregon,* 1849), 27:366

Shoemaker (place), 35:98

Shokadjal (Indian village), 26:209

Shondon, James, 15:29

Shorb, Ethel R., obit. of Mrs. Alexander Garceau, 16:190-91; obit., 38:361-63

Shorb, James A., 19:320, 321; 38:322(?)

Shorb, James de Barth, 1:13; 27:342; 38:322, 361, 362

Shorb, Mrs. James de Barth (María Jesús Wilson), 38:322

Shorb, Joseph Campbell and Mrs., 11:127

Shores, M. T., 21:235

Short (S.F., 1856), 20:308

Short, Miss J. B., 25:31

Short, John, Jr., 10:285

Short, Patrick, 15:286; 30:98

Short, W. H., 22:251

Short History of California, A, by Hunt and Sánchez, rev., 8:380-81

Shortridge, Samuel Morgan, 36:254

Shotwell, Randolph Abbott, 31:235

Show, W. I., 15:368

Showalter, Daniel, 9:198; 32:147-48, 158; 34:136, 141, 142; 39:297, 306; 40:294; art. on, 40:309-25

Shreve, C. S., 34:337

Shreve, George C., 17:314; 29:253, 254

Shriver, A. F., 33:276

Shropsline, George, 15:278

Shubert, Helen V., "The Men Who Met the Yankees in 1846," 13:43-55

Shubrick, William Bransford, 1:231; 2:250, 351; 8:261; 10:18-19, 25; 12:343, 345-46, 348, 351; 13:151, 153; 16:196; 18:52, 62; 21:194; 22:50, 65; 30:234; 33:108-9, 269, 338; 35:107

Shubrick (ship), 26:14-15; 33:235-36; 37:206, 208, 210

Shuck, Oscar Tully, 20:368; 36:328-29

Shuey, Dr. (Sierra Madre, 1890s), 31:22

Shuey, Mrs. Clarence A. (née Hayden), 25:95

Shufelt, S., 23:179

Shuk (Indian, 1849), 11:268-70

Shuki Nakamura, 28:186

Shuler, Marion, 8:344

Shultz, Theodore, 5:27

Shuman, John Franklin, obit. of Mrs. Alexander F. Morrison, 18:381-82

Shumate, Albert, 17:359

Shumway (Kern R., 1850), 11:256

Shumway, Jacob, 29:56

Shurtleff (C.P.R.R., 1869), 5:183

Shurtleff, Benjamin, 10:372

Shurtleff, George A., 4:183; 23:368, 376

Shustor, Fred, 10:184, 185

Shutes, Milton Henry, 15:100; 26:284; "Abraham Lincoln and the New Almaden Mine," 15:3-20; "Afterword on Col. Edward Dickinson Baker," 22:26; "Col. E. D. Baker," 17:303-24; "'Fighting Joe' Hooker," 16:304-20; "Henry Douglas Bacon," 26:193-200; "Henry Wager Halleck, Lincoln's Chief of Staff," 16:195-208; "Republican Nominating Convention of 1860," 27:97-103; addresses, "Lincoln's California Contacts," 22:183; "Lincoln's Chief-of-Staff, Henry Wager Halleck," 16:89

Shvetsov (fur hunter, 1803), 12:219, 221, 223, 227

Siamese Twins, 38:339-40

Sibley, George C., 23:298

Sibley, Henry H., 34:131-39 *passim*

Sibley, Hiram, 29:345, 346, 352, 353; 33:11, 12

Sicard, Theodore, 8:120; 9:75; 12:280; 14:205-12 *passim*, 219, 227, 383; 30:3-4

Sicard Flat, 14:205, 207

Sickels, Daniel E., 15:17

Sickels, John, 17: opp. 200

Sickness, *see* Diseases

Siebert, A., *see* Liebert

Siegrist, Rosa, 21:157

Sienkiewicz, Henryk, "The Chinese in California," as reported by, ed. and trans. Charles Morley, 34:301-16

Sierra, Benito de la, "Account of the Hezeta Expedition," ed. Henry R. Wagner, trans. A. J. Baker, 9:201-42

Sierra Blanca (ship), 22:353

Sierra Buttes Mine, 3:259-60; 8:388

Sierra Buttes Quartz Mill, 33:193, 199

Sierra Citizen, Downieville, 9:135, 173; 17:178

Sierra Club, 4:22, 32, 41-54 *passim*; 25:190; 28:190; 36:113; 38:250, 251; *Bulletin*, rev., 7:92-93; 8:89; 9:186-87

Sierra de Santa Clara, 9:233, 234

Sierra Estrella (ship), 22:353

Sierra Flume and Lumber Co., 27:343

Sierra Grays, 29:236

Sierra Guard, Downieville, 38:19

Sierra Madre (town), 31:18, 20-22, 27

Sierra Madre Villa, 31:21-22

Sierra Madre Water Co., 31:20

Sierra National Forest, 4:51

Sierra Nevada, 4:3-58; 7:3-19; 13:359; 28:185-86; 34:216

Sierra Nevada (prop. Terr.), 18:305; 21:228-32

Sierra Nevada (brig, 1850), 5:252, 254, 342-43

Sierra Nevada (transport, 1851), 22:4, 7, 20, 168

Sierra Nevada (str., 1854), 11:152; 15:88, 159, 165, 166, 170, 180, 184, 266, 271, 277, 280, 366, 371, 372, 374; 16:82, 182, 282; 17:75, 81, 172; 20:260

Sierra Nevada Hotel, Coloma, 27:281

Sierra Nevada Mountain Lake Water & Mining Co., 10:177

Sierra Park Colony, 25:174

Sierra Railway, by Deane, rev., 40:249-50

Sierras Nevadas (Santa Cruz Mts.), 4:3

Sierra Valley, 10:249, 262; 27:194; Swiss in, 30:312

Sierra Ventana (ship), 22:353

Sigler, H., 36:104
Sigler, William, 6:88; 18:299
Signal Hill, 31:15-16
Signal Rock, Yosemite, 1:277-78
Sign painting, 8:25; 25:106
Sigondis, Lépine de, 18:6
Sikes, Zenus, *see* Sykes
Silas J. Lewis (barge), 22:156, 163, 167, 168
Silberio (Indian, 1790s), 1:164
Silk and silkworms, 23:343; 25:15; 28:5; 31:335-42; 32:249, 253
"Silk in Piedmont," by Evelyn C. Pattiani, 31:335-42
Sill, Benjamin H., 32:17, 28, 34, 41
Sill, Daniel, 14:128, 202, 226; 17:295, 301; 18:297, 311; 21:2, 10; 25:144; 28:265; 30:54, 63
Sill, Mount, 5:48, 54
Sillem, William, 11:127
Siller Bros., 30:69
Silliman (Benicia, 1849), 29:255
Silliman, Benjamin, Jr., 4:67
Silliman, Mount, 4:17
Silly, Lea, 21:167
Silsbee, Joshua S., 17:180
Silva, Antonio E., 35:241
Silva, Jackson, 33:94
Silva, Louis Jackson, 33:94
Silva, Mariano, 3:110, 180, 186; 7:84; 8:72; 9:82; 17:146; 25:197
Silva family, 35:241
Silveira family, 35:235
Silver: coins, 12:12; in Death Valley, 18:197, 213; mines and mining, 11:42; 12:12, 328, 329, 330; 13:58; 15:324; 17:00, 18.307, 314; 27:116, 121; 32:1-41; 34:220; as political issue, 27:313, 315, 316; 28:48-50
Silver Bow, Mont., 15:324, 326, 327; *see also* Butte
Silver City, Nev., 17:80
Silver District, Los Angeles Co., 32:328
Silver Lake, Amador Co., 28:190; 34:219
Silver Mill Co., 31:295
Silver Mountain, Alpine Co., 30:246-47; 34:219, 220, 221
Silvers, Pablo, phot., 36: opp. 320
Silver Saddle Lease, 32:15
Silver Stampede, by Wilson, rev., 16:85
Silver Zone Pass, 32:198
Sime, John, 15:164; 18:55; 28:293, 295; 37:368; 40:204
Sime, Mrs. John (Mary L. Toland), 28:293

Simmerley, Samuel, 15:29, 54
Simmonds (auth. of burlesque, 1855), 15:270
Simmonds (S.F., 1855), 15:375
Simmonds, James, 10:200; 15:270(?)
Simmonds, John J., 2:128
Simmons (S.F., 1849), 29:170
Simmons (Marysville, 1858), 9:374
Simmons (Long Bar, 1859), 10:168
Simmons, Bezer, 16:76; 20:45; 22:69, 81; 25:104; *see also* Simmons, Hutchinson & Co.
Simmons, Edward, 16:283
Simmons, John C., 32:55, 121, 128, 130; 40:328, 334
Simmons, Orrin, 17:44
Simmons, Richard R., 14:223
Simmons (Lew) and (E. N.) Slocum Minstrels, 21:168, 169
Simmons, Hutchinson & Co., 20:30, 35, 45; 22:69-70, 81; 25:104, 108, 111, 117, 257, 338; 27:127-28; 30:100
Simmons *v.* Carr, 10:183, 184
Simms (S.F., 1850s), 16:130
Simon, Capt. (S.F., 1849), 2:201
Simon, Lt. (S.F., 1850), 5:26
Simon, Mrs. Estelle, 5:21, 26
Simon, Lucy, 35:269
Simonds, James, 29:337
Simonds, Samuel D., 31:1-2; 40:331
Simonds, William Day, 33:224
Simoneau, Jules, 3:292, 294, 295, 296
Simonis (Cordua's Bar, 1850s), 12:303
Simons, John, 18:154
Simons, John E., 34:35
Simons, Solon S., 9:260, 269
Simonsen, James, 35:333
Simonsen, Martin, 14:392; 15:46; 16:283, 337, 344; 17:82
Simonton, James W., 7:281; 20:334, 336-37; 30:148; 32:224; 33:216
Simoons, Frederick J., 32:383; "Development of Transportation Routes in the Clear Lake Area," 32:363-71
Simpson, A. J., 29:110
Simpson, Alexander, 28:98, 106, 109, 110, 111
Simpson, Cyrus M., 19:65; 27:318
Simpson, Sir George, 1:171; 8:125; 10:411; 11:197, 198; 12:199, 239, 249, 274; 13:226; 17:68, 142-44; 18:141, 327; 22:98; 28:99, 104-5, 110, 117-20 *passim*, 226, 243-58 *passim*; 29:149, 158, 314-15; 30:379; 33:83

Simpson, H. L., 27:95

Simpson, James, 10:173, 195-96

Simpson, Mrs. James, 10:253, 357, 385

Simpson, James H., 18:350-51, 353

Simpson, John, 27:226; 30:162, 164

Simpson, Lesley Byrd, trans. and ed.
Journal of José Longinos Martínez;
... Botanical Expedition ... 1791-1792,
rev., 40:263-65; trans. *The Laws of*
the Burgos of 1512-1513, rev.,
40:76-77; ed. *The San Sabá Papers,*
rev., 39:271-72

Simpson, M. L. and Patsy (Ritchie),
19:233

Simpson, Mary R., *see* Barker, Mrs.
Timothy

Simpson, Richard French, 21:199; 33:98,
339, 340

Simpson, Robert, 22:71

Simpson, William, 8:332

Simpton, John, 9:253; 28:34; 30:92;
31:284

Simpton, Mary Ellen, 30:92; 31:284

Sims (Camptonville, 1854), 8:199

Sims, Columbus, 29:235; 40:349

Sims, James M., 26:203

Sims, William, 4:28

Simson, Leslie, 21:370; 22:370

Simson, Robert, 21:300, 301, 302, 306,
307, 308; 22:71

Sinaloa River, *see* San Pedro y San
Pablo R.

Sinclair, Lt. (Chagres, 1845), 2:163

Sinclair, Mrs. (Sacramento, 1861),
10:279, 280, 281

Sinclair, Catharine N. (Mrs. Edwin
Forrest), 15:163, 174, 177, 181, 185,
268, 278; 20:304, 305; 37:366

Sinclair, Isabella, 28:294

Sinclair, John, 10:350; 12:267; 14:227;
16:127, 138; 18:158, 159, 173;
25:222-23; 26:123; 29:270

Sinclair, Samuel Fleming and Ellen
(Milliken), 29:93

Sinclair, Sarah, 29:93

Sinclair, William, 28:257

Sinclair, William John, 29:93

Singer, Ada, 8:197; 9:346, 356, 360,
366-77 *passim,* 397; 10:42, 43, 46, 49,
54, 55, 58, 166-74 *passim,* 178-82
passim, 188, 273, 286, 361-66 *passim,*
372, 375; phot., 9: opp. 345

Singer, Anna, 8:197; 9:346-77 *passim,*
397; 10:42-49 *passim,* 54, 55, 58, 166-74
passim, 178-88 *passim,* 192, 258, 259,

270, 273, 284, 286, 358-66 *passim,*
372, 375; phot., 9: opp. 345

Singer, Hattie, 9:357

Singer, Isaac M., sewing machine of,
36:136, 138; phot., opp. 137

Singer, William, 9:345, 348, 349, 356,
361-64, 372, 373, 377; 10:46, 53, 55, 63,
72, 170-73 *passim,* 178-87 *passim,* 194,
195, 257-58, 259, 283, 286, 357-61
passim, 369

Singer family, 9:377

Single tax, *see* George, Henry

Siniac (or Signac; d. nr. Calaveras R.,
1849), 13:375; 31:311

Sinoba, José Francisco, 14:6

Sinsheimer, A. Z. and Nettie (Weil),
35:377

Sinsheimer, Paul Ainsley, obit.,
35:377-78

Sinton, Richard H., 21:34; 23:73; *see*
also Selover & Sinton

Sipp (from Ore., 1845), 5:125

Sir Charles Coldstream (play), 16:183

Sir Francis Drake's Voyage, by Wagner,
rev., 6:93-95

Sir Knights, 10:356

Sirrine, George W., 14:176

Sirrine, John, 11:135, 143

Siskadee River, *see* Colorado River

Siskiyou County, 26:202, 292; 31:126-37
passim; 34:271-72

Siskiyou County Historical Society,
39:72

Siskiyou Daily News, 31:127-38 *passim*

Siskron, Charles, 29:291

Sisson (place), 7:124, 125

Sisson, Wallace & Co., 13:17; 37:130

Sister Beatrice (play), 20:141

Sisterna (Berkeley, 1856), 31:331

Sisters of Charity, 13:333; 15:174; 16:80,
183; 28:33

Sisters of Mercy, 31:24

Sisters of the Immaculate Heart of
Mary, 33:353, 359

Sitjar, Antonio, 23:2

Sitjar, Buenaventura, 1:165; 13:155

Sitka, 16:339; 33:147-48; 38:332

Sitka (steam launch, 1847), 7:106;
14:143-45; 19:124, 140; 27:300

Sitka (Russian ship, 1854), 15:180, 184,
185

Sit Ming Cook, 30:149

Sivey, John, 16:138

Six Horses, by Banning, rev., 9:185

Sixteen Mile House, Yuba Co., 10:254, 266

"Sixteenth (Center) St., San Francisco," address by Charles F. Griffin, 7:410

Sixth of June (ship), 13:270

Sixth Street Church, Sacramento, 31:11

"Six-toed Pete," 15:178; *see also* Badillo, Pedro

Skaggs, Chester W., 23:96

Skeantlebury, William, 4:63

Skelton (Marysville, 1858), 9:348, 374; 10:58

"Sketches of Mariposa in the Fifties," address by Homer D. Crotty, 33:276-77

Sketches of the Sixties, by Harte and Twain, rev., 5:409-12

"Sketch of the Life of Theodore D. Judah," by Carl I. Wheat, 4:219-71

Skewes-Cox, Robin Warne, 22:96

Skilling, E. W., 17:116

Skillman, Henry, 40:320

Skinker, John, 9:100, 103, 106

Skinner (S.F., ca. 1898), 35:349, 350

Skinner, Constance, 20:140

Skinner, E. C., 13:31

Skinner, Georgia, 38:343-46

Skinner, Horace A., 14:177, 182

Skinner, T. A., 13:31

Skirven, T. W., 22:251

Skis and skiing, 18:152, 153, 156; 39:80; *see also* Thompson, John A.

Slack (S.F., 1855), 15:370

Slack, Charles William, 25:15; obit., 25:87-89

Slack, Mrs. Charles William (Katherine Woolsey), obit., 17:360; 25:88-89

Slack, Edith, 25:89, 95; obit. of Marion Leale, 35:85-86

Slack, John, phot., 36: opp. 320

Slack, Uriah and Catherine (Straley), 25:87

Slack (Levi) & (Ephraim W.) Morse, 31:37

Slacum, William A., 3:77; 19:313

"Slasher, The," 28:43

Slate Creek, 9:176; 31:381

Slate Creek Canal & Mining Co., 20:43

Slate Creek Ditch Co., 9:138, 144, 153, 176

Slater, Mr. and Mrs. (Round Tent, 1859), 10:169

Slater, Jim, 10:373, 376, 377

Slater, John A., 21:233

Slater, Nelson, 22:29, 31, 32-33

Slater, William, 20:38, 44

Slate Range, Inyo Co., 17:99, 110, 116, 209, 210

Slate Range, Yuba Co., 6:214, 215-16; 8:355; 9:54; *see also* Slate Range Bar

Slate Range Bar, 8:338, 342, 344, 349, 355; 9:157, 158, 266; 10:171

Slattery, M., 9:372; 10:177

Slaughter, Henry S., 31:154

Slauson, J. S., 11:49

Slavery, 9:37, 38, 41, 100, 102, 271-72, 278, 281-82; 10:151-52, 220-31 *passim,* 234-35, 237, 268; 11:4, 15, 22, 27; 15:205, 207, 277; 16:26-28; 19:8, 16, 25-26, 348-55 *passim;* 20:103, 106, 155; 21:33, 132-33; 22:224-26, 355, 357; 23:356, 370-71; 24:65, 105, 194-202, 312; 25:65; 28:72, 155; 29:11; 30:129; 31:193-200 *passim;* 32:299, 315-16; 38:333, 359; of Indians, 5:130, 131, 257; 21:7; in Mex., 18:126

Slavyanka (Russian River), 12:189

Sledge, L. A., 25:24-25

Sleight, John, 26:204

Slidell, John, 5:306; 6:77; 11:12, 201-2; 18:220, 227; 19:44-48 *passim,* 345; 28:230

"Slim, Joshua" (Lew Walker), 20:183, 184

Slingerland, James S., 9:67, 68, 80, 130-41 *passim,* 145, 148, 150, 156, 158, 167, 254, 256, 266, 273, 349, 355, 363, 367, 375, 376, 385; 10:41, 46-54 *passim,* 69, 166-72 *passim,* 183, 194, 256, 266, 267, 273, 288, 367

Slingerland, Mrs. James S., *see* Cowell, Mary

Slingsby, William, 8:213; 9:78; *see also* Gattens, Daniel

Slinkard Creek and Valley, 26:235

Slippery Ford, 7:8, 9; 17:78

Sloan, E. W. F., 10:266; 16:81

Sloane, Norman Hinsdale, obit., 18:191

Sloane, William, 32:263, 267

Sloat, John Drake, 1:138, 139; 2:72, 162; 3:33, 105-14 *passim,* 179; 5:306; 6:77, 161, 162, 372; 7:84, 85; 8:258; 9:82, 83; 11:205-9 *passim;* 12:40-47 *passim,* 162; 13:47, 100, 109, 153; 14:148, 345; 15:58, 243, 306; 17:125, 131, 227, 271, 277, 278, 281, 282; 18:72, 217; 19:47, 52; 20:193, 215; 24:57, 63; 25:122-27 *passim;* 26:222; 29:272, 273, 274; 31:207, 210; 32:293; 35:103; 40:19; raises flag at Monterey, 1:138; 3:109,

111, 179; 4:303; 7:84; 9:82; 12:161; 13:109, 301; 14:148; 16:188; 20:233; 24:48; 25:125, 193-204; 30:224; cor. and orders, 2:71-72, 162-72, 247, 249-51, 350-56; 3:84-87, 178-79, 181-82, 184-86; 6:368-70; 7:81-83; 8:71-76; 9:85-86; 11:209-10; 15:63-65 *passim;* 18:82; procs., 2:352-54; 3:109-10, 112; 10:11-12; 18:73

Sloat, Lewis Warrington, 1:291; 3:178; 21:304, 308, 363, 364; 38:314

Slobodchikov (fur hunter, 1806), 12:220, 222, 227

Slocomb, E. H., 33:292

Slocum, E. N., 21:168

Slocumb, R. W., 9:109; 15:281, 364, 370, 372; 16:342; 17:179

Slooman (Yuba Co., 1859), 10:58, 169

Sloss, Henry C., 10:43, 44, 47, 57, 62, 70, 184, 189

Sloss, Joseph, 25:381; 35:256, 257; obit., 18:383

Sloss, Mrs. Joseph (Edith Esberg), 18:383; obit., 21:381

Sloss, Leon, 25:230, 231, 232

Sloss, Louis, 19:156; 29:286; 35:307; 37:21

Sloss, Mrs. Louis (Sarah Greenebaum), 37:182

Sloss, Louis, Jr., collection of, 37:19-38; phot., opp. 24

Sloss, Mrs. Louis, Jr. (Eleanor Fleishhacker), 37:21

Sloss, Louis B., 15:76

Sloss, Marcus Cauffman ("Max"), obit., 37:182-83

Sloss, Mrs. Marcus Cauffman (Hattie Lina Hecht), 25:233

Slough, J. P., 34:138

Slough City (ship), 23:367

Slover, Isaac, 2:10; 12:117; 15:109, 133; illus., 15: opp. 110

Sly, James C., 14:278; 26:122; 32:195

Slye (Marysville, 1851), 15:54

Smal, Jake, 19:296

Small, Clement, 13:296

Small, Henry ("Hank"), 18:355

Small, Mrs. Ina E., 29:294

Small, W. H., 13:32

Smallpox, 1:222; 4:152, 168, 286; 10:373; 14:303, 322-23; 16:360; 18:68, 69; 24:62-63, 240; 25:256; 27:382; 29:27; 35:215; 36:145; 39:297

Smart (on *California*, 1849), 27:38

Smart, George, 7:112

Smart, George R., 26:383

Smart, Robert B., 2:113, 122

Smartsville, 5:293; 6:221; 9:351, 376; 10:56, 169, 251, 255-56; 28:235, 241

Smedberg, Cora, *see* Felton, Mrs. Charles N. [Jr.]

Smedberg, William Renwick, 4:45; 20:383

Smiley, Thomas J. L., 6:36; 9:27; 17:177, 179; 32:149, 150

Smiley, Yerkes & Co., 15:269

Smilie, Robert S., 24:189-90

Smith (Peru, 1843), 18:66

Smith (S.F., 1849), 35:17

Smith, Maj. (Monterey, 1849), 35:17

Smith (brickyard, Marysville, ca. 1850), 14:398

Smith, Dr. (S.F., 1850), 2:117, 118

Smith (S.F. and Carson Creek, 1850), 7:400-401; 8:263

Smith (S.F., 1851), 28:40

Smith (on *Westward Ho*, 1853), 28:322

Smith, Dr. (Placerville, 1854), 11:58

Smith (Camptonville, 1856), 9:60

Smith, Mrs. (Yuba Co., 1856), 9:65, 66, 67, 132, 134; 10:256

Smith (Grass Valley, ca. 1859), 6:335

Smith (Siberia, 1865), 33:149

Smith (Philippines, 1898), 31:65

"Smith" (L.A. lawyer, 1919), 32:4, 11, 12-13

Smith, Albert, "scenorama" of, 10:196

Smith, Albert A., 21:232, 238

Smith, Alek, 23:229

Smith, Alfred Emanuel, 39:121-22, 129, 131

Smith, Andrew, 19:144-45; 25:1; *see also* Hallidie, Andrew Smith

Smith, Andrew Jackson, 1:148, 238, 241, 244, 250, 251; 28:223, 231; 29:29, 34; 33:101, 112, 249, 254, 264, 341; 34:35; 40:349; letter from, 33:344-45

Smith, Anna, 28:294

Smith, Ann Elisabeth, 28:292

Smith, Archibald, 23:171

Smith, Austin E., 16:183

Smith, Azariah, 14:269, 273-74, 282; 26:109, 112-15, 122-23, 128, 131

Smith, "Badger" (Robert?), 29:267, 269

Smith, Benjamin, 19:231

Smith, Betty, 14:74

Smith, C. C. (Sutter's Fort, 1848), 11:42, 136; 16:138; (called George) 26:121

Smith, C. C. (Grass Valley, 1861), 10:192

Smith, Mrs. C. C. (Virginia Vineyard), 10:169, 192; phot., 10: opp. 170

Smith, C. C. (Alaska, 1867), 35:298

Smith, C. W., 13:296

Smith, Caroline, 28:292

Smith, Carrie Amelia, 25:190

Smith, Charles (Yuba Co., 1850), 14:224

Smith, Charles (mate on *Peerless*, 1887), 22:352

Smith, Charles K., 29:253, 254

Smith, Charles M., 22:163

Smith, Charles Rand, 23:203, 215

Smith, Charles W., 17:318; 33:374

Smith, Clarence Mark, obit., 5:106

Smith, Mrs. Clarence Mark (Alice Elizabeth Prescott), 18:384; obit. of Clarence M. Smith, 5:106

Smith, David R., 19:149

Smith, E., 21:235

Smith, E. J., 15:173

Smith, Edward, 33:352

Smith, Edward P., 28:162-63

Smith, Emery, 30:298

Smith, Erwina Dunbar, 35:183

Smith, Esther Ruth (Mrs. Elmer G.), 35:381; "The First Crescent City Lighthouse," 35:325-34

Smith, Florence, 21:227

Smith, Frances Norris Rand (Mrs. James P.), 23:94; "The Mission of Nuestra Señora de la Soledad," 23:1-18; obit., 17:191-92

Smith, Francis Marion, 17:116; 19:76

Smith, Mrs. Francis Marion (Mary R..), 19:76

Smith, Frank (Russian America, 1865), 33:12

Smith, Frank (d. 1873), 30:33-34, 37

Smith, Frank (Redwood City, 1875), 34:80, 82

Smith, Frank Meriweather, 8:364

Smith, Frederick M., 33:6, 7, 12, 149, 167; 35:291-307 *passim*; phot., 33: opp. 1

Smith, G. C., 21:107

Smith, George A., 14:63, 64

Smith, George Dillon, 15:163

Smith, Grafton, 33:12

Smith, Grant Horace, "Bodie, the Last of the Old-Time Mining Camps," 4:64-80; as address, 3:398; address, "John W. Mackay," 16:88

Smith, Gustavus, 34:66, 82

Smith, Guy B., 26:204

Smith, Hamilton, Jr., 29:200-201

Smith, Henry (Yerba Buena, 1847), 6:141

Smith, Capt. Henry (of *Edward Everett*, 1849), 20:27

Smith, Henry and Emily (Alexander), 28:292

Smith, Henry Clay, 12:173, 174; 30:4-5

Smith, Mrs. Henry Clay (Mary van Gordon), 30:4

Smith, Hiram (Mormon), 26:291

Smith, Hiram (Napa Co. pioneer), 16:131

Smith, Hobart, 25:132

Smith, Horace (Sacramento, 1855), 9:36; 10:277

Smith, Horace (Auburn and S.F., 1861), 39:300

Smith, Howard Van Arsdale, 28:381

Smith, I. L., 29:231

Smith, Ina Donna, *see* Coolbrith

Smith, Isaac William, 9:269

Smith, J. B., 9:157, 266, 359, 360, 369

Smith, J. Connor, 15:164; 24:263(?); 25:335

Smith, J. H. (d. Coloma, 1855), 35:77

Smith, J. H. (Mono Co., 1865), 26:247

Smith, Mrs. J. Howard, 33:314; *see also* Jewett, Mrs. William Smith

Smith, J. Langdon, 11:8, 9

Smith, J. Mortimer, 9:272

Smith, J. Mott, 13:32

Smith, James (Sutter's Fort, 1845), 19:119, 138

Smith, James (wounded, 1846), 3:118

Smith, James (of Sutter Creek), 27:382

Smith, James (Marysville, 1851), 15:29

Smith, James (S.F., 1854), 15:178

Smith, James (Marysville, 1859), 10:185, 186

Smith, James Caleb, 20:314; 38:207-8; 40:207-8, 213

Smith, James H., 31:37

Smith, James Jerome, 33:374

Smith, James K., 9:116, 269; 11:9

Smith, Mrs. James Perrin, *see* Smith, Frances Norris Rand

Smith, Jeannette, 31:15

Smith, Jedediah Strong, 1:16, 118; 2:34-36, 46; 4:5, 140; 10:4, 27; 11:389; 12:113, 364; 13:209; 14:195-96; 18:348; 19:311; 22:98, 102, 348; 25:286; 26:164, 172; 28:118, 119-20; 32:376; 37:265;

34:221; arts. on, 2:228-36, 344-49;
4:25-29; exped. of 1823-24, 4:110, 116,
119, 120-39; gold discovered by, 2:35,
36; routes in 1826-27, 2:228-36, (map)
opp. 236, 344-49; 3:25-29; 4:5;
26:234-35, 246; bk. on, rev., 13:410;
letters of, 2:233-36, 345-46
Smith, John (Monterey, 1835), 16:326,
327, 331, 332
Smith, John ("Jack," 1845), 14:205, 227
Smith, John (Sutter's Fort, 1847),
16:136, 138
Smith, John (U.S. dragoon, 1847),
1:242, 243; 33:254, 255, 256
Smith, John (Sacramento, 1849), 23:357
Smith, John (stage driver, 1850s),
13:258
Smith, John (S.F., 1855), 15:368; 20:304,
305
Smith, John, Jr., *see* Miller, Joaquin
Smith, John C., 5:339, 341
Smith, John F., 31:231
Smith, John G., 10:266; 14:394; 15:23,
24, 29, 49
Smith, Joseph (Mormon), 15:245;
26:291
Smith, Joseph (on *Galindo*, 1849),
22:251
Smith, Joseph F., 6:69
Smith, Joseph H. and Sarah B., 12:29
Smith, Josephine D., *see* Coolbrith, Ina
Donna
Smith, Joshua, 22:251
Smith, Julia, 34:66, 82
Smith, Julia A. (Fink), 25:31
Smith, Justin H., 8:251
Smith, Miss K., 11:127
Smith, Laura Cuppy, 21:49-50, 71
Smith, Leah Margaret, 33:351-52
Smith, M., 22:251
Smith, McDuffee, 26:204
Smith, Mary F., 30:16, 37
Smith, Mrs. Maurice D., 26:190
Smith, Mix, 8:338, 356; 9:54, 157, 163
Smith, Miss N., 11:127
Smith, N. P., 15:179
Smith, Napoleon B., 15:370; 30:4-5;
31:327
Smith, Mrs. Napoleon B. (Margelina
Brown), 30:4
Smith, Nick, 2:203
Smith, Noyes, 4:321
Smith, Oliver and Sarah Amelia
(Smith), 30:32, 37
Smith, Orson K., 9:107; 10:278

Smith, Oscar, 37:140
Smith, P., 9:253
Smith, Pat, 9:139, 161, 162
Smith, "Peg Leg," *see* Smith, Thomas L.
Smith, Persifor Frazer, 6:151, 286-87;
10:144, 148; 11:105, 365, 382; 13:363,
381, 389-91; 16:304, 305, 318; 17:3;
20:120, 125; 21:312; 24:59, 62; 26:328;
27:35, 37, 42-43, 251; 28:327; 29:165;
30:56, 62, 329; 33:344, 345, 346; 34:25,
29-30; 35:12; 40:124
Smith, Mrs. Persifor Frazer, 23:51;
33:344, 345
Smith, Peter, 2:117(?), 118(?); 6:41;
28:116; 33:324; lawsuit, 34:251
Smith, Richard, 30:5
Smith, Robert (on *Brooklyn*, 1846),
37:230
Smith, Robert (L.A., 1851), 13:333
Smith, Samuel, Jr., 2:122
Smith, Samuel B., 9:40, 100, 251, 349;
10:43; 11:6
Smith, Seth, 32:126
Smith, "Slung Shot," 15:167
Smith, Stephen (1841), 3:173, 174, 177;
11:130; 13:34-35; 16:143, 344; 17:145,
154, 297, 299, 300; 18:65-69 *passim*;
19:127; 26:207; 33:64; letter, 37:13-14
Smith, Stephen (Big Bend, 1855),
26:203, 204
Smith, Stephen C., 2:122
Smith, Stephen Sears, art. on, 33:321-28;
34:65-82; phot., 34: opp. 65
Smith, Mrs. Stephen Sears (Cornelia
Josephine Child), 33:326; 34:66, 79,
82; phot., 34: opp. 65
Smith, Susan Teegarden, 10:264
Smith, T. C., 29:225
Smith, "Texas" (Egbert Olcott), 4:312
Smith, Thomas (d. 1847), 21:350, 351,
357; 33:105
Smith, Thomas (S.F., 1854), 9:27
Smith, Thomas Boarman and Muriel
Catherine (Turner), 27:382
Smith, Thomas F., 21:154, 156
Smith, Thomas L. ("Peg Leg"), 2:9, 10;
4:157; 16:141; 20:343, 347; 22:200, 209,
217, 219-20; 23:37, 125, 127; 30:53
Smith, Thomas N. and Edith Alvord
(Bowman), 27:382
Smith, Tim, 9:58, 156
Smith, Tom (Yuba Co., 1857), 9:144;
10:256
Smith, W. (Yuba Co., 1855), 8:346, 347
Smith, W. A., 13:335

Smith, W. C. S., 15:24, 28
Smith, W. W., 33:166; 35:296-304 *passim*
Smith, W. Wilson, 15:21, 28
Smith, Waddell F., 28:286; address, "The Eastern End of the Pony Express," 29:73-75; obit. of Henry H. Arnold, 29:83-84
Smith, William (San Jose, 1830s), 14:17
Smith, William (London, 1842), 28:247-49, 257
Smith, William (Isthmus, 1851), 12:109
Smith, William ("desperado," 1855), 15:271; 16:83
Smith, William (Philippines, 1898), 31:60, 64, 65, 173
Smith, William A., 3:116, 118
Smith, William F. (Monterey, 1847), 25:96
Smith, William F. (Yuba Co., 1856), 9:53, 54, 64, 72
Smith, Gen. William F. (1861), 31:232, 233
Smith, William Fowle, 11:179, 180, 181
Smith, William H. (d. 1854), 15:176
Smith, William H. (S.F., 1864), 21:66, 161
Smith, William M. ("Jim Crow"), 11:135
Smith, Mrs. William M., *see* Hinckley, Mrs. William S.
Smith, William W. (New York of the Pacific, 1849), 12:29, 30
Smith, William W. (Marysville, 1852), 8:363
Smith & Co., 15:170
Smith, Bensley & Co., 11:107
Smithers (on *London*, 1849), 7:213, 215, 221, 398
Smith River, 26:5, 7, 8, 11, 207; 30:285
Smith's Bar, 30:111
Smith's Flat, 10:309
Smith's Pomological Gardens, Sacramento, 10:278, 292; 15:173
Smith's River (San Joaquin), 8:115; (Stanislaus), 23:127
Smith's Temperance House, San Francisco, 22:263
Smithwick, Mrs. Charles A., 32:9
Smoke Creek Canyon, 39:264-66
Smoky Valley, Nev., 6:347
Smoot, George, 26:302
Smuggling, 12:145; 13:208, 223; 14:15; 15:275; 16:84; 22:319
Smyrna (ship), 23:308

Smyrniote (ship), 34:319-20
Smyth, William, drawings by, 14: opp. 109, opp. 147
Smyth, William H., 36:110
Snake River expeditions, 28:118-20 *passim*
Snakes, 5:173, 225; 8:171, 180; 12:305; 17:29, 33; 32:252; *see also* Rattlesnakes
Sneath, Richard G., 20:266; 22:17-18; 27:69-70, 272-73; 29:253-54; 31:290
Snelling, Benjamin, 27:130
Snelling, James, 23:90
Snelling's, Merced Co., 12:6
Snider, George G., 14:177
Snider, John, 33:364
Snodgrass, David E., 25:192
Snodgrass, Harold G., 25:192
Snook, J. S., 20:115
Snook, Joseph Francis, 19:210, 216; 26:22, 45, 61
Snook, Mrs. Joseph Francis (María Antonia Alvarado), 26:61
Snooks, P. (?; overland, 1844), 4:310
Snow, Capt. (in mines, 1849), 20:38, 40, 42
Snow, Albert, 5:339
Snow, Arthur P., 24:190
Snow, Howard A., 15:88
Snow, Joseph C., 38:166
Snow, Robert, 14:305, 306, 307
Snow, S. A., 22:251
Snowden, Richard, 11:122
Snowdon, Col. (prison director, 1855), 16:339
Snowhite, Edward S., 9:355, 386; 10:199
Snowhite, Harmon, 10:177, 199
Snowshoe, 18:365, 366 67, 368
Snow Storm Canyon, 39:264-66
Snow Tent, 29:194
Snowville, 32:202
Snowy Butte (Mount Shasta), 5:117, 257
Snug Harbor saloon, San Diego, 22:350
Snug Saloon, San Francisco, 10:393; 20:308; 21:40, 44
Snyder (Yuba Co., 1857, 1859), 9:149; 10:168, 372, 383, 384; lawsuits, 9:144
Snyder, A. J., 34:57
Snyder, Mrs. A. J. (née Chappelet), 17:48
Snyder, Albert, 38:32
Snyder, H. M., 9:99
Snyder, Jacob Rink, 10:156, 158, 160, 190; 11:84; 18: foll. 72; 19:7, 116, 131, 135, 136, 138, 142; 23:370; 28:373;

29:166, 336; 30:56; fac. sig., 10: opp. 159
Snyder, John, 10:349-50
Snyder, Joseph, 21:308
Snyder, M., 25:175
Snyder, S. L., 17:84
Soap, 2:55; 5:259, 269; 6:261; 13:215; 29:25, 320
Soap Lake, 29:25
Soberanes, Carmen, 1:234(?), 258
Soberanes, Feliciano, 1:258; 23:10, 13, 348
Soberanes, Gabriela, 1:234(?), 258
Soberanes, José María, 13:198
Soberanes, María Ignacia, *see* Bale, Mrs. Edward Turner
Soberanes, Mrs. Mariano (Maria Isidora Vallejo), 29:318
Soberanes, Panfilo, 23:12
"Social Life in Spanish California," address by Nellie V. Sanchez, 6:380-81
Socialism, 40:215-36; *see also* George, Henry
Socialist Party, 38:350
Sociedade Portuguesa Rainha Santa Izabel, 35:244
Sociétaire, Le (monthly), 39:316-19, 346
Société californienne de 1850, d'après Bret Harte, by Réau, rev., 1:102-4
Société de Commerce de San Francisco, 22:303, 308
Société des Lingots d'Or, *see* Lingots d'Or
Société des Mines d'Or de la Californie, 22:300
Société Française de Bienfaisance Mutuelle, San Francisco, 22:213; 35:315; 39:153, 170, 227, 230-31, 234, 238, 242-43, 256
Société Immobilière de San Francisco, 22:309
Société Nationale, 22:296-97
Societies, *see* names of organizations
Society for the Preservation of National Parks, 38:254
Society of California Pioneers, 6:197-98; 13:225; 15:166, 174, 301, 370, 373; 16:82, 200, 316; 17:74; 18:32, 36, 45; 21:369; 22:147, 275; 23:75, 173-74; 25:103; 26:107, 108, 129, 131, 133, 152, 158, 159; 27:106, 111; 28:65, 291; 30:55, 358; 30:358; 31:207, 208, 214; 33:311; 36:348; 37:216, 361; 38:28, 305
"Society of California Pioneers and

Pioneer Days," address by C. S. Cushing, 6:197-98
Society of California Volunteers, 15:301
Society of Old Californians, New York, 17:205; resolution, opp. 200
Society of Pacific Coast Pioneers, 11:51
Society of the Golden Ingots, *see* Lingots d'Or
Society of Thirty-two, 5:21
"Society's New Quarters [1938], The," by Douglas S. Watson, 17:74
Soda Bay, 32:366
Soda Lake, 2:235
Soda Springs, Nevada Co., 18:179
Soda Springs, Riverside Co., 12:9
Sofre (S.F., 1854), 30:254, 264
Soher, Lewis, 13:32
Sohr, Dr. (Calaveras Co., 1856), 7:13
Sokol, A. E., 28:92; "California: A Possible Derivation of the Name," 28:23-30
Solá, Pablo Vicente de, 2:341-43; 6:255; 12:231, 234, 235, 242; 13:205, 206, 209; 14:15, 123; 15:141-42; 16:105, 106, 109; 17:246; 20:239; 23:5; 24:291, 308; 25:60, 76, 149, 362; 27:333; 28:258; 37:123, 246
Solano, Francisco, 4:286; 12:133, 198; 16:244, 245, 250, 348, 355, 356, 360-61, 370; 17:52, 146-50, 155; 20:234; 23:295; 28:264; 29:311-12, 314
Solano, Francisco II, 16:351, 370
Solano County Courthouse, 24:64
Solano County Herald, Benicia, 16:340; 30:363
Solano House (or Hotel), Benicia, 14:364, 367; 15:73-74; 27:302, 308
Soldados de cuera, see Leather-jacket soldiers
"Soldiers of the Overland," address by Fred B. Rogers, 18:286
Soledad (Indian), 23:1
Soledad, Los Angeles Co., 17:113, 208, 209, 215
Soledad, Monterey Co., 17:100, 101; 30:311
Soledad (ship), 11:342; 12:147
Soledad Mission, *see* Missions: Nuestra Señora de la Soledad
Soledad Valley, 26:59
Soler, Pablo, 4:145-46
Solerer y Sinton, 30:258
Solinsky, Frank J., Jr., obit., 29:378-79
Solís, Joaquín, 16:219, 222; 27:337
"Solitaire" (pseud.), *see* Robb, John S.

Solitude (ship), 8:234, 248

Solomon, P. L., 10:170; 32:146, 148, 152

Solomons, Theodore Seixas, 4:39, 46-47, 48

Solvay Process Co., 17:117

"Some Anthropological Perspectives on California History," address by Robert F. Heizer, 33:85-88

"Some Bibliographical Notes Concerning Jerónimo de Ripalda's *Catecismo,*" by Henry R. Wagner, 16:373-75

"Some California Dates of 1859," comp. Mrs. Harold David *et al.*, 38:25-30

"Some California Dates of 1860," comp. Gordon C. Roadarmel, 38:329-40; "... of 1861," 39:289-308

"Some California Place Names," address by Aubrey Drury, 15:89

"Some California Politics about 1860," address by George T. Clark, 9:90-91

"Some Detached Notes by Henry Chapman Ford on the Missions of California," 3:238-44

"Some Early Botanical Explorers of California," address by Alice Eastwood, 18:376

"Some Engineering Works on the Comstock," address by John D. Galloway, 19:187

"Some Facts Concerning Leland Stanford ... in Placer County," by Boutwell Dunlap, 2:203-10

"Some Footnotes to Sutter's Fort," address by Carroll D. Hall, 30:375-76

"Some Forgotten Characters of Old San Francisco," address by Robert E. Cowan, 13:88

Some Imaginary California Geography, by Wagner, rev., 6:95-96

"Some Letters of George Sterling," ed. John R. Dunbar, 40:137-55

"Some Letters of William S. Jewett, California Artist," ed. Elliot Evans, 23:149-77, 227-46

"Some Notes with Regard to Drake's Plate of Brass," by Allen L. Chickering, 16:275-81

"Some Oatman Documents," ed. Alice B. Maloney, 21:107-12

"Some Observations of California Mission Life," address by Edward T. Planer, Jr., 30:84-86

"Some Phases of California Literature," address by Br. Leo, 8:283

"Some Phases of French Society in San Francisco in the 'Fifties," from Journal of Ernest de Massey, trans. Blanche C. Wagner, 32:105-18

"Some Pioneer Artists of California," address by Eugen Neuhaus, 15:383

Somero, Ángel, 23:371

"Some Romantic Realities in the History of California," address by Robert E. Cowan, 8:90

Somers, Fred W., 28:10

Somers, George B. and Mary McIntyre (Hooper), 31:302

Somerset House, El Dorado Co., 20:158; 27:86

"Some Russian Influences on the History of California," address by E. O. Essig, 8:90

Somerville (Yuba Co., 1857), 9:134, 135; & Co., 9:134, 136

Somes, George A., 26:204

"Some Shadows of the San Francisco Stage," by James Madison, 4:59-63

Sommers, Capt. (of *Swallow,* 1861), 10:283, 286, 356

Sommers, Charles, 3:118

Songer, W. F., 21:130

Songs: sung in 1827, 8:147; in 1844, 4:309-10; by Mormons, 1846, 37:234; in 1849, 2:99-100; in the '50's, 9:391; 22:30-31; in the '60's, 36:297; words by Bret Harte, 4:207; by Stephen Massett, 14:387, 388; 22:31; by Frank Soulé, 22:38

Songster, J. T., 31:232

Sonoma, 1:29, 31; 12:255; 16:114, 236; 17:66, 141, 155, 235, 236, 274, 281, 294; 25:122, 123, 124, 29:149 54 *passim;* 30:363; 36:242, 243; barracks, 16:236; 17:143; 21:13; churches, 26:171; 27:308; in 1840s, 12:255; 13:266; 16:101, 250; 17:55, 141-49; 19:198; 21:10, 11; 23:294; 29:316; in 1850s, 2:136; 17:237-38; 23:259-60; 24:58-63, 64, 67, 169; in 1860s, 17:236, 238; 36:245; 1870-1919, 17:238-39; founding of, 16:99-100, 114, 242-45; 24:57; guns at, 2:362; 15:64, 65, 69; 17:164, 278; 24:57; mail service, 10:353, 354; military post, 15:61; 16:100, 242, 243; 17:143-48 *passim,* 164; 21:13; 24:57, 59; 34:25, 27; name, 16:112; newspapers, 17:239-40; 18:277; 23:259-60; 24:58; printing at, 12:128, 133-34; thespian club, 9:79; U.S. flag raised at, 2:357, 361; 3:84; 16:100, 101;

17:275-76; letters from, 29:149-51, 153, 157; bk on, rev., 2:364-65; *see also* Bear Flag revolt; Missions: San Francisco Solano

Sonoma County, 15:161; 24:58; fair, 36:245; newspaper, 22:361; Swiss in, 30:310, 311; tannery in, 33:63-64

Sonoma [County] Democrat, Santa Rosa, 20:165; 22:361

Sonoma Hotel, 24:49, 57

Sonoma Mission, *see* Missions: San Francisco Solano

Sonoma Valley, 13:266; 16:112-13; 27:308; 29:319; 36:241-44 *passim*

Sonoma Valley railway cos., 17:238

Sonora, Calif., 1:98; 8:87; 10:45-46, 68; 11:164-69 *passim*, 331, 336; 13:373, 383; 15:273; 17:6-7, 10-17 *passim*; 19:325; 20:101, 256; 22:71, 73, 82; 30:110, 259, 266; 32:53, 55, 125-30 *passim*, 138; 34:213, 215, 293-95; 35:40, 41; 38:38, 309; letters from, 35:213-19, 221-31; newspapers, 1:98; 5:311; 7:277; illus., 10: opp. 58

Sonora, Mex., 5:372; 9:281, 364, 369, 370, 391; 21:297, 328; 21:297, 328; 27:205, 206, 214, 353-54; 34:134-37 *passim*; Crabb's exped. to, 9:144, 176; 21:32-33; French filibusters in, 18:3-21; 23:174; 35:319-20; gold rush from, 13:363; 19:324-25; 27:162, 164; 35:37; newspapers, 1:98; 5:311; 7:277; Walker's exped. to, 27:145-46, 147, 203-4, 204-5

Sonora (ship, 1775), 9:205-32 *passim*, 240-42

Sonora (small str., 1852), 18:6

Sonora (Panama str., 1850s), 4:237; 11:10-11; 15:164, 166, 169, 176, 182, 186, 269, 270, 273, 278, 279; 16:84, 285, 338; 17:179; 26:305; 27:327; 29:103, 116; 32:209, 310, 312; 34:336; 38:337; 39:297

Sonora Emigrant Road, 34:213, 215-17

Sonora Greys, 37:366

Sonora Junction, 36:360-61

Sonoranian (Sonorian, Sonoran) Camp, Tuolumne Co., 3:373, 383, 384; 19:325; *see also* Sonora

Sonorans, 4:170; 5:354, 372; 13:165, 225, 277, 383; 17:4, 15; 19:325-26; 21:358; 23:367; 26:124; 27:162, 164; 31:310; 35:37-46 *passim*; *see also* Mexicans

Sonora Pass, 4:8; 26:236, 244; 34:216

Sonorian Camp, Yuba Co., 15:39-40

Sons of Revolutionary Sires, 29:290-94

Sons of Temperance, 2:119; 9:157, 177; 15:45, 180; 16:81; 20:373; 32:131-32, 137; 38:311

Sons of the American Revolution, 29:289-95

Sontag, John, 8:281-82

Sophie (riv. str., 1851), 2:138

Sophie (brig, 1855), 15:272

Sophie B. (schr., 1864), 22:170

Soquel (ship), 31:295

Sorbier, Cecile M., 31:377; 32:186

Sorbier, Louise Agathe J. (Bacon), 31:377; 33:374

Sorbier, Louis Jules, port., 38: opp. 160

Sorcey, W. B., 9:61

Sorcière, La (play), 20:140; 33:45

Soria, Rafael de Jesús, 23:9

Sorrel, Francis, 28:352

Soscol, *see* Suscol

Soteaux (d. 1832), 22:198, 199

Soto, Antonio, 14:22

Soto, Felipe, 17:250

Soto, Francisco (3 of this name?), 1:167; 2:346; 14:99

Soto, Guillermo, 13:203

Soto, Hernando de, 1:44; 6:299

Soto, Ignacio (S.F., 1776), 14:99

Soto, Ignacio (quicksilver mine, 1848), 13:60, 78

Soto, Josefa, 6:270

Soto, Juan (farmer nr. San Jose, 1841), 13:269, 278

Soto, Juan (outlaw, 1860s), 17:115

Soto, Mrs. Juan (Petra Pacheco), 13:278

Soto, Lorenzo, 21:351; 26:29, 42, 54, 58

Soto, Pepita, 9:275

Soto, Rejis, 13:203

Soucha (Yuba Co., 1857), 9:148

Souffrey (ship), 5:141

Soulé, Frank, 7:281; 8:361, 362; 13:299; 14:74; 15:165, 174, 186, 272; 16:336; 20:336; 22:38, 260, 275; 26:344; 29:260; 30:252, 256; 38:310

Soulé, Frank, Jr., 4:31; 35:255, 260, 263

Soulé, Henry Douglas Bacon, 26:197, 200; "Old California Market, San Francisco," 5:85-86; bk. rev. by, 6:99-101

Soule, Robert S., 22:78-79

Soulié, Maurice, *The Wolf Cub*, trans. Symons, rev., 7:198-99

"Source of the Sutter Myth, The," by Erwin G. Gudde, 9:398-99

Souris (Mouse, now Mary's) River, 23:143

South Africa, gold in, 28:277-78

South America, emigrants from, 19:326-27, 334

Southampton (ship), 6:151; 33:341; 36:310

Southard, L., 13:32

South Carolina, 16:154-60, 170

South Carolina (ship, 1836), *see Sarah and Caroline*

South Carolina (ship, 1849), 27:362

South Dome (Half Dome), Yosemite, 1:279

Southern, May Hazel, obit., 22:381-82

"Southern and Northern Methodism in Civil War California," by Barbara McClung MacVicar, 40:327-42

Southern and Western Hotel, Marysville, 14:394, 404

Southern California Gas Co., 31:176

Southern California, Los Angeles, 13:336, 337; 29:245

Southern Counties Gas Co., 31:176

Southerner (ship), 15:268, 270; 32:353, 360-61

Southern News, Los Angeles, 13:347; 32:327, 344; 39:289

Southern Pacific Railroad, 4:93, 225-26; 7:292; 8:282; 15:190, 380; 17:238; 18:373, 384; 22:162, 164; 24:91; 28:94; 30:341; 32:342-44, 366, 368, 369; 35:263-64; 36:104, 105, 375-77

Southern Rifles, 29:234-39 *passim*

Southern Sierras of California, The, by Saunders, rev., 3:92

Southern Syndicate, San Diego, 36:75-76

Southern Title & Trust Co., 36:76, 156-60, 163-64

Southern Trust & Savings Bank, Southern Trust & Commerce Bank, 35:363; 37:353-54

Southern Vineyard, Los Angeles, 13:337

Southfork, Madera Co., 38:223-24

Southgate, Horatio, 12:100

Southgate & Mitchell, 19:146

South Pacific Coast Railroad, 18:373

South Park, San Francisco, 10:44, 67; 16:182, 195, 341; 17:85; 19:231-32, 238; 36:212; 39:304; illus., 19: opp. 225

South Pass, 1:64; 3:53; 4:127-28, 134, 139, 279, 338; 5:117, 362; 6:117; 22:137; 27:182; 38:275; 40:161

Southport Land and Improvement Co., 12:33

South San Francisco, 5:376; 17:245, 254, 255; 25:264

South Vallejo, 27:194, 197, 200, 201; phot., 27: opp. 200

Southwester (ship), 22:162, 166, 167

Southwest Museum, Los Angeles, 4:215; 13:151; 31:18

Southwick, John (Stockton's bat., 1846), 21:354, 357

Southwick, John (Grass Valley, 1850s), 6:339

Southwick, Willard, 16:283

Southworth, Eli, 11:381(?); 12:138; 14:320, 322, 324, 328, 329, 330

South Yuba Canal, 18:154; 29:193, 199-200

"Souvenirs of an Interesting Family," by Helen T. Pratt, 7:282-85, 406

Soverano, Francisco, 13:78

Sovereign (ship), 22:154, 170, 171

Sovereign of the Seas (ship), 10:294

Sowers, Lewis, 6:350

Sowers, William, 31:171

Spafford (Calaveras Co., 1852), 22:78

"Spain Delayed Occupation of California," address by David P. Barrows, 26:374-76

Spalding, Albert, 25:236

Spalding (or Spaulding), Charles C., 37:271

Spalding, Georgiana Lacy (Thompson), 27:286

Spalding, Henry Harmon, 4:353; 10:402; 15:283, 285; 20:25; 25:141, 142, 143

Spalding, Josiah, 12:244-45; 17:83; 18:310; 28:108

Spalding, Z. N., 18:306-7

Spangenberg, E. M., 22:32, 39

Spangled Gold Gulch, 28:335

"Spanish Anchorage in San Francisco Bay, The," by J. N. Bowman, 25:319-24

Spanish Arcadia, by Sánchez, rev., 9:87

Spanish Bar, 2:138; 19:134, 143

Spanish Californians, 8:309-12; 15:231-34, 237-38; 25:313, 314; soldiers, 8:310-11; women, 8:311; *see also* Mexican Californians

Spanish Camp, on Spanish Creek, 32:376

Spanish expeditions and explorations, 3:262-67 *passim;* 4:142-43; 10:313-45; 26:375-76; 32:43-48 *passim; see also* Anza; Atondo y Antillón; Bodega y

Quadra; Cabrillo; Cermeño; Fages; Garcés; Goycoechea; Hezeta; Malaspina; Portolá; Ulloa; Unamuno; Vizcaíno
Spanish Flat, 8:201, 210; 38:307
Spanish language newspapers, 37:199
Spanish Mine, 11:61
Spanish period in California, 1:157-67, 169; 4:142-50; 15:139-42; 17:118-22, 246-48; 32:43-48 *passim*
Spanish River (Sacramento R.), 24:232
Spanish Songs of Old California, ed. Lummis, rev., 2:363-64
Spanish Southwest, The, by Wagner, rev., 3:290-91
Spanish trail, bet. Santa Fe and Los Angeles, 1:119, 121, 123, 148; 2:39; 10:27-39, 89; 14:348; 22:12; 34:212; map, 10: opp. 27; *see also* Santa Fe trail
"Spanish Voyages to the Northwest Coast in the 16th Century," by Henry R. Wagner, 6:293-331; 7:20-77, 132-93, 228-76, 295-394; 8:26-70
Spark, Anna Maria, 7:108-10
Sparks (Stockton, 1892), 34:351, 354
Sparks, G. S., 14:177
Sparks, Isaac J., 1:170; 2:45; 4:157; 18:162, 164, 175, 256; 27:135
Sparks, Matthew, 28:237, 242
Sparks, Quartus S. and Mary (Hamilton), 14:73, 176, 182
Sparlin (Mt. Shasta, 1856), 6:74
Sparrow, A. R., 39:159
Sparrow (ship), 22:172
Spaulding (New York Flat, 1855), 8:342, 348
Spaulding (Marysville, 1859), 10:173, 195
Spaulding, Miss (nr. Placerville, 1865), 20:256-57
Spaulding, Charles A., 30:102, 107, 113
Spaulding, De Forest Wells and Letitia Jane (Joiner), 31:190
Spaulding, Nathan Weston, 29:381
Spaulding, Lake, 29:199
Spaulding & Martin, 30:103
Spear (2d mate *Westward Ho*, 1852), 26:227; 28:322; 29:39
Spear (Marysville, 1859, 1861), 10:363, 375; lawsuit, 10:188
Spear, Nathan, 3:32; 4:169-70; 5:255, 305; 8:124; 10:91; 11:73, 75, 130, 135; 12:146; 14:80, 121-29 *passim*, 342; 16:58, 106, 324-26, 329-31; 17:54, 157,

293-95, 297, 300; 18:67, 70; 28:113, 253, 257, 266-67; 30:1, 3; 35:200
Spear, Mrs. Nathan (Jane Holmes), 14:127
Spear, Thomas G., 23:272, 279, 280; 30:247
Spear, William N., 14:128
Spearman, Arthur D., 37:303-4
Spears, John Randolph, 17:117
Spear's Bank, Georgetown, 17:78
Speckles *v.* R. R. Merrill, 10:174
Spect, Jonas, 14:212; 23:349, 369
Spectateur, Le, 39:153, 350
Spectre Bridegroom (play), 15:48
Spects (Placerville, 1854), 11:58
Spee (from Ore., 1848), 24:27
Speedy (ship), 6:257, 259, 261
Speer, William, 15:163; 30:251; 32:130
Speiden, William, 18:52, 62; 29:275
Speilbergen, Joris van, 8:36, 50, 54
Spence, Clark C., 35:381; "The Mining Bureau of the Pacific Coast," 35:335-44
Spence, David, 3:182; 4:170; 6:262; 8:101, 105, 128, 301; 12:345; 13:34; 14:318, 343; 15:123, 234; 16:106, 222; 17:138-39, 146, 157, 231; 28:100, 102, 108, 246, 260-62; 29:23, 27; 35:107, 110
Spence, Mrs. David (Adelaida Estrada), 29:27
Spence, Edward Fallis, 36:330
Spence, J. F., 13:32
Spence, John F., 34:245, 246
Spence, Robert, 19:126, 140
Spence, Thomas, 11:369
Spencer, Miss (Yuba Co., 1857), 9:148
Spencer (alias Herrick, 1859), 10:177
Spencer, A. J., 29:237
Spencer, Dorcas J. (Barber), 6:332
Spencer, Elizabeth (Durham), 20:255
Spencer, Ephraim V., 18:307, 314
Spencer, Hamilton, 2:216
Spencer, Jeannette (Dyer), obit. of Mrs. Charles N. Felton, 20:383
Spencer, O. W., 26:73, 74, 175, 176
Spencer, Stephen, 9:134, 135, 139, 148, 173, 267, 371, 373; 10:46
Spencer, Mrs. Stephen (Carrie Green), 9:173
Spencer, W. R., 30:367; *see also* Kendall (E. A.) and Spencer
Spencer & Adkinson, 9:79
Sperry, Austin, 27: opp. 97, 194
Sperry, Ethel W., *see* Crocker, Mrs. William H.

Sperry, James L., 22:192

Sperry, R. A., 22:192

Sperry Flour Co., 27:194-95, 200; 30:285

Sperry Hotels, Calaveras Co., 22:192

Spice Islands, *see* Moluccas

Spicer, Edwin and Mary Ann (Burke), 28:292

Spicer, Henry, 30:8

Spiders and scorpions, 17:28-29; 21:206

Spier, Dr. (San Juan del Sur, 1852), 36:143-44, 146

Spier, Robert F. G., 37:91; "Food Habits of Nineteenth-Century California Chinese," 37:79-84, 129-36

Spiers, Mrs. Samuel (Sarah Graves Fosdick Ritchie), 19:139

Spies brothers (1849), 23:161

Spikes, railroad ceremonial, 3:398; 19:186; 24:365, 368; art. on, 36:97-106, 263-74; phot., 36: opp. 97

Spiller, J. C., 4:36

Spillman, B. R., 9:151, 163, 170, 248, 269, 349, 353, 385

Spink, John, 13:258

Spink, R., lawsuits, 9:153, 154

Spinney, Mrs. Charles (Salista Bosqui), 21:332

Spinney, Frank Oakman, 20:287-88; "A New Hampshire Minstrel Tours the Coast: Rhodolphus Hall and His Letters," 20:243-58

Spinney, William, 26:204

Spirit of the Age, Sacramento, 9:275

Spirit of the Times, San Francisco, 10:68; 23:261; 25:336, 344

Spiritual Bookstore, Sacramento, 30:355

Spiritualism, 9:144, 169, 170, 179, 361; 10:186, 187, 201, 246, 247, 260, 261, 386; 14:74; 30:356; 31:6; 36:344-45

Spoehr, Mrs. H. A. (Florence Mann), 29:382-83

Spoiled Child, The (play), 15:48

Spokane House, 28:117-18; 33:82, 83, 84

Spon, Henry, 2:128

"Sponge, The: James King of William, His Surgeons and the Vigilantes," address by George D. Lyman, 7:95-96

Sponknabel, William, 28:239

Spooner, J. Pitcher, 35:48, 55

Spooner, John A., 13:296

Sports, 9:145, 147, 156, 157; billiards, 246, 251

Sportsman's Hall, 20:158

"Spotlights on the Political History of

California from 1887 to 1898," by Donald W. Wheaton, 5:283-88

Spotts *v.* Hanley, 21:118-19

Sprague, Charles A., 31:125, 128

Sprague, Richard Homer, obit., 18:95

Sprague, Royal T., 10:362

Spreckels, Adolph Bernard, 40:42

Spreckels, Claus, 35:265; 38:259, 260; art. on, 40:33-48; port., 40: opp. 40

Spreckels, Claus Augustus ("Gus"), 40:42, 43

Spreckels, John Diedrich, 30:195; 35:362, 363; 36:69, 76, 156; 38:354; 40:43

Spreckels, Rudolph, 31:303-4; 36:183, 255; 40:42, 43

Spreckels, Mrs. Rudolph (Eleanor Joliffe), 36:183

Spreckels Oceanic Steamship Line, 40:38

Spreckels Sugar Co., 36:110

Spreckels Theater, San Diego, 36:156

"Spreckelsville Plantation, The: A Chapter in Claus Spreckels' Hawaiian Career," by Jacob Adler, 40:33-48

Spring (Marysville, 1860), 10:246; lawsuit (Sacramento, 1861), 10:356

Spring, Francis S., 32:236, 238-39

Spring, Mrs. George, 16:137

Spring, John, 10:246(?), 276

Spring, John H., 31:297

Spring and Autumn (play), 16:339

Spring Creek Mining Co., 32:359

Springer (Coloma, 1851), 22:29

Springer, Charles, 24:127

Springer, James Peter, 10:62

Springer, Robert, 24:127

Springer, Thomas, 2:103, 117, 118, 121

Springfield, 11:332, 336; 32:132

Spring Valley, Mono Co., 26:242

Spring Valley, Yuba Co., 3:149-51; 8:344, 360

Spring Valley Canal and Mining Co., 29:196-97

Spring Valley School, San Francisco, 33:308

Spring Valley Water Co., 9:96, 259, 283; 10:391; 21:380; 25:241; 31:297, 301; 37:224-25; 38:251-53

Sproul, Robert Gordon, 19:188; 36:151; phot., 37: opp. 208

Sproule, William, 25:232, 239, 246, 247

Sproule, Mrs. William, 25:233

Sprowl *v.* Woods *et al.*, 9:130

Spruce Gulch, 22:78, 83

"Spurious Californiana: *Four Months among the Gold-Finders*," by Douglas S. Watson, 11:65-68

Spy (schr., 1825), 8:290

Spy (brig, 1846), 3:108, 113

Spyns (on *London*, 1849), 7:210

Squatters: 2:65, 119; 5:367, 376-77; 8:268; 9:256, 259, 281; 14:389-390; 15:8, 52, 163, 165, 179, 181; 17:233, 235, 253; 20:29, 109, 260, 333; 21:120, 226-27; 22:62, 361-62; 24:193; 26:70; 27:128; 29:323-24; 33:307; 35:7, 157; *see also* Settlers' League of California

Squaw Man, The (play), 34:364

Squaw Valley, 7:14; CHS Olympic Games luncheon, phot., 39: opp. 80

"Squibob" (pseud.), *see* Derby, George Horatio

Squire, Henry Charles, 36:184

Squires, George D., 20:337, 339

Squires, Henry, 10:265; 21:51; 29:119

Squires, Ogden, 10: opp. 48, 62, 70; 26:131

Squirrels, 2:287; 12:304; 20:42; 23:297; 32:264

S. S. Lewis (ship), 27:293; 36:135, 139

Stace, Elizabeth, 28:292

Stacey, May Humphreys, *Uncle Sam's Camels*, ed. Lesley, rev., 9:182-84

Stackhouse, Robert, 20:308

Stackpole, Ralph, 38:1, 2, 4; phot., 38: opp. 8

Stacy (Smartsville, 1859), 10:169

Stacy & Grant, 30:366

Stadmuller, Edwin W., 23:96

Stafford, Daniel, 23:192

Stafford, Helen Cortez, bk. rev. by, 16:85

Stafford, J., 8:201, 205, 206

Stafford, James, 23:192

Stafford, Mrs. Mallie, quoted, 8:356-57

Stafford, Morris G., 8:201, 205, 209

Stafford, Mrs. Morris G. (later Mrs. Mix), 8:344, 347, 360; 9:52

Stafford, R., 13:32

Stafford, Walter B., 31:134, 135

"Stage-Coach Days in California: Reminiscences of H. C. Ward," ed. Oscar O. Winther, 13:255-61; as address, 14:186-87

Stagecoaches, 3:170; 13:255-61; 14:160-61, 187; 16:32-33; 18:359; 38:335; illus., 13: opp. 255

Stage companies and routes, 3:170; 6:71; 7:13-19 *passim*; 8:345, 360; 13:255-61;

14:160-62, 187, 385, 402; 15:166, 328; 17:33-34, 43, 108, 109; 18:262, 359; 22:76, 162, 368; 26:244; 38:219; *see also* Butterfield Overland Mail; California Stage Co.

Stage Drivers' Retreat, Columbia, 24:268

Stage Hotel, Angel's Camp, 11:326

Stage Hotel, Sonora, 11:331

Stagg, Cornelius, 40:213

Staghound (ship), 15:172; 17:75

Stair, Alexander, 4:13; 23:376

Stakes, A. G., 9:249, 251-59 *passim*, 269, 274

Staley, Thomas Nettleship, 34:318-19, 321

Stambaugh, S. C., 15:24

Stampede Lake, 22:202, 214

Stamp mills, *see* Quartz mills

Stamps (Nevada City, 1851), 8:359

Stanbery, Henry, 21:120

Standard, Capt. (Colorado R., 1863), 22:170, 172, 173

Standard Mining Co., 4:68, 75-76

Standard Oil Co. of California, 17:94, 115; 36:112

Standard Theater, San Francisco, 21:259; 35:142

Standish, Miles, obit., 11:296

Stanely (ship), 13:358, 382

Stanfield, Miss (Yuba Co., 1859), 10:170

Stanfield House, Yuba Co., 8:340, 356, 358; 9:53

Stanford, Josiah, 26:181

Stanford, Josiah W., obit., 16:384

Stanford, Leland, 5:94; 7:17; 10: opp. 48, 392; 12:76; 19:249-54 *passim*; 21:369; 23:246; 24:98; 26:181; 27:17, 170, 171, 274; 31:337; 33:173; 38:311; Central Pacific RR, 4:219, 245, 246, 258-68 *passim*; 5:178-83; 19:249; 21:328; 24:367; 27:271, 272, 339; 30:136; 36:98, 99, 100, 263-72 *passim*; 38:352; gov. of Calif., 4:258; 10:373, 387, 388, 390; 19:250-53; 22:147; 23:109, 260; 26:16; 29:239, 241, 326; 30:134; 33:231; 34:51, 52; 36:318; 40:297; houses of, 19:234, 238, (phot.) opp. 245, 245, 249-53; 39:197-98; in Placer Co., 2:203-10; in politics, 5:94; 9:90-91, 116; 10:78, 195, 369; 22:146, 229, 230; 27:97, 99, 318; 32:159, 299; 39:299, 302; 40:291-92; university founder, 10:392; 15:98; 33:169, 173; letters to Hopkins, 5:178-83; bk. on, rev., 10:407

Stanford, Mrs. Leland (Jane Lathrop), 2:208-10; 8:87; 10:379, 392; 19:240, 249-54 *passim;* 31:8

Stanford, Leland, Jr., 2:209-10; 10:392; 19:253

Stanford, Philip, 2:209; 26:181

Stanford, Mount, 4:47, 54

Stanford-Lathrop Memorial Home, Sacramento, 19:245

Stanford University, 7:412; 10:392, 407; 13:86; 15:98; 19:76; 23:180; 31:5, 8-9; 36:97-106 *passim;* 37:41-42, 45

Stanger, Frank Merriman, "A California Rancho [Buri Buri] under Three Flags," 17:245-59; " 'The Hospice' or 'Mission San Mateo,' " 23:247-58, 287; ed. "Letters of an Artist in the Gold Rush," 22:235-52; address: "The Portolá Discovery Site," 27:377

Stanhope, George, 14:211

Stanislaus City, 5:34

Stanislaus County, bk. on, rev., 3:90-92; Swiss in, 31:312

Stanislaus Diggings, 24:344

Stanislaus River, 16:219, 220; 22:102; 23:60; 34:24, 222; 38:336, mining on, 13:173; 20:119; 23:60

Stanislaus Water Co., 24:269

Stanley (stage driver, 1850), 13:256

Stanley, Emma, 21:42

Stanley, F., 9:100

Stanley, H.H., 9:38

Stanley, J. L., 40:218

Stanley, John Mix, 21:200, 205, 222; 25:294, 304-5; 26:40, 43

Stanley, Larkin, 29:342

Stanley, Leo Leonidas, address, "History of San Quentin Prison," 13:88

Stanley, Peter, 13:20-23

Stanley, R. H., 26:181-82

Stanley, Reva (Holdoway), "First Utah Coins Minted from California Gold, The," 15:244-46; "Sutter's Mormon Workmen at Natoma and Coloma," 14:269-82; coed. "A Mormon Mission to California in 1851 ... Parley Parker Pratt," 14:59-73, 175-82

Stanley, Wyland, 17:287, 359

Stanlili (ship), see *Stanely*

Stanly, Edward, 6:11; 9:113, 115, 116, 153, 177; 16:81, 82; 17:177, 309, 320-21; 31:236

Stanly, John Alexander, 21:328

Stanner (San Luis Obispo Co., 1860s), 18:265

Stansbury, B. B., 9:394

Stansbury, J. J., 9:283

Stanton, Charles H., 9:26

Stanton, Charles Tyler, 10:348, 350; 19:121, 138

Stanton, Edwin L., 29:81

Stanton, Edwin McMasters, 15:5, 6, 15, 19; 16:197, 202, 203; 19:163; 22:13

Stanton, Henry Whiting, 21:197, 221

Stanton, Mrs. Lewis E., 24:93

Stanton, Phil, 39:21, 22

Stanwood, Capt. (of *Favorite*), 14:305

Stanwood, Edward B., 10:270; 14:225; bk. rev. by, 9:87-88

Stanwood, Richard Goss, 6:69; 10:259, 270, 286, 357; "An Ascent of Mt. Shasta in 1861," from Journal of, 6:69-76

Staples, Mrs. (on *Westward Ho*, 1853), 28:322; 29:39, 55

Staples, Charles, 2:122

Staples, David Jackson, 10:359; 26:355; 27:97, 102, 166; Journal, ed. Harold F. Taggart, 22:119-50; phot., 22: opp. 119

Staples, Mrs. David Jackson (Mary Pratt Winslow), 22:119, 146

Staples, Fred, 22:127, 130, 144, 146

Staples, Joseph M., 20:158

Star, Columbia, 24:269; 34:343

Star, Los Angeles, 13:319-20, 336; 20:186; 22:361; 33:198; 39:289

Star, North San Juan, 9:168, 181; 10:395; 30:126

Star (weekly, 1890), San Francisco, 27:318

Star and Ryer, 13:348

Starbird, Ellen Alicia, 27:285

Starbuck house, Green Valley, 27:281

Star Co., mining claim of, 11:233

Stark (left Calif., 1849), 12:109

Stark, Benjamin, 15:208; 19:3

Stark, Daniel, 5:407; 14:177(?); 30:99; 33:65

Stark, Mr. and Mrs. James, 7:117; 9:371, 385, 394; 10:42, 52, 65, 75, 246, 254, 260; 15:48, 166, 168, 266, 278; 16:182, 283, 285, 339, 341; 20:294-97, 304; 21:46, 53, 64; 39:298

Stark and Ryer, 13:348

Starke, D. Frederick, 19:128, 141

Starkey (S.F., 1850), 7:227, 398, 400;

8: 180, 182, 264, 266, 267; store, 7:397; wharf, 7:399

Starkey, Janion & Co., 8:264; 23:277, 278

Starkweather, McClenachan & Co., 6:38; 15:170

Starlight (ship), 16:81

Star of Italy (ship), 22:353

Star of Oregon (ship), 19:197, 214; 23:291

Star of the West (ship), 5:132-33; 26:178-79; 34:119

Starr, Abraham Dubois, 27:193-202, 284; phot., 27: opp. 193

Starr, Mrs. Abraham Dubois (Mary Anna Teegarden), 27:194, 202

Starr, Augustus W., 27:196, 197

Starr, Elizabeth, 27:382

Starr, Henry, 9:394; 11:9

Starr, J. B., 9:346; 10:293

Starr, Walter Augustus, 27:283-84; 36:93; "Abraham Dubois Starr, Pioneer California Miller," 27:193-202 "Drake in California...," 36:31-34; obits. of Everett J. Brown, 26:90-91; Allen L. Chickering, 37:86-88; Aubrey Drury, 39:75-77; Harry H. Fair, 40:84-85; Olive H. Palmer, 37:181; Henry H. Patterson, 35:183-84

Starr, William M., 27:197, 199, 200, 202

Starr, Mrs, William M. (Kate Florence Calkin), 27:283-84

Starr & Co., 27:197-202 *passim*

Starr King (ship), 15:172

"Starr Kings Heads List; Subscribers to First Unitarian ... Building Fund," ed. Clothilde G. Taylor, 29:251-54

Starr Mills, South Vallejo, 27:194-200 *passim;* phot., opp. 200

State Board of Silk Culture, 31:337

State debts, 15:272; 19:10; Civil: 15:267; War, 15:173, 267

State Fair, 9:385; 1854, 9:385; 15:177; 1858, 9:354, 385; 1859, 9:385; 10:174, 196, 198; 1860, 36:245-46; 1861, 10:361, 370; *see also* California State Agricultural Society

State Educational Convention, 15:268

State General Hospital, Stockton, 10:67

State Government and Finance (newsp.), 36:255

State House, Benicia, art. on., 17:260-70; *see also* California: capitols

State Journal, Sacramento, 20:334-35; 21:31

State Library, *see* California State Library

State Marine Hospital, *see* Marine Hospital

State of California (ship), 29:225

"State of Jefferson," by William N. Davis, Jr., 31:125-38

State printer, 30:129-34, 146-47

State Reform School, Marysville, 10:258, 265, 269, 273, 288, 375, 388

Statesman, Sacramento, *see California Statesman*

State Tribune, Sacramento, 17:178-79

Stationers' Hall, San Francisco, 30:356

Staunton, George, 10:255

Stealey, Emma, 20:286

Stealey, Thomas and Mary Louise (Sanders), 20:286

Steamboats: on Colorado R., 22:1-25, 151-74; first on Calif. inland waters, 14:143-46; 27:366, 370; to Orient, 19:169, 172, 260; 28:357, 359; *see also* names of ships

Steamboat Springs, Nev., 6:343; 17:77

Steam engines, 38:335; *see also* Steam paddy

"Steam Navigation on the Colorado River," by Francis H. Leavitt, 22:1-25, 151-74

"Steam paddy," 22:257; 29:148

Steamship companies: Australian, 27:267; *see also* Calif. Steam Navigation Co.; Independent Opposition Line; Pacific Mail

Steam wagons, 9:374, 396

Stearns, Abel, 1:236, 251; 4:159, 170; 6:269-71; 12:295; 13:212, 216, 220-31 *passim,* 308-21 *passim,* 330, 336, 344, 349, 350; 14:126; 16:5, 225; 22:2; 23:197, 211, 213, 327, 332, 333; 25:197; 26:22, 23, 52; 27:105, 108; 28:196, 260; 29:234, 242; 32:327; 33:345, 346; letters from Larkin, 3:180-81, 288; 6:77-79

Stearns, Mrs. Abel (Arcadia Bandini), 1:236, 244, 251, 257, 258; 13:216, 344, 346; 33:109, 345, 346

Stearns, Charles, 20:37, 44

Stearns, Robert E. C., 30:145

Stearns, Thomas, 20:45

Stebbins (S.F., 1854), 14:74

Stebbins, Charles M., 29:349

Stebbins, Francis, 20:45

Stebbins, Horatio, 18:384; 19:153-54;

20:2, 3, 5, 8; 23:246; 26:200; 29:377; 32:244-45; 34:180

Stebbins, Mrs. Horatio (Lucy Elizabeth Ward), 34:180

Stebbins, Ira, 17:240; 24:58, 71

Stebbins, James C., 9:27; 16:341

Stebbins, James G., 8:202, 211; 9:261, 262, 284, 350, 362, 372, 373

Stebbins, Lucy Ward, 18:384; obit., 34:180-81

Stebbins, William P., 20:308

Stedman, Henry B., 31:29

Steel, James, 8:113

Steel, Thomas, 8:342, 358

Steel, *see* Iron and steel

Steele, Catherine Baumgarten (Mrs. William F.), 20:288; "The Steele Brothers, Pioneers ... Dairy Industry," 20:259-73; obits. of Arnold M. Baldwin, 34:82-83; Theodore J. Hoover, 35:179-80

Steele, Edgar Willis, 20:259-73 *passim*

Steele, Elijah, 10:191; 26:202, 207; 31:137

Steele, Frederick, 20:259, 265, 266, 271; 21:312

Steele, G. W., 30:115

Steele, George, 20:259-73 *passim*

Steele, George C. (or D.), 21:308

Steele, Isaac Chapman, 20:259-73 *passim;* port., 20: opp. 259

Steele, Mrs. Isaac Chapman (Hulda Emeline Steele), 20:272

Steele, John, *In Camp and Cabin,* ed. Quaife, rev., 8:87-88

Steele, John A., 10:269

Steele, John W., 33:296

Steele, Joseph, 4:170; 14:126, 342; 23:319, 322, 323, 327, 333, 334

Steele, Nathaniel III, 20:259, 260, 264, 271

Steele, Mrs. Nathaniel III (Dameras Johnson), 20:259, 264, 271

Steele, O. G., 31:127, 131, 134

Steele, Rensselaer E., 20:259-73 *passim*

Steele, Mrs. Rensselaer E. (Clarissa A. Jameson), 20:260, 261, 272

Steele, Robert J., 21:78

Steele, Mrs. Robert J., *see* Granice, Rowena

Steele, Seymour G., 1:248

"Steele Brothers, The, Pioneers in ... Dairy Industry," by Catherine B. Steele, 20:259-73

Steen, Edward T., *see* Gordon & Steen

Steen, Leslie, 15:277

Steeple Rocks, 6:113, 122; 22:144; 32:199, 203, 206; illus., 6: foll. 112

Steere, George, 13:31

Steeving, 6:262-63

Steffens, Joseph Lincoln, 25:285

Steger, Gertrude A., 20:384; 24:384; "A Chronology of the Life of Pierson Barton Reading," 22:365-71

Steiff (North San Juan, 1854), 8:200

Stein, Christine, 29:225

Stein, Fritz, 25:233, 243

Stein, William, 33:364

Stein & Co., 10:189

Steinberger, Baron, 15:266; 16:347; 21:327; 23:171, 176

Steinberger, John A., 33:374

Steinberger, Justus, 40:343

Steindorff, Paul, 25:237

Steiner (Stockton, 1858), 33:66

Steinhart (Marysville, 1851), 15:38

Steinhart, Ignatz, 21:370

Steller, George Wilhelm, 23:219, 221-22

"Stellifer, the King" (D. S. Moulton), 2:240-41

Stenberg, Richard R., 18:288; introd. to "Further Letters of Archibald H. Gillespie," 18:217

Stent, *see* Poverty Hill

"Stephen Hodge Mann, Stockton Pioneer," based on his correspondence, 31:271-77

Stephen J. Field, by Swisher, rev., 10:85

Stephens (Mt. Shasta, 1856), 6:74

Stephens (Marysville, 1858), 9:265

Stephens (or Stevens), Alexander, 14:269, 276; 26:110-23 *passim*

Stephens, Henry Morse, 1:18; 23:189; 29:285; 32:98-99; 36:72, 237

Stephens, William Barclay, 27:92; 34:381; 37:380; 38:76; "Hermann Wenzel and His Air Clock," 27:1-8; "Time and the Old California Missions," 37:289-310; "A Watch and Its Owners," 34:323-32

Stephens, William Dennison, 27:183; 36:251; 37:273; 39:31, 32

"Stephen Sears Smith, Hardwood Lumber Dealer of San Francisco," by Paul O. Clark, 33:321-28; 34:65-82

Stephenson, Terry Elmo, 22:191

Stephenson, William, 21:58

Stepp, Joseph, 1:129, 132, 137; 6:88, 142, 182

Steptoe, Edward J., 27:217; 38:82

Sterett, Benjamin F., 27:4

Sterling, George, letters of, ed. John R. Dunbar, 40:137-55; ed. *Continent's End*, rev., 5:90-98; phot., 38: foll. 8; 40: opp. 137

Sterling, Mrs. George (Caroline Rand), 40:137

Sterling, John Ewart Wallace, 28:381

Sterling (ship), 8:297, 301; 12:166; 17:339, 340; 18:68, 70, 161, 166, 174; 29:335, 336

Stern, Isaac, 34:181

Stern, Jacob, 35:124

Stern, Mrs. Louis, 24:288

Stern, Madeline B., 28:92; "Anton Roman, Argonaut of Books," 28:1-18

Stern, Sigmund, 25:230, 232

Stern, Mrs. Sigmund (Rosalie Meyer), obit., 35:184-87

Sterritt, J. W., 9:166, 180

Sterritt, John, 8:360

Stetson, B., 13:31

Stetson, James Burgess, 27:350

Stetson, Capt. John (1835), 14:316

Stetson, John (1881), 21:257

Stetson, John Walter, 39:21

Stettinius, Alexander, 27:361

Stettinius, Edward R., Jr., 24:162

Steuart, Robert, 6:361, 363

Steuart, William Mott, 10:152; 28:195

Steven, William and Isabella (Sinclair), 28:294

Stevens (Brandy City, 1855), 8:338, 355

Stevens, Miss (Marysville, 1858), 9:354

Stevens (Sutter Co., 1858), 9:352

Stevens, Ashton, 20:138-39

Stevens, B. C., 9:358, 364

Stevens, Bruce, 36:202

Stevens (or Stephens), Elisha, 4:278; 17:156; 32:197; *see also* Stevens-Townsend-Murphy party

Stevens, Fernando, 2:92, 121

Stevens, Frederick, 21:350; 33:105

Stevens, George, 6:152

Stevens, George S., 2:121

Stevens, Henry P., 12:138

Stevens, Isaac Ingalls, 15:179; 35:23-27

Stevens, J. B., 9:62, 75

Stevens, John (Bodega, 1840), 18:294

Stevens, John (Santa Barbara, 1846), 18:174

Stevens, John ('49er), 21:302, 308

Stevens, John L., 18:217

Stevens, John T., 9:64, 348

Stevens, L., 8:358

Stevens, Lemuel, 14:296-97, 298

Stevens, Levi, 26:264; 29:253, 254

Stevens, Robert J., 10:294

Stevens, Samuel S., 24:288

Stevens, Thomas H., 16:345

Stevens, William (owner of *Daphne*, 1882), 14:298

Stevens, William (fought Indians, 1846), 12:310, 311

Stevens, William (Monoville, 1859), 7:112

Stevens, William H., 15:270, 371

Stevenson (Galena Hill, 1857), 9:159, 160, 161

Stevenson, Mrs. Amelia, 9:159, 160, 161

Stevenson, Andrew M., 9:107, 112; 23:295

Stevenson, Edward A., 11:6, 9, 22

Stevenson, G. Bush, 23:295

Stevenson, Jonathan Drake, 1:208, 231, 238-39, 244, 246-47, 252-67 *passim*; 11:142; 12:26-32 *passim*; 13:305, 306-7, 381; 14:387; 15:290; 16:184; 17:321; 18:166, 167, 177; 22:51; 23:160, 163-64; 24:48; 27:368; 28:60; 33:113, 114, 118, 119, 122, 269, 338-45 *passim*; 34:21, 22; 40:20; letters of, 24:343, 345-46, 352-53, 358, 363-64; regiment of, *see* New York Volunteers

Stevenson, Joseph, 21:308

Stevenson, Matthew R., 1:238, 242; 33:254, 345

Stevenson, Robert Louis, 3:43, 44; 6:380; 18:181-82; 20:376-77; 21:81; 23:179-80; 24:88; 32:238; 37:215; bk. on, rev., 3:291-96

Stevenson, Sophie (Edwin), *see* Edwin, Sophie

Stevenson, Wesley, 9:180

Stevenson, William, 21:150

Stevenson & McLean, Stockton, 30:258

"Stevenson and Silverado," address by Anne R. Issler, 23:180

Stevenson House, San Francisco, 26:15

Stevenson's California, by Bland, rev., 3:291-96

Stevens-Townsend-Murphy party, 4:10, 171, 278

Steward (Stockton, 1858), 33:65-66

Steward, William M., 12:199

Stewart (w. Vancouver, 1792), 2:275

Stewart (Sacramento, 1849; Lake Co., 1850), 23:354; 24:49, 54

Stewart (nr. San Joaquin R., 1849), 27:162
Stewart (Marysville, 1858), 9:359
Stewart, C. S., 35:193
Stewart, D. M., 34:158
Stewart, Daniel, 13:32
Stewart, George Rippey, 14:192; 30:364; fellow of CHS, 39:70; "Dumas's *Gil Blas en Californie*," 14:132-42; "The Bret Harte Legend," rev., 7:278-88; *Ordeal by Hunger: The Story of the Donner Party*, rev., 40:251-53; address: "Personal View of the Literature of California," 14:410; bk. revs. by, 14:185-86; 39:364-66; phot., 39: opp. 72
Stewart, George William, 4:43; 8:385; address, "Yokut Indians of the San Joaquin Valley," 4:301; *Big Trees of the Giant Forest*, rev., 9:185-86; obit., 10:309-10
Stewart, Mrs. George William (Martha L. Rowland), 10:309
Stewart, H. J., 32:238
Stewart, J. M., 9:115
Stewart, L. E., 18:299
Stewart, M., 16:82
Stewart, Mark, 29:381
Stewart, Victor B., obit. of Llewellyn Bixby, 21:92
Stewart, W. Frank, 12:329
Stewart, William and Eliza (Ennison), 10:309
Stewart, William Drummond, 3:76
Stewart, William Morris, 3:144; 6:343, 351; 9:42; 10:61, 78, 152; 11:48; 17:218; 19:237; 21:120; 28:195-96; 36:36, 40
Stickney, John I., 33:374
Stidger, Oliver Perry, 9:181; 10:194, 385, 394, 395; 14:377, 397-98, 407; 15:34; 28:238
Stidger, Mrs. Oliver Perry (Eliza Haun), 10:395; (Almira H. Lyon), 10:395
Stiles, Anson Gale, 2:204; 16:40
Stiles, C. O., 5:343
Stiles, Edwin B., 20:45
Stiles, Harriet Waters, *see* Blake, Mrs. Charles T.
Stiles, S., 10:77
Stiles' Nevada Book Store, 30:266, 366
Still, John Hamilton, 28:378; 30:100, 101, 102, 113, 114, 253, 256, 264, 354, 364; *see also* Burgess, Gilbert & Still

Still, Mrs. John Hamilton (Jane N.), 30:256
Still, Robert H., 30:114
Still, W. G., 29:245
Still & Thomas, 30:113-14
Still, Conner & Co., 30:102, 105, 113, 114
Stille, Henry ('49er), 21:308
Stillman, Mrs. (S.F., 1850), 12:99; 14:74
Stillman (Gilman?; S.F., 1854), 15:170
Stillman, Jacob Davis Babcock, 4:188-90, 198; 19:325; 23:279; 28:3; 36:29-30, 105
Stillman, James W., 16:84
Stillman, Stanley, 25:230, 232, 237
Stimson, Marshall, address, "Clipper Ships," 30:276-77
Stipp, George W., ed. Bradford, *Historical &c Notes*, rev., 11:386-87
Stivers, Charles A., 2:244
Stivers, Daniel A., 21:308
Stivers, William D., 21:308
Stockdale, James, 15:182
Stocker, James T., 9:253, 269, 283
Stockfleth, N. T., 39:290
Stockman, L. E., 29:107
Stockton, Col. (S.F., 1855), 17:177
Stockton, Mrs. (Marysville, 1858), 9:263, 264, 345, 346, 348
Stockton, Annis, 26:287
Stockton, H. C., 10:71
Stockton, John Edmonston, 22:367
Stockton, R. P., 15:19
Stockton, Robert Field, 2:163-72 *passim*; 3:115; 12:290, 345, 346; 14:345; 17:277-84 *passim*, 325-29 *passim*; 19:47, 170; 20:226; 25:129; 26:22, 287; 28:342; 33:115, 117, 374; 35:102, 103; 37:230; 38:41; com. U.S. forces in Calif., 1:138, 142, 146, 171, 248; 3:113, 120-24 *passim*, 125; 8:252; 9:85; 10:118, 120-22, 353; 11:209; 12:41-48 *passim*, 52, 53, 57, 58, 161, 163, 334-37 *passim*, 340, 344; 13:47, 112, 113, 150, 151, 152, 301-6 *passim*, 313; 17:228-31 *passim*, 340, 344; 18:75, 82; 20:233; 21:2, 10, 20-21, 193, 194, 199, 343-49 *passim*, 354; 22:41; 25:127; 26:287; 29:274-75; 31:210; 35:103
controversy w. Kearny, 8:251-61; 13:150; 16:196; 22:45, 46, 64; 33:106, 108; land owned by, 2:194; 14:19; 16:199, 285; 27:107; march to Los Angeles, 1:46; 3:124-25; 12:335; 17:349; 30:51, 52; at L.A. and San Pedro, 1:146; 13:100, 133, 302-6

passim; 14:328; 17:339, 345, 346;
20:233; 21:354; 25:128, 129; 29:333;
30:53; mil. gov. of Calif., 8:251-61
passim; 10:13-15, 18, 22; 18:35;
20:216; 21:11, 15; 22:50-51; 25:129;
at Monterey, 1:138; 3:187; 12:169;
17:277; 21:2; 25:126; 29:334; orders
and appointments by, 12:344, 345;
21:10, 11, 14, 194; 22:45, 65; 25:128,
129, 130; 27:106; 29:275, 335; 35:104;
proclamations, 3:113, 188-90; 12:47,
53; 13:123-24; 18:79; 20:215; 22:54,
56; 25:127, 129; 32:293; relations w.
French consulate, 11:205; 12:40-45,
56, 60, 161-62, 169; ret. East, 12:315;
18:299; at San Diego, 1:142, 146;
3:120-24 *passim;* 12:334; 26:22, 24,
47, 49; 21:333, 337; 28:342; at S.F.,
6:145; 11:130; 12:56, 57, 162; 17:296;
25:131; cor., 1:82-83; 3:188; 8:76-77;
10:10-11, 120, 122; 12:41-42, 169;
13:115-17; 17:228; 21:356
Stockton, William R., 18:202
Stockton (place), 6:248-49; 7:10, 12,
277; 10:44-45, 403; 12:27, 312-13;
13:356, 364, 372, 379; 14:17, 415;
15:277, 290, 383; 16:138; 18:11, 27,
166, 267; 20:100, 141, 166, 251, 376;
22:146; 23:367; 26:99, 169, 171; 27:161,
314, 379; 30:197, 311; 31:274-76, 311;
33:65-66, 376; 34:22, 342, 343; 38:311;
39:43, 44; book dealers, 30:109-10,
258, 359; fires, 12:108; 15:272; 22:76;
insane asylum, 10:44, 45, 67; 20:252;
newspapers, 7:277; 15:163; 19:63, 68;
20:162, 164-65; 25:192; 26:244;
34:341-55; fac., 7: opp. 277
Stockton and Aspinwall mine, 12:75
Stockton and Tulare Railroad, 25:175
Stockton Blues, 10:198; 38:18, 22
Stockton Electric Railway Co., 31:298
Stockton Gas Co., 18:100
Stockton House, Stockton, 6:249;
22:76, 77
Stockton Lumber Co., 31:294
"Stockton schooner," 11:232
Stockton Street House, San Francisco,
20:310
Stockwell, Mrs. (N.Y., 1860), 11:11
Stockwell & Co., 30:254, 264
Stoddard (Graham's Ranch, 1859),
10:169
Stoddard, Charles Warren, 1:301;
3:292-94; 5:88, 202; 10:201; 28:6, 8;
37:215; *A Bit of Old China,* rev., 5:88

Stoddard, J. R., 13:17, 28
Stoddard, Joel, 9:349, 357, 379; 10:254,
256, 281
Stoddard, S. B., 26:232
Stoddard, Mrs. S. B., 24:262
Stoddard (R. R.) & Co., 10:189; lawsuit,
10:178, 179
Stoddard Well (Mojave Desert),
27:116
Stodder, George G. S., 15:281
Stoepel, F., 9:388
Stoepel, Matilda, *see* Heron, Matilda
Stokely, John, 33:256, 257
Stokes, Adolphus, 26:52
Stokes, Aristides ("Reestis"), 26:52
Stokes, Charles, 10:362; 14:394
Stokes, Edward (1840s), 19:209, 216;
21:333, 334, 355; 26:23, 24, 25, 52
Stokes, Mrs. Edward (Refugio Ortega),
26:24
Stokes, Edward S., 38:381
Stokes, James, 3:85; 4:152-53, 156; 8:74,
109; 11:206; 13:48; 14:148, 318, 343;
25:126; 28:261, 268; 30:98; 34:119
Stokes, Mrs. James (Josefa Soto), 6:270
Stombs, Daggett & Co., 9:395
Stone, Dr. (S.F., 1849), 22:69
Stone (Philippines, 1898), 31:58
Stone, Andrew L., 29:377; 31:185
Stone, C. E., 9:79, 287; 10:255, 366
Stone, Mrs. C. E., *see* Phillips, Caroline
Stone, Charles, 11:266-73 *passim;*
24:49-54 *passim*
Stone, Charles P., 4:225; 8:339
Stone, Charles Pomeroy, 15:207; 17:320;
31:233-37 *passim*
Stone, E. W., 15:377
Stone, Frederick P., 29:99-100, 221, 225,
361
Stone, J., 13:32
Stone, J. P. ("Jerry"), 6:227
Stone, John, 6:341
Stone, John A., 22:31, 36
Stone, Lucy, 34:44
Stone, M. C., 24:45, 124
Stone, Nathan, 29:100
Stone, Raymond M., 29:186
Stone, Mrs. Rockwell L., 28:93
Stone, S., 4:127, 138
Stone, William Hamilton, 11:9
Stone and Kelsey "massacre," 1849,
24:49-54 *passim;* "The Indian
Viewpoint," ed. Max Radin,
11:266-73
Stoneman, George, 1:238-43 *passim,*

255; 16:305, 310, 315, 317, 318; 20:344;
22:52, 65; 24:59, 61; 28:340; 29:34-35;
32:341; 33:111, 112, 117, 119, 120, 255,
258, 263-64, 267, 339, 343, 345
Stoner, Victor R., 30:227
Stonewall Mine, 34:201; 36:124, 125
Stoney Creek and Ford, 32:376
Stonington (ship), 3:119, 120, 121, 125;
21:339, 356; 22:46; 29:335; 30:52
Stony Bar, Placer Co., 2:206
Stony Bar, Yuba Co., 8:201, 206, 210,
345; 11:55
Stopes, Fisher, 2:116
Storch, Louis, 30:228
"Storeman in San Francisco," (pseud.),
24:359-60
Storer, Si, 9:348
Storer, Tracy Irwin, 22:194; coauth.
Animal Life in the Yosemite, rev.,
3:299-300
Storey, W. H., 30:262
Stories of Stanislaus, by Elias, rev.,
3:90-92
Storke, Thomas More, 25:287; 39:133
Storm, Peter, 17:240; 24:58, 72; 29:276
Storm Cloud (ship), 22:24, 169, 170
Storms, S. P., 27:215; 30:161, 164; his
"mile track," 27:222
Story, Charles Robinson and Caroline
Pillsbury (Bailey), 28:293
Story, D. W. C., 12:327, 329
Story, George L., house of, 34:347
Story, Robert, 22:351
Story, Stephen C., 16:137
Story, William F., 9:26; 15:367
"Story of a Gold Miner, The,"
reminiscences of Edwin F. Morse,
6:205-37, 332-59
Story of Inyo, The, by Chalfant, rev.,
2:178-79
Story of Rancho San Antonio, The, by
De Veer, rev., 4:93
"Story of San Jose, 1777-1869, The,"
by Oscar O. Winther, 14:3-27, 147-74
"Story of the Last Expedition of Dr.
Josiah Gregg, The," address by
Charles P. Cutten, 6:197
"Story of the Wreck of the *Rio de
Janeiro*, The," address by Mrs. Arthur
A. O'Neill, 19:282
Stott & Co., 33:68
Stout (Nev., 1861), 4:250
Stout, Arthur B., 4:194; 13:249, 253,
387, 394; 15:179, 370; 19:237; 27:346;
28:17

Stout, Moses, 9:116, 250, 256, 258, 269
Stout, William, 14:175, 180, 182
Stout, William C., 13:251, 398
Stoutenberg, 22:72, 82; *see also*
Murphy's
Stoutenburgh, John J., *Dictionary of
the American Indian*, rev., 39:274
Stovepipe Wells, 17:196, 214
Stover, David B., 15:370
Stover, Jacob Y., 18:196, 215
Stover, S., 9:68
Stow (Sacramento, 1858), 9:250, 261
Stow, Joseph W., 27:68; 33:374
Stow, Nellie, obit. of Mrs. Edwin R.
Dimond, 13:288
Stow, William W., 9:42; 15:269
Stowe, H. K., 15:76, 146
Stowell, Levi, 13:392-404; 26:85;
"Bound for the Land of Canaan, Ho!,"
Diary, ed. Marco G. Thorne,
27:33-50, 157-64, 259-66, 361-70;
28:57-68
Stowell, William H., 20:30; 25:103
Stoy *v.* Jones, 9:165
Strahle & Hughes, 36:103
"Straight toward His Heart: George
Wilkes' Eulogy of David C.
Broderick," by Donald E. Hargis,
38:197-217
Strain, Isaac, 10:180
Strain, James, 10:269
Strain, R. R., 29:291
Strait, J. H., 31:31
Strakosch, Maurice, 15:165, 167, 169;
21:243
Strakosch, Max, 21:245; Company,
21:258
Stranger, The (play), 15:48
Stranger's Friend Society, 32:119
Stranglers of Paris, The (play), 21:257
Strangman (S.F., 1850), 8:267-72 *passim*
Strassburger, Isaac, 15:384
Strassburger, Lawrence, obit., 15:384-85
Stratton, George Malcolm, 37:39
Stratton, James, 21:121, 126
Stratton, Royal B., 21:99-100
Stratton, W. C., 4:215
Stratton, William C., 9:269, 276, 278;
10:40, 44, 52-53, 62, 67, 70, 75, 76
Strawberry Valley, El Dorado Co.,
17:75, 78
Strawberry Valley, Siskiyou Co., 6:72;
7:124, 125
Strawberry Valley, Tuolumne Co.,
34:213

Strawberry Valley, Yuba Co., 8:343;
9:51, 52; 10:171, 255, 359
Strawbridge, Justus C., 31:337
Strawbridge, William, 11:163
Street, Charles R., 9:250, 269; 10: opp.
48, 53, 62, 65; 11:9
Street, G. D., 16:79
Street, James, 29:346, 350
Streeter, David, 18:167, 265; 21:339-44
passim; 22:48-58 *passim*; 33:111
Streeter, Thomas Winthrop, 30:353;
36:177; obit. of Henry R. Wagner,
36:165-75
Streeter, William A., 4:157-58; 15:237;
16:58; 27:337; 28:263; 33:111;
"Recollections of Historical Events
in California, 1843-1878," ed. William
H. Ellison, 18:64-71, 157-79, 254-78;
phot., 18: opp. 64
Streets, Walter, 16:346
Strentzel, Louise Wanda, *see* Muir, Mrs.
John
Stretch, R. H., 18:210-11
Strickland, J., 33:200
Stridwick (Fresno Co., 1868), 25:25
Strikes: hod-carriers' and tenders',
15:168, 273; iron moulders', 21:67;
longshoremen's, 16:81; plasterers',
39:305; Pullman employees', 35:271;
sailors', 12:99; street construction
workers', 39:299; teamsters', 35:66, 68,
145-52
Stringham, Roland Irving, 25:93; "A
Note on Antecedents and Trends in
the Domestic Architecture of
California," 25:54-56
Stringham, Washington Irving, 1:13;
25:93
Strobridge, James Harvey, 4:300;
36:268-69, 272
Strobridge, Tullius Albert, 33:380;
38:75; "Anderson Valley, Mendocino
Co.," 33:361-67
Strobridge, Tullius Washington and
Sarah (Marvin), 33:380
Strode (S.F., 1852), 12:174
Strode, Col. (S.F., 1854), 16:346
Strode, John A., 21:335
"Stroll through San Francisco in the
Long Ago, A," address by Charles B.
Turrill, 2:369-70
Strong, Charles L., 17:76, 77, 79; 19:231;
see also LeCount & Strong
Strong, Daniel W., 4:240-47 *passim*, 250,
260-64 *passim*, 300; 5:178

Strong, Demas, 30:21, 27
Strong, Joseph D., 19:107
Strop (or Stroh; on *London*, 1849),
7:210
Strother, Fleet F., 13:237
Stroud, Mary, 9:149
Stroud, Robert, 8:208, 213; 9:267; 10:56
Stroud's (hotel), Yuba Co., 8:208, 213,
338, 340; 9:50; 10:256
Strout & Sargent, 30:359
Struck Oil (play), 4:212
"Struggle for Civil Government in
California, The," by Joseph Ellison,
10:3-26, 129-64, 220-44
"Struggle for the Valley, The:
California's Hetch Hetchy
Controversy, 1905-1913," by Elmo R.
Richardson, 38:249-58
Stuart (Sonoma Co. and S.F., 1870s),
20:269
Stuart, A. H. H., 9:15
Stuart, Charles V., 9:27
Stuart, James (d. Ore., 1851), 28:213,
229
Stuart, James (hanged, S.F., 1851),
2:136; 6:49; 12:106; 15:34-37 *passim*;
28:43
Stuart, Reginald R., 23:287; 28:378; ed.
"The Burrell Letters," 28:297-322;
29:39-59, 173-79
Stuart, Robert, 14:409; 27:181-82;
Discovery of the Oregon Trail, The,
ed. Rollins, rev., 15:191
Stuart, William W., 26:2, 4-5, 7
Stuart, Mrs. William W. (née Basye),
26:7
Stubbe, A., 22:251
Stubborn Motor Car, The (play),
34:364
Stubbs, J. C., 28:375
Stubbs, Mary, 28:375
Studebaker, John M., 15:380; 30:208;
33:327
Sturdavant, B. F., 33:374
Sturges, George, 36:75-76
Sturgis, William, 8:289; 19:49, 56;
23:193
Sturtivant, Henry, 2:128
Sturzenneger, John and Rosina (Zopfe),
28:292
Suárez, Cayetano, 13:107; 17:155
Suárez, Crecencio, 25:363
Suárez del Real, *see* Real
Sublett, Susan, 3:156, 158, 160
Sublette (San Jose, 1853), 13:29-30

Sublette, Andrew Whitley, bk. on, rev., 40:256-57
Sublette, Milton G., 2:35
Sublette, William Lewis, 2:10, 34; 4:107, 120, 127-33 *passim*, 139, 140, 278, 279, 319, 322, 323, 324, 337; 17:161; 19:135; 28:119
Succara (Indian, 1834), 16:236, 245, 355, 356, 371; 29:312
Succès (ship), 5:28, 37
Such, John, 7:398
Sucker Bar, 8:338, 345, 355
Sucker Flat, 9:351, 355, 376, 384, 386; 10:55, 56, 169, 173, 251, 255, 256, 257, 358
Sudden & Christenson, 31:295, 296, 303
Suenz, Domingo, 16:249
Sugar, Carl, 25:383
Sugar, 13:8; 18:95; 26:249; 27:117, 200; 36:110; 40:33-48; beets, 27:117, 121; 30:311; cane, 5:138; 13:8
Sugar Factors Co., Ltd., 27:200
Sugar Loaf (Liberty Cap), Yosemite, 1:281
Suicides, 15:176, 277, 376; 16:83; 21:248, 258; 24:131; 28:252-53; 33:254
Suisun Bay, 10:213, 214, 405
Suisun, Berryessa & Clear Lake Railroad, 32:366
Suisun Gun Club, 32:375
Sullers (Sutter Co., 1858), 9:263, 264, 346; lawsuit, 9:264, 265
Sullivan (cigar store, S.F., 1851), 30:109
Sullivan (hotel prop., S.F., 1851), 19:228
Sullivan (S.F., 1855), 16:82
Sullivan, Anne, 19:96
Sullivan, Barry, 21:241, 247
Sullivan, Catherine, 33:352
Sullivan, Charles A., obit., 7:413
Sullivan, Dennis T., 15:315, 322; phot., 15: opp. 316
Sullivan, Elizabeth (alias Howard), 15:267
Sullivan, Eugene Lemuel, 2:67; 8:187, 284; 19:237; 33:374
Sullivan, Mrs. Eugene Lemuel, *see* Davis, Mrs. John Calvert
Sullivan, Georgina Frances, *see* Jones, Mrs. John P.
Sullivan, Isaac W., 19:128, 141
Sullivan, J. W., 30:261
Sullivan, James V., 20:36, 45
Sullivan, Jerry, 6:15
Sullivan, John, 5:407; 19:231, 237

Sullivan, Mrs. John (Ada E. Kenna), 7:413
Sullivan, Mrs. John A., 25:287
Sullivan, John L., 21:263
Sullivan, Maurice S., *Travels of Jedediah Smith*, rev., 13:410
Sullivan, "Yankee" (Frank Murray), 8:364, 372; 9:75; 15:171; 16:347; 17:182; port., 8:368
Sullivan & Leland, 30:254, 264
Sullivan (G.T.) & (K.) Root, 5:42, 140
Sullivan's Camp, 20:100; 23:54; *see also* Sullivan's Creek
Sullivan's Creek and Diggings, 4:165; 11:168, 169, 171; 13:373, 383; 34:222; *see also* Sullivan's Camp
Sulphur, 15:235; 32:363
Sulphur (ship), 18:344; 19:213
Sulphur Bank, 32:365, 366
Sulphur Creek, 32:365
Sulphur Mountain, 17:28
Summers, H. B., 9:366
Summers, John E., 33:344
Summers, Pete, 8:352, 363
"Summers with Our Neighbor Authors, A," address by Eudora Garoutte, 13:411
Summit (RR station), 22:178-80; 23:117-22 *passim*
Summit City (Meadow Lake), 18:154
Summit of Sierra Nevada, 6:126-27, 363; illus., 6: opp. 124, opp. 126
Summit Soda Springs, 34:19-20
Summit Water and Irrigation Co., 29:197
Sumner, Charles A., 10:393
Sumner, Edwin Vose, 1:144; 10:282; 13:39; 21:198, 200, 222; 24:276; 26:261, 363; 28:166, 168-71 *passim*; 29:239, 240, 243; 33:230; 34:136, 150-55 *passim*; 40:343
Sumner, J. W., 31:93
Sumner, Lowell, 26:134
Sumner, Owen, 5:123, 125, 276
Sumner, Owen, Jr., 5:123
Sumner, R. R., 33:3
Sumter (ship), 26:18
Sun, San Francisco, 16:399
Sunday: in the mines (illus.), 6: opp. 252; 15: opp. 295; laws, 9:255, 280-81; 10:362, 370; 14:165; 15:25, 280, 368; 16:80; 20:302, 304; 21:45, 49, 66; 31:7-8; 39:301, 302, 303
Sunday Dispatch, San Francisco, 13:299

"Sunday Morning in the Mines," by Charles Nahl, 15: opp. 295
Sunday schools, 15:165, 168; 27:125; 29:121; 32:128; 39:293
Sundials, 36:77; 37:301-2, 308-9
Suñer, Francisco, 25:135
Sunny South (ship), 15:279
Suñol, Antonio María, 5:130, 305; 8:122; 12:247, 263, 266-67; 13:78, 167, 269, 270, 278; 14:19; 15:18; 17:67, 152; 20:108-9; 23:211, 218
Suñol v. Hepburn, 20:108; 34:98, 240-41
Sunset Development & Transportation Assoc., San Francisco, 33:376
Sunset Telephone and Telegraph Co., 2:205
Sun Sun Wo Co., Coulterville, 33:375
Superior (ship), 13:251, 397
Supreme Court, California, *see* Courts
Suría, Tomás de, 15:214-15, 380; 16:87; 24:292, 308; 25:60, 277, 363; sketches by, 15: opp. 213, foll. 214; 39: foll. 180
Suriano, Juan Francisco, 7:299, 300, 334, 347, 377, 378, 385
"Surmounting the Sierras," by Chester L. White, 7:3-19
Surprise, The (juvenile newsp.), 6:380
Surprise (clipper), 8:384; 10:294
Surprise (side-wheel str., 1852), 11:153
Surprise (riv. str., 1854), 15:267, 278, 377; 16:79
Surprise Valley, 31:137
Surprise Valley Mill and Water Co., 17:210, 218
"Surrender of Monterey by ... Gutierrez, The," by George Tays, 15:338-63
Surveying, 11:161-63, 360; 13:177-78; 18:296, 304; 24:166-67, 171, 176-78; 34:1-17, 22; *see also* names of surveyors
Susan Abigail (ship), 15:271; 34:254
Susan Ann (ship), 27:157, 163
Susan Drew (ship), 1:208, 210-32; 22:65; 24:48, 70; 25:130
Susan E. Owens (ship), 11:358; 23:376
Susanita (ship), 16:127; 24:63
Susannetta (launch), 27:163
Susan River, 7:14; 30:58, 66
Susanville, 18:304, 308, 313; 30:60
Suscol (or Soscol), 36:295, 296, 305
Suscol House, 16:134
Suspension Flume, 9:66
Susquehanna (ship), 15:183, 185
Sussman, Emilie, 18:182

Sussman, Mrs. Samuel, 25:233
Sutch, John, *see* Such, John
Sutherland, Judge (S.F., 1855), 15:366
Sutherland, Daniel, 26:204
Sutherland, David, 26:204
Sutherland, Edwin S., 25:7; 30:382
Sutherland, John, 26:204
Sutherland, Roderick, 26:204
Sutherland, T. W., 31:45
Sutil (ship), 3:233; 10:316, 320, 332, 334, 338-41 *passim*; 15:215; 38:275
Sutlej (ship), 33:235-36
Sutro, Adolph, 4:62; 15:381; 18:192; 21:373; 32:234-35, 262; 33:374
Sutro, Alfred, obits. of Horace D. Pillsbury, 19:85-86; Kenneth R. Kingsbury, 17:94-95; obit., 24:89-90
Sutro, Mrs. Alfred (Rose Newmark), 24:90; 25:95
Sutro, Oscar, obit., 14:287
Sutro, Mrs. Oscar (Mary O'Sullivan), 32:191
Sutro Heights, San Francisco, 4:62
Sutro Library, 7:111
Sutro Tunnel, 20:83
Sutter, Adolphus, 17:172
Sutter, Eliza, 8:25, 172-73; 14:217, 407; 29:300
Sutter, John Augustus, 1:98, 121, 139, 182; 3:89-90; 5:36-37, 96, 305; 6:141, 153, 198-99, 239, 241, 273, 369; 8:97, 101, 120, 121, 123, 127-28, 168-74 *passim*, 181, 268; 9:75, 270, 395, 398-99; 10:292, 299; 11:67, 121, 141, 144, 349-50, 355; 12:280-85 *passim*, 295, 299, 301, 313, 357; 13:13, 262-63; 14:128, 197-99, 217, 219, 220, 378, 390; 15:4, 173, 179, 226-27, 236, 369, 370; 16:127, 129; 17:58, 69, 141, 145, 149, 150, 154-62 *passim*, 224-25, 231, 232, 273; 18:158, 159, 173, 293, 295; 19:22-23, 116-24 *passim*, 131-35 *passim*, 236; 20:36, 120, 148; 21:1, 5, 7, 9, 16; 22:33, 366; 23:245; 24:331-32; 25:123, 126; 26:109-18 *passim*, 124; 27:136, 140, 243; 28:245, 254; 29:303, 314; 30:3, 36, 98, 375-76; 37:363, 364, 366 aids Donner party, 10:348-49, 350; aids Micheltorena, 12:149, 288; 13:229-30, 231; 15:228, 229, 230; 16:56-58; 17:157-59; 18:296-97; 20:151; 29:134-35; at Constitutional Convention, 10:163; 17:234; 19:7; buys Ft. Ross property, 12:189, 194, 199, 246, 247-48, 263-76 *passim*, 347;

14:199; 16:100; 17:23, 66-68, 162;
18:160; 28:110; 30:324; 33:64, 311,
315-16; 39:98-99, 110, 193
cor., 5:77-78, 124, 184; 6:80-83, 184-85;
11:42-43; 14:198; 17:69; 23:293-94;
26:208; 28:56; 36:245; Diary, 1:124;
11:386 (*see also* New Helvetia
Diary); gun of, 26:29, 54
land grants and claims, 5:96; 11:349;
12:283-84; 13:262; 14:199; 15:279,
280; lawsuit, 14:378-79; list of
immigrants from Ore., 5:125;
Mormon workmen of, 14:269-82;
15:244; 19:134, 143; 22:141;
26:109-17 *passim*, 122, 123, 124;
32:194-95; treatment of Indians,
12:309; 16:129
arts. on, 14:28-46, 269-82; 38:321-27;
bks. about, 9:398-99; 10:90; 12:179;
14:82, 185-86; 15:187, 379; 18:279;
21:276; ports., 14: opp. 28; 23: opp.
227; 38: opp. 321; fac. sig., 10: opp.
159
see also New Helvetia; Sutter's flour
mill; Sutter's Fort; Sutter's Sawmill
Sutter, Mrs. John Augustus (Anna
Dübeld), 8:172, 173; 14:37-38, 39, 41,
42; 27:243
Sutter, John Augustus, Jr., 8:170-74
passim; 12:300; 23:178; 36:245, 250
Sutter, W. Alphonse, 10:177, 199
Sutter Buttes, 3:271; 9:366; 10:184, 382;
11:113-14, 122; 13:173; 14:197;
22:325-27, 331-34; 25:122, 123; 29:262;
illus., 22: opp. 323
Sutter Creek, 18:22; 31:190
Sutter House, Eliza City, 8:25
Sutter Rifles, 9:244, 268, 270; 10:69, 198,
277, 291; 17:268; 24:172, 174-76
passim; 37:363, 364, 366; 38:19
Sutter's Fort, 1:97, 296; 3:89, 90; 4:163;
5:124, 128-29, 264; 6:141, 239, 272;
8:127; 10:9, 111, 299, 301, 348, 353;
11:88, 136; 12:281, 295, 337; 13:12, 13,
20, 21, 25, 43, 262-64, 372; 14:271;
15:226, 237; 16:56, 57, 127, 129, 212;
17:158, 161, 162, 273, 275, 360; 18:173,
293, 297; 19:116, 119, 131-38 *passim*;
20:36, 120, 217; 21:1-2, 10, 11, 13, 82;
22:366; 23:291, 369; 24:22-28 *passim*,
324, 336, 353; 25:123-29 *passim*, 144-47
passim, 220; 26:109-13 *passim*, 118-23
passim; 28:324; 29:133, 257; 30:376;
32:194; aid to Donner party from,
10:348, 350; Frémont at, 1:121, 124,

126, 127, 137; 4:9; 5:264; 6:140-41;
prisoners of Bear party at, 1:75, 97,
293-94; 10:114; 12:337; 15:230;
17:222-30 *passim*; 19:118; 29:321-22;
views of, 13: opp. 265; 23: opp. 352;
see also New Helvetia
Sutter's flour (grist) mill, 11:42; 14:269,
273, 276, 278, 280, 281; 16:127, 138,
142; 19:133, 139, 143; 26:109, 110, 118,
123
Sutter Slough, 23:349
"Sutter's Mormon Workmen at Natoma
and Coloma," by Reva H. Stanley,
14:269-82
Sutter's sawmill, 2:186; 3:128; 5:96;
6:247; 8:210; 10:298, 299, 348, 350;
11:42; 12:295, 357; 13:56, 164, 169,
170, 172, 175; 14:269, 273-82 *passim*;
15:298; 16:127, 140; 19:124, 125, 133;
28:295; 30:26, 36; 32:195; arts. on,
26:107-62; illus., 6: opp. 205; 26: opp.
111, foll. 126, opp. 128, foll. 132
"Sutter's Sawmill," by Aubrey
Neasham, 26:109-33
Sutter the Man, by Zollinger, rev.,
18:279
Sutterville, 8:22; 9:252, 277; 10:391;
11:42-43, 106; 12:300-303; 13:367,
371, 372, 381, 382; 14:202; 19:127, 141;
21:82
"Sutter Writes of the Gold Discovery,"
ed. Charles L. Camp, 11:42-43
Sutton, Charles, 21:169
Sutton, Cornelius, 21:290
Sutton, Mrs. John (Anna B.), 27:32
Sutton, Joseph, 6:13
Sutton, Owen Paul, 15:370; 27:159, 160,
163, 259, 260, 265, 368-69; 28:58
Sutton, Samuel S., 9:264
Suwerkrop, E. A., 2:188; 14:333, 335-36,
346
Swaffield, Roland George, 26:190
Swagert, S. Laird, 32:95; "British
Comment—as of 1849-1851," 32:81-
86, 269-75; 33:23-28
Swain, Capt. (of *Crescent City*, 1849),
29:18
Swain, J. W., 33:68
Swain, Lizzie, 10:171
Swain, Robert B., 4:208; 29:253, 254
Swain, William B., 33:374
Swain, William Caldwell, 9:156, 178,
264; 10:250
Swaine (w. Vancouver, 1792), 2:297
Swain's (S.F., 1860), 29:110, 121

Swallow (riv. str.), 10:273-86 *passim*, 380

Swan (master of *Sarah*, 1867), 27:68

Swan, George W., 12:328

Swan, James C. (G.?), 21:368

Swan, James G., 21:4

Swan, John A., 29:25

Swan, John M., 1:144

Swan, Thomas M., 11:9

Swan, W., 16:282

Swansea, Inyo Co., 17:115

Swart, Jan Lows de, 27:136, 140

Swartwout, Henry, 28:221, 230

Swartzlow, Carl R., 18:384

Swartzlow, Mrs. Carl R. (Ruby Johnson), 18:384; "Peter Lassen," 18:291-314

Swasey, Henry S., 18:384

Swasey, William F., 1:138; 2:369; 5:308; 16:79; 18:384; 28:290; 29:156, 342; 31:44; letter to, 29:157

Swasey, Mrs. William F. (née Bascom), 18:384

Swasey-Todd (or Snyder-Blackburn) party, 17:161; 19:135

Swat (Schwartz or Swart), George, 27:136

Swat, Juan de, *see* Swart, Jan Lows de

Swayne, Noah Haynes, 15:8, 13

Swayne, Robert H., obit. of Arthur L. Duncan, 9:293

Swayne (R. H.) & Co., 34:330

Swearingen, Belle, *see* McCreery, Mrs. Andrew B.

Swearingen, Mary Lewis, *see* Whitney, Mrs. George E.

Swearingen, Mrs. Richard S. (Isabella Virginia), 36:41, 44

Swearingen, Sarah, *see* Condit-Smith, Mrs. J.

Swearingen, Sue Virginia, *see* Field, Mrs. Stephen J.

Swearinger, Miss (Sacramento, 1859), 10:44

Sweasey, Esther, 27:189

Sweasey, Louisa, 29:284

Sweasey, William John, 9:26; 27:189; 29:284

Sweat houses, 2:325; 8:315; 15:111-12, 134; 17:293; 24:50

Sweden (ship), 1:208; 33:261-62

Swedenborgian Society, San Francisco, 38:306

Swedes, 20:67, 76; 30:305

Sweem, J. B., 25:20-21

Sweeney, George F., 22:33

Sweeny, Thomas William, 22:4, 5, 20

Sweet, Mrs. (clairvoyant, 1857), 9:163

Sweet, Capt. (Colorado R., 1863), 22:170, 171

Sweet, Lulu, 21:63

Sweet, Paul, 33:64, 65

Sweet, S., 18:26, 27

Sweetheart, The (play), 35:142

Sweeting's Hotel, San Francisco, 11:65

Sweetland, Henry P., 3:144-45, 153-60 *passim;* 8:209

Sweetland (place), 3:144, 156, 161; 8:199, 209; 28:234, 236

Sweetland's Crossing, 9:162

Sweet potatoes, 2:321; 23:371; 35:242

Sweetser, Albion Chase, 22:127, 129, 147; 38:33, 36, 39

Sweetser, Joseph B., 9:277

Sweetser (James E.), (U. P.) Hutchings & Co., 15:172

Sweetwater Reservoir, 34:159; 35:269

Sweetzer, A. J., 23:71

Swenson, Mrs. Bert Edward (Stella Spillner), 28:190

Swett, Frank, 33:306

Swett, James, 15:174, 180, 267

Swett, John, 4:29; 15:174, 180, 267; 16:283; 30:135; "Diary . . . 1853," ed. Will S. Cluff, Jr., 33:289-308; fac. of p. from "Pocket Memorandum," 33: opp. 289

Swett, Leonard, 15:7-20 *passim*

Swezy, Charles E., 9:391

Swezy, Gabriel N., 3:149; 8:346, 361; 9:65, 257, 260, 364, 365, 390-91; 10:183, 194, 280, 382, 383, 384; 14: opp. 209, 382-83, 389, 403; 15:21, 23, 29, 33, 53, 54; family, 9:391

Swift, Capt. (of *Derby*, 1807), 12:221

Swift, Mrs. (Sacramento, 1859), 10:176

Swift (S.F., 1864), 24:263

Swift, Andrew M., 13:31

Swift, C. A., 13:296

Swift, C. H., 26:262

Swift, Granville P., 1:134; 6:273; 11:184; 17:155, 240; 18:81, 158, 172; 21:14, 15; 24:58; 29:134, 262, 266-67, 271-72, 275, 333, 335, 339; 30:53-55, 169

Swift, Harry G., 23:96

Swift, John Franklin, 14:86; 27:93, 173; 35:259

Swift, John H., 27:222

Swift, Richard, 30:5

Swig, Benjamin H., 26:287-88

Swindlehurst, Lizzie, 21:152, 178

Swindler, Frank P., 25:96

Swine, 1:169; 2:41, 42, 310; 12:193, 287, 293; 14:6, 9, 200; 16:119; 21:209; 23:252; 27:298; 38:119, 120

Swinerton, G. H., 33:333

Swingle, John, bk. revs. by, 38:274-75, 371; 39:366-67; 40:170-71

Swinnerton, James, 38:2

Swinnery (Marysville, 1858), 9:364

Swisher, Carl Brent, *Stephen J. Field*, rev., 10:85

Swiss, 15:46-47, 226; 20:69-70, 77, 81; 28:293; 30:305-14; *see also* Italian Swiss

Switzler, Simeon, letters, 24:135, 259, 353

Sword, presented to Gen. Hooker, 16:310-11

Sword Fish (ship), 10:294; 15:373

Swords, Thomas, 1:240; 21:201, 208, 211, 218, 221, 222, 335, 341, 356; 22:51-52; 25:297, 307, 371; 26:34; 33:103-4, 107, 109, 113-14, 117, 262, 266-67, 338-39

Swycaffer, Jeff, 36:123-24

Swycaffer, Joseph, 36:119, 124

Sybil (play), 10:51, 57, 75

Sycamore (or Sycamous) River (Battle Creek?), 22:211, 216, 217; 23:134

Sycamore Slough Co. *v.* Dry Slough Co., 10:274

"Sydney coves" (or "Ducks"), 3:40; 6:226; 15:32; 19:328-29; 22:269; 24:169; 30:242

Syer, Robert Reay, obit., 21:382

Sykes, F., 2:175

Sykes, Zenas (or Zenus), 29:42, 46, 49, 50, 55, 178

Sykes, Mrs. Zenas (Eliza Burrell), 28:316; 29:42, 46-55 *passim*, 174, 178

Sylph (ship), 12:11; 13:7-10, 31-33

Sylve, Madora, 28:294

Sylvestro, Clement M., phot., 39: opp. 80

Sylvie's (or Sylvaille's) River, 22:101, 199

Symmes, Anita Day, 35:7

Symmes, Loring P., 2:121

Symonds, Rev. Mr. (Sonoma, 1851), 24:60

Symons, Farrell, trans. Soulié, *The Wolf Club*, rev., 7:198-99

Syndicate Mining Co., 4:68

Symington, Mrs. Powers (Maud Fay), 25:94, 236

Szabo, Janos, 28:130, 133, 141

T

Taaffe, G. O'Hara, 15:53, 57; 17:176; 27:170

Taaffe, William, 17:176

Taba, La (ship), 38:105

Tabasacca (place), 12:10, 14

Tabb, John Bannister, 40:137

Taber, John, 11:56

Taber, Loren B., 18:288; 30:191; coauth. "College of Physicians and Surgeons of San Francisco," 30:67-71

Taber, Louise Eddy, 23:346; address, "Four Interesting Pioneer Personalities," 17:186

Taber, William H., 20:45

Table Mountain, Butte Co., 6:243; view, 6: opp. 243

Table Mountain, Tuolumne Co., 11:335-36; 16:338; 35:227, 229

Taboada, Luis, *see* Gil y Taboada

Taboga (island), 20:20, 227-28; 27:38

Tabor, B., 13:32

Tabor, John, 15:270, 274, 376

Tacamas, Ecuador, *see* Atacames

Taché Lake, *see* Tulare Lake

Tacna (ship), 22:303

Tacubaya, Bases of, 1:31

Taffe (Colorado R., 1850), 22:20

Taft (Calaveras Co., 1850), 22:74, 75, 76

Taft, William Howard, 36:70; 38:233-34, 237-38, 252

Taggart, Harold Francis, 19:95; 22:181; 27:381; 33:93; "The Senatorial Election of 1893 in California," 19:59-73; "Thomas Vincent Cator, Populist Leader," 27:311-18; 28:47-55; ed. "California Soldiers in the Philippines . . . Correspondence of Howard Middleton," 30:289-304;

31:49-67, 163-73; "Journal of David Jackson Staples," 22:119-50; "Journal of George Russell Adams," 35:291-307; "Journal of William H. Ennis," 33:1-12, 147-68

Taggart, J. E., 13:32

Tagle (ship), 37:119

Tagus (ship), 25:331

Tahiti, 12:155, 156, 160; 14:320, 322, 323; 15:269; 18:315, 317

Tahoe, Lake, 4:9, 10; 7:7, 8; 9:187, 307; 12:324; 17:76, 77-78; 22:191

Tail, George, 15:376

Tailer (ship), 31:63

Tailholt, 28:377-78

Tak, Eduard, 25:233

Talamantes, Tomás, 13:212-13

Talbert, T. A., 10:78

Talbot (San Blas, 1849), 29:14

Talbot, C. F. A., 31:300, 301

Talbot, Frederick, 21:380

Talbot, James W., 10:265, 363-67 *passim*, 375, 381

Talbot, Mrs. James W., *see* Trego, Laura

Talbot, Marcus H., 34:113

Talbot, Mary, 32:375

Talbot, Samuel, 34:112

Talbot, Theodore, 1:125-26; 3:270, 271, 272; 4:9; 6:183; 12:166, 168; 18:161, 174, 266; 21:354, 357; 29:335; 30:51

Talbot, William Chaloner, 21:380; 26:264; 32:375

Talbot (ship), 3:108; 17:125

Talcott (S.F., 1855), 15:282

Talcott, William M., 10:394

Taliaferro, Alfred W., 9:251

Tallant, D. J., 15:272; 19:233; 28:116

Tallant & Wilde (bank), 15:272

Tallmadge, D. P., 9:113-14

Tallman, B., 15:23, 24; 26:127-28

Tallman, Mrs. Beverly Lamar (Lydia Alcinda Clyman), 4:106; 6:63, 65

Tallmann, John H., 9:116, 269

Tallman, Wilbur Lamar, 4:106; 6:63

Tallot, A., 5:13, 42, 346

Tallow, *see* Hides and tallow

Talmage, William H., 9:26

Tamalpais, Mount, 27:293

Tamaral, Nicolás, 5:196; 8:375-76

Tamariz, Francisco de Paula, 24:290-91, 292, 308; 25:60, 74, 267, 277, 351, 356, 361, 362, 366-67; 27:336; plans for colonization and trade, 25:69-72, 149, 150-66

Tamiet, F., 39:324, 325, 328

"Tammany" Democrats, *see* Democratic Party

"Tammany Hall," San Francisco, 3:39

Tampico, Mex., 23:262-63, 267; 30:238; 34:157

Tam-Tam, Le (semi-weekly), 39:149, 246, 350

Tanforán, Mrs. Toribio (María Sánchez), 17:255

Tanguy, P. Louis, 14:142

Tannahill, Alec, 7:117

Tanner, Herman J., 20:192

Tanner, J., 8:7

Tanner, Zera L., 31:154, 157

Tanner fishing bank, 31:158

Tanning, 5:64; 12:194; 13:25; 29:133; 33:59-72; 34:80, 82; 36:135, 136, 137

Tansill, Robert, 1:233

Taos, N.M., 1:111, 112, 113, 117, 118, 124-25, 149; 2:31; 10:88, 90, 202

Taperin (S.F., 1850s), 32:111-14 *passim*

Tapía, Andrés de, 19:242; 30:279-80

Tapía, Bartolome, 13:205

Tapía, Felipe, 14:6

Tapía, José Bartolomé, 30:336; 38:172

Tapía, Mrs. José Bartolomé (María Lobo), 38:172

Tapía, Tiburcio, 4:159; 12:112; 13:217, 220, 223; 21:320; 38:172

Tapís, Estevan, 6:159; 12:123, 124; 16:115; 25:134, 135, 138; 36:334-35; 37:117, 152

Taplin, Dr. (S.F., 1854), 15:172

Taplin, Dewitt, 30:258

Tappaan, Clair Sprague, 4:52

Tar, 16:14-15; 23:350

Tarabal, Sebastián, 10:216

Tarakanov, Boris, 13:205

Tarakanov, Vasilii Petrovich, 12:221, 223, 231; 13:205

Taranto (ship), 22:22, 168

Tarasov, Boris, 12:232-33

Taraval, Sigismundo, 8:374-77; *Indian Uprising in Lower California*, ed. Wilbur, rev., 11:86

"Tar Flat," San Francisco, 37:215

Tarquina (ship), 3:93

Tartary, Sea of, 25:357, 364

Tasheira, George, 33:374

Tassin (S.F., 1850s), 32:116

Tassin, Augustus G., 27:223

Tasso (ship), 5:255; 8:297-300 *passim*; 12:150-51; 23:202; 28:110, 111; 31:216

Tatem (Indian village) 26:209
Tatnall, Josiah, 23:335, 344
Taubeneck, H. E., 19:66
Tavernier (from France, 1849), 22:304
Tavernier, Jules, 19:107; 21:329;
37:36-37; painting by, 37: foll. 24
Taxation, 5:258; 8:109; 19:13-14; 21:328;
24:319-20; 28:70; 31:316-17; 32:378-
79; *see also* Foreign Miner's Tax
Tay (Marysville, 1850), 15:43
Tay (ship), 32:84
Taylor (Weaverville, 1849), 24:124,
135
Taylor, Mrs. (Yuba Co., 1855), 8:350
Taylor, Mrs. (S.F., 1861), 10:276
Taylor, Mrs. (S.F., 1864), 24:263
Taylor (S.F., 1867), 11:127
Taylor, Alexander Smith, 1:9; 3:101,
248-49; 7:23, 61, 278; 10:91; 12:18-24;
15:377; 20:171-80; 22:34; 30:251,
262, 263
Taylor, Augustus C., 29:292
Taylor, Bayard, 3:37-39; 4:189; 6:155;
9:7; 12:28; 14:165; 15:331-32; 16:61,
64, 86; 17:352; 20:102; 23:254; 27:369;
30:321; 32:297, 301; 38:27, 114
Taylor, C. T., 15:275
Taylor, Charles (to Calif., 1847), 16:136
Taylor, Charles (Monterey, 1855),
16:346
Taylor, Charles L., 27:350
Taylor, Charles Lassell, 29:253, 254
Taylor, Clotilde (Grunsky), 29:284;
ed. "Starr King Heads List:
Subscribers to First Unitarian
Society's Building Fund," 29:251-54
Taylor, E. A., 22:139
Taylor, Mrs. E. C., *see* McDowell,
Mrs. James
Taylor, E. H., 17:176
Taylor, E. W., 9:26, 29; 16:79
Taylor, Edith, *see* Pope, Mrs. George A.
Taylor, Edward Robeson, 1:15, 16, 17;
poem by, 4:271; obit., 2:262-63
Taylor, Frances, 22:94
Taylor, George B., 10:54, 55, 76, 190;
39:293
Taylor, H. C., 7:61
Taylor, J. H., 10:386, 395
Taylor, J. P., letters from, 24:124, 135
Taylor, James M., 10:62; 13:32
Taylor, Jarvis, 21:237
Taylor, Jobe T., 7:14, 17
Taylor, John (Oregon Bar and
Sacramento, 1849), 30:238-39

Taylor, John (Salt Lake City, 1849),
22:141, 150
Taylor, John F., 9:319
Taylor, Knowles, 15:19
Taylor, Levi W., 14:378; 15:29, 52
Taylor, Mary Ellen, 24:88
Taylor, "Mart," 9:144, 176
Taylor, Nelson, 1:238, 259-60; 20:115;
33:254-55
Taylor, Paul Schuster, 24:285;
"Foundations of California Rural
Society," 24:193-228
Taylor, Phoebe, 7:284
Taylor, Ray W., *Hetch Hetchy*, rev.,
5:316-17
Taylor, Richard, 15:169
Taylor, Robert Higgins, 10:186; 14:
opp. 209, 385-89 *passim*; 15:21-29
passim, 34-38 *passim*, 47-53 *passim*
Taylor, Stuart, 13:305
Taylor, Thomas, 10:168, 170(?), 172,
246, 248
Taylor, Mrs. Thomas, 10:246, 248, 250,
251, 255, 273
Taylor, W. H., 9:55
Taylor, W. S., 16:341
Taylor, William (Contra Costa Co.,
1849), 30:7
Taylor, Rev. William (S.F., 1849),
3:36-37; 6:284; 15:165, 335; 16:130;
22:260; 26:169, 170, 172; 27:124, 131,
231; 28:291; 30:5-6, 358, 359; 31:1;
32:135-36; 40:328
Taylor, William E., 11:164, 169, 172
Taylor, William H., 29:253, 254
Taylor, William Henry and Mary
Ellen, 24:88
Taylor, Mrs. William John (Myra
Hopkins), 25:103; 27:348, 351
Taylor, Zachary, 2:119-20; 3:41, 270;
8:270; 9:5, 18; 10:111, 147, 220, 221,
231; 12:99-100; 14:393; 17:307, 308;
19:1, 2, 15, 17, 174, 351; 23:259, 261,
263, 267, 359; 26:321-33 *passim*
Taylor (F. B.) & Co., 29:254
Taylor's Ferry, 11:103
Taylor's Ranch, Cold Springs, 7:7
Tays, George, 14:192, 288; "California
Never Was an Independent
Republic," 15:242-43; "Capt. Andrés
Castillero, Diplomat," 14:230-68;
"Commodore Edmund B. Kennedy
... versus Governor Nicholas
Gutiérrez," 12:137-46; "Mariano
Guadalupe Vallejo and Sonoma,"

16:99-121, 216-55, 348-72; 17:50-73, 141-67, 219-42; "The Passing of Spanish California," 15:139-42; "The Surrender of Monterey by . . . Gutiérrez," 15:338-63; ed. "Pio Pico's Correspondence with the Mexican Government," 13:99-149; trans. "Record of Padre Fray Junípero Serra's Death," 13:155-58; address, "How Revolutions against Mexican Control Held California for the U.S.," 14:283

Tea, 13:8; 28:5; 37:132

Teague, Charles C., 25:287

Teal, Hiram, 28:104, 111

Teal, Lewis, 15:175

Teal (ship), 2:103

Teamsters, 35:59-69, 145-53; *see also* Freight

Tearle, Osmund, 21:257

Techatacup Mine, 3:163-70 *passim*

"Techniques and Implements of the American Whale-Fishery, from an Early Japanese Account," ed. Robert F. Heizer, trans. Hitoshi Watanabe, 32:225-29

Tecumseh (ship), 20:195

Tedro, Philip, *see* Ali, Hadji

Teed, H. W., 9:250, 276; 10:172, 189, 194

Teed, Matthew, 38:32, 34

Teegarden, Eli, 10:198, 264, 365, 367; 27:194

Teegarden, Mrs. Eli (Deborah Anna Carr), 27:194

Teegarden, Mary Anna, 27:194, 202

Teegarden & Co., 27:194

Teegarden, Susan, 10:251, 264

Teel, H. J., 7:117; 26:247

Tefft, Henry A., 10:151, 156; 18:255, 258-59, 275; 19:8-9; 20:105-6; 24:196-97; 28:193, 195-96, 361-62

Tefft, Mrs. Henry A. (née Dana), 18:259

Teggart, Frederick John, 1:108; ed. "The Gold Rush: Extracts from the Diary of C. S. Lyman," 2:181-202; ed. Lyman, *Around the Horn to . . . California*, rev., 4:91-92

Tehachapi Mountains, 17:208, 213

Tehama, 6:69; 15:161; 18:311; 21:9; 22:211-12; 30:158, 159

Tehama Company, 15:48; *see also* Stark, James

Tehama House, San Francisco, 9:253, 278; 19:229; 26:70, 74; 28:33

Tehama Theater, Sacramento, 28:295

Tehipite Valley, 4:26, 37

Teichen, Charles, 11:174

Teignemouth (ship), 8:335

Teiser, Ruth, 25:93; 26:308; "The Charleston: An Industrial Milestone," 25:39-53; bk. rev. by, 38:271-72

Teixeira, Pedro, 27:290

Tejon Pass, 10:214-15, 218; 11:256, 262; 29:29, 35, 36

Telegraph, in Calif., 2:205; 34:346, 348; 38:29; bet. Calif. and Nev., 12:323; 15:95; 29:346; Columbia and Stockton, 15:272; L.A. and S.F., 13:347-48; 38:338; Marysville and Sacramento, 34:346; 38:25; Red Mt., 18:366

Telegraph: ocean, bill to establish, 19:263 in Russian America (exploration), 33:1-12, 147-68; 35:291-307 transcontinental, 6:350; 15:95; 24:365-68 *passim*; 26:357, 359; 29:345-56 *passim*; 34:348 (*see also* Western Union); legislation for, 11:14; 15:170; 19:169-73 *passim*, 360; *see also* Pacific Telegraph bills

Telegraph (newsp.), San Jose, 14:157; 22:223; quoted, 14:162

Telegraph (ship), 15:278

Telegraph Hill, San Francisco, 15:62, 370; 17:292, 301, 315; 25:126; 29:318

Telephone and telegraph cos., 18:365-66, 384; 28:234, 237, 241; 29:199, 206; 31:301; 33:366; 34:354

Telescope Mining District, 18:202, 204

Telescope Peak, 18:200, 213

Tellegen, Lou, 20:141

Teller (d. 1849), 21:308

Teller, John de P., 32:238

Telles, Rafael, 13:45

Tellurium Mine, 20:183

Temécula (rancheria), 3:242-43; 25:300

Temescal, 4:211; 30:220, 222, 224, 230

Temescal, Encinal del (Oakland), 31:326

Temescal Creek, 30:219, 224, 225

Temescales, see Sweat houses

Temperance Hill, 10:251

Temperance movement, 2:182; 8:212, 356; 15:377; 16:80, 81; 22:263; 24:165; 27:45, 50, 302; 30:247; 38:306; in politics, 9:44; 15:367, 377; 16:80;

20:368; *see also* Dashaway Association; Prohibition; Sons of Temperance

Temple, Francis Pliny Fisk, 13:224, 326, 336; 32:331

Temple, John (Juan), 13:210, 218, 220, 224, 302, 311, 319, 325-26, 345, 349; 14:317, 324, 342; 23:208, 217; 26:23; 30:99; 32:340; 34:33-34; 38:28; 39:175

Temple, Mrs. John (Rafaela Cota), 34:21-22, 33-34, 39

Temple, Thomas Workman II, 39:215; "Lanterns at Monterey: Serra's Description of the Founding of Monterey," 11:274-79; trans. "La Carta de Flores," ed. Douglas S. Watson, 12:147-54

Temple Block, Los Angeles, 13:325-26

Templeman, Eleanor Lee (née Redding), 22:370, 371

Temple of Music, San Francisco, 21:161

Temple's Ranch, Merced Co., 12:6

Templeton, Alice V., 21:172

Templeton, Fay, 21:172

"Templeton Crocker Collection of Californiana, The," by Henry R. Wagner, 19:79-81

Tenaya (or Ten-ie-ya; Indian), 1:272, 273; 5:330-33 *passim*, 336; 26:236; 28:332

Tenaya, Lake, 1:272, 280; 4:7, 13, 31, 41; 5:331

Ten Broek, George W., 14:394

"Tenderfoot's Adventures in Hunting California History, A," address by Rodman W. Paul, 20:283

Tendiso, Jesús, 15:356

Ten Eyck, Anthony, 6:364-65

Ten Mile, Mendocino Co., 30:164, 168

Ten Mile River, 23:26; 27:216; 30:163

Tennent, Miss (S.F., 1861), 10:276

Tennent, James, 9:188

Tennent, John H., 8:351, 362; 9:57, 73; 10:362; *see also* Fall, Eckman & Co.

Tennent, May, 10:251, 264

Tennent, Sally, 10:251, 264

Tennent, Samuel J., 4:162-63; 9:188; 19:126, 140

Tennent, Thomas, 22:35; 23:339; 30:256

Tennent, William, 16:84

Tennent, William R., 9:317

Tennessee (ship), 2:107; 7:399; 8:7, 14-16, 263; 11:302; 12:372; 20:192; 27:293; 31:142, 147; 32:145

Tennessee Jubilee Singers, 21:242

"Tennessee Tom," 9:62

Ten Nights in a Bar-Room (play), 39:298

Tent City, 26:53

Tepic, Mex., 14:334; 15:130, 225, 234, 238, 239, 241; 17:125, 128-29; 23:273-74; 27:40; 29:14, miners from, 24:64, 344

Tepusquet (place), 38:261

Tequila, Mex., 23:270-71

Terboy, Richard, 9:319

Teredos, 16:342

Terrapin, *see* Turtles

Terrazas, Francisco de, 3:310, 313, 347, 363-66; 19:242

Terrell, James E., 23:18

Terrill, Charles C., 19:156

Territorial Enterprise, Virginia City, 11:48, 190; 12:84, 323-24; 21:141, 142; 31:185; 34:317; 36:365; quoted, 11:51, 52; 21:27, 147

Territorial Pioneers of California, 33:376

Territories, in U.S., 32:291, 315-16

"Territory of California," 32:293

"Territory of Nataqua, The," by William N. Davis, Jr., 21:225-38; as address, 21:184

Terry, David Smith, 3:42; 4:184, 185; 6:11, 16; 9:39, 42, 45, 174, 244, 270, 277, 285, 389, 390, 397; 10:63, 70, 78, 85, 197, 199; 12:179; 14:351, 358, 364-65, 367-68; 15:70, 73, 77, 78, 85-86, 146-52 *passim*, 156-61 *passim*, 247, 248, 259, 377, 382-83; 17:180, 313; 19:167, 347-48, 353; 20:310, 371; 21:27-28, 96; 24:174; 25:22; 29:20-21; 32:223; 34:139, 142; 36:42; 38:28, 206, 212-15, 336; 40:203, 315, 321, 323, 324; cor., 15:70, 78-79, 259; illus., 15: opp. 143

Terry, Mrs. David Smith, 15:159; 40:320

Terry, E. G., 22:251

Terry, Real, 21:96

Terwer (Indian camp site), 20:173; 26:10; *see also* Fort Ter-Waw

Teschemacher, Henry Frederick, 5:305; 14:342; 16:139; 18:40, 47, 50, 52, 59; 23:339, 344; 26:264; 27:107, 250, 251, 252; 30:165

Teschemacher, S. E., 13:296

Tetlow, Samuel, 4:61, 62, 63; 21:66, 159

Tetrazzini, Mme. Luisa, 25:238

Tevatcon, T., 22:196, 199, 200, 201, 206, 209, 217, 218, 222

Tevis, Lloyd, 8:212; 11:127; 17:175, 191;

19:232, 233, 238; 25:224-25; 26:199; *see also* Haggin & Tevis

Tevis, Robert, 8:212

Tewksbury, Jacob M., 9:109; 15:280, 364

Texans: in Calif. mines, 23:351-52

Texan Santa Fe expedition, 18:235, 245, 247

Texas, 18:57; 31:195, 200; in Civil War, 34:125-42 *passim;* proposed colonization of, 18:137, 138, 140; emigration from, 12:115; 40:161-62; 1849 journey through, 18:101-35; new State, 10:111; 28:74

Texas & Pacific Railroad, 32:343, 344, 348

Texas Bar, 8:199, 209

Texas Rangers, 8:367; 18:122

Thacher, Elizabeth, 23:95

Thaddeus (ship), 35:193, 198

Thames (ship), 17:78

Thane, Arthur F., 30:286

Thanksgiving Day: in the mines, 1849, 20:40; Marysville, 1860, 10:258; San Francisco (1854), 15:184; Visalia (1862), 20:161; proclamation, 10:135; sermon, 19:299-307

Tharp, Eugene H., 28:63

Tharp, Hale, 4:15, 29, 30, 41

Thauillon (S.F., 1850s), 6:55

Thayer, George A., 20:114

Thayer, I. E., 24:368; 36:103

Thayer, Isaac, 2:108

Thayer, James B., 20:1; 33:244

Thayer, Moses, 18:201

Thayer, Philip R., 24:368; 36:103

Thayer, William H., 13:296

Theall, Hiram W., 20:114, 115

Thearle Music Co., 29:92

Theaters:
　Marysville, 8:213, 363; 15:47-48; 21:69-70
　Oakland, 20:39; 33:44-45
　Sacramento, 4:60; 9:251, 252, 273, 276, 277, 279, 377, 394; 10:41, 42, 51, 63, 74, 270, 272, 274, 279, 281, 289, 361, 368; 20:37, 46, 314; 21:43, 44, 160; 23:355
Theaters and opera houses, San Francisco, 4:59-63 *passim;* 6:48; 7:283, 406; 10:276, 281, 290, 294, 368, 371, 376, 378, 381, 388-95 *passim;* 14:74, 133, 411; 15:163-88 *passim,* 266-81 *passim,* 364-75 *passim;* 16:84, 182, 183, 184, 283, 285, 301, 303, 339-47 *passim;* 17:81, 315; 18:286, 376; 19:107; 20:2, 31, 129-30,

135, 138, 293-308 *passim,* 314, 375; 21:40-69 *passim,* 77, 141-79 *passim,* 240-64 *passim,* 274; 22:113, 260, 266; 23:73, 97-116 *passim;* 28:36-37, 133-34; 33:39-47; 35:142; 37:227; *see also* names of playhouses

Thelen, Rosemary, 33:19

Theller, Edward A., 39:15

Theller, Samuel L., 11:9

Théodora (play), 20:131, 137

Théologne (S.F., 1849), 5:21, 346-47

Thérèse, Capt. (of *Rose,* 1827), 8:222

Thérèse (ship), 13:382

Therrill, J. B., 13:32

Thespian clubs: Sonoma, 9:79; Young's Hill, 8:196; 9:66, 67, 79, 129-36 *passim,* 141, 144

Thétis (ship), 14:319, 342; 20:59; 21:373

Thevelin (Paris, 1849), 22:301

Thiaud brothers, 6:55

Thibault, Frederick I., 31:312, 314, 322; son of, 31:312, 314, 315

Thibault (G.) & Co., 31:312, 315; *see also* Fortune, La

Thickens, Virginia Emily, 25:93; 31:189; "Pioneer Agricultural Colonies of Fresno Co.," 25:17-38, 169-77; coed. and trans. "Putting a Lid on California ... Diary of the Portolá Expedition by José de Cañizares," 31:109-24, 261-70, 343-54

Thiele, Théodore, 39:149, 151, 153, 160, 167, 221-22, 238

Thieme, Fred H., 28:93

Thierry, Mme. (S.F., 1854), 15:174, 179; 32:110

Thillon, Anna, 15:88; 19:229; 22:272

"Third Map of Yerba Buena, The," by J. N. Bowman, 26:267-68

Thom (Yuba Co., 1861), 10:363, 376(?), 383

Thom, Cameron E., 9:253, 254, 255; 10: opp. 48, 62, 376(?); 13:336, 338; 32:332

Thomälen (mining region, 1859), 11:327

Thoman, Jacob W., 9:275; 10:65

Thoman, Mrs. Jacob W. (Julia), 16:283

Thomas, Rev. Mr. (San Jose, 1851), 27:301

Thomas, Alfred Barnaby, *Forgotten Frontiers,* rev., 11:387-88

Thomas, Charles C., 29:298, 300, 306

Thomas, Charles L., 10:284, 358, 359

Thomas, Charles W., 34:163

Thomas, Daniel J., 15:377

Thomas, Rev. E. (Petaluma, 1855), 38:312

Thomas, Rev. Eleazer, 28:163; 31:7; 40:329, 332

Thomas, Mrs. Eleazer, 24:262

Thomas, Elisha, 16:138

Thomas, Eugene, 39:231

Thomas, Frederick Folger, 25:383; 31:290

Thomas, George, 16:205; 21:111

Thomas, George F., 13:258

Thomas, George W., 9:254(?); 10:52(?), 62

Thomas, Mrs. George W. (?), 9:254; 10:44, 52, 176, 178

Thomas, Helen (Marye), 23:96

Thomas, Hugh, 28:239

Thomas, I. R., Jr., 12:138

Thomas, J. A., 31:152

Thomas, James A., 29:109-10

Thomas, Jeanne, 30:286

Thomas, John, 37:210

Thomas, John Hudson, 25:383

Thomas, John S., 13:32

Thomas, John Wickson, 25:383

Thomas, Joseph B., 11:10; 19:233

Thomas, L. W., 10:173, 179, 200

Thomas, Martin E., 16:288

Thomas, Massey, 19:60, 61, 63, 64, 69, 72; 27:316; phot., 19: opp. 59

Thomas, Nathaniel S., library of, 8:78

Thomas, O. H., 4:234

Thomas, Richard, 35:298

Thomas, Robert, 30:16, 19-28 *passim*

Thomas, Thomas (Tepic, 1840), 15:240

Thomas, Thomas (from N.Y., 1849), 30:21, 22

Thomas, Townsend A., 9:103; 24:166

"Thomas A. Ayres, Artist-Argonaut of California," by Jeanne Van Nostrand, 20:275-79

Thomas Cope (ship), 16:337

Thomas H. Benton (ship), 33:252

Thomas H. Perkins (ship), 1:208, 210, 231; 22:58, 65; 24:48, 70; 25:130

Thomas Hunt (ship), 15:365; 32:358

Thomas Nowlan (ship), 14:345; 16:223; 18:176; 23:206, 210, 216, 217-18

"Thomas Oliver Larkin in 1831," ed. Robert J. Parker, 16:263-70

"Thomas Sim King, Vigilante Editor," by George D. Carter, 21:23-38

"Thomas Vincent Cator, Populist Leader of California," by Harold F. Taggart, 27:311-18; 28:47-55

Thomas Walters (ship), 23:259, 261, 279; 30:237

Thomas Woodward (ship), 35:305

Thomasset, A., 39:343

Thomes, Robert Hasty, 18:56; 22:366; 30:54; 35:105, 110

Thomes, William Henry, 17:293; 18:283; 20:44

Thomes Creek, 27:215; 30:160, 161; 32:376

Thommen (Thomen, Thomann), Henrich, 11:43; letter to, 11:42

Thompson (Grass Valley, 1851), 6:229

Thompson (Sacramento, 1853, 1859), 10:49, 53; 36:146

Thompson (Yuba Co., 1854), 8:203, 341; 9:52

Thompson, Capt. (of *Georgina*, 1855), 17:84, 168

Thompson (East on *Northern Light*, 1852), 36:135

Thompson, A. W. (surveyor, 1850s), 16:79; 19:369

Thompson, A. W. (editor, 1893), 19:66; 28:48

Thompson, Alpheus Basil, 2:52; 8:106, 299; 12:138-45 *passim*; 14:342; 15:121; 17:253; 18:70, 162, 164, 175; 23:215, 322, 332; 27:286, 337; 28:114, 123, 254, 258; 29:94; 34:118, 119

Thompson, Mrs. Alpheus Basil (Francisca Carrillo), 18:175; 27:286, 339; 29:94

Thompson, Alvah, 30:239, 244, 245

Thompson, Ambrose W., 28:359

Thompson, Augusta Batchelder, *see* Warren, Augusta

Thompson, Bluford K., 25:145; 29:335, 337-39; 30:54

Thompson, Carolyn Mabel, *see* Haas, Mrs. Edward F.

Thompson, Carrie Batchelder, 30:246, 247

Thompson, Charles S., 40:343

Thompson, D. W. (carpenter, 1850), 2:127, 128, 137

Thompson, David, 22:97-98

Thompson, Dewitt Clinton, 15:281; 40:298, 345, 350

Thompson, Dixey Wildes, 27:286

Thompson, Edward Batchelder, 30:246

Thompson, Elena Anita, 29:94

Thompson, Francis Alexander, 23:200, 214, 321, 324, 333; 27:286

Thompson, Frank, painting by, 8: opp. 289

Thompson, G. L., 19:2

Thompson, G. W., 6:49

Thompson, H. F., 10:70

Thompson, Hugh, 10:356

Thompson, I. B., 13:296

Thompson, Ira, 21:99, 100-101

Thompson, Isaac and Petronilla, 28:292

Thompson, J. F., 15:29

Thompson, James (dragoon sgt., 1846), 18:81

Thompson, James (L.A. sheriff, 1855), 29:235, 247

Thompson, James Alden, 25:287

Thompson, John A. ("Snowshoe"), 7:13, 16; 12:323; 15:190; 18:152, 155; 30:246, 377

Thompson, John Chatten and Mary Adams (Williams), 36:374

Thompson, John Chatten, Jr., and Carolyn (Rutledge), 36:374

Thompson, Joseph P., 11:142; 18:39, 40, 44-52 *passim*, 56, 59; 27:107-8

Thompson, Joseph Sexton, 25:242, 249, 287

Thompson, Josiah, 12:146; 14:342

Thompson, Lewis, 20:22, 25

Thompson, Lucius, 29:254

Thompson, Lydia, 21:165

Thompson, Manley S., 21:227-28, 238

Thompson, Percy, 36:75-76

Thompson, Peter (Sonoma, 1853), 24:169

Thompson, Peter (Yuba Co., 1857), 9:167

Thompson, R. Augustus, 9:260, 284; 14:354; 15:79, 80, 83, 169; 17:178; report by, 15:249-51

Thompson, R. B., 16:138

Thompson, Robert (overland, 1849), 30:56

Thompson, "Judge" Robert, 23:274, 279, 280, 356, 382; art. on, 30:237-48

Thompson, Mrs. Robert (Caroline Batchelder), 30:237-47 *passim*

Thompson, Robert A. (Santa Rosa, 1870s), 3:174-75, 177; 12:197; 19:113; 21:138

Thompson, Robert A. (S.F., 1889), 1:16, 18

Thompson, Roy Gaige, 25:96

Thompson, Samuel ("Buckle," 1841), 30:98

Thompson, Samuel (Mormon, 1848), 14:278

Thompson, Simpson, 16:134

Thompson, Theodore, 2:121, 122

Thompson, Thomas, 26:170

Thompson, Thomas L., 3:174, 175

Thompson, Thomas R., 26:204

Thompson, W. P., 9:169, 181, 372

Thompson, Waddy, 10:6, 7, 9; 11:198; 37:12

Thompson, Walter Parmelee, 22:243

Thompson, Web, 22:243

Thompson, Wildes, 27:286

Thompson, William Fletcher, Jr., 32:190; "M. S. Latham and the Senatorial Controversy of 1857," 32:145-59

Thompson, William H., 3:123; 22:44, 64; 26:49

Thompson, Mrs. William Henry (Celia Crocker), 23:96

Thompson, William Neely, *see* Thompson (William Neely) & Co.

Thompson family, 30:246

Thompson (ship), 7:217-18, 221

Thompson & Co., 21:323

Thompson (William Neely) & Co., 15:177, 271; 17:197

Thompson (Lydia) Burlesque Company, 21:165

Thompson *v.* Bealer, 9:67

Thompson, Wilcox & Taylor, 30:238-39

Thompson's Dry Diggings, *see* Yreka

Thoms Creek, *see* Thomes Creek

Thomson, Virginia, 31:287; 32:286; "Note on George Nidever," 32:263-68

Thong (Chinese, S.F., 1868), 23:111

Thorn (d. on Isthmus, 1849), 27:36

Thorn, Herman, 21:299, 304

Thorn, Hiram, 30:8, 9, 10

Thorn, Steven, 22:159

Thornburgh, William, 9:40

Thornburgh, William B., 8:360

Thornbury, Delmar L., *California's Redwood Wonderland*, rev., 3:203

Thorne (S.F., 1853), 2:238

Thorne, Charles Robert, 15:164-65; 16:184, 283, 285; 20:297; 21:63, 64, 165

Thorne, Charles Robert, Jr., 21:63, 165

Thorne, Edwin, 7:285

Thorne, Emily, 21:142, 147; 28:294, 295

Thorne, Isaac N., 17:174, 256-57

Thorne, Marco G., 27:92; ed. "Bound for the Land of Canaan, Ho! The

California Historical Society Quarterly

Diary of Levi Stowell," 27:33-50, 157-64, 259-66, 361-70; 28:57-68

Thorne, William ("Billy the Cooper"), 19:132, 138; 29:338

Thornhill Canyon, 30:10

Thornley, William H., obit., 11:94

Thorn Road, Alameda Co., 30:10; phot., opp. 1

Thornton (S.F., 1855), 15:370

Thornton, Harry Innes, 14:364; 16:183; 19:230, 236

Thornton, Harry Innes [Jr.], 10:262, 274, 289

Thornton, J., 7:11

Thornton, James Dabney, 29:108

Thornton, Jessy Quinn, 28:324; 30:329

Thorp, John, 4:277-78

Thorp, Lindsay, 5:125

Thorpe, Caroline M., 14:176

Thorpe, Moses, 22:68

Thorpe, Theodore, 14:176, 177

Thousand Springs Valley, 32:199, 203

Thrall, Stephen Chipman, 14:76; 34:233, 235

"Threatened Invasion of California, A," 13:38-42

Three Brothers, Yosemite, 1:278

Three Fast Young Men, The (play), 10:277

"Three-Fingered Jack," *see* García, Bernardino; McDonald, Jack

"Three Letters of John Gantt," ed. Alice B. Maloney, 20:147-53

Three-Mile House, Alameda Co., 31:331, 333

Threlkeld, Mrs. Melville Calvert (Annie Rogers Fryer), 21:284; obit., 28:375-76

Thresher, Minord S., 8:211; 9:77

Thresher, Mrs. Minord S., *see* Rideout, Hannah Jane

Threshing (1837), 8:237

Throop, Helen, *see* Pratt, Helen Throop

Throop, Origen B., 23:226

Thrum, D., painting by, 14: opp. 291

Thumb, Tom and Mrs., 6:65

Thurlow, John M., 14:223

Thurman, Allen G., 24:270

Thursby, Emma, 21:80

Thurston, Marion, 11:192

Thurston, Samuel Royal, 10:231

Thurston, Thomas G., 16:7-8, 9, 161-64, 170, 171

Tiareng, W., 31:333

Tibbett, William E., 32:2

Tibbett, Lawrence, 32:2

Tibbetts, Charles, 21:155-59 *passim*

Tibbetts' Opera House, 21:179

Tibbey, Edney Stagg and Emily (Chase), 36:208, 210, 212

Tibbey, Mrs. M. A., 27:369

Tiburcio, José, 14:6

Tiburon Island, 3:323; 11:370, 378

Tiburon Point, 27:271, 273

Tichenor, H. B., 26:264; 32:330-39 *passim*, 344

Tichenor, William, 25:112

Ticó, Fernando, 24:91; 27:335-36, 337

Ticó, Joaquín, 27:337

Tidball (Marysville, 1858), 9:363, 369-70

Tide Land Reclamation Co., 24:212

Tides: at mouth of Colorado R., 22:159-60; San Francisco Bay, 11:314

Tiernan, Patrick Henry, 22:23

Tierney, Joe, 3:259-60

Tiffany (S.F., 1849), 27:129

Tiffany, Robert J., 21:151

Tiffany, W. G., 7:119

Tiffony, W. B., 24:76

Tiger, American, 16:80

Tiger Flat Mining Co., 33:375

Tijuana River, 31:354

Tikhmenef, P., 12:195, 215; 30:335

Tilden, Mrs., boardinghouse of (Sacramento, 1861), 10:272, 288; 26:181

Tilden, (S.F., 1867), 11:127

Tilden, A. F., 38:336

Tilden, Alphonso F., 22:24

Tilden, Bessie, 37:217

Tilden, Charles Lee, 34:323, 328-32; 35:145, 152; 37:217; address, "William C. Ralston," 17:185-86; letter from, 34:323-25

Tilden, Mrs. Charles Lee (Lily F. von Schmidt), 34:328

Tilden, Harmon J., 34:328

Tilden, Leslie, 37:217

Tilden, W. P., 15:376

Tilden, William P., 10:276-79 *passim*, 292

Tilden (place), 34:330

Tilden Regional Park, 34:332

Tile (roofing), 1:163-64; 23:348

"Tiles from Mission Soledad," by Paul P. Parker, 23:348

Tilfair, J., 13:32

Tilford, Frank, 8:370; 9:26, 27, 46, 47, 72;

10:191, 255; 16:80, 82, 84, 336; 17:83; 22:112; 32:147, 151-52, 155; 34:243

Tilghman, Richard L., 3:112, 123; 17:345; 26:49

Tillamook Head, 10:328

Tillchson (Alameda Co., 1851), 12:173

Tillinghast, William De Silver, obit., 13:92

Tillinghast, William H., 13:92

Tillman (Tillmann?) brothers, Fris (Frederick?) and Tom, 6:15

Tillmann & Bendel, San Francisco, 35:305

Tilton, A. E., 40:212

Tilton, C. E., 40:212

Tilton, Cecil Gage, 32:286; *William Chapman Ralston*, rev., 15:191

Tilton, S. S., 11:9

Timandra (ship), 22:171

Timber, 12:194, 203, 204; 22:318; 27:260; *see also* Lumber

Timber Point, 25:322

Timbuctoo, Yuba Co., 9:264, 285, 351, 355, 356, 373, 375, 376; 10:55, 56, 167, 168, 169, 173, 247, 251, 253, 255, 265, 367; 33:202; phot., 9: opp. 376

Timbuctoo Rescue Hose Co. No. 1, 10:253, 258, 265; illus., 10: opp. 252

"Time and the Old California Missions," by W. Barclay Stephens, 37:289-310

Times, Aurora, 7:117; 26:241

Times, Los Angeles, 37:176-77; cited, 31:26-27; 37:171, 351; 38:131-32, 236, 237, 240, 243, 253

Times, North San Juan, 14:398; 28:238

Times (Sun.), San Francisco (1856), 21:25

Times (daily), San Francisco (1860s), 33:209, 210; 39:302

Times, Santa Ana, 18:384

Times, Stockton, 7:277; 34:342, 343; fac. page, 7: opp. 277

Times and Transcript, see Placer Times and Transcript

Timlow, Emily Carolan, 27:190

Timlow, William Ferree and Evelyn (Carolan), 27:190

Timms, George, 8:196; 9:133, 147, 161-62

"Timothy Dwight Hunt and His Wedding Records," by Clifford M. Drury, 28:289-96

Tindal, J. C., 9:366

Tingley, George Brown, 4:207; 9:42;

14:376; 15:202, 211; 16:336; 17:81; 26:344; 30:131; 34:248

Tingley, Mary Viola, *see* Lawrence, Mary V. (Tingley)

Tinker, D. B., 18:22

Tinker, James, 33:365

Tinker, P., 13:32

Tinling, Mrs. Marion, 27:137

Tinnemann, Mrs. Otto (Sue Parrish), 23:288

Tin plate, 30:350

Tioga Mine, 4:40

Tipton, J. S., 9:269; 10:62, 70

Tirrell & Co.'s Panorama, 10:250, 263

Tirrell *et al. v.* Townsend *et al.*, 9:129, 131

Tisdale, W. L., 9:69

Titcomb, Charles, 12:138

Titcomb, Rufus, 28:111

Title insurance company, proposed, 26:261

Tittmann, H., 30:40, 41

Titus, Isaac S., 10:62; 11:7, 9

Titus, Nat, 35:361

Titus, Warren I., 39:358; ed. "Two Unpublished Letters of Jack London," 39:309-10

Tivoli Garden, San Francisco, 19:231; 21:259; 35:142

Tivoli Theater, San Francisco, 25:235; 33:41

Tivy (from Liverpool, 1824), 6:259

Toana Range, 32:198

Toando (or *Towanda*; ship), 22:170, 171

Tobacco, 5:131; 10:382, 383; 12:29; 13:8; 22:319; 25:350; 26:183, 249; 33:197; 38:40; art. on, 40:97-107; Indian, 10:335; 12:293; 18:337; 40:97

Tobacco Plant (ship), 26:175, 183

Tobar y Tamariz, José, 10:317-18, 320; 38:275

Tobin, Mr. and Mrs. (S.F., early 50s), 19:230, 237

Tobin, James, 27:217, 220-21; 30:164, 165

Tobin, Richard Montgomery, 25:230-34 *passim*, 238, 242, 248, 249, 251

Tobin, Robert J., 9:109; 15:281, 364; 19:156

Toca, Manuel, 29:310

"To California through Texas and Mexico: The Diary and Letters of Thomas B. and Joseph G. Eastland,"

ed. Dorothy H. Huggins, 18:99-135, 229-50

Tocqueville, Alexis Charles Henri de, 36:337-38

Tod, John, 22:100-106 *passim*

Todd (Negro, Yuba Co., 1857), 9:144, 146

Todd, Alexander H., 30:65

Todd, Charles Burr, *The Battles of San Pasqual*, rev., 4:291

Todd, E. H., 30:58, 59, 61, 62

Todd, F. Walton, 2:204

Todd, Harry L., address, "Washington the Patriot," 7:96

Todd, Samuel, 2:205; 10:72

Todd, William L., 1:84, 90; 10:10; 17:240; 24:58; 25:123, 190; 29:265-70 *passim*

Todd's Valley, 2:204

Todos Santos, islands of, 31:349

Todos Santos Bay, 1:157; 31:119, 346, 353

"To Europe via Promontory in 1869," recollections of Mary Gamble, 24:365-68

Tofft, Peter, 24:265; 30:126

Toft, Mrs. S. H., 25:32

Tognazzi, Peter, 19:322

Tognazzini, Roland, 25:192

Toison d'Or, La (company), 22:309

Tojetti, Amelia Musto, 25:252

Toland, Hugh Huger, 4:187, 192, 195, 196-200, 202; 5:93; 17:176; phot. of bust, 4: opp. 200

Toland, Mrs. Hugh Huger (1, Mary Goodwin; 2, Mary Avery; 3, Mary V. B.), 4:199

Toland, Mary L., 28:293

Toland Hall, 32:251

Toland Medical College, 4:191, 192, 197-98, 199; 5:93; 27:187

Tolay Lake, 16:112

Toledo, Cabo, *see* Blanco, Cape

Toler, Charlotte Catherine, *see* Hastings, Mrs. Lansford W.

Toler, Hopeful, 22:35

Toler, James Hoyt, 30:229

Toler, William Pinckney, 4:303; 23:358; 25:125, 195, 196, 199, 374; 30:224; 31:37, 38

Toler, Mrs. William Pinckney (Antonia María Peralta), 30:224; 31:77

Tolle, Mrs. Mary A., 28:292

Tolles, John, 8:346, 350, 360

Tolles Dry Diggings, 15:52

Tolles' New Diggin's, *see* Indiana Ranch

Toll House, Yuba Co., 10:57, 77

Toll roads, *see* Roads

Tolmie, William Fraser, 22:103

Tolmie, Mrs. William Fraser (Jane Work), 22:104, 107

Tolson, Hillory A., 25:203

Toma de Razón, 21:311-20

Tomales Bay, 2:304, 335; 9:242; 10:319, 331, 334, 337-45 *passim*; 11:314; map, 10: opp. 337

Tomás de Aquino, Fr., 7:298, 300, 332, 337, 349, 357, 359, 370, 376; 8:54; 36:228, 230

Tomé, New Mex., 25:300, 306

"Tom Hill—Delaware Scout," by Francis Haines, 25:139-48

Tomki Creek, 27:220

Tomlinson, Ambrose G., 12:146

Tomlinson, O. A., 25:200, 203

"Tom Maguire, Napoleon of the Stage," by Lois F. Rodecape, 20:289-314; 21:39-74, 141-82, 239-75

Tomo (Indian), 4:286

Tompkins (or Thomkins; S.F., 1851), 14:73

Tompkins, Christopher Q., 1:233, 234; 22:65

Tompkins, Edward, 11:51

Tompkins, Harry James, 38:157, 158, 222, 223, 226

Tompkins, Mrs. Harry James, 38:157; 222-23

Tompkins, Schuyler C., 8:204, 212; 9:141, 157, 161, 167, 257, 267, 381, 384; 10:72, 183, 367; 14: opp. 209, 378; 15:24, 29, 53; lawsuit, 10:167

Tompkins (or Thompkins), Thomas, 14:177

Tompkins, Walker A., *Santa Barbara's Royal Rancho*, rev., 40:265-66

Toms (Berkeley, 1850s), 31:333

Tondel, Healey, 24:288

Tone, John Henley, 21:306-7, 308-9, 384

Tone, Mrs. John Henley (Alice Walsh), 21:309, 384

Tone, John N., 21:307, 309, 384; 22:81

Toney, John A., 10:370

Tong Hook Tong Company, 23:101-2

Tonquin (ship), 15:191; 27:182

Ton Taché Lake, *see* Tulare Lake

Tooker, J., 9:40

Tooker, Lansing, 9:42

Toole, J. Lawrence, 20:141

Toomes, Albert G., 18:56, 82; 22:366; 29:135; 30:54; 35:105, 110
To Oregon by Ox-team in '47, by Lockley, rev., 3:90
Toplin, Charles, 4:376
"Topographical Reports of Lt. George H. Derby, The," ed. Francis P. Farquhar, 11:99-123
Toppan (Tappan?), B., 9:63
Torbert, Charles J., 9:270
Torch Hill, 29:109
Torchiana, Henry Albert William van Coenen, address on history of Santa Cruz, 12:366; obit., 19:87
Toro (Japanese, 1858), 23:336
Toro's (Riverside Co., 1863), 12:9
Toroso, El, by Sharpsteen and Neelands, rev., 6:99-101
Torquemada, Juan de, writings of, 7:267, 269-70; 10:83; 26:310
Torrance (place), 30:347, 349, 350, 351
Torre, Bernardo de la, 6:321; 7:147
Torre, Estevan de la, 13:48, 55; 29:28
Torre, Gabriel de la, 1:167; 12:151; 16:221, 248, 348; 25:145; 29:28
Torre, Hernando de la, 6:311, 321
Torre, Joaquín de la, 1:135, 136, 137, 289; 3:180-81; 9:81-82; 15:62, 127, 129, 138, 230-31; 16:346; 17:275-76; 18:277; 25:123-24, 145; 29:23, 28, 268-71 *passim;* 31:215
Torre, María Ramona Antonio de la, 12:135
Torre, P. de la, 9:104
Torre, Raimundo de la, 1:167; 16:221
Torrence, John, 15:177; 20:308; 21:52-53
Torrence, Mrs. John, *see* Judah, Mrs. Marietta
Torrence, W., 13:32
Torres, Alonso de, 10:315
Torres, Francisco, 13:217
Torres, Joaquín, 31:77
Torres, Manuel (surg. gen., 1802), 4:145, 146
Torres, Manuel (Muñiz Rancho, 1845), 12:200; 13:35, 54; assemblyman (1859), 10: opp. 48, 62
Torres, Mrs. Manuel (Mariana Richardson), 13:35, 235, 238-39
Torres family, 13:239
Torrey, Delia C., 32:90
Torrey, E. W., 9:244, 269
Torrey, John, 18:343-44; 24:339
Torrey, Mrs. Mary A., 9:170, 181,

244-52 *passim*, 255, 257, 371, 376, 397; 10:67
Torrey, S. F., 13:31
Torrey, Susan, 33:375
Torrubia, Giuseppe [José], *I Moscoviti nella California*, 1:192-93; 10:80
Tortolas, Rio de las, 9:220, 221
Tortoni's restaurant, San Francisco, 3:38
Tosca, La (play), 20:132; 33:45
Toste, Manuel, 35:243
"To the Fraser River!" Diary and letters of Cyrus Olin Phillips, ed. Frederic W. Howay, 11:150-56
Totten, Enoch, 31:47
Totten, Joseph G., 11:10-11
Toubin, Adolph, 35:313; 39:6, 15, 147-50 *passim*
Touchard, Gustave, 17:85; 26:265; 27:350
Toulmin, Mrs. Henry W. (Alice Sistare Larkin), 16:321
Toupin, J., 22:196, 198, 201, 203, 207-8, 217, 218, 220, 324, 325, 330; 23:125
Tour de Nesle, La (play), 10:274, 289
Tournache, Mlle. (Monterey, 1851), 31:313
Tourney, Miss (S.F., 1864), 24:263
Tournoux, A. L., 39:343
Tourny, George, obit., 12:184
Toussaint, (S.F., 1850s), 32:116
Tovar y Tamariz, José, *see* Tobar y Tamariz
Towle, B., 8:343
Towle, G. W., 2:121
Towle, Helen, 36:153
Towle, John, 2:110, 121
Towle, John A., 2:121
Towle, Katherine Amelia, 27:190
Towle, William, 2:101, 104, 109, 122
Towle, William C., 2:122
Towle, William M., 2:113, 116, 117, 121
Towle Brothers Co., 36:110
Towles, W., 8:341, 343, 353
Towne, Capt. (Death Valley, 1850), 18:198, 200-201
Towne, Alban N., 23:118, 121
Towne, Arthur W., 10:90; obit. of James K. Moffit, 34:281-82
Towne, Smith D., 30:363
Towne & Bacon, 30:358; 31:381
Towne's Pass, 18:200
Townsend (Inyo Co., 1849), 18:214
Townsend, Capt. (of *John Stuart*, 1851), 25:331, 332

Townsend (Yuba Co., 1857), 9:130;
　lawsuit, 129, 131
Townsend, Edward D., 28:204, 355
Townsend, Mrs. E. J., 27:255
Townsend, Edward S., 11:358-62; 23:376
Townsend, Henry, 11:358
Townsend, Isaac, 11:11
Townsend, John, 1:234; 4:170-73, 175,
　177; 5:132; 11:134, 141, 143; 16:212-13;
　18:37; 19:77; 33:103; phot., 4: opp. 172;
　see also Stevens-Townsend-Murphy
　party
Townsend, Mrs. John (Elizabeth Louise
　Schallenberger), 1:234; 4:171; 5:132
Townsend, John H. M., 4:173
Townsend, John K., 3:74
Townsend, Sidney, 11:358, 360
Town Talk, San Francisco, 15:182
Toye, Harry F., 9:27
Toye, Henry H. F., 9:27(?); 12:29, 31,
　32; "Celebration of the Fourth of July
　at Ciudad de Los Angeles . . . 1847,"
　1:238-39
Tozer (Sacramento, 1861), 10:272, 282
Tozer, Mary, 15:164
Trabucco, Louis and Eleanor
　(Lambroscini), 33:94
Trabucco, Louis J., 33:94
Trabuco (place), 21:329
"Tracing the Coronado Trail," address
　by Aubrey Neasham, 25:372
Tracy, E. W., 21:128
Tracy, Edward W., 14: opp. 209, 403;
　21:128(?)
Tracy, Felix, 15:368
Tracy, Frederick Palmer, 9:104; 17:323;
　27:97-101, 102, 103; 28:59, 66
Traders' Association of the City and
　County of San Francisco, 33:376
Trade Wind (ship), 24:95
Tragedy Springs, 14:279-80; 32:196
Trahern, G. W., 27:382
"Trailing the Forty-niners through
　Death Valley," address by Carl I.
　Wheat, 17:356
Trails: Coronado, 25:372; Franciscan,
　29:57; fur traders', 18:328; Indian (*see*
　Indians: trails); Noble Pass, 18:302;
　Santa Fe to Los Angeles, 18:328;
　Sonora, 7:113; in Yosemite, 1:283;
　4:13; 5:337; *see also* Lassen trail;
　Mormon trail; Oregon trail; Santa Fe
　trail; Spanish trail
Traits of American Indian Life, by
　Ogden, rev., 12:364-65

Tramezini, Michael, 8:38
Trancas ford and bridge, 29:319
Transcontinental railroad, *see* Railroads:
　transcontinental
Transcript, Boston, 30:256
Transcript, Nevada City, quoted,
　28:233-42 *passim*; 29:199-200, 207
Transcript, Sacramento, 10:239-42
　passim; 13:297-98; 20:332-33; *see also*
　Placer Times and Transcript
Transcript and Times, Nevada City,
　10:394
"Transport Case" (shipping), 27:67-68
Trapier, Richard S., 3:113
Trappers and trapping, 1:15, 111, 112-19;
　2:7-51 *passim*; 4:5-6; 5:146, 229-31;
　6:102; 8:97, 101-2, 120; 10:3-4, 27, 28;
　13:210-11; 14:195-96, 252; 15:105-13,
　133, 134; 17:54, 57, 68; 18:174; 19:135;
　24:231-33, 332; 26:235-36; 32:263-68;
　see also Bridger, James; Campbell,
　Richard; Gantt, John; Nidever,
　George; Ogden, Peter S.; Pattie,
　James O.; Smith, Jedediah
Trask, Capt. (Colorado R., 1855), 22:22,
　168, 170
Trask, John Boardman, 8:355; 21:309,
　363, 365; 22:34, 35
Travaillot, Capt. (S.F., 1851), 6:56
Travels of Jedediah Smith, The, by
　Sullivan, rev., 13:410
Travers, William B., 1:246; 33:256-57
Traviata, La, (opera), 21:68
Traynor party, 34:216
Treador (American R., 1847), 26:110
Treadwell, L. L., 27:67-68
Treadwell Hardware Co., 15:40
Treanor, James Henry and Mary
　(Harrington), 14:414
Treanor, John, obit., 14:414-15
Treasure City, Nevada, 11:49
"Treasure Expresses of the Old West,"
　address by Neill C. Wilson, 15:192
Treasure Island, 32:184
Treat, Archibald and Helen (Bosqui),
　21:332; 22:96
Treat, George, 21:118-19, 122-23
Treat, Mrs. George (Clarinda Littlefield
　Batchelder), 21:123
Treat, John, 21:119, 123
Treat, May Benton, *see* Morrison, Mrs.
　Alexander F.
Treat, Payson Jackson, 23:346; address,
　"First Californian . . . at the Court of
　the Tenno, The," 14:86

Treat family, 21:123

Treaty of Guadalupe Hidalgo, 1:195; 5:322; 9:3-4, 11, 13; 10:129, 140, 142, 152, 153, 154, 233; 13:308; 14:149; 15:243, 306; 19:217, 218, 368; 22:22; 27:206; 28:325, 328; 33:264; 40:24; address by F. L. Paxson, 27:87-89

Trébaol, Jean, 39:337-41

Trees:
mentioned by early explorers, 2:225, 286, 320; 14:10; 18:328, 335-44 *passim;* in Portsmouth Square, S.F., 15:185; on Yerba Buena I., 32:234-35 acacias, 26:280; 32:246, 247; alders, 5:265; 13:232; 18:337, 342; 26:3; 34:200; 36:241; mountain ash, 12:190; Oregon ash, 18:342; box elder, 18:339; buckeye, 5:266; 6:244; 18:342; 36:241; cedars, 17:43; 18:336, 344; 28:218; cottonwood, 8:113; cypress, 12:203; 13:21; 17:43; 18:336, 338, 342, 343; 32:235; firs, 5:47; 12:195, 293; 18:339, 341, 342; 33:60; Joshua, 10:215; juniper, 18:339; 26:245; laurel, 15:185; 18:336; 36:241; madrone, 18:336; 20:39-40; 33:60; maple, 14:10; 18:339; pepperwood, 25:4; plane, 2:320; poplar, 2:320; 14:10, 14; spruce, 18:336, 337; sycamore 13:21, 214, 232; 18:342; walnut, 18:344; 21:202; willow, 8:113; 14:10, 14; yew, 18:339; *see also* Eucalyptus; Fruit; Oaks; Palms; Pines; Redwoods

Treganza, Adan E., 26:136, 156

Tregloan (in mines, 1853), 11:172

Trego, Ellen, 10:264-65

Trego, Laura, 10:252-59 *passim,* 271-85 *passim,* 356-65 *passim,* 375, 380-81

Trego, Nancy, 10:252, 259, 265

Trego, William, 10:264

Tréhouart (on *Hèros,* 1827), 8:150, 222

Trembley, David and Mary Matilda (Kroh), 28:294

Tremmels, William R., 1:227

Tremont House, Marysville, 8:202, 211; 14:394, 404; illus., 14: opp. 209

Trench, Joseph R., 15:368; 16:80; 20:304

Trenor, Dr. and Mrs. (S.F., 1867), 11:127

Trent, Le (ship), 31:141

Trény (Fr. auth.), 22:289, 298; "California Unveiled," trans. Desiré Fricot, 23:41-68; fac. cover of his *La Californie Devoilée,* 23: opp. 40

Trescony, Alberto, 29:22, 27

Tresidder, Donald Bertrand, 22:96, 191; address, "Early History of Stanford University," 23:180-81

Tresidder, Mrs. Donald Bertrand (Mary Curry), 22:96

Trespass Act, *see* "No fence" law

Tres Reyes (ship), 7:271, 300-377, 382-90 *passim;* 8:26, 28; 10:337; 20:319; 36:228, 230

Treutline, Theodore Edward, 35:75

Trevett, Mrs. Theodore Brooks (Mary Melissa Bancroft), 29:98-123 *passim,* 221, 222, 223, 226, 363, 365

Trevor, Frank, 10:196

Triad Society, San Francisco, 15:177

"Trial of the Hounds, 1849, The," ed. Earl S. Pomeroy, 29:161-66

Trías, Ángel, 18:233-34, 247

Tribune, Oakland, 11:190; 38:236, 237, 243; quoted, 30:197, 199, 200, 204; 31:9, 126-28 *passim,* 297, 304, 340

Tribune, Sacramento, 9:39; 16:339

Tribune, San Jose, 20:162; 22:224, 230, 356, 360

Tribune-Index, Sonoma, 17:239-40

Tricou, Henry P., 11:127

Trimble, John, 13:29

Trimingham, James and Augusta J. F. (Rathke), 27:383

Trimingham, Robert, 27:283, 383

Trinidad (town), 5:145, 146, 147, 154, 161, 220, 225, 232, 248, 253-54; 18:5; 22:247, 252; 34:269

Trinidad, Punta de la (Point Tosco), 3:342, 343, 344, 349, 350, 366

Trinidad (ship, 1500s), 3:316-62 *passim,* 367; 7:134, 147, 187; 19:240-44

Trinidad (ship, 1842), 13:280; 18:179

Trinidad Bay, 2:296-97; 3:200; 5:140, 145, 147, 154, 155, 161, 219, 230, 252; 9:208, 217-23; 10:319, 330, 334, 335; 11:302; 12:220; 16: No. 1, Pt. 2, pp. 6, 15; 20:316; 22:252; 23:176; 25:110, 118; 27:294; 28:245, 255; map, 9:219

Trinidad Head, 9:208, 221; 34:266-67

Trinidad Mill Co., 31:293

Trinity Bay, 5:160, 164; *see* Humboldt Bay; Trinidad Bay

Trinity Center, 6:70

Trinity City, *see* Trinidad (town)

Trinity County, 15:195; 20:80; 21:127-28; 31:130, 133; 34:267, 268, 271

Trinity Episcopal Church, San Francisco, 12:95, 99; 23:157, 176;

26:169, 171, 361; 27:111, 112; 28:33, 291; 34:233, 235

Trinity Journal, Weaverville, 21:383; 29:91; 30:361

Trinity River, 5:145, 161-66 *passim*, 170, 177, 240, 246; 19:313; 20:149, 357, 364; 22:366, 379; 23:165; mining on, 5:139, 146, 170, 177, 219-36 *passim*; 13:384-85; 35:156

Trip (Tripp?; Yuba Co., 1850), 10:77

Tripler, Charles Stuart, 34:34

Tripp, Cal. L., 2:128

Tripp, Robert Orville, 9:27

"Trip to the Colorado Mines in 1862, A," from reminiscences of Mahlon Dickerson Fairchild, 12:11-17

"Trip to the Mining Regions in ... 1859, A," by Eduard Vischer, trans. Ruth Frey Axe, 11:224-46, 321-38

"Trip to the Yosemite Falls, A" (prob. by Warren Baer), 1:274-85

Trist, Nicholas P., 5:323-24; 27:88-89

Trivett, Theodore, 15:317

Trocadero, The, San Francisco, 35:185

Trollope, Henry, 15:175

Tromelin, *see* Legoarant de Tromelin

Trona (place), 17:116-17

Tropic Bird (ship), 40:2

Troubador (ship), 14:336

Troupers of the Gold Coast, by Rourke, rev., 8:84

Trovatore, Il (opera), 21:47, 68, 162; 38:338

Trow, Henry, 19:117, 136, 142

Trowbridge, Mrs. (Jackson, 1850s), 32:128

Trowbridge, William Petit, 11:303

Troxel (Camptonville, 1857), 9:177

Troy (Slate Range, 1857), 9:155

Troy, Daniel Q., 8:279; addresses: "Early Day Political Bosses," 5:94-95; "The Old Cocktail Route," 12:180; "Recollections Inspired by a San Francisco Directory," 13:188; "Recollections of Contra Costa," 9:188; obits. of Fred M. DeWitt, 23:90-91; Luke Fay, 12:183; William M. Fitzhugh, 8:189; Theodore W. Hubbard, 6:200; Eusebius J. Molera, 11:94-95; account of luncheon meeting, 12:180; Rep. of Exhibit Com., 4:403

Troy, Robert P., 19:67, 71, 72; 27:316

Trubody, John, 6:62; 16:122-43 *passim*

Trubody, Josiah Palmer, 16:123-34 *passim*, 143

Trubody, Mrs. Josiah Palmer (Sophronia Ament), 16:143

Trubody, Josiah Simmons, 16:131, 140, 142

Trubody, William Alexander, art. on, 16:122-43; phot., 16: opp. 122

Trubody, Mrs. William Alexander (Lura Jane Grigsby), 16:122, 131; phot., 16: opp. 122

Trubody family, 16:122-23, 143

Truckee, 23:117, 119, 121; 24:74, 75

Truckee Lake, *see* Donner Lake

Truckee River and Valley, 3:137-38; 5:280-82, 378; 6:362; 7:14; 10:347, 348; 16:126; 24:120; 32:198, 203, 207

Trudel, Jean B., 13:345

True, Jack, 16:134

True Californian, San Francisco, 17:80; 21:28

True Standard, San Francisco, 6:46; 32:108; 39:13, 14

"True Tales of Early California Days," address by Noel H. Jacks, 15:193

True to the Core (play), 21:159, 256

Truett, Miss (Sacramento, 1861), 10:282, 377

Truett, H. B., 16:183

Truett, J., 15:182

Trueworthy, Thomas E., 10:293; 22:14-19 *passim*, 25, 155, 159, 165

Trujillo, Lorenzo, 12:114-20 *passim*

Truman, Jacob M., 14:278

Truman, John H., 31:151

Trumbaugh (Hitt's co., 1849), 24:117

Trumbull, Mrs. Henri (Emily Pope), 23:94; obit. of Mrs. George A. Pope, 24:88-89

Trumbull, Joseph, 13:296

Truorgy (mate on *Glencoe*, 1849), 11:157

"Truth about Frémont, The," address by Ernest A. Wiltsee, 11:88

Truth about Frémont, The, by Wiltsee, rev., 15:191

Tryon, Ely, 3:163, 168

Tryon, Joseph, 15:51

Tryon, Thomas E., 25:192

Tryon, W. M., 25:96

T'Scharner, Théodore, 37:312; 38:141-42; drawing by, 38: opp. 145

Tschernikh (or Tschernich), George, 12:197-209 *passim*, 271, 272, 273; ranch of, 12:193, 209, 257

Tsukahara Jugoro Masayoshi, 23:342
Tubbs, Alfred L. and Elizabeth R. (Chapin), 28:294
Tubutama (place), 33:16-17
Tucker, Mrs. (Augusta?; S.F., 1861), 10:276
Tucker, E. H., 25:175
Tucker, Miss E. Havemeyer, 31:177
Tucker, G. L., 10:76
Tucker, John W., 7:117; 15:181; 16:310; 19:232; 34:323, 327-28; bldg. on site of store, 34: opp. 329
Tucker, Joseph C., 4:187
Tucker, Reasin P., 10:350, 351
Tucker, Thomas (1846), 6:374
Tucker, Thomas (Sacramento, 1859), 10:59, 70, 165
Tucker's Academy of Music, San Francisco, 10:374; 17:315; 23:344; 29:112, 114, 122; 39:302
Tucson, 21:101, 105; 34:126, 127, 135, 137, 391
Tudor (Yosemite, 1852), 5:332-35
Tudor *v.* G. W. Butler, 9:130
Tueros, Pedro, 33:15-16; 34:195, 206
Tuesday Club, San Diego, 35:354-55
Tuffs (or Tufts), L., 30:55
Tufts, Mrs. (Yuba Co., 1855), 8:350
Tukey, Francis, 9:36, 38
Tulamniu (Indian village), 10:213, 215, 219
Tulare, 18:27
Tulare County, 28:334; canals, 9:256, 282; Confed. feeling in, 20:160-64; plaque marking organization of, 28: opp. 334
Tulare County Historical Society, 29:90, 93-94
Tulare Lake, 11:136, 247, 248, 252, 254; 18:27, 348; on map, 11: opp. 247
Tulare Post, Visalia, 20:160; *see also Equal Rights Expositor*
Tulare Valley Citizen, 19:68, 72; 27:318
Tule Lake, 28:228
Tule River, 11:253, 256; 12:6; war on, 28:338
Tule Shooting Club, 29:365
Tuley, Samuel P., 26:203
Tull, S. R., 14:399
Tully, E. C., 10:62; 27:313
Tully, Eugene, 38:226-27
Tulocay Cemetery, Napa, 16:122, 133; 29:329
Tuohy, John, 4:43

Tuolumne City, 15:290
Tuolumne County, 15:155; 40:249; water companies in, 21:288; 24:269; 35:208
Tuolumne Hydraulic Association, 37:139
Tuolumne Meadows, 4:40
Tuolumne River, 11:359-62 *passim*, 390; 20:101, 114, 115; 23:369, 376; 34:212; mining on, 24:131; 35:208
Tuomey, Honoria Rosalie Pamela, 12:197-98; "Historic Mt. St. Helena," 3:171-77; coauth. *History of . . . Sonoma,* rev., 2:364-65
Tupper, Chester, 30:8, 10
"Turk, The" (Indian), 3:264; 6:316
Turk, Charles A., 18:206
Turk, Frank, 9:27; 11:126-27; 15:180; 19:4, 237
Turnbull, James, 22:4-6, 21
Turnbull, W., 16:81
Turnbull, Walter, 30:293, 295, 300, 304; phot., 30: opp. 289
Turner (Coloma, 1848), 19:125
Turner (Death Valley, 1850), 18:197-98
Turner (Sonoma, 1850), 24:59-60
Turner, Mrs. (Plumas Co., 1853), 28:322; 29:39
Turner, Mrs. and sister (Sacramento, 1861), 10:361
Turner, Miss (S.F., 1862), 10:379
Turner (S.F., 1867), 11:127
Turner, A., 29:120
Turner, A. W., 9:368, 370
Turner, Albert D., 9:265, 286
Turner, Archibald G., 10:372, 376, 377, 381, 387
Turner, Bob and brother, 10:173, 179, 200, 253
Turner, Charles C., 28:342
Turner, David S., 9:29; 15:163, 180, 181, 280, 373-74; 38:300
Turner, Frederick Jackson, 5:288; 32:43, 291; 36:214; 38:370
Turner, Garrison and Elizabeth (Starr), 27:382
Turner, George, 15:10; 26:241
Turner, George F., 33:266, 267, 344; 34:27, 28, 30
Turner, Gustavus James, 31:378
Turner, H. Foote, 24:171
Turner, Henry Garrison, 27:382
Turner, Henry Smith, 1:142; 3:122; 17:344; 21:202, 221, 222, 345; 22:46,

49, 64; 25:306; 26:44, 45, 47, 50, 54;
33:101-2, 108-10, 266-67; *see also*
Lucas, Turner & Co.
Turner, Capt. I., 14:309-10
Turner, James, 15:174, 178
Turner, John (from Ore., 1850), 27:382
Turner, John (S.F., 1876), 29:291
Turner, John N., 9:105, 106
Turner, John S., 22:331, 344, 348
Turner, Justin G., 28:190; obit. of
　　Marco Newmark, 39:175-76
Turner, Mary, 19:125
Turner, Matthew, 22:353
Turner, Theodore, 27:382
Turner, Vi, 20:302
Turner, William, 13:32
Turner, R. M., 8:360
Turner, Judge William R. (Marysville,
　　1850), 9:174; 14:378-82 *passim*, 386,
　　391, 397; 15:28, 30
Turner, William R. (S.F. Recorder,
　　1854), 9:26
Turner & Co. *v.* Lewis & Co., 10:383
Turn Verein, San Francisco, 15:171,
　　268
Turn-Verein Guard, Sacramento,
　　10:198
Turpentine, 16:14, 15; 21:356
Turrill, Charles Beebe, 18:334;
　　"Deuteronomy Brown," 6:169-80;
　　addresses: "Celebrations in San
　　Francisco," 4:400; "The First
　　Transcontinental Railroad," 3:398;
　　"A Stroll through San Francisco in
　　the Long Ago," 2:369-70; obit., 6:202
Turrill, Joel, 6:365
Turtles, 5:173; 12:14, 305; 15:279;
　　26:218; 28:39
Tuscarora (ship), 20:194
Tusitala (ship), 36:380
Tustin, Columbus, 20:261
Tustin, William Isaac, 6:147; 27:62;
　　29:136
Tuthill, Franklin, 30:148
Tutnall, Josiah, 16:83
Tuttle, Capt. (Benicia, 1862), 10:387
Tuttle, Capt. (Colorado R., 1865),
　　22:171
Tuttle, Anson Akenside Hull, 9:256, 269
Tuttle, Charles Albion, 2:204; 9:369,
　　393; 18:361; 27: opp. 97
Tuttle, Charles M., 10:412
Tuttle, F. P., 9:393
Tuttle, L., 26:247

Tuttle, Raglan, 9:393
Tuttle, William H., 37:198
Tutusí (Indian, 1793), 10:323
Twain, Mark, *see* Clemens, Samuel
Tweed (ship), 39:37
Tweet, Fred, 11:161
"Twenty-four Minutes in El Dorado,"
　　address and film by G. W. Wickland,
　　16:286
"Twenty Rarest and Most Important
　　Works Dealing with the History of
　　California, The," 10:79-83
*Twenty Years in the Backwoods of
　　California*, by Shay, rev., 3:93-94
Twigg, C. A., 9:180
Twigg, D. E., 34:125
Twins (or Two Sisters), Yosemite,
　　1:278
Twin Star Republic, 12:318
Twist, William W., 18:267-68;
　　29:230-35 *passim*, 239, 243, 244
Twitchell, Caesar, 18:202-3, 204
Twitchell, Theodore M., 14:220, 222,
　　229
Two Bonnycastles, The (play), 15:186
Two Christmas Eves (play), 34:367
"Two Fourgeaud Letters," by John F.
　　McDermott, 20:117-25
Two Friends (ship), 17:78; 20:365
"Two Letters of Lafayette Maynard,"
　　16:71-76
"Two Men and a Mill: John Dolbeer,
　　William Carson, and the Redwood
　　Lumber Industry in California," by
　　H. Brett Melendy, 38:59-71
Two Men of Sandy Bar (play), 34:361
Twomley, Richard, 8:357
"Two Remarkable California Baskets,"
　　by Zelia Nuttall, 2:341-43
Two Rock Valley, 20:260, 268, 271
Two Sisters, Yosemite, 1:278
"Two Unpublished Letters of Jack
　　London," ed. Warren I. Titus,
　　39:309-10
Tyler, Asher, 38:159
Tyler, Mrs. Asher (Sarah Worth),
　　38:159
Tyler, C. W., 30:265, 365
Tyler, Edwin ("Ned"), 2:204, 208;
　　12:94; 16:31, 40, 42, 172-78
Tyler, George E., 27:36, 38
Tyler, J. W., 22:251
Tyler, John, 5:77; 10:8; 18:142; 37:11-12,
　　15

Tyler, Julia, *see* Shinn, Mrs. Charles H.

Tyler, O. B., 34:257, 258

Tyndall, Mount, 4:19, 28, 54; phot., opp. 18

Tyng, Francis, 29:94

Tyng, George and Elena Anita (Thompson), 29:94

Typhoid fever, 22:50, 56, 61; 33:252, 258-59

Typographical Unions: 1859, 38:28; 1862, 34:347, 349

Tyre, John, 3:118

Tyro (ship), 14:295, 299

Tyrolese Singers, 15:47

Tyrrell, Samuel and Mary Alice (Jones), 28:93

Tyson, Charles, 22:156

Tyson, James L., 4:181-82; 12:28

U

Ubiquitous (journal), 6:5, 12-14; illus., opp. p. 3

Udell, Joseph H., 22:39

Ugarte y Loyola, Jacobo, 1:169

Ugly Club, Camptonville, 9:57, 58, 59, 73

Ukiah, 32:364; newspaper, 20:165

Ukiah Valley, 26:209-15

Ullman, M., 30:256

Ulloa, Alonso de, 19:242-43

Ulloa, Francisco de, 1:36, 38, 42-43, 45; 2:258-59; 3:388; 6:299, 301, 308, 325; 7:71, 72; 36:218; "Voyage of," by Henry R. Wagner, 3:307-83

Ulloa, Lope de, 27:290

Ulph, Owen, bk. rev. by, 40:69-71

Ultimo (play), 21:174

Umber, Charles, 15:281, 364

Umbsen (S.F., 1855), 15:368

"Umpqua City," 25:257

Umpqua Mountains, 28:209, 212, 228

Umpqua River and Valley, 22:343; 23:293; 25:102; 28:119, 209, 251, 256; 30:340; exped. to, 25:102, 110-16, 255-63

Unamuno, Pedro de, 7:245, 251; 27:290-91; 36:226-27, 239; "Narrative," trans. Irene A. Wright, 2:145-60; art. on, 2:140-60

Uncas (ship), 22:305-7 *passim*

Uncle John (play), 10:254

Uncle Sam (magazine), 30:253

Uncle Sam (steam tug, 1852), 22:1, 5, 6, 21

Uncle Sam (str., 1852-1876), 15:165, 168, 173, 178, 184, 267, 269, 273, 279, 365, 371, 377; 16:79, 83, 338; 22:10, 22, 154, 167, 169; 26:176, 177, 183; 27:154; 32:355, 356, 361; 38:340

Uncle Sam's Camels, by Stacey, ed. Lesley, rev., 9:182-84

Uncle Tom's Cabin (book), 11:167-68; (play), 9:385; 10:258, 269; 21:78; 38:337

Unda, Pedro, 31:331

Underhill, Jacob, 26:71, 75

Underhill, Mrs. Jacob, 19:229

Underhill, Reuben Lukens, "Frederick S. Dellenbaugh, 1853-1935," 14:347-49

Underwood (Grass Valley, 1850), 11:244

Underwood, Dr. (Marysville, 1860), 10:247

Underwood, Joseph R., 19:21

Underwood, N. I., 30:355(?); 31:6

Underwood, N. J., 10:43, 65

Unequal Match, An (play), 9:360, 389

Unger, Mrs. Frank B. (Minna C. Buchanan), 9:273

Unicorn (ship), 2:201; 28:59, 62

Uniforms: Calif. Battalion, 29:340; Californian soldiers (1842-46), 13:49-50; 17:144; mining co., 27:369; N.Y. Volunteer (illus.), 1:203; private military cos., 2:119; 37:364; 38:17; S.F. police, 16:340

Union, L' (weekly), Los Angeles, 39:1, 324-26, 329, 350

Union (U.S.): advocates of preservation of, 9:16-17, 22, 37, 38; 349, 351, 360-61; 10:296, 394; 22:228 (*see also* King, Thomas Starr); conventions and meetings, 9:119; 10:282, 283, 284, 295, 296, 355, 367; 22:232; demonstrations, 10:282, 295; newspapers, 10:394 (*see also Union*, Sacramento; *Union*, San Diego); resolutions in Legis., 10:271-74 *passim*, 280, 281, 287-88, 289; 39:291

Union, Sacramento, 4:228; 7:277-81
  passim, 286; 9:179; 10:196, 198; 11:190;
  14:80; 15:8, 202, 205, 208; 17:78,
  176-77, 300; 21:147; 30:195-202
  passim; 31:5-6; 32:299, 301, 315-21
  passim; 33:204-9 *passim*, 329-32
  passim; 34:55, 56, 57, 318; quoted,
  15:206; 21:332; 31:315-21 *passim*
Union, San Diego, quoted, 31:151-59
  passim; 32:335
Union, Yreka, 28:230
Union (ship), 15:51
Union Association (reading room),
  San Francisco, 38:314
Union Band, San Francisco, 15:267;
  24:263
Union Book Store, San Francisco, 30:356
Union City, 12:173-75 *passim;* 14:160
Union Club, San Francisco, 32:215, 221,
  223; 37:198; 38:307, 334
Union clubs or leagues (Civil War),
  10:283, 284, 289, 367; 15:49; 20:157;
  22:232, 358, 360; 27:152; *see also*
  Union Club, San Francisco
Union Colony, Fresno Co., 25:174
Union Co. *v.* The Ridge Co., 10:384,
  385, 386
Unione Nazionale, L', San Francisco,
  39:221
Union Fire and Marine Insurance Co.
  of New Zealand, 27:349-50
Union Franco-Américaine, L', San
  Francisco, 39:154, 158-59, 164, 171, 350
Union Guard, Sacramento, 10:296
Union Guards, Los Angeles, 29:236-37
Union Guards, Marysville, 38:22
Union Guards, San Jose, 22:360
Union Hall, San Francisco, 23:237, 246;
  24:262-65; 26:15
Union Hotel, Camptonville, 10:359, 368
Union Hotel, Mariposa, 1:274
Union Hotel, Sacramento, 6:10; 9:54,
  72; 10:53, 75-76, 174, 191
Union Hotel, San Francisco, 6:251;
  10:198; 15:178, 280; 16:344; 19:228,
  236; 22:263-64
Union Hotel, Smartsville, 10:251
Union Hotel, Sonoma, 24:60, 169-70;
  28:382
Union Insurance Co., San Francisco,
  26:265; 27:168, 270
Union Iron Works, San Francisco,
  7:292; 18:100; 25:39-53 *passim;*
  27:179; 30:344; 33:236
Union List of Newspapers, 39:1

Union Lumber Co., 27:218
Union Mine, 31:94
Union Nationale, L', San Francisco, 39:
  221, 349, 350
Union Nouvelle, L' (weekly), 39:1, 167,
  329, 334-46 *passim*, 350
Union Pacific Railroad, 3:251; 4:255,
  299; 5:181, 182; 32:368-69; *see also*
  "Last Spike"
Union parties (political), 10:369, 394;
  15:205; 21:358; 22:231; 30:135;
  34:51-59 *passim*
Unions (labor), 35:59-69, 145-53;
  Brotherhood of Teamsters, 35:61-67
  passim, 145-52 *passim;* Carpenters and
  Joiners, 40:258; Carriage Blacksmiths,
  Woodworkers and Painters, 35:65;
  Coal Yard Teamsters', 35:67; Coast
  Seamen's, 35:60; Draymen's and
  Teamsters', 35:59-60, 61; Hackmen's,
  35:67; Laundry Wagon Drivers',
  35:67; Milk Wagon Drivers, 35:67;
  Plasterers' Protective, 21:151, 305;
  Porters' and Packers' and Ware-
  housemen's, 35:67; Retail Delivery
  Drivers', 35:67; Riggers' and
  Stevedores' Association, 15:168, 173,
  174; Sailors', 35:67; Sand Teamsters',
  35:64-65, 67, 150; Sanitary Wagon
  Drivers', 35:67; Stevedores', 35:67;
  Team Drivers' International, 35:61;
  Typographical, 34:347, 349
Union Saloon, Sacramento, 33:330
Union Saloon, San Francisco, 15:369-70
Union Square Theatre Co., 21:245-46
Union Theatre, San Francisco, 15:165,
  169; 16:84, 182, 183, 184, 283, 285, 339,
  341; 20:305; 23:107-8, 110, 112; 38:330
Union Title Co., San Diego, 36:159
Union Town, 2:124; 5:145, 248-52
  passim; 13:411; *see also* Arcata
Union Volunteers, Arcata, 34:269
Union Water Co., 11:329-30
Unitarian churches and societies, 10:282,
  295; 15:169; 19:153, 299, 300; 20:2-7
  passim; 25:334, 341; 26:71, 171, 361;
  27:350; 29:251-54; 31:248-49; 38:34;
  phot., 20: opp. 1; 38: foll. 40
United Land Association *v.* Knight,
  21:121
United Nations, 24:1-4, 7-8, 72, 162, 163
United Pacific Gold Co., 25:99
United States (ship), 4:303; 34:320
United States Arsenal, 14:356; 15:83, 84;
  20:154; 33:232

United States Board of Land
   Commissioners, 13:322, 339; 15:4, 5,
   164, 169, 172, 176, 183, 269, 277, 279,
   280, 364, 365, 366, 370; 16:82, 197,
   235, 306, 339, 342, 347; 17:169, 172-78
   passim, 182-83, 253, 254; 19:163, 182;
   21:120, 123, 318; 25:221-24 *passim;*
   26:210, 253; 27:134-35; 30:330
United States Bonded Warehouse, San
   Francisco, 8:275
United States Circus, 10:280
United States Coast and Geodetic
   Survey, 4:42; 19:165, 369, 370; 20:194;
   29:185-86
United States Coast Guard, 25:320
United States Congress, measures
   relating to Calif., 19:16-23, 26, 157-84,
   256-77, 344-67
United States Consualte in California,
   37:1-17; *see also* Larkin, Thomas O.
United States Customs, *see* Customs
United States Engineers, 30:320, 327,
   328, 337
United States Forest Service, 4:51-52
United States Geological Survey,
   4:33-37 *passim*, 42, 50-51; 7:121; 9:401;
   15:290; 18:214
United States Hotel, Camptonville,
   9:129, 150, 151, 172
United States Hotel, Los Angeles,
   13:339
United States Hotel, Marysville, 8:340;
   9:365, 391; 10:252, 257, 356, 382;
   14:215, 392, 393, 394, 402; 15:41-46
   passim
United States Hotel, Sacramento, 2:137;
   9:35; 24:357; 28:254
United States Hotel, San Francisco,
   28:254; 36:309
United States Hotel, Young's Hill, 9:61
United States Land and Colonization
   Co., Ltd., 35:344
United States Land Association *v.*
   Knight, 21:121
United States Land Offices, 19:18;
   24:176-78; 35:157-58
United States Life Insurance Co., 26:256
United States Mail Steamship Co., 8:7,
   10; 13:389
United States Marines, 18:82; 24:48
United States Mint, 15:246; San
   Francisco Branch, 2:188; 10:190, 281,
   294; 11:175; 12:12; 15:173, 182, 273,
   277, 384; 16:32-36 *passim*, 342-43;

17:83, 184; 19:164, 169, 170, 183;
   36:297-98
United States Silk Culture Experimental
   Station, 31:335, 339-40
United States Steel Corp., 30:351
United States Topographical Engineers,
   18:116, 124; 39:83-84; *see also* Abert,
   John J.; Derby, George Horatio;
   Emory, William H.; Frémont, John
   C.; "International Boundary Survey";
   Ives, Joseph C.; Whipple, Amiel W.
United States *v.* Andrés Castillero, 3:194;
   10:191; 15:19
United States *v.* Limantour, 1:32; *see
   also* Limantour, José Yves
United States *v.* Perot, 30:333, 337-38
Universalist Church, 15:45
University Club, San Diego, 35:356
University Gardens Tract, Berkeley, 30:
   opp. 225, 227
University Hotel, Berkeley, 31:329
University of California: proposed,
   12:93; 21:330; 36:350; as College of
   Calif., 16:336-37; 17:49; 31:329;
   36:349; in 1860s and '70s, 17:47, 49;
   19:152-53; 20:2, 9; 25:12; 31:328-30;
   36:350; in 1880s, 35:144, 253-61;
   36:350-51; in 1890s, 25:12-13; 30:67;
   37:39; in 1900s, 35:260; 37:45;
   architectural plans, 25:12; buildings,
   26:193, 196, 200; 31:329; dental and
   medical depts., 30:67; faculty clubs,
   35:152; gifts to, 36:151-52, 200, 350;
   at Los Angeles, 36:150; Philosophy
   Dept., 33:350-51; regents, 19:152-53,
   155; 25:15
University of California Alumni Assoc.,
   36:150-52
University of San Francisco, 37:43;
   38:26; *see also* St. Ignatius
University of Santa Clara, 3:209; 30:307;
   37:43; *see also* Santa Clara College
University of Southern California,
   36:328-29; 37:42-43
University of the Pacific, 4:177, 191;
   14:157; 16:131; 28:142; 29:55, 59;
   30:249; 31:2-4, 10; 33:73; 36:349
Unknown River, *see* Humboldt River
Unmack, Mrs. William, 26:95
Unona (ship), *see Juno*
"Unveiling at Columbia," 35:77-78
Up and down California, by Brewer, ed.
   Farquhar, rev., 9:401
Upham, Samuel Curtis, 13:297, 298,
   300; 20:332, 338

Upper Corral, *see* Illinoistown
Upper Hotel (Hutchings House),
	Yosemite, 5:338
Upper Lake, 23:297; 32:364
Upper San Joaquin Canal Co., 25:173
Upson, Lauren, 17:78
Upson, Lauren A., 4:228; 17:75, 77, 78
Upson, Warren, 17:78
Upton, Bruce, 13:293
Upton, Isaac J., 38:60
Upton, Mattias Gilbert, 10:69
Urançu, Joanes de, 2:154, 156
Uranium claims, 32:4, 28, 29, 33, 34
Urbana (L.A., 1848), 33:268, 338
Urdaneta, Andrés, 2:140; 3:266;
	6:310-11; 7:137-51 *passim*, 169, 172-73,
	181, 182, 233
Urgideo, Encarnación, 13:211
Uría, Francisco Javier de, 23:6, 13
Urilda (riv. str.), 9:72

Urio, José Antonio, 37:108, 126
Urioste, Rosita de, 31:280
Urquhart, C. F., 4:50
Urrea, José, 14:259
Urrutia, José de, 3:319
U. S. Grant Hotel, San Diego, 35:365
Ustel (Yuba Co., 1857), 9:167
Usury, bill to prevent, 10:42, 63
Utah, 22:29; 29:291; coal and iron,
	30:346-50 *passim;* coins from Calif.
	gold, 15:244-46; trade bet. Calif. and,
	22:12-17; *see also* Mormons; Salt Lake
	City
Utah Lake, 11:53
Utica Mine, 20:184
Uvas, Cañada de las, *see* Grapevine
	Canyon
Uznay, Károly, 21:327; 28:126, 130-31,
	137, 141

V

Vaca, Manuel, 13:278; 16:249; 23:295;
	ranch of, 13:264, 265, 266; 29:256
Vacaville, 13:278; 17:224; 26:381
Vaccination, 2:256; 4:168; 9:137; 18:68;
	36:146
Vachel, Horace A., 31:25, 26
Vadugo, Sra. Ignacia, 16:285
Vaidis Sisters, 4:61
Vail (Wilde's bus. mgr.), 19:105
Vail, E. J., 32:165, 167
Vaillant, Clothilde A. (Hossefross),
	23:75
Vaillant, J. Louis, 14:142
Vaillant (ship), 7:212, 213, 214, 220;
	12:37
Valdés, Antonio, 3:215, 236; 40:118
Valdés, Basilio, 4:159
Valdés, Dorotea, 23:5
Valdés (or Valdez), Melecio, ranch of,
	13:203
Valdés Flores Bazán y Peón, Cayetano,
	10:313, 315-16, 324; 15:214, 215;
	40:117, 118, 119, 122; map of
	explorations, foll. 112
Valdez, Feliciana, 12:117
Valdez family, 13:349
Valencia, Calendario and Paula
	(Sánchez), 17:255

Valencia, Mrs. José Jesús (Julia
	Sánchez), 17:256
Valencia, Pedro de, 3:309
Valencia (ship), 31:59
Valentine, Charles, 21:308, 309
Valentine, Matthias B., 21:309
Valentine, Thomas B., 21:309
Valentine & Co., 30:355, 356
Valenzuela (bandit, Mex. War), 16:258
Valenzuela, Francisca Xaviera, 14:8;
	30:217
Valenzuela, Joaquín, 18:162-63, 175;
	26:41
Valenzuela, Ramón, 13:326
Valerio (Indian, 1827), 8:216-17
Valladares, Manuel, 31:267, 270
Valladares, Arroyo, 31:270
Valle, del, *see* Del Valle
Valleau, T. B., 15:179
Valleau, Thomas P., 9:26; 15:179(?)
Vallecito, Calaveras Co., 11:166, 331;
	22:74, 82
Vallecito, San Diego Co., 21:219;
	25:298-302 *passim,* 307, 308; 34:198;
	36:117, 118-19, 123, 124, 125
Vallecito Hill, 25:302
Vallecito Springs, 1:145
Vallejeda, Gerónimo de, 2:156

Vallejo, Adelayda Rosario, 16:351;
17:235
Vallejo, Andronico, 4:284; 16:232, 235
Vallejo, Andronico II, 16:235; 17:236;
29:159
Vallejo, Encarnación, 17:142, 145
Vallejo, Enrique and Antonia, 29:326
Vallejo, Epifania Gertrudis, 16:244;
17:235; 25:340
Vallejo, Francisca, *see* McGettigan,
Mrs. Charles D.
Vallejo, Guadalupe (dau. of J. de J.),
29:310
Vallejo, Guadalupe (s. of M. G.),
17:150, 231; 29:159
Vallejo, Ignacio Loyola, 29:326
Vallejo, Ignacio Vicente Ferrer, 1:165;
14:9; 16:101-2, 103, 106; 29:309
Vallejo, Mrs. Ignacio Vicente Ferrer
(María Antonia Lugo), 16:102; 29:309
Vallejo, José de Jesús, 8:112; 12:261;
13:51, 107; 16:103, 247, 354; 17:51, 54,
55, 149, 151, 226; 21:320; 25:382;
29:309, 310; 33:350; 40:98
Vallejo, José Manuel Salvador, 12:134;
13:36; 16:133, 237, 240, 250, 350-56
passim, 359, 368, 369, 370; 17:142-51
passim; 20:96; 21:13, 17, 20; 28:259-60;
29:157, 158, 263, 264-65; 40:348; art.
on, 29:309-31; Bear Flag prisoner,
1:72-73, 79, 90-95 *passim*, 135, 179, 186,
286; 2:69; 6:140, 272, 273; 7:79; 10:105;
13:107-9 *passim;* 16:100; 17:220-29
passim, 275; 19:118, 132; 24:57; 25:123;
29:264-65; expeds. against Indians,
16:250, 351, 355; 20:234; 24:49-50, 51;
ranchos and land grants, 5:273; 6:63;
21:317, 320; 24:49; 26:267; 27:107;
29:318; residence, 4:285; 17:143;
25:124; trouble w. Dr. Bale, 4:153;
17:155-56; 28:263-66; port., 16: opp.
236
Vallejo, Mrs. José Manuel Salvador
(María de la Luz Carrillo), 27:107;
29:311-12
Vallejo, José Mariano, letter to,
29:149-51
Vallejo, Jovita Francisca, 17:154, 237,
239
Vallejo, Juan Antonio, 27:107; 28:114;
29:318; 30:98
Vallejo, Luisa, *see* Emparan, Mrs.
Ricardo
Vallejo, Manuel (or Avril), 29:326
Vallejo, María Isidora, 29:318

Vallejo, Maria Ygnacia, 17:237
Vallejo, Mariano Guadalupe, 1:180, 233;
2:53; 4:225, 284-89 *passim*; 5:269,
415-16; 6:142, 153; 7:80; 8:128; 9:90;
11:142; 12:38, 198, 199, 244, 345; 13:34,
35-36, 170, 267; 14:22, 101, 144, 231,
247-52 *passim*, 255, 258, 259, 264; 15:61,
141, 176, 183, 340; 16:305; 17:248;
18:294; 19:127; 20:108; 22:346; 23:39,
259, 328; 24:47, 63; 25:122; 26:121;
28:104, 111, 113, 243, 245, 260-66
passim; 29:309-29 *passim;* 30:321;
32:235; 35:109; 36:341; 37:195, 361;
38:338; arts. on, 16:99-121, 216-55,
348-72; 17:50-73, 141-67, 219-42;
29:146-60; 36:241-50
Bear flag prisoner, 1:72-73, 79-97
passim, 135, 137, 179, 180, 182, 189,
286, 292-94; 2:69-73 *passim;*
6:137-41, 272-74, 277; 7:79; 9:81;
10:10, 105, 106, 114; 11:136; 12:39,
337; 13:107, 108, 109; 14:147; 15:230;
17:219-30, 275; 19:118, 132; 24:57;
25:123; 29:264-65; 31:209
interest in Benicia, 6:146; 11:133;
13:267; 17:301; 20:152
comandante general of Calif., 2:255;
8:103, 120, 121, 123; 10:9; 11:197;
12:244, 245; 14:232, 249, 255;
15:355; 23:334
comandante linea miltar, 4:85; 13:44,
45; 29:262
at Constitutional Convention, 19:7;
24:63; 28:193
cooperation w. U.S., 21:11-12, 13, 17
offers land for capital, 12:30; 17:260,
263
at 1846 *junta*, 4:286; 5:188-89, 193-95;
7:93-94
library, 4:284; 20:108; 29:149, 151;
30:98, 101
press, 12:128, 133-34
ranchos, 4:284; 5:273; 13:267; 14:37;
15:280; 26:210; 36:242
relatives, 4:153, 284-89; 11:69, 142;
13:267, 348; 14:125; 17:265; 29:159;
see also Vallejo family
residences, 17:142, 143, 235; 29:149,
151; illus., 4: opp. 286; *see also*
Lachryma Montis
state senator, 14:197; 24:58
vineyards, 17:144; 36:241-50
correspondence, 1:292-95; 4:380-82,
390; 5:184-86, 188-89; 6:184-85;
12:246-69 *passim;* 14:247-49;

15:341-42; 17: opp. 224, 230;
29:149-57
poems, 4: (fac.) opp. 289, 289; 29:152
proclamations, 4:387-89; 12:132
fac. sig., 10: opp. 159
ports., 4: opp. 284; 14: opp. 230; 16:
opp. 99; 17: opp. 141; 29: opp. 153
Vallejo, Mrs. Mariano Guadalupe
(Francisca Benicia Carrillo), 1:180;
4:284, 285, 286; 6:146; 16:222-29
passim; 29:159, 310; 17:150, 224, 226,
231-36 *passim,* 301-2; letter to,
1:184-85; port., 16: opp. 216
Vallejo, María Ynez Telecillia, *see*
Frisby, Mrs. William Edward Rose
Vallejo, Napoleon P., 4:284; 17:234, 239;
36:246, 247
Vallejo, Mrs. Napoleon P. (Martha
Brown), 17:239
Vallejo, Natalia, 16:359; 17:237; 29:159
Vallejo, Platón, 4:152; 6:138; 17:145,
236, 237, 239; art. on, 4:284-89; phot.,
4: opp. 284
Vallejo, Mrs. Platón (Lilly Poole
Wiley), 4:288; 17:237
Vallejo, Platón C., 29:326
Vallejo, Plutarco, 16:367; 17:145, 232
Vallejo, Rosalia, *see* Leese, Mrs. Jacob
Primer
Vallejo, Salvador, *see* Vallejo, José
Manuel Salvador
Vallejo, Uladislao E., 17:160; 29:159;
36:246, 247; 37:194, 205, 211
Vallejo family, 16:101-2; 17:142, 145,
234-39 *passim;* 18:265; 29:159, 309, 310,
326; 37:194; crest, 16: opp. 112; *see
also* individual names
Vallejo (place), 2:136; 5:94-95; 11:163;
12:30; 15:280; 17:234, 260-64; 24:63,
64; 27:196, 303, 306; 29:159; 31:294;
38:50-51, 312; newspaper, 8:285; *see
also* South Vallejo
Vallejo Savings and Commercial Bank,
29:155
Vallet (S.F. and Yuba R., 1850), 5:17,
18, 23, 34, 38
Valleyfield (ship), 28:247, 248
Valley Forge (ship), phot., 22: opp. 349
Valley Lumber Co., 31:294
"Valley of Dry Bones, The," address
by Robert G. Cleland, 29:375-76
Valley Springs, 11:182; 31:143, 148; *see
also* Double Springs
Valota Park, 31:298
Valparaiso, Chile, 1:224-27; 2:104-9;

6:212; 7:218-21; 14:315; 16:283;
20:205-6; 22:241-43, 302; 23:331;
28:101; 29:149; 37:13
Van Alen, William Knickerbocker,
23:229, 245
Van Allen, L. C., 29:107, 110, 122;
30:359; *see also* Rosenbaum and Van
Allen
Van Amringe, Edwin Verne, obit.,
36:184-85
Van Arsdale, J. A., 28:381
Van Arsdale, William Wilson, 28:381
Van Avery, Mrs. (Sacramento, 1858),
9:371
Van Beck, Pvt. and Mrs. (L.A., 1847),
1:243
Van Bergen, John, 26:264
Van Bokkelen, George A., 9:100, 101;
29:124
Van Bokkelen, Jacob Lorillard, 9:26;
10:76; 15:276, 281
Van Brunt & Johnson, 14:385, 402
Van Buren, George F., 21:309; 22:80
Van Buren, Martin, 37:9-10
Van Buren, Thomas B., 11:177-78, 181
Van Caneghan, Dr. P. N., 16:337
Van Caneghem, Peter C. L., 14:163
Vance, James M., 10:274, 289, 291; 11:8,
9, 21
Vance, James R., 8:204; 9:180; 10:186,
200
Vance, Robert H., 34:295; 35:48
Vance Mill, Eureka, 38:62
Vance's Bar, 21:128
Vance's Daguerrean Gallery, San
Francisco, 34:295
Vance's Panorama, 11:229
Van Choate, Sylvanus Frederick,
29:355
Vancij (or Vancy), Gaspard, Duché
de, 3:224; 15:213, 215; painting by,
15: opp. 213
Van Cleft, George H., 19:368-69
Van Cortlandt, Augustus, 9:75
Van Court (Crescent City, 1856), 35:326
Vancouver, George, 2:256; 8:136, 233;
9:223; 10:88, 313, 314, 316, 320, 321,
325, 328, 335; 15:59; 18:336-37; 23:250;
25:319-24 *passim;* 28:21; quoted,
14:10-11, 111-20; bk. on, rev.,
39:368-71; Menzies' journal of his
voyage, 2:256-57, 265-340
Vancouver, Wash., 22:213; 28:210; *see
also* Fort Vancouver

Vancouver (ship), 5:304; 6:189; 28:249-50, 252, 253

Vancouver Island, 9:233; 10:323; 11:150-51; 28:111

Van Crombrugghe, Alfred, 22:303

Van Curen, Paul, 18:212, 213

Vandalia (ship, 1840s), 3:115, 117, 118; 8:75, 297, 298; 12:168; 17:332-40 *passim*; 18:59; 22:56; 29:335; 37:306

Vandalia (ship, 1889), 30:153

Vandenberg, F. L., 36:104

Vanderbeck, James and Mrs., 1:243-44

Vanderbilt, Mrs. (Benicia, 1852), 27:302

Vanderbilt, Cornelius, 31:37; 33:206

Vanderbilt Independent Line, 28:309, 313, 320; 31:37; 33:206; 36:136, 140

Vanderslice & Co., 36:103

Vandervoort, Paul, 19:66; 28:54

Van der Weyden (artist), 37:38

Vandever, William, 4:44; 31:136

Vandewater, John, 9:109; 15:281, 364

Vandewater, Mrs. R. J., 19:229

Van Dorn (Death Valley, 1861), 18:206

Van Dorn, Earl, 34:125-26

Van Dyke (S.F., 1849), 23:159

Vandyke (Mariposa, 1856), 1:274

Van Dyke, Theodore Strong, 31:13, 29

Van Dyke, Walter, 10:372, 377; 34:269

Vane, William, 33:64

Vanegas, José, 13:200, 203

Van Ess, Miss (Marysville, 1861), 10:280

Van Fleet, William Cary, 9:396

Van Guelpen, Mme. (S.F., 1854), 15:175

Van Gundy (Yuba Co., 1855), 8:347

Van Heusen, Henry, 9:135, 139, 143, 147, 150, 152, 268, 349, 362, 363, 373; 10:187

Van Heusen, I. N., 9:75; *see also* Van Heusen, Henry

Van Heusen, Mary, 9:62, 75

Van Heusen, S. H., 9:143; *see also* Van Heusen, Henry

Van Horn, Jefferson, 18:111, 130, 134

Vanin, Theresa, 34:181

"Vanished Waters of Southeastern San Francisco," by William C. Sharpsteen, 21:113-26

Vann, W. A., 19:60, 64, 66, 69; 27:316; phot., 19: opp. 59

Van Natter (RR conductor, 1870s), 18:360

Van Ness, Mrs. (Grass Valley, 1851), 6:231

Van Ness, James P., 9:26, 27, 108; 14:75, 354; 15:281, 282, 369, 370; 21:124

Van Ness Ordinance, 15:367; 16:342; 21:119, 124

Van Nortwick, J. L., 22:251

Van Nostrand, Jeanne (Skinner), 19:384; 21:382; 23:286; 24:83, 84; "Audubon's Ill-Fated Western Journey," 21:289-310; "American Occupations of Rancho Santa Margarita de las Flores," 22:175-77; ed. "The Diary of a 'Used-up' Miner," 22:67-83; "Thomas A. Ayres, Artist-Argonaut of California," 20:275-79; obit. of Vera Mae (Shafford) Sharritt, 22:286

Van Noy, A. R., 27:286-87

Van Nuys, Ezra, 26:95

Van Nuys, Isaac N., 25:287

Van Pelt, John, 9:277; 27:302

Van Pragg (or Van Praag), Samuel, 13:32

Van Rensselaer, Mrs. (S.F., 1867), 11:127

Van Reynegom, Francis William, 1:16; 24:80

Van Sandt, J. W., 15:164

Van Sickles (Nev., ca. 1859), 6:342-43

Van Sloun, Frank, 38:3

Van Sooy, Neal, 23:384; address, "California Newspaper Centennial," 26:83-84

Van Tassel, A. J., 22:251

Van Tassell, John A., 22:251

Vantine, James, 30:8

Van Vleck, Miss (S.F., 1864), 24:263

Van Vleck, Fred B., 15:375

Van Voorhies, William, 10:50, 295; 12:31, 32; 17:176; 27:34, 36, 37, 44, 45, 46, 157-63 *passim*, 262, 368-69; 28:58-64 *passim*, 67

Van Waler (or Van Valer), Andrew J., Jr., 22:251

Van Winkle, P. Warren, 7:110; 11:10; 15:179, 376; 17: opp. 168, 177

Van Wormer, Martin, 13:18-23

Van Wyck, H. D. (or John), 28:219, 230

Van Wyck, Sidney, 30:104; 38:314

Van Zandt, J., 16:79

Vaquero (ship), 32:361

Varela, Sérbulo, 17:328; 18:174; 25:130-31; 26:32; 29:335

Varelas, Casimiro, 13:207

Vargas, Francisco de, 7:20, 61, 76

Variael (or Veriael), Manuel, 26:215
Variel, J. H., 8:358; 9:62, 150-51, 264, 360
Varieties, The (theater), San Francisco, 10:381; 21:55, 78
Varina (ship), 20:194
"Various Phases of Marin County History," address by Robert H. Menzies, 29:373-74
Varney, Jeremiah, 14:176
Varney, Samuel, 6:364, 368; 19:327
Varnum (Yuba Co., 1854), 8:204-7 *passim*, 337
Varsi, Aloysius, 1:12-17 *passim*; 24:79
Vas, Count Samu, *see* Wass, Count Samu
Vásquez, Francisco ("Chico"), 17:100
Vasquez, Louis, 4:342; 26:324, 325
Vásquez, Tiburcio (bandit), 10:86; 13:344; 17:100-102, 106-10 *passim*, 114-15, 116; 25:191; 29:27; 30:377; bks. on, rev., 7:195; 40:260-61
Vásquez, Tiburcio (of Rancho Corral de Tierra), 17:252-53
Vásquez de Coronado, Francisco, *see* Coronado
Vásquez del Mercado, Jesús María, 17:153; 23:8
Vassar (Philippines, 1898), 30:300
Vassar *v.* Vassar, 9:362
Vassault, Ferdinand, 9:26; 15:167, 177, 181; 17:173, 177; 31:44
Vastan de Santiago, Felipe, 7:271
Vatican Circus, Risley's, 9:152, 177; 16:183, 285
Vaugh, Henry, 15:169
Vaughan, A. M., 21:238
Vaughan (or Vaughn), C. L. N., 9:376; 10:50, 62
Vaughn, Charles, 12:117
Vaughn, Henry, 15:269
Vaughn, William F., 9:40
Vázquez Mexía, Diego, 2:149-50
Veagas (barge), 22:156, 168
Veal (New York Flat, 1855), 8:341-42
Veatch, John Allen, 21:373
Veazie, John, 2:122
Vedder, Charles A., 26:256
Veeder, Peter, 15:174
Vega, Benito de la, *see* Díaz de la Vega
Vega, Plácido, 37:193-214; phot., opp. 193
Vegetables, 2:520; 5:131, 135, 186, 266, 269; 8:21; 10:414; 14:20, 22; 20:31; 24:189; raised by Chinese, 34:308-9; raised at Missions, 1:166; 2:321; 4:369,

370; 5:217; 8:319; by Portuguese, 35:242; by Russians, 12:193, 243; by Swiss, 30:310-12 *passim; see also* Beans; Corn; Onions; Peas; Potatoes; Sweet Potatoes
Veiga, Dominic, 35:243
Veitch, William, 18:343, 346
Vejar, Pablo, 16:218, 221; 26:25, 29-35 *passim*, 40-41, 46-47, 52, 55
Vejar, Ricardo, 13:349
Vejar, Salvador and María Josefa (López), 26:32
Velasco, Luis de (1550s), 7:139-42 *passim*, 145, 146
Velasco, Luis de (1590s), 3:3-4; 7:257-62 *passim*, 266, 267; 8:47, 48, 49; 20:315-16
Velasques (or Velásquez), José, 34:196, 197, 204, 208; 36:120, 121
Velasquez (or Velázquez), Joseph, 11:275; 31:121
Velásquez, Romualdo, 37:201, 204
Velicatá, Lower Calif., 31:113-18 *passim*
Vellati, Louis, 17:255
Venard, Stephen, 18:359
"Vendéen, Le" (pseud.; Mokelumne Hill, 1851), 35:317
Venegas, Miguel de, 1:52; 3:335; 6:161-62, 166; 8:374-77 *passim*; 9:206; 15:190; 24:316
Venetian Restaurant, San Francisco, 28:39
Veniaminov, Ivan, 12:196, 200
Venice, Calif., 20:139-40, 142
Venice Island, 17:46, 47
Venting of brands, 20:344-45; 23:360, 371
Ventura: 17:40; natural history soc., 17:32; newspaper, 19:63, 72; *see also* San Buenaventura
Ventura County, 18:275; rainfall in, 16:299
Venus, transit of (1769), 11:315; 31:111
Vénus (ship), 8:117; 12:49
Vera, Santiago de, 2:142, 144
Vera Cruz, 16: No. 1, Pt. 2, p. 5; 18:219-22; 33:49; 34:158; 37:292
Veranda Hotel, San Francisco, 8:273
Verástegui, Martín de, 26:315; 27:310
Verbarg, Leonard H., obit. of Dozier Finley, 40:272-73
Verde Ranch, 27:116, 121, 122
Verdenal, D. F., 21:264-65, 268
Verdenal, J. M., 39:160
Verdugo, José María, rancho of, 13:203

Verdugo, Juan Diego, 20:238

Verdugo, Julio, 13:315

Verdugo, Mariano de la Luz, 13:203, 207; 20:238; ranch of, 13:203

Verdugo, Mrs. Mariano de la Luz (María Guadalupe), 20:238

Verduzco, Francisco, 16:239-40

Vérité, La, San Francisco, 39:258-59, 312-15 *passim*, 350

Ver Mehr, John L., 8:284; 10:290; 11:146, 326; 12:96, 99, 106; 26:170, 171, 172; 28:35; 30:39, 46; 32:122; 36:243-44, 310

Vermeule, Thomas Lloyd, 1:246-47, 254; 20:115; 28:195-96; 33:254; fac. sig., 10: opp. 159

Vermilion, John, 15:240

Vermilion Sea, *see* California, Gulf of

Vermilion Valley, 4:46

Vernaci (or Vernacci), Juan, 10:316; 40:121

Vernal Falls, Yosemite, 1:280-81

Vernon, Los Angeles Co., 38:131

Vernon, Sutter Co., 4:204; 8:23; 11:117; 14:212, 218, 375, 384, 402, 405; 23:349, 369; 25:104; 27:128

Vernon House, Sacramento, 10:41, 63

Véron, Pierre, 39:160, 170

Veron, Prosper Alexandre, 5:5, 17, 21, 22, 23, 29, 31, 36, 42, 142, 144, 153-58 *passim*, 220, 227-28, 233, 235, 246, 348; 6:38, 56; 39:10

Verplank, Philip, 17:179

Ver Planck, William E., 39:117, 119; *Salt in California*, rev., 37:373-74

Vert (S.F., 1850), *see* Virt

Very True Public Balance, 6:45; 39:13

Vesey, Louis, *see* Xánthus, János

Vesian (or Versian; S.F., 1853), 39:160

Vessels, *see* name of vessel

Vesta (ship), 15:278; 26:176

Vestal, Stanley, *Kit Carson*, rev., 7:194-95

Vestments, 37:109, 121-22, 246, 256

Vestvali, Félicité de, 21:146-47

"Vétille" (pseud.), 39:160

Vevis, Joseph, 1:235

Viader, José, 8:153, 236, 237; 10:99; 23:210, 217; 37:102, 117; 38:102-3, 105

"Viator" (pseud.), 24:138

Vice, Martin, 22:23

Vick, Mrs. (Marysville, 1860), 10:258

Victoria (Indian, 1888), 3:244

Victoria, Guadalupe, 24:289; 27:333; port., 24: opp. 289

Victoria, Manuel, 12:237-38; 13:211-13; 16:223-26 *passim*; 23:197, 303, 304, 305, 331; 26:249, 250, 251; 27:337; 33:279; rebellion against, 13:211-13

Victoria, B.C., 11:153, 307

Victoria (Magellan's and Loaysa's ship, 1522), 6:294; 7:134, 135

Victoria (Cabrillo's ship, 1542), 7:20, 55

Victoria (British ship, 1849), 27:48

Victoria (Amer. schr., 1850), 7:404; 8:17-24, 167

Victoria (barge-schr., 1864), 22:14, 15, 23, 156, 166, 169, 170

Victorine (ship), 13:382

Victorine Mine, 6:347

"Victor J. Fourgeaud, M.D.," by George D. Lyman, 11:138-49

Victorville, 27:113, 116, 121

Vidal, Francisco, 7:376

Videau, Henry, 14:395; 15:49; restaurant of, 10:255, 267

Viejas Indian Reservation, 34:203

Vienna Café, San Francisco, 35:126, 140

Vigil, Francisco Esteban, 10:33-36 *passim*; 12:113-14

Vigil, José María, 37:199

Vigilance Committee, Aurora, Nev. (1863), 7:115-16, 119

Vigilance Committee, Los Angeles, (1836), 13:218-21; 23:324

Vigilance Committee, Marysville (1851), 15:30-41 *passim*, 36, 56; (1856), 31:5-6

Vigilance Committee, in mining region, 18:265; 30:239-43

Vigilance Committee, San Francisco (1851); 2:135-36; 3:40; 6:49, 51; 12:106, 157; 15:36, 38-39; 18:371; 19:167-69, 291; 21:26; 22:112-14, 263, 275; 23:72; 25:331; 28:42-43; 29:161; 30:55, 208, 275-76; 31:140, 290, 319; 32:133; 33:323; 34:243-49 *passim*; 35:314; 37:330; 38:296, 299; bk. on, rev., 1:99-101

Vigilance Committee, San Francisco (1856), 3:41-42, 101; 4:192; 6:3-14 *passim*, 49, 50; 8:382; 9:48, 61, 75, 103, 106, 250, 275, 276, 283; 13:82, 83; 15:205, 301; 16:344-47 *passim*; 17:310; 18:259, 276, 372, 373; 19:169, 291; 20:260, 306, 307, 371; 21:26-28, 30, 37, 365; 22:39, 40; 23:74; 24:173-76 *passim*; 26:259, 260; 28:71, 151-53; 29:175-76; 31:5, 291; 32:133, 149-50; 37:30-31; 39:143, 153; arts. on,

8:364-73; 14:350-74; 15:70-87,
143-62, 247-65; illus., 6:6, 50;
8:368; 15: opp. 143
Vigilance Committee, San Luis Obispo
(1856), 18:270
"Vigilance Committee of 1851," address
by Peter T. Conmy, 30:185, 275-76
Vigilance organization, San Joaquin
Valley (1879), 3:91
Vigilante Days at Virginia City, by
Dosch, ed. Lockley, rev., 3:297
Vigneaux, Ernest, 18:5, 10, 17, 19, 21
Vignes, Jean Louis, 1:235, 236; 12:282,
295; 13:213, 214, 230, 336, 345; 17:331;
21:313; 33:341, 342; 37:71
Vignes, Pierre E., 12:333
Vila, Vicente, 4:143; 31:110, 121, 123
Villa Capt. (1837), 14:249; 15:341;
16:354, 359, 360; *see also* Villavicencio,
José María
Villa, Francisco, 34:161
Villa, José, 13:203
Villa, María del Rosario, 13:218-21
Villa, Rafael, *see* Villavicencio, Rafael
Villa (institution), 1:25
Villaceque (San Andres, 1851), 35:317
Villa de Branciforte, *see* Branciforte
Villalobos, Juan de, 1:45; 6:318, 319
Villalobos, López de *see* López de
Villalobos
Villalon (New Almaden, 1860s), 37:201
Villamanrique, Marqués de, 2:140, 142,
144; 3:3; 7:238
Villapando, Jesús, 10:29, 30
Villa-Puente, Marqués de, 5:197
Villavicencio, Antonio and María (de
los Santos), 13:200
Villavicencio, José María, 1:170; 14:258;
see also Villa, Capt.
Villavicencio, Rafael (San Jose, 1811),
14:14
Villavicencio, Rafael (San Luis Obispo
Co., 1842), 18:162, 163, 175
Ville du Havre, A la (restaurant),
28:46
Villela, Juan Manuel, 14:6
Villeneuve (S.F., 1850), 5:139, 228, 232,
235
Viña Ranch (Stanford's), 16:136, 137;
18:302, 313; *see also* Ranchos:
Bosquejo
Viñals, José, 37:304; letters to.
37:100-108
Vincennes (ship), 16:182; 24:324; 35:193

Vincent (S.F., 1850s), *see* Quintin,
Vincent
Vincent (Berkeley, 1855), 31:331
Vincent, George W., 8:296, 297, 301;
18:68, 70
Vincent, Joshua, 31:72; 33:374
Vincent & Co., Coloma, 30:259
Vincent & Payot, 30:265
Vine (sailboat), 20:135
Vines, George Yount, 2:67
Vines, William Bartlett, 2:63, 67; 16:132;
17:240; 24:58, 72
Vines, Mrs. William Bartlett (Frances
Yount), 2:63, 67
Vine Spring Garden, 11:164-65
Vineyard, Caroline, *see* Whiteside, Mrs.
Ninian E.
Vineyard, Elida (Mrs. Charles E. De
Long), 8:194, 196; 9:245-53 *passim*,
261, 263, 268, 270, 271, 277, 348, 356,
361, 362; 10:41, 42, 48, 56-61 *passim*,
69, 77, 166, 176-88 *passim*, 200, 246-54
passim, 259, 357, 365, 372-85 *passim*,
391, 395; 11:47, 50, 51, 61; diary of,
10:386-87; letters to, 10:269-70; 11:60,
64; phot., 10: opp. 170, opp. 378
Vineyard, James R., 8:194, 359; 9:77,
274, 277, 361, 387; 10:56, 60, 61, 77,
78, 192, 247, 248, 253, 372-77 *passim*,
386, 387; 11:61
Vineyard, Jenny, *see* Hays, Mrs. R. T.
Vineyard, Nellie, *see* Woods, Mrs.
Matthew
Vineyard, Virginia, 10:169, 192; phot.,
opp. 170
Vineyard, William B., 9:387; 10:192;
lawsuit, 10:183
Vineyard family, 8:194; 9:358; 10:192
Vineyard, Lake, 26:22
Vineyards, *see* Grapes; Wines and wine
making
"Vineyards of Gen. M. G. Vallejo,
The," by Madie D. Brown, 36:241-50
Vineyard Sound, 29:11
Viniculture, *see* Wines and wine making
Vining, Leroy, 4:13; 5:335-36; 26:236
Vining River, 26:236
Vinson, James H., 21:160
Vinsonhaler, L. D., 28:334
Vioget, Jean Jacques, 3:32; 11:69, 76,
134; 12:248, 272; 13:236; 14:226, 326,
328, 330, 341, 345; 17:67, 296, 297, 298;
19:198, 214; 30:325, 326; 38:327; 39:5
Violé, Felix, 39:332, 338-39

Violette, La, San Francisco, 39:246, 350

Violin City, 24:167, 169

Viot, E., 30:357, 366

Virago (ship), 15:181

Vírgenes, Ensenada de las (San Quintín Bay), 31:119

Vírgenes, Ensenada de las (Todos Santos Bay), 31:119, 346

Virgin, George W., 18:331

Virginia, overland party from (1849), 22:127, 128, 130, 131

Virginia Block, San Francisco, 19:230

Virginia City, Mont., 15:324, 326, 328

Virginia City, Nev., 2:260-61; 3:297; 4:64, 66, 74, 77; 6:342-43; 7:92; 9:312; 10:260, 266; 11:47-51; 12:327, 330; 15:381; 17:76-77; 19:187; 20:250; 21:56-60, 67, 141-42, 164, 165, 176, 288; 34:317-18; letters from, 11:60-64; newspapers, 11:48, 51-52, 190; 12:84, 323-24; 21:57, 141, 142, 147; 31:185; 34:317; 36:35-40

Virginia Creek, 26:236

Virginie (ship), 3:108

Virginius (play), 15:48

Virgin River, 1:123; 2:37, 40, 41; 28:121, 124

Virgo, Joseph H., 9:181, 270, 377, 397

Virmond, Henry, 6:263; 8:106; 17:55, 65; 19:193, 214, 215, 216; 23:206, 209, 216, 217, 305, 331, 332, 333; 37:254-58 *passim*

Virt, Auguste, 6:42

Visalia, 1:271; 12:6; 18:26-28, 29, 201; 39:213; 40:293; Confed. feeling in, 20:160-64; newspapers, 10:309; 20:160-64

Vischer, Eduard (or Edward), 9:183, 184, 342; 15:164, 370; 16:286; 30:165; "First Visit to California," ed. and trans. E. G. Gudde, 19:193-216; "A Trip to the Mining Regions in . . . 1859," trans. Ruth Frey Axe, 11:224-46, 321-38; drawings by, 9: opp. 299, opp. 306, opp. 312, opp. 332; *Pictorial of California,* 4:26; 9:184, 312, 332-35; port., 19: opp. 193

"Visit to Monterey in 1786, A," by Jean F. G. de Lapérouse, 15:216-23

"Visual Knowledge of California to 1700, The," by Arda M. Haenszel, 36:213-40

Viticulture, *see* Grapes and Vineyards

Vitoria (island), 7:46, 73

Vivasseur, Paul, 10:77

Vizcaíno, Juan, 31:121

Vizcaíno, Sebastián, 1:158, 192; 2:144, 295; 3:5; 7:62, 256-76, 295-394; 8:26-70; 13:196; 20:222, 234, 319; 23:220; 25:363; 27:289, 290, 291; 31:110, 111, 354; 36:227-32

Vizcaino, Cabo, 9:208; 10:330

Vizetelly, Henry (J. Tyrwhitt Brooks, pseud.), 4:182; 13:175; 33:126; art. on, 11:65-68

Voce del Popolo, San Francisco, 39:221

Vörös, Jozsef, 28:137-38, 142

Vogan, James H., 26:204

Vogel, Mrs., *see* Gantner, Mrs. John O.

Voiles, Mrs. William H. (Jane), 21:384; address, "Old Homes of El Dorado [County]," 27:280-82

Volante (ship), 27:48

Volcano (place), 32:55; church, 15:164; 32:55; newspapers, 16:339; 20:185

Volcanoes, 27:137; 28:206, 227; 29:2; *see also* Lassen Peak

Volga (ship), 12:194

Volkmann, George Frederick, 21:96; 23:188; obit., 25:86-87

Volkmann, Mrs. George Frederick (Louisa M. Daegener), 23:188; 25:87

Volkmann, William George, obit., 23:187-88

Volkmann, William George, Jr., 21:96; 23:188; 25:87

Volkmann family, 23:188; 25:87

Volks, Voulks, *see* Foulkes

Volunteer (ship), 14:342, 343; 16:4; 23:305, 331; 26:164; 31:33; 35:199

Volunteer Guards of Yerba Buena, 3:85; *see also* Militia

Von Carnap, Robert, 28:294

Von Geldern, Charles, 25:287; 29:329

Von Geldern, Charles E., 25:287-88

Von Geldern, Otto, 9:90; 36:247

Von Hafften, Alexander, 27:191

Von Hamme (dancer, 1869), 21:163

Von Leicht, Ferdinand, survey by, 21:121

Von Pfister, Edward H., 6:147, 148; 27:62

Von Rosen, Jonas F. C., 24:190

Von Schmidt, Alexis Waldemar, 19:370, 372; 23:275, 281; 30:338

Von Schmidt, Lily F., 34:328

Von Schrader, Frederick, 13:80

Von Schroeder, Baroness (Mary Ellen Donahue), 7:292; 10:389

Voorhies (S.F., 1861), *see* Van Voorhies
Voorhies, Margaret (Sinclair), 15:163; 16:344; 17:82
Voorman, Henry, 25:169
Vorian (or Voriau; Indian, 1833), 22:200; 23:38
Vosbrough, A. S., 15:280
Vosnesensky, I. G., 12:197, 198, 209; 18:338
Votaw, Homer C., 26:191; 36:380; coauth. "More on the Ewing Mutiny," 36:307-11
"Voyage from the Columbia to California in 1840, A," from Journal of Sir James Douglas, ed., Herman Leader, 8:97-115
"Voyage of Pedro de Unamuno to California in 1587, The," by Henry R. Wagner, 2:140-60
"Voyage to California of Sebastian Rodríguez Cermeño, The," by Henry R. Wagner, 3:3-24
Voz de México, La, San Francisco, 37:199
Voz Portugueza, A, San Francisco, 35:244
Vulcan Foundry, San Francisco, 8:276
Vulture (ship), 23:216

W

W., E. M. rev. of Edwards, *Desert Voices*, 38:77-80
Waack, William, 24:384
Wachs, Aaron Nathan, 26:383
Wachs, Lionel, 26:383
Wackenreuder, Vitus, 14: opp. 209, 398; 22:37
Waddams, N., 22:73
Waddell, Archibald, 33:120-23 *passim*
Waddell, J. P., 13:32
Waddell, James Iredell, 26:356; 27:180; 33:238, 240; 40:301
Waddell, William Bradford, 28:286; 29:73, 74, 75
Wade, James M., 9:42
Wade, Japtha Homer, 29:343, 36
Wade, John, 6:259
Wade, Richard, 8:346; 9:166, 181; 10:165, 170, 171
Wade, Robert E., Jr., 26:383
Wade's Opera House, 25:235; *see also* Grand Opera House, San Francisco
Wadham, Ed, 35:351
Wadleigh, J.W., 14:220
Wadsworth, Charles, 24:263; 28:10
Wadsworth, E., 13:296
Wadsworth, James C. L., 26:71
Wadsworth, Lysander, 14:180
Wadsworth, Mary E., 9:384; 14:397
Wadsworth, William R., 22:23-24; 27:69; 36:306
Wadsworth, Nev., 32:203
Wadsworth's *National Wagon Road Guide* (1858), 3:46

Wagener, S.H., 30:363; & Co., 29:107
Wages and salaries: in 1792, 2:323; in 1830s, 2:53; 16:322-32; in 1840, 8:109; in 1846, 13:48; in 1848-49, 4:204; 12:29; 13:84, 166, 263, 279, 357, 365, 368, 369-70, 377, 379, 397, 401; 16:140; 21:363; 22:70; 23:53, 56; 24:23, 24, 26, 126, 133, 348, 354, 359; 26:110; 27:43; 28:66; 30:24; in 1850-55, 11:54, 161, 162; 26:302; 27:232
Waggoner, W. W., 10:352; "The Donner Party and Relief Hill," 10:347-52
Wagner (Sacramento, 1858), 9:244
Wagner, Blanche Henriette Collet (Mrs. Henry R.), 32:190, trans. "Some Phases of French Society in San Francisco in the 'Fifties,'" from journal of Ernest de Massey, 32:105-18; obit., 36:185-86
Wagner, H., 9:67, 347; 10:246, 260; 30:359; lawsuit, 9:346
Wagner, Harr, 7:88; 32:234
Wagner, Henry Raup, 1:19, 20; 3:249-50; 6:91; 10:306; 12:86; 16:288; 17:87; 19:288; 20:191, 325; 21:183; 23:287; 24:80; 25:378-79; 27:291; 32:44, 190; 36:27, 175, 176, 215, 217, 218, 237

"Albert Little Bancroft," 29:97-128, 217-27, 357-67; "Another Huntington Acquisition," 5:196-97; "Bibliographical Note," 1:192-93;

"California Historical Society, 1852-1922," 1:9-22; "The Descent on California in 1683," 26:309-19; "The Discovery of California," 1:36-56; "Edward Bosqui," 21:321-32; "Four Early Sketches of Monterey Scenes," 15:213-15; "Francisco de Ulloa Returned," 19:240-44; "George Davidson, Geographer," 11:299-320; "The Journal of John Wood," 6:361-63; "The Last Spanish Exploration of the Northwest Coast," 10:313-45; "The Last Will of Pedro de Alvarado," 25:309-10; "The Life of Ferdinand C. Ewer," 13:291-300; 14:74-79; "A Map of Cabrillo's Discoveries," 11:44-46; "Monterey in 1796," 1:173-77; "Quivira, a Mythical California City," 3:262-67; "A Recently Discovered Account of the Atondo Expedition . . . 1683," 8:80; "Recollections of Templeton Crocker," 28:364-66; "Some Bibliographical Notes Concerning Jerónimo de Ripalda's *Catecismo*," 16:373-75; "Spanish Voyages to the Northwest Coast in the 16th Century," 6:293-331; 7:20-77, 132-93, 228-76, 295-394; 8:26-70; "The Templeton Crocker Collection of Californiana," 19:79-81; contrib. to "Twenty Rarest . . . Works," 10:79-80, 83

ed. and trans. "California Voyages, 1539-1941," 3:307-97; ed. "Extracts from the Log of the . . . *Savannah*," 3:105-25; ed. and trans. "Fray Benito de la Sierra's Account of the Hezeta Expedition," 9:201-42; ed. "Journal of John McHenry Hollingsworth," 1:207-70; ed. "Memoirs of Lemuel Clark McKeeby," 3:45-72, 126-70; ed. and trans. "Memorial of Pedro Calderón y Henríquez," 23:219-25; ed. and trans. "The Voyage of Pedro de Unamuno to California in 1587," 2:140-60; ed. and trans. "The Voyage to California of Sebastián Rodríguez Cermeño," 3:3-24

introductions to "Adventures on the Plains," 1:57-59; "A David Douglas Letter," 2:223; "Some Phases of French Society in San Francisco in the 'Fifties,'" 32:105-6

addresses: "California History and Our Own Society," 19:89; "California Material in the Archives of Spain," 2:258-60; "The Discovery of California," 1:20; "Drake's Voyage around the World," 3:204-7; "The Hartnell School," 15:286-87

bk. revs. by, 1:194-97, 199-200; 2:256-57; 9:401-2; 24:77-78

bks. by, rev.: *Sir Francis Drake's Voyage*, 6:93-95; *Some Imaginary California Geography*, 6:95-96; *The Spanish Southwest*, 3:290-91

gifts from, 4:97; 11:82, 83; 13:285, 412; 14:93, 189; 15:94, 194, 215, 287-88, 386; 16:93, 189-90, 287, 381; 17:88, 190, 286, 358, 359; 18:92, 93-94, 186, 284, 285, 378; 19:83, 190, 283-84, 377-78; 20:90, 189, 284; 21:90, 186, 280, 375; 22:189, 282-83, 376

rep. of Publication Com., 4:99

obits. of William A. Bowen, 17:94; G. R. G. Conway, 30:278-80; Robert E. Cowan, 21:282-83; Frederic W. Howay, 22:380-81; Henry E. Huntington, 6:200-202; Walter A. Nimocks, 7:100; Glenn A. Schaefer, 18:382-83; arts. on, 36:79-82, 165-75

Wagner, Mrs. Henry Raup, *see* Wagner, Blanche Collet

Wagner, Jacob C., 33:66

Wagner, John, 4:71-72

Wagner, Joseph Anthony, 33:284; "The Oratory of Thomas Starr King," 33:219-27

Wagner, Kate, 9:255; 10:173

Wagner, William A., 3:113

Wagner Memorial Award, 38:358; 39:62-63; 40:366-69; phot., 40: opp. 360

Wagon Road Act (1855), 7:6, 10-11; (1857), 7:17-18

Wagons, manufacture of, 13:314; 33:327-28

Wagontire Mountain, 22:215

Wahl, John C., 10:166; lawsuits, 9:367; 10:54; 10:178

Wainwright, James E., 17:256; 28:35; *see also* Wainwright, Randall & Co.

Wainwright, Byrne & Co., 28:35
Wainwright (James E.), (Albert G.) Randall & Co., 15:183, 368; 17:181, 256
Wair, J. W., 4:360
Wait, Frona Eunica, *see* Colburn, Mrs. Frederick H.
Waite, Edwin G., 9:46, 107; 27:315; 30:146
Waitt, Daniel, 12:12
Wakeman, Abe, 8:366, 367
Wakeman, Edgar ("Ned"), 10:193; 15:267; 17:77, 80; bk. on, rev., 38:377-78
Wakeman, Mrs. Ferdinand O. (Mary Eliza Wilson), 26:336; 30:56, 65, 167-68, 169
Wakeman, Mrs. Robert, 19:229
Wakker, Micheltum, 40:63
Walbridge, Dunstan S., 22:38
Walbridge, H. C., 17:179
Waldeck, Herman, 35:124
Walden, Minor, 11:9
Waldo, Daniel, 5:73-74
Waldo, David, 20:342
Waldo, William, 17:353; 24:169, 170; letter, 24:246-47
Waldo, Ore., 19:370; 21:128, 129, 136
Waldorf, Dolores, *see* Bryant, Dolores Waldorf
Waldron, Asa, 12:329
Waldron, W. C., 18:199
Waldron (Daniel G.), & Co., 30:111, 259
Waldteufel, A., 30:367
Wales, F. H., 4:38, 55
Wales, Henry, 18:359
Wales, Prince of (Edward VIII), 36:114
Walker (San Diego, 1847), 22:57
Walker (Mariposa Mine, 1850), 12:75
Walker (Colusa Co., 1855), 17:177; ranch of, 17:176-77
Walker (Marysville, 1858), 9:346, 347
Walker, Lt., (S.F., late 1850s), 19:237
Walker, A. B., 9:269
Walker, Ben Randal, 21:96; obit. of George Cosgrave, 24:375-76
Walker, Courtney M., 3:74
Walker, Mrs. Cyrus, 25:233
Walker, Cyrus B., 13:31
Walker, Edith Marion, 32:375
Walker, Edyth, 33:40
Walker, Elkanah, 4:279
Walker, Frank J., 4:43
Walker, Franklin Dickerson, fellow of CHS, 39:70; "Ridge's Life of Joaquin

Murieta," 16:256-62; address, "Frank Norris," 26:277-79; *San Francisco's Literary Frontier*, rev., 18:280-81; phot., 39: opp. 72
Walker, Hartwell, 20:28, 44
Walker, James, 24:373
Walker, James T., 6:61
Walker, Joel P., 4:352; 5:69, 110; 17:233; 23:291; 24:321; 28:196; fac. sig., 10: opp. 159
Walker, Mrs. Joel P. (Mary Young), 5:110
Walker, John (Columbia, 1850), 24:269
Walker, John (nr. Sebastopol, 1850s), 19:129, 141
Walker, Joseph Reddeford, 1:125, 126, 138, 271; 3:270, 272; 4:6-12 *passim*, 210; 5:328; 8:17; 10:33, 38; 13:224; 16:56; 18:328; 20:343, 344; 22:57(?), 366; 24:46; 26:235; 32:266-67; 34:212, 221; phot., 4: opp. 6
Walker, K. (Robert?), 4:310
Walker, Lew, 20:183, 184
Walker, Percival John, 30:222
Walker, Robert J., 15:4, 15, 19
Walker, S., 31:333
Walker, Sam (Mex. War, 1847), 23:351
Walker, Samuel (Oregon trail, 1844), 4:310
Walker, W. C., 11:127
Walker, W. W., 21:309
Walker, William, 1:15; 9:75, 249, 274; 10:267; 12:318, 319, 321, 329; 14:397; 15:88, 163-64, 178-79, 278, 370, 377; 17:172, 178, 179, 285; 18:16; 21:31, 32, 328; 22:112; 24:165, 179; 25:336; 26:176; 27:145, 146, 148, 203, 204, 206; 30:65; 35:220, 320, 322; fac. agreement, 12: opp. 318
Walker, William C., 11:127; 33:375
Walker, William W., 36:137; letters from, 140-41
Walker & Co. (Yuba Co., 1857), 9:151
Walker (J. M.) & Co., San Francisco, 27:5
Walker Lake, 4:9; 34:214
Walker Pass, 1:126; 4:8, 9, 11; 13:224; 19:312; 22:366; 34:210
Walker River, 4:10; 12:325-26; 26:233; 34:213, 215, 216, 219, 223; diggings, 12:324, 325, 326
Walkington, Mrs. M. O., 32:193
Walkinshaw, Miss (S.F., 1867), 11:127
Walkinshaw, Robert, 13:59, 78; 16:347; 39:42, 49, 50

Walküre (ship), 31:296

Walkup, Joseph, 9:116, 177, 244, 265, 269-70; 19:347; port., 9:245

Wall, Capt. (of *Alabama*, 1851), 25:329

Wall, Isaac B., 16:342, 346; 27:213, 214, 308; 29:23

Wall, James R., 17:82

Wall, John, 15:169

Wall, Joseph G., 32:162

Wall, Lot, 17:37, 38, 39

Wallace, A. D., 30:115

Wallace, Alfred Russel, 32:181, 256

Wallace, Charles W., 17:85

Wallace, F., 24:37

Wallace, George (S.F., 1855), 34:257

Wallace, George (Latham's sec'y., 1860), 11:7, 8, 10, 24

Wallace, George W., 20:34, 45

Wallace, James (from Philadephia, 1849), 23:266, 276, 277, 353

Wallace, James (Anderson Valley, 1862), 33:364

Wallace, John T., 16:81, 341

Wallace(William, 9:369

Wallace, William B., 4:38, 55

Wallace, William J., 25:194

Wallace, William T., 15:257; 18:95; 19:232; 34:98, 242; 38:49, 54

Wallace Guards, San Francisco, 9:244, 270; 15:375; 16:336; 38:17

Wallack, Mr. and Mrs. James W., 9:257, 258, 263, 283; 21:43, 45, 46

Walla Walla, Wash., 29:142; letter from, 16:172-74

"Walla Walla Indian Expeditions to the Sacramento Valley," by Robert F. Heizer, 21:1-7

Waller, Alvin F., 4:356; 5:58

Waller, Edwin, 34:130

Waller, H. B., 15:176

Waller, Royal Hiram, 9:29; 15:176; 27:150; art. on, 22:110-18

Waller, Mrs. Royal Hiram (Elizabeth A. Hodges), 22:110-16 *passim*

Wallis, Joseph Sawyer, 18:49, 61; 19:137

Wallis, Mrs. Joseph Sawyer, 18:49; *see also* Green, Mrs. Talbot H.

Wallis, Talbot H., 18:37, 43, 49, 61

Wallot, Paul, 25:12-13

Walls, Jim, *Chinatown San Francisco*, rev., 39:367-68

Walnut, California, 18:344

Walpole, Frederick, 6:142; 18:75; 29:29, 274

Walsh (S.F., 1854), 15:181

Walsh, Capt. (Colorado R., 1857), 22:169, 170

Walsh (Marysville, 1858), 9:363

Walsh, Henry L., 30:377

Walsh, James (Nevada Co., 1850s), 3:154; 6:229, 336; 11:243, 245

Walsh, James (Philippines, 1898), 30:295

Walsh, John, 10:77

Walsh, Nicholas J., 21:300, 303, 309, 384

Walsh, Tim, 32:30, 35, 37

Walsworth, Edward B., 10:76, 190, 198, 286, 361-64 *passim*, 370; 36:208

Walsworth, Mrs. Edward B., (Sarah P.), 10:370

Waltemann, Louis, 14:142

Walter, Charles, 9:195

Walter, Charles Lewis, 25:174

Walter, Edgar, 38:2, 7

Walter, Gertrud, 29:225-26

Walter, Isaac Nathan and Caroline (Greenbaum), 9:295

Walter, John Isidor, obit., 9:295

Walter, Max, 21:142, 153

Walter Colony, 25:174

Walter Colton (ship), 21:373

"Walter Colton, Chaplain and Alcalde," by Clifford M. Drury, 35:97-117

Walther, Eric, 32:184

Walton, Henry Gordon, 19:229

Walton, Mrs. Henry Gordon, *see* Wills, Elizabeth Maria Bonney

Walton, J. W., 15:371

Walton, Mrs. Robert (Georgina Frances Jones), 2:68

Walton, Samuel, 3:92

Walton, Stanley V., 25:96

Walton, T. H. O., 8:358

Walton, William E., 9:315-16

Walton, William F., 19:233

Walton, William N., 9:173

Walton & Walton (lawsuit, 1859), 10:167, 183

Waltz, S. W., 25:170

Walworth (Yosemite, 1856), 5:337

Wambaugh, M. M., *see* Wombough

Wambaugh's (or Wambo's) Bar, 8:338, 345, 347, 355; 9:76

Wambold, David, 21:64, 264

Wandesforde, Juan B., 30:137; 36:199

Wandle, Charles Westey, 14:72, 176

Wangenheim, Alice, *see* Heyneman, Mrs. George

Wangenheim, Emil S., 35:271; 36:163

Wangenheim, Julius, "Autobiography,"

35:119-44, 253-74, 345-66; 36:63-78,
149-64; phot., 35: opp. 120
Wangenheim, Mrs. Julius (Laura
Klauber), 35:269-74 *passim*, 351-54
passim, 364; 36:70-73 *passim*, 77, 78,
153-54, 163
Wangenheim, Sol, 35:119-23 *passim*,
359
Wangenheim family, 35:119, 124;
36:163
Wankowski, Robert, 34:160
Wanzer (Marysville, 1858), 9:373, 374
Wanzer, Harry S., 19:96
War and the Far West, 1861-1865, by
Lewis, rev., 40:351-53
Warbass, Thomas A., 9:27; 16:182
Warburton, Austen D., bk. rev. by,
39:274
Ward, Abba, 28:293
Ward, Allen Thomas H., 29:324
Ward, Andrew J., 19:139
Ward, Artemus (pseud.), *see* Browne,
Charles Farrar
Ward, Charles, 5:39
Ward, Frank, 5:39; 11:135, 142, 146;
14:278; 27:264, 266, 352
Ward, George R., 6:9; 15:255; 21:37
Ward, Harriet (Sherrill), *Prairie
Schooner Lady*, rev., 38:378-79
Ward, Henry C., "Stage-Coach Days in
California," reminiscences of, ed.
Oscar O. Winther, 13:255-61
Ward, J. N., 9:269
Ward, James C., 5:38, 39; 11:141, 142,
144; 19:4; 27:266
Ward, Lucy Elizabeth, 34:180
Ward, Michael R., 25:204
Ward, Samuel, 11:11, 14, 17-18, 19, 25,
124, 125; 13:402; 19:4
Ward, Mrs. Samuel (née Grimes),
19:229, 232
Ward, Mrs. Samuel (née Astor), 11:125
Ward, Thomas H., 29:324
Wardall, E. M., 19:63, 72; 27:313, 314;
28:52
Wardell, Justus S., 39:123, 126-30
passim
Warden, William, 23:218
Ward House, San Francisco, 7:396
Ward's Furnishing Store, 28:7
Wardwell, A., 17:174
Wardwell, Mollie, 29:226
Ware, Mr. and Mrs. George, 21:175
Ware, Joseph E., 10:83; 32:199-200
Ware, William, 18:295, 311

Warfield, Dr. (Sacramento, 1849), 11:36
Warfield (Marysville, 1859), 10:56
Warfield, David, 21:266
Warfield, Jacob Bigelow, 9:170, 181,
243, 250, 267, 269, 281, 365, 366, 376,
391; 10:174, 276-82 *passim*, 290, 358,
373-81 *passim*; 14:396; 15:29; 33:294,
305
War Hawk (ship), 15:375
Waring, George, 35:263
Wark, Alex, 32:27
Wark, David and John, 22:99
Warmcastle, F. M., 9:269
Warm Springs, 10:358, 368; 36:294
Warm Springs Hotel, 33:375; 36:294
Warne, Lt., *see* Warner, William
Horace
Warner, Capt. (of *Isabel*, 1850), 5:147
Warner, Alice, 5:289, 292
Warner, Col. (S.F., 1854), 15:177
Warner, Charles, 24:173
Warner, Eric G., 32:286-87
Warner, Francisco, 37:199
Warner, Franklin, 4:211
Warner, J. B., address, "Early Day
Shipping," 5:415
Warner, James, 21:309
Warner, John, 15:239
Warner, John Joseph, *see* Warner,
Jonathan Trumbull
Warner, Jonathan Trumbull, 1:15, 111,
118; 2:36; 4:170; 5:109; 6:79; 11:21;
13:213, 214, 223, 224, 337; 19:312;
20:342; 21:224, 333; 23:19, 39, 146;
25:302; 26:21, 22, 23; 31:44; 36:316;
38:184; 40:314; letters from, 26:23;
37:9-10; *see also* Warner's Hot
Springs; Warner's Ranch
Warner, Juan José, *see* Warner,
Jonathan Trumbull
Warner, Miron and Sarah, 14:73, 182
Warner, William and Sarah, 5:289;
letter from, 5:289-92
Warner, William Horace, 1:249, 256;
11:101, 107, 247, 264; 17:343; 21:216,
221; 22:49; 24:23-24; 25:294, 305;
26:37; 29:32; 30:57-58; 33:268-69, 337,
341; 39:193
Warner, William W., 9:27
Warner Lakes, 22:203
Warner's Hot Springs, 20:235, 239;
21:333; 25:303; *see also* Warner's
Ranch
Warner's Pass, 17:325, 340
Warner's Ranch, 1:140, 146; 13:214;

17:325, 340; 20:157; 21:220, 333-34, 342, 345, 355, 356; 22:47; 25:298, 299, 302-3, 308; 26:21, 23-24; 31:40; 34:136; bk. on, rev., 7:86-87; *see also* Warner's Hot Springs

Warnersville, *see* Trinidad

Warnock, Samuel, 36:119-20

Warren, Capt. (of *Roman*, 1854), 15:183

Warren, Miss (S.F., 1861), 10:281-82

Warren, Augusta Batchelder (Thompson), 30:246, 284; " 'Judge' Robert Thompson," 30:237-48

Warren, Earl, 24:2, 267-68; 36:260, 317; 39:33

Warren, Frederic W., 30:247

Warren, Gilbert R., 10:374; 30:134

Warren, Henry S., 20:332; 28:293

Warren, Mrs. Henry S. (Maria L. Hamblin), 28:293

Warren, James, 14:71

Warren, James H., 3:159, 160, 161; 32:54, 125, 129

Warren, Mrs. James H., 3:159; 32:125

Warren, James Lloyd LaFayette, 12:21; 19:250; 30:114

Warren, John, 26:301-2

Warren, Mary, *see* Howard, Mrs. William Davis Merry

Warren, O. P., 33:289, 292, 294, 296, 300, 305

Warren, Stafford L., 33:188

Warren, Timothy, 9:61, 133, 144, 150, 158, 165; *v.* Joel H. Seabury, 9:132, 133, 134

Warren, Viola Lockhart (Mrs. Stafford L.), 33:188; ed. "Dr. John S. Griffin's Mail, 1846-53," 33:97-124, 249-70, 337-47; 34:21-39

Warren, William M., 12:146

Warren, William R., 1:235; 14:128; 16:328; 18:70; 27:105

Warren, William S., 29:242

Warren (ship), 2:166-71 *passim*, 188; 3:39, 108, 113; 5:132; 10:107; 12:351, 357; 13:272; 14:149, 327, 336, 342; 17:125, 130; 18:265; 20:215, 232-33; 22:65; 24:364; 25:128, 129; 26:221, 230; 27:264, 266; 29:169-70, 213; 30:21, 43; 31:207, 210, 216; 33:251, 268, 340; 34:119; 36:310

Warren & Co., 15:173; 30:103; 38:315

Warren Engine Co. No. 4, Marysville, 9:354, 366, 386, 391; 10:54, 55, 57, 165, 174, 179, 181, 182, 186, 246, 250, 257,

258, 259, 263-64, 265, 268, 285, 365, 380, 381, 382

Warren House, Portland, 2:130

Warrior Queen (ship), 27:293

Wartenberg (L.A., 1868), 33:66

Warwick, James H., 10:63, 65, 274, 289, 382, 394; 21:69, 74

Waseurtz af Sandels, *see* Sandels

Washburn, Benjamin, 18:80

Washburn, C. E., 4:29, 35

Washburn, Charles Ames, 10:268; 27: opp. 97; 38:214-15

Washburn, Chester A., 27:346

Washburn, I. & J. H., 14: opp. 209

Washburn, Mrs. Israel (née Brown), 31:292

Washburn and Moen Co., 19:153

Washburne, Rev. Mr. (Marysville, 1850), 15:41

Washington, Benjamin Franklin, 9:54; 10:257; 11:6-7; 15:280, 369; 16:79; 19:232; 20:334-45; 29:302, 306; 32:148, 149, 151, 158; 38:214-15

Washington, Fannie Wallace, 22:369

Washington, George, 11:29

Washington, Henry, 34:11-17

Washington, John A., 29:380; ed. "Noblet Herbert to Mrs. John Augustine Washington," 29:297-307

Washington, Ovid, 13:85

Washington, Samuel, 33:374

Washington, Nevada Co., 13:28

Washington, Yolo Co., 4:225; 8:22, 201-2, 210; 9:259; 16:66; 23:365-66, 375; 25:329

Washington (schr., 1821), 12:230; 18:175; 23:203, 215, 217

Washington (str., 1850), 18:302

Washington City and California Mining Assoc., 22:128; 27:363, 369

Washington Continental Guards, San Francisco, 9:244, 270

Washington Grove, 10:165, 189

Washington Guards, San Francisco, 37:362

Washington Hall, San Francisco, 3:35; 20:293

Washington Hotel, Boston Ravine, 6:225

Washington Hotel, Monterey, 29:22, 27

Washington Irrigated Colony, 25:23, 32-35

Washington Marine Insurance Co., 26:355

Washington Market, San Francisco, 5:86

Washington Mill (Yuba Co.), 9:52, 70

Washington Monument Fund, 38:330-31

"Washington the Patriot," address by Harry L. Todd, 7:96

Washoe, 4:66, 241, 257; 6:343-44; 9:312, 332; 10:246, 249, 260, 262, 392; 11:47; 12:11, 327-30; 23:229; 36:365-70; *see also* Comstock Lode; Virginia City

"Washoe's First Literary Journal," by Franklin R. Rogers, 36:365-70

Wasp, The, 19:102-3, 107; 21:249-50, 252; fac. cover, 21: opp. 239

Wass, Count Samu, 21:327; 28:126, 130, 131, 137, 141

Wassen, Warren, 21:238

Waste, William Ewing, 28:381-82; address, "Photographs of California Missions," 34:87

Waste, William Harrison, 28:381; 34:87; address, "Romance Period of California History," 9:292

Watanabe, Hitoshi, trans. "Techniques and Implements of the American Whale-Fishery, from an Early Japanese Account," ed. Robert F. Heizer, 32:225-29

W. A. Tarlton (ship), 15:279

"Watch and Its Owners, A," by William Barclay Stephens, 34:323-32

Watch Dog, Sacramento, 9:246, 272-73

Watches, *see* Clocks and watches

Wateman (Marysville, 1859), 10:42

Water birds, 2:52, 58, 200, 270, 285, 287, 298, 303; 5:44-45, 49, 50, 53, 64, 71, 155, 273, 275, 367; 7:361; 8:146, 147; 10:213; 12:208, 305; 13:20, 21; 21:349; 25:2; albatrosses, 30:243, 244; 35:13; bitterns, 13:21; booby, 30:244; cormorants, 13:21; cranes, 2:200; 5:50; 7:361; 8:147; 10:213; 12:208; 13:21; curlews, 2:303; 5:45, 155; 13:20; curly-jacks, 7:361; herons, 5:45; 8:147; 12:305; ibis, 12:305; pelicans, 2:303; 7:302; 12:305; 13:21; plover, 2:303; 5:44; sandpipers, 2:298; sea eagle, 8:166; snipe, 5:53, 64; swans, 5:44, 45; 12:305; 13:20, 21; whalebirds, 30:244; *see also* Birds

Waterbury (mate on *Salem*, 1849), 30:21, 22

Wateree (ship), 27:179

Water Fount and Home Journal, San Francisco, 17:177

Waterhouse, Lillian F., 32:239

Waterman, Misses (Sacramento, 1861), 10:274-75

Waterman, Benjamin, 2:128

Waterman, Edwin R., 13:31

Waterman, Gordon B., 16:182; 32:358(?)

Waterman, Robert H., 20:46; 35:304

Waterman, Robert Whitney, 27:174; 33:374; 35:260

Waterman, Waldo, 35:345, 353

Water rights, 24:194; 25:23, 28-29

Waters, Clara, 21:257

Waters, Eliza, 28:294

Waters, Eva, 21:191

Waters, G. L., 9:369

Waters, James, 4:350, 352

Waters, Jane A., 2:88

Waters, Joseph N. H. and Mary Louisa (Barker), 28:294

Waters, Thomas J., 9:181

Waters, Willard Otis, comp. "California Bibliographies," 3:245-58

Waters, William, 18:201-2

Waters, William P., 27:35-44 *passim*, 157-62 *passim*, 362, 364, 365, 370; 28:57-62 *passim*, 64-65

Water supply, 25:17; 30:343-44; Columbia, 24:269; Fresno Co., 25:20-28 *passim*, 34, 169-75 *passim*; Los Angeles, 2:178; 13:201, 205, 311-12, 339; 17:232; 29:247; mining region, 24:269 (*see also* Aqueducts; Canals; Dams); Marysville, 10:262; 15:54; Oakland, 36:113; Philippines (1898), 31:52; San Bernardino Co., 27:113, 117; San Francisco, 11:390; 17:175, 180, 181; 22:253 (*see also* Hetch-Hetchy; Mountain Lake; Spring Valley Water Co.); Vallejo, 22:372; *see also* Irrigation

"Water Supply of San Francisco," address by Michael M. O'Shaughnessy, 11:390

Water wheels, 29:203, 208; illus., 11:325

Water Witch (ship), 15:371

Water Works Co. of San Francisco, 17:175

Water Works Hall, Marysville, 10:249, 252, 259, 262, 366

Watford, W. H., 34:190; "The Far-Western Wing of the Rebellion, 1861-1865," 34:125-48

Watkins, Capt. (of *Constitution*, 1865), 6:350, 351

Watkins, Andrew, 20:36, 37, 44, 45

Watkins, Carleton E., 4:23; 15:190;
26:133; 29:204; 35:50; phot. by, 26:
opp. 128, 147; 29: foll. 200
Watkins, Henry P., 9:353, 357; 10:72,
77, 166, 171, 191, 195, 285; 11:7, 8, 9;
14:397; 15:28, 51, 281
Watkins, James T., 2:83(?), 10:389;
16:184; 17:168; 19:232; 33:316;
36:207, 212
Watkins, Lewis D., 24:65
Watkins, W. T., 28:337
Watkins, William F., 10:62, 70, 71, 74;
31:137
Watkinson, Joseph S., 21:309; 22:71, 76
Watmough, James T. Horatio, 2:359,
362; 3:123; 6:269; 8:74; 10:109; 15:64;
18:80, 81; 21:12, 14, 15; 26:49
Watmough, Pendleton G., 3:118
Watoka (Indian, 1852), 28:335-36
Watriss, George E., 16:306, 316
Watrous, Charles, 27:97, 101
Watson (Sacramento, 1849), 26:171
Watson (Napa, 1878), 35:8, 158
Watson (Calif. Naval Militia, 1914),
34:158
Watson, Charles, 24:173
Watson, Douglas Sloane, 8:185; 10:307;
18:288; "Did the Chinese Discover
America?," 14:47-58; "The First Mail
Contract in California," 10:353-54;
"The First Mention of George
Washington in California History,"
11:29; "The Great Express Extra of
the *California Star*," 11:129-37;
"Herald of the Gold Rush—Sam
Brannan," 10:298-301; "An Hour's
Walk through Yerba Buena,"
17:291-302; "An Inquiry into the
Significance of the Raising of the
American Flag at Yerba Buena,"
15:306-10; "The San Francisco
McAllisters," 11:124-28; "San
Francisco's Ancient Cannon,"
15:58-69; "The 1781 Cañizares Map of
San Francisco Bay," 13:180; "The
Society's New Quarters [1938],"
17:74; "Spurious Californiana: 'Four
Months among the Gold-Finders,'"
11:65-68; "Meetings of the Society,"
10:307; 14:86; ed. "La Carta de
Flores," 12:147-54; trans. "Millions
for a Cent!," 11:40-41; foreword to
Thomas B. and Joseph G. Eastland,
"To California through Texas and
Mexico," 18:99-100; addresses; "More

Yerba Buena Days," 10:91-92; "The
Old 'Enterprise' Gang," 12:84; "San
Francisco's Old Spanish Cannon,"
15:90; "Yerba Buena's Village Days,"
8:387; ed. Powell, *Santa Fe Trail to
California*, rev., 10:406-7; ed. *Diary of
Johann August Sutter*, rev., 11:386-87;
bk. revs. by, 13:409; 18:279; obit. of
Mrs. Theodore J. Hoover, 19:287
Watson, Elizabeth (Lowe), 33:374
Watson, Henry B., 2:165(?), 358, 362;
3:84, 85, 123; 17:298; 26:49; orders to,
2:360-61
Watson, J. A., 13:338
Watson, J. M., 31:137
Watson, James, 14:318, 343; 29:26, 274;
34:119
Watson, Job H., 15:51
Watson, James H., 11:9, 23
Watson, John H., 10:272, 273, 274, 278,
282, 288, 289; 11:7, 9; 14:376; 28:59, 66
Watson, Joseph D., 23:366; 24:166
Watson, Maud, 2:67
Watson, Michael, 12:222
Watson, Nick, 9:142, 147, 176
Watson, Sereno, 18:344; 32:255
Watson, William, 6:152
Watson, Mrs. William Campbell
(Elizabeth Ann Davis), 2:67
Watson, William S., 4:226, 250
Watsonville, 16:354; 28:66
Watt, Janet McAlpin, 31:177
Watt, Robert, 6:335
Watt, William, 6:335
Wattles, Will, 37:53
Watts, Mrs. (Monoville, 1860), 26:237
Watts (Alaska, 1867), 35:294, 303
Watts, Frances Ann, *see* Bancroft, Mrs.
Albert Little
Watts, John William, 33:374
Watts, S. T., 9:51; 10:362; 14:395-96;
15:28, 44-45, 53, 54
Watts, Samuel, 30:162
Waugh, Lorenzo, 31:9
Wave (schr., 1841), 28:104, 256
Wave (skiff, 1850), 5:352
Waverly (ship), 2:45; 8:245, 250, 322,
335; 14:342; 18:175; 23:217
Wawona, 4:24; 5:330, 334, 337, 341
Way, Capt. (Colorado R., 1859),
22:169, 170
Way, William S., 15:168
Waybur, Mrs. Arnold (Marjorie
Stanton), 29:191

Waybur, Julius R., 29:191; *see also* Weber, Julius R.

Wayland, Mr. and Mrs. (Santa Cruz Mts., 1854), 29:47, 55

Wayland, J. Harold, 40:259; bk. rev. by, 40:258-59

Wayman, Theodore, 28:238, 242

Wayman, Willard O., 19:96

Waymire, James, 19:64; 27:318

Wayne, Henry C., 9:300, 301, 302, 313, 314; 16:341

Way Sketches, by Sawyer, ed. Eberstadt, rev., 5:404-5

W. D. Rice (ship), 22:170

Weapons, of Mexican Californians, 13:50-51; *see also* Cannons; Guns; Howitzers; Lances

Weathered, T. H., 30:17

Weatherlow, William, 18:304, 307-8, 313, 314; 21:237

Weaver (Yuba Co., 1853, 1857), 9:169; 10:186; 11:53-56 *passim*

Weaver, Franklin (or Miles), 14:278; 19:134, 143

Weaver, James B., 19:62, 66; 27:315-16

Weaver, Miles (or Franklin), 14:278; 19:134, 143

Weaver, P. L., 29:253, 254

Weaver, Pauline, 12:112

Weaver, Thomas, 8:6

Weaver's Creek, *see* Weber Creek

Weavertown, *see* Weberville

Weaverville, El Dorado Co., *see* Weberville

Weaverville, Trinity Co., 16:82; 30:251, 259, 261, 361; 32:131; 40:61; newspaper, 11:383; 29:91; 30:361

Weaving, 5:257; 36:6; 37:120

Webb, C. C., 30:254, 264

Webb, Charles Henry, 5:409-10, 412; 21:65; 28:7

Webb, Edward C., 21:310

Webb, Henry J., 36:93; "The Long Drive on the Hastings Cut-off," 36:57-62

Webb, Henry Livingston, 21:290-93, 303

Webb, J. C., 29:235

Webb, Lispenard S., 21:310

Webb, Samuel, 30:365

Webb, Sidney P., 7:5; 9:28, 29, 32, 108; 15:176, 178, 180, 182, 266, 272, 280

Webb, Thompson, 22:96

Webb, W. S., 10:64

Webb, Watson, 21:310

Webb, William H., 13:249; 27:267

Webber, R. N., 8:200, 203, 209; 9:132, 137, 163, 174; lawsuit, 9:132

Webb Sisters (Emma and Ada), 21:46

Webb Street House, San Francisco, 20:310

Weber (Shasta, ca. 1851), 30:112

Weber (on *Azalene*, 1889), 31:156

Weber, Anna Barbara, 28:293

Weber, Charles María, 18:173-74; 20:376; 26:54; land claim, 6:249; 15:277; against Micheltorena, 16:57; 18:173; in the mines, 2:187, 188, 189, 194, 198; prisoner, 8:73, 76; 14:148; 18:159, 173; in San Jose, 5:134, 305; 10:125; 14:17, 19, 149, 151; 16:57; 20:376; in Stockton, 6:249; 10:67; 13:379; 14:17, 415; 15:290; 16:138; 18:166, 173; 20:166; 26:99; 27:379; aids U.S. forces, 19:132; descendants, 6:249; 13:191-92; 14:415; 20:376; 24:381; *see also* Weberville

Weber, Charles Maria (grandson), address on life of his grandfather, 20:376

Weber, Julia Helen, 13:191-92; obit., 14:415

Weber, Julius R., 25:252; *see also* Waybur

Weber and Fields, 4:61-62

Weber Canyon, 5:181, 182

Weber Creek, 2:187, 194; 24:25; 26:125; 30:36

Weber House, Stockton, 10:44, 45, 67

Weber's Camp, 2:187, 188, 189, 194; *see also* Weberville

Weberville, 6:238; 20:38, 39, 42, 46; 24:252; 30:36; illus., 6: opp. 238; *see also* Weber's Camp

"Webfoot," *see* Phelps, William D.

Webster (on *London*, 1849-50), 7:212, 213, 217, 219

Webster, Charles A., 22:62-63

Webster, Daniel, 6:368; 10:7, 142, 222-31 *passim*; 19:15-16, 266; 20:111, 112; 37:12-13, 15

Webster, George Gideon, 2:208; 16:31

Webster, Jonathan V., 28:48, 49, 53

Webster, Kimball, 22:147

Webster, Marcus L., 22:2

Webster, Noah, 17:44

Webster, Noah C., 20:44

Webster, William, 14:337

Wecter, Dixon, address, "Mark Twain and the Mark Twain Papers," 29:77-80

Weddell, P. M., 24:93; "Location of the Donner Family Camp," 24:73-76

Weddings: in North Carolina, 16:16-17; at Rose's Bar (1849), 23:352-53; in San Francisco (1850), 26:338; in Santa Barbara (1842), 12:282; Yerba Buena (1846), 37:235; De Long-Vineyard, 10:379, 392; Jeffers-Willey, 35:11-21; Semple-Cooper, 6:151-52; 20:152; Vallejo-Carrillo, 16:227-28; tin, 11:127-28; *see also* Marriages

Weed (S.F., 1858), 9:255, 280

Weed, Charles L., 5:337

Weed (or Wead), George, 21:310

Weeds, 5:135; 29:27; found in adobe bricks, 4:362-65, 370; *see also* Mustard

Weed's Daguerrean Gallery, San Francisco, 34:295

Weeds Point, 8:203, 212

Weekly Ledger, see Amador Weekly Ledger

Weekly Occidental, see Occidental

Weekly Visitor, San Jose, 14:157; 22:223

Weeks, Capt. (Colorado R., 1869), 22:172, 173, 174

Weeks, Alanson, 23:192

Weeks, Charles Peter, 38:3

Weeks, George F., *California Copy*, rev., 8:82-83

Weeks, James W., 14:17

Weeks, William H., 9:394; 10:252, 264; 27: opp. 97; 30:134

Wee-mah (Indian, 1850), 6:235

Weer, William, 4:321

Wee Willie Winkie (pantomime), 20:2

Wehr, Mrs. Charles D., 25:192

Weib & Beecher, 8:199

Weick, Charles H., 28:337

Weightman, Richard Hanson, 25:371

Weights and measures, 2:199; 6:261; 24:318-19; 25:78; almud, 25:78; 30:315-18 *passim*; arroba, 2:261; 17:118; 25:78; 30:315, 318, 335, 336; brazo, 30:324; bushel, 30:335; cordel, 24:319; 30:326; cuarto, 25:78; dedo, 30:319, 327; fanega, 12:293; 17:118; 25:78; 28:109; 30:315-24 *passim*, 336; league (legua), 24:319; 30:315, 325, 335; marine league, 3:9, 332; 7:71; 9:10; square league, 30:315, 326; libra, 25:78; milla, 24:310, 318-19; 30:315, 325; onza, 25:78; pulgada, 30:315, 325, 327; quintal, 25:78; sitio, 24:319; 30:315, 326-27, 335; tierce, 28:110;

vara, 24:318, 319; 30:315, 327-38 *passim*

"Weights and Measures of Provincial California," by J. N. Bowman, 30:315-38

Weil, Adolph L. and Florence (Greenebaum), 28:382

Weil, Martin J., 28:382

Weill, Alexander, 27:170

Weill, M. (from Frankfurt, 1850), 22:305

Weill, Raphaël, 39:229, 236-37, 238, 253, 257, 311; phot., 39: foll. 232

Weimar, *see* Wee-mah

Weingand, Alvin Carl, 28:286

Weir, B. G., 9:103

Weir, J. M., 5:46, 396

Weissenhagen, Capt. (of *Caesar*, 1852), 12:304

Weitchpec, 26:201-2

Welch, Pvt. (L.A., 1847), 33:257

Welch (Yuba Co., 1857), 9:140, 352

Welch, C. W., 29:225

Welch, Charles, 33:68

Welch, G. W., 30:360

Welch, J. C., 10:178, 180

Welch, Presley, 3:89; 19:135

Welch, John, 15:269

Welch, Pat (San Jose, 1849), 14:153

Welch, Patrick J., 10:177, 199, 255, 285(?)

Welch, Thaddeus, 37:37

Welcker, W. T., 1:16; 24:80

"Welcome to the Czar's Fleet," by Benjamin F. Gilbert, 26:13-19

Weld, Gilbert Cumming, 20:332

Weldon, T. J., 26:213, 215

Welland, Mrs. (Santa Clara Co., 1853), 29:40, 56

Weller, Charles L., 15:165, 170; 16:338; 17:177; 20:156, 167

Weller, Mrs. Charles L. (Elizabeth McMullin), 27:382

Weller, John B., 2:207, 212, 214; 6:9; 7:15; 8:342, 359; 9:4-14 *passim*, 113, 115, 116, 150, 155, 157, 177, 178, 244, 250, 253, 259, 260, 261, 269, 270, 277, 281, 357, 381, 397; 10:49, 52, 59, 70, 71, 198, 240, 246, 260; 11:6, 7, 8; 13:402; 15:180, 182, 205, 280; 16:184, 305; 19:3, 173, 174, 263, 268, 276; 20:107; 27:221, 382; 29:14, 195, 237; 30:161; 31:136, 217; 32:146, 148, 318, 319; 34:346; 37:166-68; 38:28; cor., 31:214-15; port., 9: opp. 244

Welles, Gideon, 15:5, 10, 19; 16:203, 204, 207; 26:14
Welles, Nathaniel, 13:296
Wellman, Chauncey R., 40:315, 316
Wellman, Peck & Co., 24:378; 34:184
Wells (Yuba Co., 1856), 9:67
Wells, Dr. (Sonoma, 1876), 29:329
Wells (Sonora, 1860s?), 34:295
Wells, Alexander, 15:181, 182; 20:366; 34:252-53
Wells, Benjamin F., 3:123; 26:49
Wells, Evelyn, address, "Characters of the Champagne Period in San Francisco," 18:185
Wells, Gaylord S., 22:34; 30:110
Wells, Henry Jackson, 9:109; 15:169, 364, 370
Wells, Henry S., 4:234
Wells, James, 20:183
Wells, Jerry, 9:67(?), 136, 137
Wells, S. T., 27:150
Wells, Samuel A., 9:273; 10:200; 20:305; 21:41, 42, 64, 67; Melodeon, 10:289
Wells, Thomas (?), 9:369
Wells, W. S., 30:69
Wells, Nev., 32:199
Wells & Co. Bank, 23:176
Wells (Robert) & Co., 5:12
Wells and well drilling, 27:118
Wells, Fargo & Co., 8:212; 9:363, 390; 11:54, 331; 13:255, 261, 339-40; 14:169; 15:76, 99, 192, 271, 272, 273, 328, 376; 16:30-42 *passim*, 88, 172-81 *passim*, 286; 17:79, 169, 212; 18:70, 359, 360, 361; 19:292, 297; 20:158; 22:224; 23:188, 236; 24:268; 25:87; 26:199; 30:266; 33:275
Wells Fargo Bank, 5:103; History Room, 15:196; 29:377; *see also* Wells, Fargo & Co.
Wells Fargo Building, Columbia, 23:188; 24:268
Welsh, J. C., 29:237
Welsh, P. J., 9:390
Welsh, William, 23:210, 218
Welty, Daniel W., 11:9; 12:200
Wemys (on *Camilla*, 1850), 21:321
Wendell, George H., 15:371, 372, 374
Wendell, Joseph F., 32:163, 167
Wenderoth, A., 15:297, 305
Wendling (now Navarro), 33:366
Wendte, Charles William, 33:221
Wentworth, Dan, 13:258
Wentworth, Frank W., 23:192

Wentworth, John Parker Hale, 25:325-26, 340
Wentworth, May, 28:5, 7
Wenzel, Caroline, "Finding Facts about the Stanfords," 19:245-55; as address, 19:282; obits. of George G. Pollock, 29:84-85; Albert F. Zangerle, 22:286; obit., 38:176-77; phot., 38: opp. 112
Wenzel, Edward, 27:8
Wenzel, Hermann, art. on, 27:1-8; phot., opp. 1; of clock made by, opp. 4
Wenzel, Mrs. Hermann (Marie Mocker), 27:2
Wenzell, William T., 32:251
Werner, E. P., 27:285
Werner, John, 32:239
Werth, John J., 22:30, 33; 24:105
Wertheimer, Henry, 39:151
Wertheimer, Monroe and Annetta, 36:78
Wescoatt, Jonas, 10:77; 11:9
Wescoatt, N., map by, 8: opp. 199
Wessel, Frederick F., 31:381-82
Wessel, Peter and Mrs. (née Masten), 381-82
Wessells, Henry W., 3:26; 27:224; 28:231; 34:32
West (Mariposa Co., 1853), 11:174
West (d. Nevada Co., 1853), 11:233
West, Francis T., 14:19
West, Frank, 21:96
West, George (newspaperman), 40:142, 154
West, George (vintner and viticulturist), 21:96; 27:379
West, Harriot, 27:379
West, John, 9:154, 347; 10:56
West, Joseph B., 8:373; 15:282
West, Joseph R., 15:147, 149, 164; 22:37; cor., 15:149-50, 256
West, Joseph Rodman, 40:315, 348, 349
West, Olive, 21:251
West (San Jose, 1849), *see* West, Thomas M.
West, Thomas (Marysville, 1850), 14:394
West, Thomas M., 14:19; 34:22(?)
West, W. B., 27:379
West, William Marcus (Mark), 16:249, 324, 329, 330, 331
West family (nr. San Joaquin R., 1848), 2:195; 14:19
West Berkeley, 31:328, 330-33
Westbrook, Henry, Jr., 26:11
West Coast Lumber Co., 38:68

Westcott, George, 16:82
Westcott, George Clinton, 11:103, 121;
    19:22; 35:11, 14, 15
Westcott, Mrs. George Clinton (Lottie
    Jeffers), letter of, 35:11-21
Westdahl, Ferdinand, 35:292-304
    passim; drawing by, 35: opp. 291
Westend, San Bernardino Co., 17:117
Western, Helen, 21:44, 158, 255, 272
Western, Lucile, 21:44, 72
Westerners, The, Los Angeles Corral,
    39:71
Western House, Marysville, 8:341, 349,
    350, 357; 9:51, 357; 10:261, 280, 359,
    369
Western Nursery, 31:378
Western Pacific Railroad, 5:179; 29:382
"Western Rendezvous of the Fur
    Trappers," address by George L.
    Gary, 32:174
Western Salt Co., 35:350
Western Shore (ship), 27:293
Western Star Lodge, F. & A. M., 18:299,
    312; phot. of bldg. at Shasta, 18:
    opp. 304
Western Union Telegraph Co., 18:366;
    24:367-68; 29:200, 345-56 *passim;*
    36:104, 266-69 *passim;* exped. to
    Russian America, 33:1-12, 147-68;
    35:291-307
Western Watchman, Eureka, 19:68;
    27:318
Western World Institute, San
    Francisco, 38:314
Westervelt (S.F., 1867), 11:127
Westfall, Jacob (?), 33:265
Westhoff, Rudolf, 12:301
Westlake, Richard, 15:239
Westmoreland, Charles, 2:205; 9:46,
    346, 378
West of the Great Divide, by Kenneth
    Bjork, rev., 37:372
Weston, Benjamin Frank and Abbie
    May (Bunker), 27:191
Weston, F. E., 32:170
Weston, H. L., 3:176; 12:197, 198
Weston, J. M., 18:199-200
Weston, William B., 27:191
West Park, 25:174
West Point (riv. str.), 25:325
Westrope, Mrs. (Yuba Co., 1857), 9:163
West Sanger Colony, 25:175
West Walker River, 4:8; 34:213, 223;
    see also Walker River

Westward Ho (ship), 26:226, 227;
    28:314-16. 320
West Winds: An Anthology of Verse,
    rev., 5:90-92
"Wet Diggings," 31:253, 260
Wetherbee, Seth H., 29:253, 254
Wetmore (lawsuit, Marysville, 1861),
    10:278, 279, 280
Wetmore, Lt. (Calif. Vols., 1862), 26:3
Wetmore, C. A., 31:47
Wetmore, Charles A., 36:247-48
Wetmore, Chauncey E., 6:151; 28:290
Wetmore & Gray, 30:100
Wetzel, Francis Theodore and
    Frederika W. Amalia (Merkel),
    28:293
Wetzlar, Gustavus, 27:174
Whalen, John, 33:257
Whaler's Island, 3:8
Whales and whaling, 1:224; 2:298; 5:64;
    7:211, 212, 331; 8:324-25; 12:141, 142;
    13:7; 14:320; 15:235, 276; 16:284, 344;
    17:23, 183-84; 21:323; 22:319; 25:258;
    26:183, 217-19; 27:180; 29:1, 15;
    30:212; 33:151; 35:194, 237-39;
    37:14-15, 74-75; 39:110, 111-12, 304;
    art. on, 32:225-29; implements, illus.,
    32: foll. 244
Whaling, J. W., 15:366
Whannel, P. B., 6:20-23, 26, 27, 28
Wharton, James, 14:215
Wharves:
    in San Diego, 22:350, 354; 31:34-35,
        36, 41-47 *passim*
    in San Francisco, 16:183-84; 19:228,
        235; Broadway, 15:282; 17:315;
        Central (*see* Long Wharf); Clay
        St., 15:175; 16:83, 340, 342; 38:207;
        Cunningham's, 16:284; East St.,
        15:176; Flint's, 16:182; Folsom St.,
        17:314; Jackson St., 15:170, 184,
        375; Market St., 15:165, 337; 16:184,
        337; Niantic, 5:140; P.M.S.S. Co.'s,
        16:337; Pacific St., 15:168, 277;
        16:337; Sacramento St., 15:275;
        Shaw's, 16:82; Steuart St., 15:170,
        180, 272; 16:337; Vallejo St., 15:373;
        see also Long Wharf; Meiggs'
        Wharf
What Cheer House, Gold Hill, Nev.,
    17:76
What Cheer House, San Francisco,
    11:152; 15:375; 38:306; 39:289; illus.,
    38: opp. 310

"What It Means to Be a Californian," by Marion Clawson, 24:139-61

"What the Indians Remember of ... Jedediah Smith," address by David R. Jones, 11:389

Whatcom, Wash., 11:152

Whealdon, John, 9:349, 352, 357-58, 376, 379, 384; 10:41, 47-55 *passim*, 62, 70, 189, 358

Wheat, Alexander R., 11:181-82

Wheat, C. R., 15:169

Wheat, Carl Irving, 14:96; 17:288; 18:288; 35:74; 39:63; fellow of CHS, 38:74; "Ned, the Ubiquitous," 6:3-36; "Pioneer Visitors to Death Valley after the Forty-niners," 18:195-216; "The Rocky-Bar Mining Co.," 12:65-76; "A Sketch of the Life of Theodore D. Judah," 4:219-71; ed. "The California Letters of James Carr," 11:157-75; ed. "California's Bantam Cock: The Journals of Charles E. De Long, 8:193-213, 337-63; 9:50-80, 129-81, 243-87, 345-97; 10:40-78, 165-201, 245-97, 355-95; 11:47-64; ed. "The Old Ames Press," 9:193-200; introd. to "A Glimpse of San Francisco in the '50's," by Murray Morrison, 13:80; addresses: "Early Mapping of the American West," 35:75; "Fact vs. Fancy in California History," 7:289; "Pioneers ... Three Early California Printing Presses," 11:389; "The Post Gold-Rush Era," 9:408; "Santa Barbara's Place in California's Background," 32:174; "Trailing the Forty-niners through Death Valley," 17:356; bk. revs. by, 4:299-300; 5:203-4, 316-17, 402-3; 7:92-94, 197-99, 286, 408, 409; 8:87-89, 186, 280-81, 384-85; 9:88-89; 10:85, 205, 406-7; 11:87; 12:177; 38:275-76; note and reports by Publication Com., 8:93; 9:93; 9:99; 12:187; obits. of Arthur M. Ellis, 11:191; Thomas W. Norris, 31:177; Henry Root, 7:100-101

Wheat, Francis Millspaugh, "Senator Benton Lays His Plans," 13:150-54

Wheat, Marvin, 22:40

Wheat, Robert Cheatham, 11:11

Wheat, 1:166; 2:278; 3:223, 224; 4:199, 362-68 *passim;* 5:47, 127, 131, 135, 217; 8:108, 111, 112; 12:193, 195, 251, 256, 270, 275, 287, 293; 14:11, 21, 168, 201,

202, 203; 16:346; 17:183; 18:23, 298; 20:270, 352; 21:333-34; 22:318, 319; 23:295, 300; 24:216; 25:340; 27:163, 194-98 *passim;* 28:101, 102, 108, 109; 29:320; 30:197; 32:196; 36:3; 37:69, 71; 38:103-4, 108, 110; 40:99; *see also* Flour; Grist- and flour mills

Wheatleigh, Charles, 10:362, 364, 376; 16:183, 283, 285; 21:51-54, 64, 145-46, 159

Wheatleigh, Mrs. Charles, 16:183, 285, 344; 17:82

Wheaton, Donald W., "Spotlights on the Political History of California from 1887 to 1898," 5:283-88

Wheatport, 27:197-200; phot., opp. 197, opp. 200; *see also* Crockett

Wheeler (Marysville, 1851), 15:54

Wheeler (Sacramento, 1851), 28:304

Wheeler, Alfred, 13:339; 15:175; 16:82; 19:230; 22:37; 33:375

Wheeler, Mrs. Alfred (née Sanders), 19:230

Wheeler, Benjamin Ide, 1:19; 24:193; 35:150, 260; 38:251

Wheeler, Burton K., 39:129

Wheeler, Charles Stetson, 25:88

Wheeler, Cyrus T., 10:190-91

Wheeler, Edwin D., 9:349-55 *passim,* 361, 362, 365, 379, 383-84, 385, 389; 10: opp. 48, 62, 173, 195, 198, 252, 266, 276, 279; 11:9; 14:377-78; 15:29, 33, 43

Wheeler, G. H., 17:177

Wheeler, George, 33:346

Wheeler, George H., 31:231

Wheeler, George Montague, 4:36; 18:214

Wheeler, John O., 13:323, 337; 29:232, 234, 235, 245, 246

Wheeler, Osgood Church, 12:96-97, 103; 20:266; 22:34; 24:47, 48; 26:168, 169, 171, 172, 348; 27:41, 44, 261, 370; 28:291; 31:1; 32:139; 36:310; "Selected Letters," ed. Sandford Fleming, 27:9-18, 123-31, 229-36, 301-9

Wheeler, Mrs. Osgood Church (Elizabeth Hamilton), 26:168; 27:10, 14, 125, 130, 131

Wheeler, William (Amador Co., 1850s), 20:183

Wheeler, William (S.F., 1854), 15:183, 185

Wheeler, Zenas, 6:336-37

Wheeler, Mrs. Zenas, 6:226, 337

Wheeler & Wilson, 24:263

Wheeler Survey, *see* United States
Geological Survey
Wheelock (A.A.) & (B.) Wilcocks,
28:142
Wheelock's Trading Station, 28:228;
see also Fort Jones
Wheelright, Alfred, 13:296
Wheelwright, Mrs. Joseph B. (née
Hollister), 27:287
Wheelwright, William, 13:248
Whelan (S.F., 1855), 16:346
Whelan, George J., 16:79
"When I Think Back to San Francisco"
[poem], by Harry W. Frantz,
24:163-64
"When the French Came to California,"
by Gilbert Chinard, 22:289-314
*When the Pack Mule Express Was the
U.S. Mail*, by Wiltsee, rev., 8:385
When the West Was Young, by
Bechdolt, rev., 5:312-15
Whepley (S.F., 1849), 27:157
Whidbey, Joseph, 2:282, 335; 10:321,
325
Whiffen, Thomas, 21:172
Whig Party, 3:81, 83; 8:366; 9:24-49
passim, 105, 119; 15:27-30 *passim*, 33,
168, 171, 172, 181, 200-201, 202; 16:79,
80, 81, 82; 17:309; 19:256, 261, 265-70
passim, 344; 20:109, 111; 22:115, 223,
228, 368; 23:74; 24:169, 170; 26:293,
345; 28:58; 31:38, 194; 32:295
Whipple (Sacramento, 1858), 9:258
Whipple, Albert, 10:381, 383
Whipple, Amiel Weeks, 9:6, 7, 10, 11,
14; 19:3; 20:187; maps: boundary w.
Mex., 9: opp. 12; mouth of Gila R.,
19: opp. 217
Whipple, Frank ("Big"), 10:370
Whipple, J. C., 20:28, 44
Whipple, Stephen, building of, 16:345;
37:156
Whipple, Stephen Girard, 13:411;
26:203; 40:350
Whirlwind (ship), 30:243-44
Whiskey Diggings, 11:240
Whiskey Flat and Gulch, 22:79-80, 83
Whiskey Hill, 29:24
Whisman (or Whistman), John W.,
13:256; 14:160; 16:127, 136, 137;
27:163, 164, 260, 370; ranch of, 22:245,
246, 251
Whisman (or Whistman), Lorenzo,
27:164
Whitaker (S.F., 1867), 11:127

Whitaker, Herman, 31:340
Whitaker & Ray, 18:23
Whitcher, Jeremiah E., 25:321
Whitcomb, Mrs. (Yuba Co., 1856), 9:66
Whitcomb, Adolphus Carter, 26:216;
33:375
Whitcomb, C. G., 9:147, 153, 160, 161;
lawsuit, 9:136
Whitcomb, Caroline (Peralta), 30:224,
229
Whitcomb, Clem, 9:57, 156
Whitcomb, Frank, 8:211
Whitcomb, J. L., 3:79
Whitcomb, Jonadab B., 8:199, 202, 211,
340; 9:50, 67, 130, 132, 138, 139, 144,
145, 153-59 *passim*, 166, 167, 168;
lawsuits, 9:64, 139, 145, 147, 152, 154,
155
Whitcomb, Walter F., 34:328
Whitcomb (J. B.) & Co., 9:155, 167;
lawsuits, 9:148, 153, 154, 155, 166, 167
Whitcombe, Mr. and Mrs. (Marysville,
1859), 10:55
Whitcomb Excursions, 31:20
Whitcomb's, Foster's Bar, 8:202, 211;
9:135, 139, 153, 156, 161, 162; *see also*
Whitcomb (J. B.) & Co.
White (S.F., 1849), 5:17, 18, 23; *see also*
Blanc
White (overland, 1849), 22:138
White, Capt. (of *Wm. G. Hackstaff*,
1849), 25:120
White (Marysville, 1858), 9:359
White, A. F., 16:337
White, A. M. (Merced R., 1849), 20:114
White, A. M. (S.F., 1855), 15:281, 364
White, Annie, 30:66
White, Asa, 26:168, 169; 27:307
White, B., lawsuit (Yuba Co., 1856),
9:66
White, Caleb E., 32:185
White, Charles, 22:345
White, Charles Corwin, address,
"California's Place in the Tapestry of
History," 26:280-81
White, Charles L., 9:26
White, Chester Lee, 10:306;
"Surmounting the Sierras," 7:3-19
White, Edward, 19:60, 61
White, Elijah, 4:280-81; 5:65, 69, 74, 76,
82, 132, 255; 21:2, 82; letter to, 5:79-80
White, Ernest E., 35:353, 354; 36:63
White, Fannie, 10:267; 13:80
White, Felix B., 21:53
White, George, 26:204

White, George Cossitt, 26:191; 30:185
White, George E., 27:224
White, George R., 2:122
White, Gerald T., 36:112; bk. rev. by, 37:373-74
White, H. B., 17:176
White, J. and Mary J., 6:74
White, J. E., 29:119
White, J. H., 13:32
White, J. Q., 26:213
White, James, 22:251
White, James E., 33:293-304 *passim*
White, James L., 22:9
White, Jason, 13:11, 31
White, John (newsp. pub., 1850s), 14:371, 373; 34:342
White, John (Assemblyman, 1860), 10:280; 11:9
White, John Roberts, coauth. *Big Trees*, rev., 9:185-86
White, L. E., 20:114
White, Laura (Retting), 15:99; "Meetings of the Society," 15:89-90, 192-93, 286-87, 382-83; 16:88-89
White, Lynn Townsend, Jr., 19:288; 21:384; 22:191; "Changes in the Popular Concept of 'California,'" 19:219-24; addresses, "A Century of Mills College," 31:85-88; "Is History Becoming Less Interesting?," 23:380
White, M. Catherine, ed. *Journal of Richard Owen Hickman*, rev., 8:185-86
White, Martin, 38:60
White, Michael C. (Miguel Blanco), 10:32; 12:111-20 *passim;* 13:211, 230
White, Milton, 15:139
White, Robert (from New Zealand, 1849), 19:192
White, Robert (Fort Bragg, 1850s), 27:226; 30:162, 164
White, S. P., 9:27
White, Stephen Mallory, 5:94; 19:59-72 *passim;* 26:85; 27:316, 317; 28:47, 48, 51; 38:56, 355
White, Stewart Edward, 36:74; 38:221, 228, 372; phot., 40: opp. 137
White, Mrs. Stewart Edward (Elizabeth Grant), 28:186
White, T. C., 25:31
White, Thomas J., 4:188; 9:27, 42; 10:267, 296; 13:80, 83; 28:63; 36:243
White, W. A., 9:30
White, W. L., 11:369
White, Walter H., 19:192

White & Friant Lumber Co., 38:220
White Cloud (str., 1858), 32:217, 223
White Cloud (cutter, 1946), 26:189
White Fawn (barge), 22:156, 168
Whitehall Hotel, Butte Co., 8:340, 356
Whitehouse, Joseph, 15:239
Whitelaw, Thomas P. H., 33:375
Whiteman (on *Westward Ho*, 1853), 28:322
Whiteman (or Whitman), Gid, 26:238
Whiteman, William, 2:195
White Maple Springs, 8:208; 9:51, 138
Whitemore, F. W., 13:296
White Mountains, 26:239, 243
Whitenight (Aspinwall, 1860), 11:11
White Pine, Nev., 11:49-50; 30:247
White River, 12:8
White Rock Canyon (nr. Placerville), 3:127
White Rock Mining Co., 6:243
White Rock Springs, 20:39
White's Ferry, 10:251
Whiteside, Elvira, *see* Marshall, Mrs. Jacob
Whiteside, Harrison, 3:149
Whiteside, Ninian E., 3:147; 8:194, 203; 9:54, 151, 157, 170, 244-51 *passim*, 256, 259, 260, 269, 345, 349-56 *passim*, 361, 373; 10:54-59 *passim*, 168, 173, 189, 253-57 *passim*, 367, 383, 394; 19:347
Whiteside, Mrs. Ninian E. (Caroline Vineyard), 8:194; 9:274, 354, 360, 362, 373, 376; 10:58, 251, 255, 259, 370, 384
Whiteside, Samuel, 3:149; 8:203, 212
Whitestine, Jerry, 5:289
Whitestine, Mrs. Jerry, 5:289, 290
White Sulphur Springs, 36:295, 305
White Swallow (ship), 35:47
Whiting (Tepic, 1846), 17:128, 129
Whiting (mate on *Oregon*, 1849), 29:212
Whiting, Capt. (of *Golden Gate*, 1854), *see* Isham
Whiting (S.F., early '50's), 16:130
Whiting, Mrs. (S.F., 1855), 16:347
Whiting, B.C., 9:44, 45; 10:48(?), 53, 189
Whiting, Charles J., 11:161
Whiting, Fenton B., 29:306
Whiting, H. A., 13:31
Whiting, Jefferson, 11:168
Whiting, M. S., 26:232
Whiting, R. L., 16:285
Whiting, Richard, 19:229, 232
Whiting, William H. C., 15:179; 18:130

Whitman, Bernard C., 9:102, 103, 106

Whitman, G. N., 10:62, 70

Whitman, G. W., 15:78

Whitman, George (Yuba Co., 1854), 8:200, 203

Whitman, George N. (L.A., 1855), 29:234, 237, 242, 243, 248

Whitman, George S., 29:243

Whitman, George W., 9:42, 45, 111, 113, 116

Whitman, Marcus, 4:279, 326, 353; 10:402; 15:285, 380; 16:53, 55, 87; 20:25; 21:1, 4; 24:61; 25:143-44

Whitman, S. P., 15:281

Whitmore, Capt. (of *Charon*, 1812), 12:226

Whitmore, Capt. (of *New Star*, 1850), 14:161

Whitmore, D. W., 36:146

Whitmore, H. M., 26:253-54

Whitmore, John, 20:45

Whitmore's Ferry, 12:6

Whitney (Stockton, 1849), 27:159, 161, 162

Whitney (m. Emma Jane Merrill, S.F., 1850), 28:292

Whitney, Mrs. (S.F., 1851), 28:39

Whitney, Asa, 2:211; 13:241

Whitney, C. S., 9:27

Whitney, Charlotte Anita, 36:47, 48, 52, 55

Whitney, Cleora M., 10:95

Whitney, Emma Jane (Merrill), 29:292

Whitney, Frank, 15:88

Whitney, Franklin E. R., 10:77; 15:314, 316, 322; 23:72; phot., 15: opp. 316

Whitney, Mrs. George E. (Mary Lewis Swearingen), 36:44, 45, 52

Whitney, George O., 15:172; 28:38

Whitney, George W., 10:62

Whitney, J. P., 25:33

Whitney, James P., 4:194

Whitney, Mrs. James P., 10:290

Whitney, Josiah Dwight, 1:284; 4:16-18, 24, 33, 34, 55, 67, 295; 7:121, 123, 126-29, 410; 28:186; 32:249; 34:220; *see also* Calif. State Geological Survey

Whitney, Sumner, 29:99, 361; *see also* Bancroft-Whitney Co.

Whitney, Walter, 25:34

Whitney, William (Grass Valley, 1852), 6:334; 12:71, 72

Whitney, William (S.F., 1854), 9:26, 29

Whitney, William W., bk. revs. by, 37:372-73; 38:382-83

Whitney & Sutton, 27:159, 161, 162

Whitney, Mount, 4:18, 19-20, 29, 32-36, 38, 54; 7:125; 28:186; phot., 4: opp. 3

Whitney Survey, *see* Calif. State Geological Survey

"Whitney Survey on Mount Shasta, 1862, The," ed. Francis P. Farquhar, 7:121-31

Whitney's Wharf (San Diego), 31:155

Whit's Bar, Mokelumne R., 30:246

Whitsell, Leon Otto, addresses: "Humor of the Mines," 11:295; "Lansford W. Hastings," 21:82

Whitson, J. E., 25:175

Whittaker, Mrs. Elmer H., 26:288

Whittaker, Robert, 3:123; 26:49

Whittaker, Samuel, 22:113-14; 25:331, 340; 28:43

Whittemore (William and F. H.) & Co., 30:244

Whittier (overland, 1849), 22:134

Whittier, John Greenleaf, 31:241, 251; letters from, 31:249-50

Whittier, Mrs. William R. (née Carroll), 13:192; 24:89

Whittier (place), 25:286; 31:294; 39:213

Whittimore (Marysville, 1858), 9:348

Whittle, J. S., 3:115; 24:321

Whittlesey, Edward W., 21:291, 310

Whittlesey, Gilbert B., 21:310

Whittlesey, William, 21:310

Whittock, Capt. (Plumas Co., 1862), 10:387

Whitton, Abel, 15:376

Whitton family, 16:132

Whitton, Towne & Co., 17:173; 30:358; 31:381

Whitwell, F. S., 27:254

Whitwell, Gertrude Howard (Mrs. F. S.), "William Davis Merry Howard," 27:105-12, 249-55, 319-32

Whitzel, Adam, 8:6

Whymper, Frederick, 33:12, 166, 168; 35:292, 304

Wicher, Edward Arthur, *Presbyterian Church in California*, rev., 6:282-84

Wichs, Chris, 18:203

Wickersham (Yuba Co., 1858), 9:264; 10:41, 52, 171

Wickersham, W. R., 10:190

Wickham, Harvey, 25:244

Wickland, G. W., address and film, "Twenty-Four Minutes in El Dorado," 16:286

Wicklow Rebel, The (play), 21:146

Wickman (S.F., 1862), 9:319
Wickoff (Woods Cr., 1853), 11:169-70
Wicks (S.F., 1860), 29:113
Wickson, Edward James, 25:283; 30:195; 31:336; obit., 2:263
Wickson, Mrs. Edward James (Ednah Newell Harmon), 24:94-95
Wickson, Gladys Clare, 24:84; 37:92; 38:76; obit. of Marion Leale, 35:85-86
Widdleton, William J., 28:11
Wide Awake Club, San Francisco, 17:315
Widenham, A. W., 25:235
Wide West, 15:301; 30:252-53; fac., 32: opp. 291
Wide West Mine, 7:115, 116
Widney, Joseph Pomeroy, 13:351; 31:16
Widney, R. M., 19:65, 67, 73; 27:318
Widow's Victim, The (play), 15:48
Wiegand, Conrad, 10:281, 294; (W. Carroll, pseud.), 22:39
Wieghtman (lawsuit, Marysville, 1859), 10:185
Wiehe, Elise Christian, *see* Hittell, Mrs. Theodore H.
Wiel, Eli Hecht, 22:96
Wienholz, Paul, obit. of Alexander S. Keenan, 37:375-76
Wier, Jeanne Elizabeth, 22:192
Wierzbicki, Felix Paul, 4:202; 13:56, 76, 296; 14:78; 30:101, 113; *California as It Is and as It May Be,* rev., 12:364-65
Wiesenthal (S.F., 1851), 20:296, 313; 23:100
Wife, The (play), 3:35
Wiggenstein, Sam, 10:277, 280, 282
Wiggin, Charles L., 29:290
Wiggins (Sacramento, 1861), 10:279
Wiggins, Frank, 31:17-18
Wiggins, George, 9:36
Wiggins, Lewis N., 27:383
Wiggins, Oliver, 1:151
Wiggins, Robert, 33:323
Wiggins, William, 18:292-94, 310; 23:291
Wigginton, Peter Dinwiddie, 18:26-27; 20:168
Wight, George J., 21:164
Wigman, Lewis, 18:82
Wigwam, The (theater), 14:411
Wilber (S.F., 1858), 9:250
Wilber, James, 34:246
Wilbur, J. Q., 15:53
Wilbur, James Harvey, 26:165
Wilbur, Marguerite (Eyer), 23:287;

trans. "A Frenchman in the Gold Rush," 5:3-43, 139-77, 219-54, 342-77; 6:37-57; trans. Ludwig Salvator, *Los Angeles in the Sunny Seventies,* rev., 8:379-80; ed. Taraval, *Indian Uprising in Lower California,* rev., 11:86
Wilbur, Ray Lyman, 22:96; 36:151; obit., 28:279-81
Wilbur, Mrs. Ray Lyman (Marguerite M. Blake), 28:280
Wilbur, Mrs. Van Rensselaer, *see* Wilbur, Marguerite (Eyer)
Wilburn, Misses (Yuba Co., 1855), 8:350
Wilburn, Mrs. (Sacramento, 1858), 9:371; 10:272
Wilburn, R. B., 38:330
Wilcocks, Dr. (S.F., 1850), 2:118
Wilcocks, B., 28:142
Wilcox (Sacramento, 1849), 30:238
Wilcox, Alfred H., 11:365, 366, 375, 377, 378, 382; 22:3, 4, 6, 24, 159, 165, 168, 170
Wilcox, Charles Winthrop, 31:190
Wilcox, George, 8:196; 9:62, 63, 133, 134
Wilcox, Harry M. and Emma E. (Spaulding), 31:190
Wilcox, James Smith, 36:183
Wilcox, Tulita, 36:182
Wilde, John Walker, 15:272
Wilde, Jonathan, 9:26, 32; 15:276, 277, 279, 281, 365
Wilde, Louis J., 35:365; 36:155-56
Wilde, Oscar, 18:369; 19:97-112; caricature, 19: opp. 97
Wilder (Yuba Co., 1854), 8:206
Wilder, A. H., 14:396; 15:43
Wilder, C. R., 22:251
Wilder, Edward, 13:31
Wilder, F. B., 9:99
Wilder, Hasen, 21:111
Wilder, Henry, 2:122
Wilder, Willard, 21:111
Wilder (ship), 35:302, 303, 304
Wildes (fur trade, 1820s), 23:215, 217
Wildes, Green, 10:277, 291
Wildflower Colony, 25:175
Wildflowers, 2:289, 302, 321, 334, 336, 338; 5:274, 266; 18:335-46 *passim;* 27:130; 28:217; *see also* Mustard
Wild Hunter (ship), 37:82
Wildred, Robert, 15:34
Wild Rose Canyon, 17:107, 116
Wilds, Eliza Cambridge, *see* Yount, Mrs. George Concepcion

Wild Wave (ship), 33:376

Wiley, Mrs. (S.F., 1864), 24:263

Wiley, Hugh, 10:131, 135, 154

Wiley, Lilly Poole, 4:288; 17:237

Wiley, William Halstead, 32:37, 39

Wilfred, Robert, *see* Windred

Wilgus, Mrs. William John, Jr. (Hilda K.), 27:191; address, "17 Years with the Rollins Collection of Western Americana," 27:181-83

Wilkerson, H. H., 24:237

Wilkes (to mines, 1848), 2:183, 187, 188, 197, 199, 200

Wilkes (Cape San Lucas, 1850), 11:368

Wilkes, Charles, 2:232; 3:29; 4:4, 161; 8:125; 10:6; 14:324, 344; 17:55, 141-42; 23:44, 47; 24:321-42; 25:321; 29:320; port., 17: opp. 50

Wilkes, George, 38:197-98; 40:205, 210, 212; eulogy of Broderick, 38:199-217

Wilkes, Mary, 21:251

Wilkins (English Bar, 1852), 8:355

Wilkins (Marysville, 1858), 9:373

Wilkins (Sierra Co., 1860), 33:200-201

Wilkins, Calvin, 2:122

Wilkins, Charles P., 11:9

Wilkins, E. T., 10:259

Wilkins, Edward, 16:138

Wilkins, James F., "Moving Mirror" of the overland trail, described, 33:29, 32-38; adv. for, 33:35

Wilkins, Thurman, *Clarence King: A Biography*, rev., 38:164-65

Wilkinson (to mines, 1848), 35:111

Wilkinson (overland, 1849), 13:84

Wilkinson, N. N., 8:339; store, illus., 9: opp. 62

Wilks, Thomas E., 9:80

Willamette (ship), 2:88, 130, 134

Willamette Cattle Co., 3:77

Willamette River and Valley, 2:166, 168, 171; 17:69; 23:144, 293; 23:142, 144; 31:287

Willapa (ship), 31:295

Willapa Bay, 10:326; 31:295

Willard, Charles Dwight, 31:18, 29

Willard, E. L., 30:367

Willard, Emory L., 29:289, 290, 291

Willard, H. P., 11:127

Willaume, Prosper, 39:343, 345

Willet, Lawry, 2:122

Willet, William, 9:35

Willey, Annie Brewster, 35:12

Willey, O. F., 27:172-73

Willey, Samuel Hopkins, 1:14; 12:93; 13:389; 15:185; 16:198; 21:83, 330; 24:79; 25:191; 26:168, 170, 172; 27:47; 30:157; 31:75, 328, 332; 32:49, 133; 33:225, 292, 295, 301, 302; 35:11-20, 112-13; 38:312

Willey, Mrs. Samuel Hopkins (Martha Jeffers), 35:11; letter of, 35:12-21

William (Indian, 1845), 18:174

William (ship, 1820s), 14:300-302, 309

William (ship, 1847), 12:349

"William Alexander Trubody and the Overland Pioneers of 1847," by Charles L. Camp, 16:122-43

William Chapman Ralston, by Tilton, rev., 15:191

"William C. Ralston and His Times," address by Charles L. Tilden, 17:185-86

"William Davis Merry Howard," by Gertrude H. Whitwell, 27:105-12, 249-55, 319-32

"William Dunbar Jewett," address by Elliot A. P. Evans, 32:174

William G. Davis (ship), 22:353

William G. Hackstaff (pilot boat), 25:116, 120

"William Heath Davis and the Founding of American San Diego," by Andrew F. Rolle, 31:33-48

"William Herman Rulofson, Pioneer Daguerreotypist," by Robert B. Haas, 34:289-300; 35:47-58

William H. Russell, by Berthold, rev., 8:186

William H. Starbuck (ship), 22:353

William Irelan (ship), 22:171

"William Keith," address by Br. Cornelius, 21:278

William Little (ship), 23:301, 330

William L. Marcy (ship), 32:149

William Penn (ship), 16:83

Williams, Sgt. (S.F., 1849), 33:344

Williams (Marysville, 1850-51), 15:38; 24:348

Williams, Dr. (S.F., 1855), 17:176

Williams (Portuguese, Yuba Co., 1857), 9:152

Williams, Miss (Marysville, 1859), 10:186

Williams, Dr. (Philippines, 1898), 31:173

Williams, A. A. C., 37:203-10 *passim*

Williams, A. B., 26:243

Williams, A. Bascom, 18:277

Williams, A. F., 8:360

Williams, A. M., letters of, 24:248-52, 255-56, 257-58, 350-51
Williams, Albert (Tepic, 1840), 15:240
Williams, Rev. Albert (S.F., 1849), 3:35, 40; 12:105; 15:174; 20:13, 15, 22; 22:11, 113, 115; 26:168, 172; 27:260, 265; 28:34, 291; 30:46; 32:122, 126; 33:325; 34:65, 70; 38:304
Williams, Barney, 15:175; 20:291, 304; 24:69
Williams, Mrs. Barney, 15:175; 24:69
Williams, Baylis, 19:139
Williams, C. F., 25:195-96
Williams, Charles, 15:240
Williams, Charles H. S., 9:178; 10:62; 16:80, 81
Williams, Charles L., 35:359; 36:65, 69
Williams, David A., "The Forgery of the Broderick Will," 40:203-14
Williams, Delia F., 28:294
Williams, Edward, 1:254; 33:254
Williams, Edward H., 31:293
Williams, Edwards C., 21:383; 25:342
Williams, Eliza, 19:139
Williams, Elsie B., 18:262-65 *passim*
Williams, Ezekiel, 2:21; 4:126
Williams, Frank, 1:274
Williams, George, 15:169
Williams, George E., 9:155, 178
Williams, George W., 1:134; 24:58; 29:269
Williams, Gordon (Thomas B. Godden), 29:21, 25
Williams, Henry, 15:368
Williams, Henry Fairfax, 15:281; 17:33 44 *passim*, 259, 261, 264, 265, 361, 368, 369, 370; 28:58-67 *passim*
Williams, Henry G., 25:7
Williams, I. M., 13:296
Williams, Isaac (or Julián), 11:367, 382; 13:215, 336, 348, 349; 28:189; 33:249; ranch of, 1:71; 13:215; 14:69; 25:131; 27:135
Williams, Mrs. Isaac (María de Jesús Lugo), 13:215; 28:189
Williams, J., 18:306; 21:238
Williams, J. Milton, 9:103; 11:9
Williams, J. S., 30:46
Williams, James, 5:77; 27:260; 28:293
Williams, Mrs. James (Mary Patterson), 28:293
Williams, James and Harriet (Lewis), 28:293
Williams, James G. and Marie, 28:382

Williams, John, 26:336
Williams, John S., 29:134; 30:53
Williams, Julian, *see* Williams, Isaac
Williams, Mary Floyd, 3:101, 255; "Mission, Presidio, and Pueblo: ... Local Institutions under Spain and Mexico," 1:23-35; address, "Pushing the Frontier Westward," 9:292; bk. rev. by, 1:102-4; *History of the San Francisco Committee of Vigilance of 1851*, rev., 1:99-101
Williams, Patrick, 33:364
Williams, Peter, 16:79
Williams, Poe, 4:321
Williams, R. F., 22:251
Williams, R. L., 2:205
Williams, R. O., 13:259
Williams, Richard, 21:343; 26:31, 32
Williams, Samuel, 30:148; *The City of the Golden Gate*, rev., 1:199
Williams, Stephen (or Steven), 18:262, 264, 265, 272
Williams, Stephen Heddon, 38:32
Williams, Thomas H., 9:116, 273; 11:48; 27:281; 40:206
Williams, Thomas S., 14:177
Williams, Virgil M,., 24:265, 266; 30:139; 36:199-200; 37:21
Williams, Mrs. Virgil M., 24:88
Williams, W. J., 26:243
Williams, W. R., 37:353, 354, 355
Williams, W. W., 7:113
Williams, Wade Hampton, 32:2-10 *passim*, 17-21 *passim*, 24, 36
Williams, William (San Diego Co., 1857), 36:128
Williams, William (Santa Barbara, 1864), 18:262-64
Williams, Mrs. William E. (Helen Follett), 27:287; address, "Richmond's Golden Anniversary," 35:75
Williams, William Sherley, 2:20-21; 14:409; 26:56
Williams (S. H.) & Co., 8:299; 14:333, 346
Williams (ship), 11:208; 12:62; 13:59, 138, 139
Williams and Kellinger Gold, Silver and Copper Mining Co., 22:369
"William S. and William D. Jewett," by Elliot Evans, 33:309-20
William S. Clark (ship), phot. of launching, 22: opp. 383
William's Fork, 22:157

Williamson, Mrs. Albert, 10:291
Williamson, C. V., 10:272, 375
Williamson, Frederick Warren, obit.,
  21:286-87
Williamson, Henry, 4:320
Williamson, Isaac H. (or J. A.), 21:310
Williamson, J. C., 4:212
Williamson, James, 18:77
Williamson, John (lawsuit), 10:186
Williamson, John Marshall, obit., 11:192
Williamson, Lindley, 9:375, 376
Williamson, Robert Stockton, 4:10-11;
  11:316; 27:71; 28:214, 229
Williamson, Thomas S., 16:342, 346;
  27:213, 214; 29:23
Williamson, Victoria, 25:383
Williamson, William F., 9:258; 10:44, 46,
  47, 70
Williamson, Mount, 4:54; phot., opp. 18
"William Walker, Filibusterer," address
  by Aubrey Drury, 35:75
Williard (lawsuit, Yuba Co., 1857),
  9:142
Willie Boy: A Desert Manhunt, by
  Lawton, rev., 39:371-74
Willis (to mines, 1848), 2:182
Willis, Edward, 4:179-81
Willis, Edward B., 29:236
Willis, Edward J., 15:164, 186; 27:305,
  309
Willis, Ira J., 14:277, 278; 22:141, 150;
  26:110, 113, 122; art. on his "Best
  Guide to the Gold Mines,"
  32:193-207; phot., 32: opp. 193
Willis, Sidney S. (or W. S. S.), 14:277,
  278; 22:141, 150; 26:110, 112, 121, 122;
  32:194-95
Willis, Talbot H., 10:76
Willis, W. H., *see* Willis, Ira
Willis, William, 14:17
Williston, Henry C., 22:30, 36; 30:251,
  364; *see also* Bonestell & Williston
Willmot (Auburn, 1875), 18:361
Willoughby, F. S. M., 27:38, 48
Willoughby, Howard, 24:288; address,
  "From Quill and Pen to Typewriter,"
  32:174
Willow Bar, Yuba Co., 8:338, 345, 347,
  355
Willow Creek, Yuba Co., 8:340, 344,
  356; 9:64, 353
Willows, The, San Francisco, 10:276,
  282, 285, 290, 379; 36:209

Willow Springs, Kern Co., 17:104, 216,
  217, 218
Willow Springs (Folsom), 8:210
Willow Springs Hotel, Folsom, 8:201
Wills, Elizabeth Maria Bonney (Mrs.
  W. R. D.), 4:406; 6:40; 16:83; 19:229;
  28:34, 45; 30:105, 114; *see also* Parker,
  Mrs. Elizabeth Maria
Wills, G. W., 24:238
Wills, Marianna A., 6:40; obit., 4:406
Wills, Robert W., 26:204
Willson, Israel C., 9:246, 247, 251, 269,
  375
Willys, *see* Wyllys
Wilmarth (or Wilmot), A., 9:372;
  lawsuits, 9:148, 149, 152, 166
Wilmerding Training School, 19:153
Wilmington, 13:325; 29:246; 31:294;
  32:327-48 *passim*
Wilson (overland, 1849), 22:126
Wilson (Santa Barbara Co., d. 1852),
  13:329
Wilson (S.F., 1855), 15:270
Wilson (Sutter Co., 1858), 9:264, 265
Wilson, Dr. (Yuba Co., 1858), 9:348
Wilson, A. Jeffery, 25:383
Wilson, Andrew, " 'Jottings' on Civil
  War California," ed. John H. Kemble,
  32:209-24, 303-12
Wilson, Ann, 40:213
Wilson, Benjamin Davis (Benito),
  4:165; 9:46, 47, 48; 10:375; 12:111,
  115-20 *passim*; 13:223-24, 230, 302, 318,
  319, 321, 335; 17:330, 331; 21:223;
  25:131; 26:22, 51; 29:234, 235, 245-48
  passim; 30:99; 32:345; 38:361-62;
  dictation about Sutter, 38:322-24
Wilson, Mrs. Benjamin Davis (Ramona
  Yorba), 13:224; 38:361-62
Wilson, "Bob" (in mines, 1853), 35:210,
  212, 218, 219
Wilson, Carol (Green), 25:288; 30:376;
  address, "Adventures of a Botanist,"
  32:180-85
Wilson, Caroline, 28:294
Wilson, Charles, 9:109; 15:281, 364
Wilson, Charles H., 20:265
Wilson, Charles Lincoln, 4:221, 226;
  11:11; 30:63, 66; 38:352
Wilson, Dan, 10:184, 255
Wilson, David J., 40:218
Wilson, Ezekiel, 9:42, 45
Wilson, Francisca Peralta, 31:190
Wilson, George, 21:250

Wilson, George Osborne (1849), 33:375
Wilson, Mrs. George Osborne (1946),
  see Wilson, Carol (Green)
Wilson, Henry Clay, 19:65, 67; 27:317,
  318
Wilson, Herbert Earl, *The Lore and the
  Lure of the Yosemite*, rev., 1:199-200
Wilson, Horatio Gates, 31:77
Wilson, Gen. James (S.F., 1851),
  26:253, 254; 27:250
Wilson, James (S.F. and San Mateo
  Co., 1855, 1867), 11:127; 17:254, 255;
  27:250(?)
Wilson, James (Merced Co., 1860s),
  20:168
Wilson, Jo, 11:161, 172
Wilson, Capt. John (1826), 1:170; 8:106;
  11:247, 264; 14:325, 345; 17:26; 18:157,
  160, 163, 172, 176; 19:201, 202, 215;
  23:217; 28:115, 246, 255
Wilson, Mrs. [Capt.] John (Ramona
  Carrillo de Pacheco), 1:170; 11:264;
  14:345; 18:172; 28:255
Wilson, John (nr. Sonoma, 1837),
  16:249; 27:108
Wilson, "Gen." John (S.F., 1849), 9:42;
  30:56-65 *passim*, 157-60 *passim*; art.
  on, 26:321-48; family of, 26:328, 338;
  30:56, 65, 157, 167
Wilson, Mrs. ["Gen."] John (Anne R.
  Pulliam), 26:333, 334, 337-38, 346;
  30:56, 60, 65, 157, 168, 169, 172; letters
  of, 26:334-40
Wilson, John (Carson Hill, 1852),
  11:165, 172
Wilson, John (S.F., 1854), 22:192
Wilson, John (Sacramento and S.F.,
  1858), 9:394; 18:270(?); 21:43-44, 45,
  46
Wilson, Gen. John A. (Sacramento,
  1855), 15:367
Wilson, John K., 3:111, 113; 33:112-13
Wilson, Josefa (Peralta), 30:218, 221,
  228; 31:77, 190
Wilson, Joseph (surgeon, 1846), 18:81
Wilson, Joseph (seaman, 1847), 33:105
Wilson, Joseph (purser, 1848), 28:113
Wilson, Joshua, 15:41, 42, 45
Wilson, Lewis, 26:204
Wilson, Luzena (Stanley), 16:186
Wilson, Mary, 15:371
Wilson, Mary Eliza, *see* Wakeman, Mrs.
  Ferdinand O.

Wilson, Matty, 27:366; 28:57-61 *passim*,
  64
Wilson, Micajah D., 26:339, 345; 30:56,
  60, 62, 65
Wilson, Neill Compton, 15:99; address,
  "Treasure Expresses of the Old
  West," 15:192; *Silver Stampede*, rev.,
  16:85
Wilson, Obed G., 30:261, 362; 38:309
Wilson, Oliver C., 33:263
Wilson, Percy, 21:249
Wilson, R. A., 14:222
Wilson, R. M., 26:239, 242, 247
Wilson, R. P., 13:32
Wilson, Robert, 30:56
Wilson, S. H., 29:235
Wilson, Samuel (d. 1849), 24:119
Wilson, Samuel (Calaveras Co., 1860),
  11:9
Wilson, Samuel M., 10:295, 296, 380,
  393; 26:358; 33:333
Wilson, Santa, 36:320
Wilson, Susan Anne, *see* Ford, Mrs.
  Henry Lewis
Wilson, Sherman, 36:322
Wilson, Thomas Ware, 14:391, 406
Wilson, W. H., port. of Edwin F.
  Morse, 6: opp. 332
Wilson, Mrs. Wesley (Belle
  McDonald), 10:265
Wilson, William Frederick, 19:87
Wilson, William Henry, 26:341; 30:56,
  60-65 *passim*
Wilson, Woodrow, 36:154
Wilson, Zeke, 19:229
Wilson & Spaulding, 30:102, 107, 113
Wilson, Mount, 13:224; 31:20
Wilson G. Hunt (ship), 9:55; 15:277;
  17:268
Wilson's Exchange, San Francisco,
  15:267, 271, 376
Wilson's Mastodon Champion Circus,
  21:145
Wiltsee, Ernest Abram, 17:288; "The
  British Vice Consul in California ...
  1846," 10:99-128; "The City of New
  York of the Pacific," 12:25-34;
  "Double Springs, First County Seat
  of Calaveras County," 11:176-83;
  "The Emigrant's Dream," 15:324-28;
  "Hawes & Co.'s San Francisco and
  New York Express," 11:30-32;
  "Meetings of the Society," 9:408;
  10:413; 13:284; addresses: "Gold Rush

Steamers," 17:285; "Gregory's Express," 13:88-89; "The Pioneer Miner and the Pack Mule Express," 9:407; "The Truth about Frémont," 11:88; *The Truth about Frémont*, rev., 15:191; *When the Pack Mule Express Was the U.S. Mail*, rev., 8:385; coauth. *Early California . . . Post Office Cancellations*, rev., 8:385; obits. of Everett N. Bee, 15:95-96; Mrs. Richard T. Carroll, 13:191-92; Boutwell Dunlap, 10:95; John H. Hammond, 15:290-91; obit., 26:377

Wim-mel-che (or Wim-mul-che) River, 2:236, 345-49 *passim*, 3:25-26, 28

Wimmer, John, 26:110-15 *passim*

Wimmer, Martin, 26:118, 119

Wimmer, Peter L., 4:89; 14:273, 275; 19:125, 140; 26:110-19 *passim*; 27:281

Wimmer, Mrs. Peter L. (Elizabeth Jane Bays), 19:124-25, 126, 140; 26:110-17 *passim*, 131, 161

Wimmer family, 11:136; 19:124, 125, 140; 26:110, 111, 118, 131-32

"Wimmer nugget," 4:89

Winans, Joseph W., 1:10; 16:183; 17:182; 23:373; 26:200

Winants, A., 16:84

Winants, Augusta, *v.* Alvin Winants, 10:54, 55

Winants, Newel, 10:54, 55

Winblad, Sig, 25:170

Winchell, E. C., 4:26, 39

Winchell, Lilbourne Alsip, 4:26, 37, 38, 39, 55

Winchester (d. 1834), 14:314, 315

Winchester, Ezra H., 29:253

Winchester, Heman, 25:110-11, 113, 258, 260, 264, 265; *see also* Winchester, Paine & Co.

Winchester, Jonas, 13:297; 23:279; 25:257, 265, 266; 30:131, 132, 146

Winchester, Paine & Co., 25:257-63 *passim*, 334

Winchester, Ore., 25:255, 256-57

Winckler, Ad, 31:137

Windeler (or Windler), Dr. (Tuolumne Co., 1859), 11:229, 333

Winder, William A., 22:9; 26:16; 33:233, 235; 34:47-48

Winding, Capt. (Colorado R., 1862), 22:170, 171

"Windjammer Days in San Diego," by Jerry MacMullen, 22:349-54

Windred, Robert, 6:49; 12:106

Wines and wine making, 2:55; 11:19; 13:166, 274; 17:144, 237, 238; 21:329, 334, 338, 353, 355; 22:319; 28:138-41; 30:309-10; 31:258; 34:22; 36:241-50; *see also* Grapes

Winfield Scott (ship), 21:321; 24:64; 35:217

Wing, W. P., 10:62

Wing's House, 10:172

Wing's Ranch, 10:366

Wingate, Caleb C., 2:113, 116, 117, 121

Wingate, Charles D., 2:117, 121

Wingate, Richard P., 2:118, 121

Winged Racer (ship), 4:223

Wingman, Miss (Marysville, 1857), 9:151, 169

Wing Souey, 23:109

Winkley, John W., 22:371; 26:95, 163; address, "Gold and Ghost Towns," 27:85-87

Winkley, P. William ("Dutch Bill"), 8:205; 9:57, 73; 10:362, 370

Winman, Gertrude, *see* Glover, Mrs. J. T.

Winn, Abel T. ("Fussy"), 35:139-40

Winn, Adolphus Gustavus and Agnes T. (Hilsee), 13:92; 28:94; 39:177

Winn, Albert Maver, 24:172, 174, 175; 28:93-94, 190; 29:290, 291; 39:177; report, 29:292-93; phot., 29: opp. 289

Winn, Mrs. Albert Maver (Catherine Gaffney), 28:94; (Charlotte [Libbey] King), 28:94

Winn, J. M., 9:180

Winn, M., 17:174

Winn, M. L., 15:369, 370; 27:307; *see also* Fountain Head

Winn, William Watkin, 13:92; 28:93-94; 32:286; "California Society, Sons of the American Revolution," 29:289-95; "The Joaquin Miller Foundation," 32:231-41; "Joaquin Miller's 'Real Name,'" 33:143-46; obit. of George D. Louderback, 36:88-90; obit., 39:177-78

Winne *v.* McKeebe & Co., 10:174

Winnemucca (Indian), 12:326; 18:306, 314

Winnemucca, Sarah, 38:153-54

Winner, Emma Jane, 14:73, 182

Winner, George K., 14:72, 73, 176, 182; 37:234

Winner, Hannah P., 14:72, 73, 182
Winner, Lizzie (Mrs. Basil Hall), 37:235
Winner, Moroni, 14:174
Winner family, 8:276; 14:72, 73, 175, 176, 182; 37:234, 235
Winnett, P. G., 25:288
Winn Park, Sacramento, 28:94
Winn's Bookstore (Iowa Hill), 30:367
Winn's Serenaders, 20:314
Winrow, J., 15:171
Winship, George Parker, 3:264, 370, 372, 384; 6:303, 306
Winship, Jonathan, 12:220-24 *passim*
Winship, Nathan, 12:223-24
Winslow, Capt. (Winslow Bar, ca. 1850), 8:355
Winslow, Charles Frederick, 15:177(?); 29:1-4, 259; 31:5; 33:375; 36:346; letters and diary of, 29:4-18, 167-72, 255-60; phot., 29: before 1
Winslow, Mrs. Charles Frederick (Lydia Coffin Jones), 29:1, 3; letters to, 29:7-8, 11-14, 168-70
Winslow, Chauncey R., 31:185
Winslow, Elos, 13:32
Winslow, George, 22:124-27 *passim*
Winslow, Jesse, 22:127
Winslow Bar, 8:338, 344, 348, 355; 9:53
Winsor, Upton B., 8:360
Winsted, James, 3:259
Winston, I., 9:306
Winston, Dr. James B., 12:12; 13:319
Winston, Joseph, 9:103; 15:153; 17:266
Winter, Henry, 11:127
Winter, J. D., 15:29
Winter, J. W., 14:396 97; 15:43
Winters, John B., 11:48
Winters, John D. (Coloma, 1848), 26:125; 30:36
Winters, John D. (Nev., 1850s), 12:328
Winters, Theodore, 9:100; 12:328
Winters, William H., 2:75
Winter's Tale, A, 9:258; 16:84
Winther, Oscar Osburn, 14:86; 40:250; "The Story of San José, 1777-1869," 14:3-27, 147-74; ed. "Stage-Coach Days in California: Reminiscences of H. C. Ward," 13:255-61; address, "Stage Coach Days in California," 14:186-87; bk. rev. by, 40:249-50
Winthrop, Francis B., 21:310
Winthrop House, Yuba Co., 10:171
Wipley, Daniel H., 27:45, 157
Wire rope, 19:146, 149, 153; 25:4

Wisconsin Co., 9:158
Wisconsin House, Yuba Co., 9:51, 69
Wise, Daniel P., 20:45
Wise, Henry Augustus ("Harry Gringo"), 4:285; 13:34, 36
Wise, John H., 19:156
Wise, Marion, 17:240; 24:58, 71
Wishar, Emile Beauchamp, 33:190
Wislizenus, F. Adolph, 18:245, 246, 292, 309-10, 344, 346; 32:249
Wistar, Isaac Jones, 15:76, 83-85; 17:310, 318, 319; 31:230-37 *passim*
Witchcraft (ship), 15:172
Witch Creek (resort), 35:352
Witch Creek (San Diego Co.), 26:25, 28
Witcher, James, 16:177
Witherall, Joseph, 30:8
Withered, T. H., 30:17
Within an Inch of His Life (play), 21:256
Witowski (Grass Valley, 1855), 30:266
Witt, Margaret, 33:144
Witte, H. H. (lawsuit), 10:167
Wittenbach, Dr. (Grass Valley, 1850), 6:229
Wittmer, Jacob, 14:277-78; 26:121
Wittram, Charles, 29:108, 118
Wittram Colony, 25:174
Wittschen, Theodore Peter, 23:192
"Wives of the 'Big Four,' " address by Mrs. Frederick H. Colburn, 12:84
W. L. Capps (ship), 23:189
W. L. Marcy (ship), 15:172, 185; 16:83
W. L. Richardson (ship), 22:170, 171
Wöhler, *see* Wohler
Wogitiu (Indian village), 10:219
Wohler, Herman, 9:26; 10:43(?); 12:303(?); 15:172; 16:81, 84
Wohlgemuth, O. J., 23:192
Wolcott, Marjorie Tisdale, ed. Hayes, *Pioneer Notes*, rev., 8:280-81
Woldenberg, David, 19:291
Wolf, Mrs. J. L., 27:383
"Wolf Cub," *see* Raousset-Boulbon
Wolf Cub, The, by Soulié, trans. Symons, rev., 7:198-99
Wolfrum, Philip, 25:233
Wolfskill, John, 26:38
Wolfskill, John Reed (or Reid), 2:65; 5:123, 126, 273-74; 6:152; 10:28, 31; 23:291, 293, 295, 364
Wolfskill, Mrs. John Reed (or Reid), *see* Cooper, Susan

Wolfskill, William, 2:10, 36-41; 3:164; 5:109; 10:28; 13:213, 224, 325, 339; 18:175, 176, 328; 23:295; 27:108, 109, 110; 32:332, 339

Wolfskill, trail, *see* Spanish trail

Wolfstein, H., 30:361-62

Wolf Tone Guard, 10:390

Wolter, Charles (or Carl C.), 19:197, 214; 29:22, 27

Wolter, Mrs. Charles (née Estrada), 29:27

Wolters, Henry, 25:173

Wolverine Mine, 20:184

Wolverton, James, 4:41

Woman of the World, The (play), 10:361, 370

Woman's suffrage, 9:59; 21:79; proposed, 1878, 5:283; voted down, 1896, 5:284

Wombough (Wambaugh, Wornbaugh), M. M., 1:77; 4:320

Women, 28:31-32; economic status (1850), 34:70; influence of, 28:31, 32, 77; 32:125-27; "Mercer girls," 40:255-56; in mining region, 3:128-29, 155-56; 4:78-79; in S.F. (1849-51), 24:360; 32:114; scarcity of, 13:357; 20:31; 27:261, 368; 34:70; on shipboard, 1:227-28; 24:69; Spanish Californian, 8:311; suffrage, 5:283, 284; 9:59; 21:79; in wartime, 24:261-66; *see also* Chinese; Farnham, Eliza; Indians

"Women in War-Time, San Francisco, 1864," by Dorothy H. Huggins, 24:261-66

Women's Auxiliary Silk Culture Association of California, 31:335-42 *passim*

Wong Fong, 23:109

Wong On (Ah Louis), 37:130-31

Wood (Negro, Yuba Co., 1857), 9:167

Wood, A., 22:251

Wood, Abram Epperson, 4:44

Wood, Allen, 10:271, 272

Wood, Charles, 11:166

Wood, Charles S., 30:256

Wood, David I., 28:242

Wood, Delia Williams, 2:181, 201

Wood, Elizabeth, 7:412

Wood, Ellen (Lamont), 23:383; "Samuel Green McMahan," 23:289-300

Wood, Frank S., 29:253, 254, *see also* Hodge & Wood

Wood, Henry (?), 5:73

Wood, Jake, 3:259

Wood, James, 8:357

Wood, John (overland, 1850), Journal of, rev., 6:360-63; family of, 6:361

Wood, Mrs. John (Eliza Jane Slagle), 6:361

Wood, John (actor, 1858), 9:279, 280; 21:43, 46, 71

Wood, Mrs. John (Matilda), 9:254, 255, 279, 280, 360, 389; 10:47, 69; 21:43, 45, 46, 71, 164

Wood, John Henry, 22:37

Wood, Philo B., 14:61, 69, 71, 73

Wood, R. N., 9:42, 100, 103

Wood, Richard Coke, 31:287

Wood, Robert S. S. and Frances E. (Merril), 28:292

Wood, Rose, 21:246, 256

Wood, Samuel A., 33:68

Wood, Mrs. Samuel A. (Susan Torrey), 32:90; 33:375

Wood, Thomas, 25:258

Wood, William (on *Columbia*, 1840), 8:98

Wood, William, 21:327

Wood, William Bussy, 24:67, 172

Wood, Mrs. William Bussy (Annie Harding), 26:172

Wood, William Christopher, 36:252, 253, 257-58; 37:352-56 *passim*

Wood, William Graham, 15:368; 27:93

Wood, William H. R., *Digest of the Laws of California*, 9:140, 175

Wood, William Maxwell, 29:337; quoted, 13:49

Wood, William W., 24:67

Wood family (from Ky.), 35:352

Woodall, John, 10:63

Woodard, John, 4:60-61

Woodbeck (fight w. Joaquin), 16:260

Woodbridge, Sylvester, Jr., 6:63; 20:166; 26:168, 172; 27:36, 37, 43, 47, 49, 302-3; 29:109-10, 115, 117

Woodbury, Stillman, 14:61, 73

Woodbry (Woodbury?), Henry, 2:121

Woodcock, William, 9:252

Woodcuts, in Stockton newspapers, 34:341-55 *passim*

Woodlief, Deveraux Jerome, 15:182; 35:317-18

Woodman, Charles, 8:202

Woodman, L. C., 38:314

Woodruff, A., 19:230

Woodruff, Charles A., 1:16; 24:80
Woodruff, Edward C., 27:223
Woodruff, Edwards, 14:400; 15:21, 24, 28
Woodruff's steam mill, 7:11
Woodruff *v.* North Bloomfield Gravel Mining Co., 29:202
Woods (Yuba Co., 1850s), 8:345; 10:57; lawsuits, 8:345, 347; 9:130
Woods, Miss (Marysville, 1858), 9:263
Woods, Miss (Sacramento, 1859), 10:176
Woods, Chaplin (on *Powhatan*, 1860), 23:342
Woods, Cad (Carl?), 10:46
Woods, D. W., 27:287
Woods, Daniel B., 23:262, 279, 280; 30:105; quoted, 38:37
Woods, Francis H., 29:253, 254
Woods, George Lemuel, 35:338-39, 341, 343
Woods, Isaiah Churchill, 15:177, 269, 277, 368, 371, 372, 377; 16:83, 184; 17:170, 171, 172, 180; 26:195; 31:40; report, 36:118, 121-29 *passim*, 37:139
Woods, James, 13:333, 334, 383 (?); 15:168; 23:279; 26:173; 28:325; 38:36; 39:51 (?)
Woods, Lottie G., 31:340
Woods, Martha Elizabeth, 19:148
Woods, Mrs. Mary E., 29:294
Woods, Matthew, 8:194, 343, 347, 359; 9:53, 77, 149, 151, 254, 255, 259-62 *passim*, 265, 274, 279, 352, 358, 373, 396; 10:56, 61, 165, 166, 183, 370, 383
Woods, Mrs. Matthew (Nellie Vineyard), 8:194, 359; 9:248-54 *passim*, 259-67 *passim*, 274, 346, 352, 354, 362, 367; 10:56, 167, 168, 179, 269, 370
Woods, Robert E., 16:81, 84; 17:172
Woods, Saschel, 18:299
Woods & Purdy, Sonora, 30:266
Wood's Bridge, Yuba Co., 8:338, 355
Woods (Wood's, Woods') Camp, Tuolumne Co., 13:383; 24:345
Woods (Wood's, Woods') Creek Diggings, 11:164-73 *passim;* 13:383; 18:166; 20:101, 114; 22:70; 23:60; 30:112; 39:45, 51; 40:99; illus., 11: opp. 157
Woods (Wood's, Woods') Crossing, Tuolumne Co., 13:383; 28:325

Wood's Dry Diggings, *see* Auburn
Woodside, Preston K., 15:167
Woodside (place), 17:254
Woodson (Sharon Valley, 1859), 10:58
Woodson, Warren N., 30:158
Wood's Ranch, 8:342, 359
"Woods' Shorter Mountain Trail to San Diego," by Hero E. Rensch, 36:117-32
Woodville, Joseph Shannon, 28:292
Woodville House, Yuba Co., 8:357
Woodward, Capt. (on *Valleyfield*, 1842), 28:247
Woodward (North San Juan, 1854), 8:200, 201
Woodward, Absalom, 6:122
Woodward, Arthur, 25:218, 379; 38:75; "Lances at San Pascual," 25:289-308; 26:21-62; bk. revs. by, 38:371-73; 40:162-65
Woodward, Chesley, 26:205, 207
Woodward, D. S., 9:36
Woodward, Mrs. Elizabeth, 16:283, 339; 20:296; 28:37
Woodward, F. M., 26:205, 207
Woodward, Gideon, 24:382
Woodward, J. M., 13:252
Woodward, Mrs. Mary, 20:296
Woodward, Robert B., 3:260; 38:306; *see also* What Cheer House; Woodward's Gardens
Woodward, Thomas, 13:187
Woodward, William, 26:205
Woodward's Gardens, San Francisco, 3:260; 10:368; 30:68; 35:130, 135; 37:217
Woodward's House, 34:345; *see also* What Cheer House
Woodworth, Benjamin R., 25:35
Woodworth, Frederick A., 15:164, 270; 28:38
Woodworth, H. ("Woody"), 13:258
Woodworth, John D., 32:330, 333
Woodworth, Selim E., 25:336, 343; 26:113, 119; 28:35; 29:27; 30:131; 33:340; 38:299
Woodworth, Wallace, 13:331, 336
Wool, John E., 14:356-57, 360-68 *passim*, 372; 15:70, 71, 75-85 *passim*, 158, 173, 180, 181, 272, 282, 367, 369, 373; 16:339; 17:175; 19:229(?); 23:245; 24:174; 27:207; 30:161, 162; 35:320-21, 322; cor., 14:361-64; port., 14: opp. 350

Wool, 5:257, 258; 12:243; 20:343;
23:242; 32:335; blankets made from,
2:273; 5:131, 257; 14:118; *see also*
Sheep

Woolen factories, 10:276, 291, 373;
20:343; 32:306

Woolenschneider (Yuba Co., 1857),
9:131-32

Wooll, John, 25:7; 30:382

Woollarha (ship), 30:211

Woolley, Charles, 30:254

Woolley, G. W., 9:36

Woolley, Robert W., 39:133

Woolroofe & Thornton, 33:375

Woolsey, James B., 17:44, 360; 25:95

Woolsey, John L., 28:294

Woolsey, Katherine, *see* Slack, Mrs.
Charles W.

Woolworth, S. B., 12:71

Wooster, Charles W., 11:141

Wooster, Clarence Marshall, 18:192;
"Building the Railroad down the San
Joaquin in 1871," 18:22-31;
"Compound Interest: Alvinza
Hayward Pays a Debt," 20:181-85;
"Early Days on the Mountain
Division," 23:117-22; "Meadow Lake
City and a Winter at Cisco in the
Sixties," 18:149-56; "More about
Railroading in California in the
Seventies: The Fire Train,"
22:178-80; "Railroading in California
in the Seventies," 18:355-68

Wooster, Edwin Clough, 18:22, 151

Wooster, Ernest, 40:231

Wooster, Fletcher Lewis, 18:22, 28, 30,
151, 360

Wooster, John Marshall, 18:22, 149-56
passim; 20:181, 182

Worden, J. B., 29:291

Worden, J. D., 8:346

Wores, Joseph (Jósef Vörös),
28:137-38, 142

Wores, Theodore, 37:26, 37

Work, Jane, 22:104, 107

Work, John, 19:313, 315; 24:230; 25:264;
arts. on, 22:97-109, 193-222, 323-48;
23:19-40, 123-46; Journal, 22:195-213,
323-43; 23:19-39, 123-45; map, 22: opp.
193; phot., 22: opp. 97

Work, Mrs. John (Josette Legace),
22:100-106 *passim,* 218; phot., 22: opp.
104

Work family, 22:107

"Working for Wells Fargo, 1860-1863:
Letters of Charles T. Blake," ed.
Anson S. Blake, 16:30-42, 172-81; as
address, 16:88-89

Workingmen's Party, 21:248; 37:218,
222-24, 339-40

Workman, David, 29:29

Workman, William (Julian), 3:164, 170;
10:34; 12:115-16, 335; 13:223-24, 230,
335, 343, 349; 21:348-49, 357; 22:64;
27:135; 38:25; *see also* Workman-
Rowland party

Workman, William H. ("Uncle Billy"),
13:343

Workman-Rowland party, 10:33-36;
17:152; 18:172

Works, Mrs. (Yuba Co., 1857), 9:150

Works, Hiram, 8:341, 356

Works, John Downey, 26:85; 38:255

Worland, Charles W., 26:247

World Beater Mine, 18:204

*World Encompassed by Sir Francis
Drake, The,* from notes of Francis
Fletcher, 3:205; 16:273, 279; 17: No.
4, Pt. 2, p. 7; 36:23-24; excerpts from,
16: No. 1, Pt. 2, pp. 4-11 *passim,* 14,
23, 32-46, 52

Wornbaugh, M. M., *see* Wombough

Worrell, Franklyn, 26:291

Worrell Sisters, 4:60

Worth, Andrew I., 9:313, 325, 330-31

Worth, George F., 38:158-59

Worth, Sarah, 38:159

Worth, W., 13:32

Worth, William J., 18:130; 23:259, 370

Worth a Million (play), 34:367

Worthington, Robert, 15:281

Wozencraft, Oliver Meredith, 3:26;
4:185-86; 7:4, 6; 10:151; 15:267;
20:101-2, 114, 115; 22:368; 24:197,
198; 28:328-40 *passim;* 36:314-15

Wozencraft's boardinghouse, San
Francisco, 19:230, 236

Wrangell, Baron Ferdinand P., 2:227;
12:191, 198, 199, 209, 237, 238, 243-44;
17:62; 28:109

Wren, Mrs. (laundress, 1863), 26:9

Wren, Thomas, 11:49, 51

Wright, Mr. and Mrs. (Halo Chamo,
1849), 20:34

Wright (d. Mex., 1850), 1:60

Wright (S.F., 1860), 29:120

Wright, A. S., 15:273; bank, 3:37;
15:268, 272, 274

Wright, Adaline M., 30:285

Wright, Allen, 30:302
Wright, Clarissa, *see* Burrell, Mrs. Lyman J.
Wright, Daniel (David?), 27:108
Wright, Daniel E., 1:60
Wright, Doris Marion, 19:383; 29:383; "The Making of Cosmopolitan California," 19:323-43; 20:65-79
Wright, Elizabeth C. ("Carrie Carlton"), 28:5, 6
Wright, Elizur and Clarissa (Richards), 28:297
Wright, Elizur, Jr., 28:297, 305, 314, 320
Wright, F., 28:59, 66
Wright, F. L., 39:247
Wright, G. B., 11:151, 153
Wright, George (S.F., 1849), 27:45, 50
Wright, George (overland and Calif., 1850-51), 3:45-72 *passim*, 126-34 *passim*
Wright, Gen. George, 15:9, 10, 11; 20:162; 22:224, 360; 24:278; 26:2, 5, 7, 9, 360, 363; 27:217, 222, 227; 28:168, 212, 214, 220, 228; 29:245; 33:230-36 *passim;* 34:136-37; 40:317, 343, 344
Wright, George H. Burwell, 18:384; obit., 22:93
Wright, George M., 33:5, 7, 8, 12, 152
Wright, George S., 9:313
Wright, George W., 10:163, 238; 14:164; 17:84; 19:14; 33:375
Wright, Gus, 9:63, 65
Wright, Henry C., 14:379
Wright, Irene A., 3:314; trans. Unamuno narrative, 2:145-60; trans. Ulloa narrative, 3:315-67
Wright, J. (to Calif., 1840), 18:292-94, 309
Wright, J. (Grass Valley, 1850), 6:229
Wright, J. T., 6:17
Wright, James Richards, 28:300, 310, 318, 320
Wright, James William Abert, 4:38, 55; 26:237, 238, 247
Wright, John, 27:174
Wright, Leroy A., 36:63
Wright, O. P., 9:144
Wright, Patrick, 26:300, 302, 303, 304
Wright, Philo, 28:302, 305, 309, 312
Wright, S. H., 14: opp. 209
Wright, Silas, 38:54
Wright, T. T. and Rachel McCreary (McKnight), 2:21
Wright, Thomas F., 40:349

Wright, W. T., 8:348
Wright, Washington, 9:275
Wright, William (S.F., 1854), 15:163
Wright, William ("Dan De Quille"), 15:381; 21:141, 142; 36:35, 39, 365-70 *passim*
Wright, William B., 16:282
Wright & Sanders, 27:173, 174
"Writing an Epic of the California Gold Rush," address by Robin Lampson, 14:283
"Writing Local History," by W. W. Robinson, 39:209-17
Wroth, Lawrence Counselman, 36:172-74; bk. rev. by, 6:93-95; "Early Cartography of the Pacific," rev., 24:77-78
Wunderlich (S.F., 1864), 24:263
Württemberg, Prince Paul Wilhelm, Herzog von, 8:180, 181; 12:301-2; 16:380
Wyandotte (place), 15:52; 29:104
Wyatt (Yuba Co., 1856), 9:65
Wyatt, Christopher B., 13:299; 15:373; 34:233
Wyatt, Dorothea, 11:3
Wyatt, Lemericus, 18:307-8, 314
Wyche (S.F., 1861), 29:127
Wyeth, E. R., address, "Early Associations between California and Australia," 26:279-80
Wyeth, Nathaniel Jarvis, 3:74, 75, 76, 279; expedition, 18:342
Wyllie, Robert Crichten, 17:21, 22, 132; 18:142-44; letter to, 17:22-26
Wylly, Charles G., 26:256
Wyllys, Rufus Kay, "French Imperialists in California," 8:116-29; *French in Sonora*, rev., 11:388
Wyman, George F., 17:158; 19:119, 137
Wyman, Mrs. George F. (America Kelsey), 19:119, 137
Wyman, L., 13:32
Wyman, Rufus P., 20:45
Wyman, S. B., 4:250
Wyman, Walker D., 24:93; comp. "California Emigrant Letters," 24:17-46, 117-38, 235-60, 343-64
Wynn, Charles H. and Euphemia (Rittenhouse), 28:189
Wynn, Wilbur Webster and Mabel Jessamyn (Heaton), 28:189
Wynne, Sedman W., 4:52
Wyoming (ship), 28:179

X

Xántus de Vasey, János, "California for Hungarian Readers," Letters of, ed. Henry M. Madden, 28:125-42; port., 28: opp. 128

Xaramillo, Lope, 3:389

Xexo (Cojo Anchorage), 7:49, 75

Ximénez de Bertandona, Ortuño, 1:39-40, 45-51 *passim;* 6:298, 307

Xucu (Indian village), 7:23, 48, 49

Xylon (ship), 14:344

Y

Yabit (Indian rancheria), *see* Yang Na

Yacht racing, 15:278, 369

Yaeger, *see* Jaeger

Yager, Cornelius, 11:9

Yah-Fee-Pah (Indian, 1890), 26:201, 206

Yainax Butte, 24:231

Yale, Charles P., obit. of Edwin V. Van Amringe, 36:184-85

Yale, Gregory, 10:375; 11:11; 16:79; 28:4; 34:252

Yamamoto Kusu, 28:349-50

Yamhill River, 23:143, 144

Yanaga, Chitoshi, 23:346

Yanagawa Masakiyo, 23:346

Yancey, F., 11:9

Yáñez, José María, 18:17, 18

Yáñez, Juan, 7:172

Yang Na (Indian village), 13:195, 202, 204, 206, 211, 310, 344

Yankee (ship), 8:371; 15:158, 280; 16:83, 347

Yankee Blade (ship), 15:88, 165, 169, 173, 176, 178, 179, 185, 269, 270, 271; 16:183, 347; illus., 15: opp. 364

Yankee [mining] Company, 3:143, 144, 145

Yankee Jim's, 2:203-8 *passim;* 7:17; 16:31; 24:252; 30:261, 285; 32:133

"Yank's" (store at Smith's Bar), 30:111

Yanovski, Semion, 12:191, 234, 235

Yanson, Capt. (d. Gila R., 1850), 15:374

Yaqui (place), 14:132, 141

Yard, Edward M., 20:234

Yarrow (L.A., 1850), 13:319

Yarwood, Charles M., 9:19

Yates, Capt. (Marysville, 1851), 15:49

Yates, Mrs. A. J. (Matilda H.), 19:236

Yates, Charles H., 26:215

Yates, Frederick, 32:261, port. of Hans H. Behr, 32: opp. 248

Yates, Lorenzo G., 1:15; 24:79

Yates & Co., 14: opp. 209

Ybarra, Desiderio, 13:211

Ybarra, Gerónimo, 29:236

Ybarra, Gil, 13:222-23

Ybarra, Hilario, 29:236

Ybarra, Juan María, 14:257

Yeager (overland, d. 1849), 22:143

Yeatman, William, 18:244, 250

Yeatman, Woods, 18:244, 250

Yee Chi, 23:111

Yee Teen, 23:111

Ye Liberty Playhouse, *see* Liberty

Yelland, Raymond Dabb, 37:37

Yellow Aster Mine, 32:1, 31

Yellow Bird, *see* Ridge, John R.

Yellow Jacket Silver Mining Co., 33:375

Yellow Serpent, 5:77, 79; 21:1-6 *passim,* 9, 16, 17; 25:144, 147; 29:323, 327, 334; port., 21: opp. 1

Yelverton, Theresa, 28:186

Yeomans, Capt., 4:184-85

Yerba Buena, 1:31; 3:30-34; 4:169; 6:381; 8:98, 107, 120, 122, 141, 146, 148, 234, 238, 244, 387; 10:7, 19, 91; 11:69-78; 12:59, 161, 283, 341, 350, 353; 13:63, 65, 235-36, 272-76 *passim,* 343, 355, 357, 365, 367, 378; 14:121-31; 15:59, 309; 16:209, 243, 249-50, 343; 17:230, 273, 274, 279, 291-302; 18:293; 19:197; 20:216, 291, 292; 21:11, 12; 23:210, 372; 24:47, 324, 335; 26:267-68; 27:61; 28:246, 247, 250-54 *passim,* 266, 289; 32:234; 37:314; cove, 14:111; 17:291, 301; 20:291; 25:319-23; 27:59-60; 28:258; early settlers in, 14:121-31;

17:291-301; (*see also* Leese, Jacob P.;
  Richardson, William Antonio); first
  houses in, 3:31; 11:69, 73-78; 13:238;
  14:100, 125, 186; 16:249-50, 343;
  17:292; U.S. flag raised at, 15:63-64,
  306, 310; maps of, 17: opp. 291; 25:125;
  26:267
"Yerba Buena Biographies," 14:123-31
Yerba Buena Cemetery, San Francisco,
  15:172, 277
Yerba Buena Island, 5:7, 178; 8:382;
  10:91; 14:129, 144; 15:280; 17:174, 293;
  32:234; 33:231, 234; *see also* Goat
  Island; Limantour Claim
"Yerba Buena's Village Days," address
  by Douglas S. Watson, 8:387
Yerba santa, 31:25-26
Yerington, H. M., 7:118; 19:95
Yerkes (S.F., 1855), 15:269
"Yipsels," 40:218
Ynitía, José Camilo (Indian, 1843),
  29:268, 277
Ynfanzón, Cristóbal, 2:150, 155
Yoell (lawsuit, 1850s), 38:52
"Yokayo Rancheria," by Charles Kasch,
  26:209-15
"Yokuts Indians of the San Joaquin
  Valley, The," address by George W.
  Stewart, 4:301
Yollo Bolly Mountains, 32:376
Yontez, John, 14:164
Yorba, Bernardo, 13:224, 349
Yorba, Isabel, 18:264
Yorba, José Antonio, 13:198
Yorba, Ramona, *see* Wilson, Mrs.
  Benjamin D.
Yorba, Teodosio, 13:349
Yorba, Tomás, 19:208, 211, 215
Yorba, Mrs. Tomás (Doña Vicenta
  Sepúlveda), 19:208
York (Weaverville, 1855), 30:261
York, John (in mines, 1848), 2:183, 187,
  194; ranch of, 24:57; 29:263
York, Mrs. John (Lucinda Hudson),
  19:142
York, John (San Francisco, 1854),
  15:175
York (ship), 13:296
Yorke, Peter C., 28:55, 190
Yorkinos, Los, 8:223, 238
Yorktown (ship), 34:116
Yosemite (ship), 21:58
Yosemite Falls, 1:274-79
Yosemite Guide Book, 4:16

Yosemite National Park, 4:43;
  38:249-58; *see also* Yosemite Valley
"Yosemite Pioneers," address by Ansel
  F. Hall, 4:210
Yosemite Valley, 4:12-13, 24, 195;
  13:186, 224; 14:78; 15:190, 286, 379;
  23:368, 376; 28:332-33; 30:274-75,
  284; 32:193; 36:72-73; arts. on,
  1:272-85; 5:328-41; Ayres in, 5:336-37;
  Emerson in, 20:2, 7; 33:245; granted to
  State, 1:24; 30:275; Roosevelt and
  Muir in, 17:18-19; bk. on, rev.,
  1:199-200; Ayres' sketch of, 5: opp.
  336; *see also* Yosemite National Park
Yoshida Ichitaro, 28:349-50
Yoshida Yohei, 28:349-50
Youghl, George, 13:30
Youghl, John Alexis, 13:29-31
Youmans, E. S., 13:32
Young (relief exped., 1849), 30:60
Young (Yuba Co., 1857), 9:138, 139, 161
Young (S.F., 1862), 10:377
Young (son of Brigham, 1868), 5:181
Young, B., 13:32
Young, Brigham, 5:181, 290; 9:90, 180;
  11:132; 14:271, 272, 279; 15:244, 245;
  21:228, 236; 22:12, 141; 26:326-27,
  329, 333, 347; 30:57; 33:247; 37:230,
  238
Young, "Caddie," 9:172
Young, Clement Calhoun, 30:350;
  34:330; 36:55, 152, 252-58 *passim*;
  37:273, 347-58 *passim*; 39:28
Young, E. D., 13:32
Young, Ewing, 1:111-18 *passim*, 143,
  150; 2:7, 10, 37; 3:77-79; 4:5-6, 170;
  8:98; 10:28; 12:176; 13:211; 14:22, 346;
  18:175, 328, 349-50; 19:313; 20:341-42;
  22:102, 208, 323, 326, 347; 23:25, 39,
  140; 28:122
Young, Fanny, 21:171
Young, Francis G., 31:231, 234, 235
Young, Fuller B., 26:10
Young, G. W., 33:375
Young, George A., 9:269; 10:62, 377(?)
Young, George E., 26:1-10 *passim*;
  sketches by, 26: opp. 1
Young, Gordon, *Days of '49*, rev.,
  5:312-15
Young, Herbert, 31:155
Young, J., 22:251
Young, J. W., 34:246
Young, Jacob C., 22:36
Young, John Philip, 32:236
Young, Levi, 22:346

Young, Lorenzo D., 14:270
Young, Lucy, "Out of the Past, a True Indian Story," told to Edith V. A. Murphey, 20:349-64
Young, N. G., 8:358
Young, Nicodemus, 9:172
Young, Mrs. Nicodemus, 9:66, 131, 140, 143-51 *passim*, 172, 267
Young, Pedro Lewis, 39:56
Young, Richard, 3:114
Young, Romualdo, 26:41
Young, Sam, 20:358
Young, Sheldon, 18:196, 214
Young, Stephen, 20:248
Young, Thomas, 23:339, 344
Young, Thomas A., 7:14, 15, 17
Young, William, 8:211
Young, William M., 26:203
Young & Co., 9:142
Young America (riv. str.), 10:281, 285, 294, 375
"Young Chief" (Indian, 1845), 21:5, 6
Younger, Coleman and Augusta (Peters), 19:191, 192
Younger, Rosalie, 19:191-92
Younger, William John, 29:82
Young Ladies' Seminary, Benicia, 24:63, 64, 165, 179; 26:354; 27:67, 303; 29:55, 59; 30:262; 31:85-86; 32:90
Young Ladies' Seminary, Sacramento, 10:287
Young Men's Christian Association, San Francisco, 14:75; 15:376; 17:177; 31:4-5, 24; Library Association, 38:304
Young's Ferry, 34:269
Young's Hill, 3:148-49; 8:193, 196, 203-4, 211, 337-38, 342, 349, 350, 352; 9:51, 54-68 *passim*, 78, 79, 129-69 *passim*, 172, 262, 266, 352-53; 10:56, 63, 170-71, 256, 359
Young's River (Putah Cr.), 22:345
Young Tartar (ship), 6:257, 258
Yount, A. K., 12:329
Yount, Frances, 2:63, 67
Yount, George Concepción, 5:127, 135-36, 272-73; 6:40; 11:136; 13:54; 15:370; 16:129, 132, 249, 355; 20:82, 150-51, 153; 22:31-32, 37, 341, 345; 23:294, 296; 25:94; 28:262, 264, 266; 29:319, 325; 35:1; "The Chronicles of," ed. C. L. Camp, 2:3-66
Yount, Mrs. George Concepción (Eliza Cambridge Wilds), 2:6, 67; 20:153
Yount, Mrs. George Concepción (formerly Mrs. Gashwiler), 2:66; 20:153
Yount, Elizabeth Ann, 2:4, 63, 67; 8:284
Yount, Hattie Emma, 23:296
Yount, Jacob, 2:5
Yount, John Burnette and Lavenia Ellen (Clarke), 23:295-96
Yount, John Burnette, Jr., 23:296
Yount, Robert W., 2:67
Yountville, 16:59; Cemetery, 16:132-33
Yousef Bey, 15:377
Yreka, 3:90; 6:71, 76; 26:201, 292; 28:210, 213, 219; 30:260, 362, 367; 31:125-38 *passim*; 38:308; letters from, 26:301-4; 28:214, 223, 356; the name, 26:292, 306; newspaper, 28:230; *see also* Shasta Butte City
Ysunza, Juan A., 30:230
Yuba (riv. str.), 14:384, 406
Yuba City, 9:163, 264-67 *passim*, 356, 366, 373; 10:186, 280, 360, 386; 13:297; 14:212, 213, 216, 218, 384, 403, 405; 15:41-42; 23:369
Yuba County: creation of, 14:375-78; politics in, 8:194, 204, 206; 9:66; 14:375-78, 383, 391-92; in 1850s, 6:214-21; 8:193, 199-213 *passim*, 337-63 *passim*; 9:50-80 *passim*, 129-81, 261-68, 285-87, 347-97 *passim*; 10:53-61 *passim*; map, 8: opp. 199; *see also* Marysville
Yuba County Cavalry Co., 10:360, 369
Yuba Hose Co. No. 2, Marysville, 9:263; 10:258; 15:369
Yuba House, Marysville, 14:394
Yuba Light Infantry, Camptonville, 9:74; 38:22
Yuba Mining Co., 3:93
Yuba Ranch, 10:385, 395
Yuba River, 6:214, 244; 10:347, 349, 352; 11:110, 111, 112, 117; 12:284, 292, 301; 14:195-96, 198, 206-21 *passim*, 383-85, 389, 403, 406; 15:22, 50-51; 23:131; 28:233-42; 29:203; 33:51; early settlers on, 14:198-200; ferry, 14:403; mining on, 5:38, 293-95; 6:215-21; 8:193, 199-213 *passim*, 337-63 *passim*; 9:50-79 *passim*, 129-81 *passim*, 285; 13:170, 171, 174, 175; 14:203-11 *passim*, 244; 15:331; 20:119; 23:349, 350; 39:102-3; the name, 12:284; 14:196, 198; 26:307; map, 14: opp. 224; views, 6: opp. 242, opp. 244; *see also* Bridges; Dams; Floods; Indians

Yuba River Bridge Co., 15:53
Yuba Telegraph, Marysville, 15:29, 56
Yubaville (Marysville), 14:218, 219, 220, 376; 34:66
Yukichi, Fukuzawa, 23:346
Yulee, David Levy, 10:231, 237

Yulupa, Straits of, 3:173
Yuma, 22:162-67 *passim;* 36:219; *see also* Colorado City; Fort Yuma
Yuma (barge), 22:156, 168
Yun Sing Ping Company, 23:112
Yuttan, Joseph, 14:207

Z

Zabala, Pedro (Monterey, 1849), 29:22, 26
Zabala, Mrs. Pedro (Anna Hartnell), 29:26
Zabala, Pedro (Salinas, 1913), 23:348
Zabriskie, A. C., 8:360
Zabriskie, A. L., 8:360; 10:170, 362; lawsuit, 10:362, 370; *see also* Zabriskie's Hotel
Zabriskie, Christian Brevoort, 15:152
Zabriskie, James C., 10:63(?); 15:151-57 *passim*
Zabriskie, William M., 9:26, 27
Zabriskie, Zayda, 21:379
Zabriskie's Hotel, Yuba Co., 8:343, 349, 360; 9:154, 350, 367, 376; 10:56, 170, 172, 255(?), 370; 33:202
Zachrisson and Nelson, 13:391
Zadig & Weil, 27:5
Zahn, Mrs. Otto J., 36:253
Zakheim, Boruch Barnard, painting by, 33: opp. 97
Załᵣ... Alexander, ..136
Zaldo, Ramón de, 37:199
Zaltieri, Bolognino, 3:267; 7:234, 250; map by, 7: opp. 250
Zalvidea, José María, 3:241; 6:258, 259; 10:219; 12:115, 123; 13:210; 19:209, 215
Zamora, Manuel, 15:356
Zamorano, Agustín Vicente, 1:258; 6:143; 12:126-29 *passim*, 140, 149; 13:86, 411; 14:233-38 *passim*, 243-50 *passim*, 255, 267; 15:341, 347-48; 16:222, 229, 230-31, 245, 356, 375; 23:216; 28:257; 33:188; 35:193, 199, 201; bk. on, rev., 13:409; document (forged), 15:276; *see also* Zamorano press
Zamorano, María de Guadalupe, *see* Dalton, Mrs. Henry

Zamorano, María Dolores, *see* Flores, Mrs. José María
Zamorano, Nicolás, 3:386
Zamorano, Rodrigo, 7:62
Zamorano press, 6:143; 7:277; 12:126-31; 13:53; 16:351; 25:129; 35:104, 199, 200, 201
Zampay (Indian, 1835), 16:250, 350-51, 353, 355; 29:312, 327
Zampillaerostation, 21:178
Zamudio, Alonso de, 1:39
Zander, L. T., 15:164
Zanjas, 13:201, 311
Zane, John P., 27:97, 99, 101-2
Zanetta, Angelo, 33:352
Zanetta, Mary, 33:352
Zangerle, Albert Frederick, obit., 22:286
Zapeda, Pedro, 30:317-18, 321, 336
Zárate Salmerón, Gerónimo de, 8:38, 42; 36:232
Zavaleta, Antonio María, 14:237
Zavalishin, Dmitry, 12:195, 198
Zavitowski Sisters, 21:164, 167
Zayante (or Sayante), 14:346; 15:121, 227, 233, 235; 29:135; *see also* Ranchos: Zayante
Zayas, Juan, *see* Martínez y Zayas
Zealandia (ship), 31:60, 62
Zean, Dusu, 15:377
Zeigler, Charles, 24:275
Zeilin, Jacob, 3:123; 17:344; 21:345, 356; 26:49
Zelee (ship), 31:296
Zellerbach, Anthony, 31:186; 33:375
Zellerbach, Isadore, 22:96
Zellerbach, James David, 22:96
Zellerbach, Marks, 31:186
Zenobia (ship), 15:184; 16:337
Zermenyo, *see* Cermeño
Zimmerman (miner, 1848), 11:42

Zimmerman, Peter, 8:204; 9:180

Zoe, Marie, 21:172

Zoe, 32:180-82 *passim*

Zollinger, James Peter, 14:96; "John Augustus Sutter's European Background," 14:28-46; *Sutter the Man*, rev., 18:279

Zook, Edgar T., obit. of Charles W. Slack, 25:87-89

Zook, Mrs. Edgar T. (Ruth Slack), 25:89

Zopfe, Rosina, 28:292

Zorer, Max, 9:274; 20:305

Zornow, William Frank, 29:380-81; 33:93; 34:92; "California Sidelights on the Presidential Election of 1864," 34:49-64; "Jeptha H. Wade in California," 29:345-56, ed. "Prospecting on the Pacific Coast, 1848-1864," as recollected by Orlando J. Hodges, 33:49-58

Zouaves, 10:360

Zoyara, Ella, 21:145

Zumwalt, D. K., 4:38, 41, 43

Zumwalt, John R., 4:38

Zúñiga, José, 2:332-39; 13:199; 34:204

Zúñiga y Acevedo, Gaspar de, Conde de Monterey, 7:259, 260-68 *passim*, 295-99 *passim*, 377-78; 8:43, 44, 50, 69; 23:222

Zweig, Stefan, *Die Entdeckung Eldorados*, 9:398